Street by Street

HAMPSHIRE

PLUS BOURNEMOUTH, CAMBERLEY, CHRISTCHURCH, FARNHAM, FERNDOWN, HASLEMERE, NEWBURY, NORTH TIDWORTH, POOLE, SOUTHBOURNE, VERWOOD, WIMBORNE MINSTER

Enlarged Areas Aldershot, Andover, Basingstoke, Fareham, Gosport, Havant, Portsmouth, Southampton, Winchester

Ist edition May 2001

© Automobile Association Developments Limited 2001

This product includes map data licensed from Ordnance Survey® with the permission of the Controller of Her Majesty's Stationery Office. © Crown copyright 2000. All rights reserved. Licence No: 399221.

Published by AA Publishing (a trading name of Automobile Association Developments Limited, whose registered office is Norfolk House, Priestley Road, Basingstoke, Hampshire, RG24 9NY.
Registered number 1878835).

Mapping produced by the Cartographic Department of The Automobile Association.

ISBN 0 7495 2360 3

A CIP Catalogue record for this book is available from the British Library.

Printed in Italy by Printer Trento srl

The contents of this atlas are believed to be correct at the time of the latest revision. However, the publishers cannot be held responsible for loss occasioned to any person acting or refraining from action as a result of any material in this atlas, nor for any errors, omissions or changes in such material. The publishers would welcome information to correct any errors or omissions and to keep this atlas up to date. Please write Publishing, The Automobile Association, Fanum House, Basing View, Basingstoke, Hampshire, G21 4EA.

: MX008

Key to map pages	ii-iii
Key to map symbols	iv-1
Enlarged scale pages	2-23
Street by Street	24-457
Index – towns & villages	458-460
Index – streets	461-506
Index – featured places	506-513

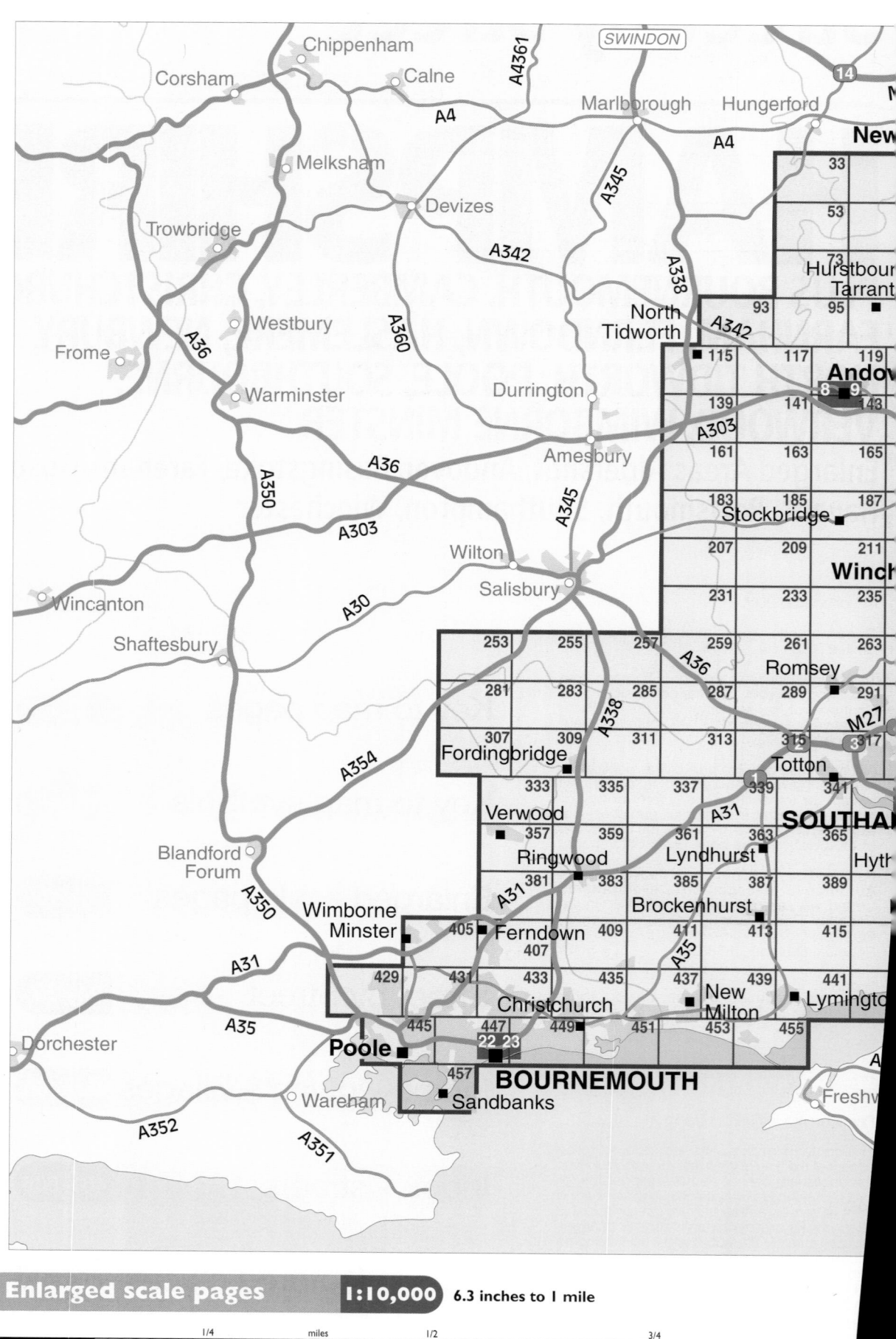

Enlarged scale pages   1:10,000   6.3 inches to 1 mile

| 0 | 1/4 | miles | 1/2 | | 3/4 | |
| 0 | 1/4 | 1/2 | kilometres | 3/4 | 1 | 1 1/4 |

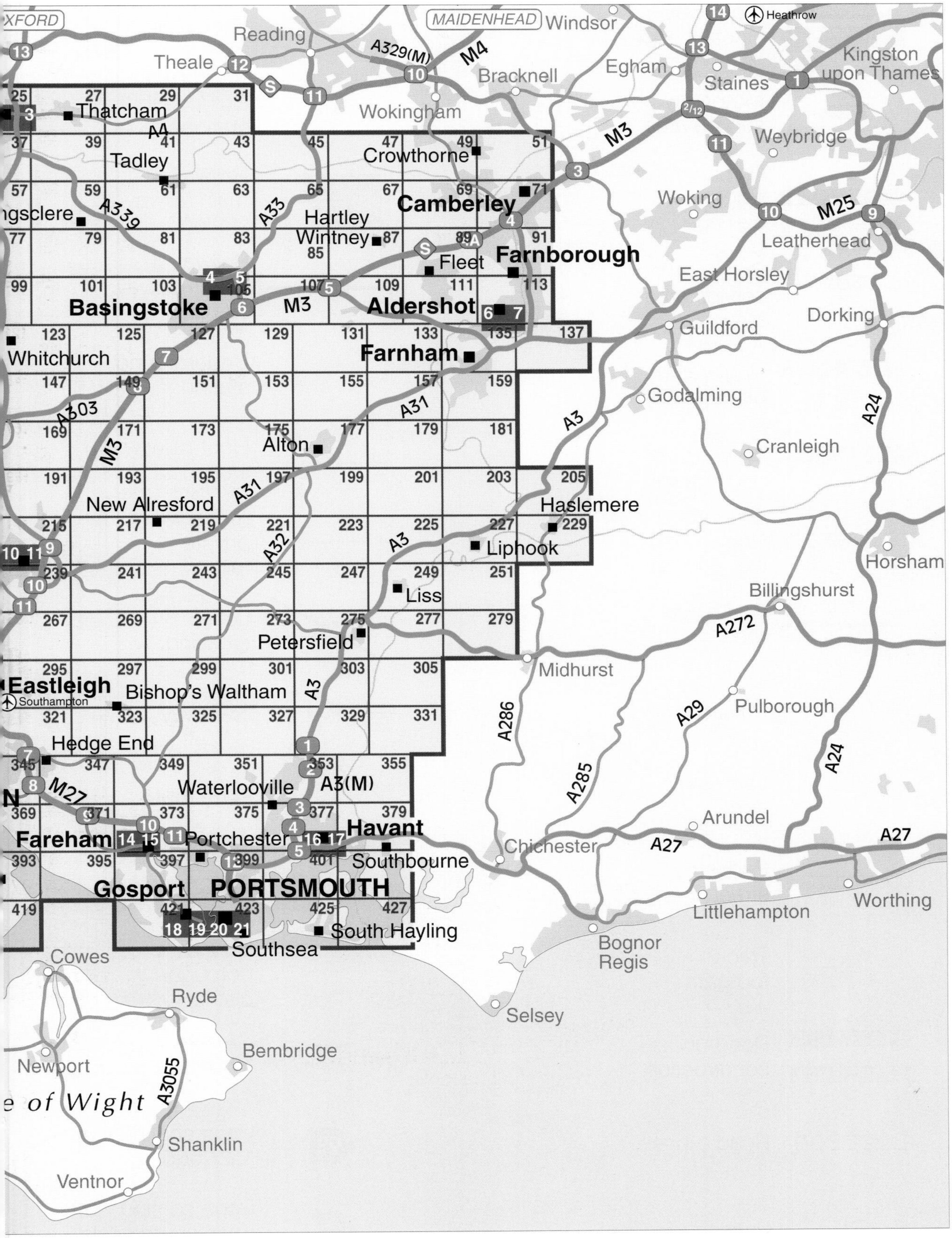

XFORD

Reading

MAIDENHEAD Windsor

14 ✈ Heathrow

13

Theale

12

A329(M)

10

M4

Bracknell

Egham

13

Staines

Kingston upon Thames

1

25 27 29 31

3 Thatcham

S

11

Wokingham

Woking

2/12

11

Weybridge

37 39 41 43 45 47 49 51

A4

Tadley

Crowthorne

M3

3

10

M25

9

ngsclere

A339

57 59 61 63 65 67 69 71

A33

Hartley Wintney

Camberley

4

Farnborough

Leatherhead

East Horsley

Dorking

77 79 81 83 85 87 89A 91

S

Fleet

A

Guildford

99 101 103 105 107 109 111 113

4 5

Basingstoke

6

M3

5

Aldershot

6 7

123 125 127 129 131 133 135 137

Whitchurch

7

Farnham

Godalming

147 149 151 153 155 157 159

A303

A31

A3

Cranleigh

A24

169 171 173 175 177 179 181

M3

Alton

191 193 195 197 199 201 203 205

A31

Haslemere

215 217 219 221 223 225 227 229

New Alresford

A32

A3

Liphook

Horsham

239 241 243 245 247 249 251

9

Billingshurst

10

11

267 269 271 273 275 277 279

Liss

A272

Petersfield

295 297 299 301 303 305

Midhurst

Pulborough

Eastleigh

Bishop's Waltham

A3

A286

A29

A24

Southampton

321 323 325 327 329 331

A285

Hedge End

1

345 347 349 351 353 355

7

Waterlooville

2

A3(M)

Arundel

8

M27

N

369 371 373 375 377 379

3

Chichester

A27

A27

N

10

4

Havant

14 15

11

Portchester

16 17

Fareham

Bognor Regis

393 395 397 399 401

Southbourne

1

Littlehampton

Worthing

Gosport

PORTSMOUTH

419 421 423 425 427

18 19 20 21

South Hayling

Southsea

Cowes

Ryde

Bembridge

Selsey

Newport

A3055

e of Wight

Shanklin

Ventnor

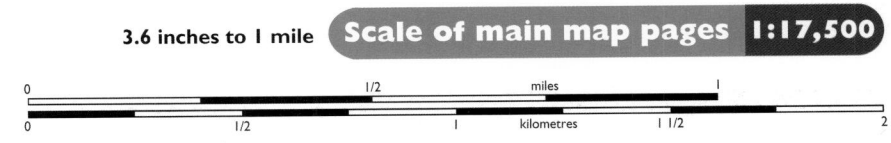

3.6 inches to 1 mile **Scale of main map pages** 1:17,500

0 1/2 miles 1

0 1/2 1 kilometres 1 1/2 2

Junction 9	Motorway & junction
Services	Motorway service area
	Primary road single/dual carriageway
Services	Primary road service area
	A road single/dual carriageway
	B road single/dual carriageway
	Other road single/dual carriageway
	Restricted road
	Private road
← ←	One way street
	Pedestrian street
	Track/ footpath
	Road under construction
	Road tunnel
P	Parking

P+	Park & Ride
	Bus/coach station
	Railway & main railway station
	Railway & minor railway station
	Underground station
	Light railway & station
+++++++++	Preserved private railway
LC	Level crossing
•–•–•–•–	Tramway
---------------	Ferry route
....	Airport runway
–·–·–·–·–	Boundaries- borough/ district
vvvvvvvvvv	Mounds
93	Page continuation 1:17,500
7	Page continuation to enlarged scale 1:10,000

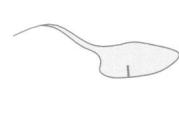 River/canal lake, pier

 Aqueduct lock, weir

 Peak (with height in metres)

465
▲
Winter Hill

 Beach

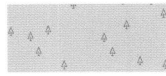 Coniferous woodland

 Broadleaved woodland

 Mixed woodland

 Park

 Cemetery

 Built-up area

 Featured building

ᴪᴪᴪᴪᴪᴪᴪᴪ City wall

A&E Accident & Emergency hospital

🚻 Toilet

♿ Toilet with disabled facilities

⛽ Petrol station

PH Public house

PO Post Office

📖 Public library

i Tourist Information Centre

♜ Castle

🏛 Historic house/ building

Wakehurst Place NT — National Trust property

Ⓜ Museum/ art gallery

✝ Church/chapel

♈ Country park

🎭 Theatre/ performing arts

🎥 Cinema

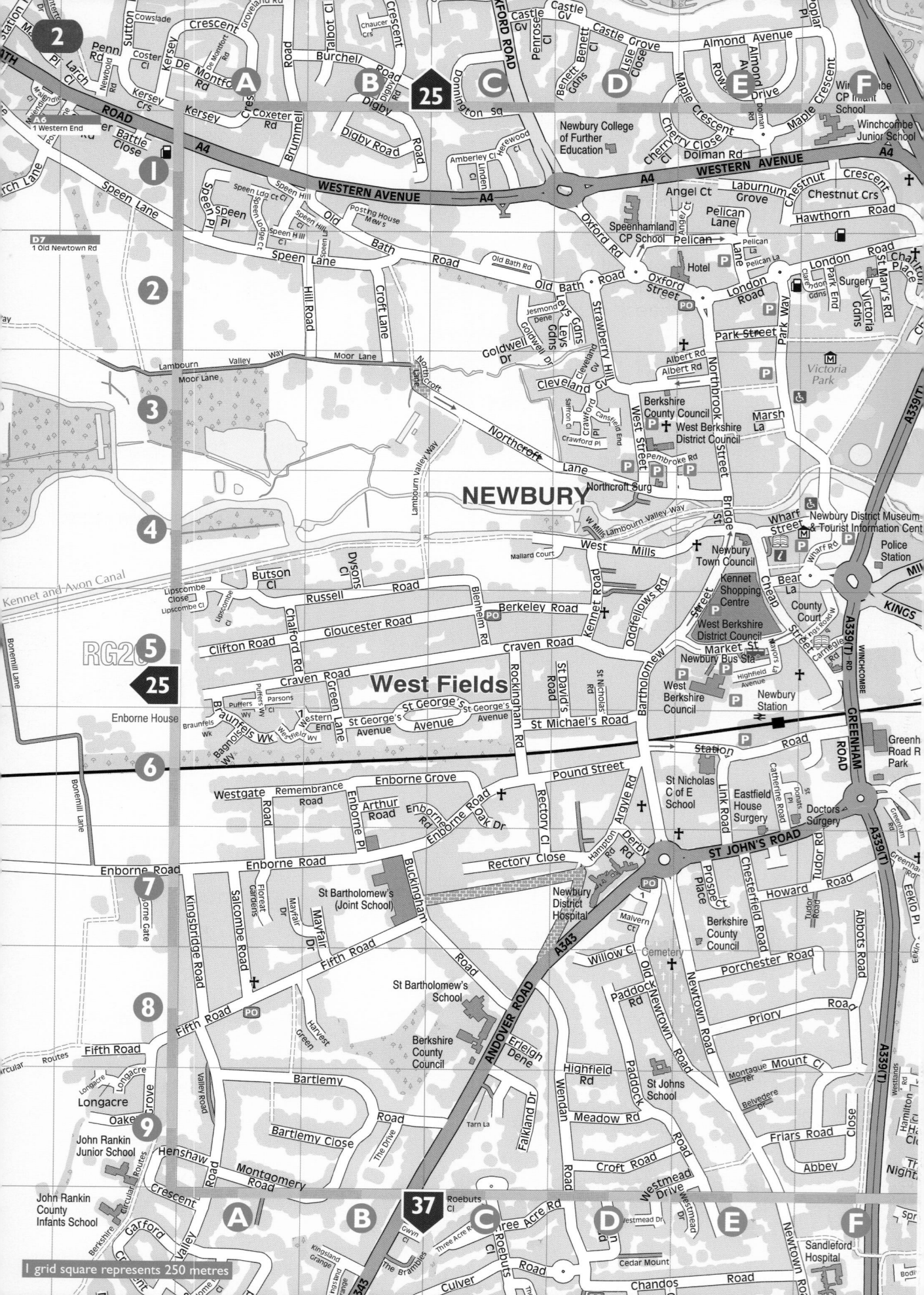

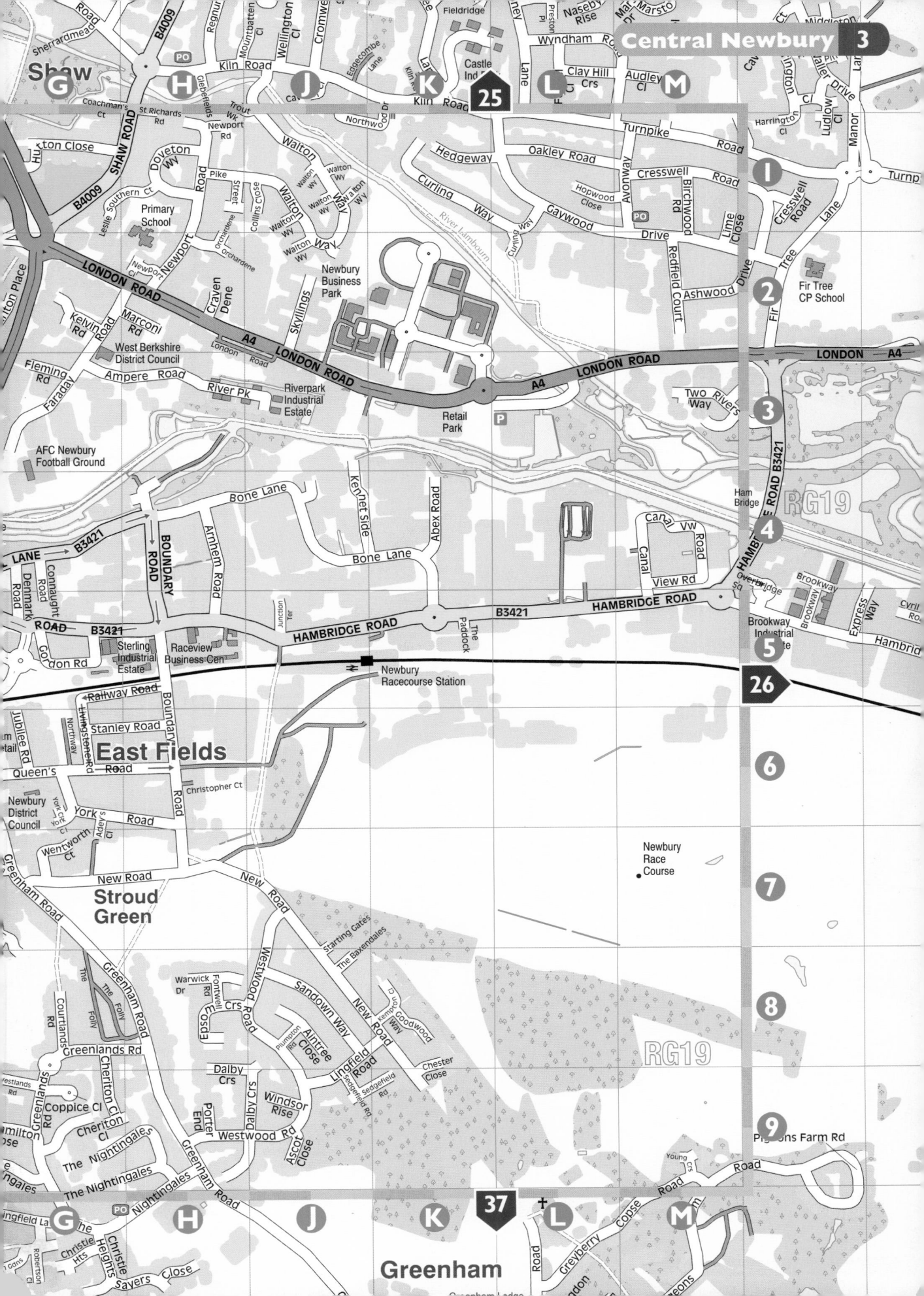

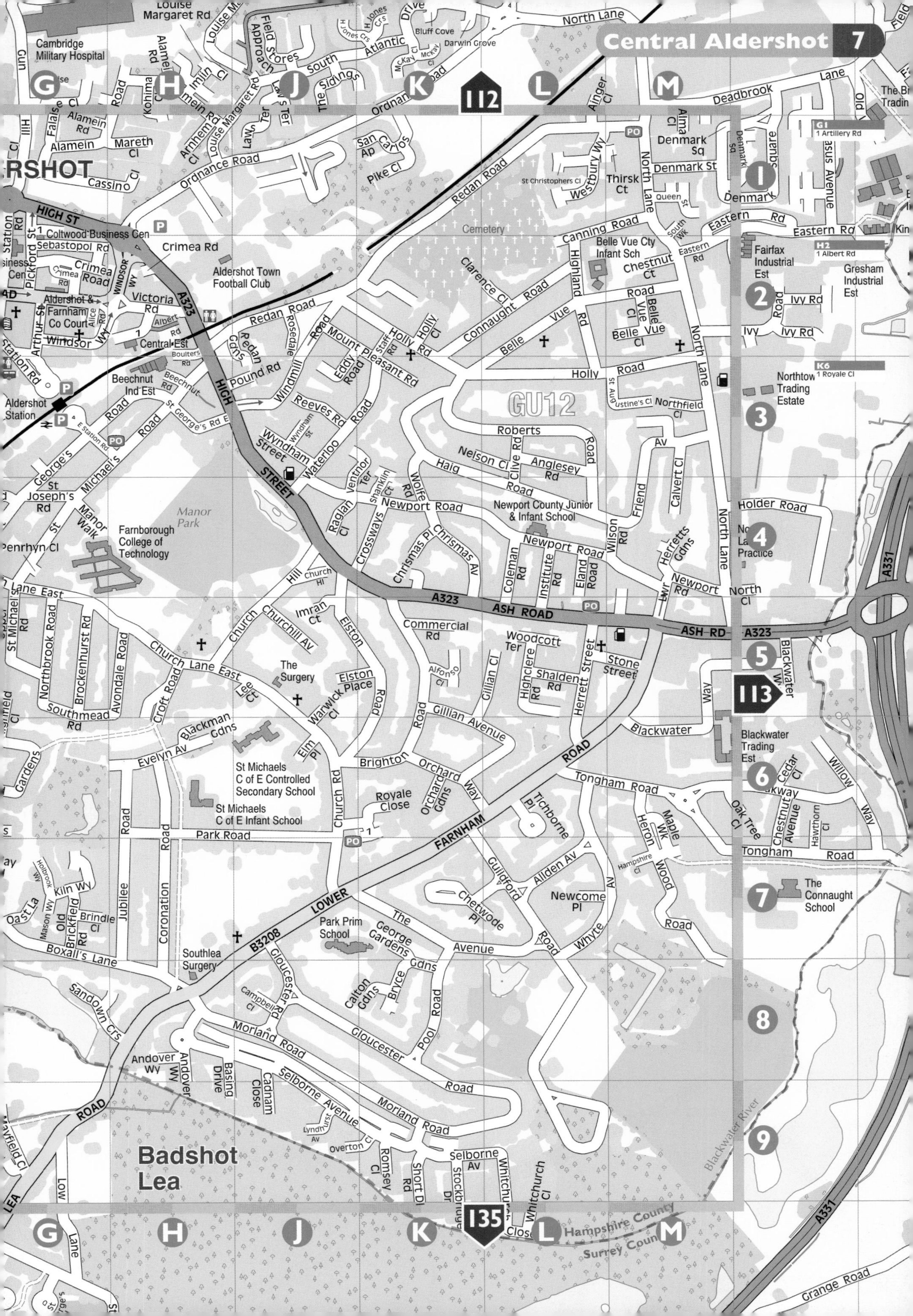

Cambridge Military Hospital
Louise Margaret Rd
Field Stores Approach
South
Atlantic Drive
Bluff Cove
Darwin Grove
North Lane
Ordnance Road
112
Deadbrook Lane
Alamein Rd
Mareth Cl
Falaise Cl
Kohima Cl
Imjin Cl
Arnhem Cl
Louise Margaret Rd
The Sidings
Lawn Ter
Ordnance Road
San Carlos Ap
Pike Cl
Cassino Cl
Redan Road
Ainger Cl
Alma Cl
Denmark Sq
Denmark St
Denmark Square
Pegasus Avenue
G1 1 Artillery Rd
St Christophers Cl
Westbury Wy
Thirsk Ct
North Lane
Queen St
Eastern Rd
HIGH ST
Coltwood Business Cen
Sebastopol Rd
Crimea Rd
Pickford St
Aldershot Town Football Club
Cemetery
Canning Road
Belle Vue Cty Infant Sch
Chestnut Ct
Fairfax Industrial Est
H2 1 Albert Rd
Gresham Industrial Est
Ivy Rd
Aldershot & Farnham Co Court
Victoria Rd
Albert Rd
Central Est
Windsor Wy
Arthur St
Station Rd
Aldershot Station
Beechnut Ind Est
Beechnut Rd
Boulters Rd
Redan Gdns
Pound Rd
Rosedale
Windmill Road
Mount Pleasant Rd
Eddy Road
Holly Rd
Holly Cl
Staff Rd
Clarence Cl
Connaught Road
Highland Rd
Belle Vue Road
Belle Vue Cl
Holly Road
St Augustine's Cl
Northfield Cl
Northtown Trading Estate
K6 1 Royale Cl
GU12
Roberts Road
Clive Rd
Nelson Cl
Anglesey Rd
Haig Road
Wolfe Rd
Friend Av
Calvert Cl
Reeves Rd
Waterloo Road
Wyndham Street
Wyndham St
E Station Rd
St George's Rd E
Michael's Road
George's Road
St Joseph's Rd
Manor Walk
Manor Park
Farnborough College of Technology
Penrhyn Cl
Ventnor Ter
Shanklin Ct
Raglan Cl
Crossways
Newport Road
Chrismas Pl
Chrismas Av
Newport County Junior & Infant School
Coleman Rd
Institute Rd
Eland Road
Wilson Rd
Herretts Gdns
Newport Rd
Holder Road
North Lane Practice
North Cl
A331
Church Hill
Imran Ct
Elston Road
A323 ASH ROAD
ASH RD A323
Commercial Rd
Woodcott Ter
Stone Street
Blackwater Way
113
Church Lane East
St Michael's Rd
Northbrook Road
Brockenhurst Rd
Avondale Road
Churchill Av
The Surgery
Elston Place
Warwick Place
Lee Ct
Croft Road
Alfonso Cl
Gillian Cl
Highclere Rd
Shalden Rd
Herrett Street
Gillian Avenue
Southmead Rd
Blackman Gdns
Evelyn Av
Elm Pl
Brighton Road
Orchard Way
Orchard Gdns
Blackwater Trading Est
Cedar Cl
Willow Way
Tongham Road
Oakway
St Michaels C of E Controlled Secondary School
St Michaels C of E Infant School
Church Rd
Royale Close
Tichborne Pl
Heron Wk
Maple Wk
Oak Tree Cl
Chestnut Avenue
Hawthorn Cl
Park Road
Jubilee Road
Coronation Road
FARNHAM ROAD
Tongham Road
Hampshire Cl
Wood Road
The Connaught School
Holbrook Wy
Kiln Wy
Oast La
Mason Wy
Old Brickfield Rd
Brindle Cl
B3208 LOWER
Park Prim School
The George Gardens
Guildford Road
Allden Av
Chetwode Pl
Newcome Pl
Whyte Av
Boxall's Lane
Southlea Surgery
Gloucester Rd
Campbell Cl
Calton Gdns
Bryce Gdns
Avenue
Pool Road
Sandown Crs
Morland Road
Gloucester Road
Andover Wy
Basing Drive
Cadnam Close
Selborne Avenue
Morland Road
Lyndhurst Av
Overton Cl
Romsey Cl
Short Rd
Stockbridge Dr
Selborne Av
Whitchurch Cl
Blackwater River
Badshot Lea
ROAD
LEA
Low Lane
135
Hampshire County
Surrey County
Grange Road

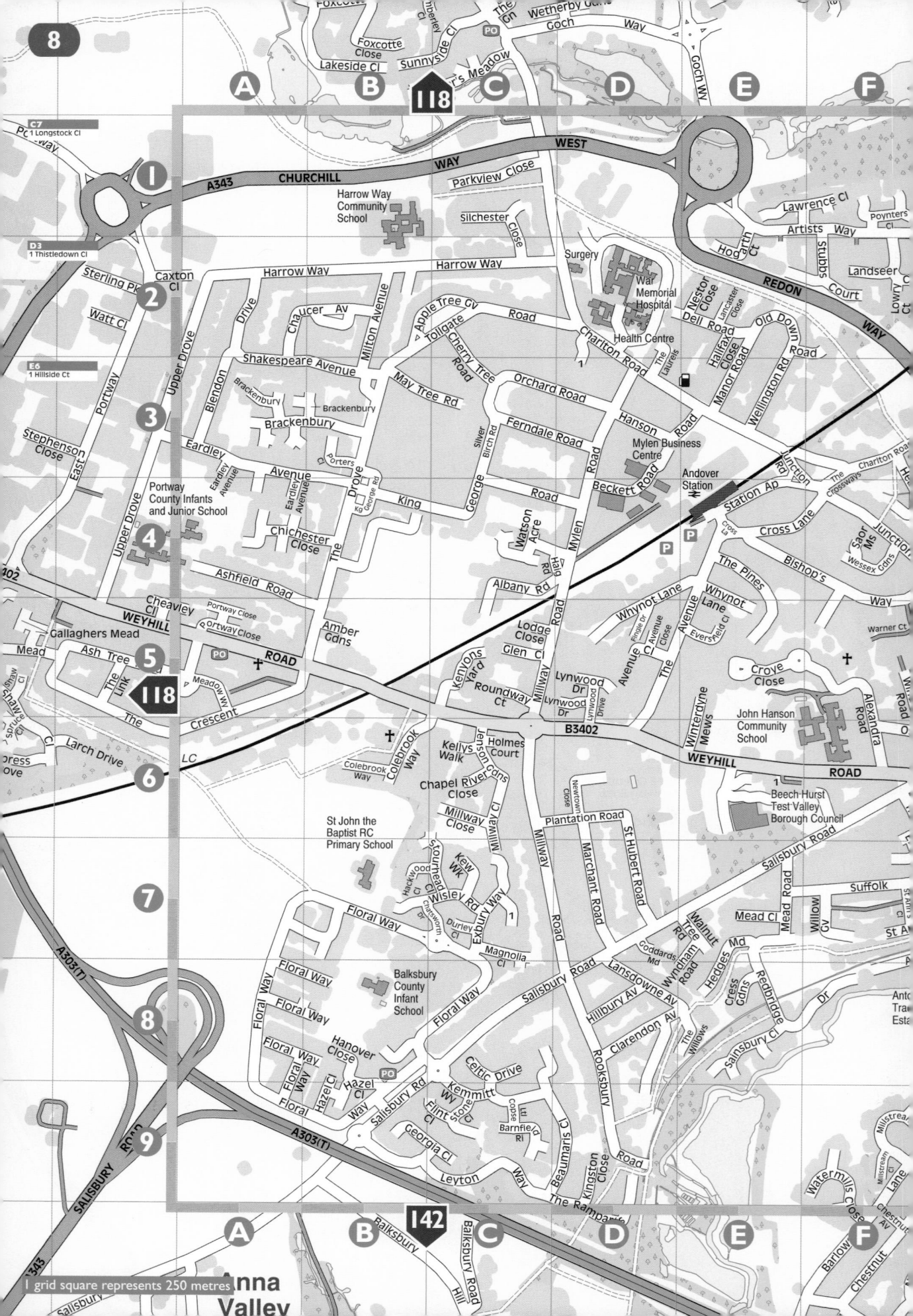

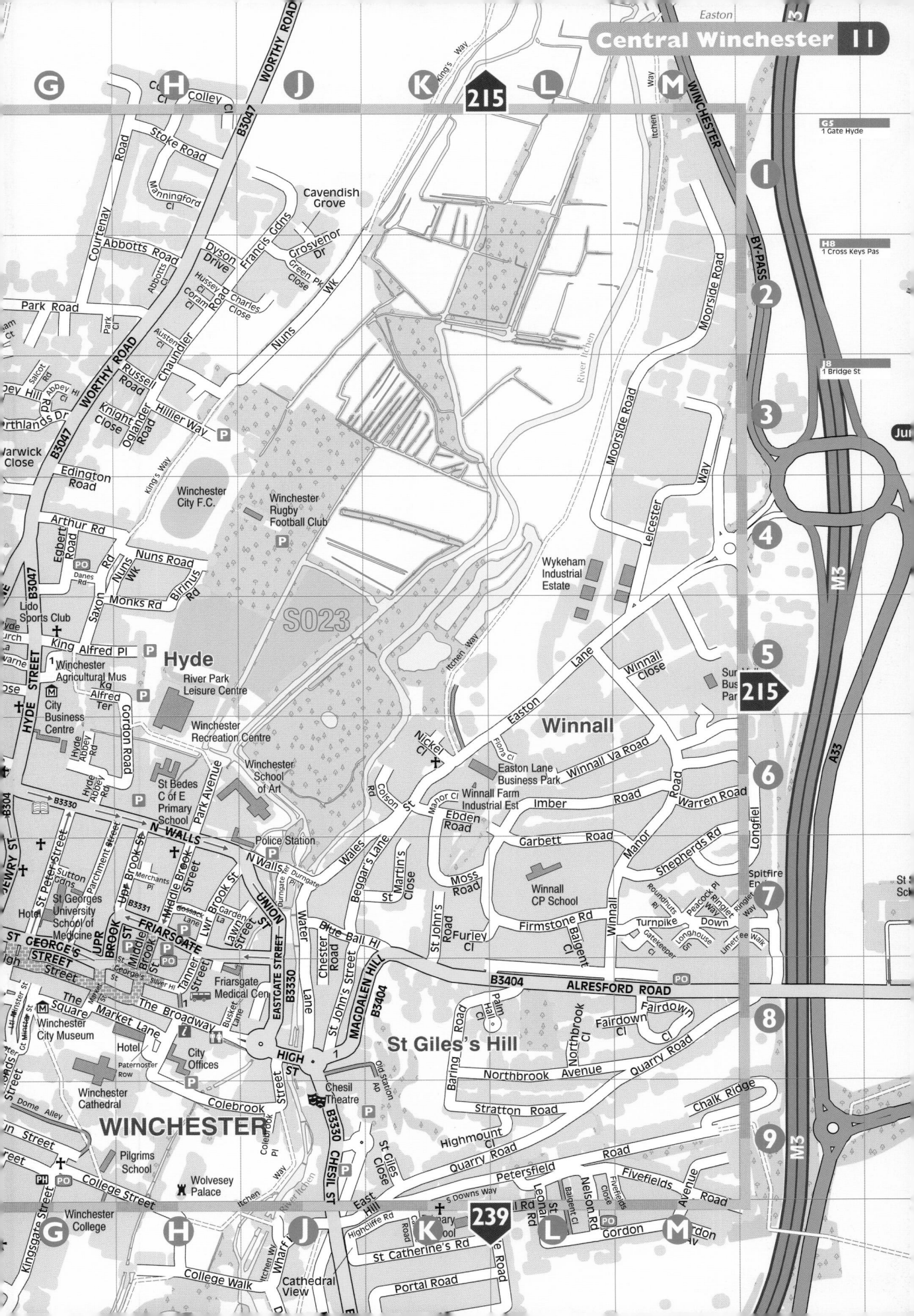

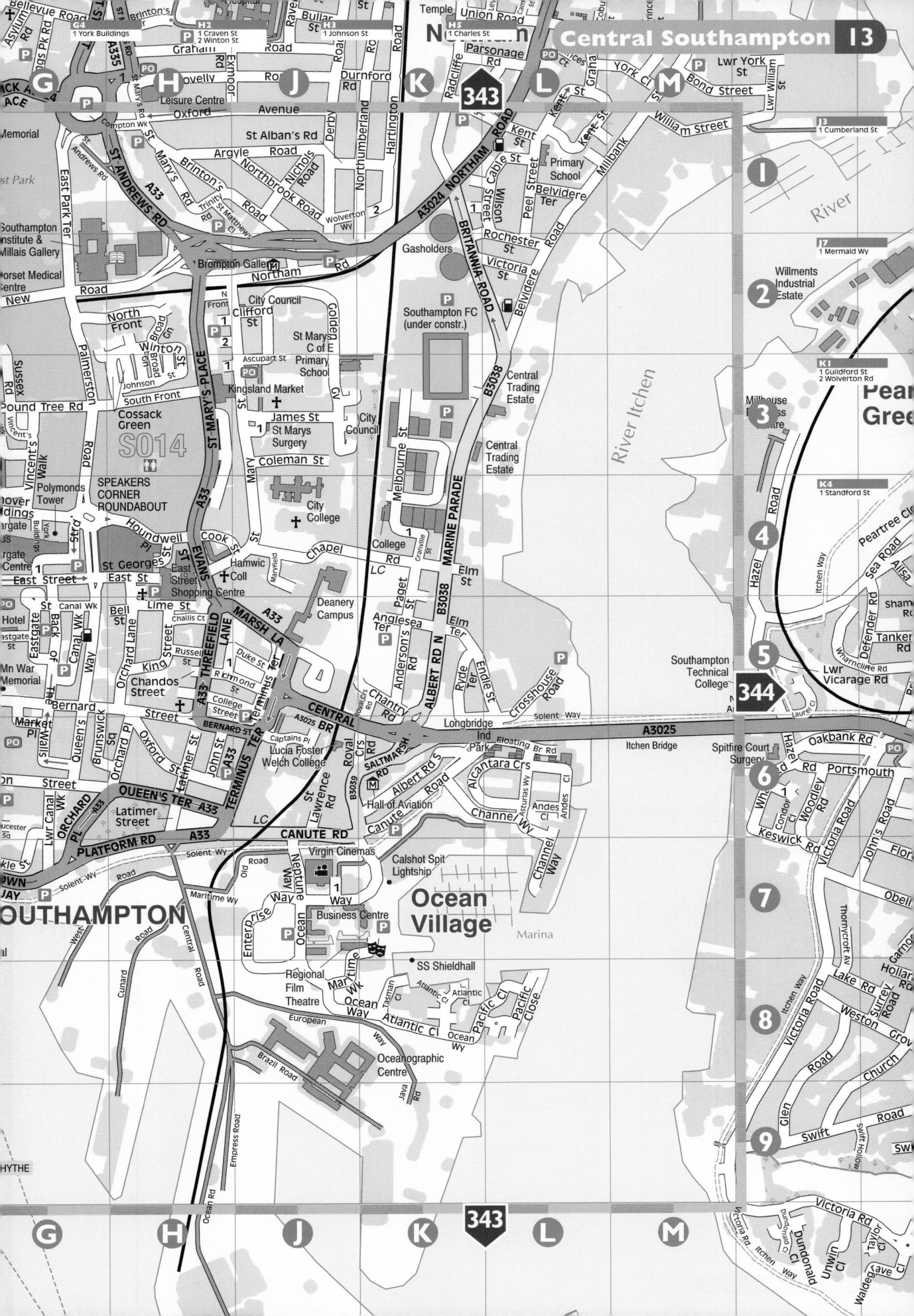

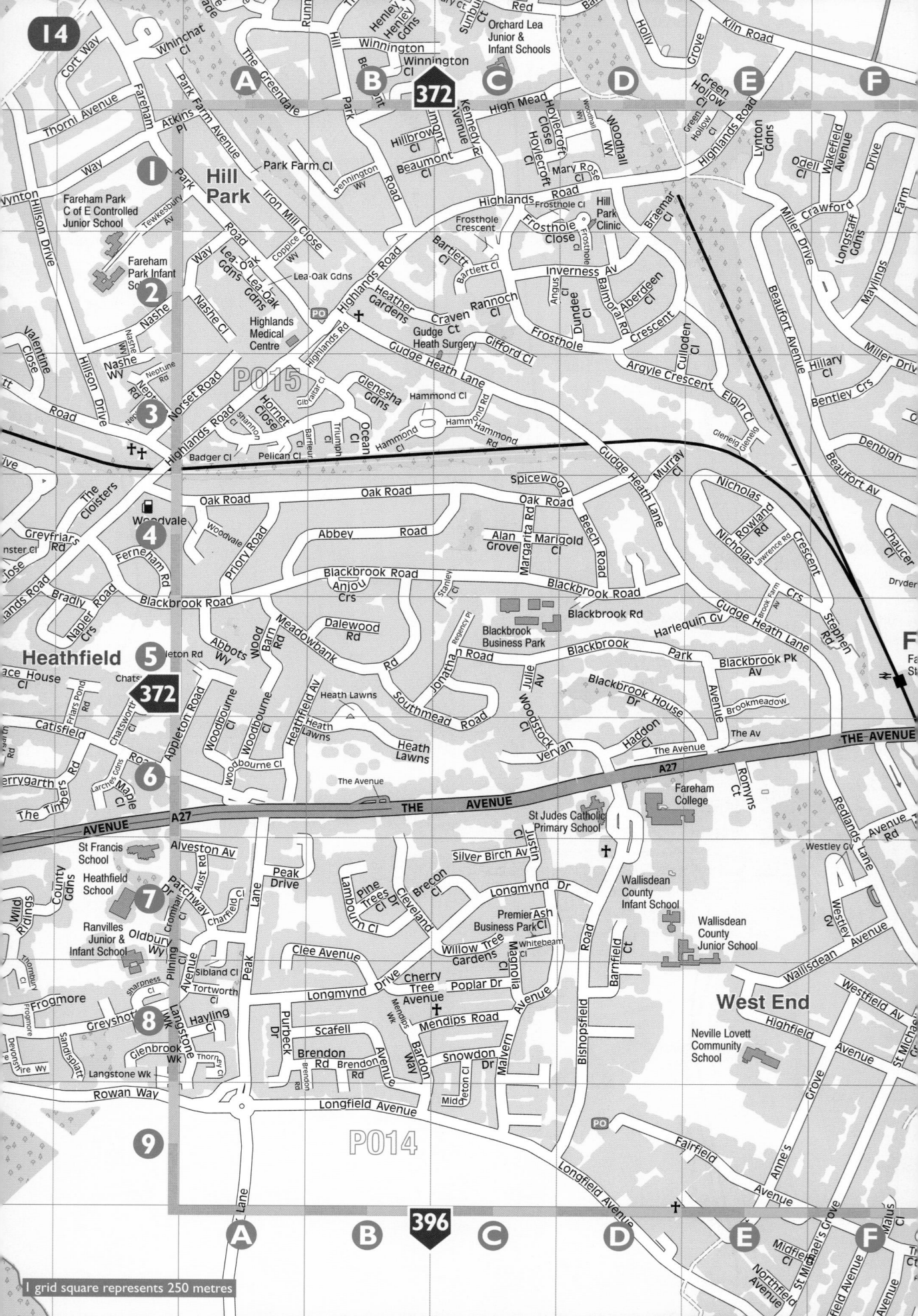

G2 1 Battenburg Rd

G4 1 Leventhorpe Ct
2 Molesworth Rd
3 Shaftsbury Rd
4 Woodley Rd

H3 1 Henery St
1 Joseph St
3 Pr of Wales Rd

H5 1 Thornbrake Rd

K3 1 Thorngate Wy

City of Ports
pshireCounty

G H J K L M

422

Mary Ros
hip Hall

HMS
Victory

Ma
Ro

1

2 Portsmouth Harbour

The Ha
Bus &

3

4 Bath Sq

Bathing La
West St

5

20

6

7

8

9

G H J K L M

422

Salt Meat

Weevil

Weevi

Brewhouse
Sq

Jamaica Road

Osborne   Road

Yacht
Marina

FORTON   ROAD

Fe
Road

Parham Road

Albert St

Victoria St

Leonard
Road

George St

Pearce
Court

A32

GOSPORT

MUMBY

King Street

Clarence Road

North St

N Cross
Street

ROAD

Harbour Rd

Minnitt Rd

Grove   Av

Carlton
Wy

Carlton

Spring Garden Lane

Avenue

Fey
Rd

Peel
Road

Blake
Road

Queen's
Road

Percy
Road

Jamacia
Rd

Strathmore
Rd

Oak St

Holly
Rd

Stoke
St

3

1

Richard Martin
Gallery &.Bookshop

Ordnance   Rd

Willis   Road

Creek Rd

Gosport
Museum

High   Street

PO

Town Hall

1

SOUTH   ST

B3333

SOUTH   STREET

Church Pth

Trinity
Cl

Trinity   Gn

The Esplanade

Gosport Museum

Minnitt Rd

Bus Station

Jamaica
Place

PO

3

Jamaica

STREET

B3333

Endeavour Cl

Shamrock
Cl

Nyria
Wy

Dock   Road

Willis
Rd

Hampshire
County Council

SOUTH

4

Kensington
Road

Shaftsbury
Road

Cranbourne   Rd

Old Road

1

Old

Woodstock
Road

Dolman
Rd

Dolman   Road

Mariners
Wy

Dolman Rd

The
Anchorage

Haslar   Road

Solent Way

PO

Crescent

Crossland Cl

Royal Navy Submarine
Museum Offices

Haslar Road

Haslar Road

Clayhall

Cem

Royal
Hospital
Haslar

Mabey
Cl

Mabey Cl

Mabey Cl

Clayhall   Road

Wilberforce
Rd

St Francis
Rd

Waterloo Rd

Dolphin   Way

St Francis
Rd

Spithead
Av

The Redan

Lind
Rd

Gilkicker

able

Golf Club

Military   Rd

Fort Rd

ISLE OF WIGHT

The Solent

Portsea

Old Portsmouth

ST GEORGE'S RD

Portsmouth Harbour

Portsmouth Harbour Station

The Hard Interchange Bus & Coach Station

Royal Naval Museum

Dockyard Apprentice Exhibition

Mary Rose Exhibition

HMS Victory

HMS Warrior

HMS Nelson

City of Portsmouth Hampshire County

Isle of Wight Car Ferry Terminal

Bath Sq

Bathing La

West St

East Street

Round Tower

Town Walls

Square Tower

Battery Row

Grand Pde

The Long Curtain (Old Town Defences)

Captains Rw

Camber Place

Cathedral Church of St Thomas of Canterbury

Goldfield Gallery

Portsmouth City Council

City Museum & Art Gallery

Chadderton Gdns

City Museum

St Judes C of E Primary School

Hotel

Chatham Dr

Gordon Road

Clarence Pier & Amusement Centre

Clarence Esplanade

Hovercraft Terminal

Southsea Common

Solent

Bus Station

Royal Navy Submarine Museum Offices

Primary School

Old Star

College

St Georges Business Centre

United Services Cricket Ground

United Services Rugby Club

University of Portsmouth

HMS Temeraire

Portsmouth Grammar School

The Pascoe Practice

Portsmouth Natural Hea

University Practice

Doctors Surgery

Lion St

Portland St

Richmond Place

Clock St

North Street

Treadgold Museum

Prince George

Victoria Swim Centr

Portsmouth Natural Heal

Long Curtain Road

GUERNSEY; JERSEY

I grid square represents 250 metres   Solent

19

422

G3
1 Coster Cl
2 Cowslade
3 Majendie Cl
4 Marshalls Ct
5 Newbold Rd

G4
1 Caunter Rd

H4
1 Posting H Ms
2 Speen Hill Cl
3 Speen La
4 Speen Lodge Ct
5 Speen Pl

H6
1 Parsons Cl
2 Puffers Wy
3 Western End

I1
1 The Chase

H3
1 Sylvester Cl

A B C D E F

Bagnor

Woodspeen

Lambourn Valley Way

Woodspeen Farm

Watermill Theatre
& Restaurant

PH

I

RG20

B4000

Snake Lane

A34(T)

Lambo

2

Cricketers
Chapel Road
Stockcross School
Rookswood

PO

Deanwood Farm

Church Road
Glebe Lane

✝

Stockcross

B4000

Spee

3

GRAVEL HILL

Benham Cha

Milkhouse Rd

A4

A4

Speen House

4

Benham Park

Elmore House

Marsh Benham

5

Benham Marsh Farm

6

Enborne Road

7

Enborne Copse

8

✝

Church Lane

Enborne

Berkshire Circular Routes

A34(T)

Skinners Green

M7
1 Plumpton Rd

A

M6
1 Junction Ter
2 The Paddock

M4
1 Collins Cl

B C

36

D

L7
1 Fontwell Rd
2 Wentworth Ct

E

L6
1 Adey's Cl

F

M3
1 Fieldridge
2 Mountbatten Cl
3 Wellington Cl

L8
1 Coppice Cl
2 Robertson Cl

Cope Hall

1 grid square represents 500 metres

C4
1 Southdown Rd

C5
1 Foxhunter Wy

B6
1 Overbridge Sq

B4
1 Cresswell Rd
2 Ludlow Cl

B3
1 Fairfax Pl
2 Pindar Pl

A3
1 Clay Hill Crs
2 Preston Pl

A8
1 Blagdon Cl

A B C D E F

Ashmore Green

1

Mousefield Farm

Stoney Lane

PH

Stone Copse

Hatchgate Farm

Hatchgate Close

2

Sycamore Rise

Henwick Cl

Henwick Manor

Hotel

Pear Tree Lane

3

Wansey Gdns
Fleetwood Cl
Yates Copse
Waller

Naseby Rd
Marston
Wyndham Rd
Sorrel Cl
Audley Cl
Fennel
Cavendish Dr
Middleton
Harrington Close
Manor Road

Lower Henwick Farm

Bowling Green
Elmhurst Rd
Severn Ct
Trent Cl
Thames Rd
Dart Cl
Tyne Wy
Conway Dr
Humber Close
Medway Cl
Elm Gv

Gordon Road
Calard Dr
Westfield
The Close
Bally Avenue
Westfield Rd
Henwick Lane
Roman Way
Loundyes Cl
Link Way
Barfield Rd
Bourne Arch

Norlands
Whitelands Park CP School
Shakespeare Rd
Kendal
Brown Cl
Lancaster
Stirling Wy
Coopers Crs
Beverley Close

THAT

3

Castle Ind Park
Hedgeway
Oakley Road
Turnpike Road
3
Cresswell Road
PO
Birchwood
Lime
Drive
Fir Tree Lane
Turnpike Rd

THAT

Curling Way
Hopwood Cl
Gaywood
Redfield Ct
Ashworth
Fir Tree CP School

4

25

London Road

Retail Park
P
Two Rivers Wy
Hambridge Road

Bath Rd
Lower Way
Robertsfield
Arle Ct
Winston
Pegasus Cl
Doublet
Pound Lane
Rival Dr
Coniston
Derwent Rd
Ulswater Close
Heron Wy
Parsons Down Infant School
Windermere Wy
Bourne Rd
Paynesdown Rd
Cygnet Cl
Pipit Cl
Crowfield Dr
Maple

A4 Bath Road

St John's Rd
Rope Walk
St Mary's Lane
Greenly
Glebelands

5

Abex Lane

Canal Vw Rd
Ham Bridge

Mill Reach
Pr Hld Rd

Junior School

Lower Way
Low

Fylingdales
Rosedale Gdns
Denton
Aston Cl
Bodmin
Keighley Cl

6

Newbury Racecourse Station

HAMBRIDGE ROAD B3421

Brookway Industrial Est
Brookway
Express Wy
Cyril Vokins Rd
Hambridge Lane

LC

7

Kendales
Kempton Cl
Chester Cl
Cogwood

Lower Farm
Lower Farm Ct

Newbury Race Course

Kennet and Avon Canal

River Kennet

8

Greenham
Greenham Lodge

Young Crs
Greyberry Copse Road
New Road
Farm Rd
Pigeons

Pigeon's Farm

Bowdown House

D5
1 Clerewater Pl
2 Ennerdale Wy
3 Saxon Ct

E4
1 Westland

B5
1 Kestrel Cl
2 Matthews Cl

F3
1 Flecker Cl
2 Hardy Cl

F4
1 Halifax Pl
2 Sunderland Pl
3 Wordsworth Rd

F5
1 Crown Acre Cl
2 Curlew Cl
3 The Turnery

F6
1 Ashworth Dr

Bury's Bank

Wat
Bury's Bank

1 grid square represents 500 metres

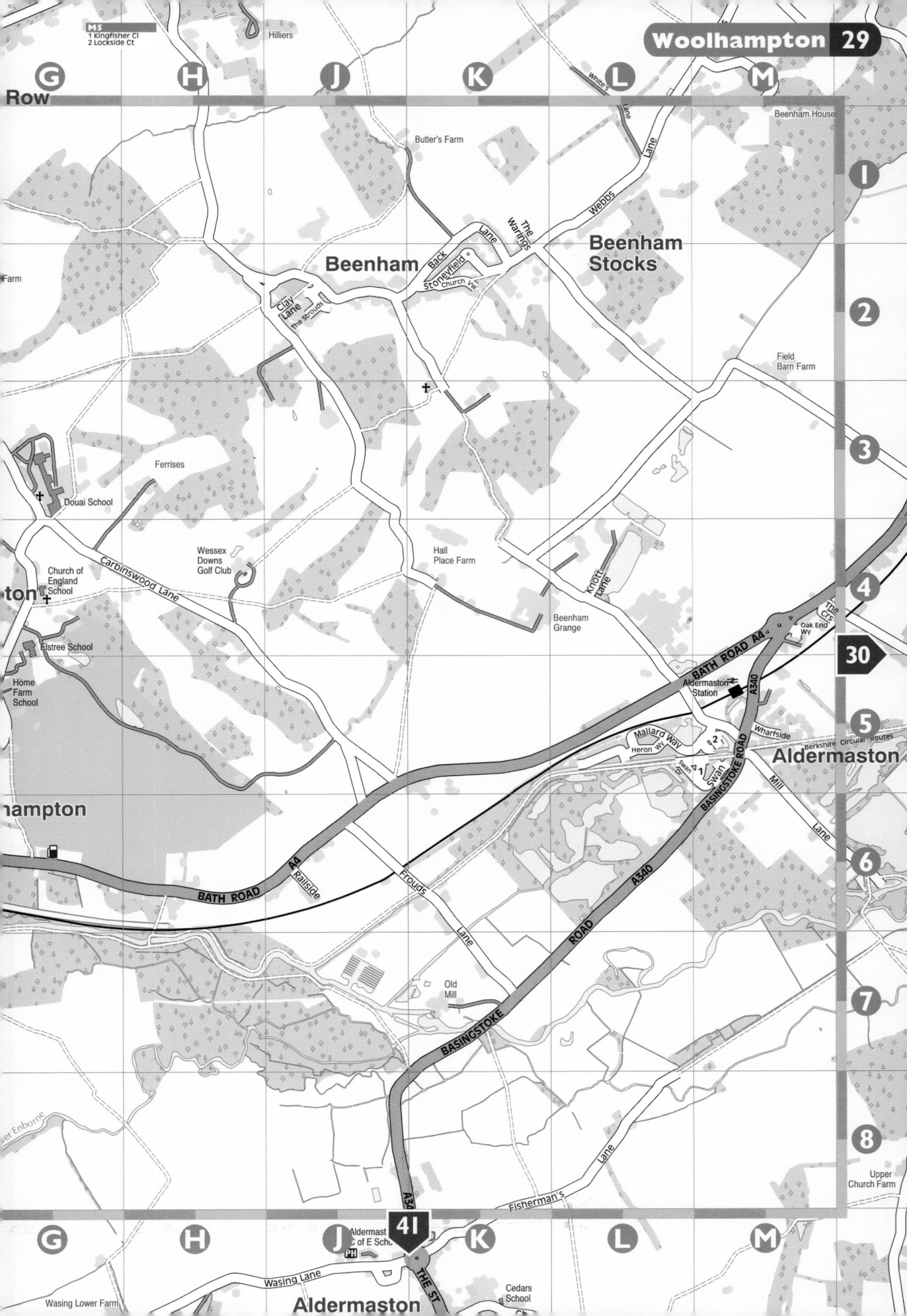

G H J K L M

1 Kingfisher Cl
2 Lockside Ct

Hilliers

Butler's Farm

Beenham House

Beenham

Beenham
Stocks

Field
Barn Farm

Ferrises

Douai School

Wessex
Downs
Golf Club

Hall
Place Farm

Knott
Lane

30

Church of
England
School

Carbinswood Lane

Beenham
Grange

BATH ROAD A4

Aldermaston
Station

A340

The
Crs

Oak End
Wy

Elstree School

Mallard Way

Heron Wy

Swan

1
2

Wharfside

Berkshire Circular Routes

Aldermaston

Home
Farm
School

Mill
Lane

hampton

A4

Railside

BATH ROAD

Frouds
Lane

A340

BASINGSTOKE ROAD

5

6

Old
Mill

7

BASINGSTOKE

ROAD

Upper
Church Farm

8

Lower Enborne

41

Aldermast
of E Schoo

PH

Wasing Lane

Cedars
School

Wasing Lower Farm

Aldermaston

THE ST

G H J K L M

Row

Farm

ton

Clay
Lane

The Strouds

Stoneyfield

Back
Lane

Church Vw

The
Warings
Lane

Webbs
Lane

White's
Lane

I

2

3

4

5

6

7

8

A   B   C   D   E   F

Lambden's Farm

Beenham House

1

Lambdens Hill

Tyle Mill

Sulhamstead

2

Field Barn Farm

LC

Berkshire Circular Routes

Ufton Bridge

King

BATH ROAD

Berkshire Circular Routes

Avon Way

Bath Road

3

LC

Hart's Lane

Ufton Green

Lower Padworth

River Kenner

Berkshire Circular Routes

Middle Farm

Church Lane

Ufton Parock Prima School

4

The Cre

Oak End Wv

29

Berkshire Circular Routes

5

harfside

Berkshire Circular Routes

Aldermaston Wharf

Mill Lane

Padworth Lane

Berkshire Circular Routes

Green

6

Lodge Farm

Berkshire Circular Routes

The Ark School

Old Farm

School Road

7

Padworth House College

Padworth

Berkshire Circular Routes

Silver Lane

Upper Church Farm

8

The Old Rectory

A   B   C   42   D   E   F

Rectory

West Berkshire Count

Hatch

Hampshire

I grid square represents 500 metres

A B C D E F

Stype Grange

Bagshot

Upper Slope End Farm

Prosperous Home Farm

I

Annett's Lane

The Lilley Clinic

2

Eastcourt Farm

Polesdon House

Six Acre Lane

Bitham Lane

3

ROAD

A338

4

Cutting Hill

Shalbourne C of E School

Cemetry

Mill Lane

Ham Road

SALISBURY

5

Road

Shalbourne

Manor House

Church Road

Ham

Kingston

Cox's Lane

PO

Carvers Hill

Burr Lane

River Road

Little Mead

The Lynch

6

Manor Farm

7

8

Rivar

A B C D E F

Wood

Anvilles

G H J K L M

I

2

3

4

34

5

6

7

8

Balsdon Farm

Totterdown House

Little Common

Sadlers

Sadlers Road

Anville's Copse

perous

Berkshire Circular Routes

West Berkshire
Wiltshire County

Lower Spray Farm

Spray Road

Ham Spray House

Northcroft Farm

Folly Road

Inkpen

Craven Road

PH

Lower Green

Bitham Lane

Cemetery

Manor Farm

Upper

Combe Gibbet

Test Way

Combe Gibbet

Town Farm

Downs Lane

Ro

Buttermere

Heat

Wright's Farm

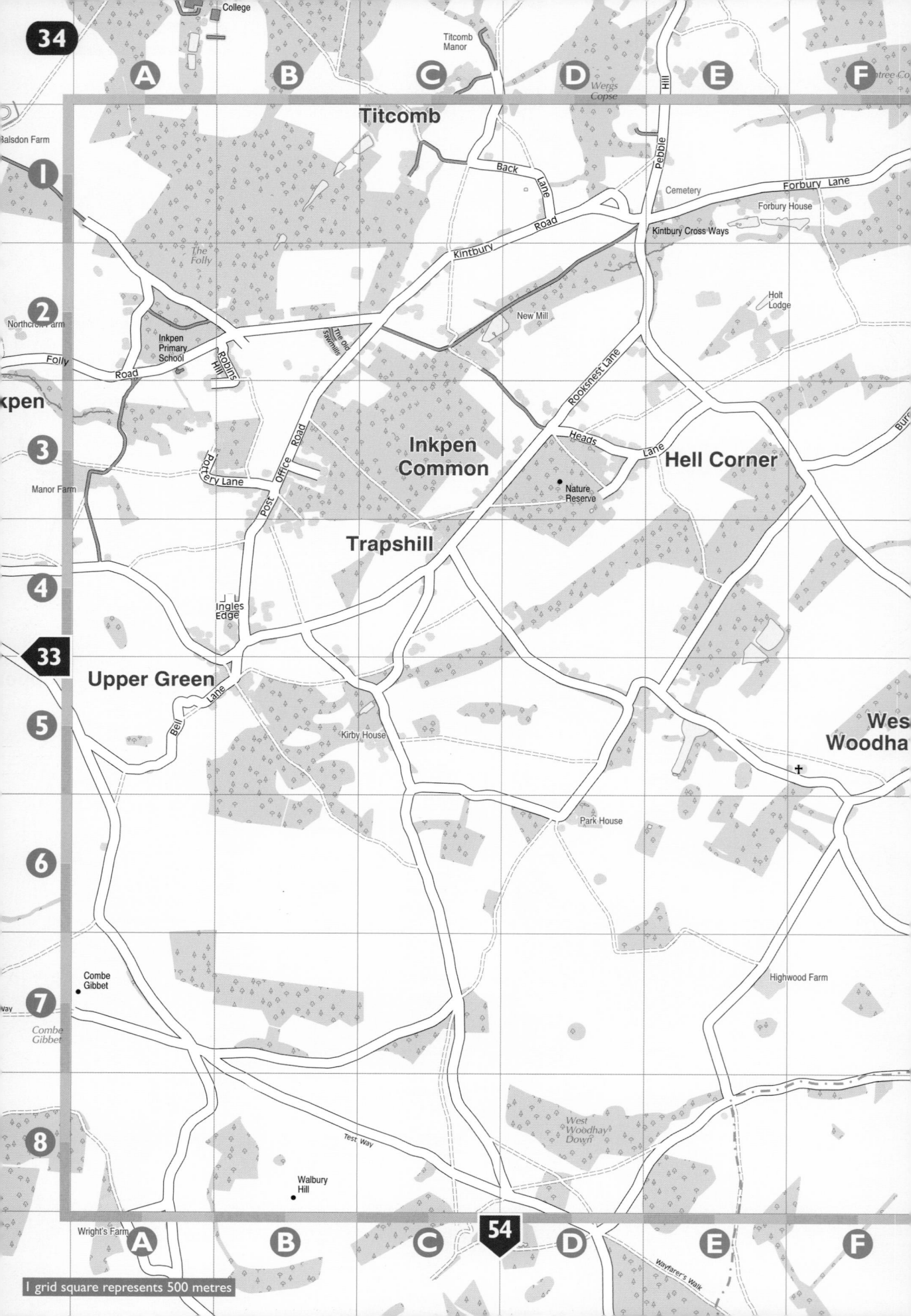

34

A　　B　　C　　D　　E　　F

Titcomb

College

Titcomb
Manor

Wergs
Copse

Balsdon Farm

1

Back Lane

Forbury Lane

Cemetery

Forbury House

Kintbury Cross Ways

Pebble Hill

The
Folly

Kintbury

New Mill

Holt
Lodge

2

Northcroft Farm

Folly

Road

Inkpen Primary
School

Robins Hill

The Old
Sawmills

Rooksnest Lane

kpen

3

Manor Farm

Pottery Lane

Post Office Road

**Inkpen
Common**

Nature
Reserve

Heads
Lane

Hell Corner

Burr

Trapshill

4

Ingles
Edge

33

Upper Green

Bell Lane

Kirby House

**Wes
Woodha**

5

Park House

†

6

Combe
Gibbet

Highwood Farm

7

Combe
Gibbet

way

Test Way

West
Woodhay
Down

8

Walbury
Hill

Wright's Farm

A　　B　　C　　**54**　　D　　E　　F

Wayfarer's Walk

I grid square represents 500 metres

G H J K L M

I

Kintbury
Holt Farm

Hamstead Marshall PH

Plumb's Farm

Great
Holt
Copse

Ash Tree
Grove

2

Holtwood Road

Redhill
Wood

Waterman's Farm

Vanne

3

Holt
Manor Farm

Watery   Lane

Holtwood

Malt House

West Berkshire
Hampshire County

4

Hatt Common

Gore End

36

Hazelby House

Gore End Road

Knights
Lea

Knights Lane

Ball Hill

5

Fishponds Farm

Gravelly
Cl

**North
End**

Burlyns

Oakhurst

6

Woo
Hou

Hatch
House Farm

Northenby

Hayes

**Heath
End**

7

Woolton
House

Copse Farm

8

Doctors
Surgery

Barn
Croft

Fullers Lane

Malverleys

Copnor
Close

G H J **55** K L M

East Woodhay

St Martins East Woodhay
College of Education
Primary School

East

G H J 25 K L M **Meenham**
Greenham Lodge

John Rankin Junior School
1 Monkswood Cl
2 Monument Cl
John Rankin County Inf School

G3
1 Bledlow Cl

Bartlemy

Tarn Lane

Croft Road

Friars Rd
Abbey

Springfield La

PO

Gringales

Greyberry

New Road

Wormery Rd

H1
1 Sutherlands

Monkswood Cl
Montgomery Rd

Three Acre
The Marlowes
Roberts Rd

Culver Rd

Brian Rd

Sandleford Hospital

Christie Hts

Bodin Gdns

Savers Cl

Water Lane

Bury's

Middle Fields
Home
Island

Sandleford Rise

Robins Cl

Sandleford

PO

Sandleford Rise

Newbury Retail Park

Equine Wy

Equine W

Deadmans Lane

Pinchington Lane

The Triangle

Rokeby Cl

I

Barn Crse
Elizabeth
Hill Cl

Essex St

Cary Cl

Road

Battery End

Falkland CP School

Spencer Rd

Middle Avenue
Woodside
Sidestrand Rd

ANDOVER ROAD

Tydehams

AppleTree Cl

Pond Cl

Wood Rdg

Monks Lane

The Natural Health Cen

Kennedy

Falkland Rd

Charles St

St Gabriels

Falkland Garth

Dormer Rd

Park House School

Falkland Memorial

Sunley

Warren Road

Warren Lodge

Round End

Kendrick Rd

The Gabriels

The Hollies

A343

ANDOVER

Ladwell Cl

Garden Close Lane

Wash Common

Newbury Rugby Football Club Ltd

NEWTOWN ROAD

St Gabriels School

2

3

A339(T)

Sandleford Place

Newbury Retail Park

Meenham

Bury's

Falkland Farm

West Berkshire County
Hampshire County

River Enborne

B4640

Newtown House

Newtown

PO

Jonathan Hill

Adbury

4

38 Adbury

5

Horris Hill Preparatory School

B4640

Newtown Common

Broken Way

Burghclere Common

Adbury Park

Adbury F

6

7

Tot Hill

A34(T)

Woodbine La

Deadmoor Lane

Sheepwash Lane

Pinewood Dr

Yeomans La

Heatherwold

Earlstone Common

Ayres

Breachfield

8

G H J 57 K L M

Burghclere
B4640

The Clere Secondary School

Limes Av

L
1 The Halters
2 Horseshoe End
3 Stirrup Pightle

K1
1 Pinchington La

Palmer's Hill House

A1
1 Marchant Cl
2 Pritchard Cl

Greenham
Greenham Lodge

A **B** **C** **26** **D** **E** **F**

Young
Crs

Greyberry Copse Road

Farm
Rd

New Road
Wormersley
Rd
1
2
Pigeons

Water Lane

Bury's Bank Road

Golf Course

Pigeon's Farm

Bowdown House

River Kennet

I

The
Round House

**Bury's
Bank**

2

Greenham Common
Airfield (disused)

Bury's Bank Road

3

Watermill Theatre

Seventh
St
Sixth St
Fifth
St
Warehouse Rd
Third Street
Barracks Rd
Third St
Second street
Second
Main
St
Ministry Road
First St
Street
New Greenham Park
Leisure Cen

**Goldfinch
Bottom**

Foxhold

A339(T)

4

River Enborne

Thornford Road

37

Adbury House

Aldern
Bridge House

Sydmonton
Common

**Bishop's
Green**

Knightsbridge
House

Knightsbridge
Dr

5

Ash
Rd
Beech Rd
Ash
Rd
Willow
Rd
Eagle Road

Rooksfield

6

A339(

Adbury Farm

Hyde Lane

Headley Stud

7

North
Sydmonton House

North
Ecchinswell Farm

8

Frith

A **B** **C** **58** **D** **E** **F**

**Brock's
Green**

Hyde
Farm

A B C D E F

Sawyers Ley
Wokefield Rw
Cross Lane
Bloomfield Hatch
Cross Lane

I

Mortimer Lane
Mortimer Ho
Mortimer Park
Wokefield Park

2

Nightingale Lane
Wheat's Farm
Berkshire Circular Routes
Great Park Farm
Trunkwell House

Monktons Lane

3

The Street
St Marys School
Church Barns
Mortimer Lodge
Stratfield Mortimer
Station Road
Mortimer Station

Circular Routes

4

The Forehead
Perrins Farm

43

5

Little Park Farm

Park Lane

6

Butlers Lands
West Berkshire
Hampshire County
Park Lane
Home

7

Wigmore Farm
Forelands
New Street
New Street

8

Lavell's Lane
The Springs
Mortimer Lane
Green Lane
West End Green
Green Lane
Stratfield Saye
Herriot's

A B C D E F

Fair Oak Lane
Kings Farm

1 grid square represents 500 metres

A B C D E F

I

The
Street

2

Trowe's Lane

3

45

4

5

6

7

8

Swallowfield Medical Practice

PO 1

The Naylors

Foxborough

Part Lane

Brookside Business Centre

Swallowfield

PH

Rowe's Farm

Cemetery

Swallowfield Park

Swallowfield Road

Swallowfield Road

Tanner's Farm

Kiln Hill

Castle Hill

A2 1 Curleys Wy

The Chatters

Bungler's Hill

Farley Court

Nuthean Lane

Sandpit Lane

The Broadwater

Ford Lane

Trowe's Lane

Riseley Farm

Part Lane

School Lane

School Road

Benham La

Part Lane

Wokingham

Hampshire County

Wellington Country Park

Cordery's Farm

Well House Lane

Well House

Bramshill Plantation

Riseley Mill

ODIHAM ROAD

Hall's Farm

Ford Lane

Springwater Farm

Park Farm

River Whitewater

A B C D E F

Bramshill

I grid square represents 500 metres

G H I J K L M

ROAD
Vennin... Rd
Isaac Newton Rd
HEME Museum
...field
Biggs Lane
Baird
...shill Close
Whitehall
Buttenshaw Avenue
But...
Tope Rd
Parsons
Stephen's

**Arborfield
Garrison**

I

Eversley
Baird
Fleming Tcl
2
1
Tyler Dr
Sheerlands
Road
Barker... Dr
Princess Marina Drive
Rowcroft Rd
Nuffield   Road
Whitworth Rd
James Watt Road

California
Country
Park

Long
Moor

Parsons Farm

Westwood
Farm

Sheerlands   Road

Weller Dr
Hogwood La
Marino Way
Ivanhoe Road

Coleshill Farm

2

Nine Mile

A327

Hogwood Farm

Park Lane

White Horse Lane

3

Farley Hill

...urch
Lane

Larchwood Farm

West Court

Park Lane

Wheatlands
Manor

4

READING

The
Leas

Bulloway's Farm

Lea Farm
Park Lane

Banisters Farm

48

5

Blackwater River

New Mill

New Mill Lane

New
Mill
Lane

ROAD

The   Rise

Fleet Lane

Fincha

FLEET   HILL

6

Oaklea
Drive

Fleethill Farm

7

Lower
Common
Road

Mud La

Lower Common

Warbrook Lane

EVERSLEY STREET

Eversley

Wokingham
Hampshire County

St Neots
Preparatory
School

Neot's

St

Warbrook

8

B3272

READIN

Glaston Hill Road
Kingsley Road

Charles
Kingsley
School

G H J K L M

Glaston
Hill House

Three

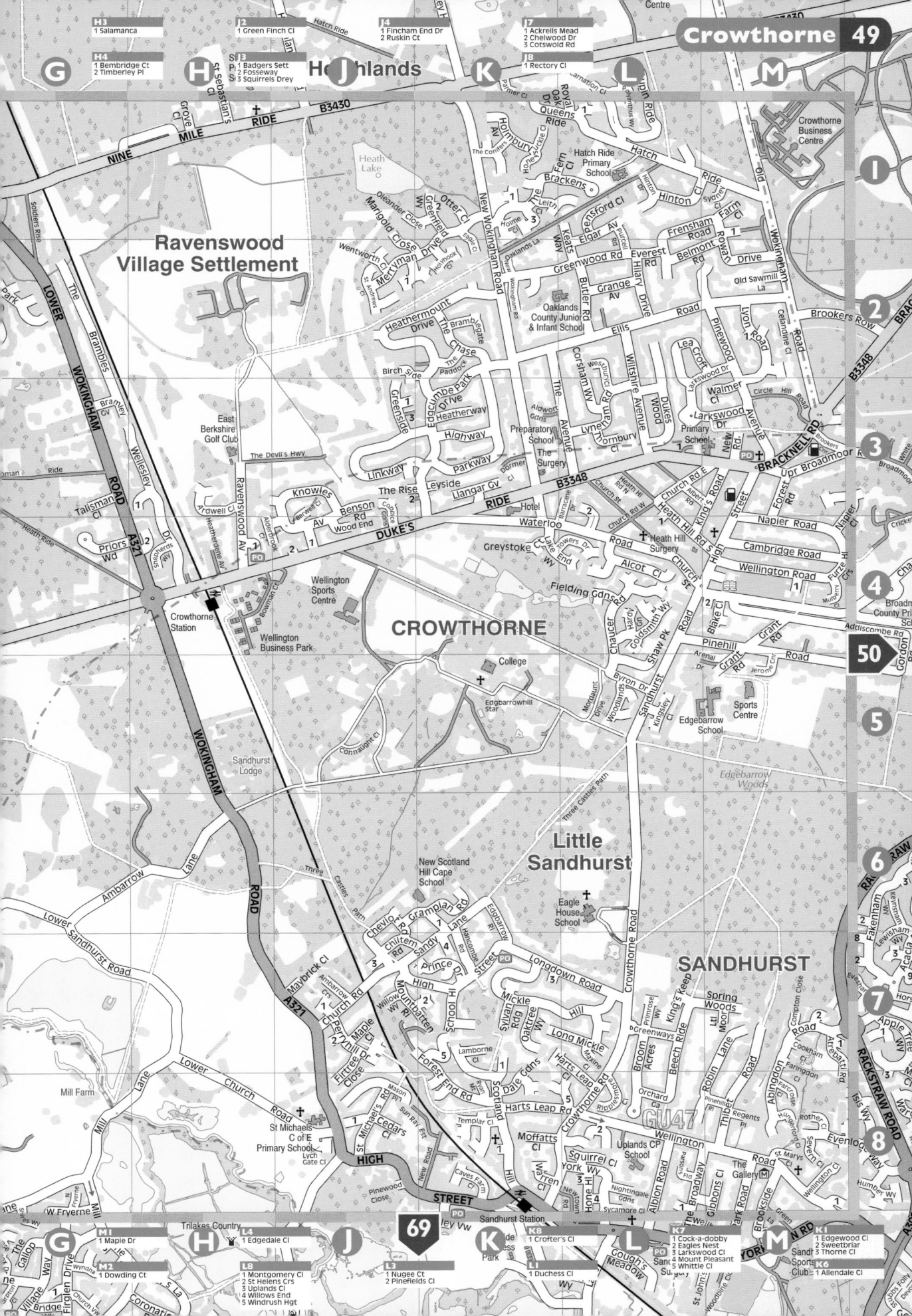

Highlands

Ravenswood
Village Settlement

East
Berkshire
Golf Club

The Devil's Hwy

Crowthorne
Station

Wellington
Business Park

Wellington
Sports
Centre

CROWTHORNE

College

Edgbarrowhill
Star

Sandhurst
Lodge

New Scotland
Hill Cape
School

**Little
Sandhurst**

Eagle
House
School

Edgbarrow
School

Sports
Centre

Edgbarrow
Woods

SANDHURST

Crowthorne
Business
Centre

Oaklands
County Junior
& Infant School

Preparatory
School

The Surgery

Hotel

Heath Hill
Surgery

Spring
Woods

Mill Farm

St Michaels
C of E
Primary School

Sandhurst Station

GU47

G M1
1 Maple Dr
M2
1 Dowding Ct

H L4
1 Edgedale Cl

J 69

K

L L7
1 Montgomery Cl
2 St Helens Crs
3 Uplands Cl
4 Willows End
5 Windrush Hgt
L8
1 Nugee Ct
2 Pinefields Cl

K7
1 Cock-a-dobby
2 Eagles Nest
3 Larkswood Cl
4 Mount Pleasant
5 Whittle Cl
K8
1 Crofter's Cl
L6
1 Duchess Cl

M M1
1 Edgewood Cl
2 Sweetbriar
3 Thorne Cl
M6
1 Allendale Cl

A　　　**B**　　　**C**　　　**D**　　　**E**　　　**F**

1

Crowthorne
Business
Centre

2

BRACKNELL ROAD
B3348

RG45

FORESTERS WAY
A3095

Crowthorne
Wood

3

Upr Broadmoor Rd
Broadmoor Rd
White City
Kentigern Drive
The Terrace
Cricket Fld-Gv
Napier

Three Castles Path

4

Chaplain's Hill
Broadmoor Hospital
School Hill
Broadmoor County Primary School
Lower Broadmoor Road
Eastern Lane

49

Addiscombe Rd
Gordon Rd
South Meadow
Three Castles Path
Broadmoor Farm

5

South Road
A3095
FORESTERS WAY

6

RACKSTRAW ROAD
A3095
Copperfield Av
Magdalene Road
Owlsmoor
Fakenham
Lewisham Wy
Acacia Av
Union
Church Road
Durham Rd
Oxford Rd
Rowood Av
Cambridge Road
Owlsmoor Primary School
Merton Cl
Trinity
Yale Cl
Peterhouse
Nuffield
Waltham

7

Compton Close
Road
Cookham
Faringdon
Apple Tree Wy
Oak Avenue
Owlsmoor
Evenham Wy
Horsham
May Cl
Millns Cl
Victoria Rd
PO
Yeovil
The Surgery
Brook
Balliol Way
Girton
Birkbeck Pl
Harvard Rd

College Town

8

RACKSTRAW ROAD
A3095
Attebatti Rd
Wellington
St Marys
Avocet Crs
Bittern Cl
Blackbird
Blackcap Pl
Sandhurst School
Silver Hl
Hallmark Cl
Cannon Close
Range Vw
College Crs
The Close
Junior School
Richmond Rd
Windsor Ride
The Hospital
Epsom Close
Goodwood
DAWNAY ROAD
Matthews

A　　　**B**　　　**C**　　　70　　　**D**　　　**E**　　　**F**

VN RD
A3095
Sandhurst Sports Club
Branksome Hill Road
College Road
The Breach
Clarke Crs
Pine Cl
Range Ride
Wood Road
Egerton Road
Hillside
Dawnay Road
Old Green Lane

J8
1 Horseshoe Cl

K8
1 Caesar's Cl

L8
1 Maultway Cl
2 Ramsay Cl

G   H   J   K   L   M

1

Rapley Farm

2

Rapley Lake

3

Bracknell Forest
Surrey County

4

BAGSH

Bagshot
Heath

Vicarage Road

Connaught Rd
Wellesley Cl
Ride

Higgs La
St Annes
Grd
Chur

5

Pinewood Gdns

College

Heywood Dr
Yaverland Dr

Hotel

JENKINS HILL LONDON RO

6

Lupin Cl

7

Bracknell Road

Pineridge County First School

Mitcham Road

Subiton Rd
Kingston Rd
Esher Rd
Sutton Rd
Carshalton Rd
Wychwood Pl
Mitcham Rd
Maultway N

Highview Crs
Wimbledon Road
Bracknell Cl

First School

Collingwood College

LONDON ROAD
B3015 THE MAULTWAY

Collingwood Gra
Maultwa
Foxhill Crs
B3015

7

Queen Elizabeth Rd
Everest Rd
Duke of Cornwall Av

Olddean Common

Academy Close

Larch Av
Birch Rd
Saddleback Road
Star Post Road
Wishmoor Ct

Hampshire Road
Middle School

Horseshoe Crs
Berkshire Road
Kingston
Ballard Road
Paschal Rd
Caesar's Rd

Lorraine Rd

College
Highland Road
Poophills Rd
Rapley Cl
Rowan

Turf Hill Rd
Cordwallis Rd

Deer Rock Rd
Upper
Wickham Rd

PO
1

Ltl Paddock

The
Buchan

Tree Tops Av
Buchan

Seymour Dr
Ellis

Wishmoor Bottom

8

Whitehill Cl
College
Barossa
College Cl
Fosswood Cl
Upland Road
Old Dean
Diamond Ridge
Diamond Hl

G   H   **71**   J   K   L   M

CAMBERLEY
ROAD

Crosby Hill Dr
Crawley Ridge

A325
Gibbet La
Beaufront

Hillcrest Road
Waterloo
Paget
Clarence Dr

Oaken Copse
Heathside

A B C D E F

Rivar

32

Wood

1

Rivar
Down

2

New
Buildings

Ashley Drove

Hung

3

n's Farm

Bishop's Barn

4

Manor Farm

Ashley   Drove

Moordown Farm

5

Smay
Down

Smay Down Lane

PO

Oxenwood

Henley

6

Pearce's Farm

Fosbury House

†

Upper
Row Farm

7

Church Farm

Beacon Farm

Fosbury

Wiltshire County
Hampshire County

8

Vernham
Row

A B C D E F

72

Tunball Lane

East
Down

Bowers Lane

G H J K L M

33

Wright's Farm

1

Town Farm
Road
Downs Lane
Buttermere
Heath Lane
Grange Farm
Church Lane
Farm Lane
White
Manor Farm
Buttermere Wood
Ballyack House
Upper ns Farm
Rockmoor Down
Wiltshire County
Hampshire County
Rockmoor Lane
Winterside Farm
Littledown
Vernham Street
Box Farm
n Lane

Test Way
Test Way
Combe Wood
Test Way
Hart Hill Down
Manor House
PO
Manor Farm
Test Way

Link

2

3

4

54

5

6

7

8

G H J K L M

73

54

A B Walbury Hill C **34** D E F

Test Way

West Woodhay Down

Wright's Farm

Lower Farm

Wayfarer's Walk

Combe

Manor Farm

Church Lane

Hampshire County West Berkshire

Eastwick

Hogs Hole

53

West Berkshire
Hampshire County

Test Way

Faccombe

Manor House

Linkenholt

PO

Netherton

Manor Farm

A B C **74** D E F

I grid square represents 500 metres

G   H   J   **35**   K   L   M

Doctors
Surgery

Copnor
Close

East Woodhay

Barn
Croft

Fullers L

Malverleys

St Martins East Woodhay
College of Education
Primary School

**East
End**

Stargrove

I

Hotel

2

Tower House

Hollington Lane

Wayfarer's Walk

Wayfarer's
Walk

Jones' Farm

3

Wayfarer's Walk

Hollington Lane

Hollingto   **4**

Kinghams Farm

56

5

6

Coles
Wood

Wayfarer's Walk

7

Curzon
Street Farm

Privet
Copse

Manor Farm

8

Bath Close Lane

Cross Lane

HILL

G   H   J   **75**   K   L   M

PO

Ashmansworth

Steeles Farm

Three Ashes

hmere Green

Bramley
Corner

Bramley

Bramley Gree

Cufaude

G H J K L M

K5
1 Pheaben's Fld

L5
1 Jibbs Meadow
2 Longbridge Rd

M6
1 Beech Cl

kledon's Farm

Lavell's

Lavell

The
Springs

Clappers Farm

43

64

83

Bramley Road

Lower Farm

Haines Farm

Barefoot
House

Holly
Cross

Bramley
Lane

Bramley C of E
Primary School

Clift
Surgery

Minchens Lane

Minchens Lane

Moat Close

Browns
Cl

Bramley

Meitner Cl

Tottenham Cl

Bromelia
Close

PO

Osler Cl

Strawberry Fields

Oliver's Farm

Oliver's Lane

Stratfield Saye Road

Folly

Folly Farm

Bramley
Station

The Street

Pound Cl

Ringshall
Gdns

Ringshall Gdns

Ellen Gdns

Coopers Lane

LC

Sherfield Road

Longbridge Rd

Dollis
Gn

Coopers Ct

The
Smithy

Farriers Cl

Silchester

Middle Farm

Beaurepaire Cl

Church Lands

The Street

The Maltings

Lane End

Lane End

End

3

Pigeon
Green

Forge
Road

Bramley
Green

Holly

1
2
4

German
Road

St John
Road

Taylor Dr

Campbell

The
Lime
Av

St Mar

Wallis Dr
sims

Officers Row

Locksbridge Lane

Vyne Road

Bow Brook

Watford
Copse

Baker's
Farm

Vyne
Lodge Farm

Ragg
Copse

G H I 2 3 4 5 6 7 8

M

G H J K L M

45

I
2
3
4
66
5
6
7
8

85

G H J K L M

Heckfield

Stratfield Saye

River Loddon

Stratfield Saye Park

Wellington Monument

The Causeway

Church Lane

B3349

Highfield House

Hotel

Park Pitham Copse

BASINGSTOKE ROAD

A33

Lower Pitham

Hotel

PH

Lawn Farm

Daneshill School

Home Farm

Bylands Farm

Sheldons Farm

Hartley House

Chandlers Green

Vicarage Lane

Thackham's Farm

Blue House Farm

Bottle Lane

rtley espall

Rotherwick Lane

Rotherwick Lane

Frog Lane

Mill Farm

Black Wood

READING

G H J K L M

47

B3272

Glaston Hill Road

Charles Kingsley School

St Neots Preparatory School

Warbrook

Kingsley Road

Three Cas

Glaston Hill House

1

Church Farm

A3272

2

Heath Warren

Bus

3

Three Castles Path

Warren Heath

4

68

5

A327

6

B3016

Hulford's Copse

HARTFORD BRIDGE FLATS

7

Purdies Farm

Star Hill Plantation

Hulfords Lane

STAR HILL

Springwell Lane

Hare's Lane

LONDON ROAD

Hartfordbridge

Elvetham Lane

8

Hares Farm

River Han

G H J K L M

87

Three Castles Path

B3011

Arrow Lane

Trefoil Cl

Franklin Av

BRACKNELL

Heather Gv

Heather Grove

Springfield

primr

Campion Wy

Harebell Cl

Hawkes

Hayward'n

Hare's La

The Paddock

Home Farm Rd

Elvetham Farm

Ivy

Lakeside Dr

Mansion Drive

Pool Road

River Hart

A **B** **C** **D** **E** **F**

50

69

90

A **B** **C** **D** **E** **F**

D7
1 Claydon Gdns

E2
1 Willington Cl

C5
1 Campion Cl

C7
1 Cypress
2 Fernhill Wk
3 Recreation Cl

C1
1 Church Rd

B3
1 Chestnut Cl

B4
1 Broom Cl
2 Glenhurst Cl
3 Ryecroft Gdns

B1
1 Rosedene La

B2
1 Hepworth Cft
2 Brown End
3 Seebys Oak
4 Thorburn Cha

A1
1 Balintore Ct
2 Burghead Cl
3 Castlecraig Ct
4 Findhorn Cl
5 Fortrose Cl
6 Hopeman Cl
7 Watern'se Mead

A2
1 Bacon Cl
2 Reynolds Gn

A3
1 Clanfield Ride
2 Russell Ct
3 Tichborne Cl

A4
1 Harlech Rd
2 Jays Nest Cl
3 Quebec Gdns
4 Springcross Av

A5
1 Belvedere Ct
2 Clarendon Ct

E3
1 Hatfield Ct
2 Heatherley Cl
3 Hollyfields Cl
4 Montague Cl
5 St Michaels Rd
6 Woodway

E4
1 Burford Rd
2 Butterfield
3 Crandall Ct
4 Donnington Cl

E5
1 Dorcas Ct

E6
1 Bramley Rd

E7
1 Mayfield Rd

E8
1 Prentice Cl

E9
1 St Mary's Rd

F1
1 Albert Rd
2 Bennett Ct
3 Park La

F3
1 Birchfields

1 grid square represents 500 metres

A B C **52** D E **Vernham RoF**

I

The Slay

Turnball Lane

East Down

Oakhill Wood

Fosbury Farm

2

Vernham Bank

Hippenscombe

254
▲
Haydown Hill

3

Conholt Hill

Cleves Copse

4

Little Down

Middle Conholt Farm

Chute Causeway

5

Conholt House

Du... Lane

6

Conholt Park

Hungerford Lane

Wiltshire County
Hampshire County

7

Hampshire Gate

Brean La

Standen House

Chute Standen

Cathanger Wood

8

Dummer Lane

Chute CCey **94** D E F

Dowlands Far

A B Chute C D E F

Lower Chute

†

Tangley

A   B   C   56   D   E   F

Cross Lane

Three Legs House

Wayfarer's Walk

1

HILL

A343

RED

Grotto
Copse

Highclere Stud

2

Mopper's Barn

ux Easton

3 †

Upper
Woodcott
Down

Wayfarer's Walk

4

Beech
Hanger
Copse

Lower
Woodcott
Down

75

Hook
Copse

5

Woodcott

Easton
6

†

Lower Woodcott Farm

7

Paul's
Copse

Stubb's
Copse

Woodcott House

8

Buckets Down Farm

Dunley

A   B   C   98   D   E   F

I grid square represents 500 metres

G H J K L M

57

99

Sydmonton

78

A B C **58** D E F

1

Watership Down

Wayfarer's Walk

2

Wayfarer's Walk

Cannon Heath Down

3

4

Ashley Warren Farm

77

Cannon Heath Farm

5

Hare Warren Farm

6

Polhampton Lodge Stud

B3051

Robley Belt

7

8

Caesar's Belt

A B C **100** D E F

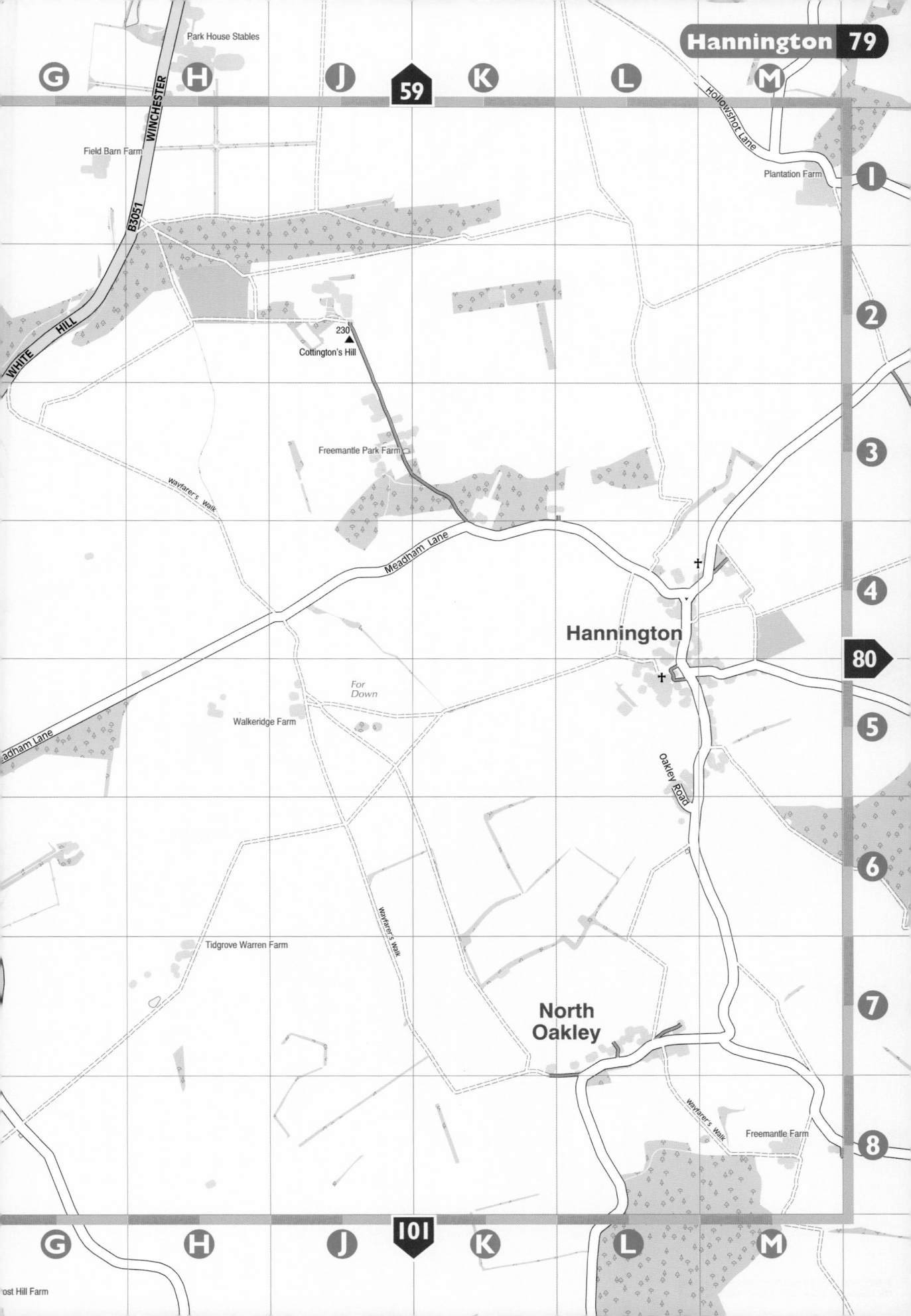

G   H   J   **59**   K   L   M

Park House Stables

WINCHESTER

Field Barn Farm

B3051

WHITE HILL

Hollowshot Lane

Plantation Farm

1

2

230
Cottington's Hill

3

Wayfarer's Walk

Freemantle Park Farm

Meadham Lane

4

Hannington

80

Meadham Lane

For
Down

Oakley Road

5

Walkeridge Farm

6

Tidgrove Warren Farm

Wayfarer's Walk

7

**North
Oakley**

Wayfarer's Walk

Freemantle Farm

8

G   H   J   **101**   K   L   M

ost Hill Farm

G6
1 Carpenter's Dn

G8
1 Lansley Rd
2 Normanton Rd
3 Stratfield Rd

H6
1 Falkland Rd
2 Montserrat Pl
3 Tasmania Cl

H8
1 Myland Cl

K5
1 Aghemund Cl
2 Southlands

K6
1 Great Oaks Cha
2 Longacre Ri
3 Minden Cl

L4
1 Greenwood Dr
2 Parkwood Cl
3 Renown Wy

L6
1 Bracken Bank
2 Clover Fld
3 Crofters Meadow
4 Dragonfly Dr

L7
1 Hazeldene
2 Remember. Gdns
3 St Joseph's Crs
4 Wallins Copse

M3
1 Brookfield Cl
2 Gilbard Ct
3 Guinea Ct
4 Nursery Cl
5 Warbleton Pl

M4
1 Belvedere Gdns
2 Copse View Cl
3 Summerfields
4 Woodlands

M5
1 Birchwood
2 Larchwood
3 Martins Wd
4 Thurnwood

M6
1 Merrydown La

M7
1 Beddington Ct

Cufaude

Upper Cufaude Farm

Cufaude Lane

Vyne (NT)

Vyne Farm

Razor's Farm

Carpenters Down Wood

Chineham
Whitewood

Popley
Fields House

Popley

Marnel Infant & Junior Schools

John Hunt of Everest Community School

Longfellow Parade Clinic

Bilton Industrial Estate

Superstore

Binfields Cl

Basingstoke & Deane Borough Council

Daneshill

Pyott's Hill

Foxs Furlo

Lovegroves

Four Lanes End

Pyotts Court

RINGWAY NORTH

A339

A33

Daneshill Industrial Estate

65

L7
1 Bowling Green Dr
2 Garden Cl
3 Shaw Pightle
4 Trust Cl
5 Whites Cl

L8
1 Froud Cl
2 Newnham Pk
3 Seton Dr

M6
1 Broad Leaze
2 Chalky Copse
3 Elms Rd
4 Ferndale Gdns
5 Hatchgate Mead
6 John Morgan Cl
7 Nursery Cl
8 Reading Rd
9 Wash Brook

G H J K L M

1

2

3

4

86

5

6

7

8

Lyde Green

Rotherwick

Lampards Cl

Wedman's Lane

Cowfold Lane

Street End Copse

Reaon Pond

Black Wood

Whitewater C of E (Controlled) Primary School

The Street

Hook Road

Mill Farm

Mill Lane

Frog Lane

Summerstead Farm

Lyde River

The Old House

Tylney Park Golf Club

Post Horn Lane

Newnham

Hotel

Tylney House

Ridge Lane

Tylney Lane

Newnham Lane

Manor Farm

Owen's Farm

Crown Lane

Newnham Road

Nately Scures

107

Old School Rd

Morris Street

London Road A30

Hook Common

A287

Hook Station

Osborn Way Industrial Est

Reading Road

Coppice

Great Sheldons Coppice

Elms Road

Dorchester Road

Sheldon's Rd

Carleton

Memorial Road

Rectory Road

Bell Meadow

Station

M7
1 Butts Meadow
2 Harfield Cl
3 Middle Mead

G H J K L M

B3349

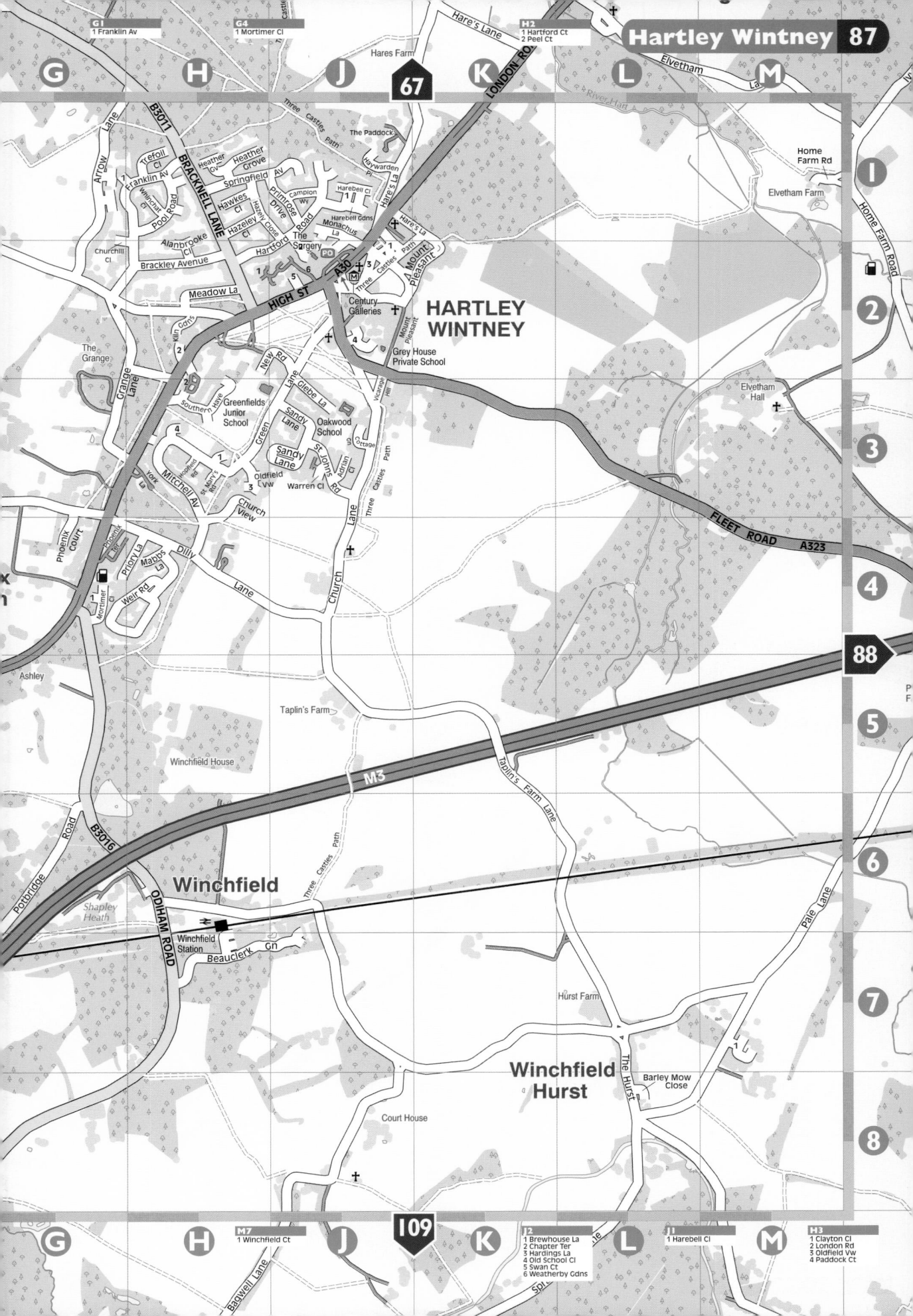

Map Grid References

Brook House

MINLEY ROAD A327

Junction 4a

M3

Pinewood Park

Guillemont County Junior School

Sandy Lane

Nightingale Close

Bramshot Lane

Minley Rd

Marlborough

Guillemont Flds

Juniper Rd

Herbs End

Broadhurst

Fennel Cl

Howard Dr

Lindsey Cl

Brownsover Rd

Whetstone ROAD

Holmbrook Close

GU

Jubilee Clo

Apollo

Armstrong M

Aldrin Place

Doctors Surgery

Chiltern

Harvest Crs

Barley Wy

Ancells

Shetland Way

Rifle Road

Oasthouse Dr

Angora Way

Swaledale

Ellen Dr

Drovers End

Falkners Cl

Friesian Cl

Chessum Cl

Galloway Cl

Sussex Gdns

Devon

Farm

Guernsey

Highland Dr

Hanover

Forest Dean

shire Av

South

Sankey Lane

Great Bramshott Farm

B3014   FLEET

Summit Rd

Columbus Drive

SUMMIT AVE

Gleneagles Wy

Long Beech Dr

Laurel

Links

Fox Heath

Randolph Dr

Deiville Cl

Copse

Southwood

COVE ROAD

COVE ROAD A3013

FLEET ROAD

Southwood Lane

A327

Old Cove Rd

Lakeside Ct

Waterside Court

Attenborough

Fleet Station

Fleet Pond

Station Industrial Estate

Kennels Lane

Chestnut Grove

Brookly Gdns

Pondview Cl

Kenilworth Crs

Fugelmere Rd

Kenilworth ROAD

Monteir Gdns

Woodside Gdns

Weir

Constant Road

Bramshott Road

Roxbee Cox Rd

The Romany

The Howe

Donlan Dr

Ively Road

Westover

Lestock Wy

Williams Way

Cypress Dr

Lyndale Road

Rowan Cl

Farnham Road

Marlborough Gdns

Westbury Gdns

Barford

The Fairway

Armstrong Way

Ively Road

Boundary Road

Vulcan Way

Victor

Kevins Dr

Southby Dr

KINGS

Adams Drive

Camden Walk

Howard Cl

Cedar Dr

Guildford Road

Alton Road

Albany Cl

Elms Road

PO

ROAD

A323

St Michaels Cl

Pondtail Gdns

Pondtail

Crown Gdns

The Aloes

Firtree Way

Priors Keep

Velmead Rd

NORRIS ROAD

Norris Bridge

69

90

III

G6
1 St Nicholas Cl

G   H   J   K   L   M

Chute Down

ngbourne

1 owe

Coldridge Wood

Honey Bottom

2

Jolly's Farm

Forest House

3

Stert Copse

Coldridge Down

4

94

Long Bottom

5

Longbottom Farm

Biddesden House

6

Biddesden Lane

Crawlboys Lane

Wiltshire County

Hampshire County

7

Wiltshire

Hampshire

Maple Crs
Elm Cl
Abbatt Cl
Spray Leaze
1

Biddesden Lane

Grasslan Rd
Pretoria Rd

Faberstown

ROAD
A342

8

Redenham Drove

New House

Tilly Down

ANDOVER ROAD
A3

116

Redenham House

Redenham

G H J 73 K L M

I
2
3
4
96
5
6
7
8

Locke's Drove

Whistler's Farm

Pill
Heath Farm

Tangley
Farm

Blagden
Copse

Blagden House

Doles Farm

Wildhern

The Avenue

Plough Farm

Hatherden
Manor

Hungerford Lane

The Close

Hatherden
House

Hungerford Lane

Cemetery

Hatchet Lane

Hatherden C of E
Primary School

Hatherden

Goddards Farm

Pigeon
House Farm

Charlton Down
Farm

Greer

A343 NEWBURY ROAD

Cullum
more
Close

NEWBURY

Newbury
Road

PO

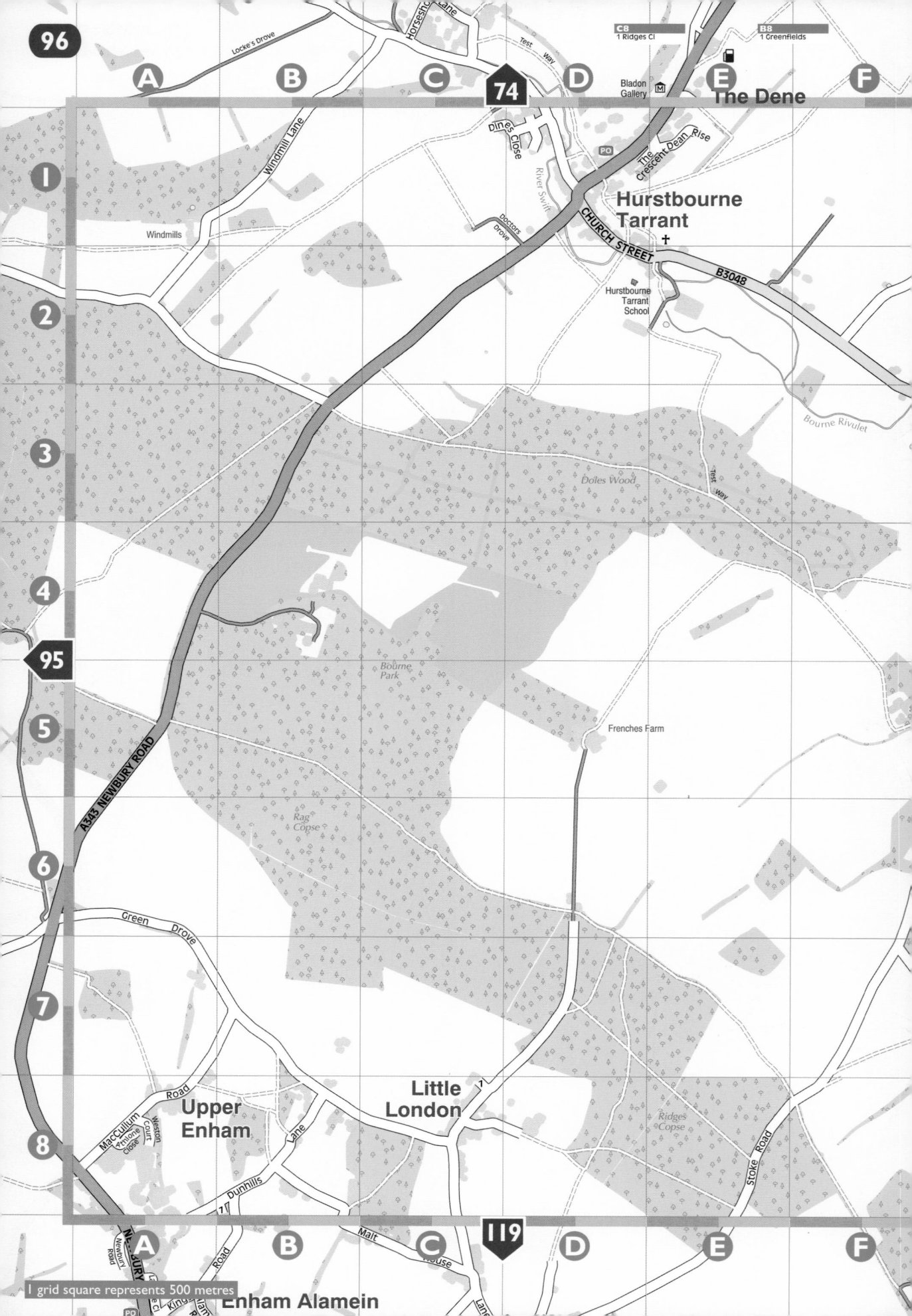

A B C D E F

74

C8
1 Ridges Cl

B8
1 Greenfields

The Dene

1

Windmills

Windmill Lane

Horseshoe Lane

Test Way

Dines Close

Bladon
Gallery

PO

The Crescent

Dean Rise

River Swift

PO

Hurstbourne
Tarrant

Doctors
Drove

CHURCH STREET

†

B3048

Hurstbourne
Tarrant
School

Bourne Rivulet

2

3

Doles Wood

Test Way

4

95

Bourne
Park

5

Frenches Farm

A343 NEWBURY ROAD

6

Green Drove

Rag
Copse

7

Upper
Enham

MacCullum

Weston
Court

Antons
Close

Little
London

Ridges
Copse

Stoke Road

8

NEWBURY

Newbury
Road

Road

Lane

Dunhills

Malt House

Lane

A B C 119 D E F

Enham Alamein

PO

Kingsmill

G H J 75 K L M Binley

I

2

3

4

98 Cold H

5

6

7 Bourne

8

Prior's Farm

Slade Bottom Farm

Elm Farm

Binley Bottom

ANE

B3048

Long Leaze Chapel La

Stoke

Stoke Hill

Gangbridge Lane

Wakeswood

Wadwick Bottom

Swampton

Spring Hill Lane

Oak Tree Farm

Test Way

School

Baptist Hill

Batsford

Hurst Copse

Edbury

PO

PH

Upper Wyke

Stevens Green

St Mary Bour

Bourne Meadow

B3048

Test Way

Derry Down Health Clinic

South Vw

wood

Middle W Farm

Derrydown Farm

G H J 120 K L M

Road

Test Way

Wormley Copse

Litchfield

G H J **77** K L M

I

2

3

4

I00

5

6

7

8

G H J **I22** K L M

Angledown Copse

Clap Gate

Twinley Manor

Cole Henley Manor Farm

Cole Henley

RG28

Larks

Barrow

Hill

A34(T)

Newbury Road

Harroway

Down Farm

Wooldings Farm

The Orchards

Watch Lane

Harroway

Priory Lane

Watch Lane

Vw Cottages

Home F

Farm

100

A   B   C   78   D   E   F

1

I

Ridgeway Farm

Willesley Warren Farm

2

3

4

99

Whitnal

New Barn

5

Court Drove

6

Hill Meadow

Watch Lane

7

Primary School

Court Fa

Lordsfield Gdns

Glebe Meadow

Lynch

White Hart Gallery

8

Watch Lane

The Lynch

Southington Close

Silk Mill Lane

Southington Lane

Court Drove

Red Lion Lane

HIGH ST

Harvey's Fld

Oak Close

S VW Cottages

A   B   C   123   D   B3400   E   F

Southington

Deiiands Lane

1 grid square represents 500 metres

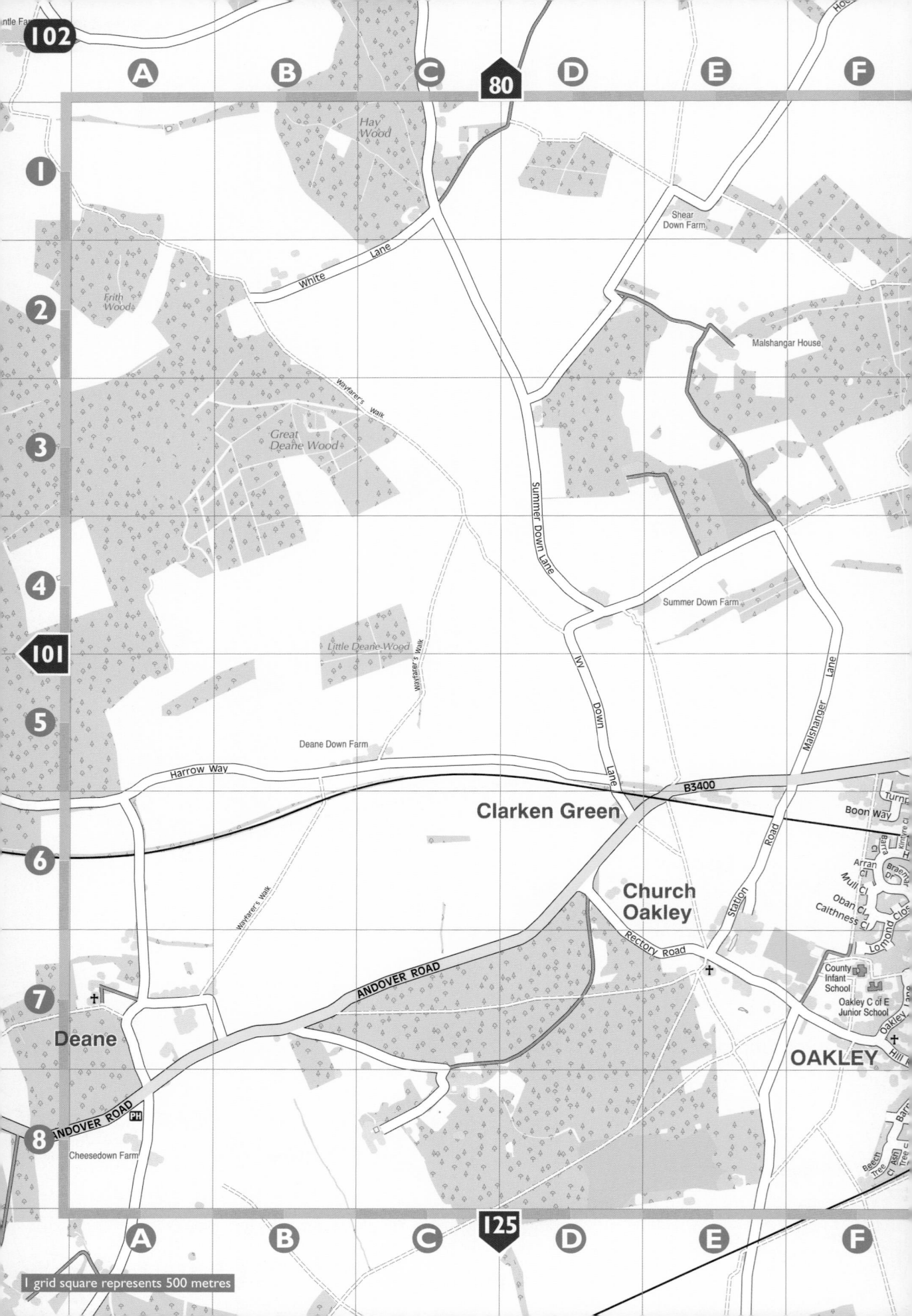

G6
1 Marlbo. Gdns

G7
1 Blackwater Cl
2 Hamble Cl
3 Medina Gdns

L8
1 Eagle Cl
2 Hawk Cl
3 Seagull Cl

G   H   J   **81**   K   L   M

I

Tangier

PO

✝

Wootton St Lawrence

Worting Wood Farm

2

3

Roman Way
Tiverton
Aylings Cl
Ways

Worting

Worting House

Wykeham Drive

Glebe Lane

Church La

West

RG23

B3400   WORTING   ROAD   B3400   WORTING   ROAD

✝

PO

Worting County Infant School

Cotswold

Junior School

4

✝

Mourne

B

104

Hampshire

Highlands Rd

Chiltern

5

Newfound

Dell Farm

Foxmoor
Tollgate
Hunters Cl
Dellfield
Fox Lane

Lightsfield
Pack Lane

Berwyn
Malvern
Mendip

Kempshott

Old

Lowland's Rd

Melford Gdns
Melford Gdns

Chilterns

Dalewood Wy

Cleveland

Buckskin Lane

Stratton

6

Pack Lane   Pack Lane

Pack La

PO

East Oakley

Well's Copse

Oakley Road
Cadnam Cl
Tanner's Cl
Dever Way
Aston
Itchen Cl
Springfield
Medway Av
Meon Cl
Avon Cl
Lyde Close
Kennet Rd
Lifton Cres
Stour
Severn Gdns
Matthews Way
Frome Close
John's Rd
Hoopers Way
Link Way
The Drive
Oak Hazel
Kings Orchard
St John's Piece
Goddard's Firs
St John's Road
Hill
Water Ridges
Sunny
Saltram Lane
Pardown

Battledown Farm

Windermere Av

Kestrel Road

Linnet Cl

Curlew
Plover

Kestrel Rd
Dove Cl
Kingfisher Close
Kestrel Cl

✝

Windermere Av
Derwent Rd
Derwent Rd
Derwent Rd
Coniston Rd

Homestead Road

Holy Barn

Kenda Gdns

Pack Lane

7

Con900
Conwy Rd
Conwy Rd
Conwy Rd

Kempshott

Osprey Cl

Osprey Rd

Falcon Cl

Heron Wy

Robin Cl

Kempshott County Infant School

Merriels
Homestead

Junior School

8

Lark
Starling Close
Swallow Close
Chaffinch Cl

Pheasant Close
Magpie Close
Woodpecker Close
Blackbird

Heron Way

Fuzzy Drove

Petunia Drive

Columbine Rd

Daffodil
Marigold

Hollyhock
Rose Cl

Jasmine Road

Breach Farm

Fairview Meadow
The Surgery

Lupin Cl
Lily Cl
Begonia Cl

Veronica
Foxglove

Lavender
Heather

G   **H**   **J**   **126**   **K**   **L**   **M**   **9**

M8
1 Dahlia Cl
2 Honeysuckle Cl
3 Hyacinth Cl
4 Kempshott Gdns
5 Petrel Cft
6 Snowdrop Cl

M5
1 Sidlaw Cl

M4
1 Kempshott Gv

A30

G   H   J   87   K   L   M

Court House

Bagwell Lane

Sprat's Hatch Lane

Basingstoke Canal

Swan's Farm

Dogmersfield C of E Primary School

1

Dogmersfield

2

Sprat's Hatch Farm

Tundry Pond

3

Sprat's Hatch Lane

Odiham Common

Great Park

Ormersfield Farm

Three Castles Path

Dogmersfield Lake

4

Dogmersfield Park

110

Chalky Lane

Coxmoor Wood

5

Farnham Rd

A287

FARNHAM ROAD

Coxmoor Farm Light Industrial Est

6

Bullock's Farm

Small Acres Farm

Rye Common

Mill Lane

7

Buttridge

8

G   H   J   132   K   L   M

Roke Lane

Home Farm

Roke Farm

1 Brisbane Cl
2 Sydney Cl

G **H** **J** 92 **K** **L** **M**

DWORTH

**Perham
Down**

Lambdown Terrace

Lambdown Terrace

Kemmel Rd

Somme Road

Wouldham Cl

Hatton Rd

Adelaide Cl

Upnor
Close

Perm

2 1

Benn Rd

Tobruk Rd

Fyfield
Way

Furze Dr

Appleshaw
Way

Downsview
Way

Lamb
Down

South
Park

Andover

Lane

I

Great Shod 2 sde **2**

Wiltshire County

Hampshire County

Newdown
Copse

3

4

116 **116**

Kimpton
Down Farm

Down Road

Dc

5

Kimpton
Wood

Ox Drove

6

Ox Drove

7

Old Coach Road

8

G **H** **J** 139 **K** **L** **M**

Snoddington

G7
1 Aelmas Mich Dro

L5
1 Ramblers Mead

G **H** **J** **94** **K** **L** **M**

I

2

3

4

118

5

6

7

8

Nutbane

Nutbane Lane

Clanville

Clanville Lodge

Penton Lane

Chalk Croft Farm

Chalkcroft Lane

Back Lane

Appleshaw School

Ragged Appleshaw

ppleshaw

st Park

ft

Ramridge House

Ramridge Cott

Pent Cop

The Grove

Trinity Rise

Penton Mewsey

Penton Grafton

St Benedicts Convent School

NDOVER ROAD A342

Tittymouse Lane

Rectory Place

Hardyfair Close

Lodge Drive

Weyhill

Weyhill Gardens

Fairways

Road

WEYHILL

ROAD

A342

Short Lane

Harroway

Harrow Way

Beech Close

Penton Corner

West Portway Industrial Estate

Hopkins

A303(T)

Red Post Lane

Weyhill Service Area

WEYHILL ROAD

Joule Rd

West Pt Business Park

Whit Roa

The Hawk Conservancy

G **H** **J** **141** **K** **L** **M**

Douglas Rd

Monxton

Dickson Rd

Pattinson

PH

Opp. Enham

London

G2
1 Chapel La

G3
1 Icknield Wy
2 Lillywhite Crs

G4
1 Corinthian Cl
2 Danegeld Cl
3 Olaf Cl

G6
1 Blackbird Ct
2 Dove Cl
3 Martin Wy
4 Plover Ct

G **H** **J** **K** **L** **M**

96

I

2

3

4

120

5

6

7

8

Enham Alamein

Woodhouse

Tobruk Close

Knightsbridge Rd

Smannell & Enham Primary School

Smannell

Finkley House

Finkley Road

Finkley Manor Farm

East Anton

Smannell Road

Farm Park

Picket Piece

Walworth Road

Ox Drove

Shepherd Spring Medical Centre

Infants School

Swallowfields

Cricketers

Icknield School

PO

Andover Down

Down House

LONDON ROAD

B3

CHURCHILL WAY A3093

Pilgrims Way

Itchen Court

Churchill Way

North Way

South Way

Central Way

Focus 303 Business Cen

West Way

New Street

Watery Lane

Majorca Av

Colenzo Drive

Madrid Road

Vigo Road

Batchelors Barn Road

Vigo County Infant School

Mark Way School

Winton Play School

The Winton School

Admirals

London Road

Springfield Close

Pearman Drive

Stiles Drive

Andover Mus & the Mus of the Iron Age

The Manse
Health Cen

Adelaide Medical Cen

Eastfield Rd

Wolversdene Road

Micheldever Road

Picket Twenty Farm

The Grange

143

H6 cont.
8 Forth Ct
9 Helford Ct
10 Hendren Sq
11 Humber Ct
12 Jardine Sq
13 Larwood Sq
14 Nene Ct

H6
1 Avon Ct
2 Beaulieu Cl
3 Bourne Ct
4 Calder Ct
5 Clyde Ct
6 Dart Ct
7 Derwent Ct cont.

G7
1 Barcelona Cl
2 Dances Cl
3 Spring Ms

G8
1 Bracher Cl
2 Silkweavers Rd

H8
1 Eastfield Cl

ANDOVER

1 Charlotte Cl
2 Palmer Dr

J6
1 Thames Ct
2 Tyne Ct

120

A   B   C   **97**   D   E   F

Hackwood Copse

Derrydo Farm

Middle Wyke Farm

1

Finkley Road

Test Way

Test Way

Lower Wyke Farm

2

Harroway

3

Apsley Farm

4

Walworth Road

Test Way

◀119

Faulkner's Down Farm

Ox Drove Rise

✝ **5**

Tinker's Hill

Harewood Peak

Fox Cottages

Test Way

6

B3400

7   B3400   LONDON ROAD

ROAD

House

Andover Down

The Middleway

8

A   B   C   **144**   D   E   F

Test Way

G H J K L M

98

I

2

3

4

122

5

6

7

8

G H J K L M

145

East

B3048

Chapmansford Farm

New
Barn Farm

Harroway

Cowdown
Copse

Dirty Corner

Bloswood Lane

Skylark
Rise

Bloswood Lane

nor Far

Bourne Rivulet

The
Mansion

Hurstbourne
Park

The
Common

B3048

B3400

Hurstbourne
Priors

Budgett Farm

LONGPARISH ROAD

Drury
Cl

Tracy's
Dell

Testbourne

Paper
Mill Farm

Ho

Ce

T

G   H   J   100   K   L   M

H2
1 Marsden Ct

The Lynch   Silk   Mill

Southington Close

LONDON

PO

Battens Avenue

HIGH ST

Southington

Red Lion Lane

Woolands

Oak Close

Lion

Greyhound La

Alexander Road

Two

Winchester Street

I

Home Farm

Laverstoke Ho

Dellands

Sapley Lane

Charledown Close

Charledown Road

Poultons Road

Dellands Lane

Crawts Road

Pond Close

ROTTEN HILL

Vinns Lane

B3400

Southington La

2

LONDON ROAD

†

†

Laverstoke

1

Laverstoke Lane

Coine Valley Way

Turrill Hill Farm

3

Florence Portal Ct

4

124

Lower Whitehill Cottag

5

Spring Pond Farm

New Barn Cotts

6

Laverstoke Grange Farm

Upper Whitehill Farm

7

Laverstoke Lane

Micheldever Road

New Barn Farm

Laverstoke Wood

8

G   H   J   147   K   L   M

124

101

123

148

London Road B3400
B3400

OVERTON

Station Road
Winchester Street
Red Lion Lane
Woodlands
Poultons Road
Charledown Road
Two Gate Lane
Nightingale Rise
Paperworkers
Made Close
Pound Road
Waltham Road
The Green
Battens Avenue
Alexander Road
Greyhound La

Berrydown Lane
Berrydown Court
Berrydown Farm

Source of
the River Test

Ashe Park

Burley Wood

Burley Lane

Sapley Farm House

Waltham Lane

Bramdown Copse

Basset's Farm

Lower Whitehill Cottages

Southley Farm

Upper Whitehill Farm

Pilgrim's Farm

Burley Lane

Golf Course

Steventon Warren Farm

1 grid square represents 500 metres

G **H** **J** 102 **K** **L** **M**

I

Pardo

2

3

4

126

5

6

7

8

Steventon

Wayfarer's Walk

Bull's Bushes Copse

Bull's Bushes Fo

Dean Heath Copse

Stubb's Copse

West Wood

Village Farm

Nor Bus Cer

North Waltham

Mary Lane

Waltham Lane

Manor Farm

North Waltham School

Steventon Rd

Folly Farm

Church Cl

Cuckoo Cl

Cuckoo Cl

St Michael's Close

Church Road

Yew Tree Lane

Chapel St

Elizabethan Rise

Well Close

Longfield Cl

Smith's Md

Home Md

Up St

Coldharbour

Maidenthorn Lane

Popham Lane

PH

A30

M3

Fairview Meadow
The S

Water Ridge

Brighton Hill

G1
1 Chantry Ms
2 Fayrewood Cha
3 Matilda Dr
4 Paxton Cl
5 Sandbanks Dr
6 Westminster Cl
7 Wights Wk

G2
1 Petworth Cl

K
1 Burrowfields
2 Grosvenor Cl

Viabies
Industrial

G   **H**   **J**   **K**   **L**   **M**

Manorfield
Infant
School

Hatch Warren
County Junior
School

Hatch Warren County
Infant School

St Marks
Primary
School

I

Cliddesden

Manor Farm

2

Cliddesden
Primary School

3

FARLEIGH ROAD B3046

Broadmere

4

128

5

6

Northgate Farm

The
Avenue

**Farleigh
Wallop**

Grammarsham Lane

Bedlam
Bottom

Manor Farm

Farleigh
House School

Inwood
Copse

Great
Wood

7

B3046

**Gobley
Hole**

Norton's
Wood

Green Lane

Farler's
Field

8

Nutley
Wood

G   **H**   **J**   **K**   **L**   **M**

K1
1 Hatchwar. Gdns

J1
1 Arne Cl

H3
1 Tamarisk Cl
2 Tithe Meadow

H2
1 The Brackens
2 Holmes Cl
3 Whitestones

H1
1 Mitchell Gdns

Upper Common

128

A B C **105** D E F

Wood

Hackwood House

1

Hoddersmead Lane

Station Road

Hackwood Park

2

Hackwood Lane

Cliddesden Primary School

3

Winslade

A339

Swallick Farm

4

127

5

Allwood Copse

Three Castles Path

6

Northgate Farm

Northgate Lane

Bushywarren Lane

7

Herriard

Church Lane

Ellisfield

Elisfield Manor

Manor Farm

8

Three Castles Path

Furze Lane

A B C **152** D E F

Furze Lane

Merritts Farm

Herriard Grange

1 grid square represents 500 metres

G Roundtown
H
J unworth H 106 Down K L M

I

Three Castles Path

2
Cleves
Upton Grey House

Tunworth

†

The Dower House

Upton Grey
†

3

4

Weston Road

130

5

Weston
Corbett

Weston Patrick
†

6

Herriard
Park

Herriard House
Park Farm

7

8

A339

G
H
J 153
Lee Farm
K
L Wood
M
New Farm

Nash's Green

G H J K L M

108

RG29

Down Farm

Barbour
Close

Readon
Farm House

ALTON ROAD

B3349

Long Lane

Four
Lanes End

Hayley Lane

Stapely
Down Farm

132

Wood Hill Lane

Leaden Vere

Long
Sutton

Andrew's
Farm

Ham
Copse

nborough

The Street

Andrew's Lane

Long Lane

Wells
Hill Farm

Copse

Wingate Rd

Longsutton
Primary
School

Summers Farm

Lord
Wandsworth
College

Hesters
Copse

echaffers Cl

Lord
Wandsworth
College

Lord
Wandsworth
College

Hyde Farm

New Farm

Lord Wandsworth
College

Sheephouse Copse

Vinney
Copse

G H J K L M

155

Sutton
Common

Highnam Copse

I 1 2 3 4 5 6 7 8

132

A   B   109   D   E   F

[109]

I

Roke Lane

Itchel
Home Farm

Roke Farm

2

Penn
Croft Farm

Park
Corner Farm

Newlands Farm

3

Horsedown
Common

Swanthorpe Farm

Stapely Farm

4

131

Thorn's Farm

5

Ham
Copse

Travers Farm

6

White Hill

PH

Montgomery's Farm

Well

7

Well Lane

Hole Lane

Glade
Farm

8

ephouse Copse

156   Isnage Farm

Bury
Cou

A   B   C   D   E   F

1 grid square represents 500 metres

Hill Farm

ODIHAM ROAD

G H J **110** K L M

H2
1 Hannam's Farm

J3
1 Ravelin Cl

Hannam's
Copse

Eastbridge

Lea Farm

Broomhill

Church

Hyde Lane

Lefroy's
Fld

Hancroft

Green Springs

The Surgery

Redlands La

Redlands Lane

Warren
Corner

Redlands

Heath Lane

1

Itchel Lane

Ash Rly Ct D Se

Ashley Cl

Pankridge Street

Crondall

Warren
Corner

Ewshot
Hall

PO

Oak Park
Golf Club

Dora's Green Lane

Dora's
Green

Well Road

Church Street

Dippenhall Lane

Glebe Rd

Heath La

Heath Lane

Crondall CP
School

St Cross Rd

Chaundlers

Heath Street

1

Croft

Farm La

Cliff

Dippenhall Street

Upper
Clare Farm

Clare
Park

Lower
Old Park

134

Lee
Wood

Dora's Green Lane

Crondall Lane

swanthorpe House

Dippenhall

Dora's Green Lane

Dippenhall
Road

Wimble Hill

Hampshire County
Surrey County

Clarks

Dippe

Hill

Runwick

Old Farnham Lane

Runwick Lane

Cheeks Farm

Grovers Farm

Chamber

Hotel

Willey
Place

ay Hous

G H J **157** K L M

Hill Farm

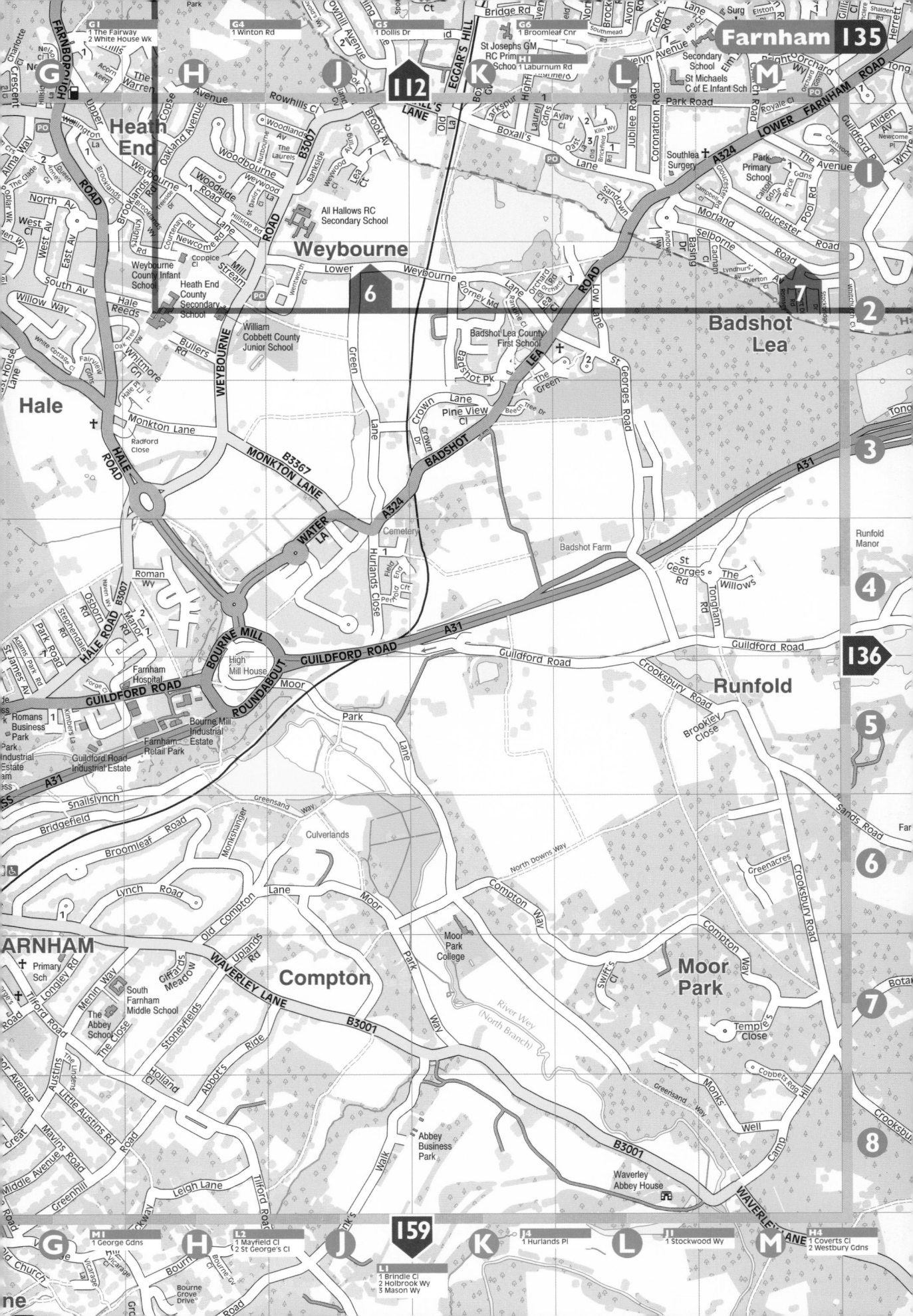

K4
1 M Boro Rd

G h
Green

Green Lane West

Farm

Green Lane East

H

J

K

L

Westwood Lane

M

I 1

Wanborough
Wood

Wanborough
Manor

Wanborough

Wanborough Hill

✝

2

Inwood Farm

Hog's Back

B3000

3

A31(T)

B3000 PUTTENHAM HILL

Puttenham

Puttenham
C of E
School

School Lane

✝

am   Road

Totford Lane

Seale Lane

Munday's
Boro

Dark   La

The   Street

PUTTENHAM

Putte
Golf
Club

4

Shoelands

Lascombe Lane

Suffield Farm

North Downs Way

Highfield   Lane

Lascombe

5

Hampton

Puttenham
Common

Church
Croft

Hook Lane

6

General's
Pond

Puttenham   Lane

7

mpton
k

Warren
Pond

Lydling Farm

Suffield Lane

The
Tarn

Rodsall
Manor

8

Littleworth Road

Cutt Mill Ho

G

H

J

K

L

M

Aldro
School

PD **Sha**

Roker
La

A   B   C   114   D   E   F

D1
1 Gilbert's Gn
2 Kingfishers

C1
1 Goodwyns Cl
2 Muscott Cl

Bulford Road

1

Muscott Close
Primary School
Hedges Road
Threadgill Way
Muscott
Parkhouse
Mayfair Cl
Sarum Cl
Gardener's Green
High Street
Manor Cl
St Peter's
Kingfishers
Bourne La

Shipton Bellinger

2

Hampshire County
Wiltshire County

SALISBURY ROAD
A338

Snoddington Manor

Althorne

3

4

Park House
A338

Thruxton Farm

5

A303(T)

River Bourne

A338

Home Farm

6

Choderton House

7

Amesbury Road

Cholderton

Edric's Gn
Beech Hanger
Grateley
Cholderton Road
Cholderton Lodge

Cholderton Road

8

Quarley Down Farm

A   B   C   160   D   E   F

Pit
Wilbury House

G H J K L M

117

163

I
2
3
4
142
5
6
7
8

M4
1 St Mary's Mdw

The Hawk
Conservat

Sarson
Cl
Chapel
Cl
ed)

Sarson

Pillhill-Brook

Sarson Lane

Monxton

Green Lane

Abbotts Ann Road

Chalkpit Lane

Pillhill-Brook

Andover Road

Sunnybank

Monxton

Red Post Lane

Red Post Lane

Farm Road

Little
Park Farm

Cattle Lane

**Little
Ann**

Hillside

Abbotts Ann Primary School

PO

Abbotts
Close

Hill

Old Salisbury

Manor
Close

Warren
Drive

Bulbery

**Abbotts
Ann**

Dunkirt Lane

Broad Road

Great
Wood

Monxton Farm

St John's Cross

Eastover Farm

SALISBURY ROAD

Eastover
Copse

Stonehanger
Copse

Prospect Farm

Stockbridg

Douglas Rd

Monxton

Pattinson

Dickson Rd
Newall
Newall

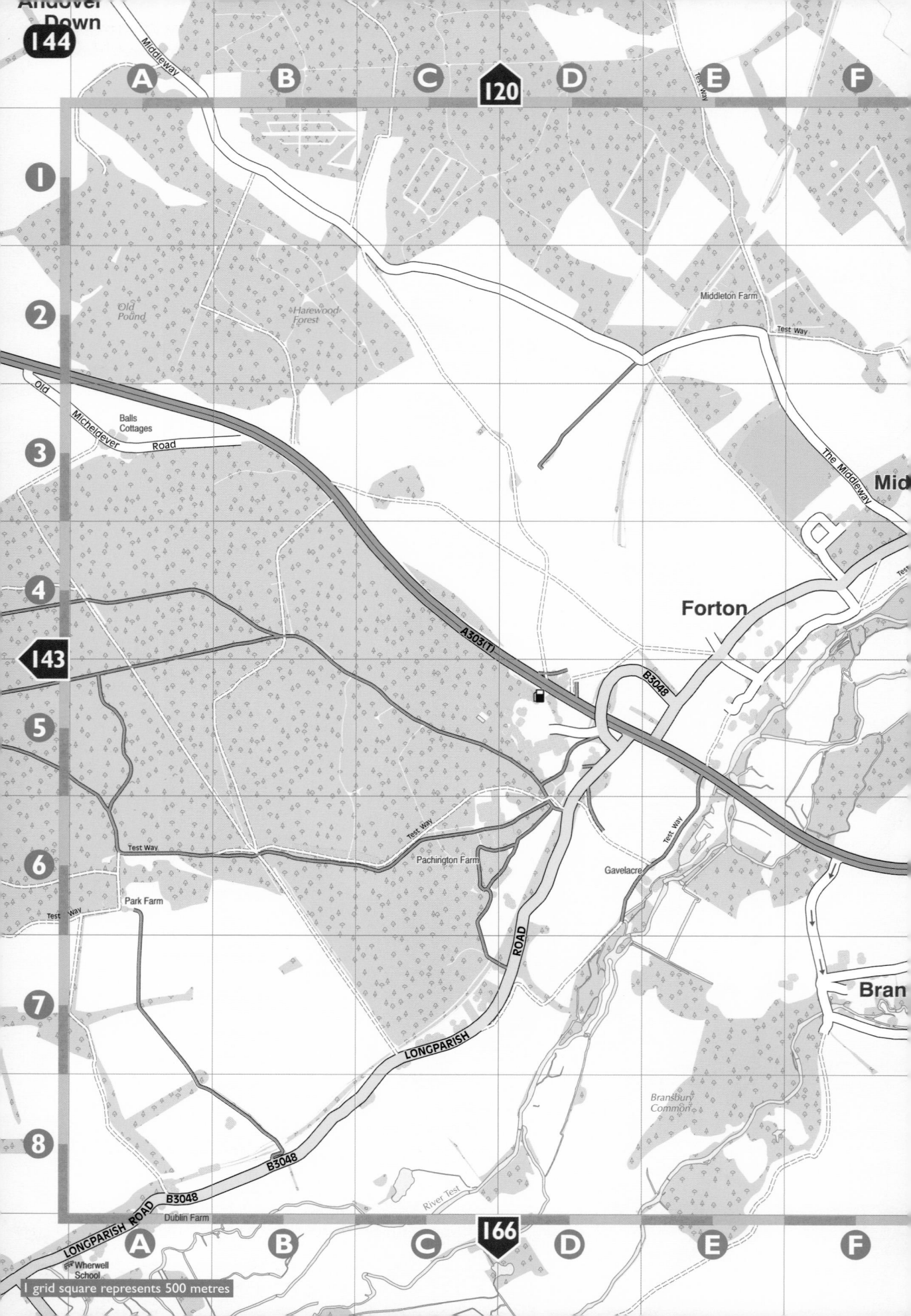

G Tracy's Dell

H

J

121

K

Paper Mill Farm

L

M

I

River Test

2

East Aston

B3048

Longparish Ho

Larkwhistle Farm

Longparish

3

Lower Mill

Vale Farm

on

Test Way

PH

Southside

146

Longparish School

Road

Mill Lane

4

Southside Farm

The Avenue

5

Montier William Rd

Dawson Rd

Hill Rd

Stevenson Rd

Carpenter Rd

Thuillier Rd

6

A303(T)

Campbell Road

A303(T)

7

River Dever

ry

8

Roberts Road

Tidbury Common

Barton Stacey C of E Primary School

G

H

J

167

The Green

K

Pheasant Cl

Roman Way

East Rd

L

M

West Road

Partridge

Bullington Lane

Lower

146

A B C 122 D E F

1

2 Firgo Farm Tufton Warren Farm

3

4

145

5

6 Upper Norton Farm

7 Tidbury Farm A30 A3 A30
Bullington Cross Inn
A303(T)

8 Upper Bullington

A B C 168 D E F

1 grid square represents 500 metres

wer

G H J 123 K L M

I

Roundwood Farm

2

Freefolk Wood

3

4

148

5

Bru... C...er R...
Ando... R...

6

Warren Farm

7

A303(T)

Upper
Cranbourne Farm

8

Hunton
Down Farm

148

Ⓐ Ⓑ Ⓒ 124 Ⓓ Ⓔ Ⓕ

Golf Course

Deveton Warren Farm

1

2

Cobley Wood

Bellevue Plantation

3

A303(T)

Popham Beacons

4

147

5

Black Wood

Overton Road

Brunel Road

Andover Road

New Road

Micheldever Station

⇄

6

Micheldever Station

Warren Farm

Northbrook Farm

Larkwhistle Farm Road

7

8

Ⓐ Ⓑ Ⓒ 170 Ⓓ Ⓔ Ⓕ

A33

1 grid square represents 500 metres

A   B   C   126   D   E   F

1

Dummer
Down Farm

Dummer Down

Lane

2

Dummer Grange

Wayfarer's Walk

3

Dummer Grange Farm

4

The
Holt

149

Flockmoor
Cottage

Breach Farm

Wayfarer's Walk

5

6

7

8

A   B   C   172   D   E   F

Chilton
Wood

G   H **Gobley Hole**   J   **127**   K   L   M

Upper Common

I

Farrier's Field

Nutley Wood

2 Low Com

Nutley Down

High Wood

3

Nutley

Berrydown Farm

4 Pres Oak Hill

152

Axford

Moundsmere Manor

5

Damsel Lane

Fawkners

6

Southwood Farm

B3046

Preston House

7

Garden Ct

PO

Preston Candover Primary School

Preston Candover

Stenbury Drive

8 **Bradle**

G   H   J   **173**   K   *Preston Down* L   M

A   B   C   128   D   E   F

1

Furzen Lane

Elisfield Manor

Lane

Three Castles Path

Merritts Farm

Herriard Grange

Oxlease Lane

Hurst Farm

Bagr

Bell Lane

Lower Common

College Farm

College Lane

Three Castles Path

Bagmore Lane

2

Gre
Ma
Cot

3

Berrydown Lane

Herriard Common

4

Preston Oak Hills

Red Lane

151

5

wood Farm

6

Burkham House

Spain Lane

A359

Three Castles Path

7

8

Bradley

A   B   174   C   D   E   F

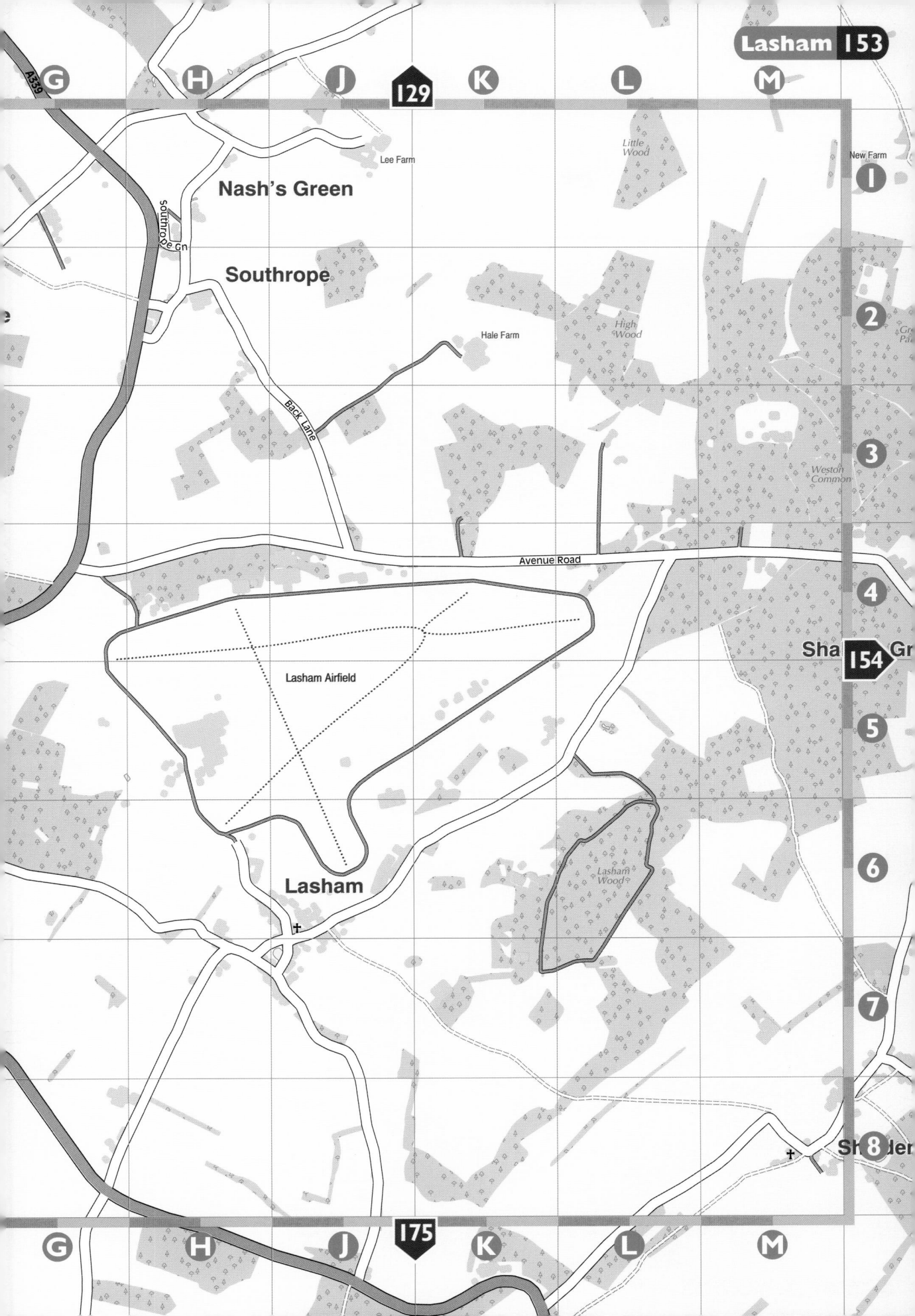

G H J **129** K L M

I

2

3

New Farm

Little Wood

High Wood

Gre Pa

Weston Common

Lee Farm

Nash's Green

Southrope Gn

Southrope

Back Lane

Hale Farm

Avenue Road

4

Sha **154** Gr

5

Lasham Airfield

6

Lasham Wood

Lasham

7

8

Sh der

154

A   B   C   130   D   E   F

New Farm

1

Great
Park

2

Weston
Common

3

Humbly
Grove
Copse

oly
Grove

Blounce

Powntley
Copse

Swainshill Farm

Swaines
Hill Manor

Pickaxe Lane

Sowcroft

Lan

B3349

153 Iden Green

4

Avenue Rd

Shalden
Park Farm

Golden
Pot

B3349

5

Brockham Hill Lane

B3349

Shalden Park
Wood

6

Stancombe Lane

7

Golf
Club

Golf
Course

Fiddlers Fld

NEW ODIHAM ROAD

Old Odiham Road

+ 8 Shalden

Southwood

Old Odiham Road

Anstey Lane

B
H

A   B   C   176   D   Gree   Farm   E   A   F

New Farm

Vinney Copse

Froyle Lane

Sheephouse Copse

Sutton Common

Highnam Copse

I

2

3

Yarnhams

Hawkins Wood

Bambet

4

156

5

Ham Wood

Spollycombe Copse

Upper Froyle

Holybourne Down

Mayor ar Colle ower Schoo

6

7

Bonham's Farm

8

Brockham Hill Lane

Cuckoo's Corner

Howard's La

Church

Holybourne

London Road

River Wey

A31

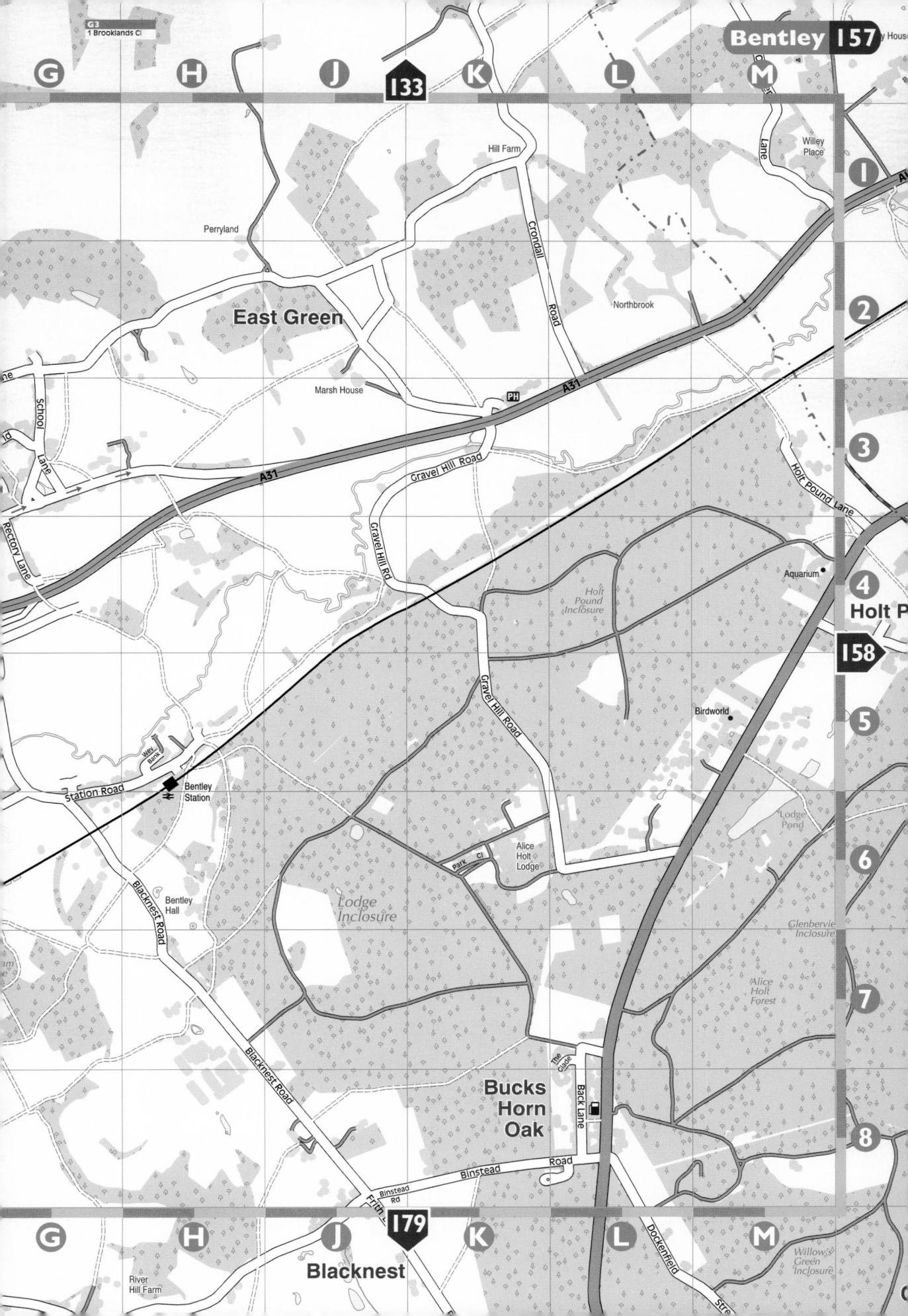

G3
1 Brooklands Cl

G   H   J   133   K   L   M

I

2

3

Perryland

Hill Farm

Crondall Road

Northbrook

Willey Place

Holt Pound Lane

East Green

Marsh House

PH

A31

Gravel Hill Road

Gravel Hill Rd

A31

School Lane

Rectory Lane

4

Holt P

158

5

6

7

8

Holt Pound Inclosure

Aquarium

Birdworld

Lodge Pond

Gravel Hill Road

Glenbervie Inclosure

Alice Holt Forest

Bentley Station

Station Road

Well Bank

Bentley Hall

Blacknest Road

Lodge Inclosure

Park Cl

Alice Holt Lodge

Alice Holt Forest

The Clade

Back Lane

Bucks Horn Oak

Binstead Road

Binstead Rd

Frith End

G   H   J   179   K   L   M

Blacknest

River Hill Farm

Dockenfield

Willow's Green Inclosure

A B C 138 D E F

Quarley
Down Farm

1

Cemetery

Wilbury House

Pit   Walk

River Bourne

Three
Corner Hat

2

Beechfield

PO

Newton Tony

The Croft

Newton
Tony
School

St Just Cl

3

4

River Bourne

5

Hampshire County
Wiltshire County

6

7

Allington Farm

8

A B C 182 D E F

Boscombe
Down
East

1 grid square represents 500 metres

& Infant School

G H Portway Farm J OLDER 139 K L M

Wallop Rodu

1

Station Road

Grateley Business Park

Grateley Station

Olc

Campbell Cl

Station Ap

B3084

Streetway Road

Streetway Road

Salisbury Road

2

Mount Hermon Road

Palestine Road

Zion Road

Palestine

Bournemouth Road

Red Lodge Farm

Orange Grove

Orange Grove

Olive Grove

Peach Grove

Peach Grove

3

Mount Carmel Road

4

Castle Farm

162

WALLOP ROAD

B3084

5

Martin's Clump

6

Pottery Drove

Croft Farm

7

8

G H J 183 K L M

A343

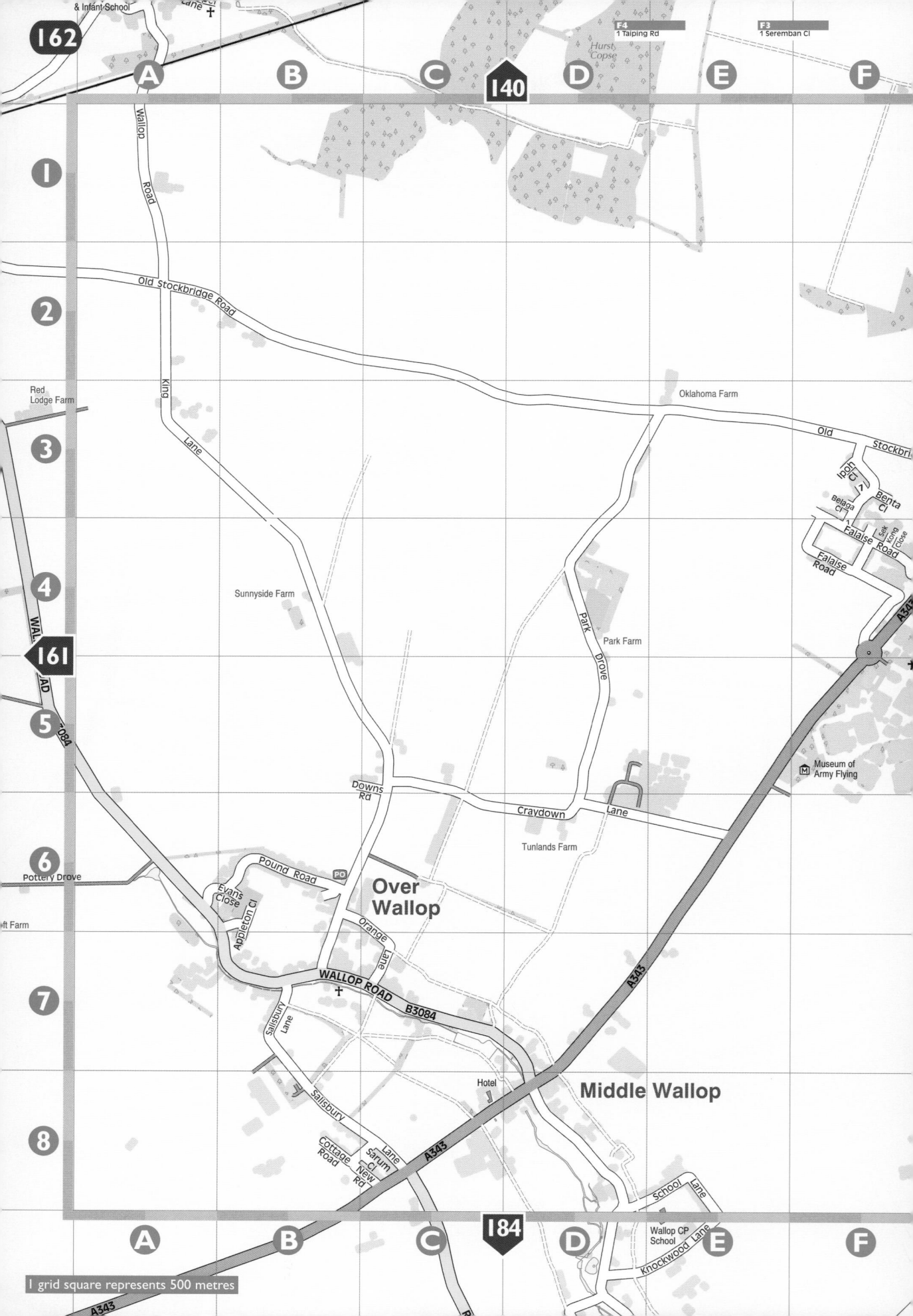

A B C **140** D E F

I

2

Old Stockbridge Road

Red
Lodge Farm

3

Oklahoma Farm

Old
Stockbri

Ipoh
Cl

Benta
Cl

Belaga
Cl

Falaise
Road

Sek
Kong
Close

Falaise
Road

4

Sunnyside Farm

Park Farm

Wallop Road

161

Park
Drove

King
Lane

Wallop
Road

5

Downs
Rd

Craydown   Lane

Museum of
Army Flying

B3084

6

Pound   Road

PO

**Over
Wallop**

Tunlands Farm

Pottery Drove

Evans
Close

Appleton Cl

Orange
Lane

ft Farm

7

Salisbury
Lane

WALLOP ROAD

B3084

A343

Hotel

Middle Wallop

8

Salisbury
Lane

Cottage
Road

Sarum
Cl

New
Rd

A343

School
Lane

Knockwood Lane

Wallop CP
School

A343

A B **184** C D E F

& Infant School

F4
1 Taiping Rd

F3
1 Seremban Cl

Hurst
Copse

G H J **141** K L M

I

Stockbridge Road

Prospect Farm

Stonehanger Copse

Down Farm

A343

Dipden Bottom

2

Road

Saxley Farm

3

Kentsboro

Maple Cl

Sycamore

Birch
Willow Way
Avenue
Larch
Elm
Oak
Pine Cl
Chestnut Crescent

Beech Cl

4

Clatford Oakcuts

164

Stockbridge Road

5

6

Down Farm

7

143
Danebury Hill

P

The Turret

8

G H J **185** K
Danebury Down
L M

G H J K L M

Roberts Road

Tidbury Common

145

Barton Stacey
C of E
Primary School

Roman Way

The Green

Pheasant Cl

East Rd

West Road

Partridge Cl

Bullington Lane

Lower
Bullington

I

King's Elms

King's Elms

Gravel Lane

PO

Barton Stacey

Ashfields

Greenacres

Hill Barn

Hill Barn

2

Barton

3

Barton Drove

4

168

Cocum Farm

5

Moody's Down Farm

A30

6

B3420

A30

7

A30

A272

8

Hill Farm

Sutton Down Farm

189

G H J K L M

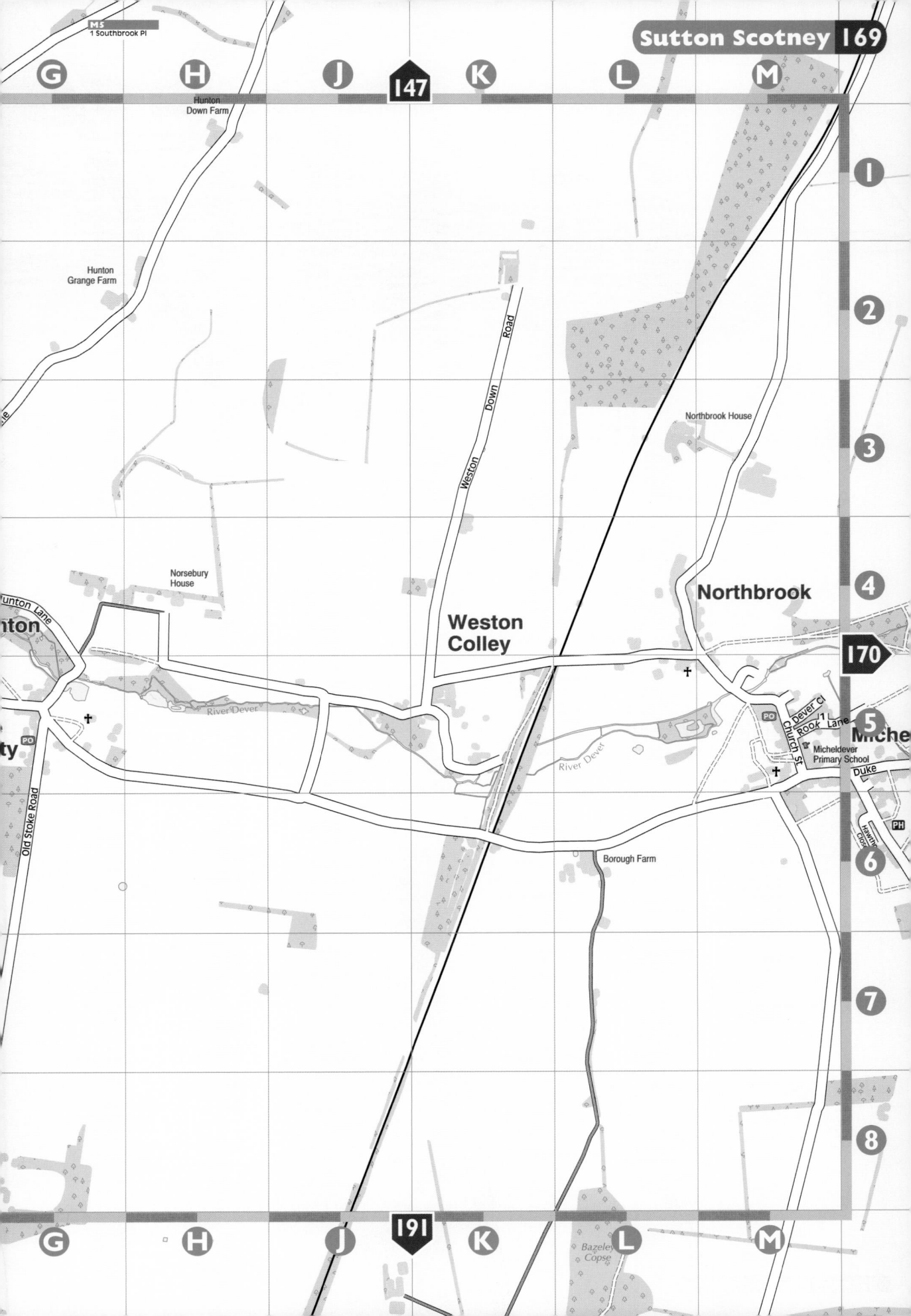

G H J **147** K L M

1 Southbrook Pl

Hunton
Down Farm

Hunton
Grange Farm

Northbrook House

Norsebury
House

Northbrook

170

Weston
Colley

River Dever

PO

Dever Cl

Rook Lane

Micheldever
Primary School

Miche

River Dever

Duke

PH

Borough Farm

Old Stoke Road

Hunton Lane

nton

ty

PO

Bazeley
Copse

G H J **191** K L M

I 1

2

3

4

5

6

7

8

G H J **149** K L M

1

2

3

4

172

5

6

7

8

G H **193** J K L M

Lone Farm

Whiteway Farm

Lone Barn

Gunners Lane

Warfarers W.

Candover Copse

Thorny Down Wood

Foxhill

t Stratton

Copse Lane

Copse Lane

Bryces Lane

Burcot Farm

Totford Farm

Stratton Lane

Totford

Northington Down Farm

Northington

Swarraton

Candover

Primary School

Stenbury Drive

Bradle

G   H   J   **151**   K   L   M

I

Preston Grange

Preston Down

Oxdrove Way

Three Castles Path

Berry Road Lane

2

Down Farm

3

Oxdrove Way

4   PH

174

Three Castles Path

5

Wield Wood

Upper Wield

PO

Home Close

6

Pound Cl

Three Castles Path

Barton Copse

7

Ferney Lane

Armsworth Hill Farm

Barton Industrial Estate

Newmer Farm

8

Armsworth Ho

Ferney Lane

Upper Wield Lane

Hoggs Lodge

Heath Green Lane

Heath

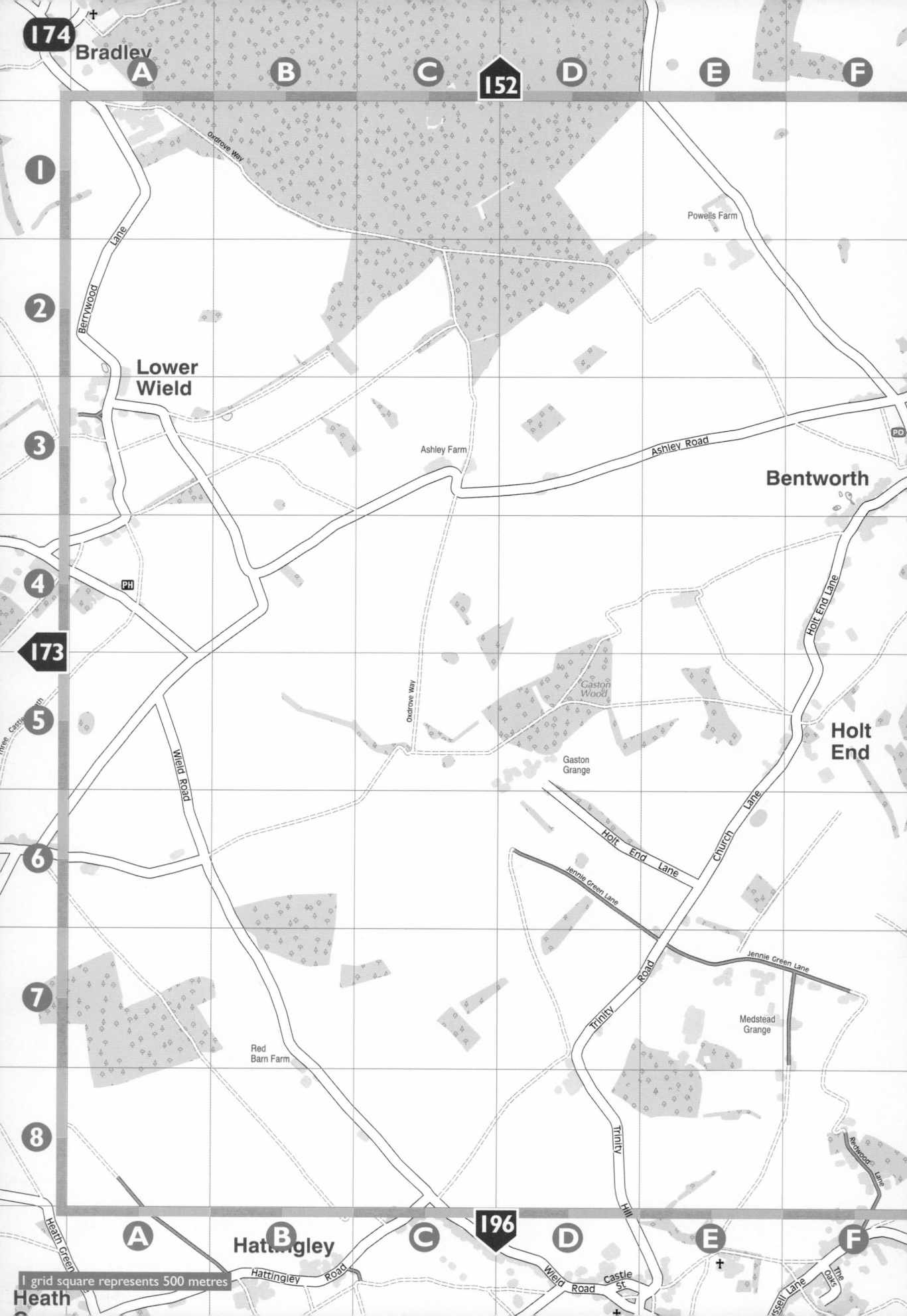

A B C 152 D E F

1

2

Lower
Wield

3

Bentworth

4

PH

173

5

Holt
End

6

7

8

A B 196 D E F

Hattingley

Heath

Berrywood Lane

Oxdrove Way

Ashley Farm

Ashley Road

PO

Holt End Lane

Oxdrove Way

Gaston
Wood

Gaston
Grange

Wield Road

Holt End Lane

Church Lane

Jennie Green Lane

Jennie Green Lane

Medstead
Grange

Redwood Lane

Trinity Road

Trinity Hill

Red
Barn Farm

Heath Green

Hattingley Road

Wield Road

Castle St

Russell Lane

The Oaks

Powells Farm

Three Castles Path

1 grid square represents 500 metres

G   H   J   K   L   M

153

I

2

Wadgett's Copse

3

Warren Farm

Bentworth
Lodge

*Thedden
Copse*

BASINGSTOKE ROAD

Childer
Hill Farm

Heathcroft Farm

176

4

5

Snode   Hill

Wivelrod Road

Medstead Road

Thedden
Grange

Bentworth
Hall

Wellhouse   Road

Crematory

Beech

6

*Ackender
Wood*

Summerley

PH

...rys Primary
...ol

...ge Street

Lane
Glebe Cl
Glebe
Flds

Wivelrod

Medstead Road

*Bushy
Leaze
Wood*

7

Wivelrod Road

King's   Hill

The
Abbey

Cem

Abbey   Road

Old
Park Farm

Chawton
Park Farm

8

Jennie Green Lane

...ssell Lan

G   H   J   K   L   M

197

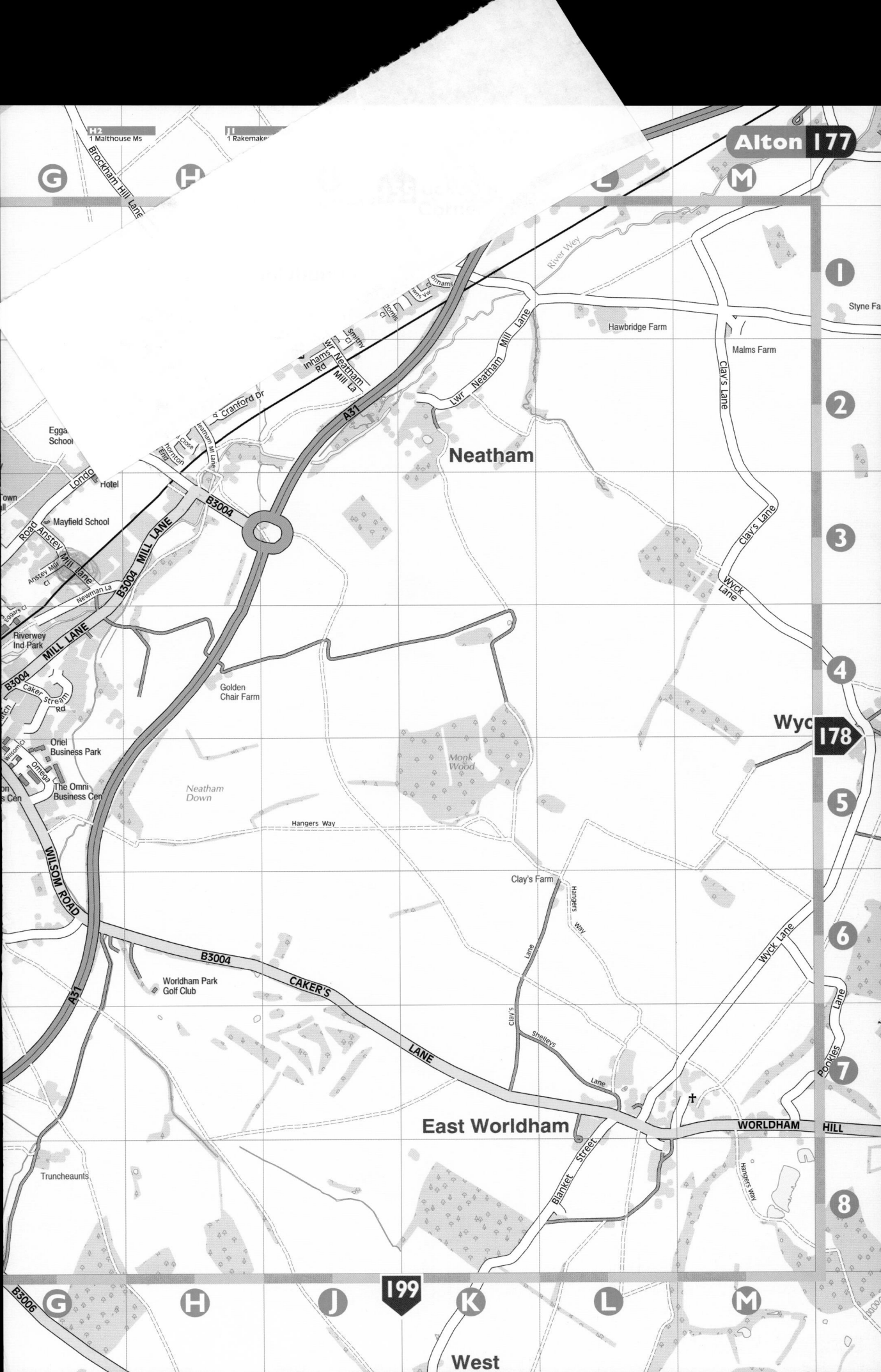

G   H

H2
1 Malthouse Ms

J1
1 Rakemaker

Brockham Hill Lane

L   M

I

Styne Far

River Wey

Hawbridge Farm

Malms Farm

Clay's Lane

2

Onhams

Smithy
Cl

Wr Neatham
Mill La

Lwr Neatham Mill Lane

Boms
Cl

Innams
Rd

Cranford Dr

Neatham Ml Lane

Thornton
End

Close

A31

Egga
School

Londo
Hotel

B3004

Mayfield School

Anstey Mill Lane

Road

Neatham

Clay's Lane

3

WYCK
Lane

MILL LANE

Anstey Mill
Cl

Newman La

B3004 MILL LANE

Riverwey
Ind Park

MILL LANE

Eggar's Cl

Wilson

4

B3004

Caker Stream
Rd

Golden
Chair Farm

Wyc

178

Oriel
Business Park

omega

The Omni
Business Cen

n Cen

Monk
Wood

5

Neatham
Down

Hangers Way

WILSOM ROAD

Clay's Farm

Hangers

6

Hangers
Way

Lane

B3004

CAKER'S

Worldham Park
Golf Club

LANE

Clay's

Wyck Lane

A31

Shelleys

Lane

Bonkies Lane

7

Lane

†

East Worldham

Blanket Street

WORLDHAM

HILL

Truncheaunts

Hangers Way

8

West

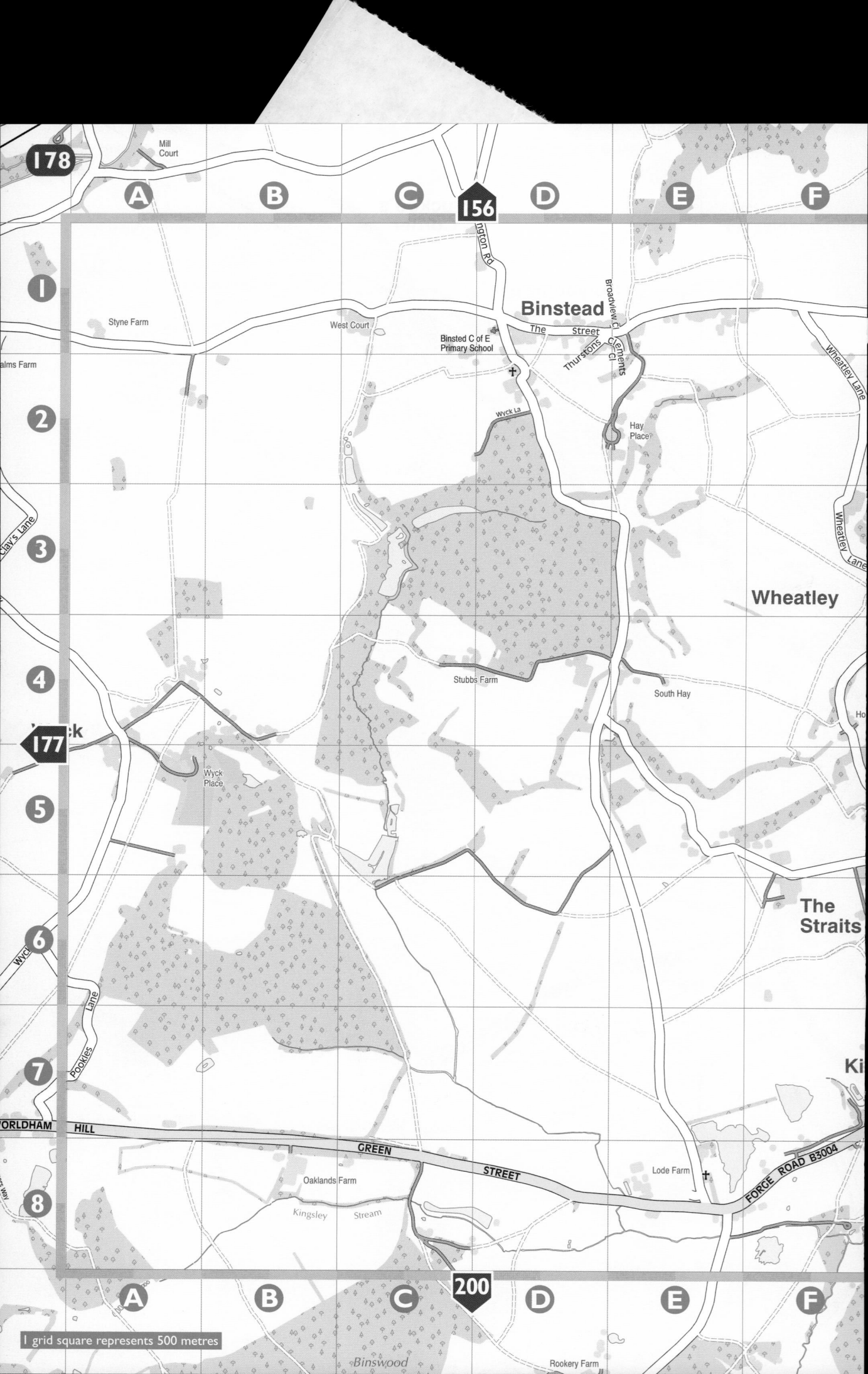

178

A B C **156** D E F

I

Mill Court
Styne Farm
West Court
Binstead
The Street
Binsted C of E Primary School
Broadview Cl
Clements Cl
Thurstons
alms Farm
ngton Rd
Wheatley Lane

2

Wyck La
Hay Place
Clay's Lane

3

Wheatley

4

Stubbs Farm
South Hay
Ho
:k
177
Wyck Place

5

Wyc

6

The Straits

Pookles Lane

7

Ki

ORLDHAM HILL
GREEN STREET
Oaklands Farm
FORGE ROAD B3004
Lode Farm

8

Kingsley Stream

A B C **200** D E F

Binswood
Rookery Farm
Way

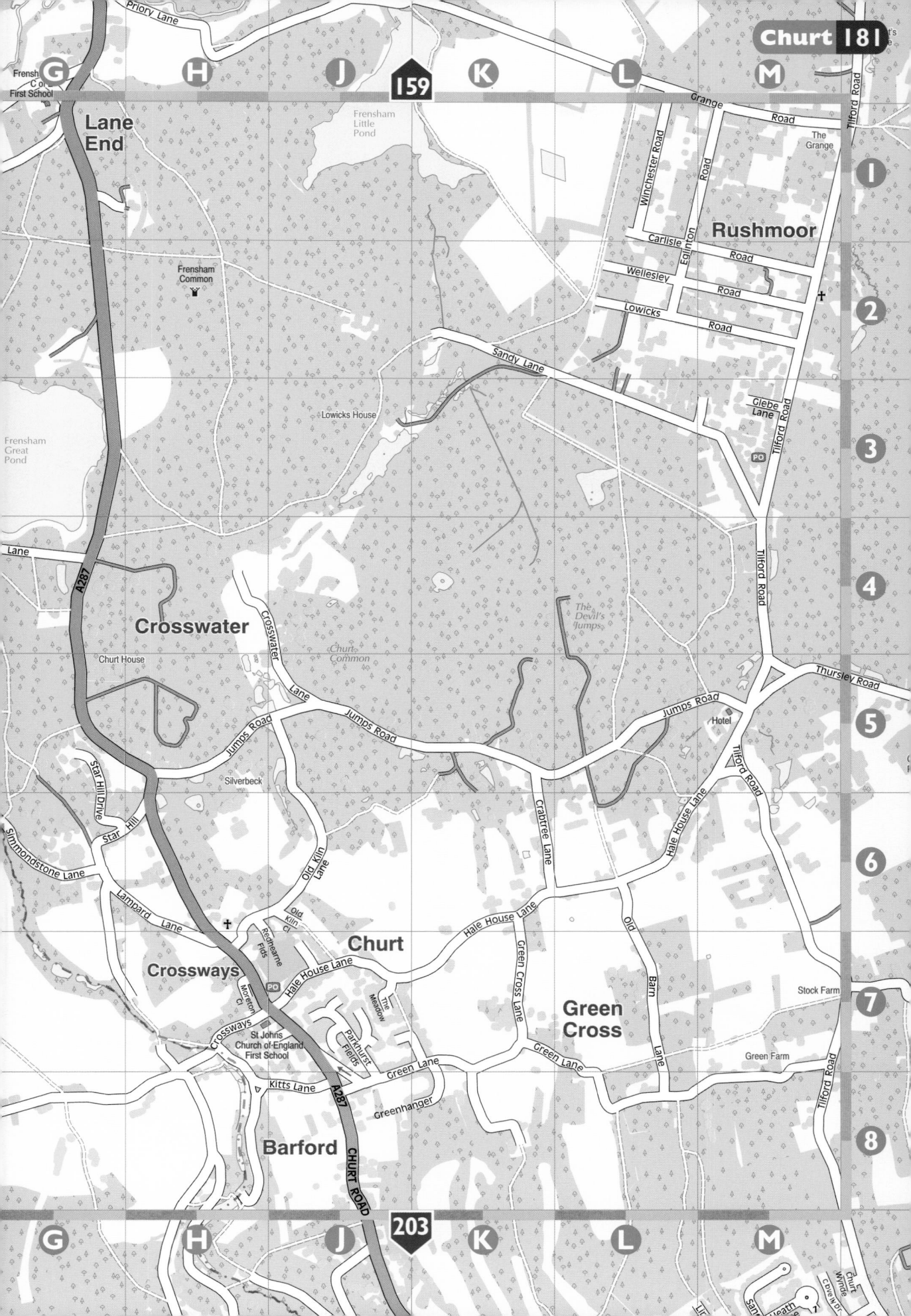

Priory Lane

G **H** **J** 159 **K** **L** **M**

Frensham
C of E
First School

**Lane
End**

Frensham Little
Pond

1

Grange Road

Winchester Road

Eglinton Road

The Grange

Tilford Road

Rushmoor

Carlisle Road

2

Wellesley Road

Frensham Common

Lowicks Road

†

Sandy Lane

Glebe Lane

3

Lowicks House

PO

Tilford Road

**Frensham
Great
Pond**

Lane

4

A287

Crosswater

Crosswater Lane

Churt House

Churt Common

The Devil's Jumps

Tilford Road

Thursley Road

5

Jumps Road

Jumps Road

Hotel

Star Hill Drive

Silverbeck

Old Kiln Lane

Crabtree Lane

Hale House Lane

Tilford Road

6

Simmondstone Lane

Star Hill

Lampard Lane

†

Old Kiln

Redhearne Flds

Churt

Hale House Lane

Hale House Lane

Green Cross Lane

Old Barn Lane

Stock Farm

7

Crossways

PO

Moreton Cl

Crossways

St Johns
Church of England
First School

The Meadow

Parkhurst Fields

Green Lane

**Green
Cross**

Green Lane

Green Farm

Kitts Lane

A287

Greenhanger

8

Barford

CHURT ROAD

203

G **H** **J** **K** **L** **M**

Churt Wynde

C Dyke In Dr

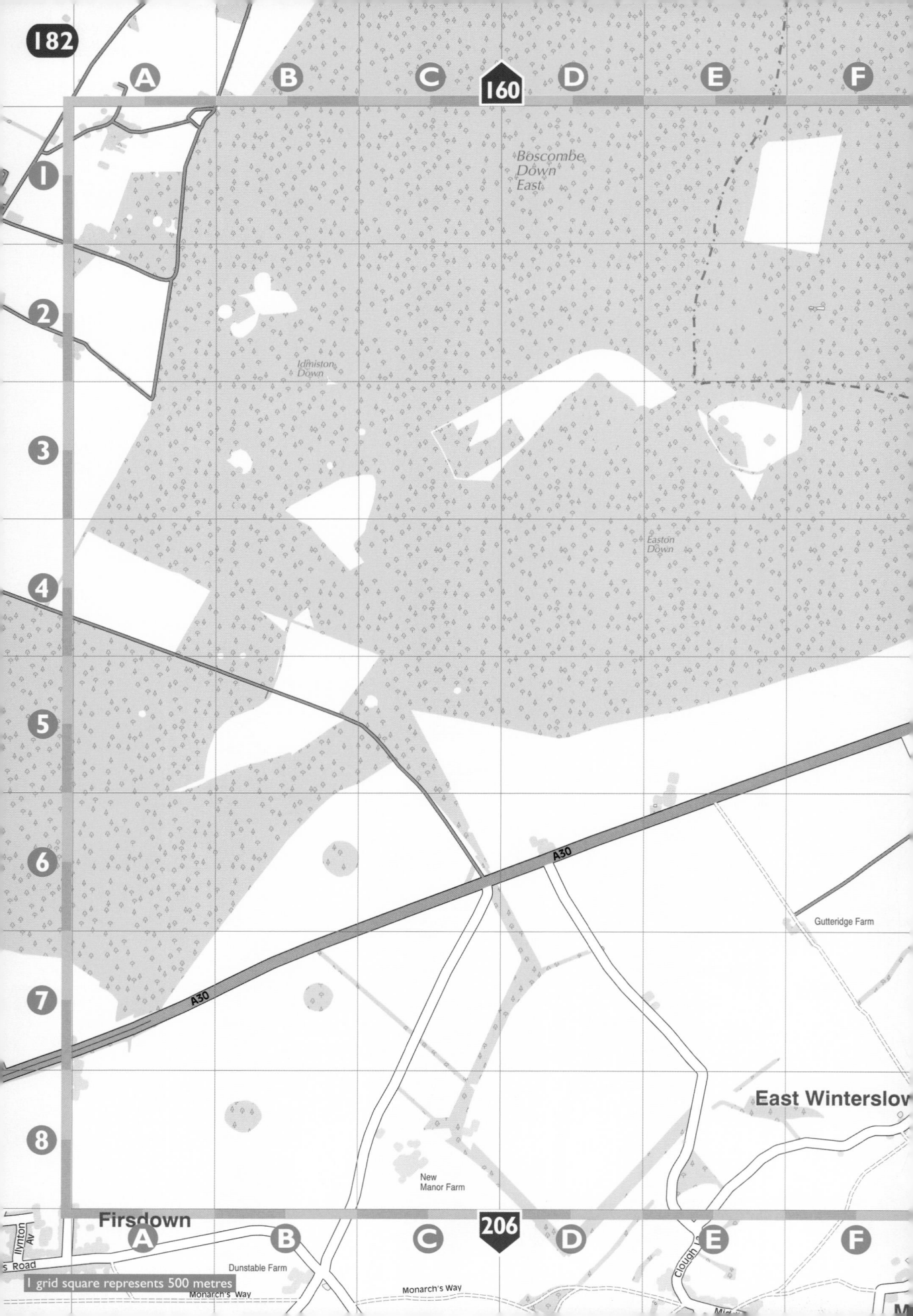

182

A   B   C   160   D   E   F

1

Boscombe
Down
East

2

Idmiston
Down

3

Easton
Down

4

5

6   A30   Gutteridge Farm

7   A30

East Winterslow

8

New
Manor Farm

Firsdown

A   B   206   D   E   F

Dunstable Farm

1 grid square represents 500 metres

Monarch's Way   Monarch's Way

184

A   B   C   162   D   E   F

1

A343

A343

ROMSEY

Bent Street   Farley   Street

Benham   Drove   Wallop Brook

Wallop House

Wallop Brook

2

ROAD

B3084

Hosketts Lane   Heathman   Street

Ducks Lane   1   Church Lane

PO   High Street   Church Hill

Avlwards   WY

Bells

Five

3

Sheep Drove

Berry
Court Farm

Wallop Drove

Gar

4

183

Beech Farm

5

A30

A30

A30

6

SALISBURY ROAD

B3084

7

Waterloo Farm

8

Broughton
Down Farm

Broughton
Down

B3084

A   B   C   208   D   E   F   SALISBURY

1 grid square represents 500 metres

G H J 163 K L M

I
2
3
4
186
5
6
7
8

Danebury Hill

Turret

Danebury
Down

Danebury

Nether
Wallop

Houghton
Down

Chattis
Hill Ho

A30

A30

Hou
Down

Darfield Farm

Broughton Road

ine Mile
ter Farm

Wallop Brook

Manor Farm

G H J 209 K L M

ughton Co
nary Scho

High St

Dixons Lane

Hinwood

+

Eveley Farm

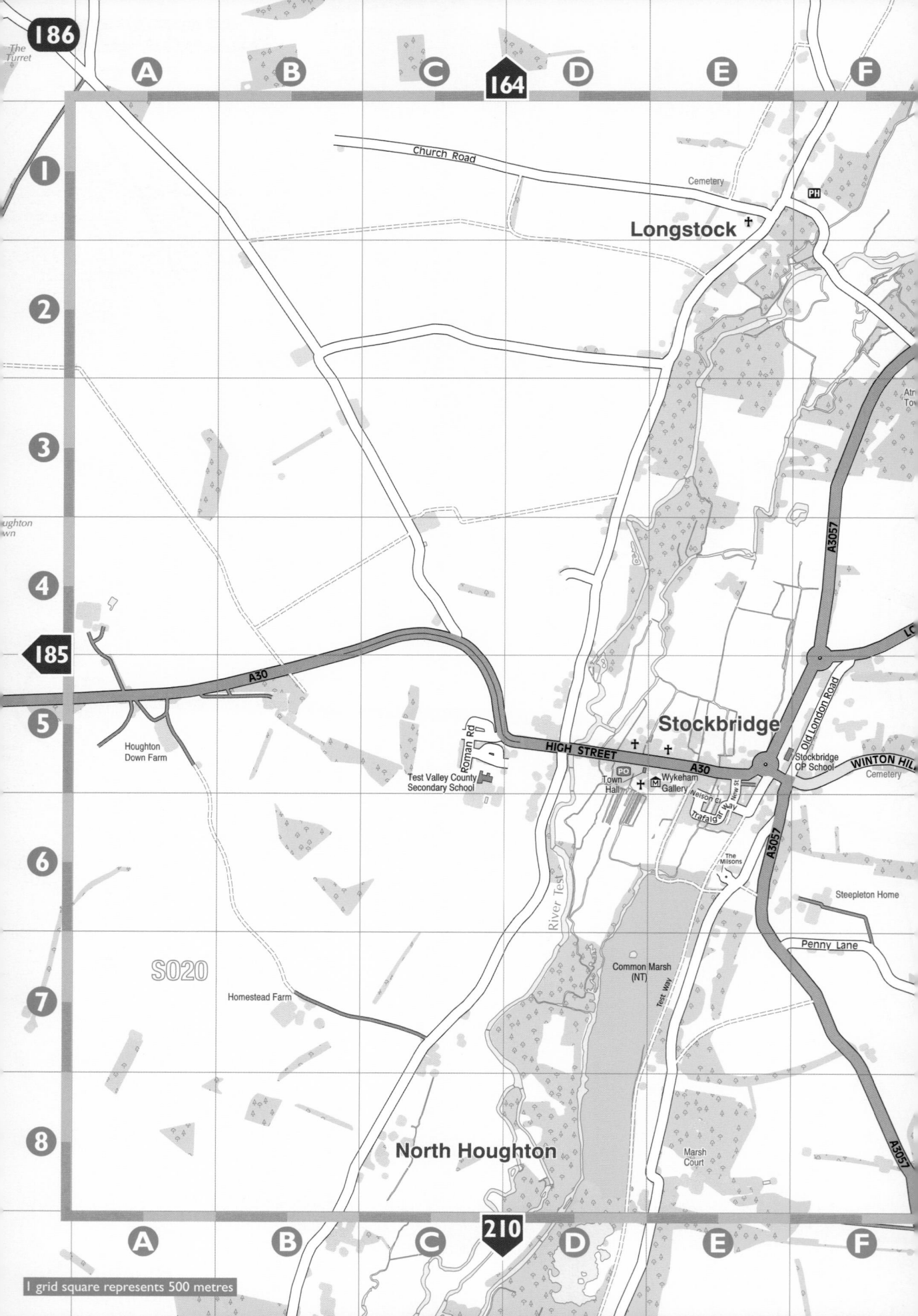

G   H   J   K   L   M

Leckford
PO

165

Leckford Abbas

LECKFORD LANE

A3057

leaf Way

1

2

New Farm

A30

3

A30

4

Fairview Farm

188

Sandydown Farm

Heath House

5

DAD

Stockbridge
Down

6

Bushy
Copse

B3049

B3049

7

Somborne Park Road

Whitehall Road

North
Park Farm

8

Winter
Down
Copse

North
Park Wood

G   H   J   K   L   M

211

G H J **167** K L M

1
2
3 rkwhistle
4
190
5
W
D
6
7
8

Hill Farm

Sutton Down Farm

A272

Crawley Down

Warren Wood

A272

Crawley

New Barn

Beeches Farm

Littleton House

Long Park

G H J **213** K L M

A   B   C   170   D   E   F

I

Newdown Farm

2

3

BASINGSTOKE ROAD

M3

Oxdrove Way

Shroner Wood

Itchen Wood

Micheldever Wood

Chillandham Lane

Chillandham Lane

4

191

5

M3

6

Bridgets Lane

7

Bridgets Farm

Oxdrove Way

Lone Farm

Oxdrove

Rectory Lane

8

A   B   C   216   D   E   F

Baring Cl

Old Station

A B C **172** D E F

I

2 Swarraton Farm

3 Abbotstone Down Abbotstone Woods Spiers Lane

4 Wayfarer's Walk

193

5 Coombe Farm

6 Oxdrove Way

7 **Old Alresford** Southdowns Colden Lane

obdown Farm Green Cl Kiln Lane Colden La

The Brook

8 Oxdrove Way B3046 Alresford House

A B C **218** D E F

Godsfie Farm

Copse Three Castles Path

Three Castles Path

Nettle Fa

Colden L

Pinglestone Farm SOKE Old Alresford SO24

G H J **173** K L M

Armsworth Ho

I

Heath
Green

Upper Lanham Lane

Hoggs
Lodge

Oxdrove Way

Heath Green Lane

Chalky Hill

Upper
Lanham Farm

2

Lower
Lanham
Copse

3

Lower
Lanham

Oxdrove Way

Breach Farm

4

Bighton
House

196

Broadlands

5

Nettlebeds Lane

6

High
Dell Farm

Bighton
Manor

7

Bighton Dean Lane

Bighton
Dean La

Malthouse La

Bighton

Bighton Lane

Barnetts
Wood Farm

Barnetts Wood Lane

8

Sutton Wood Lane

G H J **219** K L M

Gundleton

Sutton
Beech
Wood

Berry Hill

A   **B**   **C**   **174**   **D**   **E**   **F**

E6
1 Drummond Ci

Trinity

1
Heath
Green

Heath Green Lane

Hattingley

Hattingley Road

Wield Road

Castle St

High St

PO

Gn Stile

Hill

The Oaks

Redwood Lane

Hussell Lane

Foul Lane

Medstead

Common Hill

South Town Road

Cem

Roe Downs Road

2

Chalky Hill

Grove Farm

Medstead School

3

Bighton Road

Goatacre Rd

Goatacre Farm

Homestead Road

Dry Hill

South Town

South Town Road

West End

West End Lane

4

Paice Lane

Five

Ash

Lymington Bottom Road

195

Lower Paice Lane

Stancombe Lane

Soldridge Road

Broadlands

5

Rookwood Lane

Stancomb Farm

Stancomb Broad Lane

Upper Soldridge Road

Soldridge

Lymington Farm Industrial Est

Tawny G

6

Grosvenor Road

Kingswood Rise

7

A31

Gloucester

Winchester Road

Bishop's Wy

Hotel

7

Rookwood Lane

Gravel La

Barn Lane

Uplands Lane

Cem

SOKE HILL

Green Lane

Brislands Lane

Gradwell

8

Wo... Lane

Ranscombe Farm

Ropley Soke

Old Down Wood

A   Bowers   Grov.. La   **B**   **North Street**   **C**   **220**   **D**   **E**   **F**

Horse T

Brislands Lane

Kitwoo...

G6
1 Chalk Cl
2 Thorn Crs
3 Thorn Dr

H4
1 Chawton End Cl

H5
1 Fairlight Gdns
2 Hazel Rd

G H J 175 Old Park Fm K L M Chawton Park Farm

I
2
3
4
198
5
6
7
8

Abbey
Road

Chawton Park Wood

Roe Downs Farm

A31

Bricklin Lane

Woodside Lane
Woodside Farms

sell Lane

Red Hill
The Crs
Beechlands Rd
Stoney Lane
Windsor Road
Boyneswood Cl
Boyneswood
Boyneswood Lane
Boyneswood Road

The Shrave

Watercress Line

A31

WINCHESTER ROAD

1
7
Windmill Flds
Station Approach
Approach
Rise
inston
ton
Winston
Spencer
Blenheim Cl
PO
Pine Rd
Thorn Lane
2
Badger
Bray Lane
Blackberry Cl
Fairfield Gn
Mulberry
Boundaries Surgery
Abbotsford Farm Business Centre

Telegraph Lane

Kitcombe Lane

Common Barn Farm

Bogmoor Rd
Merlin Rd
Brambles
Yarmans Cl
Reads Fld
Cozgluun
Bernard Avenue
St Aubins
3
2
Thorn
Blackberry Lane

Four Marks

Weathermore Lane

Telegraph Lane

Pies Farm

Brightstone Lane

Headmore Lane

Willis Lane

Headmore Farm

us Lane
Lymington Bottom
Alton Lane
Bottom

Hawthorn Lane

Mary Lane

Newton Common

Lane
ld Farm
Road
Hawthorn Road

Kitwood
Kitwood Lane

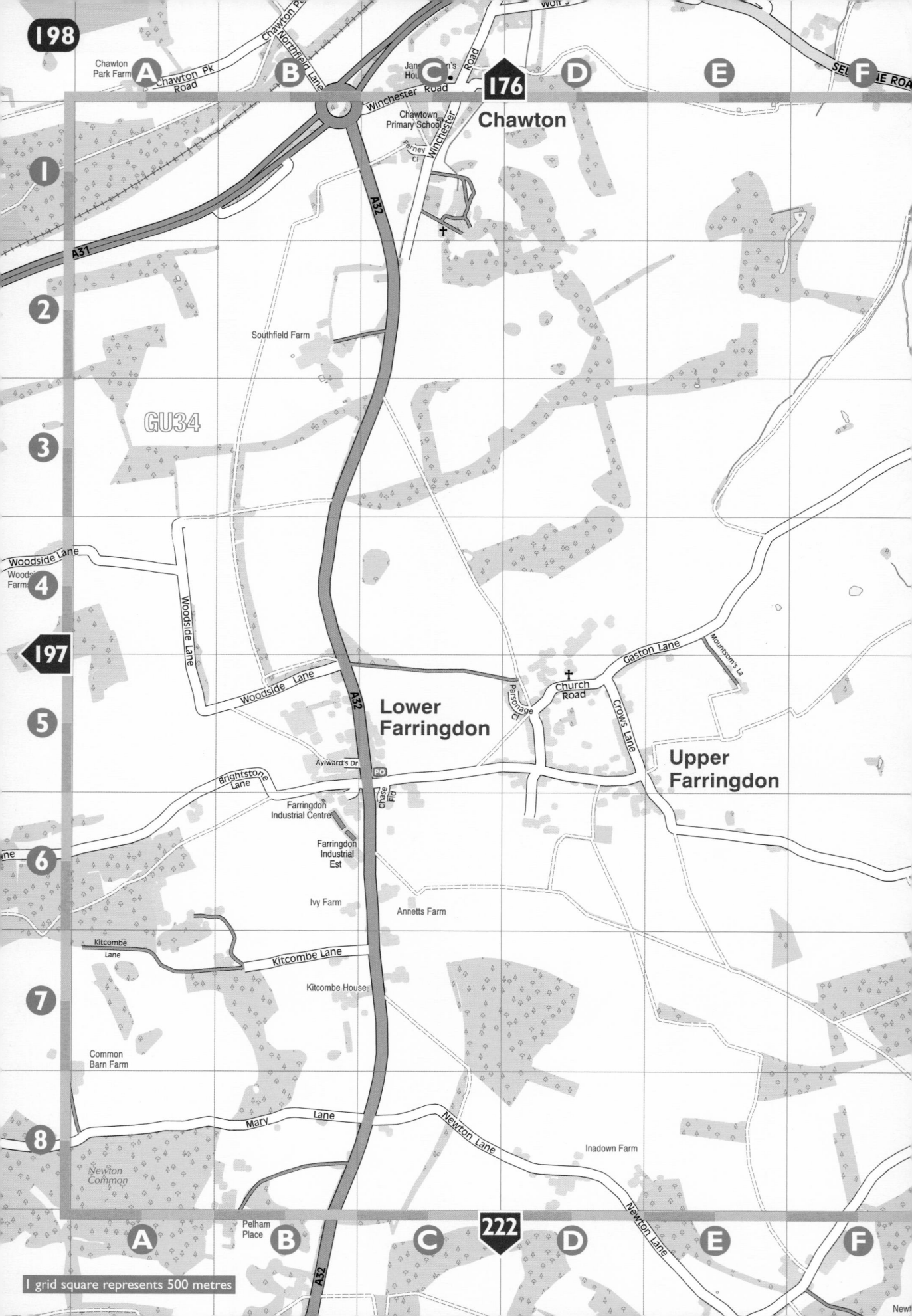

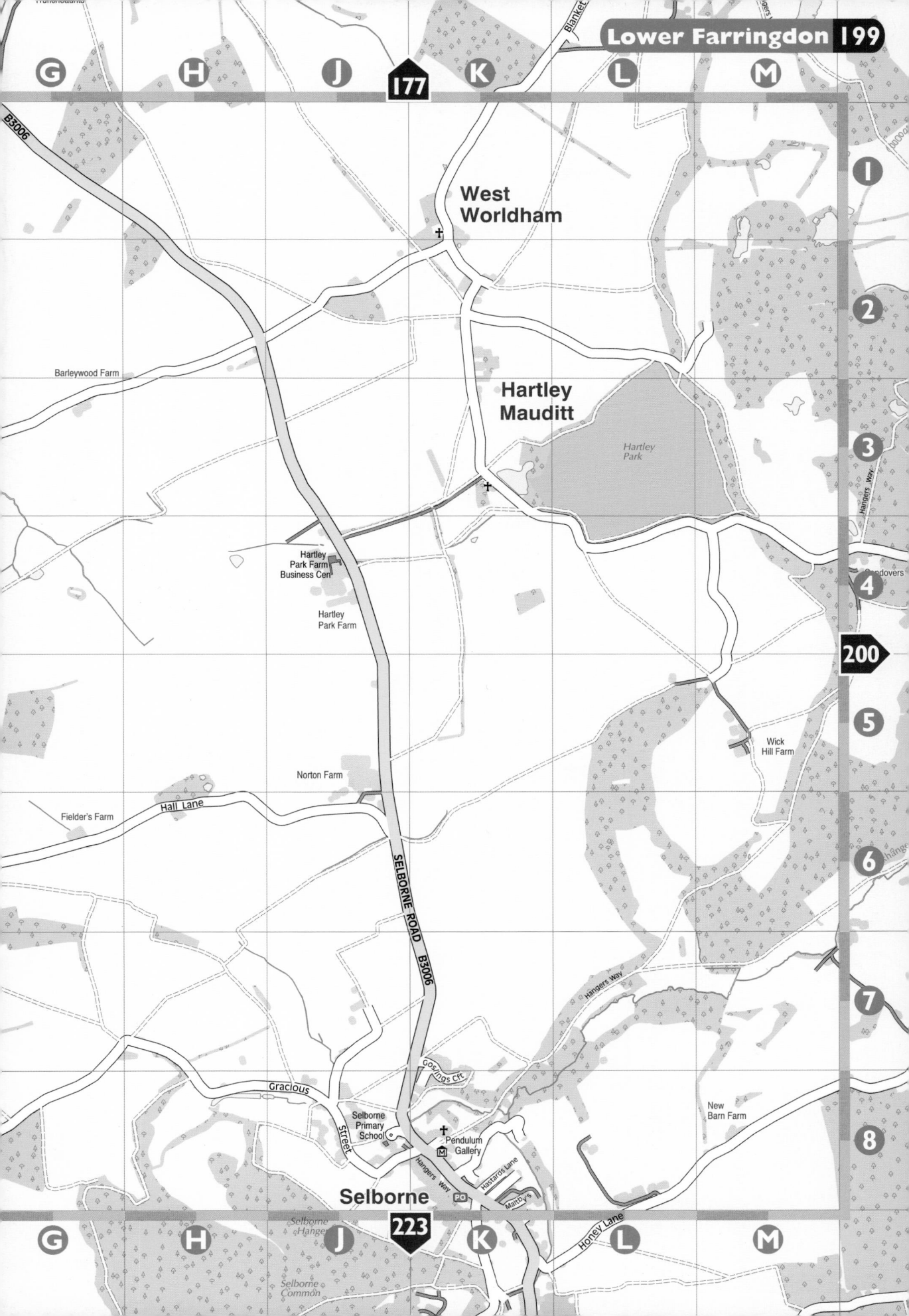

G   H   J   **177**   K   L   M

I

2

West
Worldham

Barleywood Farm

3

Hartley
Mauditt

*Hartley
Park*

Sandovers

4

Hartley
Park Farm
Business Cen

200

Hartley
Park Farm

Wick
Hill Farm

5

Norton Farm

6

Fielder's Farm   Hall Lane

SELBORNE ROAD

B3006

Hangers Way

7

Goslings Cft

New
Barn Farm

8

Gracious

Selborne
Primary
School

Pendulum
Gallery

Hangers Way

Hazards Lane

Selborne
Hanger

Selborne

223

PO

Malteys

Honey Lane

G   H   J   **223**   K   L   M

Selborne
Common

Oxney
Street
179
Broxhead
Common
G H J K L M
I
2
3
4
202
5
6
7
8

Oxney Farm
River Wey
Oxney Pool

Amherst Road
Louisburg Road
Western Rd
North Parade
Stable Road
Southern Road
Eastern Road
Central Parade
STATION ROAD
B3002
FARNHAM RD
CAMP ROAD

Broxhead Trading Est
Frensham Lane
B3004
GU35
HEADLEY RD
MILL LANE
He

LINDFORD ROAD B3002
Lindford Chase
Heather Dr
PO
Forest La
Azalea Av
B3002
B3004
Lindford Wey
Mount Pleasant
Clover Rd
Bluebell Road
Elderberry Rd
Mimosa
Rosewood
Campion
Pryor Rd

Canes La
Taylors Lane
Windsor Road
Pear Tree La
Lands End Lane
Imadene Crescent
LIPHOOK ROAD
Mill Lane

Ladysmith Pl
Oakley
Beaufort Rd
Coniston Rd
Ennerdale Rd
Ullswater
Rydal
Haweswater Cl
Kildare Rd
Bordon County Junior & Infant School
Lamerton Rd
Essex Rd
School Rd
Ramsey Rd
BUDDS LANE
A325
Canada
Car Dr
Maple Cl

Road
B3002
Bolley Av
Cem
Pearl
Road

Waterside Close
Junior School
Rivermede
Waterside
Mill
Washford La
Meadow Vw
Weford County Infants School
Hamilton Close
Chase Road
The Meadow School
Whitehill Cemetery
STANDFORD

Lindford
Deadwater
Mill Chase County Secondary School

Bordon
Whitehill

Woolmer Way
HIGH STREET
Lynton Road
Ashmead
Park St
Somerset Rd
Devon Cl
Woodside Pk
Sydney
Forest Surg
Savile Crs
Saville Crs
Chalet Hill
Varna Rd
Alma Road
Elm Cl
Willow Dr
Lake Dr
Horseshoe
Hollybrook Park
Marsh Close
Waterman
HOLLYWATER ROAD

Sunbury
Heathcote
Birch Cl
Woolmer
PO
Pinehill Rd
Jacaranda Rd
Lilac Cl
Wisteria
Woodpecker Rd
Pinehill Surgery
Hendon Rd
Apollo Drive
Hibiscus Grove
Robinson Wy
Way

Chase Community Hosp
Conde Way
Wellington Av
Kent Rd
York Cl
Argyll
Ashbury
Gainey Rd
Conde Way
Grafton Cl
Roxburghe
Sutherland
Chase
Montrose

Mainsbury Road
Dudley
Cornwall Rd
South Hurst
Alpine Rd
Aspen
Monument Way
Whitehill Road
Standford Hill
Standford

Stubbington Av
Sutton Field
New Road
Lemon Grove
Forest Road
Walldown Rd
Woodlea Primary School
Hollywater

Champney Cl
Fir Grove
Heather Cl
Princes Cl
Corner Close
Champney Cl
PO
Oak Tree Gv
Birch Gv
Pelham Cl
The Woodlands
Liphook Road
Walldown Road

The Fairway
The Links
Firgrove Road
Hogmoor Rd
Broomfield Rd
Eveley Cl
Drift Road
Spruce Avenue
Hogmoor Inclosure

Passfield Common

G8
1 Bartholomew Cl

J7
1 Ash Tree Cl
2 Williamson Cl

G   H   J   Park Lane   K   L   M

Park Copse

I

Park Lane

A286

Witley Farm

2

Creedhole Farm

High Button

Holmen's Grove

Littlebrook Farm

3

Hurthill Copse

Lower Birtley Farm

4

South Park Farm

A286

5

Prestwick Lane

High Prestwick Farm

6

Church Cl

Grayswood C of E School

PH

Lower Road

Paddock Wy

The Mount

Park Cl

1
2

Upper Mt

Grayswood

Frillinghurst Wood

7

GRAYSWOOD ROAD

A286

Sandy Lane

Grayswood Common

Holdfast Lane

St End Lane

8

Highercombe Rd

Grays Cl

Three Gates La

Imbhams Farm

Uplands Cl

Beech Road

Haslemere Health Centre & District Hospital

Kernal Pk

Three Gates Lane

G   H   J   229   K   L   M

Holdfast

Furnace Place

G2
1 Glenfield Cl

M8
1 The Withies

G   H   J   183   K   L   M

I

2

3

4

208

Yew Tree Lane

5

6

7

8

Hill Farm

Warren Farm

Causeway

The Flashett Gunville Hill

Easton Common Hl

Gunville Rd

The Common

Witt
Way

Bentley
Way

Tytherley
Road

Road

Clarendon Way

Monarch's Way

Noad's
Copse

Picked
Copse

Hedgemoor
Copse

Bentley
Wood

Norman
Court
School

North
Lane

Park   Lane

Park Lane

Park
Copse

alpits
pse

Park Lane

Standing   Hill

Home Farm

Dean Road

Pug's Hole

North La

North Lane

Rectory Hill

PO

Chalk

West Tytherley
Primary School

We
Tyt

The Green

Pug's Hol

The Coa

G   H   J   231   K   L   M   The Gree

G **H** **J** 185 **K** **L** **M**

I

2

Manor Farm

oughton County
mary School

High St

Dixons Lane

Hinwood

Paynes

Chapel
Lane

Paynes Ct

eshoot

Plough
Cons

Queenwood Rd

PH

Broughton

PO

PO

Rectory Lane

Eveley Farm

Queenwood
Rise

Beechcroft
Cottages

Coolers
Farm

Rookery

Lane

Monarch's Way

South
Road

3

The   Hollow

Roake Farm

ROMSEY ROAD

B3084

Horsebridge Road

Wallop Brook

Faithfulls

Drove

4

Horsebridge Road

210
Bossir

Beech Tree Walk

5

6

Crown Farm

River T

7

8

Bentley
Farms

B3084

Pittleworth Farm

G **H** **J** 233 **K** **L** **M**

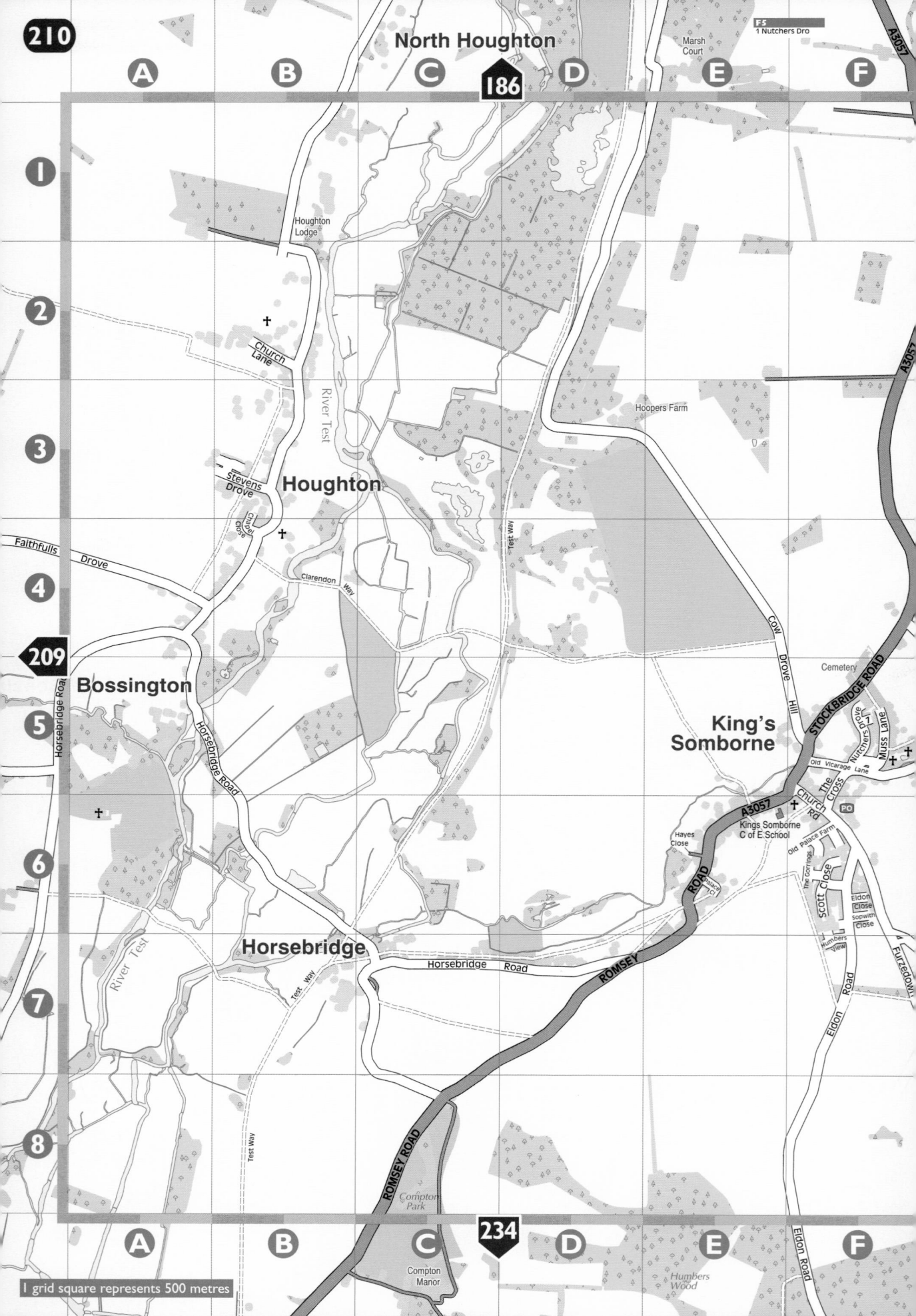

A   B   C   **188**   D   E   F

B3049

STOCKBRIDGE ROAD

Kirton Fa

1

Rookley
Manor

2

CourtLane

● **Somborne**

3

Sparsholt College
Hampshire

4

◀**211**

5

Great Up
Somborne Wood

Ashley
Wood

6

Well
Copse

7

Forest of Bere Farm

Farley
Mount

West
Wood

Farley Mount
Country Park

8

A   B   C   **236**   D   E   F

Clarendon W.

1 grid square represents 500 metres

Clarendon Way

G H J K L M

189

Long Park

Littleton House

I

Church Lane

2

New Road

Main Road

Rozelle Close
Holm Oak Cl
Fairclose
The Hall

Litt

Hilden Way

Dale Close
Valley Road

Eyre

3

South Drive

4

214

STOCKBRIDGE ROAD B3049

B3049

Westley Lane

Northwood Park

Lainston House Hotel

Watley Lane

Westley Lane

Moor Court Farm

Lock's Lane

Lock's Lane

Lane

PH

Church Lane

Home Lane

Woodman Lane

Dean

5

Moor Court Lane

Lambourne Close

PO

Sparsholt

Sparsholt Primary School

Bostock Close

Woodman Close

Dean Lane

Westview Road

6

Littleton Lane

Lanham Lane

7

Burrow Road

Beec Copse

Lanham Lane

8

Crab Wood

Crabwood Farm House

Teg Dow

Clarendon Way

Royal Winchester Golf Club

G H J K L M

237

Clarendon Way

Sarum Road

Sarum Road

G5
1 Cavendish Gv

G6
1 Green Park Cl

H1
1 Felmer Dr
2 Field End
3 Holdaway Cl

191

G H J K L M

I

B3047

2

KINGS WORTHY

Hinton House

Kingsworthy Primary School

Springvale Av

Bentley Cl

Hinton Fields

Mt. Pleasant

Abbots Worthy

Princes Mead School

Worthy Park

Itchen Way

Easton Lane

3

Easton

PH PH PH

Three Castles Path

Church Lane

Malthouse Cl

216

4

St Mary's

King's Way

Itchen Way

Three Castles Path

Lone Barn

Easton Lane

5

BASINGSTOKE ROAD

WINCHESTER BY-PASS

A33

B3047

Park Lane

London Road

Bedfield Lane

B3047

Easton Down

Long Walk

M3

II

Long Walk

Chapel Lane

6

Harfield

River Itchen

Itchen Way

Moorside Road

Leicester Way

Winchester Rugby Football Club

Fair Lane

7

Larkwhistle Farm

WINCHESTER BY-PASS

A272

Junction 9

Wykeham Industrial Estate

Son Valley Business Park

Winnall Down Farm

8

Winnall

Easton Lane

Easton Lane Business Park

Winnall Valley Road

Imber Road

Manor Road

Warren Road

Shepherds Road

Longfield Road

Garbett Road

Winnall CP School

Turnpike

St Swithuns School

No Man's Land

G St Giles's Hill H

ALRESFORD ROAD

239

J K L M

A33

Old Station Approach

Chesil Theatre

Northbrook Avenue

Stratton Road

Magdalen Hill Down

Cemetery

J8
1 Limetree Wk
2 Spitfire End

J2
1 Old Rectory Gdns

H8
1 Baigent Cl
2 Gatekeeper Cl
3 Longhouse Gn
4 Peacock Pl
5 Ringlet Wy
6 Roundhuts Ri

C3
1 Carpenters
2 Ellingham Cl
3 Meadow Cl
4 Searles Cl

B3
1 Maple Cl
2 Robertson Rd

B3
1 Lovells Wk

A4
1 Watercress Mdw

A   B   C   D   E   F

194

I

S024

Pinglestone Farm

2

Arle Cl   Arle Gdns   Mallard Cl

NEW ALRESFORD

Baytree Gallery   Candover Gallery

PH   The George Yard

WEST ST   EAST ST

POUND HL   Hotel   The Alresford Surg

B3047

B3047 THE AVENUE

Perins County Secondary School

Station Ap   Haig Rd

MANCHESTER RD

De-Lucy Av   Grange   Nursery Road   Watercress Line

3

Bridge Rd   Road   Roseley Rd   Lime Rd   Beech Rd   Western Court

Ashburton   Salisbury Rd   Hawthorn   Oak Hill   Mill Lane

South Cl   South Road   Ashburton Rd   Elm Road   Alresford County Junior School

Jesty Rd   Windsor Rd   Beneden Gn   Oak Hill   Sun Hill Infant School

Covey Wy   Mervon Rd   Jacklyn Cl   Culley VW   Beneden Gn   Sun Lane

JACKLYNS LANE   Russell Rd   Lindley Gdns   Derwent Gdns   Crescent

4

Prospect Road   Prospect Business Cen   Linnets   Hasted Dr   Corfe Cl   Down   Appledown   Tichborne Down

Spring Gdns   Paddock Wy   Shepherds   Tichborne   Down   Orchard Cl   Bell Ho   Whitehill Lane

217

A31   A31

5

Alresford Golf Club

Vernal Farm

Wayfarer's Walk

Appledown Lane

Scrubbs Lane

6

Tichborne Park   B3046   Scrubb Farm   Dark Lane

chborne

7

Wayfarer's Walk   Cheriton La   Cheriton

8

Itchen Way   River Itchen

Sevington Farm   Cheriton Mill   Bighton Lane   Bighton End Lane

242

A   B   C   D   E   F

C4
1 Arundel Cl
2 Buttermere Gdns
3 Carisbrooke Cl
4 Coniston Gv
5 Dickenson Wk
6 Ennerdale Gdns
7 Ullswater Gv
8 Win'mere Gdns
9 Witton Hl

1 grid square represents 500 metres

NORTH   B3046   Middle Farm

G   H   J   **195**   K   L   M

1

2

A31

3

Watercress Line

Berry Hill

Bighton Hill

Gundleton

Goscombs Lane

Sutton Beech Wood

Sutton Wood Lane

Bighton Bottom Farm

Northside Farm

Northside Lane

Northside Lane

Bighton Lane

Green Lane

North Street

Church La

School La

Home Close

Riverhead

Hobbs Cl

Water Lane

B3047

Bishop's Sutton

THE DENE

Station Hill

Darvil Rd

Dene

PO

Ropley Lodge

Dean Surgery

Ropley Dean

Hook

Lane

Berry Hill

Petersfield Rd

4

220

5

Park Lane

Manor House Farm

Tegg Down Road

Old Park Road

Parkside Lane

6

7

Common Farm

Old Park Wood

Old Park Road

8

Bramdean Common

G   H   J   **243**   K   L   M

Cheriton Wood

Wood Lane

1 grid square represents 500 metres

Selborne Primary School

† Pendulum Gallery

Selbo 199

Street

Hangers Way

PO

K

Crss Lane

MaltDys

Honey Lane

New Barn Farm

G H J K L M

Selborne Hanger

Selborne Common

Newton Valence

Longhope

Lane

Hangers Way

Ketchers Fld

Sotherington Lane

Burhunt Farm

1

2

Lower Noar Hill Farm

Hangers Way

3

Charity Farm

Hangers Way

4

Mill Lane

224

5

Empshott Green

Empshott

†

Churc

Goleigh Farm

Hangers Way

Lythanger

6

Button's Lane

Vann Farm

Keyham Farm

Mill Lane

Hawkley Hurst

7

Mill Lane

Eames Lane

8

Manor House

†

Lowergreen Farm

G H J K L M

Hangers Way

247

Hawkley

Upland Lane

Hawkley Ro

† PH

Scotland Farm

G   H   J   **201**   K   L   M

I
2
3
4
5
6
7
8

Liphook   Road

Hollywater Road

Cranmer
Bottom

Linchborough
Park

Brimstone
Inclosure

Woolmer
Forest

Forkedpon
Inclosure

A325

PETERSFIELD ROAD

Woolmer
Pond

WOOLMER ROAD

PORTSMOUTH   ROAD

Longmoor Road

226

A3(T)

A3(T)

Old
& Co

Queens   Road

Plumer
Road

French Rd

Railway Rd

Kitchener   Road

Methuen

Rd

Roberts   Rd

Warren   Road

Hunters
Rd

Avenue

White

Longmoor Camp

Hamilton
Rd

Kimberley Rd

Paterson   Rd

Baden Powell Rd

Pretoria

Jan Smuts Cl

Union   Cl

Cr

Weavers
Down

Moor Road

Palmer's
Ball

Longmoor
Inclosure

Sussex   Border   Path

Fo
M

Fo

G   H   J   **249**   K   L   M

G4
1 Hawkshaw Cl
2 Wey Lodge Cl
3 Wykwood

G5
1 Enfield Cl
2 Willow Cl

H4
1 Collyers Crs

G Downlands **H** **J** 203 **K** Bramshott Common **L** Knocknundred Lane **M** Woolmer Hill Road

PORTSMOUTH ROAD

Woolmer H **I**

Rectory Lane

Sandy Lane

Hatchetts Drive

Lower Hanger

Fir A Sur **2**

Oak

nshott

A3(T)

Cold Ash Hill

Hewshott Lane

Hewshott Lane

Hewshott Cr

Hampshire County

West Sussex County

Hammer Lane

Hammer Bottom

Hammer Lane

Moor Rd

Hammer

Cemetery

Copse Heath

Roa

B2. **3**

Hewshott House

Gillham's Lane

Gillham's Lane

ROAD

Linchmere Road

Hammer Hill

Locke Rd

Stonehouse Rd

The Maltings

B2131 ROAD

ASLEMERE

Hazelbank Cl

Manor Flds

LIPHOOK

Linchmere Common

4

228

Devils Lane

Highfield Lane

Sussex Border Path

Danley Lane

Linchmere

Linchmere †

5

Willow Ash Gdns Golden Flds Chestnut Cl Lane

Chiltley Way Chiltley Lane

Littlefield School

Highfield Lane

Brookham School

Highfield School

Sussex Border Path

Sussex Border Path

6

7

Stanley Common

sheeps

Stanley Farm

8

G Hollycombe **H** **J** 251 **K** Parkgate Rough **L** **M**

G H J 205 K L M

1

Haslemere Health Centre District Hospital

Three Gates Lane

G 1 Cobden La

Uplands Cl

Highercombe Rd

Three Gates La

Holdfast La

Imbhams Farm

Furnace Place

Killinghurst Lane

Kemnal Pk

Haslemere Museum

HASLEMERE

Well La

Collards Lane

epherd's Hill

2

Swan Barn Road

Holdfast

Holdfast Lane

PETWORTH ROAD B2131

PETWORTH ROAD

Ansteadbrook

3

Hotel

B2

Haste Hill

Haste Hill

mere ratory ool

Denbigh Rd

Lane

Lythehill House

4

Chase Lane

Tennyson's Lane

Surrey County

West Sussex County

Home Wood

5

Sussex Border Path

Tennyson's Lane

Barfold

Jay's Lane

Chase Lane

Tennyson's Lane

6

Valewood Ho

Aldworth Ho

Roundhurst Common

Roundhurst Farms

7

Fernden Lane

Black Down

Sussex Border Path

Tennyson's Lane

8

Black Down

▲ 280
Blackdown Hill

Cotchet Farm

Abesters

Jobson's Lane

G H J K L M

G H J K L M

207

I
The
Green

2

Frenchmoor

3

4

232

5

6
East
Dean

7

8

259

G H J K L M

Park

Copse

Standing Hill

Dean

Tyth

The Coach

Pug's Hole

Red Lane

Bulls

Drove

Dean Road

Tytherley Common

Dean Road

Frenchmoor Lane

Drove Farm Ho

Howe
Copse
East

Wiltshire County
Hampshire County

Dean
Copse

Pilgrims
Croft

PO

Hill

River Dunn

Rectory

West
Dean

Frenchmoor La

Park Farm

Dean
Station

Dean Road

Moody's Hill

Hillside Close

Ashmore Lane

Glebe Mdw

Deanhill
Barn

Gatmore
Copse

Hampshire County
shire County

Mean
Wood

Ashmore Lane

Tytherley

Stride's Farm

208

nor Farm

Manor Rd

Manor
Rd

**East
Tytherley**

Cedars Vw

The Green

The Coach Road

The Coach Road

Pug's Hole

Drove

Pug's Hole

Lockerley Hall

Lain
Copse

Pug's
Hole Farm

231

Holbury Farm

Holbury La.

Holbury Lane

Holbury
Mill

Lockerley
Water Farm

River Dunn

River Dun

LC

Road

East

Dean

PO

**East
Dean**

Glebe Mdw

Lockerley

Lockerley
C of E
Primary School

Lockerley Rd

Pendle Gn

Butt'
Gree

Cooks Lane

Butlers
Close

Oval Rd

Clem's Wy

Deanhill
Barn

**Critchell's
Green**

Cooks Lane

260

Hampshire County
Wiltshire County

Mount
Lane

F7
1 Butlers Cl

G H J 209 K L M

I
2
3
4
234
5
6
7
8

Bentley Farms
Pittleworth

B3084

Back Lane

River Test

Spearywell Wood

Test Way

Oakley Fm

Cadbury Fm

Spearywell

Oakley Rd

Test Way

Mottisfont Abbey

Mottisfont Abbey Garden House & Estate (NT)

Keepers Lane

Benger's Lane

Mottisfont Club House

A3057

B3084

Hatt Lane

PO

Church Lane

Mottisfont

Church Lane

Hatt Hill

Stonyma

LC
Dunbridge Station

Dunbridge

PH
Russell Dr
Mill Rise

River Dun

Lockerley Road

Staff F

Canefield

DUNBRIDGE

Kimbridge Lane

Kimbridge

Monarch's Way

Kimbri Lane LC

River Test

LANE

I

2

3

4

5

6

7

8

A B C D E F

Romsey Road

Compton Park

Compton Manor

Compton

Test Way

Brook

A3057

Test Way

A3057

Humbers Wood

Eldon Road

Lower Brook

Lower Eldon Fm

Michelmersh Wood

Park Fm

Stubb's Copse

Parnell Lane

Mesh Road

Church Rd

Monarch's Way

Monarch's Way

Stonymarsh

Staff Road

Manor Fm

Lane

Monarch's Way

Staff Road

Michelmersh

Hackupos Lane

Farm

Staff Road

Manor Road

Rudd Lane

PO

Hill View Road

New Road

Chapel La

ge La

STOCK... BRIDGE ROAD

A505...

Mannyngham Way

Timsbury

A B C D E F

I grid square represents 500 metres

G   H   J   **211**   K   L   M

I
2
3
4
236   †
5
6
7
8

Clarendon Way

Luke Copse

Furzedown

Parnholt Wood

Farley Down

Bailey's Down

Fishponds Fm

Farley Fi

Farley Ho

Oakfield

Dore

Ho

Furzedown Road

Eldon Road

Eldon Road

Hall Place

Monarch's Way

Kings Somborne Road

Pitt Fm

Farley Lane

Upper Slackstead

Monarch's Way

Braishfield Road

Paynes Hay Road

Paynes Hay Farm

Monarch's Way

Hill Lane

Fern

Church Lane   †

G   H   J   **263**   K   L   M   **Lower Slackstead**

Braishfield   Dummers   res Lane

Farley
Mount

Wood

Farley Mount
Country Park

A   B   C   D   E   F

Clarendon Way

1

Clarendon Way

Pitt
Down

2

Mount
Down

Farley Mount Road

3

Farley
Down

South
Lynch

4

Farley Fm

Berrydown Farm

5

Southlynch
Plantn

Dores Lane

Dores   Lane

6

Gudge
Copse

Merdon Manor Farm

7

ope
ackstead

Dores   Lane

8

A   B   C   D   E   F

Home Farm

Clap

Mon

Hursley Park

1 grid square represents 500 metres

G H J K L M

I

2

3

4

238

5

6

7

8

213

265

Crab Wood

Crabwood Farm House

Lanham Lane

Dow

Royal Winchester Golf Club

Clarendon Way

Sarum Road

Clarendon Way

Sarum Road

Sarum Road

Sparsholt Road

Clarendon Way

Kilham

Sarum View

Enmill Farm

Enmill Lane

Pitt

A3090

Seldon Close

Grovelands Copse

Sparsholt Road

unt Road

A3090

andon

Millers Lane

Oliver's Battery

Sunnydown Road

Broad View Lane

Beyne Road

shepherds

Rose Braeside

Close

ford Road

Pine Close

Beech Cl

Prio

Texas

old Kennels Close

Wedmore Close

Lisle Cl.

Down Farm

Lane

Old Kennels Lane

Silkstead Lane

Port Lane

Heathcote Place

Collins Lane

Shawlan Lane

Cemetery

Monarch's Way

Huxley

PO

G H J **217** K L **M** Sevington Farm

Barley
Down House

...ley
...od

King's
Way

River Itc...

1

Rodfield Lane

Ovington
Down Farm

2

Hill Houses

3

Westfield
Farm

King's Way

4

South Downs Way

242

A2...

Gander
Down

Ganderdown
Farm

Hockley House

5

...field Lane

A272

A272

Holding Lane

Holden Farm

6

New
Warren Farm

Rabbit
Copse

7

Lane
End
Down

South Downs Way

Westfield Drove

Beauworth

Hamilton Farm

8

Lane End

G H J **269** K L **M** Yew Tree Farm

Lane End Farm

Holden

G H J K L M

219

Old Park Wood

Park Road

Bramdean Common

1

Cheriton Wood

Wood Lane

Marriners Farm

Wood Farm

2

3

Bramdean

The Spinney

Wood Lane

Woodlane Close

Slys Farm

Church Lane

A272

PH

Woodcote Manor House

Tithelands Lane

4

244

Hinto Woo

5

The Dean

A272

6

Joan's Acre

Brockwood Bottom

Brockwood Park

7

Joan's Acre Wood

Brockwood Bottom

8

Black House Farm

G H J K L M

271

Bere Farm

Mardell Farm

Bramdean
Common

① West Tisted

220

Clinkley
Road

† PO

Brick Kiln Lane

② Wolfhanger Farm

Punsholt Lane

The Jumps

Green La

③

④ Slys Farm

Punsholt Farm

Purser's

243

Hinton
Woodlands Farm

Punsholt Lane

Filmore Hill

A32

Filmorehill Lane

⑤

Three Horse
Shoes Farm

Three Horse Shoes Lane

The
Dean

A272

Lane

Kitt's

**West Meon
Woodlands**

⑥

Woodlands Farm

⑦ Shutt's
Copse

West
Meon Hut

A272

Sto

⑧

Highfield

Marlands

272

Vinnells

Hayling
Wood

G H J **221** K L M

Brick Kiln Farm

Brick Kiln Lane

Lane End

Colemora Common

Basing Park

Basing Home Farm

A32

Sages Lane

Ashen Wood House

Basing Dean

Coles

Basing Dean

Fawley Lane

Fawley Farm

Hempland Lane

Ilmorehill Lane

Bailey Green

Church Lane

PO

Farnfield Farm

Merepond Lane

Hurst Farm

Hurst

246

Stocks Lane

k Farm

Privett

Bower Far

A272

A272

Pe G H J **273** K L M

1
2
3
4
5
6
7
8

222

245

274

Colemore
Common

A B C D E F

I

2

3

4

5

6

7

8

Field Farm

Hermitage Farm

Five
Ash

PH

Claypitt Lane

Claypit Farm

Barnet
Side

Barnet
Side

Ragmore Lane

Green Lane

Wa
Co

Alexander's Farm

Coles

Basing Dean

King's Lane

Ivyhouse Lane

Blackmore Lane

Ivyhouse Farm

Bensgreen Farm

Hu

Hurst

Woolfield Lane

King's Lane

The
Slade

High Cross Lane

Week Green Fa

Bower Farm

Privett Road

High
Cr

Dellfield

Dellfield

PO

High Cross

Froxfield
Endowed Controlled
Infant School

Deans
Dell

Bydean Farm

High Cross Lane

Soalwood Lane

High Cross Lane

Broadhanger

King

Lane

Bro

Broad   Way

† Froxfield
Green

Staple Ash Lane

er's Farm

Ridge Top Lane

1 grid square represents 500 metres

G   H   J   223   K   L   M   1

Mill Lane

Eames Lane

Manor House

Scotland Farm

Lowergreen Farm

Hawkley

Hangers Way

Upland Lane

2

Pococks Lane   PH

Hawkley Road

Farm

Hawkley Road

3

Ba   Farm

The Warren

Oakshott Farm

Hangers Way

Oakshott Stream

Warren Lane

Cottage Lane

4

Oakshott

248

Hill Farm

Wheatham Farm

Lane

5

PH   Honeycritch   Old Litten Lane   Old Litten Lane

Coldh

Lane   Lane

Cockshott   Lane

6

Hangers Way

Bushy Hill

Steep Marsh Farm

Steep Marsh

Ashford Chace   Hangers Way   Mill Lane   7

Hangers Way   Brickyards Ind Estate

Stoner Hill

8

Lane

Church Common

Island   Mill Lane   Hangers Way   **Steep**   Steep Farm

Steep   275   Church   Steep School   Steep School

Stonerwood Park

G   H   J   K   L   M

PH   A3(T)

G H J 227 K L M

I
2
3
4
5
6
7
8

Hollycombe

Parkgate
Rough

Home
Farm

Elmers
Copse

Elmers
Marsh

Minepit
Copse

ley

Northend Farm

✝

Lambourne Lane

Linch Road

Woodmansgreen

Upper North
Park Farm

Inholms
Copse

Redford

Lambourne Lane

PO

Hurst
Farm

Titty Hill

Linch Road

Woolbeding
Common

Queen's
Corner

sheeps

Iping Road

ns

High Road

The Alley Netton St

Butt Lane

The Croft

The Styles

ne

Hill Lane

G **H** **J**

Bishopstone

Chapel La

Bridge The Cross

Croucheston Drove

K **L** **M**

I

2

3

Faulston Down

A354 **4**

254

Faulstone Down Farm

Jervoise Farm

5

Croucheston Down Farm

A354

Toyd Clump

Toyd Clump

6

Hampshire County

Wiltshire County

Swayne's Firs

7

A354

Grimsdyke Granaries

Little Toyd Down

Toyd Farm

8

G **H** **J** **281** **K** **L** **M**

254

A   B   BLANDFORD   C   D   E   F

1

2
Coombe Bissett Down
Homington
Down

A354

3
Stratford
Tony Down
Down Bar

Southdown Farm

4
A354
Pennings Farm
SP5

Greenacres Farm

253

5
'Great
Yews'
Grims
Lodge Farm
Wiltshire County
Hampshire County

6
Black
Hill
Round
Clump

7

8
arm
Tenantry Farm
Whitsbury Down

A   B   C   282   D   E   F

Rockbourne
Down

G H J K L M

I
2
3
256
4
5
6
7
8

Odstock

Odstock Down

Little
Yews

Nunton Drove

Yews Farm

New Court
Down Barn

New Court Down

Wick Lane

Wick
Down

G H J 283 K Botley's Farm L M

Wiltshire County
Hampshire County

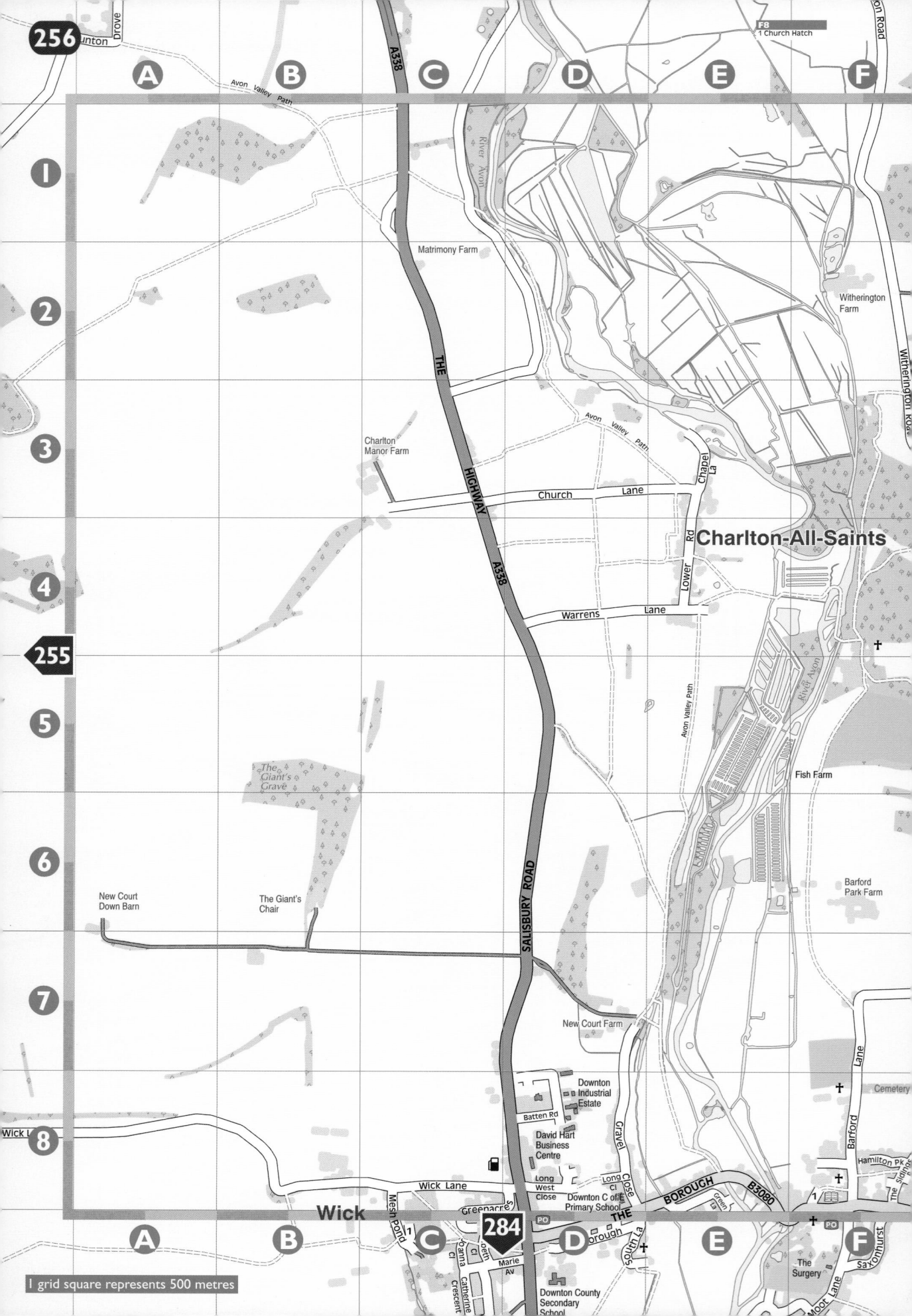

G H J K L M

1

Windwhistle Lane

A36(T)

Witherington Down

2

3

Standlynch Farm

Privett Farm

4

258

5

Standlynch Down

Langford   Lane

Barford Down Farm

Barford Down

Langford Lane

6

7

Muddyford Road

Templeman Farm

Down House

8

Langford La

Low Pensworth Farm

DE HILL B3080

ow G n

285

H

J

The Business Centre

The Row

K

PH

L

Grove   Lane

M

Chalk's Rd

Morgans

Rise Road

Down

Bowers Hill

Prince

Petticoat La

Sa

1

G4
1 The Triangle

G H J **231** K L M

Gatmore Copse

Hampshire County
Wiltshire County

1

Mean Wood

2

Cowesfield House Farm

3

Rowden's Farm

Ashmore Lane

Miles's Lane

Miles's Lane

more Ho

Ashmore Green

Highlands Way

The Green

Dean La

A27 ROMSEY ROAD

Meadow Ct

Miles's Lane

Bunny

Morrisholt Farm

4

260

Whiteparish Surgery

Croft Hts

Whiteparish All Saints C of E Primary School

The Bramleys

Cowesfield Green

THE STREET

A27

5

Common Rd

Common Fm

Parkwater Road

6

The Drive

The Drive

Whiteparish Common

Common Road

Parkwater Road

Melchet Court (St Edwards School)

lchet Cl

7

arldoms odge

Common

8

A36(T)

Stock Lane

La rdw d

Stock La

Park Water

Canefield

G   H   J   **233**   K   Kimbridge   L   M

I

Mount Fm

2

Hyde Fm

Awbridge Ho

Carter's

Saunders Lane

Lockerley Road

Kents Oak

3

Clay

Road

Awbridge County School

Danes Road

Awbridge

Test Way

Cooks

Lane

4

262

STANBRID

The Square

Newtown

Church

Upper Ratley

Lane

Newtown Road

Awbridge Danes

Lower Ratley

Coombe Lane

5

South Drive

Dunwood Manor Golf Club

Danes Road

6

Dunwood Manor

SALISBURY ROAD

The Frenches

Old Salisbury Lane

Test   Way

Frenches Lane

Shootash

7

Rok

Stanbridge Ranvilles Fm

Squabb Wood

Tanners Lane

A27

8

G   H   J   **289**   K   L   M

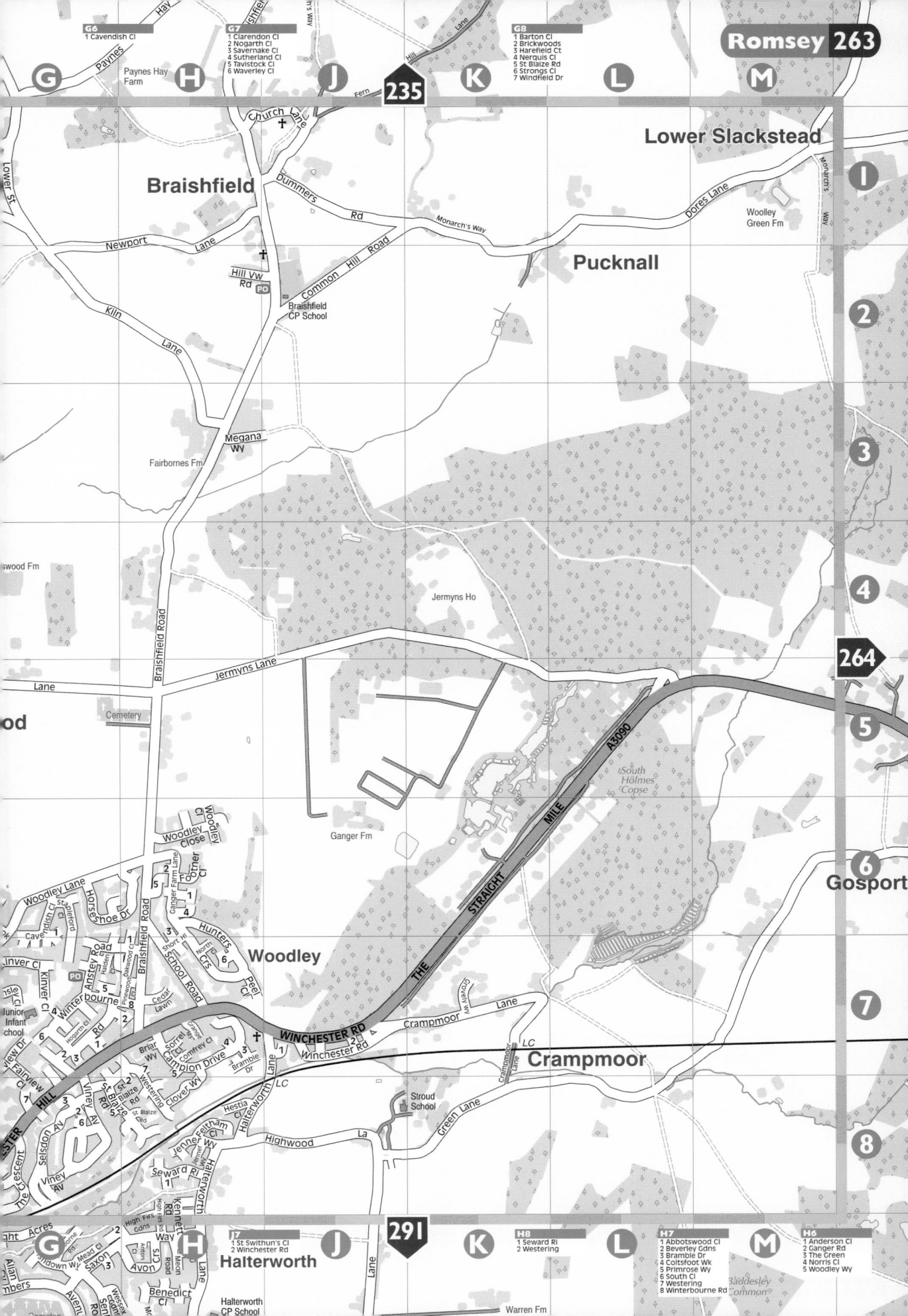

235

264

291

G H J K L M

I 2 3 4 5 6 7 8

Lower Slackstead

Braishfield

Pucknall

Paynes Hay Farm

Woolley Green Fm

Newport Lane

Monarch's Way

Dores Lane

Monarch's Way

Hill VW Rd PO

Braishfield CP School

Kiln Lane

Megana Wy

Fairbornes Fm

Jermyns Ho

South Hölmes Copse

Braishfield Road

Jermyns Lane

Cemetery

Ganger Fm

A3090

THE STRAIGHT MILE

Woodley Close

Woodley Lane

Horseshoe Dr

Woodley

Ganger Farm Lane

Hunters

North Crs

Grovely Lane

Gosport

Junior Infant chool

Winter bourne

School Road

Braishfield Road

Cedar Lawn

Pinewood

Oakwood

WINCHESTER RD

Crampmoor Lane

Crampmoor Lane

Crampmoor

Winchester Rd

Stroud School

Green Lane

Briar Wy

Campion Drive

Clover Wy

Bramble Dr

Halterworth Lane

Hestia

Highwood

La

Selsdon Av

Viney Av

Jenne Feltham Wy

Seward Ri

HILL

The Crescent

Halterworth Av

Kennett Rd

Saxon

Avon

Meon

Benedict Cl

Halterworth CP School

Warren Fm

G6
1 Clevelands Cl
2 Rothville Pl
3 Tithewood Cl

G7
1 Albury Pl
2 Apsley Pl
3 Chillingfield Gdns
4 Lauriston Dr
5 Stratfield Dr
6 The Tanyards
7 Vanburgh Wy

G8
1 Balmoral Cl
2 Barford Cl
3 Drummond Wy
4 Polesden Cl

G   H   J   237   K   L   M

Port Lane
Heathcote Place
Collins Lane
Shawlands Farm

Cemetery
Monarch's Way

Hursley

Bunstead Lane

PO
Merdun Close
South End Close

A3090
Keble Memorial Primary School

B3043

Poles Lane

Bunstead

Shepherds Lane

Silkstead Lane

Silkstead

Four Dell Farm

Poles Lane

Ladwell

HURSLEY ROAD

B3043

Field House

Freemantles Copse

266

Cranbury House

Home Farm

Cranbury Park

Otterbourne Primary School

M3

Hill

Hocombe Road

Hocombe Park Close

Ashdown

Hocombe

Charnwood Cl
Charnwood Crs

Ashdown Close
Maytree Rd

Hiltingbury

Randall Road

Hocombe Road

Coultas Road

Hocombe Road

Otterbourne Lane

Boyatt Lane

HURSLEY ROAD

Hocombe Drive

Ashdown Road
Hazel Close
Heathfield Road
Walnut Close
Woodlands Close

Sycamore Avenue

PO

Nichol Road
Queen's Road

Gordon Road

Lakewood Road

Malcolm Road
Sherwood Road
Western Road
Marlborough Road

Kingsway

Wood Thornley
Thornly The Glade
Thornbury Heights

Wessex Nuffield Hospital

Junction 12

A335

Boyatt Crescent
Lincolns Rise
Pitmore Close
PO

Crescent

Rosebmoor Grove
Cranbome Close

Millers Dale Surgery

Hiltingbury County Junior & Infant School

Hiltingbury Road

Pine Crescent

Hiltingbury Road

Grosvenor Rd

Winchester Road

Thornden School

Pitmore School

ALLBROOK WAY

A335

Pitmore Close
Pitmore

Dale
Mesh Drive

Leigh House
Leigh House Hospital

Cuckoo Bushes Lane

Pine Road

Beech Road
Forest Road
Adamson Close

Oakwood Road

Lakewood Close

Chandler's Ford

Sherborne House School

Lake Road

Kingsway

Kingsway Gardens

Alexandra Road

Linden Grove

B3043

Common Road

Heathlands Close

Park Road

Lakewood Road

Merdon Close

Merdon

Westwood Gardens

G   H   J   293   K   L   M

Cemetery
Valley Road
Brownhill

Woodhill Prep School

Kingsway

Winchester Avenue

Merdon Junior School

Scantabout Avenue

Scantabout Primary School

Panther Road

H6
1 Charnwood Gdns

S053

The Fryern

G H J 239 K L M Morestead

Hazeley Down

I

thfields

arnefields

Hazeley Road

Hazeley

Mare Lane

Jackman's

Hill

Hill Farm

2

Love Lane

Monarch's Way

Monarch's Way

Hazeley Farm

Morestead House

Watley Lane

Monarch's Way

Stags La

Owslebury

Bottom

3

Knighton

Hatchers

Lane

Bottom Farm

Gabriel's Copse

Mare Lane

Whites

Monarch's Way

Hill Cl

Beech Cl

4

Owslebury CP School

268

Owslebury

PO

5

Hensting Lane

Hill

PH

tcott La

Watley Lane

Lower Farm

6

Whaddon Farm

Hensting Farm

Hensting Lane

7

Hensting

Whaddon Lane

PO

Marwell Zoological Park

8

G H 295 J Hotel K L M Marwell House

b's

ok

B3354

MAI

rook

Hensting Lane

Swifts Farm

Thompson's Lane

Lane

Hurst

A   B   C   **240**   D   E   F

Farm

Honeyman Farm

1

Hill Farm

Old Down

Warren

Old

2

Hill

Longwood
House

Stags La

3

Owslebury

Bottom Farm

Bottom

Longwood

Road

Belmore Lane

King's Way

4

Rd

Hilly Cl

Baybridge House

Owslebury
CP School

Beech

Main

PO

†

Pitcot Lane

5

Baybridge

King's Way

6

haddon
arm

Baybridge Lane

Blackdown Farm

7

Lower Baybridge Lane

King's Way

Rowhay
Wood

8

Woodcote

Marwell House

Woodlock's
Down Farm

Woodcote Lane

A   B   C   **296**   D   E   F

onarch's Way

1 grid square represents 500 metres

Hamilton Farm

Lane End

G H J 241 K L M

Lane End Farm

Yew Tree Farm

I

Longwood Dean Lane

Holden Lane

Greendowns

2

PH

Lancen Cotts

Salt Lane

South Downs Wy

3

Longwood Dean Farm

Dür Wood

4

270

Preshaw House

5

The Holt

Salt Lane

Walk

Lane

Valley

Stony Hard Farm

6

Monarch's Way

Belmore House

Preshaw

7

Lower Preshaw Lane

Ower Farm

Stephen's Castle Down

8

G H J 297 K L M

Monarch's Way

Stake's Lane

G · Black House Farm · H · J · 243 · K · L · M

1

Bere Farm

Marldell Farm

2 · Lippen Cotts

3

Wheely Farm

We

4 · A32

Warnford

Lippen Lane

272

Wheely Down

5

Monarch's Way

Monarch's Way

Old Winchester Hill Lane

Warnford Park

6 · Old Winc

Monarch's Way

7

†

Peake New Road

8 · Peake Farm

A32

G · H · J · 299 · K · L · M

Exton

South Downs Way

Monarch'

A B Highfield C   D E F

Marlands

1

Hayling
Wood

Lippen
Cotts

2

Long Priors

3

Knapps Hard

Headon Vw

Church Lane

Floud La

West Meon
Controlled
Primary School

Doctors Lane

The Surgery

East End

Vinnells Lane

Vinnells Lane

PO

High Street

Meonwara Crs

West Meon

Love Lane

Station Road

Lynch Lane

Coombe Lane

Westbury House

River Meon

Ripling

4

A32

5

Old Winchester Hill Lane

6

Monarch's Way

Old Winchester Hill Lane

Hen
Wood

7

8

Peake Farm

A B C   South Downs Way D E F

South Downs Way

Whitewool Farm

South Downs Way

I grid square represents 500 metres

G   H   J   245   K   L   M

Peak Farm

Old Down Farm

Lower Bordean

A272

Tigwell Farm

Bereleigh House

GU32

274

Drayton

Park Farm

Pidham Farm

The Cross

East Meon Controlled Primary School

Worknouse Lane

Chapel St

Chidden

Cl

Duncombe Rise

Garston Cl

Hill View

Glenthorne Meadow

Temple Lane

Church Street

PH

PO

High Street

East Meon

Coombe Road

Duncombe Farm

Lower House Farm

South Downs Way

G   H   J   301   K   L   M

Oxenbourne House

1   2   3   4   5   6   7   8

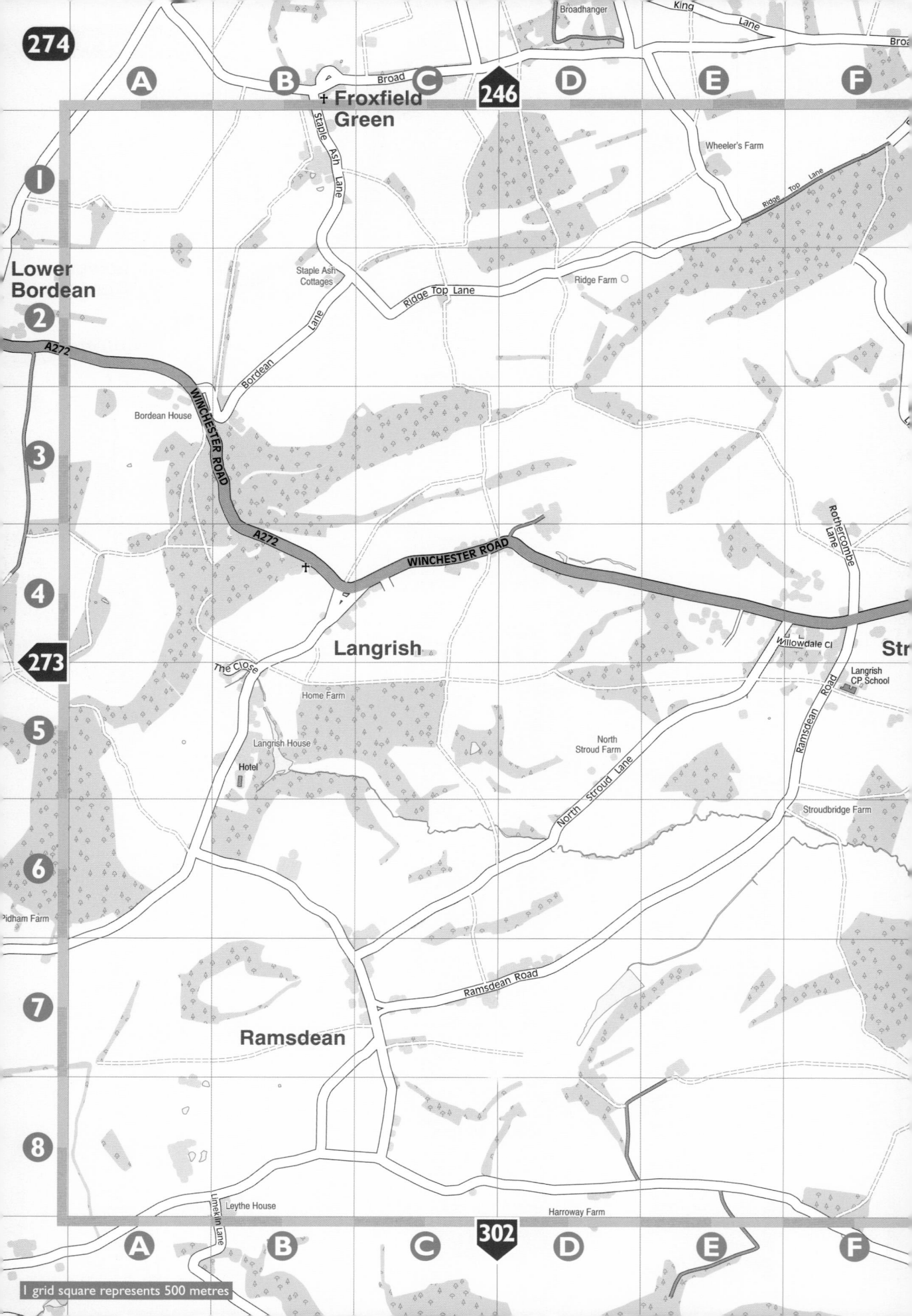

Ⓐ   Ⓑ   Ⓒ   **246**   Ⓓ   Ⓔ   Ⓕ

Broadhanger

King   Lane

Broad

✝ **Froxfield Green**

Wheeler's Farm

Ⓘ

Ridge Top Lane

Staple Ash Lane

Lower Bordean

Staple Ash Cottages

Ridge Farm

Ridge Top Lane

⓶

A272

Bordean Lane

WINCHESTER ROAD

⓷

Bordean House

Rothercombe Lane

A272

WINCHESTER ROAD

⓸

✝

273

Willowdale Cl

Str

The Close

Langrish

Langrish CP School

⓹

Home Farm

Langrish House

North Stroud Farm

Hotel

North Stroud Lane

Ramsdean Road

Stroudbridge Farm

⓺

Pidham Farm

⓿7

Ramsdean

Ramsdean Road

Harroway Farm

Ⓜ8

Limekiln Lane

Leythe House

Ⓐ   Ⓑ   Ⓒ   **302**   Ⓓ   Ⓔ   Ⓕ

I grid square represents 500 metres

G H J **249** K **Tullecon** L M

Durford Wood

I

Rogate Common

2

Rogate Lodge

Ter

Halecommon

3

Fyning

Slade Lane

Slade Farm

4

Sussex Border Path

PO

urleighmarsh Farm

Red House Ct

Rogate C of E Controlled School

278

A272

Parsonage Est

Wenham Manor Farm

urleighmarsh

Rogate

Habin

Carbitts Lane

Hill

5

er Rother

Haben Farm

West Heath Common

Sussex Border Path

6

Habin

Fair Oak

Wak

Sandhill House

7

Down Park Farm

Dumpford Lane

Little B

GU31

8

Greenfields Ct

Furze Meadow

Nyewood

G H J **305** K L M

Hill Ash Farm

A   B   C   250   D   E   F

Trotten Marsh

Borden Wood

Rondle Wood

Borden Lane

Borden

Dangstein

Gatehouse Lane

Chithurst Lane

Kingsham Wood

Hammer Stream

Bobbolds Farm

ok's Pond Road

R

Terwick Common

Fyning

Cumber's Farm

Gatehouse Farm

Chithurst Lane

Cemetery

Ch

Manor House

Wakeham Farm

Gatehouse Lane

A272

Trotton

Trotton Common

Oak

River Rother

Rother Lane

Mill La

Mill Lane

Terwick Lane

Lane

Little Barn

Hotel

Dumpford

Dumpford Park Farm

Trotton Road

Goldrings Farm

Bridgelands

A   B   C   D   E   F

Woolbeding Common

Titty Hill

I

Queen's Corner

Robins Lane

Iping Road

Bowley Farm

Pound Farm

Pound Common

2

St Cuthmans School

Tote Hill

Eastshaw Farm

Tentworth

Tote Lane

Linch Road

3

Woodgate Farm

Eastshaw Lane

Ash House

Iping Lane

4

Hammer Lane

Stanwater Lane

Stedham Lane

Woolbeding Lane

Hammerwood House

Crouchhouse Farm

Brambling Lane

5

Hollist Lane

Iping Lane

Stedham Lane

Woolbeding

6

River Rother

Iping

Rotherhill Ho

Mill Lane

Queens St

Crowshole Farm

Common View

PH

School Lane

Stedham CP School

The Alley

The Street

Stedham

7

Iping Common

Elsted Road

A272

Stedham Common

Minsted Road

Severals Road

Sandy Lane

8

Quags Corner

Andrews Lane

Midhurst Common

252

A B C D E F

I

2

3

4

5

6

7

8

A354

Verndtich Chase

Wiltshire County
Hampshire County

Martin Drove End

A354

Martin Drove End

Martin L End

Townsend Lane

Martin Down

Silien Lane

Earthpits Lane

Jubilee Trail

Hampshire County
Dorset County

Bokerley Down

Whitey Top

organ's Lane

Pentridge

A B C D E F

306

Blagdon Farm

Kites est Farm

G   H   J   **253**   K   L   M

I

2

3

Paradise

St Brides Farm

Knap
Barrow

Grans
Barrow

Toyd
Down

4

282

**East
Martin**

5

† **Martin**

Allen River

Tidpit

Knoll
Down

6

North Allenford Farm

7

*Damerham
Knoll*

*Tidpit
Common
Down*

8   Knoll Far

*Blackheath
Down*

South
Allenford Farm

258

285

312

Glazier's
Copse

Scotland Lane

N_Com
Lane

Bagfield
Copse

Whitterns
Hill Farm

East
Copse

Shearwood
Copse

Langley
Wood

Hamptworth Road

Coles's Lane

Hamptworth Road

Black Lane

Black Lane

Hamptworth
Lodge

Lyburn Road

ehanger Copse

Cloven
Hill
Plantation

Golden
Cross

Pound
Bottom

Timberley Lane

ge Road

rch

B3080

Franchises

1 grid square represents 500 metres

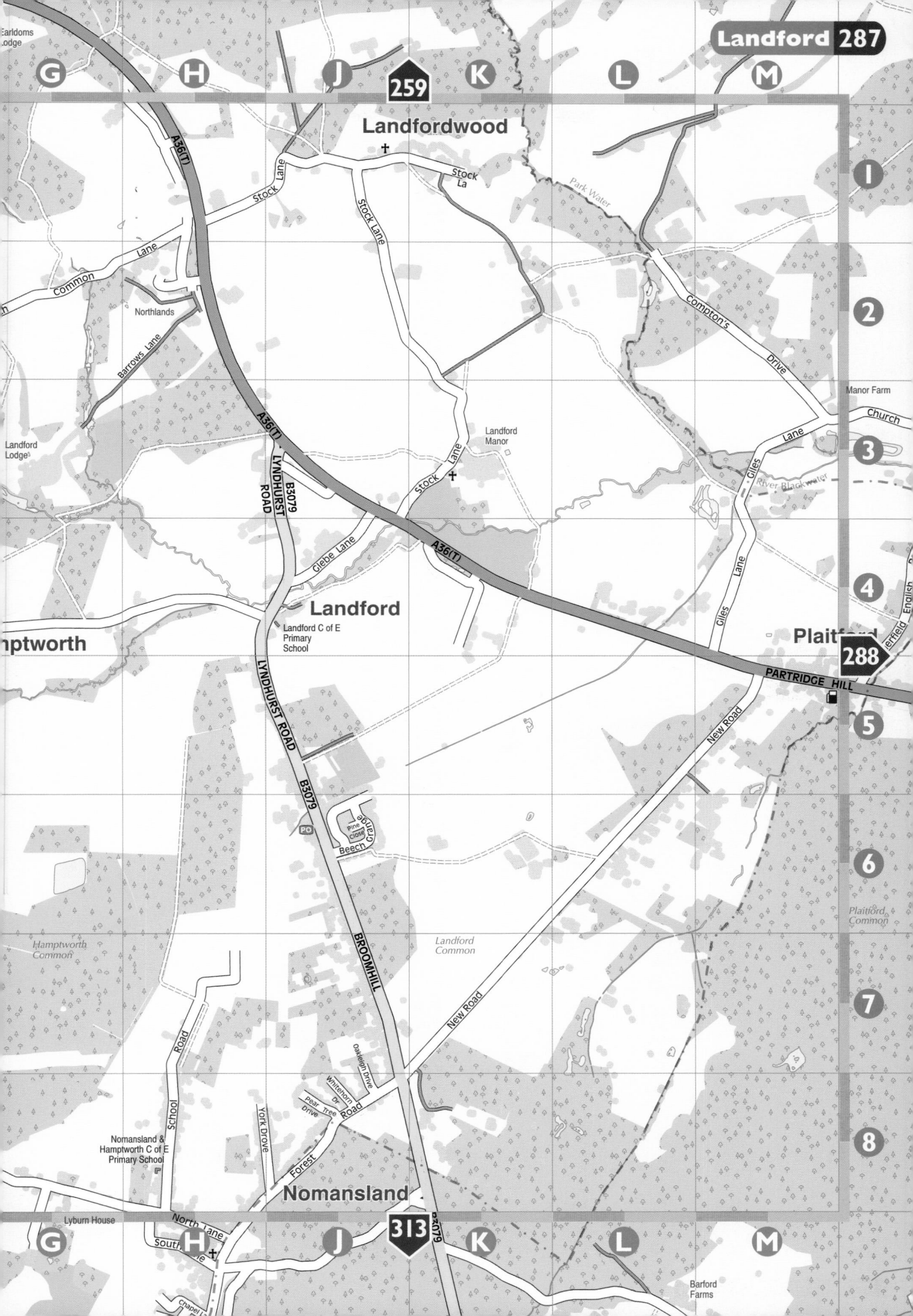

G H J 261 K L M

I

Spursholt Ho

A27

Woodington

Woodington Road

Embley Lane

Embley Park School

2

st llow

Gardeners Lane

Hall Copse

Burnt Grove

3

Lane

Woodington Rd

Ryedown Lane

4

Warners Fm

River Blackwater

290

Kentford Lake

5

Whinwhistle Road

Hamdown Crs

Florence Cl
Crasfield
Chichester

Hammonds Fm

Embley Wood

Ranw

6

A3090

Whinwhistle Road

Semple Ho

Ridge

7

Shelley Lane

SALISBURY ROAD

8

Bricky Lake Lane

Shelley Fm

Old Salisbury

Hotel

A   B   C   D   E   F

262

F2
1 Petty Cl
2 St Barbe Cl
3 Sydmanton Cl
4 The Tyleshades

F1
1 Jacobs Cl
2 Nursery Gdns
3 Oakleigh Gdns
4 Tadburn Cl

1 Fleming Pl
2 Knatchbull Cl
3 Palmerston St
4 Pembroke Cl

1 Abbey Water
2 Corn Market
3 Narrow La
4 Palmerston St
5 Spring Pl

Romsey County
Junior School

The Romsey
School

ROMSEY

Romsey Industrial
Est

Station Rd

Romsey Infant
School

Plaza
Theatre

Russell Hicks
& Temple

Mill
Primary School

Abbey Mead
Surg

The Meads

Abbey
Chiropractic
Clinic

Love

Alma
Road Surg

The Bus
Station

THE HUNDRED

The Harrage

BROADWATER RD

Romsey Town
Football Club

Romsey Sports
Centre

Romsey Rugby
Football Club

Romsey Cricket
Club

Spursholt Ho

MILLSTREAM RISE

Millstream Rise

A27

A27

Burnt
Grove

River Test

Broadlands
House

PAUNCEFOOT HILL — MAINSTONE

A3090

Pauncefoot Ho

Test Way

289

Cutters
Barn

River Test

Lee Ho

Spaniard's

Yewtree
Copse

Ranvilles Fm

A3090

Ridge Lane

Ridge

Lee Park Fm

Lee Church Lane

Lee

Moorcourt
Copse

Test Way

A27

SOUTHAMPTON ROAD

WINCHESTER RD

Botley Road

Tadfield Rd

316

A   B   C   D   E   F

1 grid square represents 500 metres

Moorcourt

G · H · J · **263** · K · L · M

G1
1 Eight Acres
2 Halterworth Cl
3 Hereward Cl
4 Nightingale Cl
5 The Vikings

H1
1 Montfort Heights

H2
1 The Thicket

I

Halterworth

Whitenap

Baddesley Common

Cemetery

Halterworth CP School

Warren Fm

2

Botley Road

Sycamore

Northlands Rd

Whitenap

The Thicket

Mountbatten Secondary School

Premier

BOTLEY ROAD A27

BOTLEY ROAD

S052

LUZBOROUGH LANE

West Lane
Broad La
Andrews
Ringwood Drive
Hillcrest
The Birches

Cedar

Juniper

Ash

Crescent

Spring Gdns

Firgrove Road
Camelia
Laburnum
SIX OAKS Rd

3

N

LUZBOROUGH LANE

A27

Ringwood

Cerne Cl

Ringwood Drive

Firgrove Cl Rd

Rosslyn

PO

A27

North Baddesley

The Vineyards

Church Cl

4

Ashfield

Queens Ride

Torny

Sylvan

Drive

Hylles Wy

Seymour La

Christophers

Rownhams Lane

Ennel Copse

Rownhams Road

Brownhill Road

Fleming

292

Hoe Fm

Sylvan Drive

Mortimer Gdns
Lavington
Launcelyn

Proctor Dr
Dibble Dr

Bracken
Heath Road
Bracken Road

5

Hoe Lane

6

Telegraph Wood

Tanner's Brook

Toothill Road

Toothill

Packridge

Lane

Rownhams Lane

7

Drove

A3057

Nightingale Wood

Upper Toothill Road

Greenhill Lane

Rownhams Service Area

M27

Rownhams Service Area

8

M3
1 Emer Cl

L4
1 Heatherb. Gdns
2 Northerwood Cl
3 Tutland Rd
4 Woodside Rd

L3
1 Heatherview Cl
2 Pine Cl

L2
1 Stragwyne Cl

K3
1 Broad La
2 Highlands Cl
3 Overbrook Wy

Upton

Highbridge

Stoke Common

EASTLEIGH

293

Bishopstoke

266

Allbrook

ambDge

320

S050

1 grid square represents 500 metres

G5
1 Brunswick Cl
2 Olympic Wy
3 Wooderson Cl

G6
1 Grangewd Gdns
2 Newbury Cl
3 Stoke Wood Cl
4 Torch Cl

G7
1 Goodison Cl

H5
1 Ridgeway Cl
2 Winifred Cl

G   H   J   **267**   K   L   M   Marwell House

Swifts Farm

Marwell Zoological Park

Hotel

Thompson's Lane   Hurst Farm

1

Hensting Lane

PORTSMOUTH   ROAD

B2177

Marwell Manor

PORTSMOUTH   **2**

ROAD

3

B2177

fisher's Pond

MAIN   ROAD   B3354

Low Hill Farm

Crowdhill

Park Hills Wood

4

Stroudwood Lane

296

Pylehill

Upr Barn Copse

Harding La

Hall Lands House

Stroudwood Dairy Farm

5

WINCHESTER   ROAD   B3354

Stoke Hts

Pilchards Av

Victena Rd

Fair Oak

Hall Lands Lane

Camellia Cv

Glenwood Court

Magnolia

High Trees

MORTIMERS

Mortimers Farm

6

Brunswick Rd

Ormond Cl

Latham Cl

Sandys

Brookfield Rd

Campbell Way

Spring Cl

Clifford

Orchard Rd

Glebe Ct

B3037

MORTIMERS   LANE

Rustan Cl

Michaels Way

Scotland Cl

Osborne Gardens

Knowle Lane

East Horton Farm

7

FAIROAK   ROAD

Sandy La

Shorts Road

Fairoak Road

Kimberley

Ashlea Cl

Noyce Dr

Stubbington Wy

Farley Heath

Alma La

EASTLEIGH   RD

White Hart Rd

Oak Rd

Cotsails

Fratton Wy

Selhurst Way

Fair Oak Cem

Roker Way

Trafford Way

St Ninian Cl

Anfield Cl

Dean

Highburn

Allington Lane

Kings School

The Wyvern Community Secondary School

Fair Oak Junior & Infant School

Pavilion Close

B3354

Greenwood Farm

Greenwood Lane

8

e Farm

BOTLEY

Knowle Lane

321

The Cockpit Farm

Durley

Greenwood

G   **K6**   H   J   **321**   K   L   M   **H6**
1 Bradshaw Cl

J7
1 The Beeches
2 Carroll Cl
3 The Martins
4 Osborne Gdns

J6
1 F Routh Gdns
2 Mortimers Dr
3 Palmers Cl
4 Upper Mead Cl
5 Walkers Cl

H7
1 Eastville Rd
2 Stamford Wy

1 Hawthorn Cl
2 Malmesbury Cl

G8
1 Claylands Rd
2 Edington Cl
3 Princes Cl
4 St Swithun Cl

H8
1 Denewulf Cl
2 Middlebrook
3 St Bonnet Dr

G · H · J · K · L · M

269

I · 2 · 3 · 4 · 298 · 5 · 6 · 7 · 8

Stake's Lane

Monarch's Way

Bigpath Farm

Dean Farm

Corhampton Down

Franklin Farm

Monarch's Way

Dean Lane

B3035

Street End

Peak Lane

Limekiln Lane

Little Ashton Lane

Dean

Highfield Farm

Galley Down

Ashton

Dean Lane

The Hangers

S032

New Rd

Beeches Hill

Lane

Shipcote

Vernon Hill House

Vernon Hill

The Hangers B3035

Bishopsdown Stud Farm

Roke Farm

Pondside Lane

Northbrook

Duncombe

The Coach Station

Dundridge Lane

BISHOP'S WALTHAM

Gravatom Business Centre

Merlin

Claylands Rd

Blanchard Rd

Greens Cl

PH

PO

Priory

The Priory

Elizabeth Wy

Victoria Rd

Martin Street

Station Road

Pondside Lane

Langton Road

Weymans Drive

Beaufort Drive

Brooklands Road

Garfield Rd

Andrewes Cl

Garfield Close

LOWER LANE

Free Street

Chalky Lane

Colville Dr

Hall Close

Infant School

Ridgemede Junior School

The Surg

St Peter's Street

Brook Street

High St

Houndon St

Basingwell St

Mavern Cl

Shore La

Meon Valley Police Station

Oak Road

Pine Rd

Sycamore Rd

Elm Rd

Bank Street

Hoe Rd

Tennyson Cl

Wordsworth Cl

Byron Close

Rareridge Lane

Cemetery

West Hoe Lane

Swanmore

Hill Top

Jervis Court Lane

Hoe Road

Hoe

Bishop's Palace (remains of)

Bishop's Lane

COPPICE HI

Crickmede

Hamble Springs

Polly Field

Cherry Gro

323

G · H · J · K · L · M

271

G H J K L M

I

Exton

White Way

S Downs Way

Beacon Hill Lane

River Meon

South Downs Way

Shavards Farm

Shavard Lane

Stock's Lane

The Butts
De P
H PO

Corhampton

Allens Lane

Meonvale Farm

Shavard Lane

Rectory Lane

Pound Cottages
Bridge Md
Pound

Stock's Lane

Harvestgate Farm

N LANE

PH
Bucks Head Hill

Hill Rise

Fry's Lane

Lane

Stock's Lane

Stocks Fm

A32

High Street

Fry's Lane

Meonstoke School

Chapel Road

New Road

Stock's Lane

300

Pondside Fm

Lane Cut Throat La

Cem

Watton Lane

Watton Lane

GARRISON HILL

A32

Mill Lane

Brockbridge

B2150

Sheardley Lane

Stoke

PO

High St

Mill La

Park La
Wayfarer's Wk

Station Road

Bushy Down Fm

Wallops Wood Fm

Sheardley Lane

A32

B2150

Cutts

G H J K L M

325

Grenville Hall

2

3

4

5

6

7

8

300

A B C **272** D E F

South Downs Way

1

Monarch's Way

South Downs Way

Whitewool Farm

2

South Downs Way

South Downs Way

Monarch's Way

South

Coombe

Monarch's Way

199
▲
Old Winchester Hill

3

Monarch's Way

Rocks Fm

4

Lane

Teglease
Down

299

Little West End
Fm

5

Chi

Westend
Down

6

Teglease Fm

Sheardley Lane

Stoke Wood

Whiteleaf

7

Lane

Big West
End Fm

Chidden

8

Stoke Wood

Whiteleaf

Lane

Green Lane

A B C **326** D E F

Green Lane

Hermitage

Monarch's Way

ville

1 grid square represents 500 metres

East Meon

Coombe

Duncombe Farm

Lower House Farm

273

Oxenbourne House

Coombe Cross

South Downs Way

South Farm

Stonylands Farm

233 Salt Hill

302

South Downs Way

South Downs Way

Old Hambledonians Cricket Club

Hyden Farm Lane

Coombe Wood

Hyden Wood

Hyden Farm Lane

Hyden Farm

327

North Fm

Harvesting Lane

Little Hyden Lane

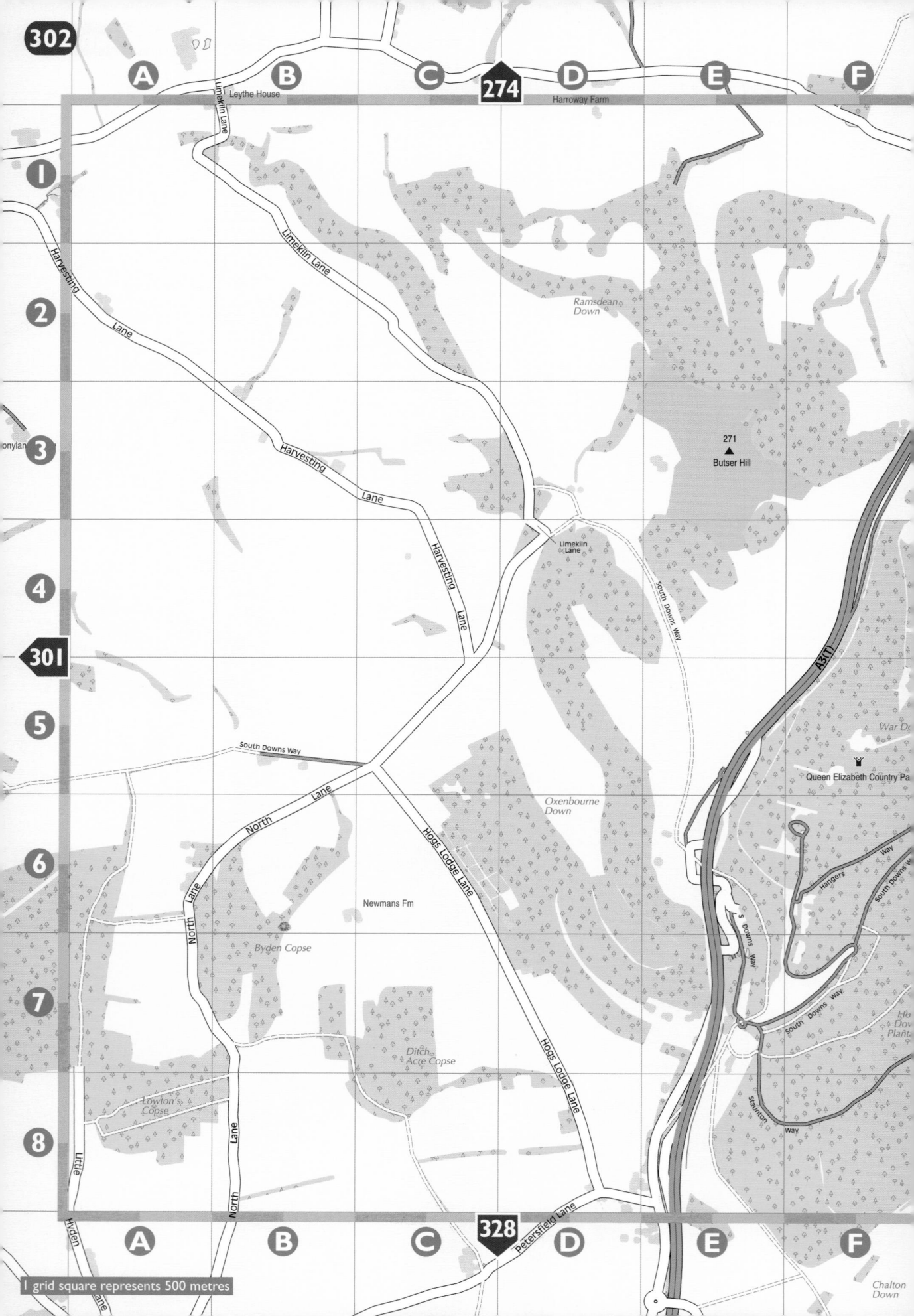

A **B** **C** **D** **E** **F**

276

Stanbridge Farm

Hampshire County
West Sussex County

Goose
Green

Manor Farm

Quebec

Collins Lane

Sussex Border Path

1 SUSSEX ROAD

Nursted

Westons

Putmans Lane

2

Hurst
Farm

B2146

3

Old
Ditcham

Sussex Border Path

4

B2146

B2146

South L

Leith
Copse

Cow Lane

Cow
La

5 Forty Acre
Lane

Sunwood Fm

South Downs Way

B2

6

Hampshire County

West Sussex County

Sussex Border Pth

South Downs Way

Foxcombe Fm

7

West
Harting
Down

Round
Down

8

Sussex Border Path

NT Uppark

B2146

A **B** **C** **D** **E** **F**

330

G H J K L M

I

277

Nyewoo

Hill
Ash Farm

Upperton

2

Woodhouse Farm

3

Manor House

North Lane

North Lane

4

Elsted

East Harting St

Orchard Cl

orchard Cl

uth Harting

The Square

Hollist Lane

Harting Street

Lane

PO

Mill Lane

Culvers

Eastfield Lane

East

Turkey Island

East Harting

5

Pease Cft

Tipper

Lane

S Acre

Warren Side

ren e

Telegraph Lane

New Lane

6

Hill Lane

Down Place

South Downs Way

South Downs Way

South Downs Way

7

B2141

South Downs Way

South Downs Way

south Down

Round Down

8

Telegraph House

Up Park

B214

280

A B C D E F

I
2
3
4
5
6
7
8

Longpits Lane

Kites
Nest Farm

Blagdon Farm

Penbury
Knoll

West
Blagdon

Jubilee Trail

Jubilee Trail

Blackbush
Down

Toby's
Bottom

Bowldish
Pond

River Crane

Jubilee

Trail

Bove

Cranborne Farm

Burwood

Nine Yews

Manor Farm

Cranborne

Jubilee Trail

The Surgery

Grugs La

Rew s La

Penny's Md

The
Square crane

Salisbury St

Water St

School

Swan
St
Church
St

Castle
St

1
2
RG

Water St

CASTLE STREET

HIBD

A B C D E F

Creech
Hill House

Jubilee Trail

Ⓐ   Ⓑ   Ⓒ   **282**   Ⓓ   Ⓔ   Ⓕ

Ⓘ

2

3

4

◀**307**

5

6

7

8

Knoll Farm

Allen River

Allen River

Pound Lane

High Street

Littlemill La

West Park Lane

North End

West Park Drive

Damerham

Browns Lane

Browns Lane

Court Farm

Court Hill

Stony Lane

Steels La

Church Lane

Western Downland Primary School

Mill End

Cornpits Lane

Ashley Park Farm

South End

Ashridge Copse

Hawkhill Ditch

Hampshire County

Dorset County

Bull Hill Farm

Rockbourne Lane

West Park

Roman Villa

Marsh Farm

Cl

West Park Farm

Lower Court Wood

Lower Court Wood

Tanners Lane

Sandleheath

Alderholt Road

Ashford Water

Alderholt Mill Farm

Sandleheath Road

Home Farm

Ⓐ   Ⓑ   Ⓒ   **333**   Ⓓ   Ⓔ   Ⓕ

Hart's Farm

High Wood

Alderholt Park

Sandleheath Road

I grid square represents 500 metres

G   **H**   **J**   283   **K**   **L**   **M**

1

Rockstead Farm

Green Lane

Flood Street

I

Radnall Wood

Peasash Farm

2

SP6

Brookheath

**Upper
Burgate**

Lane

Green La

Fryern Court Road

3

Fryern Court

Fryern Court Road

Allen's Farm

4

Avon Valley Path

310

Wilkins's Coomb

Lane

Sweatsfords Water

**Lower
Burgate**

Sandle Dairy Farm

Puddleslosh

Fordingbridge Junior & Infant School

The Burgate School

Hertford Cl

Dudley Av

Penny's Crescent

Burgate Flds

5

Arch Farm Industrial Est

Sandleheath Industrial Est

Marl Lane

Whitsbury

Beacon

Sharpley Cl

Charnwood Dr

Pennys La

Waverley

Waverley Road

Player Ct

Langley Gdn

Penbridge

Old Brickyard Rd

Sandle Manor School

Willow Av

Rivergale

Georges Rd

Orchard Cl

Albion Road

Salisbury Road

Lyster Rd

Bruyn Rd

6

Station Road

Sandle Manor

Elmwood Av

Downwood Cl

Brympton

Normandy Way

Picket Cl

Queens Cdns

Alexandra Rd

Park Rd

Manor

A338

FORDINGBRID

Sandle Copse

Mayfield Rd

Manor Farm Road

Station Road

Ashford Close

Ashford

Marl Lane

Green La

Lwr Bartons

Fordingbridge Hospital

Salisbury St

B3078

7

Jubilee Rd

Victoria Rd

Station Road

Victoria Gdns

Beechwood

Hotel

Bartons Rd

Flatfields

West St

Shaftesbury St

Council Office

High St

Town Hall

Bridge St

Ringwood Road

Stuckton Road

Ashford Road

BOWERWOOD ROAD

Padstow Pl

Mulberry Gdns

Church St

Provost St

Church Farm

Cemetery

8

310

A B C Woodgreen D E F

C of E Primary School

C6
1 Woodfern

Lwr Densome Wd

284

Higherend Farm

Love La

Imm's Grove

steels Dro

Little Grove

1

The Shallows

Marsh Lane

The Shallows

Brook

Avon Valley Path

Godshill Inclosure

2

3

Folds Farm

4

Avon Valley Path

309

River Avon

5

Brune's Purlieu

ROGER PENNY WAY

6

Woodling Crescent

Larch Rd

1

Field Wy

The Pines

Well Lane

Godshill

B3078

Sandy Balls

Avon View

Newground

ORDINGBRIDGE

7 8

SOUTHAMPTON ROAD

Criddlestyle

Cemetery

Stuckton Road

Broadhill Lane

Blissford Road

Long Bottom

8

The Merrie Thought

Blissford Cross

Blissford

A B Stuckton C 335 D E F

Stuckton Rd

Ditchend Brook

Abbotswell Road

ssford Hill

1 grid square represents 500 metres

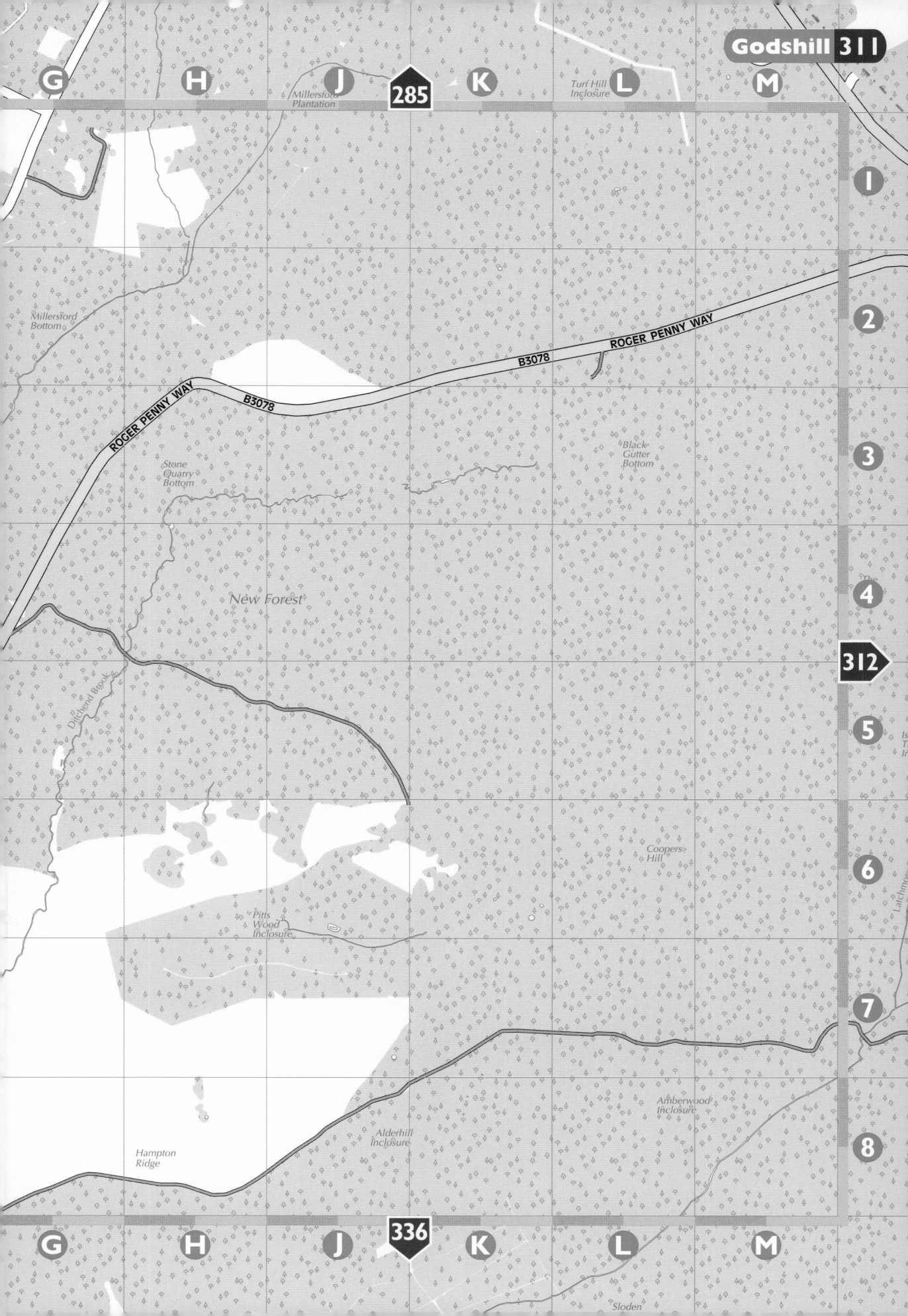

G   H   J   **285**   K   Turf Hill L   M
                              Inclosure

I

Millersford
Plantation

2

Millersford
Bottom

ROGER PENNY WAY
B3078   B3078   ROGER PENNY WAY

Stone   Black
Quarry   Gutter
Bottom   Bottom   3

New Forest   4

312

Ditchend Brook   5
                                                                                      Is
                                                                                      T
                                                                                      Ir

Coopers   6
Hill   Latchmore

Pitts
Wood
Inclosure

7

Amberwood
Inclosure

Hampton   8
Ridge   Alderhill
             Inclosure

G   H   J   **336**   K   L   M

Sloden

312

A   B   C   286   D   E   F

1

B3080

2
B3078   Hope
                         Cottage

Picket
Corner

3   Wiltshire County
                                                     Hampshire County   Crow's
                                                                         Nest
                                                          B3078   Bottom

                                              New
The
Butts

4   Forest

311

                                          Eyeworth
                                          Wood

5
Islands   Longcross
Thorns   Plain
Inclosure

                                          Irons
                                          Well

6
                                                                     Fritham
Latchmore Brook   Eyeworth   Lodge
                                   Lodge

7   Fritham
                                                         Fritham   House

                                                         Fritham

                         Hiscocks
                         Hill   The
                                                                                 Bu
8

A   B   C   337   D   E   F

Franchises
Wood

Pound
Bottom

Fritham
Plain

North
Bentley
Inclosure

1 grid square represents 500 metres

G   H   **Nomansland** 287   K   L   M

Nomansland & Hamptworth C of E Primary School

Lyburn House

North Lane
South Lane

Chapel La

Forest

York Drive
Scho

Tree Road

B3079

Barford Farms

Penn Commi

1

2

Bramshaw Wood

Bloodoaks Farm

3

Black Bush Plain

Bramble Hill Hotel

Bramshaw

B3079

Vice Lane

4

B3078

Long Cross

Broom Hill

314

5

Warrens

6

Salisbury Trench

PO

Brook Hill

B3078

B3079

Bramshaw Golf Club

Hotel
PH

7

Round Hill

Brook Common

Brook

8

Blackthorn Copse

Canterton Manor

Pipers Copse

Canterton Lane

King's Garn Gutter Inclosure

King's Garn Gutter

G   H   J   **338**   K   L   M

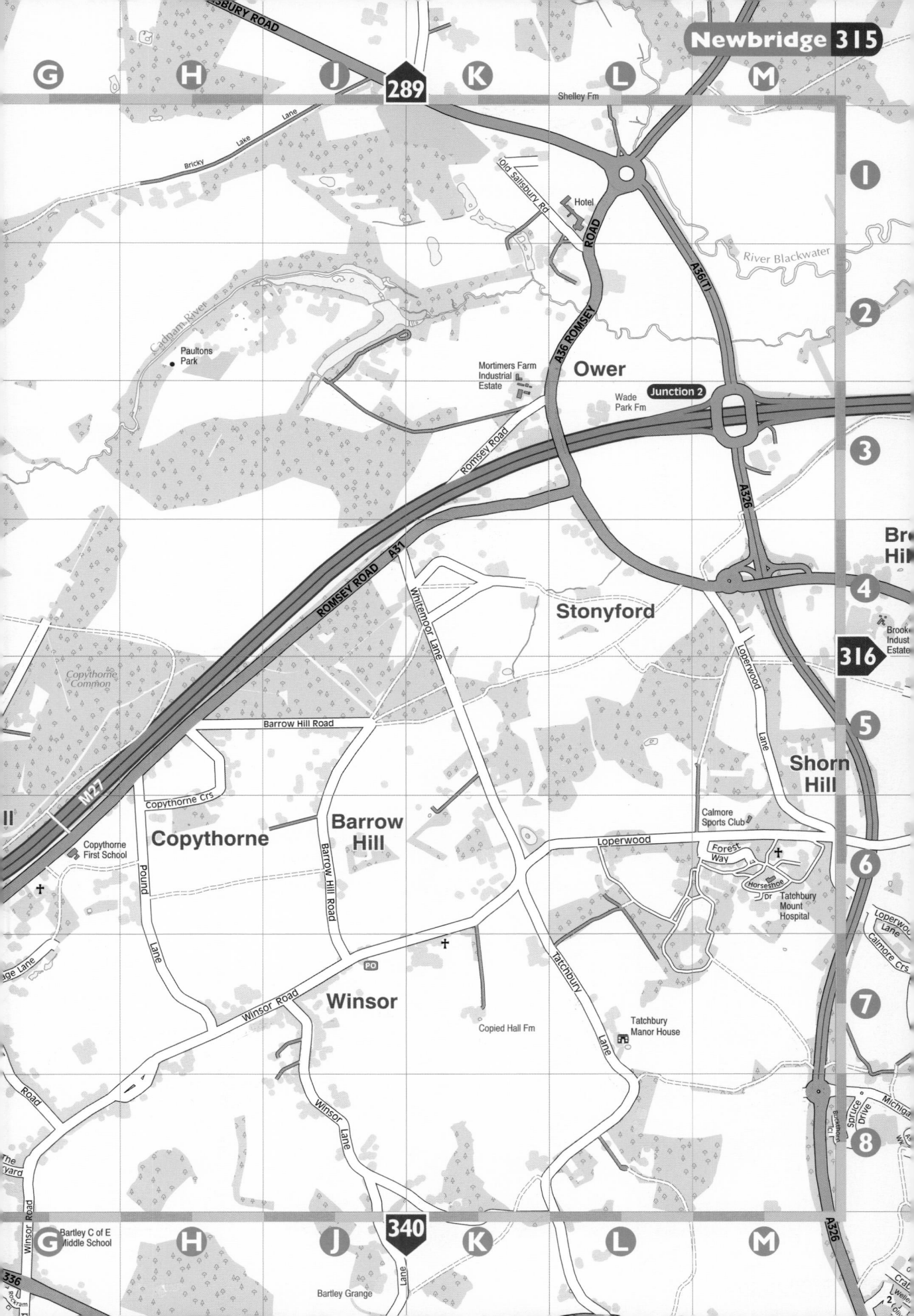

G H J 289 K L M

1

2

Ower

Junction 2

3

Br
Hil

4

316

Stonyford

5

Shorn
Hill

Copythorne

Barrow
Hill

Calmore
Sports Club

Forest
Way

Loperwood

Horseshoe
Tatchbury
Mount
Hospital

6

7

Winsor

Copied Hall Fm

Tatchbury
Manor House

8

G Bartley C of E
Middle School
H J 340 K L M

Bartley Grange

G   H   J   299   K   L   M

I
2
Home
Down
3

Stoke Wo

Grenville
Hall

B2150

East Hoe Road

East
Ma

Wayfarer's Wak

326

4

5

6

7

8

Cutts

Arch

Soberton Towers

Station Road

School Hill

Long   Road

Soberton

West Street

Hill

Wayfarer's Wak

West
St

Cole   Hill

Chalk   Hill

High St

High Street

Peststead   Lane

Webbs Green
Fm

air's Fm

eon
lley

Senworth   Lane

Webbs   Green

Taplands

Hambledon Lane

Plough Lane

Roy's   Lane

Horns   Hill

Chapel Road

Bush   Lane

Goldfield
Gallery

Ingoldfield Lane

May

Kiln Hill

Dradfield Lane

Southend Lane

Southend

Wayfarer's Wak

King's   Way

Broom Fm

Hambledon   Lane

Amsworth   Lane

Russell's Fm

Amsworth   Lane

Hill View
Farm

Hole Farm

Hoe Lane

Menslands
Lane

Hoe Cross
Fm

Hoe Street

King's Way

King's Way

King's Way

PO   Church Road   Ingoldfield Lane   Huntboun

Hoe Gate

King's   Way

G H J 301 K L M

North Fm

Monarch's Way

Hyden Farm Lane

Stoneridge Fm

Clanfield

I

2

Hambledon Road

Peak Rd

Pipers

South

3

Old Mill Lane

Broadhalfpenny
Down

Hinton Manor Lane

Drift

Downhouse Road

4

328

5

Hinton
Manor

Dogkennel Lane

Monarch's Way

Lane

Old Mill Lane

Whit

Glamorg

6

Harrowgate Lane

Catherington
Down

Catherington Lane

Catherington
C of E Controlle
Infant School

7

Denmead Mill

Monarch's Way

Broadway Lane

Hinton
Daubnay

Roads

Hill

Cathering

Five

Hea

Lane

Ham

8

Old Mill Lane

Monarch's Way

Lovedean Lane

Tagdell

Lane

Lychgate

Drive

Crouch

Road

G H J 352 K L M

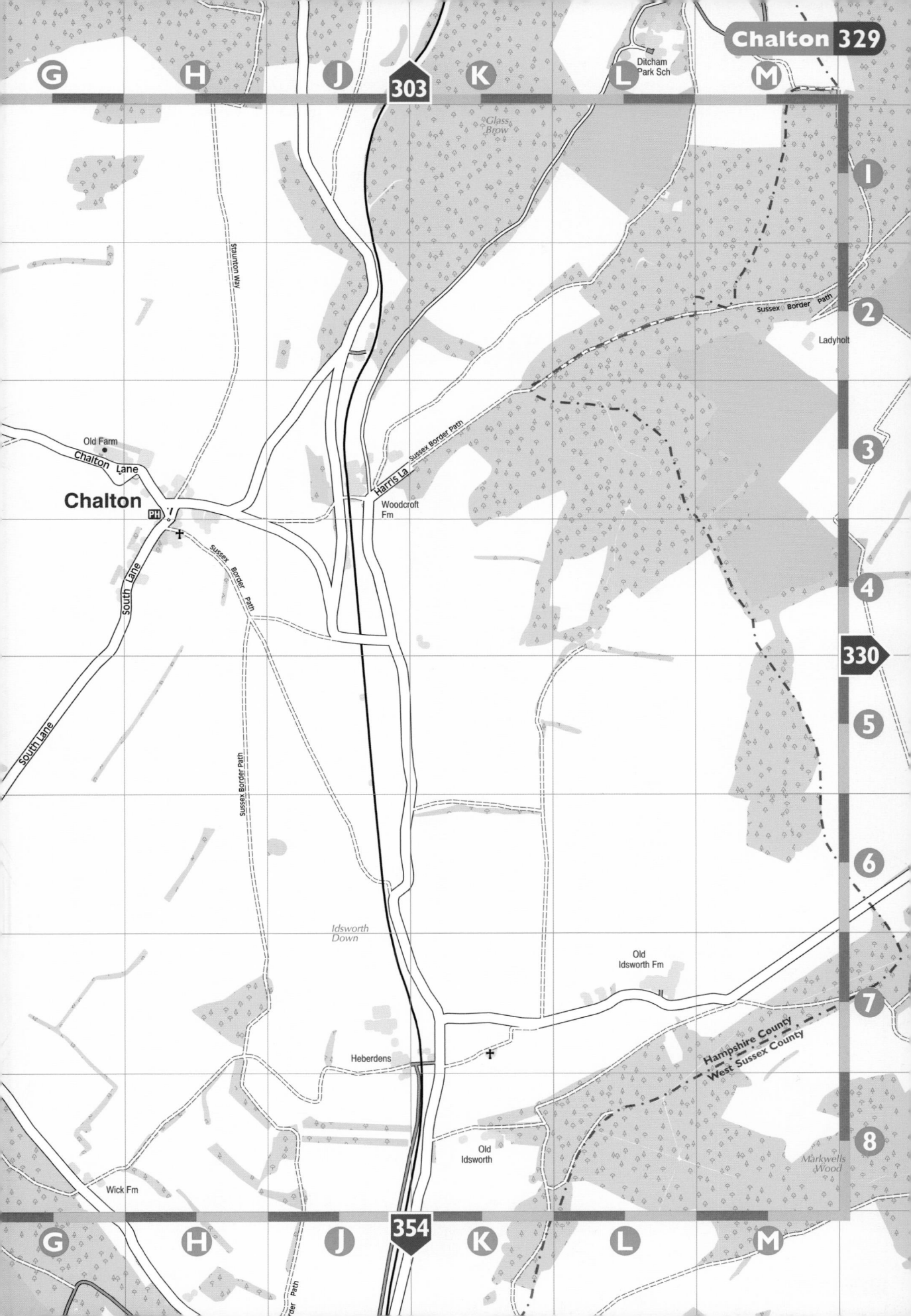

G H J K 303 L M

Glass Brow

1

Sussex Border Path

2

Ladyholt

3

4

330

5

6

Staunton Way

Old Farm
Chalton Lane

Chalton
PH
†

South Lane

Sussex Border Path

Harris La. Sussex Border Path

Woodcroft Fm

Sussex Border Path

Idsworth Down

Old Idsworth Fm

7

Hampshire County
West Sussex County

Heberdens
†

Wick Fm

Old Idsworth

8

Markwells Wood

A　　B　　C　　D　　E　　F

304

NT Uppark

0

I

2

Ladyholt

Eckensfield

Hale Wood

3

Hucksholt Fm

B2146

Cowdown   Lane

4

Cowdown Fm

Little Green School

329

5

B2146

6

Compton

PO

PH School Lane

Compton & Upmarden C of E Primary School

7

County
County

8

Markwells Wood

Horsley Farm

Locksash Lane

Locksash Fm

West Marden

355

North Down Way

B2146

A　　B　　C　　D　　E　　F

G   H   J   K   L   M

305

B2141

Up Park

Telegraph House

North Marden Down

Pads Wood

Hooksway

North Marden

Hill Lands Farm

Fernbeds Down

Fernbeds Fm

Bevis's Thumb

Long Lane

Long Lane

East Marden

East Marden Down

Up Marden

Grevitts Copse

Wildhams Wood

G   H   J   K   L   M

I
2
3
4
5
6
7
8

H2
1 Highwood Cl

K2
1 Lime Tree Cl

L2
1 Camel Green Rd
2 Down Lodge Cl
3 Fir Tree Hl
4 Silverdale Crs

G H J **308** K L M

Home Farm

FORDINGBRIDGE ROAD

Dorset County
Hampshire County

I

Alderholt Park

Sandleheath Road

High
Wood

2

Windsor Wy
2
Coppers Cl
Hayters
Alderholt
STATION ROAD
Hillbury Road
**Camel
Green**

Camel
Way
Green Road
St James
Ce (VC)
First Sch
Anterls Wy
South
Hill
7
Wren Gdns
Drive

Station
Road
Station
Yd
B3078
Pear
Tree
Cl
7
Park Lane
3
4 7
Tudor
Cl

DAGGONS
ROAD
1
Apple
Tree Rd
Alder Dr
Birchwood
1
2
5
4

Daggons

Churchill
Cl
Blackwater Gv
Atwood Cl
Earlswood Dr
Oak Road
Broomfield Dr
Fern Cl
4

Charing
Cross
Pine Rd
Ringwood Road

Hillbury Road

3

Ringwood Road

Drove
End Farm

4

Sleep Brook

Warren
Park Farm

334

Drove

Alderholt
Common

5

Cranborne
Common

Whitefield
Bottom

Dorset County
Hampshire County

Sleep Brook

6

North Plumley Farm

Hamer Brook

7

Boveridge
Heath

Plumley
Wood

8

M3
1 Kestrel Wy

M2
1 Camel Green Rd
2 Gilbert Cl

L3
1 Ash Cl
2 Beech Cl
3 Bramble Cl
4 Hazel Cl
5 Saxon Wy

Harefield
Plantation

Broadhill

G The Merrie Thought

H

J Blissford Cross

310

Blissford

K

L

M

Stuckton

Ditchend Brook

I

Flaxfields

Frogham Hill

Pentons Lane

Hyde Hill

Blissford Hill

Frogham

Abbotswell Road

The Paddock

Abbotswell Road

Abbots Well

Abbots Well Road

2

Hyde

Hyde Common

Ogdens Farm

Latchmore Bottom

Hungerford Hill

Gorley Lynch

Hyde (C of E Controlled) Primary School

Ogdens

3

Hungerford

Ringwood Road

Gorley Lynch

4

Buddle Hill

New

336

Forest

5

Ogden's Purlieu

Furze Hill

Huckles Brook

Gorley

Brookside

Black Barrow

6

Newtown Lane

Ibsley Common

Dockens Water

7

Linwood

Toms Lane

Avon Valley Path

Whitefield Plantn

Toms Lane

8

Linwood Farm

Avon Valley Path

Dockens

336

A B C 311 D E F

I

2

3

4

335

5

6

7

8

A B C 360 D E F

Hampton Ridge

Alderhill Inclosure

Sloden Inclosure

New

Forest

Latchmoor Brook

Hasley Inclosure

Holly Hatch Cottage

Holly Hatch Inclosure

New

Forest

Broomy Inclosure

Broomy Lodge

Broomy Plain

Black Barrow

High Corner Inn

Toms Lane

Linwood

Lane

Milkham Inclosure

Linwood Farm

King's

1 grid square represents 500 metres

G H J 312 K L M

The Butt

I

2

3

4

338

5

6

7

8

Fritham Plain

North Bentley Inclosure

Janesmoor Plain

South Bentley Inclosure

Anses Wood

Cadman's Pool

Ocknell Inclosure

Ocknell Plain

Slufters Inclosure

A31(T)

Fritham Cross

Bratley Water

A31(T)

Highland Water

F

G H J 361 K L M

Bratley A

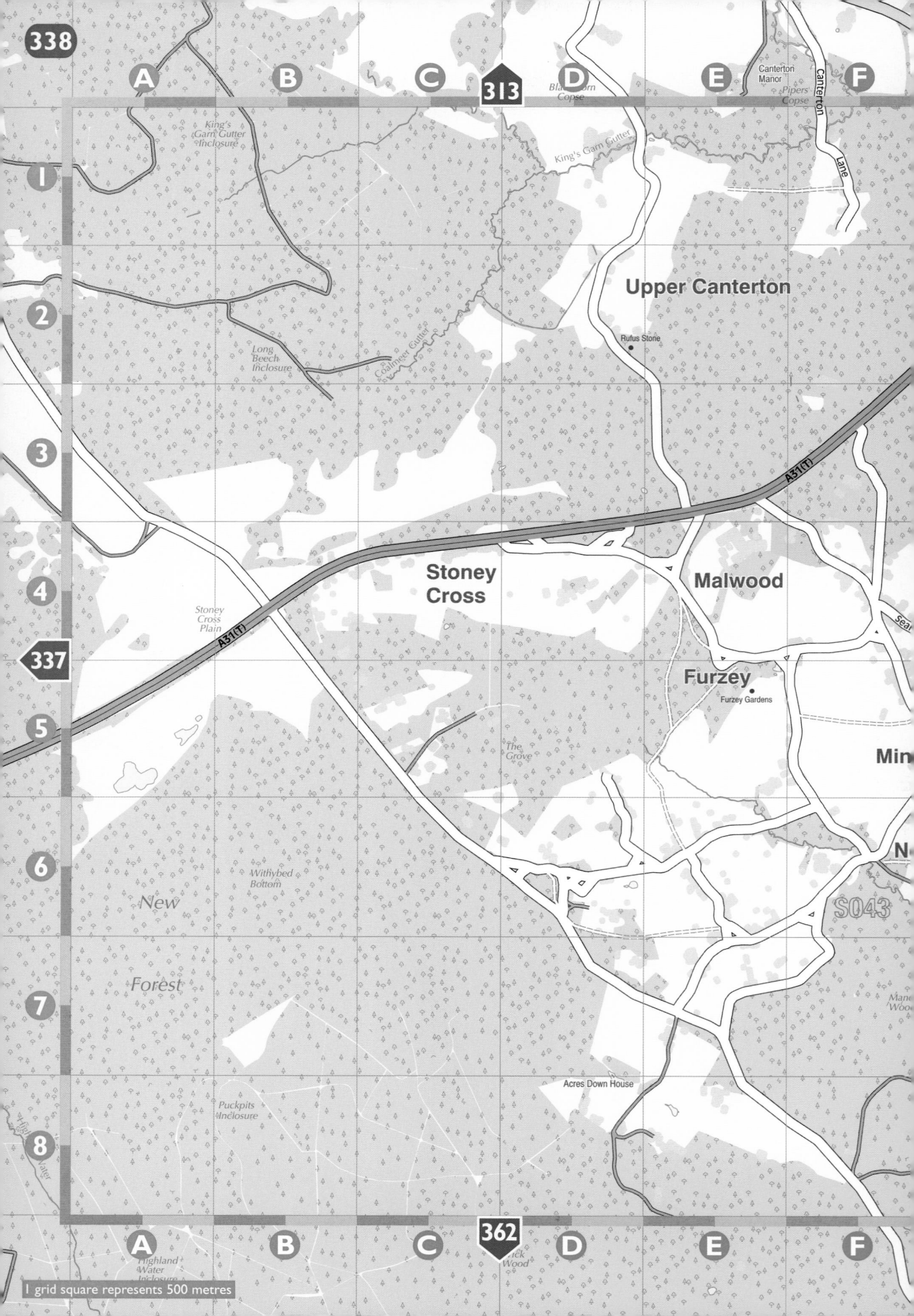

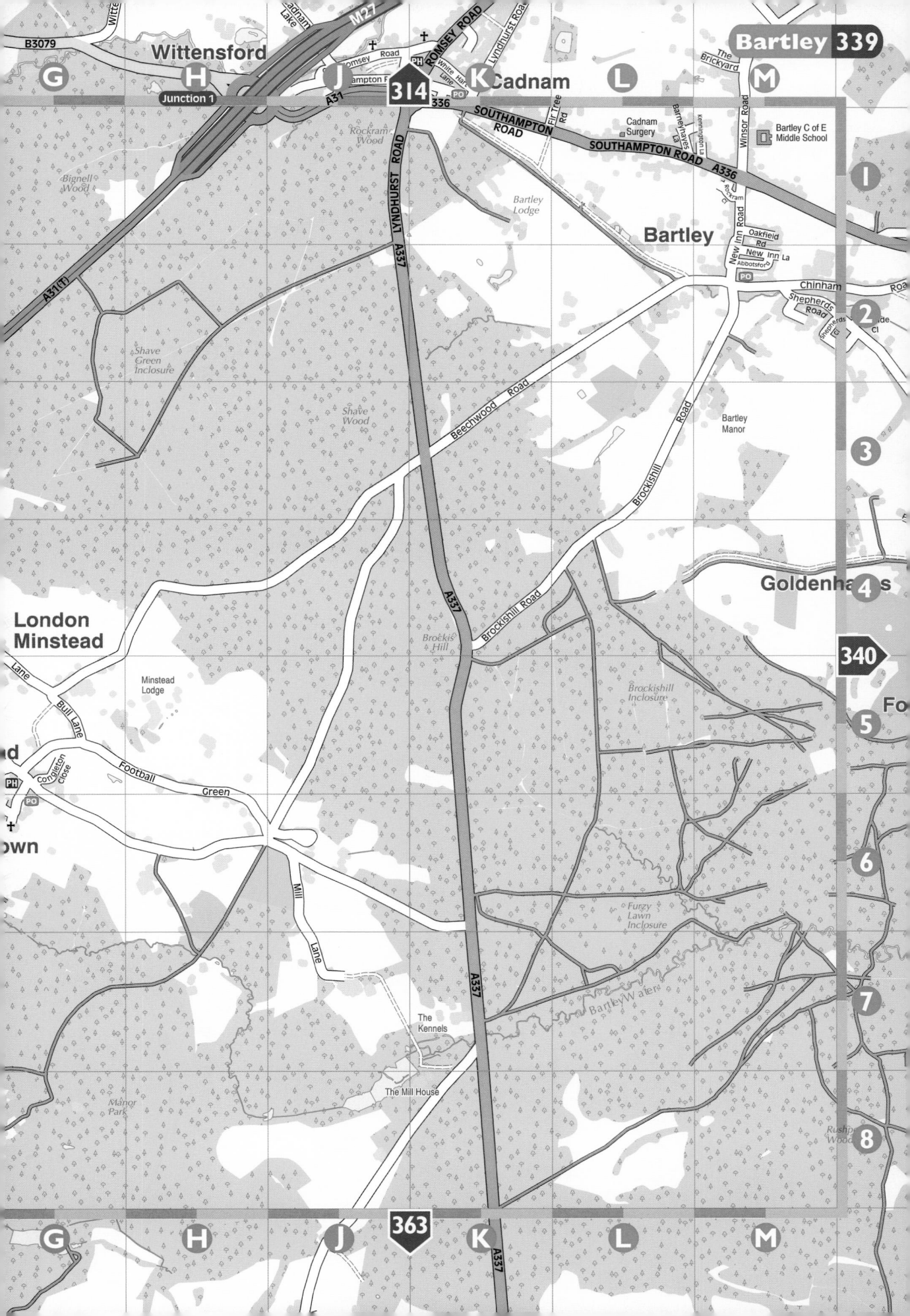

NETLEY MARSH

Woodlands

Foyers

LYNDHURST

315
339
364

Bartley C of E Middle School
Bartley Grange
Netley Marsh C of E Controlled Infant School
Carlton Ho
Willswood Fm
Great Fletchwood Fm
Busketts Wood
Busketts Lawn Inclosure
Ironshill Lodge
Ironshill Inclosure
Rushpole Wood
Ashurst Hospital
Ashurst (New Forest) Station
Lodgehill Cottage

F 1 Nickleby Gdns 2 Shawford Cl
G 1 Alfred Cl 2 Bullfinch Cl 3 Cherrywd Gdns 4 Crabapple Cl 5 Cypress Gdns 6 Milkwood Ct 7 Teal Cl 8 Watson Wk 9 Winchester Wy

1 grid square represents 500 metres

316

Totton
Recreation
Centre

Abbotswood Junior School

Forest
Edge
School

Lydlynch
County First
School

Test Vale
Surg.

Police Station

Salterns
School

COMMERCIAL ROAD

Testwood

Associated Football Club

RINGWOOD ROAD

First School

Forest Gate School

Calmore Gdns

Andrew

Coplands Av

Magpie Dr

Plover Cl

Forest Farm

Hazel La

Barnsfield Crescent

Frith La

Longstock

Testbourne Av

Testbourne Crs

Sheridan

Browning

Bronte

Itchin

Lydlynch Rd

Water La

Maynard Road

Totton Station

Mill Rd

LC

Junction Road

HIGH STREET

BY-PASS

Kinross Rd

Avenue

Lackford

Brokenford Lane

Jackie Wigg Gdns

Osbom

PO

Winsor

RUMBRIDGE STREET

TOTTON

Rose Rd

Fisher's Rd

School Road

Eling County Infant School

Eling
Lane

River Test

I 1

2

RINGWOOD ROAD

Redwood Gdns

Larchwood Rd

Harold Rd

Briarmead Road

Eastmead Ct

Myrtle Av

Doriana

Deerhurst Cl

Rowan

Eyre Cl

BartleyWater

Culford Avenue

Manor Cl

Rushington Av

Frampton Wy

Lane

Hemming

Bartley Av

Oakley Crs

Culford Crs

Rushington Gdns

Manor Cl

Rushington

Spicer's Wy

Players Crs

Cooke Cl

SPICER'S HILL

Roberts Rd

The Drive

Battram Rd

Leaby Rd

M

Down's Park Avenue

Crown's Pk Rd

Down's Pk Crs

The Heritage Centre & Museum
Tide Mill

Eling

Cemetery

Hill

Bury Lane

2

3

Ashurst Bridge Road

A326

Ashurst Bridge

Denbigh

Reynolds Dr

Surrey

Ibbotson Way

Perry Vale

Birchlands

Mill Way

Cocklydown Lane

Totton Coll

Chapel Lane

Rushington Business Park

Spicer's Hill

Hounsdown Av

Valley Rd

Powell Crs

Brookside

Riverview

The Retreat

Kirk Gdns

The Retreat Lane

MARCHWOOD

BY-PASS

A326

3

A326

Foxhills

Foxhills County First School

Kneller's Lane

HUNTERS HILL

MAIN ROAD

Jacob's Wk

Moorcrofts

Jacob's Gutter Lane

LC

Hampshire Co Council

Hounsdown School

Hounsdown

4

342

MAWOOD

Trotts Lane

5

Foxhills
SO40

Wharfons

Cooper Road

Chestnut Av

Lakewood Road

Rye Cl

Dene Way

Dene Rd

Cecil Av

A35

Colbury Fm

Pound Lane

LC

Tr

5

Colbury

ROAD

Ashurst

Hunters Inn Hill

Pound Lane

Durley Fm

Longdown Dairy Fm

6

MA

OOD

6

Deerleap Lane

Churchplace Inclosure

Deerleap Fm

Longdown Estates

Langley Wood

Langley Lodge

7

8

Deerleap Lane

G   H   J   K   L   M

320

G1
1 Holmsley Cl
2 Mountain Ash Cl

G4
1 Butt's Crs
2 Imber Cl

G5
1 Grainger Gdns
2 Heathfield Cl
3 Orpen Rd

G6
1 Dawson Rd
2 Stubbs Rd

H2
1 Masefield Gn

H4
1 Butt's Cl
2 Butt's Rd
3 Lydgate Rd
4 Quilter Cl
5 Walton Rd

J1
1 Haselfoot Gdns

Harefield

Thornhill Park

Woodlands Community School

HEDGE END

Junction 7

CHARLES WATTS WAY A334

THORNHILL PK RD

Thornhill Park Surgery

Kanes Hill Primary School

Upper Northam Drive

UPPER NORTHAM ROAD B3036

Freegrounds

Police Station

Thornhill Clinic

Thornhill Junior School

Thornhill First School

Thornhill

Hightown Primary School

Netley Hill

South West Health Authority

BURSLEDON ROAD

Botley Road

WEST END ROAD B3033

Hightown

on Common

Surrey House Health Cen

Surrey House First School

Solent Peoples Theatre

Heathfield Infant & Middle School

City of Southampton Hampshire County

Junction 8

A3024

A3025

A27

Bursledon Windmill Museum

Old Netley

HAMBLE LANE

PROVIDENCE HILL

Lowford

Bursledon C of E Junior & Infant School

Cemetery

OAKHILL BRIDGE ROAD

Bursledon Station

Bursledon

369

H5
1 Botley Rd
2 Montague Cl
3 Sullivan Rd
4 Vardy Cl
5 Warlock Cl

L6
1 Ashley Ct
2 Cambrian Cl
3 Devonshire Gdns

M1
1 Downscroft Gdns

L7
1 Estridge Cl
2 Humber Gdns
3 Lancaster Cl
4 Phoenix Cl
5 Sunnyfield Ri

M2
1 Chalice Ct
2 Little Park Gdns
3 Oak Tree Gdns
4 Rustan Cl
5 Wheatsheaf Ct
6 Yew Tree Cl

M3
1 New Cliffe Gdns

L8
1 Batchelor Gn

M4
1 Foord Rd

Bursledon Heath

L2
1 Buttercup Cl
2 Clover Wy
3 St Catherines Vw

L3
1 Norman Gdns

K8
1 Ash Cl
2 Chamberlayne Rd
3 Pilands Wood Rd

L1
1 Goodlands V

K4
1 Mosaic Cl
2 Tumulus Cl

K6
1 Devonshire Gdns

J5
1 Adela Verne Cl
2 Botley Gdns
3 Killarney Cl

K5
1 Kinsbourne Cl

J4
1 Fairfax Ct
2 Kinsbourne Wy

J4
1 Warburton Cl

G8
1 Barrie Cl
2 Bronte Gdns
3 Chesterton Pl
4 Fitzgerald Cl
5 John Bunyan Cl

The Vine School

BOTLEY ROAD

Reading Room

Vicarage

LOCK?

Lake Road

322

OCKS HILL

A334

Row Ash

G

H

J

K

L

M

Botley Station

STATION HILL

A334

Kitnocks

Outlands Lane

Raglington Farm

Hall Court

1

A3051

2

Fairthorne Manor

Mansfield Lane

3

Barn Farm

4

Curbridge

348

Ridge La

5

Bury Farm

Ridge Farm

Dimmock's Moor

6

Whiteley Lane

Titc...

Browning Close

Whiteley La

Botley Wood

7

Dickens Drive

Austen Gdns

Andersen Cl

Rattigan

Christie Gdns

Conrad Way

Buchan Av

Whiteley

Coriander Way

Angelica Way

8

Steinbeck Cl

Thyme Avenue

Rosemary Gdns

Flagpond Copse

3

Hemmingway Gardens

Fyfield Close

Saffron Way

Marjoram

Caraway

Way

Lovage Road

Hyssop Close

371

Hispano Av

Java Drive

Hanoverian Way

Drive

Sorrel Drive

Whiteley

Parkway

Lee Ground

Arabian

Whiteley County Primary

Hotel

G

H

J

K

L

M

G · H · J · 324 · K · L · M

I

New

A32

Kingsmead

ingsmead

Lane

Heath

Woodend

Road

Liberty

Road

Dradfield Lane

PO

Church Road

Newtown Sob
County Primary

Church Ro

2

3

Hundred   Acres   Road

West
Lodge

Hundred Acres Road

Hundred Acres

Trampers Lane

Goathouse
Fm

4

350

Rookesbury
Park
School

5

LittleForest

OUTHWICK

ROAD

B2177

Hundred Acres Road

North
Boarhunt

6

Wickham
Common

Wickham
Riding
School

Firgrove La

Trampers Lane

Lane

Bonhams

*Orchard
Copse*

South Hants
Country Club

PO

B2177

P017

7

Blackhouse Lane

Staple Cross

8

Bere Farm La

Blackhouse Lane

re Farm l

King's   Way

G   H   J   K   L   M

Grevitts Copse

1

2

3

4

5

6

7

8

Horsley Farm

Locksash Lane

We330arden

B2146

Nore Down Wy

Nore Down

oldhouse Lane

Lodge Fm

Lodge Lane

Locksash Lane

Watergate

Watergate Hanger

Broadreed Fm

Lumley Seat

Monarch's Way Lane

Woodlands

Monarch's Wy

Woodlands Cotts

B2146

Monarch's Way

Monarch's Way

Cooks Lane

Monarch's Wy

Walde

Stanstead House

B2146

Newbarn Lane

Park Lane

B2146

Sindle's Fm

Monument La

G   H   J   379   K   L   M

†

B2146

G   H   J   K   L   M

333

1 Lavender Cl

Plumley Wood

Plumley Farm

Harefield Plantation

Home Farm

Shepherds Lane

shepherds

Chestnut Ave

I

2

3

Ringwood Forest

Nea Drive

Somerl Par

Rd

The Chase

Hunters Cl

Barberry Wy

Fairwood Rd

Laburnum Cl

Magnolia Cl

Acacia Cl

Wisteria Dr

Black Moor Rd

Brunel Cl

RINGWOOD ROAD

The Forestside

Rosebery Close

Parsane Cl

Ebblake

Cemetery

Forest Cl

Bessemer Close

Ebblake Industrial Est

B3081

Nea Drive

Duncombe Drive

4

358

5

6

Hampshire County
Dorset County

Moors Valley Country Park

VERWOOD ROAD B3081

7

Baker's Hanging

8

G   H   J   K   L   M

381

Watchmoor Wood

River

ey Heath
strial Est

Avon Valley

G7
1 Frobisher Cl
2 Hawkins Cl
3 Padget Rd

G8
1 Cunningham Cl
2 Hudson Cl
3 Pilgrim Pk
4 Pipers Ash
5 Raleigh Cl
6 Whitehart Flds

Whitefield Plantn

G   H   J   **335**   K   L   M

Mockbeggar

Digden Bottom

Dockens Water

1

Avon Valley Path

Appleslade Inclosure

2

Moyles Court School

Dockens Water

Red Shoot Wood

Ellingham Drove

Rockford Common

3

Rockford

Great Linford Inclosure

4

360

Highwood

Highwood Lane

5

Little Linford Inclosure

Highwood Lane

Lin Brook

Linford

6

Corley Road

Cowpitts

Old Farm Close

North Poulner

Lane

Hangersley

Shaw Rd

Junior & Infant School

Lawrence Rd

St Aubyns Lane

Ross Rd

Forestside Gdns

Dene Cl

Holm Croft

Denholm

Road

Road

Shobley

7

Fairlie

Butlers La

Linford

Poulner Pk

Road

BH24

Link Rd

Corley Road

Chester Rd

Drake Cl

Grenville Cl

Narrow La

Anson Cl

Poulner

Somerville Rd

Cook

Beatty Cl

A31(T)

8

Eastfield La

Audener Ct

Jubilee Cl

The Mount

Narrow La

Chapel

A31(T)

POULNER HILL

Picket Hill

G   H   J   **383**   K   L   **Ioulford**   M

Toms Lane

Linwood Farm

I

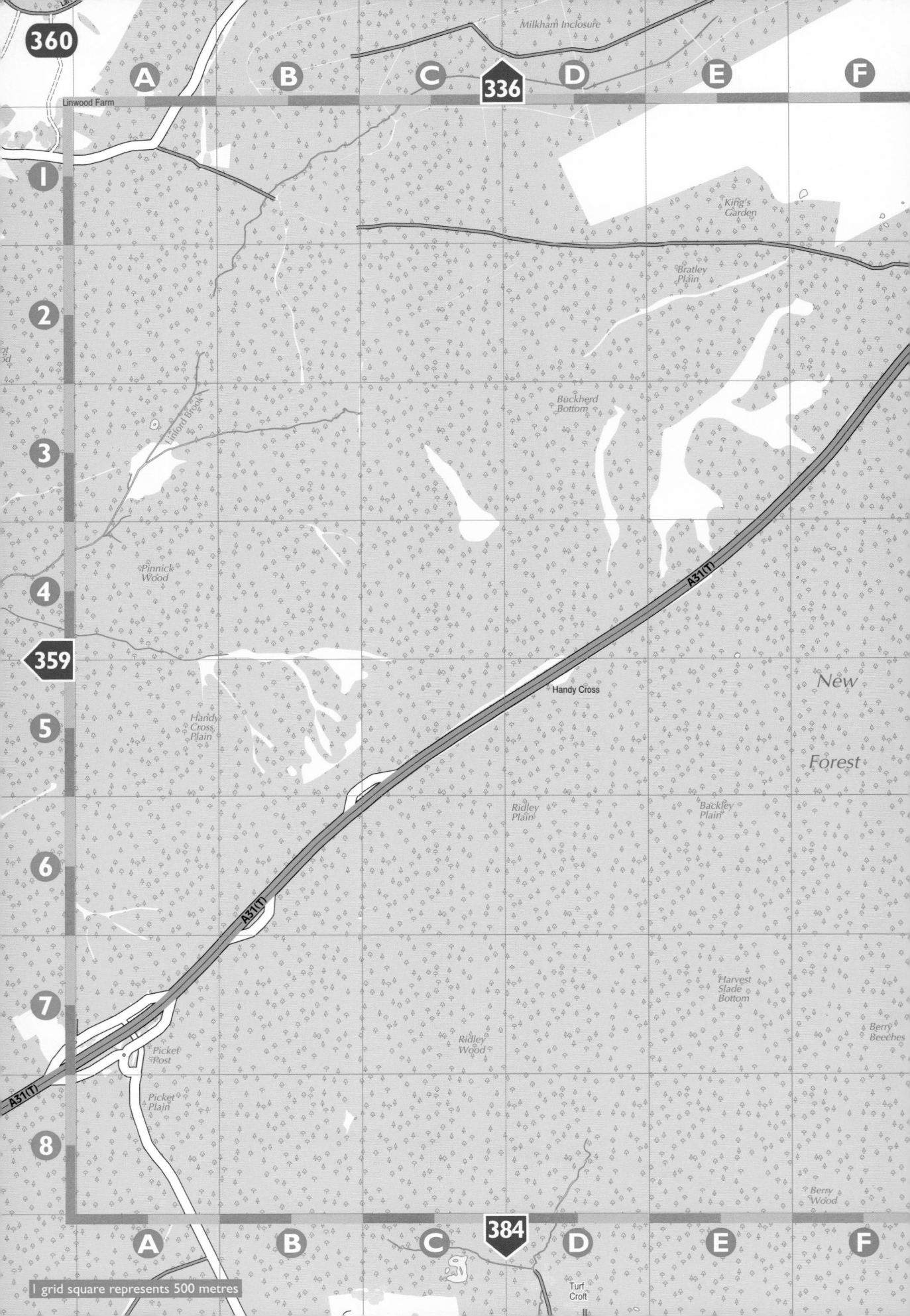

A   B   C   336   D   E   F

Linwood Farm

1

Milkham Inclosure

King's Garden

Bratley Plain

2

Buckherd Bottom

Linford Brook

3

Pinnick Wood

4

A31(T)

359

Handy Cross

New

Handy Cross Plain

5

Ridley Plain

Backley Plain

Forest

6

A31(T)

Harvest Slade Bottom

7

Picket Post

Ridley Wood

Berry Beeches

A31(T)

Picket Plain

8

Berry Wood

A   B   C   384   D   E   F

Turf Croft

I grid square represents 500 metres

338

386

A **B** **C** **D** **E** **F**

1
2
3
4
5
6
7
8

Highland
Water
Inclosure

Inclosure

Wick
Wood

Acres
Down

Pilmore
Gate
Heath

Holmhill
Inclosure

Highland   Water

Wood
Crates

White Moor

Millyford Bridge

Portuguese Fireplace

Holidays Hill
Inclosure

Allum
Gree

Barrow
Moor

Wooson's
Hill
Inclosure

Church
Moor

Warwick
Slade

Winding
Shoot

Bolderwood Arboretum Ornamental Drive

Knightwood
Oak

A35

Knightwood
Inclosure

Eagle
Oak

Warwickslade Cutting

Great
Huntley
Bank

Brinken
Wood

Highland

New

Fletchers
Thorns
Inclosure

Vinney
Ridge

1 grid square represents 500 metres

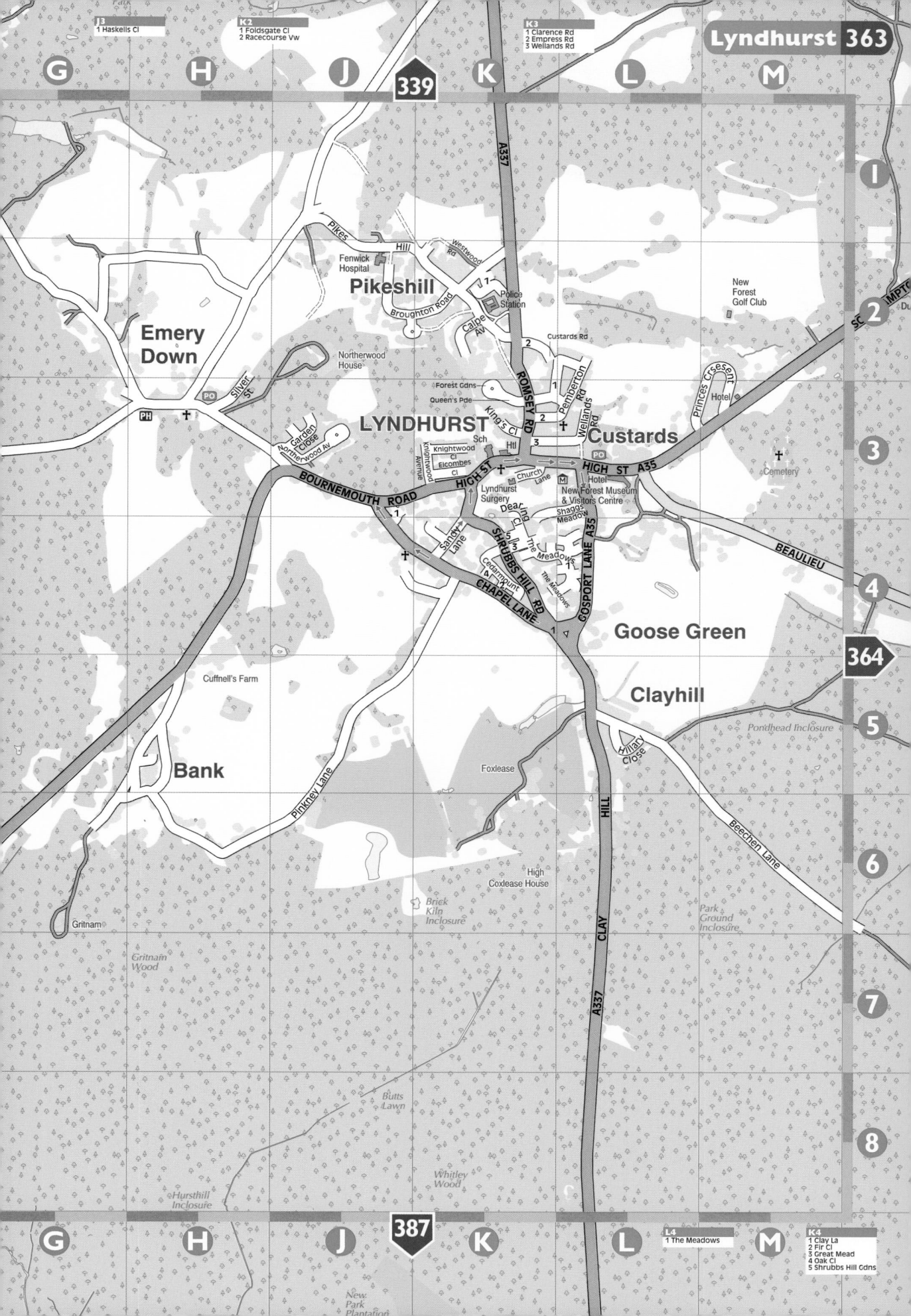

A   B   340   C   D   E   F

340

I

2

3

Ironshill
Inclosure

Lodgehill
Cottage

A35

SOUTHAMPTON   ROAD

Dunces Arch

Mallard
Wood

White
Moor

Beaulieu River

Ashurst
Wood

Ashurst Lodge

†
netery

BEAULIEU

4

ROAD

363

5

B3056

Hotel

ead I

Matley
Wood

Matley
Heath

Matley
Passage

6

Little
Holmhill
Inclosure

Denny
Inclosure

7

Park Hill

8

Denny
Wood

Denny
Lodge

A   B   C   388   D   E   F

388

1 grid square represents 500 metres

G   H   J   341   K   L   M

Churchplace
Inclosure

Deerleap
Lane

Longdown
Estates

Langley
Wood

Staplewood Lane

I

Deerleap Inclosure

Arters

2

Longdown
Inclosure

Twiggs

3   Farm

4   Inclosure

366

Decoy
Pond Farm

5

Yew
Tree
Heath

6

Black
Down

7

Beaulieu
Road Station   Hotel

Ferny
Crofts

8

New
Forest

G   H   J   389   K   L   M

BEAULIEU ROAD B3056

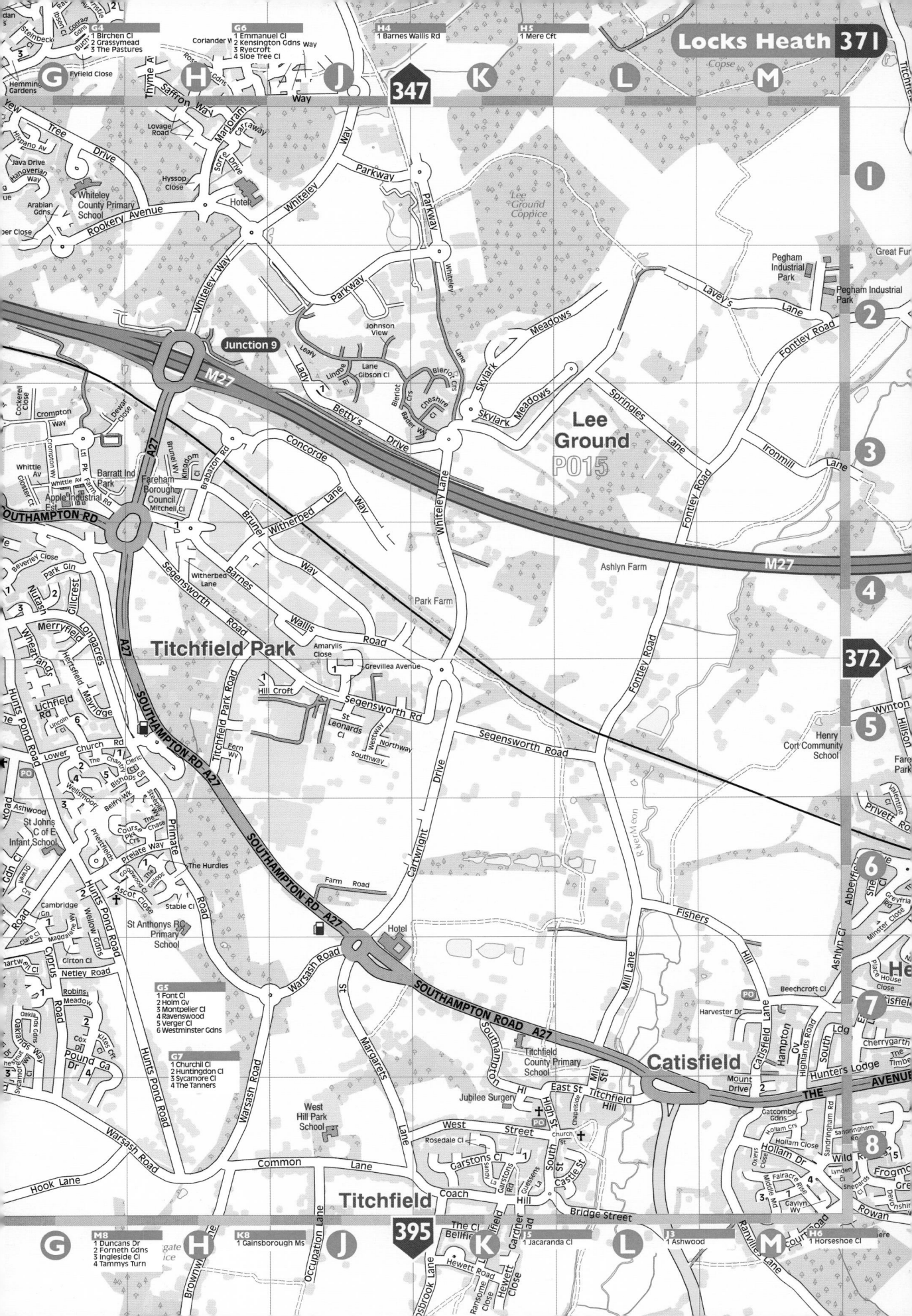

G   H   J   355   K   L   M

Sindle's Fm

Park Lane

Monument   La

B2146

I

The

†

Racton
Park Fm

B2146

HARES

2

Otanes Fm

B2147

Aldsworth

Ractonpark
Wood

3

Common Road

Common Road

B2147

LANE

FOXBURY

Marlpit Lane

Hambrook Business
Cen

4

y School

Woodmancote

Cemetery

Cemetery Lane

Woodmancote Lane

Woodmancote Lane

Cheesemans

La

Woodmancote Lane

Duffield Lane

Walnut
Tree
Dr

South La

W Ashling Rd

5

Hambrook HI
(North)

Nightingale Lane

Devils Copse

A27(T)

A27(T)

Farm   Lane

A27(T)

Lane

Stein Rd

South Av
W Ashling

Hither
Gn

Lauder
Cl

Fraser
Gdns

Hambrook

6

Scant   Road (West)

conifer
Dr

Hambrook HI (South)

Broad Road

Bourne
Road

Haslemere
Road

Bourne
Vw Cl

Breach Avenue

East
Fld
Cl

The Avenue

PO

Park   Road

Clovelly Road

Mountwood
Road

Smallcutts Av

Glenwood
Rd

Kelsey
Av

Barnfield

Funtston
Cl

Priors Leaze Lane

Oak Tree
Farm

7

The Bourne Community
College

St John's Rd

Hartland
Ct

PO

Priors
Cl

Priors Leaze

Yeomans Fld

Breach

Manor Road

Cooks   Lane

Priors Leaze Lane

LC

Manor
Gdns

Manor
Way

Hurstwood Av

LC

Guildford
Cl

Inlands   Road

LC

Nutbourne
Station

Broad Rd

8

Tuppenny Lane

Lazy
Acre

First Av

Second Av

Lodgebury
Close

Southbourne County
Junior & Infant School

Southbourne Station

LC

Flatt Rd

Alfrey
Cl

Carsons Road

Longlands
Road

The Drive

New Rd

Goodwood
Court

Mosdell
Rd

Southbourne

Flatt
La

Flatt
Rd

MAIN ROAD

A259

Ham La

Prinsted Lane

Frarydene

The
Crescent

Church Rd

Surgery

MAIN RD

Schools Rd

PO

A259

Pottery
La

†

MAIN

Nutbourne

Maybush
Dr

Iydene
Crescent

Maybush   Drive

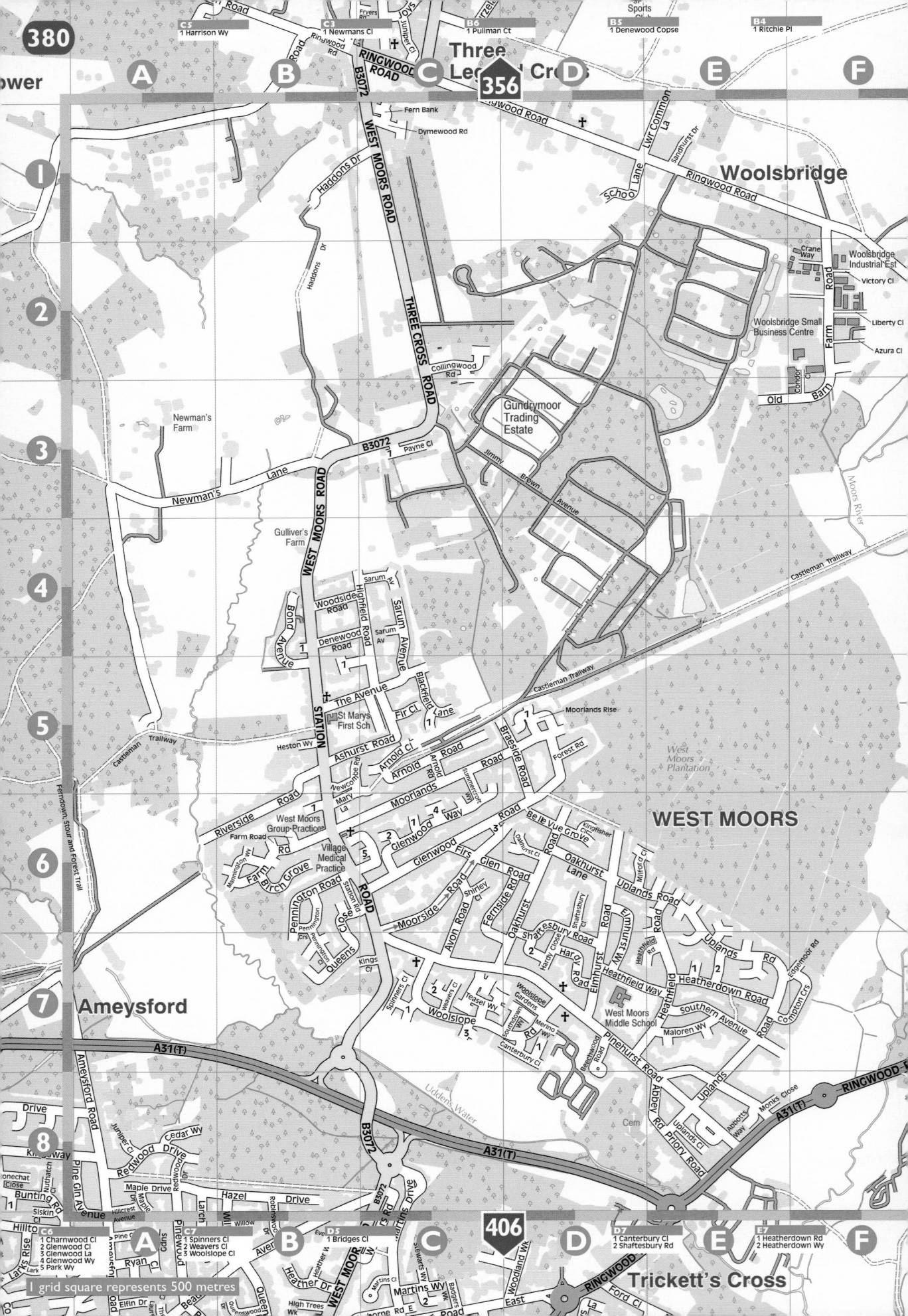

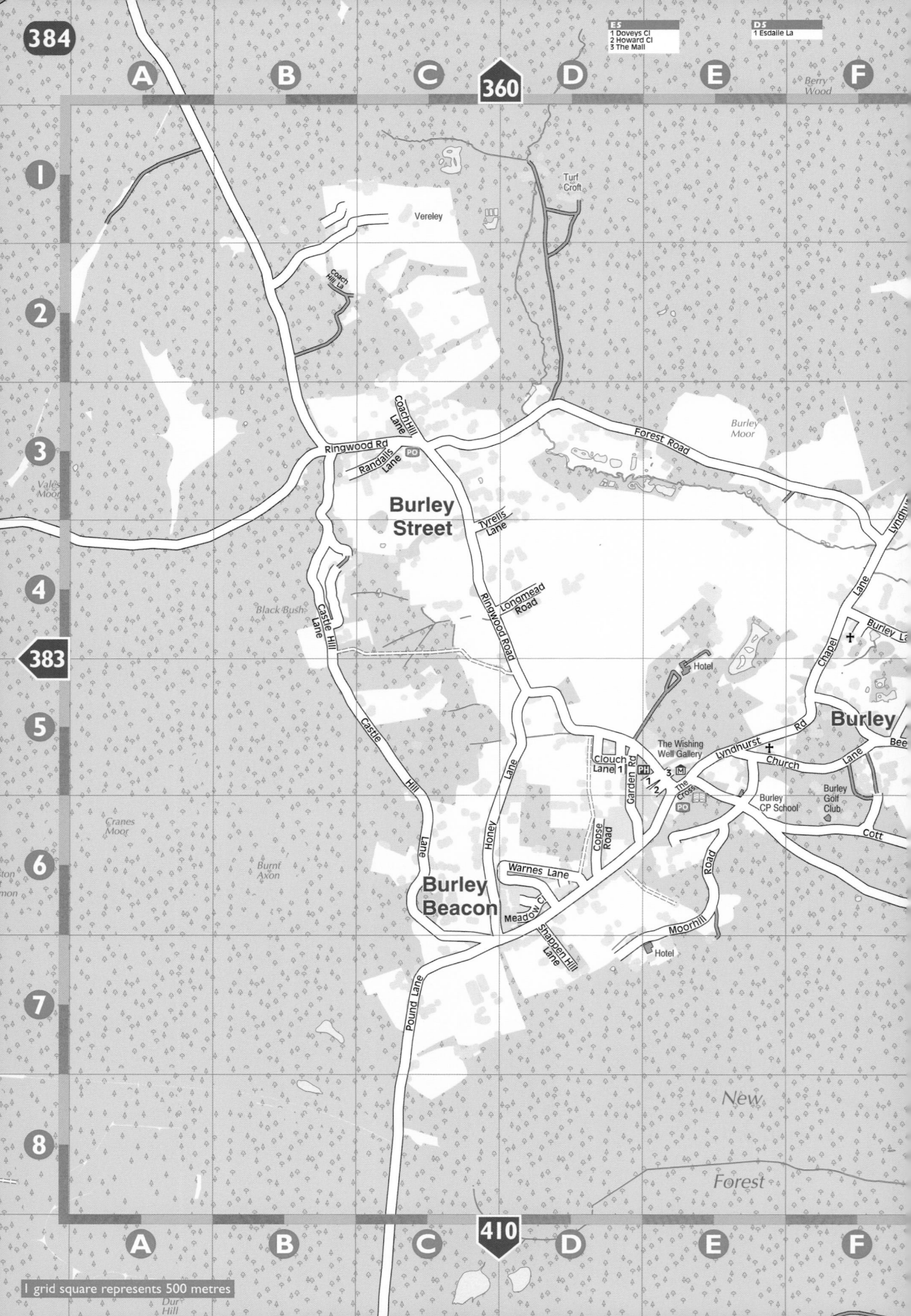

G H J 361 K L M

I
2
3
4
386
5
6
7
8

South
Oakley
Inclosure

Burley
Lodge

Dames
Slough
Inclosure

Burley
New
Inclosure

Burley
Old
Inclosure

Red
Rise

Mill Lane

Mill Lawn Brook

Burley Lawn

Lane

Bennetts Lane

Southfield

Lane

Bisterne Close

Bisterne Close

Shoot
Wood

Markway
Inclosure

A35

A35

A35

Goatspen
Plain

Clayhill
Bottom

Station Road

Wilverley
Post

Naked
Man

enberry
ge

G H J 411 K L M

A B C 362 D E F

New

Forest

Brinken Wood

Highland

Wickslade Cutting

Fletchers Thorns Inclosure

1

Vinney Ridge Inclosure

Poundhill Inclosure

2

Rhinefield Ornamental Drive

3

Rhinefield Sandy's Inclosure

A35

4

385

Hotel

Aldridgehill Inclosure

5

Markways Inclosure

Ober Water

6

Crab Tree Earth

Duck Hole

7

White Moor

Five Thorns Hill

8

Wilverley Plain

Hincheslea Moor

Burley Road

A B C 412 D E F

1 grid square represents 500 metres

G   H   J   K   L   M

K7
1 Culverley Cl
2 The Paddock
3 Wide Lane Cl

L6
1 Horlock Rd
2 Waters Gn
3 Waters Green Ct

L7
1 Auckland Pl
2 Forest Hall
3 Greenways Rd
4 Sutton Pl

363

Whitley Wood

1

Hursthill Inclosure

2

New Park Plantation

Hollands Wood

Poundhills Heath

New Park

Hotel

Ramnor Inclosure

3

Black Water

Hotel

Bolderford Bridge

Ober Heath

Balmer Lawn

4

Ober Water

Highland Water

Black Knowl

388

5

Hotel

Balmerlawn

BALMER LAWN ROAD

Beachern Wood

Butts Lawn

Meerut Road

Butts Lawn

Carey's Cottages

Martin's

Hth Waters Gn

Park Cl

Hotel

Brockenhurst College

6

Ober House

The Coppice

Oberfield Rd

Whitemoor Road

New Forest Drive

Broadlands Rd

Forest Park Road

Knowle Rd

Hotel

Ober Rd

Brookside Road

Fathersfield

CRIGG LANE

Chestnut Rd

Burford La

LYNDHURST ROAD A337

Hotel

Moorlands Cl

New Forest Dr

BROCKENHURST

Filbards Road

North Rd

MILL LANE

7

Forest Dr

New Close Rd

Forest Vw

Armstrong Road

Armstrong Lane Armstrong Cl

Broadlands Rd

Wilverley Road

Brookley Road

The Rise

PO

Hotel

Brookley Rd

North Rd

LC

North Weirs

North Weirs

Brockenhurst Primary School

Avenue Rd

E Bank Rd

Auckland

Brockenhurst Station

Church Lane

Brockenhurst Park

Burley Road

South Weirs

Partridge Rd

Highwood Rd

The Surgery

Tattenham Rd

Addison Road

Collyers Rd

8

SWAY ROAD

A337

Tilebarn Lane

413

G   H   J   K   L   M

A B C 364 D E F Denny Lodge

I

2 Ramnor Inclosure

Parkhill Inclosure

3 Pignal Inclosure

Stubby Copse Inclosure

Balmer Lawn

4 Perrywood Haseley Inclosure

387

5 Balmerlawn

BALMER LAWN ROAD

Hotel

New Copse Inclosure

S042

6 Ladycross Lodge

B3055 B3055

7 B3055

Perrywood Ironshill Inclosure

Brockenhurst Park

8 Round Hill

Lymington River

A B C 414 D Dilton E F

G H J 365 K L M

New
Forest

LIEU ROAD B3056

I

Pig
Bush

Culverley Farm

2

Shepton Bridge

3

Rowbarrow

Tantany
Wood

ure

LC

4

Pe
Lo

390

Frame
Heath
Inclosure

Stubbs
Wood

Frame
Wood

5

Moon
Hill

6

Hawkhill
Inclosure

Furzey
Lodge

Stockley
Inclosure

7

Furzey
Lane

Hatche
Gate

B3055

8

G H J 415 K L M

Masseys La

B3054

EAST

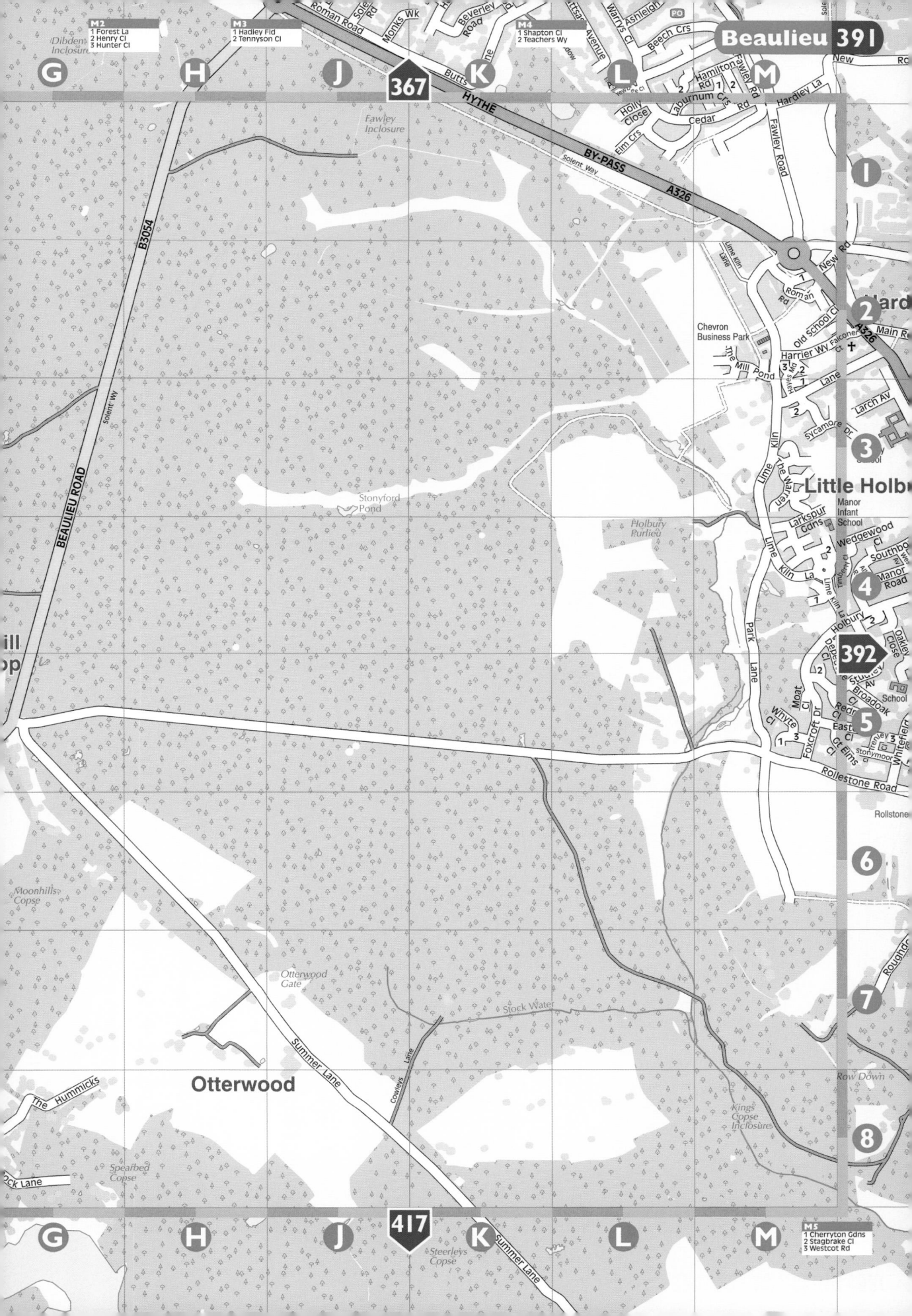

G H J K L M

M2
1 Forest La
2 Henry Cl
3 Hunter Cl

M3
1 Hadley Fld
2 Tennyson Cl

M4
1 Shapton Cl
2 Teachers Wy

367

Roman Road

Monks Wk

Beverley Road

Warn's Avenue

Beech Crs

HYTHE

BY-PASS

A326

Fawley Inclosure

Solent Way

Holly Close

Cedar

Elm Crs

Laburnum Crs

Hamilton Rd

Fawley Road

Hardley La

New

I

2

Hard

A326

Main R

Lime Kiln Lane

Roman Rd

Old School Cl

Chevron Business Park

The Mill Pond

Harrier Wy

Falconer

Larch Av

Sycamore Dr

Hayes Lane

3

School

Little Holb

B3054

Solent Wy

BEAULIEU ROAD

Stonyford Pond

Holbury Purlieu

Lime Kiln

The Warren

Park Lane

Lime Kiln La

Manor Infant School

Larkspur Gdns

Wedgewood

Cl

Southbo

Manor Road

4

392

Holbury

Depe Cl

Studley Av

Broadoak

School

5

ill op

Moat Cl

Redr

Gt Elms

Whyte Cl

Foxcroft Dr

Easte

Cl

Whitefield

stonymoor

Henley Cl

Oakley Close

Rollestone Road

Rollstone

6

Roundo

7

Moonhills Copse

Otterwood Gate

Summer Lane

Cowleys Lane

Stock Water

Kings Copse Inclosure

Row Down

8

Otterwood

The Hummicks

ck Lane

Spearbed Copse

G H J K L M

417

Summer Lane

Steerleys Copse

M5
1 Cherryton Gdns
2 Stagbrake Cl
3 Westcot Rd

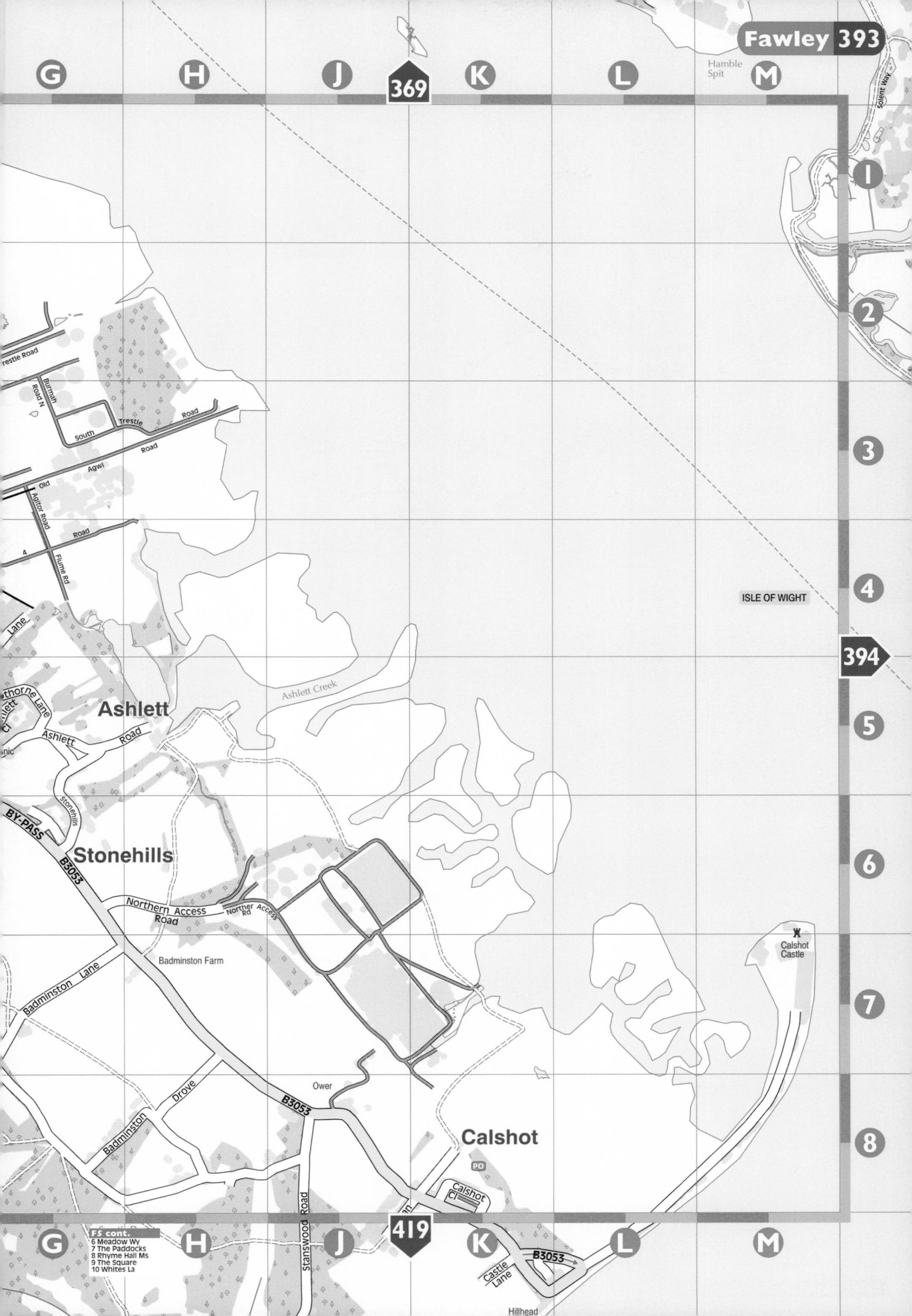

G H J 369 K L M

Hamble
Spit

1

2

3

ISLE OF WIGHT 4

394

5

Trestle Road

Burmah
Road N

South   Trestle   Road

Road

Old   Agwi

Road

Ashton Road

Flume Rd

4

Lane

Cawthorne Lane

Ashlett

Ashlett

Road

Ashlett Creek

clinic

Ashlett

Stonehills

BY-PASS

B3053

Stonehills

6

Northern Access
Road   Norther Access
Rd

Badminston Farm

Calshot
Castle

7

Badminston Lane

Badminston

Drove

Ower

B3053

Calshot

8

PO

Stanswood Road

419

Calshot
C

Castle
Lane

B3053

Hillhead

F5 cont.
6 Meadow Wy
7 The Paddocks
8 Rhyme Hall Ms
9 The Square
10 Whites La

Abshot

A   Newtown   B   C   370   D   E   F

Queen's Rd
Osborn
Meadcroft Cl
Pitchponds Rd
Hook with Warsash Primary School
Oakwood Cl
Hook Cl
New Rd
New Rd
Oakwood Ci
New   Rd   Rd
Fleet End Bottom

Solent Way
Newtown
Hewetts Rd
Lower Spinney
Jumar Close
Rossan Av
Remford Rd
Hornby Cl
Hook
Hook Park Rd
Hook La
Abshot Ltd

Gilchrist Gdns
Hook
Hook Lane

1   Solent Court

Pk
Hook Park Road
Solent Drive
Road
Hook

2   Hook Park   Cowes Lane   Workman's   Lane   Hook   Lane

Solent Way

3   Solent Way   Workman's La   Chilling   Lane   Chilling

4   OF WIGHT   Solent Way

393

5

6

Calshot Castle

7

8

A   B   C   D   E   F

Warbling

Brockhampton

G   H   J   377   K   L   M   I

Southbrook Road

Longmead Gdns

Rectory Rd

Woodbury

Regents Ct

South Cl

Norris Gdns

Penner Road

Farm Way

Havant Business Center

Southmoor Lane

Brook

The Mallards

Langstone Av

Wade Lane

Solent Way

Cemetery

Solent Way

16   **17**

Langstone Lane

Mill

Langstone High

St Cdns

PH

Tower

Harbourside

Langstone

The Saltings

2

LANGSTONE ROAD

Langstone Bridge

Broad Lake

A3023

Northney Road

Hotel

3

Long Island

Northney Road

Northney La

St Peter's

4

402

Clover Rd

Pycroft Close

New Cut

Island Cl

Kingsway

Queensway

St Peter's Rd

5

HAVANT ROAD

A3023

Avenue Road

Meadow Cl

Rogers M

Victoria Road

6

HAYLING ISLAND

Mill Close

Stoke

Croft Lane

Northwood Lane

Castlemans Lane

T

Woods

7

West Lane

Copse Lane

8

PO

Fleet

Yew Tree Rd

Daw Lane

HAVANT ROAD

G   H   J   **425**   K   L   M

A3023

Mill Rythe

378

Cemetery

Solent Way

17

EMSWORTH

Conigar
Point

2

Fowley
Island

Sweare
Deep

3

Wickor
Point

Great Deep

Spinnaker
Grange

Northney La

Northney

North   Road

Northney

4

Clovelly
Rd

401

Pycroft
Close

5

Church Lane

St Peter's Rd

North Hayling

St Peter's Av

Hampshire County
West Sussex County

Hunter

Swift   Road

Javelin
Road

Spartan Cl

Sabre Rd

S Bay

N Bay

Meteor
Road

Canberra Rd

Hornet Road

6

Thorney County
Primary School

Chichester Road

Tye

Woodgason Lane

Gutner Lane

St Peter's Road

7

Marker Point

Emsworth Channel

Sussex Border Path

Emsworth Road

Emsworth Rd

8

426

1 grid square represents 500 metres

West Rd

Beach

Knkby

Clovelly Road

Valetta Road

Lane End
Drive

Waters
Edge
Gdns

Bridgefoot Path

St Peter's Sq

Swan Cl

Warblington Road

Western Parade

Wayfarer's Walk

Solent Way

The Promenade

Creek
End

Beacon

Roundhouse
Meadow

Heron Quay

Mill Quay

Osprey Quay

Avocet Quay

Osprey

Thorney Road

Thorney Road

Sussex Border Path

Slipper Road

Gordon Road

Apple
Grove

Southbourne

Prinsted

Nutbourne

G H J K L M

Ham La
Prinsted Lane
The Drive
New Rd
Mosdell Rd
Longlands Road
Carsons Road
The Crescent
Frarydene
Church Rd
Surgery
Alfrey Cl
Tuppenn
MAIN ROAD
A259
Lodgebury Close
Southbourne County Junior & Infant School
Goodwood Court
379
School La
Farm
MAIN RD
A259
PO
Pottery La
Flatt Rd
Nutbourne Station
Rd
Maybush Drive
Cot Lane
Ivydene Crescent
A259
MAIN

I

2

3

4

5

6

7

8

Prinsted Point

Chidham Point

C

Sussex Border Path
Lane

Marsh Lane
Marsh La
PH

C

St Lane

Cobnor Fm

Cobnor Ho

Thorney Island

Stanbury Point

Thorney Island Airfield

West Thorney

Smith Lane
Church
Victor Rd
Vulcan Road
Valiant Road
Valetta Road
Pleasant Lane
Thorney Old Pk
Road
Varsity Road

Thorney Channel

New Barn

Ch ester

Sussex Border Path

G H J K L M

427

Matcham's House

A   B   C   382   D   E   F

Upper
Bisterne Farm

1

Avon Valley Path

Dragon Lane

Avon Valley Path

2

Bisterne Manor

Bisterne

River Avon

3

Lower
Bisterne Farm

Week Farm

Matchams Lane

Week Common

4

407

Church Leisure Centre

Hotel

Anna Lane

Avon Valley Pth

5

Avon Tyrrell Farm

6

London Lane

London Lane

Avon Valley Path

Avon
Common

Avon

7

River Avon

Court Farm

Pithouse Farm

8

Pithouse Lane

Avon Causeway

434

RINGWOOD ROAD

Meadow Cl

Avon Causeway

Sopley

Matchams Lane

A   B   C   434   D   E   F

Sop

I grid square represents 500 metres

Sandford

L7 1 Brookside Cl
L8 1 Woodlands Cl

M7
1 Bramble Wy
2 Rosehill Cl
3 Shackleton Sq
4 Shears Brook Cl

G H J **383** K L M

I
2
3
4
410
5
6
7
8

Bisterne Common

Avon Tyrrell

Ripleys Wood

Anna Lane

North Ripley

Shirley Common

Purlieu

Martin's Copse

Thatchers Lane

Ripley

Shirley

Sopley CP School

Thatchers Lane

Farm

Burnt House Lane

Cedar

Rosehill Drive

Ringwood Road

Shirley Holms

Tyrrells Court

Betsy Lane

The New Medical Cen

Canute Drive

Whistler's Road

Brantsg Gdns

Cuckoo Hi Way

Poplar Lane

Black

Derritt Lane

The Wishing Well Gallery

Wiltshire Gdns

Chapel Lane

Brookside Road

Peace Cl

Clare Cl

Tuck's Cl

Hungerfield Close

Pear Tree Cl

Colbourne Close

Twin Oaks Medical Cen

St Georges

St Mary's Close

Ringwood Road

Poplar

West Road

Merryfield Close

West Hill Lane

Westlands Ct

Hill Cl

Wiltshire Rd

BRANSGORE

Bransgore Primary School

Stubbs Way

G H **435** J K L M
M8 1 Halton Cl

Hampshire County
Dorset County

Derritt Lane

Burley Road

Westbury Cl

Meyrick Close

Brook

North

385

G H Station Road J K L M

Naked

1

Wilverley
Inclosure

2

Station
Road

3

A35

412

Holmsley
Inclosure

Wootton
Coppice
Inclosure

4

Brownhill
Inclosure

5

Wootton
Old Farm

Brownhill   Road
Wootton Farm Road

Rhinefield Road

Wilverley Road

Eastley
Wootton

6

HOLMSLEY

ROAD

Wootton

Manor Farm

B3058

North Drive

Ossemsley

†

7

Bashley Common Road B3058

Marlpit Lane

Wootton
Rough

Tiptc

Ossemsley

South

8

North Drive

Drive

437

St Johns

Bashley

G H J K L M

ane

G H J **389** K L M

B3055

Hatch-
Gate

Hatchet
Pond

I a

East
Heath La

Whitne

Boldre

Pa

2

HATCHET

LANE

B3054

3

Hatchet
Moor

Beaulieu Heath

4

416

5

B3054

Crockford Bridge

Crockford Stream

6

Norley
Inclosure

7

B3054

Norley Farm

Main

Road

Norleywood Road

Norleywood

Joys La

Thatchers Lane

St Leonards Rd

8

Norleywood Road

Brook

Rowes

Lane

Broom Hill

on Road

G H J **441** K L M

E

Hatchet Gate

HATCHET LANE B3054

A   B   C   390   D   E   F

I

Masseys La

East Heath La

Whithers La

Swinesleys Farm

Beufre Farm

Keeping Copse

Solent Way

Pages Lane

Gaza Av

Matthews Lane

Boldre Road

Swems Lease

Chapel Warton Cl

PO

Lane

Lodge Lane

2

Wallace La

Knights Copse

Ashen Wood

New Inn La

Cripple Gate Lane

East Boldre

Church La

3

Little Purnel

4

Newhouse Copse

Lodge Farm

Tylers Copse

415

5

6

Newlands

Coopers Wood

Horsemoor Copse

Newlands Plantation

7

Bergerie

St Leonards Road

8

Beck Farm

Solent Way

Main Road

St Leonards Rg

A   B   C   442   D   E   F

Sowley Lane

Thorns Lane

Park Lane

G H J K L M

391

Spearbed Copse

Steerley's Copse

Yard Wood

Summer Lane

Summer Lane

Beaulieu River

I

2

Keeping

Main Drive

3

Bucklers Hard

Gilbury Hard

Exbury House

Exbury

PH Hotel

Maritime Museum

4

418

Saltershill Copse

5

Clobb

Saltershill

Drokes

Lower Exbury

6

Gins

Beaulieu River

St Leonards Grange

Gins Lane

7

Gins House

Warren Lane

Ne
Ore Point

8

The Log House

G H J K L M

443

Warren Lane

Warren Farm

Blackfield

D1
1 Foxglade
2 Foxlands
3 Fox's Wk
4 Foxy Paddock
5 Langley L Gdns
6 The Mews

Tom's Down

C1
1 Bowland Wy
2 St Francis Cl

A   B   C   D   E   F

Cem.

Hampton Gdns
Hampton Cl
Northampton La
Chapel Lane
Holly Rd
pton Lane

Thornbury Avenue

Viking Cl
South

392

Langley

The Glade
Lea Road
Kings Ride
Charnwood Way
Foresters
W Common

Nicholas Rd
Chalewood Road
St Francis Rd
Hursley
Wychwood

Lepe Road

Clare Gdns
Mopley Cl
Walker's La

Mopley
Forest Ga
Foxhaves
2/La

Forge Road

1 Langley

I

Dark Water

2

West Common

West Common
Homer Farm Lane

Whitefield Farm

3

Exbury

Dark Water

East Hill Farm

4

Lepe Road

Stanswood Road

417

Stanswood

Haxland Pits

Lepe Farm

5

6

Inchmery House

Lepe

Ston

7

8

Needs Ore Point

The Solent

A   B   C   D   E   F

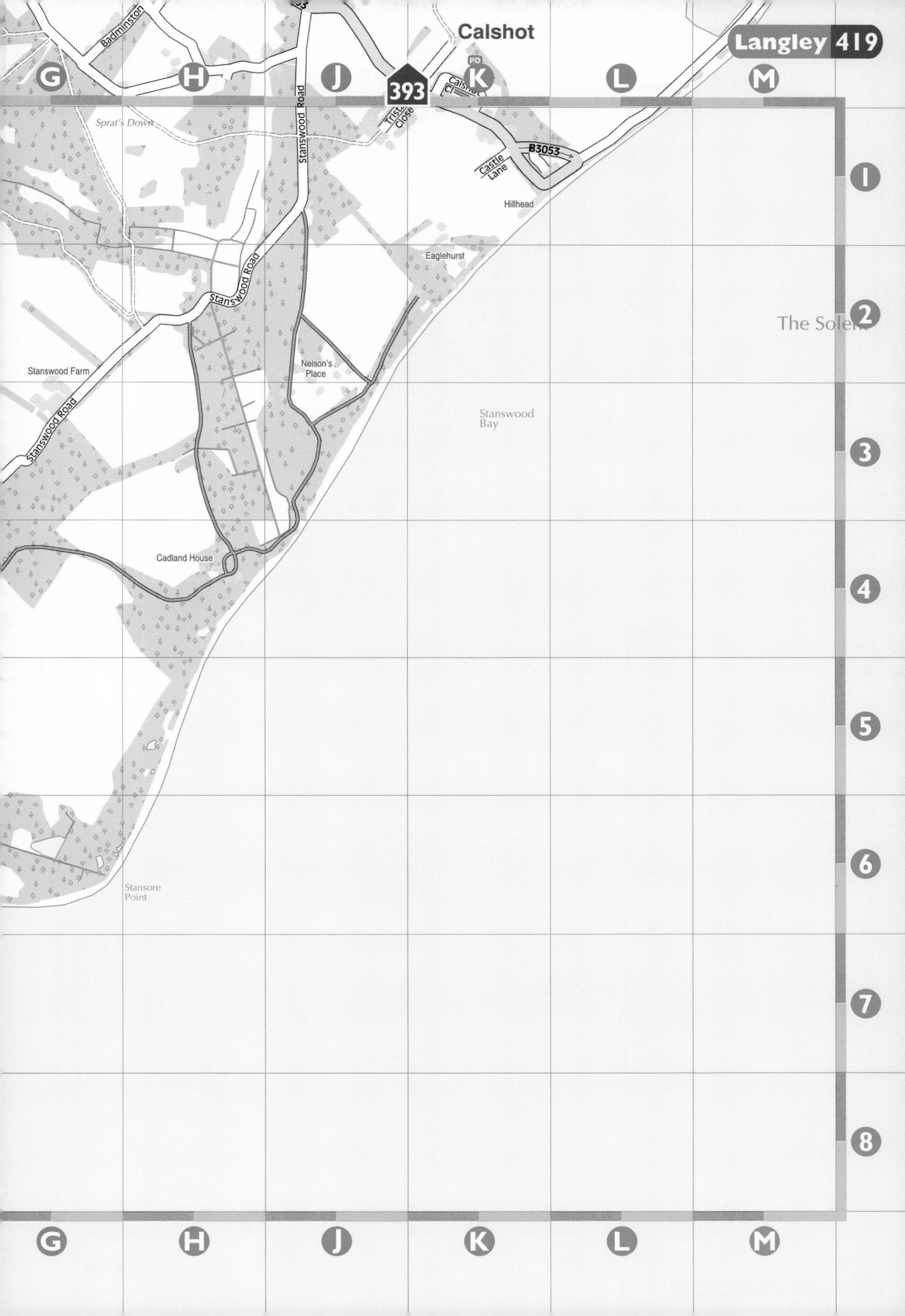

Calshot

393

Calshot Cl

PO

K

Castle Lane

B3053

Hillhead

Eaglehurst

The Solent

Badminston

Sprat's Down

Stanswood Road

Stanswood Road

Stanswood Road

Nelson's Place

Stanswood Bay

Stanswood Farm

Cadland House

Stansore Point

G H J K L M

I

2

3

4

5

6

7

8

G H J K L M

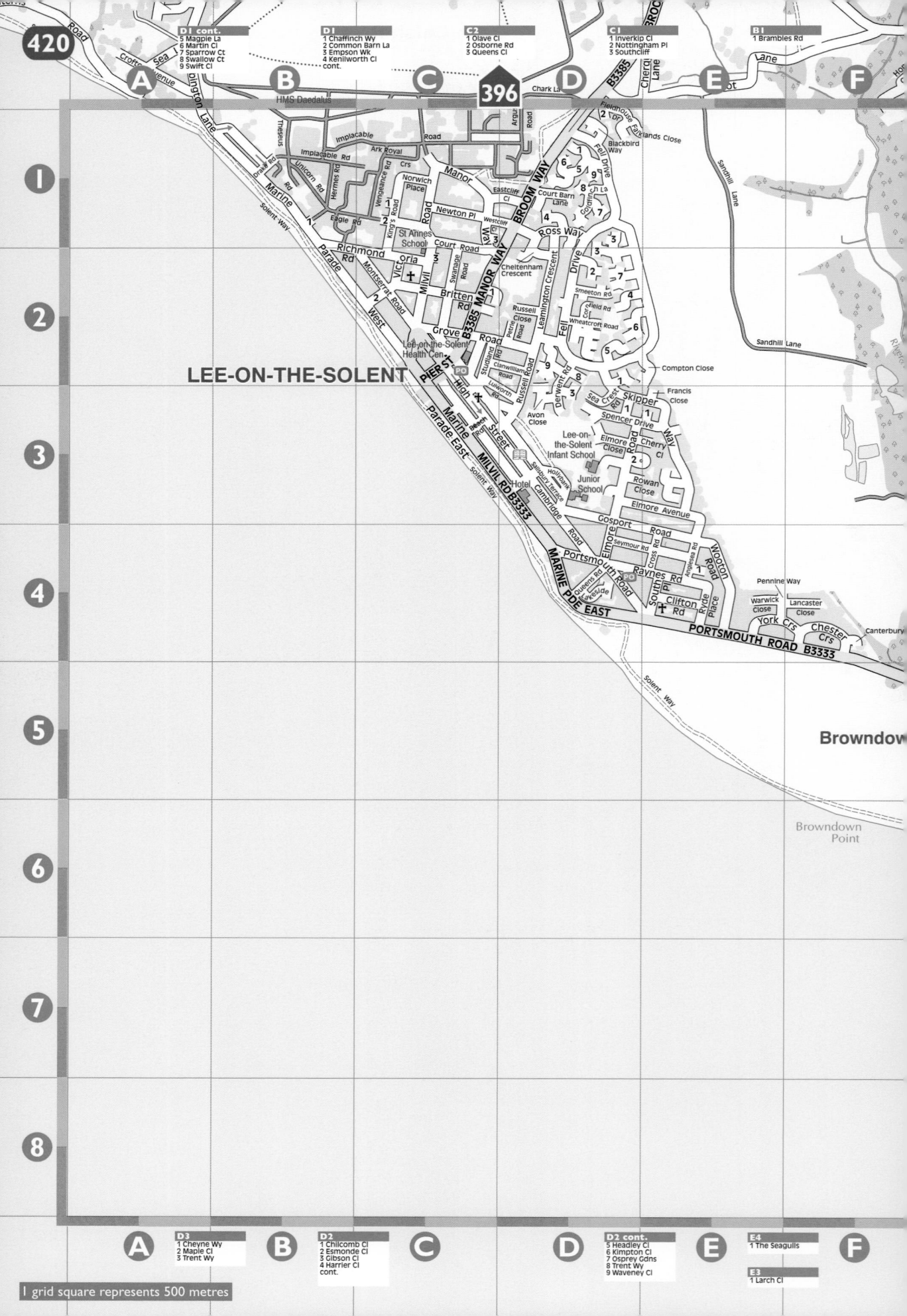

LEE-ON-THE-SOLENT

Browndow

Browndown
Point

D1 cont.
5 Magpie La
6 Martin Cl
7 Sparrow Ct
8 Swallow Ct
9 Swift Cl

D1
1 Chaffinch Wy
2 Common Barn La
3 Empson Wk
4 Kenilworth Cl
cont.

C2
1 Olave Cl
2 Osborne Rd
3 Queens Cl

C1
1 Inverkip Cl
2 Nottingham Pl
3 Southcliff

B1
1 Brambles Rd

D3
1 Cheyne Wy
2 Maple Cl
3 Trent Wy

D2
1 Chilcomb Cl
2 Esmonde Cl
3 Gibson Cl
4 Harrier Cl
cont.

D2 cont.
5 Headley Cl
6 Kimpton Cl
7 Osprey Gdns
8 Trent Wy
9 Waveney Cl

E4
1 The Seagulls

E3
1 Larch Cl

398

A **B** **C** **D** **E** **F**

1 Hardway

St Johns C of E
Primary School

2 Forton

St Vincent College

19

3

4 Newtown

Gosport Museum

Walpole Rd

Town Hall

Hampshire Co Council

Richard Martin Gallery & Bookshop

SOUTH STREET

The Anchorage

SOUTH ST

421

SOUTH ST

Cranbourne Rd

Mayfield Road

Haslet Road

Portsmouth Harbour

Burrow Island

City of Portsmouth / Hampshire County

Yacht Marina

Portsmouth Harbour

MUMBY ROAD A32

Clarence Rd

Bus Station

The Esplanade

Trinity Cl

Shipbuilding Rd

Boiler Rd

Victoria

HM Naval Base

Mary Rose Ship Hall
HMS Victory

Murray's La
Queen's Rd
King's Rd
The Pde
Sampson Rd
Scott Rd
Jago Rd

Royal Naval Museum
Dockyard Apprentice Exhibition
Mary Rose Exhibition

HMS Nelson

20 Portsea

HMS Warrior
Portsmouth
Harbour Station

St Georges Beneficial C of E Prim Sch

University

St Georges Park Road

Portsmouth Harbour Business Cen

Isle of Wight Car Ferry Terminal

Fish Market

Armory La

CAMBRIDGE RD

MUSEUM RD

University of Portsmouth

HMS Temeraire

United Services Rugby Club

Portsmouth City Council

OLD PORTSMO

City Mus & Art Gallery

5

Dolphin Crescent

Haselworth County Primary Sch

Leyland Cl

Sunbeam Way

Royal Navy Submarine Museum Offices

HMS Dolphin

West St

BROAD STREET

HIGH ST

Goldfield Gallery

St Nicholas St

Portsmouth Cathedral Church of St Thomas of Canterbury

Chatham Dr

Pembroke

SOUTHSEA TER
BELLEVUE TERR

PIER ROAD

6 Clayhall

Cemetery

Cemetery

Haslar Road

Royal Hospital Haslar

Dolphin Way

Clarence Pier and Amusement Centre

Hovercraft Terminal

Southsea Common

Clarence Esplanade

Royal Nav Memoria

7

Clayhall Rd

Waterloo Rd

St Francis Rd

The Redan

Fort Road

Dolphin Way

ISLE OF WIGHT

ISLE OF WIGHT

8

Fort Monckton

Long Water Dr

Golf Club

A **B** **C** **D** **E** **F**

1 grid square represents 500 metres

A   B   C   D   E   F

402

402

I

2

Mill Rithe

Pilsey Sand

3

Stocker's Lake

4

425

5

Mengham Salterns

ngham

Black Point

Simmons Gdn
Salterns Cl
Salterns   Lane
Marine   Walk
Weavers Rd
Seaview   Road
Blackthorn Dr
Selsmore Avenue
Seaview   Road
Avisford
Bourdale
Ilex Walk
Blackthorn Rd
Kingfisher
North Crs
Norman Rd
Silversands Gdns
Rails   Lane
Fishery   Lane
Foreland Ct
St Hermans   Rd
Ashurst Rd
1

Selsmore

Eastoke

Old School Dr
PO
Southwood   Road
Sea Front
The Glade
Culver Dr
Meath Cl
The Strand
Bembridge Drive
Eastoke   Avenue
Rowin Close
West   Haye   Road
Burgess Cl
Creek   Rd
Birdham Rd
Sandy
Nutbourne Road
Point
Coronation Rd
1
Winsor Cl
Wheatlands   Avenue
Treloar Rd
Treloar   Rd

6

7

Southwood   Road

Eastoke
Creek
Haven Road
Haven   Road
Bosmere   Rd
Haslemere Gdns
Fishermans Wk
Avenue
Earnley
Witterings   Road
Selsey Cl
Sidlesham Cl
Pagham Gdns
Itchenor Rd
Bracklesham   Road
Road

Bracklesham Rd

West Sussex County
Hampshire County

Eastoke Point

8

A   B   C   D   E   F

G   H   J   403   K   L   M

I
2
3
4
5
6
7
8

Longmere
Point

Pilsey
Island

Chichester Harbour

East Head

Sussex Border Path

Rookwood Lane

Rookwood Lane

Sheepwash Lane

Rookwood Road

Ellanore Lane

Summerfield Rd

Roman Landing

Roman Landing

Roman Landing

Summerfield Road

ROOKWOOD RD

Elmstead Park Road

Cunliffe Close

Locksash C

Elmstead Pk Rd

Elmstead Gdns

Elms Wy

Meadow

Nunnington Farm

Coastguard Lane

West Wittering
Parochial School

Pound Rd

B2179

Royce Close

Royce Wal

Elms Ride

Elms Ride

The Byeway

Elms Lane

Elms Lane

West Wittering

The Wad

Middlefield

Wellsfield

Seaward Dr.

CAKEHAM ROAD

West Strand

Berrybarn

Lane

East Strand

East
Wittering

B2179

Howard Avenue

Jolliffe Road

Southcote Avenue

Marine Dr West

Owers

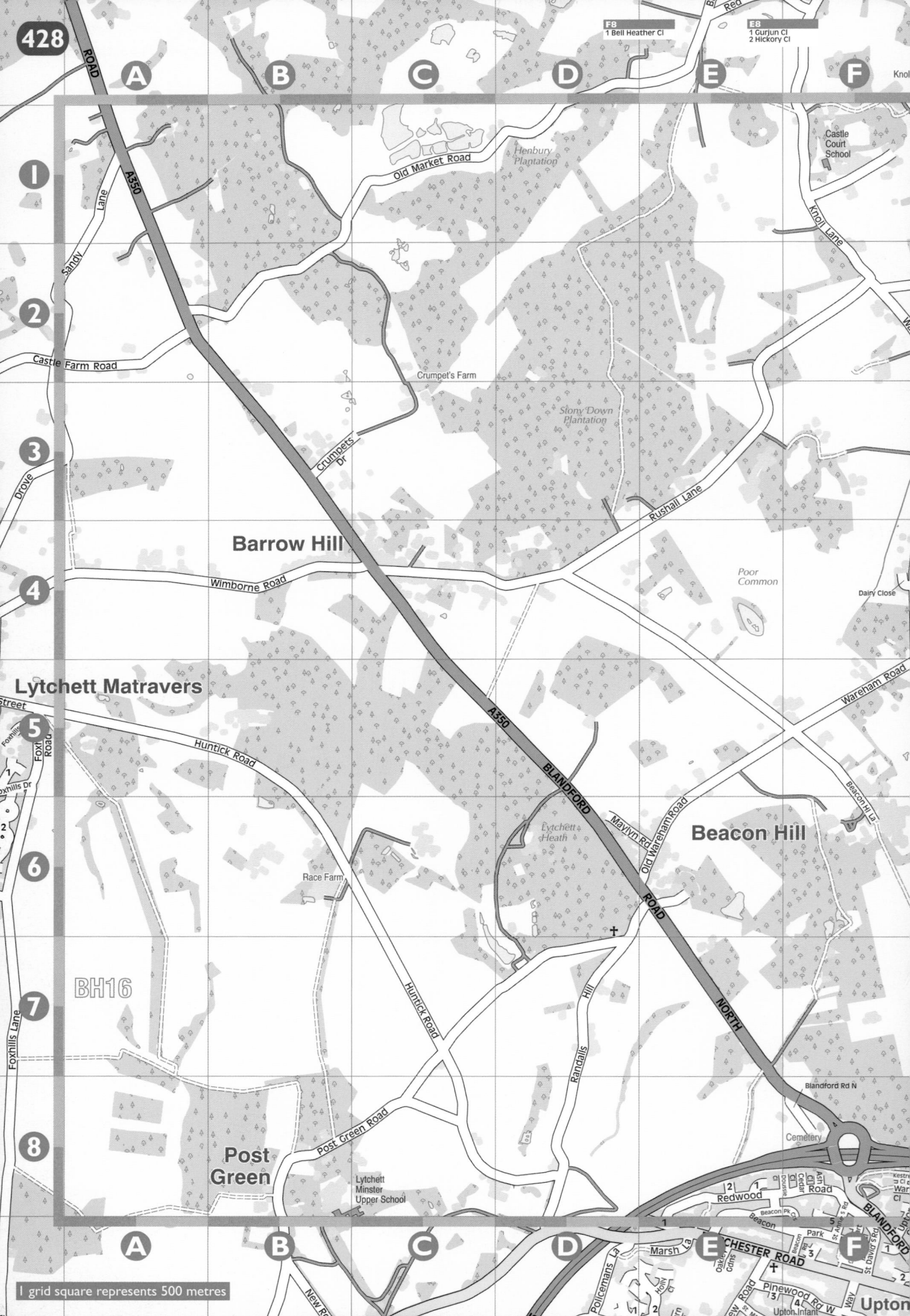

A   B   C   D   E   F

F8
1 Bell Heather Cl

E8
1 Gurjun Cl
2 Hickory Cl

I

Castle Court School

ROAD

A350

Sandy Lane

Old Market Road

Henbury Plantation

Knoll Lane

Knol

2

Castle Farm Road

Crumpet's Farm

Stony Down Plantation

3

Drove

Crumpets Dr

Rushall Lane

Poor Common

Dairy Close

Barrow Hill

4

Wimborne Road

Lytchett Matravers

Wareham Road

5

Foxhi...

Foxl Road

Huntick Road

A550

BLANDFORD

Old Wareham Road

Beacon Hil Ln

Foxhills Dr

Lytchett Heath

Mavlyn Rd

Beacon Hill

1

2

6

Race Farm

Huntick Road

ROAD

7

BH16

Foxhills Lane

Randalls Hill

NORTH

Blandford Rd N

8

Post Green Road

Cemetery

Post Green

Lytchett Minster Upper School

BLANDFORD

A   B   C   D   E   F

Marsh La

CHESTER ROAD

Redwood

Cedar Road

Ash Road

Park

War

Upton

Policemans

Beacon Pk Cl

Beacon

St Ann's Rd

Pinewood Rd W

Upton Infant

New Ro

Upton

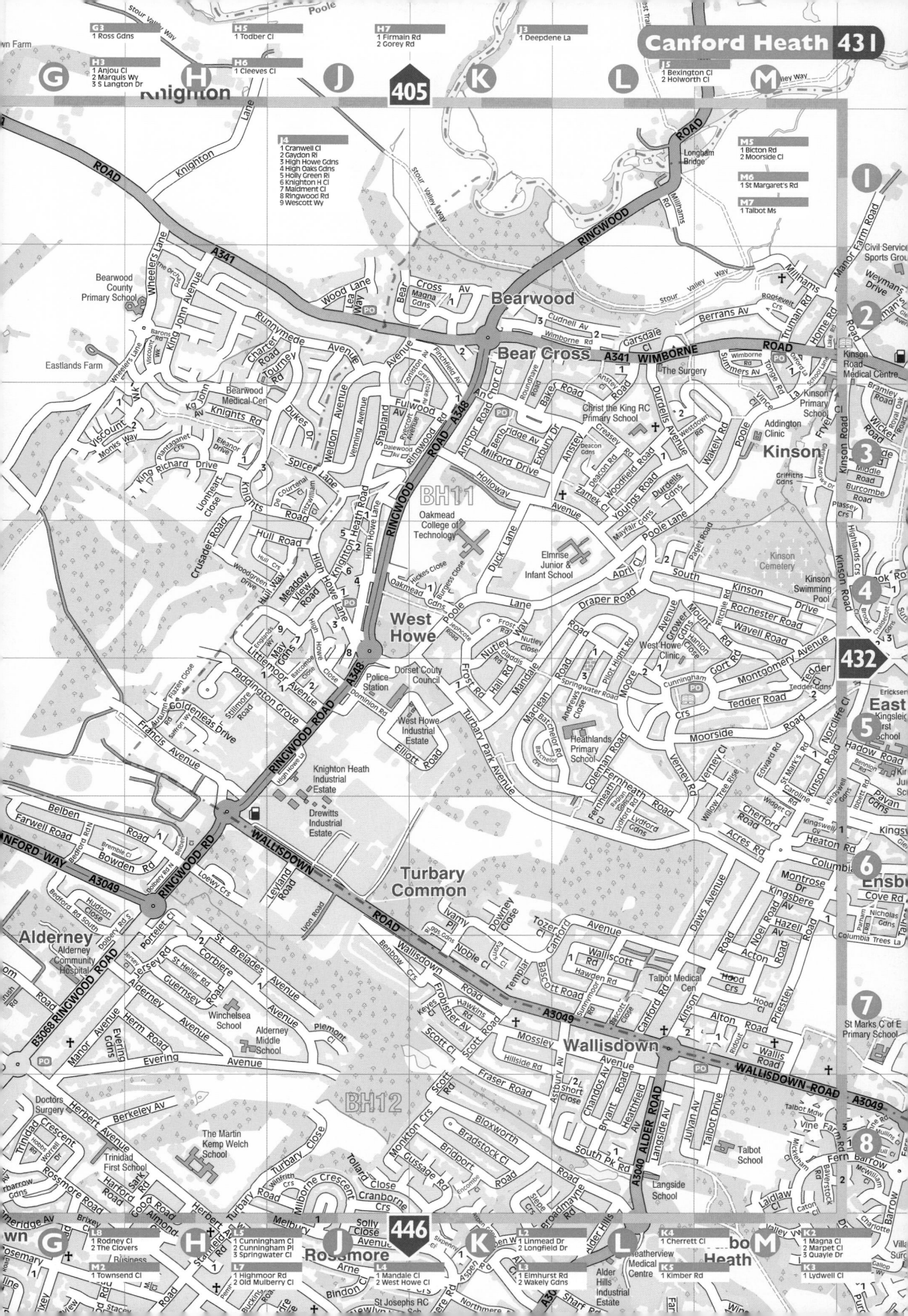

G3 1 Ross Gdns

H5 1 Todber Cl

H7 1 Firmain Rd
2 Gorey Rd

J3 1 Deepdene La

G
H3 1 Anjou Cl
2 Marquis Wy
3 S Langton Dr

H
H6 1 Cleeves Cl

J
405

K

L5 1 Bexington Cl
2 Holworth Cl

M

I

J4 1 Cranwell Cl
2 Gaydon Rl
3 High Howe Gdns
4 High Oaks Gdns
5 Holly Green Rl
6 Knighton H Cl
7 Maidment Cl
8 Ringwood Rd
9 Wescott Wy

M5 1 Bicton Rd
2 Moorside Cl

M6 1 St Margaret's Rd

M7 1 Talbot Ms

2

3

Knighton

Knighton

ROAD

Ringham Bridge

Longham Bridge

RINGWOOD ROAD

Civil Service Sports Grou

Weymans Drive

Manor Farm Road

Milhams

Bearwood County Primary School

Eastlands Farm

A341

Wood Lane

Bear Cross

Bearwood

Kinson Road Medical Centre

Wicker Road

Bear Cross

A341 WIMBORNE

ROAD

Kinson

Kinson

BH11

Oakmead College of Technology

Elmrise Junior & Infant School

Christ the King RC Primary School

Kinson Cemetery

Kinson Swimming Pool

4

432

West Howe

Police Station

Dorset Couty Council

West Howe Industrial Estate

West Howe Clinic

Heathlands Primary School

5 East Kingslie First School

6 Ensb

Knighton Heath Industrial Estate

Drewitts Industrial Estate

CANFORD WAY

A3049

RINGWOOD RD

WALLISDOWN

Turbary Common

Cove Rd

Columbia Trees La

Alderney

Alderney Community Hospital

B3068 RINGWOOD ROAD

Winchelsea School

Alderney Middle School

WALLISDOWN ROAD

A3049

Wallisdown

7 St Marks C of E Primary School

Talbot Medical Cen

Talbot School

8

BH12

The Martin Kemp Welch School

Trinidad First School

Langside School

A3049

Doctors Surgery

G
L8 1 Rodney Cl
2 The Clovers

H
J5 1 Cunningham Cl
2 Cunningham Pl
3 Springwater Av

J
446

K
K5 1 Linmead Dr
2 Longfield Dr

L
Heatherview Medical Centre

M
K4 1 Cherrett Cl

K2 1 Magna Cl
2 Marpet Cl
3 Quayle Dr

M2 1 Townsend Av

L7 1 Highmoor Rd
2 Old Mulberry Cl

Rossmore

L4 1 Mandale Cl
2 West Howe Cl

Alder Hills Industrial Estate

L1 1 Kimber Rd

Heath

K3 1 Lydwell Cl

G
G4 1 Gillingham Cl
G5 1 Durweston Cl

H
G6 1 Charminster Pl
H4 1 Barrowgate Rd

J
East Parley

H5 1 Blackfield Rd 2 Bramshaw Gdns 3 Calmore Cl 4 Hungerford Rd

407

K

H6 1 Copythorne Cl 2 Landford Gdns 3 Michelmersh Gn 4 Shawford Gdns 5 Sherfield Cl 6 Whitsbury Cl

Dorset County Police

L

I6 1 Brendon Cl 2 Craigmoor Wy

M

International Airport

PARLEY LANE

B3073

Merritown La

Merritown

PARLEY LANE

B3073

Hurn

PO

Hurn Bridge

I

Parley Green

River Stour

Dales Lane

West Hurn

Hurn Court Lane

CHRISTCHURCH

2

Stour Valley Way

Dorset County Bournemouth

Hurn Court Lane

Shoot Lane

Hurn Court

ROAD

3

Muscliffe

Lane

Boleyn Crescent

Throopside Av

Willow Mead

Stour Wk

Lavender Rd

Pig

Mill Throop

Throop Road

Stour Valley Way

Hurn Court

Blackwat

4

Muscliff C Primary School

Bradford Rd

PO

Broadway

Taylor

Drive

Careys Road

Mill Road (North)

New Bridge

Holdenhurst Road

434

Shillingstone

Charlton

Stratton Rd

Heather Cl

Ashurst

Downton

Barrowgate Rd

Ampfield Rd

Bucklers Wy

Broadlands Cl

Axford Cl

Road

Yeomans

Road

Valley

Road

Holdenhurst

5

Tweddle

Road

Bradbourne Lane

Harbeck Rd

Rowmans Rd

Chesildene

Cadnam Wy

Ibberton

Fritham Gdns

Holbury Cl

Selby Rd

Holdenhurst

6

Mag Pie Greenways

Codsnll Rd

Fawley Gn

Hurstdene Av

Ferris Chesildene Av

Nursling

Brasfield Gdns

Sway Gdns

Yeomans Wy

Yeomans Way

Yeomans Wy

Yeomans Industrial Park

Stacey Gdns

Watton Cl

Jewell Road

Tyrrell Gdns

Birch Dr

Hopkins Cl

Swansbury Dr

A338

6

Castle Gate Close

CASTLE LANE WEST A3060

Belmont Av

Landford Gn

Ytherley Gn

Mill Rd

Landford Gdns

Yeomans Road

Woodbury

Barrow Road

Barrow Dr

Hastings Road

Throop Rd

Cheshire Dr

Jewell Road

Noyce Gdns

Vickers Cl

PO

7

Charminster

Bournemouth School for Girls

Curlew Road

Mallard Road

Craigmoor Avenue

Woodlea House Surgery

A3060

CASTLE LANE WEST

Ibberton Road

Jewell

Wilkinson Dr

Royal Bournemouth Hospital A&E

WESSEX WAY

Deansleigh Rd

Bournemouth Crown & Cou Courts

7

Bournemouth School for Boys

Seagull Rd

Mallard Close

Summerbee Secondary School

Cattistock Road

Evershot Road

PO

Stroudon Park Medical Centre

BH8

Bradpole Road

Vanguard Rd

Balmoral

Inglewood

Mount Pleasant

Cooper Dean Drive

CASTLE LANE E.

A306

8

North Cemetery

Strouden

Wordsworth Avenue

Normanhurst Avenue

Feversham

Av

Hightrees Av

Queenswood Avenue

Sandy Md Rd

Leyedene Av

Midwood Av

Crosswood

Littledown Leisure Centre

Hatfield Gdns

Howell Gdns

Walkwood Av

St Peters School

Chertfon

Strouden Avenue

Brackendale

Bower Road

Brand Avenue

Hadden Rd

Queen's Park Avenue

Parkway

Linkside Av

WESSEX WAY

Chaseside

Cowell Road

Evesham Cl

Beauchamp Av

Cowell Gdns

Harbourne Gdns

Hares Green

Sevenoaks Dr

Trentham Close

Bartlett Dr

Colen

Queen's Park Avenue

West Drive

Queen's Park

448

WESSEX WAY

A338

Regent Cl

The Springbank Surgery Springbank Road Springvale Av Doctors Surg

Woodcocks Crs

Littledown

Avonbourne Girls School

G
M8 1 Bourton Gdns 2 Chandlers Cl 3 Eltham Cl 4 Perryfield Gdns 5 Sparkford Cl

H
L8 1 The Beeches 2 Eastcott Cl 3 Hazelton Cl

J

K

L
L7 1 Longbarrow Cl

M
BH7

K8 1 Countess Gdns 2 Sovereign Cl

K6 1 Cowdrey Gdns 2 Crantock Gv 3 Culford Cl 4 Mountbatten Rd

St Alban's Avenue

Richmond Park Avenue

Richmond Wood Road

St George's Av

Burntiram Dr

Portchester School

Durrington Rd

G   H   J   415   K   L   M

Joys La

Thatchers Lane

Norleywood

St. Leonards Rd

Rowes Lane

East End

I

Brook Hill

Broom Hill

Newtown Park

† **South Baddesley**

Lymington Road

PH

2

South Baddesley C of E Primary School

Solent Way

3

Solent Way

boks Farm

Road

Mill   Lane

Sowley Lane

Pitts

Deep Lane

Shotts Lane

Tanners Lane

4

442

Lisle Court

Road

5

6

7

The Solent

8

YARMOUTH

Ore Point

G The Log House

H Warren Lane

J 417

K

L

M

Warren Farm

Warren Lane

Little Marsh

Park Shore

I
2
3
4
5
6
7
8

G H J K L M

448

C4
1 Hengist Rd
St Albans
Medical
1 Palmerstone Ms
2 Shelley Cl

A

B

C2
1 Avon Cl
2 Bethia Cl
3 Egerton Gdns
4 Richmond Pk Cl
5 Richmond Pk Rd
6 St Ledger's Pl

C

433

Queen's Park

A5
1 The Lan. Rbt
2 Meyrick Rd
3 Weston Dr

D

A3
1 Ascham Rd

E

A4
1 B. Stn Rbt
2 Oxford Rd
3 St Paul's Pl
Doctors Surg.

F

WESSEX WAY

Littledown

Portchester
School

B2
1 Lawrence Ct
2 Malmesbury Ct
3 Melbourne Rd
4 Nortoft Rd
5 Shelbourne Cl

B3
1 Corporation Rd
2 Elwyn Rd
3 Henville Rd
4 Lowther Gdns
5 Mlmsbry Pk Pl
6 Methuen Cl
7 Methuen Rd
8 Stewart Cl

C3
1 Austin Cl

I

A3049

Linwood School

ROAD

Cemetery

Richmond Wood
Road

RICHMOND PK RICHMOND PARK
ROAD
A3049

2

23

Springbourne

HOLDENHURST RD

ASHLEY ROAD

King's Park

Dean Court
(Bournemouth FC)

East
Cemetery

Newlands
Rd

Harewood

Kings Park
Primary School

Kings Park
Community
Hosp

The Bournemouth
Nuffield Hospital

3

Lansdowne
Clinic

WESSEX WAY

Bournemouth &
East Dorset Hosp
Management Committee

BH1

Parkway Retail
Park
Bournemouth
Station

Central
Business Park

Boscombe

Boscombe Manor
Medical Centre

BH5

4

447

Bournemouth Co
Court

Bournemouth
Business Cen

CHRISTCHURCH RD

A35   CHRISTCHURCH

Bournemouth
College

Boscombe
Dental Health
Centre

Police
Stn

CHRISTCHURCH

Po

Shelley
Museum

5

University

College
Hotel

Doctors
Surgery

Gervis

The Marina

6

BOURNEMOUTH

Poo

7

8

D4
1 Carnarvon Rd
2 Palmerston Rd
3 Randolph Rd
4 Salisbury Rd

A

D5
1 Michelgro. Rd

B

C

E4
1 Grantley Rd

D

F1
1 Henley Gdns

E

F

E3
1 Ashley Rd
2 Haviland Rd West
3 Tamworth Rd

E5
1 Woll'craft Rd

1 grid square represents 500 metres

A

B

C

D

E

F

435

River Avon

Briar Park
Business Cen

Southern Electric Museum

Fairfield Cl

The Bold Gallery

Police Station

Stour Surg

Purewell

B3059

PUREWELL CROSS RD

Christchurch Medical Centre

Somerford

Grange Comprehensive School

Somerford Business Park

Hughes Business Cen

Silver Business Park

Beaver Industrial Est

Ambassador Industrial Est

Sea Vix Industri Est

I

BARGATES B3073

FOUNTAIN WAY

A35

Dorset County Council

Primary Sch

Red House Mus & Gardens

Christchurch Castle

Two Riversmeet Leisure Centre

Civic Offices

Stony La South

Purewell

Groveley Business

Mudeford La

Stanpit

Queen's Road

Mudeford Junior School

SOMERFORD ROAD

2

Comprehensive School

St Margaret's Avenue

CHRISTCHURCH

River Stour

Pelham Close

Gladstone Close

Disraeli Rd

Stanpit Marsh

3

Wick Lane

Wick

St Katherines C of E Primary School

Stour Valley Way

Shermin's Bank

Coastguard Way

Waterside

Rushford Warren

Hotel

4

449

Braemar

Saxon

Rolls Drive

5

Clowes Avenue

Southbourne Coast Road

Broadway

Christchurch Harbour

Dorset County
Bournemouth

6

Stour Valley Way

Hengistbury Head

Stour Valley Way

7

8

A

B

C

D

E

F

1 grid square represents 500 metres

A B C 437 D E F

Waterford
Gardens

Police Station
Stuart Road
The
Lawns
Montagu Road
Bute Drive
Waterford Place
Walnut Brook
Glenside
Chewton Lodge
Mill Lane
Loraine Avenue
Glendrive
Abingdon Drive
The Dell
Bartonside Rd
The Crescent
The Park
Pinecliffe Road
East Av
Island Road
Island View Rd
Seaview Rd
Southcliffe Rd
Cul-De-Sac
Field Place
Burley
Milly Ford
studley Ct
Glen Cl
Western
Barton
Knight Park
Dolphin Pl
Seacroft Av
Pine Cl
Waventon Avenue
Hengistbury Road
Seafield Road
Heathy Close
Barton Dr
Blythswood Ct
Highlands
Durlston
Court School

Vectis Road
Naish Road
Fairfield Road
Seafield Close
Keysworth
Barton Close
Homeopathic Surgery
Durlsto
Court
Schoo

Purbeck Rd
Cleveland Cl
Powerscourt Rd
Cliffe Rd
Seaward Avenue
Christchurch Bay Rd
Beach Avenue
Seafield Avenue
Barton Court
Lynric Ct
White Knights
Dilly
Mitchell Cl
Solent

Marine
Drive
West
Barton Rd
Wd
Marine Prospect
Cliff Crs
First Marine Av
Grove
Farm Lane South
Greenacr
Inla

Hotel
Marine
Drive
Second Marine Av
Marine Drive

Barton on Sea

Christchurch
Bay

451

A B C D E F

1 grid square represents 500 metres

G H J K L M

1 SilverDl

M3
1 Lydgate
2 Seawinds

438

A337 CHRISTCHURCH ROAD

Downton

Ashley
Clinton House

Newton Rd

Greenfield
Gdns

Royston
place

The Willows

Silverdale

The Martells

1

The Fairway

1

Maple

Barton

Common

MILFORD

Road

ROAD

Angel

Common Lane

Taddiford
Fm

Danes Stream

Downton

Lane

Shorefield Rd

Seabreeze
Wy.

Warren
Pk.

Shorefield Rd

Dane
Rd

Shore
R

Hordle
House
School

CLIFF

N Head

West Road

The
Bucklers

1

2

Pless Road

Wh

ROAD

Westminister
d

1

2

3

4

454

5

6

7

8

G H J K L M

Lower Pennington

440

The Salterns

PH

Woodside

Platoff

Woodside

Solent Way

Iley Lane

Pennington House

Lwr Pennington Lane

Avon Water

Pennington Marshes

Solent Way

Keyhaven Marshes

Farm

rewood Gn

Solent Way

Solent Way

Solent Way

G H J K L M

1 2 3 4 5 6 7 8

G H J K L M

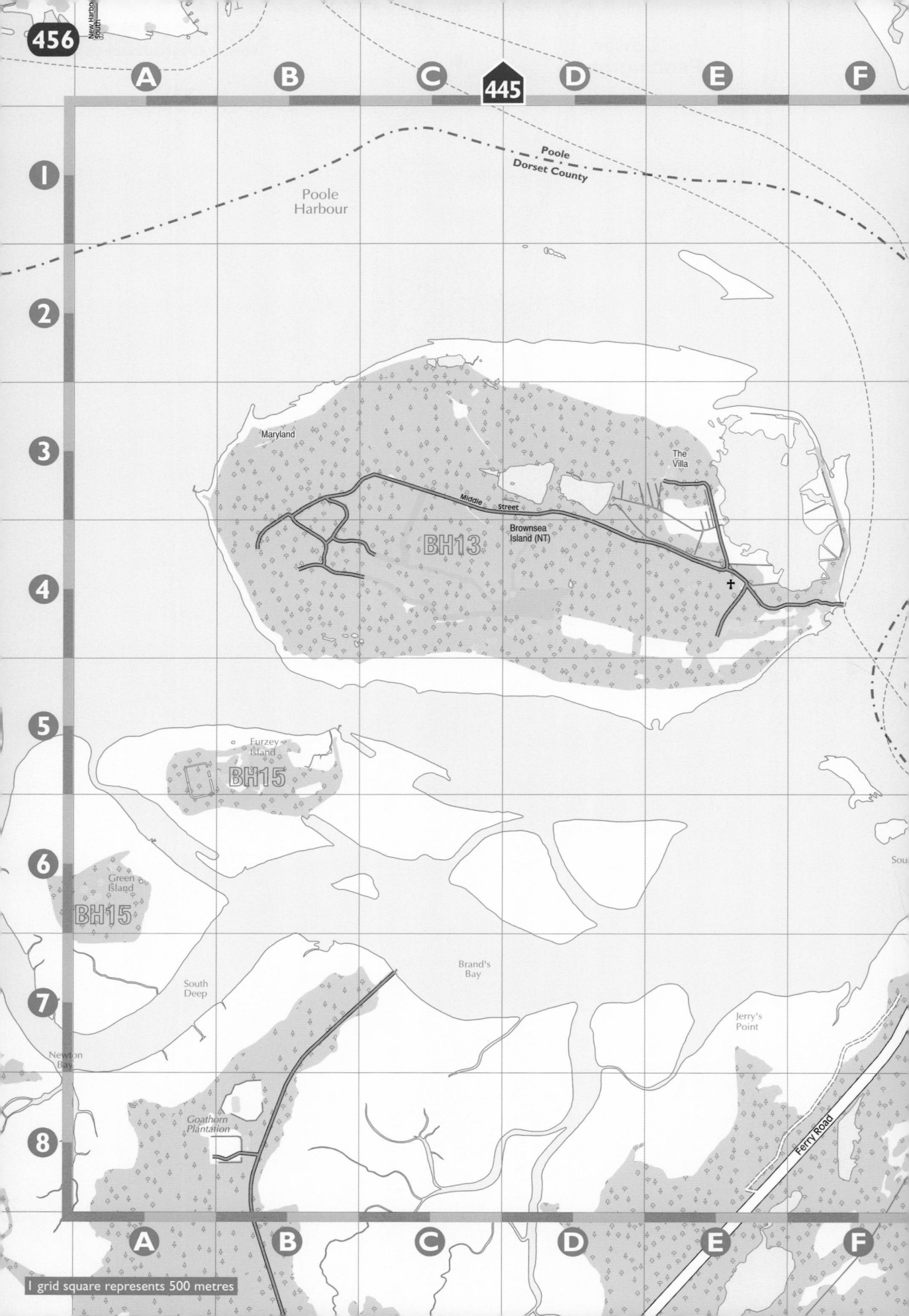

445

A   B   C   D   E   F

Poole
Dorset County

Poole
Harbour

Maryland

The
Villa

Middle
street

Brownsea
Island (NT)

BH13

✝

Furzey
Island

BH15

Green
Island

BH15

Sou

Brand's
Bay

Jerry's
Point

South
Deep

Newton
Bay

Goathorn
Plantation

Ferry Road

A   B   C   D   E   F

G   H   J   K   L   M

446

Branksome

Lilliput

Canford Cliffs

1 Beaumont Rd
2 Bodley Rd
3 Macandrew Rd

1 Harbour Cl
1 Chad. Wood Rd

Oratory Garden

Marina

WESTERN RD

HAVEN ROAD

B3065

B3369

SHORE ROAD

St Anns Hospital

Canford Cliffs Chine

Flag Head Chine

Poole Head

BANKS ROAD

B3369

Coastguard Road

PANORAMA ROAD

B3369

Sandbanks

Grasmere

Seacombe Road

Brownsea Road

Salter Rd

BANKS ROAD

FERRY WY

Ferry Wy

Hotel

Point

Shell Bay

CHERBOURG

GUERNSEY AND JERSEY
SUMMER ONLY

SANTANDER
VIA JERSEY
WINTER ONLY

South West Coast Path

Studland Bay

I   2   3   4   5   6   7   8

Abbotstone	193	L6
Abbotswood	262	F5
Abbots Worthy	215	J2
Abbotts Ann	141	K5
Abshot	370	E8
Alderholt	333	K2
Aldermaston	41	J1
Aldermaston Soke	42	C5
Aldermaston Wharf	29	M5
Aldermoor	317	M5
Alderney	431	G7
Aldershot	6	F1
Allbrook	293	M2
Alton	176	D5
Alverstoke	18	B7
Ameysford	380	A7
Ampfield	264	B5
Amport	140	F3
Anchorage Park	400	A5
Andover	9	J5
Andover Down	119	M8
Andwell	106	F3
Anmore	351	M4
Anna Valley	142	C3
Ann's Hill	18	A1
Ansteadbrook	229	M3
Anthill Common	351	H2
Applemore	366	E4
Appleshaw	117	G2
Arborfield Garrison	47	K1
Arford	202	B2
Ash	113	K5
Ashe	101	K8
Ashfield	291	G4
Ashford	309	J7
Ashford Hill	40	B7
Ashlett	393	G5
Ashley	211	L5
Ashley	382	A3
Ashley	438	A5
Ashley Heath	381	K2
Ashmansworth	75	L1
Ashton	297	G5
Ashurst	341	G6
Ashurst Bridge	341	G3
Ash Vale	113	K2
Avington	216	D3
Avon	408	D6
Awbridge	261	K4
Axford	151	H5
Axmansford	60	F1
Badshot Lea	135	M2
Baffins	423	M1
Bagmore	152	F2
Bagshot	32	C1
Bagshot	51	M5
Bailey Green	245	H5
Ball Hill	35	M5
Balmerlawn	387	M5
Bank	363	H5
Bar End	239	G2
Barford	181	H8
Barrow Hill	315	J6
Barrow Hill	428	B4
Bartley	339	L1
Barton on Sea	452	E2
Barton Stacey	167	J2
Bashley	437	L1
Bashley Park	437	M2
Basingstoke	4	C6
Bassett	318	F3
Bassett Green	318	F3
Battramsley	413	L6
Battramsley Cross	414	A7
Batt's Corner	180	A1
Baughurst	61	G1
Baybridge	268	B5
Beacon Hill	204	A1
Beacon Hill	428	E6
Bear Cross	431	K2
Bearwood	431	K2
Beaulieu	390	C7
Beauworth	241	M8
Beckley	437	G3
Bedhampton	377	G7
Beech	175	M7
Beech Hill	44	F3
Beenham	29	J2
Beenham Stocks	29	L2
Bell Hill	275	K3
Bentley	156	E3
Bentworth	174	E3
Bickton	334	D2
Bidden	130	C1
Bighton	195	H7
Binley	75	L8
Binstead	178	D1
Birchy Hill	413	G7
Bishop's Green	38	D5
Bishop's Sutton	219	G4
Bishopstoke	294	B6
Bishop's Waltham	297	G7
Bisterne	408	D2
Bisterne Close	385	H6
Bitterne	344	C1
Bitterne Park	319	J7
Black Dam	105	J5
Blackfield	392	E8
Blackhill	288	F7
Blackmoor	224	E1
Blacknest	179	J1
Blackwater	70	A4
Blackwater	433	M3
Blashford	358	D5
Bleak Hill	334	A5
Blendworth	353	J1
Blissford	310	D8
Boarhunt	373	M3
Bohemia	285	L4
Boldre	414	B7
Boorley Green	321	K6
Borden	278	C2
Bordon	201	H5
Boscombe	448	D4
Bossington	210	A5
Botley	346	F2
Boundstone	158	E4
Bournemouth	23	G6
The Bourne	158	F2
Bourne Valley	446	F2
Boveridge	306	F6
Bowling Alley	110	B8
Bowling Green	439	K2
Boyatt Wood	293	L3
Bradley	152	A8
Braishfield	263	H1
Brambridge	266	C8
Bramdean	243	H3
Bramley	63	K4
Bramley Corner	63	G5
Bramley Green	63	M6
Bramshaw	313	L4
Bramshill	66	E1
Bramshott	226	F2
Branksome	446	D3
Branksome Park	446	E6
Bransbury	144	F7
Bransgore	409	M8
Breach	379	H7
Breamore	283	M7
Bridgemary	396	F5
Brighton Hill	104	C8
Brimpton	40	B2
Brimpton Common	40	F6
Broad Chalke	252	A1
Broadgate	264	D6
Broad Layings	36	B7
Broadmere	127	J4
Broad Oak	108	F4
Broadoak	346	C1
Broadstone	429	M4
Brockbridge	299	J6
Brockenhurst	387	J7
Brockhampton	16	A7
Brockhurst	421	H2
Brock's Green	58	D1
Brook	234	B2
Brook	313	M8
Brooke's Hill	316	A4
Brook Hill	313	M6
Broughton	209	H2
Brown Candover	172	A5
Browndown	420	F5
Brown Heath	322	B3
Browninghill Green	61	J5
Bucket Corner	292	B1
Buckland	440	A3
Bucklers Hard	417	G3
Bucks Horn Oak	157	K8
Buckskin	103	M4
Bull Hill	414	F7
Bunker's Hill	314	F6
Bunstead	265	H2
Burgates	248	D2
Burghclere	57	J1
Burghclere Common	37	K7
Burghfield	31	M3
Burghfield Common	31	K6
Burghfield Hill	31	M5
Buriton	303	K3
Burley	384	F5
Burley Beacon	384	C6
Burley Lawn	385	G5
Burley Street	384	C3
Burridge	346	F7
Bursledon	345	L8
Burton	435	G7
Bury's Bank	38	B1
Butlocks Heath	369	H1
Buttermere	53	H1
Buttsash	367	M8
Butt's Green	232	F7
The Butts	176	D6
Cadnam	314	E8
Calmore	316	B7
Calshot	393	K8
Camberley	71	H1
Camel Green	333	M2
Camelsdale	228	D3
Canada	288	C7
Canford Cliffs	457	J1
Canford Heath	430	C7
Canford Magna	404	A8
Carter's Clay	260	F2
Catherington	327	M7
Catisfield	371	L7
Causeway	275	K6
Causeway	352	F3
Chalton	329	G3
Chandlers Green	65	J6
Charlton	118	D6
Chandler's Ford	265	J8
Charlton-All-Saints	256	E4
Charlwood	221	H5
Charminster	433	G7
Charter Alley	61	L8
Chawton	198	C1
Cheriton	242	C3
Chidden	300	E8
Chilbolton	165	M4
Chilbolton Down	188	D2
Chilcomb	239	L3
Chilton Candover	172	D3
Chilworth	292	C7
Chilworth Old Village	292	B6
Chineham	83	L5
Chithurst	278	F5
Cholderton	138	B7
Christchurch	450	A3
Church Common	247	G8
Church Crookham	110	E3
Church End	84	B2
Church Oakley	102	D6
Churt	181	J7
Chute Cadley	94	C1
Chute Standen	72	A8
Clanfield	327	M2
Clanville	117	J1
Clarken Green	102	C6
Clatford Oakcuts	163	M4
Clayhall	19	G8
Clayhill	363	L2
Cliddesden	127	L1
Cold Ash	26	F1
Cold Ash Hill	227	H3
Golden Common	266	F7
Cole Henley	99	J5
Colehill	404	D1
Colemore	222	C6
College Town	50	B8
Colt Hill	108	E5
Colthrop	27	L5
Combe	54	A2
The Common	206	F2
Compton	135	J7
Compton	234	B1
Compton	266	C1
Compton	330	D6
Compton End	238	B7
Conford	226	C1
Coombe	300	E2
Copnor	399	L7
Copythorne	315	H6
Corfe Mullen	429	G2
Corhampton	299	G3
Cosham	375	L8
Cottonworth	165	K4
Couch Green	216	B1
Court Corner	62	A5
Cove	90	B2
Cowesfield Green	259	H5
Cowplain	352	D5
Coxford	317	M6
Crab Orchard	356	C6
Crampmoor	263	K7
Cranborne	306	C8
Cranbourne	104	E6
Crawley	189	G6
Crawley Hill	71	H3
Creekmoor	429	L8
Crendell	332	D1
Cricket Hill	69	H3
Criddlestyle	310	A7
Cripplestyle	332	E3
Critchell's Green	232	E8
Critchmere	228	B1
Crockerhill	372	E1
Crockham Heath	36	C2
Crondall	133	H1
Crookham	39	L3
Crookham Village	110	B2
Crosswater	181	H4
Crossways	181	H7
Croucheston	252	F1
Crow	383	G4
Crowdhill	295	H3
Crowthorne	49	J4
Crux Easton	75	M3
Cuckoo's Corner	155	K8
Cufaude	83	K1
Cupernham	262	F7
Curbridge	347	H4
Curdridge	322	D8
Custards	363	L3
Daggons	333	G3
Damerham	308	C3
Daneshill	5	M2
Darby Green	69	K2
Deadwater	201	L5
Dean	213	K5
Dean	297	K5
Deane	101	M7
Deanlane End	354	B3
Deepcut	91	M2
The Dene	74	E8
Denmead	351	K3
Denvilles	17	L2
Dewlands Common	356	B3
Dibden	367	H3
Dibden Purlieu	367	G7
Dilton	414	D1
Dipley	66	D8
Dippenhall	134	A6
Dockenfield	180	C2
Dogmersfield	109	M2
Donnington	25	G2
Dora's Green	133	M3
Downton	285	G1
Downton	453	L1
Drayton	376	A8
Droxford	298	F7
Dry Hill	196	D3
Dudsbury	406	A7
Dummer	126	C7
Dumpford	278	D8
Dunbridge	233	H7
Dundridge	298	A7
Dunley	76	F8
Durleighmarsh	276	F5
Durley	322	A2
Durley Street	296	B8
Durns Town	413	G6
Durrants	353	M8
East Winterslow	182	E8
East Woodhay	55	H1
East Worldham	177	K7
Ebblake	357	H4
Ecchinswell	58	D5
Egbury	98	B2
Egypt	168	C3
Eling	341	M3
Ellingham	358	C3
Ellisfield	128	A8
Elmers Marsh	251	K3
Elson	397	L8
Elsted	305	M4
Elvetham	88	D3
Emery Down	363	H2
Empshott	223	M5
Empshott Green	223	L5
Emsworth	402	C1
Enborne	24	C8
Enborne Row	36	E4
Enham Alamein	119	H1
Ensbury	432	C2
Ensbury Park	432	A6
Eversley	47	L7
Eversley Centre	48	A8
Eversley Cross	48	C8
Everton	439	J7
Ewshot	110	F8
Exbury	417	M3
Exton	299	H1
Faberstown	93	G7
Faccombe	54	E7
Fairmile	434	D7
Fair Oak	60	B1
Fair Oak	295	H6
Fair Oak Green	64	A2
Fareham	14	F5
Farleigh Wallop	127	K6
Farley	206	C8
Farley Hill	47	G3
Farlington	376	B8
Farnborough	90	D5
Farnborough Green	90	F3
Farnborough Park	91	G5
Farnborough Street	90	F3
Farnham	135	G7
Fawley	392	F6
Ferndown	405	M3
Filmore Hill	244	F4
Finchampstead	48	A5
Finchdean	354	B2
Firsdown	206	A1
Fisher's Pond	295	G2
Fleet	88	F7
Fleet	401	K8
Fleetend	370	D7
Fleetlands	397	G3
Flexford	264	E8
Flood Street	309	L1
Folly Hill	134	D3
Fordingbridge	309	M7
Forest Gate	351	H1
Forestside	354	F2
Forton	144	E4
Forton	421	M2
Fosbury	52	C7
Foulford	383	L1
Four Houses Corner	31	H8
Four Marks	197	H6
Foxdown	101	H6
Foxhills	341	H5
Fox Lane	70	C7
Foyers	340	A5
Fratton	423	J2
Freefolk	122	E2
Freemantle	343	G2
The Frenches	261	G6
Frenchmoor	231	L2
Frensham	180	E1
Friars Cliff	451	H2
Frimley	71	K6
Frimley Green	91	J1
Frimley Ridge	71	K5
Fritham	312	E7
Frithend	179	M5
Frogham	335	J2
Frogmore	69	L2
Frostlane	368	A6
Froxfield Green	246	B8
Fryern Hill	293	J2
Fulflood	10	B6
Fullerton	165	H5
Funtley	372	C3
Furzedown	235	G1
Furze Hill	335	J5
Furzeley Corner	351	K7
Furzey	338	E5
Furzey Lodge	389	M7
Furzley	314	C3
Fyfield	116	D6
Fyning	277	M3
Gilbert Street	220	E2
Glebe	323	H5
Gobley Hole	127	H8
Godshill	310	D6
Godswinscroft	435	M3
Goldenhayes	339	M4
Golden Hill	438	B5
Golden Pot	154	C5
Goldfinch Bottom	38	F3
Goodworth Clatford	142	E7
Goose Green	363	L4
Goose Hill	39	L5
Gore End	35	L4
Gosport	19	H2
Gosport	263	M6
Gotham	332	C5
Grange Estate	381	K8
Grateley	139	M7
Grayshott	203	L5
Grayswood	205	K7
Greatham	224	E7
Great Shoddesden	115	M2
Green Cross	181	L2
Greenham	25	M8
The Green	282	A1
Greywell	107	K5
Griggs Green	226	C4
Gundleton	219	J1
Habin	277	L6
Hale	135	C3
Hale	285	G7
Halecommon	277	K3
Halterworth	291	H1
Ham	32	F6
Hambledon	326	A6
Hamble-le-Rice	369	K5
Hambrook	379	L6
Hammer	227	M3
Hammer Bottom	227	L3
Hampreston	405	J6
Hampton Park	319	J5
Hamptworth	286	F4
Hamstead Marshall	35	J1
Hamworthy	444	D5
Hangersley	359	J6
Hannington	79	L4
Harbridge	334	C7
Harbridge Green	334	B6
Hardley	392	A2
Hardway	421	M1
Harefield	345	G1
Harestock	214	B5
Hartfordbridge	67	L8
Hartley Mauditt	199	K3
Hartley Wespall	65	C7
Hartley Wintney	87	K2
Haslemere	229	G2
Hatch	106	B3
Hatch Bottom	320	C6
Hatchet Gate	390	A8
Hatchet Green	285	H5
Hatch Farm Hill	228	F8
Hatch Warren	126	F2
Hatherden	95	H7
Hatt Hill	233	J7
Hattingley	196	B1
Haughurst Hill	40	F7
Havant	16	E1
Hawkley	247	K1
Hawley	70	B5
Hawley Lane	90	E1
Hawthorn	221	H6
Hayling Island	401	M6
Hazeley	66	D5
Hazeley Bottom	66	F7
Hazeley Lea	66	E5
Headbourne Worthy	214	E3
Headley	39	H7
Headley	202	A3
Headley Down	202	E4
Hearn	202	E1
Heath End	35	K7
Heath End	41	J8
Heath End	135	G1
Heather Row	107	J2
Heatherside	71	M4
Heathfield	372	A7
Heath Green	195	M1
Heckfield	65	M1
Hedge End	345	M1
Hell Corner	34	E8
Henley	52	D5
Hensting	267	J3
Hermitage	378	E7
Herriard	128	E7
Hides Close	390	D4
Highbridge	294	E3
Highbury	399	G2
Highclere	56	C3
Highclere Street	56	A5
Highcliffe	436	E6
High Cross	246	E6
Highfield	318	F6
Hightown	345	J4
Hightown	383	H2
Highwood	359	H4
Hillbourne	429	L6
Hill Brow	249	H6
Hill Head	395	K7
Hill Park	14	A1
Hillpound	324	D4
Hillside	108	F6
Hill Side	248	F4
Hillstreet	316	A3
Hill Top	391	C4
Hill View	429	H4
Hillyfields	317	H4
Hilsea	399	K4
Hiltingbury	265	J6
Hindhead	204	C4
Hinton	436	E4
Hinton Ampner	242	D4
Hocombe	265	G6
Hoe	323	L1
Hoe Gate	350	D1
Hog Hatch	134	C2
Holbury	392	A5
Holdenhurst	433	L5
Hollington	55	M4
Hollington Cross	56	A5
Hollywater	201	L7
Holt	86	C7
Holt End	174	F5
Holt Pound	158	A6
Holybourne	177	H1
Hook	86	A7
Hook	394	C1
Hook Park	394	B8
Hooksway	331	M3
Hordle	438	E4
Horndean	353	G2
Horsebridge	210	B7
Horton Common	356	A6
Horton Heath	321	J1
Houghton	210	B3
Hound	369	J2
Hound Green	66	B5
Houndmills	104	D1
Hounsdown	341	J4
Hungerford	335	G3
Hunton	168	F4
Hurn	433	M1
Hursley	265	G1
Hurstbourne Priors	121	H6
Hurstbourne Tarrant	96	D1

Hyde 11 H5
Hyde 335 G2
Hyde End 40 B4
Hythe 367 M4
Ibsley 358 E1
Ibthorpe 74 B8
Ibworth 80 E6
Iford 449 J1
Inhurst 40 F8
Inkpen 33 M3
Inkpen Common 34 C3
Iping 279 H6
Isington 156 D7
Itchen 344 C5
Itchen Abbas 216 D2
Itchen Stoke 217 J2
Jumpers Common 434 C8
Kempshott 103 M7
Kents Oak 261 K3
Keyhaven 454 F5
Kiff Green 28 E2
Kilmeston 242 C7
Kimbridge 233 K8
Kimpton 116 A6
Kingsclere 59 H7
Kingsclere Woodlands 39 K8
King's Furlong 104 D4
Kingsley 178 F7
Kingsley Green 228 C6
Kingsmead 324 B8
King's Somborne 210 E5
Kingston 382 C7
Kingston 423 K1
Kings Worthy 215 H2
Kinson 431 M3
Kitwood 220 F1
Knapp 264 C4
Knighton 405 H8
Knights Enham 118 F3
Ladwell 265 G4
Lake 444 C7
Landford 287 J4
Landfordwood 287 J1
Lane End 181 G1
Lane End 241 H8
Lane End 245 J1
Langdown 367 M5
Langley 249 L2
Langley 418 B1
Langrish 274 B4
Langstone 401 J2
Lasham 153 J6
Latchmere Green 62 F3
Laverstoke 123 H3
Leagreen 438 E8
Leckford 165 J8
Lee 290 F8
Lee Ground 371 L3
Lee-on-the-Solent 420 A2
Leigh 404 D4
Leigh Park 377 H4
Lepe 418 E6
Lilliput 457 H1
Linchmere 227 K5
Lindford 201 L4
Linford 359 L6
Linkenholt 54 A7
Linwood 335 M8
Liphook 226 D5
Liss 248 F5
Liss Forest 248 E1
Litchfield 77 H8
Little Ann 141 M4
Little Canford 405 G4
Littledown 53 J8
Littledown 448 F1
Little Hoddington 130 B3
Little Holbury 391 M3
Little London 62 C5
Little London 96 C8
Little Posbrook 395 J3
Little Sandhurst 49 K6
Little Shoddesden 116 B2
Little Somborne 211 J2
Littleton 214 A3
Lockerley 232 D7
Locks Heath 370 F4
London Minstead 339 G4
Long Common 321 L7
Longfleet 445 H4
Longham 405 M7
Longparish 145 G2
Long Park 189 K8
Longstock 186 D1
Long Sutton 131 K5
Lord's Hill 317 M4
Lordswood 318 C4
Lovedean 352 C3
Lover 285 L3
Lower Bordean 273 M2
Lower Bourne 159 H2
Lower Brook 234 A4
Lower Buckland 440 C3
Lower Bullington 167 M1
Lower Burgate 309 L4
Lower Chute 94 A1
Lower Common 47 J7
Lower Common 152 A2
Lower Daggons 332 E1
Lower Farringdon 198 C5
Lower Froyle 156 B3
Lower Green 33 L3
Lower Hamworthy 444 F7
Lower Holwell 332 B2
Lower Padworth 30 A3
Lower Pennington 440 A4
Lower Ratley 261 L5
Lower Slackstead 263 L1
Lower Swanwick 346 A8
Lower Turmer 358 B1
Lower Upham 296 C4
Lower Wield 174 A2
Lowford 345 L7
Ludgershall 92 F5
Lumley 378 E7
Lyde Green 85 J1
Lymington 440 B4
Lymore 454 E2

Lynch 100 D8
Lynch Hill 122 C3
Lyndhurst 363 J3
Malwood 338 E4
Mapledurwell 106 D5
Marchwood 342 C6
Marley Heights 228 C7
Marsh Benham 24 A5
Martin 281 H5
Martin Drove End 280 B1
Martyr Worthy 216 A2
Mattingley 66 A8
Maybush 317 K6
Mead End 412 C7
Medstead 196 D2
Mengham 425 M5
Meon 395 J5
Merley 404 C7
Merritown 433 J1
Merry Oak 344 C3
Meyrick Park 22 C1
Micheldever 170 A5
Micheldever Station 148 A6
Michelmersh 234 B7
Midanbury 319 L8
Middle Bockhampton 435 K2
Middle Bourne 158 F1
Middleton 144 F3
Middle Wallop 162 D8
Middle Winterslow 206 F1
Midgham 28 B5
Midgham Green 28 E3
Miles's Green 27 M1
Milford on Sea 454 A5
Milland 250 D6
Millbridge 159 G7
Millbrook 342 C1
Mill Green 39 J5
Mill Lane 109 M7
Mill Throop 433 J4
Milton 424 A4
Minstead 338 F5
The Mint 248 F3
Mockbeggar 359 H1
Monk Sherborne 82 A2
Monkwood 220 F6
Montgomery Lines 112 F4
Monxton 141 H3
Moorcourt 316 B1
Moordown 432 E7
Moorgreen 320 E5
Moor Park 135 L7
Moortown 382 E3
Morestead 239 L8
Morgan's Vale 285 H1
Mortimer 43 K2
Mortimer West End 43 G4
Mottisfont 233 K6
Mount Sorrel 252 A2
The Mount 56 C1
Mudeford 450 F3
Mullenspond 116 D8
Murrell Green 86 D5
Muscliff 432 F3
Mytchett 91 H5
Mytchett Place 91 K6
Nash's Green 153 H1
Nately Scures 107 H1
Neacroft 435 M2
Neatham 177 K2
Netherton 54 C8
Nether Wallop 185 G3
Netley 368 F2
Netley Hill 345 L4
Netley Marsh 340 E2
New Alresford 218 B2
Newbridge 314 D5
New Brighton 378 E5
Newbury 2 C4
New Cheriton 242 C4
Newfound 103 G5
Newgrounds 310 F6
New Milton 437 L4
Newnham 85 J8
Newnham 258 E6
Newton 166 D3
Newton Stacey 160 A3
Newton Tony 223 G2
Newton Valence 37 L4
Newtown 176 C6
Newtown 226 E6
Newtown 261 G4
Newtown 296 E8
Newtown 338 F6
New Town 344 E7
Newtown 350 A1
Newtown 394 B1
Newtown 446 A1
Nob's Crook 294 F1
No Man's Land 215 L8
Nomansland 287 J8
Norleywood 415 K8
North Baddesley 291 M4
North Boarhunt 349 L6
North Bockhampton 435 J1
Northbourne 432 B4
Northbrook 169 L4
Northbrook 297 H7
North Camp 112 E2
North Charford 285 H4
North End 35 J6
North End 242 B1
North End 308 B3
North End 399 K6
Northfields 266 F1
North Gorley 334 F5
North Hayling 402 A5
North Houghton 186 C8
Northington 171 L8
North Kingston 383 G6
North Marden 331 L4
Northney 402 A4
North Oakley 79 K7
North Poulner 359 H6
North Ripley 409 H4
North Stoneham 319 J1
North Street 220 C1
North Street 284 A6

North Tidworth 114 F1
North Town 113 H6
North Waltham 125 K6
North Warnborough 108 B4
North Weirs 387 G7
Nursling 317 H3
Nursted 304 B1
Nutbourne 403 K1
Nutburn 292 A3
Nutcombe 204 A6
Nutley 151 H5
Nyewood 277 K8
Oakdale 445 K2
Oakhanger 200 C4
Oakley 102 F7
Oakley 404 B7
Oakridge 4 E3
Oakshott 247 J4
Ocean Village 13 K7
Odiham 108 D6
Ogdens 335 K3
Old Alresford 194 B7
Old Basing 105 M2
Old Burghclere 57 H8
Old Milton 437 J7
Old Netley 345 J7
Old Portsmouth 20 C3
Old Shirley 317 M7
Oliver's Battery 237 M5
Ossemsley 411 J7
Otterbourne 266 A4
Otterwood 391 H8
Outwick 283 K8
Overton 124 A1
Over Wallop 162 C6
Ovington 217 K4
Ower 315 L2
Owlsmoor 50 A6
Owslebury 267 L5
Oxenwood 52 A5
Padworth 30 B7
Padworth Common 42 C2
Palestine 161 K2
Pamber End 62 A7
Pamber Green 62 B4
Pamber Heath 42 A6
Pardown 126 A2
Park Gate 370 F3
Parkstone 446 A5
Parley Green 433 G1
Passfield 202 C7
Paulsgrove 374 E8
Peartree Green 344 B4
Peel Common 396 D6
Pennington 440 A6
Penton Corner 117 M7
Penton Grafton 117 K5
Penton Mewsey 117 M4
Pentridge 280 A8
Penwood 56 C1
Perham Down 115 H1
Petersfield 275 J5
Pheonix Green 86 F4
Picket Hill 359 L8
Picket Piece 119 M6
Pikeshill 363 J2
Pilley 414 F6
Pilley Bailey 414 D6
Pitt 237 M3
Plaitford 287 M4
Plaitford Green 260 B8
Plastow Green 59 K1
Pokesdown 448 F3
Pondtail 89 J8
Pooksgreen 342 B6
Poole 445 G6
Popham 149 K4
Popley 83 G7
Portchester 373 M8
Portmore 440 E1
Portsea 20 E1
Portsea Island 399 M8
Portswood 319 G7
Post Green 428 B8
Potbridge 86 F8
Poulner 359 H8
Pound Green 61 G5
Pound Street 56 F1
Powntley Copse 154 C3
Preston Candover 151 H8
Prince's Marsh 248 E6
Prinsted 403 G1
Privett 245 H6
Privett 421 J5
Pucknall 263 L2
Purbrook 376 B3
Purewell 450 B1
Puttenham 137 L3
Pylehill 295 H5
Pyott's Hill 83 M7
Quarley 139 M4
Queen's Corner 251 H8
Quidhampton 101 G7
Racedown 139 K2
Rafborough 90 B5
Ragged Appleshaw 117 H2
Rake 249 K4
Ramsdean 274 B7
Ramsdell 81 K1
Ratlake 264 D5
Ravenswood Village
    Settlement 49 H2
Redbridge 317 H4
Redenham 116 F1
Redford 251 K7
Red Hill 353 M7
Redhill 432 D4
Redlynch 285 K1
Red Rice 142 B8
Ridge 290 B7
Ridge Common 275 H3
The Ridges 48 E4
Ringwood 358 C3
Ripley 409 G6
Riseley 45 M5
Rivar 32 C8
Robins 278 F1
Rockbourne 282 D7

Rockford 359 G3
Rogate 277 K5
Romsey 290 D1
Ropley 220 D1
Ropley Dean 219 M3
Ropley Soke 196 D8
Rossmore 446 D1
Rotherwick 85 K3
Rotten Green 88 C3
Round Hill 388 D8
Row Ash 322 F8
Rowland's Castle 354 B6
Rowledge 158 C5
Rowner 397 G5
Rownhams 317 L1
Runfold 135 M5
Rushcombe Bottom 429 J1
Rushington 341 K2
Rushmoor 181 M1
Rushmore 326 D6
St Austins 413 M8
St Catherine's Hill 434 C5
St Cross 238 E3
St Denys 319 H8
St Giles's Hill 11 K8
St Ives 381 L3
St Leonards 381 L4
St Mary Bourne 97 M3
Salters Heath 62 C8
Sandbanks 457 H5
Sandford 383 G8
Sandhurst 49 L7
Sandleheath 308 E6
The Sands 136 B6
Sandy Cross 136 C4
Sandy Down 414 A4
Sarisbury 370 C3
Sarson 141 G2
Seale 136 E4
Selborne 199 J8
Selsmore 426 B6
Setley 413 L3
Shalbourne 32 C5
Shalden 153 M8
Shalden Green 153 M4
Shaw 25 L3
Shawford 266 D1
Shedfield 348 B1
Sheet 276 A3
Shepherd's Hill 228 F2
Sherborne St John 82 C5
Sherfield English 260 C7
Sherfield on Loddon 64 D8
Shipton Bellinger 138 C1
Shirley 318 C8
Shirley 409 L6
Shirley Holms 413 L7
Shirley Warren 318 D7
Shirrell Heath 323 M7
Shobley 359 L7
Sholing 344 F4
Sholing Common 344 E3
Shootash 261 J7
Shorley 243 G8
Shorn Hill 315 M5
Shortfield Common 158 E6
Shortheath 158 E2
Shortheath 200 D2
Shottermill 228 B2
Silchester 42 E8
Silkstead 265 K5
Skinners Green 24 E8
Sladen Green 75 L7
Sleaford 179 K7
Sleepers Hill 238 C2
Smannell 119 K2
Smoake 351 M5
Soberton 325 H2
Soberton Heath 324 F7
Soldridge 196 D6
Somerford 450 E1
Sopley 434 F1
Southampton 12 F7
South Baddesley 441 J2
South Bockhampton 435 H4
Southbourne 379 J8
Southbourne 449 K5
South Down 266 C3
South End 308 B5
South Farnborough 91 G7
South Gorley 334 F6
South Ham 104 C5
South Harting 304 F4
South Hayling 425 J6
Southington 123 L1
Southrope 153 H2
South Tidworth 114 E4
South Town 196 D3
South View 4 E4
South Warnborough 130 F5
South Weirs 387 H8
Southwick 373 H4
South Wonston 190 B3
Southwood 89 L5
Spanish Green 64 C5
Sparsholt 213 H5
Spearywell 233 J5
Speen 24 F3
Spreakley 158 D3
Springbourne 23 M1
Stamshaw 398 F2
Standford 201 M6
Standon 236 F6
Stanford End 45 H5
Stanley Green 445 G2
Stanmore 238 C3
Stanpit 450 D1
Stapehill 405 J3
Stedham 279 K7
Steep 275 K1
Steep Marsh 247 M7
Sterte 445 G4
Steventon 125 G4
Stockbridge 186 E5
Stockcross 24 C3
Stockheath 377 J5
Stoke 97 H4
Stoke 401 L6

Stoke Charity 168 F5
Stoke Common 294 B3
Stonehills 393 G6
Stoner Hill 247 G8
Stoney Cross 338 C4
Stony Batter 208 B8
Stonyford 315 L4
Stony Heath 61 G7
Stonymarsh 233 M7
The Straits 178 F6
Stratfield Mortimer 44 A3
Stratfield Saye 44 E8
Stratfield Turgis 64 F4
Street End 297 H4
Stroud 274 F4
Strouden 433 H7
Stroud Green 3 G7
Stubbermere 354 E8
Stubbington 396 B5
Stuckton 335 G1
Sulhampstead Abbots 31 J4
Sulhampstead
    Bannister Upper End 31 G3
Sulhamstead 30 E2
Sutton Scotney 168 C4
Swallowfield 46 A2
Swampton 97 L5
Swanmore 324 A3
Swanwick 370 E1
Swarraton 193 L1
Sway 412 E7
Swaythling 319 K5
Sydmonton 58 A8
Tadley 61 M1
Talbot Heath 447 G1
Talbot Village 432 A8
Talbot Woods 447 J1
Tangley 94 D2
Tapnage 348 A7
Terwick Common 278 A3
Testwood 316 D6
Thatcham 26 F4
Thorney Hill 410 C4
Thorney Island 403 G5
Thornhill 345 J3
Thornhill Park 345 H1
Thorns Beach 442 F2
Three Ashes 63 G1
Three Legged Cross 356 C8
Thruxton 116 C8
Tichborne 217 M7
Tidpit 281 J6
Tilford Common 159 L7
Tilford Reeds 159 L5
Tilly Down 116 F1
Timsbury 262 B1
Tipner 398 F5
Tiptoe 412 B8
Titchfield 371 J8
Titchfield Common 370 E2
Titchfield Park 371 H5
Titcomb 34 B1
Titty Hill 251 H8
Tongham 136 C2
Toothill 291 K7
Tote Hill 279 K3
Totford 171 M8
Tot Hill 37 H7
Totton 316 F8
Townhill Park 319 L6
Towns End 60 D6
Trapshill 34 B4
Trash Green 31 K1
Trickett's Cross 406 D1
Trotten Marsh 278 B1
Trotton 278 D7
Trotts 342 A5
Tuckton 449 L3
Tufton 122 A6
Tullecombe 249 K8
Tunworth 129 H2
Turbary Common 431 J6
Turgis Green 64 F5
Turkey Island 348 D1
Turlin Moor 444 A4
Turmer 334 B8
Turner's Green 27 L1
Twyford 266 F2
Tye 402 A7
Ufton Green 30 E3
Ufton Nervet 31 G4
Up Green 68 B2
Upham 296 E2
Up Marden 331 J8
Up Nately 107 G4
Upper Bucklebury 27 M2
Upper Bullington 146 B8
Upper Burgate 309 M2
Upper Canterton 338 D2
Upper Clatford 142 D4
Upper Common 151 L1
Upper Enham 96 A8
Upper Farringdon 198 E5
Upper Froyle 155 M6
Upper Green 34 A5
Upper Hale 134 E2
Upper Pennington 439 L5
Upper Ratley 261 L4
Upper Shirley 318 C6
Upper Slackstead 235 M7
Upper Street 283 L6
Upper Swanmore 298 B8
Upper Wardley 250 F3
Upper Wield 173 L6
Upper Woolhampton 28 E4
Upper Wootton 81 H6
Up Somborne 211 M3
Upton 73 L5
Upton 317 J1
Upton 444 A1
Upton Grey 129 M3
Vernham Bank 72 F2
Vernham Dean 73 G2
Vernham Row 52 E8
Vernham Street 53 J8
Verwood 356 D2
Wadwick 98 B2
Walhampton 440 E3

Walkford	436 F7	West Common	418 C2	Weston Patrick	129 M6	Wickham	348 E5	Woodgreen	284 C8
Wallington	15 M4	West Dean	231 J5	West Parley	406 D8	Wick Hill	48 D2	Woodhouse	119 H2
Wallisdown	431 L7	West Down	165 L6	West Southbourne	449 J3	Widley	376 A6	Woodington	289 G2
Waltham Chase	323 K5	West End	14 E8	West Stratton	170 D3	Wildern	346 A1	Woodlands	340 C5
Walton Heath	374 A1	West End	158 C8	West Thorney	403 H6	Wildhern	95 K6	Woodley	263 H7
Wanborough	137 L2	West End	196 A4	West Tisted	244 D1	Wildmoor	84 D3	Woodmancote	379 K4
Warblington	17 K6	West End	320 D8	West Town	425 J5	Wilsom	176 F4	Woodmancott	149 K7
Wardley	250 F4	West End Green	44 A8	West Tytherley	208 A8	Wimble Hill	133 K6	Woodmansgreen	251 K3
Warnborough Green	108 A4	Westfield	425 J6	West Wellow	288 D5	Wimborne Minster	404 A3	Woodside	440 C7
Warnford	271 K4	West Fields	2 B5	West Winterslow	206 C3	Wimpson	317 K7	Woodspeen	24 D7
Warren Corner	133 M1	West Green	86 E3	West Wittering	427 L7	Winchester	11 G9	Woolbeding	279 L6
Warren Corner	246 F3	West Ham	104 C3	West Woodhay	34 F5	Winchfield	87 H6	Woolhampton	28 F6
Warsash	370 B7	West Harting	304 F1	West Worldham	199 K1	Winchfield Hurst	87 K8	Woolmer Hill	227 M1
Wash Common	37 G3	West Heath	61 K7	Weybourne	6 C8	Winklebury	104 A2	Woolsbridge	380 E1
Wash Water	36 E5	West Heath	90 B3	Weyhill	117 H6	Winkton	435 G3	Woolston	344 C6
Wasing	41 G3	West Howe	431 J4	Wheat Hold	60 B2	Winnall	11 L6	Woolton Hill	56 B7
Waterditch	435 L3	West Hurn	433 K2	Wheatley	178 F3	Winslade	128 E3	Wootton	411 L6
Water End	107 G2	West Leigh	377 L5	Wherwell	165 K2	Winsor	315 J7	Wootton St Lawrence	103 J7
Waterford	440 E6	West Liss	248 E3	Whitchurch	122 B3	Wintershill	296 C7	Worlds End	350 D5
Waterloo	429 M8	West Marden	330 D8	Whitehall	108 E2	Winton	447 L1	Worting	103 H5
Waterlooville	352 D8	West Meon	272 A4	Whitehill	201 H6	Wittensford	314 C8	Wrecclesham	158 C2
Wecock	352 C4	West Meon Woodlands	244 B6	Whitehouse Green	31 K2	Wivelrod	175 H7	Wyck	177 M4
Weeke	10 B4	West Moors	380 E6	Whitenap	291 H1	Wolverton	60 C7	Wymering	375 J8
Well	132 B6	Weston	275 G8	Whiteparish	258 F4	Wolverton Common	60 D5	Yateley	69 G2
Wellow Wood	260 C8	Weston	344 C7	Whitsbury	282 F5	Wonston	168 E5	York Town	70 D4
Westbourne	378 F4	Weston Colley	169 K4	Whitway	57 G4	Woodcot	396 E5		
Westbourne	447 G6	Weston Common	344 F4	Wick	284 B1	Woodcott	76 C6		
West Cliff	22 B8	Weston Corbett	129 L6	Wick	450 A4	Woodfalls	285 H3		

USING THE STREET INDEX

Street names are listed alphabetically. Each street name is followed by its postal town or area locality, the Postcode District, the page number, and the reference to the square in which the name is found.

Example: **Abbey Cl** *FAWY* SO45 .... **367** L5 🗓

Some entries are followed by a number in a blue box. This number indicates the location of the street within the referenced grid square. The full street name is listed at the side of the map page.

GENERAL ABBREVIATIONS

ACC	ACCESS	CUTT	CUTTINGS	HOL	HOLLOW	NW	NORTH WEST
ALY	ALLEY	CV	COVE	HOSP	HOSPITAL	O/P	OVERPASS
AP	APPROACH	CYN	CANYON	HRB	HARBOUR	OFF	OFFICE
AR	ARCADE	DEPT	DEPARTMENT	HTH	HEATH	ORCH	ORCHARD
ASS	ASSOCIATION	DL	DALE	HTS	HEIGHTS	OV	OVAL
AV	AVENUE	DM	DAM	HVN	HAVEN	PAL	PALACE
BCH	BEACH	DR	DRIVE	HWY	HIGHWAY	PAS	PASSAGE
BLDS	BUILDINGS	DRO	DROVE	IMP	IMPERIAL	PAV	PAVILION
BND	BEND	DRY	DRIVEWAY	IN	INLET	PDE	PARADE
BNK	BANK	DWGS	DWELLINGS	IND EST	INDUSTRIAL ESTATE	PH	PUBLIC HOUSE
BR	BRIDGE	E	EAST	INF	INFIRMARY	PK	PARK
BRK	BROOK	EMB	EMBANKMENT	INFO	INFORMATION	PKWY	PARKWAY
BTM	BOTTOM	EMBY	EMBASSY	INT	INTERCHANGE	PL	PLACE
BUS	BUSINESS	ESP	ESPLANADE	IS	ISLAND	PLN	PLAIN
BVD	BOULEVARD	EST	ESTATE	JCT	JUNCTION	PLNS	PLAINS
BY	BYPASS	EX	EXCHANGE	JTY	JETTY	PLZ	PLAZA
CATH	CATHEDRAL	EXPY	EXPRESSWAY	KG	KING	POL	POLICE STATION
CEM	CEMETERY	EXT	EXTENSION	KNL	KNOLL	PR	PRINCE
CEN	CENTRE	F/O	FLYOVER	L	LAKE	PREC	PRECINCT
CFT	CROFT	FC	FOOTBALL CLUB	LA	LANE	PREP	PREPARATORY
CH	CHURCH	FK	FORK	LDG	LODGE	PRIM	PRIMARY
CHA	CHASE	FLD	FIELD	LGT	LIGHT	PROM	PROMENADE
CHYD	CHURCHYARD	FLDS	FIELDS	LK	LOCK	PRS	PRINCESS
CIR	CIRCLE	FLS	FALLS	LKS	LAKES	PRT	PORT
CIRC	CIRCUS	FLS	FLATS	LNDG	LANDING	PT	POINT
CL	CLOSE	FM	FARM	LTL	LITTLE	PTH	PATH
CLFS	CLIFFS	FT	FORT	LWR	LOWER	PZ	PIAZZA
CMP	CAMP	FWY	FREEWAY	MAG	MAGISTRATE	QD	QUADRANT
CNR	CORNER	FY	FERRY	MAN	MANSIONS	QU	QUEEN
CO	COUNTY	GAL	GALLERY	MD	MEAD	QY	QUAY
COLL	COLLEGE	GDN	GARDEN	MDW	MEADOWS	R	RIVER
COM	COMMON	GDNS	GARDENS	MEM	MEMORIAL	RBT	ROUNDABOUT
COMM	COMMISSION	GLD	GLADE	MKT	MARKET	RD	ROAD
CON	CONVENT	GLN	GLEN	MKTS	MARKETS	RDG	RIDGE
COT	COTTAGE	GN	GREEN	ML	MALL	REP	REPUBLIC
COTS	COTTAGES	GND	GROUND	ML	MILL	RES	RESERVOIR
CP	CAPE	GRA	GRANGE	MNR	MANOR	RFC	RUGBY FOOTBALL CLUB
CPS	COPSE	GRG	GARAGE	MS	MEWS	RI	RISE
CR	CREEK	GT	GREAT	MSN	MISSION	RP	RAMP
CREM	CREMATORIUM	GTWY	GATEWAY	MT	MOUNT	RW	ROW
CRS	CRESCENT	GV	GROVE	MTN	MOUNTAIN	S	SOUTH
CSWY	CAUSEWAY	HGR	HIGHER	MTS	MOUNTAINS	SCH	SCHOOL
CT	COURT	HILL	HILL	MUS	MUSEUM	SE	SOUTH EAST
CTRL	CENTRAL	HLS	HILLS	MWY	MOTORWAY	SER	SERVICE AREA
CTS	COURTS	HLS	HILLS	N	NORTH	SH	SHORE
CTYD	COURTYARD	HO	HOUSE	NE	NORTH EAST	SHOP	SHOPPING

SKWY	SKYWAY
SMT	SUMMIT
SOC	SOCIETY
SP	SPUR
SPR	SPRING
SQ	SQUARE
ST	STREET
STN	STATION
STR	STREAM
STRD	STRAND
SW	SOUTH WEST
TDG	TRADING
TER	TERRACE
THWY	THROUGHWAY
TNL	TUNNEL
TOLL	TOLLWAY
TPK	TURNPIKE
TR	TRACK
TRL	TRAIL
TWR	TOWER
U/P	UNDERPASS
UNI	UNIVERSITY
UPR	UPPER
V	VALE
VA	VALLEY
VIAD	VIADUCT
VIL	VILLA
VIS	VISTA
VLG	VILLAGE
VLS	VILLAS
VW	VIEW
W	WEST
WD	WOOD
WHF	WHARF
WK	WALK
WKS	WALKS
WLS	WELLS
WY	WAY
YD	YARD
YHA	YOUTH HOSTEL

POSTCODE TOWNS AND AREA ABBREVIATIONS

ALDT	Aldershot	CHIN	Chineham	HLER	Hamble-le-Rice	NTHA	Thatcham north
ALTN	Alton	CHOB/PIR	Chobham/Pirbright	HORN	Horndean	NTID	North Tidworth
AMSY	Amesbury	CWTH	Crowthorne	HSEA	Hilsea	NWBY	Newbury
AND	Andover	DEAN	Deane/Oakley	HTWY	Hartley Wintney	ODIM	Odiham
ASC	Ascot	ELGH	Eastleigh	HUNG	Hungerford/Lambourn	OVTN	Overton/Rural Basingstoke
ASHV	Ash Vale	EMRTH	Emsworth/Southbourne	ITCH	Itchen	PLE	Poole
BAGS	Bagshot	ENEY	Eastney	KEMP	Kempshott	PSEA	Portsea
BDST	Broadstone	EPSF	Petersfield east	KSCL	Kingsclere/Rural Newbury	PSF	Petersfield
BFOR	Bracknell Forest/Windlesham	EWKG	Wokingham east	LIPH	Liphook	PSTN	Parkstone
BKME/WDN	Branksome/Wallisdown	FARN	Farnborough	LISS	Liss	PTSW	Portswood
BLKW	Blackwater	FAWY	Fawley/Hythe	LSOL/BMARY	Lee-on-the-Solent/	RAND	Rural Andover
BMTH	Bournemouth	FBDG	Fordingbridge		Bridgemary	RCCH	Rural Chichester
BOR	Bordon	FERN	Ferndown/West Moors	LTDN	Littledown	RDGW	Reading west
BOSC	Boscombe	FHAM	Fareham	LTWR	Lightwater	RFNM	Rural Farnham
BPWT	Bishop's Waltham	FHAM/PORC	Fareham/Portchester	LYMN	Lymington	RGUW	Rural Guildford west
BROC	Brockenhurst	FHAM/STUB	Fareham/Stubbington	LYND	Lyndhurst	RGWD	Ringwood
BSTK	Basingstoke	FLET	Fleet	MARL	Marlborough	ROMY	Romsey
BWD	Bearwood	FNM	Farnham	MFD/CHID	Milford/Chiddingfold	ROWN	Rownhams
CBLY	Camberley	FRIM	Frimley	MIDH	Midhurst	RSAL	Rural Salisbury
CCLF	Canford Cliffs	GPORT	Gosport	MOOR/WNTN	Moordown/Winton	RWIN	Rural Winchester
CFDH	Canford Heath	GSHT	Grayshott	NALR	New Alresford	SBNE	Southbourne
CHAM	Cosham	HASM	Haslemere	NBAD	North Baddesley	SELS	Selsey
CHAR	Charminster	HAV	Havant	NBNE	Northbourne	SHAM	Southampton
CHCH/BSGR	Christchurch/Bransgore	HEND	Hedge End	NEND	North End	SHST	Sandhurst
CHFD	Chandler's Ford	HISD	Hayling Island	NMIL/BTOS	New Milton/Barton on Sea	SSEA	Southsea

STHA	Thatcham south
STOK	Stockbridge
SWGE	Swanage
TADY	Tadley
THLE	Theale/Rural Reading
TOTT	Totton
TWDS	Talbot Woods
UPTN	Upton
VWD	Verwood
WBNE	Westbourne
WCLF	West Cliff
WEND	West End
WHAM	Wickham
WHCH	Whitchurch
WHIT	Whitley/Arborfield
WIMB	Wimborne Minster
WINC	Winchester
WINW	Winchester west
WSHM	Southampton west
WVILLE	Waterlooville/Denmead
YTLY	Yateley

10th St FAWY SO45 .... 392 B4
11th St FAWY SO45 .... 392 B3
12th St FAWY SO45 .... 392 B2
13th St FAWY SO45 .... 392 B2
14th St FAWY SO45 .... 392 A3
1st St FAWY SO45 .... 392 E5
2nd St FAWY SO45 .... 392 E3
3rd St FAWY SO45 .... 392 D4
4th St FAWY SO45 .... 392 D3
5th St FAWY SO45 .... 392 D3
6th St FAWY SO45 .... 392 D2
7th St FAWY SO45 .... 392 C2
8th St FAWY SO45 .... 392 C4
9th St FAWY SO45 .... 392 B4

A

Aaron CI CFDH BH17 .... 445 L1
Aaron Ct TOTT SO40 .... 342 D6
A Av FAWY SO45 .... 392 B4
Abbatt CI RAND SP11 .... 93 G6
Abbetts La CBLY GU15 .... 70 F5
Abbey CI FAWY SO45 .... 367 L5 回
NWBY RG14 .... 2 F9
Abbeydore Rd CHAM PO6 ..... 375 G7
Abbeyfield Dr FHAM PO15 ..... 372 E4
Abbeyfields CI HLER SO31 ..... 369 H2
Abbey Gdns WIMB BH21 .... 405 H3
Abbey HI ITCH SO19 .... 344 C8
Abbey Hill CI WINC SO23 .... 11 G3
Abbey Hill Rd WINC SO23 .... 10 F3
Abbey Pk THLE RG7 .... 31 J5
Abbey Rd ALTN GU34 .... 175 H8
CHAM RG24 .... 4 C2
FERN BH22 .... 380 E8
FHAM PO15 .... 14 B4
Abbey St FNM GU9 .... 134 F7
Abbey Water ROMY SO51 ...... 290 D1
Abbotsbury Rd BDST BH18 .... 429 J3
ELGH SO50 .... 294 B4
Abbots CI CHCH/BSGR BH23 .. 451 L1 回
FLET GU13 .... 88 F7
WVILLE PO7 .... 376 A4
Abbotsfield TOTT SO40 .... 341 J1
Abbotsfield CI ROWN SO16 ... 318 B3
Abbotsford TOTT SO40 .... 339 M2
Abbot's Ride FNM GU9 .... 135 H8
Abbots Rd NWBY RG14 .... 2 F7
THLE RG7 .... 31 J5
Abbotstone Av HAV PO9 .... 377 L4
Abbotts Wy FHAM PO15 .... 14 A5
HLER SO31 .... 369 H2
Abbots Well Rd FBDG SP6 .... 335 K4
Abbotswood CI ROMY SO51 .. 263 H7 回
Abbott CI KEMP RG22 .... 104 B6
Abbott Rd MOOR/WNTN BH9 . 432 E4
Abbotts Ann Rd WINW SO22 .. 214 C5
RAND SP11 .... 141 H3
Abbotts CI NTID SP9 .... 114 D1
RAND SP11 .... 141 M4
WINC SO23 .... 11 H2
Abbotts Dro ROMY SO51 .... 288 D7
Abbotts HI RAND SP11 .... 141 M5
Abbotts Rd ELGH SO50 .... 293 K7
NTID SP9 .... 114 D1
WINC SO23 .... 11 G2
Abbotts Wy FERN BH22 .... 380 E8
PTSW SO17 .... 319 G2
Abbottswood CI TADY RG26 .... 61 L1 回
Abercrombie Gdns
ROWN SO16 .... 317 M4
Aberdare Av CHAM PO6 .... 375 M7
Aberdare Rd NBNE BH10 ...... 432 C5
Aberdeen CI FHAM PO15 .... 14 D2
Aberdeen Rd PTSW SO17 ...... 319 H7
Aberdour CI WEND SO18 .... 320 A8
Abex Rd NWBY RG14 .... 3 K4
Abingdon Dr
CHCH/BSGR BH23 .... 437 G8
Abingdon Gdns ROWN SO16 .. 318 D3 回
Abingdon Rd CFDH BH17 ...... 430 B7
SHST GU47 .... 49 M8
Abinger Rd LTDN BH7 .... 448 F7
Abney Rd NBNE BH10 .... 432 B5
Above Bar St SHAM SO14 .... 12 F1
Above Town RAND SP11 .... 142 D4
Abraham CI HEND SO30 .... 346 B3
Abshot CI FHAM/STUB PO14 .. 370 F7
Abshot Rd FHAM/STUB PO14 . 370 F7
Acacia CI SHST GU47 .... 50 A7
VWD BH31 .... 357 G4
Acacia Gdns HORN PO8 .... 352 F3
Acacia Rd ITCH SO19 .... 344 D3
LYMN SO41 .... 438 D4
Academy CI CBLY GU15 .... 51 H8
Accentors CI ALTN GU34 .... 176 E2
Acer Wy HAV PO9 .... 377 M4
Acheulian CI FNM GU9 .... 158 F1 回
Achilles CI CHAM RG24 .... 83 L4
Ackender Rd ALTN GU34 .... 176 D5
Ackrells Md SHST GU47 .... 49 J7 回
Ackworth Rd HSEA PO3 .... 399 L3
Acland CI MOOR/WNTN BH9 .. 432 F8
Acorn CI CHAM PO6 .... 376 C8 回
CHCH/BSGR BH23 .... 434 D8
WINW SO22 .... 10 A3
LSOL/BMARY PO13 .... 397 H7
NMIL/BTOS BH25 .... 438 A4 回
RGWD BH24 .... 381 J5
TOTT SO40 .... 342 E7 回
Acorn CI HLER SO31 .... 369 K5 回
Acorn Dr NTHA RG18 .... 27 C3
ROWN SO16 .... 317 K1
Acorn Gv NBAD SO52 .... 292 E4
Acorn Keep FNM GU9 .... 112 A8
Acorn Rd BLKW GU17 .... 69 L3 回
The Acorns HLER SO31 .... 345 K8
WIMB BH21 .... 404 E4
Acorn Wy VWD BH31 .... 356 E2 回
Acre La HORN PO8 .... 353 H7
Acre Pth AND SP10 .... 9 K5
Acres Rd BWD BH11 .... 431 M6
Acton CI NBNE BH10 .... 431 M7
Adair Rd ENEY PO4 .... 423 L6
Adam CI TADY RG26 .... 41 H7

Adames Rd PSEA PO1 .... 423 J2
Adampur Rd NTID SP9 .... 114 B4
Adams CI HEND SO30 .... 321 G5
Adams Dr FLET GU13 .... 89 G7
Adamson CI CHFD SO53 .... 265 J8
Adams Park Rd FNM GU9 ...... 135 G4
Adams Rd FAWY SO45 .... 367 L6
Adams Wy ALTN GU34 .... 176 H4
Adams Wood Dr TOTT SO40 .. 342 D7
Adastral Rd CFDH BH17 .... 430 C8
Adderbury Av EMRTH PO10 .. 378 D4
Addiscombe Rd CWTH RG45 ... 49 M4
Addison Gdns ODIM RG29 ..... 108 D5
Addison Rd BROC SO42 .... 387 K8
ELGH SO50 .... 294 A3 回
ENEY PO4 .... 21 L5
FRIM GU16 .... 71 H8
HLER SO31 .... 370 D2
Addison Sq RGWD BH24 .... 382 F1
Addlestone Rd WINW SO22 ... 238 B3
Adelaide CI RAND SP11 .... 115 J1
Adelaide Rd AND SP10 .... 9 J5
PTSW SO17 .... 319 H8
Adela Verne CI ITCH SO19 .... 345 J5 回
Adeline Rd BMTH BH1 .... 448 D4
Adey CI ITCH SO19 .... 344 F6
Adey's CI NWBY RG14 .... 3 G7
Adhurst Rd HAV PO9 .... 377 L4
Adlam's La LYMN SO41 .... 412 D5
Adlington PI FARN GU14 .... 91 H6 回
Admers Crs LIPH GU30 .... 226 F6
Admirals CI FAWY SO45 .... 392 F5 回
Admirals Rd HLER SO31 .... 370 F4
Admirals Wk GPORT PO12 ...... 18 A4
Admiralty Rd PSEA PO1 .... 20 C1
Admiralty Wy CBLY GU15 .... 70 C4
TOTT SO40 .... 342 D5
Adrian CI HTWY RG27 .... 87 J3
Adsdean CI HAV PO9 .... 377 J4 回
Adstone La HSEA PO3 .... 400 A4 回
Adur CI GPORT PO12 .... 421 K1 回
Adwood Ct STHA RG19 .... 27 H5
Aelmas Mich Dro RAND SP11 . 117 G7 回
Aerodrome Rd
LSOL/BMARY PO13 .... 397 H1
FARN GU14 .... 112 C1
Aerospace Bvd ALDT GU11 ... 112 D1
Africa Dr TOTT SO40 .... 342 D7
Agars La LYMN SO41 .... 438 E1
LYMN SO41 .... 438 F3
Agarton La LYMN SO41 .... 454 E2
Aggis Farm Rd VWD BH31 .... 356 C2
Aghemund CI CHAM RG24 ...... 83 K5 回
Agincourt Rd NEND PO2 .... 423 H1
Agitor Rd FAWY SO45 .... 393 G3
Agnew Rd LSOL/BMARY PO13 . 397 G5
Agra Rd NTID SP9 .... 114 B4
Agravaine CI AND SP10 .... 118 F5 回
Agricola Wy STHA RG19 .... 27 J6
Aikman La TOTT SO40 .... 340 F1
Ailsa La ITCH SO19 .... 344 B4
Ainsdale Rd CHAM PO6 .... 376 B7
Ainsley Gdns ELGH SO50 ...... 293 M3
Aintree CI ELGH SO50 .... 321 J1 回
NWBY RG14 .... 3 J8
Aintree Dr WVILLE PO7 .... 352 F7
Aintree Rd TOTT SO40 .... 316 B7
Aircraft Esp FARN GU14 .... 90 F7 回
Aird CI KSCL RG20 .... 36 B8
Airetons CI BDST BH18 .... 430 A5
Airfield Rd CHCH/BSGR BH23 . 450 E1
Airfield Wy CHCH/BSGR BH23 . 450 E1
Airport Service Rd HSEA PO3 . 399 M5
Ajax CI CHAM RG24 .... 83 L4
FHAM/STUB PO14 .... 396 B7
Akeshill CI NMIL/BTOS BH25 . 437 M3
Alameda Rd WVILLE PO7 .... 376 B4
Alameda Wy WVILLE PO7 ...... 376 B4
Alamein CI ALDT GU11 .... 7 G1
RAND SP11 .... 119 G1
Alanbrooke CI HTWY RG27 ..... 87 H2
Alanbrooke Rd ALDT GU11 .... 113 G2
Alandale Rd ITCH SO19 .... 345 H4
Alan Drayton Wy ELGH SO50 . 294 D6
Alan Gv FHAM PO15 .... 14 C4
Albacore Av HLER SO31 .... 370 C7 回
Albany CI FLET GU13 .... 89 G8
NMIL/BTOS BH25 .... 437 K7
Albany Ct BPWT SO32 .... 296 F8
Albany Dr BPWT SO32 .... 296 F8
WIMB BH21 .... 356 C8
Albany Gdns PLE BH15 .... 444 E6
Albany Pk FRIM GU16 .... 70 F7
Albany Rd AND SP10 .... 8 C4
BPWT SO32 .... 296 F8
FAWY SO45 .... 392 A8
FLET GU13 .... 88 F8
ROMY SO51 .... 290 D1
SSEA PO5 .... 21 J6
WSHM SO15 .... 343 G2
Albatross Wk
LSOL/BMARY PO13 .... 396 F6
Albemarle Av FHAM PO15 ..... 372 A8
Albemarle Rd TWDS BH3 ...... 447 L1
Albert CI HLER SO31 .... 369 G3
Albert Gv SSEA PO5 .... 21 K6
Albert Rd ALDT GU11 .... 7 H2 回
ALTN GU34 .... 176 D6
BKME/WDN BH12 .... 446 C4
BMTH BH1 .... 22 E5
BPWT SO32 .... 323 C1
CBLY GU15 .... 70 F3 回
CWTH RG45 .... 49 L3
ELGH SO50 .... 294 A3
FARN GU14 .... 90 F6
FERN BH22 .... 406 B3
FHAM/STUB PO14 .... 396 D6
HEND SO30 .... 345 M3
NMIL/BTOS BH25 .... 437 K6
NWBY RG14 .... 2 E5
SSEA PO5 .... 21 K7
STHA RG19 .... 29 H1
Albert Rd North SHAM SO14 ... 13 K5
Albert Rd South SHAM SO14 .. 13 K6

Albert St FLET GU13 .... 88 E7
GPORT PO12 .... 19 G2
Albion CI CHCH/BSGR BH23 .. 434 D7
FBDG SP6 .... 309 L6
SHST GU47 .... 69 L1
Albion Wy VWD BH31 .... 356 B2
Albretia Av HORN PO8 .... 352 B5
Albury PI CHFD SO53 .... 265 G7 回
Alby Dr LIPH GU30 .... 226 E3 回
Alcantara Crs SHAM SO14 ...... 13 K6
Alcester Rd BKME/WDN BH12 . 446 C2
Alcot CI CWTH RG45 .... 49 L4
Alderbrook CI CWTH RG45 ..... 49 H4
Alder CI ALTN GU34 .... 176 D3
ASHV GU12 .... 113 K1 回
CHCH/BSGR BH23 .... 435 H7
FAWY SO45 .... 367 G5
ROMY SO51 .... 291 J2
RWIN SO21 .... 266 F8
TOTT SO40 .... 342 D6
Alder Dr FBDG SP6 .... 333 K3
Alderfield PSF GU32 .... 275 K5
Alder Gld THLE RG7 .... 31 J5
Alder Gv YTLY GU46 .... 68 F3 回
Alder Hill Dr TOTT SO40 .... 316 A8
Alder Hills BKME/WDN BH12 . 446 F1
Alderholt Rd FBDG SP6 .... 308 D7
Alder La LSOL/BMARY PO13 .. 421 H3
Alderley Rd NBNE BH10 .... 432 B4
Aldermaston Rd TADY RG26 ... 62 A3
Aldermaston Rd South
BSTK RG21 .... 4 A4
Aldermoor Av ROWN SO16 .... 317 M4
Aldermoor CI ROWN SO16 .... 318 B4
Aldermoor Rd
LSOL/BMARY PO13 .... 421 H1
ROWN SO16 .... 317 M4
WVILLE PO7 .... 376 B4
Aldermoor Rd East
WVILLE PO7 .... 376 B3 回
Alderney Av BKME/WDN BH12 . 431 H7
KEMP RG22 .... 127 C1
Alderney CI ROWN SO16 .... 317 K4
Alder Rd BKME/WDN BH12 ... 431 L8
BOR GU35 .... 202 E2
ROWN SO16 .... 317 L5
Alders Rd FHAM/PORC PO16 . 396 F1
The Alders NTHA RG18 .... 27 G4
Alderwood Rd CHAM RG24 ..... 83 L5
Alderwood Av CHFD SO53 ..... 292 F2
Alderwood CI HAV PO9 .... 376 E5
Alder Wood Dr HTWY RG27 .... 86 A6
Aldis Gdns PLE BH15 .... 444 D5 回
Aldrich Rd PSEA PO1 .... 422 E2
Aldridge La FERN BH22 .... 406 C5
NBNE BH10 .... 432 A3
Aldrin CI AND SP10 .... 118 D5
Aldrin PI FARN GU14 .... 90 A4
Aldroke St CHAM PO6 .... 399 K1 回
Aldsworth CI CHAM PO6 .... 376 B7
Aldsworth Gdns CHAM PO6 .. 376 A8 回
Aldwell St SSEA PO5 .... 21 J3 回
Aldwick CI HAV PO9 .... 90 D2
Aldworth Crs KEMP RG22 ..... 104 D2
Aldworth Gdns CWTH RG45 .... 49 K3
Alec Rose La PSEA PO1 .... 21 G2
Alecto Rd GPORT PO12 .... 18 E6
Alencon CI GPORT PO12 .... 398 A8 回
Alencon Link BSTK RG21 .... 4 D7
Alexander CI TOTT SO40 .... 316 B3 回
WVILLE PO7 .... 376 B3 回
Alexander Gv
FHAM/PORC PO16 .... 15 H8
Alexander Rd OVTN RG25 ..... 123 M1
HISD PO11 .... 425 K6
Alexandra CI FAWY SO45 ...... 367 L4 回
BOR GU35 .... 201 J5
Alexandra La FARN GU14 .... 90 F7 回
Alexandra Rd ALDT GU11 .... 6 B3
ALTN GU34 .... 176 E3
AND SP10 .... 8 F5
ASHV GU12 .... 113 J7
BSTK RG21 .... 4 B8
CHFD SO53 .... 265 L8
FARN GU14 .... 90 F6
FAWY SO45 .... 367 L4
FBDG SP6 .... 309 L8
HEND SO30 .... 345 M3
LYMN SO41 .... 440 A3
PSEA PO1 .... 423 H2
PSTN BH14 .... 446 D4
SBNE BH6 .... 449 G3
WSHM SO15 .... 343 G1
Alexandra St GPORT PO12 .... 421 L2 回
Alexandra Ter WINC SO23 ...... 10 E9
Alexandria Rd RWIN SO21 ..... 168 C3
Alfonso CI ASHV GU12 .... 7 K5
Alford Rd TWDS BH3 .... 447 L1
Alfred CI TOTT SO40 .... 316 B8 回
TOTT SO40 .... 341 G1 回
Alfred Rd FHAM/STUB PO14 .. 396 B5
FNM GU9 .... 134 F7
PSEA PO1 .... 20 F1
Alfred Rose Ct WEND SO18 .. 319 K4 回
Alfred St SHAM SO14 .... 343 M2
Alfrey CI EMRTH PO10 .... 379 G8
Alfriston Gdns ITCH SO19 ..... 344 F5
Alfriston Rd FRIM GU16 .... 91 M1
Algiers Rd HSEA PO3 .... 399 M8
Alhambra Rd ENEY PO4 .... 21 L9
Alice Rd ALDT GU11 .... 7 G2
Alington CI PSTN BH14 .... 457 H1
Alington Gn PSTN BH14 .... 457 H1
TWDS BH3 .... 447 M2
Alipore CI PSTN BH14 .... 446 C5
Alison CI FARN GU14 .... 90 C5
Alison Dr CBLY GU15 .... 71 J3

Alison's Rd ALDT GU11 .... 112 D3
Alison Wy ALDT GU11 .... 6 C2
Allan Gv ROMY SO51 .... 291 G1
Allaway Av CHAM PO6 .... 374 D8
Allbrook Ct HAV PO9 .... 377 H2
Allbrook HI ELGH SO50 .... 294 A1
Allbrook Wy ELGH SO50 .... 265 M8
Allcot Rd HSEA PO3 .... 399 K6
Allden Av ASHV GU12 .... 7 L7
Allee Dr LIPH GU30 .... 226 E3 回
Allenby Gv FHAM/PORC PO16 . 398 A1
Allenby Rd CBLY GU15 .... 70 D2
CFDH BH17 .... 429 M7
GPORT PO12 .... 421 J2
Allen CI ALTN GU34 .... 176 D1
ASHV GU12 .... 104 E5
Allen Ct WIMB BH21 .... 404 A3
Allendale Av EMRTH PO10 .... 378 D4
Allendale CI SHST GU47 .... 49 K6 回
Allen Rd HEND SO30 .... 346 A1
WIMB BH21 .... 404 A4
Allens La BPWT SO32 .... 296 C4
Allen's Rd SSEA PO5 .... 21 L7
Allenview Rd WIMB BH21 ..... 404 A3
Allerton CI TOTT SO40 .... 316 C7
Alliance CI WIMB BH21 .... 404 A3
Alliance La HEND SO30 .... 320 D3
Allington La HSEA PO3 .... 400 A3
Allington Rd WSHM SO15 ..... 342 B1
Alliston Wy KEMP RG22 .... 104 B5
WHCH RG28 .... 122 C4
Allmara Dr WVILLE PO7 .... 376 C3
Allnutt Av BSTK RG21 .... 5 H8
Allotment Rd HLER SO31 ...... 370 C3
All Saints Crs FARN GU14 ...... 70 B7
All Saints Rd LYMN SO41 ..... 440 C6
PSEA PO1 .... 423 H1
Alma CI ASHV GU12 .... 113 C5
FNM GU9 .... 134 F1
Alma La BPWT SO32 .... 296 C5
BOR GU35 .... 201 K5
MOOR/WNTN BH9 .... 447 M1
ROMY SO51 .... 290 E1
SHAM SO14 .... 318 F8
Alma St GPORT PO12 .... 421 L2
Almatade Rd WEND SO18 ..... 344 E1
Alma Ter ENEY PO4 .... 423 L5
Alma Wy FNM GU9 .... 135 G2
Almer Rd PLE BH15 .... 444 D5
Almond Av NWBY RG14 .... 25 J3
Almond CI CHAM RG24 .... 105 M2
CHAM PO6 .... 376 D8
FARN GU14 .... 90 D1
HORN PO8 .... 353 C4
Almond Dr NTHA RG18 .... 27 G4
Almond Gv BKME/WDN BH12 . 446 C1
Almond Rd WSHM SO15 .... 343 G3
Almondsbury Rd CHAM PO6 .. 374 D6
Almondside
LSOL/BMARY PO13 .... 397 J7
Almswood Rd TADY RG26 ...... 41 K6
The Aloes FLET GU13 .... 89 C8
Alphington Av FRIM GU16 ...... 71 J7
Alphington Gn FRIM GU16 ..... 71 H7
Alpine CI FARN GU14 .... 90 A8
WEND SO18 .... 320 A8
Alpine Ct KEMP RG22 .... 103 M5
Alpine Rd BOR GU35 .... 201 J7
RGWD BH24 .... 382 A6
WEND SO18 .... 320 A8
Alresford Dro RWIN SO21 ..... 190 D3
Alresford Rd HAV PO9 .... 377 J4 回
NALR SO24 .... 217 M4
RWIN SO21 .... 239 L1
WINC SO23 .... 11 L8
Alsford Rd WVILLE PO7 .... 376 B3
Alston Ms STHA RG19 .... 26 F5
Alten Rd WVILLE PO7 .... 352 A6
Althorpe Dr HSEA PO3 .... 400 A4
Altona Gdns AND SP10 .... 118 C5
Alton CI ELGH SO50 .... 295 G6
Alton Gv FHAM/PORC PO16 .. 398 A2
Alton La ALTN GU34 .... 197 G8
Alton Ride BLKW GU17 .... 69 G2
Alton Rd FLET GU13 .... 89 H7
NBNE BH10 .... 431 M7
RFNM GU10 .... 158 A1
ODIM RG29 .... 131 G4
PSTN BH14 .... 446 A5
Alton Rd East PSTN BH14 ..... 446 C6
Alum Chine Rd WBNE BH4 .... 447 G6
Alum CI FAWY SO45 .... 392 B6
Alumdale Rd WBNE BH4 .... 447 G6
Alumhurst Rd WBNE BH4 ..... 447 G6
Alum Wy FHAM/PORC PO16 .. 373 J7
WEND SO18 .... 344 F1
Alvara Rd GPORT PO12 .... 18 D7
Alvercliffe Dr GPORT PO12 .... 18 B8
Alver Rd GPORT PO12 .... 18 F5
PSEA PO1 .... 423 J2
Alverstoke Gdns ALDT GU11 .... 6 B4
Alverstone Rd ENEY PO4 ...... 423 L4
Alverton Av PLE BH15 .... 445 L5
Alveston Av FHAM/STUB PO14 . 372 A8
Alwin PI FNM GU9 .... 134 F1 回
Alyth Rd TWDS BH3 .... 447 L2
Amarylis CI FHAM PO15 .... 371 J4
Amazon CI BSTK RG21 .... 4 A9
Ambarrow Crs SHST GU47 ...... 49 J7 回
Ambarrow La CWTH RG45 ...... 49 J6
Amber CI BOR GU35 .... 201 K6 回
Amber Gdns AND SP10 .... 8 B5
Amber HI CBLY GU15 .... 51 L4 回
Amberley CI CHCH/BSGR BH23 . 436 C5
HEND SO30 .... 321 L8
NBAD SO52 .... 291 K3
NWBY RG14 .... 2 C5
Amberley Ct TOTT SO40 .... 341 J2
Amberley Gra ALDT GU11 .... 6 C5
Amberley Rd GPORT PO12 .... 397 L8
HORN PO8 .... 328 C3
NEND PO2 .... 399 K5
Amber Rd WIMB BH21 .... 429 C4

Amberslade Wk FAWY SO45 .. 367 K7
Amberwood FERN BH22 .... 406 C1 回
Amberwood CI TOTT SO40 .... 316 B6
Amberwood Dr CBLY GU15 ..... 71 J1
CHCH/BSGR BH23 .... 436 E6
Amberwood Gdns
CHCH/BSGR BH23 .... 436 E6
Ambledale HLER SO31 .... 370 C4
CHCH/BSGR BH23 .... 434 B5
HEND SO30 .... 346 B3
Ambleside CI FARN GU14 .... 90 B4
FRIM GU16 .... 91 K6
Ambleside Crs FNM GU9 ...... 134 D2 回
Ambleside Gdns ITCH SO19 .. 344 E5
Ambleside Rd LYMN SO41 .... 440 C6
Ambrose Rd TADY RG26 .... 41 L8
Ambury La CHCH/BSGR BH23 . 435 K8
Amersham CI GPORT PO12 ... 421 J4
Amery HI ALTN GU34 .... 176 E4
Amery St ALTN GU34 .... 176 E5
Amesbury Rd RAND SP11 ..... 116 F7
Amethyst Gv WVILLE PO7 ..... 352 F8
Amethyst Rd
CHCH/BSGR BH23 .... 450 E1
Ameysford Rd FERN BH22 .... 380 A7
Ameys La FERN BH22 .... 406 D1 回
Amherst Rd BOR GU35 .... 201 H2
Amoy St WSHM SO15 .... 343 K2
Ampere Rd NWBY RG14 .... 3 G3
Ampfield CI HAV PO9 .... 376 F4 回
Ampfield Rd CHAR BH8 .... 433 H7
Amport CI CHAM RG24 .... 83 M8 回
WINW SO22 .... 214 B5
Amport Ct HAV PO9 .... 377 H2
Ampthill Rd WSHM SO15 ...... 342 F1
Amyas Ct ENEY PO4 .... 424 A2
Ancasta Rd SHAM SO14 ...... 343 M1 回
Ancells Rd FARN GU14 .... 89 C3
Anchorage Rd HSEA PO3 ...... 399 M5
The Anchorage GPORT PO12 .. 19 H4
Anchor CI BWD BH11 .... 431 H4
Anchor Ga PSEA PO1 .... 422 E2
Anchor La PSEA PO1 .... 422 E2
Anchor Meadow FARN GU14 .. 90 C4
Anchor Ms LYMN SO41 .... 440 C4
Anchor Rd BWD BH11 .... 431 K3
KSCL RG20 .... 59 J6
Anchor Yd BSTK RG21 .... 4 F7
Andalusian Gdns HLER SO31 . 346 F8
Andeferas Rd AND SP10 .... 118 C5
Anderby Rd ROWN SO16 ...... 317 J6
Andersen CI HLER SO31 .... 347 G8
Anderson CI HAV PO9 .... 17 G1
ROMY SO51 .... 263 H6 回
Anderson's Rd SHAM SO14 .... 13 K5
Anders Rd RWIN SO21 .... 190 D4
Anderwood Dr LYMN SO41 ... 412 D4
Andes CI SHAM SO14 .... 13 L6
Andes Rd ROWN SO16 .... 317 G5
Andlers Ash Rd LISS GU33 ... 248 B6
Andover CI CHCH/BSGR BH23 . 451 G1
Andover Dro KSCL RG20 .... 36 E4
Andover La RAND SP11 .... 115 M1
Andover Rd BLKW GU17 .... 69 M2
DEAN RG23 .... 102 C7
ENEY PO4 .... 423 K6
WINW SO22 .... 10 F3
KSCL RG20 .... 36 E6
NWBY RG14 .... 101 M8
OVTN RG25 .... 101 M8
RAND SP11 .... 141 K2
RAND SP11 .... 141 M2
RWIN SO21 .... 148 A6
WSHM SO15 .... 343 H2
Andover Rd North WINW SO22 . 214 B1
Andover Wy ALDT GU11 .... 7 H8
FNM GU9 .... 7 H8
Andrewartha Rd FARN GU14 .. 91 H6 回
Andrew Bell St PSEA PO1 ..... 423 G2 回
Andrew CI FAWY SO45 .... 367 L7 回
PSEA PO1 .... 423 K2
TOTT SO40 .... 341 H1
Andrew Crs WVILLE PO7 .... 352 B7
Andrewes CI BPWT SO32 ...... 297 H7
Andrew La NMIL/BTOS BH25 . 438 B6
Andrew PI FHAM/STUB PO14 . 395 M6
Andrews CI BWD BH11 .... 431 L5
FLET GU13 .... 110 L5
Andrew's La NALR SO24 .... 220 E3
ODIM RG29 .... 131 L5
Andrews Rd FARN GU14 .... 90 B3
Andromeda Rd ROWN SO16 .. 317 K4
Andwell La HTWY RG27 .... 106 F2
Anfield CI ELGH SO50 .... 295 H7
Angel Ct NWBY RG14 .... 2 E2
Angel Crs ITCH SO19 .... 344 D2
Angelica Gdns ELGH SO50 ... 321 H1
Angelica Wy FHAM PO15 ...... 371 J4
Angeline CI
CHCH/BSGR BH23 .... 436 D8 回
Angel La FERN BH22 .... 405 M5
NMIL/BTOS BH25 .... 438 B8
Angel Md THLE RG7 .... 28 F3
Angel Mdw ODIM RG29 .... 108 D5
Angelo CI WVILLE PO7 .... 352 B8
Angelus CI FHAM/STUB PO14 . 396 A6
Angerstein Rd NEND PO2 ..... 399 H7
Anglers Wy HLER SO31 .... 346 B8
Anglesea Rd
LSOL/BMARY PO13 .... 420 C8
PSEA PO1 .... 20 F2
WSHM SO15 .... 318 A7
Anglesea Ter SHAM SO14 ...... 13 K5
Anglesey Arms Rd GPORT PO12 . 18 C8
Anglesey Av FARN GU14 .... 90 C1
Anglesey CI AND SP10 .... 142 F3
CHAM RG24 .... 83 H6
Anglesey Rd ASHV GU12 .... 7 L3
GPORT PO12 .... 18 C8
Angora Wy FARN GU14 .... 89 G4
Angus CI FHAM PO15 .... 14 C2
Anjou Crs FHAM PO15 .... 14 B4
Anker La FHAM/STUB PO14 .. 396 A4
Ankerwyke
LSOL/BMARY PO13 .... 396 F7 回
Anmore Dr WVILLE PO7 .... 352 B6
Anmore La WVILLE PO7 .... 352 A4
Anmore Rd WVILLE PO7 .... 351 L4

Anna La CHCH/BSGR BH23 408 E4
Annandale Dr RFNM GU10 159 G3
Anne Armstrong Cl ALDT GU11 113 G3
Anne Cl CHCH/BSGR BH23 434 E7
Anne Crs WVILLE PO7 376 C2
Annerley Rd BMTH BH1 23 L4
Annes Wy FLET GU13 111 G2
Annet Cl PLE BH15 444 D6
Annettes Cft FLET GU13 110 D4
Annett's La HUNG RG17 32 C1
Ann's Hill Rd GPORT PO12 18 C4
Ansell Rd FRIM GU16 71 H8
Anson Cl CHCH/BSGR BH23 450 E2
LSOL/BMARY PO13 421 H3
RGWD BH24 359 G8
Anson Dr ITCH SO19 345 G3
Anson Gv FHAM/PORC PO16 374 B7
Anson Rd ELGH SO50 321 H1
ENEY PO4 423 K3
Anstey Cl BSTK RG21 104 F6
BWD BH11 431 L2
NALR SO24 218 B2
Anstey La ALTN GU34 154 E8
Anstey Mill Cl ALTN GU34 177 G3
Anstey Mill La ALTN GU34 177 G3
Anstey Pl THLE RG7 31 K5
Anstey Rd ALTN GU34 176 F4
BWD BH11 431 L3
ROMY SO51 263 G7
Antar Cl BSTK RG21 4 A9
Antell's Wy FBDG SP6 333 L2
Anthill Cl WVILLE PO7 351 G2
Anthony Gv GPORT PO12 397 K7
LSOL/BMARY PO13 397 K7
Anthony's Av PSTN BH14 446 B7
Antler Dr NMIL/BTOS BH25 437 J4
Anton Cl DEAN RG23 103 G7
ROMY SO51 291 H1
Anton La RAND SP11 119 G2
Anton Mill Rd AND SP10 8 F8
Anton Rd AND SP10 9 G8
Antrim Cl KEMP RG22 104 A5
Anvil Cl HORN PO8 353 G7
Anvil Crs BDST BH18 429 J3
Anzac Cl FHAM/STUB PO14 396 A4
Anzio Cl ALDT GU11 6 F1
Apex Dr FRIM GU16 71 G7
Apless La WVILLE PO7 350 D4
Apollo Dr BOR GU35 201 K6
WVILLE PO7 376 D5
Apollo Ri FARN GU14 90 A4
Apollo Rd CHFD SO53 293 L1
Appelford Cl STHA RG19 27 G6
Apple Cl BKME/WDN BH12 446 F4
Appledore Ms FARN GU14 90 D1
Appledown Cl NALR SO24 218 C4
Appledown La NALR SO24 218 D5
Applegarth Cl BSTK RG21 105 H5
Apple Gv CHCH/BSGR BH23 434 C6
EMRTH PO10 378 F8
Applelands Cl RFNM GU10 158 D4
Appleshaw Cl WINW SO22 214 C4
Appleshaw Wy RAND SP11 115 J2
Appleslade Wy
NMIL/BTOS BH25 437 M3
Appleton Cl STOK SO20 162 B7
Appleton Rd FHAM PO15 372 A7
WEND SO18 319 K7
Appleton Vw ALTN GU34 222 C3
Apple Tree Cl NWBY RG14 37 H1
RSAL SP5 285 J1
Appletree Cl DEAN RG23 103 G8
NMIL/BTOS BH25 437 L7
TOTT SO40 316 B8
Appletree Ct HEND SO30 346 E1
Apple Tree Gv AND SP10 8 B2
FERN BH22 406 C3
Apple Tree Rd FBDG SP6 333 K3
Appletree Rd RSAL SP5 285 J1
Apple Tree Wy SHST GU47 50 A7
Apple Wy CHAM RG24 106 A3
Applewood Gdns ITCH SO19 344 E5
Applewood Gv WVILLE PO7 376 A6
Applewood Pl TOTT SO40 341 G2
Applewood Rd HAV PO9 377 G5
Appley Dr CBLY GU15 70 E3
Approach Rd FNM GU9 134 F7
PSTN BH14 446 A5
April Cl BWD BH11 431 L4
CBLY GU15 70 F6
WEND SO18 344 F1
April Gv HLER SO31 370 C5
April Sq PSEA PO1 423 H2
Apsley Cl AND SP10 142 E3
Apsley Crs CFDH BH17 430 A7
Apsley Pl CHFD SO53 265 G7
Apsley Rd ENEY PO4 423 L4
Aquila Wy HLER SO31 369 K6
Arabian Gdns FHAM PO15 371 G1
Aragon Wy MOOR/WNTN BH9 432 F3
Arcadia Av CHAR BH8 448 A1
Arcadia Cl ROWN SO16 318 A5
Arcadia Rd CHCH/BSGR BH23 434 D7
Archangel Wy NTHA RG18 27 J4
Archdale Cl NBNE BH10 432 B6
Archers Cl TOTT SO40 316 B6
Archers Rd ELGH SO50 293 M4
WSHM SO15 343 J2
Archery Flds ODIM RG29 108 E5
Archery Gdns ITCH SO19 344 D6
Archery Gv ITCH SO19 344 C6
Archery La FHAM/PORC PO16 15 L4
WINC SO23 10 E8
Archery Ri ALTN GU34 176 D6
Archery Rd ITCH SO19 344 C7
Archway Rd CCLF BH13 446 D4
Arcot Rd NTID SP9 114 C5
Arden Cl WEND SO18 320 A7
Arden Rd MOOR/WNTN BH9 432 D5
Arden Wk NMIL/BTOS BH25 437 M6
Ardglen Rd WHCH RG28 122 A3
Ardingly Crs HEND SO30 321 J6
Ardington Ri WVILLE PO7 376 C5
Ardmore Rd PSTN BH14 446 A4
Ardrossan Av CBLY GU15 71 K3
Ardwell Cl CWTH RG45 49 H3
Arena La ALDT GU11 112 B4
Arenal Dr CWTH RG45 49 L5
Arford Common BOR GU35 202 C2
Arford Rd BOR GU35 202 C2
Argente Cl FARN GU14 89 G4
Argosy Cl HLER SO31 370 D7
Argus Rd LSOL/BMARY PO13 420 D1
Argyle Cl BOR GU35 201 J6
Argyle Crs FHAM PO15 14 D3
Argyle Rd CHCH/BSGR BH23 450 D3
NWBY RG14 2 D6
SHAM SO14 13 H1
Argyll Rd BKME/WDN BH12 446 C2
BOSC BH5 448 D4
Ariel Cl SBNE BH6 450 A3
Ariel Dr SBNE BH6 450 A4
Ariel Rd FARN GU14 90 D6
PSEA PO1 21 L1
Arkle Av STHA RG19 26 C5
Ark Royal Crs
LSOL/BMARY PO13 420 C1
Arkwright Cl KSCL RG20 56 C2
Arle Cl HORN PO8 328 B4
NALR SO24 218 B2
Arle Gdns NALR SO24 218 C2
Arley Rd PSTN BH14 445 M6
Arlington Ct
NMIL/BTOS BH25 437 M8
Arlington Ter ALDT GU11 6 D2
Arliss Rd ROWN SO16 317 M7
Arlott Ct WSHM SO15 343 J1
Arlott Dr BSTK RG21 4 F4
Armada Cl ROWN SO16 317 K1
Armada Dr FAWY SO45 367 K6
Arminers Cl GPORT PO12 18 E9
Armitage Av FAWY SO45 367 K7
Armitage Dr FRIM GU16 71 J7
Armory La PSEA PO1 20 D4
Armstrong Cl BROC SO42 387 J7
RWIN SO21 190 D4
WVILLE PO7 352 B7
Armstrong Ct ROWN SO16 317 L3
Armstrong La BROC SO42 387 J7
Armstrong Ml FARN GU14 90 A4
Armstrong Ri AND SP10 118 D5
Armstrong Rd BROC SO42 387 J7
CHAM RG24 5 L4
Armstrong Wy FARN GU14 89 L7
Armsworth La BPWT SO32 325 J6
Arnaud Cl NEND PO2 423 H1
Arne Av BKME/WDN BH12 446 D1
Arne Cl KEMP RG22 127 J1
Arne Crs BKME/WDN BH12 446 D1
Arnett Av EWKG RG40 48 B1
Arnewood Bridge Rd
LYMN SO41 438 D1
Arnewood Rd SBNE BH6 449 H3
Arnheim Cl ROWN SO16 318 B4
Arnheim Rd ROWN SO16 318 C4
Arnhem Cl ALDT GU11 7 H1
Arnhem Rd NWBY RG14 3 H4
Arnold Cl FERN BH22 380 C5
Arnold Rd ELGH SO50 293 M8
FERN BH22 380 C5
PTSW SO17 319 H6
Arnolds Cl NMIL/BTOS BH25 437 K8
Arnside Rd WVILLE PO7 352 C8
Arnwood Av FAWY SO45 367 K8
Aron Cl PSF GU32 275 K6
Arragon Ct WVILLE PO7 352 E8
Arran Cl CHAM PO6 375 K7
DEAN RG23 102 F6
Arran Wy CHCH/BSGR BH23 436 F6
Arreton HLER SO31 369 G2
Arrow Cl ELGH SO50 293 M4
ITCH SO19 344 B7
Arrow La HTWY RG27 87 G1
Arrow Rd FARN GU14 90 C6
Arrowsmith La WIMB BH21 430 C1
Arrowsmith Rd WIMB BH21 430 B2
Arrow Smith Wy STHA RG19 27 J6
Arters Lawn TOTT SO40 365 M2
Arthur Cl FNM GU9 134 E7
WCLF BH2 22 F2
Arthur Rd CHCH/BSGR BH23 449 M1
ELGH SO50 293 M4
FNM GU9 134 F7
NWBY RG14 2 B6
WINC SO23 11 G4
WSHM SO15 343 H1
Arthurs Gdns HEND SO30 321 G5
Arthur St ALDT GU11 7 G3
NEND PO2 423 J1
Artillery Cl CHAM PO6 375 G8
Artillery Rd ALDT GU11 7 G1
Artists Wy AND SP10 8 E1
Arun Cl EPSF GU31 275 K6
Arundel Cl FLET GU13 89 G8
LIPH GU30 202 A8
NALR SO24 218 C4
NMIL/BTOS BH25 437 J5
Arundel Dr FHAM/PORC PO16 15 G4
Arundel Gdns DEAN RG23 104 A1
Arundel Rd CBLY GU15 71 M4
ELGH SO50 293 M2
GPORT PO12 18 B1
TOTT SO40 316 F8
Arundel St PSEA PO1 21 K1
Arundel Wy CHCH/BSGR BH23 451 L1
Arun Rd WEND SO18 320 A6
Arun Wy ROMY SO51 288 C5
Arwood Av TADY RG26 42 A7
Ascension Cl CHAM RG24 83 H7
Ascham Rd CHAR BH8 23 J2
Ascot Cl ALTN GU34 176 F6
FHAM/STUB PO14 371 G6
NWBY RG14 3 J9
Ascot Ct ALDT GU11 6 F3
Ascot Rd BDST BH18 429 L4
ELGH SO50 321 J1
HSEA PO3 423 L1
Ascupart St SHAM SO14 13 J3
Asford Gv ELGH SO50 294 C4
Ashbarn Crs WINW SO22 238 C3
Ashbourne Cl ASHV GU12 113 M5
Ashbourne Wy STHA RG19 26 E5
Ashbridge Ri CHFD SO53 264 F7
Ashburn Garth RGWD BH24 383 H2
Ashburnham Cl ITCH SO19 344 B3
Ashburton Cl FAWY SO45 367 H5
NALR SO24 218 B3
Ashburton Rd GPORT PO12 18 B8
NALR SO24 218 B3
SSEA PO5 21 G7
Ashbury Dr FARN GU14 70 D7
Ashbury Rd BOR GU35 201 J6
Ashby Pl SSEA PO5 21 H8
Ashby Rd ITCH SO19 344 F5
TOTT SO40 341 H1
Ash Church Rd ASHV GU12 113 L6
Ash Cl ASHV GU12 113 L5
BLKW GU17 69 M3
FAWY SO45 367 L8
FBDG SP6 333 L3
FHAM/STUB PO14 14 C7
GPORT PO12 18 E4
HLER SO31 345 K8
HORN PO8 352 C5
ITCH SO19 345 G2
NBAD SO52 291 L3
NTID SP9 114 F1
ROMY SO51 291 H2
RWIN SO21 266 E8
UPTN BH16 428 F8
Ash Copse HORN PO8 352 D3
Ashcroft La HORN PO8 354 B2
Ashdale Pk EWKG RG40 48 F1
Ashdell Rd ALTN GU34 176 F5
Ashdene WSHM SO15 318 A8
Ashdene Cl WIMB BH21 404 B3
Ashdene Crs ASHV GU12 113 K5
Ashdene Rd ASHV GU12 113 K5
TOTT SO40 340 F6
Ashdown FAWY SO45 392 D5
LSOL/BMARY PO13 397 H7
Ashdown Av FARN GU14 91 H6
Ashdown Cl CHFD SO53 265 H6
Ashdown Dr CHFD SO53 265 H6
Ashdown Rd CHFD SO53 265 H7
FAWY SO45 392 D6
Ashdown Ter NTID SP9 114 E3
Ashdown Wk
NMIL/BTOS BH25 438 A6
Ashdown Wy ROMY SO51 291 G1
Ashen Cl CHFD SO53 265 H8
Ashe Rd HAV PO9 377 M3
Ashfield CHAM RG24 83 L5
Ashfield Gn YTLY GU46 69 J3
Ashfield Rd AND SP10 8 A4
Ashfields RWIN SO21 167 J2
Ashford Cl CHAM PO6 375 J7
FBDG SP6 309 J7
Ashford Crs FAWY SO45 367 M5
Ashford Hill Rd STHA RG19 39 G6
Ashford Rd FBDG SP6 309 H8
SBNE BH6 449 J1
Ash Ga NTHA RG18 27 J4
Ash Green La East ASHV GU12 113 M8
Ash Green La West ASHV GU12 113 J8
Ash Green Rd ASHV GU12 113 M7
Ash Gv CHAM RG24 106 B2
KSCL RG20 59 J6
LIPH GU30 227 G5
LYMN SO41 439 H8
RGWD BH24 383 G1
TOTT SO40 341 G6
Ash Hill Rd ASHV GU12 113 L5
Ashington Cl HORN PO8 352 E5
Ashington Pk
NMIL/BTOS BH25 437 M7
Ash La TADY RG26 41 H7
TADY RG26 63 G3
THLE RG7 31 K4
Ashlawn Gdns AND SP10 9 J8
Ashlea HTWY RG27 86 J6
Ashlea Cl ELGH SO50 295 J6
Ashleigh Cl FAWY SO45 367 L8
Ashlet Gdns NMIL/BTOS BH25 438 B4
Ashlett Cl FAWY SO45 393 G5
Ashlett Rd FAWY SO45 393 G5
Ashley Cl BMTH BH1 448 C2
FRIM GU16 91 K2
WINW SO22 214 B5
HAV PO9 377 H4
HLER SO31 370 F1
HORN PO8 352 D3
RFNM GU10 133 J1
RGWD BH24 383 H2
Ashley Common Rd
NMIL/BTOS BH25 438 A4
Ashley Ct HLER SO31 345 L6
Ashley Crs ITCH SO19 345 G6
Ashleycross Cl FAWY SO45 392 B5
Ashley Dr BLKW GU17 69 M4
RGWD BH24 358 A8
Ashley Dr North RGWD BH24 381 K3
Ashley Dr South RGWD BH24 381 K3
Ashley Dr West RGWD BH24 381 K3
Ashley Dro MARL SN8 52 C4
Ashley Gdns BPWT SO32 323 K5
CHFD SO53 293 K3
Ashley La LYMN SO41 440 C4
NMIL/BTOS BH25 438 B4
Ashley Mdw ROMY SO51 262 F8
Ashley Meads
NMIL/BTOS BH25 438 B4
Ashley Pk RGWD BH24 381 L2
Ashley Rd ALTN GU34 174 E3
BMTH BH1 448 D2
FARN GU14 91 G4
NMIL/BTOS BH25 437 L6
PSTN BH14 446 B3
Ashling Cl CHAR BH8 433 G8
WVILLE PO7 351 K4
Ashling Gdns WVILLE PO7 351 K4
Ashling La NEND PO2 399 H8
Ashling Park Rd WVILLE PO7 351 K4
Ash Lodge Cl ASHV GU12 113 K7
Ash Lodge Dr ASHV GU12 113 K7
Ashlyn Cl FHAM PO15 371 M7
Ashman Rd STHA RG19 27 J5
Ashmead BOR GU35 201 J5
Ashmead Rd ROWN SO16 317 L5
Ashmeads Cl WIMB BH21 404 E2
Ashmeads Wy WIMB BH21 404 E2
Ashmoor La CHAM RG24 106 D2
Ashmore WIMB BH21 404 B4
Ashmore Av NMIL/BTOS BH25 437 M8
PLE BH15 444 E7
Ashmore Cl RSAL SP5 259 G4
Ashmore Green Rd NTHA RG18 26 D1
Ashmore Gv CHCH/BSGR BH23 436 C7
Ashmore La RSAL SP5 259 G3
Ashmore Rd WINW SO22 214 B7
Ashridge FARN GU14 90 C1
Ashridge Av NBNE BH10 432 B3
Ashridge Cl WSHM SO15 318 E8
Ash Rd ASHV GU12 7 L5
KSCL RG20 38 C5
TOTT SO40 340 F6
Ash St ASHV GU12 113 K7
Ashtead Cl FHAM/PORC PO16 373 L8
Ashton Cl BPWT SO32 296 F7
Ashton Cross ROMY SO51 288 F6
Ashton La BPWT SO32 296 F6
Ashton Rd MOOR/WNTN BH9 432 D6
Ashton Wy FHAM/STUB PO14 396 B8
Ash Tree Cl DEAN RG23 102 F8
FARN GU14 89 M5
HASM GU27 205 J7
Ashtree Cl NMIL/BTOS BH25 438 B6
Ash Tree Gv KSCL RG20 35 L1
Ash Tree Rd AND SP10 118 B8
WEND SO18 319 K7
Ashurst Bridge Rd TOTT SO40 341 G2
Ashurst Cl WINW SO22 214 C5
ITCH SO19 344 E7
TADY RG26 41 K8
TOTT SO40 340 F6
Ashurst Rd ASHV GU12 113 J4
CHAM PO6 375 J8
CHAR BH8 433 H5
FERN BH22 380 B5
Ashwell Av CBLY GU15 71 J2
Ashwood FHAM PO15 371 J3
HLER SO31 371 G6
Ashwood Cl HAV PO9 376 F5
HISD PO11 425 L5
Ashwood Dr BDST BH18 430 A4
NWBY RG14 3 M2
Ashwood Gdns ROWN SO16 318 D5
TOTT SO40 341 G2
Ashwood Wy DEAN RG23 104 C1
Ashworth Dr STHA RG19 26 F6
Aspen Av HLER SO31 370 B8
Aspen Cl HEND SO30 346 B1
BOR GU35 201 J7
RWIN SO21 266 F8
Aspen Dr VWD BH31 356 F2
Aspen Gdns BKME/WDN BH12 446 E1
HTWY RG27 86 A6
Aspengrove
LSOL/BMARY PO13 397 J7
Aspen Holt ROWN SO16 318 F3
Aspen Pl NMIL/BTOS BH25 437 M7
Aspen Rd BKME/WDN BH12 446 E1
Aspen Wk TOTT SO40 316 A8
Aspen Wy BKME/WDN BH12 446 E1
HORN PO8 352 E3
Aspin Wy BLKW GU17 69 L3
Astbury Av BKME/WDN BH12 431 L8
Aster Rd KEMP RG22 126 F1
ROWN SO16 319 H4
Astley St SSEA PO5 21 G4
Aston Md CHCH/BSGR BH23 434 C4
Aston Rd WVILLE PO7 352 B7
Astor Crs RAND SP11 92 D6
Astra Ct FAWY SO45 367 L3
Astral Gdns HLER SO31 369 K5
Astrid Cl HISD PO11 426 A5
Asturias Wy SHAM SO14 13 L6
Asylum Rd WSHM SO15 343 L2
Atalanta Cl ENEY PO4 424 A3
Atbara Rd FLET GU13 110 F4
Atheling Rd FAWY SO45 367 L4
Athelstan Rd ITCH SO19 344 C1
SBNE BH6 449 K3
Athena Av WVILLE PO7 376 D5
Athena Cl ELGH SO50 294 F5
Atherfield Rd ROWN SO16 317 K5
Atherley Ct WSHM SO15 318 D8
Atherley Rd HISD PO11 425 J3
WSHM SO15 343 H2
Athlone Ct RAND SP11 96 A8
Atholl Ct AND SP10 118 F5
Atholl Rd BOR GU35 201 J7
Atkinson Cl GPORT PO12 18 D8
Atkins Pl FHAM PO15 372 A5
Atlantic Cl SHAM SO14 13 K8
Atlantic Park Vw
WEND SO18 319 M6
Atlantis Av WVILLE PO7 376 D6
Atrebatti Rd SHST GU47 49 M7
Attenborough Cl FARN GU14 89 G5
Attfield Cl ASHV GU12 113 J7
Attlee Gdns FLET GU13 110 E4
Attwood Cl BSTK RG21 4 A9
BSTK RG21 104 E4
FBDG SP6 333 K3
Attwoods Dro RWIN SO21 238 C8
Aubrey Cl HISD PO11 425 J4
LYMN SO41 454 E4
Auchinleck Wy ALDT GU11 6 B2
Auckland Cl NTID SP9 114 F2
Auckland Pl BROC SO42 387 L7
Auckland Rd WSHM SO15 342 D1
Auckland Rd East SSEA PO5 21 H8
Auckland Rd West SSEA PO5 21 G8
Auclum Cl THLE RG7 31 L6
Auclum La THLE RG7 31 L6
Audemer Ct RGWD BH24 359 G8
Audley Cl NWBY RG14 26 A3
Audret Cl FHAM/PORC PO16 397 M2
Augustine Rd CHAM PO6 376 A7
SHAM SO14 343 M2
Augustine Wy AND SP10 118 C5
Augustus Dr DEAN RG23 104 B1
Augustus Gdns CBLY GU15 71 M3
Augustus Wy CHFD SO53 293 K1
Aukland Av BROC SO42 387 L7
Auklet Cl KEMP RG22 126 E1
Auriol Dr CHAM PO6 376 E8
Austen Av WINW SO22 238 B5
Austen Cl TOTT SO40 341 H2
WINC SO23 11 H2
Austen Gdns HLER SO31 347 G8
Austen Gv KEMP RG22 104 D6
Austen Rd FARN GU14 90 D2
Austerberry Wy
LSOL/BMARY PO13 397 H8
Auster Cl CHCH/BSGR BH23 451 G1
Austin Av PSTN BH14 446 A6
Austin Ct CHAM PO6 374 F7
Australia Cl PSEA PO1 21 J1
Aust Rd FHAM/STUB PO14 14 A7
Autumn Cl FERN BH22 405 M1
Autumn Rd BWD BH11 431 H5
TOTT SO40 342 E7
Avalon PSTN BH14 446 B8
Avebury Av NBNE BH10 432 C2
Avebury Gdns CHFD SO53 264 F7
Aveley La FNM GU9 158 E1
Avenger Cl CHFD SO53 293 G3
Avens Cl ELGH SO50 321 H2
Avenue C FAWY SO45 368 C8
Avenue Cl AND SP10 8 D5
LIPH GU30 226 E4
Avenue Ct GPORT PO12 18 C7
Avenue D FAWY SO45 368 C8
Avenue De Caen SSEA PO5 21 H9
Avenue E FAWY SO45 368 C8
Avenue La WCLF BH2 22 D6
Avenue Rd ALTN GU34 153 K4
BROC SO42 387 K7
CHCH/BSGR BH23 437 G7
CHCH/BSGR BH23 449 L1
FARN GU14 91 G4
FHAM/STUB PO14 14 F6
FLET GU13 88 E6
WINW SO22 10 D6
GPORT PO12 19 G2
GSHT GU26 204 A5
HISD PO11 401 K5
LYMN SO41 440 B4
NMIL/BTOS BH25 437 L5
SHAM SO14 318 F8
WCLF BH2 22 D6
WIMB BH21 404 B4
Avenue Sucy CBLY GU15 70 D4
The Avenue ALDT GU11 7 K7
AND SP10 8 D5
BPWT SO32 297 G8
CBLY GU15 70 E4
CCLF BH13 446 F8
CWTH RG45 49 K3
EPSF GU31 275 L5
FERN BH22 380 B5
FHAM PO15 14 E6
FHAM/STUB PO14 14 F6
FLET GU13 88 D7
GPORT PO12 18 C7
GSHT GU26 204 A5
HASM GU27 228 C1
LIPH GU30 226 D4
MOOR/WNTN BH9 432 D5
NALR SO24 218 A3
RFNM GU10 158 B5
NTID SP9 114 D4
OVTN RG25 127 J5
PTSW SO17 318 E6
RAND SP11 95 K6
RCCH PO18 379 M7
RWIN SO21 145 H5
RWIN SO21 266 F2
THLE RG7 43 L3
Avery Cl EWKG RG40 48 C2
Avery La GPORT PO12 421 K1
Avington Cl ELGH SO50 294 C3
Avington Ct ROWN SO16 318 E4
Avocet Crs SHST GU47 50 A8
Avocet Quay EMRTH PO10 402 E1
Avocet Wk LSOL/BMARY PO13 396 E6
Avon Av RGWD BH24 382 B5
Avonborne Wy CHFD SO53 265 G8
Avon Buildings
CHCH/BSGR BH23 450 A1
Avon Castle Dr RGWD BH24 382 B4
Avon Cswy CHCH/BSGR BH23 433 M1
Avon Cl ASHV GU12 113 J7
FARN GU14 90 B1
LSOL/BMARY PO13 420 D3
LYMN SO41 440 A5
PSF GU32 275 K6
Avon Crs ROMY SO51 291 H1
Avondale ASHV GU12 113 J1
Avondale Rd ALDT GU11 7 H5
FLET GU13 88 F6
PSEA PO1 423 K1
WVILLE PO7 352 D8
Avon Gdns CHCH/BSGR BH23 409 M7
Avon Gn CHFD SO53 293 J3
Avon Meade FBDG SP6 309 K6
Avon Pk RGWD BH24 382 B2
Avon Rd CHAR BH8 448 B2
DEAN RG23 103 G7
FERN BH22 380 C7
FNM GU9 134 F7
NTID SP9 114 D3
WEND SO18 319 L7
Avon Rd East
CHCH/BSGR BH23 434 E8
Avon Rd West
CHCH/BSGR BH23 434 D8
Avon Run Cl CHCH/BSGR BH23 451 G3
Avon Run Rd
CHCH/BSGR BH23 451 G3
Avon Valley Pth RGWD BH24 382 D4
RSAL SP5 256 E5
Avon Vw FBDG SP6 310 C7
Avon Wy HEND SO30 320 D6
Avonway NWBY RG14 3 M1
Avon Wy THLE RG7 30 B2
Award Rd FLET GU13 110 E3
WIMB BH21 405 K3
Awbridge Rd HAV PO9 377 G4
Axford Cl CHAR BH8 433 H5
Ayesgarth FLET GU13 111 G3
Ayjay Cl ALDT GU11 7 G7
Aylen Rd HSEA PO3 399 L6
Aylesbury Rd BMTH BH1 448 C4
NEND PO2 399 K8
Aylesford Wy STHA RG19 27 K6
Aylesham Wy YTLY GU46 68 E2
Ayling Cl LSOL/BMARY PO13 421 G1
Ayling Ct FNM GU9 6 D7

Ayling Hl *ALDT* GU11............... 6 C4
Ayling La *ALDT* GU11............... 6 D5
Aylings Ct *DEAN* RG23......... 104 A4
Aylward's Dr *ALTN* GU34...... 198 A5
Aylward St *PSEA* PO1............. 20 D1 🄳
Aylwin Cl *BSTK* RG21........... 104 F4
Ayres La *KSCL* RG20................ 37 J8
Ayrshire Gdns *FARN* GU14....... 89 G4
Aysgarth Rd *WVILLE* PO7...... 352 D4
Aysha Cl *NMIL/BTOS* BH25.... 437 M7
Azalea Av *BOR* GU35............. 201 M3
Azalea Cl *HAV* PO9............... 378 A4
   RGWD........................ 381 L3
Azalea Dr *HASM* GU27......... 204 C8 🄳
Azalea Gdns *FLET* GU13....... 111 G3
Azalea Wy *CBLY* GU15............ 71 L2

B

Babbs Md *FNM* GU9............. 134 D6
Babs Flds *RFNM* GU10......... 156 F5
Bach Cl *KEMP* RG22............. 127 J1
Back La *HUNG* RG17............... 34 C1
   LYMN SO41...................... 413 G6
   RFNM GU10.................... 157 L8
   OVTN RG25..................... 153 J3
   RAND............................... 73 G2
   RAND SP11..................... 117 H1
   ROMY SO51.................... 233 J3
   THLE RG7......................... 29 K2
   THLE RG7......................... 40 E5
   THLE RG7......................... 42 F4
   WHAM PO17.................... 374 C2
Back of the Walls *SHAM* SO14... 13 C5
Back St *WINC* SO23............. 238 E4
Bacon Cl *ITCH* SO19............ 344 D7
   SHST GU47........................ 70 A2
Bacon La *HISD* PO11........... 425 H5
   RFNM GU10.................... 180 F4
Badbury Cl *BDST* BH18......... 430 A5
Badbury Vw *WIMB* BH21...... 404 B3
Baddeley Cl *NBAD* SO52...... 291 L3
Baddesley Rd *CHFD* SO53.... 264 F7
Baden Cl *NMIL/BTOS* BH25.. 437 M7 🄳
Baden Powell Rd *LISS* GU33... 225 H6
Bader Cl *HEND* SO30........... 321 H8 🄳
Bader Rd *CFDH* BH17........... 430 C8
Bader Wy *FHAM* PO15......... 371 J7
Badger Brow *WVILLE* PO7.... 376 E2
Badger Cl *ALTN* GU34.......... 197 H5
   ELGH SO50....................... 294 E6
   FHAM PO15...................... 14 A3
Badger Farm Rd *WINW* SO22... 238 A3
Badger's Bank *CHAM* RG24.... 83 L8
Badgers Cl *FLET* GU13............ 88 E8
   LYMN SO41..................... 413 G6
   RGWD............................ 381 K3
Badgers Copse *CBLY* GU15...... 71 H5
   NMIL/BTOS BH25............ 438 A2
Badgers Gld *THLE* RG7........... 31 K6
Badgers Holt *YTLY* GU46...... 68 E3 🄳
Badgers Run *HLER* SO31...... 370 C2
Badgers Sett *CWTH* RG45....... 49 J5 🄳
The Badgers *HLER* SO31....... 369 G2 🄳
Badgers Wk *FAWY* SO45...... 367 K6 🄳
   FERN............................... 406 C1
Badger Wy *RFNM* GU10....... 111 C8
   VWD BH31...................... 356 D3
Badgerwood Dr *FRIM* GU16.... 71 J6
Badminston Dro *FAWY* SO45... 393 G8
Badminston La *FAWY* SO45... 393 G7
Badshear La *NALR* SO24...... 242 D1
Badshot Lea Rd *FNM* GU9.... 135 K3
Badshot Pk *FNM* GU9.......... 135 K2
Baffins Rd *HSEA* PO3.......... 423 L2
Bagber Rd *TOTT* SO40......... 341 K1
Bagmore La *OVTN* RG25...... 152 D3
Bagnols Wy *NWBY* RG14......... 2 A4
Bagwell La *ODIM* RG29....... 109 H1
Baigent Cl *WINC* SO23.......... 11 L7
Bailey Cl *FRIM* GU16............. 71 J8
   WINW SO22..................... 238 C2
   HEND SO30..................... 346 D2
   NMIL/BTOS BH25............ 438 B4 🄳
Bailey Crs *PLE* BH15............ 445 H1
Bailey Dr *CHCH/BSGR* BH23... 449 L1
Baileys Rd *BLKW* GU17.......... 69 L4
Bailey's Rd *SSEA* PO5............ 21 J3
Baily Av *NTHA* RG18............. 26 E7
Bain Av *CBLY* GU15................ 70 E7
Baird Av *KEMP* RG22............ 127 H6
Baird Rd *FARN* GU14.............. 90 F2
Baker Cl *BWD* BH11............. 431 K3
Bakers Dro *ROWN* SO16....... 317 K3
Bakers Farm Rd *VWD* BH31... 356 C1 🄳
Bakers Fld *LISS* GU33.......... 224 E6
Baker St *NEND* PO2.............. 423 H1
Balaclava Rd *WEND* SO18.... 344 E1
Balcombe Rd *CCLF* BH13..... 446 F5
Balderton Cl *NEND* PO2...... 399 K4 🄳
Baldreys *FNM* GU9.............. 134 D8
Baldwin Cl *CHCH/BSGR* BH23... 450 C2
Balfour Cl *CHCH/BSGR* BH23... 450 A4
   LSOL/BMARY PO13......... 421 H2 🄳
Balfour Crs *NWBY* RG14........ 36 F3
Balfour Dr *LISS* GU33.......... 248 A4
Balfour Rd *ITCH* SO19......... 344 F3
   MOOR/WNTN BH9............ 432 D7
   NEND PO2....................... 399 J2
Balintore Ct *SHST* GU47........ 70 A1 🄳
Balksbury Hl *RAND* SP11...... 142 C3
Balksbury Rd *RAND* SP11.... 142 D3
Ballam Cl *UPTN* BH16.......... 444 B1
Ballantyne Rd *FARN* GU14...... 90 D2
Ballard Cl *KEMP* RG22......... 104 B5
   NMIL/BTOS BH25............ 437 M4
   ROWN SO16.................... 317 H1
Ballard Rd *CBLY* GU15........... 51 K8
   PLE BH15........................ 445 J7
Balliol Cl *FHAM/STUB* PO14... 371 G7
Balliol Rd *NEND* PO2........... 423 H1
Balliol Wy *SHST* GU47............ 50 B7
Balloon Rd *FARN* GU14.......... 90 E6
Balmer Lawn Rd *BROC* SO42... 387 M5

Balmoral Av *CHAR* BH8........ 433 J7
Balmoral Cl *ALTN* GU34....... 176 C5
   CHFD SO53...................... 265 C8 🄳
   LSOL/BMARY PO13........ 397 H5
   ROWN SO16................... 318 B3
Balmoral Crs *FNM* GU9....... 134 E2 🄳
Balmoral Dr *FRIM* GU16........ 71 H8
   WVILLE PO7.................... 376 A4
Balmoral Rd *AND* SP10............ 9 G5
   ASHV GU12..................... 113 K4
   FHAM PO15...................... 14 D2
   PSTN BH14..................... 446 B5
Balmoral Wk
   NMIL/BTOS BH25............ 437 K5 🄳
Balmoral Wy *KEMP* RG22.... 126 F1
   PSF GU32........................ 275 L4
   ROWN SO16.................... 317 J2
Balston Rd *PSTN* BH14........ 445 M3
Baltic Rd *NEND* PO2............ 320 D6
Bamber La *ALTN* GU34......... 156 A4
Banbury Av *ITCH* SO19........ 345 G4
Banbury Cl *FRIM* GU16.......... 91 K1 🄳
Bangor Rd *WSHM* SO15....... 342 F2
Banister Gdns *WSHM* SO15.. 343 K1
Banister Rd *WSHM* SO15..... 343 K1
Bankhill Dr *LYMN* SO41....... 440 B3
Bank Side *EWKG* RG40.......... 48 C2
Bankside *FNM* GU9................. 6 C8
Bank Side *WEND* SO18......... 319 J4
Bankside Rd
   MOOR/WNTN BH9............ 432 E5
Banks Rd *CCLF* BH13........... 457 G5
The Banks *ROMY* SO51........ 260 F3
Bank St *BPWT* SO32............ 323 J1
Bankview *LYMN* SO41.......... 440 B2
Bannerman Rd *PSF* GU32..... 275 L4 🄳
Banning St *ROMY* SO51....... 290 D2
Bannister Gdns *HTWY* RG27... 48 B8 🄳
   YTLY GU46........................ 69 J3 🄳
Bannister Pl *THLE* RG7.......... 40 C2 🄳
Bannister Rd *THLE* RG7......... 31 J6
Banstead Rd *WIMB* BH21..... 429 L3
Bapaume Rd *HSEA* PO3....... 399 K3
Baptist Hl *RAND* SP11........... 97 L6
Barbara Cl *FLET* GU13.......... 111 G2
Barbe Baker Av *HEND* SO30.. 320 B6
Barbel Av *BSTK* RG21.............. 5 K7
Barberry Cl *FLET* GU13......... 110 F2
Barberry Wy *BLKW* GU17....... 70 C5
   VWD BH31...................... 357 G3
Barbour Cl *ODIM* RG29........ 131 H1
Barcelona Cl *AND* SP10............ 9 K3
Bardon Rd *FHAM/STUB* PO14... 14 B8
Bardsley Dr *FNM* GU9.......... 134 D8
Bardwell Rd *KEMP* RG22..... 104 B4
The Baredown *HTWY* RG27... 107 J1
Bar End Rd *WINC* SO23........ 239 G3
Barfield Cl *WINC* SO23......... 239 G2
Barfield Rd *NTHA* RG18......... 26 D4
Barfields *LYMN* SO41........... 440 C4
Barfleur Cl *FHAM* PO15........ 14 A3
Barfleur Rd *FHAM/STUB* PO14... 396 E3
   FLET GU13........................ 89 J8
Barford La *RSAL* SP5........... 256 F8
Bargates *CHCH/BSGR* BH23.. 449 M1
Bargate St *SHAM* SO14......... 12 F4
Barge Cl *ALDT* GU11............ 113 H3
Barge La *THLE* RG7................ 45 K3
Barham Cl *GPORT* PO12....... 421 M2 🄳
Barham Rd *PSF* GU32........... 275 L5
Barham Wy *NEND* PO2......... 399 H4
Baring Cl *RWIN* SO21........... 170 F4
   RWIN SO21...................... 216 F1
Baring Rd *SBNE* BH6............ 449 M4
   WINC SO23...................... 11 K9
Barker Cl *WHIT* RG2.............. 47 H1
Barker Mill Cl *ROWN* SO16... 317 K2
Barkis Md *SHST* GU47............ 50 B6 🄳
Barle Cl *WEND* SO18............ 320 A7
Barley Down Dr *WINW* SO22... 238 C4
Barley Mow Cl *HTWY* RG27.... 87 L8
Barley Mow Hl *BOR* GU35.... 202 C2
Barley Wy *FARN* GU14............ 89 G3
Barlow Cl *FHAM/STUB* PO14... 395 M6
Barlows La *AND* SP10........... 142 E3
Barlows Rd *TADY* RG26.......... 61 L1
Barnard Cl *FRIM* GU16........... 71 J8
Barnbrook Rd *HLER* SO31.... 370 C4
Barn Cl *CBLY* GU15................ 71 H2
   EMRTH PO10.................... 378 B8
Barn Close La *KSCL* RG20..... 55 L8
Barn Crs *NWBY* RG14............ 37 G1
Barncroft *FNM* GU9............. 134 F7 🄳
   RAND............................. 116 F3
Barncroft Wy *HAV* PO9........ 377 H5
Barnes Cl *FARN* GU14............ 91 J4
   HLER SO31...................... 370 B4
   ITCH SO19...................... 345 G4
   NBNE BH10...................... 432 B5
   WINC SO23...................... 238 D3
Barnes Crs *NBNE* BH10........ 432 B5
   WIMB BH21..................... 404 C4
Barnes La *HLER* SO31.......... 370 C3
   LYMN SO41..................... 439 G8
Barnes Rd *FRIM* GU16............ 71 H8
   ITCH SO19...................... 345 G2
   NBNE BH10...................... 432 B5
   PSEA PO1........................ 423 J2
Barnes Wallis Rd
   FHAM PO15..................... 371 H4 🄳
Barnes Wy *HAV* PO9............ 377 G5
Barnet Side La *PSF* GU32..... 246 C3
Barnetts Wood La *NALR* SO24... 195 M8
Barney Evans Crs *HORN* PO8... 352 B5
Barneyhayes La *TOTT* SO40... 314 F8
Barnfield *CHCH/BSGR* BH23.. 436 B8
   YTLY GU46........................ 69 G3 🄳
Barnfield Cl *ALTN* GU34....... 156 B4 🄳
   EMRTH PO10.................... 379 J6
   ITCH SO19...................... 344 C7
Barnfield Ct *FHAM/STUB* PO14... 14 D8
   ITCH SO19...................... 344 D7
Barnfield Ri *AND* SP10............ 8 C9
Barnfield Rd *EPSH* GU31...... 276 B5
   ITCH SO19...................... 344 C7

Barnfield Wy *ITCH* SO19...... 344 D7
Barn Fold *HORN* PO8............ 352 F7
Barn Green Cl *WVILLE* PO7... 351 K4
Barn La *ALTN* GU34.............. 196 C7
   DEAN RG23..................... 102 F8
Barn Meadow Cl *FLET* GU13... 110 E5
Barn Owl Wy *THLE* RG7......... 31 L5
Barn Piece *NBAD* SO52........ 292 C2
Barn Rd *BDST* BH18............. 429 M5
Barnsfield Crs *TOTT* SO40.... 341 G1
Barnsfield Rd *RGWD*............ 381 L7
Barnside *LISS* GU33............. 248 E5
Barnsland *HEND* SO30......... 320 B6
Barnsley Cl *FRIM* GU16.......... 91 L7
Barns Rd *FERN* BH22........... 406 E2
The Barns *OVTN* RG25......... 126 C8
Baroda Rd *NTID* SP9............ 114 B4
Baron Rd *HLER* SO31........... 369 K5
Barons Md *ROWN* SO16....... 317 K5
Barons Rd *BWD* BH11.......... 431 H2
Barossa Rd *CBLY* GU15.......... 71 G1
Barracane Dr *CWTH* RG45..... 49 L4
Barrack La *RGWD* BH24....... 383 H4
Barrack Rd *ALDT* GU11............ 6 C2
   CHCH/BSGR BH23........... 434 C8
   FERN BH22...................... 406 E6
Barracks Rd *STHA* RG19........ 38 C4
Barra Cl *DEAN* RG23........... 102 F6
Barrie Cl *HLER* SO31............ 347 G8 🄳
Barrie Rd *FNM* GU9.............. 134 D1
Barrington Cl *ELGH* SO50..... 293 L3
Barron Pl *CHAM* RG24........... 82 A8
Barrow Down Gdns *ITCH* SO19... 345 J5
Barrow Dr *CHAR* BH8........... 433 K6
Barrowgate Wy *CHAR* BH8... 433 H5
Barrow Hl *RAND* SP11......... 142 D8
Barrow Hill Rd *TOTT* SO40... 315 J5
Barrow Rd *CHAR* BH8.......... 433 K6
Barrows La *LYMN* SO41........ 438 F1
   RSAL SP5......................... 287 G2
Barrow Vw *FERN* BH22........ 405 L2 🄳
Barrow Wy *CHAR* BH8.......... 433 K6
Barrs Av *NMIL/BTOS* BH25.. 437 L4
Barrs Wood Dr
   NMIL/BTOS BH25............ 437 M4
Barrs Wood Rd
   NMIL/BTOS BH25............ 437 M4
Barry Gdns *BDST* BH18........ 429 K3
Barry Rd *ITCH* SO19............ 344 F3
Barry Wy *KEMP* RG22.......... 127 J1
Barters Cl *ROWN* SO16........ 317 L7
Barters La *BDST* BH18.......... 429 K4
Bartholomew Cl *HASM* GU27... 205 G8 🄳
Bartholomew St *NWBY* RG14... 2 D6
Bartlemy Cl *NWBY* RG14......... 2 A9
Bartlemy Rd *NWBY* RG14....... 2 A9
Bartlett Cl *FHAM* PO15.......... 14 C2
Bartlett Dr *LTDN* BH7........... 433 M8
The Bartletts *HLER* SO31..... 369 L6
Bartley Av *TOTT* SO40......... 341 J2
Bartley Rd *TOTT* SO40......... 340 A5
Bartley Wy *HTWY* RG27......... 86 B8
Bartok Cl *KEMP* RG22.......... 104 D7
Barton Cl *ALDT* GU11.............. 6 A3
   AND SP10........................ 118 C5 🄳
   ROMY SO51.................... 263 G8 🄳
Barton Common La
   NMIL/BTOS BH25............ 437 M8
Barton Common Rd
   NMIL/BTOS BH25............ 453 G1
Barton Court Av
   NMIL/BTOS BH25............ 452 E1
Barton Court Rd
   NMIL/BTOS BH25............ 452 F1
Barton Crs *WEND* SO18....... 319 L7
Barton Cft *NMIL/BTOS* BH25... 452 F1
Barton Cross *HORN* PO8...... 352 F5
Barton Dr *HEND* SO30......... 346 B1
   HLER SO31...................... 369 K5
   NMIL/BTOS BH25............ 437 K8
Barton Dro *RWIN* SO21........ 167 M4
Barton Gn *NMIL/BTOS* BH25... 452 F2
Barton La *NMIL/BTOS* BH25... 437 K8
Barton Rd *ELGH* SO50.......... 294 B5
Barton's Dr *YTLY* GU46.......... 69 G4
Bartonside Rd
   NMIL/BTOS BH25............ 437 G8
Bartons La *CHAM* RG24......... 83 M8
Bartons Rd *FBDG* SP6.......... 309 L7
   HAV PO9......................... 377 L3
Bartons Wy *FARN* GU14......... 89 M1
Barton Wy *NMIL/BTOS* BH25... 437 K8
Barton Wood Rd
   NMIL/BTOS BH25............ 452 D1
Bartram Rd *TOTT* SO40........ 341 L2
Barwell Cl *CWTH* RG45.......... 49 J4
Barwell Gv *EMRTH* PO10..... 378 C5 🄳
Bascott Cl *BWD* BH11........... 431 L7
Bascott Rd *BWD* BH11......... 431 K7
Bashley Common Rd
   NMIL/BTOS BH25............ 411 L8
Bashley Cross Rd
   CHCH/BSGR BH23........... 437 H3
Bashley Dr *NMIL/BTOS* BH25... 437 M2
Bashley Rd *NMIL/BTOS* BH25... 437 L1
Basingbourne Cl *FLET* GU13... 110 F2
Basingbourne Rd *FLET* GU13... 110 E3
Basing Dean *ALTN* GU34...... 245 K3
Basing Dr *ALDT* GU11.............. 7 H8
Basing Rd *CHAM* RG24............ 5 M6
   HAV PO9......................... 377 J3
Basingstoke Rd *ALTN* GU34... 176 A5
   HTWY RG27...................... 65 J2
   KSCL RG20....................... 59 K6
   RWIN SO21..................... 191 M4
   TADY RG26....................... 41 K3
   THLE RG7......................... 29 K7
   WINC SO23..................... 215 J2
Basing Vw *BSTK* RG21............. 5 H5
Basingwell St *BPWT* SO32.... 323 H1
Basin St *NEND* PO2.............. 399 H8
Bassenthwaite Gdns
   BOR GU35....................... 201 J3 🄳
Bassett Av *ROWN* SO16....... 318 E3
Bassett Cl *FRIM* GU16............ 71 H8

   ROWN SO16.................... 318 E4
Bassett Crs East *ROWN* SO16... 318 E3
Bassett Crs West *ROWN* SO16... 318 E3
Bassett Dl *ROWN* SO16........ 318 E2
Bassett Gdns *ROWN* SO16... 318 D4
Bassett Gn *ROWN* SO16....... 319 G3
Bassett Green Cl *ROWN* SO16... 318 F3
Bassett Green Dr *ROWN* SO16... 318 F3
Bassett Green Rd *ROWN* SO16... 318 F2
Bassett Heath Av *ROWN* SO16... 318 E1
Bassett Meadow *ROWN* SO16... 318 E3
Bassett Ms *ROWN* SO16...... 318 E3
Bassett Rd *BKME/WDN* BH12... 446 A2
Bassett Rw *ROWN* SO16....... 318 E2
Bassett Wood Dr *ROWN* SO16... 318 E1
Bassett Wood Rd *ROWN* SO16... 318 E2
Bat & Ball La *FNM* GU9........ 158 D2
   RFNM GU10.................... 158 D3
Batchelor Crs *BWD* BH11..... 431 K5
Batchelor Dr *CHAM* RG24...... 106 B5
Batchelor Gn *HLER* SO31..... 345 L8 🄳
Batchelor Rd *BWD* BH11...... 431 K5
Batcombe Cl *BWD* BH11...... 431 J5
Bath Cl *ITCH* SO19.............. 344 F7
Bath Hill Rbt *BMTH* BH1........ 22 F7
Bathing La *PSEA* PO1............ 20 A1
Bath La *FHAM/PORC* PO16.... 15 M6
Bath Lane (Lower)
   FHAM/PORC PO16........... 15 M7
Bath Rd *BMTH* BH1............... 22 F7
   CBLY GU15........................ 70 F2
   EMRTH PO10.................... 378 D8
   ENEY PO4....................... 425 K5
   ITCH SO19...................... 344 D7
   LYMN SO41..................... 440 D5
   NTHA RG18....................... 26 C4
   NWBY RG14...................... 37 G2
   THLE RG7.......................... 28 C6
Bath Sq *PSEA* PO1................ 20 B4
Bath St *SHAM* SO14............ 343 L1
Bathurst Cl *HISD* PO11........ 425 J5
Batsford Rd *RAND* SP11......... 97 L6
Battenburg Av *NEND* PO2.... 399 K6
Battenburg Rd *GPORT* PO12... 19 G2 🄳
Batten Cl *CHCH/BSGR* BH23... 435 H8
Batten Rd *RSAL* SP5............. 256 D8
Battens Wy *HAV* PO9........... 377 K4
Batterley Dro *WIMB* BH21.... 332 D4
Battery End *NWBY* RG14........ 37 G2
Battery Hl *BPWT* SO32......... 297 G8
Battery Rw *PSEA* PO1............ 20 C6
Battle Cl *HLER* SO31............ 370 D4
   NWBY RG14...................... 25 G4
Battle La *NWBY* RG14............ 36 F2
Baughurst Rd *TADY* RG26....... 41 H8
   THLE RG7.......................... 42 D2
B Av *FAWY* SO45................. 392 B3
Baverstock Rd
   BKME/WDN BH12............ 431 M8
Baverstocks *ALTN* GU34...... 176 F2
The Baxendales *NWBY* RG14.... 3 J8
Baxter Rd *ITCH* SO19........... 345 J4
Baybridge La *BPWT* SO32.... 268 D6
Baybridge Rd *HAV* PO9........ 377 M3
Bay Cl *ITCH* SO19................ 344 E5
   UPTN BH16..................... 444 A2
Bayfield Av *FRIM* GU16.......... 71 H6
Bayford Cl *FARN* GU14........... 70 D7
Bayly Av *FHAM/PORC* PO16... 398 D2
Baynard Cl *BSTK* RG21............ 5 G4
Bay Rd *GPORT* PO12............ 18 A6
   ITCH SO19...................... 344 E5
Bays Rd *LYMN* SO41............ 440 A5
Baythorn Cl *NEND* PO2....... 423 H1 🄳
Bay Trees *ITCH* SO19........... 345 J1
Bay Tree Wy *CHCH/BSGR* BH23... 436 F2
Baywood Cl *FARN* GU14........ 89 M3 🄳
Bazaar Rd *EMRTH* PO10....... 90 D8
Beach Av *NMIL/BTOS* BH25... 452 E1
Beach Dr *CHAM* PO6............ 374 D8
Beach Rd *CCLF* BH13........... 446 F8
   EMRTH PO10.................... 378 C8
   HISD PO11...................... 425 J5
   LSOL/BMARY PO13......... 420 C3
   SSEA PO5........................ 21 K9
Beach's Crs *TADY* RG26......... 62 D5
Beacon Bottom *HLER* SO31... 370 E1
Beacon Cl *HLER* SO31.......... 370 E2
   LYMN SO41..................... 439 H7
   RFNM GU10.................... 158 D3
Beacon Ct *FBDG* SP6........... 309 K5
Beacon Dr *CHCH/BSGR* BH23... 451 L1
Beacon Gdns *BDST* BH18..... 429 J5
Beacon Hill Ct *GSHT* GU26... 204 A2
Beacon Hill La *BPWT* SO32... 270 E8
   BPWT SO32..................... 299 G2
   UPTN BH16..................... 428 F5
Beacon Hill Rd *FLET* GU13... 111 G4
   GSHT GU26..................... 203 M2
Beacon Mt *HLER* SO31......... 370 E2
Beacon Park Crs *UPTN* BH16... 428 E8
Beacon Park Rd *UPTN* BH16... 428 E8
Beacon Rd *BDST* BH18........ 429 H5
   FARN................................. 90 E8
   HEND SO30..................... 320 C8
   UPTN BH16..................... 444 A1
   WCLF BH2........................ 22 D7
Beaconsfield Av *CHAM* PO6... 399 L1
Beaconsfield Rd
   BKME/WDN BH12............ 446 C3
   BSTK RG21...................... 105 G4
   CHCH/BSGR BH23........... 450 A1
   FHAM/PORC PO16........... 15 J8
   WVILLE PO7.................... 352 C8 🄳

Beam Hollow *FNM* GU9....... 134 F1 🄳
Beamish Rd *CFDH* BH17....... 430 D8
Beancroft Rd *STHA* RG19....... 27 G6
Bear Cross Av *BWD* BH11.... 431 J2
Bear Hl *KSCL* RG20................ 59 H7
Bear La *FNM* GU9................ 134 E5
   NWBY RG14........................ 2 E4
Bearslane Cl *TOTT* SO40...... 316 C7
Bearwood *FLET* GU13............ 88 F7
Beatrice Rd *ENEY* PO4........... 21 M7
   WSHM SO15.................... 343 G1 🄳
Beattie Ri *HEND* SO30......... 321 H6 🄳
Beatty Cl *HLER* SO31........... 370 F4
   RGWD BH24.................... 359 G8
Beatty Dr *GPORT* PO12......... 18 B7
Beatty Rd *MOOR/WNTN* BH9... 432 F7
Beauchamp Av
   LSOL/BMARY PO13......... 397 G6
Beauchamps Gdns *LTDN* BH7... 433 L8
Beauclerk Gn *HTWY* RG27..... 87 H7
Beaucroft La *WIMB* BH21..... 404 C2
Beaucroft Rd *BPWT* SO32.... 323 K5
   WIMB BH21..................... 404 B2
Beaufighter Rd *FARN* GU14.... 90 D8
Beaufort Av *FHAM/PORC* PO16... 14 C2
Beaufort Dr *BPWT* SO32...... 297 H8
   WIMB BH21..................... 404 A3
Beaufort Rd *FLET* GU13....... 111 G1
   FNM GU9........................ 134 F5
   HAV PO9........................... 16 A3
   BOR GU35....................... 201 J3
   SBNE BH6........................ 449 H5
   SSEA PO5.......................... 21 K9 🄳
   WINC SO23..................... 238 C2
Beaufoys Av *FERN* BH22...... 406 A1
Beaufoys Cl *FERN* BH22...... 406 A1
Beaufront Cl *CBLY* GU15........ 71 K1
Beaufront Rd *CBLY* GU15....... 71 K1
Beaulieu Av *CHCH/BSGR* BH23... 449 K1
   FHAM/PORC PO16........... 373 L8
   HAV PO9......................... 377 H2
Beaulieu Cl *WINW* SO22...... 214 C4 🄳
   ROWN SO16.................... 318 A3
Beaulieu Ct *AND* SP10......... 119 H6 🄳
Beaulieu Gdns *BLKW* GU17.... 69 M3
Beaulieu Pl
   LSOL/BMARY PO13......... 397 G6 🄳
Beaulieu Rd *BROC* SO42...... 365 K8
   BROC.............................. 391 G4
   CHCH/BSGR BH23........... 449 K1
   ELGH SO50..................... 293 M4 🄳
   FAWY SO45...................... 367 J7
   LYND SO43...................... 363 M4
   NEND PO2....................... 399 J7
   TOTT SO40...................... 366 B3
   WBNE BH4........................ 447 G7
Beaumaris Cl *AND* SP10.......... 8 D9
Beaumaris Gdns *FAWY* SO45... 367 K4
Beaumaris Pde *FRIM* GU16.... 71 J8
Beaumond Gn *WINC* SO23.... 10 F8
Beaumont Cl *FHAM* PO15..... 14 B1
   ROWN SO16.................... 318 D5 🄳
Beaumont Ct *GPORT* PO12... 397 L8 🄳
Beaumont Gv *ALDT* GU11....... 6 B2 🄳
Beaumont Ri *FHAM* PO15.... 372 B4 🄳
Beaumont Rd *CCLF* BH13..... 457 L1 🄳
   TOTT SO40...................... 341 L1
Beaurepaire Cl *TADY* RG26.... 63 J5
Beauworth Av *WEND* SO18... 320 B8
Beaver Dr *ELGH* SO50.......... 294 F6
Beaver La *YTLY* GU46............ 69 H3
Beavers Cl *ALTN* GU34......... 176 D4
   FNM GU9........................ 134 D6
   TADY RG26....................... 41 J7
Beavers Hl *FNM* GU9............ 134 D6
Beavers Ms *BOR* GU35......... 201 K4 🄳
Beavers Rd *FNM* GU9........... 134 D6
Beccles Cl *PLE* BH15............ 444 E6
Becher Rd *PSTN* BH14.......... 446 D4
Beck Cl *HLER* SO31.............. 370 C5
Beckett Cl *DEAN* RG23......... 103 M3
Beckett Rd *AND* SP10............. 8 D4
Beckford La *WHAM* PO17..... 350 C7
Beck Gdns *FNM* GU9............ 134 D2 🄳
Beckham La *PSF* GU32......... 275 J4
Beckhampton Rd *PLE* BH15... 444 D5 🄳
Beckley Copse
   CHCH/BSGR BH23........... 436 E6 🄳
Beck St *PSEA* PO1................ 20 E1
Becton La *NMIL/BTOS* BH25... 453 C1
Becton Md *NMIL/BTOS* BH25... 437 M7
Bedale Wy *PLE* BH15........... 445 L3
Beddington Ct *CHAM* RG24... 83 M7 🄳
Bede Dr *AND* SP10.............. 118 C5
Bedenham La
   LSOL/BMARY PO13......... 397 J5
Bedfield La *WINC* SO23........ 215 J5
Bedford Av *FRIM* GU16.......... 91 J3
   ITCH SO19...................... 344 C6
Bedford Cl *FBDG* SP6........... 309 L5 🄳
   HAV PO9........................... 17 J3
   HEND SO30..................... 346 B2 🄳
   BOR GU35....................... 201 J7 🄳
   NWBY RG14...................... 36 F3 🄳
Bedford Crs *FRIM* GU16......... 91 J3
   LTDN BH7........................ 449 H1
Bedford La *FRIM* GU16........... 91 J2
Bedford Pl *WSHM* SO15....... 343 K2
Bedford Rd *PSF* GU32.......... 275 J5
Bedford Rd North
   BKME/WDN BH12............ 431 G6
Bedford Rd South
   BKME/WDN BH12............ 431 G6
Bedford St *GPORT* PO12...... 421 L2
   SSEA PO5.......................... 21 G3
Bedhampton Hl *CHAM* PO6... 376 E7
Bedhampton Hill Rd
   HAV PO9......................... 376 F7 🄳
Bedhampton Rd *HAV* PO9.... 377 G6
   NEND PO2....................... 399 K7
Bedhampton Wy *HAV* PO9.... 377 K4
Bedwell Cl *ROWN* SO16....... 317 L3
Beecham Berry *KEMP* RG22... 127 J1
Beech Av *CBLY* GU15............. 71 G4
   CHCH/BSGR BH23........... 434 B8
   RFNM GU10.................... 158 F3
   SBNE BH6........................ 449 H4

WEND SO18 344 C1
Beechbrook Av YTLY GU46 69 G3
Beech Cl BDST BH18 429 H4
CHFD SO53 265 J8
FBDG SP6 333 L3 2
WINW SO22 238 A5
HLER SO31 369 J6
HORN PO8 352 D6
LYMN SO41 439 H8 1
OVTN RG25 101 G6
RAND SP11 116 D8
ROMY SO51 291 H2
STOK SO20 163 G4
TADY RG26 63 M6 1
TLHT RG30 31 L4
VWD BH31 356 C3 1
Beech Copse WINW SO22 214 A7
Beech Ct WIMB BH21 404 C4
Beech Crs FAWY SO45 367 L8
Beechcrest Vw HTWY RG27 86 A6 2
Beechcroft Cl CHFD SO53 293 J3
FHAM PO15 371 M7
LIPH GU30 226 A5 1
Beechcroft Cottages
STOK SO20 209 G2
Beechcroft La RGWD BH24 358 F8
Beechcroft Rd GPORT PO12 18 D6
Beechcroft Wy CHFD SO53 293 J2 1
Beechdale Cl TOTT SO40 316 B6
Beech Dr BLKW GU17 70 A4
Beechen La LYND SO43 363 M6
Beeches Hl BPWT SO32 297 J6
The Beeches ASHV GU12 91 J7 1
ELGH SO50 295 J7 1
KEMP RG22 127 J2
ROMY SO51 288 C5
Beechey Rd BMTH BH1 23 H2
CHAR BH8 23 H1
Beechfield AMSY SP4 160 A2
Beechfield Ct WSHM SO15 317 M8
Beech Gdns HLER SO31 369 J6
Beech Gra RSAL SP5 287 J6
Beech Gv GPORT PO12 18 D5
HISD PO11 425 M4
RAND SP11 165 L2
RWIN SO21 267 M4
Beech Hanger AMSY SP4 138 C7
Beech Hanger End GSHT GU26 203 L5
Beech Hl BOR GU35 202 E4
Beech Hill Rd BOR GU35 202 C2
NTID SP9 114 F1
THLE RG7 45 H2
Beeching Cl ASHV GU12 113 L5
Beechlands Rd ALTN GU34 197 G4
Beech La GSHT GU26 203 L4
RGWD BH24 381 J6
Beechmount Rd ROWN SO16 318 E3
Beechnut Dr BLKW GU17 69 L2
Beechnut Rd ASHV GU12 7 H3
Beech Ride FLET GU13 110 E1
SHST GU47 49 L8
Beech Rd CHFD SO53 265 J8
FARN GU14 90 E1
FHAM PO15 14 D4
FRIM GU16 91 J2
HASM GU27 229 G1
HEND SO30 346 B1
HORN PO8 328 C3
KSCL RG20 38 D6
NALR SO24 218 C3
TOTT SO40 340 F6
WSHM SO15 342 F2
Beech Tree Cl DEAN RG23 102 F8
Beech Tree Dr FNM GU9 135 K3
Beech Tree Wk ROMY SO51 209 H5
Beech Wk STHA RG19 27 H6
Beech Wy DEAN RG23 104 B1
HORN PO8 352 F3
Beechwood FBDG SP6 309 J7
Beechwood Av BOSC BH5 448 E4
NMIL/BTOS BH25 437 J4
WVILLE PO7 376 C2
Beech Wood Cl BDST BH18 429 L5
Beechwood Cl CHFD SO53 264 F7
FLET GU13 110 D2
HLER SO31 370 B8 1
KEMP RG22 127 H2
Beechwood Ct LISS GU33 248 F2 1
Beechwood Crs CHFD SO53 264 F6
Beechwood Gdns BOSC BH5 448 F4
WEND SO18 319 K8
Beechwood La RGWD BH24 384 F5
Beechwood Ri WEND SO18 320 B7
Beechwood Rd ALTN GU34 176 C6
FAWY SO45 392 A5
FERN BH22 380 D8
NEND PO2 399 J4
TOTT SO40 339 K3
Beechwood Wy FAWY SO45 367 G6
Beechworth Rd HAV PO9 17 G4
Beehive Wk PSEA PO1 20 D4 1
Beethoven Rd KEMP RG22 104 D8
Beeton's Av ASHV GU12 113 K4
Beggar's La WINC SO23 11 J7
Beggarwood La DEAN RG23 126 F3
KEMP RG22 127 J2
Begonia Cl KEMP RG22 126 F1
Begonia Rd ROWN SO16 319 G4
Behrendt Cl GPORT PO12 421 L2
Belaga Cl STOK SO20 162 F3
Belben Cl BKME/WDN BH12 431 H6
Belben Rd BKME/WDN BH12 431 G6
Belbins ROMY SO51 262 E4
Beldham Rd RFNM GU10 158 C1
Belfield Rd SBNE BH6 449 M4
Belfry Wk FHAM/STUB PO14 371 G6
Belgrave Ct BLKW GU17 70 A5
Belgrave Rd CCLF BH13 446 F6
PTSW SO17 319 H6
Belgravia Rd NEND PO2 399 K7
Bellair Rd HAV PO9 17 G5
Belland Dr ALDT GU11 6 B3
Bell Cl FARN GU14 90 F2
Bell Crs WVILLE PO7 376 C2
Bell Davies Rd
FHAM/STUB PO14 395 M7
Bellemoor Rd WSHM SO15 318 C7
Bellever Hl CBLY GU15 71 H3
Bellevue WHCH RG28 122 B3
Belle Vue Cl ASHV GU12 7 M2
SBNE BH6 449 J4
Belle Vue Crs SBNE BH6 449 L4
Belle Vue Gv FERN BH22 380 D6
Bellevue La EMRTH PO10 378 D6
Belle Vue Rd AND SP10 9 J8
PSTN BH14 446 B5
SBNE BH6 449 J5
ASHV GU12 7 L2
CHAM RG24 106 A2
Bellevue Rd ELGH SO50 293 M5
WSHM SO15 343 L2
Bellevue Ter SSEA PO5 20 E6
Belle Vue Wk FERN BH22 406 C6
Bellew Rd FRIM GU16 91 L2
Bellflower Wy NBAD SO52 292 E1
Bell Heather Cl UPTN BH16 428 F8 1
Bell Hl PSF GU32 275 J3
Bell Hill Rdg PSF GU32 275 K3
Bell Holt NWBY RG14 36 F3
Bell House NALR SO24 218 C4
Bellingham Cl CBLY GU15 71 M4
Bell La BLKW GU17 69 M3
HUNG RG17 34 A5
RFNM GU10 158 B5
OVTN RG25 152 C2
Bell Meadow Rd HTWY RG27 86 A7
Bell Rd AND SP10 9 L6
CHAM RG24 5 L5
CHAM PO6 375 H8
HASM GU27 228 D5
Bells La FHAM/STUB PO14 396 A6
Bell St RAND SP11 92 F6
ROMY SO51 290 D1
SHAM SO14 13 H5
WHCH RG28 122 B3
Bell Vale La HASM GU27 228 E4
Belmont Av CHAR BH8 433 G6
Belmont Cl AND SP10 9 K8
FARN GU14 90 C1
FAWY SO45 367 L6
FHAM/STUB PO14 396 B5 1
HORN PO8 328 B6
VWD BH31 356 E3
Belmont Gv HAV PO9 377 G6 1
Belmont Hts KEMP RG22 127 H3
Belmont Ms CBLY GU15 70 F5
Belmont Pl SSEA PO5 21 H5
Belmont Rd AND SP10 9 J8
CBLY GU15 70 F4
CHFD SO53 293 J5
CWTH RG45 49 L2
NMIL/BTOS BH25 438 A4
PSTN BH14 446 A3
PTSW SO17 319 G8
Belmont St SSEA PO5 21 H5
Belmore Cl PSEA PO1 423 J1
Belmore La LYMN SO41 440 C5
RWIN SO21 268 C3
Belmore Rd LYMN SO41 440 B5
Belney La WHAM PO17 351 J8
Belsize Rd FARN GU14 90 F7 1
Belstone Ms FARN GU14 90 D1 2
Belstone Rd TOTT SO40 341 J1
Belton Rd CBLY GU15 71 H3
ITCH SO19 344 F5
Belvedere Cl FLET GU13 88 B7 1
Belvedere Ct BLKW GU17 70 A5 1
Belvedere Dr NWBY RG14 2 E9
Belvedere Gdns CHAM RG24 83 M4 1
Belvedere Rd
CHCH/BSGR BH23 449 M1
FARN GU14 90 F6 1
FAWY SO45 367 L6
TWDS BH3 447 M2
Belverdere Cl PSF GU32 275 L4 2
Belvidere Rd SHAM SO14 13 L2
Belvidere Ter SHAM SO14 13 L1
Belvoir Cl FHAM/PORC PO16 15 J7
FRIM GU16 71 J7
Bembridge HLER SO31 369 G2
Bembridge Cl ROWN SO16 319 H3 1
Bembridge Ct CWTH RG45 49 H4 1
Bembridge Crs ENEY PO4 21 L9
Bembridge Dr HISD PO11 426 A7
Bemister Rd
MOOR/WNTN BH9 432 E8
Benbow Cl HORN PO8 353 G1
Benbow Crs BKME/WDN BH12 431 J7
Benbow Pl PSEA PO1 20 C1 1
Benbridge Av BWD BH11 431 K3
Bendigo Rd CHCH/BSGR BH23 434 C8
Beneden Gn NALR SO24 218 C3
Benedict Cl ROMY SO51 291 H1
Benedict Wy
FHAM/PORC PO16 374 C6
Beneficial St PSEA PO1 20 C2 1
Benellen Av WBNE BH4 447 H4
Benellen Gdns WBNE BH4 447 H4
Benellen Rd WBNE BH4 447 H3
Benenden Gn NALR SO24 218 C4
Benett Cl NWBY RG14 25 J3
Benett Gdns NWBY RG14 25 J3
Bengal Rd MOOR/WNTN BH9 432 C7
Benger's La ROMY SO51 233 J6
Benham Cha KSCL RG20 24 B3
Benham Dr HSEA PO3 399 K4 2
Benham Dro STOK SO20 184 C2
Benham Gv FHAM/PORC PO16 398 B2
Benham Hl NTHA RG18 26 D4
Benham La THLE RG7 46 A5
Benhams Farm Cl
WEND SO18 319 M7 1
Benhams La LISS GU33 224 E4
Benhams Rd WEND SO18 319 M6 2
Benin Rd RAND SP11 115 J2
Benjamin Rd PLE BH15 444 D6
Ben La RSAL SP5 230 C1
Benmoor Rd CFDH BH17 429 L8
Benmore Cl NMIL/BTOS BH25 438 A6
Benmore Gdns CHFD SO53 265 G8
Benmore Rd
MOOR/WNTN BH9 432 E7
Bennet Cl ALTN GU34 176 D4
BSTK RG21 5 H4
Bennett Cl RSAL SP5 285 J2 1
Bennett Ct CBLY GU15 70 F3 2
Bennett Rd CHAR BH8 448 B2
Bennett's Hl TLHT RG30 31 L1
Bennetts La RGWD BH24 385 G6
Bennion Rd NBNE BH10 432 A5
Benridge Cl BDST BH18 429 L5
Benson Cl CHCH/BSGR BH23 409 M7
Benson Rd CWTH RG45 49 J3
WSHM SO15 318 A8
Benta Cl STOK SO20 162 F3
Bentham Rd GPORT PO12 18 E6
Bentham Wy HLER SO31 346 B8
Bentley Cl HORN PO8 328 B8
WINC SO23 215 G2
Bentley Copse CBLY GU15 71 L4 2
Bentley Ct HAV PO9 377 M3 2
Bentley Crs FHAM/PORC PO16 14 F3
Bentley Gn WEND SO18 320 B8
Bentley Rd MOOR/WNTN BH9 432 D5
Bentley Wy RSAL SP5 207 G3
Bent St STOK SO20 184 D2
Benwell Cl ODIM RG29 108 B8
Bepton Down EPSF GU31 275 M5
Berber Cl FHAM PO15 371 G1
Bercote Cl WINW SO22 214 A3
Bere Cl CFDH BH17 430 B6
CHFD SO53 264 F8
WINW SO22 10 A3
Bere Farm La WHAM PO17 349 K8
Bere Hl WHCH RG28 122 B2
Bere Hill Cl WHCH RG28 122 C2
Bere Hill Crs AND SP10 9 L7
Berehurst ALTN GU34 176 D6
Bere Rd WVILLE PO7 351 L4
Beresford Cl AND SP10 142 F3 1
CHFD SO53 293 K3 1
FRIM GU16 91 J2
WVILLE PO7 376 C2
Beresford Gdns
CHCH/BSGR BH23 450 D2
CHFD SO53 293 K3 2
Beresford Rd
BKME/WDN BH12 446 C2
CHFD SO53 293 K3
FHAM/STUB PO14 396 B5
LYMN SO41 440 A4
NEND PO2 399 J6
SBNE BH6 449 G4
Bereweeke Av WINW SO22 10 C1
Bereweeke Cl WINW SO22 10 C4
Bereweeke Rd WINW SO22 10 C4
Bereweeke Wy WINW SO22 10 D3
Berewyk Cl KEMP RG22 126 F1 1
Bergen Crs HEND SO30 346 A3
Berkeley Av BKME/WDN BH12 431 G8
Berkeley Cl FHAM/STUB PO14 395 M6
FLET GU13 89 G7 1
VWD BH31 356 C1
WSHM SO15 343 J1
Berkeley Crs FRIM GU16 71 K8
Berkeley Dr KEMP RG22 104 E8
Berkeley Gdns HEND SO30 346 A3
Berkeley Rd NWBY RG14 2 C5
TWDS BH3 447 K1
Berkeley Sq HAV PO9 17 J4
Berkley Av FERN BH22 406 B6
Berkshire Circular Routes
HUNG RG17 33 H3
KSCL RG20 24 D8
THLE RG7 30 B2
THLE RG7 43 L4
Berkshire Cl PSEA PO1 21 K2
Berkshire Corpse Rd
ALDT GU11 112 B1
Berkshire Dr STHA RG19 27 K6
Berkshire Rd CBLY GU15 51 J8
Bermuda Cl CHAM RG24 83 H7
Bernard Av ALTN GU34 197 G6
CHAM PO6 375 L8
Bernard St SHAM SO14 13 G5
Bernersh Cl SHST GU47 49 M7 1
Berney Rd ENEY PO4 424 A4
Bernina Av WVILLE PO7 352 A6
Bernina Cl WVILLE PO7 352 A6
Bernstein Rd KEMP RG22 104 B8
Bernwood Gv FAWY SO45 418 C1
Berrans Av BWD BH11 431 M2
Berrybank SHST GU47 70 B2
Berrybarn La SELS PO20 427 K8
Berry Cl HEND SO30 346 B2
Berrydown La OVTN RG25 124 B1
OVTN RG25 152 B4
Berrydown Rd HAV PO9 377 G1
Berryfield Rd LYMN SO41 438 E6
Berry Hl NALR SO24 219 M3
Berrylands LISS GU33 248 F1
Berry La FHAM/STUB PO14 395 L6
RWIN SO21 266 F1
Berrywood Gdns
HEND SO30 321 G8 1
HEND SO30 345 M1
Berrywood La NALR SO24 174 A2
Bertie Rd ENEY PO4 423 M4
Bertram Rd NMIL/BTOS BH25 438 A4
Berwick Rd TWDS BH3 447 K2
Berwyn Cl KEMP RG22 103 M5
Beryl Av GPORT PO12 397 K8
Beryton Cl GPORT PO12 421 L2 2
Beryton Rd GPORT PO12 421 L2
Besomer Dro RSAL SP5 285 L4
Bessborough Rd CCLF BH13 457 K1
Bessemer Rd BSTK RG21 104 E6
Beswick Av NBNE BH10 432 B6
Beta Rd FARN GU14 90 C3
Bethel Cl FNM GU9 135 G2
Bethel La FNM GU9 135 G2
Bethia Rd CHAR BH8 448 C2
Betjeman Wk YTLY GU46 68 E4
Betsy Cl CHCH/BSGR BH23 409 M7
Betsy La CHCH/BSGR BH23 409 M7
Betteridge Dr ROWN SO16 317 J2
Betteridge Rd STHA RG19 27 J6
Bettesworth Rd PSEA PO1 423 J1
Bettiscombe Cl CFDH BH17 430 B6
Betula Cl WVILLE PO7 376 E2 1
Beulah Rd ROWN SO16 317 M7
Bevan Cl ITCH SO19 344 C7
Bevan Rd HORN PO8 352 D3
Beveren Cl FARN GU14 89 G4
Beverley Cl ASHV GU12 113 J7
BSTK RG21 105 G7
CBLY GU15 71 M2
HLER SO31 371 G4
NTHA RG18 26 F4
Beverley Crs FARN GU14 90 C5
Beverley Gdns BPWT SO32 324 A3 1
HLER SO31 345 J7
NBNE BH10 432 B5
ROMY SO51 263 H7 2
Beverley Hts WEND SO18 319 L5
Beverley Rd FAWY SO45 367 K8
FHAM/STUB PO14 396 A7
Beverly Cl LSOL/BMARY PO13 397 H6
The Bevers THLE RG7 43 K2
Beverston Rd CHAM PO6 374 E7
Bevis Cl FAWY SO45 392 D6
HLER SO31 370 B8
Bevis Rd GPORT PO12 18 F2
NEND PO2 399 H7
Bevois Gdns SHAM SO14 343 L1
Bevois Hl PTSW SO17 319 G8
Bevois Valley Rd SHAM SO14 343 M1
Bexmoor CHAM RG24 105 M2
Bexmoor Wy CHAM RG24 105 M2
Beyne Rd WINW SO22 238 A5
Bible Flds OVTN RG25 126 B8
Bicester Cl WHCH RG28 122 B3
Bickerley Gdns RGWD BH24 382 D2
Bickerley Rd RGWD BH24 382 D2
Bicknell Rd FRIM GU16 71 H6
Bidbury La HAV PO9 377 G7
Biddenfield La WHAM PO17 348 B4
Bidden Rd ODIM RG29 107 M6
OVTN RG25 130 A3
Biddesden La RAND SP11 93 G6
Biddlecombe Cl
LSOL/BMARY PO13 397 G8
Bideford Cl FARN GU14 90 D1
ROWN SO16 317 K7
Bighton Dean La NALR SO24 195 J7
Bighton Hl NALR SO24 219 M2
Bighton La NALR SO24 219 H2
Bighton Rd ALTN GU34 196 B3
Bilbao Ct AND SP10 119 J7
Bilberry Cl HLER SO31 370 D6
Bilberry Dr TOTT SO40 342 C6
Billett Av WVILLE PO7 352 D7
Billing Av EWKG RG40 48 B2
Billing Cl ENEY PO4 423 M5 1
Billington Gdns HEND SO30 321 J7
Billington Wy NTHA RG18 26 F2
Billy Lawn Av HAV PO9 377 K4
Bilton Wy HSEA PO3 400 A6
Bindon Cl BKME/WDN BH12 446 D1
ROWN SO16 317 M6
Bindon Rd ROWN SO16 317 M6
Binfields Cl CHAM RG24 83 L7
Bingham Av PSTN BH14 457 J1
Bingham Dr LYMN SO41 440 C5
Bingham Rd CHCH/BSGR BH23 450 D1
MOOR/WNTN BH9 432 E8
VWD BH31 356 E4
Bingley Cl ALTN GU34 176 D4
Binley Bottom RAND SP11 97 K3
Binnacle Wy CHAM PO6 374 F8
Binness Wy CHAM PO6 400 C1
Binnie Rd BKME/WDN BH12 446 D3
Binsey Cl ROWN SO16 317 K8
Binstead Cl ROWN SO16 319 H3
Binstead Rd ALTN GU34 157 J8
RFNM GU10 157 K8
Binsted Dr BLKW GU17 70 A3
Binsteed Rd NEND PO2 399 J8
Binton La RFNM GU10 136 B6
Birch Av CHCH/BSGR BH23 435 G5
FERN BH22 406 D7
FLET GU13 88 E7
NMIL/BTOS BH25 437 H2
STOK SO20 163 G4
Birch Cl CBLY GU15 51 H8
HORN PO8 352 C5
BOR GU35 201 K6
LISS GU33 248 F4
RFNM GU10 158 D4
PSTN BH14 446 D5
RGWD BH24 381 H5
ROMY SO51 291 H2
ROWN SO16 317 M6
WIMB BH21 429 H2 1
Birch Dl FAWY SO45 367 M6
Birchdale Cl HLER SO31 370 B8 2
Birchdale Rd WIMB BH21 404 B3
Birch Dr BLKW GU17 70 A5
CHAR BH8 433 L6
LSOL/BMARY PO13 397 G4
Birchen Cl HLER SO31 371 G4 1
The Birches Cl NBAD SO52 291 L3
Birches Crest KEMP RG22 127 J2
The Birches BLKW GU17 69 L3
FARN GU14 90 A4
WEND SO18 320 A8 2
Birchett Rd ALDT GU11 6 E2
FARN GU14 90 B3
Birchfields CBLY GU15 70 F4 1
Birch Gv ELGH SO50 293 L2
FERN BH22 380 B6
HTWY RG27 86 A6
BOR GU35 201 J7
STOK SO20 166 A6
Birchland Cl THLE RG7 43 H2
Birchlands TOTT SO40 341 H3
Birch La THLE RG7 43 J3
Birchmore Cl
LSOL/BMARY PO13 397 G6 2
Bircholt Rd LIPH GU30 226 A4
Birch Rd EWKG RG40 48 D1
HEND SO30 346 B1
BOR GU35 202 E2
RGWD BH24 381 M4
ROWN SO16 292 F8
ROWN SO16 317 M6
TADY RG26 41 H6
THLE RG7 31 J5
Birch Side CWTH RG45 49 J2
Birch Tree Cl EMRTH PO10 378 D4
Birch Tree Dr EMRTH PO10 378 D4
Birchview Cl YTLY GU46 68 F4
Birch Wy ASHV GU12 113 K1
Birchwood CHAM RG24 83 L5 1
Birch Wd ITCH SO19 345 J3
Birchwood Cl
CHCH/BSGR BH23 436 C7 1
Birchwood Dr FBDG SP6 333 L3
Birchwood Gdns HEND SO30 321 H8 2
Birchwood Rd NWBY RG14 3 M1
PSTN BH14 446 C5
UPTN BH16 444 A2
Birchy Hl LYMN SO41 413 G7
Birdham Rd HISD PO11 426 C6
Birdhaven RFNM GU10 158 D3
Birdlip Cl HORN PO8 352 E2
Birdlip Rd CHAM PO6 374 F7
Bird's Hill Rd PLE BH15 445 K4
Birds La THLE RG7 28 B5
Birdwood Gv
FHAM/PORC PO16 373 K8
Birdwood Rd CBLY GU15 70 C2
Birinus Rd WINC SO23 11 H5
Birkbeck Pl SHST GU47 50 B7
Birkdale Av CHAM PO6 376 A7
Birkdale Ct WIMB BH21 429 L3
Birkdale Rd WIMB BH21 429 L3
Birkenholme Cl BOR GU35 202 F4
Biscay Cl FHAM/STUB PO14 395 M5 1
Bishearne Gdns LISS GU33 248 D3 1
Bishop Ct RGWD BH24 382 E1 1
Bishop Rd MOOR/WNTN BH9 432 E8
Bishops Cl FLET GU13 110 F1
LTDN BH7 448 E2
NTID SP9 114 E4
TADY RG26 41 K7
TOTT SO40 316 D8
Bishops Ct ELGH SO50 294 C3
Bishops Crs ITCH SO19 344 D4
Bishopsfield Rd
FHAM/STUB PO14 14 D8
Bishops Ga FHAM/STUB PO14 371 G5
Bishop's La BPWT SO32 323 H1
BPWT SO32 324 A7
Bishop's Md FNM GU9 134 E6
Bishops Rd FNM GU9 134 E2
ITCH SO19 344 C5
Bishopstoke La ELGH SO50 294 D2
Bishopstoke Rd ELGH SO50 294 B5
HAV PO9 377 J3
Bishop St PSEA PO1 20 D1
Bishop Sumner Dr FNM GU9 134 F2 1
Bishop's Vw ALTN GU34 196 E6
Bishop's Wy AND SP10 8 E4
Bishopswood La TADY RG26 41 H7
Bishop's Wood Rd BPWT SO32 324 A5
Bishopswood Rd TADY RG26 41 J7
Bisterne Cl RGWD BH24 385 H6
Bitham La HUNG RG17 32 E3
Bittern Cl GPORT PO12 421 M1
KEMP RG22 103 L8
SHST GU47 50 A8
Bitterne Cl HAV PO9 377 K2
Bitterne Crs ITCH SO19 344 E2 1
Bitterne Rd East WEND SO18 344 E2
Bitterne Rd West WEND SO18 344 C1
Bitterne Wy ITCH SO19 344 C2
LYMN SO41 440 B6
VWD BH31 356 E3
Blackberry Cl ALTN GU34 197 H5
Black Berry Cl HORN PO8 328 C4
Blackberry La ALTN GU34 197 H6
CHCH/BSGR BH23 450 E2
Blackberry Ter SHAM SO14 343 M1 1
Blackberry Wk CHAM RG24 5 M4
Blackbird Cl CFDH BH17 429 J8
HORN PO8 352 D4
KEMP RG22 103 L8
SHST GU47 50 A8
THLE RG7 31 L5 1
Blackbird Ct AND SP10 119 G6 1
Blackbird Rd ELGH SO50 293 J6
Blackbird Wy
CHCH/BSGR BH23 410 A8
LSOL/BMARY PO13 420 D1
Blackbrook House Dr
FHAM PO15 14 D5
Blackbrook Park Av
FHAM PO15 14 C5
Blackbrook Rd FHAM PO15 14 D5
Blackburn Rd
BKME/WDN BH12 446 A2
Blackbushe Cl ROWN SO16 317 L3 2
Blackbushes Rd HTWY RG27 88 D2
Blackbush Rd LYMN SO41 454 A2
Blackcap Cl HAV PO9 353 L7
Blackcap Pl SHST GU47 50 B8
Blackdown Cl FAWY SO45 367 H6 1
KEMP RG22 103 M5
Blackdown Crs HAV PO9 377 J4
Blackdown Rd FRIM GU16 91 M1
Blackdown Wy STHA RG19 26 F6
Blackfield La FERN BH22 380 C5
Blackfield Rd FAWY SO45 392 C7
Blackfriars Cl SSEA PO5 21 J3 2
Blackfriars Rd SSEA PO5 21 J2
Blackheath Rd FNM GU9 134 D1
Black Hl VWD BH31 356 E2
Blackhill Rd ROMY SO51 288 E8
Black Horse La BPWT SO32 323 K7
Blackhouse La WHAM PO17 349 L8
Blacklands Rd THLE RG7 27 M3
Black La RSAL SP5 285 M3
Blackman Gdns ALDT GU11 7 H6
Blackmoor Rd LISS GU33 224 F2
Blackmore La MARL SN8 92 E3
PSF GU32 246 D4
Blacknest Rd ALTN GU34 157 H6
Black Pond La RFNM GU10 158 F2
Blacksmith Cl WIMB BH21 429 H3
Blackstocks La HTWY RG27 107 G3
Blackstone Cl FARN GU14 90 A2
Blackthorn Cl ITCH SO19 344 D3 1
LYMN SO41 439 M6
RWIN SO21 190 B4
Blackthorn Crs FARN GU14 70 C8
Blackthorn Dr GPORT PO12 397 L7
HISD PO11 426 A5
NTHA RG18 27 G3
Blackthorne Cl BOR GU35 201 K5 1

Blackthorn Gn RWIN SO21 266 F8
Blackthorn Rd HISD PO11 426 A5
ITCH SO19 344 D3
Blackthorn Wy DEAN RG23 104 B2
VWD BH31 356 F3
Blackwater Cl ASHV GU12 113 K7 1
BSTK RG21 5 H8
CHAM PO6 375 H8 1
DEAN RG23 103 G7 1
Blackwater Dr TOTT SO40 316 C7
WIMB BH21 430 B1
Blackwater Gv FBDG SP6 333 J3
Blackwater Ms TOTT SO40 316 C7
Blackwater Vw EWKG RG40 48 D6
Blackwater Wy ASHV GU12 7 M6
Blackwell Rd RWIN SO21 190 B6
Bladon Cl HAV PO9 17 L1
Bladon Rd ROWN SO16 318 B6
Blagdon Cl STHA RG19 26 A8 1
Blair Av PSTN BH14 446 B4
Blair Cl NMIL/BTOS BH25 437 J5
Blaire Pk YTLY GU46 48 E8
Blair Rd BSTK RG21 104 F5
Blaise Cl FARN GU14 91 G5
Blake Cl CWTH RG45 49 M4
ODIM RG29 108 B8 1
ROWN SO16 317 H3 1
Blakedene Rd PSTN BH14 446 A7
Blake Hill Av PSTN BH14 446 B7
Blake Hill Crs PSTN BH14 446 B7
Blakemere Crs CHAM PO6 375 G7
Blakeney Rd ROWN SO16 317 J6
Blake Rd CHAM PO6 376 B7
GPORT PO12 19 G2
Blake's La TADY RG26 41 L7
Blakesley La HSEA PO3 400 A4
Blakes Ride YTLY GU46 68 E2
Blanchard Rd BPWT SO32 297 G8
Blandford Cl PLE BH15 444 E6
Blandford Rd PLE BH15 444 F7
RSAL SP5 254 C1
UPTN BH16 444 B2
Blandford Rd North
UPTN BH16 428 D5
Bland's Cl THLE RG7 31 J6
Blaney Wy WIMB BH21 429 G2
Blanket St ALTN GU34 177 L8
Blankney Cl
FHAM/STUB PO14 395 M6 1
Blann Cl ROWN SO16 317 H3 2
Bleaklow Cl ROWN SO16 317 L8
Blechynden Ter WSHM SO15 12 D2
Bledlow Cl NWBY RG14 37 G3 1
Blencowe Dr NBAD SO52 292 D3
Blendon Dr AND SP10 8 A3
Blendworth Crs HAV PO9 377 J5
Blendworth La HORN PO8 353 H1
WEND SO18 345 G1
Blendworth Rd ENEY PO4 423 M3 1
Blenheim Av PTSW SO17 318 F7
Blenheim Cl ALTN GU34 176 F5 1
ALTN GU34 197 G5
NBAD SO52 292 E4
RFNM GU10 136 B1 1
TOTT SO40 341 H2
Blenheim Ct ENEY PO4 423 L5 1
FARN GU14 91 G6
Blenheim Crs FNM GU9 134 D2
LYMN SO41 438 C4
Blenheim Dr CHCH/BSGR BH23 451 G1
Blenheim Gdns FAWY SO45 367 H6
GPORT PO12 397 M8
HAV PO9 17 L2
PTSW SO17 319 G6
Blenheim Pk ALDT GU11 112 F1
Blenheim Rd ALDT GU11 112 F1
CHAM RG24 106 B3
ELGH SO50 293 M6
HORN PO8 352 E3
NWBY RG14 2 C4
Bleriot Crs FHAM PO15 371 K2
Blighmont Crs WSHM SO15 342 F2
Blighton La RFNM GU10 136 A6
Blind La BPWT SO32 321 H3
FBDG SP6 335 G7
WHAM PO17 348 D3
Bliss Cl KEMP RG22 104 D7
WVILLE PO7 376 C3
Blissford Cl HAV PO9 377 M2 1
Blissford Cross FBDG SP6 310 D8
Blissford Hl FBDG SP6 335 J2
Blissford Rd FBDG SP6 310 C7
Bloomfield Av
MOOR/WNTN BH9 432 D6
Bloomsbury Wy BLKW GU17 69 M5
Blossom Cl HEND SO30 346 C2
Bloswood Dr WHCH RG28 122 A3
Bloswood La WHCH RG28 98 E8
Blount Rd PSEA PO1 20 E5
Bloxworth Rd
BKME/WDN BH12 431 K8
Blue Ball Hl WINC SO23 11 J7
Bluebell Cl CHCH/BSGR BH23 435 M8
WVILLE PO7 376 D2
Bluebell Copse HLER SO31 370 D6
Bluebell Dr THLE RG7 31 J5
Bluebell La CFDH BH17 429 J7
Bluebell Rd BOR GU35 201 M3
ROWN SO16 319 G4
Bluebell Wy NTHA RG18 27 G3
Bluecoats NTHA RG18 27 G4
Bluestar Gdns HEND SO30 321 H6
Bluethroat Cl SHST GU47 50 B8 1
Bluff Cove ALDT GU11 112 F5 1
Blundell La HLER SO31 346 A6
Blunden Cl BSTK RG21 104 E7
Blunden Rd FARN GU14 90 C3
Blyth Av STHA RG19 27 H6
Blyth Cl CHCH/BSGR BH23 434 B4
ROWN SO16 317 J6
Blythe Rd WIMB BH21 429 H2
Blythswood Ct
NMIL/BTOS BH25 452 E1 1
Blythwood Dr FRIM GU16 71 G6
Boakes Pl TOTT SO40 341 G6 1
Boames La KSCL RG20 36 C3
Boarhunt Cl PSEA PO1 21 J1 1
Boarhunt Rd WHAM PO17 373 L4
Boar's Br TADY RG26 62 D6
Bob Hann Cl BKME/WDN BH12 446 D3
Bockhampton Rd
CHCH/BSGR BH23 435 J3
Bodin Gdns NWBY RG14 25 K8
Bodley Rd CCLF BH13 457 L1 2
Bodmin Cl KEMP RG22 104 A5
STHA RG19 26 F6
Bodmin Rd CHAM PO6 374 E8 1
ELGH SO50 294 D5
Bodorgan Rd WCLF BH2 22 E4
Bodowen Cl CHCH/BSGR BH23 435 H6
Bodowen Rd
CHCH/BSGR BH23 435 H6
Bodycoats Rd CHFD SO53 293 J2
Bofors Rd FARN GU14 90 D8
Bogmoor Cl ALTN GU34 197 G6
Bognor Rd BDST BH18 429 K4
Bohemia La RSAL SP5 285 L5
Boiler Rd PSEA PO1 422 D2
Bolde Cl HSEA PO3 399 M5
Boldens Rd GPORT PO12 18 E9
Bolderford Br BROC SO42 387 J3
Bolderwood
Arboretum Ornamental Dr
LYND SO43 361 L4
RGWD BH24 362 A6
Bolderwood Cl ELGH SO50 294 E5
Boldre Cl BKME/WDN BH12 446 D1
HAV PO9 377 G4 1
NMIL/BTOS BH25 437 H8
Boldre La LYMN SO41 440 B1
Boldrewood THLE RG7 31 J6 1
Boldrewood Rd ROWN SO16 318 D4
Boleyn Crs MOOR/WNTN BH9 433 G4
Bolhinton Av TOTT SO40 342 B7
Bolingbroke Wy STHA RG19 27 J5
Bolle Rd ALTN GU34 176 C6
Bolley Av BOR GU35 201 G3
Bolton Crs FERN BH22 406 E2
KEMP RG22 104 D5
The Boltons WVILLE PO7 376 C5 1
Bonchurch Cl ROWN SO16 319 H3 2
Bonchurch Rd ENEY PO4 423 L3
Bond Av FERN BH22 380 B4
Bond Cl CHAM RG24 5 M1
LYMN SO41 412 F5
Bondfields Crs HAV PO9 377 K2
Bond Rd PLE BH15 445 L3
WEND SO18 319 K7
Bond St SHAM SO14 344 A2
Bone La NWBY RG14 3 H4
Bonemill La KSCL RG20 25 G6
Bones La EPSF GU31 303 J3
Bonfire Cnr PSEA PO1 422 E2
Bonhams Cl ALTN GU34 177 K1
Boniface Cl TOTT SO40 316 C8 1
Boniface Crs ROWN SO16 317 K5
Bonners Fld RFNM GU10 156 F3
Boon Wy DEAN RG23 102 F6
Boothby Cl TOTT SO40 341 L2 1
Bordean La PSF GU32 274 A3
Borden Gates AND SP10 9 H7
Borden La LIPH GU30 278 C2
Border Dr UPTN BH16 444 B3
Border Rd HASM GU27 228 A2
UPTN BH16 444 B3
Borderside YTLY GU46 68 D2
Bordon Cl TADY RG26 41 K8
Bordon Rd HAV PO9 377 K3
The Boreen BOR GU35 202 E3
Boreham Rd SBNE BH6 449 J3
Borkum Cl AND SP10 118 E5
Borley Rd CFDH BH17 429 L8
Borman Wy RWIN SO21 190 D4
Borodin Cl KEMP RG22 104 E8
Borough Gv PSF GU32 275 K6
Borough Hl PSF GU32 275 K5
Borough Rd PSF GU32 275 J6
The Borough FNM GU9 134 E6
RFNM GU10 133 H2
RSAL SP5 284 D1
Borovere Cl ALTN GU34 176 D6
Borovere Gdns ALTN GU34 176 D6
Borovere La ALTN GU34 176 D6
Borrowdale Rd ROWN SO16 317 K7
Borsberry Cl AND SP10 9 K4
Borthwick Rd BMTH BH1 448 D3
Boscawen Wy STHA RG19 27 K5 1
Boscobel Rd WINW SO22 10 E4
Boscombe Cliff Rd BOSC BH5 448 D5
Boscombe Grove Rd
BMTH BH1 448 C3
Boscombe Overcliff Dr
BOSC BH5 448 E5
Boscombe Spa Rd BOSC BH5 448 C4
Bosham Rd NEND PO2 399 K8
Bosham Wk
LSOL/BMARY PO13 396 F6
Bosley Cl CHCH/BSGR BH23 434 C6
Bosley Wy CHCH/BSGR BH23 434 C6
Bosmere Gdns EMRTH PO10 378 C7
Bosmere Rd HISD PO11 426 C6
Bossington Cl ROWN SO16 317 K3 1
Bostock Cl RWIN SO21 213 J5
Boston Rd CHAM PO6 375 J7
Bosuns Cl FHAM/PORC PO16 396 F2
Bosville ELGH SO50 293 M2
Boswell Cl HEND SO30 346 D1
ITCH SO19 345 G2
Botany Bay Rd ITCH SO19 344 D3
Botany Cl STHA RG19 27 J5 1
Botany Hl RFNM GU10 136 A7
Botisdone Cl RAND SP11 73 G2
Botley Dr HAV PO9 377 H3
Botley Gdns ITCH SO19 345 J5 2
Botley Rd BPWT SO32 322 C8
ELGH SO50 295 J8
HEND SO30 320 E7
HEND SO30 347 H2
HLER SO31 346 E8
ITCH SO19 345 H5 1
NBAD SO52 291 L3
Bottle La HTWY RG27 65 M8
Bottom La ROMY SO51 288 D4
Boulnois Av PSTN BH14 446 D5
Boulter La WHAM PO17 374 E1
Boulters Rd ASHV GU12 7 H3
Boulton Rd SSEA PO5 21 L6
Boundary Cl WSHM SO15 342 D2
Boundary Dr WIMB BH21 404 B2
Boundary La RGWD BH24 381 H7
Boundary Rd FARN GU14 89 M7
GSHT GU26 204 A5
HLER SO31 345 K8
MOOR/WNTN BH9 432 B8
NBNE BH10 432 B7
RFNM GU10 180 A2
NWBY RG14 3 H5
Boundary Wy CHAM PO6 375 M6
HAV PO9 16 D4
Bound La HISD PO11 425 L6
Boundstone FAWY SO45 367 K5 1
Boundstone Cl RFNM GU10 158 E3 1
Boundstone Rd RFNM GU10 158 C4
Boundway LYMN SO41 412 B7
Bounty Ri BSTK RG21 104 F4
Bounty Rd BSTK RG21 104 F4
Bourley La RFNM GU10 111 J6
Bourley Rd FLET GU13 111 H4
Bourne Arch NTHA RG18 26 E4
Bourne Av WCLF BH2 22 C5
WSHM SO15 318 B7
Bourne Cl HORN PO8 352 F2
ROMY SO51 288 C5
RWIN SO21 266 A4
WBNE BH4 22 A5
Bourne Ct ALDT GU11 6 E5
AND SP10 9 L1
WIMB BH21 404 B3
Bourne Dene RFNM GU10 158 D3
Bourne Fld CHAM RG24 82 D4
Bournefields RWIN SO21 267 G1
Bourne Firs RFNM GU10 159 G3
Bourne Gv RFNM GU10 159 H1
Bourne Grove Cl FNM GU9 159 H1
Bourne Grove Dr RFNM GU10 159 H1
Bourne La NTID SP9 138 E1
RWIN SO21 266 F1
TOTT SO40 340 B3
Bourne Meadow RAND SP11 97 M7
Bourne Mill Rbt FNM GU9 135 H5
Bournemouth Av GPORT PO12 421 L1
Bournemouth
International Centre Rbt
WCLF BH2 22 E7
Bournemouth Rd CHFD SO53 293 G5
LYND SO43 363 J3
PSTN BH14 446 B4
RAND SP11 161 K3
ROWN SO16 292 F8
Bournemouth Road Castle Hl
PSTN BH14 446 A4
Bournemouth Station Rbt
BMTH BH1 23 J4
Bourne Rd CHAM PO6 374 F8
NTID SP9 114 E2
STHA RG19 26 E4
TOTT SO40 340 A3
WSHM SO15 12 B1
The Bourne FLET GU13 110 F2
Bourne Valley Rd
BKME/WDN BH12 446 F3
Bourne View Cl EMRTH PO10 379 H6
Bournewood Dr WBNE BH4 447 H4
Bouverie Cl NMIL/BTOS BH25 437 K7
Boveridge Gdns
MOOR/WNTN BH9 432 F4
Bovington Cl CFDH BH17 430 D7
Bowater Cl TOTT SO40 316 B7
Bowater Wy TOTT SO40 316 B7
Bowcombe HLER SO31 369 G1
Bowcott Hl BOR GU35 202 C3
Bowden La PTSW SO17 319 H6
Bowden Rd BKME/WDN BH12 431 G6
Bow Dr HTWY RG27 64 C8
Bowenhurst Gdns FLET GU13 110 F4
Bowenhurst Rd FLET GU13 110 F3
Bowenhust La RFNM GU10 110 B5
Bower Cl FAWY SO45 392 A5
ITCH SO19 344 D7
Bower Rd CHAR BH8 433 H8
RFNM GU10 158 D3
Bowers Cl HORN PO8 352 E4
Bowers Grove La ALTN GU34 220 B1
Bowers Hl RSAL SP5 285 K1
Bowers La RAND SP11 72 F1
Bowerwood Rd FBDG SP6 309 H8
Bowes Hl HAV PO9 354 A5
Bowes Rd STHA RG19 27 G6
Bow Fld HTWY RG27 86 B7
Bow Gdns HTWY RG27 64 C8 1
Bow Gv HTWY RG27 64 C7
Bowland Ri CHFD SO53 292 F1
NMIL/BTOS BH25 438 A6
Bowland Wy FAWY SO45 418 C1 1
Bowler Av PSEA PO1 423 K2
Bowler Ct HSEA PO3 423 K2
Bowling Court Gn FRIM GU16 91 H1
Bowling Green Dr HTWY RG27 85 L7 1
Bowling Green Rd NTHA RG18 26 D3
Bowman Ct CWTH RG45 49 H4
Bowman Rd CHAM RG24 83 L4
Bowmonts Rd TADY RG26 42 A8
Bow St ALTN GU34 176 D6
Boxall's Gv ALDT GU11 6 E6
Boxall's La ALDT GU11 6 F7
FNM GU9 6 D6
Box Cl CFDH BH17 445 G1
Boxwood Cl
FHAM/PORC PO16 373 M7 1
WVILLE PO7 376 C2
Boyatt Crs ELGH SO50 265 M8
Boyatt La CHFD SO53 265 M7
ELGH SO50 266 A7
Boyce Cl KEMP RG22 104 B8
Boyd Cl FHAM/STUB PO14 395 M7 1
Boyd Rd BKME/WDN BH12 446 E2
LSOL/BMARY PO13 396 F5
Boyes La RWIN SO21 266 F7
Boyle Crs WVILLE PO7 376 B3
Boyne Mead Rd WINC SO23 215 G1
Boyne Ri WINC SO23 191 G8
Boyneswood Cl ALTN GU34 197 H4
Boyneswood La ALTN GU34 197 G4
Boyneswood Rd ALTN GU34 197 H4
Boynton Cl CHFD SO53 265 G8
Brabant Cl HLER SO31 370 F1
Brabazon Dr CHCH/BSGR BH23 451 G1
Brabazon Rd FHAM PO15 371 H3
WIMB BH21 404 D7
Brabon Rd FARN GU14 90 C3
Brabourne Av FERN BH22 406 A4
Bracebridge CBLY GU15 70 D3
Bracher Cl AND SP10 9 J4
Bracken Bank CHAM RG24 83 L8 1
Brackenbury AND SP10 8 A3
Bracken Cl NBAD SO52 291 M5
RGWD BH24 381 H4
Bracken Crs ELGH SO50 294 E6
Brackendale Cl FRIM GU16 71 H5
Brackendale Ct WIMB BH21 356 B8 1
Brackendale Rd CBLY GU15 71 G4
CHAR BH8 433 G8
Brackendene ASHV GU12 113 M5
Bracken Gln PLE BH15 445 K4
Bracken Heath HORN PO8 352 F7
Brackenhill CCLF BH13 446 F7
Brackenhill Rd WIMB BH21 404 E1
Bracken La BOR GU35 200 F8
ROWN SO16 317 M7
YTLY GU46 68 D2
Bracken Pl ELGH SO50 318 F1
Bracken Rd EPSF GU31 276 B6
FERN BH22 405 M1
NBAD SO52 291 M5
SBNE BH6 449 H4
The Brackens CWTH RG45 49 K1
FAWY SO45 367 H5 2
HLER SO31 370 F6
KEMP RG22 127 H2 1
Brackens Wy LYMN SO41 440 D6 1
Bracken Wy CHCH/BSGR BH23 436 F7
THLE RG7 31 K6 1
Brackenway Rd CHFD SO53 265 H8
Bracklesham Cl FARN GU14 90 D1
ITCH SO19 344 D5
Bracklesham Rd HISD PO11 426 D7
LSOL/BMARY PO13 397 H8
Brackley Av ELGH SO50 295 G6
HTWY RG27 87 H2
Brackley Cl CHCH/BSGR BH23 407 L8
Brackley Wy KEMP RG22 104 B7
TOTT SO40 316 C8
Bracknell Cl CBLY GU15 51 J7
Bracknell La HTWY RG27 87 H1
Bracknell Rd CBLY GU15 51 K6
CWTH RG45 49 M3
Bradburne Rd WCLF BH2 22 C5
Bradbury Cl WHCH RG28 122 A3 1
Bradford Rd
MOOR/WNTN BH9 433 G4
SSEA PO5 21 K3
Brading Av ENEY PO4 423 L6
LSOL/BMARY PO13 397 G6
Brading Cl ROWN SO16 319 H3
Bradley Ct HAV PO9 377 M3
Bradley Gn ROWN SO16 318 A4
Bradley-Moore Sq NTHA RG18 27 H3
Bradley Peak WINW SO22 214 B7
Bradley Rd WINW SO22 214 B5
Bradly Rd FHAM PO15 372 A7
Bradpole Rd CHAR BH8 433 J7
Bradshaw Cl ELGH SO50 295 K6 1
Bradstock Cl BKME/WDN BH12 431 K8
Bradwell Cl AND SP10 118 C5
Braehead FAWY SO45 367 K6
Braemar Av CHAM PO6 399 M1
SBNE BH6 449 M4
Braemar Cl FHAM PO15 14 D1
FRIM GU16 71 J7
LSOL/BMARY PO13 397 H6
SBNE BH6 449 M4
Braemar Dr CHCH/BSGR BH23 436 D7
DEAN RG23 102 F6
Braemar Rd
LSOL/BMARY PO13 397 H5
Braemore Cl STHA RG19 27 G7
Braeside Cl WINW SO22 238 A4
HASM GU27 204 C8
Braeside Crs ITCH SO19 344 C3 1
Braeside Rd FERN BH22 380 C5
ITCH SO19 344 C3
RGWD BH24 381 J4
Brahms Rd KEMP RG22 104 D8
Braidley Rd WCLF BH2 22 D3
Brailswood Rd PLE BH15 445 J4
Braintree Rd CHAM PO6 375 H7
Brairwood Gdns HISD PO11 425 K5
Braishfield Cl ROWN SO16 317 L7
Braishfield Gdns CHAR BH8 433 H6
Braishfield Rd HAV PO9 377 L4
ROMY SO51 263 H7
Brake Rd FARN GU14 90 B7
Bramber Rd GPORT PO12 421 L1
Bramble Bank FRIM GU16 91 K2
Bramble Cl ELGH SO50 294 A3 2
FAWY SO45 392 A5
FBDG SP6 333 L3 3
FHAM/STUB PO14 395 L7
Bramble Dr ROMY SO51 263 H7 3
Bramblegate CWTH RG45 49 K2
Bramble Hl CHFD SO53 293 G2
NALR SO24 218 C3
Bramble La CHCH/BSGR BH23 436 F7
HLER SO31 370 C3
HORN PO8 328 A1
Bramble Ms WEND SO18 319 M8 1
Bramble Rd ENEY PO4 21 L4
EPSF GU31 276 B5
Brambles Cl ALTN GU34 197 G6
ASHV GU12 113 L7
RWIN SO21 266 F8
Brambles Rd
LSOL/BMARY PO13 420 B1 1
The Brambles CWTH RG45 49 G2
NWBY RG14 25 H8
Brambleton Av FNM GU9 158 E1
Bramble Wk LYMN SO41 440 A4 1
Bramble Wy CHAM RG24 106 B2
LSOL/BMARY PO13 396 E6
Bramblewood Pl FLET GU13 88 D7
Brambling Cl KEMP RG22 126 E1 1
ROWN SO16 318 A2 1
Brambling La MIDH GU29 279 L5
Brambling Rd HAV PO9 353 M7
The Bramblings TOTT SO40 316 B8 2
Bramblys Cl BSTK RG21 4 D9
Bramblys Dr BSTK RG21 4 C9
Bramcote CBLY GU15 71 M3
Bramdean Dr HAV PO9 377 H3
Bramdean Rd WEND SO18 345 H1
Bramdown Hts KEMP RG22 127 G2
Bramham Moor
FHAM/STUB PO14 395 M6 2
Bramley Cl ALTN GU34 176 F4 1
LYMN SO41 440 C6 1
WVILLE PO7 352 D8
Bramley Crs ITCH SO19 344 F6
Bramley Gdns EMRTH PO10 378 F8
GPORT PO12 421 L7
Bramley Green Rd TADY RG26 63 M6
Bramley Gv CWTH RG45 49 G3
Bramley La BLKW GU17 69 L3
TADY RG26 63 L4
Bramley Rd CBLY GU15 70 E6 1
FERN BH22 406 B2 1
HTWY RG27 64 C7
NBNE BH10 432 A3
TADY RG26 62 C7
THLE RG7 42 E7
The Bramleys RSAL SP5 259 G5
Bramley Wk BOR GU35 201 G6
Bramling Av YTLY GU46 68 E2
Brammpton Gdns KEMP RG22 127 G3
Brampton La HSEA PO3 400 A4
Brampton Rd PLE BH15 445 J2
Bramshaw Cl WINW SO22 214 B5
Bramshaw Ct HAV PO9 377 M3 3
Bramshaw Wy
NMIL/BTOS BH25 437 H8
Bramshot Dr FLET GU13 88 F6
Bramshot La FARN GU14 89 K3
Bramshott Dr HTWY RG27 86 A7
Bramshott Rd ENEY PO4 423 K4
FARN GU14 89 K7
ITCH SO19 344 D7 1
Bramston Rd WSHM SO15 318 B8
Bramwell Cl STHA RG19 27 J6 2
Brancaster Av AND SP10 118 C5 3
Branches La ROMY SO51 260 E6
Branders Cl SBNE BH6 449 M4
Branders La SBNE BH6 449 M3
Brandon Cl ALTN GU34 176 C4
Brandon Rd FLET GU13 110 D3
SSEA PO5 21 J8
Brandy Mt NALR SO24 218 C2
Branksea Av PLE BH15 444 C7
Branksea Cl PLE BH15 444 D7
Branksome Av STOK SO20 165 M5
WSHM SO15 318 B7
Branksome Cl CBLY GU15 71 H2 1
WINW SO22 238 A2
NMIL/BTOS BH25 437 M6
STOK SO20 165 L5
Branksome Dene Rd
WBNE BH4 447 G6
Branksome Hill Rd SHST GU47 70 B1
WBNE BH4 447 G3
Branksome Park Rd CBLY GU15 71 H2
Branksome Towers CCLF BH13 447 G8
Branksome Wood Gdns
WCLF BH2 22 B3
Branksomewood Rd FLET GU13 88 D7
Branksome Wood Rd
WBNE BH4 447 H3
Bransbury Cl ROWN SO16 318 B4 1
Bransbury Rd ENEY PO4 423 M5
Bransgore Av HAV PO9 377 G4
Bransgore Gdns
CHCH/BSGR BH23 409 M7
Bransley Cl ROMY SO51 263 G7
Branson Rd BOR GU35 201 K5
Branton Cl KEMP RG22 104 B5
Branwell Cl CHCH/BSGR BH23 434 E7
Branwood Cl LYMN SO41 439 J7 1
Brasenose Cl
FHAM/STUB PO14 371 G7
Brasher Cl ELGH SO50 294 F6
Brassey Cl MOOR/WNTN BH9 432 F7
Brassey Rd WINW SO22 10 E4
MOOR/WNTN BH9 432 D7
Brasted Ct ENEY PO4 424 A3 1
Braunfels Wk KSCL RG20 2 A6
NWBY RG14 2 A5
Braye Cl SHST GU47 49 M7 2
Brazil Rd SHAM SO14 13 J8
Breach Av EMRTH PO10 379 H6
Breachfield KSCL RG20 57 J1
Breach La HTWY RG27 64 D8
RAND SP11 72 A8
Breamore Cl ELGH SO50 293 M2 1
NMIL/BTOS BH25 437 J5 1
Breamore Rd RSAL SP5 284 C2
WEND SO18 345 H1
Brean Cl ROWN SO16 317 K5
Brecon Av CHAM PO6 375 M7
Brecon Cl CHFD SO53 293 G5 1
FARN GU14 90 A1
FAWY SO45 367 J5
FHAM/STUB PO14 14 B7
NBNE BH10 432 C2
NMIL/BTOS BH25 438 A6
Brecon Rd ITCH SO19 345 G3
Bredenbury Crs CHAM PO6 375 G7
Breech Cl HSEA PO3 399 K4 3
The Breech CBLY GU15 70 B1
Bremble Cl BKME/WDN BH12 431 G6
Bremen Gdns AND SP10 118 E6
Brenchley Cl
FHAM/PORC PO16 397 L1
Brendon Cl FAWY SO45 367 H6 2
Brendon Gn ROWN SO16 317 L8
Brendon Rd FARN GU14 90 A1
FHAM/STUB PO14 14 B8
Brent Cl STHA RG19 27 G6
Brent Ct EMRTH PO10 378 C8
Brentwood Crs WEND SO18 319 M7
Bret Harte Rd FRIM GU16 71 H7
Breton Cl FHAM PO15 370 F1
Brewells La LISS GU33 249 K2
Brewer Cl HLER SO31 370 F4

KEMP RG22 .... 104 B5
Brewers Cl FARN GU14 .... 90 D3
Brewers La LSOL/BMARY PO13 .. 397 G6
NALR SO24 .... 221 J7
RWIN SO21 .... 266 E3
Brewery Common THLE RG7 .... 43 L2
Brewhouse Sq GPORT PO12 .... 19 J1
Brewhouse La HTWY RG27 ...... 87 J2 🔲
Brewster Cl HORN PO8 .... 352 B5
Briar CHCH/BSGR BH23 .... 450 E2
GPORT PO12 .... 421 J5
HORN PO8 .... 352 F3
PLE BH15 .... 445 K3
Briardene Ct TOTT SO40 .... 341 J1 🔲
Briarfield Gdns HORN PO8 ..... 352 F3
Briar La ALTN GU34 .... 197 H5
Briarlea Rd THLE RG7 .... 43 J2
Briars Cl FARN GU14 .... 90 A5
Briarswood ROWN SO16 .... 318 A7
Briarswood Ri FAWY SO45 ...... 367 H6
Briarswood Rd UPTN BH16 ...... 444 B1 🔲
Briar Wy ROMY SO51 .... 263 H7
TADY RG26 .... 41 M8
WIMB BH21 .... 404 F3
Briar Wy LISS GU33 .... 248 F1
Briarwood Cl FHAM/PORC PO16.. 15 J7
Briarwood Dr EWKG RG40 .... 48 B2 🔲
Briarwood Rd TOTT SO40 .... 341 G4
LYMN SO41 .... 440 D3
Brickfield La CHFD SO53 ...... 293 G5
LYMN SO41 .... 440 D3
Brickfield Rd PTSW SO17 ...... 319 H6
Brickfields Cl CHAM RG24 ..... 83 M8 🔲
Bricklin La ALTN GU34 .... 197 L2
Brick Kiln La ALTN GU34 ...... 176 B4
NALR SO24 .... 244 E1
Brick La CHCH/BSGR BH23 ...... 410 C4
FLET GU13 .... 88 C6
Brickmakers Rd RWIN SO21 .... 266 E8
Bricksbury HI FNM GU9 .... 134 F1
Brickwoods ROMY SO51 .... 263 G8 🔲
Brickworth Rd RSAL SP5 .... 258 D4
Brickworth Rd RSAL SP5 .... 258 D4
Brickyard La WIMB BH21 .... 405 L2
Brickyard Rd BPWT SO32 .... 323 L5
The Brickyard TOTT SO40 ...... 315 H1
Bricky Lake La ROMY SO51 ..... 315 H1
Bridefield Cl HORN PO8 .... 352 B5
Bridefield Crs HORN PO8 ...... 352 B5
Bridge Ap PLE BH15 .... 445 G7
Bridge Cl HLER SO31 .... 345 M7
Bridge End CBLY GU15 .... 70 E4
Bridgefield FNM GU9 .... 135 G6
Bridgefoot Dr
  FHAM/PORC PO16 .... 15 M5
Bridgefoot Pth EMRTH PO10 ... 378 D8
Bridgemary Av
  LSOL/BMARY PO13 .... 397 H5
Bridgemary Gv
  LSOL/BMARY PO13 .... 397 G4
Bridgemary Rd
  LSOL/BMARY PO13 .... 397 G3
Bridgemary Wy
  LSOL/BMARY PO13 .... 397 G3 🔲
Bridge Md BPWT SO32 .... 299 J3
Bridgemead FRIM GU16 .... 71 J8
Bridge Mdw LISS GU33 .... 248 E4
Bridge Pl NBNE BH10 .... 432 B1
Bridge Rd ALDT GU11 .... 6 F5
  CBLY GU15 .... 70 E5
  EMRTH PO10 .... 378 D7
  FARN GU14 .... 90 C4
  HASM GU27 .... 228 F1
  HLER SO31 .... 345 M7
  HLER SO31 .... 370 C2
  ITCH SO19 .... 344 B5
  LYMN SO41 .... 440 D4
  NALR SO24 .... 218 A3
  ODIM RG29 .... 108 B4
  ROMY SO51 .... 290 E1
  RSAL SP5 .... 253 C1
Bridgers Cl ROWN SO16 .... 317 K3
Bridges Cl ELGH SO50 .... 293 L5
  FERN BH22 .... 380 D5 🔲
Bridgeside Cl PSEA PO1 .... 21 K1
The Bridges RGWD BH24 .... 382 C1
  THLE RG7 .... 42 F3
Bridge St AND SP10 .... 9 H6
  CHCH/BSGR BH23 .... 450 B4
  FBDG SP6 .... 309 L7
  FHAM/STUB PO14 .... 371 L8
  NWBY RG14 .... 2 E4
  OVTN RG25 .... 100 F8
  WHAM PO17 .... 348 E4
  WHAM PO17 .... 374 B2
  WINC SO23 .... 11 J8 🔲
Bridget Cl HORN PO8 .... 353 G1
Bridgetts La RWIN SO21 .... 192 A6
Bridge Wk YTLY GU46 .... 69 L1
Bridgwater Ct WSHM SO15 ..... 12 A1
Bridle Cl ALTN GU34 .... 222 C3
  GSHT GU26 .... 203 K5
  UPTN BH16 .... 444 C1
Bridle Ct ALDT GU11 .... 6 B2
Bridle Crs LTDN BH7 .... 434 A8
Bridle Wy WIMB BH21 .... 404 F2
Bridleways VWD BH31 .... 356 C2
Bridlington Av WSHM SO15 .... 318 C8
Bridport Rd BKME/WDN BH12 .. 431 K8
  VWD BH31 .... 356 C2
Bridport St PSEA PO1 .... 21 H1
Brierley Av FERN BH22 .... 406 C4
Brierley Cl NBNE BH10 .... 432 C3
Brierley Rd NBNE BH10 .... 432 C4
Briff La THLE RG7 .... 27 L2
Brigantine Rd HLER SO31 ..... 370 C1
Brighstone Cl ROWN SO16 ..... 319 H3 🔲
Brightlands Av SBNE BH6 ..... 449 L4
Brighton Av GPORT PO12 ...... 397 K8
Brighton Rd ALDT GU11 .... 7 K6
  LYMN SO41 .... 412 L5
  WSHM SO15 .... 343 K1
Brighton Wy KEMP RG22 ...... 104 C7
Bright Rd PLE BH15 .... 445 J2
Brightside WVILLE PO7 .... 376 B2
Brightside Rd ROWN SO16 ..... 317 L6
Brights La HISD PO11 .... 425 K3

Brightstone La ALTN GU34 .... 197 M6
Brightstone Rd CHAM PO6 ..... 399 J1
Brightwells Rd FNM GU9 ...... 134 F6 🔲
Brimpton Rd THLE RG7 .... 28 B7
  THLE RG7 .... 40 F6
Brindle Cl ALDT GU11 .... 7 G7
  ROWN SO16 .... 318 F3
Brinksway FLET GU13 .... 88 F8
Brinn's La BLKW GU17 .... 69 M3
Brinsons Cl CHCH/BSGR BH23.. 435 G5
Brinton La FAWY SO45 .... 367 L3
Brinton's Rd SHAM SO14 ...... 13 H1
Brinton's Ter SHAM SO14 ..... 343 L2 🔲
Brisbane Rd RAND SP11 .... 115 J1 🔲
Brisbane Rd CHCH/BSGR BH23 . 434 C7
Brislands La ALTN GU34 ...... 220 L1
Bristol Rd ENEY PO4 .... 423 K6
Bristow Rd CBLY GU15 .... 70 G5
Britain St PSEA PO1 .... 20 D7
Britannia Cl BOR GU35 .... 201 L5 🔲
Britannia Gdns HEND SO30 ... 321 G5 🔲
Britannia Rd PSTN BH14 ...... 445 M5
  SHAM SO14 .... 13 K1
  SSEA PO5 .... 21 K4 🔲
Britannia Rd North SSEA PO5 .. 21 K4
Briton St SHAM SO14 .... 12 F6
Britten Cl ASHV GU12 .... 113 L6
Britten Rd LSOL/BMARY PO13.. 420 C2
Britten Wy WVILLE PO7 .... 376 C4
Brixey Cl BKME/WDN BH12 .... 446 B1
Brixey Rd BKME/WDN BH12 .... 446 B1
Broadacres FLET GU13 .... 88 C8 🔲
Broad Av CHAR BH8 .... 433 H8
Broadbent Cl ROWN SO16 ..... 317 J2
Broad Chalke Down
  WINW SO22 .... 238 B4
Broadcut FHAM/PORC PO16 ... 15 M3
Broadfields LYMN SO41 .... 454 C3
Broad Gdns CHAM PO6 .... 376 C8
Broad Gn SHAM SO14 .... 13 H2
Broadhalfpenny La TADY RG26. 41 M7
Broadhill Rd FBDG SP6 .... 310 C8
Broadhurst FARN GU14 .... 89 M4
Broadhurst Av NBNE BH10 .... 432 C4
Broadhurst Gv CHAM RG24 ... 105 L1
Broadlands FARN GU14 .... 91 H6 🔲
  FRIM GU16 .... 71 J8
Broadlands Av ELGH SO50 .... 293 M3
  SBNE BH6 .... 449 L4
  WVILLE PO7 .... 376 C2
Broadlands Cl CHAR BH8 ...... 433 H5
  CHCH/BSGR BH23 .... 436 F6
Broadlands Rd BROC SO42 .... 387 J6
  PTSW SO17 .... 319 G5
Broad La BPWT SO32 .... 323 M3
  LYMN SO41 .... 440 D5
  NBAD SO52 .... 291 K3 🔲
  THLE RG7 .... 27 L2
  WVILLE PO7 .... 350 F2
Broad Leaze HTWY RG27 .... 85 M6 🔲
Broadley Cl FAWY SO45 .... 392 A4 🔲
Broadly Cl LYMN SO41 .... 439 M6
Broadmayne Rd
  BKME/WDN BH12 .... 446 E1
Broadmead FARN GU14 .... 90 A5
Broadmeadow Cl TOTT SO40 .. 341 J1
Broadmeadow End NTHA RG18 . 27 J5
Broadmeadows La
  WVILLE PO7 .... 376 E1 🔲
Broadmead Rd ROWN SO16 .... 317 J2
Broad Mead Rd WIMB BH21 ... 356 C7
Broadmere Av HAV PO9 .... 377 K3
Broadmoor Rd WIMB BH21 .... 429 G2
Broad Oak HEND SO30 .... 346 C1
Broadoak TADY RG26 .... 42 A8 🔲
Broadoak Cl FAWY SO45 .... 392 A5
Broad Oak La ODIM RG29 ...... 108 F5
Broad Rd RAND SP11 .... 141 G5
  RCCH PO18 .... 379 M8
Broadsands Dr GPORT PO12 .. 421 K6
Broadshard La RGWD BH24 ... 358 E7
Broadstone Wy BDST BH18 .... 429 K7
Broad St NALR SO24 .... 218 C2
  PSEA PO1 .... 20 B5
Broadview Cl ALTN GU34 ...... 178 D1
Broad View La WINW SO22 .... 237 M5
Broad Wk FRIM GU16 .... 71 H6
Broadwater Av PSTN BH14 .... 446 A6
Broadwater Rd ROMY SO51 ... 290 D2
  WEND SO18 .... 319 L5
Broad Wy HLER SO31 .... 369 J3
  FARN GU14 .... 90 D8
  PSF GU32 .... 246 C8
  THLE RG7 .... 45 C5
Broadway SBNE BH6 .... 449 M4
  STHA RG19 .... 27 G5
  WHCH RG28 .... 122 C4
Broadway La CHAR BH8 .... 433 G5
  HORN PO8 .... 352 B2
The Broadway NBNE BH10 .... 432 B2
  SHST GU47 .... 69 L1
  WINC SO23 .... 11 H8
Broadwell Rd RFNM GU10 .... 158 C2
Broad Woods La ROMY SO51 .. 288 F1
Brocas Dr BSTK RG21 .... 5 H4
Brocas Rd THLE RG7 .... 31 J7
Brockenhurst Av HAV PO9 .... 377 H2
Brockenhurst Dr YTLY GU46 .. 69 G3 🔲
Brockenhurst Rd ALDT GU11 ... 7 G5
  MOOR/WNTN SO9 .... 432 F6
Brockham Hill La ALTN GU34 .. 154 F5
Brockhampton La HAV PO9 .... 16 D5
Brockhampton Rd HAV PO9 ... 16 B5
Brockhills La NMIL/BTOS SO25. 438 A3
Brockhurst Ldg FNM GU9 .... 158 E1
Brockhurst Rd GPORT PO12 ... 421 K1
Brockishill Rd LYND SO43 .... 339 K4
  TOTT SO40 .... 339 L3
Brocklands HAV PO9 .... 16 B4
  YTLY GU46 .... 68 L4 🔲
Brockley Rd NBNE BH10 .... 432 B4
Brocks Cl FAWY SO45 .... 367 H6
Brocks Pine RGWD BH24 ...... 381 K5
Brockwood Bottom
  NALR SO24 .... 243 K7
Brodrick Av GPORT PO12 ...... 18 D6

Brokenford Av TOTT SO40 .... 341 L1
Brokenford La TOTT SO40 .... 341 K1
Bromelia Cl TADY RG26 .... 63 L4
Bromley Rd WEND SO18 .... 319 L7
Brompton Rd ENEY PO4 .... 423 K6
Bromyard Crs CHAM PO6 ...... 375 G8
Bronte Av CHCH/BSGR BH23 .. 434 E7
Bronte Cl TOTT SO40 .... 341 H2
Bronte Gdns FHAM PO15 ...... 347 G8 🔲
Brook Av FNM GU9 .... 6 D7
Brook Av North
  NMIL/BTOS BH25 .... 437 M3
Brook Cl FLET GU13 .... 88 F8
  HLER SO31 .... 370 B5 🔲
  NBAD SO52 .... 291 M5
  NBNE BH10 .... 432 A4
  SHST GU47 .... 50 B7
Brookdale Cl WIMB BH21 ...... 429 L4
  WVILLE PO7 .... 352 C8
Brook Dr VWD BH31 .... 356 F4
Brooke Cl WINC SO23 .... 191 G8
Brookers Cnr CWTH RG45 .... 49 M3
Brookers La
  LSOL/BMARY PO13 .... 396 E5
Brookers Rw CWTH RG45 ...... 49 M2
Brook Farm Av FHAM PO15 ... 14 E5
Brookfield Cl CHAM RG24 ..... 83 M5 🔲
Brookfield Gdns HLER SO31 .. 370 D4
Brookfield Rd ASHV GU12 .... 113 H6
  ELGH SO50 .... 295 G6
  PSEA PO1 .... 423 J2
Brookfields ROMY SO51 ...... 288 C5
Brook Gdns EMRTH PO10 ...... 378 B8
  FARN GU14 .... 90 C6
Brook Gn TADY RG26 .... 42 A8
Brookhouse Rd FARN GU14 .... 90 C5
Brookland Cl LYMN SO41 ..... 440 A5 🔲
Brooklands ALDT GU11 .... 6 B3 🔲
Brooklands Cl FNM GU9 ...... 135 G1
  RFNM GU10 .... 157 G3 🔲
Brooklands Rd BPWT SO32 ... 297 H8
  HAV PO9 .... 376 F6
Brooklands Wy FNM GU9 .... 6 A8
Brook La CHCH/BSGR BH23 ... 435 L1
  FBDG SP6 .... 310 D1
  HEND SO30 .... 346 D2
  HLER SO31 .... 370 A7
  WIMB BH21 .... 429 G2
  WVILLE PO7 .... 326 A2
Brookley Rd BROC SO42 .... 387 K7
Brookly Gdns FLET GU13 ...... 89 G6
Brooklyn Cl RWIN SO21 .... 266 B5
Brooklyn Ct
  NMIL/BTOS BH25 .... 437 K5 🔲
Brooklyn Dr WVILLE PO7 ...... 352 D8 🔲
Brooklynn Cl BPWT SO32 ...... 323 K6
Brookmeadow FHAM PO15 ..... 14 E5
Brookmead Wy HAV PO9 .... 16 E8
Brooksby Cl BLKW GU17 .... 69 L3 🔲
Brooks Cl RGWD BH24 .... 382 F2
Brookside FBDG SP6 .... 335 G6
Brook Side
  NMIL/BTOS BH25 .... 437 K5 🔲
  LSOL/BMARY PO13 .... 396 F3
  SHST GU47 .... 69 M1
  TOTT SO40 .... 341 K3
Brookside Av WSHM SO15 .... 342 D1
Brookside Cl WVILLE PO7 ..... 351 K4
Brookside Rd BROC SO42 ..... 387 K6
  CHCH/BSGR BH23 .... 409 L8
  HAV PO9 .... 16 B6
  HAV PO9 .... 377 G6
  WIMB BH21 .... 404 C4
Brookside Wy
  CHCH/BSGR BH23 .... 436 F6
  HEND SO30 .... 320 D5 🔲
  WEND SO18 .... 319 K4
Brooks Rd NTHA RG18 .... 27 H4
Brook St BPWT SO32 .... 323 H1
  FBDG SP6 .... 309 L8 🔲
The Brook NALR SO24 .... 194 C8
Brookvale Rd PTSW SO17 ..... 318 F7
Brook Va ROWN SO16 .... 317 M6
Brook Wy CHCH/BSGR BH23 .. 451 H1
Brookway NWBY RG14 .... 26 B5
  RAND SP11 .... 142 B4
Brook Wy ROMY SO51 .... 262 F7
Brookwood Av ELGH SO50 .... 293 L5
Brookwood Rd FARN GU14 .... 91 G4
  ROWN SO16 .... 317 J8
  SHST GU47 .... 49 L8
Broom Cl BLKW GU17 .... 70 B4 🔲
  ENEY PO4 .... 424 D4
  WVILLE PO7 .... 376 E3
Broome Cl YTLY GU46 .... 68 F1
Broomfield Crs
  LSOL/BMARY PO13 .... 420 F1
Broomfield Dr FBDG SP6 ...... 333 L3
Broomfield La LYMN SO41 .... 440 C4
  RFNM GU10 .... 158 D7
Broomfield Rd BOR GU35 ..... 201 D7
Broom HI NMIL/BTOS SO4 ..... 441 M1
Broomhill RFNM GU10 .... 111 G8
  RSAL SP5 .... 287 J7
Broomhill Rd FARN GU14 ..... 90 A3
Broom Hill Wy ELGH SO50 .... 293 L1
Broomleaf Cnr FNM GU9 ..... 135 G6 🔲
Broomleaf Rd FNM GU9 ...... 135 G6
Broomrigg Rd FLET GU13 .... 88 C6
Broom Rd BKME/WDN BH12 .. 431 G2
  EPSF GU31 .... 276 B6
Brooms Gv ITCH SO19 .... 345 H5

Broom Sq ENEY PO4 .... 424 B4
Broom Wy LSOL/BMARY PO13 . 420 D1
Broomwood Wy RFNM GU10 .. 158 F2
Broomy Cl FAWY SO45 .... 367 G4 🔲
Brougham La GPORT PO12 .... 421 J2 🔲
Brougham Pl FNM GU9 .... 134 E1
Brougham Rd SSEA PO5 .... 21 G4
Brougham St GPORT PO12 .... 421 J2 🔲
Broughton Av BH10 .... 432 C4
Broughton Cl HSEA PO3 ..... 400 A4 🔲
Broughton Ct HSEA PO3 ..... 400 A4 🔲
Broughton Ms FRIM GU16 ..... 71 J7 🔲
Broughton Rd LYND SO43 .... 363 J2
  STOK SO20 .... 185 K6
Brown Cft HTWY RG27 .... 85 L7
Browndown Rd
  LSOL/BMARY PO13 .... 421 G5
Brownen Rd
  MOOR/WNTN BH9 .... 432 F8
Brownhill Cl CHFD SO53 ..... 293 F1
  ROWN SO16 .... 317 K5
Brownhill Rd CHFD SO53 ..... 293 H1
  NBAD SO52 .... 292 A4
  NMIL/BTOS BH25 .... 411 H5
Brownhill Wy ROWN SO16 .... 317 H5
Browning Av BOSC BH5 .... 448 E4
  CHAM PO6 .... 374 C7
  ITCH SO19 .... 345 H2
Browning Cl CBLY GU15 .... 71 M4
  CHAM RG24 .... 5 G1
  ELGH SO50 .... 293 L5 🔲
  HLER SO31 .... 347 G8
  NTHA RG18 .... 26 F4
  TOTT SO40 .... 341 H1
Browning Dr WINW SO22 ..... 10 B6
Browning Rd FLET GU13 ..... 110 D5
Brownings Cl LYMN SO41 .... 439 L4
Brownlow Av ITCH SO19 ...... 344 E2
Brownlow Gdns ITCH SO19 ... 344 E2
Browns Cl TADY RG26 .... 63 K4
Brownsea Av WIMB BH21 .... 429 H2
Brownsea Cl NMIL/BTOS BH25 .. 437 J5
Brownsea Rd CLCH PO13 ..... 457 C5
Brownsea View Av PSTN BH14 . 446 F4
Brownsfield Rd NTHA RG18 .. 26 F5
Browns La FBDG SP6 .... 308 A3
  LYMN SO41 .... 442 A3
Brownsover Rd FARN GU14 ... 89 M4
Browns Wk RFNM GU10 .... 158 C3
Brownwich La
  FHAM/STUB PO14 .... 395 H3
The Brow WVILLE PO7 .... 376 A6
Broxburn Cl CHFD SO53 ...... 265 K7
Broxhead Farm Rd BOR GU35 . 179 K8
Broxhead Rd HAV PO9 .... 377 L2 🔲
Brtten Rd KEMP RG22 .... 104 D8
Bruan Rd NWBY RG14 .... 25 J8
Bruce Cl FHAM/PORC PO16 ... 15 H2
Bruce Rd ENEY PO4 .... 423 K6
Brudenell Av CCLF BH13 ..... 457 J1
Brudenell Rd CCLF BH13 ..... 457 J1
Brue Cl CHFD SO53 .... 293 C1
Brummell Rd NWBY RG14 ...... 2 A1
Brune La LSOL/BMARY PO13 .. 396 E7
Brunel Cl HEND SO30 .... 321 J7 🔲
  RWIN SO21 .... 148 A6
Brunel Rd BSTK RG21 .... 104 D2
  NEND PO2 .... 399 J5
  TOTT SO40 .... 316 C5
  WSHM SO15 .... 342 A1
Brunel Wy FHAM PO15 .... 371 H3
Brunstead Pl
  BKME/WDN BH12 .... 447 G4
Brunstead Rd
  BKME/WDN BH12 .... 446 F4
Brunswick Cl ELGH SO50 .... 295 G5 🔲
Brunswick Gdns HAV PO9 .... 16 A3
Brunswick Pl LYMN SO41 .... 440 C4
  WSHM SO15 .... 343 K2
Brunswick Rd ELGH SO50 .... 295 G5
  FRIM GU16 .... 91 M2
Brunswick Sq SHAM SO14 .... 13 H8
Brunswick St SSEA PO5 ...... 21 G4 🔲
Bruntile Cl FARN GU14 ...... 91 G7
Bruyn Rd FBDG SP6 .... 309 M7
Bryanston Cl FLET GU13 .... 110 F2
Bryanston Rd TWDS BH3 ..... 447 K1
Bryanston Rd ITCH SO19 .... 344 B4
Bryant Rd BKME/WDN BH12 .. 431 G8
Bryce Gdns ALDT GU11 .... 7 K8
Bryces La NALR SO24 .... 171 M5
Brydes Rd RAND SP11 .... 92 E6
Bryher Island CHAM PO6 .... 398 F3
Brympton Cl FBDG SP6 ...... 309 H6
Bryn Rd RFNM GU10 .... 158 E1 🔲
Bryon Rd WIMB BH21 .... 404 A2
Bryony Cl BDST BH18 .... 429 K5
  HLER SO31 .... 370 D6 🔲
Bryony Gdns ELGH SO50 ..... 321 H2 🔲
Bryony Wy WVILLE PO7 .... 376 E2
Bryson Rd CHAM PO6 .... 375 H8 🔲
Bubb La CHCH/BSGR BH23 ... 450 D2
  HEND SO30 .... 321 G5
Bub La CHCH/BSGR BH23 ..... 450 D2
Buccleuch Rd CCLF BH13 .... 446 F7
Bucehayes Cl
  CHCH/BSGR BH23 .... 436 E8
Buchanan Av LTDN BH7 ...... 448 C1
Buchanan Dr EWKG RG40 ..... 48 B1
Buchanan Rd ROWN SO16 .... 317 L3
Buchanan Sq STHA RG19 ..... 27 H7
Buchan Av FHAM PO15 .... 347 G8
Buchan Ct FAWY SO45 .... 367 G6
The Buchan CBLY GU15 .... 51 K8
Buckby La BSTK RG21 .... 5 K7
  HSEA PO3 .... 400 A4
Bucketts Farm Cl BPWT SO32 . 324 A3
Buckfast Cl CHAM RG24 ...... 82 F7
Buckholt Rd STOK SO20 ..... 208 F2
Buckhurst Rd FRIM GU16 .... 91 J2
Buckingham Cl ALTN GU34 .. 176 C5 🔲
Buckingham Ga WSHM SO15 . 318 D8 🔲
Buckingham Rd
  BKME/WDN BH12 .... 446 C1
  NWBY RG14 .... 2 B7
  PSF GU32 .... 275 J5
Buckland Av KEMP RG22 .... 104 C7

Buckland Cl ELGH SO50 ...... 293 M3
  FARN GU14 .... 90 F1
  WVILLE PO7 .... 352 B6
Buckland Dene LYMN SO41 .. 440 B6
Buckland Gdns TOTT SO40 ... 316 B6
Buckland Gv CHCH/BSGR BH23. 436 C6
Buckland Rd BKME/WDN BH12. 446 B3
Buckland St NEND PO2 .... 423 J1 🔲
Buckland Ter
  BKME/WDN BH12 .... 446 B3
Bucklers Cl HAV PO9 .... 377 H1
  NEND PO2 .... 399 H7 🔲
Bucklers Rd GPORT PO12 .... 398 A8
The Bucklers LYMN SO41 .... 453 K6
Bucklers Wy CHAR BH8 ...... 433 H5
Buckmore Av PSF GU32 ...... 275 J4
Bucksey Rd
  LSOL/BMARY PO13 .... 397 G8
Bucks Head HI BPWT SO32 ... 299 H3
Buckskin La KEMP RG22 ..... 103 M5
Buckstone Cl LYMN SO41 .... 439 L7
Buckthorn Cl TOTT SO40 .... 315 M8
  WIMB BH21 .... 429 K6 🔲
Budden's La WHAM PO17 .... 324 F2
Buddens Rd WHAM PO17 ..... 348 L4
Buddle HI FBDG SP6 .... 335 G4
Buddlesgate RWIN SO21 .... 168 C5
Budd's Cl BSTK RG21 .... 4 C7
Budds La BOR GU35 .... 201 H4
  ROMY SO51 .... 262 D7
Bude Cl CHAM PO6 .... 374 D7
Buffbeards La HASM GU27 ... 228 B1
Buffins Rd ODIM RG29 .... 108 B6 🔲
Bugdens La VWD BH31 .... 356 D2
Bugkingham Wy FRIM GU16 ... 71 J8
Bugle St SHAM SO14 .... 12 F6
Bulbeck Rd HAV PO9 .... 16 E5
Bulbery RAND SP11 .... 141 L5
Buldowne Wk LYMN SO41 .... 412 F5
Bulford Rd NTID SP9 .... 114 A7
  NTID SP9 .... 114 D8
Bullar Rd WEND SO18 .... 344 C1
Bull Dro WINC SO23 .... 239 G5
Buller Ct FARN GU14 .... 90 F7 🔲
Buller Rd ALDT GU11 .... 112 E4
Bullers Rd FNM GU9 .... 135 H2
Bullfinch Cl CFDH BH17 ..... 429 K7
  SHST GU47 .... 50 B8 🔲
  TOTT SO40 .... 341 G1 🔲
Bull HI LISS GU33 .... 249 K1
  LYMN SO41 .... 414 F7
Bullington La RWIN SO21 .... 167 K1
Bull La BPWT SO32 .... 323 J5
  LYND SO43 .... 339 G5
  RSAL SP5 .... 45 L5
Bullrush Cl FAWY SO45 ...... 367 G4
Bulls Copse La HORN PO8 ... 352 L2
Bulls Down Cl HTWY RG27 ... 64 B7
Bulls Dro RSAL SP5 .... 231 M2
Bulls La RSAL SP5. .... 252 A1
Bulpits HI RAND SP11 .... 73 H2
Bunces La THLE RG7 .... 31 K6
Bunch La HASM GU27 .... 228 D1
Bunch Wy HASM GU27 .... 228 D2
Bungalow Rd FARN GU14 .... 90 E6
Bungler's HI THLE RG7 .... 46 E2
Bunkers HI NWBY RG14 .... 36 F5 🔲
  WVILLE PO7 .... 351 H5
Bunnian Pl BSTK RG21 .... 4 F6
Bunns La WVILLE PO7 .... 350 C3
Bunny La ROMY SO51 .... 262 G2
  RSAL SP5 .... 259 M4
Bunstead La RWIN SO21 .... 265 J3
Bunting Cl KEMP RG22 ...... 126 E1
Bunting Gdns HORN PO8 .... 352 D4
Bunting Ms KEMP RG22 ..... 126 F1 🔲
Buntings ALTN GU34 .... 176 C2
Burbidge Gv ENEY PO4 ...... 423 L6
Burbush Cl FAWY SO45 ...... 392 A5
Burchell Rd NWBY RG14 ..... 25 H3
Burcombe Rd NBNE BH10 .... 432 A4
Burcote Dr HSEA PO3 .... 399 M4
Burdale Dr HISD PO11 .... 426 B5
Burdens Heath NTHA RG18 ... 27 K1
Burdock Cl CHCH/BSGR BH23 . 435 M7
  RAND SP11 .... 142 B8
  THLE RG7 .... 31 L6
Bure Cl CHCH/BSGR BH23 .... 451 G2
Bure Haven Dr
  CHCH/BSGR BH23 .... 450 F2
Bure Homage La
  CHCH/BSGR BH23 .... 450 F2
Bure Pk CHCH/BSGR BH23 ... 451 G3
Bure Rd CHCH/BSGR BH23 ... 451 G2
Burfield KSCL RG20 .... 56 B3
Burford Cl CHCH/BSGR BH23. 434 D7
Burford La BROC SO42 .... 387 G4
Burford Rd CBLY GU15 .... 70 E4 🔲
Burgate Cl HAV PO9 .... 377 H5
Burgate Flds FBDG SP6 ..... 309 M5
Burgess Cl BWD BH11 .... 431 K4
  HISD PO11 .... 426 B7
  ODIM RG29 .... 108 B6 🔲
Burgess Gdns ROWN SO16 ... 318 D5 🔲
Burgess La KSCL RG20 .... 34 F5
Burgess Rd BSTK RG21 .... 4 D5
  PTSW SO17 .... 319 G4
  WSHM SO15 .... 318 C6
Burghclere Rd HAV PO9 ..... 377 M2
  ITCH SO19 .... 344 D8 🔲
Burghead Cl SHST GU47 ..... 70 A1 🔲
Burgh Hill Rd LIPH GU30 ... 226 C1
Burgoyne Rd CBLY GU15 ..... 71 K2
  ITCH SO19 .... 345 J4
  SSEA PO5 .... 423 H7
Burgundy Cl HLER SO31 .... 370 D6 🔲
Buriton Cl FHAM/PORC PO16. 374 B7
Buriton Rd WINW SO22 ...... 214 C4
Buriton St PSEA PO1 .... 423 H2
Burke Dr ITCH SO19 .... 345 G2
Burleigh Rd FRIM GU16 ...... 71 J8
  NEND PO2 .... 399 K8
  SBNE BH6 .... 449 J2
Burley Cl CHFD SO53 .... 293 G4
  HAV PO9 .... 377 M2 🔲

NMIL/BTOS BH25 437 H8
VWD BH31 356 C3
Burley Down CHFD SO53 293 G4
Burley La OVTN RG25 124 C7
Burley Lawn RGWD BH24 384 F4
Burley Rd BKME/WDN BH12 446 B2
BROC SO42 412 E1
CHCH/BSGR BH23 410 B3
CHCH/BSGR BH23 435 G3
WINW SO22 214 C4
Burley Wy BLKW GU17 69 M2
Burlington Ct BLKW GU17 69 M5
Burlington Rd NEND PO2 399 J7
WSHM SO15 343 J2
Burmah Rd North FAWY SO45 393 G2
Burmah Rd South FAWY SO45 392 F3
Burma Wy TOTT SO40 342 D8
Burmese Cl FHAM PO15 371 G1
Burnaby Cl KEMP RG22 104 B5
Burnaby Rd PSEA PO1 20 E2
WBNE BH4 447 H7
Burnbake Rd VWD BH31 356 D3
Burnbank Gdns TOTT SO40 341 J1
Burnbrae Rd FERN BH22 406 B7
Burn Cl VWD BH31 356 F4
Burne Cl RWIN SO21 190 C6
Burne-Jones Dr SHST GU47 70 A2
Burnett Av CHCH/BSGR BH23 449 K1
Burnett Cl FAWY SO45 367 M6
WINW SO22 214 B6
WEND SO18 319 K7
Burnett Rd CHCH/BSGR BH23 449 L1
GPORT PO12 421 K2
Burnetts Flds ELGH SO50 321 H1
Burnetts Gdns ELGH SO50 321 J1
Burnetts La HEND SO30 321 G4
Burney Bit TADY RG26 42 B8
Burney Rd GPORT PO12 421 J5
Burngate Rd PLE BH15 444 D6
Burnham Beeches CHFD SO53 293 G2
Burnham Cha WEND SO18 344 F1
Burnham Dr CHAR BH8 448 B1
Burnham Rd CHAM PO6 376 B7
CHCH/BSGR BH23 435 G6
FBDG SP6 309 L5 2
TADY RG26 41 J6
Burnhams Cl AND SP10 118 F5
Burnham Wd
FHAM/PORC PO16 15 G1
Burnleigh Gdns
NMIL/BTOS BH25 438 A4 2
Burnley Cl TADY RG26 61 L1
Burnmoor Meadow
EWKG RG40 48 B6
Burnsall Cl FARN GU14 90 E2
Burns Av FLET GU13 111 G2
Burns Cl CHAM RG24 5 H2
ELGH SO50 293 K7
FARN GU14 90 C2
RWIN SO21 190 D4
Burnside LSOL/BMARY PO13 396 F3
WVILLE PO7 352 E7
Burns Pl ROWN SO16 317 M6
Burns Rd ELGH SO50 293 L7
ITCH SO19 345 H3
SBNE BH6 449 J1
Burnt Hill Rd RFNM GU10 158 F2
Burnt Hill Wy RFNM GU10 158 E3
Burnt House La
CHCH/BSGR BH23 409 M7
FHAM/STUB PO14 396 B5
LYMN SO41 414 D7
Burrard Gv LYMN SO41 440 D6
Burr Cl RWIN SO21 266 E8
Burrell Rd FRIM GU16 70 F8
Burrfields Rd HSEA PO3 399 M7
Burridge Rd HLER SO31 346 E6
Burrill Av CHAM PO6 375 L8
Burr La MARL SN8 32 B6
Burrowfields KEMP RG22 127 G3 1
Burrow Rd RWIN SO21 213 H7
Burrows Cl HAV PO9 17 H1
Burrows La VWD BH31 332 D8
Burrwood Gdns ASHV GU12 113 K4
Bursledon Hts HLER SO31 345 M7
Bursledon Pl WVILLE PO7 376 B3
Bursledon Rd HEND SO30 345 M3
ITCH SO19 344 E2
WVILLE PO7 376 B3
Burtley Rd SBNE BH6 449 K5
Burton Cl RGWD BH24 381 H3
Burtoncroft CHCH/BSGR BH23 435 G5
Burton Rd CCLF BH13 446 F5
CHCH/BSGR BH23 450 D1
WSHM SO15 343 J1
Burton's Gdns CHAM RG24 106 A1
Burt's Hl WIMB BH21 404 A2
Burwood Gv HISD PO11 425 L4
Bury Cl GPORT PO12 18 F4
Bury Crs GPORT PO12 18 E4
Burydown Cl OVTN RG25 125 L7 1
Buryfields ODIM RG29 108 D6
Bury Hall La GPORT PO12 18 A5
Bury Hill Cl RAND SP11 142 C4
Bury La TOTT SO40 341 M3
Bury Rd CCLF BH13 446 E7
DEAN RG23 104 C2
GPORT PO12 18 E4
TOTT SO40 342 C6
Bury's Bank Rd STHA RG19 27 H8
STHA RG19 38 A1
Bushell Rd PLE BH15 445 H1
Bushells Farm FBDG SP6 309 K8 1
Bushey Rd CHAR BH8 433 G7
Bushmead Dr RGWD BH24 381 J3
Bushnells Dr KSCL RG20 59 H6 1
Bush Saint West SSEA PO5 21 G5 1
Bush St East SSEA PO5 21 G5
Bushy Md WVILLE PO7 376 A5
Bushywarren La OVTN RG25 128 E7
Busk Crs FARN GU14 90 C5
Busket La WINC SO23 11 H8
Busketts Wy TOTT SO40 340 E6
Butcher St PSEA PO1 20 C2
Bute Dr CHCH/BSGR BH23 452 A1
Butler Cl KEMP RG22 104 B4
Butler Rd CWTH RG45 49 L2
Butlers Cl ROMY SO51 232 F7 1
Butlers La RGWD BH24 359 G7
Butson Cl NWBY RG14 2 A4
Butt Cl RAND SP11 92 D5
Buttercup Cl FAWY SO45 367 L7 2
HEND SO30 345 L2 1
BOR GU35 201 M3 1
Buttercup Dr
CHCH/BSGR BH23 435 M7
Buttercup Pl NTHA RG18 27 G4
Buttercup Wy HLER SO31 370 C5
Butterfield CBLY GU15 70 E4 2
Butterfield Rd ROWN SO16 318 D4
Butterfly Dr CHAM PO6 374 E6
Buttermer Cl RFNM GU10 158 B1
Buttermere Cl FARN GU14 90 B4
BOR GU35 201 J3 2
ROWN SO16 317 K6
Buttermere Dr KEMP RG22 103 M7
Buttermere Gdns
NALR SO24 218 C4 2
The Buttery CHCH/BSGR BH23 450 C1
Button's La ALTN GU34 223 G6
ROMY SO51 288 D5
Buttsash Av FAWY SO45 367 L8
Butts Ash Gdns FAWY SO45 367 L7
Butts Ash La FAWY SO45 367 L7 3
Butts Bridge Hl FAWY SO45 367 L6
Buttsbridge Rd FAWY SO45 367 L7
Butts Cl WINW SO22 10 B4
ITCH SO19 345 H4 1
Butt's Crs ITCH SO19 345 G4 1
Butts La BPWT SO32 297 J8
Butts Lawn BROC SO42 387 K6
Butts Meadow HTWY RG27 85 M7 1
Butts Ms ALTN GU34 176 D6
Butts Paddock BROC SO42 387 K6
Butts Rd ALTN GU34 176 D7
ITCH SO19 344 F5
ITCH SO19 345 H4 2
Butt's Sq ITCH SO19 345 G4
The Butts BPWT SO32 299 H2
THLE RG7 42 E8 1
Butt St RAND SP11 92 D6
The Butty BSTK RG21 5 K7
Byerley Cl EMRTH PO10 378 F3 1
Byerley Rd PSEA PO1 423 K2
Byes La THLE RG7 62 E1
Byeways FAWY SO45 367 K6 2
KSCL RG20 56 B3
The Byeway SELS PO20 427 L7
Byfields Rd KSCL RG20 59 H6
Byfleet Av CHAM RG24 106 A3
By-pass Rd ROMY SO51 290 D2
By Pass Rd RWIN SO21 168 A4
Byrd Cl WVILLE PO7 376 C3
Byrd Gdns KEMP RG22 127 H1
Byron Av FRIM GU16 71 L5
WINW SO22 10 A7
Byron Cl BPWT SO32 297 K8
CHAM RG24 83 H7
FHAM/PORC PO16 15 G3
FLET GU13 88 F8
NWBY RG14 37 J1
RAND SP11 92 E6
YTLY GU46 68 E4 2
Byron Dr CWTH RG45 49 L5
Byron Rd BOSC BH5 448 E4
ELGH SO50 294 A4
ITCH SO19 345 H2
NEND PO2 399 K8
NMIL/BTOS BH25 437 J8
Byways YTLY GU46 68 E3
Byworth Cl FNM GU9 134 C6
Byworth Rd FNM GU9 134 C6

C

Cable St SHAM SO14 13 L1
Cabot Dr FAWY SO45 367 G5
Cabot La CFDH BH17 429 L8
Cabot Wy NMIL/BTOS BH25 437 K5
Cabrol Rd FARN GU14 90 D3
Cabul Rd NTID SP9 114 C3
Cadet Wy FLET GU13 111 G4
Cadgwith Pl CHAM PO6 398 F1
Cadhay Cl NMIL/BTOS BH25 437 J5
Cadland Rd FAWY SO45 392 B1
Cadlands Park Est FAWY SO45 392 A2
Cadnam Cl ALDT GU11 7 J8
DEAN RG23 103 G6
Cadnam La TOTT SO40 314 E5
Cadnam Rd ENEY PO4 423 M5
Cadnam Wy CHAR BH8 433 H5
Cadogan Rd RGWD BH24 382 F1
Cadogen Rd ALDT GU11 113 G1
Cador Dr FHAM/PORC PO16 397 M2
Caerleon Av ITCH SO19 345 G2
Caerleon Cl GSHT GU26 203 M2 1
Caerleon Dr AND SP10 118 F4
ITCH SO19 344 F2
Caernarvon FRIM GU16 71 J8
Caernarvon Cl DEAN RG23 104 B3 1
Caernarvon Gdns
CHFD SO53 292 F4 1
Caesar Ct ALDT GU11 6 B2
Caesar Rd AND SP10 119 G5
Caesar's Camp Rd CBLY GU15 51 K8
Caesar's Cl CBLY GU15 51 K8 1
Caesar's Wy WHCH RG28 122 A2
WIMB BH21 429 J4
Cains Cl FHAM/STUB PO14 396 A5
Caird Av NMIL/BTOS BH25 437 M5
Cairn Cl FRIM GU16 71 L5
Cairngorm Cl KEMP RG22 104 A4 1
Cairngorm Pl FARN GU14 90 B1 1
Cairngorm Rd STHA RG19 27 G6 1
Cairns Cl CHCH/BSGR BH23 434 D8
Cairo Ter NEND PO2 423 H1
Caister Cl FERN BH22 406 A2
Caistor Cl ROWN SO16 317 M4
Caithness Cl DEAN RG23 102 F6
Cakeham Rd SELS PO20 427 L8
Caker's La ALTN GU34 177 J6
Caker Stream Rd ALTN GU34 177 G4
Calabrese HLER SO31 370 F1
Calard Dr NTHA RG18 26 D3
Calbourne HLER SO31 369 G1 1
Calcot Hl BPWT SO32 322 D5
Calcot La BPWT SO32 322 D6
Calcott Pk YTLY GU46 68 F2
Calder Cl ROWN SO16 317 K8
Calder Ct AND SP10 119 H6 1
Calder Rd CFDH BH17 430 D8
Calderwood Dr ITCH SO19 344 E4
Caledonia Dr FAWY SO45 367 H5
Caledon Rd PSTN BH14 446 C5
Calender Cl ALTN GU34 176 E6 1
Calkin Cl CHCH/BSGR BH23 434 E7
Calleva Cl KEMP RG22 127 G1
Calluna Rd BKME/WDN BH12 430 F7
Calmore Crs TOTT SO40 316 A7
Calmore Dr TOTT SO40 316 B6
Calmore Gdns TOTT SO40 341 G1
Calmore Rd TOTT SO40 316 A7
Calpe Av LYND SO43 363 K2
Calshot Cl FAWY SO45 393 K8
Calshot Dr CHFD SO53 292 F4
Calshot Rd FAWY SO45 392 F5
HAV PO9 377 G1
Calshot Wy FRIM GU16 91 K1
LSOL/BMARY PO13 396 F7 2
Calthorpe Rd FLET GU13 88 D6
HTWY RG27 88 D5
Calton Gdns ALDT GU11 7 J8
Calvecroft LIPH GU30 226 F4
Calvert Cl ASHV GU12 7 M4
Calvin Cl CBLY GU15 71 L4
Calvin Rd MOOR/WNTN BH9 432 D8
Camargue Cl HLER SO31 346 F8
Camber Pl PSEA PO1 20 B5
Camberry Cl BSTK RG21 105 H5
Cambria Dr FAWY SO45 367 H5
Cambrian Cl CBLY GU15 70 E3
HLER SO31 345 L6 2
Cambrian Rd FARN GU14 90 A1
Cambrian Wy KEMP RG22 104 A5
Cambridge Dr CHFD SO53 293 H5
Cambridge Gdns
CHCH/BSGR BH23 434 D6
Cambridge Gn
FHAM/STUB PO14 371 G6
Cambridge Rd ALDT GU11 6 C2
CWTH RG45 49 M4
GPORT PO12 421 J2
LSOL/BMARY PO13 420 D4
PSEA PO1 20 E4
SHAM SO14 318 F8
SHST GU47 50 B7
WCLF BH2 22 B5
Cambridge Rd East
FARN GU14 90 F7 5
Cambridge Rd West FARN GU14 90 F7
Camcross Cl CHAM PO6 374 F7 1
Camden St GPORT PO12 421 L2
Camden Wk FLET GU13 89 H7
Camel Green Rd FBDG SP6 333 L2 1
FBDG SP6 333 M2 1
Camelia Cl HAV PO9 377 M5
NBAD SO52 291 M3
Camelia Gdns WEND SO18 319 M6 1
Camelia Gv ELGH SO50 295 K6
Camellia Cl WIMB BH21 356 C7 1
Camellia Gdns
NMIL/BTOS BH25 437 M6
Camelot Cl AND SP10 118 F6
Camelot Crs FHAM/PORC PO16 373 M7
Camelsdale Rd HASM GU27 228 C3
Camel Wy FARN GU14 90 D8
Cameron Cl
LSOL/BMARY PO13 397 G5 1
Cameron Rd ALDT GU11 113 G1
Camfield Cl BSTK RG21 105 H5
Camlea Cl BSTK RG21 105 H5
Camley Cl ITCH SO19 344 C7
Cammel Rd FERN BH22 406 B6
Camomile Dr RAND SP11 92 E6
Campbell Cl ALDT GU11 7 H8
FLET GU13 88 D7
RAND SP11 161 K1
YTLY GU46 69 J2
Campbell Pl FRIM GU16 71 J5
Campbell Rd ALDT GU11 112 D5
BMTH BH1 448 D3
CHCH/BSGR BH23 435 G5
ELGH SO50 294 A7
RWIN SO21 145 H6
SSEA PO5 21 K5
TADY RG26 64 A6
Campbell St SHAM SO14 344 A2 1
Campbell Wy ELGH SO50 295 H6
Camp Farm Rd ALDT GU11 113 G3
Camp Hl RFNM GU10 135 M8
Campion Cl BLKW GU17 70 C5 1
ELGH SO50 321 H2 2
HLER SO31 370 C7
BOR GU35 201 M4
LYMN SO41 440 C3 1
WVILLE PO7 376 E2 2
Campion Dr ROMY SO51 263 H7
Campion Gv CHCH/BSGR BH23 450 E2
Campion Rd ITCH SO19 345 H3
Campion Wy HTWY RG27 87 J1
LYMN SO41 440 C3
WINC SO23 215 H2
Camp Rd FARN GU14 90 F8
BOR GU35 201 J3
LSOL/BMARY PO13 397 H5
THLE RG7 30 F5
Campsie Cl KEMP RG22 104 A4
Camrose Wy BSTK RG21 105 H5 1
Cams Bay Cl
FHAM/PORC PO16 373 K7 1
Cams Hl FHAM/PORC PO16 373 J7
WVILLE PO7 326 A7
Camus Cl FLET GU13 110 C3
Camwood Cl BSTK RG21 105 H5
Canada Rd ITCH SO19 344 C6
ROMY SO51 288 C7
Canada Wy BOR GU35 201 J4
Canal Cl ALDT GU11 113 G3
ODIM RG29 108 B4 1
ROMY SO51 262 F7
Canal View Rd NWBY RG14 3 M4
Canal Wk ROMY SO51 262 E8
SHAM SO14 13 G5
SSEA PO5 21 J2
Canberra Cl GPORT PO12 18 B4
HTWY RG27 68 D1
Canberra Rd CHCH/BSGR BH23 434 C7
EMRTH PO10 402 E5
ROWN SO16 317 G4
Canberra Wy FARN GU14 90 C8
Candover Cl TADY RG26 61 L1 2
Candy La WEND SO18 345 J1
Canes La BOR GU35 201 L3
Canford Av BWD BH11 431 K7
Canford Bottom WIMB BH21 405 G2
Canford Cliffs Av PSTN BH14 446 C6
Canford Cliffs Rd CCLF BH13 446 D6
Canford Cl BPWT SO32 348 C1
ROWN SO16 317 J6
Canford Crs CCLF BH13 457 K1
Canford Heath Rd CFDH BH17 430 B7
Canford Rd BWD BH11 431 L7
PLE BH15 445 J4
Canford View Dr
WIMB BH21 404 F2 1
Canford Wy BKME/WDN BH12 431 K6
Canhouse La LISS GU33 249 L5
Canning Rd ASHV GU12 7 L2
Cannon Cl BDST BH18 429 K7
SHST GU47 50 C8
Cannon Hill Gdns
WIMB BH21 404 F1 1
Cannon Hill Rd WIMB BH21 404 E1
Cannon St LYMN SO41 440 C4
WSHM SO15 318 B8
Canoe Cl HLER SO31 370 D7
Canon's Barn Cl
FHAM/PORC PO16 374 A7 1
Canons Cl NTID SP9 114 E4 1
Canon's Ct KSCL RG20 59 H6
Canon St WINC SO23 10 F9
Cansfield End NWBY RG14 2 D3
Canterbury Av ITCH SO19 345 G5
Canterbury Cl FERN BH22 380 D7 1
KEMP RG22 104 A8 1
LSOL/BMARY PO13 420 F4
Canterbury Dr FAWY SO45 367 G5
Canterbury Rd ASHV GU12 113 K5
ENEY PO4 423 K5
FARN GU14 91 G6
FHAM/STUB PO14 396 A5
Canterton La LYND SO43 314 A8
Canton St WSHM SO15 343 K2
Canute Dr CHCH/BSGR BH23 409 M7
Canute Rd SHAM SO14 13 K6
WINC SO23 239 G2
Capella Gdns FAWY SO45 367 H5 3
Capel Ley WVILLE PO7 376 C4
Capers End La BPWT SO32 322 D7
Capesthorne
CHCH/BSGR BH23 451 G3
Capper Rd CBLY GU15 70 D1
Capstone Pl CHAR BH8 448 C2
Capstone Rd CHAR BH8 448 B2
Captains Pl SHAM SO14 13 J6
Captain's Rw LYMN SO41 440 D4
PSEA PO1 20 B5
Carberry Dr FHAM/PORC PO16 397 M1
Carbery Av SBNE BH6 449 J4
Carbery Ct HAV PO9 377 H1
Carbery Gdns SBNE BH6 449 K3
Carbinswood La THLE RG7 29 G4
Carbis Cl CHAM PO6 398 E1
Carbonel Cl DEAN RG23 103 M3
Cardew Rd LISS GU33 248 F5
Cardiff Rd NEND PO2 399 H6
Cardigan Rd
MOOR/WNTN BH9 432 D8
Cardinal Dr WVILLE PO7 352 F7
Cardinal Wy HLER SO31 370 F5
Carey Rd ITCH SO19 345 G3
MOOR/WNTN BH9 432 D6
Careys Cottages BROC SO42 387 K6
Careys Rd CHAR BH8 433 H4
Carfax Av RFNM GU10 113 J8
Cargate Av ALDT GU11 6 E3
Cargate Gv ALDT GU11 6 D4
Cargate Hl ALDT GU11 6 D3
Cargate Ter ALDT GU11 6 D4
Carisbrooke FRIM GU16 71 J8
HLER SO31 369 G1 2
Carisbrooke Av
FHAM/STUB PO14 395 L6
Carisbrooke Cl DEAN RG23 104 B2
HAV PO9 17 J3
NALR SO24 218 C4 3
Carisbrooke Ct
NMIL/BTOS BH25 437 K5
ROMY SO51 262 F7 1
Carisbrooke Crs CHFD SO53 293 K3
PLE BH15 444 D5 3
Carisbrooke Dr ITCH SO19 344 D2
Carisbrooke Rd ENEY PO4 423 L4 1
LSOL/BMARY PO13 396 F5
Carisbrooke Wy
CHCH/BSGR BH23 436 C7
Carless Cl LSOL/BMARY PO13 421 H1
Carleton Cl HTWY RG27 85 L7
Carlinwark Dr CBLY GU15 71 J1
Carlisle Cl DEAN RG23 104 B2
Carlisle Rd RFNM GU10 181 L1
ROWN SO16 318 A8
SSEA PO5 21 K2
Carlton Av NMIL/BTOS BH25 452 C1
Carlton Cl FRIM GU16 71 L5
Carlton Crs FLET GU13 111 G2
WSHM SO15 343 K2
Carlton Gv PSTN BH14 446 C3
Carlton Pl WSHM SO15 343 K2
Carlton Rd BMTH BH1 23 M3
FHAM/PORC PO16 374 B7
GPORT PO12 19 H3
BOR GU35 202 F4
WSHM SO15 343 K1
Carlton Wy GPORT PO12 19 H2
Carlyle Rd GPORT PO12 18 E1
SBNE BH6 449 J2
Carlyn Dr CHFD SO53 293 J1
Carlyon Cl FARN GU14 90 F4
FRIM GU16 91 J4
Carmans La RWIN SO21 266 C1
Carmarthen Av CHAM PO6 375 M7
Carmarthen Cl FARN GU14 90 C1
Carmichael Wy KEMP RG22 104 B8
Carnarvon Rd GPORT PO12 18 C3
NEND PO2 399 K8
Carnation Rd ROWN SO16 319 H4
Carne Cl CHFD SO53 265 H8
Carnegie Rd NWBY RG14 2 F5
Carolina Pl EWKG RG40 48 B1
Caroline Av CHCH/BSGR BH23 450 D3
Caroline Rd BWD BH11 431 M5
Caroline Wy FRIM GU16 71 J7
Carolyn Cl ITCH SO19 344 C6
Carpathia Cl WEND SO18 319 M6 3
Carpenter Cl ENEY PO4 423 L5 2
FAWY SO45 367 L4 2
LYMN SO41 440 B3 1
Carpenter Rd RWIN SO21 145 H6
Carpenters NALR SO24 218 C3 1
Carpenters Cl HTWY RG27 64 C7
Carpenter's Down
CHAM RG24 83 G6 1
Carraway FHAM PO15 371 H1
Carrbridge Cl TWDS BH3 447 J1
Carrbridge Rd TWDS BH3 447 J1
Carrick La YTLY GU46 69 H2
Carrick Wy NMIL/BTOS BH25 438 A6
Carrington Cl LYMN SO41 454 D4
Carrington Crs TADY RG26 41 L8
Carrington La LYMN SO41 454 D3
Carrinton La ASHV GU12 91 J8
Carroll Av FERN BH22 406 B3
Carroll Cl BKME/WDN BH12 446 F2
ELGH SO50 295 J7 2
Carronade Wk HSEA PO3 399 K3
Carshalton Av CHAM PO6 375 M8
Carshalton Rd CBLY GU15 51 K7
Carters Av PLE BH15 444 C4
Carter's Clay Rd ROMY SO51 261 G3
Carter's Cl FBDG SP6 285 J5
Cartersland LIPH GU30 250 E5
Carter's La TOTT SO40 366 C3
Carter's Meadow AND SP10 118 C6
Carters Wk FNM GU9 112 A8 1
Carthage Cl CHFD SO53 293 L1
Carthagena RWIN SO21 168 C4
Carthona Dr FLET GU13 110 E1
Cartref Cl VWD BH31 356 D2
Cartwright Dr FHAM PO15 371 K6
Carvers Hl MARL SN8 32 A6
Carvers La RGWD BH24 382 E1
Cary Cl NWBY RG14 37 G2
Carysfort Rd BMTH BH1 448 C4
Cask St PSEA PO1 423 G2
Caslake Cl NMIL/BTOS BH25 437 K7
Caspar John Cl
FHAM/STUB PO14 395 M7
Caspian Cl HLER SO31 370 F1
Cassel Av WBNE BH4 447 G7
Cassino Cl ALDT GU11 7 G1
Castle Av CHCH/BSGR BH23 436 C8
HAV PO9 17 K5
Castle Cl CBLY GU15 71 J4
LYMN SO41 454 D5
SSEA PO5 21 G5
Castle Ct RAND SP11 92 D5 1
WSHM SO15 342 E2
Castlecraig Ct SHST GU47 70 A1 3
Castledene Crs PSTN BH14 445 M6
Castle Farm La WHAM PO17 348 F6
Castle Gate Cl CHAR BH8 433 G6
Castle Gv FHAM/PORC PO16 398 B1
NWBY RG14 25 J3
Castle Hl FNM GU9 134 E5
THLE RG7 46 F1
Castle Hill La RGWD BH24 384 B4
Castle La CHFD SO53 292 F4
FAWY SO45 419 K1
NBAD SO52 292 A4
NWBY RG14 25 H2
SHAM SO14 12 F4
Castle Lane East LTDN BH7 433 M8
Castle La West CHAR BH8 433 K6
MOOR/WNTN BH9 432 E4
Castlemain Av SBNE BH6 449 H3
Castlemans La HISD PO11 401 L7
Castleman Trailway
CFDH BH17 429 J8
FERN BH22 380 A5
RGWD BH24 381 H3
WIMB BH21 404 E5
Castleman Wy RGWD BH24 382 E2
Castlemews RGWD BH24 382 A3
Castle Ri ODIM RG29 108 B4
WINC SO23 191 H7
Castle Rd ALDT GU11 112 B4
BSTK RG21 105 G5
CBLY GU15 71 H4
HAV PO9 353 L6
HLER SO31 368 F2
MOOR/WNTN BH9 432 D7
SSEA PO5 20 F6
WEND SO18 319 K6
WHAM PO17 374 D2
Castleshaw Cl ROWN SO16 342 D1 1
Castle Sq SHAM SO14 12 F5
Castle St ALTN GU34 196 D1
CHCH/BSGR BH23 450 A2
FHAM/PORC PO16 398 B1
FHAM/STUB PO14 371 K8
FLET GU13 110 E1
FNM GU9 134 E5
PLE BH15 445 H7
RAND SP11 92 D5
SHAM SO14 343 L1
Castleton Av NBNE BH10 432 B2
Castle Vw GPORT PO12 397 M8
Castle View Rd
FHAM/PORC PO16 398 B2
Castleway HAV PO9 17 K5
Castle Wy SHAM SO14 12 F4
Castlewood RGWD BH24 382 B3
Castle Woods RSAL SP5 285 J2 2
Castor Ct FLET GU13 111 G3 1
YTLY GU46 68 E1
Caswall Ride YTLY GU46 69 J3 2
Caswell Cl FARN GU14 90 C2

Catalina Cl *CHCH/BSGR* BH23 ..... 450 F2
Catalina Dr *PLE* BH15 .... 445 K7
Catamaran Cl *ROWN* SO31 ...... 370 D7
Cateran Cl *ROWN* SO16 .... 317 L8 🔢
Catesby Gdns *YTLY* GU46 .... 68 D3
Cathay Gdns *FAWY* SO45 .... 367 G5
Cathedral Vw *WINC* SO23 .... 239 C2
Catherine Cl *HEND* SO30 .... 320 D6
Catherine Crs *RSAL* SP5 .... 284 C1
Catherine Gdns *HEND* SO30 .... 320 D6
Catherine Rd *NWBY* RG14 .... 2 E6
Catherington La *HORN* PO8 .... 352 F1
Catherington Wy *HAV* PO9 .... 377 K4
Catisfield La *FHAM* PO15 .... 371 M7
Catisfield Rd *ENEY* PO4 .... 423 M4 🔢
FHAM PO15 .... 372 A7
Catkin Cl *CHAM* RG24 .... 83 L5
Caton Cl *CHAR* BH8 .... 433 J7
Cattistock Rd *CHAR* BH8 .... 433 J7
Cattle La *RAND* SP11 .... 141 M4
Caunter Rd *NWBY* RG14 .... 25 G4 🔢
Causeway Crs *TOTT* SO40 .... 316 F8
Causeway Farm *HORN* PO8 .... 352 F3
The Causeway *EPSF* GU31 .... 275 K6
FHAM/PORC PO16 .... 573 J7
HTWY RG27 .... 65 M1
RSAL SP5 .... 206 F2
STOK SO20 .... 184 E2 🔢
Cavalier Cl *CHAM* RG24 .... 106 B2
FAWY SO45 .... 367 G5
NWBY RG14 .... 25 M3
Cavalier Rd *CHAM* RG24 .... 106 B2
Cavalier Wy *ALTN* GU34 .... 176 C6
Cavalry Cl *ALDT* GU11 .... 6 B2
Cavan Crs *CFDH* BH17 .... 429 M7
Cavanna Cl *LSOL/BMARY* PO13 ... 396 F5
Cavan's Rd *ALDT* GU11 .... 112 F7
Cavel Ct *CHAM* RG24 .... 83 M8 🔢
Cavell Dr *CHAM* PO6 .... 375 J7
Cavendish Cl *ROMY* SO51 .... 263 G6 🔢
WVILLE PO7 .... 352 D8 🔢
NWBY RG14 .... 26 B3
Cavendish Ct *BLKW* GU17 .... 70 A5
NWBY RG14 .... 26 B3
Cavendish Dr *WVILLE* PO7 .... 376 D1
WSHM SO15 .... 318 E8
Cavendish Gv *WINC* SO23 .... 11 J1
WSHM SO15 .... 318 E8
Cavendish Ms *WSHM* SO15 .... 318 E8
Cavendish Pl *BMTH* BH1 .... 23 G2
Cavendish Rd *ALDT* GU11 .... 6 F3
BMTH BH1 .... 23 G2
FLET GU13 .... 110 D5 🔢
SSEA PO5 .... 21 J6
WCLF BH2 .... 22 F7
C Av *FAWY* SO45 .... 392 B3
Caversham Cl *HEND* SO30 .... 320 C7 🔢
ITCH SO19 .... 344 E4
PLE BH15 .... 444 D5
Caves Farm Cl *SHST* GU47 .... 49 K8
Cawdor Rd *TWDS* BH3 .... 447 J1
Cawte Rd *WSHM* SO15 .... 343 G2
Caxton Av *ITCH* SO19 .... 344 F2
Caxton Cl *AND* SP10 .... 118 B7
CHCH/BSGR BH23 .... 450 E1
Cayman Cl *CHAM* RG24 .... 83 H7
Cecil Av *CHAR* BH8 .... 433 G8
ROWN SO16 .... 318 A4
TOTT SO40 .... 341 G6
Cecil Cl *WIMB* BH21 .... 429 J2
Cecil Gv *SSEA* PO5 .... 20 F6
Cecil Pl *SSEA* PO5 .... 20 F6 🔢
Cecil Rd *BKME/WDN* BH12 .... 446 C2
BOSC BH5 .... 448 D4
ITCH SO19 .... 344 D5
Cedar Av *BLKW* GU17 .... 70 A3
CHCH/BSGR BH23 .... 434 B8
NBNE BH10 .... 432 B2
RGWD BH24 .... 381 J5 🔢
WSHM SO15 .... 318 C8
Cedar Cl *ASHV* GU12 .... 113 H8
GPORT PO12 .... 397 L7
HEND SO30 .... 346 A1
HLER SO31 .... 345 K8
TADY RG26 .... 62 A2
UPTN BH16 .... 428 F8
WINC SO23 .... 191 G8
WVILLE PO7 .... 376 C2
Cedar Crs *HORN* PO8 .... 353 F8
NBAD SO52 .... 291 L3
Cedar Dr *FLET* GU13 .... 89 H7
KSCL RG20 .... 59 H6
LYMN SO41 .... 439 H8 🔢
WIMB BH21 .... 404 F3
Cedar Gdns *HAV* PO9 .... 17 G2
Cedar Gv *HSEA* PO3 .... 423 M1
STHA RG19 .... 26 F5
Cedar Lawn *ROMY* SO51 .... 263 H7
Cedarmount *LYND* SO43 .... 363 K4
Cedar Mt *NWBY* RG14 .... 25 J8
Cedar Pl *CHCH/BSGR* BH23 .... 409 M7
Cedar Rd *ELGH* SO50 .... 293 K7
FARN GU14 .... 90 F5
FAWY SO45 .... 391 L1
SHAM SO14 .... 318 F8
Cedars Cl *SHST* GU47 .... 49 J8
The Cedars *FLET* GU13 .... 89 G8
Cedars Vw *RSAL* SP5 .... 232 D1
Cedar Tree Cl *DEAN* RG23 .... 102 F8
FERN BH22 .... 380 A8
Cedarways *FNM* GU9 .... 158 E1
Cedarwood *WINC* SO23 .... 215 H1
Cedar Wood Cl *ELGH* SO50 .... 295 K6
TOTT SO40 .... 316 B8 🔢
Cedric Cl *FAWY* SO45 .... 392 D8
Celandine Av *HLER* SO31 .... 370 D6
HORN PO8 .... 353 F8
Celandine Cl *CHCH/BSGR* BH23 ... 435 M8
CWTH RG45 .... 49 M2
NBAD SO52 .... 292 E3 🔢
Celandine Ct *YTLY* GU46 .... 68 D1
Celandine Gv *HORN* RG18 .... 27 J3
Celia Cl *WVILLE* PO7 .... 352 F8
Cellars Farm Rd *SBNE* BH6 .... 449 M5
Celtic Dr *AND* SP10 .... 8 C3
Cement Ter *SHAM* SO14 .... 12 F5 🔢
Cemetery Av *HORN* PO8 .... 445 L2
Cemetery Hl *ODIM* RG29 .... 108 D6

Cemetery La *EMRTH* PO10 .... 379 G5
OVTN RG25 .... 130 A3
WVILLE PO7 .... 351 K3
Cemetery Rd *FLET* GU13 .... 110 D1
WSHM SO15 .... 318 D8
Centaur St *NEND* PO2 .... 399 H8
Centaury Gdns *ELGH* SO50 .... 321 H1 🔢
Centenary Cl *LYMN* SO41 .... 413 G6
Centenary Wy *BMTH* BH1 .... 448 D3
Central Av *WIMB* BH21 .... 429 H1 🔢
Central Br *SHAM* SO14 .... 13 J5
Central Dr *WCLF* BH2 .... 22 D1
Central Rd *CHAM* PO6 .... 400 A1
FHAM/PORC PO16 .... 397 M1
BOR GU35 .... 201 J2
SHAM SO14 .... 13 H7
Central Station Br *WSHM* SO15 ... 12 C2
Centre Dr *CHAM* RG24 .... 83 L7
Centre La *LYMN* SO41 .... 439 J7
Centre Pl *RGWD* BH24 .... 382 D1 🔢
Centre Terrace Rd *FARN* GU14 .... 90 D8
Centre Wy *HLER* SO31 .... 370 E5
Centurion Cl *SHST* GU47 .... 50 A8 🔢
Centurion Wy *KEMP* RG22 .... 127 G2
Cerdic Ms *HLER* SO31 .... 369 L4
Cerne Cl *NBAD* SO52 .... 291 K4
WEND SO18 .... 320 A7
Chadderton Gdns *PSEA* PO1 .... 20 E5
Chaddesley Gln *CCLF* BH13 .... 457 J2
Chaddesley Wood Rd
CCLF BH13 .... 457 K3 🔢
Chadwell Av *ITCH* SO19 .... 344 F4
Chadwick Rd *ELGH* SO50 .... 293 K6
Chafen Rd *WEND* SO18 .... 319 J8
Chaffers Cl *ODIM* RG29 .... 131 J6
Chaffey Cl *RAND* SP11 .... 139 G4 🔢
Chaffinch Cl *CFDH* BH17 .... 429 K6 🔢
KEMP RG22 .... 103 M8
NMIL/BTOS BH25 .... 437 K6
SHST GU47 .... 50 B8 🔢
TOTT SO40 .... 316 B8 🔢
Chaffinch Gn *HORN* PO8 .... 352 C4
Chaffinch Wy
FHAM/PORC PO16 .... 373 K8
LSOL/BMARY PO13 .... 420 D1 🔢
Chalbury Cl *CFDH* BH17 .... 430 C6
Chalcraft Cl *LIPH* GU30 .... 226 D4 🔢
Chalcrafts *ALTN* GU34 .... 176 F3
Chale Cl *LSOL/BMARY* PO13 ...... 397 G4
Chalet Hl *BOR* GU35 .... 201 K5
Chalewood Rd *FAWY* SO45 .... 418 C1
Chalfont Av *CHCH/BSGR* BH23 .... 434 B5
Chalfont Dr *FARN* GU14 .... 90 F6
Chalford Rd *NWBY* RG14 .... 2 K8
Chalice Ct *HEND* SO30 .... 345 M2 🔢
Chalk Cl *ALTN* GU34 .... 197 G6 🔢
Chalkcroft La *RAND* SP11 .... 117 L4
Chalk Hl *BPWT* SO32 .... 325 H3
STOK SO20 .... 211 L3
WEND SO18 .... 320 B7
Chalk La *WHAM* PO17 .... 372 F1
Chalkpit La *RAND* SP11 .... 141 J3
Chalk Pit La *RSAL* SP5 .... 208 A2
Chalkpit Rd *CHAM* PO6 .... 374 F6
Chalk Rdg *HORN* PO8 .... 328 C5
WINC SO23 .... 11 M9
Chalkridge Rd *CHAM* PO6 .... 375 L7
Chalk's Cl *RSAL* SP5 .... 285 J1
Chalk V *CHAM* RG24 .... 106 B3
Chalky Copse *HTWY* RG27 .... 85 M6 🔢
Chalky Hl *ALTN* GU34 .... 195 M2
Chalky La *BPWT* SO32 .... 297 J8
HTWY RG27 .... 109 L5
Challenger Wy *FAWY* SO45 .... 367 H4
Challenor Cl *EWKG* RG40 .... 48 C1 🔢
Challis Cl *KEMP* RG22 .... 104 B6
Challis Ct *RAND* SP11 .... 92 F6
SHAM SO14 .... 13 H5
Challoner Cl *KEMP* RG22 .... 104 B5
Chalmers Wy *HLER* SO31 .... 369 L6
Chaloner Crs *FAWY* SO45 .... 367 L7 🔢
Chalton Crs *HAV* PO9 .... 377 H3
Chalton La *HORN* PO8 .... 328 E2
Chalvington Rd *CFDH* SO53 .... 293 H3
Chalybeate Cl *ROWN* SO16 .... 318 A6

Chapel Cl *OVTN* RG25 .... 126 C7
RAND SP11 .... 141 G2
STOK SO20 .... 210 B3
WIMB BH21 .... 429 G2
Chapel Crs *NTHA* RG18 .... 27 H4
Chapel Dro *ELGH* SO50 .... 321 H1
HEND SO30 .... 345 M2
Chapel Gdns *BOR* GU35 .... 201 L3
Chapel Hl *BSTK* RG21 .... 4 D6
Chapel La *BPWT* SO32 .... 322 D8
BROC SO42 .... 416 A2
CHCH/BSGR BH23 .... 407 G5
CHCH/BSGR BH23 .... 409 L8
ELGH SO50 .... 266 A7
FARN GU14 .... 70 C8
FAWY SO45 .... 392 C8
FAWY SO45 .... 392 E5
LYMN SO41 .... 413 H7
LYND SO43 .... 363 K4
RAND SP11 .... 92 D6
RAND SP11 .... 97 H4
RAND SP11 .... 119 G2 🔢
RAND SP11 .... 140 A8
RGWD BH24 .... 384 F5
ROMY SO51 .... 234 C8
RSAL SP5 .... 253 G1
RSAL SP5 .... 256 E3
RSAL SP5 .... 285 K2
RSAL SP5 .... 313 H1
RWIN SO21 .... 215 M6
STHA RG19 .... 40 C7
STOK SO20 .... 209 G1
TADY RG26 .... 60 C4
THLE RG7 .... 42 C3
TOTT SO40 .... 341 J3
WIMB BH21 .... 429 G3
Chapel Md *HTWY* RG27 .... 48 B8 🔢
Chapel Pond Dr *ODIM* RG29 .... 108 B5
Chapel Ri *RGWD* BH24 .... 382 B6
Chapel River Cl *AND* SP10 .... 8 B6
Chapel Rd *BPWT* SO32 .... 299 H5
BPWT SO32 .... 324 A3
BPWT SO32 .... 325 G6
CBLY GU15 .... 70 E3
HEND SO30 .... 320 D6
HLER SO31 .... 370 C2
KSCL RG20 .... 24 B2
RGWD BH24 .... 383 J6
ROWN SO16 .... 317 K6
SHAM SO14 .... 13 J4
Chapelside *FHAM/STUB* PO14 ..... 371 L8
Chapel Sq *CBLY* GU15 .... 70 C2
Chapel St *FARN* GU14 .... 91 G2
GPORT PO12 .... 397 M8
NEND PO2 .... 399 H8 🔢
NTHA RG18 .... 27 H3
OVTN RG25 .... 125 K7
PSF GU32 .... 273 J8
PSF GU32 .... 275 L4
SSEA PO5 .... 20 F5 🔢
Chaplains Av *HORN* PO8 .... 352 B5
Chaplains Cl *HORN* PO8 .... 352 B4
Chaplain's Hl *CWTH* RG45 .... 50 A4
Chapman Wk *NTHA* RG18 .... 26 E4
Chappell Cl *LIPH* GU30 .... 226 F4
Chapter Ter *HTWY* RG27 .... 87 J2 🔢
Charborough Rd *BDST* BH18 ...... 429 M5
Charden Rd *ELGH* SO50 .... 294 F7
LSOL/BMARY PO13 .... 397 H8
Charfield Cl *FHAM/STUB* PO14 ... 14 A7
Charfield Cl *FHAM/STUB* PO14 ... 14 A7
Charing Cl *RGWD* BH24 .... 382 E2 🔢
Chark La *LSOL/BMARY* PO13 ...... 396 D8
Charlcot Cl *WHCH* RG28 .... 122 B5
Charlcot Farm *WHCH* RG28 .... 122 B5
Charldon Gn *CHAM* RG24 .... 83 M8 🔢
Charlecote Cl *FARN* GU14 .... 91 G5
Charlecote Dr *CHFD* SO53 .... 264 F8
Charledown Cl *OVTN* RG25 .... 123 M1
Charledown Rd *OVTN* RG25 .... 123 M1
Charlesbury Av *GPORT* PO12 ...... 18 A4
Charles Cl *HTWY* RG27 .... 85 M7
WINC SO23 .... 11 H2
WVILLE PO7 .... 376 B2
Charles Crs *NMIL/BTOS* BH25 .... 437 H2
Charles Dickens St *PSEA* PO1 .... 21 G2 🔢
Charles Gdns *NBNE* BH10 .... 432 A4
Charles Knott Gdns
WSHM SO15 .... 343 K1
Charles Richards Cl
BSTK RG21 .... 104 F5 🔢
Charles's La *RGWD* BH24 .... 383 H6
Charles St *CBLY* GU15 .... 70 F3
KEMP RG22 .... 104 C4
NWBY RG14 .... 37 G2
PSEA PO1 .... 423 H2
PSF GU32 .... 275 K5
SHAM SO14 .... 13 H5 🔢
Charleston Cl *HISD* PO11 .... 425 J4
Charleston Rd *FAWY* SO45 .... 368 B8
Charles Watts Wy
HEND SO30 .... 345 J1
Charlesworth Dr
WVILLE PO7 .... 352 B7 🔢
Charlesworth Gdns
WVILLE PO7 .... 352 B7
Charliejoy Gdns *SHAM* SO14 ...... 344 A2 🔢
Charlock Cl *NTHA* RG18 .... 27 H3
Charlotte Cl *AND* SP10 .... 119 J8 🔢
BKME/WDN BH12 .... 447 H1
CHCH/BSGR BH23 .... 450 F2
FNM GU9 .... 112 A8
Charlotte Pl *SHAM* SO14 .... 343 L2 🔢
Charlton Cl *LYMN* SO41 .... 438 D5 🔢
MOOR/WNTN BH9 .... 433 G4
Charlton Ct *SHST* GU47 .... 50 A7
Charlton La *THLE* RG7 .... 45 M3
Charlton Pl *NWBY* RG14 .... 2 E2
Charlton Rd *AND* SP10 .... 8 D2
WSHM SO15 .... 343 H1
Charlwood La *ALTN* GU34 .... 221 H4
Charminster Av
MOOR/WNTN BH9 .... 432 F7
Charminster Cl *WVILLE* PO7 ...... 352 C8

Charminster Rd *CHAR* BH8 .... 432 F7
Charmouth Gv *PSTN* BH14 .... 445 M4
Charmus Rd *TOTT* SO40 .... 316 A6
Charmwen Crs *HEND* SO30 .... 320 B6
Charnwood Cl *NWBY* RG14 .... 25 J3 🔢
Charnwood
LSOL/BMARY PO13 .... 397 H6
Charnwood Cl *AND* SP10 .... 9 K8
CHFD SO53 .... 265 H6
FERN BH22 .... 380 C6 🔢
KEMP RG22 .... 104 A4 🔢
TOTT SO40 .... 316 C7
Charnwood Crs *CHFD* SO53 .... 265 H6
Charnwood Dr *FBDG* SP6 .... 309 K6
Charnwood Gdns
CHFD SO53 .... 265 H6 🔢
Charnwood Wy *FAWY* SO45 .... 418 B1
Charterhouse Wy *HEND* SO30 .... 321 C7
Charter Rd *BWD* BH11 .... 431 H2
NWBY RG14 .... 25 J8
Chart House Rd *ASHV* GU12 ...... 113 K1
Chartwell *FRIM* GU9 .... 158 C2
FRIM GU16 .... 91 H3
Chartwell Cl *ELGH* SO50 .... 294 A2
FHAM/STUB PO14 .... 371 G7
Chartwell Dr *HAV* PO9 .... 17 L1
Chartwell Gdns *ALDT* GU11 .... 112 F1
Chase Cl *LISS* GU33 .... 248 F4
Chase Farm Cl *BPWT* SO32 .... 323 K5
Chase Fld *ALTN* GU34 .... 198 C6
Chase Gv *BPWT* SO32 .... 323 K5
Chase La *HASM* GU27 .... 229 H4
Chase Rd *BOR* GU35 .... 201 L3
LISS GU33 .... 248 F4
Chaseside *LTDN* BH7 .... 433 L8
The Chase *CWTH* RG45 .... 49 K2
FARN GU14 .... 91 G2
FHAM/STUB PO14 .... 371 H6
GPORT PO12 .... 18 A4
NWBY RG14 .... 25 J1 🔢
RGWD BH24 .... 382 B3
VWD BH31 .... 356 F2
Chasewater Av *HSEA* PO3 .... 423 L1
Chatburn Av *HORN* PO8 .... 352 C5
Chatfield Av *NEND* PO2 .... 398 E7
Chatfield Cl *FARN* GU14 .... 90 F6
Chatfield Rd
LSOL/BMARY PO13 .... 397 G4
Chatham Dr *PSEA* PO1 .... 20 E5
Chatham Rd *WINW* SO22 .... 238 E3
Chatsworth Av *CHAM* PO6 .... 399 L2
HASM GU27 .... 204 F8
Chatsworth Cl *FHAM* PO15 .... 372 A7
Chatsworth Dr *AND* SP10 .... 8 A7
Chatsworth Gn *KEMP* RG22 ...... 127 H2
Chatsworth Gv *FNM* GU9 .... 134 E2 🔢
Chatsworth Hts *CBLY* GU15 ...... 71 K1
Chatsworth Rd *CHAR* BH8 .... 448 A2
ELGH SO50 .... 294 A2
FARN GU14 .... 91 H5
ITCH SO19 .... 344 E3
PSTN BH14 .... 446 A3
Chatsworth Wy
NMIL/BTOS BH25 .... 437 J5
The Chatters *THLE* RG7 .... 46 F1
Chaucer Av *AND* SP10 .... 8 A7
CHAM PO6 .... 374 C7
RWIN SO21 .... 190 D3
WIMB BH21 .... 404 A2 🔢
WVILLE PO7 .... 352 C6
Chaucer Cl *FARN* GU14 .... 90 F6
FHAM/PORC PO16 .... 14 F4
RWIN SO21 .... 190 D3
WIMB BH21 .... 404 A2 🔢
WVILLE PO7 .... 352 C6
Chaucer Crs *NWBY* RG14 .... 25 H3
Chaucer Dr *LYMN* SO41 .... 454 C3
Chaucer Gv *CBLY* GU15 .... 71 G3
Chaucer Rd *CCLF* BH13 .... 446 E8 🔢
CWTH RG45 .... 49 L4
FARN GU14 .... 90 C2
ITCH SO19 .... 345 H2
Chaundler Rd *WINC* SO23 .... 11 H3
Chaundlers Cft *RFNM* GU10 ...... 133 J3
Chauntsingers Rd *ALTN* GU34 ... 176 E4
Chaveney Cl *FAWY* SO45 .... 367 K7 🔢
Chawton Cl *WINW* SO22 .... 214 C4
WEND SO18 .... 320 C8 🔢
Chawton End Cl *ALTN* GU34 ...... 197 H4 🔢
Chawton Park Rd *ALTN* GU34 .... 176 A8
Cheam Rd *BDST* BH18 .... 429 K4
Cheam Wy *TOTT* SO40 .... 316 C7
Cheap St *NWBY* RG14 .... 2 E4
Cheavley Cl *AND* SP10 .... 118 B8
Cheddar Cl *ITCH* SO19 .... 344 C5 🔢
Cheddington Rd
MOOR/WNTN BH9 .... 432 E4
Chedington Cl *CFDH* BH17 .... 430 C6
Chedworth Crs *CHAM* PO6 .... 374 E7
Cheesecombe Farm La
LISS GU33 .... 247 L2
Cheetah Rd *FARN* GU14 .... 90 E6
Chelmsford Rd *NEND* PO2 .... 399 K6
UPTN BH16 .... 444 A1
Chelsea Rd *SSEA* PO5 .... 21 K6
Cheltenham Crs
LSOL/BMARY PO13 .... 420 D2
Cheltenham Gdns
HEND SO30 .... 321 H5 🔢
Cheltenham Rd
BKME/WDN BH12 .... 446 B3
CHAM PO6 .... 375 G8
Chelveston Crs *ROWN* SO16 ...... 317 L4
Chelwood Dr *SHST* GU47 .... 49 J7 🔢
Chene Rd *WIMB* BH21 .... 404 B4
Cheping Gdns *HEND* SO30 .... 346 C2
TOTT SO40 .... 316 B8 🔢
Chepstow Cl *CFDH* SO53 .... 293 H3
Chepstow Ct *WVILLE* PO7 .... 352 F7
Chequer La *THLE* RG7 .... 45 H6
Chequers Cl *HTWY* RG27 .... 68 J3
Chequers Rd *BSTK* RG21 .... 4 F8
Cherberry Cl *FARN* GU14 .... 89 C4 🔢
Cherbourg Rd *ELGH* SO50 .... 293 L7
Cherford Rd *BWD* BH11 .... 431 M6
Cherita Ct *PLE* BH15 .... 445 J1
Cheriton Av *LTDN* BH7 .... 434 A8
WEND SO18 .... 345 G1
Cheriton Cl *WINW* SO22 .... 10 B5
HAV PO9 .... 377 H4 🔢

Cheriton La *NALR* SO24 .... 218 C3
Cheriton Rd *ELGH* SO50 .... 293 L5
WINW SO22 .... 10 C5
GPORT PO12 .... 18 B3
Cheriton Wy *BLKW* GU17 .... 70 A3
FARN GU14 .... 404 A2
Cherque La *LSOL/BMARY* PO13 ... 396 F5
Cherries Dr *MOOR/WNTN* BH9 ... 432 C6
Cherrimans Orch
HASM GU27 .... 228 C2 🔢
Cherry Cl *HTWY* RG27 .... 86 A6
LSOL/BMARY PO13 .... 420 D3
NWBY RG14 .... 2 D1
PSTN BH14 .... 446 A4
RWIN SO21 .... 190 C5
Cherry Dro *ELGH* SO50 .... 321 H2
Cherry Gdns *BPWT* SO32 .... 323 J4
Cherrygarth Rd *FHAM* PO15 ...... 372 A7
Cherry Gv *FERN* BH22 .... 406 A2
Cherryhill Gv *ALDT* GU11 .... 6 C4
Cherryton Gdns *FAWY* SO45 ..... 391 M5 🔢
Cherry Tree Av
FHAM/STUB PO14 .... 14 B8
HASM GU27 .... 228 C6
HORN PO8 .... 352 F6
NTID SP9 .... 114 F1
Cherry Tree Cl *FARN* GU14 .... 89 M3 🔢
LYMN SO41 .... 439 H8 🔢
RGWD BH24 .... 381 H5
SHST GU47 .... 50 A7 🔢
Cherry Tree Dr
NMIL/BTOS BH25 .... 437 J3 🔢
Cherry Tree Rd *AND* SP10 .... 8 C2
RFNM GU10 .... 158 B5
Cherry Wk *WSHM* SO15 .... 318 B8
Cherryway *ALTN* GU34 .... 176 D3
Cherrywood *HEND* SO30 .... 345 M2
Cherrywood Gdns
TOTT SO40 .... 341 G1 🔢
HISD PO11 .... 425 K4
Cherrywood Rd *FARN* GU14 ...... 90 D1
Chervil Cl *ROWN* SO16 .... 328 B7
Cherville St *ROMY* SO51 .... 262 C4
Chervil Wy *THLE* RG7 .... 31 L6
Cherwell Crs *ROWN* SO16 .... 317 K8
Cherwell Gdns *CHFD* SO53 .... 293 J3
Cheshire Cl *FHAM* PO15 .... 371 K3
Cheshire Dr *CHAR* BH8 .... 433 L6
Cheshire Wy *EMRTH* PO10 .... 379 J6
Chesildene Av *CHAR* BH8 .... 433 H6
Chesildene Dr *CHAR* BH8 .... 433 H6
Chesil St *WINC* SO23 .... 11 J9
Chesilton Crs *FLET* GU13 .... 110 F4
Cheslyn Rd *HSEA* PO3 .... 423 M2
Chessel Av *BOSC* BH5 .... 448 E4
ITCH SO19 .... 344 C1
Chessel Crs *ITCH* SO19 .... 344 C1
Chester Cl *ASHV* GU12 .... 113 L6
NWBY RG14 .... 3 G8
Chester Crs *LSOL/BMARY* PO13 . 420 F4
Chesterfield Cl *CCLF* BH13 .... 446 E8
HSEA PO3 .... 423 L1
NWBY RG14 .... 2 E7
Chesterfield Rd *BSTK* RG21 ...... 105 H5 🔢
HSEA PO3 .... 423 L1
Chester Pl *BSTK* RG21 .... 104 F4
SSEA PO5 .... 21 J7
Chester Rd *ASHV* GU12 .... 113 L5
CCLF BH13 .... 446 F6
WEND SO18 .... 319 M7
WINC SO23 .... 11 J3
Chesters Rd *CBLY* GU15 .... 71 L3
Chesterton Gdns *HORN* PO8 ..... 352 C5
Chesterton Pl *FHAM* PO15 .... 347 G8 🔢
Chesterton Rd *NTHA* RG18 .... 26 F3
Chester Wy *RFNM* GU10 .... 136 C2
Chestnut Av *AND* SP10 .... 142 E3
ASHV GU12 .... 136 B1
CBLY GU15 .... 71 K2
CHCH/BSGR BH23 .... 434 B8
CHFD SO53 .... 293 H5
ELGH SO50 .... 293 K7
ENEY PO4 .... 423 K4 🔢
FNM GU9 .... 134 D8
WINW SO22 .... 214 A4
HASM GU27 .... 228 F1
HAV PO9 .... 376 F5
HORN PO8 .... 353 G3
NMIL/BTOS BH25 .... 437 L8
NTID SP9 .... 114 E1
RGWD BH24 .... 357 M2
RWIN SO21 .... 266 E7
SBNE BH6 .... 449 H4
TOTT SO40 .... 341 G5
Chestnut Cl *ALTN* GU34 .... 176 D3
BLKW GU17 .... 70 B3 🔢
CHFD SO53 .... 293 H6
FARN GU14 .... 89 H4
GSHT GU26 .... 203 L5
LIPH GU30 .... 227 C5
ROMY SO51 .... 291 J2
WVILLE PO7 .... 351 K4
Chestnut Ct *ASHV* GU12 .... 7 M2
BOR GU35 .... 201 K6 🔢
Chestnut Crs *NWBY* RG14 .... 2 E1
STOK SO20 .... 163 G4
Chestnut Dr *TLHT* BG30 .... 31 L4
Chestnut End *BOR* GU35 .... 202 C4
Chestnut Gv *FLET* GU13 .... 89 G6
WIMB BH21 .... 405 F2
Chestnut Ri *BPWT* SO32 .... 298 F7
ELGH SO50 .... 293 J7 🔢
Chestnut Rd *BROC* SO42 .... 387 L7
FARN GU14 .... 90 D3
ROWN SO16 .... 317 M6
The Chestnuts *HLER* SO31 .... 370 F4
Chestnut Wk *GPORT* PO12 .... 397 M7
Chestnut Wy
CHCH/BSGR BH23 .... 435 G5
FHAM/STUB PO14 .... 371 G7
Cheswell Gdns *FLET* GU13 .... 110 D2
Chetnole Cl *CFDH* BH17 .... 430 D7
Chettle Rd *ITCH* SO19 .... 345 J3
Chetwode Pl *ALDT* GU11 .... 7 K7
Chetwode Ter *ALDT* GU11 .... 6 A3

Che - Clo 469

Chetwode Wy CFDH BH17 429 M6
Chetwynd Dr ROWN SO16 318 E4
Chetwynd Rd ENEY PO4 21 L5
ROWN SO16 318 E4
Chevening Ct ENEY PO4 423 M3 2
Cheviot Cl CBLY GU15 71 M4
FARN GU14 90 B1
KEMP RG22 104 A5
NWBY RG14 36 F3
Cheviot Dr FARN GU14 89 G4
FAWY SO45 367 H5
Cheviot Gn HLER SO31 370 B8 3
Cheviot Rd ROWN SO16 317 K8
SHST GU47 49 J7
Cheviot Wy VWD BH31 356 D3
Chewter Cl SSEA PO5 21 L9
Chewton Common Rd
CHCH/BSGR BH23 436 E7
Chewton Farm Rd
CHCH/BSGR BH23 437 G7
Chewton Ldg
CHCH/BSGR BH23 436 F8
Chewton Wy
CHCH/BSGR BH23 436 F7
Cheyne Gdns WBNE BH4 447 H6
Cheyne Wy FARN GU14 90 C1
LSOL/BMARY PO13 420 D3 1
Chichester Av HISD PO11 425 K6
Chichester Cl AND SP10 8 A4
HEND SO30 321 H7
HLER SO31 370 C5
LSOL/BMARY PO13 396 F6
ROMY SO51 289 G6
Chichester Pl KEMP RG22 104 D6
Chichester Rd ASHV GU12 113 K5
HISD PO11 402 A7
NEND PO2 399 J8
RGWD BH24 359 G8
WEND SO18 344 E1
Chichester Wk WIMB BH21 404 C7
Chickenhall La ELGH SO50 294 B6
Chidden Cl PSF GU32 273 J7
Chidden Holt CHFD SO53 292 F3
Chidham Cl HAV PO9 16 D2
Chidham Dr HAV PO9 16 C2
Chidham Rd CHAM PO6 375 L7
Chidham Sq HAV PO9 16 C3
Chigwell Rd CHAR BH8 433 G7
Chilbolton Av WINW SO22 10 A6
Chilbolton Ct HAV PO9 377 M2 1
Chilcomb Cl
LSOL/BMARY PO13 420 D2 1
Chilcombe Cl HAV PO9 377 J5
Chilcomb La RWIN SO21 239 K3
WINC SO23 239 G3
Chilcomb Rd WEND SO18 320 B8
Chilcote Rd HSEA PO3 423 L1
Chilcroft La HASM GU27 228 E7
Chilcroft Rd HASM GU27 228 C1
Chilcrofts Rd HASM GU27 228 D7
Childerstone Cl LIPH GU30 226 E4 1
Childe Sq NEND PO2 399 G6
Chilfrome Cl CFDH BH17 430 A7
Chilgrove Rd CHAM PO6 376 A8
Chilham Cl ELGH SO50 293 M1 1
FRIM GU16 71 J8
Chillandham La RWIN SO21 192 B5
Chilland La RWIN SO21 216 B2
Chillenden Ct TOTT SO40 341 H2 2
Chillerton HLER SO31 369 G2
Chillingham Wy CBLY GU15 70 F4
Chilling La HLER SO31 394 C3
Chillington Gdns CHFD SO53 265 G7 3
Chilsdown Wy WVILLE PO7 376 C3
Chiltern Av FARN GU14 90 A4
Chiltern Cl FARN GU14 89 M4
FLET GU13 111 G3
HASM GU27 228 E3
NMIL/BTOS BH25 437 K7
NWBY RG14 36 F3
TOTT SO40 341 H3 1
WBNE BH4 447 G3
Chiltern Dr NMIL/BTOS BH25 437 J8
VWD BH31 356 D2
Chiltern Gn ROWN SO16 317 K8
Chiltern Rd SHST GU47 49 J7
Chiltern Wy KEMP RG22 103 M5
Chiltlee Cl LIPH GU30 226 F5
Chiltlee Mnr LIPH GU30 226 F4
Chiltley La LIPH GU30 227 G6
Chiltley Wy LIPH GU30 226 F6
Chilton Rdg KEMP RG22 127 G3
Chilworth Cl ROWN SO16 292 C7
Chilworth Dro ROWN SO16 292 B8
Chilworth Gdns HORN PO8 328 C4 1
Chilworth Gv GPORT PO12 18 D1
Chilworth Rd ROWN SO16 292 D7
Chine Av ITCH SO19 344 C2
Chine Cl HLER SO31 370 E4
Chine Crs WCLF BH2 22 B7
Chine Crescent Rd WBNE BH4 22 B7
Chineham La CHAM RG24 5 H2
CHAM RG24 82 F6
Chineham Park Ct CHAM RG24 5 J1
The Chine LSOL/BMARY PO13 397 J7 1
RFNM GU10 158 C3
Chine Wk FERN BH22 406 C7
Chingford Av FARN GU14 90 F3
Chinham Rd TOTT SO40 339 M2
Chinnock Cl FLET GU13 110 E1
Chipstead Rd CHAM PO6 375 K8
Chisels La CHCH/BSGR BH23 435 M2
Chisholm Cl ROWN SO16 317 L3
Chiswell Rd CFDH BH17 430 B7
Chithurst La LIPH GU30 278 E2
Chitty Rd ENEY PO4 423 L6
Chivers Cl KEMP RG22 104 A5
SSEA PO5 21 H5 1
Chivers Dr EWKG RG40 48 B1 1
Chobham Rd FRIM GU16 71 H6
Cholderton Rd AMSY SP4 138 D7
RAND SP11 139 J5
Cholsey Cl STHA RG19 27 J5
Chopin Rd KEMP RG22 104 C8
Chorley Cl PLE BH15 445 H2
Chrismas Av ASHV GU12 7 K4
Chrismas Pl ASHV GU12 7 K4
Christchurch Bay Rd
NMIL/BTOS BH25 452 E1
Christchurch By-pass
CHCH/BSGR BH23 435 J8
Christchurch Cl FLET GU13 110 E4 1
Christchurch Dr BLKW GU17 69 M2
Christchurch Gdns
CHAM PO6 375 M6 1
WINC SO23 238 D3
Christchurch Rd BMTH BH1 23 M5
BOSC BH5 448 F3
CHCH/BSGR BH23 433 M2
FERN BH22 405 M6
LYMN SO41 453 L1
NMIL/BTOS BH25 437 J8 1
RGWD BH24 382 D1
WINC SO23 238 E2
Christie Av HLER SO31 347 G8
Christie Hts NWBY RG14 25 L8
Christie Wk YTLY GU46 68 F4
Christine Cl ASHV GU12 113 J7
Christmas Hl RWIN SO21 168 B6
Christopher Ct NWBY RG14 3 H6
Christopher Crs PLE BH15 445 H2
Christopher Wy EMRTH PO10 378 D6
Christy Ct TADY RG26 61 M1 1
Church Av FARN GU14 90 F6
Church Bank Rd RWIN SO21 170 E3
Church Barns Farm THLE RG7 44 A3
Church Brook TADY RG26 61 K2
Church Cir FARN GU14 90 F7
Church Cl AND SP10 9 J5
ELGH SO50 294 B4
HASM GU27 205 J6
HLER SO31 370 F5
HORN PO8 328 A2
KSCL RG20 36 B2
NBAD SO52 291 M4
Churcher Cl GPORT PO12 421 H5
Churcher Rd EMRTH PO10 378 F4
Church Farm FBDG SP6 309 L8
Church Farm Cl FAWY SO45 366 F2
OVTN RG25 125 K6
Churchfield VWD BH31 356 C2 1
Churchfield Crs PLE BH15 445 K4
Churchfield La RGWD BH24 334 C6
Churchfield Rd EPSF GU31 276 A4
PLE BH15 445 K5
Churchfields FAWY SO45 392 F5 1
BOR GU35 179 G7
Church Flds BOR GU35 202 B3
Churchfields Rd RWIN SO21 266 E2
Church Ga STHA RG19 27 G5
Church Gv FLET GU13 88 D7
Church Hams EWKG RG40 48 A2
Church Hatch RSAL SP5 256 F8 1
Church Hl ALDT GU11 7 J5
ASHV GU12 7 J4
CBLY GU15 71 H3
HEND SO30 320 B7
LYMN SO41 454 D3
RSAL SP5 285 L3
STOK SO20 184 F3
VWD BH31 356 C2
Churchill Av ASHV GU12 7 J5
BPWT SO32 296 F7
ODIM RG29 108 B7
Churchill Cl ALTN GU34 176 E6 2
ALTN GU34 197 G5
FBDG SP6 333 J3
FHAM/STUB PO14 371 G7 1
HTWY RG27 87 G2
ODIM RG29 108 C8
TADY RG26 62 A1
WINC SO23 191 G7
Churchill Ct HORN PO8 352 E2 1
Churchill Crs BKME/WDN BH12 446 B2
FARN GU14 70 E8
BOR GU35 202 C4
Churchill Dr EMRTH PO10 378 D4
Churchill Rd BKME/WDN BH12 446 B3
BMTH BH1 448 C3
WIMB BH21 404 B5
Churchill Wy AND SP10 9 L2
BSTK RG21 4 E7
Churchill Wy East BSTK RG21 5 H7
Churchill Wy West AND SP10 8 A1
BSTK RG21 4 A8
KEMP RG22 104 C3
Church Lands TADY RG26 63 J5
Church La ALTN GU34 174 E6
ALTN GU34 177 H1
ALTN GU34 245 H5
ASHV GU12 113 L6
BPWT SO32 321 L2
BPWT SO32 322 C8
BPWT SO32 324 B2
BROC SO42 387 L8
BROC SO42 416 B3
CHAM RG24 106 A2
CHCH/BSGR BH23 450 A2
DEAN RG23 103 M4
ELGH SO50 266 D8
EWKG RG40 48 B4
FARN GU14 90 B4
FAWY SO45 392 E5
FBDG SP6 308 C4
FERN BH22 432 D1
WINW SO22 213 M2
GSHT GU26 203 M5
HASM GU27 228 F1
HAV PO9 17 K7
HEND SO30 345 M3
HEND SO30 346 E3
HISD PO11 402 A5
HLER SO31 345 M8
HTWY RG27 65 M2
HTWY RG27 87 J4
HUNG RG17 54 A2
KSCL RG20 36 A8
KSCL RG20 57 K1
BOR GU35 202 A2
LIPH GU30 226 E2
LISS GU33 224 A5
LISS GU33 224 C6
LYMN SO41 412 F7
LYMN SO41 414 B5
LYMN SO41 440 C5
LYND SO43 363 K3
MARL SN8 53 H2
NALR SO24 219 G4
NALR SO24 220 B4
NALR SO24 243 H4
RFNM GU10 134 A1
RFNM GU10 156 F2
RFNM GU10 158 B5
RFNM GU10 158 C1 2
NMIL/BTOS BH25 437 K7
NTID SP9 114 E4
NWBY RG14 25 G4
OVTN RG25 127 M1
OVTN RG25 128 A7
PSF GU32 272 A3
PTSW SO17 319 G6
RAND SP11 52 F8
RAND SP11 92 D6
RAND SP11 142 F7
RGWD BH24 384 E5
ROMY SO51 233 L6
ROMY SO51 260 C5
ROMY SO51 261 K4
ROMY SO51 263 H1
ROMY SO51 288 A3
ROMY SO51 290 D1
ROWN SO16 316 E3
RSAL SP5 256 D3
RWIN SO21 213 H5
RWIN SO21 215 L3
RWIN SO21 216 A2
RWIN SO21 238 F8
RWIN SO21 266 E8
STHA RG19 27 G5
STOK SO20 184 F3
STOK SO20 210 B2
TADY RG26 60 A6
THLE RG7 30 E4
THLE RG7 40 C2
THLE RG7 43 H7
THLE RG7 47 G2
WINC SO23 215 H2
WVILLE PO7 326 C5
Church La East ALDT GU11 6 F4
Church La West ALDT GU11 6 D4
Church Md LYMN SO41 440 C6
Church Mdw NTID SP9 114 D8 1
Churchmoor Rd WIMB BH21 404 E3
Church Pth ASHV GU12 113 K5
EMRTH PO10 378 D8
FHAM/PORC PO16 15 L5
GPORT PO12 19 K4
HORN PO8 353 H2
Church Pth North PSEA PO1 423 G2 3
Church Rd ALDT GU11 7 J6
ALTN GU34 198 D5
BPWT SO32 324 A2
BPWT SO32 348 B1
CBLY GU15 70 C1 1
ELGH SO50 294 C3
EMRTH PO10 378 F5
EMRTH PO10 403 H1
EMRTH PO10 403 H7
FERN BH22 406 A2
FHAM/PORC PO16 398 C2
FLET GU13 88 D6
FRIM GU16 71 G8
GPORT PO12 18 C7
HASM GU27 228 F1
HISD PO11 425 L3
HLER SO31 370 B8
HLER SO31 370 F5
ITCH SO19 344 B7
KSCL RG20 24 B3
LIPH GU30 226 F2
MARL SN8 29 H8
NWBY RG14 25 K3
OVTN RG25 100 F8
OVTN RG25 125 K7
PSF GU32 275 K1
PSTN BH14 445 M4
ROMY SO51 234 C6
ROMY SO51 290 D1
RSAL SP5 230 B1
SBNE BH6 449 L5
SHST GU47 49 J7
SHST GU47 50 A7
STOK SO20 186 C1
STOK SO20 210 F5
TADY RG26 42 B7
TADY RG26 61 L2
THLE RG7 41 K1
THLE RG7 41 M2
WHAM PO17 349 M1
WIMB BH21 356 C7
Church Rd East CWTH RG45 49 L3
FARN GU14 91 G7
Church Rd West CWTH RG45 49 L4
FARN GU14 90 F7
Church Sq BSTK RG21 4 E8
Church St ALDT GU11 6 C3
ALTN GU34 174 F3
ALTN GU34 176 E4
BPWT SO32 296 E2
BSTK RG21 4 E8
CHCH/BSGR BH23 450 A2
CWTH RG45 49 L3
FBDG SP6 309 K8
FHAM/STUB PO14 371 K8
LISS GU33 248 D2
NALR SO24 220 B4
RFNM GU10 133 H2
ODIM RG29 108 C6
PLE BH15 445 G7
PSEA PO1 423 G1 1
PSF GU32 273 J7
RAND SP11 96 D1
RAND SP11 165 M2
ROMY SO51 290 D1
RWIN SO21 169 M5
WHCH RG28 122 B4
WSHM SO15 318 A8 2
Church Street Rbt PSEA PO1 423 G1
Church Vw ASHV GU12 113 K6
EMRTH PO10 378 F5 1
ENEY PO4 423 L4
HTWY RG27 86 A7
HTWY RG27 87 H3
ODIM RG29 130 E5
THLE RG7 29 K2
YTLY GU46 69 G1
Church View Cl ITCH SO19 344 E5
Church Wk RSAL SP5 285 M3
Churchward Gdns
HEND SO30 321 H6 2
Churn Cl CHAM RG24 106 A1
Churt Rd BOR GU35 202 D1
RFNM GU10 181 J8
Churt Wynde GSHT GU26 204 A1
Chute Cswy RAND SP11 72 A5
Cibbons Rd CHAM RG24 83 L5
Cinderford Cl CHAM PO6 375 G7 1
Circle Hill Rd CWTH RG45 49 M3
The Circle SSEA PO5 21 J8
WHAM PO17 348 D4
Circular Rd PSEA PO1 422 F2
The Circus WVILLE PO7 374 E6
Cirrus Gdns HLER SO31 369 K6
City Rd WINC SO23 10 F6
Civic Centre Rd HAV PO9 16 E2
SHAM SO14 12 F2
Civic Wy FHAM/PORC PO16 15 L5
Clack La FBDG SP6 308 F2
Clacton Rd CHAM PO6 375 H8
Claire Gdns HORN PO8 328 B6
Clandon Ct FARN GU14 91 G5 1
Clandon Dr ELGH SO50 293 L2
Clanfield Cl CHFD SO53 293 J2
Clanfield Dr CHFD SO53 293 J2
Clanfield Ride BLKW GU17 70 A3 1
Clanfield Rd WEND SO18 345 G1
Clanfield Wy CHFD SO53 293 J2
Clanwilliam Rd
LSOL/BMARY PO13 420 C2
Clappers Farm Rd THLE RG7 43 K8
Clapps Gate Rd TADY RG26 42 B7
Clare Cl FHAM/STUB PO14 371 G7
Clare Gdns EPSF GU31 276 B5
FAWY SO45 418 D1
Clare Lodge Cl
CHCH/BSGR BH23 409 L8
Clare Md RFNM GU10 158 C5
Claremont Av CBLY GU15 71 J3
MOOR/WNTN BH9 432 F6
Claremont Cl ELGH SO50 293 M2 2
Claremont Crs WSHM SO15 342 E1
Claremont Gdns WVILLE PO7 376 C4
Claremont Rd
MOOR/WNTN BH9 432 F6
PSEA PO1 21 L2
WSHM SO15 342 E1
Clarence Cl ASHV GU12 7 K2
RAND SP11 92 D6
Clarence Dr CBLY GU15 71 L1
Clarence Esp SSEA PO5 20 E7
Clarence Pde SSEA PO5 20 F7
Clarence Park Rd LTDN BH7 448 F2
Clarence Rd FLET GU13 88 E8
GPORT PO12 19 K2
LYND SO43 363 K3 1
PSTN BH14 445 M5
SSEA PO5 21 J9
Clarence St PSEA PO1 423 G2
Clarendon Av AND SP10 8 D8
Clarendon Cl BDST BH18 429 L4
ROMY SO51 263 G7 1
Clarendon Ct BLKW GU17 70 A5 2
Clarendon Crs
FHAM/STUB PO14 370 F7
Clarendon Gdns NWBY RG14 2 F2
Clarendon Pk LYMN SO41 440 B6
Clarendon Pl PSEA PO1 21 H1 1
PSEA PO1 423 H2 3
Clarendon Rd BDST BH18 429 J5
CHCH/BSGR BH23 449 M1
HAV PO9 16 D5
ROWN SO16 317 M8
SSEA PO5 21 H7
WBNE BH4 22 A7
Clarendon St PSEA PO1 423 H2
Clarendon Wy RSAL SP5 207 K2
STOK SO20 208 E2
STOK SO20 210 B4
STOK SO20 236 B1
Clarewood Dr CBLY GU15 71 H2
Clarke Crs CBLY GU15 70 B1
Clarke's La RAND SP11 94 E2
Clarkes Rd PSEA PO1 423 K2
Clark's Cl RGWD BH24 382 E1 2
Clarks Hl RFNM GU10 133 M6
Claude Ashby Cl WEND SO18 319 K4
Claudeen Cl WEND SO18 319 K3
Claudia Ct GPORT PO12 421 K2 1
Claudius Cl AND SP10 119 G4
CHFD SO53 293 L1 1
Claudius Dr DEAN RG23 104 B1 1
Claudius Gdns CHFD SO53 293 L2
Clausentum Cl CHFD SO53 293 K1
Clausentum Rd SHAM SO14 343 L1
WINC SO23 238 E3
Clausen Wy LYMN SO41 440 A7
Claxton St PSEA PO1 21 J1
Claybank Sp HSEA PO3 399 L7
Claycart Rd ALDT GU11 112 A5
Claydon Av ENEY PO4 423 L4
Claydon Gdns FARN GU14 70 D7 1
Clayford Av FERN BH22 405 M1
Clayford Cl CFDH BH17 430 B6
Clayhall Rd GPORT PO12 18 D8
Clay Hl BROC SO42 363 L7
Clayhill Cl BPWT SO32 323 J4 1
Clay Hill Crs NWBY RG14 26 A3 1
Clayhill Rd THLE RG7 31 J5
Claylake Dr VWD BH31 356 E3
Claylands Ct BPWT SO32 297 G8
Claylands Rd BPWT SO32 297 G8 1
Clay La LYND SO43 363 K4 1
THLE RG7 29 J2
Claypit Rd ROMY SO51 264 A1
Claypits La FAWY SO45 367 G4
Claypitt La ALTN GU34 246 B2
Clay's La ALTN GU34 177 K7
Clay St RSAL SP5 258 F5
Claythorpe Rd KEMP RG22 104 A5
Clayton Barracks ALDT GU11 113 G4
Clayton Cl HTWY RG27 87 H3 1
Clayton Rd FARN GU14 70 C7
Cleasby Cl ROWN SO16 342 C1
Clease Wy RWIN SO21 266 B1
Clee Av FHAM/STUB PO14 14 A7
Cleethorpes Rd ITCH SO19 344 F4
Cleeve Cl CHAM PO6 374 F7 2
The Cleeves TOTT SO40 341 G2
Clegg Rd ENEY PO4 423 L5
Clemence Gdns WHCH RG28 122 B3 1
Clement Attlee Wy CHAM PO6 374 F8
Clements Cl ALTN GU34 178 D1
Clem's Wy ROMY SO51 232 F7
Clere Gdns CHAM RG24 83 L6
Clerewater Pl STHA RG19 26 D5 1
Cleric Ct FHAM/STUB PO14 371 H5
Clevedge Wy ODIM RG29 108 B4
Clevedon Ct FARN GU14 91 G5 2
FRIM GU16 71 K8
Cleveland Cl KEMP RG22 104 A5
NMIL/BTOS BH25 452 C1
Cleveland Dr FAWY SO45 367 H6
FHAM/STUB PO14 14 B7
Cleveland Gdns BMTH BH1 23 M1
Cleveland Gv NWBY RG14 2 D3
Cleveland Rd BMTH BH1 448 C3
GPORT PO12 18 F5 1
SSEA PO5 21 L4
WEND SO18 319 L6
Clevelands Cl CHFD SO53 265 G6 1
Cleves La OVTN RG25 130 A2
Clewborough Dr CBLY GU15 71 L2
Clewers Hl BPWT SO32 323 J4
Clewers La BPWT SO32 323 J4
Cliddesden Ct BSTK RG21 105 G6
Cliddesden La KEMP RG22 127 G3
Cliddesden Rd BSTK RG21 105 G5
Cliff Crs NMIL/BTOS BH25 452 E1
Cliff Dr CCLF BH13 457 K2
CHCH/BSGR BH23 451 H2
Cliffe Av HLER SO31 369 J5
Cliffe Rd NMIL/BTOS BH25 452 D1
Clifford Dibben Ms
SHAM SO14 318 F8 1
Clifford Pl ELGH SO50 295 H6
Clifford Rd MOOR/WNTN BH9 432 E7
Clifford St SHAM SO14 13 J2
Cliff Rd FHAM/STUB PO14 395 K7
LYMN SO41 453 M3
WSHM SO15 12 A1
Cliff Wy RWIN SO21 266 C2
Clifton Cl RFNM GU10 158 D4
Clifton Crs WVILLE PO7 351 M4
Clifton Gdns FERN BH22 406 A4
FRIM GU16 91 J2
WEND SO18 320 B7
Clifton Hl WINW SO22 10 E7
Clifton Rd WINW SO22 10 D6
LSOL/BMARY PO13 420 E4
NWBY RG14 2 A5
PSTN BH14 446 C6
SBNE BH6 449 J5
SSEA PO5 21 G8
WSHM SO15 317 M8
Clifton St GPORT PO12 421 K2
PSEA PO1 423 J2
Clifton Ter BSTK RG21 4 F6
WINW SO22 10 E7
Clingan Rd SBNE BH6 449 J2
Clinkley Rd NALR SO24 244 C1
Clinton Cl CHCH/BSGR BH23 436 F6 1
Clinton Rd LYMN SO41 440 C3
WVILLE PO7 352 A5
Clipper Cl HLER SO31 370 C7
Clitheroe Rd FARN GU14 69 J7
Cliveden Cl FERN BH22 406 A1
Clive Gv FHAM/PORC PO16 398 A1
Clive Rd ASHV GU12 7 L4
CHCH/BSGR BH23 436 C6
MOOR/WNTN BH9 432 D7
PSEA PO1 423 J2
Clockhouse Rd FARN GU14 90 E4
Clock St PSEA PO1 20 C2
Clocktower Dr ENEY PO4 423 M6
The Cloisters FHAM PO15 372 A6
FRIM GU16 71 G7
RGWD BH24 383 G2 1
ROMY SO51 262 D8 1
ROWN SO16 318 F4
The Close Bellfield
FHAM/STUB PO14 395 K1
The Close BDST BH18 429 J5
CHAM PO6 399 L1 1
FAWY SO45 392 B5
FHAM/PORC PO16 374 A8
FNM GU9 135 G7
FRIM GU16 70 F8
HEND SO30 345 M2
LYMN SO41 412 E6
NMIL/BTOS BH25 437 L8
NTHA RG18 26 E4
PSF GU32 274 B5
RAND SP11 95 H6
RGWD BH24 381 L4 1
RGWD BH24 382 D1 2
RSAL SP5 285 J1
SHST GU47 50 B8
TADY RG26 82 A2
THLE RG7 31 K5
WEND SO18 345 H1
Closewood Rd WVILLE PO7 351 L7
Closeworth Rd FARN GU14 91 H8
Clouch La RGWD BH24 384 D5
Clough La RSAL SP5 206 E1
Clough's Rd RGWD BH24 382 F1
Clouston Rd FARN GU14 90 C3
Clovelly Dr GSHT GU26 203 M1
Clovelly Rd EMRTH PO10 378 C8
EMRTH PO10 379 H7
ENEY PO4 423 L4
GSHT GU26 203 M2
HISD PO11 402 A4
SHAM SO14 343 L2
Cloverbank WINC SO23 191 G6
Clover Cl CHCH/BSGR BH23 435 M8
HLER SO31 370 C6
BOR GU35 201 M3
LSOL/BMARY PO13 397 G6 3
Clover Ct NMIL/BTOS BH25 438 B4

Clover Dr CFDH BH17 .... 429 K7
Clover Fld CHAM RG24 .... 5 M3
Clover Gdns HORN PO8 .... 352 D4
Clover Sq SP11 .... 92 E6
Clover La YTLY GU46 .... 68 D2
Clowes Av SBNE BH6 .... 450 A5
  ROMY SO51 .... 263 H8
Club House La BPWT SO32 .... 323 J5
Clubhouse Rd ALDT GU11 .... 112 C3
Club La CWTH RG45 .... 50 A3
  NTID SP9 .... 114 D4
Clumps Rd RFNM GU10 .... 159 H4
Clydebank Rd NEND PO2 .... 399 H8
Clyde Ct GPORT PO12 .... 421 K2
Clyde Rd GPORT PO12 .... 421 K2
Clydesdale Dr TOTT SO40 .... 316 A8 🔟
Clydesdale Rd HLER SO31 .... 370 F1
Clydesdale Wy TOTT SO40 .... 316 A8
Coach HI FHAM/STUB PO14 .... 371 K8 🔟
  RAND SP11 .... 94 A4
Coach Hill Cl CHFD SO53 .... 293 G1
Coach Hill La RGWD BH24 .... 384 B2
Coach House Cl FRIM GU16 .... 71 H5
Coach House Gdns FLET GU13 .... 88 F5
Coach House Pl BMTH BH1 .... 23 H2
Coachmans Copse
  WEND SO18 .... 319 M6
Coachman's Ct NWBY RG14 .... 25 L3 🔟
Coach Rd HLER SO31 .... 369 J6
The Coach Rd RSAL SP5 .... 208 A8
Coachways AND SP10 .... 9 G8 🔟
Coal Park La WVILLE PO7 .... 376 B7
Coalville Rd ITCH SO19 .... 344 F4
Coastguard Cl GPORT PO12 .... 18 A8
Coastguard La SELS PO20 .... 427 J7
Coastguard Wy
  CHCH/BSGR BH23 .... 450 E4
Coate Dr RWIN SO21 .... 190 C6
Coates Cl KEMP RG22 .... 104 E7
Coates Rd ITCH SO19 .... 345 H4
Coates Wy WVILLE PO7 .... 376 H4
Coat Gdns FAWY SO45 .... 367 L5 🔟
Cobbets Rdg RFNM GU10 .... 135 M7
Cobbett Cl WINW SO22 .... 238 B3
Cobbett Gn KEMP RG22 .... 104 D6
Cobbett Rd WEND SO18 .... 344 C1
Cobbett's La BLKW GU17 .... 69 J4
  YTLY GU46 .... 69 J3
Cobbetts Wy FNM GU9 .... 158 C2
Cobbett Wy HEND SO30 .... 346 C1
Cobblers Cnr LYMN SO41 .... 413 L5
Cobblewood EMRTH PO10 .... 378 D5
Cobbs La PLE BH15 .... 445 K2
Cobb's Rd WIMB BH21 .... 404 C2
  WEND SO18 .... 319 J8
Cobden Av HSEA PO3 .... 399 L8
  WEND SO18 .... 319 J8
Cobden Crs WEND SO18 .... 319 J8
Cobden Gdns WEND SO18 .... 319 K7
Cobden La HASM GU27 .... 229 G1 🔟
Cobden St GPORT PO12 .... 18 E1
Cobham Cl MOOR/WNTN BH9 .... 432 E5
  WIMB BH21 .... 405 K1
Cobham Wy WIMB BH21 .... 404 C7
Coblands Av TOTT SO40 .... 341 H1
Coburg St PSEA PO1 .... 21 K1
  SHAM SO14 .... 344 A2
Cochrane Cl
  LSOL/BMARY PO13 .... 421 H2
Cochrane Cl STHA RG19 .... 27 H5 🔟
Cock-a-dobby SHST GU47 .... 49 K7
Cockerell Cl WIMB BH21 .... 404 D7
Cockleshell Gdns ENEY PO4 .... 424 A5
Cocklydown La TOTT SO40 .... 341 J3
Cockshott La PSF GU32 .... 247 H6
Cody Cl ASHV GU12 .... 113 J3
Cody Rd FARN GU14 .... 90 C5
Coe Cl ALDT GU11 .... 6 E3
Cogdeane Rd CFDH BH17 .... 430 B6
Coghlan Cl FHAM/PORC PO16 .... 15 J3
Cokenor Wd RFNM GU10 .... 158 C2
Coker Cl WINW SO22 .... 10 D6
Colbeck FLET GU13 .... 111 G4
Colborne Av WIMB BH21 .... 404 D3
Colborne Cl LYMN SO41 .... 440 C3
Colbourne Cl
  CHCH/BSGR BH23 .... 409 L8
Colbred Cnr FARN GU14 .... 89 H4 🔟
Colburn Cl ROWN SO16 .... 317 J6
Colbury Gv HAV PO9 .... 377 G4
Colchester Av ELGH SO50 .... 294 D4
Colchester Rd CHAM PO6 .... 375 H7
Cold East Cl HLER SO31 .... 370 D3
Coldeast Wy HLER SO31 .... 370 D3
Colden La NALR SO24 .... 194 D7
Coldharbour Cl WHAM PO17 .... 348 D4
Coldharbour Farm Rd
  EMRTH PO10 .... 378 D7
Cold Harbour La FARN GU14 .... 70 C8
Coldharbour La ROWN SO16 .... 290 F8
Coldhill La HORN PO8 .... 352 C1
Colebrook Av HSEA PO3 .... 423 M1
  WSHM SO15 .... 318 B7
Colebrook Pl WINC SO23 .... 11 J9
Colebrook Wy AND SP10 .... 8 B6
Cole Cl AND SP10 .... 118 F4
Coleford Bridge Rd
  FRIM GU16 .... 91 H4 🔟
Coleford Cl FRIM GU16 .... 91 J5
Coleford Paddocks
  FRIM GU16 .... 91 H4 🔟
Cole HI BPWT SO32 .... 325 G3
Colehill Crs MOOR/WNTN BH9 .... 432 F5
Colehill La WIMB BH21 .... 404 C1
Coleman Cl BSTK RG21 .... 5 H3
  BWD BH11 .... 431 L5
Coleman Rd ASHV GU12 .... 7 L4
Coleman St SHAM SO14 .... 13 J3
Colemere Gdns
  CHCH/BSGR BH23 .... 436 D7
Colemore Rd LTDN BH7 .... 449 H1
Colemore Sq HAV PO9 .... 377 K4 🔟
Colenso Rd FHAM/PORC PO16 .... 15 H4
Colenzo Dr AND SP10 .... 9 K2
Coleridge Av YTLY GU46 .... 69 H3
Coleridge La CWTH RG45 .... 49 M4 🔟
  HLER SO31 .... 370 B7

Coleridge Gdns HORN PO8 .... 352 D4
Coleridge Rd CHAM PO6 .... 374 D7
Coles Cl RWIN SO21 .... 444 D6
Colesbourne Rd CHAM PO6 .... 374 D7
Coles Ct WINC SO23 .... 266 F1
Coles Gdns PLE BH15 .... 444 A5
Coles Mede OVTN RG25 .... 266 A5
Coleson Hill Rd RFNM GU10 .... 158 C3 🔟
Coleson Rd WEND SO18 .... 319 K8
Coleville Av FAWY SO45 .... 392 F5
Coleville Rd FARN GU14 .... 90 C3
Coley La STOK SO20 .... 165 L4
Colin Cl WIMB BH21 .... 429 H3
Colinton Av
  FHAM/PORC PO16 .... 374 B7
Collards La HASM GU27 .... 229 G2
Collaroy Rd NTHA RG18 .... 26 F1
College Cl CBLY GU15 .... 51 G8
  HAV PO9 .... 354 A7
  HLER SO31 .... 369 K6 🔟
College Crs SHST GU47 .... 50 B6
College Gdns FNM GU9 .... 134 E6 🔟
College HI HASM GU27 .... 228 F2
College Hill Ter HASM GU27 .... 228 F2
College La OVTN RG25 .... 152 A2
  PSEA PO1 .... 20 C2 🔟
College Piece THLE RG7 .... 43 J2
College Ride BAGS GU19 .... 51 M6
  CBLY GU15 .... 71 G1
College Rd ASHV GU12 .... 113 K5
  BOSC BH5 .... 448 F4
  BSTK RG21 .... 4 B7
  ITCH SO19 .... 344 C6
  PSEA PO1 .... 20 C1
  RGWD BH24 .... 382 E1
  SHST GU47 .... 70 B1
  WVILLE PO7 .... 376 C6
College St EPSH GU31 .... 275 L5
  PSEA PO1 .... 20 C2
  SHAM SO14 .... 13 H5
  WINC SO23 .... 11 G3
College Wk WINC SO23 .... 238 F2
Collett Cl HEND SO30 .... 321 G6
Collier Cl FARN GU14 .... 91 G4
  PTSW SO17 .... 319 H8 🔟
Collingbourne Av SBNE BH6 .... 449 J2
Collingbourne Dr CHFD SO53 .... 292 F2
Collington Crs CHAM PO6 .... 374 F7
Collingwood FARN GU14 .... 91 H4
Collingwood Grange Cl
  CBLY GU15 .... 51 L8
Collingwood Ri CBLY GU15 .... 71 K1
Collingwood Rd SSEA PO5 .... 21 K7
  WIMB BH21 .... 380 C2
Collingworth Cl HLER SO31 .... 370 F2
Collins Cl AND SP10 .... 118 D5
  NBAD SO52 .... 292 E2 🔟
  NWBY RG14 .... 3 J1
Collins Gdns ASHV GU12 .... 113 L6
Collins La EPSH GU31 .... 304 E1
  RGWD BH24 .... 382 E1
  RWIN SO21 .... 265 H1
Collins Rd ENEY PO4 .... 423 L4
Collis Rd HSEA PO3 .... 399 L8
Collwood Cl PLE BH15 .... 445 H1
Collyers Crs LIPH GU30 .... 227 H4 🔟
Collyers Rd BROC SO42 .... 387 K8
Colne Av ROWN SO16 .... 317 J5
Colne Valley Wy WHCH RG28 .... 123 G3
Colne Wy ASHV GU12 .... 113 K7
  BSTK RG21 .... 5 J8
Colpoy St SSEA PO5 .... 20 F4
Colson Rd WINC SO23 .... 11 K6
Colt Cl ROWN SO16 .... 317 L3 🔟
  WIMB BH21 .... 404 F2
Colthrop La STHA RG19 .... 27 L6
Coltsfoot Cl HEND SO30 .... 345 M1
  THLE RG7 .... 31 L5
Coltsfoot Dr HLER SO31 .... 370 C6
  WVILLE PO7 .... 376 D3
Coltsfoot Pl HTWY RG27 .... 86 B6 🔟
Colts Foot Rd BOR GU35 .... 201 M3 🔟
Coltsmead CHAM PO6 .... 374 D8
Colts Rd ROWN SO16 .... 317 K1
Columbia Cl EWKG RG40 .... 48 B1 🔟
Columbia Rd NBNE BH10 .... 431 M6
Columbia Trees La NBNE BH10 .. 432 A4
Columbine Rd KEMP RG22 .... 103 M8
Columbus Dr FARN GU14 .... 89 M5
Columbus Wy AND SP10 .... 119 K8
Colville Cl BOSC BH5 .... 448 F5
Colville Dr BPWT SO32 .... 297 J8
Colville Rd BOSC BH5 .... 448 F5
  CHAM PO6 .... 375 L8
Colwell Cl ROWN SO16 .... 317 J8
Colwell Rd CHAM PO6 .... 399 K1
Colwyn Cl YTLY GU46 .... 68 E2
Colyer Cl KEMP RG22 .... 104 B5 🔟
Combe La FARN GU14 .... 90 D2 🔟
Combe Ri RFNM GU10 .... 159 G3
Combe Rd LISS GU33 .... 249 G7
Comber Rd MOOR/WNTN BH9 .... 432 F5
Comet Wy CHCH/BSGR BH23 .... 450 F2
Comfrey Cl FARN GU14 .... 89 M3
  HORN PO8 .... 328 B7 🔟
  ROMY SO51 .... 263 H9
Comines Wy HEND SO30 .... 345 J2
Comley HI HAV PO9 .... 378 A1
Comley Rd MOOR/WNTN BH9 .... 432 F5
Commercial Pl PSEA PO1 .... 423 G2 🔟
Commercial Rd ASHV GU12 .... 7 K5
  PLE BH15 .... 445 H3
  PSEA PO1 .... 21 G1
  PSEA PO1 .... 423 G2 🔟
  TOTT SO40 .... 341 L1
  WCLF BH2 .... 22 C6
  WSHM SO15 .... 12 F1
Commercial St WEND SO18 .... 344 F1
Common Barn La
  LSOL/BMARY PO13 .... 420 D1 🔟
Common Cl CHFD SO53 .... 265 H8
Common Gdns CHFD SO53 .... 265 H8
Common HI ALTN GU34 .... 196 C2
Common Hill Rd ROMY SO51 .... 263 J2
Common La FHAM/STUB PO14 .. 371 H8

WHAM PO17 .... 350 C7
  RCCH PO10 .... 379 K3
  RSAL SP5 .... 259 G5
  STHA RG19 .... 39 H8
Commonside EMRTH PO10 .... 378 F3
Common St PSEA PO1 .... 423 H2 🔟
The Common RSAL SP5 .... 207 J8
Common Vw MIDH GU29 .... 279 J7
Compass Cl
  LSOL/BMARY PO13 .... 421 H2 🔟
Compass Fld HTWY RG27 .... 86 A7 🔟
Compass Rd CHAM PO6 .... 374 F8
Compton Av PSTN BH14 .... 446 C6
Compton Beeches
  RGWD BH24 .... 381 L3 🔟
Compton Cl ELGH SO50 .... 293 L2
  FLET GU13 .... 111 G3
  WINW SO22 .... 238 A5
  HAV PO9 .... 16 E1
  HTWY RG27 .... 86 A8
  LSOL/BMARY PO13 .... 420 E2
  SHST GU47 .... 49 M7
  VWD BH31 .... 356 D2
Compton Crs FERN BH22 .... 380 E7
Compton Dr PSTN BH14 .... 446 B6
Compton Gdns PSTN BH14 .... 446 B6
Compton Rd FLET GU13 .... 111 G3
  NEND PO2 .... 399 K5
  NMIL/BTOS BH25 .... 437 L6
  TOTT SO40 .... 316 F8
  WINW SO22 .... 238 A5
Compton's Dr ROMY SO51 .... 287 L2
Compton Wk SHAM SO14 .... 13 G1
Compton Wy WINW SO22 .... 238 A5
  RFNM GU10 .... 135 K6
Conan Rd NEND PO2 .... 399 J4
Concorde Wy FHAM/PORC PO16 .. 371 J3
Conde Wy BOR GU35 .... 201 H5
Condor Av FHAM/PORC PO6 .... 373 K8
Condor Cl ITCH SO19 .... 344 B5 🔟
Condor Rd FARN GU14 .... 90 E6
Coneygar La FHAM/PORC PO16 .. 405 L5
Conference Dr HLER SO31 .... 370 F5 🔟
Conference Pl LYMN SO41 .... 440 D6 🔟
Conford Ct HAV PO9 .... 377 M1
Conholt HI BSTK RG21 .... 72 E3
Conholt La RAND SP11 .... 73 G5
Conholt Rd AND SP10 .... 142 F3
Conifer Av PSTN BH14 .... 446 A6
Conifer Cl CHCH/BSGR BH23 .... 434 B5
  FAWY SO45 .... 367 K5 🔟
  FERN BH22 .... 406 D7
  FLET GU13 .... 110 E3
  WINW SO22 .... 10 D5
  HORN PO8 .... 352 E6
  BOR GU35 .... 201 H7
  RGWD BH24 .... 381 H4
  TADY RG26 .... 41 H7
Conifer Crs LYMN SO41 .... 439 M5
Conifer Crest NWBY RG14 .... 36 F4
Conifer Dr CBLY GU15 .... 71 K2
Conifer Gv LSOL/BMARY PO13 .. 397 G4
Conifer Ms
  FHAM/PORC PO16 .... 374 B7 🔟
Conifer Rd ROWN SO16 .... 317 M4
The Conifers CWTH RG45 .... 49 K1
Conigar Rd EMRTH PO10 .... 378 D5
Coniston Av BWD BH11 .... 431 J3
  HSEA PO3 .... 399 L8
Coniston Cl CBLY GU15 .... 71 M5
  FARN GU14 .... 90 B5
  STHA RG19 .... 26 D5
  VWD BH31 .... 356 C3
Coniston Dr FNM GU9 .... 134 D2
Coniston Gdns HEND SO30 .... 345 M3
Coniston Gv NALR SO24 .... 218 C4 🔟
Coniston Rd ELGH SO50 .... 293 L6
  KEMP RG22 .... 104 A7
  BOR GU35 .... 201 H3
  RGWD BH24 .... 382 F2 🔟
  ROWN SO16 .... 317 H8
Coniston Wy FLET GU13 .... 110 D3
Connaught Barracks
  ALDT GU11 .... 113 G2
Connaught Cl BOR GU35 .... 201 J6 🔟
  NMIL/BTOS BH25 .... 437 J5
  YTLY GU46 .... 68 E2
Connaught Crs
  BKME/WDN PO12 .... 446 D2
Connaught Rd ASHV GU12 .... 7 K2
  BAGS GU19 .... 51 M5
  CBLY GU15 .... 71 J3
  FLET GU13 .... 88 F8 🔟
  HAV PO9 .... 17 G4
  NEND PO2 .... 399 H6 🔟
  NWBY RG14 .... 3 J4
  RWIN SO21 .... 190 B6
Connell Rd PLE BH15 .... 445 H3
Connemara Crs HLER SO31 .... 370 F1
Connigar Cl
  LSOL/BMARY PO13 .... 421 G1 🔟
Connop Wy FRIM GU16 .... 71 J5
Conqueror Wy
  FHAM/STUB PO14 .... 396 B6
Conrad Gdns FHAM PO15 .... 347 G8
Consort Dr CBLY GU15 .... 71 M1 🔟
Consort Rd ELGH SO50 .... 294 A3
Constable Cl BSTK RG21 .... 105 J5
  GPORT PO12 .... 18 F9
  ITCH SO19 .... 345 G6
Constable Ct AND SP10 .... 9 G3
Constable's Ga WINC SO23 .... 10 B8
Constable Wy SHST GU47 .... 70 B2
Constantine Av CHFD SO53 .... 293 K2
Constantine Wy KEMP RG22 .... 126 C1
Constant Rd FARN GU14 .... 89 K6
Constitution Hill Rd
  PSTN BH14 .... 445 L4
Convent La EMRTH PO10 .... 378 D8
Conway Cl CHFD SO53 .... 293 G5
  NMIL/BTOS BH25 .... 437 M5

Conway Dr FARN GU14 .... 90 A3
  NTHA RG18 .... 26 E3
Cook Cl RGWD BH24 .... 359 G8
Cooke Rd BKME/WDN BH12 .... 446 E2
Cookham Cl SHST GU47 .... 49 M7
Cooks La EMRTH PO10 .... 379 J7
  RCCH PO18 .... 355 M6
  ROMY SO51 .... 260 C1
  ROMY SO51 .... 261 M4
  TOTT SO40 .... 316 B6
Cook's Pond Rd LIPH GU30 .... 250 D8
Cook St SHAM SO14 .... 13 H4
Coolarne Ri CBLY GU15 .... 71 K2
Coolers Farm STOK SO20 .... 209 H2
Coombe Av NBNE BH10 .... 432 C6
Coombe Cl FRIM GU16 .... 71 G8
Coombe Ct NTHA RG18 .... 27 H5
Coombedale HLER SO31 .... 370 F6 🔟
Coombe Dr FLET GU13 .... 89 H7
Coombe Farm Av
  FHAM/PORC PO16 .... 15 H8
Coombe Gdns NBNE BH10 .... 432 B6
Coombehurst Dr BSTK RG21 .... 105 C6
Coombe La FHAM/STUB PO14 .... 14 A2
  PSF GU32 .... 272 D4
  ROMY SO51 .... 261 L5
Coombe Rd GPORT PO12 .... 421 M1
  PSF GU32 .... 273 G8
  YTLY GU46 .... 68 E1
Coombe Sq STHA RG19 .... 27 H5
Coombs Cl HORN PO8 .... 328 B7 🔟
The Cooperage ALTN GU34 .... 176 D5 🔟
Cooper Dean Dr CHAR BH8 .... 433 K7
Cooper Gv FHAM/PORC PO16 .. 398 B2
Cooper Rd HSEA PO3 .... 423 M1
  TOTT SO40 .... 341 G5
Cooper's Cl ROMY SO51 .... 289 G6 🔟
  RWIN SO21 .... 190 C6
  WEND SO18 .... 320 B7
Coopers Crs TADY RG26 .... 63 L5
Coopers Crs NTHA RG18 .... 26 F4
Cooper's HI HTWY RG27 .... 66 D1
Cooper's La ITCH SO19 .... 344 B5 🔟
  TADY RG26 .... 63 K5
  VWD BH31 .... 356 D1
Cope Hall La NWBY RG14 .... 36 E1
Copeland Dr PSTN BH14 .... 446 A6
Copeland Rd ROWN SO16 .... 317 J7
Copes La HTWY RG27 .... 66 D1
Copinger Cl TOTT SO40 .... 341 G2 🔟
Copland Cl KEMP RG22 .... 104 B8
Copnor Cl KSCL RG20 .... 35 M8
Copnor Rd NEND PO2 .... 399 K4
Copped Hall Dr CBLY GU15 .... 71 M2
Copped Hall Wy CBLY GU15 .... 71 M2
Copper Beech Cl
  BKME/WDN BH12 .... 446 F4
Copper Beech Dr CHAM PO6 .. 376 C8 🔟
Copper Beech Gdns
  NBNE BH10 .... 432 B6
Copperfield Av SHST GU47 .... 50 B6
Copperfield Rd ROWN SO16 .... 318 F3
Copperfields TOTT SO40 .... 340 F1
Coppers Cl FBDG SP6 .... 333 L2
Copper St SSEA PO5 .... 20 F5
Coppice Av FERN BH22 .... 405 M2
Coppice Cl FNM GU9 .... 6 B9
  WINW SO22 .... 214 B7
  NMIL/BTOS BH25 .... 438 B4
  NWBY RG14 .... 3 G9
  RGWD BH24 .... 381 K4
  TADY RG26 .... 41 G8
Coppice Gdns CWTH RG45 .... 49 J3
  YTLY GU46 .... 68 F3
Coppice HI BPWT SO32 .... 323 H1
Coppice Ms DEAN RG23 .... 104 B2
Coppice Rd KSCL RG20 .... 59 K6
  TOTT SO40 .... 316 B6
The Coppice BROC SO42 .... 387 H6
  HORN PO8 .... 352 E2
  LSOL/BMARY PO13 .... 397 H6 🔟
Coppice Vw NBNE BH10 .... 432 C5
Coppice Wy FHAM PO15 .... 14 A2
Coppins Gv FHAM/PORC PO16 .. 398 A2
Copse Av FNM GU9 .... 6 A7
  NMIL/BTOS BH25 .... 437 M6
Copse Cl CBLY GU15 .... 71 K3
  EPSH GU31 .... 276 B4
  LISS GU33 .... 248 F4
  NBAD SO52 .... 291 L4
  PLE BH15 .... 445 L5
  RWIN SO21 .... 266 B4
  TOTT SO40 .... 341 K2
  WVILLE PO7 .... 376 B6
Copse End CBLY GU15 .... 71 J2
Copse La HISD PO11 .... 401 L8
  HLER SO31 .... 369 K6
  LSOL/BMARY PO13 .... 397 H7
  NALR SO24 .... 171 K5
  ODIM RG29 .... 131 J5
  ROWN SO16 .... 292 E7
Copse Rd HASM GU27 .... 228 A3
  NMIL/BTOS BH25 .... 437 M6
  OVTN RG25 .... 101 G6
  RGWD BH24 .... 384 D8
  VWD BH31 .... 356 D2
  WEND SO18 .... 319 L6
Copse Vw ITCH SO19 .... 344 F5
Copse View Cl CHAM RG24 .... 83 M4 🔟
Copse Wy CHCH/BSGR BH23 .... 436 C8
  EWKG RG40 .... 48 B1 🔟
  RFNM GU10 .... 158 C2
Copsewood Av CHAR BH8 .... 433 J7
Copsewood Rd FAWY SO45 .... 367 K5
  TOTT SO40 .... 341 G5
  WEND SO18 .... 319 K6
Copsey Cl CHAM PO6 .... 376 B5
Copsey Gv CHAM PO6 .... 376 B8
Copthorne La FAWY SO45 .... 392 F5
Copythorne Crs TOTT SO40 .... 315 M6
Copythorn Rd NEND PO2 .... 399 K5

Coracle Cl HLER SO31 .... 370 D7
Coral Cl FHAM/PORC PO16 .... 398 A2
Coralin Gv WVILLE PO7 .... 352 F7
Coram Cl WINC SO23 .... 11 H2
Corbar Rd CHCH/BSGR BH23 .... 434 C8
Corbett Rd WVILLE PO7 .... 376 B2
Corbiere Av BKME/WDN BH12 .. 431 H7
Corbiere Cl ROWN SO16 .... 317 K5
Corbin Av FERN BH22 .... 406 E2
Corbin Rd LYMN SO41 .... 439 M6
Corbould Rd FAWY SO45 .... 367 K8 🔟
Corby Crs HSEA PO3 .... 399 H4
Cordale Rd BSTK RG21 .... 104 F5
Cordelia Cl FAWY SO45 .... 367 H5
Cordelia Gdns ASHV GU12 .... 91 J8 🔟
Corderoy Cl STHA RG19 .... 27 J6 🔟
Cordwalles Rd CBLY GU15 .... 51 J8
Corfe Cl FHAM/STUB PO14 .... 395 K4
  NALR SO24 .... 218 B4
Corfe Gdns FRIM GU16 .... 71 J8
Corfe Lodge Rd WIMB BH21 .... 429 G4
Corfe View Rd PSTN BH14 .... 446 B5
  WIMB BH21 .... 429 G3
Corfe Wy BDST BH18 .... 429 J2
  FARN GU14 .... 91 H7
Corfield Cl EWKG RG40 .... 48 B5
Corhampton Crs HAV PO9 .... 377 H4
Corhampton La BPWT SO32 .... 298 C3
Corhampton Rd SBNE BH6 .... 449 H2
Coriander Cl FARN GU14 .... 89 M4 🔟
Coriander Dr TOTT SO40 .... 340 F1
Coriander Wy FHAM PO15 .... 347 M8
Corinna Gdns FAWY SO45 .... 367 H5
Corinthian Cl AND SP10 .... 119 G4 🔟
  KEMP RG22 .... 127 H1
Corinthian Rd CHFD SO53 .... 293 K1
Cork La TOTT SO40 .... 342 C4
Cormorant Cl
  FHAM/PORC PO16 .... 373 K8 🔟
Cormorant Dr FAWY SO45 .... 367 M6
Cormorant Pl SHST GU47 .... 50 B8
Cornaway La
  FHAM/PORC PO16 .... 397 M1
Cornbrook Gv HORN PO8 .... 351 M6
Cornbunting Cl SHST GU47 .... 50 A8 🔟
Cornelia Cl FARN GU14 .... 90 A5 🔟
Cornelia Crs BKME/WDN BH12 .. 446 F2
Cornelius Dr WVILLE PO7 .... 352 F7
Corner Md WVILLE PO7 .... 351 K4
Cornes Cl WINW SO22 .... 10 A7
Cornfield FHAM/PORC PO16 .... 372 F4
Cornfield Cl NBAD SO52 .... 292 E2
Cornfield Rd
  LSOL/BMARY PO13 .... 420 D2
Cornfields AND SP10 .... 9 K9
  YTLY GU46 .... 68 E2
The Cornfields KEMP RG22 .... 127 H1
Cornflower Cl HLER SO31 .... 370 C6
Cornflower Dr
  CHCH/BSGR BH23 .... 436 A7
Cornflower Wy RAND SP11 .... 92 E7
Cornford Wy
  CHCH/BSGR BH23 .... 436 B8
Cornforth Rd TOTT SO40 .... 316 B7
Cornish Cl KEMP RG22 .... 104 B5 🔟
Cornish Gdns NBNE BH10 .... 432 C6
Corn Market ROMY SO51 .... 290 D1 🔟
Cornpits La FBDG SP6 .... 308 B5
Cornwall Cl CBLY GU15 .... 71 J1
Cornwall Crs WEND SO18 .... 319 L6
Cornwall Rd LYMN SO41 .... 454 A4
Cornwallis Crs PSEA PO1 .... 423 G2
Cornwallis Rd LYMN SO41 .... 454 A4
Cornwall Rd CHFD SO53 .... 293 H5
  BOR GU35 .... 201 J7
  PSEA PO1 .... 21 J2
  WEND SO18 .... 319 L6
Cornwell Cl LSOL/BMARY PO13 .. 421 H1
  NEND PO2 .... 398 F6
Coronado Rd GPORT PO12 .... 421 M2
Coronation Av
  MOOR/WNTN BH9 .... 432 D6
  UPTN BH16 .... 444 A1 🔟
Coronation Cl KSCL RG20 .... 57 J7
  ODIM RG29 .... 108 E5 🔟
Coronation Pde HLER SO31 .... 369 J5 🔟
Coronation Rd ALDT GU11 .... 7 H7
  BPWT SO32 .... 324 A3 🔟
  BSTK RG21 .... 5 H5
  HISD PO11 .... 426 C7
  RAND SP11 .... 92 F6
  VWD BH31 .... 356 D1
  YTLY GU46 .... 69 G1
Corporation Rd BMTH BH1 .... 23 K3
Correlli Rd KEMP RG22 .... 104 E8
Corringway FLET GU13 .... 111 G2
Corry Rd GSHT GU26 .... 203 M2
Corsair Dr FAWY SO45 .... 367 H4
Corsham Wy CWTH RG45 .... 49 L2
Corunna Main AND SP10 .... 9 K3
Corvette Av HLER SO31 .... 370 D7
Cosford Cl ELGH SO50 .... 294 F6 🔟
Cosham Park Av CHAM PO6 .... 399 H1
Cossack Gn SHAM SO14 .... 13 H3
Cossack La WINC SO23 .... 11 H7
Coster Cl NWBY RG14 .... 25 G3 🔟
Cosworth Dr FAWY SO45 .... 367 H5
Cotes Av PSTN BH14 .... 445 M3
Cotlands Rd BMTH BH1 .... 23 J4
Cot La RCCH PO18 .... 403 M3
Cotsalls ELGH SO50 .... 295 H7
Cotswold Cl FARN GU14 .... 90 B1
  FAWY SO45 .... 367 H5 🔟
  HAV PO9 .... 377 J2 🔟
  KEMP RG22 .... 104 A4
  VWD BH31 .... 356 D3 🔟
Cotswold Rd ROWN SO16 .... 317 L8
  SHST GU47 .... 49 J7 🔟
Cottage Cl WVILLE PO7 .... 351 K5
Cottage Gdns
  BKME/WDN BH12 .... 446 B3
  FARN GU14 .... 90 C4 🔟
Cottage Gn HTWY RG27 .... 87 J3
  RAND SP11 .... 142 E8
Cottage Gv GPORT PO12 .... 18 E2
  SSEA PO5 .... 21 H4

Cottage La *LISS* GU33 .... 247 L4
Cottage Ms *FBDG* SP6 .... 309 K6 🔢
RGWD BH24 .... 382 D1 🔢
Cottage Rd *STOK* SO20 .... 162 B8
Cottagers La *LYMN* SO41 .... 438 E5
Cottage Vw *PSEA* PO1 .... 21 J1
Cottes Wy *FHAM/STUB* PO14 ... 395 L7
Cottesway East
FHAM/STUB PO14 .... 395 L7
Cottington Cl *KSCL* RG20 .... 59 K6 🔢
Cott La *RGWD* BH24 .... 384 F6
Cottle Cl *BSTK* RG21 .... 104 F6
Cotton Cl *BDST* BH18 .... 429 K3
ELGH SO50 .... 294 D5
Cotton Dr *EMRTH* PO10 .... 378 C5
Cott St *BPWT* SO32 .... 324 F4
Cott Street La *BPWT* SO32 ...... 324 F4
Cotwell Av *HORN* PO8 .... 352 F4
Coulmere Rd *GPORT* PO12 .... 421 J2
Coultas Rd *CHCH/BSGR* BH23 265 K6
Council Rd *BSTK* RG21 .... 105 G4
Countess Cl *WIMB* BH21 .... 404 C7
Country Vw *FHAM/STUB* PO14 .. 395 M4
ROMY SO51 .... 288 D5
County Gdns
FHAM/STUB PO14 .... 372 A8
Course Park Crs
FHAM/STUB PO14 .... 371 G7
Court Barn La
LSOL/BMARY PO13 .... 420 D1
Court Cl *CHAM* PO6 .... 399 M1
LIPH GU30 .... 226 E5
LYMN SO41 .... 440 B6
TOTT SO40 .... 316 B6
Court Dro *OVTN* RG25 .... 100 F8
Courtenay Dr *WBY* PO14 ...... 404 A2 🔢
Courtenay Pl *LYMN* SO41 .... 440 C6
Courtenay Rd *FNM* GU9 .... 6 A9
PSTN BH14 .... 446 A4
WINC SO23 .... 11 G2
Court Gdns *CBLY* GU15 .... 71 G3
Court Hl *FBDG* SP6 .... 308 D4
Courthill Rd *PSTN* BH14 .... 446 B4
Court House Cl *FAWY* SO45 ..... 367 L4 🔢
Courtland Gdns *ROWN* SO16 ... 319 G3
Courtlands Rd *NWBY* RG14 .... 3 G8
Court La *ALTN* GU34 .... 220 C2
CHAM PO6 .... 399 M1
STOK SO20 .... 212 A2
Court Md *CHAM* PO6 .... 399 M1 🔢
Courtmoor Av *FLET* GU13 .... 110 E1
Courtmount Gv *CHAM* PO6 ..... 375 L8
Court Rd *ALDT* GU11 .... 6 F1
LSOL/BMARY PO13 .... 420 C1
MOOR/WNTN BH9 .... 432 F7
WINC SO23 .... 215 H3
WSHM SO15 .... 343 K1
Court Royal Ms *WSHM* SO15 ... 318 E8 🔢
Courts Hill Rd *HASM* GU27 ..... 228 C2
Courts Mount Rd *HASM* GU27 . 228 C2
The Courtyard *EPSF* GU31 ...... 275 L5
Cousins Gv *ENEY* PO4 .... 423 L6
Covena Rd *SBNE* BH6 .... 449 J1
Coventry Cl *KEMP* RG22 ...... 104 A8 🔢
WIMB BH21 .... 429 G4
Coventry Crs *CFDH* BH17 .... 429 L7
Coventry Rd *WSHM* SO15 .... 343 K2
Coverack Wy *CHAM* PO6 .... 398 F1
Cove Rd *FARN* GU14 .... 89 G5
NBNE BH10 .... 432 C6
Covert Cl *WVILLE* PO7 .... 376 C3
Coverts Cl *FNM* GU9 .... 135 H4 🔢
The Covert *FARN* GU14 .... 70 B8
ROMY SO51 .... 291 G2
Covey Cl *FARN* GU14 .... 70 B8
Covey Wy *NALR* SO24 .... 218 A4
Covington Rd *EMRTH* PO10 .... 378 F3
Cowan Rd *WVILLE* PO7 .... 376 B3
Coward Rd *GPORT* PO12 .... 18 B4
Cowdown La *RAND* SP11 .... 143 J5
RCCH PO18 .... 330 B4
Cowdrey Cl *ELGH* SO50 .... 294 E6 🔢
ROWN SO16 .... 318 A4
Cowdray Pk *ALTN* GU34 .... 176 L6
FHAM/STUB PO14 .... 5 H3
Cowdrey Cl *BSTK* RG21 .... 5 H3
Cowdrey Hts *CHAM* RG24 .... 5 L6
Cow Drove HI *STOK* SO20 .... 210 E4
Cowell Dr *LTDN* BH7 .... 433 L8
Cowes La *HLER* SO31 .... 394 B2
Cowfold La *HTWY* RG27 .... 85 M2
Cow La *CHAM* PO6 .... 399 H1
EPSF GU31 .... 304 F4
FHAM/PORC PO16 .... 398 C1
RAND SP11 .... 116 A5
Cowley Cl *ROWN* SO16 .... 317 K6
Cowley Dr *RWIN* SO21 .... 190 C6
Cowley Rd *LYMN* SO41 .... 440 A4
Cowleys La *BROC* SO42 .... 391 J3
Cowleys Rd *CHCH/BSGR* BH23 435 G6
Cowper Av *NMIL/BTOS* BH25 ... 437 L5
Cowper Rd *ITCH* SO19 .... 345 H2
MOOR/WNTN BH9 .... 432 E7
PSEA PO1 .... 423 J1 🔢
Cowpitts La *RGWD* BH24 .... 359 H6
Cowslade *NWBY* RG14 .... 25 G3 🔢
Cowslip Bank *CHAM* RG24 ...... 105 L1
Cowslip Cl *HLER* SO31 .... 370 C1
BOR GU35 .... 201 M4 🔢
LSOL/BMARY PO13 .... 397 G5
Cowslip Rd *WIMB* BH21 .... 429 J6 🔢
Cox Av *MOOR/WNTN* BH9 .... 432 F5
Coxbridge Dr *FNM* GU9 .... 134 C7
Coxbridge Mdw *FNM* GU9 .... 134 C7
Cox Cl *MOOR/WNTN* BH9 .... 432 F4
Cox Dl *FHAM/STUB* PO14 .... 371 G7
Coxes Meadow *PSF* GU32 .... 275 K3
Coxeter Rd *NWBY* RG14 .... 3 L5
Coxford Cl *ROWN* SO16 .... 317 M6
Coxford Dro *ROWN* SO16 .... 317 L6
Coxford Rd *ROWN* SO16 .... 317 L5
Coxgreen *SHST* GU47 .... 70 A2
Coxheath Rd *FLET* GU13 .... 110 D4
Coxmoor Cl *FLET* GU13 .... 111 H3
Cox Rw *CHFD* SO53 .... 293 G5
Cox's Dr *ITCH* SO19 .... 344 F6

Coxs Hl *RWIN* SO21 .... 238 F8
Cox's La *MARL* SN8 .... 32 C5
THLE RG7 .... 28 A5
Coxstone La *RGWD* BH24 .... 382 E2
Coy Pond Rd
BKME/WDN BH12 .... 446 F3
Cozens Cl *ITCH* SO19 .... 344 C7 🔢
Crabapple Cl *TOTT* SO40 ...... 341 G1 🔢
Crabbe Ct *SSEA* PO5 .... 21 H4 🔢
Crabbs Wy *TOTT* SO40 .... 340 F1
Crabbswood La *LYMN* SO41 .... 412 C8
Crabden La *HORN* PO8 .... 328 D8
Crableck La *HLER* SO31 .... 370 A3
Crab Orchard Wy *WIMB* BH21 . 356 C6
Crabs Hl *TADY* RG26 .... 60 A7
Crabthorne Farm La
FHAM/STUB PO14 .... 395 M5 🔢
Crabton Close Rd *BOSC* BH5 ... 448 E3
Crabtree *ROWN* SO16 .... 317 L7 🔢
Crabtree Gdns *BOR* GU35 .... 202 B3
Crabtree La *BOR* GU35 .... 202 B3
Crabtree Rd *CBLY* GU15 .... 70 E6
Crabtree Wy *CHAM* RG24 .... 106 A4
Crabwood Cl *HAV* PO9 .... 377 H1 🔢
Crabwood Dr *HEND* SO30 .... 320 D7
Crabwood Rd *ROWN* SO16 .... 317 K6
Cracknore Hard *TOTT* SO40 .... 343 G6
Cracknore Hard La *TOTT* SO40 343 G6 🔢
TOTT SO40 .... 343 G6 🔢
Craigmoor Av *CHAR* BH8 .... 433 J7
Craigmoor Cl *CHAR* BH8 .... 433 K7
Craigside Rd *RGWD* BH24 .... 381 H4
Craigwell Rd *WVILLE* PO7 .... 376 B4
Craigwood Dr *FERN* BH22 .... 406 C4
Crake Pl *SHST* GU47 .... 50 A8
Crammpour La *ROMY* SO51 ..... 263 J7
Cramptons *ALTN* GU34 .... 175 M6
Cranberry Cl *TOTT* SO40 .... 342 D7
Cranborne Crs
BKME/WDN BH12 .... 431 J8
Cranborne Gdns *CHFD* SO53 ... 265 G8
Cranborne Rd *CHAM* PO6 .... 375 L7
FBDG SP6 .... 332 E3
WCLF BH2 .... 22 D7
Cranbourne Cl *WSHM* SO15 .. 318 C7 🔢
Cranbourne Dr *RWIN* SO21 ..... 266 A5
Cranbourne La *BSTK* RG21 .... 104 E6 🔢
Cranbrook Ct *FLET* GU13 .... 88 F5
Cranbrook Rd
BKME/WDN BH12 .... 446 A2
Cranbury Av *SHAM* SO14 .... 343 M4
Cranbury Cl *RSAL* SP5 .... 284 E2
RWIN SO21 .... 266 A5
Cranbury Gdns *HLER* SO31 ..... 345 K7
Cranbury Pl *SHAM* SO14 .... 343 L2
Cranbury Rd *ELGH* SO50 .... 293 M6
ITCH SO19 .... 344 D5
Crane Cl *VWD* BH31 .... 356 C1
Crane Ct *SHST* GU47 .... 50 A8
Crane Dr *VWD* BH31 .... 356 C2
Cranemoor Av
CHCH/BSGR BH23 .... 436 C6
Cranemoor Cl
CHCH/BSGR BH23 .... 436 C6
Cranemoor Gdns
CHCH/BSGR BH23 .... 436 D6
Cranesfield *CHAM* RG24 .... 82 D4
Cranes Rd *CHAM* RG24 .... 82 D4
Craneswater Av *ENEY* PO4 .... 21 M8
Craneswater Ga *ENEY* PO4 ...... 21 M9 🔢
Craneswater Pk *ENEY* PO4 .... 21 M9
Cranfield Av *WIMB* BH21 .... 404 B3
Cranford Av *FLET* GU13 .... 110 D3
Cranford Dr *ALTN* GU34 .... 177 M1
Cranford Gdns *CHFD* SO53 ...... 265 G8
Cranford Park Dr *YTLY* GU46 ..... 69 G2
Cranford Rd *PSF* GU32 .... 275 K6
Cranford Wy *PTSW* SO17 .... 318 F6
Cranleigh Av *PSEA* PO1 .... 423 J2
Cranleigh Cl *SBNE* BH6 .... 449 K3
Cranleigh Ct *FARN* GU14 .... 90 C4 🔢
Cranleigh Gdns *SBNE* BH6 ...... 449 K3
Cranleigh Rd
FHAM/PORC PO16 .... 397 L1
HEND SO30 .... 346 A2
PSEA PO1 .... 423 J2
SBNE BH6 .... 449 J2
Cranmer Dr *ROWN* SO16 .... 317 H3
Cranmer Rd *MOOR/WNTN* BH9 432 E7
Cranmore *HLER* SO31 .... 369 G1
Cranmore Cl *ALDT* GU11 .... 6 A4
Cranmore Gdns *ALDT* GU11 .... 6 A4
Cranmore La *ALDT* GU11 .... 6 A4
Cranmore Rd *FRIM* GU16 .... 91 J4
Cranwell Cl *CHCH/BSGR* BH23 409 M7
Cranworth Rd *WINW* SO22 .... 10 E5
Crasswell St *PSEA* PO1 .... 423 J2
Craven Cl *RFNM* GU10 .... 158 F2
Craven Pl *FHAM* PO15 .... 14 B2
Craven Dene *NWBY* RG14 .... 3 H2
HUNG RG17 .... 33 L2
NWBY RG14 .... 2 A5
Craven St *SHAM* SO14 .... 13 H2 🔢
Crawford Cl *ROWN* SO16 .... 317 K6
Crawford Dr *FHAM/PORC* PO16 . 14 E1
Crawford Gdns *CBLY* GU15 .... 70 E3
Crawford Pl *NWBY* RG14 .... 2 D3
Crawlboys La *RAND* SP11 .... 92 E5
Crawley Av *HAV* PO9 .... 377 L2
Crawley Dr *CBLY* GU15 .... 71 J2
Crawley Hl *CBLY* GU15 .... 71 J3
ROMY SO51 .... 288 E6
Crawley Rdg *CBLY* GU15 .... 71 J2
Crawley Wood Cl *CBLY* GU15 .. 71 J5 🔢
Crawshaw Rd *PSTN* BH14 .... 446 B4
Crawte Av *FAWY* SO45 .... 392 B6
Crawts Rd *OVTN* RG25 .... 123 M1
Craydown La *STOK* SO20 .... 162 D6
Creasey Rd *BWD* BH11 .... 431 L3
Credenhill Rd *CHAM* PO6 .... 375 G7
Credon Cl *FARN* GU14 .... 90 D1
Creech Rd *BKME/WDN* BH12 ... 446 B3

Creedy Gdns *WEND* SO18 .... 319 M5 🔢
Creek End *EMRTH* PO10 .... 402 D1
Creekmoor La *CFDH* BH17 .... 429 K7
Creek Rd *GPORT* PO12 .... 19 J3
HISD PO11 .... 426 B6
Creighton Rd *WSHM* SO15 ...... 342 D2
Cremyll Cl *FHAM/STUB* PO14 .. 396 A6
Crerar Cl *FARN* GU14 .... 90 A5
Crescent Cl *WINW* SO22 .... 238 A4
Crescent Dr *NMIL/BTOS* BH25 . 452 E1
Crescent La *ASHV* GU12 .... 113 L3
Crescent Rd *FHAM/PORC* PO16 . 15 H6
GPORT PO12 .... 18 C3
HLER SO31 .... 370 D1
NBAD SO52 .... 291 L3
PSTN BH14 .... 446 B4
VWD BH31 .... 356 C2
WCLF BH2 .... 22 C5
WIMB BH21 .... 404 A4
The Crescent *ALTN* GU34 .... 197 G4
BMTH BH1 .... 448 D4
BPWT SO32 .... 296 B6
ELGH SO50 .... 293 M4
EMRTH PO10 .... 379 H8
FARN GU14 .... 90 F5
FLET GU13 .... 110 B2
FNM GU9 .... 112 A8
HLER SO31 .... 368 F3
ITCH SO19 .... 344 E6
NMIL/BTOS BH25 .... 437 L6
RAND SP11 .... 96 D1
RAND SP11 .... 142 D4
RAND SP11 .... 142 E7
ROMY SO51 .... 263 G8
RWIN SO21 .... 266 F2
THLE RG7 .... 29 M4
THLE RG7 .... 43 K2
TOTT SO40 .... 340 C5
WVILLE PO7 .... 376 A4 🔢
Crescent Wk *FERN* BH22 .... 406 C6
Cressey Rd *ROMY* SO51 .... 290 E1
Cress Gdns *AND* SP10 .... 8 E3
Cresswell Rd *NWBY* RG14 .... 3 M1
Cressy Rd *NEND* PO2 .... 423 H1
Cresta Gdns *FERN* BH22 .... 406 C4
Crest Cl *FHAM/PORC* PO16 ...... 373 H7
Crestland Cl *HORN* PO8 .... 352 E3
Crest Rd *BKME/WDN* BH12 ..... 446 B2
The Crest *WVILLE* PO7 .... 376 A6
Crest Wy *ITCH* SO19 .... 345 G4
Crete La *FAWY* SO45 .... 367 K7
Crete Rd *FAWY* SO45 .... 367 K8
Cribb Cl *CFDH* BH17 .... 445 K1
Crichel Mount Rd *PSTN* BH14 . 446 B8
Crichel Rd *MOOR/WNTN* BH9 . 432 E8
Cricket *CHCH/BSGR* BH23 ...... 450 E3
RWIN SO21 .... 189 G6
Cricket Dr *WINW* SO22 .... 238 C3
Cricketers *KSCL* RG20 .... 24 B2
Cricketers Wy *AND* SP10 .... 119 G5
Cricket Field Gv *CWTH* RG45 ..... 50 A4
Cricket Hl *EWKG* RG40 .... 48 C6
YTLY GU46 .... 69 H3
Cricket Hill La *BLKW* GU17 .... 69 G5
YTLY GU46 .... 69 H3
Cricket La *RFNM* GU10 .... 159 G2
Cricket Lea *BOR* GU35 .... 201 L3 🔢
Cricklemede *BPWT* SO32 .... 323 J1
Cricklewood Cl *BPWT* SO32 .. 323 J1 🔢
Crigdon Cl *ROWN* SO16 .... 317 K8
Crimea Rd *ALDT* GU11 .... 7 G2
Cringle Av *SBNE* BH6 .... 449 L6
Crinoline Gdns *ENEY* PO4 .... 423 L6
Cripley Rd *FARN* GU14 .... 90 B3
Cripple Gate La *BROC* SO42 .... 416 B3
Crispin Cl *CHCH/BSGR* BH23 .. 436 D8
ELGH SO50 .... 321 H2
HLER SO31 .... 370 F4
Crispstead La *WINC* SO23 .... 238 E3
Crisspyn Cl *HORN* PO8 .... 352 F2
Critchmere HI *HASM* GU27 ...... 228 B1
Critchmere La *HASM* GU27 ...... 228 B2
Critchmere V *HASM* GU27 .... 228 A2
Crittall Cl *LYMN* SO41 .... 413 G6
Cricket Lea *LYMN* SO41 .... 413 G6
Crockford Br *LYMN* SO41 .... 415 H6
Crockford Cl *NMIL/BTOS* BH25 437 H8
Crockford La *CHAM* RG24 .... 83 K4
Crockford Rd *EMRTH* PO10 ..... 378 F2
Crocus Md *NTHA* RG18 .... 27 H4
Croft Av *AND* SP10 .... 9 H8
Croft Cl *WIMB* BH21 .... 429 H1
Crofter's Cl *SHST* GU47 .... 49 K8 🔢
Crofters Meadow *CHAM* RG24 . 83 L8 🔢
Croft Gdns *AND* SP10 .... 9 H9
Croft Hts *RSAL* SP5 .... 259 G5
Croftlands Av
FHAM/STUB PO14 .... 396 A5
Croft La *HISD* PO11 .... 401 L7
RFNM GU10 .... 133 H3
NWBY RG14 .... 2 B2
YTLY GU46 .... 68 F1
Crofton Av *LSOL/BMARY* PO13 396 A8
Crofton Cl *CHCH/BSGR* BH23 . 434 C8
PTSW SO17 .... 318 F7 🔢
WVILLE PO7 .... 376 A3
Crofton La *FHAM/STUB* PO14 .. 395 M7
Crofton Rd *ENEY* PO4 .... 423 M3
NEND PO2 .... 399 J4
Crofton Wy *BPWT* SO32 .... 323 M5
HLER SO31 .... 370 A7
Croft Rd *ALDT* GU11 .... 7 G1
BKME/WDN BH12 .... 446 A2
CHCH/BSGR BH23 .... 435 M4
CHCH/BSGR BH23 .... 450 E1
DEAN RG23 .... 102 F6
MOOR/WNTN BH9 .... 432 D6
NEND PO2 .... 399 H7 🔢
NWBY RG14 .... 3 H2
RGWD BH24 .... 359 G2
THLE RG7 .... 43 J2
The Crofts *KEMP* RG22 .... 127 H2
The Croft *AMSY* SP4 .... 160 A2
CHFD SO53 .... 293 H5 🔢
FHAM/STUB PO14 .... 396 A4
TOTT SO40 .... 316 B4
Croft Wy *FRIM* GU16 .... 71 J7
Cromarty Av *ENEY* PO4 .... 423 M4
Cromarty Cl *FHAM/STUB* PO14 . 395 M5

Cromarty Rd *ROWN* SO16 .... 317 K3
Crombie Cl *HORN* PO8 .... 352 D4
Cromer Rd *BKME/WDN* BH12 .. 446 E3
CHAM PO6 .... 375 H7
CHAR BH8 .... 448 C1
ROWN SO16 .... 317 J7
Cromhall Cl
FHAM/STUB PO14 .... 372 A8 🔢
Crompton Wy *FHAM* PO15 ...... 371 G3
Cromwell Cl *CHAM* RG24 .... 106 A2
Cromwell Rd
BKME/WDN BH12 .... 446 C3
BOSC BH5 .... 449 G3
BSTK RG21 .... 4 D5
CBLY GU15 .... 71 G1
ENEY PO4 .... 423 M6
WINW SO22 .... 238 C2
WIMB BH21 .... 404 A4
The Cross *PSF* GU32 .... 273 J7
RGWD BH24 .... 384 E5
RSAL SP5 .... 253 G1
STOK SO20 .... 210 F5
Cross Barn La *ALDT* GU11 .... 6 E2
BPWT SO32 .... 297 H8
BSTK RG21 .... 5 J4
FARN GU14 .... 90 A7
Cross Keys Pas *WINC* SO23 ..... 11 H8 🔢
Cross La *FNM* GU9 .... 135 K3
Crondall Av *HAV* PO9 .... 377 J2
Crondall Ct *CBLY* GU15 .... 70 E4 🔢
Crondall End *YTLY* GU46 .... 68 F1
Crondall Rd *RFNM* GU10 .... 133 M6
RFNM GU10 .... 110 B5
RFNM GU10 .... 157 K1
Crooked Hays Cl *TOTT* SO40 .. 342 D7 🔢
Crooked Walk La *WHAM* PO17 . 374 C5
Crookham Cl *HAV* PO9 .... 377 G4 🔢
TADY RG26 .... 61 L2 🔢
Crookham Reach *FLET* GU13 ... 110 D2
Crookham Rd *FLET* GU13 .... 110 D2
ITCH SO19 .... 344 D8 🔢
Crookhorn La *WVILLE* PO7 ...... 376 C7
Crooksbury Rd *RFNM* GU10 .... 135 L5
Crookshouse Rd *SHAM* SO14 .... 13 L6
Cross Keys *AND* SP10 .... 8 E4
Crossmead
NMIL/BTOS BH25 .... 437 L6
Cross Rd *ASHV* GU12 .... 113 L5
FARN GU14 .... 90 B7
ITCH SO19 .... 344 C1
LSOL/BMARY PO13 .... 420 E4
Cross St *ALDT* GU11 .... 6 E2
BPWT SO32 .... 297 H8
BSTK RG21 .... 5 J4
FARN GU14 .... 90 A7
SSEA PO5 .... 21 J3 🔢
Crossways *ASHV* GU12 .... 7 K4
LYMN SO41 .... 439 H7
RWIN SO21 .... 190 H1
Crossways Rd *RFNM* GU10 ...... 181 H1
Crossways *ASHV* GU12 .... 7 K4
LYMN SO41 .... 439 H7
RWIN SO21 .... 266 C3
The Crossways *AND* SP10 .... 8 F4
GPORT PO12 .... 421 M2
UPTN BH16 .... 444 B1
The Crossway
FHAM/PORC PO16 .... 374 A8
Crosswell Cl *ITCH* SO19 .... 345 G3
Croucher's Cft *WINW* SO22 .... 214 A7
Croucheston Dro *RSAL* SP5 ..... 253 G1
Crouch La *HORN* PO8 .... 352 E1
Crow Arch La *RGWD* BH24 ...... 382 F2
Crowder Ter *WINW* SO22 .... 10 E8
Crowfield Dr *STHA* RG19 .... 26 E5
Crow La *RGWD* BH24 .... 383 G2
Crowley Dr *ALTN* GU34 .... 176 F5
Crown Acre Cl *STHA* RG19 .... 26 F5
Crown Cl *BKME/WDN* BH12 .... 446 B3
WVILLE PO7 .... 376 C5
Crown La *FNM* GU9 .... 135 K3
HTWY RG27 .... 85 H8
RAND SP11 .... 92 D6
Crown Md *WIMB* BH21 .... 404 A3 🔢
Crown Pl *SHST* GU47 .... 50 B7
Crown St *PSEA* PO1 .... 423 H2
WSHM SO15 .... 318 A8
Crowsbury Cl *EMRTH* PO10 .... 378 C5
Crows La *ALTN* GU34 .... 198 D5
Crows Nest La *BPWT* SO32 ...... 321 L7
Crowsport *HLER* SO31 .... 369 L5
Crowther Cl *ITCH* SO19 .... 345 G4
Crowthorne Rd *SHST* GU47 .... 49 L8
Croyde Cl *FARN* GU14 .... 90 D2
Croydon Cl *ROWN* SO16 .... 317 M4
Croye Cl *AND* SP10 .... 8 E5
Cruickshank Lea *SHST* GU47 .... 70 B2
Crummock Rd *CHFD* SO53 ...... 292 F1
Crumpets Dr *UPTN* BH16 .... 428 B3
Crundles *EPSF* GU31 .... 275 M5
Crusader Rd *HEND* SO30 .... 346 A4
WIMB BH21 .... 431 H4
Crusaders Wy *NBAD* SO52 ...... 292 C2
Cruse Cl *LYMN* SO41 .... 412 F6
Crystal Wy *WVILLE* PO7 .... 352 F8
Cucklington Gdns
MOOR/WNTN BH9 .... 432 F5
Cuckmere La *ROWN* SO16 ...... 317 J8

Cuckoo Bushes La *CHFD* SO53 . 265 G8
Cuckoo Cl *OVTN* RG25 .... 125 K7
Cuckoo Hill Wy
CHCH/BSGR BH23 .... 410 A7
Cuckoo La *FHAM/STUB* PO14 .. 395 M4
Cuckoo Rd *BKME/WDN* BH12 .. 430 C8
Cudnell Av *BWD* BH11 .... 431 K2
Cudworth Md *HEND* SO30 ...... 321 J7
Cufaude La *TADY* RG26 .... 83 L2
Cuffelle Cl *CHAM* RG24 .... 83 M5
Cuffnells Cl *RGWD* BH24 .... 334 F8
Cul-de-sac *NMIL/BTOS* BH25 .. 437 G8
Culford Av *TOTT* SO40 .... 341 K2
Culford Wy *TOTT* SO40 .... 341 K2
Cull Cl *BKME/WDN* BH12 .... 432 A8
Cullen Cl *YTLY* GU46 .... 68 F3
Culley Vw *NALR* SO24 .... 218 C4
Culliford Crs *CFDH* BH17 .... 430 C6
Cull La *NMIL/BTOS* BH25 .... 437 M3
Culloden Cl *FHAM* PO15 .... 14 D3
Culloden Rd *FHAM/STUB* PO14 396 D2
Cullwood La *NMIL/BTOS* BH25 438 A3
Culver *HLER* SO31 .... 369 G3
Culver Cl *ROWN* SO16 .... 317 J6
Culver Dr *HISD* PO11 .... 426 A7
Culverlands Crs *ASHV* GU12 .... 113 J5
Culverley Cl *BROC* SO42 .... 387 K7 🔢
Culver Rd *BSTK* RG21 .... 104 F5
ENEY PO4 .... 423 L6
NMIL/BTOS BH25 .... 437 K6
NWBY RG14 .... 25 J8 🔢
SHST GU47 .... 50 A7
WINC SO23 .... 238 C2
Culvers *EPSF* GU31 .... 305 G5
Culverwell Gdns *WINC* SO23 ..... 10 F9
Culvery Gdns *WEND* SO18 ...... 319 M6
Cumberland Av *CHFD* SO53 .... 293 K3
EMRTH PO10 .... 378 C4
KEMP RG22 .... 104 D7 🔢
Cumberland Pl *WSHM* SO15 .... 12 E1
Cumberland Rd *CBLY* GU15 ...... 71 M4
SSEA PO5 .... 21 L2 🔢
Cumberland St *PSEA* PO1 .... 422 E2
SHAM SO14 .... 13 J3 🔢
Cumberland Wy *FAWY* SO45 .... 367 H5
Cumber Rd *HLER* SO31 .... 370 C5
Cumbria Ct *FARN* GU14 .... 91 H7
Cumbrian Wy *ROWN* SO16 ..... 317 K8
Cumnor Rd *BMTH* BH1 .... 23 G7
Cunard Av *WSHM* SO15 .... 318 B8
Cunard Rd *SHAM* SO14 .... 13 H8
Cundell Wy *WINC* SO23 .... 191 G7
Cunliffe Cl *SELS* SO20 .... 427 L6
Cunningham Av *BPWT* SO32 ... 296 F8 🔢
Cunningham Cl *RGWD* BH24 ... 359 G8 🔢
Cunningham Crs *BWD* BH11 .... 431 L5
ITCH SO19 .... 344 F4 🔢
Cunningham Dr *HLER* SO31 .... 370 E4
LSOL/BMARY PO13 .... 397 L5
Cunningham Rd *HORN* PO8 .... 353 G2 🔢
WVILLE PO7 .... 376 B3
Cunnington Rd *FARN* GU14 ...... 91 H7
Cupernham Cl *ROMY* SO51 ..... 262 F5
Cupernham La *ROMY* SO51 ..... 262 F5
Curdridge Cl *HAV* PO9 .... 377 L3 🔢
Curdridge La *BPWT* SO32 .... 322 F6
Curlew Cl *EMRTH* PO10 .... 378 C8
FERN BH22 .... 405 M1
KEMP RG22 .... 103 M7
ROWN SO16 .... 318 A3
STHA RG19 .... 26 F5 🔢
Curlew Dr *FAWY* SO45 .... 367 M6
FHAM/PORC PO16 .... 373 K8
Curlew Gdns *HORN* PO8 .... 352 D4
Curlew Rd *CHAR* BH8 .... 433 H6
CHCH/BSGR BH23 .... 450 F2
Curlews *ALTN* GU34 .... 176 C2
The Curlews *VWD* BH31 .... 356 E3
Curleys Wy *THLE* RG7 .... 46 A2 🔢
Curlieu Rd *PLE* BH15 .... 445 K2
Curling Wy *NWBY* RG14 .... 3 K1
Curly Bridge Cl *FARN* GU14 ...... 70 C8
Curtis Cl *CBLY* GU15 .... 71 M1 🔢
BOR GU35 .... 202 B2 🔢
Curtis La *BOR* GU35 .... 202 B2
Curtis Md *NEND* PO2 .... 399 K4
Curtis Rd *ALTN* GU34 .... 176 F6
BKME/WDN BH12 .... 446 B3
Curtiss Gdns *GPORT* PO12 .... 18 A3
The Curve *HORN* PO8 .... 352 D2
LSOL/BMARY PO13 .... 396 F6
Curzon Dr *FLET* GU13 .... 110 F3
Curzon Howe Rd *PSEA* PO1 ...... 20 D1
Curzon Pl *LYMN* SO41 .... 440 B6
Curzon Rd *CHAR* BH8 .... 448 C2
PSTN BH14 .... 445 M5
WVILLE PO7 .... 376 C1
Curzon Wy *CHCH/BSGR* BH23 . 436 B8
Cusden Dr *AND* SP10 .... 9 G1
Custards Rd *LYND* SO43 .... 363 K2
Cutbush La *WEND* SO18 .... 319 M5
WEND SO18 .... 320 A8
Cuthbert Rd *ASHV* GU12 .... 113 L2
PSEA PO1 .... 423 K2
Cuthburga Rd *WIMB* BH21 ...... 404 A3
Cutler Cl *BKME/WDN* BH12 ..... 447 H1
NMIL/BTOS BH25 .... 438 A5
Cutlers La *FHAM/STUB* PO14 .. 396 A5
Cutlers Pl *WIMB* BH21 .... 404 E3
Cutter Av *HLER* SO31 .... 370 C7
Cut Throat La *BPWT* SO32 .... 299 G6
BPWT SO32 .... 324 B2
Cutting HI *HUNG* RG17 .... 32 D4
Cutts Arch *BPWT* SO32 .... 325 G1
Cutts Rd *ALDT* GU11 .... 113 G1
Cuxhaven Wy *AND* SP10 .... 118 E5
Cygnet Cl *STHA* RG19 .... 26 E5
Cygnet Ct *FHAM/PORC* PO16 . 373 K8 🔢
Cygnet La *CHAM* RG24 .... 400 D1
Cygnus Gdns *FAWY* SO45 .... 367 G5
Cynthia Cl *BKME/WDN* BH12 .. 446 A1
Cynthia Rd *BKME/WDN* BH12 .. 446 A1
Cypress Av *FARN* GU14 .... 70 C7 🔢
Cypress Av *ITCH* SO19 .... 344 D3
Cypress Crs *HORN* PO8 .... 352 E4
Cypress Dr *FLET* GU13 .... 89 H7
Cypress Gdns *HEND* SO30 .... 346 E1
TOTT SO40 .... 341 G1 🔢

Cypress Gv *ASHV* GU12 .... 113 J1
  RAND SP11 .... 142 B1
Cypress Rd *BOR* GU35 .... 200 F5
Cypress Wy *GSHT* GU26 ...... 204 A6
Cyprus Rd *FHAM/STUB* PO14... 371 G7
  KEMP RG22 .... 127 H3
  NEND PO2 .... 399 J4
Cyril Rd *CHAR* BH8 .... 448 B2
Cyril Vokins Rd *NWBY* RG14... 26 B6

D

Dacombe Cl *UPTN* BH16 ...... 444 B1
Dacombe Dr *UPTN* BH16 ...... 444 B1
Dacre Cl *AND* SP10 .... 118 C5
Daffodil Cl *KEMP* RG22 .... 103 M8
Daffodil Rd *ROWN* SO16 ...... 319 H4
Daggons Rd *FBDG* SP6 .... 333 G2
Dahlia Cl *KEMP* RG22 .... 103 M8 ▣
Dahlia Rd *ROWN* SO16 .... 318 F4 ▣
Daintree Cl *ITCH* SO19 .... 345 H5
Dairy Cl *CHCH/BSGR* BH23 ... 450 C1
  RSAL SP5 .... 285 J3
  WIMB BH21 .... 428 F4
Dairy Gate Rd *FARN* GU14 .... 90 E8
Dairy La *ROWN* SO16 .... 316 F4
Dairymoor *WHAM* PO17 ...... 348 E4
Daisy La *GPORT* PO12 .... 18 D3
  HLER SO31 .... 370 F5
Daisy Md *WVILLE* PO7 .... 376 E2
Daisy Rd *ROWN* SO16 .... 319 H4
Dalby Crs *NWBY* RG14 .... 3 H9
Dale Cl *WINW* SO22 .... 213 M3
  RFNM GU10 .... 158 C1
  PLE BH15 .... 445 L2
Dale Dr *LSOL/BMARY* PO13 ... 396 F5
Dale Gdns *SHST* GU47 .... 49 K8
Dale Rd *KEMP* RG22 .... 367 K5
  FHAM/STUB PO14 .... 396 B5
  PLE BH15 .... 445 L2
  ROWN SO16 .... 318 B6
Dales Cl *WIMB* BH21 .... 405 G2
Dales Dr *WIMB* BH21 .... 404 F3
Dales La *CHCH/BSGR* BH23 ... 433 J1
Dales Wy *TOTT* SO40 .... 316 A8
The Dale *WVILLE* PO7 .... 376 A6
Dale Valley Cl *ROWN* SO16 ... 318 B6
Dale Valley Gdns *ROWN* SO16 .. 318 B6
Dale Valley Rd *PLE* BH15 ...... 445 K1
  ROWN SO16 .... 318 B5
Dale Vw *HASM* GU27 .... 228 C3 ▣
Dalewood Rd *KEMP* RG22 .... 103 M6
Dalewood Av *BWD* BH11 .... 431 J3
Dalewood Rd *FHAM* PO15 .... 14 B5
Dalkeith Rd *CCLF* BH13 .... 446 F7
  WIMB BH21 .... 429 H4 ▣
Dalley Ct *SHST* GU47 .... 70 A1
Dalling Rd *BKME/WDN* BH12 .. 446 F3
Dallington Cl
  FHAM/STUB PO14 .... 396 A7 ▣
Dalmally Gdns *WEND* SO18 ... 319 L8 ▣
Dalmeny Rd *SBNE* BH6 .... 449 M5
Damask Gdns *WVILLE* PO7 .... 352 F1
Damen Cl *HEND* SO30 .... 345 M3
Damerham Rd *CHAR* BH8 ..... 433 H5
Dampier Cl *LSOL/BMARY* PO13 .. 421 G1
Damsel La *OVTN* RG25 .... 151 J5
Damsel Pth *BSTK* RG21 .... 5 K8
Damson Hl *BPWT* SO32 .... 298 A8
Danbury Cl *HAV* PO9 .... 377 J2 ▣
Danbury Gdns *CHFD* SO53 .... 292 F4 ▣
Danbury Rd *KEMP* RG22 .... 127 G2
Danbury Wy *ROWN* SO16 ...... 317 J5
Dane Cl *FAWY* SO45 .... 392 D7
Danecourt Cl *PSTN* BH14 ...... 445 L4
Danecourt Rd *PSTN* BH14 ..... 445 L4
Danecrest Rd *LYMN* SO41 ..... 438 D5
Dane Dr *FERN* BH22 .... 406 C5
Danegeld Cl *AND* SP10 .... 119 G4 ▣
Danehurst New Rd
  LYMN SO41 .... 412 A8
Danehurst Pl *AND* SP10 ...... 118 B8
Dane Rd *LYMN* SO41 .... 453 M2
Danesbrook La *WVILLE* PO7 ... 376 E1 ▣
Danesbury Av *SBNE* BH6 ...... 449 L4
Danes Cl *NMIL/BTOS* BH25 ... 452 F5
Daneshill Dr *CHAM* RG24 .... 83 L8
Danes Rd *FHAM/PORC* PO16 .. 373 M7
  ROMY SO51 .... 261 J4
  WINC SO23 .... 11 G4
Danestream Cl *LYMN* SO41 .. 454 C4 ▣
Daneswood Rd
  NMIL/BTOS BH25 .... 438 A5 ▣
Daniell's Cl *LYMN* SO41 .... 440 C6
Daniell's Wk *LYMN* SO41 ..... 440 C6
Daniel Rd *WHCH* RG28 .... 122 C4
Dankworth Rd *KEMP* RG22 .. 104 B8
Danley La *HASM* GU27 .... 227 K5
Dansie Cl *PSTN* BH14 .... 446 A4
Danvers Cl *STHA* RG19 .... 27 G6 ▣
Danvers Dr *FLET* GU13 .... 110 C4
Daphne Dr *FLET* GU13 .... 110 D5
Dapple Pl *TOTT* SO40 .... 342 E7
Darby Pl Green La *BLKW* GU17 .. 69 L3
Darby Green Rd *BLKW* GU17 ... 69 K3
Darby's Cl *PLE* BH15 .... 445 J2
Darby's La *PLE* BH15 .... 445 J2
Dare's La *RFNM* GU10 .... 110 D7
Dark La *CHAR* RG24 .... 82 D5
  CHCH/BSGR BH23 .... 436 E4
  FAWY SO45 .... 392 D7
  NALR SO24 .... 218 D6
  NALR SO24 .... 242 C3
  RGUW GU3 .... 137 L4
Darleydale Cl *SHST* GU47 .... 50 A6 ▣
Darley Rd *FERN* BH22 .... 406 A5
Darlington Gdns *WSHM* SO15 .. 318 C8

Darlington Rd *BSTK* RG21 .... 4 D4
  ENEY PO4 .... 21 L5
Darracott Cl *CBLY* GU15 .... 71 L1 ▣
Darracott Rd *BOSC* BH5 .... 448 F4
Darren Cl *FHAM/STUB* PO14 .. 396 B4
Darset Av *FLET* GU13 .... 88 F6
Dart Cl *EWKG* RG40 .... 48 C1
  NTHA RG18 .... 26 E3
Dart Ct *AND* SP10 .... 119 H6 ▣
Dartington Rd *ELGH* SO50 .... 294 C3
Dartmouth Rd *HSEA* PO3 ..... 399 L4
Dart Rd *FARN* GU14 .... 90 A2
  WEND SO18 .... 320 A5
Darvill Rd *NALR* SO24 .... 219 M3
Darvills La *FNM* GU9 .... 134 F6
Darwin Av *CHCH/BSGR* BH23... 434 C7
Darwin Gv *ALDT* GU11 .... 112 F5
Darwin Rd *ELGH* SO50 .... 294 A4
  WSHM SO15 .... 343 H1
Darwin Wy *LSOL/BMARY* PO13 .. 421 H2
Dashwood Cl *ALTN* GU34 ..... 176 C6
Dasna Rd *NTID* SP9 .... 114 C3
Daulston Rd *PSEA* PO1 .... 423 J1
Daunch Cl *NTID* SP9 .... 114 C1
Dauntless Rd *THLE* RG7 .... 31 L5
Dauntsey Dro *RAND* SP11 ..... 116 F2
Dauntsey La *RAND* SP11 ...... 116 F2
Davenport Cl
  LSOL/BMARY PO13 .... 421 G2 ▣
  UPTN BH16 .... 444 B1 ▣
Daventry La *HSEA* PO3 .... 400 A4
D Av *FAWY* SO45 .... 392 B2
David Wy *PLE* BH15 .... 444 C6
Davis Cl *LSOL/BMARY* PO13 ... 397 G8 ▣
Davis Fld *NMIL/BTOS* BH25 ... 437 K6
Davis Gdns *SHST* GU47 .... 70 B1
Davis Rd *PSTN* BH14 .... 446 D3
Davy Cl *KEMP* RG22 .... 104 C4
Dawkins Rd *PLE* BH15 .... 444 C4
Dawkins Wy *NMIL/BTOS* BH25 .. 437 L6
Daw La *HISD* PO11 .... 401 K8
Dawlish Av *WSHM* SO15 ...... 318 C8
Dawnay Cl *ROWN* SO16 .... 319 J3
Dawnay Rd *CBLY* GU15 .... 50 D8 ▣
Dawn Cl *NBNE* BH10 .... 432 A6
Dawn Gdns *WINW* SO22 ...... 238 B2
Daws Av *BWD* BH11 .... 431 M6
Dawsmere Cl *CBLY* GU15 .... 71 M3
Dawson Rd *ITCH* SO19 .... 345 G6 ▣
  RWIN SO21 .... 145 H5
Day La *HORN* PO8 .... 352 B1
Dayrell Cl *TOTT* SO40 .... 316 A7
Day's Ct *WIMB* BH21 .... 404 B4
Dayshes Cl *LSOL/BMARY* PO13 .. 396 F5
Dayslondon Rd *WVILLE* PO7 ... 376 B3
Deacon Cl *ITCH* SO19 .... 344 E1
Deacon Crs *ITCH* SO19 .... 344 E2
Deacon Rd *BWD* BH11 .... 431 L3
Deacon Rd *BWD* BH11 .... 431 L3
  HLER SO31 .... 370 F5
  ITCH SO19 .... 344 E3
  RAND SP11 .... 116 B6
Deadbrook La *ASHV* GU12 .... 113 H5
Deadmans La *STHA* RG19 .... 37 L2
Deadmoor La *KSCL* RG20 .... 37 H6
Deal Cl *FHAM/STUB* PO14 .... 396 A4
Deal Rd *CHAM* PO6 .... 375 J7
Dean Cl *WINW* SO22 .... 214 B6
  PLE BH15 .... 444 D5
Dean Ct *HEND* SO30 .... 345 M1
Dean La *RFNM* GU10 .... 159 G2
Deane Down Dro *WINW* SO22 .. 214 A4
Dean La West *RFNM* GU10 .... 159 G3
Dene Rd *AND* SP10 .... 9 J7
  FARN GU14 .... 90 C5
  TOTT SO40 .... 341 L5
The Deanery *CHFD* SO53 ...... 265 G8
Deane's Cl *BSTK* RG21 .... 5 G5
Deane's Park Rd
  FHAM/PORC PO16 .... 373 H7
Deanfield Cl *HLER* SO31 ...... 369 K6
Dean La *BPWT* SO32 .... 297 K5
  HORN PO8 .... 354 B3
  RSAL SP5 .... 259 C4
  RWIN SO21 .... 213 K5
Dean Park Crs *BMTH* BH1 .... 22 F4
  WCLF BH2 .... 22 F4
Dean Park Rd *BMTH* BH1 ...... 22 F4
  WCLF BH2 .... 22 F4
Dean Ri *AND* SP10 .... 96 E1
Dean Rd *CHAM* PO6 .... 399 J4
  ELGH SO50 .... 295 G7
  RSAL SP5 .... 230 C5
  WEND SO18 .... 344 E1
Deans Cl *BMTH* BH1 .... 22 D2 ▣
Dean Swift Crs *PSTN* BH14 ... 446 B8
Deanswood Dr *WVILLE* PO7 ... 352 F2
Deanswood Rd *TADY* RG26 .... 41 K8
The Dean *NALR* SO24 .... 218 B2
Dear Hay La *PLE* BH15 .... 445 H6
Dearing Cl *LYND* SO43 .... 363 K3
De Courtenai Cl *BWD* BH11 .... 431 J3
Decouttere Cl *FLET* GU13 ..... 110 D3
Dee Cl *CHFD* SO53 .... 292 F3
Deedman Cl *ASHV* GU12 ...... 113 K6 ▣
Deep Dene *HASM* GU27 .... 228 B2
Deepdene La *ROWN* SO16 ..... 319 C2
Deeping Cl *ITCH* SO19 .... 344 D7 ▣
Deeping Ga *WVILLE* PO7 ...... 376 C5
Deep La *BSTK* RG21 .... 4 A8
Deep Well Dr *CBLY* GU15 .... 71 H3
Deerhurst Cl *TOTT* SO40 ...... 341 H2
Deerhurst Crs *CHAM* PO6 ..... 374 E7
Deer Leap *FHAM* PO15 .... 372 B3 ▣
Deerleap Wy *FAWY* SO45 ...... 367 L4
  NMIL/BTOS BH25 .... 437 M2
Deer Park Cl
  NMIL/BTOS BH25 .... 437 K4 ▣
Deer Rock Rd *CBLY* GU15 .... 71 J1
Dee Wy *PLE* BH15 .... 445 G6
Defender Rd *ITCH* SO19 .... 344 B5

Defiant Rd *FARN* GU14 .... 90 C8
De Grouchy La *PTSW* SO17 ... 318 F7
De Haviland Cl *WIMB* BH21 ... 404 D6
De Havilland Wy
  CHCH/BSGR BH23 .... 450 F3
Delamere Gdns *NBNE* BH10 .. 432 C5
Delamere Rd *ENEY* PO4 .... 21 M5
De La Warr Rd *LYMN* SO41 ... 454 B4
Delft Cl *HLER* SO31 .... 370 D5
Delft Gdns *WVILLE* PO7 .... 352 B6
Delhi Cl *PSTN* BH14 .... 446 C5
Delhi Rd *NBNE* BH10 .... 432 C6
Delibes Rd *KEMP* RG22 .... 104 E8
Delilah Rd *PLE* BH15 .... 444 C6
Dellcrest Pth *CHAM* PO6 ...... 375 M7
De Lisle Cl *NEND* PO2 .... 399 K4
De Lisle Rd *TWDS* BH3 .... 447 L1
Delius Av *ITCH* SO19 .... 345 H5
Delius Cl *KEMP* RG22 .... 104 D7
Dellands *OVTN* RG25 .... 123 M1
Dellands La *OVTN* RG25 .... 100 B8
Dell Cl *BDST* BH18 .... 429 J4
  CHAM PO6 .... 375 M6
  ELGH SO50 .... 295 H7
  HASM GU27 .... 228 B1
Dellfield *DEAN* RG23 .... 103 C5
  PSF GU32 .... 246 D6
Dellfield Cl *CHAM* PO6 .... 374 E7 ▣
Dell Gv *FRIM* GU16 .... 71 J6
Dell Piece East *HORN* PO8 .... 353 H5
Dell Piece West *HORN* PO8 ... 353 C3
Dell Quay Cl *FHAM/STUB* PO14 .. 396 B6
Dell Rd *AND* SP10 .... 8 C2
  EWKG RG40 .... 48 C5
  WEND SO18 .... 319 L6
  WINC SO23 .... 239 C2
The Dell *FHAM/PORC* PO16 ... 373 H7
  FNM GU9 .... 134 F1
  HAV PO9 .... 376 F6
  KSCL RG20 .... 59 J6
  NMIL/BTOS BH25 .... 437 C8
  RAND SP11 .... 73 H2
  RAND SP11 .... 140 A7
  YTLY GU46 .... 68 F3
Delme Dr *FHAM/PORC* PO16 .. 373 H6
Delphi Wy *WVILLE* PO7 .... 376 D6
Delph Rd *WIMB* BH21 .... 404 B8
Delta Cl *CHCH/BSGR* BH23 ... 450 F1
De-Lucy Av *NALR* SO24 .... 218 A3
Delville Cl *FARN* GU14 .... 90 A5
De Mauley Rd *CCLF* BH13 ..... 446 D8
De Montfort Rd *NWBY* RG14 ... 25 C3
  WIMB BH21 .... 404 B7
De Mowbray Wy *LYMN* SO41 .. 440 B6 ▣
Dempsey Cl *ITCH* SO19 .... 344 H4
Denbigh Cl *ELGH* SO50 .... 293 L3
  TOTT SO40 .... 341 H3
Denbigh Dr *FHAM/PORC* PO16 .. 14 F3
Denbigh Gdns *ROWN* SO16 ... 318 C4
Denby Rd *PLE* BH15 .... 445 J4
Dene Cl *HASM* GU27 .... 228 F2
  HLER SO31 .... 370 C4
  BOR GU35 .... 201 J5 ▣
  NALR SO24 .... 219 L3
  RFNM GU10 .... 159 G2
  RGWD BH24 .... 359 C7
  ROWN SO16 .... 318 E1
Dene Ct *AND* SP10 .... 9 J7
  PLE BH15 .... 444 D5
Dene Hollow *CHAM* PO6 ...... 376 B8
Dene La *RFNM* GU10 .... 159 G2
Dene La West *RFNM* GU10 .... 159 G3
Dene Rd *AND* SP10 .... 9 J7
  FARN GU14 .... 90 C5
  TOTT SO40 .... 341 L5
Deneside Copse *LYMN* SO41 .. 439 M7
Deneside Gdns *LYMN* SO41 ... 439 M6
The Dene *NALR* SO24 .... 219 L4
Deneve Av *CFDH* BH17 .... 430 A7
Dene Wk *FERN* BH22 .... 406 C7
  RFNM GU10 .... 159 H2
Dene Wy *NWBY* RG14 .... 25 J3
  TOTT SO40 .... 341 C5
Denewood Copse
  FERN BH22 .... 380 B5 ▣
Denewood Rd *FERN* BH22 ..... 380 B4
  WBNE BH4 .... 447 C6
Denewulf Cl *BPWT* SO32 .... 297 H8 ▣
Denham Cl *CFDH* BH17 .... 430 C5
  FHAM/STUB PO14 .... 395 M6
  WINC SO23 .... 10 F3
Denham Ct *WINC* SO23 .... 11 G2
Denham Dr *CHCH/BSGR* BH23 .. 436 D7
  KEMP RG22 .... 104 B6
  YTLY GU46 .... 69 H3 ▣
Denham Gdns *HLER* SO31 ..... 368 F3
Denhill Cl *HISD* PO11 .... 425 J3
Denholm Cl *RGWD* BH24 ...... 359 H7
Denison Rd *CFDH* BH17 .... 430 A7
Denman Cl *FLET* GU13 .... 89 H7
Denmark La *PLE* BH15 .... 445 J5
Denmark Rd
  MOOR/WNTN BH9 .... 432 D7
  NWBY RG14 .... 3 G4
  PLE BH15 .... 445 J5
Denmark Sq *ASHV* GU12 .... 7 M1
Denmark St *ASHV* GU12 .... 7 M1
Denmead *NMIL/BTOS* BH25 .. 438 B4
Denmead Cl *TADY* RG26 .... 41 L8
  WEND SO18 .... 320 B8
Denning Cl *FLET* GU13 .... 110 D1
Dennis Rd *WIMB* BH21 .... 429 H3
Dennistoun Av
  CHCH/BSGR BH23 .... 450 E1
Dennistoun Cl *CBLY* GU15 ..... 71 G3 ▣
Dennis Wy *LISS* GU33 .... 248 F5
Denny Cl *FAWY* SO45 .... 392 F5 ▣
Denton Cl *STHA* RG19 .... 26 F6
Denton Wy *FRIM* GU16 .... 71 G6
Denville Av *FHAM/PORC* PO16 .. 398 B2
Denville Cl *CHAM* PO6 .... 376 D8
Denvilles Cl *HAV* PO9 .... 17 J2
Denzil Av *HLER* SO31 .... 369 G2
Depedene Cl *FAWY* SO45 ...... 391 M4
De Port Hts *BPWT* SO32 .... 299 H2
Deptford La *ODIM* RG29 .... 107 M5
Derby Flds *ODIM* RG29 .... 108 B2

Derby Rd *BMTH* BH1 .... 23 M4
  ELGH SO50 .... 293 L6
  HASM GU27 .... 228 E1
  NEND PO2 .... 399 H7
  NWBY RG14 .... 2 D7
  SHAM SO14 .... 13 J1
De Redvers Rd *PSTN* BH14 ... 446 B6
Dereham Wy
  BKME/WDN BH12 .... 446 E2
Deridene Ct *TOTT* SO40 .... 341 H2
Derlyn Rd *FHAM/PORC* PO16 .. 15 H5
Derritt La *CHCH/BSGR* BH23 .. 435 G1
Derrybrian Gdns
  NMIL/BTOS BH25 .... 437 L6 ▣
Derry Cl *ASHV* GU12 .... 113 J3
Derry Rd *FARN* GU14 .... 70 C7
Derwent Av *ASHV* GU12 .... 113 J4
Derwent Cl *FARN* GU14 .... 90 A4
  FERN BH22 .... 406 E2
  FHAM/STUB PO14 .... 396 B4 ▣
  FNM GU9 .... 134 D2
  HORN PO8 .... 328 B6
  BOR GU35 .... 201 J3 ▣
  WEND SO18 .... 320 A1
Derwent Dr *TOTT* SO40 .... 316 A8
Derwent Gdns *NALR* SO24 .... 218 C4
Derwent Rd *KEMP* RG22 ...... 103 M7
  LSOL/BMARY PO13 .... 420 D3
  NMIL/BTOS BH25 .... 437 M3
  ROWN SO16 .... 317 K7
  STHA RG19 .... 26 D5
Derwentwater Rd *WIMB* BH21 .. 404 B6
Desborough Cl *CHAM* PO6 .... 374 E7 ▣
Desborough Rd *ELGH* SO50 ... 293 M6
Devenish Rd *WINW* SO22 .... 10 C1
Dever Cl *RWIN* SO21 .... 169 M5
Deverel Cl *CHCH/BSGR* BH23 .. 434 M5
Deverell Pl *WVILLE* PO7 .... 376 A5
Dever Wy *DEAN* RG23 .... 103 G7
The Devil's Hwy *CWTH* RG45 ... 49 H3
Devils La *LIPH* GU30 .... 227 H5
Devine Gdns *ELGH* SO50 ...... 294 D6 ▣
Devon Cl *FARN* GU14 .... 89 C7
  SHST GU47 .... 70 A1
Devon Dr *CHFD* SO53 .... 293 H5
Devon Rd *ALDT* GU11 .... 112 B1
  CHCH/BSGR BH23 .... 434 C8
  HSEA PO3 .... 399 L5
  BOR GU35 .... 201 J5 ▣
  PLE BH15 .... 445 K3
Devonshire Av *ENEY* PO4 ...... 423 L5
Devonshire Dr *CBLY* GU15 ...... 71 J1
Devonshire Gdns *FAWY* SO45 .. 367 L8 ▣
  HLER SO31 .... 345 K6 ▣
  HLER SO31 .... 345 K6 ▣
Devonshire Pl *ALDT* GU11 .... 6 C4
  BSTK RG21 .... 104 F4
Devonshire Rd *WSHM* SO15 .. 343 K2
Devonshire Sq *ENEY* PO4 ...... 423 K4
Devonshire Wy
  FHAM/STUB PO14 .... 372 A8
Deweys La *RAND* SP11 .... 92 E6
Dewlands Rd *VWD* BH31 ...... 356 B1
Dewlands Wy *VWD* BH31 ...... 356 B2
Dew La *ELGH* SO50 .... 293 L5
Dewlish Cl *CFDH* BH17 .... 430 E6
Dewpond Wk *CHAM* RG24 ..... 83 L8
Dexter Wy *FARN* GU14 .... 89 G4 ▣
Dial Cl *CHCH/BSGR* BH23 ..... 434 A6
Diamond Cl *FBDG* SP6 .... 309 K8 ▣
Diamond Hl *CBLY* GU15 .... 71 G1
Diamond Rdg *CBLY* GU15 ...... 71 G1
Diamond St *SSEA* PO5 .... 20 F5 ▣
Diamond Wy *FARN* GU14 .... 90 B8
Diana Cl *EMRTH* PO10 .... 378 C4
Diana Wy *WIMB* BH21 .... 429 J1
  GPORT PO12 .... 421 J4
  KEMP RG22 .... 104 D5
Dibble Dr *NBAD* SO52 .... 291 L5
Dibden Cl *CHAR* BH8 .... 433 H5
  HAV PO9 .... 377 C4 ▣
Dibden Lodge Cl *FAWY* SO45 .. 367 K3
Dibles Rd *HLER* SO31 .... 370 B7
Dibley Cl *KEMP* RG22 .... 104 B5
Dickens Cl *NEND* PO2 .... 423 H1 ▣
Dickens Dell *TOTT* SO40 .... 340 F5
Dickens Dr *HLER* SO31 .... 347 G8
Dickens La *CHAM* RG24 .... 105 M4
  OVTN RG25 .... 105 L6
Dickenson Wk *NALR* SO24 ... 218 C4 ▣
Dickens Rd *SBNE* BH6 .... 449 J1
Dickens Wy *YTLY* GU46 .... 68 F4
Dicker's La *ALTN* GU34 .... 176 F4
Dickson Pl *WHAM* PO17 .... 348 E4
Dickson Rd *RAND* SP11 .... 141 M1
Didcot Rd *WSHM* SO15 .... 318 B7 ▣
Dieppe Crs *NEND* PO2 .... 399 J4
Dieppe Gdns *GPORT* PO12 ..... 18 B3
Digby Rd *NWBY* RG14 .... 2 B1
Diligence Cl *HLER* SO31 .... 345 L7
Dilly La *HTWY* RG27 .... 87 H4
  NMIL/BTOS BH25 .... 452 F1
Dimond Cl *WEND* SO18 .... 319 K7
Dimond Hl *WEND* SO18 .... 319 K7
Dimond Rd *WEND* SO18 .... 319 K6
Dines Cl *RAND* SP11 .... 96 C1
Dingle Rd *BOSC* BH5 .... 449 H4
Dingle Wy *HLER* SO31 .... 370 E4
Dingley Rd *PLE* BH15 .... 445 J2
Dingley Wy *FARN* GU14 .... 90 D8
Dinham Rd *NMIL/BTOS* BH25 .. 438 B4 ▣
Dinorben Av *FLET* GU13 .... 110 D1
Dinorben Beeches *FLET* GU13 .. 110 D1
Dinorben Cl *FLET* GU13 .... 110 E1
Dippenhall Rd *RFNM* GU10 ... 133 L6
Dippenhall St *RFNM* GU10 .... 133 J2
Diprose Rd *WIMB* BH21 .... 429 J1
Discovery Cl
  FHAM/STUB PO14 .... 396 A3 ▣
Disraeli Rd *CHCH/BSGR* BH23 .. 450 C2
Ditcham Crs *HAV* PO9 .... 377 J4
Ditchbury *LYMN* SO41 .... 440 B2
Ditton Cl *FHAM/STUB* PO14 ... 396 A5
The Dittons *EWKG* RG40 .... 48 C2 ▣
Divers Cl *ALTN* GU34 .... 176 C2
Dixon Rd *HTWY* RG27 .... 64 A5
Dixons La *STOK* SO20 .... 209 G1
Dockenfield Cl *HAV* PO9 .... 377 C4 ▣

Dockenfield St *RFNM* GU10 .. 179 L1
Dock La *BROC* SO42 .... 390 F7
Dock Rd *GPORT* PO12 .... 19 H4
Doctors Dro *RAND* SP11 .... 96 C1
Doctor's HI *ROMY* SO51 .... 260 E4
Doctors La *PSF* GU32 .... 272 B3
Dodds La *BPWT* SO32 .... 324 A3
Dodgson Cl *FBDG* SP6 .... 284 D8
Dodwell La *HLER* SO31 .... 345 M5
Doe Copse Wy
  NMIL/BTOS BH25 .... 437 J4
Dogflud Wy *FNM* GU9 .... 134 F5
Dogkennel La *WVILLE* PO7 .... 326 E4
Dogwood Dell *WVILLE* PO7 ... 376 D3 ▣
Dogwood Rd *WIMB* BH21 ..... 429 J6
Doiley Bottom *RAND* SP11 ..... 75 J3
Dolbery Rd North
  BKME/WDN BH12 .... 431 H6
Dolbery Rd South
  BKME/WDN BH12 .... 431 G7
Dollis Dr *FNM* GU9 .... 135 G5 ▣
Dollis Gn *TADY* RG26 .... 63 J5
Dolman Rd *GPORT* PO12 .... 19 H5
  NWBY RG14 .... 2 E1
Dolomans La *RAND* SP11 .... 96 C1
Dolphin Av *NBNE* BH10 .... 432 C5
Dolphin Cl *ELGH* SO50 .... 294 C6
  HASM GU27 .... 228 B2
Dolphin Ct
  FHAM/PORC PO16 .... 395 M4 ▣
Dolphin Crs *GPORT* PO12 .... 18 F5
Dolphin HI *RWIN* SO21 .... 266 F5
Dolphin Pl *NMIL/BTOS* BH25 .. 452 F1 ▣
Dolphin Wy *GPORT* PO12 .... 19 H5
Dolton Rd *ROWN* SO16 .... 317 L5
Doman Rd *CBLY* GU15 .... 70 D4
Dome Aly *WINC* SO23 .... 11 G9
Dominica Cl *CHAM* RG24 .... 83 H6
Dominion Rd *BWD* BH11 ...... 431 M4
Domum Rd *NEND* PO2 .... 399 K6
  WINC SO23 .... 239 G2
Domvilles Ap *NEND* PO2 .... 398 F7
Donaldson Rd *CHAM* PO6 ..... 399 K2
Doncaster Rd *ELGH* SO50 ..... 293 M8
Donigers Dell *BPWT* SO32 ..... 323 M2
Donlan Dr *FARN* GU14 .... 89 M7
Donnelly Rd *SBNE* BH6 .... 449 L4
Donnelly St *GPORT* PO12 .... 18 C4
Donnington Cl *CBLY* GU15 ...... 70 E4 ▣
Donnington Dr
  CHCH/BSGR BH23 .... 451 G1
  CHFD SO53 .... 292 F5
Donnington Gv *PTSW* SO17 ... 319 G6
Donnington Pk *NWBY* RG14 ... 25 J2
Donnington Sq *NWBY* RG14 ... 25 J2
Donoughmore Rd *BMTH* BH1 .. 448 C4
Dora's Green La *RFNM* GU10 .. 133 M2
Dorcas Cl *WVILLE* PO7 .... 352 F7 ▣
Dorcas Ct *CBLY* GU15 .... 70 E5 ▣
Dorchester Cl *DEAN* RG23 .... 104 A3 ▣
Dorchester Gdns *PLE* BH15 ... 445 K3
Dorchester Rd *HTWY* RG27 ..... 85 M7 ▣
  PLE BH15 .... 445 K2
Dorchester Wy *ODIM* RG29 .. 107 L4 ▣
Dore Av *FHAM/PORC* PO16 .... 373 M6
Doreen Cl *FARN* GU14 .... 70 A4
  RWIN SO21 .... 236 B5
Dorian Gv *NALR* SO24 .... 218 A4
Doric Cl *CHFD* SO53 .... 293 L1
Dorking Crs *CHAM* PO6 .... 399 K1
Dorland Gdns *TOTT* SO40 ..... 341 H4
Dormer Cl *CWTH* RG45 .... 49 K3
  NWBY RG14 .... 37 H2
Dormington Rd *CHAM* PO6 ... 375 G7
Dormy Cl *LSOL/BMARY* PO13 .. 396 F7
Dormy Wy *LSOL/BMARY* PO13 .. 396 F7
Dornie Rd *CCLF* BH13 .... 457 J3
Dormere La *WVILLE* PO7 .... 376 E1 ▣
Dorothy Dymond St
  PSEA PO1 .... 21 G2 ▣
Dorrel Cl *KEMP* RG22 .... 127 G2
Dorrien Rd *GPORT* PO12 .... 421 M1
Dorrita Av *HORN* PO8 .... 352 E4
Dorrita Cl *ENEY* PO4 .... 423 K6
The Dorrits *TOTT* SO40 .... 340 F1
Dorset Av *FERN* BH22 .... 406 B4
Dorset Cl *HORN* PO8 .... 352 F4
Dorset Lake Av *PSTN* BH14 ... 446 A8
Dorset Rd *ASHV* GU12 .... 113 K3
  CHCH/BSGR BH23 .... 435 K8
  CHFD SO53 .... 293 H5 ▣
  WBNE BH4 .... 447 H3
Dorset St *PTSW* SO17 .... 343 L2
Dorset Wy *BKME/WDN* BH12 .. 430 E8
  PLE BH15 .... 445 J1
Dorstone Rd *CHAM* PO6 .... 375 G7 ▣
Doswell Wy *BSTK* RG21 .... 5 G5
Douai Cl *FARN* GU14 .... 90 F4
Doublet Cl *STHA* RG19 .... 26 D5
Doughty Wy *AND* SP10 .... 119 K7
Douglas Av *CHCH/BSGR* BH23 .. 449 L2
Douglas Cl *ITCH* SO19 .... 345 G2
Douglas Gdns
  BKME/WDN BH12 .... 446 D7
  HAV PO9 .... 377 L4 ▣
Douglas Gv *RFNM* GU10 .... 158 F3
Douglas Ride *KSCL* RG20 .... 36 E8
Douglas Rd *BKME/WDN* BH12... 446 D3
  PSEA PO1 .... 423 K1
  RAND SP11 .... 142 A1
  SBNE BH6 .... 449 K5
Douglas Wy *FAWY* SO45 ...... 367 J4
Doulton Gdns *PSTN* BH14 ..... 446 B5
Doussie Cl *UPTN* BH16 .... 428 E8
Dove Di *ELGH* SO50 .... 293 J6
Dovedale Cl *SHST* GU47 .... 50 A6 ▣
Dove Gdns *HLER* SO31 .... 370 F3 ▣
Dover Cl *CCLF* BH13 .... 446 F5
  DEAN RG23 .... 104 C2
  FHAM/STUB PO14 .... 395 M5
  NALR SO24 .... 218 C4
Dover Ct *HISD* PO11 .... 425 J3
Dovercourt Rd *CHAM* PO6 .... 399 L2

Dover Rd CCLF BH13 446 F5
HSEA PO3 399 L8
Dover St SHAM SO14 343 L1
Doveshill Crs NBNE BH10 432 B5
Doveshill Gdns NBNE BH10 432 B5
Doves La RSAL SP5 258 F5
Doveton Wy NWBY RG14 3 H1
Doveys Cl RGWD BH24 384 E5 1
Dowden Gv ALTN GU34 176 E3
Dowding Ct CWTH RG45 49 M2 1
Dowds Cl HEND SO30 321 G8
Dowlands Rd NBNE BH10 432 A4
Down End CHAM PO6 376 A7
Down End Rd CHAM PO6 376 A7
Downend Rd
FHAM/PORC PO16 373 L6
Downey Cl BWD BH11 431 K6
Down Farm La WINW SO22 190 B8
Down Farm Pl HORN PO8 328 B7 3
Down Ga NALR SO24 218 B4
Downham Cl HORN PO8 352 D5
Downhouse Rd HORN PO8 327 M4
Downing St FNM GU9 134 E6
Downland Cl HEND SO30 346 D1
HLER SO31 370 E4
Downland Pl HEND SO30 345 M4
Downlands Cl RSAL SP5 284 E2
Downlands Rd WINW SO22 238 A4
Downlands Wy RWIN SO21 190 C4
Down La OVTN RG25 106 F6
Downley Rd HAV PO9 377 M4
Down Lodge Cl FBDG SP6 333 L2 2
Down Rd HORN PO8 328 A7
RAND SP11 115 L5
Downs Cl WVILLE PO7 376 D5
Downscroft Gdns
HEND SO30 321 G8 2
HEND SO30 345 M1 1
Downside GSHT GU26 204 A1 1
LSOL/BMARY PO13 397 H6
Downside Av ITCH SO19 344 E2
Downside Rd WINW SO22 214 A6
WVILLE PO7 376 A5 1
Downsland Rd BSTK RG21 4 B9
Downs La MARL SN8 53 G1
Down's Park Av TOTT SO40 341 L2
Down's Park Crs TOTT SO40 341 L2
Down's Park Rd TOTT SO40 341 L2
Downs Rd RWIN SO21 190 B4
STOK SO20 162 B5
Down St OVTN RG25 126 C7
Downs Vw ALTN GU34 177 K1
Downsview Rd BOR GU35 202 F3
Downsview Wy RAND SP11 115 J2
Downs Wy ALTN GU34 176 C6
The Downsway
FHAM/PORC PO16 374 A8
Downton Cl CHAR BH8 433 G5
Downton Hl RSAL SP5 285 H1
Downton La LYMN SO41 453 L2
Downton Rd WEND SO18 319 L6
Downview Cl GSHT GU26 204 A2
Downview Rd FBDG SP6 280 F4
Downwood Cl FAWY SO45 367 G6 1
FBDG SP6 309 J6
Downwood Wy HORN PO8 328 B7
Doyle Av NEND PO2 399 J4
Doyle Cl NEND PO2 399 J4
Doyle Ct ITCH SO19 344 D7
Doyle Gdns YTLY GU46 68 F3 2
Doyne Rd PSTN BH14 446 D4
Dradfield La BPWT SO32 325 H8
Dragonfly Dr CHAM RG24 83 L8 4
Dragon La RGWD BH24 382 E8
Dragon St EPSF GU31 275 L6
Dragoon Cl ITCH SO19 345 G4
Dragoon Ct ALDT GU11 6 B2 2
Dragoon Wy CHCH/BSGR BH23 449 L1
Drake Av FRIM GU16 91 K7
Drake Cl EWKG RG40 48 B1
HLER SO31 370 F3
NMIL/BTOS BH25 437 K5
RGWD BH24 359 G7
TOTT SO40 342 D6
Drakeleys Fld LIPH GU30 250 E6
Drake Rd ELGH SO50 294 D4
LSOL/BMARY PO13 420 B1
Drakes Cl FAWY SO45 367 K6 3
Draper Cl STHA RG19 27 G6
Draper Rd BWD BH11 431 L4
CHCH/BSGR BH23 450 D1
Draycote Rd HORN PO8 328 B5
Draycott Rd NBNE BH10 432 B6
Drayman's Wy ALTN GU34 176 E5
Drayton Cl ITCH SO19 344 D8
Drayton La CHAM PO6 375 M7
Drayton Pl TOTT SO40 341 H1 1
Drayton Rd NEND PO2 399 J7
Drayton St WINW SO22 238 B2
Dreadnought Rd
FHAM/STUB PO14 396 C3
Dresden Dr HORN PO8 352 B6
Dreswick Cl CHCH/BSGR BH23 434 B4
Drew Cl BKME/WDN BH12 447 H1
Drift Rd FHAM/PORC PO16 15 M3
HORN PO8 328 A3
BOR GU35 201 G8
STOK SO20 166 E6
The Drift HAV PO9 353 M7
Driftway Rd HTWY RG27 86 B7
Driftwood Gdns ENEY PO4 424 A6
TOTT SO40 341 G2 4
Drill Shed Rd NEND PO2 398 F7
Drinkwater Cl ELGH SO50 293 L5
The Drive DEAN RG23 103 G7
EMRTH PO10 379 H8
FHAM/PORC PO16 15 G5
FNM GU9 158 E1
HAV PO9 16 E1
HEND SO30 320 A5
LSOL/BMARY PO13 396 E6
NWBY RG14 2 B9
ROMY SO51 259 L7
ROMY SO51 288 F6
TOTT SO40 341 K3
Drove Cl RWIN SO21 266 E3
Drove Hl STOK SO20 165 M5
Drove La NALR SO24 217 M2
Drove Rd ITCH SO19 344 F4
STOK SO20 165 M5
WHAM PO17 374 E4
Drovers End FARN GU14 89 H4
Drovers Wy ASHV GU12 113 M7
FNM GU9 134 D2
The Drove AND SP10 8 B4
BPWT SO32 296 C8
BPWT SO32 324 A3
ELGH SO50 321 J2
FAWY SO45 392 C7
HEND SO30 320 E5
ROMY SO51 288 D5
RWIN SO21 266 E3
TOTT SO40 316 A7
WEND SO18 344 E1
Droxford Cl GPORT PO12 18 B3 1
Droxford Crs TADY RG26 61 K1
Droxford Rd BPWT SO32 324 B4
LTDN BH7 449 G2
Druce Wy STHA RG19 27 G5
Druids Cl FERN BH22 406 B6
Druitt Rd CHCH/BSGR BH23 435 K8
Drum Md PSF GU32 275 K5
Drummond Cl ALTN GU34 196 E6 1
WINW SO22 238 D3 1
Drummond Rd BMTH BH1 448 C4
FAWY SO45 367 L4 4
HEND SO30 321 H7
PSEA PO1 423 H2 2
Drummond Wy CHFD SO53 265 G8 3
Drury Cl WHCH RG28 121 J8
Drury La ALTN GU34 174 F3
THLE RG7 43 L4
Dryden Av CHAM PO6 374 C7
Dryden Cl FHAM/PORC PO16 14 F4
NTHA RG18 26 F3
RGWD BH24 381 J3
WVILLE PO7 352 B6
Dryden Pl LYMN SO41 454 C3
Dryden Rd FARN GU14 90 C2
ITCH SO19 345 J3
Dryden Wy LIPH GU30 226 D3
Drysdale Ms ENEY PO4 423 M6 1
Duchess Cl ALTN GU34 176 D5 2
CWTH RG45 49 L1 1
Duchess of Kent Barracks
ALDT GU11 112 E5
Ducking Stool La
CHCH/BSGR BH23 450 A2
Duck Island La RGWD BH24 382 E2 2
Ducklands BOR GU35 201 K6 3
Duck La BWD BH11 431 K4
Duckmead La LISS GU33 249 G2
Ducks La STOK SO20 184 E2
Duddon Cl WEND SO18 320 A7
Duddon Wy BSTK RG21 5 K8
Dudleston Heath Dr
HORN PO8 352 F6
Dudley Av FBDG SP6 309 L5
LYMN SO41 438 D6
Dudley Cl DEAN RG23 104 A3
BOR GU35 201 H7
Dudley Rd HSEA PO3 423 L1 1
NBNE BH10 432 B3
Dudmoor Farm Rd
CHCH/BSGR BH23 434 D5
Dudmoor La CHCH/BSGR BH23 434 D4
Dudsbury Av FERN BH22 406 B4
Dudsbury Crs FERN BH22 406 B4
Dudsbury Gdns FERN BH22 406 C8
Dudsbury Rd FERN BH22 406 B6
Duffield La EMRTH PO10 379 H5
Dugald Drummond St
PSEA PO1 21 G2 3
Dugdell Cl FERN BH22 406 D2 1
Duisburg Wy SSEA PO5 20 E6
Duke Crs PSEA PO1 423 H1
Duke of Cornwall Av
CBLY GU15 51 G7
Duke Rd HEND SO30 346 B3
Dukes Cl ALTN GU34 176 C6
FNM GU9 134 D2 3
PSF GU32 275 J4
Dukes Dr BWD BH11 431 J3
Dukesfield CHCH/BSGR BH23 434 B6
Dukes Md FLET GU13 88 C7
Dukes Pk ALDT GU11 113 G2
Duke's Ride CWTH RG45 49 J4
THLE RG7 42 E8
Dukes Rd GPORT PO12 421 L2
SHAM SO14 319 G8
Duke St RWIN SO21 170 A5
SHAM SO14 13 J5
Dukes Wd CWTH RG45 49 L3
Dukeswood Dr FAWY SO45 367 K7
Dulsie Rd TWDS BH3 447 H1
Dumas Cl YTLY GU46 68 F3 3
Du Maurier Cl FLET GU13 110 D5
Dumbarton Cl NEND PO2 399 H8 2
Dumbleton Cl ITCH SO19 345 K4
Dummer Ct HAV PO9 377 H2
Dummer Down La OVTN RG25 150 A1
Dummer La RAND SP11 72 A8
Dummers Rd ROMY SO51 263 J1
Dumpers Dro ELGH SO50 321 J2
Dumpford La EPSF GU31 277 L8
Dump Rd FARN GU14 90 B7
Dunbar Cl ROWN SO16 317 L3
Dunbar Crs CHCH/BSGR BH23 436 D6
Dunbar Rd ENEY PO4 423 M4
FRIM GU16 91 J1
TWDS BH3 447 K2
Dunbridge La ROMY SO51 233 K8
Duncan Cl ITCH SO19 344 C8
Duncan Rd HLER SO31 370 F3
NMIL/BTOS BH25 438 B4
SSEA PO5 21 K7
Duncan's Cl RAND SP11 116 D6
Duncans Dr
FHAM/STUB PO14 371 M8 1
Duncliff Rd SBNE BH6 449 M4
Duncombe Dr RGWD BH24 357 M6
Duncombe Rd PSF GU32 273 J8
Duncton Rd HORN PO8 328 C3
Dundaff Cl CBLY GU15 71 K3
Dundas Cl HSEA PO3 399 M6
Dundas La HSEA PO3 399 M7
Dundas Rd CFDH BH17 430 C8
Dundas Sp HSEA PO3 399 M6
Dundee Cl FHAM PO15 14 D2
Dundee Rd PTSW SO17 319 H7
Dundonald Cl HISD PO11 425 L3
ITCH SO19 344 B7 1
Dundridge La BPWT SO32 297 K7
Dundry Wy HEND SO30 346 A1
Dunedin Cl FERN BH22 405 M5
NTID SP9 114 F2
Dunedin Dr FERN BH22 405 M5
Dunedin Gdns FERN BH22 405 M5
Dunedin Gv CHCH/BSGR BH23 451 H1
Dunford Cl NMIL/BTOS BH25 437 J8 2
Dunford Rd BKME/WDN BH12 446 C3
Dungells Farm Cl YTLY GU46 69 G4 1
Dungells La YTLY GU46 68 F4
Dunhills La RAND SP11 96 B8
Dunhurst Cl HAV PO9 377 L5
Dunkeld Rd GPORT PO12 421 L1
TWDS BH3 447 J2
Dunkirk Cl ROWN SO16 318 C4
Dunkirk Rd ROWN SO16 318 C4
Dunkirt La RAND SP11 141 K5
Dunley's Hl ODIM RG29 108 B5
Dunlin Cl CHCH/BSGR BH23 451 G3
ENEY PO4 424 B3
Dunmow Hl FLET GU13 88 F6
Dunmow Rd AND SP10 9 K8
Dunn Cl ENEY PO4 423 M5
Dunnings La NBAD SO52 291 K3
Dunnock Cl HAV PO9 353 M7
Dunsbury Wy HAV PO9 377 J3
Dunsell's La NALR SO24 220 C3
Dunsford Crs DEAN RG23 104 B1
Dunsmore Cl SSEA PO5 21 H4 2
Dunsmore Gdns YTLY GU46 68 D3
Dunstall Pk FARN GU14 90 D1
Dunstan Rd NTHA RG18 27 H4
Dunstan's Dro RAND SP11 74 B7
Dunstans La PSTN BH14 445 L2
Dunster Cl ROWN SO16 318 B3
Dunvegan Dr ROWN SO16 318 B3
Dunyeats Rd BDST BH18 429 M4
Durban Cl ROMY SO51 262 F7
Durban Rd PSEA PO1 423 K1
Durbidges STHA RG19 39 H8
Durdells Av BWD BH11 431 L3
Durdells Gdns BWD BH11 431 L3
Durford Ct HAV PO9 377 H2 1
Durford Rd EPSF GU31 276 B5
Durham Gdns WVILLE PO7 376 D3
Durham Rd SHST GU47 50 B6
Durham St GPORT PO12 421 L2
PSEA PO1 21 H1
Durham Wy KEMP RG22 104 A8 3
Durland Cl NMIL/BTOS BH25 437 L7
Durlands Rd HORN PO8 328 B8 1
Durley Av HORN PO8 352 D5
Durley Brook Rd BPWT SO32 321 L2
Durley Chine Rd WCLF BH2 22 B6
Durley Chine Rd South
WCLF BH2 22 B8
Durley Cl AND SP10 8 C7
Durley Crs TOTT SO40 341 H3
Durley Gdns WCLF BH2 22 B8
Durley Hall La BPWT SO32 296 A7
Durley Rd ELGH SO50 321 K1
GPORT PO12 421 L2
WCLF BH2 22 C7
Durley Rd South WCLF BH2 22 C8
Durley Rbt WCLF BH2 22 B7
Durley St BPWT SO32 322 C1
Durlston Crs CHCH/BSGR BH23 434 B4
Durlston Rd PSTN BH14 446 B6
ROWN SO16 317 H7
Durnford Cl STOK SO20 165 M4
Durnford Rd SHAM SO14 343 M2
Durngate Pl WINC SO23 11 J7
Durngate Ter WINC SO23 11 J7
Durnsford Av FLET GU13 110 F1
Durnstown LYMN SO41 413 G6
Durrant Rd PSTN BH14 446 B5
WCLF BH2 22 D4
Durrants Gdns HAV PO9 353 M8
Durrants Rd HAV PO9 377 M1
Durrant Wy LYMN SO41 412 F6
Durrington Rd LTDN BH7 449 G1
Dursley Crs CHAM PO6 375 G8
Dutton La ELGH SO50 294 A5
Duttons Rd ROMY SO51 262 D8
Dyer Rd WSHM SO15 343 G1
Dymewood Rd WIMB BH21 380 C1
Dymoke St EMRTH PO10 378 C4
Dymott Cl WSHM SO15 12 A1
Dyram Cl ELGH SO50 293 L3
Dysart Av CHAM PO6 399 M1
Dyserth Cl ITCH SO19 344 F7
Dyson Dr WINC SO23 11 H2
Dysons Cl NWBY RG14 2 B4

E

Eadens La TOTT SO40 340 B1
Eagle Av HORN PO8 352 B4
Eagle Cl ALTN GU34 176 E2
CHFD SO53 293 G4
CWTH RG45 49 K1
FHAM/PORC PO16 373 K8 3
KEMP RG22 103 L8 1
Eagle Rd BKME/WDN BH12 446 F4
FARN GU14 90 E6
KSCL RG20 38 D6
LSOL/BMARY PO13 420 B1
Eagles Nest SHST GU47 49 K7 2
Eames La LISS GU33 223 L8
Eardley Av AND SP10 8 A3
Earle Rd WBNE BH4 447 H7
Earlham Dr PSTN BH14 446 B4
Earlsbourne FLET GU13 111 G4
Earls Cl ELGH SO50 294 F6
Earlsdon St SSEA PO5 21 G4 2
Earlsdon Wy CHCH/BSGR BH23 436 D8
Earls Gv CBLY GU15 71 H2
Earls Rd FHAM/PORC PO16 15 J9
SHAM SO14 318 F8
Earlswood Dr FBDG SP6 333 K3
Earnley Rd HISD PO11 426 D6
Earthpits La RSAL SP5 280 A6
East Av FNM GU9 135 G2
NMIL/BTOS BH25 452 B1
TWDS BH3 447 H2
East Bank Rd BROC SO42 387 L8
East Boldre Rd BROC SO42 416 A1
Eastbourne Av GPORT PO12 397 L8
WSHM SO15 318 C8
Eastbourne Rd HSEA PO3 399 L8 1
Eastbrook Cl GPORT PO12 397 K8 1
HLER SO31 370 E3
Eastbrooke Rd ALTN GU34 176 F4
East Cams Cl
FHAM/PORC PO16 373 K7 2
Eastchurch Cl ROWN SO16 317 L4
Eastcliff Cl LSOL/BMARY PO13 420 C1
East Cliff Wy
CHCH/BSGR BH23 451 H1
East Cl NMIL/BTOS BH25 437 H8
East Cosham Rd CHAM PO6 375 M8
Eastcot Cl FAWY SO45 391 M5
East Ct CHAM PO6 375 M8
Eastcroft Rd GPORT PO12 18 C1
East Dean Rd ROMY SO51 232 C6
East Dr ELGH SO50 294 C4
Eastern Av AND SP10 9 J7
HSEA PO3 423 M2
Eastern La CWTH RG45 50 C4
Eastern Pde ENEY PO4 423 K7
FHAM/PORC PO16 15 K9
Eastern Rd ASHV GU12 7 M2
CHAM PO6 400 B2
ENEY PO4 423 M3
HAV PO9 17 G3
HEND SO30 320 C7
HSEA PO3 400 A4
BOR GU35 201 J2
LYMN SO41 440 B4
NEND PO2 398 F6
Eastern Villas Rd ENEY PO4 423 H7 2
Eastern Wy FHAM/PORC PO16 15 L6
LYMN SO41 454 E4
Easter Rd MOOR/WNTN BH9 432 E6
Eastfield Av BSTK RG21 5 G8
FHAM/STUB PO14 396 D2
Eastfield Cl AND SP10 9 L5
East Field Cl EMRTH PO10 379 J6
Eastfield Cl RGWD BH24 383 G1
Eastfield La EPSF GU31 305 K5
RGWD BH24 359 G8
Eastfield Rd AND SP10 9 J5
CHAM PO6 374 F6
ENEY PO4 423 L5
Eastgate St SHAM SO14 13 G5
WINC SO23 11 J8
East Gn BLKW GU17 69 M4
East Harting St EPSF GU31 305 J5
East Hl LYMN SO41 440 C4
WINC SO23 239 G2
East Hill Cl FHAM/PORC PO16 373 H6
East Hill Dr LISS GU33 248 F5
East Hoe Rd WVILLE PO7 325 M5
East House Av
FHAM/STUB PO14 396 B6
East Howe La NBNE BH10 432 A4
Eastlake Av BKME/WDN BH12 446 A2
Eastlake Cl EPSF GU31 276 B5
Eastlands NMIL/BTOS BH25 437 M7
East La LYMN SO41 439 J7
NALR SO24 217 L4
Eastleigh Rd ELGH SO50 295 H7
East Leigh Rd HAV PO9 378 A5
East Ldg FHAM PO15 372 A7
East Lodge Pk CHAM PO6 376 D8
Eastlyn Rd TADY RG26 42 B7
Eastman Cl RSAL SP5 284 F2 1
Eastmans Fld STOK SO20 165 M5
Eastmead FARN GU14 90 E4
Eastmeare Ct TOTT SO40 341 G2
Eastney Farm Rd ENEY PO4 424 A5 1
Eastney Rd ENEY PO4 423 M5
Eastney St ENEY PO4 423 M6 2
Eastoke Av HISD PO11 426 B7
Easton Common Hl RSAL SP5 207 H2
Easton La RWIN SO21 215 J6
WINC SO23 11 L6
East Overcliff Dr BMTH BH1 23 H7
Eastover Ct HAV PO9 377 H2
East Park Ter SHAM SO14 13 G1
East Portway AND SP10 118 B8
East Quay Rd PLE BH15 445 H7
East Rd FAWY SO45 368 B8
RWIN SO21 167 K1
WHAM PO17 374 E2
Eastrop La BSTK RG21 5 G8
Eastrop Rbt BSTK RG21 5 G7
Eastrop Wy BSTK RG21 5 G7
Eastshaw La MIDH GU29 279 M4
East Station Rd ASHV GU12 7 G3
East Strd SELS PO20 427 K8
East St AND SP10 9 J6
EMRTH PO10 378 F5
FHAM/PORC PO16 15 M6
FHAM/STUB PO14 371 K8
FNM GU9 134 F6
HAV PO9 16 F5
NALR SO24 218 C2
PLE BH15 445 H6
PSEA PO1 20 B4
SHAM SO14 13 G4
WVILLE PO7 326 C5
East Surrey St PSEA PO1 21 H1 2
East View Rd RGWD BH24 382 F1
Eastville Rd ELGH SO50 295 H7 1
East Wy CHAR BH8 432 F7
WIMB BH21 429 H3
Eastways BPWT SO32 323 H1
Eastwood ROMY SO51 260 B7
Eastwood Av FERN BH22 406 C2
Eastwood Cl HISD PO11 425 M4
East Woodhay Rd
WINW SO22 214 C4 2
Eastwood Rd NEND PO2 399 J4 1
Eastworth Rd VWD BH31 356 C1
Eaton Rd CBLY GU15 70 E4
CCLF BH13 446 F6
E Av FAWY SO45 392 C3
Ebble Cl NTID SP9 114 E1
Ebden Rd WINC SO23 11 K6
Ebery Gv HSEA PO3 423 M2
Ebor Cl FERN BH22 406 C6
Ebor Rd BKME/WDN BH12 446 C2
Ecchinswell Rd KSCL RG20 59 G6
Eccles Rd PLE BH15 444 F6
Echo Barn La RFNM GU10 158 B3
Ecton La HSEA PO3 400 A5
Eddeys Cl BOR GU35 202 E2 1
Eddeys La BOR GU35 202 E3
Eddy Rd ASHV GU12 7 J3
Edelvale Rd WEND SO18 320 A7
Edelweiss Cl RAND SP11 92 E7
Edenbridge Rd ENEY PO4 423 M3
Eden Gv WIMB BH21 404 B5
Eden Ri FHAM/PORC PO16 15 J8
Eden Rd WEND SO18 320 A6
Eden St PSEA PO1 423 G2 2
Eden Wk CHFD SO53 292 F3
Edgar Cl AND SP10 119 G4
Edgar Crs FHAM/PORC PO16 398 B2
Edgar Rd WINC SO23 238 E2
Edgarton Rd CFDH BH17 430 B5
Edgbarrowhill Star CWTH RG45 49 K5
Edgbarrow Ri SHST GU47 49 K6
Edgcumbe Park Dr CWTH RG45 49 K3
Edgecombe Crs
LSOL/BMARY PO13 397 G8
Edgecombe La NWBY RG14 25 M3
Edgedale Cl CWTH RG45 49 L4 1
Edgefield Gv HORN PO8 353 G7
Edgehill Cl KEMP RG22 104 A5
Edgehill Rd MOOR/WNTN BH9 432 C8
WEND SO18 319 L7
Edgell Rd EMRTH PO10 378 F4
Edgemoor Rd FERN BH22 380 F7
FRIM GU16 71 M5 1
Edgerly Gdns CHAM PO6 399 K2
Edgeware Rd ENEY PO4 423 L3
Edgewood Cl CWTH RG45 49 K1 1
Edifred Rd MOOR/WNTN BH9 432 E4
Edinburgh Rd PSEA PO1 20 F1
PSEA PO1 21 G1 1
WINC SO23 191 G7
Edington Cl BPWT SO32 297 G8 2
Edington Rd WINC SO23 11 G3
Edith Haisman Cl WSHM SO15 12 B1
Edmondsham Rd VWD BH31 332 C8
Edmund Rd ENEY PO4 21 M5
Edmunds Cl HEND SO30 346 B3
NMIL/BTOS BH25 437 L7
Edney Cl FLET GU13 111 G2
Edneys La WVILLE PO7 351 L3
Edric's Gn AMSY SP4 138 C7
Edward Av CBLY GU15 70 D3
ELGH SO50 294 C4
Edward Cl FAWY SO45 392 C7 1
Edward Gdns HAV PO9 377 G7
Edward Gv FHAM/PORC PO16 374 C7
Edward Rd ALTN GU34 176 F3
BWD BH11 431 M5
CHCH/BSGR BH23 435 K8
FAWY SO45 367 L4
FNM GU9 158 F1
PSTN BH14 446 B3
WINC SO23 238 D4
WSHM SO15 342 F1
Edwards Cl CHAM PO6 374 F7 3
WVILLE PO7 352 D6
Edward St ALDT GU11 6 D2
Edwina Cl ITCH SO19 344 D2
NBAD SO52 291 M4
RGWD BH24 359 G7
Edwina Dr CFDH BH17 429 M6
Edwin Cl STHA RG19 27 J5
Eeklo Pl NWBY RG14 2 F8
Eelmoor Br ALDT GU11 111 M2
Eelmoor Plain Rd ALDT GU11 112 A4
Eelmoor Rd ALDT GU11 112 A3
FARN GU14 90 C6
Effingham Gdns ITCH SO19 345 G4
Efford Wy LYMN SO41 439 M6
Egan Cl NEND PO2 399 K5
Egbert Rd WINC SO23 11 G4
Egbury Rd RAND SP11 97 M6
Egdon Ct UPTN BH16 444 A1 2
Egdon Dr WIMB BH21 404 C8
Egerton Rd CBLY GU15 70 C2
CHAR BH8 448 C2
SHST GU47 70 B2
Eggars Cl ALTN GU34 177 G4
Eggars Fld RFNM GU10 157 G3
Eggar's Hl ALDT GU11 6 E6
Eggleton Cl FLET GU13 110 D3 2
Eglantine Cl HORN PO8 352 F4
Eglantine Wk HORN PO8 352 F4
Eglinton Rd RFNM GU10 181 L2
Egmont Cl RGWD BH24 382 A6
Egmont Dr RGWD BH24 382 B6
Egmont Gdns RGWD BH24 382 B6
Egmont Rd UPTN BH16 444 A4
Eight Acres ROMY SO51 291 G1 1
Elaine Gdns HORN PO8 352 D3
Elan Cl WEND SO18 320 A7
Eland Rd ASHV GU12 7 L4
Elbe Wy AND SP10 118 E5
Elbow Cnr BSTK RG21 4 E8
Elcombes Cl LYND SO43 363 K3
Elderberry Bank CHAM RG24 83 L8
Elderberry Cl HORN PO8 328 C4
Elderberry La
CHCH/BSGR BH23 450 E2
Elderberry Rd BOR GU35 201 M3
Elderberry Wy HORN PO8 352 F4
Elder Cl WINW SO22 238 B4
HLER SO31 370 D6 3
TOTT SO40 342 E7
Elderfield Cl EMRTH PO10 378 E5
Elderfield Rd HAV PO9 377 H1
Elder Gn RWIN SO21 266 F8
Eldergrove FARN GU14 91 H6 4
Elder Rd HAV PO9 17 K1
Eldon Av NMIL/BTOS BH25 437 J8
Eldon Cl NMIL/BTOS BH25 437 J8
STOK SO20 210 F6
Eldon Dr RFNM GU10 159 G3

Eldon Rd MOOR/WNTN BH9 ..... 432 C7
STOK SO20 ..... 210 F7
Eldon St SSEA PO5 ..... 21 G4
Eldridge Gdns ROMY SO51 ..... 262 E8
Eleanor Cl LIPH GU30 ..... 202 A8
Eleanor Ct RAND SP11 ..... 92 D6
Eleanor Dr BWD BH11 ..... 431 H3
Electron Wy CHFD SO53 ..... 293 M6
Elettra Av WVILLE PO7 ..... 352 E8
Elfin Dr FERN BH22 ..... 406 A1
Elgar Av CWTH RG45 ..... 49 L2
Elgar Cl CHAM PO6 ..... 374 C8
GPORT PO12 ..... 18 B8
KEMP RG22 ..... 104 D8
NBNE BH10 ..... 432 B4
Elgar Rd ITCH SO19 ..... 345 G5
Elgar Wk WVILLE PO7 ..... 376 D4
Elgin Cl FAWY SO45 ..... 367 L5
FHAM PO15 ..... 14 E3
Elgin Rd BLKW GU17 ..... 69 H7
CHAM PO6 ..... 399 K2
PSTN BH14 ..... 446 A6
WBNE BH4 ..... 22 A1
WSHM SO15 ..... 12 A1
Elgin Wy FRIM GU16 ..... 91 J1
Eling Cl WINW SO22 ..... 214 C5
Eling Ct HAV PO9 ..... 377 M4
Eling Hl TOTT SO40 ..... 341 M3
Eling La TOTT SO40 ..... 341 L2
Eliot Cl CBLY GU15 ..... 71 L1
NTHA RG18 ..... 26 F3
Eliot Dr HASM GU27 ..... 228 B2
Elise Cl LTDN BH7 ..... 433 M8
Elizabethan Rd OVTN RG25 ..... 125 K6
Elizabeth Av CHCH/BSGR BH23.. 434 D8
NWBY RG14 ..... 37 G1
Elizabeth Cl HEND SO30 ..... 320 C7
RSAL SP5 ..... 284 C1
WHAM PO17 ..... 348 D4
WINC SO23 ..... 191 G7
Elizabeth Ct
FHAM/STUB PO14 ..... 396 D1
Elizabeth Crs LYMN SO41 ..... 438 E6
Elizabeth Dr FLET GU13 ..... 110 F3
Elizabeth Gdns ENEY PO4 ..... 423 K6
FAWY SO45 ..... 367 L7
Elizabeth Rd
FHAM/STUB PO14 ..... 396 B6
KEMP RG22 ..... 104 D4
PLE BH15 ..... 445 J5
WHAM PO17 ..... 348 E4
WIMB BH21 ..... 404 A3
WVILLE PO7 ..... 376 D2
Elizabeth Wy BPWT SO32 ..... 323 G1
Elkhams Cl LYMN SO41 ..... 439 H7
Elkstone Rd CHAM PO6 ..... 374 F7
Ellachie Gdns GPORT PO12 ..... 18 E9
Ellachie Ms GPORT PO12 ..... 18 E9
Ellachie Rd GPORT PO12 ..... 18 E9
Elland Cl ELGH SO50 ..... 295 H7
Ellanore La SELS PO20 ..... 427 K5
Eldene Ct TOTT SO40 ..... 341 J3
Ellen Dr FARN GU14 ..... 89 H4
Ellen Gdns CHFD SO53 ..... 292 F3
TADY RG26 ..... 63 K5
Elleray Ct ASHV GU12 ..... 113 K3
Ellerslie Cl FHAM/STUB PO14... 395 L7
Ellery Gv LYMN SO41 ..... 440 E3
Elles Cl FARN GU14 ..... 90 E5
Ellesfield Dr FERN BH22 ..... 406 B5
Ellesmere Orch EMRTH PO10 ..... 378 F4
Elles Rd FARN GU14 ..... 90 B6
Ellingham Cl NALR SO24 ..... 218 C3
Ellingham Dr RGWD BH24 ..... 358 D3
Ellingham Rd RGWD BH24 ..... 358 D3
Ellingham Rd
NMIL/BTOS BH25 ..... 437 H8
Ellington Cl RAND SP11 ..... 142 A1
Ellington Dr KEMP RG22 ..... 127 H1
Elliot Cl TOTT SO40 ..... 341 G2
Elliot Ri HEND SO30 ..... 321 H6
Elliott Rd BWD BH11 ..... 431 H5
Ellisfield Rd HAV PO9 ..... 377 J4
Ellison Wy RFNM GU10 ..... 136 C1
Ellis Rd CWTH RG45 ..... 49 L2
ITCH SO19 ..... 345 J3
Ellwood Av ITCH SO19 ..... 345 J3
Ellwood Cl ITCH SO19 ..... 345 J2
Elm Av CHCH/BSGR BH23 ..... 434 C7
LYMN SO41 ..... 440 A7
NMIL/BTOS BH25 ..... 437 L6
Elm Bank YTLY GU46 ..... 68 F1
Elm Bank Rd AND SP10 ..... 9 H7
Elm Cl HISD PO11 ..... 425 L5
BOR GU35 ..... 201 K5
RAND SP11 ..... 93 G6
RAND SP11 ..... 116 C8
STOK SO20 ..... 163 G4
Elm Crs BPWT SO32 ..... 296 D2
FAWY SO45 ..... 391 L1
FNM GU9 ..... 135 G1
Elmcroft Cl FRIM GU16 ..... 91 J1
Elmdale Cl HLER SO31 ..... 370 B8
Elmdale Gv ROMY SO51 ..... 288 F7
Elm Dr TLHT RG30 ..... 31 L3
Elmers Wy CHCH/BSGR BH23 ... 409 M7
Elmes Dr WSHM SO15 ..... 342 D1
Elmes Rd MOOR/WNTN BH9 ..... 432 C6
Elmeswelle Rd HORN PO8 ..... 352 E2
Elm Farm Gv KSCL RG20 ..... 59 J6
Elmfield Cl RSAL SP5 ..... 285 J3
Elm Gdns HEND SO30 ..... 320 C6
WBNE BH4 ..... 447 H3
Elmgate Dr LTDN BH7 ..... 448 E1
Elm Gv ELGH SO50 ..... 293 L6
FNM GU9 ..... 134 F1
GPORT PO12 ..... 18 F1
HISD PO11 ..... 425 J5
KSCL RG20 ..... 59 J6
NTHA RG18 ..... 26 E3
SSEA PO5 ..... 21 H5
Elm Grove Rd FARN GU14 ..... 90 E4
Elmhurst TADY RG26 ..... 61 L1
Elmhurst Rd FERN BH22 ..... 380 D7
FHAM/PORC PO16 ..... 15 J7
GPORT PO12 ..... 19 G3
NTHA RG18 ..... 26 E3
Elmhurst Wy FERN BH22 ..... 380 D6

Elm La HAV PO9 ..... 16 E4
RFNM GU10 ..... 113 J8
Elmleigh Rd HAV PO9 ..... 16 E2
Elmore Av LSOL/BMARY PO13... 420 D3
Elmore Cl LSOL/BMARY PO13 ... 420 D3
Elmore Dr RGWD BH24 ..... 381 J2
Elmore Rd LSOL/BMARY PO13... 420 D4
Elm Park Rd HAV PO9 ..... 16 E3
Elm Pl ALDT GU11 ..... 7 J6
Elm Rd BPWT SO32 ..... 297 K8
CHAM PO6 ..... 82 C6
FNM GU9 ..... 135 G1
WINW SO22 ..... 10 D6
HAV PO9 ..... 17 H6
NALR SO24 ..... 218 C3
OVTN RG25 ..... 101 G6
Elms Av PSTN BH14 ..... 445 M7
STHA RG19 ..... 27 H5
Elms Cl FBDG SP6 ..... 308 F6
PSTN BH14 ..... 445 M7
Elms La SELS PO20 ..... 427 L7
Elmsleigh Gdns ROWN SO16 ..... 318 F4
Elmsleigh Rd FARN GU14 ..... 90 D4
Elmslie Gdns HLER SO31 ..... 345 K7
Elms Ride SELS PO20 ..... 427 L7
Elms Rd ALDT GU11 ..... 6 F3
FHAM/PORC PO16 ..... 15 J9
FLET GU13 ..... 110 D5
HTWY RG27 ..... 85 M6
Elmstead Gdns SELS PO20 ..... 427 L6
Elmstead Park Rd SELS PO20 ..... 427 L6
Elmstead Rd CCLF BH13 ..... 446 E8
The Elms AND SP10 ..... 8 F6
RFNM GU10 ..... 136 C1
Elm St SHAM SO14 ..... 13 K4
SSEA PO5 ..... 20 F5
Elms Wy SBNE BH6 ..... 449 K4
SELS PO20 ..... 427 L6
Elm Ter TOTT SO40 ..... 340 F6
Elm Tree Cl TOTT SO40 ..... 340 F6
Elmtree Gdns ROMY SO51 ..... 291 M6
Elmtree Rd CHAM PO6 ..... 376 C8
Elm Vw ASHV GU12 ..... 113 L5
Elmwood Av FBDG SP6 ..... 309 H6
WVILLE PO7 ..... 376 C2
Elmwood Cl ALTN GU34 ..... 176 C6
Elmwood Rd NEND PO2 ..... 399 J4
Elmwood Wy
CHCH/BSGR BH23 ..... 451 L1
DEAN RG23 ..... 104 B1
Elphinstone Rd
CHCH/BSGR BH23 ..... 436 F8
SSEA PO5 ..... 21 G5
Elsenwood Crs CBLY GU15 ..... 71 K2
Elsenwood Dr CBLY GU15 ..... 71 K1
Elsfred Rd FHAM/STUB PO14 ... 395 L7
Elsley Cl FRIM GU16 ..... 91 J2
Elson La GPORT PO12 ..... 397 L8
Elson Rd GPORT PO12 ..... 397 L8
Elstead Gdns WVILLE PO7 ..... 376 A4
Elstead Rd RFNM GU10 ..... 136 D3
Elston Pl ASHV GU12 ..... 7 J5
Elston Rd ASHV GU12 ..... 7 J5
Elstree Rd ITCH SO19 ..... 344 C4
Elvetham Cl FLET GU13 ..... 88 E5
Elvetham Hts HTWY RG27 ..... 67 L8
Elvetham Pl HTWY RG27 ..... 88 D5
Elvetham Rd FLET GU13 ..... 88 C6
Elvin Cl LYMN SO41 ..... 438 D4
Elwell Gn HISD PO11 ..... 425 K5
Ely Cl CHCH/BSGR BH23 ..... 434 B3
Ely Rd BMTH BH1 ..... 23 L2
Emanuel St NEND PO2 ..... 423 H1
Embankment Wy RGWD BH24 ... 382 F2
Emberley Cl FERN BH22 ..... 406 E1
Embleton Rd BOR GU35 ..... 202 E2
Embley Cl TOTT SO40 ..... 316 C6
Embley La ROMY SO51 ..... 289 J2
Embsay Rd HLER SO31 ..... 346 B8
Emden Rd AND SP10 ..... 118 C5
Emerald Cl ITCH SO19 ..... 344 E2
WVILLE PO7 ..... 376 E1
Emer Cl NBAD SO52 ..... 291 M3
Emerson Rd PLE BH15 ..... 445 H6
Emmanuel Cl
FHAM/STUB PO14 ..... 371 G6
Emmett Rd ROWN SO16 ..... 317 L3
Emmons Cl HLER SO31 ..... 369 K7
Empress Av FARN GU14 ..... 90 E4
Empress Rd LYND SO43 ..... 363 K3
SHAM SO14 ..... 13 J9
SHAM SO14 ..... 343 M1
Empress Wy RAND SP11 ..... 92 E6
Empshott Rd ENEY PO4 ..... 423 K4
Empson Wk
LSOL/BMARY PO13 ..... 420 D1
Emsbrook Dr EMRTH PO10 ..... 378 D6
Emsworth Common Rd
EMRTH PO10 ..... 378 B3
Emsworth House Cl
EMRTH PO10 ..... 378 C7
Emsworth Rd HAV PO9 ..... 17 K5
EMRTH PO10 ..... 402 F4
HAV PO9 ..... 17 G5
LYMN SO41 ..... 440 C4
NEND PO2 ..... 399 J7
WSHM SO15 ..... 318 A8
Enborne Gv NWBY RG14 ..... 2 B6
Enborne Pl NWBY RG14 ..... 2 B6
Enborne Rd KSCL RG20 ..... 24 F7
NWBY RG14 ..... 2 B6
Enborne St KSCL RG20 ..... 36 D4
Enborne Wy THLE RG7 ..... 40 C2
Encombe Cl BKME/WDN BH12 .. 431 K8
Endeavour Cl GPORT PO12 ..... 19 J4
Enderwood Cl TOTT SO40 ..... 316 A8
Endfield Cl CHCH/BSGR BH23 .. 434 D7
Endfield Rd CHCH/BSGR BH23... 434 D7
MOOR/WNTN BH9 ..... 432 C6
Endle St SHAM SO14 ..... 13 L5
Endofield Cl FHAM/STUB PO14.. 396 D2
Enfield Av PLE BH15 ..... 445 K2
Enfield Cl LIPH GU30 ..... 227 G3
Enfield Crs PLE BH15 ..... 445 K2
Enfield Gv ITCH SO19 ..... 344 C6
Enfield Rd ASHV GU12 ..... 113 L3

PLE BH15 ..... 445 K2
Englands Wy BWD BH11 ..... 431 H4
Englefield Rd WEND SO18 ..... 344 B1
English Rd WSHM SO15 ..... 342 F1
Enham La AND SP10 ..... 118 D5
Enmill La WINW SO22 ..... 237 L3
Ennel Copse NBAD SO52 ..... 291 M4
Ennerdale Av HORN PO8 ..... 328 B6
Ennerdale Gdns NALR SO24 ..... 218 C4
WEND SO18 ..... 320 A7
Ennerdale Gv FNM GU9 ..... 134 D2
Ennerdale Rd
FHAM/STUB PO14 ..... 396 B4
BOR GU35 ..... 201 J3
ROWN SO16 ..... 317 K6
Ennerdale Wy STHA RG19 ..... 26 D5
Ensign Dr LSOL/BMARY PO13 ... 421 H2
Ensign Wy HLER SO31 ..... 369 J6
Enterprise Cl HLER SO31 ..... 370 C7
Enterprise Rd ROWN SO16 ..... 292 B7
Enterprise Wy SHAM SO14 ..... 13 J7
STHA RG19 ..... 27 K6
Epping Cl WEND SO18 ..... 320 A7
Epsom Cl CBLY GU15 ..... 50 F8
ELGH SO50 ..... 321 J1
Epsom Crs NWBY RG14 ..... 3 H8
Epsom Down ALTN GU34 ..... 176 E6
Epts Rd FARN GU14 ..... 90 D8
Epworth Rd NEND PO2 ..... 399 K7
Equine Wy NWBY RG14 ..... 37 L1
Equinne Wy NWBY RG14 ..... 37 L1
Erica Cl HLER SO31 ..... 370 D5
HORN PO8 ..... 352 F5
Erica Wy HORN PO8 ..... 352 F4
Ericksen Rd NBNE BH10 ..... 432 A5
Eric Rd FHAM/STUB PO14 ..... 396 A6
Erleigh Dene NWBY RG14 ..... 2 C8
Erles Rd LIPH GU30 ..... 226 F4
Ernest Cl EMRTH PO10 ..... 378 D7
RFNM GU10 ..... 158 E2
Ernest Rd HAV PO9 ..... 377 G4
PSEA PO1 ..... 423 J1
Erpingham Rd
BKME/WDN BH12 ..... 446 F3
Erskine Cl TADY RG26 ..... 42 C7
Erskine Rd WINW SO22 ..... 10 D9
Escombe Rd ELGH SO50 ..... 294 C5
Escur Cl NEND PO2 ..... 399 K4
Esdaile La RGWD BH24 ..... 384 D5
Esher Cl KEMP RG22 ..... 104 C7
Esher Gv WVILLE PO7 ..... 352 A6
Esher Rd CBLY GU15 ..... 51 K7
Eskdale Cl HORN PO8 ..... 328 B6
Eskdale Gdns HLER SO31 ..... 345 L7
Eskdale Wy CBLY GU15 ..... 71 K4
Esmond Cl
LSOL/BMARY PO13 ..... 420 D2
Esmonde Wy CFDH BH17 ..... 430 D8
Esplanade CCLF BH13 ..... 457 L1
ENEY PO4 ..... 423 J7
PLE BH15 ..... 445 H5
Esplanade Gdns ENEY PO4 ..... 424 A6
The Esplanade GPORT PO12 ..... 19 M4
Essex Av CHCH/BSGR BH23 ..... 434 C6
Essex Cl FRIM GU16 ..... 91 K1
Essex Rd BSTK RG21 ..... 4 D8
ENEY PO4 ..... 423 L4
BOR GU35 ..... 201 J4
Essex St NWBY RG14 ..... 37 G1
Estella Rd NEND PO2 ..... 399 H8
Estridge Cl HLER SO31 ..... 345 L7
Ethelbert Dr AND SP10 ..... 118 C5
Ethelbert Rd WIMB BH21 ..... 404 B4
Ethelburt Av ROWN SO16 ..... 319 H3
Ethelred Gdns TOTT SO40 ..... 341 G2
Ethel Rd PSEA PO1 ..... 423 J2
Eton Cl KEMP RG22 ..... 126 F2
Eton Gdns WBNE BH4 ..... 447 G4
Eton Pl FNM GU9 ..... 134 E1
Eton Rd SSEA PO5 ..... 21 L3
Etps Rd FARN GU14 ..... 90 E1
Ettrick Rd CCLF BH13 ..... 446 F7
Etwall RAND SP11 ..... 139 M4
Eucalyptus Av RGWD BH24 ..... 381 L6
Europa Cl TADY RG26 ..... 63 L5
European Wy SHAM SO14 ..... 13 J8
Euryalus Rd FHAM/STUB PO14.. 396 D2
Euskirchen Wy KEMP RG22 ..... 104 B3
Euston Gv RGWD BH24 ..... 382 F2
Euston Rd ENEY PO4 ..... 423 M3
Evans Cl BWD BH11 ..... 431 K7
NEND PO2 ..... 398 F4
RGWD BH24 ..... 381 J2
STOK SO20 ..... 162 A6
Evans Rd ENEY PO4 ..... 423 L4
Evans St SHAM SO14 ..... 13 H4
Evelegh Rd CHAM PO6 ..... 376 B8
Eveley Cl BOR GU35 ..... 201 C8
Evelyn Av ALDT GU11 ..... 7 H6
Evelyn Cl BPWT SO32 ..... 323 K4
Evelyn Crs WSHM SO15 ..... 318 C8
Evelyn Rd MOOR/WNTN BH9 .. 432 C7
Evelyn Woods Rd ALDT GU11 ... 112 F1
Evening Gld FERN BH22 ..... 406 C5
Evenlode Rd ROWN SO16 ..... 317 K7
Evenlode Wy SHST GU47 ..... 49 M8
Everdon La HSEA PO3 ..... 400 A4
Everest Cl CBLY GU15 ..... 51 G8
CHCH/BSGR BH23 ..... 435 J8
CWTH RG45 ..... 49 L2
Everglades Av HORN PO8 ..... 352 D5
Everglades Cl FERN BH22 ..... 406 B1
Evergreen Cl TOTT SO40 ..... 342 D7
WIMB BH21 ..... 356 C8
WVILLE PO7 ..... 376 B1
Evergreens RGWD BH24 ..... 381 J3
Everglade Rd FRIM GU16 ..... 71 J6
Everleigh Av SHST GU47 ..... 49 L8
Evering Gdns
BKME/WDN BH12 ..... 431 G7
Everlea Cl LYMN SO41 ..... 439 H4
Everon Gdns NMIL/BTOS BH25.. 437 M7
Eversfield Cl AND SP10 ..... 8 E5

Evershot Rd CHAR BH8 ..... 433 J7
Eversley Crs HAV PO9 ..... 377 H4
Eversley Pl WINW SO22 ..... 238 C3
Eversley St HTWY RG27 ..... 47 K7
Everton Rd LYMN SO41 ..... 438 D4
Evesham Cl LTDN BH7 ..... 433 L4
ROWN SO16 ..... 319 G3
Evesham Wk SHST GU47 ..... 49 M7
Evingar Gdns WHCH RG28 ..... 122 B2
Evingar Rd WHCH RG28 ..... 122 B2
Evreux Cl STHA RG19 ..... 27 J6
Ewart Ct FAWY SO45 ..... 367 L5
Ewart Rd PSEA PO1 ..... 423 J1
Ewell Wy TOTT SO40 ..... 316 C7
Ewhurst Cl HAV PO9 ..... 377 H4
Ewhurst Rd TADY RG26 ..... 81 H1
Ewins Cl ASHV GU12 ..... 113 K6
Ewshot La FLET GU13 ..... 110 E5
Exbury Cl ELGH SO50 ..... 294 E6
Exbury Dr BWD BH11 ..... 431 K3
Exbury Rd FAWY SO45 ..... 392 C8
HAV PO9 ..... 377 L3
Exbury Wy AND SP10 ..... 8 C7
Excellent Rd
FHAM/STUB PO14 ..... 396 D3
Excelsior Rd PSTN BH14 ..... 446 B6
Exchange Rd PSEA PO1 ..... 20 F2
Exeter Cl ELGH SO50 ..... 293 L3
EMRTH PO10 ..... 378 D5
HLER SO31 ..... 370 D5
KEMP RG22 ..... 127 G1
WEND SO18 ..... 319 M7
Exeter Crs WCLF BH2 ..... 22 C7
Exeter Gdns YTLY GU46 ..... 68 E1
Exeter Park Rd WCLF BH2 ..... 22 E7
Exeter Rd ASHV GU12 ..... 113 K5
ENEY PO4 ..... 423 K6
WCLF BH2 ..... 22 E6
WEND SO18 ..... 319 M8
Exford Av WEND SO18 ..... 320 B8
Exford Dr WEND SO18 ..... 320 B8
Exhibition Rd FARN GU14 ..... 90 D8
Exleigh Cl ITCH SO19 ..... 344 F2
Exmoor Cl KEMP RG22 ..... 104 A5
Exmoor Rd STHA RG19 ..... 26 F5
Exmouth Gdns ELGH SO50 ..... 321 H1
Exmouth Rd GPORT PO12 ..... 397 L8
SSEA PO5 ..... 21 K7
Express Wy NWBY RG14 ..... 26 A5
Exton Gdns FHAM/PORC PO16... 374 A7
Exton Rd HAV PO9 ..... 377 M3
SBNE BH6 ..... 449 J1
Eyebright Cl ELGH SO50 ..... 321 H1
Eyeworth Wk FAWY SO45 ..... 367 G4
Eynham Av ITCH SO19 ..... 345 H2
Eynham Cl ITCH SO19 ..... 344 F2
Eyre Cl TOTT SO40 ..... 341 H2

F

Faber Cl HAV PO9 ..... 377 L4
Fabian Cl WVILLE PO7 ..... 352 E8
Factory Rd ELGH SO50 ..... 293 M6
UPTN BH16 ..... 444 B2
Fairacre KSCL RG20 ..... 36 C8
Fairacre Ri FHAM/STUB PO14 ... 371 M8
Fairbairn Wk NBAD SO52 ..... 292 E2
Fairbourne Cl HORN PO8 ..... 352 E2
Fair Cl WHCH RG28 ..... 122 B4
Fairclose Dr WINW SO22 ..... 214 A3
Faircross Cl FAWY SO45 ..... 392 A5
Fairdown Cl WINC SO23 ..... 11 M8
Fairfax Cl WINW SO22 ..... 238 A3
Fairfax Ct ITCH SO19 ..... 345 J3
Fairfax Ms FARN GU14 ..... 91 G6
ITCH SO19 ..... 345 J2
Fairfax Pl NWBY RG14 ..... 26 B3
Fairfax Rd FARN GU14 ..... 90 E1
Fairfield CHCH/BSGR BH23 ..... 450 A1
Fair Fld ROMY SO51 ..... 262 F5
Fairfield WHCH RG28 ..... 122 B2
Fairfield Av FHAM/STUB PO14 .. 14 D9
Fairfield Cl EMRTH PO10 ..... 378 D6
FAWY SO45 ..... 367 L4
LYMN SO41 ..... 440 C5
WIMB BH21 ..... 404 C3
Fairfield Dr FRIM GU16 ..... 71 H5
Fairfield Gn ALTN GU34 ..... 197 H5
Fairfield Rd WINW SO22 ..... 10 D5
HAV PO9 ..... 16 F4
NMIL/BTOS BH25 ..... 452 D1
RWIN SO21 ..... 266 C3
WIMB BH21 ..... 404 B4
Fairfield Sq CHAM PO6 ..... 375 J8
Fairfields Rd BSTK RG21 ..... 105 G5
The Fairfield FNM GU9 ..... 134 F6
Fair Gn ITCH SO19 ..... 344 F3
Fairholme Gdns FNM GU9 ..... 134 F7
Fairhome Cl GPORT PO12 ..... 421 L1
Fair Isle Cl FHAM/STUB PO14.... 395 M5
Fairisle Rd ROWN SO16 ..... 317 K4
Fairland Cl FLET GU13 ..... 89 G8
Fair La RWIN SO21 ..... 215 M7
Fairlawn Cl ROWN SO16 ..... 317 L2
Fairlawn Rd TADY RG26 ..... 62 A1
Fairlead Dr
LSOL/BMARY PO13 ..... 421 H2
Fairlea Rd EMRTH PO10 ..... 378 D5
LYMN SO41 ..... 440 C4
Fairlie Rd HEND SO30 ..... 321 H5
Fairlie Pk RGWD BH24 ..... 358 G7
Fairlight Gdns ALTN GU34 ..... 197 H5
Fairlight La LYMN SO41 ..... 412 B7
Fairmead Cl SHST GU47 ..... 70 B1
Fairmead Wk TOTT SO40 ..... 341 G4
Fairmile FLET GU13 ..... 110 E4
Fairmile Rd CHCH/BSGR BH23.. 434 E8
Fair Oak HAV PO9 ..... 16 E1
Fair Oak La THLE RG7 ..... 64 B1
Fairoak Rd ELGH SO50 ..... 294 C6
Fairoak Wy TADY RG26 ..... 41 G7
Fairthorne Gdns GPORT PO12... 18 D4
Fairthorne Ri CHAM RG24 ..... 106 B3
Fair Vw NALR SO24 ..... 218 B4

Fairview Cl FAWY SO45 ..... 367 L5
ROMY SO51 ..... 263 G5
Fairview Crs WIMB BH21 ..... 429 L3
Fairview Dr FAWY SO45 ..... 367 K6
ROMY SO51 ..... 263 G8
WIMB BH21 ..... 429 L3
Fairview Gdns FNM GU9 ..... 135 G2
Fairview Meadow DEAN RG23 .. 103 G8
Fairview Pde FAWY SO45 ..... 367 L6
Fairview Rd ASHV GU12 ..... 113 L5
BOR GU35 ..... 202 E3
WIMB BH21 ..... 429 L3
Fairwater Cl
LSOL/BMARY PO13 ..... 396 F7
Fairway Cl LIPH GU30 ..... 226 A5
Fairway Dr CHCH/BSGR BH23 .. 449 L2
Fairway Gdns ROWN SO16 ..... 317 K3
Fairway Hts CBLY GU15 ..... 71 L2
Fairway Rd FAWY SO45 ..... 367 K4
PSTN BH14 ..... 446 B8
Fairways FERN BH22 ..... 406 D2
GSHT GU26 ..... 203 L2
RAND SP11 ..... 117 G6
The Fairway FARN GU14 ..... 89 L8
FHAM/PORC PO16 ..... 374 A8
FNM GU9 ..... 135 G1
FRIM GU16 ..... 71 K5
HAV PO9 ..... 354 A4
BOR GU35 ..... 201 G7
LSOL/BMARY PO13 ..... 397 G7
NMIL/BTOS BH25 ..... 453 G1
Fairwood Rd VWD BH31 ..... 357 G3
Fairy Crossway HORN PO8 ..... 352 F6
Faithfulls Dro STOK SO20 ..... 209 M4
Fakenham Wy SHST GU47 ..... 50 A7
Falaise Cl ALDT GU11 ..... 7 G1
ROWN SO16 ..... 318 B4
Falaise Rd STOK SO20 ..... 162 F4
Falcon Cl FHAM/PORC PO16 ..... 373 K8
KEMP RG22 ..... 103 L7
NTID SP9 ..... 114 E1
Falcon Coppice KSCL RG20 ..... 36 C8
Falcon Dr CHCH/BSGR BH23 .. 451 L2
Falconer Ct FAWY SO45 ..... 391 M2
Falconer Dr PLE BH15 ..... 444 D4
Falcon Flds FAWY SO45 ..... 392 F5
TADY RG26 ..... 41 L6
Falcon House Gdns KSCL RG20... 36 B8
Falcon Rd HORN PO8 ..... 352 E1
Falcon Sq ELGH SO50 ..... 293 J7
Falcon Vw WINW SO22 ..... 238 B4
Falcon Wy BPWT SO32 ..... 321 M7
YTLY GU46 ..... 68 E2
Falkland Dr NWBY RG14 ..... 2 C9
Falkland Garth NWBY RG14 ..... 37 G1
Falkland Rd CHAM RG24 ..... 83 H6
CHFD SO53 ..... 293 H5
NWBY RG14 ..... 37 G2
WSHM SO15 ..... 342 F1
Falklands Cl
LSOL/BMARY PO13 ..... 420 D1
Falklands Rd NEND PO2 ..... 399 J4
Falkner Rd FNM GU9 ..... 134 D6
Falkners Cl FARN GU14 ..... 89 H4
Fallowfield FARN GU14 ..... 89 H4
Fallow Fld WINW SO22 ..... 238 B4
Fallowfield YTLY GU46 ..... 68 C1
Falmouth Cl CBLY GU15 ..... 71 K4
Falmouth Rd CHAM PO6 ..... 374 D7
Falmouth Wy STHA RG19 ..... 27 J5
Falstaff Wy TOTT SO40 ..... 341 J3
Fancy Rd BKME/WDN BH12 ..... 430 F8
Fannys La THLE RG7 ..... 64 B3
Fanshawe St SHAM SO14 ..... 343 L2
Fantails ALTN GU34 ..... 176 E2
Faraday Cl WHIT RG2 ..... 47 H1
Faraday Rd CHAM RG24 ..... 5 K2
FARN GU14 ..... 90 F2
NWBY RG14 ..... 3 G3
Farcroft Rd PSTN BH14 ..... 446 A3
Farcrosse Cl SHST GU47 ..... 49 M8
Fareham Dr YTLY GU46 ..... 68 E1
Fareham Park Rd FHAM PO15 .. 372 A4
Fareham Rd
LSOL/BMARY PO13 ..... 397 J3
WHAM PO17 ..... 348 E5
WHAM PO17 ..... 374 C5
Faringdon Cl SHST GU47 ..... 49 M8
Faringdon Rd WEND SO18 ..... 345 H1
Farleigh La OVTN RG25 ..... 126 F7
Farleigh Ri BSTK RG21 ..... 105 K6
Farleigh Rd OVTN RG25 ..... 127 K4
Farley Cl ELGH SO50 ..... 295 J7
WINW SO22 ..... 238 A4
Farley La ROMY SO51 ..... 235 J7
Farley Mount Rd RWIN SO21... 236 F2
Farley St STOK SO20 ..... 184 E2
Farlington Av CHAM PO6 ..... 376 A7
Farlington Rd NEND PO2 ..... 399 J7
Farm Cl CWTH RG45 ..... 49 M1
RGWD BH24 ..... 358 E6
YTLY GU46 ..... 69 G3
Farm Dr FARN GU14 ..... 89 G4
Far Meadow Wy EMRTH PO10 .. 378 C4
Farm Edge Rd
FHAM/STUB PO14 ..... 396 A7
Farmers Wk LYMN SO41 ..... 439 H8
Farmery Cl ELGH SO50 ..... 319 J4
Farm Gdns HSEA PO3 ..... 399 K6
Farm Ground Cl HTWY RG27 ... 86 B7
Farmhouse Wy FLET GU13 ..... 110 D3
HORN PO8 ..... 352 E2
Farm La CHCH/BSGR BH23 ..... 450 F3
RFNM GU10 ..... 133 H7
RCCH PO18 ..... 403 K1
Farm La North
NMIL/BTOS BH25 ..... 437 L8
Farm La South
NMIL/BTOS BH25 ..... 452 F1
Farmlea Rd CHAM PO6 ..... 374 D6
Farm Rd ASHV GU12 ..... 113 H6
FERN BH22 ..... 380 B6
FHAM/STUB PO14 ..... 371 J6
FRIM GU16 ..... 71 H6
RAND SP11 ..... 141 M2
Farmside Gdns HSEA PO3 ..... 399 K4
Farm Vw EMRTH PO10 ..... 378 C4

YTLY GU46 .... 69 G3
Farm View Av HORN PO8 .... 328 A3
Farm View Dr CHAM RG24 .... 83 M3
Farnborough Rd ALDT GU11 .... 112 A7
FARN GU14 .... 90 E4
FNM GU9 .... 112 A8
Farnborough St FARN GU14 ..... 91 G3
Farnham By-pass FNM GU9 ..... 134 C8
Farnham La HASM GU27 .... 204 D7
Farnham Park Dr FARN GU14 ... 89 H1
Farnham Rd BKME/WDN BH12.. 446 F1
FLET GU13 .... 89 J7
BOR GU35 .... 201 J2
LISS GU33 .... 248 C4
ODIM RG29 .... 108 F5
PSF GU32 .... 248 A8
Farnleys Md LYMN SO41 .... 440 C6
Faroe Cl FHAM RG24 .... 83 J7
Faroes Cl FHAM/STUB PO14 ... 395 M5
Farrell Cl CBLY GU15 .... 70 F5
Farriers Cl TADY RG26 .... 63 L5
WIMB BH21 .... 404 F2
Farrier's Fld OVTN RG25 ...... 127 M8
Farriers Wy HORN PO8 .... 353 G7
Farringdon Rd HAV PO9 .... 377 L4
Farrington Wy TADY RG26 ..... 61 L1
Farringford Rd ITCH SO19 .... 345 H2
Farrs Av AND SP10 .... 9 K8
Farthing Flds BSTK RG21 ...... 202 B3
Farthings Ga WVILLE PO7 ..... 376 C5
Fastnet Cl ROWN SO16 .... 317 K3
Fathersfield BROC SO42 .... 387 K7
Fathoms Reach HISD PO11 .... 425 J4
Fay Av FAWY SO45 .... 392 D2
Faversham Rd SHST GU47 ..... 50 A7
Fawcett Rd ENEY PO4 .... 21 L3
NMIL/BTOS BH25 .... 437 K6
Fawconer Rd KSCL RG20 ...... 59 J4
Fawley Grn FAWY SO45 .... 392 C7
Fawley Ct HAV PO9 .... 377 M3
Fawley Gn CHAR BH8 .... 433 H5
Fawley La ALTN GU34 .... 245 G4
RWIN SO21 .... 239 L8
Fawley Rd FAWY SO45 .... 367 M8
FAWY SO45 .... 392 C5
NEND PO2 .... 399 J3
WHIN SO15 .... 342 E2
Fawn Gdns NMIL/BTOS BH25 .. 437 K4
Fay Cl FHAM/STUB PO14 ...... 396 A6
Fayre Rd FHAM/PORC PO16 .... 15 H9
Fayrewood Cha KEMP RG22 .... 127 G1
Fearon Rd NEND PO2 .... 399 J4
Feathers La BSTK RG21 .... 4 F9
Felbridge Cl FRIM GU16 .... 71 K6
Feld Wy CHAM RG24 .... 105 M1
Felix Rd GPORT PO12 .... 421 M1
Fell Cl HLER SO31 .... 370 E4
Fell Dr LSOL/BMARY PO13 ..... 420 D1
Fellows Rd FARN GU14 .... 91 G7
Felmer Dr WINC SO23 .... 215 H1
Feltham Cl ROMY SO51 .... 263 H8
Felton Crs FHAM/BSGR BH23 .. 436 D8
Felton Rd PSTN BH14 .... 445 L3
Feltons Rd HSEA PO3 .... 399 K3
Fen Av FHAM/PORC PO16 ...... 396 F6
Fenleigh Cl NMIL/BTOS BH25 . 437 M5
Fennel Cl CHAM RG24 .... 83 M3
FARN GU14 .... 89 L4
NWBY RG14 .... 26 A3
Fennel Gdns LYMN SO41 ...... 440 B7
Fennell Cl WVILLE PO7 .... 352 B7
Fenton Cl SBNE BH6 .... 449 H2
Ferbies FLET GU13 .... 110 F2
Ferguson Cl BSTK RG21 .... 104 F6
Fern Barrow
 BKME/WDN BH12 .... 431 M8
Fernbrae Cl RFNM GU10 .... 158 E6
Fern Cl CHCH/BSGR BH23 ..... 435 G6
CWTH GU31 .... 49 L1
EPSF GU31 .... 276 B5
FBDG SP6 .... 333 L3
FRIM GU16 .... 71 M5
Ferncote Rd BOR GU35 .... 201 K5
Ferncroft Cl
 FHAM/STUB PO14 .... 396 A7
Ferncroft Gdns NBNE BH10 ... 432 B3
Ferncroft Rd NBNE BH10 ..... 432 B3
Ferndale HEND SO30 .... 346 B3
WVILLE PO7 .... 376 D1
Ferndale Ct STHA RG19 ...... 27 G5
Ferndale Gdns HTWY RG27 ... 85 M6
Ferndale Ms
 LSOL/BMARY PO13 .... 396 F4
Ferndale Rd AND SP10 .... 8 C3
FLET GU13 .... 110 E3
NMIL/BTOS BH25 .... 437 M4
TOTT SO40 .... 342 D7
Ferndene Wy WEND SO18 ..... 319 L4
Ferndown La HASM GU27 ...... 228 A3
Ferndown Gdns FARN GU14 ... 90 B4
Ferndown, Stour &
 Forest Trail FERN BH22 .... 405 M2
WIMB BH21 .... 405 G1
Fern Dr FLET GU13 .... 110 D2
HAV PO9 .... 17 G2
Ferneham Rd FHAM PO15 ..... 372 A6
Ferney Cl ALTN GU34 .... 198 C1
Ferney La ALTN GU34 .... 173 L8
Fernglade NMIL/BTOS BH25 ... 437 L6
Fernheath Cl BWD BH11 ...... 431 L6
Fernheath Rd BWD BH11 ...... 431 L6
Fernhill Cl CFDH BH17 .... 430 E6
Fernhill Dr FNM GU9 .... 134 E2
Fernhill La FARN GU14 .... 70 C7
FNM GU9 .... 134 E1
NMIL/BTOS BH25 .... 437 L2
Fern Hill La ROMY SO51 ...... 235 J8

Fernhill Rd BLKW GU17 .... 70 B6
FARN GU14 .... 90 B1
NMIL/BTOS BH25 .... 437 L4
Fernhill Wk FARN GU14 ...... 70 C7
Fernhurst Cl HISD PO11 ...... 425 J5
Fernhurst Rd ENEY PO4 ...... 423 K4
LIPH GU30 .... 250 A1
Fernie Cl FHAM/STUB PO14 ... 395 M6
Fernlea Bdr BOR GU35 .... 201 G7
Fernlea Av FERN BH22 .... 406 B4
Fernlea Cl FERN BH22 .... 406 B4
RCWD BH24 .... 381 J4
Fernlea Gdns FERN BH22 .... 406 B4
ROWN SO16 .... 318 D5
Fernlea Wy FAWY SO45 ...... 367 H5
Fernleigh Ri FRIM GU16 ..... 91 M1
Fern Rd FAWY SO45 .... 367 H5
ITCH SO19 .... 344 D6
Fernside Av PSTN BH14 ...... 445 L4
Fernside Rd FERN BH22 ...... 380 C6
MOOR/WNTN BH9 .... 432 B8
PLE BH15 .... 445 K4
Fern Wy FHAM PO15 .... 371 H5
Fernwood Cl RGWD BH24 ..... 381 M3
Fernyhurst Av ROWN SO16 ... 317 C2
Ferrell Fld HTWY RG27 ...... 85 L7
Ferris Av CHAR BH8 .... 433 C6
Ferris Cl CHAR BH8 .... 433 H6
Ferris Pl CHAR BH8 .... 433 H6
Ferrol Rd GPORT PO12 ...... 422 A2
Ferry Rd ENEY PO4 .... 424 B5
FAWY SO45 .... 367 K5
HISD PO11 .... 424 E4
PLE BH15 .... 445 G7
SBNE BH6 .... 449 L5
Ferry Wy CCLF BH13 .... 457 G5
Festing Gv ENEY PO4 .... 423 K6
Festing Rd ENEY PO4 .... 423 K6
Feversham Av CHAR BH8 ..... 433 J7
Fey Rd GPORT PO12 .... 19 G2
Fibbards Rd BROC SO42 ..... 387 K7
Fiddlers Fld ALTN GU34 ..... 154 A8
Field Cl HLER SO31 .... 370 F6
LSOL/BMARY PO13 .... 396 F3
ROMY SO51 .... 290 F1
ROWN SO16 .... 319 H3
RWIN SO21 .... 266 B2
THLE RG7 .... 31 L6
Fielden Cl NBAD SO52 ...... 291 L4
Field End FNM GU9 .... 135 J4
Field La FRIM GU16 .... 71 H7
Fieldmore Rd GPORT PO12 ... 421 M1
Field Pl LIPH GU30 .... 226 E5
NMIL/BTOS BH25 .... 437 G8
Field Rd FARN GU14 .... 70 D8
Fields Cl FAWY SO45 .... 392 C7
Field Stores Ap ALDT GU11 .. 112 F5
Field Vw NBAD SO52 .... 292 A2
Field Wk LYMN SO41 .... 440 B3
Field Wy ASHV GU12 .... 113 H6
CHCH/BSGR BH23 .... 436 B7
FBDG SP6 .... 310 D6
RFNM GU10 .... 136 C1
RWIN SO21 .... 266 B2
WVILLE PO7 .... 351 K4
Fieldway FLET GU13 .... 88 C8
HASM GU27 .... 228 F1
RGWD BH24 .... 358 F8
Fie Yard Rd FARN GU14 ..... 90 D6
Fifield La RFNM GU10 .... 158 F6
Fifth Av CHAM PO6 .... 375 J4
HAV PO9 .... 17 K2
Fifth Rd NWBY RG14 .... 2 A1
Fifth St PSEA PO1 .... 423 K1
STHA RG19 .... 38 C3
Filmer Cl LSOL/BMARY PO13 . 397 H8
Filmorehill La ALTN GU34 ... 244 E5
Filton Cl TOTT SO40 .... 316 B8
Filton Rd LYMN SO41 .... 440 B4
Fincham End Dr CWTH GU45 . 49 J4
Finchampstead Rd
 EWKG RG40 .... 48 D1
Finch Cl TADY RG26 .... 61 M1
Finchdean Rd HAV PO9 ..... 354 A6
HAV PO9 .... 377 H4
Finches Gn ALTN GU34 ...... 176 E2
Finchfield Av BWD BH11 .... 431 K2
Finchmead La PSF GU32 .... 275 G4
Finch Rd ENEY PO4 .... 424 B5
Finch's La RWIN SO21 ...... 266 E2
Finch Wy THLE RG7 .... 31 L5
Findhorn Cl SHST GU47 ..... 70 A1
The Findings FARN GU14 .... 70 B8
Findon Rd GPORT PO12 ..... 397 M8
Fingle Dr AND SP10 .... 8 D5
Finisterre Cl FHAM/STUB PO14 . 395 M4
Finkley Rd AND SP10 .... 9 M1
Finley Rd FARN GU14 ...... 90 B1
Fintry Pl FARN GU14 .... 90 B1
Finzi Cl ITCH SO19 .... 345 G5
Fiona Cl WINC SO23 .... 11 L4
Fir Acre Rd ASHV GU12 .... 113 K2
Fir Av NMIL/BTOS BH25 .... 437 M6
Firbank Rd MOOR/WNTN BH9 . 432 F8
Fir Cl FERN BH22 .... 380 C5
FLET GU13 .... 88 B8
LYND SO43 .... 363 K4
Fir Copse Rd WVILLE PO7 ... 376 B5
Fir Croft Dr CHFD SO53 .... 293 J3
Fir Dr BLKW GU17 .... 70 A5
Firecrest Cl ROWN SO16 ... 318 A3
Firecrest Rd KEMP RG22 ... 126 E2
Fire Station Rd ALDT GU11 .. 112 E5

Fire Thorn Cl FLET GU13 .... 110 E2
Firfield Rd FNM GU9 .... 158 D1
Firglen Dr YTLY GU46 ...... 69 G1
Fir Gv BOR GU35 .... 201 G1
Firgrove Ct FNM GU9 ...... 134 F7
Firgrove Crs HSEA PO3 .... 399 K3
Firgrove Hl FNM GU9 ...... 134 F7
Firgrove La WHAM PO17 .... 349 K6
Firgrove Pde FARN GU14 ... 90 E4
Firgrove Rd FARN GU14 .... 90 E4
HTWY RG27 .... 68 B2
BOR GU35 .... 201 G7
NBAD SO52 .... 291 M3
WSHM SO15 .... 343 G1
YTLY GU46 .... 68 C7
Firlands Av CBLY GU15 .... 71 G3
Firlands Ri CHAM PO6 ..... 376 E7
Firmount Cl CHAM RG24 .... 83 J7
Firmstone Rd WINC SO23 .. 11 L7
Firs Av WVILLE PO7 .... 352 D6
Firs Cl EWKG RG40 .... 48 C1
FARN GU14 .... 90 F6
Firs Crs WINC SO23 .... 190 F8
Firs Dr HEND SO30 .... 345 L2
Fir's End THLE RG7 .... 31 K6
Firs Glen Rd FERN BH22 ... 380 C6
CHAM PO6 .... 375 K8
MOOR/WNTN BH9 .... 432 B8
VWD BH31 .... 356 D3
Firshill CHCH/BSGR BH23 .. 436 C7
Firside Rd WIMB BH21 ..... 429 G4
Firs La ODIM RG29 .... 108 B6
PSTN BH14 .... 445 J4
First Av CHAM PO6 .... 375 K8
CHAM PO6 .... 375 K8
EMRTH PO10 .... 379 H8
HAV PO9 .... 17 J3
HORN PO8 .... 328 B5
THLE RG7 .... 41 M6
WSHM SO15 .... 342 B1
First Marine Av
 NMIL/BTOS BH25 .... 452 E1
First St FAWY SO45 .... 368 C8
STHA RG19 .... 38 D3
Firs Wy DEAN RG23 .... 104 A1
Firth Cl THLE RG7 .... 42 E8
Fir Tree Av HASM GU27 ... 228 A2
Fir Tree Cl ELGH SO50 .... 321 H1
RGWD BH24 .... 381 H6
Firtree Crs LYMN SO41 .... 438 D5
Firtree Gdns HORN PO8 ... 353 C5
Fir Tree Hl HISD PO11 ... 333 L2
Fir Tree La ELGH SO50 .... 321 G1
NWBY RG14 .... 26 A4
Fir Tree Rd HISD PO11 .... 425 A6
Firtree Wy FLET GU13 .... 89 G8
ITCH SO19 .... 344 F3
Fir Vale Rd BMTH BH1 .... 22 F5
Firway CSHT GU26 .... 203 H3
Firwood Cl CHFD SO53 .... 265 H8
Firwood Dr CBLY GU15 .... 70 F3
Fisgard Rd GPORT PO12 ... 421 M1
Fisher Cl FHAM/STUB PO14 . 395 M5
Fisherman's Av SBNE BH6 .. 449 G4
Fisherman's La THLE RG7 .. 41 K1
The Fishermen
 EMRTH PO10 .... 378 E8
Fishermans Wk HISD PO11 . 426 C6
Fishermen's Cl ALDT GU11 . 113 H5
Fisher Rd LSOL/BMARY PO13 . 397 G5
Fishers Gv CHAM PO6 ..... 400 C1
Fishers Hl FHAM PO15 .... 371 L6
Fisher's Rd TOTT SO40 ... 341 L2
Fishery La HISD PO11 .... 426 A6
Fishlake Mdw ROMY SO51 . 262 E7
Fiske Cl KEMP RG22 ...... 104 B4
Fitzgerald Cl HLER SO31 .. 347 G8
Fitzharris Av
 MOOR/WNTN BH9 .... 447 M1
Fitzherbert Rd CHAM PO6 . 400 B1
Fitzherbert Sp CHAM PO6 . 400 C1
Fitzherbert St PSEA PO1 .. 423 C1
Fitzhugh Pl WSHM SO15 .. 343 K1
Fitzhugh St SHAM SO14 ... 12 E2
Fitzmaurice Rd
 CHCH/BSGR BH23 .... 434 C8
Fitzpain Cl BWD BH11 .... 431 H5
Fitzpain Rd FERN BH22 ... 406 B6
Fitzpatrick Ct CHAM PO6 . 375 H7
Fitzroy Cl ROWN SO16 ... 318 C1
Fitzroy Dr FLET GU13 ... 88 C7
Fitzwilliam Av
 FHAM/STUB PO14 .... 395 L6
Fitzwilliam Cl BWD BH11 . 431 J5
Fitzworth Av UPTN BH16 . 444 B4
Fitzwygram Crs HAV PO9 . 16 E1
Five Acres Cl BOR GU35 .. 201 L3
Five Ash Rd ALTN GU34 ... 196 F4
Five Bells La STOK SO20 .. 184 D3
Five Bridges Rd WINC SO23 . 238 D5
Five Elms Dr ROMY SO51 . 291 G2
Fivefields Cl WINC SO23 . 11 L3
Fivefields Rd WINC SO23 . 11 L3
Five Heads Rd HORN PO8 . 327 M8
Five Post La GPORT PO12 . 421 M2
Flaghead Chine Rd CCLF BH13 . 457 H3
Flaghead Rd CCLF BH13 ... 457 K1
Flag Staff Gn GPORT PO12 . 421 M2
Flag Staff Sq STHA RG19 .. 27 H7
Flag Wk HORN PO8 .... 352 D3
Flambard Av
 CHCH/BSGR BH23 .... 434 C8
Flambard Rd PSTN BH14 .. 446 B6
Flamborough Cl ROWN SO16 . 317 J4
Flamingo Ct
 FHAM/PORC PO16 .... 373 K8
Flanders Rd HEND SO30 .. 321 C6
The Flashett RSAL SP5 ... 207 G2
Flathouse Rd PSEA PO1 ... 423 G1

The Flats BLKW GU17 ...... 69 L4
Flatt Rd RCCH PO18 .... 379 M8
Flaxfield Ct BSTK RG21 ... 4 D8
Flaxfield Rd BSTK RG21 ... 4 D8
Flaxfields End FBDG SP6 .. 309 K7
Flazen Cl BWD BH11 ...... 431 H5
Flecker Cl NTHA RG18 .... 26 F3
Fleet Cl LSOL/BMARY PO13 . 397 H7
Fleet End Bottom HLER SO31 . 370 D8
Fleet End Rd HLER SO31 .. 370 D8
Fleetend Cl HAV PO9 ..... 377 J2
Fleet Hl EWKG RG40 ...... 47 M6
Fleet Rd EWKG RG40 ...... 47 L6
FARN GU14 .... 89 M4
FLET GU13 .... 88 E7
HTWY RG27 .... 87 M3
Fleets Cl PLE BH15 ...... 445 H2
Fleetwood Av FAWY SO45 . 26 A3
Fleming Av NBAD SO52 ... 291 M4
Fleming Cl FARN GU14 ... 91 G2
RAND SP11 .... 92 E6
WHIT RG2 .... 47 H1
Fleming Pl ROMY SO51 ... 290 E1
RWIN SO21 .... 266 E7
Fleming Rd WINW SO22 .. 214 B5
ROWN SO16 .... 319 J4
Flensburg Cl AND SP10 .. 118 C5
Fletcher Cl BSTK RG21 .. 104 E4
FAWY SO45 .... 367 H5
Fletcher Rd NBH10 ...... 432 B5
Fletchers Fld LIPH GU30 . 226 B5
Fletchwood La TOTT SO40 . 340 F2
Fletchwood Rd TOTT SO40 . 340 F2
Fleuret Cl FAWY SO45 ... 367 L8
Flexford Cl CHFD SO53 .. 264 F7
KSCL RG20 .... 56 C5
Flexford La LYMN SO41 .. 439 C2
Flexford Rd NBAD SO52 . 292 B2
Flint Cl AND SP10 ...... 8 B9
ITCH SO19 .... 345 J4
Flint La RAND SP11 .... 94 C8
Flint St SSEA PO5 ...... 21 K9
Floating Bridge Rd SHAM SO14 . 13 L6
The Flood RSAL SP5 .... 206 E1
Floral Farm WIMB BH21 . 404 E6
Floral Wy AND SP10 ... 8 C8
 NTHA RG18 .... 27 G3
 RAND SP11 .... 8 A9
Floreat Gdns NWBY RG14 . 2 A7
Florence Cl ROMY SO51 . 289 G6
 YTLY GU46 .... 68 F2
Florence Ct AND SP10 .. 119 G5
Florence Portal Cl WHCH RG28 . 123 G3
Florence Rd BOSC BH5 .. 448 D4
FLET GU13 .... 111 G2
ITCH SO19 .... 344 C6
PSTN BH14 .... 446 B4
SHST GU47 .... 70 B1
SSEA PO5 .... 21 K9
Florence Wy CHAM RG24 . 82 B8
Florentine Wy WVILLE PO7 . 352 E8
 WVILLE PO7 .... 376 C5
The Florins HLER SO31 . 370 E7
Floriston Gdns
 NMIL/BTOS BH25 .... 438 B5
Floud La PSF GU32 ..... 272 A3
Flowerdown Cl TOTT SO40 . 316 B8
Flower La ROMY SO51 ... 288 C2
Flowers Cl HLER SO31 .. 369 J5
Flume Rd FAWY SO45 ... 393 G4
Flushards LYMN SO41 ... 440 D5
Focus Wy AND SP10 .... 119 J7
Foden Rd ALDT GU11 ... 6 F3
Fokerham Rd STHA RG19 . 27 J6
Foldsgate Cl LYND SO43 . 363 K2
Folkestone Rd HSEA PO3 . 423 L1
Folly Cl FLET GU13 ..... 110 F1
Folly Farm La RGWD BH24 . 382 E3
Folly Fld BPWT SO32 .. 323 J1
Folly Hl FNM GU9 ..... 134 D3
Folly La EPSF GU31 ... 275 L5
 TADY RG26 .... 64 A4
 THLE RG7 .... 31 J3
Folly La North FNM GU9 . 134 E1
Folly La South FNM GU9 . 134 D2
Folly Rd HUNG RG17 ... 33 M2
The Folly NWBY RG14 .. 3 G8
Font Cl FHAM/STUB PO14 . 371 G5
Fontley Rd FHAM PO15 . 371 L5
Fontmell Cl TOTT SO40 . 316 B7
Fontmell Dr ALTN GU34 . 176 E6
Fontwell Cl TOTT SO40 . 316 B7
Fontwell Gdns ELGH SO50 . 321 J1
Fontwell Ms HORN PO8 .. 352 F7
Fontwell Rd NWBY RG14 . 3 H8
 SSEA PO5 .... 21 J7
 SSEA PO5 .... 21 J7
Foord Rd HEND SO30 .. 345 M4
Football Gn LYND SO43 . 339 G5
Footner Cl ROMY SO51 .. 263 H6
Footners La CHCH/BSGR BH23 . 435 G6
Forbes Cha SHST GU47 . 70 A1
Forbes Rd ROWN SO16 . 317 K3
Forbes Rd WINC SO23 .. 191 G8
Forbury La HUNG RG17 . 34 E8
Forbury Rd SSEA PO5 .. 21 J3
Ford Av CHFD SO53 .... 293 J4
Ford Cl FERN BH22 .... 406 D1
Fordingbridge Rd ENEY PO4 . 423 M5
 FBDG SP6 .... 333 M1
Fordington Av WINW SO22 . 10 B6
Fordington Rd WINW SO22 . 10 C6
Ford La FERN BH22 .... 406 D1
 RFNM GU10 .... 158 D2
 ODIM RG29 .... 130 F1
 THLE RG7 .... 46 D4
Ford Rd GPORT PO12 .. 421 K2
The Forehead THLE RG7 . 44 C4
Foreland Cl CHCH/BSGR BH23 . 434 B4
Foreland Rd HISD PO11 . 426 A6
Foreland Rd UPTN BH16 . 444 A4
Foreman Pk ASHV GU12 . 113 L6
Foreman Rd ASHV GU12 . 113 L7
Foreshore North FAWY SO45 . 392 F7
Foreshore South FAWY SO45 . 392 F7
Forest Av HORN PO8 ... 352 D5

Forest Cl BPWT SO32 .... 323 K5
CHCH/BSGR BH23 .... 436 B7
CHFD SO53 .... 265 H8
HORN PO8 .... 352 D5
NBAD SO52 .... 291 K3
TADY RG26 .... 41 H7
VWD BH31 .... 357 H4
Forest Cnr LISS GU33 .. 248 F1
Forest Court Hills
 RGWD BH24 .... 383 H2
Forestdale GSHT GU26 .. 204 A5
Forest Dean FARN GU14 . 89 H4
Forest Dr RG24 .... 83 L4
RFNM GU10 .... 158 F4
NTID SP9 .... 114 F1
Forest Edge FAWY SO45 . 392 E5
Forest Edge Cl RGWD BH24 . 381 H3
Forest Edge Dr RGWD BH24 . 381 H3
Forest Edge Rd RGWD BH24 . 383 J3
Forest End FLET GU13 .. 110 E2
 WVILLE PO7 .... 376 B1
Forest End Rd SHST GU47 . 49 J7
Forester Rd BPWT SO32 . 324 F7
Foresters Ga FAWY SO45 . 418 C1
Foresters Rd FAWY SO45 . 392 D6
Foresters Wy CWTH GU45 . 50 C1
Forest Front FAWY SO45 . 367 K8
Forest Gdns BPWT SO32 . 323 K5
 LYND SO43 .... 363 K3
Forest Ga FAWY SO45 .. 418 D1
Forest Gate Gdns LYMN SO41 . 440 B7
Forest Gld RFNM GU10 . 158 A5
Forest Glade Cl BROC SO42 . 387 H7
Forest Hall BROC SO42 . 387 L7
Forest Hills CBLY GU15 . 70 E4
Forest Hills Dr WEND SO18 . 319 K5
Forest Hill Wy FAWY SO45 . 367 K6
Forestlake Av RGWD BH24 . 383 H2
Forest La FAWY SO45 ... 391 M2
 BOR GU35 .... 201 M2
 RAND SP11 .... 143 L2
 RGWD BH24 .... 383 J2
 TADY RG26 .... 62 A2
 VWD BH31 .... 356 C1
 WHAM PO17 .... 348 F8
Forest Lane Ct LIPH GU30 . 226 D4
Forest Md WVILLE PO7 .. 351 K5
Forest Meadow FAWY SO45 . 367 L8
Forest Oak Dr
 NMIL/BTOS BH25 .... 437 L3
Forest Park Rd BROC SO42 . 387 J6
Forest Pines
 NMIL/BTOS BH25 .... 437 L4
Forest Ri CHCH/BSGR BH23 . 436 B6
 LISS GU33 .... 248 F2
Forest Rd BPWT SO32 .. 323 L5
 CCLF BH13 .... 446 F6
 CHCH/BSGR BH23 ...... 410 C3
 CHFD SO53 .... 265 J8
 CWTH GU45 .... 49 M3
 FBDG SP6 .... 285 J4
 FERN BH22 .... 380 D5
 BOR GU35 .... 201 J7
 LISS GU33 .... 248 E1
 RGWD BH24 .... 384 D3
 RSAL SP5 .... 287 J8
 WVILLE PO7 .... 350 E4
Forestside Av HAV PO9 . 377 L3
Forestside Gdns RGWD BH24 . 359 G7
The Forestside VWD BH31 . 357 H3
Forest Vw BROC SO42 .. 387 H7
 NMIL/BTOS BH25 .... 437 H3
 SHAM SO14 .... 12 F5
Forest View Dr WIMB BH21 . 405 L2
Forest View Rd
 MOOR/WNTN BH9 .... 432 E5
Forest Wy CHCH/BSGR BH23 . 436 B7
 LSOL/BMARY PO13 ...... 397 H6
 LYMN SO41 .... 439 H7
 TOTT SO40 .... 315 M6
 WIMB BH21 .... 405 L3
Forge Cl FNM GU9 ..... 135 G5
 HLER SO31 .... 345 L7
 TADY RG26 .... 63 M6
Forge La ALDT GU11 ... 112 C2
Forge Rd FAWY SO45 ... 418 D1
 BOR GU35 .... 175 F8
Forneth Gdns FHAM PO15 . 371 M8
Forster Rd SHAM SO14 . 343 L1
Forsyth Gdns NBNE BH10 . 432 A7
Forsythia Cl HAV PO9 .. 377 M4
 HEND SO30 .... 321 G8
Fort Cumberland Rd
 ENEY PO4 .... 424 B5
Fortescue Rd
 BKME/WDN BH12 .... 446 C1
 TWDS BH3 .... 447 M2
Fort Fareham Rd
 FHAM/STUB PO14 .... 396 D2
Forth Cl CHFD SO53 .... 293 G3
 FARN GU14 .... 90 A2
 FHAM/STUB PO14 .... 396 D2
Forties Cl FHAM/STUB PO14 . 395 M4
Forton Rd GPORT PO12 . 18 E1
 PSEA PO1 .... 423 J2
Fort Rd GPORT PO12 .. 18 C9
 ITCH SO19 .... 344 C5
Fortrose Cl SHST GU47 . 70 A1
Fortunes Wy CHAM PO6 . 376 D7
Forty Acre La EPSF GU31 . 304 A5
Forward Dr LYMN SO41 . 440 A6
Fosseway CWTH GU45 .. 49 J3
Fossewood Dr CBLY GU15 . 51 G8
Foster Cl FHAM/STUB PO14 . 396 A4
Foster Rd GPORT PO12 . 18 D5
 PSEA PO1 .... 423 H2
Foul La ALTN GU34 .... 196 E1
Founders Wy
 LSOL/BMARY PO13 ...... 397 H6
Foundry La HASM GU27 . 228 D2
 WSHM SO15 .... 318 A8
Foundry Rd RAND SP11 . 142 B4
 RSAL SP5 .... 285 J1
Fountains Cl CHAM RG24 . 82 F7
Fountain St PSEA PO1 .. 21 G1
Fountain Wy
 CHCH/BSGR BH23 .... 450 A2
Four Acre HEND SO30 .. 346 E2

Four Acre Coppice
HTWY RG27 .... 86 B6 🔢
HTWY RG27 .... 86 B7 🔢
Four Lanes Cl *CHAM* RG24 ...... 83 M5
Four Oaks *KSCL* RG20 .... 56 C2
Four Posts Hl *WSHM* SO15..... 12 C1
Fourshells Cl *FAWY* SO45 .... 392 D6 🔢
Fourth Av *CHAM* PO6 .... 375 J8
HAV PO9........................... 17 J3
Fourth St *PSEA* PO1 .... 423 K2
Four Wells Rd *WIMB* BH21..... 404 E1
Fowey Cl *CHFD* SO53 .... 293 C6
The Fowey *FAWY* SO45......... 392 C6
Fowler Av *FARN* GU14......... 90 E6
Fowler Rd *FARN* GU14.......... 90 C6
Fowler's Rd *ALDT* GU11 .... 112 F3
HEND SO30........................ 321 G8
Fowler's Wk *NBAD* SO52 ...... 292 C1
Foxborough *THLE* RG7 .... 46 A2
Foxbury Cl *FAWY* SO45 .... 367 L6
Foxbury Gv *FHAM/PORC* PO16 . 397 M1 🔢
Foxbury La *EMRTH* PO10....... 379 G4
LSOL/BMARY PO13.............. 397 H4
Foxbury Rd *RCWD* BH24 ...... 381 K7
Fox Cl *ELGH* SO50 .... 294 E6
THLE RG7 .... 31 K5
Foxcombe Cl *BPWT* SO32...... 323 M2
Foxcote *EWKG* RG40.......... 48 D1
Foxcote Gdns
NMIL/BTOS BH25 .... 437 K5 🔢
Foxcott Cl *ITCH* SO19 .... 344 D8 🔢
Foxcotte Cl *AND* SP10 .... 118 C6
Foxcotte La *RAND* SP11 ...... 118 A6
Foxcott Gv *HAV* PO9 .... 377 K3
Foxcroft Dr *FAWY* SO45 ...... 391 M5
WIMB BH21........................ 404 E1
Foxdown *OVTN* RG25 .... 100 F6
Foxdown Cl *CBLY* GU15 .... 70 D7
Fox Dr *YTLY* GU46 .... 69 C1
Foxes Cl *VWD* BH31............ 356 D3
WVILLE PO7....................... 376 C2
Foxes La *ROMY* SO51 .... 288 E4
Fox Fld *LYMN* SO41 .... 439 H7
Foxglade *FAWY* SO45 .... 418 D1 🔢
Foxglove Cl *KEMP* RG22 ...... 126 F1
Foxglove Dr *BOR* GU35 .... 201 K6 🔢
Foxglove Pl
NMIL/BTOS BH25 .... 438 B4 🔢
Foxgloves *FHAM/PORC* PO16 ... 15 L1
UPTN BH16........................ 444 A1 🔢
The Foxglove *HEND* SO30 .... 346 B3 🔢
Foxglove Wy *NTHA* RG18..... 27 H3
Foxhayes La *FAWY* SO45 ..... 418 D1
Fox Heath *FARN* GU14......... 89 M5
Foxhill Crs *CBLY* GU15........ 51 L8
Foxhills *TOTT* SO40 .... 341 G4
VWD BH31........................ 356 F2 🔢
Foxhills Cl *TOTT* SO40 .... 341 G5
Fox Hills La *ASHV* GU12...... 113 M5
Foxholes Rd *PLE* BH15........ 445 L4
SBNE BH6.......................... 449 L4
Foxhunter Wy *STHA* RG19.... 26 C5 🔢
Foxhurst Rd *ASHV* GU12 ...... 113 K3
Foxlands *FAWY* SO45 .... 418 D1 🔢
Fox La *DEAN* RG23............. 103 H5
WINW SO22........................ 238 B3
HTWY RG27........................ 48 C8
WIMB BH21 .... 405 G3
Foxlea Gdns *GPORT* PO12 .... 421 M1 🔢
Foxley Cl *BLKW* GU17 .... 69 M3
Foxley Dr *HSEA* PO3 .... 399 M4
Foxmoor Cl *DEAN* RG23 ...... 103 G5
Fox Pond La *LYMN* SO41 ..... 440 A6
Fox Rd *HASM* GU27 .... 228 B2
RFNM GU10........................ 158 F2
Foxs Furlong *CHAM* RG24 .... 84 A4
Fox's La *KSCL* RG20 .... 59 H7
Fox's Wk *FAWY* SO45 .... 418 D1 🔢
Foxtail Dr *FAWY* SO45 .... 367 K7
Fox Wy *RFNM* GU10 .... 111 G8
Foxwood *FARN* GU14 .... 89 H5 🔢
Foxwood Av
CHCH/BSGR BH23............. 450 E3
Fox Yd *FNM* GU9 .... 134 E6 🔢
Foxy Paddock *FAWY* SO45 ... 418 D1 🔢
Foye La *FLET* GU13 .... 111 G3
Foy Gdns *HLER* SO31.......... 370 A7
Foyle Pk *BSTK* RG21 .... 105 G6
Foyle Rd *CHFD* SO53 .... 293 C6
Frampton Cl *NMIL/BTOS* BH25 .. 438 A3
RWIN SO21 .... 266 E7
Frampton Pl *RCWD* BH24 .... 382 E1 🔢
Frampton Rd
MOOR/WNTN BH9 .... 432 C8
Frampton Wy *TOTT* SO40...... 341 K2
WINC SO23......................... 215 H1
France Hill Dr *CBLY* GU15..... 70 F3
Frances Rd *BMTH* BH1 .... 23 K4
BSTK RG21......................... 104 F4
WVILLE PO7....................... 376 B5
The Frances *NTHA* RG18...... 27 C4
Francis Av *BWD* BH11.......... 431 H5
ENEY PO4.......................... 423 K5
Francis Cl *LSOL/BMARY* PO13 .. 420 E3
Francis Gdns *WINC* SO23 ..... 11 J2
Francis Pl *FHAM/STUB* PO14 .. 396 B6
Francis Rd *BKME/WDN* BH12 .. 446 D5
HORN PO8.......................... 328 B5
Frankland Crs *PSTN* BH14 .... 446 D5
Frankland Ter *EMRTH* PO10 .. 378 E8 🔢
Franklin Av *HTWY* RG27 ...... 87 G1 🔢
TADY RG26......................... 41 K7
Franklin Rd *LSOL/BMARY* PO13.. 421 G1
NMIL/BTOS BH25 .... 438 A4
RWIN SO21........................ 266 F1 🔢
Franklyn Av *ITCH* SO19....... 344 B5
Franklyn Cl *UPTN* BH16....... 444 A1
Frankston Rd *SBNE* BH6....... 449 H4
Frarydene *EMRTH* PO10 ...... 379 H4
Fraser Cl *CHAM* RG24 .... 106 C2
ROWN SO16....................... 317 L2
Fraser Gdns *EMRTH* PO10 .... 379 J6
Fraser Md *SHST* GU47......... 70 B2
Fraser Rd *BKME/WDN* BH12 .. 431 K7
HAV PO9............................ 16 B2
LSOL/BMARY PO13 .... 397 G4
NEND PO2 .... 398 F6 🔢

Froxfield Gdns
FHAM/PORC PO16 .... 374 A7
Froxfield Rd *HAV* PO9......... 377 M3
Froyle Cl *HAV* PO9............. 377 M3
Froyle La *ODIM* RG29 .... 130 F5
Fry Cl *FAWY* SO45 .... 392 D6
HLER SO31......................... 369 L4
Fryer Cl *BWD* BH11............ 431 M3
Fryern Cl *CHFD* SO53 .... 293 K2
Fryern Court Rd *FBDG* SP6 ... 309 K4
Fryer's Copse *WIMB* BH21 .... 405 C2
Fryers Rd *WIMB* BH21 .... 356 C8
Fry's La *BPWT* SO32 .... 299 J4
LYMN SO41........................ 439 H7
YTLY GU46........................ 69 H1
Fugelmere Rd *FLET* GU13 ..... 89 H6
Fulbrook Wy *ODIM* RG29..... 108 C8
Fulflood Rd *HAV* PO9.......... 377 J3
Fuller Cl *STHA* RG19........... 27 J6
Fullers La *KSCL* RG20 .... 55 L1
Fullers Rd *RFNM* GU10 .... 158 A4
Fullers V *BOR* GU35 .... 202 C3
Fullerton Cl *HAV* PO9 .... 377 M3 🔢
ITCH SO19......................... 344 D8
Fullerton Rd *LYMN* SO41 ..... 440 A4
RAND SP11........................ 142 B8
Fullerton Wy *TADY* RG26..... 61 M1
Fulmar Cl *KEMP* RG22 .... 126 E1
ROWN SO16....................... 318 A3
Fulmar Dr *FAWY* SO45........ 367 M6
Fulmar Rd *CHCH/BSGR* BH23.. 450 F3
Fulmer Wk *HORN* PO8......... 352 C4
HORN PO8.......................... 352 C4
Fulwood Av *BWD* BH11........ 431 J3
Funtington Rd *NEND* PO2 ..... 399 K8
Funtley Hl *FHAM/PORC* PO16 .. 372 C4
Funtley Rd *FHAM* PO15 .... 372 B3
Furdies *WVILLE* PO7 .... 351 J4 🔢
Furley Cl *WINC* SO23 .... 11 K7
The Furlong *RCWD* BH24 ..... 382 D1
Furneaux Gdns
FHAM/PORC PO16 .... 15 J1
Furnell Rd *PLE* BH15.......... 445 J1
Furness Rd *SSEA* PO5 .... 423 H7 🔢
Furniss Wy *HISD* PO11........ 425 H4
Furnston Gv *EMRTH* PO10..... 379 J7
Furse Cl *CBLY* GU15 .... 71 L4
Furse Hill Rd *NTID* SP9 .... 114 E3
Further Vell-Mead *FLET* GU13 .. 110 D4
Fury Wy *FHAM/STUB* PO14 ... 395 M5
Furzebrook Cl *CFDH* BH17..... 430 C6
Furze Cl *ASHV* GU12 .... 113 K1
Furze Cft *NMIL/BTOS* BH25 ... 437 L7
Furzedale Gdns *FAWY* SO45 .. 367 M7
Furzedale Pk *FAWY* SO45 ..... 367 M7
Furzedown Crs *HAV* PO9 ...... 377 L3
Furzedown La *RAND* SP11..... 140 D3
Furzedown Ms *FAWY* SO45 ... 367 M7 🔢
Furzedown Rd *PTSW* SO17 .... 318 F6
STOK SO20 .... 210 F7
Furze Dr *RAND* SP11 .... 115 J2
Furzehall Av *FHAM/PORC* PO16 .. 15 L1
Furze Hill Crs *CWTH* RG45 ... 49 M4
Furze Hill Dr *PSTN* BH14...... 446 B7
Furze Hill Rd *BOR* GU35....... 202 F4
Furzelands Rd *WIMB* BH21 ... 356 C8
Furze La *ENEY* PO4............. 424 B3
Furzeley Rd *WVILLE* PO7 ..... 351 K6
Furze Meadow *EPSF* GU31 .... 277 K8
Furzen La *OVTN* RG25......... 152 A1
Furze Rd *ITCH* SO19 .... 344 E3
TADY RG26........................ 41 M8
Furze Vale Rd *BOR* GU35 ..... 202 E4
Furze Wy *HORN* PO8........... 352 F4
Furzey Cl *FAWY* SO45 .... 392 D7
Furzey Rd *UPTN* BH16......... 444 A2
Furzley La *ROMY* SO51 .... 314 C3
Furzley Rd *ROMY* SO51 .... 314 C3
Fushia Cl *HAV* PO9............. 377 G2
Fushia Gdns *ROWN* SO16 .... 318 C6 🔢
Fuzzy Dro *KEMP* RG22 .... 103 L8
Fyeford Cl *ROWN* SO16........ 317 L2
Fyfield Cl *BLKW* GU17 .... 70 A1
FHAM PO15 .... 347 G8
Fyfield La *RAND* SP11 .... 116 F6
Fyfield Rd *RAND* SP11 .... 116 F6
STHA RG19........................ 27 G6
Fyfield Wy *WINW* SO22 ...... 214 A3
RAND SP11........................ 115 J2
Fylingdales *STHA* RG19 ...... 26 F6
Fylingdales Cl *KEMP* RG22 ... 103 M5
Fyning St *PSEA* PO1 .... 423 H7

G

Gables Cl *ASHV* GU12.......... 113 K3
FARN GU14......................... 90 D4
Gables Ct *ROWN* SO16 .... 318 E3 🔢
Gables Rd *FLET* GU13 .... 110 E4
Gables Wy *STHA* RG19 .... 27 L6
Gabriel Dr *CBLY* GU15 .... 71 L4
The Gabriels *NWBY* RG14 ..... 37 G2
Gaffney Cl *ALDT* GU11 .... 113 G1 🔢
Gage Cl *CHAM* RG24 .... 105 L1
TOTT SO40......................... 342 E6
Gainsborough Av
NMIL/BTOS BH25 .... 437 M3
Gainsborough Cl *CBLY* GU15 . 71 J1 🔢
FARN GU14........................ 91 G6 🔢
Gainsborough Ms
FHAM/STUB PO14............ 371 K8 🔢
Gainsborough Rd *BSTK* RG21 . 105 H6
LTDN BH7.......................... 448 E1
RCWD BH24 .... 381 J3
Gainsford Rd *ITCH* SO19 ..... 344 C5
Gain's Rd *ENEY* PO4 .... 21 L7
Galahad Cl *AND* SP10 .... 118 F6
Galaxie Rd *HORN* PO8.......... 352 F4
Gale Moor Av *GPORT* PO12 ... 421 H5
Gallagher's Md *AND* SP10 .... 118 A8
Galleon Cl *HLER* SO31......... 370 D7 🔢
Galley La *STHA* RG19.......... 39 G7
The Gallops *FHAM/STUB* PO14 .. 371 H6
The Gallop *YTLY* GU46........ 69 G1

Gallop Wy *BKME/WDN* BH12 .. 447 H1
KEMP RG22........................ 104 A5
Galloway Cl *FARN* GU14....... 89 H4
Galloway Rd *PLE* BH15........ 444 C5
Gallows Dr *FERN* BH22........ 406 B7
Gallwey Rd *ALDT* GU11 .... 112 C5
Gally Hill Rd *FLET* GU13 ...... 110 E4
Galsworthy Rd *TOTT* SO40 .... 341 H1
Galt Rd *CHAM* PO6 .... 376 B8
Gamble Cl *ITCH* SO19.......... 344 D4
Gambledown La *ROMY* SO51 .. 260 D3
Gamblins La *BPWT* SO32 ...... 323 L8
Gander Dr *CHAM* RG24 .... 82 B8
Gangbridge La *RAND* SP11 .... 97 J5
Ganger Farm La *ROMY* SO51 .. 263 H6
Ganger Rd *ROMY* SO51 .... 263 H6 🔢
Gannet Cl *FAWY* SO45 .... 367 M6
KEMP RG22........................ 126 E1
ROWN SO16 .... 318 A3
The Gannets
FHAM/STUB BH3.............. 395 M6
Garbett Rd *WINC* SO23 .... 11 L7
Garbetts Wy *RFNM* GU10..... 136 B2
Garbitts La *EPSF* GU31 .... 277 L5
Garden City *FAWY* SO45 ...... 366 E2
Garden Cl *FARN* GU14 .... 90 B6
HISD PO11 .... 425 K5
HTWY RG27........................ 85 L7 🔢
KSCL RG20......................... 59 J6 🔢
LYND SO43........................ 363 J3
NMIL/BTOS BH25 .... 437 L7
OVTN RG25........................ 151 G7
Garden Close La *NWBY* RG14 .. 37 G4
Gardeners Gn *NTID* SP9 ...... 138 C1
Gardener's Hill Rd *RFNM* GU10.. 158 E1
Gardeners La *ROMY* SO51 .... 289 L2
Garden-lane *RGWD* BH24 .... 381 J5 🔢
Garden La *SSEA* PO5 .... 21 G6
WINC SO23........................ 11 H7
Garden Ms *HLER* SO31 .... 370 A7
Garden Rd *RGWD* BH24 .... 384 D6
Gardens Crs *PSTN* BH14 ...... 446 A8
Gardens Rd *PSTN* BH14 .... 446 A8
The Gardens *HAV* PO9 .... 17 K6
RFNM GU10........................ 136 C1
WVILLE PO7....................... 352 C8
Garden Wk *FERN* BH22........ 406 C1 🔢
Gardiner Cl *TOTT* SO40 .... 342 E6
Gardner Rd *CHCH/BSGR* BH23 .. 434 C8
FHAM/STUB PO14 .... 395 K1
RGWD BH24........................ 382 C2
Garendon Ct *FBDG* SP6 ...... 309 K6 🔢
Garfield Av *BMTH* BH1 .... 448 C1
Garfield Cl *BPWT* SO32 .... 297 H8
Garfield Rd *BPWT* SO32 .... 297 H8
CBLY GU15......................... 70 F3
HLER SO31......................... 368 E2
ITCH SO19......................... 344 C1
NEND PO2 .... 399 H8
Garford Crs *NWBY* RG14 ..... 25 C8
Garland Av *EMRTH* PO10 ..... 378 D5
Garland Rd *PLE* BH15.......... 445 J4
Garlands Cl *THLE* RG7 .... 31 K6
Garnet Fld *YTLY* GU46........ 68 D3
Garnet Rd *BOR* GU35 .... 201 K6
Garnett Cl *FHAM/STUB* PO14.. 396 A4
Garnier Pk *WHAM* PO17 ...... 348 E4
Garnier Rd *WINC* SO23 .... 238 F3
Garnier St *PSEA* PO1 .... 21 K1
Garnock Rd *ITCH* SO19 .... 344 B6
Garratt Cl *HEND* SO30 .... 321 H6
Garrett Cl *ITCH* SO19 .... 344 E7
KSCL RG20......................... 59 H5
Garrick Gdns *ITCH* SO19 ..... 344 A6
Garrick Wy *FRIM* GU16 .... 91 H2
Garrison Hl *BPWT* SO32 ...... 299 G2
Garrow Dr *LYMN* SO41 .... 440 C3
Garsdale Cl *BWD* BH11........ 431 L2
Garsons Rd *EMRTH* PO10..... 379 H8
Garston Cl *PSF* GU32 .... 273 J8
Garston Mede *STOK* SO20 .... 165 M4
Garstons Cl *FHAM/STUB* PO14.. 371 L8
Garstons Rd *FHAM/STUB* PO14.. 371 K8
Gar St *WINC* SO23 .... 10 F8
Garth Cl *FNM* GU9 .... 158 D1 🔢
RGWD BH24........................ 381 J4
Garth Rd *THLE* RG7 .... 43 K3
The Garth *ASHV* GU12 .... 113 J1
FARN GU14......................... 91 G4
Garton Rd *ITCH* SO19 .... 344 B5
Gascoigne La *NALR* SO24 ..... 220 C4
Gaskell Cl *ALTN* GU34 .... 177 H2
Gaston La *ALTN* GU34 .... 198 D5
ODIM RG29........................ 130 E2
Gatcombe *HLER* SO31.......... 369 G4
Gatcombe Av *HSEA* PO3....... 399 K6
Gatcombe Dr *NEND* PO2 ...... 399 K5
Gatcombe Gdns
FHAM/STUB PO14............ 371 M8
WEND SO18........................ 319 M6 🔢
Gatehouse Rd
FHAM/PORC PO16 .... 397 L1
Gate Hyde *WINC* SO23 .... 11 G5 🔢
Gatekeeper Cl *WINC* SO23 ... 11 M7
The Gates *FARN* GU14 .... 89 H4
Gatwick Cl *ROWN* SO16 ...... 317 M4
Gaulter Cl *HAV* PO9 .... 17 G1
Gauvain Cl *ALTN* GU34......... 176 F6
Gavan St *ITCH* SO19............ 345 H3
G Av *FAWY* SO45................ 392 C4
Gawaine Cl *AND* SP10 .... 118 F4 🔢
Gaylyn Wy *FHAM/STUB* PO14 .. 371 M8
Gaywood Dr *NWBY* RG14...... 3 L1
Gaza Av *BROC* SO42 .... 416 A2
Gazing La *ROMY* SO51 .... 288 D5
Geale's Crs *ALTN* GU34 .... 176 F3
Geddes Wy *EPSF* GU31 .... 276 B4
Gemini Cl *ROWN* SO16 .... 317 L4
Geneva Av *SBNE* BH6.......... 449 J3
Genoa Cl *LYMN* SO41 .... 440 A7
Genoa Ct *AND* SP10 .... 119 G5
Gentles La *LIPH* GU30 .... 202 D7
Gento Cl *HEND* SO30 .... 346 D5
Geoffrey Av *WVILLE* PO7 ..... 375 M6
Geoffrey Crs
FHAM/PORC PO16 .... 396 F2
George Byng Wy *NEND* PO2 .. 399 G8

George Curl Wy *ELGH* SO50 ... 319 L2 🔢
George Denyer Cl
HASM GU27...................... 228 F1 🔢
George Eyston Dr *WINW* SO22 .. 238 C2
George Gdns *ALDT* GU11 ...... 112 C5
Georgeham Rd *SHST* GU47 .... 50 A6 🔢
George Rd *FLET* GU13 .... 89 G7
LYMN SO41........................ 454 B8
George St *BSTK* RG21 .... 4 B8
ELGH SO50......................... 293 M8
GPORT PO12...................... 19 H2
KSCL RG20......................... 59 H6 🔢
PSEA PO1.......................... 423 J1
George Yd *AND* SP10 .... 9 J2
The George Yd *NALR* SO24 .... 218 C2
Georgia Cl *AND* SP10 .... 8 B7
Georgia Gdns *TADY* RG26 ..... 42 B8
Georgia La *RAND* SP11 .... 140 D7
Georgian Cl *CBLY* GU15........ 71 H1
RGWD BH24........................ 358 C6
Gerald Rd *TWDS* BH3.......... 447 M2
Gerald Sq *ALTN* GU34.......... 176 F2
Gerard Crs *ITCH* SO19 .... 345 H2
Germaine Cl *CHCH/BSGR* BH23.. 436 D5
German Rd *TADY* RG26......... 63 M6
Gershwin Rd *KEMP* RG22 ..... 104 B5
Gervis Crs *PSTN* BH14 .... 445 M4
Gervis Pl *BMTH* BH1 .... 22 E6
Gervis Rd *BMTH* BH1 .... 23 H4
Gibbet La *CBLY* GU15.......... 71 K7
Gibbons Cl *SHST* GU47 .... 69 M6
Gibbs Cl *EWKG* RG40.......... 48 B3
Gibbs' La *BOR* GU35 .... 200 F5
Gibbs Rd *SHAM* SO14 .... 12 F7
Gibbs Wy *YTLY* GU46 .... 68 E6
Gibraltar Cl *FHAM* PO15 ...... 14 A3
Gibraltar Rd *ENEY* PO4........ 424 B7
FHAM/STUB PO14............. 396 D7
Gibson Cl *FHAM* PO15 .... 371 J7
LSOL/BMARY PO13 .... 420 D2 🔢
Gibson Rd *CFDH* BH17........ 445 K4
Giddylake *WIMB* BH21 .... 404 A4
Gid La *ALTN* GU34.............. 156 A4
Giffard Dr *FARN* GU14......... 90 C2
Giffards Meadow *FNM* GU9... 135 H3
Gifford Cl *FHAM* PO15 .... 14 A5
Gilbard Ct *CHAM* RG24 .... 83 M5 🔢
Gilbert Cl *FBDG* SP6 .... 333 M2 🔢
LSOL/BMARY PO13 .... 397 H8
LYMN SO41........................ 440 B8
Gilbert Md *HISD* PO11......... 425 J2
Gilbert Rd *CHAR* BH8.......... 448 C1
FRIM GU16........................ 70 F7
Gilbert's Gn *NTID* SP9......... 138 D1 🔢
Gilberts Mead Cl *RAND* SP11 .. 142 A4 🔢
Gilbert St *NALR* SO24........... 220 C2
Gilbert Wy *WVILLE* PO7 .... 376 C3 🔢
Gilbert White Wy *ALTN* GU34.. 176 E1
Gilbury Ct *WEND* SO18 .... 319 K4 🔢
Gilchrist Gdns *HLER* SO31..... 394 A4
Giles Cl *FHAM/PORC* PO16 .... 15 K1
GPORT PO12...................... 421 L1
HEND SO30........................ 321 J7 🔢
Giles La *ROMY* SO51 .... 287 M1
RSAL SP5........................... 287 M1
Giles Rd *TADY* RG26........... 41 M1
Gilkicker Rd *GPORT* PO12 ..... 19 G5
Gillam Rd *NBNE* BH10......... 432 B8
Gillcrest *FHAM* PO15 .... 371 G4
Gillett Rd *BKME/WDN* BH12 .. 447 H4
Gilham's La *HASM* GU27 ...... 227 K2
Gillian Av *ASHV* GU12 .... 7 K7
Gillian Cl *ASHV* GU12 .... 7 L1
Gillies Dr *CHAM* RG24 .... 82 B2
The Gillies *FHAM/PORC* PO16 . 15 H6
Gillingham Cl *WINC* SO23 .... 215 H1
Gillingham Rd *LYMN* SO41 .... 454 C2
Gillman Rd *CHAM* PO6 .... 376 C4
Gilpin Cl *ITCH* SO19 .... 345 H4
LYMN SO41........................ 414 D2
Gilpin Hl *LYMN* SO41 .... 412 F6
Gilroy Cl *NWBY* RG14.......... 36 F7
Gins La *BROC* SO42 .... 417 H4
Girton Cl *FHAM/STUB* PO14 .. 371 G4
SHST GU47......................... 50 B6
Gisbourne Cl *WVILLE* PO7 .... 376 A5 🔢
Gitsham Gdns *WVILLE* PO7 .... 376 A5 🔢
Gladdis Rd *BWD* BH11......... 431 K5
Glade Cl *CHAM* RG24 .... 83 L4
Gladelands Cl *BDST* BH18 ... 429 J4 🔢
Gladelands Wy *BDST* BH18 ... 429 J4 🔢
The Glades *HLER* SO31......... 370 E6
The Glade *CHFD* SO53 .... 265 L1
FAWY SO45........................ 418 C2
FHAM PO15 .... 372 B2
FNM GU9........................... 135 G2
FRIM GU16........................ 91 J2
HISD PO11 .... 426 A4
NWBY RG14........................ 36 F7
RFNM GU10........................ 157 L2
RGWD BH24........................ 381 J2
WVILLE PO7....................... 352 F2
Gladiator Wy *FARN* GU14 .... 90 D2
Gladstone Cl *CHCH/BSGR* BH23.. 450 C2
Gladstone Gdns
FHAM/PORC PO16 .... 398 A1 🔢
Gladstone Rd
BKME/WDN BH12 .... 446 E5
GPORT PO12...................... 421 L1
ITCH SO19......................... 344 F6
LTDN BH7.......................... 448 E1
Gladstone Rd East *LTDN* BH7 .. 448 E1
Gladstone Rd West *BMTH* BH1.. 448 D1
Gladstone St *WINC* SO23 ..... 10 F7
Gladys Av *HORN* PO8 .... 352 L6
NEND PO2 .... 399 H4
Glaisdale *STHA* RG19.......... 26 F6
Glamis Av *NBNE* BH10......... 432 C2
Glamis Cl *DEAN* RG23 .... 102 F7
FRIM GU16........................ 91 J3
WVILLE PO7....................... 352 E4
Glamorgan Rd *HORN* PO8 .... 328 A4
Glasgow Rd *ENEY* PO4......... 423 M4
Glasslaw Rd *WEND* SO18 ..... 319 M2
Glasspool *WVILLE* PO7 .... 351 J7
Glastonbury Cl *CHAM* RG24 .. 4 D1
Glaston Hill Rd *HTWY* RG27 ... 47 L6
Glayshers Hl *BOR* GU35 ...... 202 D7

Gleadowe Av
CHCH/BSGR BH23 .... 449 L2
Glebe Cl ALTN GU34 .... 175 G2
HISD PO11 .... 425 J3
OVTN RG25 .... 126 C7
TADY RG26 .... 61 M1
Glebe Cnr WHAM PO17 .... 348 F5
Glebe Ct ELGH SO50 .... 295 J6
FLET GU13 .... 88 E7
HEND SO30 .... 321 M8
PTSW SO17 .... 318 F6
Glebe Dr LSOL/BMARY PO13 .... 397 G7
Glebefield Gdns CHAM PO6 .... 375 J8
Glebe Flds ALTN GU34 .... 175 G2
Glebefields LYMN SO41 .... 454 C3
NWBY RG14 .... 25 L3
Glebeland Rd CBLY GU15 .... 70 C4
Glebelands RAND SP11 .... 143 C6
STHA RG19 .... 26 F5
Glebe La DEAN RG23 .... 103 M4
HTWY RG27 .... 87 J3
KSCL RG20 .... 24 B3
RFNM GU10 .... 181 M3
RSAL SP5 .... 287 J4
BOR GU35 .... 202 B3
RFNM GU10 .... 133 J2
The Glebe BLKW GU17 .... 70 B4
FHAM/STUB PO14 .... 396 A7
Glenair Rd PSTN BH14 .... 445 M5
Glenair Rd PSTN BH14 .... 445 M5
Glenavon NMIL/BTOS BH25 .... 437 M6
Glenavon Gdns YTLY GU46 .... 69 G4
Glenavon Rd
CHCH/BSGR BH23 .... 436 D7
Glenbrook Wk
FHAM/STUB PO14 .... 372 A8
Glencarron Wy ROWN SO16 .... 318 D5
Glen Cl AND SP10 .... 8 C5
GSHT GU26 .... 203 M2
NMIL/BTOS BH25 .... 437 H8
Glencoe Cl FRIM GU16 .... 71 J8
Glencoe Rd BKME/WDN PO14 .... 446 C3
LTDN BH7 .... 448 E1
PSEA PO1 .... 423 K1
Glencoyne Gdns ROWN SO16 .... 317 L6
Glenda Cl HLER SO31 .... 370 B8
Glendale BPWT SO32 .... 324 A4
Glen Dl HAV PO9 .... 354 B7
Glendale HLER SO31 .... 370 F6
Glendale FERN BH22 .... 406 B2
NWBY RG14 .... 36 F3
Glendale Cl CHCH/BSGR BH23 .... 436 A3
WIMB BH21 .... 404 A3
Glendale Pk FLET GU13 .... 88 B6
Glendale Rd SBNE BH6 .... 449 M4
TADY RG26 .... 41 K7
Glendon Av NBNE BH10 .... 432 A2
Glendowan Rd CHFD SO53 .... 292 F1
Glendrive NMIL/BTOS BH25 .... 437 G8
Gleneagles Av PSTN BH14 .... 446 C6
Gleneagles Cl FERN BH22 .... 406 D2
Gleneagles Dr FARN GU14 .... 89 M5
HORN PO8 .... 352 F2
Glenelg FHAM PO15 .... 14 E3
Glenesha Gdns FHAM PO15 .... 14 B3
Glen Eyre Dr ROWN SO16 .... 318 E3
Glen Eyre Rd ROWN SO16 .... 318 E3
Glen Eyre Wy ROWN SO16 .... 318 E4
Glenferness Av TWDS BH3 .... 447 J2
Glen Fern Rd BMTH BH1 .... 23 G5
Glenfield Av WEND SO18 .... 344 D1
Glenfield Cl RSAL SP5 .... 207 G2
Glenfield Crs WEND SO18 .... 344 D1
Glenfield Wy WEND SO18 .... 344 D1
Glengariff Rd PSTN BH14 .... 446 B6
Glengarry NMIL/BTOS BH25 .... 438 A6
Glengarry Wy
CHCH/BSGR BH23 .... 451 H2
Glenhurst Cl BLKW GU17 .... 70 B4
Glen Innes SHST GU47 .... 50 C7
Glenives Cl RGWD BH24 .... 381 K4
Glenlea GSHT GU26 .... 204 B7
Glenlea Cl HEND SO30 .... 320 C7
Glenlea Dr HEND SO30 .... 320 C7
Glenlea Hollow GSHT GU26 .... 204 B8
Glenleigh Av CHAM PO6 .... 399 K1
Glenleigh Pk HAV PO9 .... 17 J1
Glenme Adows Dr BWD BH11 .... 431 M3
Glenmoor Rd FERN BH22 .... 406 A5
MOOR/WNTN BH9 .... 432 B8
Glenmore Cl STHA RG19 .... 27 G6
Glenmount Dr PSTN BH14 .... 446 A3
Glenmount Rd FRIM GU16 .... 91 K6
Glenn Rd HEND SO30 .... 320 C6
Glen Rd BOSC BH5 .... 448 D4
FLET GU13 .... 88 E8
GSHT GU26 .... 203 M2
HLER SO31 .... 370 C1
ITCH SO19 .... 344 B7
PSTN BH14 .... 446 A4
Glenroyd Gdns SBNE BH6 .... 449 J4
Glenside FAWY SO45 .... 367 K5
NMIL/BTOS BH25 .... 452 A1
Glenside Av ITCH SO19 .... 345 H4
Glen Spey NMIL/BTOS BH25.... 438 B6
The Glen CCLF BH13 .... 446 D8
LSOL/BMARY PO13 .... 397 J7
TADY RG26 .... 42 B7
Glenthorne Cl
FHAM/STUB PO14.... 396 B7
Glenthorne Meadow
PSF GU32 .... 273 K8
Glenthorne Rd HSEA PO3 .... 399 J1
Glenville Cl CHCH/BSGR BH23 .... 436 F6
Glenville Gdns GSHT GU26 .... 204 C4
Glenville Rd CHCH/BSGR BH23 .... 436 F6
NBNE BH10 .... 432 A6
Glenwood Av ROWN SO16 .... 318 F3
Glenwood Cl FERN BH22 .... 380 C6
Glenwood Ct ELGH SO50 .... 295 K6
Glenwood Gdns HORN PO8 .... 352 D5
Glenwood La FERN BH22 .... 380 C6

Glenwood Rd EMRTH PO10 .... 379 H7
FERN BH22 .... 380 C6
VWD BH31 .... 356 C3
Glenwood Wy FERN BH22 .... 380 C6
Glidden Cl PSEA PO1 .... 21 J1
Glidden La WVILLE PO7 .... 326 D5
Glissons FERN BH22 .... 405 L6
Globe Farm La BLKW GU17 .... 69 L3
Glorney Md FNM GU9 .... 6 E9
Gloucester Cl ALTN GU34 .... 196 F6
FRIM GU16 .... 91 H2
PSF GU32 .... 275 J5
Gloucester Dr KEMP RG22 .... 127 G1
Gloucester Rd ALDT GU11 .... 7 J7
BKME/WDN BH12 .... 446 D3
LTDN BH7 .... 448 E1
NWBY RG14 .... 2 B5
PSEA PO1 .... 422 E2
WVILLE PO7 .... 376 D2
Gloucester Sq SHAM SO14 .... 13 G6
Gloucester Ter SSEA PO5 .... 21 G5
Gloucester Vw SSEA PO5 .... 21 G5
Glyn Dr FHAM/STUB PO14 .... 396 A6
Glyn Jones Cl FAWY SO45 .... 392 D6
Glynswood CBLY GU15 .... 71 J5
RFNM GU10 .... 158 D4
Glynville Cl WIMB BH21 .... 404 E1
Glynville Rd WIMB BH21 .... 404 E1
Glyn Wy FHAM/STUB PO14 .... 396 A6
Goatacre Rd ALTN GU34 .... 196 B3
Goathorn Cl UPTN BH16 .... 444 C4
Goat La BSTK RG21 .... 5 G8
Goch Wy AND SP10 .... 118 D6
Goddard Dr THLE RG7 .... 28 C5
Goddards Cl HTWY RG27 .... 64 C8
Goddards Firs DEAN RG23 .... 103 H8
Goddards La CBLY GU15 .... 70 C3
Goddards Md AND SP10 .... 8 D7
Goddard Sq AND SP10 .... 119 G6
Godfrey Pink Wy BPWT SO32 .... 323 J1
Godmanston Cl CFDH BH17 .... 430 E7
Godshill Cl CHAR BH8 .... 433 H5
Godwin Cl EMRTH PO10 .... 378 C5
WINW SO22 .... 214 B5
Godwin Crs HORN PO8 .... 328 B4
Godwit Cl GPORT PO12 .... 397 M8
Godwit Rd ENEY PO4 .... 424 A2
Gofton Av CHAM PO6 .... 399 M1
Gogg's La RSAL SP5 .... 285 L2
Goldcrest Cl
FHAM/PORC PO16 .... 373 J8
HORN PO8 .... 352 E1
YTLY GU46 .... 68 E2
Goldcrest Gdns ROWN SO16 .... 317 M3
Goldcrest La TOTT SO40 .... 316 B8
Golden Ct HEND SO30 .... 320 E6
Golden Crs LYMN SO41 .... 439 H7
Golden Flds LIPH GU30 .... 227 G5
Golden Gv WHAM SO14 .... 13 J2
Golden Hind Pk FAWY SO45 .... 367 K6
Goldenleas Dr BWD BH11 .... 431 H5
Goldfinch Cl
NMIL/BTOS BH25 .... 437 K6
Goldfinch La
LSOL/BMARY PO13 .... 420 D1
Goldfinch Rd CFDH BH17 .... 429 J8
Goldfinch Wy RWIN SO21 .... 190 D3
Goldhill RFNM GU10 .... 158 F2
Golding Cl STHA RG19 .... 27 J5
Gold La ALDT GU11 .... 113 H4
Gold Mead Cl LYMN SO41 .... 440 C6
Goldney Rd CBLY GU15 .... 71 L4
Goldring Cl HISD PO11 .... 425 L5
Goldsmith Av ENEY PO4 .... 21 M2
Goldsmith Cl NTHA RG18 .... 26 F3
TOTT SO40 .... 341 H1
Goldsmith Rd ELGH SO50 .... 293 L7
Goldsmith Wy CWTH RG45 .... 49 L4
Gold St SSEA PO5 .... 20 F5
Goldwell Dr NWBY RG14 .... 2 C2
Golf Course Rd ROWN SO16 .... 318 D2
Golf Dr CBLY GU15 .... 71 J4
Golf La BOR GU35 .... 201 G2
Golf Links Av GSHT GU26 .... 203 L2
Golf Links Rd BDST BH18 .... 429 M3
FERN BH22 .... 406 C3
Goliath Rd PLE BH15 .... 444 C5
Gomer La GPORT PO12 .... 421 J4
Gondreville Gdns FLET GU13 .... 110 D4
Gong Hi RFNM GU10 .... 159 G5
Gong Hill Dr RFNM GU10 .... 159 G4
Goodacre Dr NBAD SO52 .... 292 E3
Goodden Crs FARN GU14 .... 90 C6
The Goodens NALR SO24 .... 242 B3
Goodison Cl ELGH SO50 .... 295 G7
Goodlands V HEND SO30 .... 345 L1
Goodman Cl BSTK RG21 .... 104 E4
Good Rd BKME/WDN BH12 .... 446 B1
Goodsell Ct
FHAM/STUB PO14 .... 395 M6
Goodwin Cl ROWN SO16 .... 317 J6
Goodwood Cl ALTN GU34 .... 176 E6
CBLY GU15 .... 50 F8
FHAM/STUB PO14.... 371 G6
GPORT PO12 .... 397 M8
THLE RG7 .... 31 J6
WVILLE PO7 .... 352 F7
Goodwood Cl EMRTH PO10 .... 379 J8
Goodwood Gdns TOTT SO40 .... 316 B8
Goodwood Pl FARN GU14 .... 91 H5
Goodwood Rd ELGH SO50 .... 293 K3
SSEA PO5 .... 21 L6
Goodwood Wy NWBY RG14 .... 3 K8
Goodwyns Cl NTID SP9 .... 138 C1
Goodyers ALTN GU34 .... 176 F5
Goose Gn HTWY RG27 .... 85 L6
Goose Green Wy STHA RG19 .... 27 H5
Goose La HTWY RG27 .... 85 M6
Gordon Av CBLY GU15 .... 70 E4
FLET GU13 .... 111 G2
SHAM SO14 .... 318 F8
WINC SO23 .... 239 H7
Gordon Cl BSTK RG21 .... 5 H5
Gordon Crs CBLY GU15 .... 70 E4
Gordon Mt CHCH/BSGR BH23 .... 436 F7
Gordon Rd ALDT GU11 .... 6 F3
BKME/WDN BH12 .... 446 D3
BMTH BH1 .... 448 C1

BPWT SO32 .... 322 E7
CBLY GU15 .... 70 F4
CHCH/BSGR BH23 .... 436 E8
CHFD SO53 .... 265 J7
CWTH RG45 .... 50 A5
EMRTH PO10 .... 402 F1
FARN GU14 .... 91 G8
FHAM/PORC PO16 .... 15 G5
GPORT PO12 .... 18 D4
LYMN SO41 .... 440 B8
NTHA RG18 .... 26 D3
NWBY RG14 .... 3 G5
PSEA PO1 .... 20 E6
WIMB BH21 .... 404 C4
WINC SO23 .... 11 H5
WVILLE PO7 .... 376 B2
Gordon Rd South
BKME/WDN BH12 .... 446 F4
Gordon Ter ITCH SO19 .... 344 E6
Gordon Wk YTLY GU46 .... 69 H3
Gore End Rd KSCL RG20 .... 35 L5
Gore Rd NMIL/BTOS BH25 .... 437 J6
Goring Av HORN PO8 .... 328 B4
Goring Fld WINW SO22 .... 214 B7
Goring La THLE RG7 .... 31 J7
Gorleston Rd
BKME/WDN BH12 .... 446 E3
NWBY RG14 .... 36 F3
Gorley Ct HAV PO9 .... 377 G1
Gorley Lynch FBDG SP6 .... 335 H4
Gorley Rd RGWD BH24 .... 359 G8
Gorran Av LSOL/BMARY PO13 .... 397 G7
The Gorrings STOK SO20 .... 210 F6
Gorsecliff Rd NBNE BH10 .... 432 B7
Gorse Cl FNM GU9 .... 158 D2
HLER SO31 .... 370 D6
NMIL/BTOS BH25 .... 438 B4
RGWD BH24 .... 381 H4
Gorsedown Cl BOR GU35 .... 201 G7
Gorsefield Rd
NMIL/BTOS BH25 .... 437 M3
Gorse Hill Cl PLE BH15 .... 445 K3
Gorse Hill Crs PLE BH15 .... 445 K3
Gorse Hill Rd PLE BH15 .... 445 K3
Gorseland Ct FERN BH22 .... 406 C2
Gorselands NWBY RG14 .... 37 G3
TADY RG26 .... 41 M8
YTLY GU46 .... 68 F4
Gorselands Cl ASHV GU12 .... 113 K3
BOR GU35 .... 202 F4
Gorselands Rd WEND SO18 .... 320 A7
Gorselands Wy
LSOL/BMARY PO13 .... 397 H8
Gorse La RFNM GU10 .... 158 D2
UPTN BH16 .... 444 A1
Gorse Ride North EWKG RG40 .... 48 B1
Gorse Ride South EWKG RG40 .... 48 B1
Gorse Rd EPSF GU31 .... 276 B5
FRIM GU16 .... 71 H6
WIMB BH21 .... 429 G3
Gorseway FLET GU13 .... 110 F1
Gort Cl ALDT GU11 .... 113 J1
Gort Crs ITCH SO19 .... 344 F4
Gort Rd BWD BH11 .... 431 M5
CFDH BH17 .... 429 L7
Goscombs La NALR SO24 .... 219 J1
Gosling Cl CFDH BH17 .... 445 L1
Goslings Cft ALTN GU34 .... 199 K7
Gosport La LYND SO43 .... 363 L4
Gosport Rd FHAM/PORC PO16 .... 15 K7
FHAM/STUB PO14 .... 396 B6
LSOL/BMARY PO13 .... 420 D7
Gosport St LYMN SO41 .... 440 D4
Gough Crs CFDH BH17 .... 429 M6
Gough Rd FLET GU13 .... 88 D6
Gough's Meadow SHST GU47 .... 69 L1
Gould Cl RAND SP11 .... 92 D6
Government House Rd
ALDT GU11 .... 112 D1
Government Rd ALDT GU11.... 113 H4
Governor's Rd CBLY GU15 .... 70 C2
Gover Rd ROWN SO16 .... 317 H7
Gower Cl BSTK RG21 .... 4 E4
Gower Crs HTWY RG27 .... 86 A7
Gower Pk SHST GU47 .... 70 A1
Grace Bennett Cl FARN GU14 .... 90 D1
Grace Dieu Gdns HLER SO31 .... 345 K7
Grace La FBDG SP6 .... 284 D8
Gracemere Crs KEMP RG22 .... 126 E1
Grace Sq AND SP10 .... 119 H6
Gracious St ALTN GU34 .... 199 J8
Graddidge Wy TOTT SO40 .... 341 H1
Gradwell La ALTN GU34 .... 196 F8
Graemar La RAND SP11 .... 260 B7
Grafton Cl BOR GU35 .... 201 K6
TWDS BH3 .... 447 M1
Grafton Gdns LYMN SO41 .... 440 A7
ROWN SO16 .... 318 B3
Grafton Rd TWDS BH3 .... 447 M2
WINC SO23 .... 238 E2
Grafton St NEND PO2 .... 423 G1
Grafton Wy KEMP RG22 .... 104 C4
Graham Cl AND SP10 .... 343 M2
Graham St SHAM SO14 .... 344 A2
Grainger Cl KEMP RG22 .... 104 D7
Grainger Gdns ITCH SO19 .... 345 G5
Grammarsham La OVTN RG25.... 127 L6
Grampian Av SHST GU47 .... 49 J6
Grampian Wy KEMP RG22 .... 104 A5
Granada Cl HORN PO8 .... 352 E5
Granada Pl AND SP10 .... 9 M3
Granada Rd ENEY PO4 .... 21 L9
HEND SO30 .... 345 L3
Granby End THLE RG7 .... 31 L5
Granby Gv STWS SO17 .... 319 G5
Granby Rd MOOR/WNTN BH9 .... 432 E4
Grand Av CBLY GU15 .... 70 E4
SBNE BH6 .... 449 H4
Grand Pde WINW SO22 .... 214 D5
HISD PO11 .... 425 L6
PSEA PO1 .... 20 D6
Grand Trunk Rd NTID SP9 .... 114 B4
Grange Av CWTH RG45 .... 49 L2
Grange Cl GPORT PO12 .... 421 K2
HAV PO9 .... 17 J3
LYMN SO41 .... 439 J8

RAND SP11 .... 116 D6
WEND SO18 .... 319 K4
Grange Crs GPORT PO12 .... 421 K2
Grange Dr HEND SO30 .... 321 J8
Grange Farm Rd ASHV GU12 .... 113 K5
Grange La HTWY RG27 .... 87 G3
LSOL/BMARY PO13 .... 397 G8
Grange Ms ROMY SO51 .... 263 H7
Grange Rd ASHV GU12 .... 113 L7
BDST BH18 .... 429 L4
CBLY GU15 .... 71 H3
CHCH/BSGR BH23 .... 451 G1
FARN GU14 .... 90 E1
FLET GU13 .... 110 E3
HEND SO30 .... 321 H8
HLER SO31 .... 368 E2
LSOL/BMARY PO13 .... 421 H4
NALR SO24 .... 218 B3
NEND PO2 .... 399 H7
RFNM GU10 .... 136 B2
RFNM GU10 .... 159 L8
PSF GU32 .... 275 K6
RGWD BH24 .... 381 H6
ROWN SO16 .... 318 A7
SBNE BH6 .... 449 J5
WINC SO23 .... 238 D4
Grangewood Gdns
ELGH SO50 .... 295 L6
Grantham Av HLER SO31 .... 369 G5
Grantham Cl SHST GU47 .... 50 B7
Grantham Rd BMTH BH1 .... 448 D3
ITCH SO19 .... 344 D2
Grantley Dr FLET GU13 .... 110 E1
Grant Rd CHAM PO6 .... 376 B8
CWTH RG45 .... 49 M5
Grant's Av BMTH BH1 .... 448 C2
Grants Cl BMTH BH1 .... 448 C2
Granville Cl HAV PO9 .... 17 H5
Granville Rd BOSC BH5 .... 448 F3
PSTN BH14 .... 446 A3
Granville St SHAM SO14 .... 13 K4
Grasdean Cl WEND SO18 .... 319 M7
Grasmere ELGH SO50 .... 293 L6
Grasmere Cl CHCH/BSGR BH23 .... 434 B5
BOR GU35 .... 201 J3
WEND SO18 .... 320 A7
Grasmere Gdns
NMIL/BTOS BH25 .... 437 M3
Grasmere Rd BOSC BH5 .... 448 F4
CCLF BH13 .... 457 G5
FARN GU14 .... 90 B5
Grasmere Wy
FHAM/STUB PO14 .... 396 B4
Graspan Rd RAND SP11 .... 93 J4
Grassington Pl STHA RG19 .... 27 G5
Grassmead STHA RG19 .... 27 J6
Grassmere Wy HORN PO8 .... 352 F7
Grassymead FHAM PO15 .... 371 G4
Grateley Crs HAV PO9 .... 377 G4
Grateley Dro RAND SP11 .... 139 L7
RAND SP11 .... 140 C6
Grateley Rd AMSY SP4 .... 138 C7
Gratton Cl RWIN SO21 .... 168 C4
Gravel Cl NALR SO24 .... 172 B4
RSAL SP5 .... 256 D8
Gravel Hl BPWT SO32 .... 324 A5
KSCL RG20 .... 24 B3
WIMB BH21 .... 404 D1
Gravel Hill Rd RFNM GU10 .... 157 J4
Gravel La ALTN GU34 .... 196 D7
RGWD BH24 .... 358 E8
RWIN SO21 .... 167 J2
Gravelly Cl KSCL RG20 .... 35 K5
TADY RG26 .... 61 M2
Gravel Rd FARN GU14 .... 91 G8
FLET GU13 .... 111 G2
FNM GU9 .... 134 E1
Gray Cl CFDH BH17 .... 430 D8
HLER SO31 .... 370 D6
Graycot Cl NBNE BH10 .... 432 A3
Grayland Cl HISD PO11 .... 425 J4
Grayling Md ROMY SO51 .... 262 E7
Grays Av FAWY SO45 .... 367 M5
Grays Cl ELGH SO50 .... 266 E8
GPORT PO12 .... 421 J5
HASM GU27 .... 205 H8
ROMY SO51 .... 290 F1
Grays Ct PSEA PO1 .... 20 D4
Grayshot Dr BLKW GU17 .... 69 M3
Grayshott Cl WINW SO22 .... 214 C4
Grayshott Laurels
BOR GU35 .... 201 M3
Grayshott Rd ENEY PO4 .... 423 K4
GPORT PO12 .... 18 B4
BOR GU35 .... 202 F3
Grayswood Dr FRIM GU16 .... 91 K7
Grayswood Rd HASM GU27 .... 205 K8
Great Austins FNM GU9 .... 135 G8
Great Binfields Crs CHAM RG24 .... 83 L8
Great Binfields Rd CHAM RG24.... 105 L1
Great Br ROMY SO51 .... 262 D4
Greatbridge Rd ROMY SO51 .... 262 D5
Great Copse Dr HAV PO9 .... 377 K3
Great Elms Cl FAWY SO45 .... 391 M6
Greatfield Cl FARN GU14 .... 70 E8
Greatfield Rd FARN GU14 .... 70 D8
Great Field Rd WINW SO22 .... 10 B1
Greatfield Wy HAV PO9 .... 353 M6
Great Gays FHAM/STUB PO14 .... 395 L7
Great Hanger EPSF GU31 .... 276 A5
Great La WHCH RG28 .... 47 H3
Great Md LYND SO43 .... 363 K4
WVILLE PO7 .... 351 L5
Great Minster St WINC SO23 .... 11 G8
Great Oaks Cha CHAM RG24 .... 83 K6
Great Sheldons Coppice
HTWY RG27 .... 85 M6
Great Southsea St SSEA PO5.... 21 G5
Great Well Dr ROMY SO51 .... 262 E8
Greatwood Cl FAWY SO45 .... 367 L6
Greaves Cl NBNE BH10 .... 432 A5
Grebe Cl ALTN GU34 .... 176 D2
CFDH BH17 .... 429 J8
FHAM/PORC PO16 .... 373 K8

HORN PO8 .... 352 C4
KEMP RG22 .... 126 E1
LYMN SO41 .... 454 D4
Green Acre ALDT GU11 .... 6 D4
NMIL/BTOS BH25 .... 437 L8
Greenacre KSCL RG20 .... 59 J6
Greenacre Cl UPTN BH16 .... 444 B2
Greenacre Gdns WVILLE PO7 .... 376 B4
Greenacres KSCL RG20 .... 36 B8
BOR GU35 .... 201 L4
RFNM GU10 .... 135 M6
RSAL SP5 .... 284 C1
RWIN SO21 .... 167 H2
Greenacres Cl NBNE BH10 .... 432 C1
Green Acres Cl RGWD BH24 .... 382 B3
Greenacres Dr RWIN SO21 .... 266 B5
Greenaway La HLER SO31 .... 370 B6
Greenbank Crs ROWN SO16 .... 318 C3
Greenbanks Cl LYMN SO41 .... 454 C3
Greenbanks Gdns
FHAM/PORC PO16 .... 373 H6
Greenbirch Cl KEMP RG22 .... 126 E1
Green Bottom WIMB BH21 .... 404 E1
Greenbury Cl DEAN RG23 .... 104 B8
Green Cl FAWY SO45 .... 367 L4
RSAL SP5 .... 259 G4
TOTT SO40 .... 340 D4
NALR SO24 .... 194 C7
RWIN SO21 .... 190 D4
Greenclose La WIMB BH21 .... 404 B4
Green Crs LSOL/BMARY PO13 .... 397 G7
Greencroft FARN GU14 .... 90 E4
Green Cross La RFNM GU10.... 181 K7
Greendale Cl CHFD SO53 .... 293 K2
The Greendale FHAM PO15 .... 372 B4
Green Dro RAND SP11 .... 96 A6
Greenfield Cl LIPH GU30 .... 226 F3
Greenfield Crs HORN PO8 .... 352 F5
Greenfield Gdns
NMIL/BTOS BH25 .... 437 M8
Greenfield Ri HORN PO8 .... 352 F5
Greenfield Rd FNM GU9 .... 158 C1
PLE BH15 .... 445 K2
Greenfields EPSF GU31 .... 305 K1
LISS GU33 .... 248 F4
RAND SP11 .... 96 B3
Greenfields Av ALTN GU34 .... 176 D4
TOTT SO40 .... 316 D7
Greenfields Cl EPSF GU31 .... 277 K8
Greenfield Wy CWTH RG45 .... 49 K1
Green Finch Cl CWTH RG45 .... 49 J2
Greenfinch Cl ELGH SO50 .... 293 J7
Greenfinch Wk RGWD BH24 .... 383 G2
Green Glades FLET GU13 .... 110 E3
Greenham Rd NWBY RG14 .... 2 F6
Greenhanger RFNM GU10 .... 181 J8
Greenhaven YTLY GU46 .... 68 E3
Greenhaven Cl AND SP10 .... 9 L6
Greenhayes BDST BH18 .... 430 A6
Greenhays Ri WIMB BH21 .... 404 A3
Greenhill Av WINW SO22 .... 10 C7
Green Hill Cl CBLY GU15 .... 71 M2
Greenhill Cl FNM GU9 .... 158 D1
WINW SO22 .... 10 C7
WIMB BH21 .... 404 B2
Greenhill La ROWN SO16 .... 291 K8
WIMB BH21 .... 404 B2
Green Hill Rd CBLY GU15 .... 71 M2
Greenhill Rd FNM GU9 .... 135 G8
WINW SO22 .... 10 B7
WIMB BH21 .... 404 B1
Greenhill Ter WINW SO22 .... 10 C7
Greenhill Wy FNM GU9 .... 158 D1
Green Hollow Cl
FHAM/PORC PO16 .... 14 C1
Green Jacket Cl WINW SO22 .... 238 D3
Greenlands KSCL RG20 .... 36 B7
Greenlands Rd CBLY GU15 .... 70 E7
KSCL RG20 .... 59 J6
NWBY RG14 .... 3 C9
Green La ALTN GU34 .... 196 E8
ALTN GU34 .... 221 H4
BLKW GU17 .... 69 L4
BLKW GU17 .... 70 B4
BPWT SO32 .... 324 B1
FAWY SO45 .... 392 D8
FBDG SP6 .... 283 H8
FERN BH22 .... 405 L7
FNM GU9 .... 6 D9
FNM GU9 .... 134 D8
GPORT PO12 .... 18 C7
HASM GU27 .... 228 E4
HISD PO11 .... 425 J6
HLER SO31 .... 345 J7
HLER SO31 .... 346 B7
HLER SO31 .... 346 E7
HLER SO31 .... 369 L6
HLER SO31 .... 370 D7
HORN PO8 .... 328 C3
HSEA PO3 .... 399 L5
HTWY RG27 .... 87 H3
NALR SO24 .... 219 H3
NALR SO24 .... 244 C2
NBNE BH10 .... 432 C4
RFNM GU10 .... 180 B2
RFNM GU10 .... 181 J8
NMIL/BTOS BH25 .... 437 M8
NWBY RG14 .... 2 B5
OVTN RG25 .... 127 M8
PSF GU32 .... 246 E8
RAND SP11 .... 141 H5
RGWD BH24 .... 382 E1
RGWD BH24 .... 382 F5
ROMY SO51 .... 263 M8
ROWN SO16 .... 292 E7
ROWN SO16 .... 317 K6
RSAL SP5 .... 256 C8
SHST GU47 .... 69 L8
STHA RG19 .... 26 F5
TADY RG26 .... 62 B4
THLE RG7 .... 30 F6
THLE RG7 .... 44 C8
TOTT SO40 .... 316 A4
WVILLE PO7 .... 325 L8
WVILLE PO7 .... 351 J3
YTLY GU46 .... 68 E1

Green Lane Cl *CBLY* GU15.............. 70 F1
Greenlea Cl *CHAM* PO6.............. 375 M6
Greenlea Crs *ROWN* SO16.............. 319 J5
Greenlea Rd *GPORT* PO12.............. 421 K1
Greenleas *FRIM* GU16.............. 71 H6
Greenleas Cl *YTLY* GU46.............. 68 F1
Green Leys *FLET* GU13.............. 110 E4
Greenmead Av *SSEA* PO5.............. 21 G5
Greenmead Av *WSHM* SO15.............. 12 D3
Green Meadows La
　RAND SP11.............. 142 F1
Green Park Cl *WINC* SO23.............. 11 J2
Green Park Rd *ROWN* SO16.............. 342 C1
Green Pond Cnr *HAV* PO9.............. 17 J5
Green Pond La *ROMY* SO51.............. 264 B5
Green Rd *FHAM/STUB* PO14.............. 396 A4
　GPORT PO12.............. 18 C7
　MOOR/WNTN BH9.............. 432 E8
　PLE BH15.............. 445 H6
　SSEA PO5.............. 21 G5
Greensand Wy *FNM* GU9.............. 135 H6
　GSHT GU26.............. 204 D6
　HASM GU27.............. 228 F1
Greens Cl *BPWT* SO32.............. 297 G8
　ELGH SO50.............. 294 F7
Greenside *CWTH* RG45.............. 49 J3
Greensleeves Av *BDST* BH18.............. 429 M2
Greens Meade *RSAL* SP5.............. 285 J2
Greensome Dr *FERN* BH22.............. 406 D2
Green Springs *RFNM* GU10.............. 133 J1
Green Stile *ALTN* GU34.............. 196 D2
Green St *BOR* GU35.............. 178 C8
The Green *AND* SP10.............. 118 D6
　FNM GU9.............. 134 F2
　FNM GU9.............. 135 K3
　FRIM GU16.............. 91 J2
　HLER SO31.............. 370 B2
　LISS GU33.............. 248 D3
　RFNM GU10.............. 136 B7
　OVTN RG25.............. 101 C8
　ROMY SO51.............. 263 H6
　RSAL SP5.............. 259 C4
　TADY RG26.............. 61 M2
　WHCH RG28.............. 122 C3
Green Wy *ASHV* GU12.............. 113 H5
Greenway *HTWY* RG27.............. 64 C8
Greenway Cl *LYMN* SO41.............. 440 A4
Greenway La *EPSF* GU31.............. 303 H2
Greenway Rd *GPORT* PO12.............. 421 M2
Greenways *BPWT* SO32.............. 324 A3
　CHCH/BSGR BH23.............. 436 D8
　CHFD SO53.............. 293 J2
　FLET GU13.............. 110 E2
　KSCL RG20.............. 36 B7
　LYMN SO41.............. 454 B3
　ROWN SO16.............. 319 J3
　SHST GU47.............. 49 L7
Greenways Av *CHAR* BH8.............. 433 C5
Greenways Rd *BROC* SO42.............. 387 L7
The Greenwich *FAWY* SO45.............. 392 C6
Greenwich Wy *AND* SP10.............. 118 F6
Greenwood Av *CHAM* PO6.............. 375 H8
　FERN BH22.............. 406 A2
　PSTN BH14.............. 446 B8
　ROWN SO16.............. 317 J1
Greenwood Cl
　FHAM/PORC PO16.............. 372 E4
　ROMY SO51.............. 262 F8
Greenwood Copse
　RGWD BH24.............. 381 L4
Greenwood Dr *CHAM* RG24.............. 83 L4
Greenwood La *BPWT* SO32.............. 295 M8
Greenwood Rd *CWTH* RG45.............. 49 K2
　MOOR/WNTN BH9.............. 432 C7
Greenwoods
　NMIL/BTOS BH25.............. 437 M7
　WHCH RG28.............. 122 B2
Greenwood Wy *RGWD* BH24.............. 381 K4
Greetham St *SSEA* PO5.............. 21 H2
Gregory Cl *BSTK* RG21.............. 5 H3
Gregory Gdns *TOTT* SO40.............. 316 B7
Gregory La *BPWT* SO32.............. 322 A3
Gregson Cl *LSOL/BMARY* PO13.............. 397 C5
Greig Rd *KEMP* RG22.............. 104 D7
Grenadier Cl *HLER* SO31.............. 370 F6
Grenadier Rd *ASHV* GU12.............. 113 L4
Grenadiers Wy *FARN* GU14.............. 89 M5
Grendon Cl *ROWN* SO16.............. 319 G3
Grenehurst Wy *EPSF* GU31.............. 275 L5
Grenfell Rd *MOOR/WNTN* BH9.............. 432 D5
Grensell Cl *HTWY* RG27.............. 48 B3
Grenville Cl *LIPH* GU30.............. 226 F4
　RGWD BH24.............. 359 C7
Grenville Dr *FLET* GU13.............. 110 D1
Grenville Gdns *FAWY* SO45.............. 367 L7
　FRIM GU16.............. 91 H2
Grenville Rd *ENEY* PO4.............. 21 L5
　WIMB BH21.............. 404 B4
Gresham Cl *MOOR/WNTN* BH9.............. 432 E7
Gresham Wy *FRIM* GU16.............. 91 H2
Gresley Gdns *HEND* SO30.............. 321 H6
Gresley Rd *BSTK* RG21.............. 5 K5
　CHAM RG24.............. 5 K4
Grevillea Av *FHAM* PO15.............. 371 J5
Greville Gn *EMRTH* PO10.............. 378 C5
Greville Rd *WSHM* SO15.............. 343 H1
Greyberry Copse Rd *STHA* RG19.. 26 A8
Greyfriars Rd *FHAM* PO15.............. 372 A6
Greyhound Cl *ASHV* GU12.............. 113 J7
　HEND SO30.............. 321 G3
Greyhound La *OVTN* RG25.............. 123 M1
Greys Ct *ALDT* GU11.............. 6 A2
Greys Farm Cl *NALR* SO24.............. 242 C4
Greyshott Av
　FHAM/STUB PO14.............. 372 A8
Greystead Pk *RFNM* GU10.............. 158 B2
Greystoke Av *BWD* BH11.............. 431 K2
Greystoke Ct *CWTH* RG45.............. 49 K4
Greywell Av *ROWN* SO16.............. 318 A4
Greywell Cl *TADY* RG26.............. 41 K8
Greywell Rd *CHAM* RG24.............. 106 C3
　HTWY RG27.............. 107 H4
Grieve Cl *RFNM* GU10.............. 136 B1
Griffen Cl *ELGH* SO50.............. 294 D6
Griffin Ct *PTSW* SO17.............. 319 H6
Griffin Wk *LSOL/BMARY* PO13.............. 421 G2
Griffin Wy South *HTWY* RG27.. 86 A5
Griffiths Cl *STHA* RG19.............. 27 J6
Griffiths Gdns *BWD* BH11.............. 431 M3

Griffon Cl *FARN* GU14.............. 90 A5
　HLER SO31.............. 345 L7
Grigg La *BROC* SO42.............. 387 L7
Grimstead Rd *RSAL* SP5.............. 230 B2
Grindle *NTHA* RG18.............. 26 F3
Gritanwood Rd *ENEY* PO4.............. 423 M5
Grosvenor Cl *KEMP* RG22.............. 127 G3
　PTSW SO17.............. 319 H6
　RGWD BH24.............. 381 H3
Grosvenor Ct *BLKW* GU17.............. 70 A5
Grosvenor Dr *WINC* SO23.............. 11 J2
Grosvenor Gdns *BMTH* BH1.............. 448 D4
　HEND SO30.............. 320 C7
　PTSW SO17.............. 319 H6
Grosvenor Rd *ALDT* GU11.............. 6 C3
　ALTN GU34.............. 196 D6
　CHFD SO53.............. 265 K7
　PTSW SO17.............. 319 H6
　WBNE BH4.............. 447 H5
Grosvenor Sq *WSHM* SO15.............. 343 K2
Grove Av *FHAM/PORC* PO16.............. 398 A2
　GPORT PO12.............. 19 G2
Grove Cl *BSTK* RG21.............. 105 H5
　EWKG RG40.............. 49 H1
Grove Cross Rd *FRIM* GU16.............. 71 G7
Grove End Rd *FNM* GU9.............. 158 E1
Grovefields Av *FRIM* GU16.............. 71 G7
Grove Gdns *ITCH* SO19.............. 344 F7
Groveland Rd *NWBY* RG14.............. 25 C3
Grovelands Rd *RFNM* GU10.............. 159 H1
Grovelands Rd *WINW* SO22.............. 214 A7
Grove La *RSAL* SP5.............. 285 L1
Grovely Av *BOSC* BH5.............. 448 L4
Grovely Wy *ROMY* SO51.............. 263 K7
Grove Pastures *LYMN* SO41.............. 440 C5
Grove Pl *ITCH* SO19.............. 344 F6
　LYMN SO41.............. 440 C5
Grove Rd *ALTN* GU34.............. 176 E4
　ASHV GU12.............. 113 K4
　BKME/WDN BH12.............. 446 A2
　BMTH BH1.............. 23 H6
　BSTK RG21.............. 105 H6
　CBLY GU15.............. 71 H3
　CHAM PO6.............. 400 A1
　FHAM/PORC PO16.............. 15 G6
　FLET GU13.............. 111 G3
　GPORT PO12.............. 421 M1
　GSHT GU26.............. 203 M2
　HAV PO9.............. 16 F5
　LSOL/BMARY PO13.............. 420 C2
　LYMN SO41.............. 440 C5
　NMIL/BTOS BH25.............. 452 F1
　NWBY RG14.............. 25 G3
　RWIN SO21.............. 266 C3
　WIMB BH21.............. 404 A4
　WSHM SO15.............. 343 G3
Grove Rd East
　CHCH/BSGR BH23.............. 434 E8
Grove Rd North *SSEA* PO5.............. 21 H5
Grove Rd South *SSEA* PO5.............. 21 H6
Grove Rd West
　CHCH/BSGR BH23.............. 434 D8
Groves Cl *RWIN* SO21.............. 190 B4
Groves Down *ROMY* SO51.............. 288 D4
Groves Lea *THLE* RG7.............. 43 J2
The Grove *ALDT* GU11.............. 6 F3
　CHCH/BSGR BH23.............. 434 C7
　EMRTH PO10.............. 378 F5
　FARN GU14.............. 91 J1
　FERN BH22.............. 406 A4
　FHAM/STUB PO14.............. 395 M6
　FRIM GU16.............. 71 G7
　HLER SO31.............. 345 L7
　HLER SO31.............. 369 H1
　ITCH SO19.............. 344 F7
　LIPH GU30.............. 226 E4
　MOOR/WNTN BH9.............. 432 D5
　NTHA RG18.............. 27 G4
　RAND SP11.............. 117 L4
　VWD BH31.............. 356 F3
Grower Gdns *BWD* BH11.............. 431 L4
Gruneisen Rd *NEND* PO2.............. 399 G6
Guardhouse Rd *PSEA* PO1.............. 422 F1
Guardroom Rd *NEND* PO2.............. 398 F7
Gudge Heath La *FHAM* PO15....... 14 B2
Guernsey Cl *CHAM* RG24.............. 83 H6
　ROWN SO16.............. 317 K5
Guernsey Dr *FARN* GU14.............. 89 C7
Guernsey Rd
　BKME/WDN BH12.............. 431 H7
Guessens La *FHAM/STUB* PO14.. 371 K8
Guest Av *BKME/WDN* BH12.............. 446 F2
Guest Rd *ELGH* SO50.............. 294 C5
　UPTN BH16.............. 444 A1
Guildford Rd *EMRTH* PO10.............. 379 H7
Guildford Dr *CHFD* SO53.............. 293 C5
Guildford Rd *ALDT* GU11.............. 7 L7
　FLET GU13.............. 89 H7
　FNM GU9.............. 135 G5
　FRIM GU16.............. 91 K3
　RFNM GU10.............. 135 K4
　PSEA PO1.............. 21 M1
Guildford Rd East *FARN* GU14..... 90 F7
Guildford Rd West *FARN* GU14.... 90 F7
Guildford St *SHAM* SO14.............. 13 K1
Guildhall Wk *PSEA* PO1.............. 20 F3
Guildhill Rd *SBNE* BH6.............. 449 K4
Guillemont Flds *FARN* GU14.............. 89 M3
Guillemot Gdns *FAWY* SO45.............. 367 M5
Guillemot Gdns
　LSOL/BMARY PO13.............. 396 F5
Guinea Ct *CHAM* RG24.............. 83 H5
Gull Cl *LSOL/BMARY* PO13.............. 396 F6
Gulley Rd *FARN* GU14.............. 90 E7
Gulliver Cl *PSTN* BH14.............. 446 B8
The Gulls *TOTT* SO40.............. 342 D6
Gullycroft Md *HEND* SO30.............. 345 M1
Gun Hl *ALDT* GU11.............. 112 C5
Gunners Cl *RWIN* SO21.............. 171 M4
Gunners Pk *WIMB* BH21.............. 297 K8
Gunners Rw *ENEY* PO4.............. 423 M6
Gunners Wy *GPORT* PO12.............. 397 K8
　LSOL/BMARY PO13.............. 397 C7
Gunns Farm *LIPH* GU30.............. 226 F6
Gunville Crs *MOOR/WNTN* BH9.. 432 F5
Gunville Hl *RSAL* SP5.............. 207 H2
Gunville Rd *RSAL* SP5.............. 207 H2

Gunwharf Rd *PSEA* PO1.............. 20 C4
Gurdons *ALTN* GU34.............. 176 C7
Gurjun Cl *UPTN* BH16.............. 428 E8
Gurnard Rd *CHAM* PO6.............. 399 J1
Gurnays Md *ROMY* SO51.............. 288 C5
Gurney Rd *ENEY* PO4.............. 429 J2
　WIMB BH21.............. 429 J2
　WSHM SO15.............. 318 B8
Gussage Rd *BKME/WDN* BH12.. 431 J8
Gutner La *HISD* PO11.............. 402 A7
Guttridge La *TADY* RG26.............. 41 K8
Gwatkin Cl *HAV* PO9.............. 377 C5
Gwenlyn Rd *UPTN* BH16.............. 444 A1
Gwyn Cl *NWBY* RG14.............. 25 J8
Gwynne Rd *BKME/WDN* BH12.. 446 D3
Gypsy La *HORN* PO8.............. 352 D3
　RGWD BH24.............. 358 F8

H

Haarlem Ms *CHCH/BSGR* BH23 .. 450 C1
Habin Hl *EPSF* GU31.............. 277 L4
Hack Dr *RWIN* SO21.............. 266 E8
Hacketts La *BPWT* SO32.............. 298 F6
Hackleys La *ROMY* SO51.............. 289 J3
Hacks La *RWIN* SO21.............. 189 G5
Hackupps La *ROMY* SO51.............. 234 B7
Hackwood Cl *AND* SP10.............. 8 B7
Hackwood La *OVTN* RG25.............. 128 A2
Hackwood Rd *BSTK* RG21.............. 105 H5
Hackworth Gdns *HEND* SO30.. 321 H6
Hadden Rd *CHAR* BH8.............. 433 H8
Haddon Cl *FHAM* PO15.............. 14 D6
Haddon Cl *ELGH* SO50.............. 293 M3
Haddons Dr *WIMB* BH21.............. 380 B1
Hadleigh Gdns *ELGH* SO50.............. 293 M3
Hadleigh Pl *BSTK* RG21.............. 4 D8
Hadleigh Rd *CHAM* PO6.............. 375 H8
Hadley Fld *FAWY* SO45.............. 391 M3
Hadleys *RFNM* GU10.............. 158 B5
Hadley Wy *BDST* BH18.............. 429 J5
Hadow Rd *BWD* BH11.............. 432 A5
Hadrian Cl *FERN* BH22.............. 406 B6
Hadrian Rd *AND* SP10.............. 119 C5
Hadrians Cl *CHFD* SO53.............. 293 K1
Hadrians Wy *DEAN* RG23.............. 104 B1
Hadrian Wy *ROWN* SO16.............. 318 D1
Haflinger Dr *HLER* SO31.............. 346 F8
Haglane Copse *LYMN* SO41.............. 439 M6
Hagley Rd *FLET* GU13.............. 88 D6
Hahnemann Rd *WCLF* BH2.............. 22 C7
Haig Av *PSTN* BH14.............. 446 D7
Haig La *FLET* GU13.............. 111 G3
Haig Rd *AND* SP10.............. 8 C4
　ASHV GU12.............. 7 K3
　CBLY GU15.............. 70 C2
　ELGH SO50.............. 294 F6
　NALR SO24.............. 218 C2
Haileybury Gdns *HEND* SO30 .. 321 H7
Hailsham Cl *SHST* GU47.............. 50 A7
Hailstone Rd *BSTK* RG21.............. 4 E2
Hainault Dr *VWD* BH31.............. 356 F2
Haining Gdns *FRIM* GU16.............. 91 K5
Halcyon Dr *RAND* SP11.............. 116 D8
Halden Cl *ROMY* SO51.............. 263 G7
Hale Av *NMIL/BTOS* BH25.............. 437 M6
Hale Gdns *NMIL/BTOS* BH25.............. 437 M6
Hale House La *RFNM* GU10.............. 181 K7
Hale La *FBDG* SP6.............. 284 E7
Hale Pl *FNM* GU9.............. 135 K4
Hale Reeds *FNM* GU9.............. 135 G2
Hale Rd *FNM* GU9.............. 135 G2
Hales Dr *HEND* SO30.............. 345 L3
Hales Fld *HASM* GU27.............. 228 F1
Hale St North *PSEA* PO1.............. 423 H4
Hale St South *PSEA* PO1.............. 423 H2
Hale Wy *FRIM* GU16.............. 71 G7
Halewood Wy
　CHCH/BSGR BH23.............. 434 D8
Half Moon Hl *HASM* GU27.............. 228 F2
Halfpenny La *PSEA* PO1.............. 20 D5
Halifax Cl *AND* SP10.............. 8 E3
　FARN GU14.............. 90 C5
Halifax Ri *NTHA* RG18.............. 26 F4
Halifax Wy *CHCH/BSGR* BH23 .. 451 C1
　FARN GU14.............. 112 C1
Halimote Rd *ALDT* GU11.............. 6 F3
Hall Cl *BPWT* SO32.............. 297 J8
　CBLY GU15.............. 71 H2
Hall Lands La *ELGH* SO50.............. 295 J6
Hall La *ALTN* GU34.............. 199 H6
　YTLY GU46.............. 68 F3
Hallmark St *SHST* GU47.............. 50 B8
Hall Rd *ALTN* GU34.............. 176 E2
　BWD BH11.............. 431 K5
　FARN GU14.............. 90 E6
Halls Farm Cl *WINW* SO22.............. 214 D5
The Hall Wy *WINW* SO22.............. 214 A3
Halsey Cl *GPORT* PO12.............. 18 B5
Halstead Rd *CHAM* PO6.............. 375 H8
　WEND SO18.............. 319 L6
Halstock Crs *CFDH* BH17.............. 430 B6
Halter Pth *PLE* BH15.............. 444 D5
Halter Ri *WIMB* BH21.............. 405 J4
Halters End *GSHT* GU26.............. 203 K5
The Halters *NWBY* RG14.............. 37 L1
Halterworth Cl *ROMY* SO51.............. 291 C1
Halterworth La *ROMY* SO51.............. 263 H8
Halton Rd *RAND* SP11.............. 115 J1
Haltons Cl *TOTT* SO40.............. 316 C7
Halyard Cl *LSOL/BMARY* PO13.. 421 H1
Hambert Wy *TOTT* SO40.............. 341 J3
Hamble Av *BLKW* GU17.............. 70 A3
Hamble Cl *DEAN* RG23.............. 103 G7

　HLER SO31.............. 370 A7
Hamble Ct *BSTK* RG21.............. 5 K8
　CHFD SO53.............. 293 J3
Hambledon Cl *WINW* SO22.............. 214 C4
Hambledon Gdns *SBNE* BH6.............. 449 H2
Hambledon La *BPWT* SO32.............. 325 H2
Hambledon Rd *HORN* PO8.............. 327 M3
　LTDN BH7.............. 449 G1
　SBNE BH6.............. 449 H2
　WVILLE PO7.............. 326 C8
　WVILLE PO7.............. 351 H1
Hamble Dr *TADY* RG26.............. 42 A8
Hamble House Gdns
　HLER SO31.............. 369 L6
Hamble La *HLER* SO31.............. 345 K6
　WVILLE PO7.............. 376 C3
Hamble Rd *GPORT* PO12.............. 18 B3
　PLE BH15.............. 445 L1
Hamble Springs *BPWT* SO32.............. 323 J1
Hambleton Cl *CBLY* GU15.............. 71 L5
Hamblewood *HEND* SO30.............. 346 D3
Hamborne Ga *NWBY* RG14.............. 25 C7
Ham Br *STHA* RG19.............. 26 B5
Hambridge Rd *NWBY* RG14.............. 3 J5
Hamdens *NWBY* RG14.............. 36 C3
Hamdown Crs *ROMY* SO51.............. 289 G5
Hameldon Cl *ROWN* SO16.............. 342 D1
Hamelyn Rd *BSTK* RG21.............. 104 F4
Hamesmoor Rd *FRIM* GU16.............. 91 H4
Hamesmoor Wy *FRIM* GU16.............. 91 J4
Hamfield Dr *HISD* PO11.............. 425 J4
Hamilton Cl *BMTH* BH1.............. 448 C3
　HAV PO9.............. 16 F7
　BOR GU35.............. 201 L4
　NWBY RG14.............. 2 F9
　PLE BH15.............. 444 D6
Hamilton Ct *LYMN* SO41.............. 454 B4
Hamilton Crs *PLE* BH15.............. 444 D6
Hamilton Gv
　LSOL/BMARY PO13.............. 396 F7
Hamilton Ms *FAWY* SO45.............. 367 M7
Hamilton Pk *RSAL* SP5.............. 256 F8
Hamilton Rd *BMTH* BH1.............. 448 C4
　CHAM PO6.............. 374 C8
　ELGH SO50.............. 294 C5
　FAWY SO45.............. 367 M8
　FLET GU13.............. 111 G2
　LISS GU33.............. 225 J6
　PLE BH15.............. 444 D6
　SSEA PO5.............. 21 J7
　WIMB BH21.............. 429 J3
Ham La *EMRTH* PO10.............. 403 H1
　GPORT PO12.............. 397 L7
　HORN PO8.............. 327 L8
　TADY RG26.............. 60 E4
　WIMB BH21.............. 404 F4
Hamlash La *RFNM* GU10.............. 158 F7
Hamlet Wy *GPORT* PO12.............. 397 L7
　LSOL/BMARY PO13.............. 397 K7
Hammer Hl *HASM* GU27.............. 227 M4
Hammer La *GSHT* GU26.............. 203 M8
　HASM GU27.............. 227 M3
　LIPH GU30.............. 227 K2
　MIDH GU29.............. 279 G4
Hammersley Rd *ALDT* GU11.............. 112 C1
Hammerwood Copse
　HASM GU27.............. 228 A3
　STHA RG19.............. 27 H6
Hammond Cl *FHAM* PO15.............. 14 B3
　FHAM PO15.............. 14 C3
Hammonds Cl *TOTT* SO40.............. 316 D8
Hammond's Gn *TOTT* SO40.............. 316 C8
Hammonds Heath *THLE* RG7.............. 43 L2
Hammond's La *NALR* SO24.............. 220 B4
　TOTT SO40.............. 316 D8
Hammonds Wy *TOTT* SO40.............. 316 D8
Hampshire Cl *ASHV* GU12.............. 7 M7
　CHCH/BSGR BH23.............. 434 C7
　KEMP RG22.............. 103 M5
Hampshire Hatches La
　RGWD BH24.............. 382 C4
Hampshire Rd *CBLY* GU15.............. 51 J8
　BOR GU35.............. 201 J4
Hampshire St *PSEA* PO1.............. 423 J1
Hampshire Ter *PSEA* PO1.............. 20 F4
Hampton Cl *FAWY* SO45.............. 392 C8
　FLET GU13.............. 110 F4
　WVILLE PO7.............. 376 E1
Hampton Dr *RGWD* BH24.............. 358 F7
Hampton Gdns *FAWY* SO45.............. 392 C8
Hampton Gv *FHAM* PO15.............. 371 M7
Hampton Hl *BPWT* SO32.............. 324 A3
Hampton La *FAWY* SO45.............. 392 C6
　WINW SO22.............. 214 B7
Hampton Rd *FNM* GU9.............. 134 D3
　NWBY RG14.............. 2 D7
Hamptworth Rd *RSAL* SP5.............. 286 C4
Ham Rd *HUNG* RG17.............. 32 D5
Hamtun Crs *TOTT* SO40.............. 316 D7
Hamtun Gdns *TOTT* SO40.............. 316 D7
Hamtun Rd *ITCH* SO19.............. 345 G6
Hamtun St *SHAM* SO14.............. 12 F5
Hanbidge Crs
　LSOL/BMARY PO13.............. 397 H4
Hanbury Wy *CBLY* GU15.............. 70 D3
Hancombe Rd *SHST* GU47.............. 49 K6
Handcroft Cl *RFNM* GU10.............. 110 C3
Handel Cl *KEMP* RG22.............. 103 M5
Handel Rd *WSHM* SO15.............. 12 E1
Handel Ter *WSHM* SO15.............. 12 D1
Handford La *YTLY* GU46.............. 69 G4
Handford Pl *WSHM* SO15.............. 343 K2
Handley La *YTLY* GU46.............. 68 F3
Hanger Rd *TADY* RG26.............. 41 J7
The Hangers *BPWT* SO32.............. 297 M4
Hangers Wy *ALTN* GU34.............. 176 F4
　EPSF GU31.............. 303 H4
　HORN PO8.............. 302 F6

The Hanger *BOR* GU35.............. 202 B1
Hanger Wy *EPSF* GU31.............. 276 A3
Hanham Rd *WIMB* BH21.............. 404 A3
　WIMB BH21.............. 429 H3
Hankinson Rd
　MOOR/WNTN BH9.............. 432 E8
Hanley Rd *WSHM* SO15.............. 318 C8
Hanlon Cl *BWD* BH11.............. 431 L4
Hanmore Rd *CHAM* RG24.............. 83 K6
Hannah Gdns *WVILLE* PO7.............. 352 D8
Hannam's Farm *RFNM* GU10 .. 133 H2
Hannay Ri *ITCH* SO19.............. 345 H3
Hannington Rd *HAV* PO9.............. 377 H1
　LTDN BH7.............. 448 F2
Hannnigtons Wy *THLE* RG7.............. 31 M5
Hann Rd *ROWN* SO16.............. 317 K2
Hanns Wy *ELGH* SO50.............. 293 M6
Hanover Buildings *SHAM* SO14.. 13 G4
Hanover Cl *AND* SP10.............. 8 B3
　FRIM GU16.............. 71 H7
Hanover Dr *FARN* GU14.............. 89 H4
Hanover Gdns *BSTK* RG21.............. 104 F6
　FARN GU14.............. 90 B2
　FHAM/PORC PO16.............. 15 J1
Hanoverian Wy *FHAM* PO15.............. 371 J5
Hanover St *PSEA* PO1.............. 20 C1
　FARN GU14.............. 90 B2
Hanson Cl *CBLY* GU15.............. 71 L1
Hanson Rd *AND* SP10.............. 8 D3
Hanway Rd *NEND* PO2.............. 399 H4
Ha'penny Dell *WVILLE* PO7.............. 376 C5
Harbeck Rd *CHAR* BH8.............. 433 C8
Harbour Cl *CCLF* BH13.............. 457 J2
　FARN GU14.............. 70 E8
Harbour Hill Crs *PLE* BH15.............. 445 L5
Harbour Hill Rd *PLE* BH15.............. 445 K5
Harbourne Gdns *WEND* SO18 .. 320 A6
Harbour Pde *SHAM* SO14.............. 12 E1
　WSHM SO15.............. 12 D5
Harbour Rd *GPORT* PO12.............. 19 K2
　HISD PO11.............. 425 C4
　SBNE BH6.............. 449 K1
Harbourside *HAV* PO9.............. 401 K2
Harbour Vw
　FHAM/PORC PO16.............. 398 A2
Harbour View Cl *PSTN* BH14.............. 445 K1
Harbour View Rd *PSTN* BH14.............. 445 K1
Harbour Wy *EMRTH* PO10.............. 378 E8
　NEND PO2.............. 399 G8
Harbridge Ct *HAV* PO9.............. 377 H7
Harbridge Dro *FBDG* SP6.............. 334 A4
Harcourt Cl *HORN* PO8.............. 352 C4
Harcourt Rd *BOSC* BH5.............. 448 F3
　CBLY GU15.............. 70 E3
　FHAM/STUB PO14.............. 395 M4
　GPORT PO12.............. 18 D2
　PSEA PO1.............. 423 J2
　WEND SO18.............. 319 J2
Harding La *ELGH* SO50.............. 295 G2
Harding Rd *GPORT* PO12.............. 421 K2
Hardings La *HTWY* RG27.............. 87 J2
Hardley La *FAWY* SO45.............. 391 M4
The Hard *PSEA* PO1.............. 20 C5
Hardwicke Cl *ROWN* SO16.............. 317 K4
Hardwicke Wy *HLER* SO31.............. 369 J5
Hardwick Rd *CHFD* SO53.............. 293 J2
Hardy Av *YTLY* GU46.............. 68 F2
Hardy Cl *FERN* BH22.............. 380 C2
　HLER SO31.............. 370 F7
　NMIL/BTOS BH25.............. 26 F3
　NTHA RG18.............. 26 F3
　WSHM SO15.............. 342 F7
Hardy Crs *WIMB* BH21.............. 404 B3
Hardy Dr *FAWY* SO45.............. 367 M7
Hardyfair Cl *RAND* SP11.............. 117 J4
Hardy Gn *CWTH* RG45.............. 49 L4
Hardy La *BSTK* RG21.............. 104 E2
Hardy Rd *CHAM* PO6.............. 400 C2
　ELGH SO50.............. 293 L1
　FERN BH22.............. 380 D2
　PSTN BH14.............. 446 C2
Hardys Fld *KSCL* RG20.............. 59 H1
Harebell Cl *FHAM/PORC* PO16.. 15 L1
　HTWY RG27.............. 87 J1
Harebell Dr *NTHA* RG18.............. 27 H4
Harebell Gdns *HTWY* RG27.............. 87 J1
Harefield Ct *ROMY* SO51.............. 263 G8
Harefield Rd *PTSW* SO17.............. 319 H4
Hare La *NMIL/BTOS* BH25.............. 438 B3
　RWIN SO21.............. 266 F1
　WIMB BH21.............. 332 C2
Hares Gn *LTDN* BH7.............. 433 L1
Hare's La *HTWY* RG27.............. 67 K2
　RCCH PO18.............. 379 M6
Harestock Cl *WINW* SO22.............. 214 C5
Harestock Rd *WINW* SO22.............. 214 C5
　HAV PO9.............. 16 B2
Harewood Av *LTDN* BH7.............. 448 E1
Harewood Cl *ELGH* SO50.............. 293 M4
Harewood Crs *LTDN* BH7.............. 448 E1
Harewood Gdns *LTDN* BH7.............. 448 E1
Harewood Gn *LYMN* SO41.............. 455 G2
Harfield Cl *HTWY* RG27.............. 85 M7
Harford Cl *LYMN* SO41.............. 439 M4
Harford Rd *BKME/WDN* BH12.. 431 G2
Harkness Dr *WVILLE* PO7.............. 352 F7
Harkwood Dr *PLE* BH15.............. 444 D6
Harland Crs *WSHM* SO15.............. 318 C4
Harland Rd *SBNE* BH6.............. 449 M4
Harlaxton Cl *ELGH* SO50.............. 293 L1
Harlech Cl *DEAN* RG23.............. 104 B2
Harlech Dr *CHFD* SO53.............. 293 C4
Harlech Rd *BLKW* GU17.............. 70 A4
Harlequin Gv *FHAM* PO15.............. 14 D7
Harleston Rd *CHAM* PO6.............. 375 H4
Harlington Wy *FLET* GU13.............. 88 D2
Harlyn Rd *ROWN* SO16.............. 317 L1
Harmsworth Rd *TADY* RG26.............. 41 L8
Harness Cl *WIMB* BH21.............. 404 F1
Harold Cl *TOTT* SO40.............. 341 H6
Harold Gdns *ALTN* GU34.............. 176 F2
Harold Rd *EMRTH* PO10.............. 378 E7
　ENEY PO4.............. 21 M4
　FHAM/STUB PO14.............. 396 B8
　HISD PO11.............. 425 M4
　WSHM SO15.............. 343 G2
Harpdon Pde *YTLY* GU46.............. 69 G1
Harper's Rd *ASHV* GU12.............. 113 M4
Harpton Cl *YTLY* GU46.............. 69 G1

Harpway La CHCH/BSGR BH23 .... 435 G2
The Harrage ROMY SO51 .... 290 E1
Harrier Cl HORN PO8 .... 352 E1
LSOL/BMARY PO13 .... 420 D2
ROWN SO16 .... 318 A2
Harrier Dr WIMB BH21 .... 404 B6
FAWY SO45 .... 391 M2
Harriet Cl FHAM/STUB PO14 ..... 395 M6
Harrington Cl NWBY RG14 .... 26 A3
Harris Av HEND SO30 .... 321 H8
Harris Hl KEMP RG22 .... 127 C1
Harris La HORN PO8 .... 329 J3
Harrison Av BMTH BH1 .... 448 C2
Harrison Rd FHAM/PORC PO16.... 15 D1
PTSW SO17 .... 319 H5
Harrison Wy FERN BH22 .... 380 C5
Harris Rd LSOL/BMARY PO13 ..... 397 G5
Harroway RAND SP11 .... 120 F3
WHCH RG28 .... 99 C7
Harroway La RAND SP11 .... 117 M6
Harrow Cl CHCH/BSGR BH23 ..... 435 M1
Harrow Down WSO22 .... 238 C4
Harrowgate La WVILLE PO7 ...... 326 E8
Harrow La PSF GU32 .... 275 L2
Harrow Rd CHCH/BSGR BH23 .... 435 L1
SSEA PO5 .... 21 L3
Harrow Wy AND SP10 .... 8 A2
OVTN RG25 .... 102 A5
RAND SP11 .... 117 M6
The Harrow Wy KEMP RG22 ..... 104 D7
Harry Barrow Cl RGWD BH24 .... 382 E2
Hart CI FARN GU14 .... 70 B8
NMIL/BTOS BH25 .... 437 K4
Hartford Bridge Flats
HTWY RG27 .... 67 M7
Hartford CI HTWY RG27 .... 87 H2
Hartford Ri CBLY GU15 .... 71 C2
Hartford Rd HTWY RG27 .... 87 H2
Hart Hl FAWY SO45 .... 368 A5
Harthill Dro RSAL SP5 .... 285 K3
Harting Cl HORN PO8 .... 328 C3
Harting Down EPSF GU31 .... 276 A5
Harting Gdns
FHAM/PORC PO16 .... 374 A7
Harting Rd SBNE BH6 .... 449 J1
Hartington Rd GPORT PO12 ..... 421 K2
SHAM SO14 .... 13 K1
Hartland CI EMRTH PO10 .... 379 H7
Hartland Pl FARN GU14 .... 90 D2
Hartland's Rd
FHAM/PORC PO16 .... 15 K6
Hartley Av PTSW SO17 .... 319 C6
Hartley CI BLKW GU17 .... 69 L3
ELGH SO50 .... 294 F7
FAWY SO45 .... 367 L7
Hartley Ct ROWN SO16 .... 318 F4
Hartley Gdns TADY RG26 .... 61 L1
Hartley La HTWY RG27 .... 64 E6
Hartley Meadow
WHCH RG28 .... 122 A3
Hartley Rd ELGH SO50 .... 294 F6
NEND PO2 .... 399 H5
Hartleys THLE RG7 .... 42 D8
Hartley Wk FAWY SO45 .... 367 K7
Hartmead Rd STHA RG19 .... 27 H5
Hart Plain Av HORN PO8 .... 352 E6
Hartsbourne Dr LTDN BH7 ..... 433 M8
Harts Farm Wy HAV PO9 .... 377 C4
Hartsgrove Cl FAWY SO45 ...... 392 C8
Harts Hill Rd NTHA RG18 ...... 27 H4
Harthill Rd TADY RG26 .... 41 J8
Harts La KSCL RG20 .... 57 H2
THLE RG7 .... 30 E3
Hartsleaf Cl FLET GU13 .... 88 E8
Harts Leap Cl SHST GU47 ...... 49 K7
Harts Leap Rd SHST GU47 ..... 49 K8
Harts Wy LYMN SO41 .... 439 H7
Hartswood CHAM RG24 .... 83 K6
The Hart FNM GU9 .... 134 E6
Hartwell Rd HSEA PO3 .... 399 M5
Hartwood Gdns HORN PO8 ..... 352 C6
Harvard St SHST GU47 .... 50 C7
Harvest Cl WINW SO22 .... 238 C4
YTLY GU46 .... 68 F3
Harvest Crs FARN GU14 .... 89 G3
Harvester Dr FHAM PO15 ...... 371 M7
Harvester Wy LYMN SO41 ...... 440 B2
Harvest Gn NWBY RG14 .... 2 M2
Harvesting La PSF GU32 .... 301 M2
Harvest Rd NBAD SO52 .... 292 E2
WVILLE PO7 .... 351 J4
Harvest Wy CHAM RG24 .... 83 L8
Harvey Ct FAWY SO45 .... 392 C6
Harvey Crs HLER SO31 .... 370 D6
Harvey Gdns FAWY SO45 ...... 367 M5
Harvey Rd BOSC BH5 .... 448 F3
ELGH SO50 .... 294 C6
FARN GU14 .... 89 M3
WIMB BH21 .... 404 E8
Harveys Fld OVTN RG25 .... 100 F8
Harwich Rd CHAM PO6 .... 375 H7
Harwood CI
LSOL/BMARY PO13 .... 397 G4
TOTT SO40 .... 316 C8
Harwood Pl WINC SO23 .... 191 H8
Harwood Ri KSCL RG20 .... 36 C7
Harwood Rd
LSOL/BMARY PO13 .... 397 G5
Haselbury Rd TOTT SO40 ...... 341 K1
Haselfoot Gdns WEND SO18 .... 345 J1
Haselsdale Dr GPORT PO12 .... 18 F9
Haskells Cl LYND SO43 .... 363 J3
Haskells Cl BKME/WDN BH12.... 446 A1
Haslar Crs WVILLE PO7 .... 352 B6
Haslar Rd GPORT PO12 .... 19 J7
Hasler Dr HASM GU27 .... 228 E3
Haslemere Av
CHCH/BSGR BH23 .... 436 D8
Haslemere Cl FRIM GU16 ...... 71 M1
Haslemere Gdns HISD PO11 .... 426 C6
Haslemere Pl
CHCH/BSGR BH23 .... 436 E8
ENEY PO4 .... 423 K6
HASM GU27 .... 228 E6
LIPH GU30 .... 227 G4
Hasler Rd CFDH BH17 .... 430 A6

Haslop Rd WIMB BH21 .... 404 D1
The Hassocks WVILLE PO7 ..... 376 E1
Hastards La ALTN GU34 .... 199 K8
Hasted Dr NALR SO24 .... 218 B4
Haste Hl HASM GU27 .... 229 H3
Hastings Av GPORT PO12 ...... 397 K8
Hastings Cl DEAN RG23 .... 104 A3
FRIM GU16 .... 91 K1
Hastings Dr CHAR BH8 .... 433 K6
Hatchbury La RAND SP11 ...... 73 H2
Hatch Cl THLE RG7 .... 28 C1
Hatch Ct HAV PO9 .... 377 C1
Hatchers La RWIN SO21 .... 267 L3
The Hatches FNM GU9 .... 134 C8
FRIM GU16 .... 91 J2
Hatchet Cl FBDG SP6 .... 285 J5
Hatchet La BROC SO42 .... 390 B8
RAND SP11 .... 95 H7
Hatchetts Dr RWIN SO21 ...... 227 M2
Hatchgate Cl NTHA RG18 ...... 26 F2
Hatch Gn CWTH RG45 .... 85 M6
Hatch Hl HASM GU27 .... 228 E7
Hatch La CHAM RG24 .... 106 A3
HASM GU27 .... 228 E6
LISS GU33 .... 249 H4
THLE RG7 .... 28 E7
Hatchley La RWIN SO21 .... 296 A2
Hatch Md HEND SO30 .... 320 B6
Hatch Ride CWTH RG45 .... 49 L1
Hatchwarren Gdns
KEMP RG22 .... 127 K1
Hatch Warren La KEMP RG22 .. 104 E7
KEMP RG22 .... 127 H1
NMIL/BTOS BH25 .... 437 J3
Hatfield Gdns FARN GU14 ..... 91 H5
LTDN BH7 .... 433 M8
Hatfield Rd ENEY PO4 .... 423 L5
Hathaway Cl ELGH SO50 ...... 294 A4
Hathaway Gdns CHAM RG24 ... 5 H1
WVILLE PO7 .... 352 F7
Hathaway Rd SBNE BH6 .... 449 J4
Hatherden Av PSTN BH14 ..... 445 L3
Hatherell Cl HEND SO30 ...... 320 C7
Hatherley Crs
FHAM/PORC PO16 .... 397 M1
Hatherley Dr
FHAM/PORC PO16 .... 373 M8
Hatherley Rd CHAM PO6 ...... 374 E7
WINW SO22 .... 10 D5
Hatherwood YTLY GU46 .... 69 J3
Hatley Rd WEND SO18 .... 320 A8
Hattem Pl AND SP10 .... 118 E6
Hattingley Rd ALTN GU34 .... 196 B1
Hatt La ROMY SO51 .... 233 K6
Haughurst Hl STHA RG19 ..... 40 E8
Havant Farm Cl HAV PO9 ..... 16 F1
Havant Rd CHAM PO6 .... 375 K8
EMRTH PO10 .... 17 M5
HAV PO9 .... 17 J6
HISD PO11 .... 401 K5
HORN PO8 .... 353 H2
NEND PO2 .... 399 H7
Havant St PSEA PO1 .... 20 C2
Havelock Rd BKME/WDN BH12.. 446 F3
HLER SO31 .... 370 A7
SHAM SO14 .... 12 E1
SSEA PO5 .... 21 K4
WSHM SO15 .... 12 E1
Havelock Wy
CHCH/BSGR BH23 .... 436 B6
Haven Crs FHAM/STUB PO14.... 395 K7
Havendale HEND SO30 .... 346 B3
Haven Gdns NMIL/BTOS BH25... 437 M6
Haven Rd CCLF BH13 .... 457 K2
HISD PO11 .... 426 C7
WIMB BH21 .... 429 G2
Havenstone Wy WEND SO18 ... 319 J4
The Haven ELGH SO50 .... 294 A3
ENEY PO4 .... 423 M3
GPORT PO12 .... 18 E8
H AV FAWY SO45 .... 392 D2
Haven Wy FNM GU9 .... 135 G4
Haverstock Rd
MOOR/WNTN BH9 .... 432 F6
Haviland Rd BMTH BH1 .... 448 C3
WIMB BH21 .... 405 L1
Haviland Rd East LTDN BH7 .. 448 E3
Havisham Rd NEND PO2 ...... 423 H1
Hawden Rd BWD BH11 .... 431 L7
Haweswater Cl BOR GU35 .... 201 J3
Hawfinch Cl ROWN SO16 ..... 318 A2
Hawkchurch Gdns CFDH BH17.. 430 C6
Hawk Cl FHAM/STUB PO14 .... 395 M6
KEMP RG22 .... 103 L8
WIMB BH21 .... 404 E1
Hawker Cl WIMB BH21 .... 404 D7
Hawker Cl ASHV GU12 .... 113 J3
Hawkes Cl HTWY RG27 .... 87 H1
Hawke St PSEA PO1 .... 20 C1
Hawkeswood Rd WEND SO18... 344 A1
Hawkewood Av WVILLE PO7 ... 352 B6
Hawkfield La BSTK RG21 ..... 104 F5
Hawkhill FAWY SO45 .... 367 L6
Hawkhurst Cl ITCH SO19 ..... 344 E7
Hawkins Cl RGWD BH24 ...... 359 G7
Hawkins Gv FLET GU13 ...... 110 C2
Hawkins Rd BKME/WDN PO13.. 431 K7
LSOL/BMARY PO13 .... 397 H6
Hawkins Wy FLET GU13 ...... 89 H8
Hawkley Cl HAV PO9 .... 377 J2
Hawkley Dr TADY RG26 ...... 61 M1
Hawkley Gn ITCH SO19 ...... 344 D8
Hawksbury CI LISS GU33 ..... 247 L3
Hawkshaw Cl LIPH GU30 ..... 227 G4
Hawkswood Av FRIM GU16 .... 91 J5
Hawksworth Rd THLE RG7 .... 31 J4
Hawkwell FHAM/PORC PO16 ... 373 K8
FLET GU13 .... 111 J4
Hawkwood Rd BOSC BH5 ..... 448 D4
Hawley Av BLKW GU17 .... 70 B5
Hawley La FARN GU14 .... 70 D4
Hawley Rd BLKW GU17 .... 70 B5
Hawlth Cl CHCH/BSGR BH23... 435 J4
Hawswater Ri ROWN SO16 .... 317 L7
Hawthorn Cl ASHV GU12 ..... 113 H8
ELGH SO50 .... 295 H6
FHAM/PORC PO16 .... 373 M7

HEND SO30 .... 346 B2
NALR SO24 .... 218 C3
NMIL/BTOS BH25 .... 438 A4
RWIN SO21 .... 170 A6
RWIN SO21 .... 266 F8
Hawthorn Crs CHAM PO6 ..... 399 L2
Hawthorn Dr CFDH BH17 ..... 429 M7
LYMN SO41 .... 412 C6
Hawthorn Cl RAND SP11 ..... 140 A8
Hawthorne Crs BLKW GU17 .... 70 B4
Hawthorne Gv HISD PO11 .... 425 L4
Hawthorne Rd STOT SO40 .... 316 C8
HLER SO31 .... 370 C3
RFNM GU10 .... 158 C5
Hawthorn Ri HTWY RG27 ..... 86 A6
Hawthorn Rd ALTN GU34 ..... 197 G8
CHCH/BSGR BH23 .... 435 J6
FAWY SO45 .... 367 K5
FRIM GU16 .... 71 J1
HORN PO8 .... 328 B6
MOOR/WNTN BH9 .... 432 D8
NTID SP9 .... 114 E1
NWBY RG14 .... 2 E1
PTSW SO17 .... 318 F6
WVILLE PO7 .... 351 H4
Hawthorn WM ALTN GU34 .... 176 D3
The Hawthorns ELGH SO50 ... 293 K7
TADY RG26 .... 41 H8
TOTT SO40 .... 342 E7
Hawthorn Wy DEAN RG23 .... 104 B2
Hayburn Rd ROWN SO16 ..... 317 C3
Haydn Cl WINC SO23 .... 191 C8
Haydn Rd KEMP RG22 .... 104 C8
Haydock Cl ALTN GU34 ...... 176 E6
TOTT SO40 .... 316 B6
Haydock Ms WVILLE PO7 ..... 352 F7
Haydon Rd CCLF BH13 .... 447 L5
Hay Down La RAND SP11 .... 140 D3
Hayes Av LTDN BH7 .... 448 D2
Hayes Cl STOK SO20 .... 210 E6
Hayes La WIMB BH21 .... 404 E4
Hayeswood Rd WIMB BH21 ... 404 E2
Hayle Rd WEND SO18 .... 320 A6
Hayley Cl FAWY SO45 .... 367 K8
Hayley La ODIM RG29 .... 131 G3
Hayling Av LU FHAM/STUB PO14 14 A8
Haymoor Rd PLE BH15 ...... 445 M1
Haynes Av PLE BH15 .... 445 J4
Haynes Wy FAWY SO45 ...... 367 J7
Haysoms Cl NMIL/BTOS BH25 .. 437 M7
Hay St PSEA PO1 .... 20 C1
Hayter Gdns ROMY SO51 .... 262 F8
Hayters Wy FBDG SP6 .... 333 L2
Hayward Ct FAWY SO45 ..... 392 A4
Hayward Crs VWD BH31 ..... 356 C3
Haywarden Pl HTWY RG27 ... 87 J1
Haywards Farm Cl
VWD BH31 .... 356 C3
The Haywards NTHA RG18 ... 27 G4
Hayward Wy VWD BH31 ..... 356 B3
Haywood Dr FLET GU13 ..... 110 F1
Hazel Av FARN GU14 .... 90 C6
Hazelbank EWKG RG40 ...... 48 A2
Hazelbank Cl EPSF GU31 .... 276 A4
LIPH GU30 .... 227 C4
Hazel Cl CHCH/BSGR BH23 ... 436 A7
CHFD SO53 .... 265 H6
DEAN RG23 .... 103 J3
FBDG SP6 .... 333 L3
RAND SP11 .... 8 B9
RWIN SO21 .... 266 F7
TLHT RG30 .... 31 L3
Hazel Coppice HTWY RG27 ... 86 A6
Hazeldean Dr HAV PO9 ...... 353 M7
Hazeldene CHAM RG24 ...... 83 L6
Hazeldene Rd LIPH GU30 .... 226 A4
Hazeldown Cl ROWN SO16 ... 317 K3
Hazel Dr FERN BH22 .... 380 B8
Hazeleigh Av ITCH SO19 .... 344 C6
Hazeley Cl HTWY RG27 ...... 87 H1
Hazeley Rd RWIN SO21 ...... 266 F2
Hazel Farm Rd TOTT SO40 .. 341 C1
Hazel Gv HLER SO31 .... 370 F6
TOTT SO40 .... 340 D5
Hazel Gn TADY RG26 .... 41 G7
Hazel Gv WINW SO22 .... 238 C3
GSHT GU26 .... 204 B7
Hazelgrove HORN PO8 ...... 328 B3
Hazel Rd ALTN GU34 .... 197 H5
ASHV GU12 .... 136 F1
FRIM GU16 .... 91 K6
HORN PO8 .... 328 B3
ITCH SO19 .... 344 B5
LYMN SO41 .... 439 L4
Hazelwood
FHAM/STUB PO14 .... 395 M3
Hazelwood Av HAV PO9 ..... 376 F5
NMIL/BTOS BH25 .... 437 J4
Hazelwood Cl DEAN RG23 ... 104 C1
Hazelwood Dr DEAN RG23 .. 104 C1
VWD BH31 .... 356 F4
Hazelwood Rd WEND SO18 .. 319 M7
Hazely Cl HTWY RG27 .... 87 H1
Hazlebury Rd CFDH BH17 ... 445 C1
Hazlemere Dr RGWD BH24 .. 381 J5
Hazleton Wy HORN PO8 ..... 352 F5
Head Down EPSF GU31 ...... 276 A7
Headington Cl KEMP RG22 .. 104 C8
Headland Dr HLER SO31 .... 370 E4
Headley Cl
LSOL/BMARY PO13 .... 420 D2
Headley Flds BOR GU35 ..... 202 B4
Headley Hill Rd BOR GU35 .. 202 C3
Headley La LIPH GU30 ...... 202 B6
Headley Rd GSHT GU26 ..... 203 J4
BOR GU35 .... 201 M5
LIPH GU30 .... 226 D2
Headmore La ALTN GU34 ... 197 K7
Headon Vw PSF GU32 .... 272 B3

Heads La HUNG RG17 .... 34 D3
NBNE BH10 .... 432 C3
Headswell Av NBNE BH10 ... 432 C4
Headswell Crs NBNE BH10 ... 432 C4
Heanor Cl NBNE BH10 .... 432 A6
Heardman Cl STHA RG19 .... 27 J6
Hearmon Cl YTLY GU46 ..... 69 G2
Hearne Gdns BPWT SO32 .... 323 M7
Hearn V BOR GU35 .... 202 D1
Hearsey Gdns BLKW GU17 ... 69 L2
Heath Av PLE BH15 .... 445 J2
Heath Cl ELGH SO50 .... 295 J7
FNM GU9 .... 134 F1
GSHT GU26 .... 203 M1
HORN PO8 .... 352 F1
WIMB BH21 .... 404 F1
Heathcote Cl RWIN SO21 .... 265 C1
Heathcote Rd ASHV GU12 ... 113 L5
BMTH BH1 .... 448 E4
BOSC BH5 .... 448 E4
CBLY GU15 .... 71 C3
CHFD SO53 .... 293 J2
BOR GU35 .... 201 K5
NEND PO2 .... 399 K7
Heathcott Ms WVILLE PO7 ... 352 F7
Heathdale Rd CBLY GU15 .... 70 F4
Heatherdeane Rd PTSW SO17. 318 F4
Heatherdell UPTN BH16 ..... 444 A2
Heatherdene Av CWTH RG45.. 49 H4
Heatherdene Rd CHFD SO53 .. 265 K7
Heatherdown Rd
FERN BH22 .... 380 E7
Heatherdown Wy
FERN BH22 .... 380 E7
Heather Dr AND SP10 .... 8 F3
FERN BH22 .... 406 B1
FLET GU13 .... 110 E3
BOR GU35 .... 201 L3
NTHA RG18 .... 27 C3
TADY RG26 .... 41 J6
Heatherfield EPSF GU31 ..... 303 J3
Heather Gdns FARN GU14 ... 90 B6
FHAM PO15 .... 14 B2
Heather Gv HTWY RG27 ..... 87 H1
Heatherlands Rd ROWN SO16. 292 E8
Heatherlea La HTWY RG27 .. 107 H3
Heatherley Cl CBLY GU15 ... 70 E3
Heatherley Rd CBLY GU15 .. 70 E3
Heather Md FRIM GU16 ..... 71 J1
Heathermount Dr CWTH RG45. 49 J2
Heather Rd EPSF GU31 ...... 276 B5
FAWY SO45 .... 392 D6
NBNE BH10 .... 432 D5
Heather Row La HTWY RG27. 107 J2
Heatherstone Av FAWY SO45. 367 K8
Heatherton Ms EMRTH PO10. 378 E3
Heatherview Cl NBAD SO52 .. 291 L3
Heather View Rd
BKME/WDN BH12 .... 446 E1
Heatherway CWTH RG45 .... 49 K3
Heather Wy FERN BH22 ..... 406 B1
GSHT GU26 .... 204 C4
KEMP RG22 .... 126 F1
Heath Farm Rd FERN BH22 .. 406 A6
Heath Farm Wy FERN BH22 . 406 A5
Heathfield FAWY SO45 ...... 367 K6
Heathfield Av
BKME/WDN BH12 .... 431 L8
FHAM PO15 .... 14 A6
Heathfield Cl ITCH SO19 .... 345 G5
Heathfield Ct FLET GU13 .... 110 D1
Heathfield Rd CHFD SO53 ... 265 H6
EPSF GU31 .... 276 B5
FERN BH22 .... 380 E7
ITCH SO19 .... 344 F5
KEMP RG22 .... 127 J1
NEND PO2 .... 399 H8
Heathfield Wy FERN BH22 ... 380 D7
Heath Gdns HLER SO31 ..... 369 H1
Heath Green La ALTN GU34 . 195 M1
Heath Hl RFNM GU10 .... 156 A2
Heath Hill Rd North CWTH RG45. 49 L3
Heath Hill Rd South CWTH RG45. 49 L3
Heath House HEND SO30 .... 345 M4
Heath House Gdns HEND SO30. 345 M4
Heathhouse La HEND SO30 .. 345 M4
Heathlands KSCL RG20 ...... 36 C8
TADY RG26 .... 41 H7
Heathlands Av FERN BH22 .. 406 B6
VWD BH31 .... 356 E2
Heathlands Cl CHFD SO53 ... 265 H6
Heathlands Rd CHFD SO53 .. 265 H6
Heathland St ALDT GU11 .... 6 C7
Heath La BROC SO42 .... 416 A1
FNM GU9 .... 134 F1
MARL SN8 .... 53 H1
RFNM GU10 .... 133 J2
NTHA RG18 .... 26 F3
Heath Lawns FHAM PO15 ... 14 B6
Heathman St BPWT SO32 ... 322 A4
Heath Ride CWTH RG45 ..... 49 C4
Heath Ri BPWT SO32 .... 324 F7
CHCH/BSGR BH23 .... 436 C5
EPSF GU31 .... 275 M5
HASM GU27 .... 228 A3
HLER SO31 .... 370 D5

ITCH SO19 .... 344 E3
LYMN SO41 .... 438 D5
NBAD SO52 .... 291 M5
RGWD BH24 .... 381 H4
TADY RG26 .... 42 B7
WHAM PO17 .... 324 E8
Heath Rd East EPSF GU31 ... 276 A6
Heath Rd North HLER SO31 .. 370 D5
Heath Rd South HLER SO31 .. 370 D5
Heath Rd West
CHCH/BSGR BH23 .... 407 J2
EPSF GU31 .... 275 M6
Heathrow Copse TADY RG26 . 41 C8
Heathside La GSHT GU26 .... 204 A2
Heathside Pk CBLY GU15 .... 71 M1
The Heath WVILLE PO7 ...... 351 L4
Heath V AND SP10 .... 9 J7
Heathvale Bridge Rd
ASHV GU12 .... 113 K2
Heathview HTWY RG27 ...... 86 B6
Heathway CBLY GU15 .... 71 G3
Heathway Cl CBLY GU15 .... 71 G3
Heathwood Av
NMIL/BTOS BH25 .... 437 J8
Heathwood Cl YTLY GU46 ... 69 G1
Heathwood Rd
MOOR/WNTN BH9 .... 432 C8
Heathy Cl NMIL/BTOS BH25 . 437 K8
Heathyfields Rd FNM GU9 ... 134 C2
Heaton Gdns GPORT PO12 ... 421 L1
NBNE BH10 .... 431 M6
Hebden Cl STHA RG19 ...... 26 F7
Hebrides Cl
FHAM/STUB PO14 .... 395 M5
Heckfield Cl HAV PO9 ...... 377 M3
Heckford La PLE BH15 ...... 445 J4
Heckford Rd PLE BH15 ...... 445 J4
WIMB BH21 .... 429 G3
Hector Cl FHAM/STUB PO14... 396 E3
Hector Rd FHAM/STUB PO14... 396 E3
Heddon Wk FARN GU14 ..... 90 D1
Hedera Rd HLER SO31 ...... 370 D5
Hedge End Rd AND SP10 .... 9 K8
Hedgehog La HASM GU27 ... 228 E5
Hedgeley NMIL/BTOS BH25 .. 437 M8
Hedgerow Cl ROWN SO16 ... 317 K2
Hedgerow Dr WEND SO18 ... 320 A7
Hedgerow Gdns EMRTH PO10. 378 D5
The Hedgerows CHAM RG24 . 83 M8
Hedges Md NTID SP9 .... 158 C1
Hedgeway NWBY RG14 ...... 3 K1
Hedley Cl FAWY SO45 ...... 392 D7
Hedley Gdns HEND SO30 ... 321 G5
Heenan Cl FRIM GU16 ...... 91 H1
Heidelberg Rd ENEY PO4 ... 423 K4
Heights Ap UPTN BH16 ..... 444 B1
Heights Rd UPTN BH16 ..... 444 B1
The Heights FHAM/PORC PO16. 373 H6
HEND SO30 .... 345 L2
Hei-Lin Wy RAND SP11 ..... 92 D6
Hele Cl BSTK RG21 .... 104 F6
Helena Rd ENEY PO4 .... 423 K6
Helen Ct FARN GU14 .... 90 E4
Helford Ct AND SP10 .... 119 H6
Helford Gdns WEND SO18 ... 320 A6
Helksham Cl SHST GU47 .... 50 A7
Hellyer Rd ENEY PO4 .... 423 L5
Helm Cl LSOL/BMARY PO13 .. 421 J2
Helsted Cl GPORT PO12 ..... 421 J4
Helston Dr EMRTH PO10 .... 378 C5
Helston Rd CHAM PO6 ...... 374 D7
Helvellyn Rd ROWN SO16 ... 317 L8
Helyar Rd CHAR BH8 .... 433 K6
Hemdean Gdns HEND SO30 . 320 C7
Hemlock Rd HORN PO8 ..... 352 C4
Hemlock Wy NBAD SO52 .... 292 E3
Hemming Cl TOTT SO40 .... 341 J2
Hemmingway Gdns
FHAM PO15 .... 347 C8
Hempland La ALTN GU34 ... 245 L2
Hempsted Rd CHAM PO6 ... 374 F7
Hemsley Wk HORN PO8 ..... 352 E4
Henbury Cl WIMB BH21 .... 429 H2
Henbury Ri WIMB BH21 .... 429 H2
Henbury View Rd
WIMB BH21 .... 429 H2
Henderson Rd ENEY PO4 ... 423 M5
Hendford Rd NBNE BH10 ... 432 B6
Hendon Rd BOR GU35 ...... 201 K6
Hendren Sq AND SP10 ..... 119 H6
Hendy Cl SSEA PO5 .... 21 J5
Henery St GPORT PO12 .... 19 H3
Hengest Cl AND SP10 ...... 118 C5
Hengistbury Rd
NMIL/BTOS BH25 .... 437 J8
SBNE BH6 .... 449 L5
Henley Cl FARN GU14 ...... 70 B8
Henley Dr FRIM GU16 ...... 91 H1
Henley Gdns FHAM PO15 ... 372 B4
YTLY GU46 .... 69 G3
Henley Rd ENEY PO4 .... 423 K5
Henning's Park Rd PLE BH15. 445 J3
Henry Cl FAWY SO45 .... 391 M2
Henry Rd ELGH SO50 .... 294 C4
WSHM SO15 .... 342 F1
The Henrys NTHA RG18 ..... 27 G4
Henry St WSHM SO15 ...... 342 E2
Henshaw Crs NWBY RG14 ... 25 G8
Henstead Rd WSHM SO15 ... 343 H2
Hensting La RWIN SO21 .... 267 K5
Henty Rd ROWN SO16 ...... 317 M8
Henville Cl LSOL/BMARY PO13. 397 H8
Henville Rd CHAR BH8 ..... 23 L1
Henwick La NTHA RG18 .... 26 D3
Henwick Rd NTHA RG18 .... 26 D3
Henwood Down EPSF GU31 .. 275 M5
Hepplewhite Cl TADY RG26 . 41 H7
Hepplewhite Dr KEMP RG22 . 126 F1
Hepworth Cl AND SP10 .... 9 H2
ITCH SO19 .... 345 G6
Hepworth Cft SHST GU47 ... 70 B2
Herbert Av BKME/WDN BH12. 431 C8
Herberton Rd SBNE BH6 .... 449 H3
Herbert Rd ENEY PO4 ...... 21 L8
FLET GU13 .... 88 D7
GPORT PO12 .... 18 B2
NMIL/BTOS BH25 .... 437 M5

RSAL SP5 .... 285 J2
WBNE BH4 .... 447 G6
Herbert St PSEA PO1 .... 423 G1
Herbert Walker Av WSHM SO15 .. 12 E5
Herbs End FARN GU14 .... 89 M3
Hercules Rd PLE BH15 .... 444 C5 🔲
Hercules St NEND PO2 .... 399 H8 🔲
Hereford Cl ODIM RG29 .... 108 B6 🔲
Hereford La FNM GU9 .... 134 E2
Hereford Md FARN GU14 .... 89 G4 🔲
Hereford Rd DEAN RG23 .... 104 B3
SSEA PO5 .... 21 J6
Hereward Cl ROMY SO51 .... 291 G1 🔲
Herewood Cl NWBY RG14 .... 2 C1
Heritage Pk DEAN RG23 .... 127 G3
Hermes Cl FLET GU13 .... 89 H7
Hermes Rd LSOL/BMARY PO13 .. 420 B1
Hermitage Cl BPWT SO32 .... 296 F8 🔲
FARN GU14 .... 91 G7 🔲
FRIM GU16 .... 71 J7
HAV PO9 .... 377 J4
Hermitage Rd PSTN BH14 .... 445 M2
Hermits Cl THLE RG7 .... 31 L5
Herm Rd BKME/WDN BH12 .... 431 G7
Herne Rd CHAM PO6 .... 375 J8
EPSF GU31 .... 275 M5
Hern La FBDG SP6 .... 334 F2
Heron Cl ALTN GU34 .... 176 E2
ENEY PO4 .... 423 M3
FLET GU13 .... 111 H3
FRIM GU16 .... 91 J4
LYMN SO41 .... 412 F6
Heron Court Rd
MOOR/WNTN BH9 .... 447 M1
TWDS BH3 .... 447 M2
Herondale HASM GU21 .... 228 B2
Heron Dr WIMB BH21 .... 404 E1
Heron La ROMY SO51 .... 262 C2
Heron Pk FARN RG24 .... 83 L7
Heron Quay EMRTH PO10 .... 402 E1
Herons FHAM/STUB PO14 .... 396 A4
Heron Sq ELGH SO50 .... 293 K7
Herons Ri AND SP10 .... 9 K9
Heron Wy KEMP RG22 .... 103 L8
LSOL/BMARY PO13 .... 396 E5
STHA RG19 .... 26 E5
THLE RG7 .... 29 L5
Heron Wood Rd ASHV GU12 .... 7 M6
Herretts Gdns ASHV GU12 .... 7 M4
Herrett St ASHV GU12 .... 7 L5
Herriard Wy TADY RG26 .... 61 L1 🔲
Herrick Cl FRIM GU16 .... 71 M5
ITCH SO19 .... 345 H4
Herriot Cl YTLY GU46 .... 68 F4
Herriott Cl HORN PO8 .... 352 E3
Herstone Cl CFDH BH17 .... 430 D7
Hertford Cl FBDG SP6 .... 309 L8
Hertford Pl PSEA PO1 .... 423 H1
Hertsfield FHAM/STUB PO14 .... 371 G4
Hesketh Cl RGWD BH24 .... 381 L3
Hester Rd ENEY PO4 .... 423 M4 🔲
Hestia Cl ROMY SO51 .... 263 H8
Heston Cl CHCH/BSGR BH23 .... 434 B4
Heston Wy FERN BH22 .... 380 B5
Hewett Cl FHAM/STUB PO14 .... 395 K1
Hewett Rd FHAM/STUB PO14 .... 395 K1
NEND PO2 .... 399 J6
Hewetts Ri HLER SO31 .... 370 A4
Hewitt Cl GPORT PO12 .... 421 L2 🔲
Hewitt Rd PLE BH15 .... 444 D4
Hewitt's Rd WSHM SO15 .... 12 B2
Hewshott Gv LIPH GU30 .... 227 H3
Hewshott La LIPH GU30 .... 227 G3
Hexham St SHST GU47 .... 50 A6
Heyes Dr ITCH SO19 .... 345 G4
Heysham Rd BDST BH18 .... 429 L5
WSHM SO15 .... 318 A8
Heyshott Rd ENEY PO4 .... 423 K4
Heyward Rd ENEY PO4 .... 21 L4
Heywood Dr BAGS GU19 .... 51 M6
Heywood Gn ITCH SO19 .... 345 J3
Hibberd Wy NBNE BH10 .... 432 B7
Hibbs Cl UPTN BH16 .... 428 E8 🔲
Hibiscus Gv BOR GU35 .... 201 K6 🔲
Hickes Cl BWD BH11 .... 431 K4
Hickory Cl UPTN BH16 .... 428 E8 🔲
Hickory Dr WINW SO22 .... 214 B4
Hickory Gdns HEND SO30 .... 320 C5
Hicks La BLKW GU17 .... 69 L3
Hides Cl WHCH RG28 .... 122 B4
Highams Cl KSCL RG20 .... 59 J6
Highbank Av WVILLE PO7 .... 375 M5
Highbank Gdns FBDG SP6 .... 309 L7 🔲
High Beeches FRIM GU16 .... 71 G6
Highbridge Rd ELGH SO50 .... 294 C1
Highbury Cl ELGH SO50 .... 295 H7
NMIL/BTOS BH25 .... 437 M5
Highbury Crs CBLY GU15 .... 71 K1
Highbury Gv CHAM PO6 .... 204 F8 🔲
HASM GU27 .... 204 F8 🔲
Highbury Rd RAND SP11 .... 142 C4
Highbury Wy CHAM PO6 .... 399 K2
Highclere Av HAV PO9 .... 377 H4
Highclere Cl CBLY GU15 .... 71 K1
Highclere Rd ASHV GU12 .... 7 L5
ROWN SO16 .... 318 C5
Highclere Wy CHFD SO53 .... 292 F5
Highcliff Av SHAM SO14 .... 318 F8 🔲
Highcliffe Dr ELGH SO50 .... 293 M1
Highcliffe Rd
CHCH/BSGR BH23 .... 435 L8
GPORT PO12 .... 18 B4
WINC SO23 .... 239 G2
Highcroft La HORN PO8 .... 328 B8
High Cross PSF GU32 .... 246 D6
High Cross La PSF GU32 .... 246 A8
Highcrown St PTSW SO17 .... 318 F6
Highdown FLET GU13 .... 88 F6
Highdowns KEMP RG22 .... 127 H2
High Dr KEMP RG22 .... 104 B6
LSOL/BMARY PO13 .... 397 G3 🔲
Higher Blandford Rd
BDST BH18 .... 429 L3
WIMB BH21 .... 429 K2
Highercombe Rd HASM GU27 .. 205 H8 🔲
Higher Md CHAM RG24 .... 83 L8
Highfield LYMN SO41 .... 440 B5

Highfield Av ALDT GU11 .... 6 F6
FHAM/STUB PO14 .... 14 E8
LYMN SO41 .... 440 A5
NWBY RG14 .... 2 C1
PTSW SO17 .... 318 E5
RGWD BH24 .... 358 E8
RWIN SO21 .... 266 F3
WVILLE PO7 .... 352 E8
Highfield Cha BSTK RG21 .... 4 B8
Highfield Cl ALDT GU11 .... 7 G6
CHFD SO53 .... 293 J2
FARN GU14 .... 90 C4
FNM GU9 .... 158 E1 🔲
LYMN SO41 .... 412 F6
PTSW SO17 .... 318 F6 🔲
WIMB BH21 .... 429 J3
WVILLE PO7 .... 352 D7
Highfield Crs GSHT GU26 .... 204 B4
PTSW SO17 .... 319 G6
RSAL SP5 .... 206 E2
Highfield Dr RGWD BH24 .... 358 E7
Highfield Gdns ALDT GU11 .... 6 F6
LISS GU33 .... 249 G4
LYMN SO41 .... 412 F6 🔲
Highfield La LIPH GU30 .... 227 G6
PTSW SO17 .... 318 F6
RGUW GU3 .... 137 K5
RSAL SP5 .... 285 J3
Highfield Pth FARN GU14 .... 90 C4
Highfield Rd CHFD SO53 .... 293 K2
FARN GU14 .... 90 C4
FERN BH22 .... 380 B4
GPORT PO12 .... 421 K2
LYMN SO41 .... 440 A4
MOOR/WNTN BH9 .... 432 C6
NWBY RG14 .... 2 D9
PSEA PO1 .... 21 K1
PSF GU32 .... 275 L4
PTSW SO17 .... 318 E7
RGWD BH24 .... 358 E8
WIMB BH21 .... 429 J3
High Firs Gdns ROMY SO51 .... 291 H1
High Firs Rd ITCH SO19 .... 344 F3
ROMY SO51 .... 263 H8
Highgate La FARN GU14 .... 90 F3
Highgate Rd HSEA PO3 .... 399 L7
Highgrove FARN GU14 .... 90 E1 🔲
Highgrove Cl TOTT SO40 .... 341 H3 🔲
Highgrove Rd HSEA PO3 .... 399 M8
High Howe Cl BWD BH11 .... 431 J4
High Howe La BWD BH11 .... 431 J4
Highland Av CHCH/BSGR BH23 .. 436 F7
Highland Cl EMRTH PO10 .... 378 C8
Highland Dr DEAN RG23 .... 102 F6
FARN GU14 .... 89 G5
Highland Rd ASHV GU12 .... 7 L2
CBLY GU15 .... 51 H8
EMRTH PO10 .... 378 C4
ENEY PO4 .... 423 K5
PSTN BH14 .... 446 A3
WIMB BH21 .... 404 B3
Highlands Cl FAWY SO45 .... 367 L6
FNM GU9 .... 158 E1
NBAD SO52 .... 291 K3 🔲
Highlands Crs NBNE BH10 .... 432 A4
Highlands Rd AND SP10 .... 9 M6
CHAM PO6 .... 376 B8
FHAM PO15 .... 14 A2
FNM GU9 .... 134 F1
KEMP RG22 .... 103 M5
NMIL/BTOS BH25 .... 437 L8
Highland St ENEY PO4 .... 423 L6
Highlands Wy FAWY SO45 .... 367 K6
RSAL SP5 .... 259 G4
Highland View Cl WIMB BH21 .. 404 B3
High La HASM GU27 .... 204 B4
High Lawn Wy HAV PO9 .... 377 J3
High Md FERN BH22 .... 405 L6
FHAM PO15 .... 14 C1
High Mead La FERN BH22 .... 405 L7
High Meadow ITCH SO19 .... 345 G2
Highmoor Cl WIMB BH21 .... 429 H3 🔲
Highmoor Rd PSTN BH14 .... 446 B5
WIMB BH21 .... 429 H3
Highmoors CHAM RG24 .... 83 K5
Highmount Cl WINC SO23 .... 11 K9
Highnam Gdns HLER SO31 .... 370 E5
High Oaks Cl HLER SO31 .... 370 E5
High Park Rd BDST BH18 .... 429 J4
FNM GU9 .... 134 C5
High Pitfold GSHT GU26 .... 204 A7
Highridge ALTN GU34 .... 176 C5
High Ridge Crs
NMIL/BTOS BH25 .... 438 A5
High Rd ELGH SO50 .... 319 J3
ROWN SO16 .... 319 J5
High St ALDT GU11 .... 6 E1
ALTN GU34 .... 176 E5
ALTN GU34 .... 196 E1
AND SP10 .... 9 H5
ASHV GU12 .... 7 H3
BPWT SO32 .... 299 G7
BPWT SO32 .... 323 H1
BPWT SO32 .... 325 G5
BPWT SO32 .... 348 C5
BROC SO42 .... 390 D8
CBLY GU15 .... 71 G2
CHAM PO6 .... 399 K1
CHCH/BSGR BH23 .... 450 A2
CWTH RG45 .... 49 M4
ELGH SO50 .... 293 M7
EMRTH PO10 .... 378 D8
EPSF GU31 .... 275 L5
EPSF GU31 .... 303 J3
FARN GU14 .... 90 F8
FAWY SO45 .... 367 L3
FBDG SP6 .... 308 B2
FBDG SP6 .... 309 L7
FBDG SP6 .... 310 D1
FHAM/PORC PO16 .... 15 L4
FHAM/STUB PO14 .... 371 K8
GPORT PO12 .... 19 K3
HASM GU27 .... 229 G2
HEND SO30 .... 320 D7 🔲
HEND SO30 .... 346 E1
HLER SO31 .... 369 M1
HTWY RG27 .... 87 J2

BOR GU35 .... 201 J5
BOR GU35 .... 202 B3
LSOL/BMARY PO13 .... 420 C5
LYMN SO41 .... 440 C5
LYMN SO41 .... 454 C4
LYND SO43 .... 363 K3
RFNM GU10 .... 158 B5
NTID SP9 .... 114 D8
ODIM RG29 .... 108 C6
OVTN RG25 .... 100 F8
PLE BH15 .... 445 G7
PSEA PO1 .... 20 C5
PSF GU32 .... 272 B3
PSF GU32 .... 273 K7
RAND SP11 .... 92 D6
RAND SP11 .... 140 A7
RGWD BH24 .... 381 J2 🔲
RGWD BH24 .... 382 D1 🔲
RWIN SO21 .... 266 F3
SHAM SO14 .... 13 G6
SHST GU47 .... 49 J8
STHA RG19 .... 27 C5
STOK SO20 .... 184 F3
STOK SO20 .... 186 D5
STOK SO20 .... 209 G1
TOTT SO40 .... 341 L1
WHAM PO17 .... 374 D3
WINC SO23 .... 10 F7
WINC SO23 .... 326 C5
High St North PLE BH15 .... 445 J5
High Thicket Rd RFNM GU10 .. 180 A4
Hightown Gdns RGWD BH24 .. 382 F2
Hightown Hl RGWD BH24 .... 383 K1
Hightown Rd RGWD BH24 .... 382 E2
Hightrees Av CHAR BH8 .... 433 J7
High Trees Dr WINW SO22 .... 10 C3
High Trees Rd ELGH SO50 .... 295 K6
WVILLE PO7 .... 352 D8
High Trees Wk FERN BH22 .... 406 B1
High Vw FHAM/PORC PO16 .. 374 A7
Highview Cl CHCH/BSGR BH23 .. 434 C5
Highview Crs CBLY GU15 .... 51 J7
Highview Gdns
BKME/WDN BH12 .... 446 B1
High Vw Rd FARN GU14 .... 90 D4
High View Wy WEND SO18 .... 319 L8
High Wy BDST BH18 .... 429 K5
Highway CWTH RG45 .... 49 K3
Highways Rd RWIN SO21 .... 266 B3
The Highway RSAL SP5 .... 256 C2
Highwood Cl FBDG SP6 .... 333 H2 🔲
NWBY RG14 .... 25 L2
YTLY GU46 .... 68 F4
Highwood La ROWD BH24 .... 359 G6
ROMY SO51 .... 263 J8
Highwood Rdg KEMP RG22 .... 127 G2
Highwood Rd BROC SO42 .... 387 K8
LSOL/BMARY PO13 .... 421 G1
Higworth La HISD PO11 .... 425 K3
Hilary Av CHAM PO6 .... 399 L1
Hilary Dr CWTH RG45 .... 49 L2
Hilary Rd CFDH BH17 .... 430 A7
Hilda Gdns WVILLE PO7 .... 351 L4
Hilda Rd BKME/WDN BH12 .... 446 D2
Hilden Wy WINW SO22 .... 213 M3
Hilder Gdns FARN GU14 .... 91 G5
Hiley Rd PLE BH15 .... 445 H2
Hilfield BLKW GU17 .... 69 J3
Hilland Ri BOR GU35 .... 202 C4
Hillary Cl FHAM/PORC PO16 .. 14 E3
FNM GU9 .... 134 E8 🔲
LYND SO43 .... 363 L5
Hillary Rd BSTK RG21 .... 4 B4
FNM GU9 .... 158 E1
Hill Barn La RWIN SO21 .... 167 M2
Hillborough Crs SSEA PO5 .... 21 J6 🔲
Hillbrook Rd CFDH BH17 .... 429 L6
Hillbrook Ri FNM GU9 .... 134 D2
Hillbrow Cl FHAM PO15 .... 14 B1
Hill Brow Cl HAV PO9 .... 353 M7
Hill Brow Rd LISS GU33 .... 248 F5
Hill Brow Rd SBNE BH6 .... 449 G2
Hillbury Av AND SP10 .... 8 D8
Hillbury Rd FBDG SP6 .... 333 L2
Hill Cl CHCH/BSGR BH23 .... 435 L1
ELGH SO50 .... 295 H5
NWBY RG14 .... 37 C1
Hill Ct FARN GU14 .... 70 C7
Hillcrest FLET GU13 .... 88 F5 🔲
FERN BH22 .... 406 A1
Hillcrest Cl MOOR/WNTN BH9 .. 432 C6
NBAD SO52 .... 291 L3
Hillcrest Ct DEAN RG23 .... 104 A2 🔲
Hillcrest Dr CHFD SO53 .... 293 J2 🔲
Hill Crest Dr RFNM GU10 .... 158 C2 🔲
Hill Crest Gdns BPWT SO32 .... 323 J4
Hillcrest Rd BKME/WDN BH12 .. 445 M3
CBLY GU15 .... 71 L1
MOOR/WNTN BH9 .... 432 C5
WIMB BH21 .... 429 G3
Hillcroft PSF GU32 .... 273 J7
Hilldean Wy HEND SO30 .... 320 D7 🔲
Hillditch LYMN SO41 .... 440 B2
Hilldown Rd PTSW SO17 .... 318 F5
Hilldowns Av NEND PO2 .... 399 G6
Hill Farm La HASM GU27 .... 228 C3 🔲
Hill Farm Rd NALR SO24 .... 221 G7
WSHM SO15 .... 343 J2
Hillgarth GSHT GU26 .... 204 A3
Hillgrove Rd WEND SO18 .... 319 L5 🔲
Hill Head Rd FHAM/STUB PO14.. 395 L7
Hill House Hl LIPH GU30 .... 226 C1
Hillhouse La STHA RG19 .... 39 K7
Hill Houses La NALR SO24 .... 242 A3
Hillier Wy WINC SO23 .... 11 H3
Hill La CHCH/BSGR BH23 .... 409 L8
CHCH/BSGR BH23 .... 435 K6
EPSF GU31 .... 305 H6
ROWN SO16 .... 318 C5
RWIN SO21 .... 266 E7
WSHM SO15 .... 318 D7
Hillman Rd PSTN BH14 .... 446 C3
Hillmead Gdns HAV PO9 .... 376 F6
Hill Meadow OVTN RG25 .... 100 F6
Hillmeadow VWD BH31 .... 356 E4
Hill Park Rd FHAM PO15 .... 372 B4

GPORT PO12 .... 421 K2
Hill Pl HLER SO31 .... 345 M8
Hill Ri BPWT SO32 .... 299 H3
RWIN SO21 .... 266 F2
Hill Rd DEAN RG23 .... 102 F1
FHAM/PORC PO16 .... 374 B7
FNM GU9 .... 135 G1
GSHT GU26 .... 203 M2
GSHT GU26 .... 203 M5
HASM GU27 .... 228 F2
NWBY RG14 .... 2 A2
RGWD BH24 .... 407 L2
RWIN SO21 .... 145 G6
Hillsborough Ct FARN GU14.... 70 B8
Hillsborough Pk CBLY GU15.... 71 M3
Hill School RFNM GU10 .... 158 C1
Hillside CBLY GU15 .... 70 C1
WINW SO22 .... 214 B3
RAND SP11 .... 141 L4
TADY RG26 .... 61 G4
THLE RG7 .... 31 H5
Hillside Av ROMY SO51 .... 290 F1
WEND SO18 .... 319 K7
WVILLE PO7 .... 375 M6
Hillside Cl ALTN GU34 .... 176 E3 🔲
CHFD SO53 .... 293 J2
FLET GU13 .... 110 B2
WINW SO22 .... 214 B6
BOR GU35 .... 202 D2
RSAL SP5 .... 231 J6
Hillside Ct AND SP10 .... 8 E6 🔲
Hillside Crs CHAM PO6 .... 374 D7
FRIM GU16 .... 91 J1
Hillside Dr CHCH/BSGR BH23 .. 434 B8
Hillside Gdns WIMB BH21 .... 429 G4
Hillside La FNM GU9 .... 135 G1
Hillside Rd ALDT GU11 .... 6 D6
ASHV GU12 .... 113 L5
BKME/WDN BH12 .... 431 K7
FNM GU9 .... 6 B8
WINW SO22 .... 214 B7
HASM GU27 .... 228 C3
LYMN SO41 .... 440 A5
RFNM GU10 .... 158 E5
ODIM RG29 .... 108 E7
VWD BH31 .... 356 E1
WIMB BH21 .... 429 G1
Hillsley Rd CHAM PO6 .... 374 D6
Hillson Dr FHAM PO15 .... 372 A5
Hill St PLE BH15 .... 445 H6
ROMY SO51 .... 316 B2
Hilltop WINW SO22 .... 214 B3
Hilltop Cl FERN BH22 .... 405 M1
Hilltop Crs CHAM PO6 .... 375 M6
Hilltop Dr ITCH SO19 .... 345 G4
Hilltop Gdns HORN PO8 .... 328 C5
Hilltop Rd FERN BH22 .... 405 M1
OVTN RG25 .... 101 G6
WIMB BH21 .... 429 J3
WVILLE PO7 .... 374 E6
Hilltop Vw YTLY GU46 .... 68 E3
Hillview HORN PO8 .... 353 G3
Hill Vw PSF GU32 .... 273 J7
Hill View Rd FERN BH22 .... 406 A2
FHAM/PORC PO16 .... 374 A7
FNM GU9 .... 134 C6
KEMP RG22 .... 104 D5
ROMY SO51 .... 234 B8
ROMY SO51 .... 263 H2
Hillview Rd FAWY SO45 .... 367 K5
NBNE BH10 .... 432 C5
Hill Wy RGWD BH24 .... 381 J3
The Hillway CHFD SO53 .... 293 J1
FHAM/PORC PO16 .... 374 A4
Hilly Cl RWIN SO21 .... 268 A4
Hillyfields ROWN SO16 .... 317 H4
Hilsea Crs NEND PO2 .... 399 J3
Hiltingbury Av HAV PO9 .... 377 L3 🔲
Hiltingbury Cl CHFD SO53 .... 265 J7
Hiltingbury Rd CHFD SO53 .... 265 G7
Hiltom Rd RGWD BH24 .... 382 F1
Hilton Cl PLE BH15 .... 445 M2
Hilton Rd GPORT PO12 .... 19 H6
NMIL/BTOS BH25 .... 437 M4
Hinaidi Wy FARN GU14 .... 90 C8
Hinchliffe Cl PLE BH15 .... 444 E6 🔲
Hinchliffe Rd PLE BH15 .... 444 E6
Hindell Cl FARN GU14 .... 70 D8
Hindhead Rd HASM GU27 .... 204 B8
Hinkler Rd ITCH SO19 .... 345 L1
Hinstock Cl FARN GU14 .... 90 D5
Hinton Cl CWTH RG45 .... 49 L1
HAV PO9 .... 377 G4
TADY RG26 .... 61 L1
Hinton Crs ITCH SO19 .... 345 J3
Hinton Dr CWTH RG45 .... 49 L1
Hinton Flds WINC SO23 .... 215 H2
Hinton HI NALR SO24 .... 242 E4
Hinton Manor La HORN PO8 .. 327 K7
Hinton Rd BMTH BH1 .... 22 F7
Hinton Wood Av
CHCH/BSGR BH23 .... 436 C7
Hintonwood La
CHCH/BSGR BH23 .... 436 C6
Hinwood Cl STOK SO20 .... 209 G1
Hipley Rd HAV PO9 .... 377 L5
Hirst Copse RAND SP11 .... 97 M6
Hirst Rd FAWY SO45 .... 367 M5
Hispano Av FHAM PO15 .... 371 G4
Hitches La FLET GU13 .... 110 B1
Hither Gn EMRTH PO10 .... 379 J1
Hitherwood Cl HORN PO8 .... 352 F7
Hives Wy LYMN SO41 .... 440 B2 🔲
H Jones Crs ALDT GU11 .... 112 F5 🔲
Hoadlands EPSF GU31 .... 275 M4
Hoad's HI WHAM PO17 .... 348 F6
Hobart Dr FAWY SO45 .... 367 M5
Hobart Rd NMIL/BTOS BH25 .. 437 K6
Hobb La HEND SO30 .... 346 B2
Hobbs Cl NALR SO24 .... 219 H4
Hobbs Pk RGWD BH24 .... 381 K4
Hobbs Rd BKME/WDN BH12 .. 431 G8
Hobbs Sq AND SP10 .... 119 H6
Hobby Cl HSEA PO3 .... 399 M8
Hobson Wy FAWY SO45 .... 392 B5 🔲
Hoburne Gdns
CHCH/BSGR BH23 .... 436 A7
Hoburne La CHCH/BSGR BH23 .. 435 M8

Hockford La THLE RG7 .... 40 D5
Hockham St HAV PO9 .... 377 G1
Hockley Cl CHAM PO6 .... 375 H8 🔲
Hockley Link RWIN SO21 .... 238 D7
Hocombe Dr CHFD SO53 .... 265 G6
Hocombe Park Cl CHFD SO53 .. 265 G6
Hocombe Rd CHFD SO53 .... 265 G6
Hocombe Wood Rd
CHFD SO53 .... 264 F6
Hodder Cl CHFD SO53 .... 293 G3 🔲
Hodges Cl CFDH BH17 .... 445 K1
HAV PO9 .... 17 G1
Hoeford Cl FHAM/PORC PO16.. 396 F2
Hoe La ROMY SO51 .... 291 H6
Hoe Rd BPWT SO32 .... 323 K1
Hoe St WVILLE PO7 .... 350 F1
The Hoe LSOL/BMARY PO13 .. 397 J7 🔲
Hogarth Cl BSTK RG21 .... 105 K4
ROMY SO51 .... 263 C7
SHST GU47 .... 70 B2
Hogarth Ct AND SO51 .... 8 E2
Hoggarth Cl EPSF GU31 .... 275 M4
Hoghatch La FNM GU9 .... 134 D2
Hogmoor Rd BOR GU35 .... 201 G4
Hogs Lodge La HORN PO8 .... 302 C6
Hogwood La EWKG RG40 .... 47 K2
HEND SO30 .... 320 D2
Holbeche Cl YTLY GU46 .... 68 D3
Holbein Cl BSTK RG21 .... 105 K4
Holborne Cl NWBY RG14 .... 36 F3
Holbrook Rd FNM GU9 .... 6 C6
Holbrook Rd FHAM/PORC PO16 .. 15 J7 🔲
PSEA PO1 .... 21 K1
Holbrook Wy ALDT GU11 .... 7 G7
Holbury Cl CHAR BH8 .... 433 L5
Holbury Ct HAV PO9 .... 377 M3 🔲
Holbury Dro FAWY SO45 .... 391 M4
Holbury La RSAL SP5 .... 232 D5
Holcombe Rd UPTN BH16 .... 400 A4
Holcot La HSEA PO3 .... 400 A4
Holcroft Rd ITCH SO19 345
Holdaway Cl WINC SO23 .... 215 H1 🔲
Holdenbury Ct HSEA PO3 .... 400 A3
Holdenhurst Av LTDN BH7 .... 449 H1
Holdenhurst Cl HORN PO8 .... 328 B7 🔲
Holdenhurst Rd BMTH BH1 .... 23 J8
CHAR BH8 .... 433 L5
CHAR BH8 .... 448 L2
Holden La RWIN SO21 .... 269 L1
Holder Rd ASHV GU12 .... 113 H7
Holdfast La HASM GU27 .... 205 J8
Holding La NALR SO24 .... 241 K6
Hole La BPWT SO32 .... 322 F7
RFNM GU10 .... 132 F7
WVILLE PO7 .... 325 L8
Holes Bay Rd PLE BH15 .... 445 G4
Holes Cl LYMN SO41 .... 438 D4
Holkham Cl ROWN SO16 .... 317 K5 🔲
Hollam Cl FHAM/STUB PO14 .. 371 H8
Hollam Crs FHAM/STUB PO14 .. 371 H8
Hollam Dr FHAM/STUB PO14 .. 371 H8
Hollam Rd ENEY PO4 .... 423 K4
Holland Cl FNM GU9 .... 135 H7
Holland Dr AND SP10 .... 118 C5
Holland Gdns FLET GU13 .... 88 F7
Holland Pk HLER SO31 .... 370 C5
Holland Pl
LSOL/BMARY PO13 .... 397 H6 🔲
ROWN SO16 .... 318 A7
Holland Rd ENEY PO4 .... 21 L4
ITCH SO19 .... 344 B6
TOTT SO40 .... 341 G1
The Hollands STHA RG19 .... 27 H5
Hollands Wood Dr
NMIL/BTOS BH25 .... 437 M3
Holland Wy BDST BH18 .... 429 K3
The Hollies Cl LYMN SO41 .... 412 F7
The Hollies NWBY RG14 .... 37 G3
Hollingbourne Cl WEND SO18 .. 319 J8
Hollington La KSCL RG20 .... 55 M4
Hollist La EPSF GU31 .... 305 J4 🔲
Hollis Wood Dr RFNM GU10 .... 158 B3
Holloway Av BWD BH11 .... 431 K3
Hollow La HISD PO11 .... 425 K5
BOR GU35 .... 202 B2
Hollowshot La TADY RG26 .... 59 H7
TADY RG26 .... 59 M8
Holly Av FRIM GU16 .... 71 L5
Hollyfields LSOL/BMARY PO13 .. 420 D3
Holly Bank Cl HORN PO8 .... 353 G3
Hollybank Crs FAWY SO45 .... 367 K4
Hollybank La EMRTH PO10 .... 378 D4
Hollybank Rd FAWY SO45 .... 367 K5
Hollybrook Av ROWN SO16 .... 318 B5
Hollybrook Cl ROWN SO16.... 318 A7
Hollybrook Gdns HLER SO31 .. 370 D3
Hollybrook Pk BOR GU35 .... 201 K5
Hollybrook Rd ROWN SO16 .... 318 B6
Hollybush La ALDT GU11 .... 91 H8
HTWY RG27 .... 48 B8
TADY RG26 .... 61 J6
THLE RG7 .... 31 J6
Hollybush Ride EWKG RG40 .... 48 F3
Holly Cl ASHV GU12 .... 7 K2
FARN GU14 .... 90 D4
FAWY SO45 .... 391 L4
HLER SO31 .... 370 C5
BOR GU35 .... 202 F3
RGWD BH24 .... 381 H4
TADY RG26 .... 63 M6
Hollycombe Cl LIPH GU30 .... 226 F6
Holly Dell ROWN SO16 .... 318 D3
Holly Dr CHAM RG24 .... 106 B2
WVILLE PO7 .... 376 E2
Hollyfields Cl CBLY GU15 .... 70 E3 🔲
Holly Gdns CHCH/BSGR BH23 .. 435 H7
HEND SO30 .... 320 C5
LYMN SO41 .... 454 B3
Holly Gv FHAM/PORC PO16 .... 372 C4
WIMB BH21 .... 356 B3
Holly Hatch Rd TOTT SO40 .... 341 J2
Holly Hedge La FRIM GU16 .... 71 H6
Holly Hedge La CFDH BH17 .... 430 A8
Holly Hedge La FRIM GU16 .... 71 H6
Holly HI ROWN SO16 .... 318 D3

Holly Hill Cl ROWN SO16 ......318 D3
Holly Hill La HLER SO31 ......370 A4
Hollyhock Cl KEMP RG22 ......103 M8
Holly La CHCH/BSGR BH23 ......437 G6
  LYMN 414 F4
  NMIL/BTOS BH25 ......438 A4
  THLE 42 E8
Holly Oak Rd ROWN SO16 ......317 M5
Hollyridge HASM GU27 ......228 F2
Holly Rd ASHV GU12 ......7 K2
  FARN GU14 ......90 C4
  FAWY SO45 ......392 C8
  TOTT SO40 ......340 F6
Holly St GPORT PO12 ......19 H3
Hollytree Gdns FRIM GU16 ......71 G8
Hollytrees FLET GU13 ......110 D3
Hollywater Rd LIPH GU30 ......201 L8
Holly Wy BLKW GU17 ......70 A4
Hollywell Dr CHAM PO6 ......398 F1
Hollywood La LYMN SO41 ......440 B3
Holman Cl HORN PO8 ......352 E6
Holmbrook Cl FARN GU14 ......89 M4
Holmbury Av CWTH RG45 ......49 K1
Holm Cl RGWD BH24 ......359 G7
Holmdale Rd GPORT PO12 ......421 K1
Holmdene THLE RG7 ......31 L5
Holme Cl CWTH RG45 ......49 K1
Holmefield FHAM/STUB PO14 ......396 D2
Holme Rd CHCH/BSGR BH23 ......436 F1
Holmhurst Av CHCH/BSGR BH23 ......436 C7
Holm Oak Cl WINW SO22 ......213 M3
Holmsley Cl LYMN SO41 ......439 M6
  WEND SO18 ......345 G1
Holmsley Rd NMIL/BTOS BH25 ......411 H6
Holmwood Garth RGWD BH24 ......383 G2
Holne Ct ENEY PO4 ......424 A5
Holnest Rd CFDH BH17 ......430 B7
Holst Cl KEMP RG22 ......127 K1
Holst Wy WVILLE PO7 ......376 D3
Holt Cl FARN GU14 ......90 F1
  WHAM PO17 ......348 D4
Holt Cottages STHA RG19 ......40 C8
Holt Ct ITCH SO19 ......344 C8
Holt Down EPSF GU31 ......276 A5
Holt End La ALTN GU34 ......174 D6
  ALTN GU34 ......174 F4
Holt Gdns HAV PO9 ......353 M5
Holt La HTWY RG27 ......108 B1
  RAND SP11 ......73 G8
  TADY RG26 ......60 C4
Holt Pound La RFNM GU10 ......157 M3
Holt Rd BKME/WDN BH12 ......446 E2
  WIMB BH21 ......356 B8
  WSHM SO15 ......343 K1
Holt Wy HTWY RG27 ......86 B6
Holtwood Rd KSCL RG20 ......35 L2
Holy Barn Cl KEMP RG22 ......103 M7
Holybourne Rd ROMY SO51 ......291 G1
Holybourne HAV PO9 ......16 E1
Holyhook Cl CWTH RG45 ......49 K2
Holyrood Av PTSW SO17 ......319 G6
Holyrood Cl WVILLE PO7 ......376 E1
Holywell Cl CFDH BH17 ......430 B5
  FARN GU14 ......90 D1
Holywell St STHA RG19 ......27 G5
Home Cl NALR SO24 ......173 M6
  NALR SO24 ......219 H3
Home Farm Cl FARN GU14 ......91 G2
  FAWY SO45 ......392 A8
Home Farm Gdns AND SP10 ......118 C5
Home Farm Rd HTWY RG27 ......88 A1
Home Farm Wy WEND BH31 ......356 C2
Homefield ROMY SO51 ......262 F7
Home Field Dr ROWN SO16 ......317 H3
Homefield CHAM PO6 ......400 A1
  EMRTH PO10 ......378 F4
Homefield Wy HORN PO8 ......328 A2
Home La RWIN SO21 ......213 H5
Homelea Cl ASHV GU12 ......91 K8
Homeleigh Crs ASHV GU12 ......91 K8
Home Md OVTN RG25 ......125 L7
  WVILLE PO7 ......351 K5
Home Mead NWBY RG14 ......25 H8
Home Park Rd YTLY GU46 ......68 F2
Homer Cl HORN PO8 ......352 E6
  LSOL/BMARY PO13 ......396 F8
Homer Farm La FAWY SO45 ......418 C2
Home Rd BWD BH11 ......431 M2
Home Rule Rd HLER SO31 ......370 E4
Homeside Rd MOOR/WNTN BH9 ......432 E6
Homestead Rd ALTN GU34 ......196 L1
Homesteads Rd KEMP RG22 ......103 M7
Home Wy EPSF GU31 ......276 B5
Homewell HAV PO9 ......16 E5
Homewood Cl NMIL/BTOS BH25 ......438 A5
Hone Hl SHST GU47 ......69 L1
Honeybottom Rd TADY RG26 ......41 L7
Honeybourne Crs SBNE BH6 ......449 M4
Honeycritch La PSF GU32 ......247 G5
Honey La ALTN GU34 ......223 L1
  FHAM PO15 ......372 B3
  RGWD BH24 ......384 C6
Honeysuckle Cl CWTH RG45 ......49 K1
  WINW SO22 ......238 C4
  HLER SO31 ......370 E3
  KEMP RG22 ......103 M8
  LSOL/BMARY PO13 ......396 F5
  YTLY GU46 ......68 D2
Honeysuckle La CFDH BH17 ......429 K7
  BOR GU35 ......202 E3
Honeysuckle Rd ROWN SO16 ......319 G4
Honeysuckle Wy NBAD SO52 ......291 H2
Honeywood Cl PSEA PO3 ......399 K4
  TOTT SO40 ......316 C7

Honister Gdns FLET GU13 ......89 H6
Hood Cl HLER SO31 ......370 F4
  NBNE BH10 ......431 M7
Hood Crs NBNE BH10 ......431 M7
Hood Rd WEND SO18 ......319 M8
Hook Cl CHFD SO53 ......264 F6
Hook Crs CHFD SO53 ......264 F6
Hooke Cl CFDH BH17 ......430 E6
Hook La HLER SO31 ......394 E1
  NALR SO24 ......219 M4
  TADY RG26 ......60 E2
  TADY RG26 ......80 F8
Hook Park Rd HLER SO31 ......394 A1
Hookpit Farm La WINC SO23 ......191 G8
Hook Rd HTWY RG27 ......85 M3
  HTWY RG27 ......107 M1
  KSCL RG20 ......59 K6
  ODIM RG29 ......107 L4
  ODIM RG29 ......108 B3
  ROMY SO51 ......264 D5
Hook's Farm Wy HAV PO9 ......16 A1
Hook's La HAV PO9 ......16 B2
Hookstile La FNM GU9 ......134 F7
Hook Water Rd CHFD SO53 ......264 F6
  ROMY SO51 ......264 D5
Hoopersmead OVTN RG25 ......127 M1
Hoopers Wy DEAN RG23 ......103 G7
Hope Fountain CBLY GU15 ......71 J4
Hope Grant's Rd ALDT GU11 ......112 D4
Hope La FNM GU9 ......134 E2
Hopeman Cl SHST GU47 ......70 A1
Hope Rd HEND SO30 ......320 D6
Hope St PSEA PO1 ......423 G2
Hopeswood LISS GU33 ......224 E5
Hopfield Ms WVILLE PO7 ......376 C2
Hopfield Rd HTWY RG27 ......87 H3
Hop Gdn FLET GU13 ......110 D4
Hop Garden Rd HTWY RG27 ......85 L7
The Hop Gdn EPSF GU31 ......304 F5
Hopkins Cl CHAM PO6 ......374 C8
  CHAM BH8 ......433 L6
Hopkinson Wy AND SP10 ......118 A7
Hopton Garth CHAM RG24 ......83 M7
Hopwood Cl NWBY RG14 ......3 L1
Horace Rd BOSC BH5 ......448 M4
Hordle La ALTN SO41 ......438 D8
Hordle Rd HAV PO9 ......377 G4
Horlock Rd BROC SO42 ......387 L6
Hormer Ct SHST GU47 ......50 A7
Hornbeam Cl FARN GU14 ......89 M3
  HEND SO30 ......346 B2
  RWIN SO21 ......190 D4
  SHST GU47 ......50 A7
Hornbeam Gdns HEND SO30 ......320 C6
Hornbeam Pl HTWY RG27 ......86 A6
Hornbeam Rd HAV PO9 ......17 K1
  NBAD SO52 ......292 D3
Hornbeams THLE RG7 ......45 M1
Hornbeam Wy WIMB BH21 ......404 B3
Hornby Cl HLER SO31 ......370 B8
Hornchurch Rd ROWN SO16 ......317 L3
Horndean Rd EMRTH PO10 ......378 B4
  HORN PO8 ......328 D8
Horne Rd STHA RG19 ......27 G6
Hornet Cl FHAM PO15 ......14 A3
  GPORT PO12 ......19 H6
Hornet Rd EMRTH PO10 ......402 E5
  FHAM/STUB PO14 ......396 D3
Horning Rd BKME/WDN BH12 ......446 E3
Horn Rd FARN GU14 ......90 B3
Horns Dro ROWN SO16 ......317 K2
Horns Hl BPWT SO32 ......325 G6
Horsa Cl SBNE BH6 ......449 K4
Horsa Ct SBNE BH6 ......449 K4
Horsa Rd SBNE BH6 ......449 K4
Horsea La NEND PO2 ......399 H4
Horsea Rd NEND PO2 ......399 J3
Horsebridge Rd HAV PO9 ......377 L4
  STOK SO20 ......209 K4
Horsebridge Wy ROWN SO16 ......317 K3
Horsecroft ROMY SO51 ......262 E8
Horsefair Ct ROMY SO51 ......290 D1
Horse La ALTN GU34 ......220 C1
Horsepost La WVILLE PO7 ......327 L6
Horse Sands Cl ENEY PO4 ......424 B5
Horseshoe Bend ROMY SO51 ......263 H6
Horseshoe Cl CBLY GU15 ......51 J8
  FHAM/STUB PO14 ......371 H6
  WIMB BH21 ......404 F2
Horseshoe Crs CBLY GU15 ......51 J8
  BOR GU35 ......201 K5
  THLE RG7 ......31 K5
Horseshoe Dr ROMY SO51 ......263 H6
Horseshoe End NWBY RG14 ......37 L2
Horseshoe La ASHV GU12 ......113 K2
  RAND SP11 ......74 C8
Horseshoe Ldg HLER SO31 ......370 C7
Horsham Av NBNE BH10 ......432 A1
Horsham Rd SHST GU47 ......50 A7
Horton Cl MOOR/WNTN BH9 ......433 C5
Horton Rd LSOL/BMARY PO13 ......397 G4
  RGWD BH24 ......381 G2
Horton Wy ELGH SO50 ......294 E7
  VWD BH31 ......356 B3
Horwood Gdns BSTK RG21 ......104 E5
Hose Hl THLE RG7 ......31 K1
Hosker Rd BOSC BH5 ......449 G3
Hosketts La STOK SO20 ......184 D5
Hospital Hl ALDT GU11 ......6 E1
Hospital La FHAM/PORC PO16 ......398 C2
Hospital Rd ALDT GU11 ......112 D5
  BPWT SO32 ......323 M7
Hostel Rd FARN GU14 ......90 B8
Hotspur Cl FAWY SO45 ......367 K3
Houchin St BPWT SO32 ......323 H1
Houghton Cl HAV PO9 ......377 M2
Houlton Rd PLE BH15 ......445 K4
Hound Cl HLER SO31 ......369 H4
Hound Green Cl HTWY RG27 ......66 A5
Houndmills Rd BSTK RG21 ......104 D2
Hound Rd HLER SO31 ......369 H2
Hound Road Gdns HLER SO31 ......369 H3
Hounds Wy WIMB BH21 ......404 F3
Hound Wy HLER SO31 ......369 H2
Houndwell Pl SHAM SO14 ......13 H4
Hounsdown Av TOTT SO40 ......341 H4

Hounsdown Cl TOTT SO40 ......341 K3
Hounslow Cl PLE BH15 ......444 D6
House Cl RWIN SO21 ......266 F7
House Farm Rd GPORT PO12 ......421 J4
Houseman Cl FARN GU14 ......90 C2
Hoveton Gv CHFD SO53 ......265 G8
Howard Cl CHCH/BSGR BH23 ......450 E2
  CHFD SO53 ......293 H3
  ELGH SO50 ......295 H6
  FLET GU13 ......89 H7
  RGWD BH24 ......384 E5
  WEND SO18 ......319 K4
Howard Cole Wy ALDT GU11 ......6 A2
Howard Dr FARN GU14 ......89 L4
Howard Rd BSTK RG21 ......105 H5
  CHAR BH8 ......448 B1
  NEND PO2 ......399 J4
  NWBY RG14 2
  VWD BH31 ......356 D2
  WSHM SO15 ......343 H2
Howard's Gv WSHM SO15 ......318 B8
Howard's La ALTN GU34 ......177 H1
Howards Md LYMN SO41 ......439 M6
Howe Cl CHCH/BSGR BH23 ......450 E3
  NMIL/BTOS BH25 ......437 K5
Howe La VWD BH31 ......356 C3
Howe Rd LSOL/BMARY PO13 ......421 G2
Howerts Cl HLER SO31 ......394 B1
Howes Gdns FLET GU13 ......110 D2
Howeth Cl NBNE BH10 ......432 B5
Howeth Rd NBNE BH10 ......432 A4
Howgare Rd RSAL SP5 ......252 A6
Howlett Cl LYMN SO41 ......440 A4
Howton Rd NBNE BH10 ......432 A3
Hoxley Rd NBNE BH10 ......432 B5
Hoyal Rd PLE BH15 ......444 C5
Hoylake Cl LSOL/BMARY PO13 ......397 G7
Hoylake Rd CHAM PO6 ......376 A7
Hoylecroft Cl FHAM PO15 ......14 C1
Hubbard Rd BSTK RG21 ......4 A4
Hubert Rd WINC SO23 ......238 D1
Huddington Gld HTWY RG27 ......68 D3
Hudson Cl BKME/WDN BH12 ......431 G6
  LSOL/BMARY PO13 ......421 G2
  RGWD BH24 ......359 G8
Hudson Ct TOTT SO40 ......341 H2
Hudson Davies Cl LYMN SO41 ......414 D3
Hudson Rd PSEA PO5 ......21 J4
Hudsons Meadow HTWY RG27 ......66 A3
Hugh's La FAWY SO45 ......392 C7
Huish La OVTN RG25 ......106 A6
Hulbert Rd HAV PO9 ......376 F3
  WVILLE PO7 ......376 E1
Hulbert Wy KEMP RG22 ......104 B6
Hulfords La HTWY RG27 ......67 K7
Hullam La ALTN GU34 ......223 G3
Hull Crs BWD BH11 ......431 H4
Hulles Wy NBAD SO52 ......291 L4
Hull Rd BWD BH11 ......431 H4
Hull Wy BWD BH11 ......431 H4
Hulse Rd WSHM SO15 ......318 E8
Hulton Cl ITCH SO19 ......344 B7
Humber Cl FHAM/STUB PO14 ......395 M5
  NTHA RG18 ......26 E3
Humber Gdns HLER SO31 ......345 L7
Humber La NTID SP9 ......114 C4
Humber Rd FARN BH22 ......406 E2
Humberstone Rd AND SP10 ......9 H5
Humbers Vw STOK SO20 ......210 F7
Humber Wy SHST GU47 ......50 A8
The Hummicks BROC SO42 ......390 F8
Hundred Acres Rd WHAM PO17 ......349 L3
Hundred La LYMN SO41 ......440 B1
The Hundred ROMY SO51 ......290 D1
  WVILLE PO7 ......352 B7
Hungerfield Cl CHCH/BSGR BH23 ......409 L7
Hungerford HLER SO31 ......369 K1
Hungerford Cl SHST GU47 ......49 M8
Hungerford Hl FBDG SP6 ......335 G5
Hungerford La AND SP10 ......118 F2
  RAND SP11 ......72 D6
Hungerford Rd MARL SN8 ......93 G6
Hunnels Cl FLET GU13 ......110 D5
Hunt Av HLER SO31 ......369 G2
Hunt Cl RWIN SO21 ......190 D4
Hunter Cl CHCH/BSGR BH23 ......450 F1
  FAWY SO45 ......391 M2
  LSOL/BMARY PO13 ......421 H1
  WIMB BH21 ......405 G2
Hunter Rd EMRTH PO10 ......402 E4
  ENEY PO4 ......423 K5
  FARN GU14 ......90 C5
Hunters Cha BPWT SO32 ......324 B5
  LIPH GU30 ......226 E3
Hunters Cl DEAN RG23 ......103 G5
  VWD BH31 ......357 G3
Hunters Crs ROMY SO51 ......263 H6
  TOTT SO40 ......340 F2
Hunter's Hl THLE RG7 ......31 J5
  TOTT SO40 ......341 H5
Hunters Ldg FHAM PO15 ......371 M8
Hunters Ride WVILLE PO7 ......376 C1
Hunters Rd LISS GU33 ......225 J6
Hunters Wy ELGH SO50 ......294 F6

PLE BH15 ......445 K4
Hunts Cl HTWY RG27 ......86 B7
Hunts La HTWY RG27 ......86 B7
Huntsman's Ms FRIM GU16 ......91 J5
Huntsmead ALTN GU34 ......176 F5
Hunts Pond Rd HLER SO31 ......370 F4
Huntvale Rd MOOR/WNTN BH9 ......432 F5
The Hurdles FHAM/STUB PO14 ......371 H6
Hurdle Wy RWIN SO21 ......238 B8
Hurland La BOR GU35 ......202 C4
Hurlands Cl FNM GU9 ......135 J4
Hurlands Pl FNM GU9 ......135 J4
Hurlingham Gdns ROWN SO16 ......318 F3
Hurn Cl RGWD BH24 ......382 B2
Hurn Ct HAV PO9 ......377 M2
Hurn Court La CHCH/BSGR BH23 ......433 K2
Hurn La RGWD BH24 ......382 B2
Hurn Rd CHCH/BSGR BH23 ......434 C5
  RGWD BH24 ......382 A8
Hurn Wy CHCH/BSGR BH23 ......434 B7
Hurricane Dr ROWN SO16 ......317 K2
Hurricane Wy FARN GU14 ......112 C1
Hursley Dr FAWY SO45 ......418 C1
Hursley Rd CHFD SO53 ......293 G1
  HAV PO9 ......377 H3
  RWIN SO21 ......265 C4
Hurstbourne Av CHCH/BSGR BH23 ......436 C7
Hurstbourne Pl HAV PO9 ......377 H2
Hurst Cl CHCH/BSGR BH23 ......437 C6
  CHFD SO53 ......292 F4
  FHAM/STUB PO14 ......395 L7
  LIPH GU30 ......226 D3
  TOTT SO40 ......316 E8
Hurstdene Rd CHAR BH8 ......433 G6
Hurst Gn Cl LSOL/BMARY PO13 ......396 F6
Hurst Green Cl HORN PO8 ......352 F6
  ITCH SO19 ......344 E7
Hurst Hl PSTN BH14 ......446 B8
Hurst La ALDT GU11 ......246 A5
  RWIN SO21 ......295 M2
Hurstmere Cl GSHT GU26 ......204 A5
Hurst Rd ALDT GU11 ......112 F5
  FARN GU14 ......70 E8
  LYMN SO41 ......454 D5
  RGWD BH24 ......358 E7
The Hurst HTWY RG27 ......87 L7
Hurstville Dr WVILLE PO7 ......376 D1
Hurstwood Av EMRTH PO10 ......379 J8
Hussar Ct ALDT GU11 ......6 A2
Hussell La ALTN GU34 ......196 E1
Hussey Cl WINC SO23 ......11 H2
Hussey's La ALTN GU34 ......156 B3
Hutton Cl NWBY RG14 ......3 G1
Hutton Rd ASHV GU12 ......113 K2
Hutton Sq AND SP10 ......119 H6
Hutwood Rd ROWN SO16 ......292 F8
Huxley Cl HLER SO31 ......370 F6
Huxley Ct FAWY SO45 ......367 G6
Hyacinth Cl CFDH BH17 ......429 K7
  KEMP RG22 ......103 M8
Hyde Abbey Rd WINC SO23 ......11 G6
Hyde Church La WINC SO23 ......11 G5
Hyde Cl LYMN SO41 ......412 F6
  TOTT SO40 ......340 F1
  WINC SO23 ......10 F5
  WSHM SO15 ......318 B7
Hyde End La STHA RG19 ......40 A3
Hyde La FBDG SP6 ......335 G3
  KSCL RG20 ......58 D2
  RFNM GU10 ......133 G2
Hyden Farm La HORN PO8 ......327 J2
Hyde Park Rd SSEA PO5 ......21 H3
Hyde Rd NBNE BH10 ......432 A4
Hydes Platt THLE RG7 ......42 E8
Hyde St SSEA PO5 ......21 G5
  WINC SO23 ......11 G5
The Hyde NMIL/BTOS BH25 ......437 J4
Hylton Rd PSF GU32 ......275 L5
Hymans Wy TOTT SO40 ......341 J1
Hynesbury Rd CHCH/BSGR BH23 ......451 H2
Hyson Crs RAND SP11 ......93 G6
Hyssop Cl FHAM PO15 ......371 H1
Hythe By-pass FAWY SO45 ......366 F4
Hythe Rd CHAM PO6 ......375 J8
  PLE BH15 ......445 M1
  TOTT SO40 ......342 D8

I

Ibbertson Cl CHAR BH8 ......433 K6
Ibbertson Rd CHAR BH8 ......433 K7
Ibbertson Wy CHAR BH8 ......433 K6
Ibbett Rd NBNE BH10 ......432 A6
Ibbotson Wy TOTT SO40 ......341 H3
Iberian Wy CBLY GU15 ......71 K2
Ibsen Cl HLER SO31 ......347 G8
Ibsley Cl CHAR BH8 ......448 B3
Ibsley Dro RGWD BH24 ......334 E7
Ibsley Gv HAV PO9 ......16 A1
Ibworth La TADY RG26 ......80 A5
Icarus Pl WVILLE PO7 ......376 D6
Icknield Wy AND SP10 ......119 G3
Iddesleigh Rd TWDS BH3 ......447 L3
Idsworth Cl HORN PO8 ......353 H2
Idsworth Rd HORN PO8 ......352 F6
  HSEA PO3 ......399 J4
Iford Ct HAV PO9 ......377 M2
Iford Gdns BWD BH7 ......449 H1
Iford La SBNE BH6 ......449 K1
Ilex Cl TADY RG26 ......42 B7
  WINC SO23 ......191 G8
  YTLY GU46 ......68 C2
Ilex Crs HLER SO31 ......370 D5
Ilex Wk HISD PO11 ......426 A5
Iley La LYMN SO41 ......455 H1
Ilford Cl SBNE BH6 ......449 L2
Ilkley Wy STHA RG19 ......26 F6
Imadene Crs BOR GU35 ......201 L4
Imber Dr CHCH/BSGR BH23 ......436 D8

Imber Rd WINC SO23 ......11 L6
Imber Wy ITCH SO19 ......345 G4
Imbrecourt CCLF BH13 ......457 K1
Imjin Cl ALDT GU11 ......112 E5
Imperial Av WSHM SO15 ......342 F1
Imperial Rd SHAM SO14 ......343 M1
Implacable Rd LSOL/BMARY PO13 ......420 B1
Impstone Rd TADY RG26 ......42 C7
Imran Ct ASHV GU12 ......7 J5
Ingersley Ri HEND SO30 ......320 C7
Ingle Dell CBLY GU15 ......71 G4
Ingledene Cl GPORT PO12 ......18 E4
  HAV PO9 ......16 A3
Ingle Gln EWKG RG40 ......48 D1
  FAWY SO45 ......367 L7
Ingle Gn TOTT SO40 ......316 A7
Ingles Edge HUNG RG17 ......34 A4
Inglesham Wy PLE BH15 ......444 D4
  PLE BH15 ......444 D5
Ingleside HLER SO31 ......369 G1
Ingleside Cl FHAM/STUB PO14 ......371 M8
Ingleton Rd ROWN SO16 ......317 J7
Inglewood Av CBLY GU15 ......71 M4
  CHAR BH8 ......433 K7
Inglewood Dr KEMP RG22 ......127 G2
  NMIL/BTOS BH25 ......437 M6
Inglis Rd SSEA PO5 ......21 L5
Ingoldfield La WHAM PO17 ......350 A1
Ingworth Rd BKME/WDN BH12 ......446 F3
Inhams La WVILLE PO7 ......351 H4
Inhams Rd ALTN GU34 ......177 J2
Inhams Wy THLE RG7 ......42 D8
Inhurst Av WVILLE PO7 ......352 M8
Inhurst La STHA RG19 ......40 F7
Inhurst Rd NEND PO2 ......399 J6
Inhurst Wy TADY RG26 ......41 J7
Inkerman Rd ITCH SO19 ......344 B5
Inkpen Gdns CHAM RG24 ......83 M8
Inlands Rd RCCH PO18 ......379 K7
Inmans La PSF GU32 ......276 A3
Innisfail Gdns ALDT GU11 ......6 C5
Insley Crs WIMB BH21 ......429 J3
Institute Rd ASHV GU12 ......7 L5
Instow Gdns FARN GU14 ......90 D1
International Wy ITCH SO19 ......344 C8
Inval Hl HASM GU27 ......204 F8
Inveravon CHCH/BSGR BH23 ......450 E4
Inverclyde Rd PSTN BH14 ......446 B4
Invergordon Av CHAM PO6 ......399 M1
Inverkip Cl LSOL/BMARY PO13 ......420 C1
Inverleigh Rd SBNE BH6 ......449 H2
Inverness Av FHAM PO15 ......14 C2
Inverness Rd NEND PO2 ......423 J1
Inverness Wy SHST GU47 ......70 A1
Invincible Rd FARN GU14 ......90 D6
Inwood Rd LISS GU33 ......248 F5
Ionic Cl CHFD SO53 ......293 L1
Iping Av HAV PO9 ......377 H3
Iping Cl HAV PO9 ......377 H3
Iping La MIDH GU29 ......279 H5
Iping Rd LIPH GU30 ......250 E6
Ipley Wy FAWY SO45 ......367 L6
Ipoh Ct STOK SO20 ......162 F3
Ipswich Rd WBNE BH4 ......447 G4
Ireland Wy WVILLE PO7 ......376 C3
Iris Cl KEMP RG22 ......126 F1
Iris Rd MOOR/WNTN BH9 ......432 D7
  ROWN SO16 ......319 G4
Ironbridge Crs HLER SO31 ......370 E2
Ironbridge La ENEY PO4 ......424 A4
Iron Mill Cl FHAM PO15 ......14 A1
Ironmill La FHAM PO15 ......371 M3
Irvine Cl FHAM/PORC PO16 ......15 G2
Irvine Dr FARN GU14 ......70 B8
Irvine Wy CHCH/BSGR BH23 ......435 J8
Irving Rd ROWN SO16 ......317 L7
  SBNE BH6 ......449 J3
Irwell Cl BSTK RG21 ......5 J8
  CHFD SO53 ......292 F3
Isaacs Cl BKME/WDN BH12 ......447 G1
Isambard Brunel Rd PSEA PO1 ......21 G2
Isington La ALTN GU34 ......156 D5
Isington Rd ALTN GU34 ......156 C8
Isis Cl ROWN SO16 ......317 K8
Isis Wy SHST GU47 ......50 A8
Island Cl HISD PO11 ......401 L5
Island Farm La THLE RG7 ......31 H7
Island View Av CHCH/BSGR BH23 ......451 G2
Island View Cl LYMN SO41 ......454 D5
Island View Rd NMIL/BTOS BH25 ......452 C1
Island View Ter NEND PO2 ......399 G7
Islay Gdns CHAM PO6 ......375 K7
Itchel La RFNM GU10 ......133 G1
Itchen Av ELGH SO50 ......294 E6
Itchen Cl DEAN RG23 ......103 G3
  PSF GU32 ......275 K6
  ROMY SO51 ......288 D3
Itchen Ct AND SP10 ......9 M1
Itchenor Rd HISD PO11 ......426 D6
Itchen Rd HAV PO9 ......377 M2
Itchenside Cl WEND SO18 ......319 L4
Itchen Vw NALR SO24 ......217 J3
Itchen Vw ELGH SO50 ......294 A2
  ITCH SO19 ......344 B5
  NALR SO24 ......218 A8
  RWIN SO21 ......215 J3
  RWIN SO21 ......216 F3
  WINC SO23 ......11 M1
Itchin Cl TOTT SO40 ......341 H2
Ithica Cl HISD PO11 ......425 L4
Ivamy Pl BWD BH11 ......431 K6
Ivanhoe Rd EWKG RG40 ......47 K2
  WSHM SO15 ......318 C7
Ively Rd FARN GU14 ......89 M7
Ives Cl YTLY GU46 ......68 C1
Ivor Cl FAWY SO45 ......392 A4
Ivor Rd PLE BH15 ......444 F5
  WIMB BH21 ......429 H4
Ivy Cl WINW SO22 ......238 D3
  RGWD BH24 ......381 H4
  TOTT SO40 ......316 D6
Ivy Ct WVILLE PO7 ......376 B4

Ivy Dene *ITCH* SO19............ 345 H4
Ivydene Crs *RCCH* PO18........ 403 M1
Ivydene Gdns *HORN* PO8......... 352 E4
Ivy Down La *DEAN* RG23........ 102 D5
Ivyhole HI *HTWY* RG27.......... 68 A8
Ivyhouse La *PSF* GU32........... 246 D5
Ivy La *FNM* GU9................ 134 E6
   HEND SO30........... 320 A6
   RGWD BH24.......... 358 E5
Ivy Rd *ASHV* GU12.............. 113 H6
   PTSW SO17............ 319 H8
   WIMB BH21........... 404 B8

J

Jacaranda Cl *FHAM* PO15........ 371 J5 🔳
Jacaranda Rd *BOR* GU35......... 201 J6
Jack Cockerill Wy *SSEA* PO5..... 423 H7 🔳
Jackdaw Cl *HORN* PO8........... 352 C4
   KEMP RG22............ 103 L8
Jackdaw Ri *ELGH* SO50.......... 293 J7 🔳
Jackie Wigg Gdns *TOTT* SO40.... 341 K1
Jacklyns Cl *NALR* SO24......... 218 B4
Jacklyns La *NALR* SO24......... 218 B4
Jackmans Cl *ITCH* SO19......... 344 B5 🔳
Jackman's HI *RWIN* SO21........ 267 M1
Jackson Cl *CHAM* PO6........... 400 A2
Jackson Rd *BKME/WDN* BH12.... 446 B2
Jacob Rd *CBLY* GU15............ 70 D7
Jacobs Cl *HORN* PO8............ 328 B3
   ROMY SO51............ 290 F1 🔳
Jacob's Gutter La *TOTT* SO40.... 341 M4
Jacobs Rd *PLE* BH15............ 444 D6
Jacob's St *PSEA* PO1............ 423 C4
Jacobs Wk *TOTT* SO40........... 341 J4
Jacomb Pl
   LSOL/BMARY PO13...... 397 H6 🔳
Jacqueline Av *WVILLE* PO7....... 376 B4
Jacqueline Rd
   BKME/WDN BH12........ 446 A1
Jagdalik Rd *NTID* SP9........... 114 D4
Jago Rd *PSEA* PO1.............. 422 D2
Jaguar Rd *FARN* GU14........... 90 C6
Jamaica Pl *GPORT* PO12......... 19 G4
Jamaica Rd *GPORT* PO12......... 19 G4
Jamaica St *GPORT* PO12......... 19 K1
James Callaghan Dr
   CHAM PO6............. 374 E6
James Cl *BSTK* RG21............ 5 G3
   HISD PO11............. 425 J5
   LSOL/BMARY PO13...... 397 C4
James Copse Rd *HORN* PO8....... 352 D3
James Grieve Av *HLER* SO31..... 370 E6
Jameson Rd *MOOR/WNTN* BH9.. 432 C7
James Rd *ALDT* GU11............ 113 C1
   BKME/WDN BH12........ 446 F3
   CBLY GU15............ 70 E6
   HAV PO9.............. 16 B2
   LSOL/BMARY PO13...... 397 G4
James St *SHAM* SO14............ 13 J3
James Wy *CBLY* GU15............ 70 A8
Jamrud Rd *NTID* SP9............ 114 C3
Janaway Gdns *PTSW* SO17....... 319 H8
Janes Cl *FAWY* SO45............ 392 D4
Jan Smuts Cl *LISS* GU33........ 225 J7
Janson Rd *WSHM* SO15.......... 343 G1
Japonica Wy *HAV* PO9........... 378 A4
Jaques's La *THLE* RG7........... 31 J2
Jardine Sq *AND* SP10........... 119 H6 🔳🔳
Jarvis Cl *HTWY* RG27........... 48 B8
Jarvis Flds *HLER* SO31.......... 345 M8
Jasmine Cl *LYMN* SO41.......... 440 C4 🔳
Jasmine Gv *WVILLE* PO7......... 376 C6
Jasmine Rd *HEND* SO30.......... 321 C8
   KEMP RG22............ 104 A8
Jasmine Wy *HORN* PO8.......... 328 B3
   BOR GU35.............. 201 K6 🔳
Jasmond Rd *CHAM* PO6.......... 399 K2
Jason Pl *WVILLE* PO7........... 376 C6
Jason Wy *GPORT* PO12.......... 397 K8 🔳
Jaundrells Cl *NMIL/BTOS* BH25.. 438 A5
Java Dr *FHAM* PO15............ 371 C1
Java Rd *SHAM* SO14............ 13 K9
Javelin Rd *EMRTH* PO10......... 402 E5
J Av *FAWY* SO45................ 392 D2
Jay Cl *FHAM/STUB* PO14......... 395 M4
   HORN PO8............. 352 E4
Jays Cl *KEMP* RG22............. 104 F7
Jay's Ct *CHCH/BSGR* BH23....... 436 F8 🔳
Jay's La *HASM* GU27............ 229 L5
Jays Nest Cl *BLKW* GU17........ 70 A4 🔳
Jealous La *LYMN* SO41.......... 413 L6
Jedburgh Cl *STHA* RG19......... 27 J5
Jefferson Av *CHAR* BH8......... 448 C2
Jefferson Rd *BSTK* RG21........ 4 F3
Jeffries Cl *ROWN* SO16......... 317 K3
Jellicoe Av *GPORT* PO12........ 18 B7
Jellicoe Cl *PSTN* BH14......... 445 L3
Jellicoe Dr *CHCH/BSGR* BH23... 450 C4
Jenkins Cl *HEND* SO30.......... 346 E1
Jenkins Gv *PSEA* PO1........... 423 M1
Jenkins' Hill London Rd
   BAGS GU19............ 51 M7
   ROMY SO51............ 263 H8
Jenner Wy *ALTN* GU34.......... 176 F2
Jennie Green La *ALTN* GU34..... 174 D6
Jennings Rd *PSTN* BH14......... 446 B6
   TOTT SO40............ 316 F8
Jenny's Wk *YTLY* GU46.......... 69 H2
Jenson Gdns *AND* SP10......... 8 C6
Jephcote Rd *BWD* BH11......... 431 K4
Jermyns La *ROMY* SO51......... 263 H5
Jerome Cnr *RFWK* RG45......... 49 M5
Jerome Cl *ITCH* SO19........... 345 H2
Jerram Cl *GPORT* PO12......... 18 A6
Jerrett's La *ROWN* SO16........ 317 H4
Jersey Brow Rd *FARN* GU14..... 90 D6
Jersey Cl *BKME/WDN* BH12..... 431 H7
   CHAM PO6............. 83 H6
   FARN GU14............ 89 G4 🔳
   FHAM/STUB PO14....... 396 B2
   ROWN SO16............ 317 K5
Jersey Rd *BKME/WDN* BH12..... 431 H7
   NEND PO2............. 399 J3
Jervis Court La *BPWT* SO32...... 297 M8

Jervis Dr *GPORT* PO12.......... 421 M2
Jervis Rd *NEND* PO2............ 399 G6
Jesmond Av *CHCH/BSGR* BH23.. 436 D8
Jesmond Dene *NWBY* RG14....... 2 C2
Jesmond Gv *HLER* SO31......... 370 E7
Jessamine Rd *ROWN* SO16....... 318 A6
Jesse Cl *BLKW* GU17............ 69 J3
Jessett Dr *FLET* GU13.......... 110 D4
Jessica Av *VWD* BH31........... 356 H1
Jessica Cl *WVILLE* PO7......... 352 F7
Jessie Rd *ENEY* PO4............ 21 M4
   GPORT PO12........... 18 D4
   HAV PO9.............. 377 G5
Jessop Cl *FAWY* SO45........... 367 K3
Jessopp Cl *NBNE* BH10......... 432 D4
Jessopp Rd *WIMB* BH21......... 404 F2
Jesty Rd *NALR* SO24............ 218 A4
Jetty Rd *FAWY* SO45............ 392 F3
Jewell Rd *CHAR* BH8............ 433 K7
Jewry St *WINC* SO23............ 11 G7
Jex Blake Cl *ROWN* SO16........ 318 A4
Jibbs Meadow *TADY* RG26....... 63 L5 🔳
Jimmy Brown Av *WIMB* BH21.... 380 C3
Jinny La *ROMY* SO51............ 262 D3
Joanna Cl *RSAL* SP5............ 284 C1
Jobson Cl *WHCH* RG28.......... 122 B3 🔳
Jobson's La *HASM* GU27......... 229 M8
Jockey La *ELGH* SO50........... 294 D3
Jodrell Cl *HORN* PO8........... 353 G1
John Bunyan Cl *FHAM* PO15..... 347 C8 🔳
John Cl *ALDT* GU11............. 112 D5
John Hunt Dr *STHA* RG19....... 27 J6
John Morgan Cl *HTWY* RG27..... 86 A5 🔳
   HTWY RG27........... 86 A5 🔳
Johnson Dr *EWKG* RG40......... 48 L1
Johnson Rd *WIMB* BH21......... 405 L1
Johnson St *SHAM* SO14.......... 13 H3 🔳
Johnson Vw *FHAM* PO15......... 371 J2
Johnson Wy *FLET* GU13......... 110 E2
Johns Rd *FHAM/PORC* PO16..... 15 J9
   ITCH SO19............ 344 B5
Johnston Rd *PLE* BH15.......... 445 J1
John St *SHAM* SO14............. 13 H6
Jolliffe Av *PLE* BH15.......... 445 J4
Jolliffe Rd *PLE* BH15........... 445 J4
Jonathan Cl *LYMN* SO41......... 440 C3
Jonathan HI *KSCL* RG20........ 37 L5
Jonathan Rd *FHAM* PO15........ 14 C5
Jones La *FAWY* SO45............ 367 K4
Jopps Cnr *CHCH/BSGR* BH23.... 435 G4
Jordans La *LYMN* SO41.......... 413 G5
   THLE RG7............. 31 K5
Joseph St *GPORT* PO12.......... 19 H3 🔳
Joshua Cl *PLE* BH15............ 444 D6 🔳
Jouldings La *HTWY* RG27........ 47 G4
Joule Rd *AND* SP10............. 118 A7
   BSTK RG21............ 4 B8
Jowitt Dr *NMIL/BTOS* BH25..... 437 K6
Joyce Dickson Cl *RGWD* BH24... 382 F7
Joys La *LYMN* SO41............. 415 J8
   STOK SO20............. 165 M4
Joys Rd *WIMB* BH21............. 356 C8
Jubilee Av *CHAM* PO6........... 374 C8
Jubilee Cl *ELGH* SO50.......... 293 L7 🔳
   FARN GU14............ 89 M4
   RGWD BH24............ 359 G8
   TADY RG26............. 42 B7
   WIMB BH21............ 429 J7
Jubilee Ct *FHAM/STUB* PO14.... 396 B2
   LYMN SO41............ 412 F7
Jubilee Dr *ASHV* GU12.......... 113 K2
Jubilee Gdns *NBNE* BH10....... 432 B6
   WEND SO18............ 344 F4
Jubilee Hall Rd *FARN* GU14..... 90 F4
Jubilee La *GSHT* GU26.......... 203 M5 🔳
   RFNM GU10............ 158 D3
Jubilee Pth *HAV* PO9........... 377 G7
Jubilee Rd *ALDT* GU11.......... 7 J1
   BSTK RG21............ 105 C4
   ENEY PO4............. 423 K5
   EWKG RG40............ 48 C5
   FBDG SP6.............. 309 H7
   FHAM/PORC PO16....... 374 B8
   FRIM GU16............. 91 K6
   GPORT PO12........... 18 E2
   NWBY RG14............ 3 G6
   PSTN BH14............ 446 C3
   ROMY SO51............ 262 D8
   WIMB BH21............ 429 J2
   WVILLE PO7........... 352 D8
Jubilee Ter *SSEA* PO5.......... 20 F5 🔳
Jubilee Trail *WIMB* BH21........ 306 D2
Julia Cl *CHCH/BSGR* BH23....... 436 D8
Julian Cl *ROWN* SO16........... 318 E2
Julian Rd *ITCH* SO19........... 344 F5
Julie Av *FHAM* PO15............ 14 C5
Juliet Cl *WVILLE* PO7........... 352 E8 🔳
Julius Cl *CHAM* PO6............. 82 B8
   CHFD SO53............ 293 K2
Julyan Av *BKME/WDN* BH12..... 431 K7
Jumar Cl *HLER* SO31............ 394 B1
Jumpers Av *CHCH/BSGR* BH23... 434 C8
Jumpers Rd *CHCH/BSGR* BH23... 434 D8
Jumps Rd *RFNM* GU10........... 181 H5
Junction Rd *AND* SP10.......... 8 C1
   TOTT SO40............ 341 L1
   UPTN BH16............ 444 C1
Junction Ter *NWBY* RG14....... 3 J5
June Dr *DEAN* RG23............. 104 A3
Juniper Cl *CHAM* PO6........... 83 M4
   FERN BH22............ 380 A8
   WINW SO22............ 238 C3
   BOR GU35.............. 200 F6
   LYMN SO41............ 439 M6
   NBAD SO52............. 291 J3
   WIMB BH21............ 356 C8
Juniper Rd *FARN* GU14......... 89 M3
   HORN PO8............. 328 B7 🔳
   WEND SO18............ 344 D1
Juniper Sq *HAV* PO9............ 16 F5
Jupiter Cl *ROWN* SO16.......... 317 K4
Jura Cl *CHAM* PO6.............. 375 K7
Jurds Lake Wy *ITCH* SO19....... 344 D7
Jurd Wy *HLER* SO31............ 345 K7
Justice Cl *STHA* RG19.......... 27 J6
Justin Cl *FHAM/STUB* PO14...... 14 C6
Justin Gdns *NBNE* BH10........ 432 C4
Justinian Cl *CHFD* SO53........ 293 L1

Jute Cl *FHAM/PORC* PO16....... 373 M7
Jutland Cl *FHAM* PO15.......... 370 F1
Jutland Crs *AND* SP10.......... 118 E4

K

Kampteo Copse
   NMIL/BTOS BH25....... 437 M2 🔳
Kanes HI *ITCH* SO19............ 345 K2
Kangaw Pl *PLE* BH15............ 444 C6 🔳
Karachi Cl *NTID* SP9........... 114 D1
Karen Av *CHAM* PO6............ 400 A2
Kassassin St *ENEY* PO4......... 423 L6
Kassel Cl *WVILLE* PO7.......... 352 F7
Kathleen Cl *BSTK* RG21......... 104 F6 🔳
Kathleen Rd *ITCH* SO19......... 344 F5
Katrina Gdns *HISD* PO11........ 425 L3
Katrine Crs *CHFD* SO53......... 292 F1
Katterns Cl *CHCH/BSGR* BH23... 434 C6
Kayak Cl *HLER* SO31............ 370 C7
Kay Crs *BOR* GU35............. 202 D2 🔳
Kayleigh Cl *TOTT* SO40......... 341 H2
Keable Rd *RFNM* GU10.......... 158 C1
Kealy Rd *GPORT* PO12.......... 421 C1
Kearsney Av *NEND* PO2......... 399 J5 🔳
Keats Av *CHAM* PO6............ 374 C7
   LYMN SO41............ 454 C3
Keats Cl *CHAM* PO6............ 83 H7
   WINW SO22............ 238 B4
   HORN PO8............. 352 D4
   RWIN SO21............ 190 C4
Keats Rd *WEND* SO18........... 345 G2
Keats Wy *CWTH* RG45........... 49 L1
   YTLY GU46............ 68 E4
Keble Cl *CHFD* SO53............ 293 H4 🔳
Keble Rd *CHFD* SO53............ 293 H4
Keble St *WINW* SO22........... 238 B2
   WB SHST GU47......... 50 B6
Keeble Cl *NBNE* BH10.......... 432 B2
Keeble Crs *NBNE* BH10......... 432 B2
Keeble Rd *NBNE* BH10.......... 432 B2
Keel Cl *HSEA* PO3.............. 400 A5
   LSOL/BMARY PO13...... 421 H1 🔳
Keepers Cl *CHFD* SO53.......... 293 C2
Keeper's HI *RAND* SP11......... 140 F3
Keepers La *ROMY* SO51......... 233 H6
   WIMB BH21............ 405 J3
Keeps Md *KSCL* RG20........... 59 H5
The Keep *FHAM/PORC* PO16..... 374 C8
   FHAM/PORC PO16....... 398 B1
Kefford Cl *HORN* PO8........... 352 D7
Keighley Av *BDST* BH11......... 429 K6
Keighley Cl *STHA* RG19......... 26 F6
Keith Cl *GPORT* PO12........... 421 M2
Keith Lucas Rd *FARN* GU14..... 90 C6
Keith Rd *TWDS* BH3............. 447 H2
Kelburn Cl *CHFD* SO53.......... 293 G1
Kellaway Rd *CFDH* BH17........ 430 D8
Kellett Rd *WSHM* SO15.......... 318 C8
Kelly Cl *CFDH* BH17............ 430 D8
Kellynch Cl *ALTN* GU34........ 176 D4
Kelly Rd *WVILLE* PO7........... 376 C3
Kellys Wk *AND* SP10........... 8 C6
Kelmscott Gdns *CHFD* SO53..... 264 F7
Kelsall Gdns *NMIL/BTOS* BH25.. 437 J4
Kelsey Av *EMRTH* PO10......... 379 J7
   EWKG RG40............ 48 B2
Kelsey Cl *FHAM/STUB* PO14..... 370 F7
   LISS GU33............ 248 F3
Kelsey Gv *YTLY* GU46........... 69 H3
Kelvin Cl *FAWY* SO45........... 367 L5
Kelvin Gv *FHAM/PORC* PO16..... 374 B8 🔳
   HLER SO31............ 369 C2
Kelvin HI *KEMP* RG22........... 104 D6
Kelvin Rd *ELGH* SO50........... 293 K6
   FARN GU14............ 90 E6
   KEMP RG22............ 103 L7
Kestrel Wy *FBDG* SP6.......... 333 M3 🔳
   THLE RG7............. 31 L4
Keswick Av *HSEA* PO3.......... 399 L8
Keswick Cl *CBLY* GU15.......... 71 M4
Keswick Rd *BOSC* BH5.......... 448 E4
   ITCH SO19............ 344 B5
   NMIL/BTOS BH25....... 437 M3
Keswick Wy *VWD* BH31......... 356 H1
Ketchers Fld *ALTN* GU34........ 223 L2
Ketelbey Ri *KEMP* RG22......... 127 L1
Kettering Ter *NEND* PO2........ 399 G8
Kevin Cl *KSCL* RG20............ 59 L6
Kevins Dr *YTLY* GU46........... 69 H1
Kevins Gv *FLET* GU13........... 89 C7
Kevlyn Crs *HLER* SO31.......... 345 K7 🔳
Kewlake La *ROMY* SO51......... 314 C6
Kew La *HLER* SO31............. 369 L1
Kew Wk *AND* SP10............. 8 C7
Keydell Cl *HORN* PO8........... 352 E3
Keyes Cl *BKME/WDN* BH12..... 431 K7
   CHCH/BSGR BH23...... 450 E2
   LSOL/BMARY PO13...... 397 G4
Keyes Rd *LSOL/BMARY* PO13.... 397 G5
Keyhaven Cl
   LSOL/BMARY PO13...... 396 E6 🔳
Keyhaven Dr *HAV* PO9.......... 377 G3
Keyhaven Rd *LYMN* SO41........ 454 D4
Keynes Cl *FLET* GU13........... 111 G4
Keynsham Rd *ITCH* SO19........ 344 F2
Keynsham Wy *SHST* GU47....... 50 A1
Keysworth Av
   NMIL/BTOS BH25....... 452 E1
Keysworth Rd *UPTN* BH16...... 444 B4
Khandala Gdns *WVILLE* PO7..... 376 D4 🔳
Khartoum Rd *PTSW* SO17........ 318 F6
Khyber Rd *BKME/WDN* BH12.... 446 B1
Kidmore La *WVILLE* PO7........ 351 K2
Kielder Cl *CHFD* SO53.......... 292 F1
Kielder Gv
   LSOL/BMARY PO13...... 397 H6 🔳
Kiel Dr *AND* SP10............. 118 E4
Kildare Rd *CHAM* PO6........... 83 J4
Kilford Ct *HEND* SO30.......... 346 E2
Kilham La *WINW* SO22.......... 238 A2
Killarney Cl *ITCH* SO19......... 345 J5 🔳
Killinghurst La *HASM* GU27..... 229 M2
Kilmartin Gdns *FRIM* GU16...... 71 J7 🔳
Kilmeston Rd *NALR* SO24....... 242 C0

Kilmington Wy
   CHCH/BSGR BH23...... 436 D8
Kilmiston Cl *PSEA* PO1......... 423 J7
Kilmiston Dr
   FHAM/PORC PO16....... 374 D7
Kilmore Dr *CBLY* GU15.......... 71 L4
Kilmuir Cl *SHST* GU47.......... 70 A1
Kiln Cl *FAWY* SO45............. 367 J3
   WIMB BH21............ 429 G4
Kiln Fld *LISS* GU33............ 248 D3
Kiln Flds *HASM* GU27........... 204 F8
Kiln Gdns *HTWY* RG27........... 87 H2
Kiln HI *BPWT* SO32............ 325 C8
   THLE RG7............. 46 E1
Kiln La *EPSF* GU31............. 303 H4
   NALR SO24............ 194 C7
   RFNM GU10............ 158 F2
   ROMY SO51............ 263 G2
   RSAL SP5............. 285 K1
   RWIN SO21............ 201 M6
   TADY RG26............ 81 M3
   THLE RG7............. 43 M3
   WVILLE PO7........... 350 B4
Kiln Ride *EWKG* RG40........... 48 B5
Kiln Ride Extension *EWKG* RG40.. 48 D2
Kiln Rd *CHAM* PO6............. 82 D5
   FHAM/PORC PO16....... 372 D4
   NWBY RG14............ 25 M3
Kilnside *WVILLE* PO7........... 351 K5
Kiln Wy *ALDT* GU11............ 7 G7
   GSHT GU26............ 203 H3
Kilnyard Cl *TOTT* SO40......... 316 C2
Kilpatrick Cl *NEND* PO2........ 399 H8 🔳
Kilwich Wy *FHAM/PORC* PO16.... 397 M1
Kimbell Rd *KEMP* RG22......... 104 E6
Kimber Cl *CHAM* RG24.......... 83 L5
Kimberley Cl *FLET* GU13........ 111 G4
Kimberley Cl *AND* SP10......... 118 C6 🔳
   ELGH SO50............ 295 J6
Kimberley Rd *ENEY* PO4......... 423 L4
   KEMP RG22............ 104 D5
   LISS GU33............ 225 H6
   PSTN BH14............ 446 A5
   SBNE BH6............. 449 H2
Kimbers *PSF* GU32............. 275 K4
Kimbers Dr *NWBY* RG14........ 24 F7
Kimbers La *FNM* GU9........... 135 G5
   TADY RG26............ 62 A3
Kimbolton Rd *HSEA* PO3........ 423 L1
Kimbridge Crs *HAV* PO9........ 377 L2
Kimbridge La *ROMY* SO51....... 261 L1 🔳
Kimmeridge Av
   BKME/WDN BH12........ 431 G8
Kimpton Cl
   LSOL/BMARY PO13...... 420 D2 🔳
Kimpton Ct *HAV* PO9........... 377 M2 🔳
Kineton Rd *WSHM* SO15......... 318 D7
King Albert St *PSEA* PO1........ 423 H2 🔳
King Alfred Pl *WINC* SO23....... 11 G5
King Alfred Ter *WINC* SO23..... 11 G5
King Arthur's Ct *CHAM* PO6..... 376 B8 🔳
King Arthur's Wy *AND* SP10..... 118 C5
King Charles St *PSEA* PO1....... 20 C4
King Cl *RGWD* BH24............ 381 K4
King Cup Av *HLER* SO31........ 370 C4
Kingcup Cl *BDST* BH18......... 429 J6
King Edward Av
   MOOR/WNTN BH9....... 432 D6
   ROWN SO16............ 317 M7
King Edward's Crs
   NEND PO2............. 399 H6 🔳
Kingfisher Cl *FARN* GU14....... 89 M2
   FERN BH22............ 380 C6
   FLET GU13............ 110 F3
   HAV PO9.............. 353 M7
   HISD PO11............ 425 G6
   HLER SO31............ 369 L4 🔳
   HORN PO8............. 352 C4
   KEMP RG22............ 103 L7
   BOR GU35............. 201 K6 🔳
   THLE RG7............. 29 M5 🔳
Kingfisher Copse *HLER* SO31.... 370 F5 🔳
Kingfisher Dr *YTLY* GU46....... 68 E2
Kingfishers *FHAM/PORC* PO16... 373 K8 🔳
   NTID SP9............. 138 D1 🔳
The Kingfishers *VWD* BH31...... 356 E3
Kingfisher Wk *ASHV* GU12...... 113 J5
Kingfisher Wy
   CHCH/BSGR BH23...... 450 F5
   RGWD BH24............ 358 F7
   ROMY SO51............ 262 E8 🔳
   TOTT SO40............ 342 C2
King George Av *EPSF* GU31..... 275 L4
   MOOR/WNTN BH9....... 432 D6
King George Rd *AND* SP10...... 8 A7
   FHAM/PORC PO16....... 398 A1
King George's Av *WSHM* SO15... 342 D2
King Henry I St *PSEA* PO1....... 20 F7
King John Av *BWD* BH11........ 431 H7
   FHAM/PORC PO16....... 397 M1
King John Rd *KSCL* RG20........ 59 J6
King Johns Rd *ODIM* RG29...... 108 B4
Kingland Rd *PLE* BH15.......... 445 J4
King La *PSF* GU32............. 246 E8
   STOK SO20............ 162 A2
King Richard 1 Rd *PSEA* PO1.... 20 F3 🔳
King Richard Dr *BWD* BH11...... 431 H1
Kings Arms La *RGWD* BH24..... 382 D1 🔳
Kings Arms Rw *RGWD* BH24.... 382 D1 🔳
King's Av *CHCH/BSGR* BH23..... 449 L1
   WINW SO22............ 238 D7
   HLER SO31............ 369 J1
   RFNM GU10............ 113 H4
   PSTN BH14............ 446 C6
Kingsbere Av *NBNE* BH10....... 431 M6
Kingsbridge HI *THLE* RG7....... 45 K2
Kingsbridge Rd *NWBY* RG14..... 2 A1
   PSTN BH14............ 446 C6
Kingsbury Rd *SHAM* SO14....... 343 M1 🔳
Kingsbury's La *RGWD* BH24..... 382 D2
Kingsclear Pk *CBLY* GU15....... 71 G4
Kingsclere Av *HAV* PO9......... 377 H1
   ITCH SO19............ 344 D7
Kingsclere Cl *ITCH* SO19....... 344 D7 🔳
Kingsclere Rd *BSTK* RG21....... 4 B5
   DEAN RG23............ 81 K4
   OVTN RG25............ 100 F1
King's Cl *CHFD* SO53........... 293 J2

FERN BH22 ... 380 B7
HAV PO9 ... 353 L6
LYND SO43 ... 363 K3
RWIN SO21 ... 266 F1
WINC SO23 ... 191 G7
Kings Copse Av HEND SO30 ... 346 B5
King's Copse Rd FAWY SO45 ... 392 A4
HEND SO30 ... 346 A3
Kingscote Rd CHAM PO6 ... 374 D6
HORN PO8 ... 352 B5
King's Ct RFNM GU10 ... 113 J8
King's Crs CBLY GU15 ... 50 F3
LYMN SO41 ... 440 B4
PSTN BH14 ... 446 B6
Kingscroft Ct HAV PO9 ... 16 B5
Kingsdown Pl PSEA PO1 ... 21 L2 □
Kingsdown Rd WVILLE PO7 ... 352 A6
Kingsdown Wy WEND SO18 ... 319 L6
King's Elms RWIN SO21 ... 167 J2
Kingsfernsden La PSF GU32 ... 275 M3
Kings Fld HLER SO31 ... 345 L7
Kingsfield LYMN SO41 ... 440 E6 □
RGWD BH24 ... 382 E1
Kings Field Gdns HLER SO31 ... 345 L7
Kingsfold Av WEND SO18 ... 319 L5
Kingsford Cl RSAL SP5 ... 285 J3 □
Kings Furlong Dr BSTK RG21 ... 104 C5
King's HI ALTN GU34 ... 175 M3
Kings Keep FLET GU13 ... 110 F2
SHST GU47 ... 49 L7
Kingsland Cl CHAM PO6 ... 375 G7
Kingsland Gra NWBY RG14 ... 25 H8
Kingsland Rd ALTN GU34 ... 176 D5
RFNM GU10 ... 158 C2
PSF GU32 ... 246 B6
RWIN SO21 ... 239 L2
Kingsley Av CBLY GU15 ... 70 F4
Kingsley Cl CWTH RG45 ... 49 L5
NWBY ... 25 L2
SBNE BH6 ... 449 M6
Kingsley Gdns TOTT SO40 ... 340 F1
Kingsley Pk WHCH RG28 ... 122 B2
Kingsley Pl WINW SO22 ... 238 D3
Kingsley Rd ENEY PO4 ... 423 M5
FARN GU14 ... 90 C2
GPORT PO12 ... 421 K1
HTWY RG27 ... 47 M8
WSHM SO15 ... 342 F1
Kingsmead ALTN GU34 ... 176 E5
FARN GU14 ... 90 E4
FRIM GU16 ... 91 H1
RAND SP11 ... 142 B4
WHAM PO17 ... 349 G1
Kingsmead Av
FHAM/STUB PO14 ... 396 B7
OVTN RG25 ... 100 F8
Kings Meadow AND SP10 ... 9 J6
Kings Mede HORN PO8 ... 352 F2
Kingsmill Cl GPORT PO12 ... 18 B4
Kingsmill Rd BSTK RG21 ... 104 F6
CFDH BH17 ... 445 K1
Kings Orch DEAN RG23 ... 103 C8
King's Paddock RSAL SP5 ... 206 D3 □
King's Park Dr LTDN BH7 ... 448 D8
King's Park Rd BMTH BH1 ... 448 C8
WSHM SO15 ... 343 L2
Kings Pightle CHAM RG24 ... 83 L5
King's Ride CBLY GU15 ... 51 G7
FAWY SO45 ... 418 C1
King's Rd ALDT GU11 ... 6 B3
ALTN GU34 ... 176 C6
CHFD SO53 ... 293 H2
CWTH RG45 ... 49 L4
EMRTH PO10 ... 378 C4
FHAM/PORC PO16 ... 15 J4
FLET GU13 ... 89 G7
WINW SO22 ... 238 B2 □
GPORT PO12 ... 18 F3
HASM GU27 ... 228 D2
HISD PO11 ... 425 L3
KEMP RG22 ... 104 D5
LSOL/BMARY PO13 ... 420 C1
LYMN SO41 ... 440 B4
NMIL/BTOS BH25 ... 438 A4
NWBY RG14 ... 2 E1
PSEA PO1 ... 422 D2
PSF GU32 ... 275 J4
RAND SP11 ... 119 G1
SSEA PO5 ... 20 F5
THLE RG7 ... 42 D7
TWDS BH3 ... 447 M1
Kings Rd West NWBY RG14 ... 2 F5
Kings & Saltern Rd LYMN SO41 ... 440 E6
Kings Somborne Rd
ROMY ... 235 J7
King's Ter EMRTH PO10 ... 378 D8 □
PSEA PO1 ... 20 F5
Kingston HLER SO31 ... 369 G1 □
Kingston Cl AND SP10 ... 8 D9
Kingston Crs NEND PO2 ... 399 H8
Kingston Gdns FHAM PO15 ... 372 B4
Kingston La THLE RG7 ... 30 F2
Kingston Pk LYMN SO41 ... 440 A6 □
Kingston Rd CBLY GU15 ... 51 K8
GPORT PO12 ... 18 B1
MARL SN8 ... 32 B6
NEND PO2 ... 399 J8
PLE BH15 ... 445 J4
SHAM SO14 ... 13 H5
WSHM SO15 ... 343 H2
King St EMRTH PO10 ... 378 C5 □
GPORT PO12 ... 19 K2
ODIM RG29 ... 108 D5
SHAM SO14 ... 13 H5
SSEA PO5 ... 20 F4
THLE RG7 ... 43 K7
Kings Wk WHCH RG28 ... 122 B3
King's Wy BPWT SO32 ... 296 D5
BPWT SO32 ... 323 M1
FHAM/PORC PO16 ... 373 K8
NALR SO24 ... 217 L6
RWIN SO21 ... 216 D2
RWIN SO21 ... 240 C4
RWIN SO21 ... 240 F2

WHAM PO17 ... 350 D7
WINC SO23 ... 11 H4
WVILLE PO7 ... 350 D3
Kingsway ALDT GU11 ... 6 C4
BLKW GU17 ... 70 B4
CHFD SO53 ... 293 J1
HISD PO11 ... 401 L5
Kingsway Cl CHCH/BSGR BH23 ... 434 D7
Kingsway Gdns CHFD SO53 ... 265 K8
The Kingsway
FHAM/PORC PO16 ... 374 A8
Kingswell Gdns NBNE BH10 ... 431 M6
Kingswell Rd NBNE BH10 ... 431 M6
NBNE BH10 ... 432 A6
Kingswell St PSEA PO1 ... 21 G1 □
Kingswood TOTT SO40 ... 342 E7
Kingswood Firs GSHT GU26 ... 203 M6
Kingswood La GSHT GU26 ... 203 M6
Kingswood Ri ALTN GU34 ... 196 E6
Kingsworthy Rd HAV PO9 ... 377 K5
King's Yd AND SP10 ... 9 J5
King William St PSEA PO1 ... 422 E2
Kinnell Cl EMRTH PO10 ... 378 D8
Kinross Crs CHAM PO6 ... 399 M1
Kinross Rd TOTT SO40 ... 341 K1
TWDS BH3 ... 447 K2
Kinsbourne Av NBNE BH10 ... 432 B6
Kinsbourne Cl NTID SP9 ... 345 K2 □
Kinsbourne Ri ITCH SO19 ... 345 K3
Kinsbourne Wy ITCH SO19 ... 345 J2 □
Kinson Av PLE BH15 ... 445 M2
Kinson Gv NBNE BH10 ... 432 A2
Kinson Park Rd NBNE BH10 ... 432 B2
Kinson Rd NBNE BH10 ... 431 L7
Kintbury Rd HUNG RG17 ... 34 C2
Kintyre Cl DEAN RG23 ... 102 F6
Kintyre Rd CHAM PO6 ... 375 F6
Kinver Cl ROMY SO51 ... 263 G7
Kipling Cl NTHA RG18 ... 26 F3
YTLY GU46 ... 68 F4 □
Kipling Ct ITCH SO19 ... 344 D7 □
Kipling Rd ELGH SO50 ... 293 L5
NEND PO2 ... 399 J5
PSTN BH14 ... 446 A3
Kipling Wk KEMP RG22 ... 104 D5
Kirby Cl PLE BH15 ... 445 L2
Kirby Rd NEND PO2 ... 399 J6
Kirby Wy SBNE BH6 ... 449 J4
Kirkee Rd NTID SP9 ... 114 D3
Kirk Gdns TOTT SO40 ... 341 K3
Kirkham Cl SHST GU47 ... 50 A6 □
Kirk Knoll BOR GU35 ... 202 C3
Kirkstall Rd ENEY PO4 ... 423 J7 □
Kirkway BDST BH18 ... 429 M4
Kirkwood Crs THLE RG7 ... 31 J5 □
Kirtley Cl CHAM PO6 ... 400 A1
Kirton Rd CHAM PO6 ... 400 A1
Kitchener Crs CFDH BH17 ... 429 M6
Kitchener Rd ALDT GU11 ... 113 G2
LISS GU33 ... 225 H6
PTSW SO17 ... 319 H5
Kitchers Cl LYMN SO41 ... 412 F5
Kitcombe La ALTN GU34 ... 198 A7
Kite Cl HORN PO8 ... 352 C4
Kites Croft Cl
FHAM/STUB PO14 ... 371 G7
Kitnocks HI BPWT SO32 ... 322 D8
Kitscroft Rd NBNE BH10 ... 432 A3
Kittiwake Cl
LSOL/BMARY PO13 ... 396 F6
Kitt's La NTID SO24 ... 244 B6
RFNM GU10 ... 181 J8
Kitwalls La LYMN SO41 ... 454 C3
Kitwood La ALTN GU34 ... 221 H1
Kitwood Rd ALTN GU34 ... 221 G1
Kivernell Rd LYMN SO41 ... 454 B4
Kiwi Cl PLE BH15 ... 445 K5
Knapp Cl CHCH/BSGR BH23 ... 434 E8
Knapp La ROMY SO51 ... 264 C4
TADY RG26 ... 62 A2
Knapp Mill Av
CHCH/BSGR BH23 ... 434 E8
Knapps Hard PSF GU32 ... 272 A3
Knatchbull Cl ROMY SO51 ... 290 E1 □
Knellers La TOTT SO40 ... 341 H4
Knight Cl FLET GU13 ... 110 B2
WINC SO23 ... 11 G3
Knighton Heath Rd BWD BH11 ... 431 J4
Knighton La BWD BH11 ... 431 H1
Knighton Pk NMIL/BTOS BH25 ... 437 J8
Knighton Rd ITCH SO19 ... 344 D5
RSAL SP5 ... 252 C1
Knights Bank Rd
FHAM/STUB PO14 ... 395 K7
Knightsbridge Dr STHA RG19 ... 38 E5
Knightsbridge Rd CBLY GU15 ... 71 H1
RAND SP11 ... 119 H1
Knights Cl HLER SO31 ... 370 C7 □
Knights La KSCL RG20 ... 35 M5
Knights Lea KSCL RG20 ... 35 L5
Knights Rd BWD BH11 ... 431 H3
RSAL SP5 ... 252 C1
Knightstone Gra FAWY SO45 ... 367 L6 □
Knight St BSTK RG21 ... 104 E4
Knights Wy ALTN GU34 ... 176 C5
CBLY GU15 ... 71 M4
Knightwood Av HAV PO9 ... 377 L3
LYND SO43 ... 363 K6
Knightwood Cl
CHCH/BSGR BH23 ... 436 C8 □
LYND SO43 ... 363 K6
TOTT SO40 ... 340 F6
Knightwood Rd FAWY SO45 ... 367 M6
NBAD SO52 ... 264 E8
Knockhundred La GSHT GU26 ... 203 L8
Knockwood La STOK SO20 ... 184 D1
Knole Gdns BMTH BH1 ... 448 C4
Knole Rd BMTH BH1 ... 448 C3
Knoll Cl FLET GU13 ... 88 F6
Knoll Gdns RGWD BH24 ... 381 K4
Knoll La WIMB BH21 ... 428 F1
Knoll Rd CBLY GU15 ... 71 G1
FLET GU13 ... 88 F6
Knollys' Rd ALDT GU11 ... 112 C5
THLE RG7 ... 42 C7
Knottgrass Rd HLER SO31 ... 370 C6
Knott La THLE RG7 ... 29 L4
Knowland Dr LYMN SO41 ... 454 B4

Knowle Crs KSCL RG20 ... 59 J6
Knowle HI ELGH SO50 ... 294 A1
Knowle La ELGH SO50 ... 295 K8
Knowle Rd BROC SO42 ... 387 G6
Knowles Av CWTH RG45 ... 49 J4
Knowles Cl CHCH/BSGR BH23 ... 450 D1
Knowles Meadow LISS GU33 ... 249 G7
The Knowlings WHCH RG28 ... 122 C4
Knowlton Rd CFDH BH17 ... 430 D6
Knowsley Crs CHAM PO6 ... 399 L1
Knowsley Rd CHAM PO6 ... 399 K1
Knox Cl FLET GU13 ... 110 C3
Knox Rd HAV PO9 ... 16 B4
NEND PO2 ... 399 G7
Knyght Cl ROMY SO51 ... 290 F2
Knyveton Rd BMTH BH1 ... 23 M4
Kohat Cl NTID SP9 ... 114 C1
Kohat Ct ALDT GU11 ... 6 C2
Kohima Cl ALDT GU11 ... 7 H1
Komat Rd NTID SP9 ... 114 D3
Kootenay Av WEND SO18 ... 345 J1
Kooyong Cl ROMY SO51 ... 289 G6
Krooner Rd CBLY GU15 ... 70 E5
Kynegils Rd WINW SO22 ... 10 B3
Kynon Cl GPORT PO12 ... 398 A8 □
Kyrchil La WIMB BH21 ... 404 C2
Kyrchil Wy WIMB BH21 ... 404 C1
Kytes La BPWT SO32 ... 322 A3

L

Labrador Dr PLE BH15 ... 445 J7
Laburnum Av CHAM PO6 ... 400 A1
Laburnum Cl ALDT GU11 ... 6 E3 □
FERN BH22 ... 405 M2
NBAD SO52 ... 291 M3
VWD BH31 ... 357 G3
Laburnum Crs FAWY SO45 ... 367 M8 □
Laburnum Dr LYMN SO41 ... 439 J8 □
Laburnum Gv ELGH SO50 ... 293 M4
HISD PO11 ... 425 M4
NEND PO2 ... 399 J7
NWBY RG14 ... 2 E1
Laburnum Pas ALDT GU11 ... 6 E3 □
Laburnum Rd ALDT GU11 ... 6 E3
FHAM/PORC PO16 ... 396 F2
FNM GU9 ... 6 A8 □
HEND SO30 ... 346 B2
ROWN SO16 ... 319 H4
WVILLE PO7 ... 376 C2
The Laburnums BLKW GU17 ... 69 L3
Laburnum Wy DEAN RG23 ... 104 C2
Lacey Crs PSTN BH14 ... 445 M2
Lackford Av TOTT SO40 ... 341 G4
Lacon Cl WEND SO18 ... 319 K8
Lacy Cl WIMB BH21 ... 404 A2
Lacy Dr WIMB BH21 ... 404 A2
Ladram Rd GPORT PO12 ... 421 J2
Ladwell Cl NWBY RG14 ... 37 G3
Ladybridge Rd WVILLE PO7 ... 376 A4
Ladycross Rd FAWY SO45 ... 367 L6
Lady Diana Ct RAND SP11 ... 92 E6
Ladygate Dr GSHT GU26 ... 203 L5
Lady Godley Cl NTID SP9 ... 114 D3
Lady Jane Wk RAND SP11 ... 92 E6 □
Ladysmith Cl
CHCH/BSGR BH23 ... 450 D1
Ladysmith Pl BOR GU35 ... 201 H3
Ladywell La NALR SO24 ... 218 C1
Ladywood ELGH SO50 ... 293 L2
Ladywood Av FARN GU14 ... 89 M4
Laffan's Rd ALDT GU11 ... 112 C3
ODIM RG29 ... 108 C3
Laffan Tr ALDT GU11 ... 111 M2
Lagado Cl PSTN BH14 ... 446 B8
Lagland St PLE BH15 ... 445 H7
Lagoon Rd PSTN BH14 ... 446 A7
Lahore Cl NTID SP9 ... 114 D1
Lahore Rd NTID SP9 ... 114 D1
Laidlaw Cl BKME/WDN BH12 ... 431 M8
Lainston Cl WINW SO22 ... 214 B6
Lake Av PLE BH15 ... 444 C7
Lake Crs PLE BH15 ... 444 D5
Lake Dr BOR GU35 ... 201 K5
PLE BH15 ... 444 C6
Lake End Wy CWTH RG45 ... 49 K4
Lake Farm Cl HEND SO30 ... 321 H8 □
Lake Grove Rd
NMIL/BTOS BH25 ... 437 L4
Lakeland Dr FRIM GU16 ... 71 H7
Lakeland Gdns TOTT SO40 ... 342 C7 □
Lakelands TADY RG26 ... 41 G7 □
Lakelands Dr WSHM SO15 ... 343 G2 □
Lake La RFNM GU10 ... 180 B2
Lake Rd BPWT SO32 ... 322 E8
BWD BH11 ... 431 M2
CHFD SO53 ... 265 K8
FRIM GU16 ... 91 K2
ITCH SO19 ... 344 B6
PLE BH15 ... 444 D6
PSEA PO1 ... 423 G2 □
VWD BH31 ... 356 E4
Laker Sq AND SP10 ... 119 H6
Lakeside ELGH SO50 ... 293 L8
LSOL/BMARY PO13 ... 420 D4
RGWD BH24 ... 383 G2
WHAM PO17 ... 372 C3
Lakeside Av HSEA PO3 ... 423 M2
ROWN SO16 ... 317 K3
Lakeside Cl FARN GU14 ... 89 G5
Lakeside Dr HTWY RG27 ... 67 G4
Lakeside Gdns FARN GU14 ... 90 A1
HAV PO9 ... 17 G2
Lakeside Rd ALDT GU11 ... 112 D1
ASHV GU12 ... 113 J4
CCLF BH13 ... 446 F7
The Lake Side BLKW GU17 ... 70 A4
Lakesmere Rd HORN PO8 ... 353 G2
The Lakes BPWT SO32 ... 323 M4
Lakeview Dr RGWD BH24 ... 383 G2
Lakewood Cl CHFD SO53 ... 265 D8
Lakewood Rd
CHCH/BSGR BH23 ... 436 D7

CHFD SO53 ... 265 J8
TOTT SO40 ... 341 G5
Lamb Cl NTHA RG18 ... 9 L6
NTHA RG18 ... 26 F3
Lambdens HI THLE RG7 ... 30 B1
Lambdens Wk TADY RG26 ... 41 L8 □
Lambdown Ap RAND SP11 ... 115 H2
Lamberhurst Cl ITCH SO19 ... 344 E8
Lambert Cl WVILLE PO7 ... 376 C3
Lambert Crs BLKW GU17 ... 69 M4
Lamborne Cl SHST GU47 ... 49 K7
Lambourn Cl FHAM/STUB PO14 ... 14 B7
Lambourne Cl FAWY SO45 ... 367 K7 □
RAND SP11 ... 116 D8
RWIN SO21 ... 213 H5
Lambourne Dr HLER SO31 ... 370 E5
Lambourne La LIPH GU30 ... 251 G5
Lambourne Rd WEND SO18 ... 320 A6
Lambourne Wy NTID SP9 ... 116 D8
RAND SP11 ... 116 D8
Lambourn Rd KSCL RG20 ... 24 F2
Lambourn Sq CHFD SO53 ... 292 F2
Lambourn Valley Wy
NWBY RG14 ... 2 B4
Lambs Cl CFDH BH17 ... 430 A7
Lambs Rw CHAM RG24 ... 105 L1
Lamden Wy THLE RG7 ... 31 L5
Lamerton Cl BOR GU35 ... 201 H4
Lammas Rd FAWY SO45 ... 367 L6
Lampard La RFNM GU10 ... 181 G6
Lampards Cl HTWY RG27 ... 85 L2
Lamp Acres NWBY RG14 ... 25 L3
Lampeter Av CHAM PO6 ... 375 M8
Lanark Cl FRIM GU16 ... 71 H6 □
Lancaster Cl AND SP10 ... 8 E2
ASHV GU12 ... 113 J3
BDST BH18 ... 429 K3
CHCH/BSGR BH23 ... 451 G1
FHAM/PORC PO16 ... 373 M7
HLER SO31 ... 345 L7 □
LSOL/BMARY PO13 ... 420 F4
NTHA RG18 ... 26 F4
Lancaster Dr BDST BH18 ... 429 J3
CBLY GU15 ... 71 G2 □
VWD BH31 ... 356 C3
Lancaster Rd BSTK RG21 ... 4 C5
FARN GU14 ... 90 E7
ROWN SO16 ... 317 L5
Lancaster Wy FARN GU14 ... 90 F1
WVILLE PO7 ... 376 D2
Lancer Cl CHCH/BSGR BH23 ... 449 L1
Lancer Ct ALDT GU11 ... 6 D2
Lance's HI ITCH SO19 ... 344 D1
Landale Cl RAND SP11 ... 119 G1
Lander Cl PLE BH15 ... 445 J7
Landford Wy CHAR BH8 ... 433 H6
Landguard Rd WSHM SO15 ... 342 C5
Landon Cl LSOL/BMARY PO13 ... 397 H8
Landport St PSEA PO1 ... 423 H2
SSEA PO5 ... 20 F4 □
Landport Ter PSEA PO1 ... 20 F4
Landport Vw PSEA PO1 ... 423 G2 □
Landsdowne St SSEA PO5 ... 20 A8 □
The Landsdown Rbt BMTH BH1 ... 23 H5
Landseer Cl BSTK RG21 ... 105 J5
SHST GU47 ... 70 J5
Landseer Rd AND SP10 ... 8 F2
ITCH SO19 ... 345 G5
Lands End La BOR GU35 ... 201 K3
Lands End Rd HLER SO31 ... 369 M1
Lane End TADY RG26 ... 63 L6
Lane End Dr EMRTH PO10 ... 378 D8
Lanehays Rd FAWY SO45 ... 367 K5
Lanesbridge Cl TOTT SO40 ... 340 D3
The Lanes NMIL/BTOS BH25 ... 437 L3
Laneswood THLE RG7 ... 43 H3
The Lane ENEY PO4 ... 423 K6
FAWY SO45 ... 392 F5 □
GPORT PO12 ... 18 D9
TADY RG26 ... 41 L8
Langbar Cl ITCH SO19 ... 344 C2
Langbrook Cl HAV PO9 ... 16 E7
Langdale Av CHAM PO6 ... 399 M1
Langdale Cl FARN GU14 ... 90 B4 □
ROWN SO16 ... 317 L8 □
Langdon Cl CBLY GU15 ... 71 M4
Langdon Rd PSTN BH14 ... 446 A4
Langdown Lawn FAWY SO45 ... 367 L6
Langdown Lawn Cl
FAWY SO45 ... 367 L6 □
Langford La RSAL SP5 ... 257 L7
Langford Rd NEND PO2 ... 399 K1
Langham Cl NBAD SO52 ... 291 G4
Langham Rd ALTN GU34 ... 176 D5
Langhorn Rd ROWN SO16 ... 319 H4
Langley Cha RGWD BH24 ... 381 L3
Langley Cl FLET GU13 ... 110 E4
Langley Dr CBLY GU15 ... 71 G2
Langley Gdn FBDG SP6 ... 309 M5
Langley Lodge Gdns
FAWY SO45 ... 418 D1 □
Langley Rd CHCH/BSGR BH23 ... 436 C7
NEND PO2 ... 399 J8
PSTN BH14 ... 446 E4
WSHM SO15 ... 342 E2
Langrish Rd ROWN SO16 ... 318 A4
Langside Av BKME/WDN BH12 ... 431 L8
Langstone Av HAV PO9 ... 16 E8
Langstone High St HAV PO9 ... 401 K2
Langstone Rd HAV PO9 ... 16 E8
HSEA PO3 ... 423 L2
Langstone Wk
FHAM/STUB PO14 ... 372 A8
LSOL/BMARY PO13 ... 396 F6
Langton Cl WINW SO22 ... 10 C5
Langton Dr BOR GU35 ... 202 D6
Langton Rd BPWT SO32 ... 297 G8
LTDN BH7 ... 448 E3
Lanham La WINW SO22 ... 213 L8
Lankhills Rd WINC SO23 ... 10 F3
Lansdown Av
FHAM/PORC PO16 ... 398 B2

Lansdowne Av AND SP10 ... 8 D8
WINC SO23 ... 238 E3
WVILLE PO7 ... 375 M5
Lansdowne Cl ROMY SO51 ... 262 D8 □
Lansdowne Gdns BMTH BH1 ... 23 H3
Lansdowne HI SHAM SO14 ... 12 F5 □
Lansdowne Rd ALDT GU11 ... 6 E3
ALTN GU34 ... 176 F3
BMTH BH1 ... 23 G1
FRIM GU16 ... 71 K8
WSHM SO15 ... 342 E1
Lansley Rd BSTK RG21 ... 4 E2
Lantana Cl WVILLE PO7 ... 376 D2 □
Lanyard Dr LSOL/BMARY PO13 ... 421 H2
Lapin La KEMP RG22 ... 127 G3
Lapthorn Cl
LSOL/BMARY PO13 ... 396 F4
Lapwing Cl GPORT PO12 ... 421 M1 □
HORN PO8 ... 352 E1
Lapwing Dr TOTT SO40 ... 316 B8
Lapwing Gv
FHAM/PORC PO16 ... 375 K8 □
Lapwing Ri WHCH RG28 ... 122 A2
Lapwing Rd WIMB BH21 ... 404 E1
Lara Cl CHAR BH8 ... 433 H5
Larch Av FAWY SO45 ... 392 A3
Larch Cl CBLY GU15 ... 51 H7
CFDH BH17 ... 429 J7
HEND SO30 ... 320 C5
LIPH GU30 ... 226 E5
LSOL/BMARY PO13 ... 420 E1 □
LYMN SO41 ... 438 D3 □
NWBY RG14 ... 25 L3
RGWD BH24 ... 381 L4
STOK SO20 ... 163 G4
TLHT RG30 ... 31 L4
WINC SO23 ... 191 G8
Larchdale Cl HLER SO31 ... 370 B8 □
KSCL RG20 ... 59 J6
Larch Dr AND SP10 ... 142 B1
KSCL RG20 ... 59 A6
Larches Gdns FHAM PO15 ... 372 A1
Larchfield Rd FLET GU13 ... 110 F1
Larchfield Wy HORN PO8 ... 353 G1
Larch Rd BOR GU35 ... 202 E2
ROWN SO16 ... 317 M5
Larch Rw FBDG SP6 ... 310 C6
Larch Wy FARN GU14 ... 89 M5
FERN BH22 ... 380 A8
HLER SO31 ... 345 K8
Larchwood CHAM RG24 ... 83 L5 □
Larchwood Av HAV PO9 ... 376 F4
Larchwood Gld CBLY GU15 ... 71 K1
Larchwood Rd TOTT SO40 ... 341 G2
Larcombe Rd PSF GU32 ... 275 J7
Larg Dr WINW SO22 ... 214 B4
Lark Cl AND SP10 ... 119 G6
KEMP RG22 ... 103 L8
NTID SP9 ... 114 E1
Larkfield CHAM RG24 ... 83 L5
Larkfield Rd FNM GU9 ... 134 C5
Lark Hill Ri WINW SO22 ... 238 C4
Larkhill Rd HSEA PO3 ... 399 K4
Lark Ri LIPH GU30 ... 226 D3
Larks Barrow HI WHCH RG28 ... 99 H6
Larks Cl FERN BH22 ... 405 M1
Larksfield Av MOOR/WNTN BH9 ... 432 E5
Larkshill Cl NMIL/BTOS BH25 ... 437 M4
Larkspur Cha ITCH SO19 ... 345 J3
Larkspur Cl ALDT GU11 ... 6 F7
BPWT SO32 ... 323 M3
HLER SO31 ... 370 D6 □
Larkspur Dr TOTT SO40 ... 342 C8
Larkspur Drive NBAD SO52 ... 292 E2
Larkspur Gdns FAWY SO45 ... 391 M4
HEND SO30 ... 346 B3 □
NTHA RG18 ... 27 J4 □
Larks Ri FERN BH22 ... 405 M1
Larkswood Cl SHST GU47 ... 49 K7 □
Larkswood Dr CWTH RG45 ... 49 L3
Larkwhistle Farm Rd
RWIN SO21 ... 148 C7
Larmer Cl FLET GU13 ... 110 C1
Larwood Sq AND SP10 ... 119 H6 □
Lascelles Rd LTDN BH7 ... 449 G2
Lascombe La RGUW GU3 ... 137 K4
Laser Cl HLER SO31 ... 370 C7
Lashly Meadow WVILLE PO7 ... 326 B5
Latchmore Dr FAWY SO45 ... 367 G4
Latchmore Forest Gv
HORN PO8 ... 352 D5
Latchmore Gdns HORN PO8 ... 352 C5
Latchwood La RFNM GU10 ... 159 G3
Latelie Cl HLER SO31 ... 369 G3 □
Latham Av FRIM GU16 ... 71 H6
Latham Cl ELGH SO50 ... 295 G6
Latham Ct WSHM SO15 ... 342 F1
Latham Rd ELGH SO50 ... 295 G6
ROMY SO51 ... 262 F8 □
Latimer Ct ROMY SO51 ... 399 M4
FRIM GU16 ... 71 H6
Latimer Rd MOOR/WNTN BH9 ... 432 D8
Latimers Cl CHCH/BSGR BH23 ... 436 D7
Latimer St ROMY SO51 ... 290 D1
SHAM SO14 ... 13 H6
Laud Cl NWBY RG14 ... 26 A3
Lauder Cl EMRTH PO10 ... 379 H6
FRIM GU16 ... 71 H6
Lauderdale FARN GU14 ... 90 A3
Launcelot Cl AND SP10 ... 118 F5
Launcelyn Cl NBAD SO52 ... 291 L5
Launceston Dr ELGH SO50 ... 293 L3 □
Laundry La CBLY GU15 ... 70 B3
HTWY RG27 ... 66 G3
LYMN SO41 ... 454 D4
Laundry Rd ROWN SO16 ... 318 A6
Laurel Cl CBLY GU15 ... 71 G4
CHCH/BSGR BH23 ... 436 B7
FARN GU14 ... 89 M5
FAWY SO45 ... 367 J5
HLER SO31 ... 370 F4 □
LYMN SO41 ... 438 C4
ODIM RG29 ... 108 B5
RGWD BH24 ... 381 J4
WIMB BH21 ... 429 H2
Laurel Dr BDST BH18 ... 429 M4
Laurel Gdns ALDT GU11 ... 6 F7
BDST BH18 ... 430 A4
HLER SO31 ... 370 F4

Laurel Gv RFNM GU10.....158 C3
Laurel La RGWD BH24.....381 J5
Laurel Rd HLER SO31.....370 F4
HORN PO8.....353 G4
The Laurels AND SP10.....8 D3
BSTK RG21.....5 H5
FERN BH22.....406 A1
FLET GU13.....88 F7
FNM GU9.....6 C7
Laurence Ct RAND SP11.....92 E6
Lauriston Dr CHFD SO53.....265 G7 🖪
Laurus Cl WVILLE PO7.....376 E3
Lavant Cl HORN PO8.....352 F7
Lavant Dr HAV PO9.....17 G1
Lavant St PSF GU32.....275 K4
Lavell's La THLE RG7.....43 M8
Lavender Cl ITCH SO19.....344 D3 🖪
VWD BH31.....357 C3 🖪
Lavender Gdns BOR GU35.....201 J5 🖪
Lavender La RFNM GU10.....158 C4
Lavender Rd CHAR BH8.....433 H4
KEMP RG22.....126 F1
LYMN SO41.....438 C5
WVILLE PO7.....376 E2
Lavender Wy BDST BH18.....429 H5
Laverock Lea
FHAM/PORC PO16.....374 A7
Laverstoke Cl ROWN SO16.....317 K2 🖪
Laverstoke La OVTN RG25.....123 H8
WHCH RG28.....123 H3
Lavey's La FHAM PO15.....371 M2
Lavington Gdns NBAD SO52.....291 L5
GPORT PO12.....18 D2
Lavinia Rd BKME/WDN BH12.....446 B1
Lawday Link FNM GU9.....134 D1
Lawday Pl FNM GU9.....134 D1 🖪
Lawday Place La FNM GU9.....134 D1
Lawford Crs YTLY GU46.....69 G2
Lawford Rd MOOR/WNTN BH9.....432 E5
Lawford Wy TOTT SO40.....316 D8
Lawn Cl LSOL/BMARY PO13.....397 H7 🖪
LYMN SO41.....454 C4
Lawn Dr HLER SO31.....370 E6
Lawn Rd ELGH SO50.....294 A3
WINW SO22.....214 B3 🖪
LYMN SO41.....439 M5
LYMN SO41.....454 C4
PTSN SO17.....319 G8
Lawns Cl WIMB BH21.....405 G2
Lawnside Rd WSHM SO15.....317 M8
Lawns Rd WIMB BH21.....404 F2
The Lawns CHCH/BSGR BH23.....436 F1
FARN GU14.....90 B5
Lawn St WINC SO23.....11 H7
Lawnswood Cl HORN PO8.....352 D6
Lawn Vw CHCH/BSGR BH23.....437 H3
Lawrence Av HORN PO8.....352 C6
CHAM PO6.....83 H7
Lawrence Cl AND SP10.....8 E1
CHAM PO6.....399 L1
Lawrencedale Ct BSTK RG21.....4 B9
Lawrence Dr PSTN BH14.....446 D7
Lawrence Gv ITCH SO19.....344 D6
Lawrence Houses RAND SP11.....140 A7 🖪
Lawrence La FBDG SP6.....334 F4
Lawrence Rd FHAM PO15.....14 E4
FLET GU13.....88 E8
RGWD BH24.....359 G6
SSEA PO5.....21 L6
Lawrences La NTHA RG18.....27 G2
Lawrence Wy CBLY GU15.....70 C4
Lawson Cl HLER SO31.....346 B8 🖪
SSEA PO5.....21 L4
Laws Ter ALDT GU11.....7 J1
Laxton Cl HLER SO31.....370 F5
ITCH SO19.....344 E6
Layard Dr WIMB BH21.....404 B7
Lay Fld HTWY RG27.....85 L7
Layton Rd BKME/WDN BH12.....446 C3
LSOL/BMARY PO13.....397 G5
Lazy Acre EMRTH PO10.....379 M8 🖪
Lea Cl ASHV GU12.....113 K7
BSTK RG21.....5 K7
FNM GU9.....6 F9
Leacock Cl BPWT SO32.....324 A4
Lea Ct FNM GU9.....6 D7
Lea Cft CWTH RG45.....49 L2
Leaden Vere ODIM RG29.....131 J4
Leafy La FHAM PO15.....371 J2
Lealand Gv CHAM PO6.....376 B8
Lealand Rd CHAM PO6.....400 B1
Leamington Crs
LSOL/BMARY PO13.....420 D2
Leamington Rd
MOOR/WNTN BH9.....447 M1
Leander Cl ELGH SO50.....293 M3 🖪
Lea-oak Gdns FHAM PO15.....14 A4
Leaphill Rd LTDN BH7.....448 F2
Lea Rd CBLY GU15.....70 E6
FAWY SO45.....418 C1
Learoyd Rd CFDH BH17.....445 J1
Lear Rd GPORT PO12.....18 C7
Leaside Wy ROWN SO16.....319 H3
Lea Springs FLET GU13.....110 C1
The Lea FLET GU13.....110 C1
VWD BH31.....356 F3
Leatherhead Gdns
HEND SO30.....321 J6 🖪
Lea Wy ASHV GU12.....113 J5
BWD BH11.....413 G4
The Leaway FHAM/PORC PO16.....374 B8
Leawood Rd FLET GU13.....110 C1 🖪
Lebanon Rd WSHM SO15.....342 B1
Le Borowe FLET GU13.....110 D4
Lechlade Gdns FHAM PO15.....372 B4
LTDN BH7.....433 L8
Leckford Cl FHAM/PORC PO16.....374 A7
WEND SO18.....320 C8 🖪
Leckford La STOK SO20.....187 C1
Leckford Rd HAV PO9.....377 M2
Ledbury Rd CHAM PO6.....375 G7
CHCH/BSGR BH23.....450 E3
Lederle La ROMY SO51.....290 E8
Ledgard Cl PSTN BH14.....446 A4
Lee Church La ROMY SO51.....290 E8
Lee Ct ALDT GU11.....7 J5
Leedam Rd NBNE BH10.....432 B4
Lee Dro ROMY SO51.....290 F7

Lee Lands LYMN SO41.....440 B7
Lee La ROMY SO51.....290 F4
Leep La GPORT PO12.....18 F8
Lee Rd ALDT GU11.....6 C2
GPORT PO12.....421 L2
Lees Cl ITCH CHCH/BSGR BH25.....434 B4
Leesland Rd GPORT PO12.....18 C1
Lees La GPORT PO12.....18 E1
Leeson Rd LTDN BH7.....448 D1
Lefroy Av BSTK RG21.....5 G4
Lefroy's Fld RFNM GU10.....110 C8
Leger Cl FLET GU13.....110 D3
Legge Crs ALDT GU11.....6 A3 🖪
Legg La WIMB BH21.....404 B4
Legion Cl PLE BH15.....444 D6
Legion La WINC SO23.....215 H1
Legion Rd HISD PO11.....425 L4
PLE BH15.....444 C6
Lehar Cl KEMP RG22.....104 C8
Leicester Pl AND SP10.....9 G6
Leicester Rd CCLF BH13.....446 E5
WSHM SO15.....318 C6
Leicester Wy WINC SO23.....11 M4
Leigham Vale Rd SBNE BH6.....449 J4
Leigh Cl AND SP10.....9 L7
Leigh Common WIMB BH21.....404 C3
Leigh Fld THLE RG7.....43 J2
Leigh Gdns AND SP10.....9 L7
WIMB BH21.....404 B4
Leigh La FNM GU9.....135 H8
WIMB BH21.....404 D3
Leigh Pk WIMB BH21.....440 A4
Leigh Rd AND SP10.....9 L7
CHFD SO53.....293 H4
ELGH SO50.....293 K5
ELGH SO50.....294 A5 🖪
FHAM/PORC PO16.....15 G4
HAV PO9.....16 F2
NMIL/BTOS BH25.....437 L4
PTSW SO17.....318 F7
WIMB BH21.....404 A4
Leighton Av WSHM SO15.....318 A8
Leighton Rd ITCH SO19.....344 C5
Leipzig Barracks FLET GU13.....111 G6
Leipzig Rd FLET GU13.....111 G5
Leith Av FHAM/PORC PO16.....374 B7
Leith Cl CWTH RG45.....49 K1
Le Marchant Rd FRIM GU16.....71 J5
Lemon Gv BOR GU35.....201 H7
Lemon Rd WSHM SO15.....342 F1
Lena Cl RAND SP11.....92 D6
Lendorber Av CHAM PO6.....399 L1
Lendore Rd FRIM GU16.....71 G8
Lennel Gdns FLET GU13.....111 H2
Lennon Wy KEMP RG22.....127 H1
Lennox Cl CHFD SO53.....265 K8
GPORT PO12.....18 F9
ROWN SO16.....317 L3
Lennox Rd North SSEA PO5.....21 J8
Lensyd Gdns HORN PO8.....352 D2
Lenten St ALTN GU34.....176 D5
Lentham Cl CFDH BH17.....430 B7
Lentune Wy LYMN SO41.....440 B6
Leofric Ct ENEY PO4.....424 A5
Leominster Rd CHAM PO6.....374 F7
Leonard Cl FRIM GU16.....71 G8
Leonard Rd GPORT PO12.....19 H2
Leopold Av FARN GU14.....90 E3
Leopold Dr BPWT SO32.....323 G1
Leopold St ENEY PO4.....21 M7
Le Patourel Cl
CHCH/BSGR BH23.....450 C1
Lepe Rd FAWY SO45.....418 D1
Lerryn Rd LSOL/BMARY PO13.....397 H6
Leslie Rd MOOR/WNTN BH9.....432 C8
PSTN BH14.....445 M5
Leslie Southern Ct NWBY RG14.....3 J2
Lester Av HAV PO9.....377 G6
Lester Rd GPORT PO12.....18 A2
Lestock Wy FLET GU13.....89 H7
Levell Ct RAND SP11.....92 E6 🖪
Leven Av WBNE BH4.....22 A2
Leven Cl CHFD SO53.....264 F8
WBNE BH4.....22 A3
Leventhorpe Ct GPORT PO12.....19 G4 🖪
Levern Dr FNM GU9.....134 F2 🖪
Leveson Cl GPORT PO12.....18 A6
Leviathan Cl FHAM/STUB PO14.....396 B6
Levignen Cl FLET GU13.....110 C3
Lewens Cl WIMB BH21.....404 A4
Lewesdon Dr BDST BH18.....429 K4
Lewin Cl RWIN SO21.....266 F3
Lewis Cl BSTK RG21.....5 H4
FAWY SO45.....367 G6
Lewisham Wy SHST GU47.....50 A7
Lewis Rd EMRTH PO10.....378 A4
Lewis Silkin Wy ROWN SO16.....317 M4
Lewry Cl HEND SO30.....346 A1
Lexby Rd TOTT SO40.....341 G7
Lexden Gdns HISD PO11.....425 J4
Leybourne Av NBNE BH10.....432 B3
WEND SO18.....319 L8
Leybourne Cl NBNE BH10.....432 A3
Leydene Av CHAR BH8.....433 K7
Leydene Cl CHAR BH8.....433 K7
Leyland Cl GPORT PO12.....18 A6
Leyland Rd BKME/WDN BH12.....431 J6
Ley Rd FARN GU14.....70 D8
Leys Gdns NWBY RG14.....2 D2
Leyside CHCH/BSGR BH23.....450 E2
CWTH RG45.....49 K3
Leyton Rd SHAM SO14.....344 A1
Leyton Wy RAND SP11.....8 C9
Liam Cl HAV PO9.....377 L4
Liberty Rd BPWT SO32.....324 F8
The Liberty WVILLE PO7.....351 J5
Library Rd BKME/WDN BH12.....446 D3
FARN GU14.....90 E6
FERN BH22.....406 A2
MOOR/WNTN BH9.....432 D7
TOTT SO40.....341 L1
Lichen Wy TOTT SO40.....342 D6
Lichfield Rd FHAM/STUB PO14.....371 G5
HSEA PO3.....423 L2
Lickfolds Rd RFNM GU10.....158 B6
Liddell Cl EWKG RG40.....48 B5
Liddel Wy CHFD SO53.....292 F3

Liddiards Wy WVILLE PO7.....376 C5
Lidiard Gdns ENEY PO4.....423 M6
Lightfoot Gv BSTK RG21.....105 G6
Lightsfield DEAN RG23.....103 G5
Lilac Cl HAV PO9.....378 A5
BOR GU35.....201 J6
RGWD BH24.....358 F8
Lilac Rd ROWN SO16.....319 G8
Lilac Wy DEAN RG23.....104 C2
Lille Barracks ALDT GU11.....91 G8
Lilliput Rd PSTN BH14.....446 B8
Lillywhite Crs AND SP10.....119 C3 🖪
Lily Av WVILLE PO7.....375 M6
Lily Cl KEMP RG22.....126 F1
Limecroft YTLY GU46.....68 F3
Lime Av ALTN GU34.....176 D3
CBLY GU15.....71 K2
ITCH SO19.....344 E3
NWBY RG14.....3 M2
PLE BH15.....445 L2
RWIN SO21.....266 F8
Lime Cl FAWY SO45.....367 J6
ITCH SO19.....344 E3
Lime Dr FARN GU14.....89 G4 🖪
Limes Av KSCL RG20.....59 K6
Lime Gdns HEND SO30.....320 C5
Lime Gv ALTN GU34.....176 D3
CHAM PO6.....374 F7
HISD PO11.....425 C5
LYMN SO41.....439 H8
Lime Kiln La FAWY SO45.....391 M4
Limekiln La BPWT SO32.....297 L5
PSF GU32.....274 A2
PSF GU32.....302 B1
Limekiln Rd RAND SP11.....94 A3
Limes Av KSCL RG20.....57 K1
Limes Cl LIPH GU30.....248 E4 🖪
LISS GU33.....248 E4
Limes Rd FARN GU14.....89 M3
The Limes LSOL/BMARY PO13.....397 H7
TADY RG26.....64 A6
TOTT SO40.....342 E7 🖪
Lime St ALDT GU11.....6 D2
SHAM SO14.....13 H5
Limetree Av KSCL RG20.....56 E6
Lime Tree Cl FBDG SP6.....333 K2 🖪
Limetree Wk WINC SO23.....11 M7
Lime Tree Wy CHAM RG24.....83 K5
Lime Wk FAWY SO45.....367 J6
Limited Rd MOOR/WNTN BH9.....432 E7
Linacre Rd ITCH SO19.....345 H4
Lin Brook Dr RGWD BH24.....359 C6
Linchmere Rd HASM GU27.....227 M5
Linch Rd HASM GU27.....251 K5
MIDH GU29.....279 L3
Lincoln Av BMTH BH1.....448 C2
Lincoln Cl ASHV GU12.....113 K3
CBLY GU15.....71 L4
FHAM/STUB PO14.....371 G5
KEMP RG22.....127 C1
Lincoln Ct WSHM SO15.....318 C6 🖪
Lincoln Gn ALTN GU34.....176 D6
Lincoln Ri HORN PO8.....352 F4
Lincoln Rd BKME/WDN BH12.....446 C1
FARN GU14.....90 D7
PSEA PO1.....21 M1
Lincolns Ri ELGH SO50.....266 C4
Linda Gv HORN PO8.....352 D5
Linda Rd FAWY SO45.....392 F5 🖪
Lindberg Ri FHAM PO15.....371 J2
Lind Cl OVTN RG25.....123 M1
Linden Av CHAM RG24.....106 A3
ODIM RG29.....108 E4
Linden Cl BPWT SO32.....323 K5
FERN BH22.....406 B2
NWBY RG14.....2 C1
RAND SP11.....92 F6
Linden Ct CBLY GU15.....71 J1
Linden Dr LISS GU33.....248 E4
Linden Gdns HEND SO30.....320 C5
RGWD BH24.....358 D8
Linden Gv CHFD SO53.....265 H8
GPORT PO12.....18 E5
HISD PO11.....425 L5
Linden Lea FHAM/PORC PO16.....374 A7
Linden Rd BKME/WDN BH12.....446 B2
FERN BH22.....406 B2
BOR GU35.....202 B3
MOOR/WNTN BH9.....432 C5
ROMY SO51.....290 E1
ROWN SO16.....317 M4
Lindens Cl EMRTH PO10.....378 D5
The Lindens CHCH/BSGR BH23.....435 H5
HAV PO9.....135 L7
Linden Wk NBAD SO52.....291 L3
Linden Wy HAV PO9.....377 K5 🖪
HORN PO8.....352 F3
LYMN SO41.....440 A4
Lindford Cha BOR GU35.....201 L3
Lindford Cl BOR GU35.....201 L2
Lindford Wey BOR GU35.....201 L3
Lindisfarne Cl CHAM PO6.....399 L1
Lindley Av ENEY PO4.....423 L6
Lindley Gdns NALR SO24.....218 C4
Lind Rd GPORT PO12.....19 C9
Lindsay Rd CCLF BH13.....446 F4
ITCH SO19.....345 J2
Lindum Dene ALDT GU11.....6 E4
Lindway HLER SO31.....370 C6
Lineside CHCH/BSGR BH23.....435 C8
The Lines KSCL RG20.....59 J5
Linford Cl NMIL/BTOS BH25.....437 L4
Linford Ct HAV PO9.....377 H1
Linford Crs ROWN SO16.....318 C5
Linford Rd RGWD BH24.....359 H7
Ling Crs BOR GU35.....202 E2
Lingdale Rd SBNE BH6.....449 J2
Lingen Cl AND SP10.....118 E5 🖪
Lingfield Cl CHAM RG24.....106 B3
Lingfield Gdns WEND SO18.....319 L6 🖪
Lingfield Rd NWBY RG14.....3 J3
Lingmala Gv FLET GU13.....111 C3 🖪
Ling Rd BKME/WDN BH12.....430 F7
Lingwood Av
CHCH/BSGR BH23.....450 E2
Lingwood Cl ROWN SO16.....318 E1

Lingwood Wk ROWN SO16.....318 E1 🖪
Linhorns La NMIL/BTOS BH25.....437 L2
Linkenholt Wy HAV PO9.....377 G3
Link Ri WIMB BH21.....429 J2
Link Rd ALTN GU34.....176 F2
CHAM PO6.....374 F6
FARN GU14.....90 A8
KSCL RG20.....59 K6
NWBY RG14.....2 E6
RGWD BH24.....359 G5
ROWN SO16.....317 L5
Links Dr CHCH/BSGR BH23.....434 B7
Linkside Av CHAR BH8.....433 J8
Linkside East GSHT GU26.....203 L1
Linkside North GSHT GU26.....203 L1
Linkside South GSHT GU26.....203 M2
Linkside West GSHT GU26.....203 L1
Links La HAV PO9.....353 M5
HISD PO11.....425 G5
Links Rd WINW SO22.....10 A5
PSTN BH14.....446 C6
The Links BOR GU35.....201 G7
LSOL/BMARY PO13.....397 G7
Links View Av PSTN BH14.....446 D7
Links View Wy ROWN SO16.....318 C6
Links Wy FARN GU14.....89 M5
The Link AND SP10.....118 B8
WVILLE PO7.....352 E7 🖪
YTLY GU46.....68 F1
Linkway CBLY GU15.....70 F4
CWTH RG45.....49 J3
FHAM/STUB PO14.....396 A7
FLET GU13.....110 E2
Link Wy NTHA RG18.....26 E4
DEAN RG23.....103 G7
Linnet Cl EPSF GU31.....276 B6
HORN PO8.....352 C4
KEMP RG22.....103 M6
RGWD BH24.....383 G2 🖪
Linnet Ct NMIL/BTOS BH25.....437 K5 🖪
Linnet Rd CFDH BH17.....429 J8
Linnet Sq ELGH SO50.....293 J7
Linnets Rd NALR SO24.....218 B4
The Linnets
FHAM/PORC PO16.....373 K8 🖪
TOTT SO40.....316 B8 🖪
Linnets Wy ALTN GU34.....176 E3
Linnies La LYMN SO41.....438 E1
Linsford La FARN GU14.....70 B8
Linstead Rd FARN GU14.....70 D8
Linthorpe Rd PLE BH15.....445 K4
Linton Cl TADY RG26.....61 M1
Linton Dr AND SP10.....8 F2
Linwood Cl FAWY SO45.....367 L6
Linwood Rd MOOR/WNTN BH9.....448 A1
Lion & Lamb Wy FNM GU9.....134 E6
Lion Cl OVTN RG25.....123 M1
Lionheart Cl BWD BH11.....431 H3
Lionheart Wy HLER SO31.....345 J4
Lion La GSHT GU26.....204 C7
Lion Rd FARN GU14.....90 E6
Lions Fld BOR GU35.....200 C4
Lions Hill Wy RGWD BH24.....381 G3
Lions La RGWD BH24.....381 H4
Lion St PSEA PO1.....20 E1
Lions Wd RGWD BH24.....381 J4
Lion Wy FLET GU13.....111 G3
Liphook Rd HASM GU27.....227 K4
BOR GU35.....201 H8
BOR GU35.....201 L3
BOR GU35.....202 B5
Lipizzaner Flds HLER SO31.....346 C1
Lippen La BPWT SO32.....271 L5
Lipscombe Cl NWBY RG14.....2 A5
Lipscombe Ri ALTN GU34.....176 E3
Lisbon Rd WSHM SO15.....343 H2
Liskeard Dr FARN GU14.....90 D2 🖪
Lisle Cl WINW SO22.....237 M5
LYMN SO41.....440 F5
NWBY RG14.....25 J3
Lisle Court Rd LYMN SO41.....440 F5
Lisle Wy EMRTH PO10.....378 C5
Lismoyne Cl FLET GU13.....88 E6 🖪
Liss Rd ENEY PO4.....423 K4
Lister Rd KEMP RG22.....104 D6
Litchfield Crs WEND SO18.....319 L7
Litchfield Rd WINW SO22.....214 C4
WEND SO18.....319 L7
Litchford Rd NMIL/BTOS BH25.....437 M4
Lith Av HORN PO8.....328 B8
Lith La HORN PO8.....328 B7
Litle Hyden La HORN PO8.....302 A8
Little Abshot Rd
FHAM/STUB PO14.....370 F8
Little Aldershot La STHA RG19.....40 F6
Little Anglesey Rd GPORT PO12.....18 C7
Little Arthur St NEND PO2.....423 J1 🖪
Little Ashton La BPWT SO32.....297 L5
Little Austins Rd FNM GU9.....135 G8
Little Barn Pl LISS GU33.....249 G4
Little Barrs Dr
NMIL/BTOS BH25.....437 M4
Little Basing CHAM RG24.....105 L1
Little Bull La BPWT SO32.....323 J6
Little Copse AND SP10.....8 C9
FLET GU13.....110 E1
YTLY GU46.....68 F1
Little Copse Cha CHAM RG24.....83 K6
Little Cnr WVILLE PO7.....351 K5
Littlecroft Av
MOOR/WNTN BH9.....432 F5
Little Dean La OVTN RG25.....130 D3
Little Dene Copse LYMN SO41.....439 M6
Little Dewlands VWD BH31.....356 B2 🖪
Littledown Av LTDN BH7.....448 D1
Littledown Dr LTDN BH7.....448 D1
Little Dro FBDG SP6.....310 D1
Little Drove Rd STOK SO20.....165 M5
Little Fallow CHAM RG24.....83 L8
Littlefield Cl ASHV GU12.....113 K7
Littlefield Crs NBAD SO52.....292 D4
Littlefield Gdns ASHV GU12.....113 K7
Littlefield Rd ALTN GU34.....176 F4
Little Forest Rd WBNE BH4.....22 B1
Little Frith EWKG RG40.....48 B1

Little Gays FHAM/STUB PO14.....395 K2
Little George St PSEA PO1.....423 J1 🖪
Little Gn GPORT PO12.....18 C7
Littlegreen Av HAV PO9.....377 L5
Little Green La RFNM GU10.....155 M4
Little Hambrook St SSEA PO5.....20 F5 🖪
Little Hayes La RWIN SO21.....216 E1
Little Hoddington Cl
OVTN RG25.....130 D3
Little Hyden La HORN PO8.....328 A1
Little Knowle Hl KSCL RG20.....59 L4
STHA RG19.....60 A2
Little Lance's Hl ITCH SO19.....344 D7
Little La GPORT PO12.....18 C7
THLE RG7.....27 M2
Little London Rd THLE RG7.....62 D2
Little Md MARL SN8.....32 C6
WVILLE PO7.....351 L5
Littlemeads ROMY SO51.....290 C1
Littlemill La FBDG SP6.....308 B3
Little Minster St WINC SO23.....11 G8
Little Moor SHST GU47.....49 M7
Littlemoor Av BWD BH11.....431 H4
Little Oak Rd ROWN SO16.....318 E4
Little Paddock CBLY GU15.....51 K8
Littlepark Av HAV PO9.....377 J4
Little Park Cl HEND SO30.....345 M2 🖪
Little Park Farm Rd
FHAM PO15.....371 G3
Little Quob La HEND SO30.....320 D6
Little Shore La BPWT SO32.....323 H1
Little Southsea St SSEA PO5.....20 F5 🖪
Little Thurbans Cl FNM GU9.....158 D2
Littleton Gv HAV PO9.....377 K4
Littleton La RWIN SO21.....213 J6
Little Vigo YTLY GU46.....68 C4
Little Wellington St ALDT GU11.....6 C2 🖪
Little Woodfalls Dr RSAL SP5.....285 J4
Littlewood Gdns HEND SO30.....320 C5
HLER SO31.....370 C5 🖪
Little Woodham La
LSOL/BMARY PO13.....421 C3
Littleworth Rd RFNM GU10.....136 C1
Litton Gdns DEAN RG23.....103 G7
Liverpool Rd
FHAM/STUB PO14.....396 D2
PSEA PO1.....21 M1
Liverpool St SHAM SO14.....343 L1
Livery Rd RSAL SP5.....206 D3
Livia Ct AND SP10.....119 G4
Livingstone Rd
BKME/WDN BH12.....446 B2
BOSC BH5.....449 G4
NWBY RG14.....3 G5
SHAM SO14.....318 F8
SSEA PO5.....21 K5
WIMB BH21.....404 C4
Llangar Gv CWTH RG45.....49 K3
Llewellin Cl WBHM BH16.....429 G8
Lloyd Av TOTT SO40.....342 C7 🖪
Lloyd's La TADY RG26.....80 F3
Loader Cl WINC SO23.....215 H4
Loane Rd ITCH SO19.....344 D5
Lobelia Rd ROWN SO16.....319 H4
Locarno Rd PSEA PO3.....399 K6
Loch Rd PSTN BH14.....446 D1
Lock Appoach CHAM PO6.....398 E1
Locke Cl RAND SP11.....161 K1
Lockerley Cl LYMN SO41.....440 C6
Lockerley Crs ROWN SO16.....317 L6
Lockerley Rd HAV PO9.....377 L5
ROMY SO51.....232 F7
ROMY SO51.....261 J3
Locke Rd HEND SO30.....321 H6
LIPH GU30.....227 G4
Lock's Dro RAND SP11.....73 J7
Lockhams Rd BPWT SO32.....322 E8
Lockram La THLE RG7.....31 M7
Lock Rd ALDT GU11.....113 G3
Locksash Cl SELS PO20.....427 K6
Locksash La RCCH PO20.....330 D8
Locksbridge La TADY RG26.....63 J9
Locksheath Cl HAV PO9.....377 H2 🖪
Locksheath Park Rd
HLER SO31.....369 M5
Lockside Ct THLE RG7.....29 M5 🖪
Lock's La RWIN SO21.....213 J5
Locksley Dr FERN BH22.....406 A5
Locksley Rd ELGH SO50.....293 K7
Locks Rd HLER SO31.....370 C4
Locksway Rd ENEY PO4.....423 K4
Lockswood Rd HLER SO31.....370 C5
Lock Vw CHAM PO6.....398 E4
Lockwood Cl FARN GU14.....70 B8
Lockyers Dr FERN BH22.....406 D2
Loddon Cl BSTK RG21.....5 J8
Loddon Dr BSTK RG21.....5 J8
Loddon Rd FARN GU14.....90 A2
Loddon Wy ASHV GU12.....113 G7
Lode Hl RSAL SP5.....285 G1
Loders Cl CFDH BH17.....430 A5
Lodge Av CHAM PO6.....375 C8
Lodgebury Pl EMRTH PO10.....379 J1
Lodge Cl AND SP10.....8 C5
PSTN BH14.....446 D4
Lodge Ct PSTN BH14.....446 D4
Lodge Dr FAWY SO45.....367 G4
RAND SP11.....117 J6
Lodge Dro RSAL SP5.....285 H1
Lodge Gdns GPORT PO12.....18 C5
Lodge Gv YTLY GU46.....69 G3
Lodge Hill Cl RFNM GU10.....159 G2
Lodge Hill Rd RFNM GU10.....159 G2
Lodge La BROC SO42.....416 C2
HAV PO9.....355 H2
RAND SP11.....94 A5
Lodge Rd CHCH/BSGR BH23.....454 C8
HAV PO9.....376 F7
HLER SO31.....370 C5
LYMN SO41.....439 M5
SHAM SO14.....343 L1
Lodge V ROMY SO51.....289 G6
Lodsworth HORN PO8.....328 C4 🖪
Lodsworth Cl HORN PO8.....328 C4 🖪
Loewy Crs BKME/WDN BH12.....431 H6
Lofting Cl ELGH SO50.....294 D6 🖪
Logan Cl ROWN SO16.....317 L3
Loggon Rd BSTK RG21.....104 F1

oman Rd FRIM GU16 ... 91 K5
omax Cl HEND SO30 ... 321 H7
ombard Av SBNE BH6 ... 449 J3
ombard St PSEA PO1 ... 20 C5
ombardy Cl
  LSOL/BMARY PO13 ... 397 J6
  VWD BH31 ... 356 F3
ombardy Ri WVILLE PO7 ... 376 D3
omer La RGWD BH24 ... 334 A5
omond Cl DEAN RG23 ... 102 F7
  NEND PO2 ... 399 H8
ondesborough Rd ENEY PO4 ... 21 M5
ondlandes FLET GU13 ... 110 D4
ondon Av NEND PO2 ... 399 H6
ondon La CHCH/BSGR BH23 ... 408 D6
ondon Rd ALTN GU34 ... 177 G3
  AND SP10 ... 9 K6
  BLKW GU17 ... 70 B4
  BSTK RG21 ... 4 F3
  CBLY GU15 ... 70 F2
  CHAM RG24 ... 106 A4
  CHAM PO6 ... 375 K8
  EPSF GU31 ... 276 A3
  HORN PO8 ... 328 B7
  HTWY RG27 ... 87 H3
  LIPH GU30 ... 226 F1
  NEND PO2 ... 399 J6
  NWBY RG14 ... 2 E2
  ODIM RG29 ... 108 D5
  OVTN RG25 ... 123 L1
  RAND SP11 ... 119 L8
  STHA RG19 ... 27 H5
  STOK SO20 ... 186 F4
  WHCH RG28 ... 122 D3
  WINC SO23 ... 215 G4
  WSHM SO15 ... 343 K2
  WVILLE PO7 ... 352 C8
  WVILLE PO7 ... 376 A4
ondon St AND SP10 ... 9 J6
  WHCH RG28 ... 122 B3
one Barn La BPWT SO32 ... 298 D1
one Pine Dr FERN BH22 ... 406 C6
one Pine Wy FERN BH22 ... 406 D6
one Va WVILLE PO7 ... 376 A5
ongacre ASHV GU12 ... 113 K6
  NWBY RG14 ... 25 C8
ongacre Cl LISS GU33 ... 248 F4
ongacre Ri CHAM RG24 ... 83 K6
ongacre FHAM/STUB PO14 ... 371 M7
ong Barrow Cl RWIN SO21 ... 190 D3
ong Beech Dr FARN GU14 ... 89 M5
  TOTT SO40 ... 341 H2
ong Bottom RAND SP11 ... 93 L5
ong Br FNM GU9 ... 134 F6
ongbridge Cl HTWY RG27 ... 64 D7
  TOTT SO40 ... 316 C6
ongbridge Rd TADY RG26 ... 63 L5
ong Cl RSAL SP5 ... 256 D8
ongclose Rd HEND SO30 ... 346 B1
ong Close West RSAL SP5 ... 256 D8
ong Copse FAWY SO45 ... 392 C5
ong Copse Cha CHAM RG24 ... 83 K6
ong Copse La EMRTH PO10 ... 378 D4
ongcroft RFNM GU10 ... 156 F3
  STHA RG19 ... 27 H6
ong Cross HI BOR GU35 ... 202 B3
ong Cross La KEMP RG22 ... 126 F2
ong Curtain Rd PSEA PO1 ... 20 D6
ongdean Cl CHAM PO6 ... 374 E7
ongdene Rd HASM GU27 ... 228 D4
ong Down EPSF GU31 ... 276 A4
ongdown Cl RFNM GU10 ... 158 F2
ongdown Rd RFNM GU10 ... 158 E3
  SHST GU47 ... 49 K7
ong Dr HEND SO30 ... 320 D6
  LSOL/BMARY PO13 ... 397 G7
ong Dro RSAL SP5 ... 230 C3
ongfield Av FHAM/STUB PO14 ... 14 B8
ongfield Cl ENEY PO4 ... 424 A3
  FARN GU14 ... 70 D8
  OVTN RG25 ... 125 K7
ongfield Rd ASHV GU12 ... 113 K6
  EMRTH PO10 ... 378 C1
  LYMN SO41 ... 438 F6
  WINC SO23 ... 215 J8
ongfleet Dr WIMB BH21 ... 430 E1
ongfleet Rd PLE BH15 ... 445 K4
ongford Cl CBLY GU15 ... 71 G4
ong Garden Wk FNM GU9 ... 134 E6
ong Garden Wk East
  FNM GU9 ... 134 E6
ong Garden Wk West
  FNM GU9 ... 134 E6
ong Garden Wy FNM GU9 ... 134 E6
ong Gv TADY RG26 ... 41 G6
ong HI RFNM GU10 ... 136 B7
onghope Dr RFNM GU10 ... 158 D2
onghouse Gn WINC SO23 ... 11 M7
onglands Rd EMRTH PO10 ... 379 H8
ong La CHAM RG24 ... 83 M6
  FAWY SO45 ... 392 A3
  HLER SO31 ... 345 L7
  NWBY RG14 ... 25 M1
  ODIM RG29 ... 108 E8
  RCCH PO18 ... 331 J5
  RGWD BH24 ... 382 F4
  TOTT SO40 ... 342 B7
  WIMB BH21 ... 404 B1
ong Lane Cl FAWY SO45 ... 392 B5
ongleat Gdns
  NMIL/BTOS BH25 ... 437 J5
  ROWN SO16 ... 318 A3
ongleat Sq FARN GU14 ... 91 H5
ong Leaze RAND SP11 ... 97 H4
ongley Rd FLET GU13 ... 135 C7
ongmead FLET GU13 ... 110 F2
  KSCL RG20 ... 36 C7
  LISS GU33 ... 248 E5
ongmead Gdns HAV PO9 ... 16 C4
ongmead La CFDH BH17 ... 429 J7
ongmeadow Gdns
  FAWY SO45 ... 367 G4
ongmeadow La CFDH BH17 ... 429 J7

Longmead Rd RGWD BH24 ... 384 D4
  WEND SO18 ... 319 L6
Long Moor Dr LIPH GU30 ... 226 A4
Longmoor La THLE RG7 ... 43 K1
Longmoor Rd BSTK RG21 ... 104 F4
  LIPH GU30 ... 225 M4
  LISS GU33 ... 224 F6
Longmore Rd ITCH SO19 ... 344 B6
Longmore Crs ITCH SO19 ... 344 B6
Longmynd Dr
  FHAM/STUB PO14 ... 14 B8
Longparish Rd RAND SP11 ... 165 M1
  WHCH RG28 ... 121 J7
Long Priors PSF GU32 ... 272 A3
Longridge Rd HEND SO30 ... 346 A2
Long Rd BPWT SO32 ... 325 H2
  NBNE BH10 ... 432 A4
  PSF GU32 ... 275 M3
The Long Rd RFNM GU10 ... 158 C5
Longroden La OVTN RG25 ... 129 G1
Longs Ct WHCH RG28 ... 122 B3
Longshore Wy ENEY PO4 ... 424 B3
Longs La FHAM/STUB PO14 ... 396 A5
Longstaff Gdns
  FHAM/PORC PO16 ... 14 F2
Long Steeple La FBDG SP6 ... 283 K6
Longstock La AND SP10 ... 8 C7
  CHAM RG24 ... 84 A4
  ITCH SO19 ... 344 B6
Longstock Crs TOTT SO40 ... 341 H1
Longstock Rd HAV PO9 ... 377 M2
  RAND SP11 ... 164 E4
Long Wk RWIN SO21 ... 215 J4
Longwater Dr EWKG RG40 ... 48 B6
Longwater Rd EWKG RG40 ... 48 C6
  HTWY RG27 ... 48 C8
Longwood Av CHAM PO6 ... 399 L1
Longwood Dean La
  RWIN SO21 ... 269 H3
Longwood Rd RWIN SO21 ... 268 B4
Lonsdale Av CHAM PO6 ... 399 L1
  FHAM/PORC PO16 ... 398 B2
Lonsdale Rd TWDS BH3 ... 447 L1
Loperwood TOTT SO40 ... 315 L6
Loperwood La TOTT SO40 ... 315 M4
Loraine Av CHCH/BSGR BH23 ... 437 G8
Lord Cl CFDH BH17 ... 445 L1
Lordington Cl CHAM PO6 ... 375 M8
Lord Montgomery Wy
  SSEA PO5 ... 20 F3
Lord Mountbatten Cl
  WEND SO18 ... 319 K4
Lordsfield Gdns OVTN RG25 ... 100 E8
Lord's Hill Centre East
  ROWN SO16 ... 317 L3
Lord's Hill Centre West
  ROWN SO16 ... 317 L4
Lord's Hill Wy ROWN SO16 ... 317 L3
Lords St PSEA PO1 ... 423 H2
Lordswood Cl ROWN SO16 ... 318 C5
Lordswood Gdns ROWN SO16 ... 318 C4
Lordswood Rd ROWN SO16 ... 318 B4
Loreille Cl ROWN SO16 ... 317 K1
Lorne Park Rd BMTH BH1 ... 23 K5
Lorne Rd SSEA PO5 ... 21 L4
Lorraine Rd ITCH SO19 ... 344 B5
Loughwood Cl ELGH SO50 ... 293 M2
Louisburg Rd BOR GU35 ... 201 J2
Loundyes Cl NTHA RG18 ... 26 E4
Lovage Gdns TOTT SO40 ... 341 G1
Lovage Rd FHAM PO15 ... 371 H1
Lovage Wy HORN PO8 ... 328 B7
Lovedean La HORN PO8 ... 352 D2
Lovedon La WINC SO23 ... 191 H8
Lovegroves CHAM RG24 ... 83 M5
Love La AND SP10 ... 9 J7
  BPWT SO32 ... 270 A5
  EPSF GU31 ... 275 M4
  FBDG SP6 ... 284 D8
  KSCL RG20 ... 59 J2
  NWBY RG14 ... 25 J2
  ODIM RG29 ... 108 D2
  PSF GU32 ... 272 B4
  ROMY SO51 ... 290 D1
  RWIN SO21 ... 267 G3
Lovell Cl RAND SP11 ... 140 C1
  RWIN SO21 ... 190 B4
Lovells Wk NALR SO24 ... 218 B3
Loveridge Cl AND SP10 ... 119 G4
  BSTK RG21 ... 104 F6
Lovers La RFNM GU10 ... 180 F1
Love's Cl THLE RG7 ... 31 J5
Loves Wd THLE RG7 ... 43 J5
Lovett Rd HSEA PO3 ... 399 K5
Lovington La RWIN SO21 ... 217 H4
Lowa Cl NTID SP9 ... 114 D3
Lowa Rd NTID SP9 ... 114 C2
Lowcay Rd SSEA PO5 ... 21 L7
Lowden Cl WINW SO22 ... 238 C4
Lower Alfred St SHAM SO14 ... 343 M2
Lower Ashley Rd
  NMIL/BTOS BH25 ... 438 B5
Lower Banister St WSHM SO15 ... 343 K4
Lower Bartons FBDG SP6 ... 309 L7
Lower Baybridge La
  RWIN SO21 ... 268 A7
Lower Bellfield
  FHAM/STUB PO14 ... 395 K1
Lower Bere Wd WVILLE PO7 ... 376 D3
Lower Blandford Rd
  BDST BH18 ... 429 M5
Lower Broadmoor Rd
  CWTH RG45 ... 50 A4
Lower Brook St BSTK RG21 ... 4 B4
Lower Brownhill Rd
  ROWN SO16 ... 317 H6
Lower Buckland Rd
  LYMN SO41 ... 440 B3
Lower Canal Wk SHAM SO14 ... 13 L4
Lower Canes YTLY GU46 ... 68 D2
Lower Chase Rd BPWT SO32 ... 323 M3
Lower Chestnut Dr BSTK RG21 ... 104 E5
Lower Church La FNM GU9 ... 134 E6

Lower Church Pth PSEA PO1 ... 21 H1
Lower Church Rd
  FHAM/STUB PO14 ... 371 G5
  SHST GU47 ... 49 H1
Lower Common La
  PLE BH15 ... 444 D7
  HISD PO11 ... 425 L3
  ROWN SO16 ... 317 K6
Lower Common La WIMB BH21 ... 380 E1
Lower Common Rd
  ROMY SO51 ... 288 D6
Lower Crabbick La
  WVILLE PO7 ... 350 F4
Lower Densome Wd
  FBDG SP6 ... 284 D8
Lower Derby Rd NEND PO2 ... 399 G7
Lower Drayton La CHAM PO6 ... 400 A1
Lower Duncan Rd HLER SO31 ... 370 F3
Lower Evingar Rd WHCH RG28 ... 122 B3
Lower Farlington Rd
  CHAM PO6 ... 376 C8
Lower Farm Ct STHA RG19 ... 26 C7
Lower Farnham Rd ALDT GU11 ... 7 J7
Lower Forbury Rd SSEA PO5 ... 21 J3
Lower Golf Links Rd
  BDST BH18 ... 429 M3
Lower Gv FBDG SP6 ... 283 G6
Lower Grove Rd HAV PO9 ... 17 G6
Lower Hanger HASM GU27 ... 227 M2
Lower Heyshott EPSF GU31 ... 275 M4
Lower Lamborough La
  NALR SO24 ... 242 C3
Lower La BPWT SO32 ... 297 J8
Lower Md EPSF GU31 ... 276 A5
Lower Mead End Rd
  LYMN SO41 ... 412 D8
Lower Moor YTLY GU46 ... 69 G3
Lower Moors Rd RWIN SO21 ... 190 A8
Lower Mortimer Rd ITCH SO19 ... 344 B5
Lower Mullin's La FAWY SO45 ... 367 J4
Lower Neatham Mill La
  ALTN GU34 ... 177 K2
  FRIM GU16 ... 91 K1
Lower Nelson St ALDT GU11 ... 6 E1
Lower Newport Rd ASHV GU12 ... 7 M5
Lower New Rd HEND SO30 ... 320 C7
Lower Northam Rd
  HEND SO30 ... 346 A1
Lower Paice La ALTN GU34 ... 196 B4
Lower Pennington La
  LYMN SO41 ... 440 B7
Lower Pool Rd HTWY RG27 ... 67 G4
Lower Preshaw La BPWT SO32 ... 269 L8
Lower Quay Cl
  FHAM/PORC PO16 ... 15 J8
Lower Quay Rd
  FHAM/PORC PO16 ... 15 K8
Lower Rd HASM GU27 ... 205 J6
  HAV PO9 ... 376 F7
  RSAL SP5 ... 256 C4
  RWIN SO21 ... 190 B4
Lower St Helens Rd
  HEND SO30 ... 346 A3
Lower Sandhurst Rd
  EWKG RG40 ... 48 D6
Lower Sandy Down La
  LYMN SO41 ... 413 M5
Lower South Vw FNM GU9 ... 134 F5
Lower Spinney HLER SO31 ... 394 A1
Lower St HASM GU27 ... 228 A2
  ROMY SO51 ... 263 G1
Lower Swanwick Rd
  HLER SO31 ... 346 B8
Lower Terrace Rd FARN GU14 ... 90 D8
Lower Turk St ALTN GU34 ... 176 E5
Lower Vicarage Rd ITCH SO19 ... 344 B5
Lower Wardown EPSF GU31 ... 276 A4
Lower Wy STHA RG19 ... 26 C5
Lower Weybourne La FNM GU9 ... 6 C9
Lower Wokingham Rd
  EWKG RG40 ... 49 G2
Lower Woodside LYMN SO41 ... 440 C8
Lower Wote St BSTK RG21 ... 4 F7
Lower York St SHAM SO14 ... 344 B4
Lowestoft Rd CHAM PO6 ... 375 H7
Loweswater Gdns BOR GU35 ... 201 J3
Lowford HI HLER SO31 ... 345 K7
Lowicks Rd RFNM GU10 ... 181 L2
Lowland Rd WVILLE PO7 ... 351 J4
Lowlands Rd BLKW GU17 ... 69 M4
  KEMP RG22 ... 103 M5
Low La FNM GU9 ... 7 G9
Lowry Cl SHST GU47 ... 70 A2
Lowry Ct AND SP10 ... 8 F2
Lowry Gdns ITCH SO19 ... 345 G6
Lowther Gdns CHAR BH8 ... 23 L1
Lowther Rd CHAR BH8 ... 447 L6
Loxwood Av FLET GU13 ... 110 D1
Loxwood Rd HORN PO8 ... 352 D5
Loyalty La CHAM RG24 ... 106 A2
Luard Rd HAV PO9 ... 17 J5
Lubeck Dr AND SP10 ... 118 E5
Lucas Cl ROWN SO16 ... 317 L3
  YTLY GU46 ... 69 G3
Lucas Fld HASM GU27 ... 228 B2
Lucas Rd BKME/WDN BH12 ... 446 B2
Luccombe Pl WSHM SO15 ... 318 C6
Luccombe Rd WSHM SO15 ... 318 C6
Lucerne Av SBNE BH6 ... 449 J3
  WVILLE PO7 ... 352 B6
Lucerne Gdns HEND SO30 ... 345 L2
Lucerne Rd LYMN SO41 ... 454 C4
Luckham Rd
  MOOR/WNTN BH9 ... 432 F6
Lucknow St PSEA PO1 ... 21 L2
Lucky La LYMN SO41 ... 414 E7
Ludcombe WVILLE PO7 ... 351 K3
Ludgershall Rd NTID SP9 ... 114 A1
Ludlow Cl DEAN RG23 ... 104 B3
  FRIM GU16 ... 91 K1
  NWBY RG14 ... 26 B4
Ludlow Gdns DEAN RG23 ... 104 B3
Ludlow Rd CHAM PO6 ... 375 G7
  ITCH SO19 ... 344 C6
Ludshott Gv BOR GU35 ... 202 E3
Ludwell's La BPWT SO32 ... 323 L4
Lugano Cl WVILLE PO7 ... 352 B7
Luke Rd ALDT GU11 ... 6 A5
Luke Rd East ALDT GU11 ... 6 B5
Lukin Dr ROWN SO16 ... 317 H3

Lulworth Av PLE BH15 ... 444 D7
Lulworth Cl CHFD SO53 ... 293 G5
  FARN GU14 ... 90 D1
  HISD PO11 ... 425 L3
  PLE BH15 ... 444 D7
  ROWN SO16 ... 317 K6
Lulworth Crs PLE BH15 ... 444 D7
Lulworth Gn ROWN SO16 ... 317 K6
Lulworth Rd
  LSOL/BMARY PO13 ... 420 C2
Lumby Dr RGWD BH24 ... 358 F8
Lumby Drive Pk RGWD BH24 ... 358 F8
Lumley Rd EMRTH PO10 ... 378 E7
Lumsden Av WSHM SO15 ... 343 G1
Lumsden Rd ENEY PO4 ... 424 B5
Lundy Cl CHAM RG24 ... 83 J7
  ROWN SO16 ... 317 K3
Lune Cl BSTK RG21 ... 5 J8
Lune Ct AND SP10 ... 9 M1
Lunedale Rd FAWY SO45 ... 367 J8
Lupin Cl BAGS GU19 ... 51 M7
  KEMP RG22 ... 103 M8
Lupin Rd ROWN SO16 ... 319 H3
Luscombe Rd PSTN BH14 ... 446 B6
Luther Rd MOOR/WNTN BH9 ... 432 D8
Lutman St EMRTH PO10 ... 378 C4
Lutyens Cl CHAM RG24 ... 83 L8
Luton Cl ITCH SO19 ... 344 F4
Luxborough La ROMY SO51 ... 291 G4
Luxton Cl HEND SO30 ... 321 L8
Lyall Pl FNM GU9 ... 134 E1
Lyburn Cl ROWN SO16 ... 318 B4
Lyburn Rd RSAL SP5 ... 286 F6
Lych Gate Cl SHST GU47 ... 50 C6
Lych Gate Ct RGWD BH24 ... 383 G2
Lychgate Dr HORN PO8 ... 352 F1
Lychgate Gn FHAM/STUB PO14 ... 396 A3
Lyde CI DEAN RG23 ... 103 G7
Lydford CI FARN GU14 ... 90 D1
Lydford Gdns BWD BH11 ... 431 L6
Lydford Rd BWD BH11 ... 431 L6
Lydgate LYMN SO41 ... 453 M3
  TOTT SO40 ... 341 H1
Lydgate Cl ITCH SO19 ... 345 H4
Lydgate Gn ITCH SO19 ... 345 H4
Lydgate Rd ITCH SO19 ... 345 H4
Lydiard CI ELGH SO50 ... 293 M3
Lydlinch CI FERN BH22 ... 406 B7
Lydlynch Rd TOTT SO40 ... 341 J1
Lydney CI CHAM PO6 ... 375 G7
Lydney Rd HLER SO31 ... 370 D6
Lye Copse Av FARN GU14 ... 70 E8
Lyell Rd BKME/WDN BH12 ... 446 B2
Lyeway La NALR SO24 ... 220 C4
Lyeway Rd ALTN GU34 ... 220 F3
Lyford Rd BSTK RG21 ... 4 F5
Lymbourn Rd HAV PO9 ... 17 G5
Lyme Cl ELGH SO50 ... 293 L3
Lyme Crs CHCH/BSGR BH23 ... 436 D8
Lymefields LYMN SO41 ... 454 D2
Lymer La ROWN SO16 ... 317 H2
Lymington Bottom ALTN GU34 ... 197 G6
Lymington Bottom Rd
  ALTN GU34 ... 196 F4
  KEMP RG22 ... 127 G2
Lymington Ri ALTN GU34 ... 197 G6
Lymington Rd BROC SO42 ... 413 G2
  CHCH/BSGR BH23 ... 451 J1
  LYMN SO41 ... 441 M8
  LYMN SO41 ... 454 D1
  NMIL/BTOS BH25 ... 437 L7
Lymington Road Shelley HI
  CHCH/BSGR BH23 ... 451 K1
Lymore La LYMN SO41 ... 439 J8
Lymore Va LYMN SO41 ... 454 D1
Lynchborough Rd LIPH GU30 ... 202 A3
Lynch Cl WINW SO22 ... 10 C3
Lynchford La FARN GU14 ... 91 H7
Lynchford Rd ALDT GU11 ... 90 F8
  FARN GU14 ... 90 F8
Lynch HI WHCH RG28 ... 122 B3
Lynch Hill Pk WHCH RG28 ... 122 C3
Lynch La PSF GU32 ... 272 B4
Lynch Rd FNM GU9 ... 135 G2
The Lynch MARL SN8 ... 32 C6
  OVTN RG25 ... 100 D8
  WHCH RG28 ... 122 C3
Lyndale Cl LYMN SO41 ... 454 D3
Lyndale Dr FLET GU13 ... 89 J7
Lyndale Rd HLER SO31 ... 370 F4
Lynden Cl FHAM/STUB PO14 ... 371 M8
Lynden Ga ITCH SO19 ... 344 E5
Lyndford Ter FLET GU13 ... 110 E1
Lyndhurst Av ALDT GU11 ... 7 J9
  BLKW GU17 ... 69 M2
Lyndhurst Dr KEMP RG22 ... 127 L6
Lyndhurst Rd BROC SO42 ... 387 L6
  CHCH/BSGR BH23 ... 410 D8
  CHCH/BSGR BH23 ... 435 M7
  GPORT PO12 ... 18 C2
  NEND PO2 ... 399 K6
  RGWD BH24 ... 384 C5
  RSAL SP5 ... 287 H5
  TOTT SO40 ... 339 J1
Lyndock Cl ITCH SO19 ... 344 C6
Lyndock Pl ITCH SO19 ... 344 C6
Lyndsey Cl FARN GU14 ... 89 L4
Lyndum Cl EPSF GU31 ... 275 L5
Lyneham Rd CWTH RG45 ... 49 G3
Lyne Pl HORN PO8 ... 352 F2
Lynes La RGWD BH24 ... 382 F2
Lynford Av WINW SO22 ... 10 C2
Lynford Wy WINW SO22 ... 10 D3
Lynn Rd CFDH BH17 ... 430 D8
  NEND PO2 ... 399 K8
Lynn Wy FARN GU14 ... 90 C1
  WINC SO23 ... 215 J8
Lyric Cl NMIL/BTOS BH25 ... 452 E1
Lynton Cl FNM GU9 ... 158 L1
Lynton Ct TOTT SO40 ... 341 J2
Lynton Crs CHCH/BSGR BH23 ... 434 E5
Lynton Gdns FHAM/PORC PO16 ... 14 E1
Lynton Gv HSEA PO3 ... 399 L8

Lynton Meadow STOK SO20 ... 165 M4
Lynton Rd HEND SO30 ... 346 A1
  BOR GU35 ... 201 J5
  PSF GU32 ... 275 K4
Lynwood Av WVILLE PO7 ... 352 B5
Lynwood Dr FERN BH22 ... 406 B1
  BOR GU35 ... 201 K5
Lynwood Dr AND SP10 ... 8 D6
  FRIM GU16 ... 91 K5
  WIMB BH21 ... 404 D7
Lynwood Gdns HTWY RG27 ... 85 M7
Lynx Cl ELGH SO50 ... 294 E6
Lyon Av NMIL/BTOS BH25 ... 437 M5
Lyon Cl STHA RG19 ... 27 J6
Lyon Rd BKME/WDN BH12 ... 431 J6
  CWTH RG45 ... 49 M2
Lyon St SHAM SO14 ... 343 L2
Lyon Wy FRIM GU16 ... 70 F7
Lysander Cl CHCH/BSGR BH23 ... 451 G1
Lysander Wy FARN GU14 ... 90 E7
  WVILLE PO7 ... 352 E8
Lysons Av ASHV GU12 ... 91 J8
Lysons Rd ALDT GU11 ... 6 F3
Lyster Rd FBDG SP6 ... 309 M6
Lystra Rd MOOR/WNTN BH9 ... 432 E5
Lytchett Dr BDST BH18 ... 429 L5
Lytchett Wy UPTN BH16 ... 444 A2
Lyteltane Rd LYMN SO41 ... 440 B6
Lytham Rd BDST BH18 ... 429 L5
  WEND SO18 ... 319 M8
Lythe La PSF GU32 ... 274 F3
Lytton Rd BMTH BH1 ... 23 L2
  BSTK RG21 ... 5 H8
  FAWY SO45 ... 367 M6

M

Mabbs La HTWY RG27 ... 87 H4
Mabey Av NBNE BH10 ... 432 B6
Mabey Cl GPORT PO12 ... 19 G8
Mablethorpe Rd CHAM PO6 ... 375 J7
Macadam Wy AND SP10 ... 8 A7
Macandrew Rd CCLF BH13 ... 457 L1
Macarthur Crs WEND SO18 ... 319 M8
Macaulay Av CHAM PO6 ... 374 D7
Macaulay Rd BDST BH18 ... 429 L4
Maccullum Rd RAND SP11 ... 96 A8
Macdonald Rd FNM GU9 ... 134 E1
Maclaren Rd
  MOOR/WNTN BH9 ... 432 D6
Maclean Rd BWD BH11 ... 431 K5
Macnaghten Rd WEND SO18 ... 344 B1
Macrae Rd YTLY GU46 ... 68 F2
Madden Cl GPORT PO12 ... 18 A6
Maddison St SHAM SO14 ... 12 F5
Maddocks HI NALR SO24 ... 220 A4
Maddoxford Wy BPWT SO32 ... 321 L7
Madeira Cl CHAM RG24 ... 83 J7
Madeira Rd BMTH BH1 ... 23 G4
  NEND PO2 ... 399 J5
Madeley Rd FLET GU13 ... 111 G2
Madeline Crs
  BKME/WDN BH12 ... 446 A1
Madeline Rd EPSF GU31 ... 275 L4
Madison Av BMTH BH1 ... 448 C2
Madison Cl
  LSOL/BMARY PO13 ... 397 J8
Madox Brown End
  SHST GU47 ... 70 B2
Madrid Rd AND SP10 ... 9 M3
Mafeking Rd ENEY PO4 ... 423 K5
Magazine La TOTT SO40 ... 342 E5
Magazine Rd FARN GU14 ... 90 A8
Magdala Rd CHAM PO6 ... 399 K1
  HISD PO11 ... 425 J5
Magdalene Rd SHST GU47 ... 50 C6
Magdalene Wy
  FHAM/STUB PO14 ... 371 G7
Magdalen HI WINC SO23 ... 11 J8
Magdalen La
  CHCH/BSGR BH23 ... 449 M2
Magdalen Rd NEND PO2 ... 399 J5
Magennis Cl
  LSOL/BMARY PO13 ... 421 H1
Magna Gdns BWD BH11 ... 431 K2
Magna Rd WIMB BH21 ... 404 F8
Magnolia Cl AND SP10 ... 8 C7
  FAWY SO45 ... 367 G4
  FHAM/STUB PO14 ... 14 C7
  SHST GU47 ... 50 A7
  VWD BH31 ... 357 G3
Magnolia Gv ELGH SO50 ... 295 K6
Magnolia Rd ITCH SO19 ... 344 D5
Magnolia Wy FLET GU13 ... 110 F1
  HORN PO8 ... 353 G4
Magnus Dr KEMP RG22 ... 127 G1
Magpie Cl CHAR BH8 ... 433 G6
  KEMP RG22 ... 103 L8
  BOR GU35 ... 201 K6
  RFNM GU10 ... 111 G8
  STHA RG19 ... 26 E5
Magpie Gdns ITCH SO19 ... 344 F4
Magpie Gv NMIL/BTOS BH25 ... 437 K6
Magpie La ELGH SO50 ... 293 K6
  LSOL/BMARY PO13 ... 420 D1
Magpie Rd HORN PO8 ... 354 D4
Magpie Wk HORN PO8 ... 352 B4
Mag's Barrow FERN BH22 ... 406 C6
Maguire Dr FRIM GU16 ... 71 M5
Mahler Cl KEMP RG22 ... 104 E8
Maida Rd ALDT GU11 ... 112 L4
Maiden La LYMN SO41 ... 440 D7
Maidenthorn La OVTN RG25 ... 125 L7
Maidford Gv AND SP10 ... 400 A4
Maidstone Crs CHAM PO6 ... 375 J7
Main Dr FAWY SO45 ... 417 L2
  WHAM PO17 ... 374 L2
Main Gate Rd FARN GU14 ... 90 G6
Main Rd EMRTH PO10 ... 379 G8
  FAWY SO45 ... 366 E1
  FAWY SO45 ... 392 A3
  WINW SO22 ... 213 M2
  LSOL/BMARY PO13 ... 397 H4
  LYMN SO41 ... 415 M8
  LYMN SO41 ... 440 E1

PSEA PO1 .... 20 B1
PSEA PO1 .... 422 D2
RWIN SO21 .... 266 A6
RWIN SO21 .... 266 E6
RWIN SO21 .... 268 A4
RWIN SO21 .... 295 G1
TADY RG26 .... 62 A2
TOTT SO40 .... 341 J4
TOTT SO40 .... 342 D7
Mainsail Dr FHAM/PORC PO16 .... 15 J8
Mainstone ROMY SO51 .... 290 C2
Mainstone Cl FRIM GU16 .... 91 M1 🔟
Mainstream Ct ELGH SO50 .... 294 C5 🔟
Main St STHA RG19 8
Maisemore Gdns EMRTH PO10 .... 378 B8
Maitland Rd FARN GU14 .... 90 E8
Maitlands Cl RFNM GU10 .... 136 B2
Maitland St PSEA PO1 .... 423 H1
Majendie Cl NWBY RG14 .... 25 G3 🔟
Majestic Cl KEMP RG22 .... 126 F3
ROWN SO16 .... 317 G4
Majorca Av AND SP10 .... 9 L2
Malan Cl CFDH BH17 .... 430 C8
Malcolm Cl CHFD SO53 .... 265 K7
HLER SO31 .... 370 F5
Malcolm Rd CHFD SO53 .... 265 K7
Malcomb Cl SBNE BH6 .... 449 M5
Malcroft Ms TOTT SO40 .... 342 E7 🔟
Maldive Rd CHAM RG24 .... 83 J7
Maldon Cl ELGH SO50 .... 294 C5
Maldon Rd CHAM PO6 .... 375 H8 🔟
ITCH SO19 .... 344 C4
Malham Gdns KEMP RG22 .... 127 G3
Malham Rd STHA RG19 .... 26 F5
Malibres Rd CHFD SO53 .... 265 K8
Malin Cl FHAM/STUB PO14 .... 395 M5
ROWN SO16 .... 317 K4
Malins Rd NEND PO2 .... 423 H1
Mallard Cl AND SP10 .... 119 G6
ASHV GU12 .... 113 J6
BPWT SO32 .... 296 F8
CHAR BH8 .... 433 G7
CHCH/BSGR BH23 .... 450 A1
HASM GU27 .... 228 B2 🔟
KEMP RG22 .... 126 E1
LYMN SO41 .... 438 E5
NALR SO24 .... 218 C2
ROMY SO51 .... 262 E8
Mallard Ct NWBY RG14 .... 2 C4
Mallard Gdns HEND SO30 .... 321 H6
LSOL/BMARY PO13 .... 396 F6 🔟
Mallard Rd CHAR BH8 .... 433 H7
ENEY PO4 .... 423 M3
HAV PO9 .... 353 M7
WIMB BH21 .... 404 E1
Mallards ALTN GU34 .... 176 E3
Mallards Rd HLER SO31 .... 369 K1
The Mallards FHAM/PORC PO16 .... 15 H1
HAV PO9 .... 16 D8
Mallard Wy THLE RG7 .... 29 L5
YTLY GU46 .... 68 E2 🔟
Mallett Cl HEND SO30 .... 321 K6
Mallory Cl CHCH/BSGR BH23 .... 435 K8
Mallory Crs FHAM/PORC PO16 .... 15 J2
Mallow Cl BDST BH18 .... 429 J5
CHAM PO6 .... 375 K8 🔟
BOR GU35 .... 201 M3 🔟
WVILLE PO7 .... 376 D2
Mallow Rd HEND SO30 .... 345 L2
The Mallows NMIL/BTOS BH25 .... 438 B4
The Mall NTID SP9 .... 114 A4
RGWD BH24 .... 384 E5 🔟
Malmesbury Cl ROWN SO16 .... 295 H6 🔟
Malmesbury Gdns WINW SO22 .... 10 A3
Malmesbury Park Pl CHAR BH8 .... 23 M1
CHAR BH8 .... 448 A2
Malmesbury Pl WSHM SO15 .... 343 H1
Malmesbury Rd RGWD BH24 .... 381 J5
ROMY SO51 .... 262 D8
WSHM SO15 .... 343 H1
Malmsbury Rd BOR GU35 .... 201 J4
Maloren Wy FERN BH22 .... 380 E7
Malory Cl ITCH SO19 .... 345 H2
Malpass Rd RWIN SO21 .... 190 B6
Malshanger La DEAN RG23 .... 102 F5
Malta Cl CHAM RG24 .... 83 H7
Malta Rd NEND PO2 .... 399 J8
Maltby's ALTN GU34 .... 199 K8
Malthouse Cl FLET GU13 .... 110 D3
ROMY SO51 .... 262 D8 🔟
RWIN SO21 .... 215 L3
Malthouse Gdns TOTT SO40 .... 342 D7
Malthouse La
FHAM/PORC PO16 .... 15 J5
NALR SO24 .... 195 H7
TADY RG26 .... 62 A2
Malt House La RAND SP11 .... 119 H1
Malthouse Mdw LIPH GU30 .... 226 F4
Malthouse Ms ALTN GU34 .... 177 H2 🔟
Malthouse Rd NEND PO2 .... 399 H8
Maltings Cl ALTN GU34 .... 176 E6
The Maltings EPSF GU31 .... 275 L5
FHAM/PORC PO16 .... 373 H6 🔟
LIPH GU30 .... 227 J4
TADY RG26 .... 63 L6
Malt La BPWT SO32 .... 297 H8
Malus Cl FHAM/STUB PO14 .... 396 D1
Malvern Av FHAM/STUB PO14 .... 14 C8
Malvern Cl BPWT SO32 .... 323 J1
KEMP RG22 .... 103 M5
Malvern Ct NWBY RG14 .... 2 D7
Malvern Dr FAWY SO45 .... 367 K5
Malvern Gdns HEND SO30 .... 321 J6
EMRTH PO10 .... 378 C7
Malvern Ms EMRTH PO10 .... 378 D7
Malvern Rd BLKW GU17 .... 69 J7
FARN GU14 .... 90 A1
GPORT PO12 .... 18 B1
LISS GU33 .... 249 G6
MOOR/WNTN BH9 .... 432 E6
ROWN SO16 .... 318 B6
SSEA PO5 .... 21 J9
Malwood Av ROWN SO16 .... 318 C5
Malwood Cl HAV PO9 .... 377 L2
Malwood Gdns TOTT SO40 .... 316 B8
Malwood Rd FAWY SO45 .... 367 K4
Malwood Rd West FAWY SO45 .... 367 J4
Manchester Rd LYMN SO41 .... 412 F5

PSEA PO1 .... 21 M1
Mancroft Av
FHAM/STUB PO14 .... 396 A7
Mandale Rd BWD BH11 .... 431 K5
Mandela Wy WSHM SO15 .... 12 C1
Manderley LYMN SO41 .... 454 D5
Mandora Rd ALDT GU11 .... 112 E4
Manfield Rd ASHV GU12 .... 113 K6
Manica Cl BOR GU35 .... 201 J5 🔟
Manley Bridge Rd RFNM GU10 .... 158 B4
Manley Rd HLER SO31 .... 345 K7
Mann Cl WHCH RG28 .... 122 C4
Manners La ENEY PO4 .... 21 L3
Manners Rd ENEY PO4 .... 21 M3
Manning Av CHCH/BSGR BH23 .... 436 A7
Manningford Cl WINC SO23 .... 11 H1
Mannings Heath Rd
BKME/WDN BH12 .... 430 F6
Mannington Pl WCLF BH2 .... 22 C6
Mannington Wy FERN BH22 .... 380 B6
Manns Cl WEND SO18 .... 320 B6
Mannyngham Wy ROMY SO51 .... 262 C1
Manor Av BKME/WDN BH12 .... 431 G7
Manor Bridge Ct NTID SP9 .... 114 E1
Manor Cl ALTN GU34 .... 176 F2
FBDG SP6 .... 309 L7
FERN BH22 .... 406 C3
HASM GU27 .... 228 B2
HLER SO31 .... 345 K7 🔟
KEMP RG22 .... 126 F2
LYMN SO41 .... 454 C3
RFNM GU10 .... 136 C1
NTID SP9 .... 138 D1
RAND SP11 .... 141 M5
TOTT SO40 .... 341 J2
WHAM PO17 .... 348 E6
WINC SO23 .... 11 K6
Manor Copse AND SP10 .... 119 G3
Manor Ct FLET GU13 .... 110 F4
RGWD BH24 .... 358 D8
VWD BH31 .... 356 D2 🔟
Manor Crs CHAM PO6 .... 399 M1
HLER SO31 .... 345 K7
Manor Farm Cl ASHV GU12 .... 113 J7 🔟
NMIL/BTOS BH25 .... 437 K7 🔟
RSAL SP5 .... 252 B1
Manor Farm Gn RWIN SO21 .... 266 E3
Manor Farm Gv ELGH SO50 .... 294 D6 🔟
Manor Farm La ROMY SO51 .... 234 C7
Manor Farm Rd FBDG SP6 .... 309 H7
NBNE BH10 .... 432 A2
WEND SO18 .... 319 J7
Manor Flds LIPH GU30 .... 227 G4
Manor Gdns EMRTH PO10 .... 379 H7
RFNM GU10 .... 159 G3
RGWD BH24 .... 358 D8 🔟
VWD BH31 .... 356 D2 🔟
Manor House Av WSHM SO15 .... 342 C2
Manor La CHAM RG24 .... 106 A2
NTHA RG18 .... 26 B4
STHA RG19 .... 40 A1
VWD BH31 .... 356 D3
Manor Lodge Rd RWIN SO21 .... 189 L4
Manor Ms NEND PO2 .... 376 A8
Manor Park Av HSEA PO3 .... 399 L8
Manor Park Dr EWKG RG40 .... 48 A2 🔟
EWKG RG40 .... 48 B2 🔟
YTLY GU46 .... 69 G3
Manor Pl NWBY RG14 .... 25 G3
Manor Ri ALDT GU11 .... 142 D4
Manor Rd ALDT GU11 .... 6 D5
ALTN GU34 .... 176 F2
AND SP10 .... 8 E3
ASHV GU12 .... 113 J7
BMTH BH1 .... 23 L6
BPWT SO32 .... 322 C1
CHAM RG24 .... 82 D5
CHCH/BSGR BH23 .... 449 M2
ELGH SO50 .... 294 D6
EMRTH PO10 .... 379 H7
FARN GU14 .... 91 G3
FAWY SO45 .... 392 A4
FNM GU9 .... 135 H4
HISD PO11 .... 425 K3
LYMN SO41 .... 454 D3
NMIL/BTOS BH25 .... 437 M5
PSEA PO1 .... 423 J1
RGWD BH24 .... 382 E1
ROWN SO16 .... 292 C7
RSAL SP5 .... 232 D1
RWIN SO21 .... 266 E3
TOTT SO40 .... 366 E3
VWD BH31 .... 356 D2
Manor Rd North ITCH SO19 .... 344 C4
Manor Rd South ITCH SO19 .... 344 C5
Manorside Cl RFNM GU10 .... 113 J8 🔟
Manor Wk ASHV GU12 .... 7 G4
Manor Wy EMRTH PO10 .... 379 H7
HISD PO11 .... 425 L6
LSOL/BMARY PO13 .... 420 C2
VWD BH31 .... 356 D1 🔟
Mans Br WEND SO18 .... 319 L4
Mansbridge Rd ELGH SO50 .... 293 M7
WEND SO18 .... 319 L4
Manse La TADY RG26 .... 62 A2
Mansel Cl BKME/WDN BH12 .... 447 H1
Mansel Ct ROWN SO16 .... 317 K6
Mansell Cl FAWY SO45 .... 367 J8
Mansell Dr NWBY RG14 .... 36 F3
Mansel Rd East ROWN SO16 .... 317 K7
Mansel Rd West ROWN SO16 .... 317 J6
Mansfield Cl FERN BH22 .... 406 B6
Mansfield La WHAM PO17 .... 347 M4
Mansfield Rd KEMP RG22 .... 104 D6
LSOL/BMARY PO13 .... 397 G8
MOOR/WNTN BH9 .... 432 C8
PSTN BH14 .... 446 B4
RGWD BH24 .... 382 D1
Man's Hl THLE RG7 .... 31 M5
Mansion Dr HTWY RG27 .... 67 J3
Mansion Rd ENEY PO4 .... 423 J7
WSHM SO15 .... 343 H2
Mansvid Av CHAM PO6 .... 399 M1
Mantle Cl LSOL/BMARY PO13 .... 421 H1
Mantle Sq NEND PO2 .... 398 F6
Manton Cl PLE BH15 .... 444 D5 🔟

Maple Cl ALTN GU34 .... 176 E3 🔟
ASHV GU12 .... 113 J1
BLKW GU17 .... 69 M3
CHCH/BSGR BH23 .... 451 L1
EMRTH PO10 .... 378 D6
FHAM PO15 .... 372 A7
LSOL/BMARY PO13 .... 420 D3 🔟
NALR SO24 .... 218 B4 🔟
NMIL/BTOS BH25 .... 453 G1
ROMY SO51 .... 291 H7
SHST GU47 .... 49 J7
STOK SO20 .... 163 G6
Maple Crs BSTK RG21 .... 4 E3
HORN PO8 .... 328 B2
NWBY RG14 .... 2 E1
RAND SP11 .... 93 G6
Maple Dr CWTH RG45 .... 49 M1 🔟
FERN BH22 .... 380 A8
WINC SO23 .... 191 G8
WVILLE PO7 .... 351 L5
Maple Gdns TOTT SO40 .... 341 G2 🔟
YTLY GU46 .... 69 G3
Maple Gv TADY RG26 .... 41 L8
Maplehurst Cha KEMP RG22 .... 127 G2
Maple Leaf Cl FARN GU14 .... 90 C5 🔟
Maple Leaf Dr BOR GU35 .... 201 J4
Maple Rd FAWY SO45 .... 367 M8 🔟
MOOR/WNTN BH9 .... 432 D8
PLE BH15 .... 445 J5
SSEA PO5 .... 21 J8
WEND SO18 .... 344 C1
Maple Sq ELGH SO50 .... 293 K7 🔟
The Maples CHFD SO53 .... 265 H8
Mapleton Rd HEND SO30 .... 346 B2 🔟
Mapletree Av HORN PO8 .... 353 G3
Maple Wk ASHV GU12 .... 7 M6
Maple Wy BOR GU35 .... 202 E2
Maplewood Cl TOTT SO40 .... 341 G2
Maplin Rd ROWN SO16 .... 317 K4
Mapperton Cl CFDH BH17 .... 430 E6
Marabout Cl CHCH/BSGR BH23 .... 450 C1
Maralyn Av WVILLE PO7 .... 376 C2
Marathon Pl ELGH SO50 .... 295 G6
Marbrean Cl FBDG SP6 .... 309 H6 🔟
Marchant Cl STHA RG19 .... 38 A1 🔟
Marchant Rd AND SP10 .... 8 D7
March Cl AND SP10 .... 9 K3
Marchwood By-pass
TOTT SO40 .... 341 L3
Marchwood Rd HAV PO9 .... 377 J2
NBNE BH10 .... 432 A5
TOTT SO40 .... 342 A4
WSHM SO15 .... 342 F2
Marconi Rd NWBY RG14 .... 3 G2
Marcus Cl ELGH SO50 .... 295 G6
Mardale CBLY GU15 .... 71 M4
Mardale Rd ROWN SO16 .... 317 J8
Marden Wy EPSF GU31 .... 275 M5
Mardon Cl ELGH SO50 .... 319 K3
Mare La RWIN SO21 .... 267 K1
Mareth Cl ALDT GU11 .... 7 H1
Margam Av ITCH SO19 .... 344 D3
Margards La VWD BH31 .... 356 C3
Margaret Cl WVILLE PO7 .... 352 B7
Margaret Rd KEMP RG22 .... 104 C4
Margarita Rd FHAM PO15 .... 14 C4
Margate Rd SSEA PO5 .... 21 J4
Margery's Ct PSEA PO1 .... 20 D2 🔟
Margha Rd NTID SP9 .... 114 D2
Marian Cl WIMB BH21 .... 429 G4
Marianne Cl WSHM SO15 .... 342 D2 🔟
Marianne Rd
BKME/WDN BH12 .... 402 A8
WIMB BH21 .... 404 E1
Marian Rd WIMB BH21 .... 429 G4
Marie Cl BKME/WDN BH12 .... 446 C1
Marie Rd ITCH SO19 .... 345 G3
Marigold Cl CWTH RG45 .... 49 J1
FHAM PO15 .... 14 C4
KEMP RG22 .... 103 M8
Marina Cl EMRTH PO10 .... 378 E8 🔟
Marina Dr PSTN BH14 .... 446 A7
Marina Gv FHAM/PORC PO16 .... 398 A2
HSEA PO3 .... 423 M2
Marina Keep CHAM PO6 .... 398 E1
The Marina BOSC BH5 .... 448 D5
Marine Cl ENEY PO4 .... 423 L6
Marine Dr NMIL/BTOS BH25 .... 452 D1
Marine Dr East
NMIL/BTOS BH25 .... 452 F2
Marine Dr West
NMIL/BTOS BH25 .... 452 C1
Marine Pde SHAM SO14 .... 13 K4
Marine Pde East
LSOL/BMARY PO13 .... 420 D4
Marine Pde West
LSOL/BMARY PO13 .... 420 B1
Marine Prospect
NMIL/BTOS BH25 .... 452 E1
Marine Rd SBNE BH6 .... 449 J5
Mariner's Cl HLER SO31 .... 369 L4
TADY RG26 .... 62 A2
Mariners Ms FAWY SO45 .... 367 L4 🔟
Mariners Wk ENEY PO4 .... 423 M3
Mariners Wy GPORT PO12 .... 19 J5
HLER SO31 .... 370 A7
Marine Wk HISD PO11 .... 426 B5
Marino Av EWKG RG40 .... 47 K2
Marion Rd ENEY PO4 .... 21 M8
Maritime Av TOTT SO40 .... 342 E5
Maritime Wk SHAM SO14 .... 13 J8
Maritime Wy SHAM SO14 .... 13 H7
Marjoram Cl FARN GU14 .... 89 L4 🔟
Marjoram Crs HORN PO8 .... 352 F5
Marjoram Wy FHAM PO15 .... 371 H1
Markall Cl NALR SO24 .... 242 C3
Mark Cl HSEA PO3 .... 399 K4
WSHM SO15 .... 342 E1
Marken Cl HLER SO31 .... 370 C4
Market Cl PLE BH15 .... 445 H6
Market La WINC SO23 .... 11 G8
Market Pde HAV PO9 .... 16 E4
Market Pl BSTK RG21 .... 4 F1
RGWD BH24 .... 382 D1
SHAM SO14 .... 13 G6
Market Sq ALTN GU34 .... 176 E5
Market St ALTN GU34 .... 176 E5

ELGH SO50 .... 294 A7
NWBY RG14 .... 2 E5
PLE BH15 .... 445 G7
WINC SO23 .... 11 G8
Marketway PSEA PO1 .... 423 G2
Market Wy WIMB BH21 .... 404 B4
Markham Av NBNE BH10 .... 432 B2
Markham Ct CBLY GU15 .... 71 G2 🔟
Markham Rd
FHAM/STUB PO14 .... 396 A3
Mark's La NMIL/BTOS BH25 .... 437 L2
Markson Rd RWIN SO21 .... 190 B4
Mark's Rd FHAM/STUB PO14 .... 396 C6
MOOR/WNTN BH9 .... 432 D5
Marks Tey Rd
FHAM/STUB PO14 .... 396 A3
Marlborough Cl FLET GU13 .... 89 J8
Marlborough Ct FAWY SO45 .... 367 J6 🔟
Marlborough Gdns
DEAN RG23 .... 103 G6 🔟
HEND SO30 .... 321 H5 🔟
Marlborough Gv
FHAM/PORC PO16 .... 398 A1
Marlborough Pk HAV PO9 .... 17 K2
Marlborough Pl LYMN SO41 .... 440 B3 🔟
WIMB BH21 .... 404 B3
Marlborough Ri CBLY GU15 .... 71 H2
Marlborough Rd CHFD SO53 .... 265 K7
GPORT PO12 .... 421 K2
WBNE BH4 .... 447 H5
WSHM SO15 .... 318 A8
Marlborough Rw PSEA PO1 .... 422 E2
Marlborough St AND SP10 .... 9 H4
Marlborough Vw FARN GU14 .... 89 M3
Maridell Cl HAV PO9 .... 377 J3
Marles Cl LSOL/BMARY PO13 .... 421 H1
Marley Av NMIL/BTOS BH25 .... 437 H4
Marley Cl NMIL/BTOS BH25 .... 437 H4
Marley Combe Rd HASM GU27 .... 228 C3
Marley Hanger HASM GU27 .... 228 D5
Marley La HASM GU27 .... 228 B3
Marley Mt LYMN SO41 .... 412 C7
Marlhill Cl ITCH SO19 .... 344 D1
Marlin Cl LSOL/BMARY PO13 .... 421 H1
Marline Rd BKME/WDN BH12 .... 446 C2
Marlow Cl FHAM PO15 .... 372 C4
Marlow Dr CHCH/BSGR BH23 .... 434 C5
Marlowe Cl CHAM RG24 .... 5 H1
Marlowe Ct WVILLE PO7 .... 352 B7
The Marlowes NWBY RG14 .... 25 J8
Marlow Rd BPWT SO32 .... 296 F7
Marlpit Dr CHCH/BSGR BH23 .... 436 E6
Marlpit La EMRTH PO10 .... 379 L4
NMIL/BTOS BH25 .... 411 L8
Marl's La CHAM RG24 .... 83 G4
Marls Rd HEND SO30 .... 346 B2 🔟
Marmion Av SSEA PO5 .... 21 J7 🔟
Marmion Rd SSEA PO5 .... 21 H7
Marne Rd WEND SO18 .... 344 E1
Marnhull Rd PLE BH15 .... 445 J4
Marples Wy HAV PO9 .... 16 B5
Marram Cl LYMN SO41 .... 440 C2
Marrels Wd WVILLE PO7 .... 376 A4
Marrowbrook Cl FARN GU14 .... 90 D5
Marrowbrook La FARN GU14 .... 90 D6
Marryat Rd NMIL/BTOS BH25 .... 437 K5
Marsden Cl WHCH RG28 .... 123 H2 🔟
Marsden Rd CHAM PO6 .... 374 F8
Marshall Cl FARN GU14 .... 90 C1
Marshall Gdns BSTK RG21 .... 4 F4
Marshall Rd HISD PO11 .... 426 A6
SHST GU47 .... 70 A1
Marshalls Ct NWBY RG14 .... 25 G3 🔟
Marsham Rd CFDH BH17 .... 429 M7
Marsh Cl CHAM PO6 .... 400 A2
BOR GU35 .... 201 L5
Marshcourt CHAM RG24 .... 83 L8
Marshfield WIMB BH21 .... 404 D1
Marshfield Cl TOTT SO40 .... 342 B7
Marsh Gdns HEND SO30 .... 321 H5 🔟
Marshlands Rd CHAM PO6 .... 400 B1
Marsh La CHCH/BSGR BH23 .... 434 D6
FAWY SO45 .... 392 F4
FBDG SP6 .... 283 M8
HTWY RG27 .... 68 B3
LYMN SO41 .... 440 C2
NWBY RG14 .... 2 E3
RCCH PO18 .... 403 L4
SHAM SO14 .... 13 H5
Marsh Rd NTHA RG18 .... 27 H4
The Marsh FAWY SO45 .... 367 L3
Marshwood Av CFDH BH17 .... 430 D6
WVILLE PO7 .... 376 E1
Marston Cl NMIL/BTOS BH25 .... 437 M3 🔟
Marston Dr FARN GU14 .... 90 E1
Marston Gv CHCH/BSGR BH23 .... 436 C7
Marston La HSEA PO3 .... 399 M4
Marston Rd FNM GU9 .... 134 C6
ITCH SO19 .... 345 H3
NMIL/BTOS BH25 .... 437 M3
Marsum Cl AND SP10 .... 118 E4
Martel Cl CBLY GU15 .... 71 M1
Martello Cl GPORT PO12 .... 421 H5
Martello Pk CCLF BH13 .... 457 L1
Martello Rd CCLF BH13 .... 446 E7
The Martells NMIL/BTOS BH25 .... 453 G1
Martin Av FHAM/STUB PO14 .... 396 B6
WVILLE PO7 .... 351 L4
Martin Cl BPWT SO32 .... 324 A4
BSTK RG21 .... 5 H3
CFDH BH17 .... 444 D1
LSOL/BMARY PO13 .... 420 D1 🔟
NTID SP9 .... 114 F2
Martindale Av CBLY GU15 .... 71 M5
WIMB BH21 .... 404 F1
Martin Dr End FBDG SP6 .... 280 F3
Martingale Cl UPTN BH16 .... 444 C1
Martingale Ct ALDT GU11 .... 6 B2 🔟
Martin Rd FHAM/STUB PO14 .... 396 B6
HAV PO9 .... 16 B8
HSEA PO3 .... 399 L8
Martins Cl ALTN GU34 .... 176 F3
BLKW GU17 .... 70 A4

FERN BH22 .... 406 C3
Martins Dr FERN BH22 .... 406 C3
Martins Flds RWIN SO21 .... 238 E2
Martins Hill Cl
CHCH/BSGR BH23 .... 435 G2
Martins Hill La
CHCH/BSGR BH23 .... 435 G1
Martins La STOK SO20 .... 166 A4
Martin's Rd BROC SO42 .... 387 L2
The Martins ELGH SO50 .... 295 J7 🔟
STHA RG19 .... 27 J8
Martin St BPWT SO32 .... 323 G2
Martins Wy FERN BH22 .... 406 C2
Martins Wd CHAM RG24 .... 83 L5 🔟
Martin Wy AND SP10 .... 119 G6 🔟
FRIM GU16 .... 71 H4
Martley Gdns HEND SO30 .... 322 D3
Marvic Ct HAV PO9 .... 377 J2 🔟
Marvin Wy HEND SO30 .... 346 B1 🔟
WEND SO18 .... 345 G2
Marwell Cl LTDN BH7 .... 448 F1
Marybridge Cl TOTT SO40 .... 341 J2
Maryfield SHAM SO14 .... 13 J3
Maryland Cl WEND SO18 .... 319 L4
Maryland Gdns LYMN SO41 .... 454 A4
Maryland Rd UPTN BH16 .... 444 B3
Mary La ALTN GU34 .... 197 L4
FERN BH22 .... 380 E3
OVTN RG25 .... 125 K4
Mary Rose Cl FHAM PO15 .... 14 C7
The Mary Rose St PSEA PO1 .... 21 G2
Masefield Av CHAM PO6 .... 374 C2
Masefield Cl ELGH SO50 .... 293 L5
Masefield Crs HORN PO8 .... 352 D2
Masefield Gn ITCH SO19 .... 345 H2
Masefield Rd NTHA RG18 .... 26 F7
Maskell Wy FARN GU14 .... 89 M7
Mason Cl YTLY GU46 .... 69 H3 🔟
Mason Pl SHST GU47 .... 49 J7
Mason Rd FARN GU14 .... 90 B7
Mason Wy ALDT GU11 .... 7 G2
Masseys La BROC SO42 .... 416 A3
Masten Crs LSOL/BMARY PO13 .... 397 G2
Matapan Rd NEND PO2 .... 399 H4
Matchams La
CHCH/BSGR BH23 .... 433 M4
RGWD BH24 .... 407 M4
Matheson Rd ROWN SO16 .... 317 L4
Mathias Wk KEMP RG22 .... 127 J2
Matilda Dr KEMP RG22 .... 127 G1 🔟
Matley Gdns TOTT SO40 .... 340 F7
Matlock Rd FERN BH22 .... 406 A4
Matthew Rd FNM GU9 .... 6 A4
Matthews Cl HAV PO9 .... 377 G2
STHA RG19 .... 26 E5
Matthews La BROC SO42 .... 416 A4
Matthews Rd CBLY GU15 .... 50 F8
Matthews Wy BROC SO42 .... 103 H4
Mattock Wy CHAM RG24 .... 83 L5
Maturin Cl LYMN SO41 .... 440 B7
Maultway Cl CBLY GU15 .... 51 L8
Maultway Crs CBLY GU15 .... 51 L7
Maultway North CBLY GU15 .... 51 L7
The Maultway CBLY GU15 .... 51 L7
Maundeville Crs
CHCH/BSGR BH23 .... 434 C1
Maundeville Rd
CHCH/BSGR BH23 .... 434 C1
Maunsell Wy HEND SO30 .... 321 H5
Maureen Cl BKME/WDN BH12 .... 430 F7
Maurepas Wy WVILLE PO7 .... 376 D4
Mauretania Rd ROWN SO16 .... 317 G3
Maurice Rd ENEY PO4 .... 424 A4
Maurys La ROMY SO51 .... 288 C2
Mavins Rd FNM GU9 .... 135 G2
Mavis Crs HAV PO9 .... 16 E2
Mavis Rd MOOR/WNTN BH9 .... 432 E7
Maw Cl KEMP RG22 .... 104 E8 🔟
Maxine Ct SHST GU47 .... 49 J7
Maxstoke Cl SSEA PO5 .... 21 J2 🔟
Maxwell Rd BDST BH18 .... 429 K7
CCLF BH13 .... 457 L3
ENEY PO4 .... 423 L4
ITCH SO19 .... 344 E3
MOOR/WNTN BH9 .... 447 M4
May Av LYMN SO41 .... 440 B7
Maybray King Wy ITCH SO19 .... 344 E1
Maybrick Cl SHST GU47 .... 49 J7
Maybrook CHAM RG24 .... 83 L5
Maybury Cl FRIM GU16 .... 71 G2
Maybush La BPWT SO32 .... 325 G3
Maybush Rd ROWN SO16 .... 317 K6
May Cl CHAM RG24 .... 106 A2
FAWY SO45 .... 392 E4
BOR GU35 .... 202 E2
SHST GU47 .... 50 A4
May Copse FAWY SO45 .... 392 E4
May Crs ASHV GU12 .... 113 H4
FAWY SO45 .... 392 E4
Maydman Sq HSEA PO3 .... 423 L1
Mayfair Ct HEND SO30 .... 346 B2
Mayfair Dr NWBY RG14 .... 2 E7
Mayfair Gdns BWD BH11 .... 431 L3
WSHM SO15 .... 343 K1
Mayfield RFNM GU10 .... 158 C3
Mayfield Av PSTN BH14 .... 446 C2
TOTT SO40 .... 316 D2
Mayfield Cl FERN BH22 .... 406 A4
FHAM/STUB PO14 .... 396 B6
FNM GU9 .... 7 G1
NTID SP9 .... 138 D1
Mayfield Ct HTWY RG27 .... 48 A3 🔟
Mayfield Dr FERN BH22 .... 406 A4
Mayfield Rdg DEAN RG23 .... 127 G2
Mayfield Rd CBLY GU15 .... 70 E7
FARN GU14 .... 90 C2
FBDG SP6 .... 309 H7
GPORT PO12 .... 18 F2
MOOR/WNTN BH9 .... 432 E6
NEND PO2 .... 399 J5
PTSW SO17 .... 319 L2
Mayfield Wy FERN BH22 .... 406 A4
Mayflower Cl CHAM RG24 .... 83 K4
CHFD SO53 .... 293 G4
FHAM/STUB PO14 .... 396 A7
LYMN SO41 .... 454 A4

Mayflower Dr *YTLY* GU46 .... 68 D1
Mayflower Rd *BOR* GU35 .... 201 H7 🔲
WSHM SO15 .... 318 B3 🔲
Mayflower Rbt *WSHM* SO15 ...... 12 E6
he Mayflowers *ROWN* SO16 .... 318 F4
Mayfly Cl *FBDG* SP6 .... 309 L6 🔲
May Gdns *BWD* BH11 .... 431 J5
CHCH/BSGR BH23 .... 436 F6
Mayhall Rd *HSEA* PO3 .... 399 L7
Mayhill La *BPWT* SO32 .... 298 F8
Mayhill Rd *BPWT* SO32 .... 324 C1
Maylands Av *ENEY* PO4 .... 423 L4
Maylands Rd *HAV* PO9 .... 376 F6
May La *LYMN* SO41 .... 414 E7
Mayles Cl *WHAM* PO17 .... 348 E5
Mayles La *WHAM* PO17 .... 348 C7
Mayles Rd *ENEY* PO4 .... 423 M3
Maylings Farm Rd
FHAM/PORC PO16 .... 14 F2
Maylyn Rd *UPTN* BH16 .... 428 D6
Maynard Cl *LSOL/BMARY* PO13 .. 397 G4
NTHA RG18 .... 26 F3
Maynard Pl *HORN* PO8 .... 352 F1
Maynard Rd *TOTT* SO40 .... 341 K1
Maynard's Wd *CHAM* RG24 ...... 83 K6
Mayo Cl *PSEA* PO1 .... 423 H1
Mayors La *NWBY* RG14 .... 2 E1
Mayow Cl *STHA* RG19 .... 27 J6
May Pl *BSTK* RG21 .... 4 F9
Mayridge *FHAM/STUB* PO14 .... 371 G5
May Rd *WSHM* SO15 .... 343 G1 🔲
Mays Firs *FBDG* SP6 .... 285 L6
May's La *FHAM/STUB* PO14 .... 396 B4
May Tree Cl *WINW* SO22 .... 238 B4
Maytree Cl *HLER* SO31 .... 370 E5
Maytree Gdns *HORN* PO8 .... 352 C5
May Tree La *AND* SP10 .... 8 B3
Maytree Rd *CHFD* SO53 .... 265 H6
FHAM/PORC PO16 .... 15 G6
HORN PO8 .... 352 C5
Mayvale Cl *TOTT* SO40 .... 342 D7
Maywood Dr *CBLY* GU15 .... 71 L1
Mccartney Wk *KEMP* RG22 .... 127 H1
Mcfauld Wy *WHCH* RG28 .... 122 B4
Mcgrigor Barracks *ALDT* GU11 .. 112 E5
Mcintyre Rd *CHCH/BSGR* BH23 .. 407 K8
Mckay Cl *ALDT* GU11 .... 112 F5
Mckinley Rd *WBNE* BH4 .... 447 H6
Mc Naughton Cl *FARN* GU14 ...... 89 M5
Mcwilliam Cl *BKME/WDN* BH12.. 432 A8
Meacher Cl *TOTT* SO40 .... 316 D8 🔲
Meadbrook Gdns *CHFD* SO53 .... 293 H2
Mead Cl *AND* SP10 .... 8 E7
CFDH BH17 .... 429 L1
ROMY SO51 .... 291 G1
Mead Crs *WEND* SO18 .... 319 J5
Meadcroft Cl *HLER* SO31 .... 370 B8
Meadend Cl *HAV* PO9 .... 377 M5 🔲
Mead End Rd *LYMN* SO41 .... 412 D7
Meadham La *OVTN* RG25 .... 79 G5
Mead Hawks *LISS* GU33 .... 248 D3
Mead La *FNM* GU9 .... 134 E7
Meadow Av *HLER* SO31 .... 370 E4
Meadowbank Rd *FHAM* PO15 .... 14 A5
Meadow Cl *ASHV* GU12 .... 91 J7
BLKW GU17 .... 23 K4 🔲
BPWT SO32 .... 323 K4 🔲
CHCH/BSGR BH23 .... 450 E1 🔲
FBDG SP6 .... 309 K6 🔲
FERN BH22 .... 406 B7
HEND SO30 .... 320 D6
HISD PO11 .... 401 K5
LIPH GU30 .... 226 F4
NBAD SO52 .... 291 M5
RAND SP11 .... 358 F7
RGWD BH24 .... 384 D6
STHA RG19 .... 26 F5
TOTT SO40 .... 341 K3
Meadow Ct *RSAL* SP5 .... 259 H4
Meadow Court Cl
MOOR/WNTN BH9 .... 432 E5
Meadowcroft Cl *RWIN* SO21 .. 266 B5 🔲
Meadow Dr *RAND* SP11 .... 142 E8
Meadow Edge *WVILLE* PO7 ...... 375 L6
Meadow Gdns *BPWT* SO32 ...... 323 K4
Meadow Gate Rd *FARN* GU14 .... 90 C7
Meadow Gv *VWD* BH31 .... 356 F3
Meadowhead Rd
ROWN SO16 .... 318 E5 🔲
CHCH/BSGR BH23 .... 450 D2
WINC SO23 .... 215 G1
Meadowlands *HAV* PO9 .... 17 H5
HAV PO9 .... 354 A5
LYMN SO41 .... 440 A4
Meadow La *CHCH/BSGR* BH23 .. 435 L6
HLER SO31 .... 369 L6
HTWY RG27 .... 87 H2
SELS PO20 .... 427 M6
Meadowmead Av *WSHM* SO15 .. 342 N1
Meadow Pound *WHCH* RG28 .. 122 C3 🔲
Meadowridge *KEMP* RG22 ...... 127 H3
HORN PO8 .... 352 F5
Meadow Ri *BDST* BH18 .... 429 K3
OVTN RG25 .... 125 L7 🔲
Meadow Rd *BSTK* RG21 .... 104 F7
FARN GU14 .... 90 E1
LYMN SO41 .... 440 A6
NMIL/BTOS BH25 .... 437 M4
NWBY RG14 .... 2 D9
RGWD BH24 .... 384 D6 🔲
he Meadows
FHAM/PORC PO16 .... 15 L1
HTWY RG27 .... 85 L3 🔲
LYND SO43 .... 363 L4 🔲
RFNM GU10 .... 181 J7
Meadow St *SSEA* PO5 .... 20 F5 🔲
Meadowsweet *WVILLE* PO7 ...... 352 F7
Meadowsweet *NTHA* RG18 .... 27 H4
Meadowsweet Rd *CFDH* BH17 .. 429 J8
Meadowsweet Wy *CHAM* PO6 .. 375 H7

ELGH SO50 .... 321 H2
The Meadow *ROMY* SO51 ...... 262 E7 🔲
WVILLE PO7 .... 351 K4
Meadow V *HASM* GU27 .... 228 D2
Meadow Vw *FLET* GU13 .... 110 D3 🔲
BOR GU35 .... 201 K5
WHCH RG28 .... 122 A3
Meadow View Rd *BWD* BH11 .... 431 J5
Meadow Wk *LISS* GU33 .... 248 E4
LSOL/BMARY PO13 .... 396 F5 🔲
Meadow Wy *AND* SP10 .... 8 A5
ASHV GU12 .... 113 J5
BLKW GU17 .... 23 K4 🔲
FAWY SO45 .... 392 F5 🔲
WINW SO22 .... 238 B4
LIPH GU30 .... 226 F3
RFNM GU10 .... 158 C5
NMIL/BTOS BH25 .... 452 F1
RGWD BH24 .... 358 F8
VWD BH31 .... 356 F4
Mead Rd *AND* SP10 .... 8 E7
CHFD SO53 .... 293 H2
GSHT GU26 .... 204 C4
LYMN SO41 .... 439 M6
WINC SO23 .... 238 D4
The Meads *CHFD* SO53 .... 292 F3
HASM GU27 .... 228 C2
ROMY SO51 .... 290 C1
The Mead *CHAM* RG24 .... 106 A2
FAWY SO45 .... 367 J5
LIPH GU30 .... 226 F3
LISS GU33 .... 248 E4
LSOL/BMARY PO13 .... 396 F5 🔲
PSF GU32 .... 275 J6
Mead Wy *FHAM/PORC* PO16 .... 15 J2
Meadway *FRIM* GU16 .... 71 J6
HASM GU27 .... 228 C2
WVILLE PO7 .... 352 E7
The Meadway
CHCH/BSGR BH23 .... 436 B6
Mears Rd *ELGH* SO50 .... 295 J6
Meath Cl *HISD* PO11 .... 426 A7
Mede Cl *OVTN* RG25 .... 124 A1
Medina Cl *CHFD* SO53 .... 293 K3 🔲
Medina Gdns *DEAN* RG23 ...... 103 G7 🔲
Medina Rd *CHAM* PO6 .... 375 H8
WSHM SO15 .... 318 A7
Medina Wy *CHCH/BSGR* BH23 .. 451 H2
Medlar Cl
CHCH/BSGR BH23 .... 435 H7
HEND SO30 .... 346 B2 🔲
Medlar Dr *BLKW* GU17 .... 70 C5
Medlicott Wy *BPWT* SO32 .... 324 A4
Medonte Cl *FLET* GU13 .... 89 G8 🔲
Medstead Rd *ALTN* GU34 .... 175 K7
HAV PO9 .... 377 N6
Medwall Gn *ITCH* SO19 .... 345 H3
Medway Av *DEAN* RG23 .... 103 G6
Medway Cl *NTHA* RG18 .... 26 E3
Medway Ct *AND* SP10 .... 119 H6
BSTK RG21 .... 5 K8
Medway Dr *CHFD* SO53 .... 264 F8
FARN GU14 .... 90 B1
Medway Rd *FERN* BH22 .... 406 C2
Meerut Rd *BROC* SO42 .... 387 K6
NTID SP9 .... 114 D2
Meeting House La
RGWD BH24 .... 382 D1 🔲
Megana Wy *ROMY* SO51 .... 263 H3
Megan Rd *HEND* SO30 .... 320 C6
Meggeson Av *WEND* SO18 .... 319 M6
Meitner Cl *TADY* RG26 .... 63 L4
Melbourne Pl *SSEA* PO5 .... 20 F3
Melbourne Rd
CHCH/BSGR BH23 .... 434 C7
HEND SO30 .... 346 A2 🔲
Melbourne St *SHAM* SO14 .... 13 K4
Melbury Av *BKME/WDN* BH12.. 446 D1
Melbury Cl *FERN* BH22 .... 406 B4
LYMN SO41 .... 440 B5 🔲
Melchet Cl *ROMY* SO51 .... 260 A7
Melchet Rd *WEND* SO18 .... 320 B8
Meldrum Cl *NWBY* RG14 .... 36 F2 🔲
Melford Gdns *KEMP* RG22 ...... 103 M6
Melick Cl *TOTT* SO40 .... 342 D6
Meliot Ri *AND* SP10 .... 118 F4
Mellor Cl *CHAM* PO6 .... 375 H8 🔲
Mellstock Rd *PLE* BH15 .... 445 H3
Melrose Av *FARN* GU14 .... 89 M3
Melrose Cl *ENEY* PO4 .... 423 N4 🔲
BOR GU35 .... 201 J6 🔲
Melrose Ct *NMIL/BTOS* BH25 .. 438 A5 🔲
TOTT SO40 .... 316 B7
Melrose Gdns *GPORT* PO12 .... 421 K1
Melrose Rd *WSHM* SO15 .... 318 A5
Melverley Gdns *WIMB* BH21 .... 404 B3
Melville Av *FRIM* GU16 .... 71 J7
Melville Cl *ROWN* SO16 .... 318 B3
Melville Rd *ENEY* PO4 .... 424 A4
GPORT PO12 .... 421 L1
MOOR/WNTN BH9 .... 432 C8
Membury Cl *FRIM* GU16 .... 91 K1 🔲
Memorial Rd *HTWY* RG27 .... 85 M8
Mendip Cl *KEMP* RG22 .... 103 M5
NMIL/BTOS BH25 .... 437 M6
VWD BH31 .... 356 D3 🔲
Mendip Gdns *FAWY* SO45 ...... 367 H6 🔲
Mendip Rd *FARN* GU14 .... 90 B1
ROWN SO16 .... 317 L3
VWD BH31 .... 356 D2
Mendips Rd *FHAM/STUB* PO14 .. 14 B8
Mendips Wk *FHAM/STUB* PO14.. 14 B8
Mengham Av *HISD* PO11 .... 425 L6
Mengham La *HISD* PO11 .... 425 L5
Mengham Rd *HISD* PO11 .... 425 L5
Menin Wy *FNM* GU9 .... 135 G7
Menslands La *WVILLE* PO7 ...... 325 L8
Menzies Cl *ROWN* SO16 .... 317 L3
Meon Cl *FARN* GU14 .... 90 A2
HORN PO8 .... 328 D4
LSOL/BMARY PO13 .... 396 F6
PSF GU32 .... 275 K4
ROMY SO51 .... 291 H1
TADY RG26 .... 41 J6
Meon Crs *CHFD* SO53 .... 293 J2
Meon Rd *DEAN* RG23 .... 103 G7
ENEY PO4 .... 423 M4

LTDN BH7 .... 449 G1
ROMY SO51 .... 291 H1
Mercer Cl *KEMP* RG22 .... 104 B4
Mercer Wy *ROMY* SO51 .... 262 E8 🔲
ROMY SO51 .... 262 F8 🔲
Merchants St *WINC* SO23 .... 11 H7
Merchistoun Rd *HORN* PO8 ...... 352 F1
Mercia Av *AND* SP10 .... 118 C5
Mercury Cl *BOR* GU35 .... 201 L5 🔲
ROWN SO16 .... 317 L4
Mercury Gdns *HLER* SO31 .... 369 L4
Mercury Pl *WVILLE* PO7 .... 376 C6
Merdon Av *CHFD* SO53 .... 265 J8
Merdon Cl *CHFD* SO53 .... 265 J8
Mere Cft *FHAM* PO15 .... 371 H5 🔲
Meredith Cl *CHCH/BSGR* BH23.. 450 C1
Meredith Gdns *TOTT* SO40 ...... 341 H2
Meredith Rd *NEND* PO2 .... 399 J5
Meredun La *RWIN* SO21 .... 265 G1
Merepond La *ALTN* GU34 .... 245 K5
Merganser Cl *GPORT* PO12 ...... 421 M1
Meriden Rd *SSEA* PO5 .... 20 F3 🔲
The Meridians
CHCH/BSGR BH23 .... 449 L3
Merino Wy *FERN* BH22 .... 380 D7
Merivale *FLET* GU13 .... 88 C8
Merlewood Cl *WCLF* BH2 .... 22 E2
Merley Dr *CHCH/BSGR* BH23 .. 436 C6
Merley Gdns *WIMB* BH21 .... 404 B7
Merley La *WIMB* BH21 .... 404 B7
Merley Park Rd *WIMB* BH21 .... 404 A8
Merley Ways *WIMB* BH21 .... 404 B5
Merlin Cl *AND* SP10 .... 118 C5
BPWT SO32 .... 297 G8
RGWD BH24 .... 383 G2
Merlin Dr *HSEA* PO3 .... 400 B4
Merlin Gdns *FHAM/PORC* PO16.. 373 M7
HEND SO30 .... 345 M1
Merlin Md *KEMP* RG22 .... 126 C2
Merlin Rd *ALTN* GU34 .... 197 G6
FARN GU14 .... 90 E6
Merlins Cl *FNM* GU9 .... 134 F7 🔲
Merlin Wy *CHCH/BSGR* BH23 .. 450 F3
Mermaid Rd *FHAM/STUB* PO14.. 396 D3
Mermaid Wy *SHAM* SO14 ..... 13 J7 🔲
Merriatt Cl *BSTK* RG21 .... 105 G6
Merrick Wy *CHFD* SO53 .... 264 E8
Merridale Rd *ITCH* SO19 .... 344 C4
Merrieleas Cl *CHFD* SO53 .... 293 H1
Merrieleas Dr *CHFD* SO53 .... 293 H1
Merriemeade Cl *FAWY* SO45 .... 367 J7
Merrifield *WIMB* BH21 .... 404 C1
Merrifield Cl *BDST* BH18 .... 429 M2
Merrileas Gdns *KEMP* RG22 .... 103 M8
Merrivale Av *SBNE* BH6 .... 449 K3
Merrivale Cl *FAWY* SO45 .... 367 J5
Merrivale Rd *NEND* PO2 .... 399 J5
Merron Cl *YTLY* GU46 .... 49 J2
Merrow Av *BKME/WDN* BH12 .. 447 G2
Merrydown La *CHAM* RG24 ...... 83 M6 🔲
Merryfield *CHAM* RG24 .... 83 K5
FHAM/STUB PO14 .... 371 G4
Merryfield Av *HAV* PO9 .... 377 H3
Merryfield Cl
CHCH/BSGR BH23 .... 409 L8
Merryfield Rd *EPSF* GU31 .... 276 A4
Merry Gdns *NBAD* SO52 .... 291 M3
Merryman Dr *CWTH* RG45 .... 49 J2
Merryoak Gn *ITCH* SO19 .... 344 D3 🔲
Merryoak Rd *ITCH* SO19 .... 344 D4
Mersea Gdns *ITCH* SO19 .... 344 E4
Mersey Wy *NTHA* RG18 .... 26 E3
Merstham Gdns *WEND* SO18 ... 344 E1 🔲
Merstone Rd
LSOL/BMARY PO13 .... 397 C6
Merthyr Av *CHAM* PO6 .... 375 M7
Merton Av *FHAM/PORC* PO16 .. 398 B2
Merton Cl *FBDG* SP6 .... 309 L5 🔲
SHST GU47 .... 50 C6
Merton Crs *FHAM/PORC* PO16.. 398 B2
Merton Rd *BSTK* RG21 .... 4 B5
PTSW SO17 .... 319 G6
SSEA PO5 .... 21 H7
Meryl Rd *ENEY* PO4 .... 424 A4
Meryon Rd *NALR* SO24 .... 218 B4
Mesh Pond *RSAL* SP5 .... 256 C8
Mesh Rd *ROMY* SO51 .... 234 B6
Meteor Rd *EMRTH* PO10 .... 402 E5
Meteor Wy *FARN* GU14 .... 90 D7
Methuen Cl *CHAR* BH8 .... 23 L2
Methuen Rd *CFDH* BH17 .... 429 M6
CHAR BH8 .... 23 J1
ENEY PO4 .... 423 L5
LISS GU33 .... 225 H5
Methuen St *SHAM* SO14 .... 343 H1
Metuchen Wy *HEND* SO30 .... 346 A4
Meudon Av *FARN* GU14 .... 90 E5
Mewsey Ct *HAV* PO9 .... 377 H1
Mews La *WINW* SO22 .... 10 D8
The Mews *FAWY* SO45 .... 418 D1 🔲
HAV PO9 .... 377 J4
ROWN SO16 .... 317 L2
TADY RG26 .... 64 A6
Mey Cl *WVILLE* PO7 .... 376 D1
Meynell Cl *ELGH* SO50 .... 293 L5
Meyrick Cl *CHCH/BSGR* BH23.. 435 L1
Meyrick Dr *NWBY* RG14 .... 36 F3
Meyrick Park Crs *TWDS* BH3 ... 447 L2
Meyrick Rd *BMTH* BH1 .... 23 J5
HAV PO9 .... 16 B4
NEND PO2 .... 399 G7
Michael Crook Cl *HAV* PO9 ...... 377 G5
Michaelmas Cl *YTLY* GU46 .... 49 J6
Michaels Wy *ELGH* SO50 .... 295 J6
FAWY SO45 .... 367 K4
Micheldever Cl *WHCH* RG28 ... 122 C5
Micheldever Rd *AND* SP10 .... 9 K6
WHCH RG28 .... 122 C4
Michelmersh Cl *ROWN* SO16 .. 317 K3 🔲
Michigan Wy *TOTT* SO40 .... 316 A8

Mickleham Cl
BKME/WDN BH12 .... 431 M8
Mickle HI *SHST* GU47 .... 49 K7
Midanbury Crs *WEND* SO18 .... 319 J5
Midanbury La *WEND* SO18 ...... 319 K8
Middle Av *FNM* GU9 .... 135 C8
Middlebere Crs *UPTN* BH16 ..... 444 B4
Middle Bourne La *RFNM* GU10 .. 158 C2
Middlebridge St *ROMY* SO51 ... 290 D2
Middlebrook *BPWT* SO32 ...... 297 H8 🔲
Middle Brook St *WINC* SO23 .... 11 H7
Middle Church La *FNM* GU9 .. 134 E6 🔲
Middle Cl *CBLY* GU15 .... 71 M2
NWBY RG14 .... 37 G1
Middle Common Rd
LYMN SO41 .... 439 K5
Middlecroft La *GPORT* PO12 .... 421 K2
Middlefield *FNM* GU9 .... 158 D1
SELS PO20 .... 427 L7
Middle Gordon Rd *CBLY* GU15 .. 70 F3
Middle HI *ALDT* GU11 .... 6 F7
Middlehill Dr *WIMB* BH21 .... 404 F2
Middlehill Rd *WIMB* BH21 .... 404 E1
Middle La *RGWD* BH24 .... 382 E1 🔲
HTWY RG27 .... 85 M7 🔲
Middle Meadow *LISS* GU33 ...... 248 F4
Middlemoor Rd *FRIM* GU16 ...... 71 H8
Middle Old Pk *FNM* GU9 .... 134 C4
Middle Park Wy *HAV* PO9 .... 377 H2
Middle Rd *WINW* SO22 .... 10 D6
HLER SO31 .... 370 F3
ITCH SO19 .... 344 E5
LYMN SO41 .... 412 E6
LYMN SO41 .... 412 F6
LYMN SO41 .... 440 B5
NBAD SO52 .... 291 M3
NBNE BH10 .... 432 A3
PLE BH15 .... 445 K2
Middlesex Rd *ENEY* PO4 .... 423 L5
Middle St *CCLF* BH13 .... 456 C5
SHAM SO14 .... 343 L1 🔲
SSEA PO5 .... 21 G3
Middleton Cl *FHAM/STUB* PO14 .. 14 C9
WEND SO18 .... 319 M6
Middleton Ct *NWBY* RG14 .... 26 B3
Middleton Gdns *BSTK* RG21 .... 4 F4
FARN GU14 .... 90 B2
Middleton Ri *HORN* PO8 ...... 328 C4 🔲
Middleton Rd *CBLY* GU15 .... 71 H2
NBNE BH10 .... 432 C6
RGWD BH24 .... 358 E6
RSAL SP5 .... 206 E1
The Middleway *RAND* SP11 ..... 120 A8
Midfield Cl *FHAM/STUB* PO14 .. 396 D1
LIPH GU30 .... 226 F3
Midhurst Rd *HASM* GU27 .... 228 E3
Midland Rd *MOOR/WNTN* BH9.. 432 D7
Midlands Est *HEND* SO30 .... 320 B6
Midlane Cl *BSTK* RG21 .... 104 F6
Midlington HI *BPWT* SO32 .... 324 F1
Midlington Rd *BPWT* SO32 ...... 325 C1
Midway *FAWY* SO45 .... 367 K5 🔲
Midway Rd *NEND* PO2 .... 399 J3
Midways *FHAM/STUB* PO14 ..... 396 A7
Midwood Av *CHAR* BH8 .... 433 K7
Mike Hawthorn Dr *FNM* GU9 .. 134 F5 🔲
Milbeck Cl *HORN* PO8 .... 352 E5
Milborne Crs *BKME/WDN* BH12.. 446 D1
Milbourne Rd *FERN* BH22 .... 406 A2
Milburn Cl *WBNE* BH4 .... 447 H4
Milburn Rd *WBNE* BH4 .... 447 G4
The Milburns *ROMY* SO51 .... 262 C1 🔲
Milbury Crs *ITCH* SO19 .... 344 C3
Milden Cl *FRIM* GU16 .... 91 K2
Milden Gdns *FRIM* GU16 .... 91 K2
Mildmay Ct *ODIM* RG29 .... 108 D6
Mildmay St *WINW* SO22 .... 238 C3
Milebush Rd *ENEY* PO4 .... 424 A3
Mile End Rd *PSEA* PO1 .... 423 C1
Miles Rd *ASHV* GU12 .... 113 L5
Miles's La *RSAL* SP5 .... 259 J4
Milestone Rd *PLE* BH15 .... 445 J2
Milford Cl *FERN* BH22 .... 380 D6
HAV PO9 .... 377 H5 🔲
Milford Crs *LYMN* SO41 .... 454 D4
Milford Dr *BWD* BH11 .... 431 K3
Milford Gdns *CHFD* SO53 .... 293 K3
Milford Rd *LYMN* SO41 .... 439 K7
NMIL/BTOS BH25 .... 438 A8
PSEA PO1 .... 21 J1
Military Rd *FHAM/PORC* PO16.. 373 H6
GPORT PO12 .... 421 J3
GPORT PO12 .... 421 M8
GPORT PO12 .... 422 A7
HSEA PO3 .... 399 K3
PSEA PO1 .... 422 F2
Milkhouse Rd *KSCL* RG20 .... 24 A2
Milkingpen La *CHAM* RG24 ..... 106 A1
Milkwood Ct *TOTT* SO40 ...... 341 G1 🔲
Millais Rd *ITCH* SO19 .... 344 C5
Milland La *LIPH* GU30 .... 250 D2
Milland Rd *LIPH* GU30 .... 250 E6
WINC SO23 .... 239 G2
Millard Cl *BSTK* RG21 .... 4 B3
Millbank St *SHAM* SO14 .... 13 L1
Millbridge Gdns *ITCH* SO19 .. 344 F4 🔲
Millbrook Cl *CHFD* SO53 .... 293 C3
LISS GU33 .... 248 F4
Millbrook Dr *HAV* PO9 .... 377 L2
Millbrook Point Rd
WSHM SO15 .... 342 C1
Millbrook Rd East *WSHM* SO15.. 343 G3
Millbrook Rd West
WSHM SO15 .... 342 C1
Mill Chase Rd *BOR* GU35 .... 201 K5
Mill Cl *HASM* GU27 .... 228 B2 🔲
HISD PO11 .... 401 K6
ROWN SO16 .... 317 J3
WVILLE PO7 .... 351 K4
Mill Copse Rd *HASM* GU27 ...... 228 A2
Mill Cnr *FARN* GU14 .... 89 H3 🔲
Mill Ct *FBDG* SP6 .... 309 K7 🔲
Mill End *EMRTH* PO10 .... 378 N4
FBDG SP6 .... 308 C1
Miller Cl *NMIL/BTOS* BH25 .... 438 A4

Miller Dr *FHAM/PORC* PO16 ..... 14 F2
Miller Rd *CHCH/BSGR* BH23 .... 450 C1
Millers La *WSHM* SO22 .... 237 L5
Millers Rd *TADY* RG26 .... 41 L8
Millfield *CFDH* BH17 .... 444 F1
Millgreen La *STHA* RG19 .... 39 J6
Millhams Rd *NBNE* BH10 .... 431 L1
Milhams St North
CHCH/BSGR BH23 .... 450 A2
Mill HI *HEND* SO30 .... 346 E1
NALR SO24 .... 218 C1
Mill Hill Cl *PSTN* BH14 .... 446 A5
Milliken Cl *FAWY* SO45 .... 392 D6
Millins Cl *SHST* GU47 .... 50 A7
Mill La *ALTN* GU34 .... 177 C4 ⬅
BPWT SO32 .... 299 H8
BPWT SO32 .... 322 C5
BROC SO42 .... 587 M7
CHCH/BSGR BH23 .... 433 M2
CHCH/BSGR BH23 .... 436 F8
EMRTH PO10 .... 378 F6
EPSF GU31 .... 278 C8
EPSF GU31 .... 305 C5
FHAM PO15 .... 371 L7
GPORT PO12 .... 421 M2
HASM GU27 .... 228 F4
HAV PO9 .... 377 G7
HAV PO9 .... 401 J2
HTWY RG27 .... 85 G1
KSCL RG20 .... 58 D3
BOR GU35 .... 201 M4
LISS GU33 .... 223 L8
LYMN SO41 .... 439 J1
LYMN SO41 .... 440 D4 🔲
LYMN SO41 .... 441 K3
LYND SO43 .... 339 J6
MARL SN8 .... 32 C4
MIDH SN20 .... 279 K6
NALR SO24 .... 218 F3
RFNM GU10 .... 180 L1
NWBY RG14 .... 2 F4
ODIM RG29 .... 108 A3
PSEA PO1 .... 423 C1
PSF GU32 .... 247 K8
PSF GU32 .... 276 A2
PSTN BH14 .... 446 A5
RAND SP11 .... 145 H5
RGWD BH24 .... 385 C3
ROMY SO51 .... 260 D8
ROMY SO51 .... 290 C1
ROWN SO16 .... 316 D4
RSAL SP5 .... 183 G8
TADY RG26 .... 64 B5
THLE RG7 .... 29 M5
THLE RG7 .... 64 B8
WHAM PO17 .... 348 E3
WVILLE PO7 .... 375 J4
YTLY GU46 .... 49 G8
Mill Meadow *LYMN* SO41 .... 454 D8
Millmere *YTLY* GU46 .... 69 G1
Mill Pond Rd *GPORT* PO12 ...... 421 M2
The Mill Pond *FAWY* SO45 .... 391 M2
Mill Quay *EMRTH* PO10 .... 402 E1
Mill Reef Cl *STHA* RG19 .... 26 C5
Mill Ri *ROMY* SO51 .... 233 J8
Mill Rd *CHAM* RG24 .... 82 B8
CHCH/BSGR BH23 .... 434 E8
EMRTH PO10 .... 378 F4
FHAM/PORC PO16 .... 15 J4
GPORT PO12 .... 421 L2
LISS GU33 .... 248 F3
TOTT SO40 .... 341 L1
WSHM SO15 .... 342 D1
WVILLE PO7 .... 351 L4
WVILLE PO7 .... 376 B2
Mill Rd (North) *CHAR* BH8 .... 433 H5
Mill Rd (South) *CHAR* BH8 ...... 433 H6
Mill Rythe La *HISD* PO11 .... 425 L1
Mills Rd *NEND* PO2 .... 399 H8
Mill Stream *FNM* GU9 .... 6 D7
Millstream Cl *AND* SP10 .... 8 F9
CFDH BH17 .... 444 F1
WIMB BH21 .... 404 A4
Millstream Ri *ROMY* SO51 .... 290 D2
The Millstream *HASM* GU27 .... 228 B3
Mill St *FHAM/STUB* PO14 .... 371 G4
Mill Vale Mdw *LIPH* GU30 .... 250 E5
Millvina Cl *TOTT* SO40 .... 340 C4
Mill Wy *TOTT* SO40 .... 341 J3
Millway Cl *AND* SP10 .... 8 C5
Millway Rd *AND* SP10 .... 8 C5
Millyford Cl *NMIL/BTOS* BH25 .. 437 H8 🔲
Milne Cl *FAWY* SO45 .... 367 G6
Milner Ct *WSHM* SO15 .... 318 B8
Milner Rd *CFDH* BH17 .... 429 M7
Milner Pl *WINW* SO22 .... 238 C3
Milner Rd *WBNE* BH4 .... 447 H6
Milnthorpe La *WINW* SO22 .... 10 D9
The Milsons *STOK* SO20 .... 186 B6
Milton Av *AND* SP10 .... 8 B3
Milton Cl *CHAM* RG24 .... 5 H1
PSTN BH14 .... 446 C5
Milton Gv *HLER* SO31 .... 370 F7
NMIL/BTOS BH25 .... 437 M6
Milton Md *NMIL/BTOS* BH25 .... 437 K6
Milton Park Av *ENEY* PO4 ...... 423 M4 🔲
Milton Rd *CHAR* BH8 .... 23 H1
ELGH SO50 .... 294 A3 🔲
ENEY PO4 .... 423 L4
HSEA PO3 .... 423 L1
PSTN BH14 .... 446 C5
WIMB BH21 .... 404 A2
WSHM SO15 .... 343 J2
WVILLE PO7 .... 352 B7
Milverton Cl
CHCH/BSGR BH23 .... 436 C7 🔲
Milverton Rd *WINW* SO22 .... 10 C6
TOTT SO40 .... 341 C4
Milvil Rd *LSOL/BMARY* PO13 ... 420 C3
Mimosa Av *WIMB* BH21 .... 404 B5
Mimosa Cl *BOR* GU35 .... 201 M3
Mimosa Dr *ELGH* SO50 .... 295 K6
Minchens La *TADY* RG26 .... 63 K5
Mincingfield La *BPWT* SO32 .... 322 C4
Minden Cl *AND* SP10 .... 118 E5 🔲
CHAM RG24 .... 83 K6 🔲

Minden Wy *WINW* SO22 .... 238 B3
Minehurst Rd *FRIM* GU16........ 91 J4
Minerva Cl *WVILLE* PO7 .... 376 C6 🔢
Minerva Rd *FARN* GU14........ 90 E7
Ministry Rd *STHA* RG19........ 38 D3
Minley Cl *FARN* GU14........ 90 B4
Minley Ct *HAV* PO9 .... 377 M3
Minley Gv *FARN* GU14...... 89 G5 🔢
Minley Rd *FARN* GU14........ 69 H7
Minnitt Rd *GPORT* PO12........ 19 L3
Minstead Av *WEND* SO18........ 320 B8
Minstead Cl *WINW* SO22 ...... 214 C4 🔢
TADY RG26........................ 61 L2
Minstead Dr *YTLY* GU46........ 68 F3
Minstead Rd *ENEY* PO4........ 423 M5
NBNE BH10........................ 432 A5
Minsted Rd *MIDH* GU29........ 279 J8
Minster Cl *FHAM* PO15........ 372 A7
Minster La *WINC* SO23........ 11 G8
Minster Vw *WIMB* BH21........ 404 A3
Minster Wy *UPTN* BH16........ 444 A1
Mintern Rd *ELGH* SO50...... 294 C3 🔢
Minterne Rd *CHCH/BSGR* BH23.. 450 D3
PSTN BH14........................ 457 H1
Mint Rd *LISS* GU33........ 249 G2
Mirror Cl *HLER* SO31........ 370 D7
Mislingford Rd *BPWT* SO32.. 324 B5
Missenden Acres
HEND SO30........................ 321 H8 🔢
Mission Rd *BDST* BH18........ 429 L6
Misslebrook La *NBAD* SO52.. 292 C4
Mistletoe Rd *YTLY* GU46........ 69 G4
Mitcham Rd *CBLY* GU15........ 51 K7
Mitchell Av *HTWY* RG27........ 87 H3
Mitchell Cl *AND* SP10........ 118 A7
NMIL/BTOS BH25........ 452 F1
Mitchell Dr *ELGH* SO50...... 295 H5
Mitchell Gdns *KEMP* RG22.. 127 H1 🔢
Mitchell Rd *CFDH* BH17........ 430 D8
ELGH SO50........................ 294 A6
HAV PO9.......................... 376 F5
WIMB BH21........................ 405 L1
Mitchells Cl *ROMY* SO51........ 290 C1
RSAL SP5.................... 285 J2 🔢
Mitchell Wy *ELGH* SO50........ 319 M1
HSEA PO3........................ 399 M5
Mitford Rd *NALR* SO24........ 218 A3
Mitre Copse *ELGH* SO50...... 294 E6
Mizen Wy
LSOL/BMARY PO13........ 421 H2 🔢
TADY RG26........................ 63 K4
Moat Cl *FAWY* SO45........ 391 M5
Moat Dr *GPORT* PO12........ 421 H5
Moat Hl *WEND* SO18........ 319 L5
Moat La *NMIL/BTOS* BH25.. 437 K7
Mockbeggar La *RGWD* BH24.. 358 C1
Moffat Rd *CHCH/BSGR* BH23.. 450 C1
Moffatts Cl *SHST* GU47........ 49 K8
Moggs Md *EPSF* GU31........ 275 M5
Mole Cl *FARN* GU14........ 90 A2
Mole Hl *WVILLE* PO7........ 376 D3
Molesworth Rd *GPORT* PO12.. 19 G4 🔢
Molyneux Rd *NMIL/BTOS* BH25..438 B5
Momford Rd *WINW* SO22 ...... 238 A5
Monachus La *HTWY* RG27........ 87 J1
Monarch Cl *HLER* SO31........ 370 E6
KEMP RG22...................... 126 F1
WVILLE PO7.................. 376 E1 🔢
Monarch's Wy *BPWT* SO32.. 296 B1
HAV PO9.......................... 354 D7
HORN PO8........................ 353 H9
ROMY SO51...................... 233 L8
RSAL SP5........................ 208 B3
STOK SO20........................ 208 E2
WVILLE PO7...................... 300 F7
Monarch Wy *WINW* SO22 ...... 238 B2
HEND SO30...................... 320 D6 🔢
Monastery Rd *WEND* SO18...... 344 C1
Monckton Rd *GPORT* PO12.. 421 H5
HSEA PO3........................ 399 K6
Mon Crs *WEND* SO18........ 345 C1
Moneyfield Av *HSEA* PO3........ 399 L8
Moneyfield La *HSEA* PO3........ 399 L8 🔢
Moneyfly Rd *VWD* BH31........ 356 F3
Mongers Piece *CHAM* RG24.. 83 M4
Monier Williams Rd
RWIN SO21........................ 145 G5
Monks Brook Cl *ELGH* SO50.. 293 K7
Monks Cl *FARN* GU14........ 90 F4
FERN BH22........................ 380 E8
NTID SP9.......................... 114 D1
Monkshanger *FNM* GU9........ 135 K4
Monk Sherborne Rd *TADY* RG26.. 81 J1
Monks La *NWBY* RG14........ 37 H1
Monks Orch *PSF* GU32........ 275 L3
Monks Pl *TOTT* SO40........ 341 H2
Monks Ri *FLET* GU13...... 88 C7 🔢
Monks Rd *HLER* SO31........ 368 F2
WINC SO23........................ 11 G5
Monks Wk *FAWY* SO45........ 367 J4
RFNM GU10...................... 159 J1
Monks Wy *ELGH* SO50........ 293 L7
FHAM/STUB PO14............ 395 M8
WEND SO18...................... 319 K4
WIMB BH21........................ 431 G3
Monks' Well *RFNM* GU10...... 135 M8
Monkswell Gn
CHCH/BSGR BH23........ 450 C2
Monks Wd *PSF* GU32........ 275 L3
Monkswood Cl *NWBY* RG14.. 37 G1 🔢
Monks Wood Crs *TADY* RG26.. 61 L1 🔢
Monkton Cl *FERN* BH22........ 406 B2
Monkton Crs
BKME/WDN BH12........ 431 J8
Monkton La *FNM* GU9........ 135 H3
TOTT SO40........................ 341 G2
Monktons La *THLE* RG7........ 43 M3
Monkwood Cl *HAV* PO9........ 377 L3
Monkworthy Dr *RGWD* BH24.. 381 K3
Monmouth Cl *CHFD* SO53...... 293 G2
VWD BH31........................ 356 F4
Monmouth Dr *VWD* BH31...... 356 F4
Monmouth Rd *NEND* PO2...... 399 H6
Monmouth Sq *WEND* SO18.. 238 A2 🔢
Monnow Gdns *WEND* SO18.. 320 A7

Monroe Cl *GPORT* PO12........ 421 J5
Monsal Av *FERN* BH22........ 406 A5
Mons Barracks *ALDT* GU11.. 112 F3
Mons Cl *ALDT* GU11........ 113 H1
Montacute Av *CHAM* RG24.. 91 G4 🔢
Montacute Dr *STHA* RG19...... 27 🔢
Montacute Wy *WIMB* BH21.. 404 C8
Montague Av *ITCH* SO19...... 345 H5
Montague Cl *CBLY* GU15........ 70 E3 🔢
ITCH SO19.................... 345 H5 🔢
Montague Gdns *EPSF* GU31.. 276 B5
Montague Pl *BSTK* RG21...... 105 C5 🔢
Montague Rd *BOSC* BH5........ 449 G4
NEND PO2........................ 399 J7
Montague Ter *NWBY* RG14...... 2
Montagu Rd *CHCH/BSGR* BH23.. 452 A1
Monteagle La *YTLY* GU46........ 68 D2
Monteray Dr *LYMN* SO41........ 438 D4
Monterey Dr *HAV* PO9........ 377 L4
HLER SO31........................ 370 E6
Montfort Cl *ROMY* SO51...... 291 H1
Montfort Hts *ROMY* SO51.. 291 H1 🔢
Montfort Rd *ROMY* SO51...... 291 H2
Montgomerie Rd *SSEA* PO5.. 21 J3
Montgomery Av *BWD* BH11.. 431 M5
TOTT SO40........................ 316 C8
Montgomery Cl *SHST* GU47.. 49 L8 🔢
Montgomery Rd *FARN* GU14.. 90 C5
HAV PO9.......................... 17 G4
LSOL/BMARY PO13........ 397 G4
NWBY RG14...................... 2 A9
WEND SO18...................... 319 M8
Montgomery Wk *WVILLE* PO7.. 376 A3
Montgomery Wy *CHFD* SO53.. 293 G5
Montpelier Cl *HLER* SO31...... 371 G5 🔢
Montrose Av
FHAM/PORC PO16........ 374 C7
Montrose Cl *FLET* GU13........ 89 G8 🔢
FRIM GU16........................ 71 H6 🔢
HEND SO30........................ 346 C2 🔢
BOR GU35........................ 201 J7
VWD BH31........................ 356 D2
Montrose Dr *NBNE* BH10...... 431 M6
Montserrat Pl *CHAM* RG24.. 83 H6 🔢
Montserrat Rd *CHAM* RG24.. 83 H6
LSOL/BMARY PO13........ 420 C2
Monument Cha *BOR* GU35.. 201 K7
Monument Cl *NWBY* RG14.. 37 G1 🔢
Monument La *LYMN* SO41...... 440 E3
RCCH PO18........................ 379 K1
WHAM PO17...................... 573 M4
Monxton Rd *RAND* SP11...... 140 B7
RAND SP11...................... 141 J1
Moody Rd *FHAM/STUB* PO14.. 395 M7
Moody's Hl *RSAL* SP5........ 231 H6
Moonhills La *BROC* SO42...... 390 F6
Moonrakers Wy
CHCH/BSGR BH23........ 436 C7
Moonscross Av *TOTT* SO40.. 341 K4
Moons Hl *RFNM* GU10........ 158 E6
Moor Cl *EWKG* RG40........ 48 B1
BOR GU35........................ 201 C5
SHST GU47........................ 50 B7
Moor Court La *RWIN* SO21.. 213 C5
Moorcroft Av
MOOR/WNTN BH9........ 432 E5
Moorcroft Cl *RWIN* SO21...... 168 C5
Moordown Cl
MOOR/WNTN BH9........ 432 E5
Moore Av *BWD* BH11........ 431 L5
Moore Cl *AND* SP10........ 9 H2
FLET GU13........................ 110 F3
RFNM GU10.................... 113 J8 🔢
NMIL/BTOS BH25............ 437 K7 🔢
Moore Crs *HLER* SO31........ 368 F2
Moore Gdns *GPORT* PO12...... 18 A3
Moore Rd *FLET* GU13........ 110 F3
Moorfield Gv
MOOR/WNTN BH9........ 432 D6
Moorfields Rd *CCLF* BH13.. 446 E8 🔢
Moorfoot Gdns *KEMP* RG22.. 104 A5
Moorgreen Rd *HAV* PO9........ 377 L3
HEND SO30...................... 320 D7
Moorhams Av *KEMP* RG22.. 126 F2
Moorhill Gdns *WEND* SO18.. 345 J1
Moorhill Rd *HEND* SO30........ 320 C8
RGWD BH24...................... 384 E6
Moorhouse La *MIDH* GU29.. 278 F2
The Moorings *BSTK* RG21...... 5 K7
FHAM/PORC PO16........ 396 F1 🔢
Moorings Wy *ENEY* PO4........ 424 A2
Moorland Av *NMIL/BTOS* BH25.. 437 K8
Moorland Cl *FAWY* SO45...... 367 H5 🔢
HLER SO31........................ 370 A4
Moorland Crs *UPTN* BH16.. 444 A1
Moorland Ga *RGWD* BH24...... 382 E3
Moorland Rd *BMTH* BH8........ 448 C4
PSEA PO1........................ 423 J2
Moorlands Cl *BROC* SO42...... 387 H7
FLET GU13........................ 89 G8 🔢
GSHT GU26...................... 204 B4
Moorlands Crs *WEND* SO18.. 319 M8
Moorlands Ri *FERN* BH22...... 380 D5
Moorlands Rd *BPWT* SO32.. 323 M4
CBLY GU15........................ 70 D4
FERN BH22........................ 380 C6
VWD BH31........................ 356 D1
Moorland Wy *UPTN* BH16.. 444 A1
Moor La *RSAL* SP5........ 258 D7
Moor Pk *HORN* PO8........ 352 F7
Moor Park La *RFNM* GU10.. 135 J5
Moor Park Wy *FNM* GU9...... 135 J6
Moor Rd *BDST* BH18........ 429 M3
FARN GU14........................ 70 D8
FRIM GU16........................ 71 J3
HASM GU27...................... 227 M3
LISS GU33........................ 225 G7
Moors Cl *CHCH/BSGR* BH23.. 433 M1
RWIN SO21........................ 266 C7
Moorside Cl *FARN* GU14........ 70 D7
Moorside Rd *BWD* BH11...... 431 L5
FERN BH22........................ 380 C6
WIMB BH21........................ 429 H3
The Moors *RFNM* GU10...... 136 C1 🔢
STHA RG19........................ 27 G6
Moortown Av *CHAM* PO6.. 376 A7

Moortown Dr *WIMB* BH21.. 404 F7
Moortown La *RGWD* BH24.. 382 F4
Moorvale Rd
MOOR/WNTN BH9........ 432 E6
Moor Vw *CHAM* RG24........ 106 A1
Moor View Rd *PLE* BH15...... 445 K4
Moot Cl *AND* SP10........ 119 G4
RSAL SP5........................ 284 F2
Moot Gdns *RSAL* SP5........ 284 E2
Moot La *FBDG* SP6........ 284 E2
RSAL SP5........................ 284 E2
Mopley *FAWY* SO45........ 418 D1
Mopley Cl *FAWY* SO45........ 418 D1
Morant Rd *RGWD* BH24...... 358 F7
Morant Cl *GPORT* PO12...... 397 M8 🔢
Morant Dr *FHAM/PORC* PO16.. 597 M2
Moray Av *SHST* GU47........ 70 A1
Mordaunt Rd *SHAM* SO14.. 343 L1
Morden Av *FERN* BH22........ 406 A4
Moreland Cl *ALTN* GU34...... 176 E6
Moreland Rd *GPORT* PO12.. 18 E2
Morelands Rd *WVILLE* PO7.. 376 C4
Morestead Rd *RWIN* SO21.. 239 G3
Moreton Cl *FLET* GU13........ 110 E4
RFNM GU10...................... 181 H7
Moreton Rd *MOOR/WNTN* BH9.. 432 F4
Morgan Rd *ENEY* PO4........ 424 A4
HEND SO30...................... 346 A3 🔢
Morgans Dr *FHAM/STUB* PO14.. 396 A3
Morgans Rise Rd *RSAL* SP5.. 285 J1
Morgans Vale Rd *RSAL* SP5.. 285 J2
Morgaston Rd *TADY* RG26.. 82 E1
Morland Rd *ALDT* GU11........ 7 H8
WSHM SO15...................... 318 B7
Morland's Rd *ALDT* GU11.. 113 C3
Morley Cl *BOSC* BH5........ 448 F3
CHCH/BSGR BH23........ 435 C5
ITCH SO19........................ 344 D2
YTLY GU46........................ 68 E3
Morley Crs *HORN* PO8........ 352 E5
Morley Dr *BPWT* SO32........ 297 H8
Morley Rd *BSTK* RG21........ 104 F7
ENEY PO4........................ 423 L6
FNM GU9.......................... 134 F7
Morningside Av
FHAM/PORC PO16........ 374 B7
Mornington Cl *AND* SP10.. 142 F3 🔢
TADY RG26...................... 41 G7
Mornington Dr *WINW* SO22.. 214 B6
Mornington Rd *BOR* GU35.. 200 F6
Mornish Rd *CCLF* BH13...... 446 E6
Morpeth Av *TOTT* SO40...... 316 E8
Morris Cl *FAWY* SO45........ 367 H4
LSOL/BMARY PO13........ 397 G4
Morrison Av *BKME/WDN* BH12.. 446 E2
Morris Rd *FARN* GU14........ 91 C8
WSHM SO15...................... 12 D1
Morris St *HTWY* RG27........ 85 K8
Morse Rd *KEMP* RG22........ 104 D4
Morshead Crs
FHAM/PORC PO16........ 14 F2
Mortimer Cl *CHCH/BSGR* BH23 .. 450 F2
HLER SO31........................ 368 F2
Mortimer La *BSTK* RG21...... 4 D8
THLE RG7.......................... 44 A1
Mortimer Rd *CHAM* PO6...... 375 G7
CHAR BH8........................ 432 F7
HEND SO30...................... 346 E2
ITCH SO19........................ 344 D1
Mortimers Dr *ELGH* SO50.. 295 J6 🔢
Mortimers La *ELGH* SO50...... 295 J6
Mortimer Wy *NBAD* SO52.. 291 L5
Mortimore Rd *GPORT* PO12.. 421 K2
Morton Cl *FRIM* GU16........ 91 J1
Morval Cl *FARN* GU14........ 90 A4
Mosaic Cl *ITCH* SO19........ 345 K4 🔢
Mosdell Rd *EMRTH* PO10.. 379 H7
Moselle Cl *FARN* GU14........ 90 A3
Moss Cl *LISS* GU33........ 248 F4
Moss Dr *TOTT* SO40........ 342 D6
Mossleigh Av *ROWN* SO16.. 317 L3
Mossley Av *BKME/WDN* BH12.. 431 K7
Moss Rd *WINC* SO23........ 11 K7
Motcombe Rd *CCLF* BH13.. 446 F7
Mottisfont Cl *WSHM* SO15.. 342 E2 🔢
Mottisfont Rd *ELGH* SO50.. 293 M4
Moulsham Copse La *YTLY* GU46 .. 68 E1
Moulsham La *YTLY* GU46...... 68 E1
Moulshay La *HTWY* RG27.. 84 B3
Mound Cl *GPORT* PO12...... 18 D5
Mountain Ash Cl *WEND* SO18.. 345 G1 🔢
Mount Av *NMIL/BTOS* BH25.. 437 L7
Mountbatten Av *ROMY* SO51.. 290 C1
Mountbatten Cl
LSOL/BMARY PO13........ 397 G4 🔢
NWBY RG14...................... 25 M3 🔢
Mountbatten Ct *WINW* SO22.. 10 C1
Mountbatten Dr *FERN* BH22.. 406 A3
WVILLE PO7...................... 376 A3
Mountbatten Pl *WINC* SO23.. 191 H8 🔢
Mountbatten Ri *SHST* GU47.. 49 J7
Mountbatten Rd *CCLF* BH13.. 447 C7
ELGH SO50...................... 293 M3 🔢
TOTT SO40........................ 316 C8
Mountbatten Sq *ENEY* PO4.. 423 M6 🔢
Mount Carmel Rd *RAND* SP11.. 161 J3
Mount Cl *WINW* SO22........ 10 C1
KSCL RG20........................ 56 C2
NMIL/BTOS BH25............ 437 L7
NWBY RG14...................... 2 E8
Mount Dr *CHFD* SO53........ 293 K4
FHAM PO15...................... 371 M8
Mounters La *ALTN* GU34...... 176 C4
Mount Av *NMIL/BTOS* BH25.. 437 L7
Mountfield *FAWY* SO45...... 367 J4
Mount Grace Dr *PSTN* BH14.. 457 H1
Mount Hermon Rd *RAND* SP11.. 161 K2
Mount House Cl *FAWY* SO45.. 367 L5 🔢
Mountjoy Cl *WIMB* BH21...... 404 D6
Mount La *ROMY* SO51........ 260 D1
Mount Pleasant *FNM* GU9.. 134 D6
HTWY RG27...................... 87 J2
RGWD BH24...................... 382 E1 🔢
SHST GU47........................ 49 K7 🔢

TADY RG26........................ 41 K8
WINC SO23........................ 215 G2
Mount Pleasant Dr *CHAR* BH8.. 432 E7
Mount Pleasant La *LYMN* SO41.. 413 K8
Mount Pleasant Rd
GPORT PO12...................... 18 E7
PLE BH15.......................... 445 J6
SHAM SO14...................... 343 M1
ALTN GU34...................... 176 E6
ASHV GU12...................... 7 J2
SSEA PO5........................ 201 L3
Mount Rd *BWD* BH11........ 431 L4
KSCL RG20........................ 56 C1
NTHA RG18...................... 27 G4
PSTN BH14........................ 446 A3
Mountsom's La *ALTN* GU34.. 198 E4
Mount Temple *ROMY* SO51.. 290 F1
The Mount *FLET* GU13........ 88 F6
HASM GU27...................... 205 J6
BOR GU35........................ 202 D2
LSOL/BMARY PO13........ 397 J7 🔢
RGWD BH24...................... 359 H8
ROWN SO16...................... 317 M7 🔢
ROWN SO16...................... 318 E4 🔢
Mount Vw *ALDT* GU11........ 6 E4
SSEA PO5........................ 294 A4
Mountview Av
FHAM/PORC PO16........ 374 C7
Mountwood Rd *EMRTH* PO10.. 379 H7
Mourne Cl *KEMP* RG22........ 104 A4
Mousehole La *FAWY* SO45.. 367 L5
HAV PO9.......................... 377 L3
Mousehole Rd *CHAM* PO6.. 374 D7
Mowbray Rd *ITCH* SO19...... 344 F4
Moxhams *FBDG* SP6........ 309 L7 🔢
Mozart Cl *KEMP* RG22........ 104 D8
Muccleshell Cl *HAV* PO9...... 377 L4 🔢
Muddyford Rd *RSAL* SP5...... 257 J7
Mudeford *CHCH/BSGR* BH23.. 450 E3
Mudeford La
CHCH/BSGR BH23........ 450 E2
Mude Gdns *CHCH/BSGR* BH23.. 450 F3
Mud La *HTWY* RG27........ 47 J7
Mulberry Av *CHAM* PO6...... 399 L1
FHAM/STUB PO14............ 396 A7
Mulberry Cl *ASHV* GU12...... 113 K4
CWTH RG45...................... 49 M4
GPORT PO12...................... 18 E4
SHST GU47........................ 50 A8 🔢
Mulberry Gdns *FBDG* SP6.. 309 K8
Mulberry La *CHAM* PO6...... 399 L1
Mulberry Rd *TOTT* SO40...... 342 D7
Mulberry Wk *WSHM* SO15.. 318 B8
Mulberry Wy *CHAM* RG24.. 83 L5
Mulfords Hl *TADY* RG26........ 41 L7
Mulgrave Rd *FRIM* GU16...... 71 J6 🔢
Mull Cl *DEAN* RG23........ 102 F6
Mullen Cl *ITCH* SO19........ 344 C4
Mullins Cl *BKME/WDN* BH12.. 432 A8
BSTK RG21........................ 4 F2
Mullin's La *FAWY* SO45...... 367 K6
Mullion Cl *CHAM* PO6........ 398 F1
Mulroy Dr *CBLY* GU15........ 71 K2
Mumby Rd *GPORT* PO12...... 19 K2
Munday Cl *FAWY* SO45........ 367 K6
Munday's Boro
RGUW GU3...................... 137 K4 🔢
Munday's Boro Rd
RGUW GU3...................... 137 K4 🔢
Mundays Rw *HORN* PO8.. 328 D7 🔢
Munkle Marsh *STHA* RG19.. 27 K5 🔢
Munnings Cl *BSTK* RG21...... 105 J5
Munnings Dr *SHST* GU47...... 70 A1
Munro Crs *WSHM* SO15...... 342 D1
Munster Rd *NEND* PO2........ 399 H6
PSTN BH14........................ 446 C5
Murefield Rd *PSEA* PO1...... 21 K1 🔢
Muriel Rd *WVILLE* PO7........ 352 C8
Murley Rd *MOOR/WNTN* BH9.. 432 E8
Murray Cl *AND* SP10........ 142 E3
FHAM PO15...................... 14 D4
ITCH SO19........................ 345 J2
Murray Rd *FARN* GU14........ 90 C5
HORN PO8........................ 352 F2
Murray's La *PSEA* PO1........ 422 D2
Murray's Rd *ALDT* GU11...... 113 G3
Murrell Green Rd *HTWY* RG27.. 86 D3
Murrell Rd *ASHV* GU12........ 113 K5
Murrells La *CBLY* GU15........ 70 E5
Mush Rd *NEND* PO2........ 399 H1
Mustang Av *FHAM* PO15...... 370 F1
Myers Cl *BPWT* SO32........ 324 A3
Myland Cl *BSTK* RG21........ 5 G3
Mylen Rd *AND* SP10........ 8 D4
My Lords La *HISD* PO11...... 425 M5
Myrtle Av *FHAM/PORC* PO16.. 398 F1
TOTT SO40........................ 341 H2
Myrtle Cl *LSOL/BMARY* PO13.. 396 F5 🔢
LYMN SO41...................... 438 D4 🔢
THLE RG7.......................... 31 M5
Myrtle Dr *BLKW* GU17........ 70 A4
Myrtle Gv *HSEA* PO3........ 423 M2
Myrtle Rd *CHAR* BH8........ 448 B2
ROWN SO16...................... 318 A4
Myvern Cl *FAWY* SO45........ 392 A5

Nadder Rd *NTID* SP9........ 114 C1
Nailsworth Rd *CHAM* PO6.. 374 F7
Naini Tal Rd *NTID* SP9........ 114 C1
Nairn Cl *FRIM* GU16........ 71 H6 🔢
Nairn Rd *CCLF* BH13........ 457 K1
TWDS BH3........................ 447 K1
Naish Ct *HAV* PO9........ 377 G2
Naish Dr *GPORT* PO12........ 397 L3
Naish Rd *NMIL/BTOS* BH25.. 452 C1
Namu Rd *MOOR/WNTN* BH9.. 432 C1
Nansen Av *PLE* BH15........ 445 J1
Napier Cl *ALDT* GU11........ 113 H1 🔢
CWTH RG45...................... 49 M4
NTID SP9.......................... 114 F1
Napier Crs *FHAM* PO15...... 372 A4
Napier Dr *CBLY* GU15........ 71 K2
Napier Rd *CWTH* RG45........ 49 M4
HORN PO8........................ 353 C2
ITCH SO19........................ 345 J1
PLE BH15.......................... 444 E8
SSEA PO5........................ 21 K3
Napoleon Av *FARN* GU14.. 90 E7
Napoleon Dr *DEAN* RG23.. 104 B3
Narrow La *RGWD* BH24...... 359 H4
ROMY SO51...................... 290 D1
Narvik Rd *NEND* PO2........ 399 H1
Naseby Ri *NWBY* RG14...... 26 A2
Naseby Rd *MOOR/WNTN* BH9.. 432 E2
Nash Cl *BSTK* RG21........ 5 C2
FARN GU14........................ 90 C5
FAWY SO45...................... 367 H4
Nashe Cl *FHAM* PO15...... 14 A5
Nashe Wy *FHAM* PO15...... 372 A4
Nash Mdw *ODIM* RG29...... 130 F7
Nash Rd *FAWY* SO45........ 367 H4
Nasmith Cl *LSOL/BMARY* PO13 .. 421 H4
Nately Rd *OVTN* RG25...... 107 J2
Nathen Gdns *PLE* BH15.. 444 C5 🔢
Nations Hl *WINC* SO23........ 215 C3
Navigator's Wy *HEND* SO30.. 321 H4
Navy Rd *PSEA* PO1........ 422 E1
The Naylors *THLE* RG7........ 46 A1
Nea Cl *CHCH/BSGR* BH23.. 436 B5
Neacroft Cl *NMIL/BTOS* BH25.. 437 H1
Nea Dr *RGWD* BH24........ 357 L3
Nea Rd *CHCH/BSGR* BH23.. 436 C5
Neath Rd *BSTK* RG21........ 5 J1
Neath Wy *CHFD* SO53........ 292 F2
Needles Point *LYMN* SO41.. 454 C4
Neelands Gv *CHAM* PO6...... 374 C4
Neilson Av *FHAM/PORC* PO16.. 397 M4
NEND PO2........................ 399 H1
Nelson Cl *ASHV* GU12........ 7 J7
FAWY SO45...................... 392 A4
FNM GU9.......................... 112 A4
NMIL/BTOS BH25............ 437 H1
ROMY SO51...................... 262 E8
ROMY SO51...................... 262 F8
STOK SO20...................... 186 E3
Nelson Ct *FHAM/STUB* PO14.. 396 C4
Nelson Crs *HORN* PO8........ 353 C2
Nelson Dr *CHCH/BSGR* BH23.. 450 E3
Nelson La *WHAM* PO17...... 374 A7
Nelson Pl *LYMN* SO41........ 440 D7
Nelson Rd *BKME/WDN* BH12.. 447 J2
ELGH SO50...................... 294 C1
FNM GU9.......................... 112 A4
GPORT PO12...................... 18 F4
PSEA PO1........................ 423 H1
SSEA PO5........................ 21 H7
WINC SO23........................ 11 J1
WSHM SO15...................... 343 C7
Nelsons Gdns *HEND* SO30.. 321 H4
Nelson St *ALDT* GU11........ 6 E8
Nelson Wy *CBLY* GU15........ 70 C5
Nene Ct *AND* SP10........ 119 H6 🔢
Nepaul Rd *NTID* SP9........ 114 D1
Nepean Cl *GPORT* PO12...... 18 E3
Neptune Rd *FHAM* PO15...... 372 A4
FHAM/STUB PO14............ 395 M8
BOR GU35........................ 201 K6 🔢
Neptune Wy *SHAM* SO14.. 13 C3
Nerissa Cl *WVILLE* PO7........ 352 F7
Nerquis Cl *ROMY* SO51...... 263 C8
Nesbitt Cl *LSOL/BMARY* PO13 .. 396 F5
Nessus St *NEND* PO2........ 399 H1
Nestor Cl *AND* SP10........ 8 E3
Netherfield Cl *ALTN* GU34.. 176 C2
HAV PO9.......................... 17 H1
Netherhall Gdns *WBNE* BH4.. 447 H7
Nether Hill La *BPWT* SO32.. 322 A4
Netherhouse Moor
FLET GU13........................ 110 C1
Netherton Rd *GPORT* PO12.. 421 H3
Netley Cl *CHFD* SO53........ 293 C5 🔢
PLE BH15.......................... 445 M4
Netley Firs Rd *ITCH* SO19.. 345 K6
Netley Hill Est *ITCH* SO19.. 345 K6
Netley Lodge Cl *HLER* SO31.. 369 H7
Netley Rd *FHAM/STUB* PO14.. 371 C7
SSEA PO5........................ 21 C7
Netley St *FARN* GU14........ 90 E7
Netley Ter *SSEA* PO5........ 21 C7
Nettlebeds La *NALR* SO24.. 195 C1
Nettlecombe Av *ENEY* PO4.. 21 H5
Nettlestone *HLER* SO31...... 369 G1
Nettlestone Rd *ENEY* PO4.. 423 L6
Nettleton Cl *CFDH* BH17...... 445 H1
Neuvic Wy *WHCH* RG28...... 122 C1
Nevada Cl *FARN* GU14........ 90 A5
Neva Rd *WEND* SO18........ 319 L1
Neville Av *FHAM/PORC* PO16.. 398 F1
Neville Cl *AND* SP10........ 9 H1
BSTK RG21........................ 105 G1
Neville Dr *ROMY* SO51...... 262 E8
STHA RG19........................ 27 J1
Neville Duke Rd *FARN* GU14.. 70 A1
Neville Gdns *EMRTH* PO10.. 378 F5
Neville Rd *HSEA* PO3........ 423 L1
Neville Shute Rd *HSEA* PO3.. 399 L8
Newall Rd *RAND* SP11...... 141 M6
Newark Rd *BLKW* GU17...... 70 F1
New Barn Cl *FLET* GU13.. 110 C1
New Barn La *ALTN* GU34...... 176 A2
RAND SP11...................... 143 C1
Newbarn La *RCCH* PO18.. 355 H7
Newbarn Rd *EPSF* GU31.. 303 L5

Newbold Rd NWBY RG14 ..... 25 G3
Newbolt Cl HORN PO8 ..... 352 C5
NTHA RG18 ..... 26 F1
Newbolt Rd CHAM PO6 ..... 374 D7
New Borough Rd WIMB BH21 ..... 404 E4
Newbridge HLER SO31 ..... 369 G2
Newbridge Rd TOTT SO40 ..... 314 C5
Newbridge Wy TOTT SO41 ..... 440 A7
New Brighton Rd
EMRTH PO10 ..... 378 D4
Newbroke Rd
LSOL/BMARY PO13 ..... 397 J8
Newburgh St WINC SO23 ..... 10 F6
Newbury Cl ELGH SO50 ..... 295 G6
Newbury Pl HLER SO31 ..... 370 D6
Newbury Rd AND SP10 ..... 118 F5
KSCL RG20 ..... 59 H5
RAND SP11 ..... 119 C1
WHCH RG28 ..... 99 J7
WSHM SO15 ..... 318 B7
Newbury St AND 9 J5
WHCH RG28 ..... 122 B5
Newchurch Rd TADY RG26 ..... 41 K7
New Cliffe Gdns HEND SO30 ..... 345 M1
Newcomb Cl AND SP10 ..... 142 E3
Newcombe Rd FERN BH22 ..... 380 B5
SBNE BH6 ..... 449 L4
WSHM SO15 ..... 343 J2
Newcomen Rd NEND PO2 ..... 399 G6
Newcome Pl ASHV GU12 ..... 7 L7
Newcome Rd FNM GU9 ..... 6 A1
PSEA PO1 ..... 423 J2
Newcroft Gdns
CHCH/BSGR BH23 ..... 434 E8
New Cut HISD PO11 ..... 401 H7
New Dawn Cl FARN GU14 ..... 90 A5
New Down La WVILLE PO7 ..... 375 L6
New Dro RAND SP11 ..... 92 D7
Newenham Rd LYMN SO41 ..... 440 C6
New Farm Rd NALR SO24 ..... 218 A3
RWIN SO21 ..... 170 E5
Newfield Av FARN GU14 ..... 90 B2
Newfield Rd ASHV GU12 ..... 113 L4
LISS GU33 ..... 248 F2
New Forest Dr BROC SO42 ..... 387 H7
Newfoundland Dr PLE BH15 ..... 445 J7
Newgate La FHAM/STUB PO14 ..... 396 C2
New Harbour Rd South
PLE BH15 ..... 445 G7
New House La RAND SP11 ..... 116 F1
New Inn La BROC SO42 ..... 416 A3
TOTT SO40 ..... 339 M2
New Inn Rd TOTT SO40 ..... 339 M2
Newland Av GPORT PO12 ..... 18 C3
Newlands FLET GU13 ..... 110 F2
Newlands Av WSHM SO15 ..... 343 G1
NBAD SO52 ..... 292 D3
YTLY GU46 ..... 69 G3
Newlands Cl FAWY SO45 ..... 392 D7
Newlands Cl ASHV GU12 ..... 113 L4
Newlands La WVILLE PO7 ..... 351 L8
Newlands Rd
CHCH/BSGR BH23 ..... 450 B1
FAWY SO45 ..... 392 C6
FRIM GU16 ..... 70 E7
LTDN BH7 ..... 448 F2
NMIL/BTOS BH25 ..... 437 M7
WVILLE PO7 ..... 376 B3
Newlands Wy BDST BH18 ..... 429 H5
New La EPSF GU31 ..... 305 G6
HAV PO9 ..... 17 G3
LYMN SO41 ..... 454 E1
NMIL/BTOS BH25 ..... 437 K2
STOK SO20 ..... 210 F4
Newlease Rd WVILLE PO7 ..... 376 D3
Newlyn Wk ROMY SO51 ..... 262 F7
Newlyn Wy BKME/WDN BH12 ..... 446 C1
CHAM PO6 ..... 398 E1
Newman La ALTN GU34 ..... 177 G3
Newmans Cl WIMB BH21 ..... 380 C3
Newmans Ct FNM GU9 ..... 134 C2
Newmans HI WHAM PO17 ..... 324 B8
Newman's La FERN BH22 ..... 380 A3
Newman St ROWN SO16 ..... 318 A3
Newmarket Cl ELGH SO50 ..... 321 J1
Newmer Ct HAV PO9 ..... 377 G2
New Merrifield WIMB BH21 ..... 404 D1
New Mill La HTWY RG27 ..... 47 H5
New Mill Rd HTWY RG27 ..... 47 H6
Newmorton Rd
MOOR/WNTN BH9 ..... 432 B4
Newney Cl NEND PO2 ..... 399 K4
Newnham Ct HAV PO9 ..... 377 M3
Newnham La CHAM RG24 ..... 84 C8
HTWY RG27 ..... 85 H7
Newnham Pk HTWY RG27 ..... 85 L8
New Odiham Rd ALTN GU34 ..... 176 C4
New Orch PLE BH15 ..... 445 G6
New Paddock Cl ALTN GU34 ..... 177 L0
New Park Rd SBNE BH6 ..... 449 H4
Newport Cl CHFD SO53 ..... 292 F4
NWBY RG14 ..... 3 G2
Newport La ROMY SO51 ..... 263 G2
Newport Rd ASHV GU12 ..... 18 A1
NWBY RG14 ..... 3 H1
GPORT PO12 ..... 18 A1
New Quay Rd PLE BH15 ..... 444 F7
New Rd BKME/WDN BH12 ..... 446 C2
BLKW GU17 ..... 70 B4
BPWT SO32 ..... 297 J1
BPWT SO32 ..... 299 J5
BPWT SO32 ..... 323 L4
BSTK RG21 ..... 4 F9
CWTH RG45 ..... 49 M3
ELGH SO50 ..... 295 G6
EMRTH PO10 ..... 378 F5
EMRTH PO10 ..... 379 J8
FAWY SO45 ..... 391 M2
FAWY SO45 ..... 392 C7
FBDG SP6 ..... 282 D7
FERN BH22 ..... 406 B3
FERN BH22 ..... 432 C1
FLET GU13 ..... 111 G2

WINW SO22 ..... 213 M2
HASM GU27 ..... 228 C3
HAV PO9 ..... 16 D2
HLER SO31 ..... 346 D8
HLER SO31 ..... 368 F2
HLER SO31 ..... 370 D8
HORN PO8 ..... 328 B3
HORN PO8 ..... 352 C2
HTWY RG27 ..... 68 B1
HTWY RG27 ..... 85 M7
HTWY RG27 ..... 87 H2
BOR GU35 ..... 201 H7
LYMN SO41 ..... 454 F4
NBNE BH10 ..... 432 C3
NEND PO2 ..... 423 J1
RFNM GU10 ..... 136 C2
NWBY RG14 3
ODIM RG29 ..... 108 B4
RGWD BH24 ..... 334 F8
ROMY SO51 ..... 262 C1
ROMY SO51 ..... 262 F8
RSAL SP5 ..... 287 K7
RWIN SO21 ..... 148 A6
RWIN SO21 ..... 266 E7
SHAM SO14 ..... 13 G2
SHST GU47 ..... 49 K8
STHA RG19 ..... 38 A1
STOK SO20 ..... 162 B8
TADY RG26 ..... 61 K1
TADY RG26 ..... 62 B5
TOTT SO40 ..... 341 G6
New East NEND PO2 ..... 399 N8
New Road HI THLE RG7 ..... 28 E5
Newstead Dr SBNE BH6 ..... 449 J4
New St AND SP10 ..... 9 J4
BSTK RG21 ..... 4 E9
LYMN SO41 ..... 440 C4
RGWD BH24 ..... 382 E2
STOK SO20 ..... 186 E6
THLE RG7 ..... 44 D8
Newton Cl FHAM/STUB PO14 ..... 396 A4
RSAL SP5 ..... 258 F5
Newton La ALTN GU34 ..... 198 D6
ROMY SO51 ..... 290 D1
RSAL SP5 ..... 258 C8
Newton Pl LSOL/BMARY PO13 ..... 420 C1
Newton Rd CCLF BH13 ..... 446 B8
FARN GU14 ..... 91 G2
NMIL/BTOS BH25 ..... 437 M8
RWIN SO21 ..... 266 F1
WEND SO18 ..... 319 K7
Newton Wy RFNM GU10 ..... 136 B1
New Town FHAM/PORC PO16 ..... 374 B8
Newtown TADY RG26 ..... 41 K7
Newtown Cl AND SP10 ..... 8 D6
RGWD BH24 ..... 335 G7
Newtown Rd ELGH SO50 ..... 293 M4
HLER SO31 ..... 370 A8
ITCH SO19 ..... 344 E5
LIPH GU30 ..... 226 E5
ROMY SO51 ..... 261 G5
SHST GU47 ..... 49 L8
VWD BH31 ..... 356 F2
New Valley Rd LYMN SO41 ..... 454 B4
New Wokingham Rd
CWTH RG45 ..... 49 K2
Nicholas Cl
CHCH/BSGR BH23 ..... 436 F6
Nicholas Crs FHAM PO15 ..... 14 E4
Nicholas Gdns NBNE BH10 ..... 432 A6
Nicholas Rd FAWY SO45 ..... 418 C1
Nicholl Pl LSOL/BMARY PO13 ..... 397 G6
Nichol Rd CHFD SO53 ..... 265 J7
Nicholson Wk ROWN SO16 ..... 317 J2
Nicholson Wy HAV PO9 ..... 16 D1
Nichols Rd SHAM SO14 ..... 13 K1
Nickel Cl WINC SO23 ..... 11 K6
Nickel St SSEA PO5 ..... 20 F5
Nickleby Gdns TOTT SO40 ..... 340 F1
Nickleby Rd HORN PO8 ..... 328 A2
Nickson Cl CHFD SO53 ..... 265 G8
Nideggan Cl STHA RG19 ..... 27 G5
Nightingale Av ELGH SO50 ..... 293 J6
Nightingale Cl FARN GU14 ..... 89 M2
WINW SO22 ..... 10 B7
GPORT PO12 ..... 421 K2
HAV PO9 ..... 17 G6
ROMY SO51 ..... 291 G1
VWD BH31 ..... 356 E3
Nightingale Crs BPWT SO32 ..... 323 L8
Nightingale Dr FRIM GU16 ..... 91 K5
TOTT SO40 ..... 316 B8
Nightingale Gdns CHAM RG24 ..... 82 B8
HTWY RG27 ..... 85 M7
SHST GU47 ..... 49 L8
Nightingale Gv WSHM SO15 ..... 343 G1
Nightingale La RCCH SO18 ..... 379 L5
THLE RG7 ..... 44 A2
Nightingale Pk HAV PO9 ..... 17 J5
Nightingale Ri OVTN RG25 ..... 124 A1
Nightingale Rd ASHV GU12 ..... 113 M5
HLER SO31 ..... 345 K8
BOR GU35 ..... 201 K6
PSF GU32 ..... 275 J6
SSEA PO5 ..... 20 F7
The Nightingales NWBY RG14 ..... 2 F9
Nightingale Wk HLER SO31 ..... 369 F9
Nightjar Cl CFDH BH17 ..... 429 J8
HORN PO8 ..... 352 E2
RFNM GU10 ..... 111 G8
Nile Rd PTSW SO17 ..... 318 F6
Nile St EMRTH PO10 ..... 378 D8
Nimrod Dr LSOL/BMARY PO13 ..... 421 J7
Nimrod Wy WIMB BH21 ..... 405 K2
Nine Elms La WHAM PO17 ..... 373 J4
Nine Mile Ride EWKG RG40 ..... 48 A1
Ninian Cl ELGH SO50 ..... 295 H7
Ninian Park Rd HSEA PO3 ..... 399 L6
Niton Cl LSOL/BMARY PO13 ..... 397 G6
Noads Cl FAWY SO45 ..... 367 K6
Noads Wy FAWY SO45 ..... 367 J6
Nobbs La PSEA PO1 ..... 20 D4
Nobes Av LSOL/BMARY PO13 ..... 397 G5
Nobes Cl LSOL/BMARY PO13 ..... 397 H6
Noble Cl BWD BH11 ..... 431 K7
Noble Rd HEND SO30 ..... 346 B5

Nob's Crook RWIN SO21 ..... 294 F1
Noel Cl BROC SO42 ..... 387 L7
Noel Rd NBNE BH10 ..... 431 M7
Nogarth Cl ROMY SO51 ..... 263 G7
Nomad Cl WEND SO18 ..... 320 A7
The Nook ELGH SO50 ..... 294 A3
LSOL/BMARY PO13 ..... 397 J7
Noon Gdns VWD BH31 ..... 356 F2
Noon Hill Dr VWD BH31 ..... 356 F2
Noon Hill Rd VWD BH31 ..... 356 F2
Norbury Cl CHFD SO53 ..... 293 G1
Norbury Gdns HLER SO31 ..... 369 J6
Norcliffe Cl BWD BH11 ..... 431 M5
Norcliffe Rd PTSW SO17 ..... 318 F8
Norden Cl BSTK RG21 ..... 4 F5
Nordik Gdns HEND SO30 ..... 346 A3
Nore Crs EMRTH PO10 ..... 378 B7
Nore Down Wy RCCH SO18 ..... 330 D8
Nore Farm Av EMRTH PO10 ..... 378 B7
Noreuil Rd PSF GU32 ..... 275 J5
Norfolk Av CHCH/BSGR BH23 ..... 434 D7
WSHM SO15 ..... 318 C8
Norfolk St SSEA PO5 ..... 21 G5
Norgett Wy FHAM/PORC PO16 ..... 397 M2
Norham Av ROWN SO16 ..... 318 B6
Norham Cl ROWN SO16 ..... 318 B6
Norland Rd ENEY PO4 ..... 21 L5
Norlands Dr RWIN SO21 ..... 266 B4
Norley Cl HAV PO9 ..... 377 J4
Norleywood
CHCH/BSGR BH23 ..... 436 D8
Norleywood Rd LYMN SO41 ..... 415 H7
Norman Av BKME/WDN BH12 ..... 446 E1
Norman Cl FHAM/PORC PO16 ..... 398 B2
BOR GU35 ..... 201 K5
Norman Court La RAND SP11 ..... 142 E4
Normandy Cl LYMN SO41 ..... 412 E6
ROWN SO16 ..... 317 J2
Normandy Dr
CHCH/BSGR BH23 ..... 450 C1
Normandy Gdns GPORT PO12 ..... 18 B3
Normandy La LYMN SO41 ..... 440 D6
Normandy Rd NEND PO2 ..... 399 H4
Normandy St ALTN GU34 ..... 176 E4
Normandy Wy FBDG SP6 ..... 309 K6
PLE BH15 ..... 444 C6
TOTT SO40 ..... 342 D5
Norman Gdns
BKME/WDN BH12 ..... 446 E1
HEND SO30 ..... 345 L3
Normanhurst Av CHAR BH8 ..... 433 H7
Norman Rd ENEY PO4 ..... 21 L6
BROC SO42 ..... 387 L7
FAWY SO45 ..... 392 D8
GPORT PO12 ..... 18 C1
HISD PO11 ..... 425 M6
WINC SO23 ..... 238 E2
Normanton Cl
CHCH/BSGR BH23 ..... 434 D7
Normanton Rd BSTK RG21 ..... 4 F1
Norman Wy HAV PO9 ..... 377 G6
Normay Ri NWBY RG14 ..... 36 F3
Normoor Rd THLE RG7 ..... 31 J7
Norn Hi BSTK RG21 ..... 5 H5
Norn Hill Cl BSTK RG21 ..... 5 H5
Norris Br FARN GU14 ..... 89 K8
Norris Cl BOR GU35 ..... 201 G7
RGWD BH24 ..... 381 J4
ROMY SO51 ..... 263 H6
Norris Gdns HAV PO9 ..... 17 H6
NMIL/BTOS BH25 ..... 437 L7
Norris Hi WEND SO18 ..... 319 K7
Norris Hill Rd FLET GU13 ..... 111 J1
Norrish Rd BKME/WDN BH12 ..... 446 B3
Norset Rd FHAM PO15 ..... 372 A6
Northam Br SHAM SO14 ..... 344 A2
Northam Ms PSEA PO1 ..... 21 J1
Northampton La FAWY SO45 ..... 392 C8
Northam Rd SHAM SO14 ..... 13 K1
Northam St PSEA PO1 ..... 21 K1
PSEA PO1 ..... 423 K1
Northanger Cl ALTN GU34 ..... 176 D4
Northarbour Rd CHAM PO6 ..... 399 H1
North Av FNM GU9 ..... 135 G1
NBNE BH10 ..... 432 B2
NEND PO2 ..... 399 J3
North Battery Rd NEND PO2 ..... 398 F6
North Bay EMRTH PO10 ..... 402 E5
North Beta Rd FARN GU14 ..... 90 E6
Northbourne Av NBNE BH10 ..... 432 B4
Northbourne Cl FAWY SO45 ..... 367 L7
Northbourne Gdns
NBNE BH10 ..... 432 C3
Northbrook Av WINC SO23 ..... 11 K8
Northbrook Cl PSEA PO1 ..... 423 H1
WINC SO23 ..... 11 L8
Northbrook Rd ALDT GU11 ..... 7 G5
BDST BH18 ..... 429 L6
SHAM SO14 ..... 13 J1
Northbrook St NWBY RG14 ..... 2 E3
North Charford Crossing
FBDG SP6 ..... 284 C7
North Charford Dro FBDG SP6 ..... 283 M3
North Cl ASHV GU12 ..... 7 M4
FARN GU14 ..... 70 D8
GPORT PO12 ..... 18 A4
HAV PO9 ..... 17 G6
LYMN SO41 ..... 440 D4
ROMY SO51 ..... 263 H7
North Common La LYMN SO41 ..... 439 M7
RSAL SP5 ..... 286 F2
Northcote Av NEND PO2 ..... 399 K8
Northcote Rd ASHV GU12 ..... 113 K1
BMTH BH1 ..... 23 L2
ENEY PO4 ..... 21 M1
FARN GU14 ..... 90 B2
PTSW SO17 ..... 319 H6
North Crs HISD PO11 ..... 425 M6
Northcroft La NWBY RG14 ..... 2 A5
Northcroft Rd GPORT PO12 ..... 421 K2
North Cross St GPORT PO12 ..... 19 K3
Northdene Rd CHFD SO53 ..... 293 H3
North Downs Wy RFNM GU10 ..... 135 K2
RGUW GU3 ..... 137 J5
North Dr WINW SO22 ..... 214 A3
North Weirs BROC SO42 ..... 387 H7
Northwood Cl ROWN SO16 ..... 318 F2
Northwood Dr NWBY RG14 ..... 3 J1

North East Cl ITCH SO19 ..... 344 F3
North East Rd ITCH SO19 ..... 344 E4
North End Av NEND PO2 ..... 399 H6
North End Gv NEND PO2 ..... 399 H6
Northend La BPWT SO32 ..... 298 F6
Northend Rd CHAM PO6 ..... 399 H1
Northern Access Rd
FAWY SO45 ..... 393 H6
Northern Anchorage ITCH SO19 ..... 13 H5
Northern Av AND SP10 ..... 9 H3
NWBY RG14 ..... 25 K2
Northern Pde NEND PO2 ..... 399 H5
Northern Rd CHAM PO6 ..... 399 H5
Northerwood Av LYND SO43 ..... 363 J3
Northerwood Cl NBAD SO52 ..... 291 L4
Northey Rd SBNE BH6 ..... 449 K2
NALR SO24 ..... 242 C1
Northfield Av
FHAM/STUB PO14 ..... 396 F7
Northfield Cl ASHV GU12 ..... 7 M3
BPWT SO32 ..... 296 F7
FLET GU13 ..... 111 G2
HORN PO8 ..... 328 B6
Northfield Rd FLET GU13 ..... 111 G2
HTWY RG27 ..... 64 C7
LYMN SO41 ..... 454 D3
NTHA RG18 ..... 26 E4
RGWD BH24 ..... 358 E4
WEND SO18 ..... 319 L5
Northfields Farm La
WHAM PO17 ..... 348 E3
North Front SHAM SO14 ..... 13 H2
North Fryerne YTLY GU46 ..... 49 G8
Northgate Dr CBLY GU15 ..... 71 K1
Northgate La OVTN RG25 ..... 128 A7
North Gate Rd FARN GU14 ..... 90 F6
North Greenlands LYMN SO41 ..... 440 A6
North Head LYMN SO41 ..... 453 M3
North HI CHAM PO6 ..... 374 F6
FHAM/PORC PO16 ..... 15 J1
North Hill Cl WINW SO22 ..... 10 F3
Northington Rd RWIN SO21 ..... 193 G7
Northlands Cl TOTT SO40 ..... 316 C8
Northlands Dr WINC SO23 ..... 11 G3
Northlands Gdns WSHM SO15 ..... 343 J1
Northlands Rd ELGH SO50 ..... 293 M5
ROMY SO51 ..... 291 H2
TOTT SO40 ..... 316 C8
WSHM SO15 ..... 343 J1
Northleigh La WIMB BH21 ..... 404 C1
North Lodge Rd PSTN BH14 ..... 446 D4
Northmead FARN GU14 ..... 90 E4
Northmead Dr CFDH BH17 ..... 429 K8
Northmere Dr
BKME/WDN BH12 ..... 446 E1
Northmere Rd
BKME/WDN BH12 ..... 446 E1
North Millers Dl CHFD SO53 ..... 264 F7
Northmore Cl HLER SO31 ..... 370 F3
Northmore Rd HLER SO31 ..... 370 F3
Northney La HISD PO11 ..... 402 A4
Northney Rd HISD PO11 ..... 401 M4
Northolt Gdns ROWN SO16 ..... 317 M4
Northover La LYMN SO41 ..... 438 C1
Northover Rd HSEA PO3 ..... 399 M8
LYMN SO41 ..... 439 L4
North Pde BOR GU35 ..... 201 J6
North Poulner Rd RGWD BH24 ..... 358 F1
North Rd ALDT GU11 ..... 113 G4
ASHV GU12 ..... 113 J4
BROC SO42 ..... 387 L7
FAWY SO45 ..... 367 H6
HORN PO8 ..... 328 B6
LTDN BH7 ..... 448 D3
PLE BH15 ..... 444 F7
PSF GU32 ..... 275 L4
PSTN BH14 ..... 445 M4
PTSW SO17 ..... 319 H8
WINC SO23 ..... 191 C8
WVILLE PO7 ..... 374 E6
North Rd East WHAM PO17 ..... 374 E2
North Rd West WHAM PO17 ..... 374 D2
North Shore Rd HISD PO11 ..... 425 H3
Northside Rd NALR SO24 ..... 219 J1
North St EMRTH PO10 ..... 378 D7
EMRTH PO10 ..... 378 F4
HAV PO9 ..... 16 A3
HAV PO9 ..... 16 F4
KSCL RG20 ..... 59 J6
LYMN SO41 ..... 440 A6
NALR SO24 ..... 219 G3
PLE BH15 ..... 445 H6
PSEA PO1 ..... 20 D1
PSEA PO1 ..... 423 H1
North Stroud La PSF GU32 ..... 274 D6
North Town RWIN SO21 ..... 266 F1
North Trestle Rd FAWY SO45 ..... 392 G1
Northumberland Rd
BOR GU35 ..... 201 J7
SHAM SO14 ..... 13 K1
SHAM SO14 ..... 343 M2
SSEA PO5 ..... 21 L2
North View Rd TADY RG26 ..... 62 A1
North Wallington
FHAM/PORC PO16 ..... 15 M3
North Walls WINC SO23 ..... 11 J7
North Warnborough St
ODIM RG29 ..... 108 A5
North Wy AND SP10 ..... 119 K6
Northway HAV PO9 ..... 16 D4
Northway HFAM PO15 ..... 371 J5
North Wy HAV PO9 ..... 16 D4
Northway NTHA RG18 ..... 26 F3
NWBY RG14 ..... 3 G6
Northways FHAM/STUB PO14 ..... 396 B6

Northwood La HISD PO11 ..... 401 L7
Northwood Rd NEND PO2 ..... 399 J4
Nortoft Rd CHAR BH8 ..... 448 A2
Norton Cl CHCH/BSGR BH23 ..... 450 C1
ITCH SO19 ..... 344 C5
NWBY RG14 ..... 36 F2
WHAM PO17 ..... 374 D2
WVILLE PO7 ..... 376 B1
Norton Dr FHAM/PORC PO16 ..... 15 H3
Norton Ride CHAM RG24 ..... 105 L1
Norton Rd CBLY GU15 ..... 71 M4
MOOR/WNTN BH9 ..... 432 E7
THLE RG7 ..... 45 M6
WHAM PO17 ..... 374 D2
Norton Welch Cl NBAD SO52 ..... 292 A4
Norway Rd HSEA PO3 ..... 399 K4
Norwich Av CBLY GU15 ..... 71 H5
WCLF BH2 ..... 22 A5
Norwich Av West WBNE BH4 ..... 22 A5
Norwich Cl HLER SO31 ..... 370 C4
Norwich Pl LSOL/BMARY PO13 ..... 420 C1
Norwich Rd CHAM PO6 ..... 375 H7
WCLF BH2 ..... 22 A5
WEND SO18 ..... 319 L6
Norwood Pl BOSC BH5 ..... 449 G3
Nottingham Pl
LSOL/BMARY PO13 ..... 420 C1
Nouale La KEMP RG22 ..... 383 H1
Novello Cl WVILLE PO7 ..... 376 C3
Novello Gdns WVILLE PO7 ..... 376 C3
Noyce Dr ELGH SO50 ..... 295 J7
Noyce Gdns BSbne BH8 ..... 433 M6
Nuffield Dr SHST GU47 ..... 50 C7
Nuffield Rd CFDH BH17 ..... 430 B8
WHIT RG2 ..... 47 J1
Nugee Ct CWTH RG45 ..... 49 L3
Nugent Rd SBNE BH6 ..... 449 L4
Nunns Pk RSAL SP5 ..... 259 G4
Nuns Cl WINC SO23 ..... 11 H4
Nuns Wk WINC SO23 ..... 11 H4
Nunton Dro RSAL SP5 ..... 255 J4
Nursery Cl CHAM RG24 ..... 83 M5
EMRTH PO10 ..... 378 D5
FLET GU13 ..... 89 J8
FRIM GU16 ..... 91 J1
HTWY RG27 ..... 85 M6
LSOL/BMARY PO13 ..... 396 F5
Nursery Fld LISS GU33 ..... 248 D5
Nursery Gdns CHFD SO53 ..... 293 H5
WINW SO22 ..... 10 B7
HORN PO8 ..... 352 E3
ITCH SO19 ..... 344 F2
ROMY SO51 ..... 290 F1
Nursery Gv HEND SO30 ..... 346 A3
Nursery La FHAM/STUB PO14 ..... 396 A7
Nursery Rd ALTN GU34 ..... 176 F4
HAV PO9 ..... 377 L3
MOOR/WNTN BH9 ..... 432 E5
NALR SO24 ..... 218 C3
RGWD BH24 ..... 382 E2
WEND SO18 ..... 319 J7
Nursling Crs HAV PO9 ..... 377 L3
Nursling Gn CHAR BH8 ..... 433 H6
Nursling St ROWN SO16 ..... 317 H3
Nutash FHAM PO15 ..... 371 G4
Nutbane La THLE RG7 ..... 46 C3
Nutbeem Rd ELGH SO50 ..... 293 M6
Nutbourne FNM GU9 ..... 6 B7
Nutbourne Rd CHAM PO6 ..... 400 B1
HISD PO11 ..... 426 C7
Nutburn Rd NBAD SO52 ..... 292 A3
Nutchers Dro STOK SO20 ..... 210 F5
Nutcombe La GSHT GU26 ..... 204 B7
Nutfield Ct ROWN SO16 ..... 317 K5
Nutfield Pl PSEA PO1 ..... 423 H1
Nutfield Rd ROWN SO16 ..... 317 J2
Nuthatch Cl CFDH BH17 ..... 444 E1
HAV PO9 ..... 353 M7
RFNM GU10 ..... 134 A1
Nutley Cl BWD BH11 ..... 431 K4
BOR GU35 ..... 201 J6
YTLY GU46 ..... 69 G3
Nutley La OVTN RG25 ..... 126 E7
Nutley Rd HAV PO9 ..... 377 H3
Nutley Wy BWD BH11 ..... 431 K5
Nutmeg Ct FARN GU14 ..... 89 M3
Nutsey Av TOTT SO40 ..... 316 C6
Nutsey La TOTT SO40 ..... 316 D6
Nutshalling Av ROWN SO16 ..... 317 K3
Nutshalling Cl TOTT SO40 ..... 316 B7
Nutshell La FNM GU9 ..... 134 F2
Nutwick Rd HAV PO9 ..... 17 K1
Nutwood Wy TOTT SO40 ..... 316 D6
Nyewood Av
FHAM/PORC PO16 ..... 374 B7
Nyria Wy GPORT PO12 ..... 19 J4

O

Oakapple Gdns CHAM PO6 ..... 376 C8
SHST GU47 ..... 50 A7
Oak Bank AND SP10 ..... 9 H8
Oakbank Rd ELGH SO50 ..... 294 B5
ITCH SO19 ..... 344 B5
Oak Cl BPWT SO32 ..... 296 E3
DEAN RG23 ..... 103 G7
FAWY SO45 ..... 367 J7
FERN BH22 ..... 406 C7
HORN PO8 ..... 352 C6
LYND SO43 ..... 363 K4
NTID SP9 ..... 114 F1
OVTN RG25 ..... 123 M1
RSAL SP5 ..... 230 B1
STOK SO20 ..... 163 G4
WIMB BH21 ..... 429 G3
WSHM SO15 ..... 342 A1
Oak Coppice Cl ELGH SO50 ..... 294 F6
Oak Ct FNM GU9 ..... 134 E7
Oakcroft La FHAM/STUB PO14 ..... 396 A3
Oakdale Pl PLE BH15 ..... 445 K2
Oakdene ALTN GU34 ..... 176 D3
LSOL/BMARY PO13 ..... 397 H7
THLE RG7 ..... 31 K5
TOTT SO40 ..... 340 F1

Oakdene Cl WIMB BH21 404 B3 1
Oakdown Rd
FHAM/STUB PO14 396 B5
Oak Dr ELGH SO50 295 H6
NWBY RG14 2 C6
THLE RG7 31 J6
Oakenbrow FAWY SO45 367 H6
LYMN SO41 412 E5
Oaken Copse CBLY GU15 71 M1
FLET GU13 111 G4
Oaken Copse Crs FARN GU14 90 E1
Oak End Wy THLE RG7 29 M4
Oaken Gv NWBY RG14 25 G8
The Oakes FHAM/STUB PO14 395 M4
Oak Farm Cl BLKW GU17 69 M3
Oakfield Ct HAV PO9 377 M3 12
Oakfield Rd BLKW GU17 70 B4
PLE BH15 445 H2
TADY RG26 42 B7
TOTT SO40 339 M1
TOTT SO40 341 K1
Oakfields ELGH SO50 293 M1
Oakfields Cl KSCL RG20 58 C4
Oak Gdns LYMN SO41 439 H8 1
Oak Green Wy WEND SO18 319 M8
Oak Grove Crs CBLY GU15 70 C2
Oakgrove Rd ELGH SO50 294 D6
Oak Hanger Cl HTWY RG27 86 A7 1
Oakhanger Rd BOR GU35 200 F3
Oakhill HLER SO31 345 M7
Oak Hl NALR SO24 218 C3
Oakhill Cl CHFD SO53 293 K3
HLER SO31 345 M7
Oakhill Rd BOR GU35 202 E3
Oakhurst GSHT GU26 204 A5
Oakhurst Cl FERN BH22 380 D6
HLER SO31 369 G2 4
Oakhurst Dr WVILLE PO7 352 E8
Oakhurst Gdns CHAM PO6 375 M6
Oakhurst La FERN BH22 380 D6
Oakhurst Rd FERN BH22 380 D7
PTSW SO17 318 F5 1
Oakhurst Wy HLER SO31 369 G2
Oakland Av FNM GU9 6 A7
Oakland Dr TOTT SO40 342 D7
Oakland Rd WHCH RG28 122 B3
Oaklands HASM GU27 228 F1 2
RWIN SO21 190 C4
YTLY GU46 69 G2
LYMN SO41 440 D6
Oaklands Av TOTT SO40 341 K1
Oaklands Cl FBDG SP6 309 K6 5
WINW SO22 238 A2
VWD BH31 356 C2
Oaklands Gdns
FHAM/STUB PO14 371 G7
Oaklands Gv HORN PO8 352 C5
Oaklands La CWTH RG45 49 K2
Oaklands Rd HAV PO9 17 H4
PSF GU32 275 K4
The Oaklands CHFD SO53 293 H5 5
Oaklands Wy DEAN RG23 104 B2
FAWY SO45 367 G6
FHAM/STUB PO14 371 G7
ROWN SO16 318 E4
Oakland Wk FERN BH22 406 C7
Oak La RGWD BH24 358 F8
Oaklea ASHV GU12 113 K3
Oaklea Dr HTWY RG27 47 H6
Oaklea Gdns TADY RG26 64 A6
Oakleigh Crs TOTT SO40 341 J2
Oakleigh Dr RSAL SP5 287 J7
Oakleigh Gdns ROMY SO51 290 F1 5
Oakleigh Wy CHCH/BSGR BH23 451 L1
Oakley Cl FAWY SO45 392 A4
Oakley Dr FLET GU13 88 F8
Oakley Hl WIMB BH21 404 B5
Oakley La DEAN RG23 103 G6
WIMB BH21 404 B6
Oakley Rd CBLY GU15 70 E4
HAV PO9 377 H3
BOR GU35 201 J3
NWBY RG14 3 L1
ROMY SO51 233 K6
ROWN SO16 317 L8
TADY RG26 79 L5
WIMB BH21 404 B6
Oakley Straight WIMB BH21 404 C7
Oakmead TADY RG26 63 K4
Oakmead Gdns BWD BH11 431 K4
Oakmeadow Cl EMRTH PO10 378 E5
Oakmead Rd CFDH BH17 444 E1
Oakmont Dr WVILLE PO7 352 D6
Oakmount Av CHFD SO53 293 J4
PTSW SO17 318 F7
TOTT SO40 316 E8
Oakmount Rd CHFD SO53 293 J4
Oak Park Dr HAV PO9 17 G1
Oakridge Rd BSTK RG21 4 B3
WSHM SO15 317 J8
Oak Rd BPWT SO32 297 J8
CHAR BH8 448 B2
FARN GU14 90 F5
FAWY SO45 367 J7
FBDG SP6 333 K3
FHAM PO15 14 A4
HLER SO31 345 J8
HORN PO8 328 B3
ITCH SO19 344 B6
NMIL/BTOS BH25 438 A4
UPTN BH16 444 B2
Oaks Coppice HORN PO8 352 E2
Oaks Dr RGWD BH24 381 H5
Oakshott Dr HAV PO9 377 J3
Oaks Md VWD BH31 356 E2 5
The Oaks ALTN GU34 196 F1
FLET GU13 88 C7
HLER SO31 345 K8
ITCH SO19 344 D3
TADY RG26 41 K8
VWD BH31 356 C1
YTLY GU46 69 G3
Oak St GPORT PO12 19 H3
Oakthorn Cl
LSOL/BMARY PO13 421 G2
Oak Tree Cl ASHV GU12 7 M6
ASHV GU12 91 J7 2
BOR GU35 202 C4
RWIN SO21 266 E8
TADY RG26 41 L7 1
Oak Tree Dr EMRTH PO10 378 C4
HTWY RG27 86 A6
LISS GU33 248 F4
Oak Tree Farm RCCH PO18 379 M7
Oak Tree Gdns HEND SO30 345 M2 1
Oak Tree La HASM GU27 228 A2
Oak Tree Rd BOR GU35 201 H7
STHA RG19 27 H6
WEND SO18 319 J7
Oaktrees ASHV GU12 113 J7
FNM GU9 134 E2 3
Oak Tree Vw FNM GU9 135 G2
Oak Tree Wy ELGH SO50 293 M3
Oaktree Wy SHST GU47 49 K7
Oak V HEND SO30 320 A5
Oakway ASHV GU12 113 H8
RFNM GU10 156 F4
Oakway Dr FRIM GU16 71 H7
Oakwood CHAM RG24 83 L5
FLET GU13 110 F4
Oakwood Av HAV PO9 376 F5
NMIL/BTOS BH25 438 A4
RWIN SO21 266 B5
Oakwood Cl HLER SO31 370 B8
ROMY SO51 263 H7
RWIN SO21 266 B4
Oakwood Ct HEND SO30 320 D6 2
Oakwood Dr ROWN SO16 318 A3
Oakwood Rd
CHCH/BSGR BH23 436 C7
CHFD SO53 265 J8
HISD PO11 425 K5
MOOR/WNTN BH9 432 E6
NEND PO2 399 J4
Oakwood Wy HLER SO31 369 L5 1
Oasthouse Dr FARN GU14 89 H4
Oast House La FNM GU9 135 G3
Oast La ALDT GU11 7 G7
Oates Rd MOOR/WNTN BH9 432 C7
Oatfield Gdns TOTT SO40 316 B7
Oatlands ROMY SO51 262 E8 6
Oatlands Cl BPWT SO32 321 L7
Oatlands Rd BPWT SO32 321 L7
Oban Cl DEAN RG23 102 F6
Oban Rd TWDS BH3 447 K1
O'bee Gdns TADY RG26 41 H7
Obelisk Rd ITCH SO19 344 B6
Obelisk Wy CBLY GU15 70 F2
Oberfield Rd BROC SO42 387 H6
Oberon Cl WVILLE PO7 352 E8
Ober Rd BROC SO42 387 J6
Oberursel Wy ALDT GU11 6 D1 1
Occupation La
FHAM/STUB PO14 395 J1
Ocean Cl FHAM PO15 14 B3
Ocean Rd FHAM/STUB PO14 396 D3
Ocean Wy SHAM SO14 13 J8
Ochil Cl KEMP RG22 104 A5
Ockendon Cl SSEA PO5 21 H4 3
Ocknell Gv FAWY SO45 367 G5
O'connell Rd ELGH SO50 293 K6
O'connor Rd ALDT GU11 113 G1
Octavia Gdns CHFD SO53 293 L1
Octavia Hl WINW SO22 238 C2
Octavian Cl KEMP RG22 127 G1
Octavia Rd WEND SO18 319 K4
Octavius Ct WVILLE PO7 352 F7
Oddfellows Rd NWBY RG14 2 D5
Odell Cl FHAM/PORC PO16 14 E1
Odette Gdns TADY RG26 41 L7
Odiham Cl ROWN SO16 317 L4
Odiham Rd HTWY RG27 46 A7
HTWY RG27 108 F1
RFNM GU10 110 E8
THLE RG7 45 M5
Odstock Rd RSAL SP5 255 K1
Officers Rw TADY RG26 64 A6
Oglander Rd WINC SO23 11 H3
Ogle Rd SHAM SO14 12 F3
O'gorman Av FARN GU14 90 E6
Okeford Rd BDST BH18 429 M6
Okement Cl WEND SO18 320 A6
Okingham Cl SHST GU47 50 A7 3
Olaf Cl AND SP10 119 G4 3
Olave Cl LSOL/BMARY PO13 420 C2 1
Old Acre Rd ALTN GU34 176 D6
Old Agwi Rd FAWY SO45 393 G3
Old Barn Cl OVTN RG25 125 K7 1
RGWD BH24 382 F1
Oldbarn Cl TOTT SO40 316 B6
Old Barn Crs WVILLE PO7 326 B6
Old Barn Farm Rd WIMB BH21 380 E3
Old Barn La RFNM GU10 181 L6
Old Barn Rd CHCH/BSGR BH23 434 B6
Old Bath Rd NWBY RG14 2 B1
Oldberg Gdns KEMP RG22 104 E8 3
Old Bisley Rd FRIM GU16 71 K6
Old Bound Rd UPTN BH16 444 B2
Old Brickfield Rd ALDT GU11 7 G7
Old Brickyard Rd FBDG SP6 309 G6
Old Bridge House Rd
HLER SO31 345 M8
Old Bridge Rd ENEY PO4 21 M8
LTDN BH7 434 B8
Oldbury Cl FRIM GU16 71 J8 1
Oldbury Ct ROWN SO16 317 J6
Oldbury Wy FHAM/STUB PO14 372 A8
Old Canal ENEY PO4 423 M4 4
Old Christchurch Rd BMTH BH1 23 G5
LYMN SO41 439 H7
Old Church La FNM GU9 159 G1
Old Coach Rd NTID SP9 115 G8
Old Coastguard Rd CCLF BH13 457 G4
Old Commercial Rd
PSEA PO1 423 G1 5
Old Common HLER SO31 370 E4
Old Common Gdns HLER SO31 370 F4
Old Common Rd BSTK RG21 105 J4
Old Common Wy RAND SP11 92 E6
Old Compton La FNM GU9 135 H7
Old Copse Rd HAV PO9 16 F2
Oldcorne Hollow HTWY RG27 68 D3
Old Cove Rd FARN GU14 89 G5
Old Cracknore Cl TOTT SO40 342 D6
Old Cross Tree Wy ASHV GU12 113 M8
Old Dean Rd CBLY GU15 71 G1
Old Down RWIN SO21 268 A1
Old Down Cl KEMP RG22 103 M7
Old Down Rd AND SP10 8 E2
Olde Farm Dr BLKW GU17 69 L3
Oldenburg HLER SO31 346 F8
Old English Dr AND SP10 118 E4
Old Farm Cl RGWD BH24 359 G6
Old Farm Dr WEND SO18 319 L6
Old Farm La EMRTH PO10 378 F5
FHAM/STUB PO14 396 A7
Old Farm Pl ASHV GU12 113 J4
Old Farm Rd PLE BH15 445 K2
Old Farm Wk LYMN SO41 440 B5
Old Farm Wy CHAM PO6 400 C1
Old Farnham La FNM GU9 134 F8
RFNM GU10 133 K7
Oldfield Vw HTWY RG27 87 H3 5
Old Forge Rd WIMB BH21 405 K2
Old Frensham Rd RFNM GU10 159 G2
Old Garden Cl
FHAM/STUB PO14 371 G6
Old Gdns WINW SO22 10 F2
Oldgate Gdns NEND PO2 399 K4 6
Old Gosport Rd
FHAM/PORC PO16 15 K8
Old Green La CBLY GU15 70 F1
Old Guildford Rd FRIM GU16 91 L3
Old Ham La WIMB BH21 405 H4
Old Haslemere Rd HASM GU27 228 F3
Old Heath Wy FNM GU9 134 F1 1
Old Hillside Rd WINW SO22 214 B7
The Old Hl RAND SP11 165 L2 1
Oldhouse La HAV PO9 355 H2
ROMY SO51 288 D1
Old Ivy La WEND SO18 320 A6
Old Kempshott La KEMP RG22 103 M5
Old Kennels Cl WINW SO22 237 M5
Old Kennels La RWIN SO21 237 K7
Old Kiln Cl RFNM GU10 181 J6
Old Kiln La RFNM GU10 181 J6
Old Kiln Rd UPTN BH16 444 B1
Old La ALDT GU11 6 E7
ASHV GU12 113 H5
RFNM GU10 180 B4
STHA RG19 40 B7
Old Litten La PSF GU32 247 H5
Old London Rd STOK SO20 186 F5
Old Lyndhurst Rd TOTT SO40 314 E8
Old Magazine Cl TOTT SO40 342 D6
Old Manor Cl WIMB BH21 404 C4
Old Manor Wy CHAM PO6 399 M1
Old Market Rd WIMB BH21 428 C1
Old Micheldever Rd
RAND SP11 143 M3
Old Mill La EPSF GU31 276 A3
HORN PO8 327 G8
Old Mill Pl HASM GU27 228 C1
Old Mill Wy ROWN SO16 317 M7
Old Milton Gn
NMIL/BTOS BH25 437 K7
Old Milton Rd
NMIL/BTOS BH25 437 K7
Old Newtown Rd NWBY RG14 2 D7 1
Old Odiham Rd ALTN GU34 154 C5
Old Orch PLE BH15 445 H7
Old Orchards LYMN SO41 440 D6
The Old Orch FNM GU9 134 C8
ODIM RG29 130 E4
Old Palace Farm STOK SO20 210 F6
Old Park Cl FNM GU9 134 D2
Old Park La FNM GU9 134 C1
Old Park Rd NALR SO24 219 K5
Old Parsonage Ct RWIN SO21 266 B5
Old Pasture Rd FRIM GU16 71 J5
Old Pharmacy Ct CWTH RG45 49 M4 2
Old Pines Cl FERN BH22 406 C4
Old Pond Cl FRIM GU16 70 E7
Old Portsmouth Rd CBLY GU15 71 K4
Old Potbridge Rd HTWY RG27 86 F7
Old Priory Cl HLER SO31 369 L6
Old Priory Rd SBNE BH6 449 L4
The Old Quarry HASM GU27 228 C4
Old Reading Rd BSTK RG21 5 G7
Old Rectory Cl EMRTH PO10 378 F5 2
Old Rectory Dr ASHV GU12 113 L6
Old Rectory Gdns FARN GU14 91 G4 2
WINC SO23 215 J2 1
Old Rectory La RWIN SO21 266 F1
Old Rectory Rd CHAM PO6 376 C8
Old Redbridge Rd WSHM SO15 317 H8
Old Reservoir Rd CHAM PO6 400 B1
Old River WVILLE PO7 351 K5
Old Rd GPORT PO12 19 H5
ROMY SO51 262 F8
SHAM SO14 13 J7
The Old Rd CHAM PO6 399 K2
Old Romsey Rd TOTT SO40 314 D8
The Old Rope Wk PLE BH15 444 E7
Old Salisbury La ROMY SO51 261 K7
Old Salisbury Rd RAND SP11 142 A5
ROMY SO51 315 K1
Old Sawmill Cl VWD BH31 356 C2
Old Sawmill La CWTH RG45 49 M2
The Old Sawmills HUNG RG17 34 B2
Old School Cl ASHV GU12 113 K5
FAWY SO45 391 M2
FERN BH22 406 A3 1
FLET GU13 88 F7 1
HLER SO31 369 H1 1
HTWY RG27 87 J2 4
Old School Dr HISD PO11 425 M6
Old School Gdns HEND SO30 320 D6
Old School La YTLY GU46 68 F2
Old School Rd HTWY RG27 85 K8
LISS GU33 248 E4
Old Shamblehurst La
HEND SO30 321 H6
Old Stacks Gdns RGWD BH24 383 G2 5
Old Star PSEA PO1 20 C1
Old Station Ap WINC SO23 11 K8
Old Station Rd RWIN SO21 216 D1
Old Station Wy BOR GU35 200 F3
Old Stockbridge Rd
RAND SP11 162 A2
STOK SO20 162 F3
Old Stoke Rd RWIN SO21 190 F2
Old St FHAM/STUB PO14 395 M5
Old Timbers HISD PO11 425 K5
Old Tpk FHAM/PORC PO16 15 J2
Old Vicarage La STOK SO20 210 F5
The Old Vineries FBDG SP6 309 J7 1
Old Vyne La TADY RG26 61 J7
Old Wareham Rd
BKME/WDN BH12 445 M1
UPTN BH16 428 E6
The Old Well Cl ITCH SO19 345 G5
Old Welmore YTLY GU46 69 H3
Old Winchester Hill La
BPWT SO32 271 L5
PSF GU32 272 B5
Old Winton Rd AND SP10 9 J7
Old Wokingham Rd CWTH RG45 49 M1
Oldwood Cha FARN GU14 89 L5
Old Worting Rd KEMP RG22 104 B4
Old Wymering La CHAM PO6 375 J8
Oleander Cl CWTH RG45 49 J1
HLER SO31 370 E3
Olive Crs FHAM/PORC PO16 398 B2
Olive Gv RAND SP11 161 K3
Olive Rd ROWN SO16 317 M4
Oliver Ri ALTN GU34 176 E4
Oliver Rd ENEY PO4 423 K5
LYMN SO41 440 A5
WEND SO18 319 J5
Oliver's Battery Crs
WINW SO22 238 A4
Oliver's Battery Gdns
WINW SO22 238 A5
Oliver's Battery Rd North
WINW SO22 238 A3
Oliver's Battery Rd South
WINW SO22 238 A5
Olivers Cl TADY RG26 63 M6
TOTT SO40 340 F1
Oliver's La TADY RG26 63 M6
Olivers Rd WIMB BH21 404 E2
Oliver's Wk CHAM RG24 105 L1
Olivers Wy WIMB BH21 404 E2 2
Olivia Cl WVILLE PO7 352 E7 5
Olympic Wy ELGH SO50 294 F5 1
ELGH SO50 295 G5 2
Omdurman Rd PTSW SO17 318 F6
Omega ALTN GU34 177 G5
Omega St SSEA PO5 21 J2
Omer's Ri THLE RG7 31 K5
Onibury Cl WEND SO18 319 M7
Onibury Rd WEND SO18 319 M7
Onslow Cl CHAM RG24 83 K7
Onslow Gdns WIMB BH21 404 B2
Onslow Rd SHAM SO14 343 L2
SSEA PO5 21 K9
Openfields BOR GU35 202 B2
Ophir Gdns BMTH BH1 23 K2
Ophir Rd CHAR BH8 23 J1
NEND PO2 399 H6
Oracle Dr WVILLE PO7 376 C5
Orange Gv
LSOL/BMARY PO13 397 H7 2
RAND SP11 161 K3
Orange La STOK SO20 162 B6
Orange Rw EMRTH PO10 378 D8 5
Oratory Gdns CCLF BH13 446 E8
Orbit Cl EWKG RG40 48 C2
Orchard Av ELGH SO50 294 E7
PSTN BH14 445 L6
Orchard Cl ASHV GU12 113 K3
CHCH/BSGR BH23 449 M2
EPSF GU31 305 K4
FARN GU14 70 C7
FAWY SO45 392 F5
FBDG SP6 309 L6
FERN BH22 406 C3
FNM GU9 6 F9
GPORT PO12 397 L7
HORN PO8 353 G2
NALR SO24 218 C4
NBAD SO52 291 L3
NWBY RG14 25 M3
RGWD BH24 358 E8
RWIN SO21 190 B4
RWIN SO21 266 F7
THLE RG7 28 F6
TOTT SO40 341 K3
WIMB BH21 429 H1
Orchard Ct HEND SO30 346 C1
VWD BH31 356 E3 2
Orchard End RFNM GU10 158 C5
Orchardene NWBY RG14 3 H2
Orchard Gdns ALDT GU11 7 K6
FBDG SP6 309 L7 4
Orchard Ga SHST GU47 49 L8
Orchard Gv FHAM/PORC PO16 397 L1
HORN PO8 352 D5
NMIL/BTOS BH25 437 L7
Orchard La ALTN GU34 176 F4
EMRTH PO10 378 E8
ROMY SO51 290 D1
SHAM SO14 13 H5
WIMB BH21 429 H1
Orchardlea BPWT SO32 324 A5
Orchard Pl SHAM SO14 13 G7
Orchard Rd AND SP10 8 C3
ELGH SO50 295 H6
ENEY PO4 21 M3
FARN GU14 90 D4
FNM GU9 6 F9
GPORT PO12 422 B2
HAV PO9 16 F6
HISD PO11 425 L6
HLER SO31 370 D6
KEMP RG22 104 B4
RSAL SP5 285 J1
RWIN SO21 190 B4
THLE RG7 43 L3
Orchard St WCLF BH2 22 D6
Orchards Wy HEND SO30 320 C7 5
PTSW SO17 318 F6
The Orchard BWD BH11 431 H2
CHAM PO6 399 K1
HASM GU27 228 C3
LYMN SO41 454 C4
OVTN RG25 100 F8
ROWN SO16 292 D7
TADY RG26 42 A8
WVILLE PO7 351 K4
Orchard Wy ALDT GU11 7 K6
CBLY GU15 70 E
FAWY SO45 367 J
Orcheston Rd CHAR BH8 448 B
Orchid Dr RAND SP11 92 E
Ordnance Rd ALDT GU11 7 H
GPORT PO12 19 J
NTID SP9 114 E
WSHM SO15 343 L
Ordnance Rw PSEA PO1 20 C
Ordnance Wy TOTT SO40 342 E
Oregon Cl ITCH SO19 344 E
Oregon Wk EWKG RG40 48 A1
Orford Cl CHCH/BSGR BH23 434 B
Oriel Dr FHAM/STUB PO14 371 G
Oriel Hl CBLY GU15 71 G
Oriel Rd NEND PO2 399 H
Orient Dr WINW SO22 214 B
Orion Cl FHAM/STUB PO14 396 B6
ROWN SO16 317 L
Orkney Cl CHAM RG24 83 J
ROWN SO16 317 K
Orkney Rd CHAM PO6 375 K
Ormesby Dr CHFD SO53 265 G
Ormond Cl ELGH SO50 295 G
Ormonde Rd CCLF BH13 446 F
Ormsby Rd SSEA PO5 21 H6
Orpen Rd ITCH SO19 345 G5
Orsmond Cl WVILLE PO7 376 D2
Orwell Cl FARN GU14 90 B
ROWN SO16 317 K7
Orwell Crs FHAM/STUB PO14 371 G
Orwell Rd PSF GU32 275 K
Osborn Crs LSOL/BMARY PO13 396 F
Osborne Cl ALTN GU34 176 C
BSTK RG21 4 C
WVILLE PO7 376 E1
Osborne Dr CHFD SO53 293 K
FLET GU13 111 G
Osborne Gdns ELGH SO50 295 J7
Osborne Rd AND SP10 8 F
FARN GU14 90 F
GPORT PO12 19 J
HLER SO31 370 A
LSOL/BMARY PO13 420 C2
MOOR/WNTN BH9 432 C
NMIL/BTOS BH25 437 M
PSF GU32 275 L
PSTN BH14 446 A
SSEA PO5 20 F
TOTT SO40 341 L
WIMB BH21 404 B
Osborne Rd North PTSW SO17 319 H
Osborne Rd South PTSW SO17 319 H
Osborne View Rd
FHAM/STUB PO14 395 L
Osborn Rd FHAM/PORC PO16 15 K
FNM GU9 135 G
Osborn Rd South
FHAM/PORC PO16 15 J
Osborn Wy HTWY RG27 86 A
Osier Cl NEND PO2 399 G
Oslands Dr HLER SO31 370 B
Osler Cl TADY RG26 63 L
Osnaburgh Hl CBLY GU15 70 E
Osprey Cl CHCH/BSGR BH23 450 F
KEMP RG22 103 L
ROWN SO16 318 A
TOTT SO40 342 C
Osprey Dr HISD PO11 425 M
Osprey Gdns
LSOL/BMARY PO13 420 D2
Osprey Quay EMRTH PO10 402 F
Osprey Rd KEMP RG22 103 L
Ossemsley South Dr
NMIL/BTOS BH25 411 J
Osterley Cl HEND SO30 346 C
Osterly Rd ITCH SO19 344 C4
Oswald Cl MOOR/WNTN BH9 432 C
Oswald Rd MOOR/WNTN BH9 432 C
Othello Dr WVILLE PO7 352 E
Otterbourne Crs HAV PO9 377 H
TADY RG26 61 L
Otterbourne Hl CHFD SO53 265 M
Otterbourne Rd RWIN SO21 266 B
Otter Cl CWTH RG45 49 K
ELGH SO50 294 F
UPTN BH16 444 A
VWD BH31 356 E
Otter Rd PLE BH15 445 L
Otters Wk NMIL/BTOS BH25 438 A
Ouse Cl CHFD SO53 264 F
Ouse Ct AND SP10 119 H
Outer Cir ROWN SO16 317 M
Outlands La HEND SO30 347 H
Outram Rd SSEA PO5 21 K
Oval Gdns GPORT PO12 18 A
Oval Rd ROMY SO51 232 E
The Oval LISS GU33 248 E
Overbridge Sq NWBY RG14 3 M
Overbrook FAWY SO45 367 K
Overbrook Wy NBAD SO52 291 K3
Overbury Rd PSTN BH14 446 B
Overcliff Ri ROWN SO16 318 D
Overcombe Cl CFDH BH17 430 C
Overdale Ri FRIM GU16 71 H
Overdale Wk BOR GU35 201 J
Over Links Dr PSTN BH14 446 C
Overlord Cl CBLY GU15 50 F8
Overstand Crs LYMN SO41 454 C
Overton Cl ALDT GU11 7 J
Overton Crs HAV PO9 377 H
Overton Rd RWIN SO21 148 A
Oviat Cl TOTT SO40 340 F
Ovington Av LTDN BH7 449 H
Ovington Gdns LTDN BH7 449 H
Owen Cl LSOL/BMARY PO13 421 G
Owen Rd ELGH SO50 293 L
NWBY RG14 25 L
Owen's Rd WINW SO22 10 E
Owen St ENEY PO4 423 L
Owlsmoor Rd SHST GU47 50 A
Owls Rd BOSC BH5 448 D
VWD BH31 356 E
Owslebury Bottom
RWIN SO21 267 M
Owslebury Gv HAV PO9 377 K
Oxburgh Cl ELGH SO50 293 L
Ox Dro RAND SP11 115 L

RAND SP11 .... 119 M6
RWIN SO21 .... 190 E4
Ox Drove Ri RAND SP11 .... 120 A5
Oxdrove Wy NALR SO24 .... 172 C6
OVTN RG25 .... 173 J2
RWIN SO21 .... 192 D6
Oxenden Ct RFNM GU10 .... 113 H8
Oxenden Rd RFNM GU10 .... 113 H8
Oxford Av SBNE BH6 .... 449 G3
SHAM SO14 .... 13 H1
Oxford Cl FHAM/PORC PO16 .... 14 F3
SHAM SO14 .... 13 H6
Oxford La BPWT SO32 .... 324 E1
BWD BH11 .... 431 H2
Oxford Rd BMTH BH1 .... 23 J4
FARN GU14 .... 90 F7
GPORT PO12 .... 2 D1
NWBY RG14 .... 2 D1
RWIN SO21 .... 168 B5
SHAM SO14 .... 343 L1
SHST GU47 .... 50 B6
SSEA PO5 .... 21 L6
Oxford St NWBY RG14 .... 2 D2
SHAM SO14 .... 13 H6
Oxlease Cl ROMY SO51 .... 262 F7
Oxlease La OVTN RG25 .... 152 D1
Oxleys Cl FHAM/STUB PO14 ...... 371 M8
Oxted Ct ENEY PO4 .... 423 M3 🖫
Oyster Cl KEMP RG22 .... 126 F1
Oyster Ms PSEA PO1 .... 20 C5 🖫
Oyster Quay PO6 .... 398 F2
Oyster St PSEA PO1 .... 20 C5
Ozier Rd WEND SO18 .... 319 M6

P

Pacific Cl SHAM SO14 .... 13 K8
Packenham Rd BSTK RG21 .... 104 E4
Pack La DEAN RG23 .... 103 C5
KEMP RG22 .... 103 M6
Packridge La ROMY SO51 .... 291 J7
Packway FNM GU9 .... 159 H1
Padbury Cl NEND PO2 .... 399 K4 🖫
Paddington Gv BWD BH11 .... 431 H5
Paddington St NEND PO2 .... 399 K7
Paddock Cl CBLY GU15 .... 71 K2
RGWD BH24 .... 381 K4
RWIN SO21 .... 190 D4 🖫
WIMB BH21 .... 405 L2
Paddock Ct HTWY RG27 .... 87 H3 🖫
Paddock End WVILLE PO7 .... 351 K5
Paddock Fld STOK SO20 .... 166 A3
Paddockfields CHAM RG24 ...... 106 A1
Paddock Gdns LYMN SO41 .... 440 B3
Paddock Gv VWD BH31 .... 356 C3
Paddock Rd KEMP RG22 .... 104 C5
NWBY RG14 .... 2 D8
The Paddocks FAWY SO45 .... 392 F5 🖫
The Paddock BROC SO42 .... 387 K7 🖫
CWTH RG45 .... 49 K2
ELGH SO50 .... 294 A2 🖫
FBDG SP6 .... 335 J2
FHAM/STUB PO14 .... 396 A4 🖫
GPORT PO12 .... 18 C5
GSHT GU26 .... 203 K4 🖫
HASM GU27 .... 204 D8
HTWY RG27 .... 87 J1
KSCL RG20 .... 59 H6
BOR GU35 .... 202 B3
NWBY RG14 .... 3 K5
TOTT SO40 .... 316 B6
WINC SO23 .... 215 H2
Paddock Wy HASM GU27 .... 205 K6
LIPH GU30 .... 226 E3
NALR SO24 .... 218 B4
PSF GU32 .... 275 J6
Padfield Cl SBNE BH6 .... 449 K2
Padget Rd RGWD BH24 .... 359 G7 🖫
Padnell Av HORN PO8 .... 352 E6
WVILLE PO7 .... 352 L8
Padnell Rd HORN PO8 .... 352 E5
Padstow Pl FBDG SP6 .... 309 K8
Padwell Rd SHAM SO14 .... 343 L1
Padwick Av CHAM PO6 .... 375 J4
Padwick Cl BSTK RG21 .... 104 F4
Padworth La THLE RG7 .... 30 B5
Padworth Rd THLE RG7 .... 31 H8
Paffard Cl LSOL/BMARY PO13 ... 421 C1
Page Cl FAWY SO45 .... 392 B6
Pages La BROC SO42 .... 416 A2
Paget Cl CBLY GU15 .... 71 L1
WIMB BH21 .... 404 E1
Paget Rd BWD BH11 .... 431 L4
GPORT PO12 .... 18 C8
Paget St SHAM SO14 .... 13 K5
Pagham Cl EMRTH PO10 .... 378 E8
Pagham Gdns HISD PO11 .... 426 D6
Paice La ALTN GU34 .... 196 D4
Paices Hl THLE RG7 .... 41 K4
Paignton Av HSEA PO3 .... 399 L8
Paignton Rd ROWN SO16 .... 317 L8
Painters Pightle HTWY RG27 .... 85 L7
Paisley Rd SBNE BH6 .... 449 H3
Palace Cl STOK SO20 .... 210 K6
Palace Ga ODIM RG29 .... 108 C5
Palace La BROC SO42 .... 390 E7
Pale La HTWY RG27 .... 88 A4
Palestine Rd RAND SP11 .... 161 J2
Palk Rd HAV PO9 .... 16 B4
Pallant Gdns
  FHAM/PORC PO16 .... 373 H6
The Pallant HAV PO9 .... 16 F4
Pallet Cl RWIN SO21 .... 266 A3
Pallot Cl HLER SO31 .... 345 K8
Palmer Cl BSTK RG21 .... 5 G2
Palmer Pl NMIL/BTOS BH25 ..... 437 L4
Palmer Rd PLE BH15 .... 445 H3
Palmers Cl ELGH SO50 .... 295 J6 🖫
Palmer's La THLE RG7 .... 31 K6
Palmer's Rd EMRTH PO10 ...... 378 D7
Palmerston Av
  CHCH/BSGR BH23 .... 450 C2

FHAM/PORC PO16 .... 15 K5
Palmerston Cl FARN GU14 .... 90 A5 🖫
UPTN BH16 .... 444 C1 🖫
Palmerston Dr
  FHAM/STUB PO14 .... 396 E1
  HISD PO11 .... 425 L4
  PSTN BH14 .... 446 C4
  SHAM SO14 .... 13 G2
  SSEA PO5 .... 21 H8
  UPTN BH16 .... 444 B1
Palmerston Rd BMTH BH1 ...... 448 D3
Palmerston St ROMY SO51 ..... 290 D1 🖫
  ROMY SO51 .... 290 E1 🖫
Palmerston Wy GPORT PO12 .... 421 J6
Palm Hall Cl WINC SO23 .... 11 L8
Palm Rd ROWN SO16 .... 317 L5
Palmyra Rd GPORT PO12 .... 421 L1
Pamber Heath Rd TADY RG26 .... 42 A8
Pamber Rd THLE RG7 .... 42 D7
Pamela Av CHAM PO6 .... 374 D8
Pamplyn Cl LYMN SO41 .... 440 A4
Pangbourne Av CHAM PO6 ...... 399 H1
Pangbourne Cl ITCH SO19 ..... 344 E4
Pankridge St RFNM GU10 ...... 133 J1
Pannall Rd GPORT PO12 .... 421 L1
Pannells RFNM GU10 .... 159 G3
Panorama Rd CCLF BH13 .... 457 G4
Pan's Gdns CBLY GU15 .... 71 J4
Pan St PSEA PO1 .... 423 G2
Pansy Rd ROWN SO16 .... 318 F4
Pantheon Cl CHFD SO53 .... 293 L1
Pantile Dr HTWY RG27 .... 86 B7
The Pantiles FBDG SP6 .... 309 J7 🖫
Pantings La KSCL RG20 .... 56 C2
Panton Cl EMRTH PO10 .... 378 C5 🖫
Panwell Rd WEND SO18 .... 344 L1
Papermakers OVTN RG25 .... 124 A1
Paper Mill La ALTN GU34 ..... 176 F4
The Parade PSEA PO1 .... 422 E2
  TADY RG26 .... 41 L7 🖫
Paradise La BPWT SO32 .... 323 K4
  EMRTH PO10 .... 378 F4
  FHAM/PORC PO16 .... 373 J6
  TOTT SO40 .... 340 B2
Paradise St PSEA PO1 .... 21 H1
Paradise Wy THLE RG7 .... 28 F1
Parchment St WINC SO23 .... 11 G7
The Parchment HAV PO9 .... 16 E5
Pardoe Ct HEND SO30 .... 346 A3
Pardown DEAN RG23 .... 126 A1
Parfitts Cl FNM GU9 .... 134 D6
Parham Dr ELGH SO50 .... 293 L4
Parham Rd GPORT PO12 .... 422 A2
  NBNE BH10 .... 432 A6
Parish Cl ASHV GU12 .... 113 L7
  FNM GU9 .... 134 D2
Parish Rd FARN GU14 .... 90 B8
  PLE BH15 .... 445 K5
Park Av CBLY GU15 .... 70 F4
  CHAM RG24 .... 106 A3
  LYMN SO41 .... 440 B4
  NBNE BH10 .... 432 A4
  NTHA RG18 .... 27 G4
  WINC SO23 .... 11 H6
  WVILLE PO7 .... 376 A5
Park Cl BROC SO42 .... 387 L6
  CHCH/BSGR BH23 .... 435 G5
  DEAN RG23 .... 102 F5
  FAWY SO45 .... 367 M4
  GPORT PO12 .... 421 J4
  HASM GU27 .... 205 J7
  BOR GU35 .... 179 F7
  LYMN SO41 .... 454 D1
  RFNM GU10 .... 157 K6
  NMIL/BTOS BH25 .... 438 A3
  TOTT SO40 .... 342 B7
  WINC SO23 .... 11 G2
The Park BPWT SO32 .... 298 F7
  NMIL/BTOS BH25 .... 452 B1
Park Vw HEND SO30 .... 345 M1
  HEND SO30 .... 346 E1
Parkview Cl AND SP10 .... 8 C1
Parkville Rd ROWN SO16 ...... 319 J4
Park Wk SHAM SO14 .... 13 G2
Parkwater Rd RSAL SP5 .... 259 H4
Park Wy FERN BH22 .... 380 C6 🖫
  HAV PO9 .... 16 D4
Parkway CBLY GU15 .... 70 F5
  CWTH RG45 .... 49 K3
  FHAM PO15 .... 371 K1
Parkway Dr CHAM RG24 .... 88 A4 🖫
Parkway Gdns CHFD SO53 ..... 293 H1
The Parkway
  LSOL/BMARY PO13 .... 396 F1
  ROWN SO16 .... 318 F3
Parkwood Cl CHAM RG24 ...... 83 L4 🖫
Parkwood Rd BOSC BH5 .... 448 B1
  WIMB BH21 .... 404 A4
Parley Cl FERN BH22 .... 406 D2
Parley La CHCH/BSGR BH23 .... 406 F8
Parley Rd MOOR/WNTN BH9 ... 432 E4
Parliament Pl WINW SO22 .... 238 B4
Parmiter Dr WIMB BH21 ...... 404 C4
Parmiter Rd WIMB BH21 ...... 404 C4
Parmiter Wy WIMB BH21 ...... 404 C4
Parnell La ROMY SO51 .... 234 F6
Parnell Rd ELGH SO50 .... 293 G6
Parr Rd CHAM PO6 .... 375 H8 🖫
Parr St PSTN BH14 .... 445 M4
Parry Cl CHAM PO6 .... 374 C8
Parry Rd ITCH SO19 .... 345 H4
Parsonage Barn La
  RGWD BH24 .... 358 E8
Parsonage Cl ALTN GU34 ..... 198 D5
  EPSF GU31 .... 276 A3
Parsonage Est EPSF GU31 .... 277 K4
Parsonage Hl RSAL SP5 ...... 230 E4
Parsonage La BPWT SO32 ..... 322 A2
Parsonage Park Dr FBDG SP6 . 309 K6
Parsonage Rd BMTH BH1 .... 23 G6
  SHAM SO14 .... 343 M2
Parsonage Wy FRIM GU16 ...... 71 H7
Parsons Cl FLET GU13 .... 110 E3
  HASM GU27 .... 204 F8
  HSEA PO3 .... 399 K4
  NWBY RG14 .... 2 A5
  WHIT RG2 .... 47 K1
Parsons Fld SHST GU47 .... 49 L8
Parsons Gn HASM GU27 .... 204 F8
Parsons Gn GSHT GU26 .... 203 M4
Part La THLE RG7 .... 45 M5
Partridge Av YTLY GU46 ...... 68 E2
Partridge Cl
  FHAM/PORC PO16 .... 373 J8 🖫
  FRIM GU16 .... 71 J8
  RFNM GU10 .... 111 G8 🖫
  RWIN SO21 .... 167 J1
Partridge Down WINW SO22 ... 238 A5
Partridge Dr PSTN BH14 ...... 446 A4
Partridge Gdns HORN PO8 .... 352 B4

MFD/CHID GU8 .... 205 H1
NALR SO24 .... 220 A5
NBNE BH10 .... 432 D4
NTHA RG18 .... 27 G3
RAND SP11 .... 139 M4
RSAL SP5 .... 206 F8
RWIN SO21 .... 215 J2
RWIN SO21 .... 266 F3
THLE RG7 .... 43 M6
TOTT SO40 .... 342 A6
WIMB BH21 .... 404 A4
Park Pde HAV PO9 .... 377 J4 🖫
Park Pl FLET GU13 .... 110 E3
Park Rd ALDT GU11 .... 7 H7
  BMTH BH1 .... 23 H3
  BPWT SO32 .... 296 F8
  CBLY GU15 .... 70 F5
  CHFD SO53 .... 265 H8
  EMRTH PO10 .... 379 M4
  FARN GU14 .... 91 H7
  FBDG SP6 .... 309 L8
  FNM GU9 .... 135 G4
  WINW SO22 .... 10 E2
  GPORT PO12 .... 18 F7
  HASM GU27 .... 228 F2
  HISD PO11 .... 425 C4
  LYMN SO41 .... 440 B1
  LYMN SO41 .... 454 D4
  NMIL/BTOS BH25 .... 437 K7
  NMIL/BTOS BH25 .... 438 A3
  NTID SP9 .... 114 E2
  PLE BH15 .... 445 L5
  PSEA PO1 .... 20 D2
  PSF GU32 .... 275 L5
  SHST GU47 .... 69 M1
  WSHM SO15 .... 343 G2
  WVILLE PO7 .... 351 K3
Park Rd North HAV PO9 .... 16 D3
Park Rd South HAV PO9 .... 16 E5
Park Rw FNM GU9 .... 134 C5
Parkside CHCH/BSGR BH23 ..... 436 B7
  FNM GU9 .... 134 F2
  HAV PO9 .... 377 G6
  RGWD BH24 .... 382 D2
  TOTT SO40 .... 341 K3
Parkside Av ROWN SO16 ...... 317 J8
Parkside La NALR SO24 ...... 219 M6
Parkside Rd BSTK RG21 ...... 105 H5
  NTHA RG18 .... 27 G3
  PSTN BH14 .... 446 B4
Parkside Gdns WINW SO22 .... 214 B5
Parkstone Av ENEY PO4 .... 21 L9
Parkstone Dr CBLY GU15 ...... 70 F4
Parkstone Hts PSTN BH14 .... 445 L3
Parkstone Rd NALR SO24 ..... 220 C6
  PLE BH15 .... 445 K5
Park St CBLY GU15 .... 70 F2
  GPORT PO12 .... 18 C2
  BOR GU35 .... 201 J5
  NWBY RG14 .... 2 B3
  ROWN SO16 .... 318 A8
  SSEA PO5 .... 20 F4
The Park NMIL/BTOS BH25 .... 452 B1
Paynesdown St STHA RG19 ..... 26 E5
Payne's Hay Rd ROMY SO51 .... 235 G3
Payne's Rd WSHM SO15 .... 342 F2
Peace Cl CHCH/BSGR BH23 .... 409 L8
Peachey Dr STHA RG19 .... 27 J6
Peach Gv RAND SP11 .... 161 K3
Peach Rd ROWN SO16 .... 317 M4
Peach Tree Cl FARN GU14 .... 90 D1
Peacock Cl FHAM/PORC PO16 .. 373 J8
Peacock La PSEA PO1 .... 20 D5
Peacock Pl WINC SO23 .... 11 M7
Peak Cl ROWN SO16 .... 317 L5
Peak Dr FHAM/STUB PO14 ..... 14 A7
Peake New Rd BPWT SO32 .... 271 J4
Peakfield RFNM GU10 .... 180 F1
  WVILLE PO7 .... 351 J4 🖫
Peak La BPWT SO32 .... 296 F3
  FHAM/STUB PO14 .... 14 A8
Peak Rd HORN PO8 .... 327 M3
The Peak HAV PO9 .... 354 A6
Pealsham Gdns FBDG SP6 ..... 309 K6 🖫
Pearce Av PSTN BH14 .... 445 M7
Pearce Ct GPORT PO12 .... 19 H7
Pearl Cl BKME/WDN BH12 .... 447 G4
Pearl Gdns NBNE BH10 .... 432 A4
Pearl Rd NBNE BH10 .... 432 A4
Pearman Dr AND SP10 .... 119 J8
Pearson Av PSTN BH14 .... 446 A3
Pearson Gdns NBNE BH10 .... 432 B2
Peartree CI LYMN SO41 ...... 440 C6 🖫
Pear Tree Av FLET GU13 ...... 88 E6 🖫
Pear Tree Cl ITCH SO19 ..... 344 C4
Pear Tree Cl BPWT SO32 ..... 321 L6 🖫
  CHCH/BSGR BH23 .... 409 L8
  FBDG SP6 .... 333 K2
Peartree Cl
  FHAM/STUB PO14 .... 396 B5 🖫
  ITCH SO19 .... 344 B4 🖫
Pear Tree Cl BOR GU35 ..... 201 L3
Peartree Ct LYMN SO41 ...... 440 C6
Pear Tree Dr RSAL SP5 ...... 287 J8
Pear Tree La RFNM GU10 .... 158 C5
Peartree Rd FAWY SO45 ...... 367 J6
Peartree Rd BOR GU35 ...... 201 L3
  NWBY RG14 .... 25 J3
Peartree Rd FAWY SO45 ...... 367 J6
  ITCH SO19 .... 344 B4
Pear Tree Rd BOR GU35 ..... 201 L3
Pease Cft EPSF GU31 .... 305 C5
Peatmoor Cl FLET GU13 ...... 88 D6
Peat Moor Cl FLET GU13 ..... 88 D6
Pebble Cl HISD PO11 .... 425 M6 🖫
Pebble Cl TOTT SO40 .... 342 D6
Pebble Hl HUNG RG17 .... 34 E1
Pebmarsh Rd CHAM PO6 ...... 375 H8 🖫
Peckham Av NMIL/BTOS BH25 . 437 L6
Pedam Cl ENEY PO4 .... 423 L5 🖫
Peddiars Gv YTLY GU46 .... 69 H2
Pedula Wy ELGH SO50 .... 294 D3
Peel Av FRIM GU16 .... 91 K1
Peel Cl BKME/WDN BH12 ..... 446 B3
  ROMY SO51 .... 263 H7
Peel Ct HTWY RG27 .... 87 H2 🖫
Peel Gdns KSCL RG20 .... 59 H5
Peel Pl SSEA PO5 .... 21 G4
Peel Rd GPORT PO12 .... 19 H2

Peel St SHAM SO14 .... 13 L1
Peewit Hl HLER SO31 .... 345 L5
Peewit Hill Cl HLER SO31 ... 345 L5
Pegasus Av ASHV GU12 .... 113 H5
  LYMN SO41 .... 438 E6
Pegasus Cl HASM GU27 .... 228 A3
  HLER SO31 .... 369 K6 🖫
  ROWN SO16 .... 317 L4
  STHA RG19 .... 26 D4
Pegasus Rd FARN GU14 .... 90 C1 🖫
  FARN GU14 .... 90 E6
Peggotty Pl SHST GU47 .... 50 B6 🖫
Pelham Cl CHAM RG24 .... 106 A3
  CHCH/BSGR BH23 .... 450 C2
  BOR GU35 .... 201 J7
Pelham Pl RFNM GU10 .... 158 D4 🖫
Pelham Rd GPORT PO12 .... 18 E2
  SSEA PO5 .... 21 G6
Pelham Ter EMRTH PO10 ..... 378 E8 🖫
Pelican Cl FHAM PO15 .... 14 A3
Pelican Ct AND SP10 .... 9 J3
Pelican La NWBY RG14 .... 2 E2
Pelican Md RGWD BH24 ...... 383 G2
Pelican Rd FHAM/STUB PO14 .. 396 D3
  TADY RG26 .... 42 B6
Pelton Rd BSTK RG21 .... 4 B6
Pembers Cl ELGH SO50 .... 295 J6
Pemberton Rd LYND SO43 .... 363 L3
Pembrey Cl ROWN SO16 ...... 317 L3
Pembridge Rd FBDG SP6 ..... 309 M5
Pembroke Broadway
  CBLY GU15 .... 70 F3
Pembroke Cl ELGH SO50 ..... 293 L8
  PSEA PO1 .... 20 D6 🖫
  ROMY SO51 .... 290 C1 🖫
  THLE RG7 .... 31 M5
  TOTT SO40 .... 316 F8
Pembroke Crs
  FHAM/STUB PO14 .... 395 L6
Pembroke Rd
  BKME/WDN BH12 .... 446 C1
  DEAN RG23 .... 104 A3 🖫
  WINW SO22 .... 214 B3
  ITCH SO19 .... 344 F4
  NWBY RG14 .... 2 D3
  PSEA PO1 .... 20 E6
  WBNE BH4 .... 447 G6
Pembury Rd
  FHAM/STUB PO14 .... 396 B4
  HAV PO9 .... 17 H6
Pemerton Rd BSTK RG21 .... 5 H4
  WINW SO22 .... 10 B1
Penarth Av CHAM PO6 .... 375 M4
Pen Cl AND SP10 .... 9 M6
Pendennis Cl DEAN RG23 .... 104 A2
Pendennis Rd CHAM PO6 ..... 374 D8
Pendle Cl ROWN SO16 .... 317 L8
Pendle Gn ROMY SO51 .... 232 E7
Pendleton Gdns FAWY SO45 .. 392 C7 🖫
Penelope Gdns HLER SO31 ... 345 K6
Penfold Cft FNM GU9 .... 135 J4
Penfords Paddock
  BPWT SO32 .... 323 J1 🖫
Pengelly Av NBNE BH10 ...... 432 C3
Pengilly Rd FNM GU9 .... 134 E6
Penhale Gdns
  FHAM/STUB PO14 .... 370 F7
Penhale Rd PSEA PO1 .... 21 M1
Penhale Wy TOTT SO40 ...... 341 J3
Penhurst Rd HAV PO9 .... 376 A4
Peninsula Rd WINW SO22 ..... 10 D9
Penistone Cl ITCH SO19 .... 344 F4
Penjar Av WVILLE PO7 .... 376 A4
Penk Rdg CHAM PO6 .... 376 D8
Pennant Hills HAV PO9 ...... 376 F6
Pennant Wy CHCH/BSGR BH23 . 450 E1
Pennard Wy CHFD SO53 ...... 292 F4
Penn Cl NMIL/BTOS BH25 .... 457 J7
Pennefather's Rd ALDT GU11 . 112 C5
Pennels Cl LIPH GU30 .... 250 E6
Pennerly Ct HAV PO9 .... 377 H1
Penner Rd HAV PO9 .... 16 C8
Pennine Gdns FAWY SO45 .... 367 H6
Pennine Rd ROWN SO16 ...... 342 D1
Pennine Wy CHFD SO53 ...... 293 J4
  FARN GU14 .... 90 A1
  KEMP RG22 .... 104 A5
  LSOL/BMARY PO13 .... 420 E4
  VWD BH31 .... 356 D2 🖫
Pennington Cl ELGH SO50 ... 266 C8
  FERN BH22 .... 380 B7
  LYMN SO41 .... 440 A6 🖫
Pennington Crs FERN BH22 .. 380 B7
Pennington Ov LYMN SO41 .. 439 M6
Pennington Rd FERN BH22 .. 380 B7
Pennington Wy FHAM PO15 ... 14 B1
Penn Rd NWBY RG14 .... 25 G3
Penns Pl EPSF GU31 .... 276 C5
Penns Rd PSF GU32 .... 275 K4
Penns Wd FARN GU14 .... 91 G7
Penns Yd FNM GU9 .... 134 E6 🖫
Penn Wy GPORT PO12 .... 421 J5
Pennycress HLER SO31 ...... 370 C5
Penny Hedge
  NMIL/BTOS BH25 .... 437 M8
Penny La EMRTH PO10 .... 378 C4
  STOK SO20 .... 186 F7
Penny Pl WVILLE PO7 .... 376 C5 🖫
Penny's Cl FBDG SP6 .... 309 L5
Penny's Crs FBDG SP6 ...... 309 L5
Penny's Hatch KSCL RG20 .... 59 K6
Pennys La FBDG SP6 .... 309 L6
  RSAL SP5 .... 230 B1
Penny St PSEA PO1 .... 20 C6
Pennywell Gdns
  NMIL/BTOS BH25 .... 438 C4
Penrhyn Cl ASHV GU12 .... 7 G4
  ELGH SO50 .... 293 L3
Penrith Cl VWD BH31 .... 356 C3
Penrith Rd BOSC BH5 .... 448 F4
  BSTK RG21 .... 4 C9
Penrose Cl NEND PO2 .... 399 H6 🖫
  NWBY RG14 .... 25 J3
Penrose Rd FRIM GU16 ...... 71 J8
Penryn Dr BOR GU35 .... 202 F3 🖫
Pensford Cl CWTH RG45 ...... 49 L1
Penshurst Ri FRIM GU16 ...... 71 J8

Penshurst Wy *ELGH* SO50 ...... 293 M2
The Pentagon *FAWY* SO45 ...... 392 E6
Pentere Rd *HORN* PO8 ...... 352 E2
Pentire Av *WSHM* SO15 ...... 318 C6
Pentire Wy *WSHM* SO15 ...... 318 C6
Pentland Cl *FAWY* SO45 ...... 367 H6
KEMP RG22 ...... 104 A5
Pentland Ri *FHAM/PORC* PO16 .. 374 B7
Penton Cl *HAV* PO9 ...... 377 M2
Penton La *RAND* SP11 ...... 117 L2
Penton Rd *WSO21* 266 F1
Pentons Hl *FBDG* SP6 ...... 335 H2
Pentridge Wy *TOTT* SO40 ...... 341 H3
Penwith Dr *HASM* GU27 ...... 228 A4
Penwood Hts *KSCL* RG20 ...... 36 D8
Penwood Rd *KSCL* RG20 ...... 36 F5
Peperham Rd *HASM* GU27 ...... 204 F8
Peper Harow *HORN* PO8 ...... 352 F2
Peppard Rd *WEND* SO18 ...... 344 E1
Peppercorn Wy *HEND* SO30 ...... 321 C5
Pepys Av *ITCH* SO19 ...... 345 H3
Pepys Cl *ENEY* PO4 ...... 423 K5
GPORT PO12 ...... 421 M7
Percival Rd *NEND* PO2 ...... 399 K8
Percy Chandler St *PSEA* PO1 .. 423 H2
Percy Cl *FAWY* SO45 ...... 367 K3
Percy Rd *BOSC* BH5 ...... 448 D5
ENEY PO4 ...... 21 L4
GPORT PO12 ...... 19 G3
ROWN SO16 ...... 317 M8
Peregrine Cl *TOTT* SO40 ...... 341 G2
Peregrine Rd
CHCH/BSGR BH23 ...... 450 F2
The Peregrines
FHAM/PORC PO16 ...... 373 K8
Pergin Crs *CFDH* BH17 ...... 445 G1
Pergin Wy *CFDH* BH17 ...... 445 G1
Perham Crs *RAND* SP11 ...... 92 F6
Perins Cl *NALR* SO24 ...... 218 A4
Periwinkle Cl *BOR* GU35 ...... 201 M3
Pern Dr *HEND* SO30 ...... 346 F1
Peronne Cl *HSEA* PO3 ...... 399 K3
Peronne Rd *HSEA* PO3 ...... 399 K3
Perowne St *ALDT* GU11 ...... 6 C2
Perran Rd *ROWN* SO16 ...... 317 J7
Perring Av *FARN* GU14 ...... 70 B8
Perring Rd *FARN* GU14 ...... 90 D6
Perry Dr *FLET* GU13 ...... 88 C7
Perry Gdns *PLE* BH15 ...... 445 H7
Perryhill Dr *SHST* GU47 ...... 49 J7
Perryvale Rd *NBAD* SO52 ...... 292 E3
Perry Wy *FNM* GU9 ...... 134 C1
BOR GU35 ...... 202 C4
Perrywood Cl *FAWY* SO45 ...... 392 A5
Perrywood Gdns *TOTT* SO40 .. 316 A8
Perseus Pl *WVILLE* PO7 ...... 376 B1
Pershore Cl *HLER* SO31 ...... 370 C5
Pershore Rd *CHAM* RG24 ...... 83 G7
Persian Dr *HLER* SO31 ...... 370 F1
Persley Rd *NBNE* BH10 ...... 432 B4
Perth Cl *CHCH/BSGR* BH23 ...... 434 C7
RAND SP11 ...... 115 J1
Perth Rd *ENEY* PO4 ...... 423 M4
LSOL/BMARY PO13 ...... 397 H5
Pervin Rd *CHAM* PO6 ...... 399 K1
Peststead La *BPWT* SO32 ...... 325 H4
Peter Ashley Rd *CHAM* PO6...... 375 J7
Peterborough Rd *CHAM* PO6 .. 375 J7
Peter Grant Wy *FARN* GU14 .... 406 A3
Peterhouse Cl *SHST* GU47 ...... 50 D1
Peters Cl *HLER* SO31 ...... 370 C5
UPTN BH16 ...... 444 B2
Peterscroft Av *TOTT* SO40 ...... 340 E7
Petersfield Cl *CHAM* RG24 ...... 84 A4
Petersfield La *HORN* PO8 ...... 328 A2
Petersfield Rd *EPSF* GU31 ...... 303 J3
HAV PO9 ...... 16 F1
BOR GU35 ...... 201 H7
LISS GU33 ...... 225 G3
LTDN BH7 ...... 448 F2
NALR SO24 ...... 219 L4
NALR SO24 ...... 242 C4
RWIN SO21 ...... 239 M2
WINC SO23 ...... 11 L9
Petersham Cl *WVILLE* PO7 ...... 352 B7
Petersham Rd *CFDH* BH17...... 429 K8
Peters Rd *HLER* SO31 ...... 370 C5
Petit Rd *MOOR/WNTN* BH9 ...... 432 E5
Petrel Cft *KEMP* RG22 ...... 103 M8
Petrel Wk *LSOL/BMARY* PO13 .. 396 F6
Petrie Rd *LSOL/BMARY* PO13...... 420 D2
Petticoat La *RSAL* SP5 ...... 285 K1
Pettinger Gdns *PTSW* SO17 ...... 319 J8
Petty Cl *ROMY* SO51 ...... 290 F2
Pettycot Crs
LSOL/BMARY PO13 ...... 396 F5
Petty's Brook Rd *CHAM* RG24 .. 83 L4
Petunia Cl *KEMP* RG22 ...... 103 M8
Petworth Cl *FRIM* GU16 ...... 71 J8
KEMP RG22 ...... 127 G2
Petworth Gdns *ELGH* SO50 ...... 293 M3
ROWN SO16 ...... 318 A3
Petworth Rd *HASM* GU27 ...... 229 C3
HSEA PO3 ...... 423 M2
Petwyn Cl *FERN* BH22 ...... 406 E2
Pevensey Cl *ROWN* SO16 ...... 317 J7
Pevensey Wy *FRIM* GU16 ...... 71 K8
Peverell Rd *UPTN* BH16 ...... 444 A4
Peverells Rd *CHFD* SO53 ...... 293 K1
Peverells Wood Cl *CHFD* SO53 .. 293 K1
Peveril Cl *RGWD* BH24 ...... 381 K2
Peveril Rd *ITCH* SO19 ...... 344 C5
Pewsey Pl *WSHM* SO15 ...... 318 C6
Pheaben's Fld *TADY* RG26 ...... 63 K5
NTID SP9 ...... 114 F2
RWIN SO21 ...... 167 J1
Pheasant Copse *FLET* GU13...... 88 C6
Pheby Rd *KEMP* RG22 ...... 104 C6
Phelipps Rd *WIMB* BH21 ...... 429 H1
Pheonix Wy
LSOL/BMARY PO13 ...... 397 G2
Philip Rd *WVILLE* PO7 ...... 376 D3
Philips Crs *BOR* GU35 ...... 202 C3
Phillimore Rd *ROWN* SO16 ...... 319 J4
Phillips Cl *BOR* GU35 ...... 202 C3
RFNM GU10 ...... 113 H8

ROWN SO16 ...... 317 K2
Philpott Dr *TOTT* SO40 ...... 342 D7
Phoenix Cl *HLER* SO31 ...... 345 L7
KSCL RG20 ...... 59 J6
Phoenix Park Ter *BSTK* RG21 ...... 4 E6
Phoenix Sq *NEND* PO2 ...... 399 J4
Phoenix Ter *HTWY* RG27 ...... 87 C4
Phyldon Cl *BKME/WDN* BH12 .... 446 A3
Phyldon Rd *BKME/WDN* BH12 .. 446 A2
Pickard Rd *FERN* BH22 ...... 406 D1
Pickaxe La *ODIM* RG29 ...... 130 E6
Pickering Cl *BDST* BH18 ...... 429 L6
Picket Cl *FBDG* SP6 ...... 309 L6
Picketts Hl *BOR* GU35 ...... 179 M7
Picket Twenty *RAND* SP11 ...... 119 K8
Pickford Rd *BKME/WDN* BH9 .. 432 C7
Pickford St *ALDT* GU11 ...... 7 C2
Pickwick Cl *TOTT* SO40 ...... 340 F1
Picton Cl *CBLY* GU15 ...... 71 M1
Picton Rd *AND* SP10 ...... 142 E3
Pier Head Rd *NEND* PO2 ...... 398 F8
Pierrefondes Av *FARN* GU14 .... 90 D3
Pier Rd *PSEA* PO1 ...... 20 E7
SSEA PO5 ...... 20 E7
Pier St *LSOL/BMARY* PO13 ...... 420 C2
Pigeon Cl *TADY* RG26 ...... 63 M6
Pigeonhouse Fld *RWIN* SO21 .. 168 B4
Pigeon House La *RWIN* SO21 .. 168 A1
Pigeons Farm Rd *STHA* RG19 .. 38 A1
Pig Shoot La *CHCH/BSGR* BH23 .. 433 K4
Pike Cl *ALDT* GU11 ...... 7 K1
Pikes Hl *LYND* SO43 ...... 363 J1
Pike St *NWBY* RG14 ...... 3 H1
Pilands Wood Rd *HLER* SO31 .. 345 K8
Pilchards Av *ELGH* SO50 ...... 295 G5
Pilcot Rd *HTWY* RG27 ...... 110 A2
Pilford Heath Rd *WIMB* BH21 .. 404 E1
Pilgrim Cl *NMIL/BTOS* BH25 .... 438 A4
Pilgrim Pk *RGWD* BH24 ...... 359 C8
Pilgrim Pl *WEND* SO18 ...... 319 K4
Pilgrims Cl *FNM* GU9 ...... 134 D8
NBAD SO52 ...... 292 E3
Pilgrims Ga *WINW* SO22 ...... 10 C5
Pilgrims Vw *ASHV* GU12 ...... 113 M8
Pilgrims Wy *AND* SP10 ...... 9 L2
FHAM/STUB PO14 ...... 395 M7
BOR GU35 ...... 202 B3
Pilley Bailey *LYMN* SO41 ...... 414 B6
Pilley Hl *LYMN* SO41 ...... 414 C7
Pilley St *LYMN* SO41 ...... 414 B6
Pill Hl *RSAL* SP5 ...... 258 F4
Pilning Cl *FHAM/STUB* PO14 .. 372 A8
Pilot Hight Rd *BWD* BH11 ...... 431 L5
Pilsdon Dr *CFDH* BH17 ...... 430 C6
Pimpern Cl *CFDH* BH17 ...... 430 C6
Pimpernel Cl *HLER* SO31 ...... 370 C6
Pimpernel Pl *NTHA* RG18 ...... 27 J4
Pimpernel Wy *CHAM* RG24 ...... 105 L1
Pinchcut *THLE* RG7 ...... 31 K5
Pinchington La *NWBY* RG14 .... 37 K1
Pindar Pl *NWBY* RG14 ...... 26 B3
Pine Av *BKME/WDN* BH12 ...... 446 E1
CBLY GU15 ...... 71 G4
SBNE BH6 ...... 449 H4
Pine Bank *GSHT* GU26 ...... 204 B4
Pinecliffe Av *SBNE* BH6 ...... 449 H4
Pinecliffe Rd *NMIL/BTOS* BH25 .. 452 B1
Pinecliff Rd *CCLF* BH13 ...... 446 F8
Pine Cl *ASHV* GU12 ...... 113 K2
CBLY GU15 ...... 70 B1
FAWY SO45 ...... 367 K6
FERN BH22 ...... 406 A1
WINW SO22 ...... 238 A5
NBAD SO52 ...... 291 L3
NMIL/BTOS BH25 ...... 437 J8
RSAL SP5 ...... 287 J6
RWIN SO21 ...... 190 D4
STOK SO20 ...... 163 G4
TOTT SO40 ...... 341 G5
Pine Crs *CHCH/BSGR* BH23...... 436 C8
CHFD SO53 ...... 265 H8
Pine Dr *BLKW* GU17 ...... 70 B5
CCLF BH13 ...... 446 E5
EWKG RG40 ...... 48 D1
RGWD BH24 ...... 381 K4
THLE RG7 ...... 43 J2
WEND SO18 ...... 345 H1
Pine Dr East *WEND* SO18 ...... 345 J1
Pinefield Rd *WEND* SO18 ...... 319 L6
Pinefields Cl *CWTH* RG45 ...... 49 L3
Pine Gv *FLET* GU13 ...... 111 C3
HAV PO9 ...... 17 H5
RFNM GU10 ...... 159 H2
Pinegrove Rd *ITCH* SO19 ...... 344 D5
Pinehill Ri *SHST* GU47 ...... 49 L8
Pinehill Rd *CWTH* RG45 ...... 49 L4
BOR GU35 ...... 201 K6
Pineholt Cl *RGWD* BH24 ...... 381 L3
Pinehurst *TADY* RG26 ...... 61 L1
Pinehurst Av
CHCH/BSGR BH23 ...... 450 E3
FARN GU14 ...... 90 E3
Pinehurst Cl *HORN* PO8 ...... 353 C6
Pinehurst Rd *FERN* BH22 ...... 380 D7
ROWN SO16 ...... 318 E1
Pinelands Rd *ROWN* SO16 ...... 292 E8
Pine Manor Rd *RGWD* BH24 .. 381 H5
Pine Mount Rd *CBLY* GU15 .... 71 G4
Pine Rdg *NWBY* RG14 ...... 25 M3
Pine Ridge Dr *RFNM* GU10 .. 158 E3
Pine Ridge Rd *THLE* RG7 ...... 31 K6
Pine Rd *ALTN* GU34 ...... 197 H5
BPWT SO32 ...... 297 J3
CHFD SO53 ...... 265 H7
FBDG SP6 ...... 333 K3
MOOR/WNTN BH9 ...... 432 E5
ROMY SO51 ...... 291 H2
Pinesprings Dr *BDST* BH18 .. 429 L6
Pines Rd *FLET* GU13 ...... 88 E6
LIPH GU30 ...... 226 B4
The Pines *AND* SP10 ...... 8 E4
CBLY GU15 ...... 71 J1
FBDG SP6 ...... 310 D6
FHAM/PORC PO16 ...... 373 L7
Pinetops Cl *LYMN* SO41 ...... 439 L5
Pine Tree Cl *WIMB* BH21 ...... 404 B3
Pine Tree Gdns *HORN* PO8...... 352 E2

Pine Tree Gln *WBNE* BH4 ...... 447 H5
Pine Trees Cl *FHAM/STUB* PO14 .. 14 B7
Pine Vale Crs *NBNE* BH10 ...... 432 D5
Pine Vw *BOR* GU35 ...... 202 E2
Pine View Cl *FNM* GU9 ...... 135 K3
HASM GU27 ...... 204 F8
Pine View Cl *HLER* SO31 ...... 345 L7
RSAL SP5 ...... 285 J4
Pine View Cl *UPTN* BH16 ...... 444 B2
Pine View Rd *VWD* BH31 ...... 356 D3
Pine Wk *HLER* SO31 ...... 370 E3
LISS GU33 ...... 248 F2
ROWN SO16 ...... 318 E1
VWD BH31 ...... 356 F3
Pine Wy *ROWN* SO16 ...... 318 E1
Pinewood *LSOL/BMARY* PO13 .. 397 J7
Pinewood Av *CWTH* RG45 ...... 49 M2
HAV PO9 ...... 376 F5
NBNE BH10 ...... 432 B3
Pinewood Cl *CHCH/BSGR* BH23 .. 436 C8
FHAM/STUB PO14 ...... 396 B4
ROMY SO51 ...... 263 H7
SHST GU47 ...... 49 J8
TADY RG26 ...... 41 G7
Pinewood Crs *FARN* GU14 ...... 89 M3
FAWY SO45 ...... 367 M6
Pinewood Dr *FAWY* SO45 ...... 367 M6
KSCL RG20 ...... 37 K6
Pinewood Gdns *BAGS* GU19 .. 51 M5
FERN BH22 ...... 406 B1
Pinewood Hl *FLET* GU13 ...... 88 F6
Pinewood Pk *FARN* GU14 ...... 89 M1
ITCH SO19 ...... 345 K3
Pinewood Rd *CCLF* BH13 ...... 447 G7
CHCH/BSGR BH23 ...... 436 D7
FERN BH22 ...... 406 A1
LYMN SO41 ...... 438 D5
RGWD BH24 ...... 381 H2
Pinkerton Rd *KEMP* RG22 ...... 104 B6
Pinkney La *LYND* SO43 ...... 363 J6
Pink Rd *NEND* PO2 ...... 399 J3
Pinks Hl *FHAM/PORC* PO16 .... 373 H6
Pinks La *TADY* RG26 ...... 41 H7
Pinnell Cl *KEMP* RG22 ...... 126 F2
Pinsley Dr *WHAM* PO17 ...... 374 E2
Pintail Cl *KEMP* RG22 ...... 126 E1
Pinto Cl *FHAM* PO15 ...... 370 F1
Pipers Ash *RGWD* BH24 ...... 359 G8
Pipers Cl *TOTT* SO40 ...... 341 H2
Pipers Cft *FLET* GU13 ...... 110 F4
Pipers Dr *CHCH/BSGR* BH23 .. 450 F1
Pipers La *STHA* RG19 ...... 27 J7
Pipers Md *HORN* PO8 ...... 327 M3
Pipers Patch *FARN* GU14 ...... 90 E4
Pipers Wy *STHA* RG19 ...... 27 K6
Piping Cl *RWIN* SO21 ...... 266 E8
Piping Rd *RWIN* SO21 ...... 266 E8
Pipit Cl *GPORT* PO12 ...... 421 M1
STHA RG19 ...... 26 E5
Pippin Cl *CHCH/BSGR* BH23 .. 434 C6
LYMN SO41 ...... 440 C5
Pipsons Cl *YTLY* GU46 ...... 69 G2
Pirbright Rd *FARN* GU14 ...... 90 F5
Pirelli St *WSHM* SO15 ...... 12 E3
WSHM SO15 ...... 12 E3
Pirrie Cl *WSHM* SO15 ...... 318 C7
Pitcairn Cl *CHAM* RG24 ...... 83 H6
Pitcairn Ms *ENEY* PO4 ...... 423 M6
Pitchponds Rd *HLER* SO31...... 370 A8
Pitcot La *HAV* PO9 ...... 268 A5
Pitcroft La *EPSF* GU31 ...... 303 J3
Pitcroft Rd *NEND* PO2 ...... 399 H7
Pitfield La *THLE* RG7 ...... 43 M4
Pitfold Av *HASM* GU27 ...... 228 A2
Pitfold St *HASM* GU27 ...... 228 B2
Pither Rd *ODIM* RG29 ...... 108 B8
Pithouse La *CHCH/BSGR* BH23 .. 408 B1
Pitman Cl *KEMP* RG22 ...... 104 A6
Pitmore Cl *ELGH* SO50 ...... 266 A8
Pitmore La *LYMN* SO41 ...... 413 H6
Pitmore Rd *ELGH* SO50 ...... 266 A8
Pitreavie Rd *CHAM* PO6 ...... 399 L2
Pittard Rd *BSTK* RG21 ...... 104 E5
Pitter Cl *WINW* SO22 ...... 214 A3
Pitt Hill La *WVILLE* PO7 ...... 326 D7
Pitt La *RFNM* GU10 ...... 180 D2
Pittmore Rd *CHCH/BSGR* BH23 .. 435 C6
Pitt Rd *RSAL* SP5 ...... 206 A8
Pitt Rd *WSHM* SO15 ...... 343 C2
Pitts Deep La *LYMN* SO41 ...... 442 A3
Pitts La *AND* SP10 ...... 9 G8
Pitts Pl *NMIL/BTOS* BH25 ...... 438 B6
Pitt Wy *FARN* GU14 ...... 90 C3
Pit Wk *AMSY* SP4 ...... 160 C1
Pitwines Cl *PLE* BH15 ...... 445 J6
Pitymoor La *WHAM* PO17 ...... 374 F4
Place Crs *WVILLE* PO7 ...... 376 D3
Place House Cl *FHAM* PO15 .. 372 A7
Place La *RWIN* SO21 ...... 238 C8
Plaitford Gv *HAV* PO9 ...... 377 G4
Plantaganet Crs *BWD* BH11 .. 431 H3
Plantation Dr
CHCH/BSGR BH23 ...... 436 E6
TOTT SO40 ...... 342 C7
Plantation Rd *AND* SP10 ...... 8 C6
CFDH BH17 ...... 430 A7
CHCH/BSGR BH23 ...... 407 M4
LISS GU33 ...... 249 G6
ROMY SO51 ...... 288 C3
TADY RG26 ...... 41 H6
The Plantation *BPWT* SO32 .. 322 D6
RSAL SP5 ...... 206 D3
Plantation Wy *BOR* GU35...... 200 F8
Plant Park Rd *RGWD* BH24 .. 382 A5
Plants Cl *ROMY* SO51 ...... 289 G6
Plassey Crs *BWD* BH11 ...... 431 M3
Plassey Rd *NTID* SP9 ...... 114 D1
Platform La *SHAM* SO14 ...... 13 C7
Platoff Rd *LYMN* SO41 ...... 440 C8
Player Ct *FBDG* SP6 ...... 309 L6
Players Crs *TOTT* SO40 ...... 341 J3
Playfair Rd *SSEA* PO5 ...... 21 J4
Playfields Dr
BKME/WDN BH12 ...... 446 D2
Pleasance Wy
NMIL/BTOS BH25 ...... 437 K5

Pleasant Hl *TADY* RG26 ...... 41 L8
Pleasant La *EMRTH* PO10 ...... 403 H7
Pleasant Rd *ENEY* PO4 ...... 423 M4
Plecy Cl *FERN* BH22 ...... 406 B5
Plemont Cl *BKME/WDN* BH12 .. 431 J7
Pless Rd *LYMN* SO41 ...... 453 M3
Plough Gdns *STOK* SO20 ...... 209 G2
Plough La *BPWT* SO32 ...... 325 H6
HTWY RG27 ...... 66 E5
Plough Rd *YTLY* GU46 ...... 69 H1
Plough Wy *WINW* SO22 ...... 238 C4
Plover Cl *AND* SP10 ...... 119 G6
FHAM/STUB PO14 ...... 395 M6
KEMP RG22 ...... 103 M7
ROWN SO16 ...... 318 A3
Plover Dr *LYMN* SO41 ...... 454 E4
Plover Reach *ENEY* PO4 ...... 423 M3
Plover Rd *TOTT* SO40 ...... 341 G1
Plovers Down *WINW* SO22...... 238 A5
Plovers Wy *ALTN* GU34 ...... 176 F2
Plovers Wy *ALTN* GU34 ...... 176 E6
P.L.P.H. Rd *FAWY* SO45 ...... 392 F3
Plumer Rd *CFDH* BH17 ...... 429 L7
LISS GU33 ...... 225 H5
Plumpton Gdns *HSEA* PO3 ...... 399 M5
Plumpton Gv *WVILLE* PO7 ...... 352 F7
Plumpton Rd *NWBY* RG14 ...... 3 J8
Plumpton Wy *ALTN* GU34 ...... 176 E6
Plymouth Dr
FHAM/STUB PO14 ...... 395 M6
Plymouth St *SSEA* PO5 ...... 21 H3
Poachers Fld *ODIM* RG29 ...... 130 F5
Pococks La *LISS* GU33 ...... 247 L1
Poets Wy *WINW* SO22 ...... 10 B6
Poffley Pl *STHA* RG19 ...... 27 K5
Pointout Cl *ROWN* SO16 ...... 318 D5
Pointout Rd *ROWN* SO16 ...... 318 D5
Poland La *ODIM* RG29 ...... 108 D2
Polden Cl *FARN* GU14 ...... 90 B1
Polesden Cl *CHFD* SO53 ...... 265 G8
Poles La *LYMN* SO41 ...... 440 C5
RWIN SO21 ...... 265 G2
Police Station La *BPWT* SO32 .. 299 G7
Polkerris Wy *CFDH* BH17 ...... 111 G4
Pollard Gv *CBLY* GU15 ...... 71 M4
Pollards Moor Rd *TOTT* SO40 .. 314 F7
Polmear Cl *FLET* GU13 ...... 111 G4
The Polygon *WSHM* SO15 ...... 12 E1
Pomona Cl *FERN* BH22 ...... 406 B2
Pompeys La *FERN* BH22 ...... 405 L4
Pond Cl *NMIL/BTOS* BH25 ...... 437 L5
NWBY RG14 ...... 37 C1
OVTN RG25 ...... 123 M2
TOTT SO40 ...... 342 D6
Pond Cft *YTLY* GU46 ...... 69 H2
Pondhead Cl *FAWY* SO45 ...... 392 A5
Pond La *HORN* PO8 ...... 328 A2
RFNM GU10 ...... 180 F4
Pond Piece *WVILLE* PO7 ...... 351 K5
Pond Rd *FARN* GU14 ...... 90 E6
HLER SO31 ...... 370 D2
BOR GU35 ...... 202 D4
TADY RG26 ...... 63 M6
Pondside La *BPWT* SO32 ...... 297 H7
Pondtail Cl *FLET* GU13 ...... 89 H8
Pondtail Gdns *FLET* GU13...... 89 H8
Pondtail Rd *FLET* GU13 ...... 89 H8
Pondview Cl *FLET* GU13 ...... 89 H6
Ponsonby Rd *PSTN* BH14 ...... 446 C4
Pony Dr *UPTN* BH16 ...... 444 C1
Pook La *HAV* PO9 ...... 17 J6
WHAM PO17 ...... 372 F4
Pookles La *ALTN* GU34 ...... 178 A7
Pooksgreen *TOTT* SO40 ...... 342 B6
Poole Hl *WCLF* BH2 ...... 22 B6
Poole La *BWD* BH11 ...... 431 K4
Poole Rd *CCLF* BH13 ...... 446 E4
ITCH SO19 ...... 344 C4
UPTN BH16 ...... 444 B1
WBNE BH4 ...... 447 G5
WCLF BH2 ...... 22 B6
WIMB BH21 ...... 404 A4
Pool Rd *ALDT* GU11 ...... 7 K8
HTWY RG27 ...... 87 H1
Poors Farm Rd *CHAM* RG24...... 84 D8
Popes Hl *KSCL* RG20 ...... 59 H6
Popes La *BPWT* SO32 ...... 296 B4
TOTT SO40 ...... 341 K1
Popes Md *HASM* GU27 ...... 228 F1
Popes Rd *PLE* BH15 ...... 445 J2
Popham Ct *HAV* PO9 ...... 377 G2
Popham La *OVTN* RG25 ...... 125 K8
Poplar Cl *CHCH/BSGR* BH23 .. 410 A8
CHCH/BSGR BH23 ...... 436 F8
FRIM GU16 ...... 91 K5
HTWY RG27 ...... 87 G2
TADY RG26 ...... 41 G8
WIMB BH21 ...... 404 B3
Poplar Crs *RGWD* BH24 ...... 382 F1
Poplar Dr *FHAM/STUB* PO14 .. 14 C8
TOTT SO40 ...... 342 B7
Poplar Gv *HISD* PO11 ...... 425 L4
Poplar La *CHCH/BSGR* BH23 .. 410 A7
Poplar Pl *NWBY* RG14 ...... 25 K3
Poplar Rd *ITCH* SO19 ...... 344 D7
NMIL/BTOS BH25 ...... 438 B4
Poplars Cl *FARN* GU14 ...... 89 M3
The Poplars *BPWT* SO32 ...... 323 J5
Poplar Wk *FNM* GU9 ...... 135 G1
Poplar Wy *HEND* SO30 ...... 346 B1
NBAD SO52 ...... 291 L3
RGWD BH24 ...... 382 F1
Popley Wy *CHAM* RG24 ...... 4 B1
Poppy Cl *CHCH/BSGR* BH23 .. 435 M8
HLER SO31 ...... 370 D6
Poppy Dr *NTHA* RG18 ...... 27 J4
Poppy Flds *CHAM* RG24 ...... 83 M8
Poppyfields *NBAD* SO52 ...... 292 F2
Poppyhills Rd *CBLY* GU15 ...... 51 J8
Poppy Rd *ROWN* SO16 ...... 319 H3
Porchester Cl *AND* SP10 ...... 118 C5
Porchester Rd *ITCH* SO19...... 344 C5
NWBY RG14 ...... 2 E8
Porlock Cl *STHA* RG19 ...... 27 G6
Porlock Rd *ROWN* SO16 ...... 317 H7
Portacre Ri *BSTK* RG21 ...... 104 E5
Portal Cl *RAND* SP11 ...... 142 A1
Portal Rd *ELGH* SO50 ...... 294 C5

...... 344 C1
LSOL/BMARY PO13 ...... 397 C5
TOTT SO40 ...... 341 H1
WINC SO23 ...... 259 G2
Portarlington Cl *WBNE* BH4 .... 22 A7
Portarlington Rd *WBNE* BH4 .. 447 H5
Portchester Ct *BMTH* BH1 ...... 23 K2
Portchester La *WHAM* PO17 .. 374 B6
Portchester Pl *BMTH* BH1 ...... 23 K2
Portchester Ri *ELGH* SO50 ...... 293 M1
Portchester Rd *CHAR* BH8 ...... 23 H1
FHAM/PORC PO16 ...... 373 L6
NEND PO2 ...... 399 J8
Portelet Cl *BKME/WDN* BH12 .. 431 J7
Portelet Pl *HEND* SO30 ...... 346 A3
Porteous Crs *CHFD* SO53 ...... 293 L2
Porter Cl *ODIM* RG29 ...... 108 B8
Porter End *NWBY* RG14 ...... 3 H1
Porter Rd *CFDH* BH17 ...... 445 G1
KEMP RG22 ...... 104 C1
Portersbridge St *ROMY* SO51 .. 290 D1
Porters Cl *AND* SP10 ...... 8 B7
OVTN RG25 ...... 126 C2
Porter's La *SHAM* SO14 ...... 12 F1
WIMB BH21 ...... 405 C2
Portesbery Rd *CBLY* GU15 ...... 71 G2
Portesbery Hill Dr *CBLY* GU15 .. 71 G2
Portesham Gdns
MOOR/WNTN BH9 ...... 432 F4
Portesham Wy *CFDH* BH17 ...... 430 C5
Portfield Cl *CHCH/BSGR* BH23 .. 434 E8
Portfield Rd *CHCH/BSGR* BH23 .. 449 L1
Portiswood Cl *TADY* RG26 ...... 42 A8
Portland Dr *FLET* GU13 ...... 110 C4
GPORT PO12 ...... 421 H8
Portland Gv *AND* SP10 ...... 9 G5
Portland Rd *MOOR/WNTN* BH9 .. 432 C8
SSEA PO5 ...... 21 H7
WVILLE PO7 ...... 376 C4
Portland's Cl *PSF* GU32 ...... 276 A3
Portland Sq *LISS* GU33 ...... 248 G4
Portland St *FHAM/PORC* PO16 .. 15 K6
PSEA PO1 ...... 20 E7
SHAM SO14 ...... 12 F1
Portland Ter *SHAM* SO14 ...... 12 F1
Port La *RWIN* SO21 ...... 265 G2
Portman Crs *SBNE* BH6 ...... 449 L5
Portman Rd *LTDN* BH7 ...... 448 E1
Portmore Cl *BDST* BH18 ...... 430 A2
Portobello Gv
FHAM/PORC PO16 ...... 374 B7
Port Royal St *SSEA* PO5 ...... 21 K2
Portsdown Av *CHAM* PO6 ...... 376 A4
Portsdown Hill Rd *CHAM* PO6 .. 375 K7
WHAM PO17 ...... 373 L4
Portsdown Rd *CHAM* PO6 ...... 374 C1
Portsmouth Rd *BPWT* SO32 .. 296 A4
CBLY GU15 ...... 71 K1
CHAM PO6 ...... 399 K4
ELGH SO50 ...... 295 M2
FRIM GU16 ...... 71 H1
HLER SO31 ...... 345 K1
HORN PO8 ...... 352 F1
ITCH SO19 ...... 344 F1
LIPH GU30 ...... 225 L1
LIPH GU30 ...... 226 E1
LSOL/BMARY PO13 ...... 420 D1
RWIN SO21 ...... 295 L1
Portsview Av
FHAM/PORC PO16 ...... 374 B7
Portsview Gdns
FHAM/PORC PO16 ...... 374 B8
Portswood Av *PTSW* SO17 ...... 319 C8
Portswood Pk *PTSW* SO17 ...... 319 C8
Portswood Rd *HAV* PO9 ...... 377 H1
NEND PO2 ...... 399 J3
PTSW SO17 ...... 319 C2
Portview Rd *WEND* SO18 ...... 319 L6
Port Wy *CHAM* PO6 ...... 374 E4
Portway *TADY* RG26 ...... 41 G7
THLE RG7 ...... 45 M4
Portway Cl *AND* SP10 ...... 8 A3
WEND SO18 ...... 344 F1
Portway Pl *DEAN* RG23 ...... 123 A4
Posbrooke Rd *ENEY* PO4 ...... 423 L4
Postern Cl *FHAM/PORC* PO16 .. 374 B7
Post Green Rd *UPTN* BH16 ...... 428 B7
Post Horn La *HTWY* RG27 ...... 85 K1
Posting House Ms *NWBY* RG14 .. 2 B5
Post Office La *OVTN* RG25 ...... 126 C2
RGWD BH24 ...... 381 L4
TLHT RG30 ...... 31 M4
Post Office Rd *HUNG* RG17 .... 34 B3
WCLF BH2 ...... 22 E4
WVILLE PO7 ...... 376 A3
Potbridge Rd *ODIM* RG29 ...... 86 D3
Pot La *CHAM* RG24 ...... 84 B4
Potley Hill Rd *YTLY* GU46 ...... 69 J2
Potteries La *FRIM* GU16 ...... 91 J2
The Potteries *FARN* GU14 ...... 90 A4
FHAM/PORC PO16 ...... 15 K4
Potterne Wy *WIMB* BH21 ...... 356 C4
Potters Crs *ASHV* GU12 ...... 113 L1
Potters Fld *LISS* GU33 ...... 248 F5
Potters Ga *FNM* GU9 ...... 134 D2
Potters Heron Cl *ROMY* SO51 .. 264 D2
Potters Heron La *ROMY* SO51 .. 264 D2
Potters La *HTWY* RG27 ...... 64 E1
Potters Wy *PSTN* BH14 ...... 446 B6
Pottery Dro *STOK* SO20 ...... 161 M4
Pottery La *HUNG* RG17 ...... 34 B3
RFNM GU10 ...... 158 C2
RCCH PO18 ...... 403 M4
Pottery Rd *PSTN* BH14 ...... 445 M6
Poulner Cl *ITCH* SO19 ...... 344 E3
Poulner Ct *HAV* PO9 ...... 377 C2
Poulner Hl *RGWD* BH24 ...... 359 H4
Poulner Pk *RGWD* BH24 ...... 359 C2
Poultons Cl *OVTN* RG25 ...... 123 M4
Poultons Rd *OVTN* RG25...... 123 M4
Pound Cl *BOR* GU35 ...... 202 C4
LSOL/BMARY PO13 ...... 397 L4
NALR SO24 ...... 173 L1
RGWD BH24 ...... 358 E2
TADY RG26 ...... 63 K7

Pound Cottages *BPWT* SO32...... 299 H3
Pound Ga *ALTN* GU34 ...... 176 F3 🖾
Pound Gate Dr
　FHAM/STUB PO14....... 371 G7
Pound HI *NALR* SO24 .... 218 C2
　ROMY SO51 .... 288 B3
Pound La *BPWT* SO32 .... 299 J3
　FBDG SP6...... 308 A3
　KSCL RG20 .... 57 H2
　NWBY RG14 ...... 25 C4
　PLE BH15 ...... 445 K3
　RGWD BH24 ...... 384 C7
　ROMY SO51 ...... 264 A6
　ROMY SO51 ...... 288 B3
　STHA RG19.... 26 D5
　TOTT SO40 ...... 315 H6
　TOTT SO40 ...... 341 J5
Pound Lea *HISD* PO11...... 425 L3
Pound Meadow *HTWY* RG27 .... 64 D6
Pound Rd *ASHV* GU12......... 7 H3
　CHAM PO6 ...... 374 F6
　HLER SO31 ...... 345 K8
　LYMN SO41 ...... 439 M5
　OVTN RG25 ...... 124 A1
　SELS PO20 ...... 427 K7
　STOK SO20 ...... 162 B6
　WINC SO23 ...... 191 H8
Pound St *NWBY* RG14 .... 2 D6
　WEND SO18 ...... 344 E1
Pound Tree Rd *SHAM* SO14 ...... 13 G3
Poveys Md *KSCL* RG20 ...... 59 K6
Powell Crs *TOTT* SO40...... 341 K4
Powell Rd *PSTN* BH14...... 446 A5
Power Rd *PSEA* PO1 ...... 423 J2 🖾
Powerscourt Rd *NEND* PO2 ...... 399 J8
Powis Cl *NMIL/BTOS* BH25 ...... 452 C1
Powle Rd *RFNM* GU10 ...... 136 D1
Poyner Cl *FARN* GU14 ...... 70 E8
Poynings Crs *BSTK* RG21 ...... 105 H6
Poynings Pl *PSEA* PO1 ...... 20 E5 🖾
Poynters Cl *AND* SP10 ...... 8 F1
Poyntz Rd *OVTN* RG25 ...... 100 F8
Precosa Rd *HEND* SO30 ...... 346 C3
Prelate Wy *FHAM/STUB* PO14.... 371 G6
Prentice Cl *FARN* GU14...... 70 E8 🖾
Preshaw Cl *ROWN* SO16 ...... 318 A4
Preston Cl *UPTN* BH16 ...... 444 B1 🖾
Preston La *CHCH/BSGR* BH23 .... 435 H5
Preston Pl *NWBY* RG14 ...... 26 A3 🖾
Preston Rd *NEND* PO2 ...... 399 K7
　PLE BH15...... 445 H2
Preston Wy *CHCH/BSGR* BH23 .. 436 B8
Prestwick La *HASM* GU27...... 205 K6
Prestwood Cl
　NMIL/BTOS BH25 ...... 437 K7 🖾
Prestwood Rd *HEND* SO30 ...... 346 A2
Pretoria Cl *LISS* GU33 ...... 225 H6
Pretoria Rd *ENEY* PO4 ...... 423 K5
　HEND SO30 ...... 345 M3
　RAND SP11 ...... 93 G7
Pricketts HI *BPWT* SO32 ...... 348 D1
Prideaux-brune Av
　LSOL/BMARY PO13 ...... 397 G4
Priest Croft Dr *FAWY* SO45 ...... 392 C6
Priestfields *FHAM/STUB* PO14 .... 371 G6
Priestlands Cl *TOTT* SO40 ...... 340 E2
Priestlands La *LYMN* SO41 ...... 440 A5
Priestlands Rd *LYMN* SO41 ...... 440 A5
Priest La *CHCH/BSGR* BH23 ...... 434 F1
Priestley Cl *TOTT* SO40 ...... 341 H1 🖾
Priestley Rd *CHAM* RG24 ...... 104 D1
　NBNE BH10 ...... 431 M7
Priestwood Cl *WEND* SO18 ...... 345 H1
Primate Rd *FHAM/STUB* PO14... 371 H6
Primrose Cl *HEND* SO30 ...... 346 A3 🖾
　LSOL/BMARY PO13 ...... 397 G3
　NBAD SO52 ...... 292 E4 🖾
Primrose Gdns *CFDH* BH17...... 429 K7
　FARN GU14 ...... 90 B5 🖾
　KEMP RG22 ...... 127 C3
Primrose La *LISS* GU33 ...... 249 J4
　RSAL SP5 ...... 285 H2
Primrose Rd *RAND* SP11 ...... 92 E6
　ROWN SO16 ...... 318 F4
Primrose Wy
　CHCH/BSGR BH23 ...... 436 A8
　HLER SO31 ...... 370 D6
　ROMY SO51 ...... 263 H7 🖾
　SHST GU47 ...... 49 L7
　WIMB BH21 ...... 429 J1
Primula Rd *BOR* GU35 ...... 201 K5 🖾
Prince Albert Rd *ENEY* PO4...... 423 L5
Prince Alfred St *GPORT* PO12 .... 18 E5
Prince Charles Cl *RAND* SP11 .... 92 E5
Prince Charles Crs *FARN* GU14 .... 70 E8
Prince Dr *SHST* GU47 ...... 49 K7
Prince George's St *HAV* PO9...... 16 F4
Prince George St *PSEA* PO1...... 20 D5 🖾
Prince Hold Rd *STHA* RG19 ...... 26 D5
Prince of Wales Av
　WSHM SO15...... 342 E1
Prince of Wales Cl
　WVILLE PO7 ...... 376 E1 🖾
Prince of Wales Rd
　GPORT PO12 .... 19 H3 🖾
　WBNE BH4 ...... 447 G4
Prince Rd *FHAM/STUB* PO14 ...... 396 D2
　ROWN SO16 ...... 317 K1
Prince's Av *ALDT* GU11 ...... 112 F3
Princes Cl *SHAM* SO14 ...... 344 A2 🖾
Princes Ct *BPWT* SO32 ...... 297 G8 🖾
　BOR GU35 ...... 201 H7
　RSAL SP5 ...... 285 K1
Princes Ct *SHAM* SO14 ...... 344 A2 🖾
Princes' Crs *KEMP* RG22 ...... 104 D5
　LYND SO43 ...... 363 L3
Princes Dr *WVILLE* PO7 ...... 352 E2
Princes HI *RSAL* SP5 ...... 285 K1
Princes Pl *WINW* SO22 ...... 238 D3
　NMIL/BTOS BH25 ...... 438 A4 🖾
Princes Rd *FERN* BH22 ...... 406 B2
　PSF GU32 ...... 275 J4
　ROMY SO51 ...... 262 D8
　WSHM SO15...... 343 H2 🖾
Princess Av *CHCH/BSGR* BH23... 450 A2
Princess Cl *HEND* SO30 ...... 320 D6

Princess Dr *ALTN* GU34 ...... 176 C5
Princess Gdns *HORN* PO8 ...... 352 F1
Princess Mary Gdns *RAND* SP11... 92 E6
Princess Rd *BKME/WDN* BH12.. 446 F1
　TOTT SO40 ...... 340 F6
　WBNE BH4 ...... 447 G4
Prince's St *PSEA* PO1 ...... 423 H1 🖾
　SHAM SO14 ...... 344 A2
Princess Wy *CBLY* GU15 ...... 70 F3
Princes Wy *ALDT* GU11 ...... 6 E1
Pringles Cl *FERN* BH22 ...... 406 C3 🖾
Pringles Dr *FERN* BH22...... 406 C3
Prinstead Cl *WINC* SO23 ...... 239 G2 🖾
Prinsted Crs *CHAM* PO6 ...... 400 B1
Prinsted La *EMRTH* PO10 ...... 403 H1
Prior Croft Cl *CBLY* GU15 ...... 71 K4
Prior End *CBLY* GU15 ...... 71 K3
Prior Rd *CBLY* GU15...... 71 L4
Priors Barton *WINC* SO23 ...... 238 E5
Priors Cl *CHCH/BSGR* BH23 ...... 451 L1
　EMRTH PO10 ...... 379 J7
　FARN GU14 ...... 70 E8
　KSCL RG20 ...... 59 J6 🖾
Priorsdean Av *HSEA* PO3 ...... 423 L2
Priorsdean Crs *HAV* PO9 ...... 377 H4
Priors Dean Rd *WINW* SO22 ...... 214 C4
Priors Keep *FLET* GU13 ...... 89 H8
Prior's La *BLKW* GU17 ...... 69 K3
Priors Leaze La *RCCH* PO18 ...... 379 K7
Priors Rd *CFDH* BH17 ...... 429 K8
　TADY RG26 ...... 41 K7
Priors Wy *WINW* SO22 ...... 238 A5
Priors Wd *CWTH* RG45 ...... 49 G4
Priory Av *PTSW* SO17 ...... 319 J7
Priory Cl *BPWT* SO32 ...... 297 G8
　FLET GU13 ...... 88 C8
　PTSW SO17 ...... 319 J7
Priory Crs *ENEY* PO4...... 423 L4
Priory Gdns *CHAM* RG24 ...... 106 A1
　FHAM/PORC PO16 ...... 374 A8
　WVILLE PO7 ...... 352 C7
Priory La *HTWY* RG27 ...... 87 H4
　RFNM GU10 ...... 159 G8
　WHCH RG28 ...... 122 F1
Priory Pl *NWBY* RG14 ...... 37 L2
Priory Rd *ELGH* SO50 ...... 293 L7
　ENEY PO4 ...... 423 L6
　FERN BH22 ...... 380 E8
　FHAM PO15 ...... 14 A4
　HLER SO31 ...... 368 F2
　NWBY RG14 ...... 2 E8
　PTSW SO17 ...... 319 H8
　WCLF BH2 ...... 22 E7
　WHAM PO17 ...... 374 D2
Priory St *FARN* GU14 ...... 91 G4
The Priory *BPWT* SO32 ...... 323 G1
Priory View Pl
　MOOR/WNTN BH9 ...... 432 E5
Priory View Rd
　CHCH/BSGR BH23 ...... 435 G6
　MOOR/WNTN BH9...... 432 E5
Pritchard Cl *STHA* RG19 ...... 38 A1 🖾
Privet La *RAND* SP11 ...... 116 E4
Privet Rd *BOR* GU35 ...... 201 M3
　MOOR/WNTN BH9 ...... 432 C8
Privett Cl *CHAM* RG24 ...... 83 M8
Privett Pl *GPORT* PO12 ...... 421 J4
Privett Rd *FHAM* PO15 ...... 372 A6
　GPORT PO12 ...... 421 J4
　LSOL/BMARY PO13 ...... 421 G5
　PSF GU32 ...... 246 C6
　WVILLE PO7 ...... 376 B5
Prochurch Rd *HORN* PO8 ...... 352 F4
Proctor Cl *ITCH* SO19 ...... 345 H3
Proctor Dr *NBAD* SO52 ...... 291 L3
Proctor La *PSEA* PO1 ...... 423 K3
Promenade *CCLF* BH13 ...... 447 G8
The Promenade *EMRTH* PO10 .... 402 D1
　FAWY SO45 ...... 367 L3
Propeller Rd *FARN* GU14 ...... 90 E6
Prospect Av *FARN* GU14...... 90 E2
Prospect La *HAV* PO9 ...... 377 M3
Prospect Pl *CHFD* SO53 ...... 293 H2 🖾
　FAWY SO45 ...... 367 L3
　NWBY RG14 ...... 2 E7
Prospect Rd *ASHV* GU12 ...... 113 K3
　FARN GU14 ...... 90 D4
　NALR SO24 ...... 218 A4
　NEND PO2 ...... 423 G1
　RFNM GU10 ...... 158 B5
Provene Cl *BPWT* SO32 ...... 323 K4
Provene Gdns *BPWT* SO32 ...... 323 J4
Providence HI *HLER* SO31 ...... 345 L6
Provident Wy *BSTK* RG21 ...... 4 E7
Provost St *FBDG* SP6 ...... 309 H8
Pruetts La *LISS* GU33 ...... 248 E7
Prunus Cl *FERN* BH22 ...... 405 M1
　ROWN SO16 ...... 318 B3
Prunus Dr *FERN* BH22...... 405 M1
Puckeridge Gate Rd *ALDT* GU11 ... 112 A2
Puckridge Hill Rd *ALDT* GU11 .... 112 B3
Puckshott Wy *HASM* GU27 ...... 205 L8
Pudbrooke Gdns
　HEND SO30 ...... 321 G8 🖾
Pudding La *WINC* SO23 ...... 215 G4
Puddleslosh La *FBDG* SP6 ...... 309 J5
Puddletown Crs *CFDH* BH17 ...... 430 D6
Puffers Wy *NWBY* RG14 ...... 2 A5
Puffin Cl *KEMP* RG22 ...... 126 E2
　ROWN SO16 ...... 318 A3
Puffin Crs *FHAM/STUB* PO14... 395 M4
Puffin Gdns
　LSOL/BMARY PO13 ...... 396 F5 🖾
Puffin Wk *HORN* PO8 ...... 352 B4
Pug's Hole RSAL SP5 ...... 207 M8
Pulens Cr *EPSF* GU31 ...... 276 A4
Pulens La *EPSF* GU31 ...... 276 A4
Pullman Cl *FERN* BH22 ...... 380 B6 🖾
Pullman Wy *RGWD* BH24 ...... 382 E2
Pump La *HORN* PO8 ...... 352 E3
　LSOL/BMARY PO13 ...... 397 G7
Punsholt La *NALR* SO24 ...... 244 D1
Purbeck Av *PLE* BH15 ...... 444 D7
Purbeck Cl *UPTN* BH16 ...... 444 A1 🖾
　VWD BH31 ...... 356 D3 🖾
Purbeck Rd *NMIL/BTOS* BH25 .. 452 C1

WCLF BH2 ...... 22 C6
Purbeck St *PSEA* PO1 ...... 20 E2 🖾
Purbrook Cl *ROWN* SO16 ...... 318 B4 🖾
Purbrook Gdns *WVILLE* PO7 ...... 376 A3
Purbrook Heath Rd
　WVILLE PO7 ...... 375 K3
Purbrook Rd *PSEA* PO1 ...... 21 M2
　TADY RG26 ...... 41 K8
Purbrook Wy *HAV* PO9...... 376 F4
　WVILLE PO7 ...... 376 D4
Purcell Cl *KEMP* RG22 ...... 104 E7
　WVILLE PO7 ...... 376 C3
Purcell Rd *CWTH* RG45 ...... 49 L1
　ITCH SO19 ...... 345 H5
Purchase Rd *BKME/WDN* BH12.. 447 H1
Purewell *CHCH/BSGR* BH23 ...... 450 C1
Purewell Cl *CHCH/BSGR* BH23 .. 450 D1
Purewell Cross Rd
　CHCH/BSGR BH23...... 450 C1
Purkess Cl *CHFD* SO53 ...... 293 G3
Purkiss Ct *TOTT* SO40 ...... 340 A3
Purley Wy *FRIM* GU16...... 71 H8
　ROMY SO51 ...... 288 A5
Purmerend Cl *FARN* GU14 ...... 89 M3 🖾
The Purrocks *PSF* GU32 ...... 275 L3
Purvis Gdns *ITCH* SO19 ...... 344 F5
Pussex La *CHCH/BSGR* BH23 .... 407 L8
Putmans La *EPSF* GU31 ...... 304 C2
Puttenham HI *RGUW* GU3...... 137 M3
Puttenham La *MFD/CHID* GU8 .. 137 M1
Puttenham Rd *CHAM* RG24...... 83 M5
　RFNM GU10 ...... 136 E4
Puttock Cl *HASM* GU27 ...... 228 A3 🖾
Pycroft Cl *HISD* PO11 ...... 402 A5
Pye Cl *WIMB* BH21 ...... 429 J1
Pye La *WIMB* BH21 ...... 332 C1
Pyestock Crs *FARN* GU14 ...... 89 M4 🖾
Pye St *PSEA* PO1 ...... 423 G2
Pyland's La *HLER* SO31 ...... 345 M5
Pyle Cl *HORN* PO8 ...... 352 E4
Pylewell Rd *FAWY* SO45 ...... 367 L4 🖾
Pyotts Copse *CHAM* RG24 ...... 83 M7
Pyotts Ct *CHAM* RG24 ...... 83 M7
Pyotts HI *CHAM* RG24 ...... 83 M7
Pyrford Cl *GPORT* PO12 ...... 421 J5
　WVILLE PO7 ...... 352 B6
Pyrford Ms *LYMN* SO41 ...... 440 C6
Pytchley Cl *FHAM/STUB* PO14... 395 L6

Q

The Quadrangle *ELGH* SO50 ...... 293 M4 🖾
The Quadrant *ASHV* GU12 ...... 113 K4
Quail Wy *HORN* PO8 ...... 352 C2
Quantock Rd *ROWN* SO16 ...... 318 B4
The Quantocks *FAWY* SO45 ...... 367 H6 🖾
　STHA RG19...... 27 G6
Quarely Rd *HAV* PO9 ...... 377 J3
Quarrington Cl *STHA* RG19...... 27 H6
Quarry La *YTLY* GU46 ...... 69 H3
Quarry Rd *WIMB* BH21 ...... 404 E1
　WINC SO23...... 11 J3 🖾
Quarterdeck Av *NEND* PO2 ...... 398 F7
Quarters Rd *FARN* GU14...... 90 F6
Quartremaine Rd *HSEA* PO3 ...... 399 M5
Quavey Rd *RSAL* SP5 ...... 285 K2
Quay Hvn *HLER* SO31 ...... 346 B8
Quay La *GPORT* PO12 ...... 397 M7
Quay Rd *CHCH/BSGR* BH23...... 450 A3
Quayside *WK* SO18 ...... 344 B1
Quayside Wk *TOTT* SO40 ...... 342 D5
Quay St *FHAM/PORC* PO16...... 15 L7 🖾
　LYMN SO41 ...... 440 D4
The Quay *PLE* BH15...... 445 H7
Quebec Gdns *BLKW* GU17 ...... 70 A4 🖾
　HLER SO31 ...... 345 K7 🖾
Queen Anne Dr *WIMB* BH21 ...... 430 C1
Queen Anne's Dr *HAV* PO9...... 377 G6
Queen Anne's Ga *FNM* GU9 ...... 135 G1
Queen Elizabeth Av
　LYMN SO41 ...... 440 B4 🖾
Queen Elizabeth Dr *ALDT* GU11 .... 6 D2
Queen Elizabeth Rd *CBLY* GU15 .. 51 G7
Queen Katherine Rd
　LYMN SO41 ...... 440 D5
Queen Mary Av *BSTK* RG21...... 4 F5
　CBLY GU15 ...... 70 D3
　MOOR/WNTN BH9 ...... 432 C6
Queen Mary Cl *FLET* GU13 ...... 88 E6
Queen Mary Rd
　FHAM/PORC PO16 ...... 398 B1
Queen Rd *FHAM/STUB* PO14 ...... 396 D2
Queen's Av *ALDT* GU11 ...... 112 E3
　AND SP10 ...... 8 F5
　CHCH/BSGR BH23 ...... 450 A3
Queensbury Pl *BLKW* GU17 ...... 69 M5
Queen's Cl *FARN* GU14 ...... 90 E8 🖾
　FAWY SO45 ...... 367 L5
　FERN BH22 ...... 380 B7
　LSOL/BMARY PO13 ...... 420 C2 🖾
　RAND SP11 ...... 92 E6
Queens Crs *FHAM/STUB* PO14... 396 B5
　HORN PO8 ...... 352 F1
　SSEA PO5 ...... 21 H6
Queensfield *OVTN* RG25 ...... 126 C7
Queens Gdns *FBDG* SP6...... 309 L6
　WBNE BH4 ...... 22 A4
Queen's Gate Rd *FARN* GU14 ...... 112 E1
Queens Gv *NMIL/BTOS* BH25 .... 458 A4
　WVILLE PO7 ...... 376 B3
　SSEA PO5 ...... 21 H7
Queensland Rd *LTDN* BH7 ...... 448 E1
Queens La *FNM* GU9 ...... 134 E1
Queens Md *WINW* SO22 ...... 238 B2 🖾
Queen's Pde *EPSF* GU31 ...... 363 K3
Queen's Park Av *CHAR* BH8...... 433 G8
Queen's Park Gdns *CHAR* BH8 .. 448 B1
Queen's Park Rd *CHAR* BH8 ...... 448 C1
Queen's Park South Dr
　CHAR BH8 ...... 448 C1
Queen's Park West Dr
　CHAR BH8 ...... 448 B1
Queen's Pl *SSEA* PO5 ...... 21 H6 🖾
Queens Ride *NBAD* SO52 ...... 291 K4
Queens Ride *CWTH* RG45 ...... 49 K1

Queens Rd *ALDT* GU11 ...... 6 C3
　ALTN GU34 ...... 176 D5
　BSTK RG21 ...... 4 B7
　CBLY GU15 ...... 70 E4
　CHCH/BSGR BH23 ...... 450 D2
　CHFD SO53 ...... 265 J7
　FARN GU14 ...... 91 G8
　FERN BH22 ...... 406 B1
　FHAM/PORC PO16 ...... 15 J6
　FLET GU13 ...... 110 F1
　FNM GU9 ...... 134 F2 🖾
　GPORT PO12 ...... 19 G2
　HLER SO31 ...... 370 A8
　KSCL RG20 ...... 59 K6
　LIPH GU30 ...... 225 M5
　LSOL/BMARY PO13 ...... 420 D4
　NEND PO2 ...... 399 J8
　NWBY RG14 ...... 3 G6
　ODIM RG29 ...... 108 B5 🖾
　PSEA PO1 ...... 422 D7
　PSF GU32 ...... 275 J4
　PSTN BH14 ...... 446 C4
　WBNE BH4 ...... 22 A5
　WHCH RG28 ...... 122 C5
　WIMB BH21 ...... 429 H3
　WSHM SO15...... 318 B6
　WVILLE PO7 ...... 352 C7
Queens St *MIDH* GU29 ...... 279 K6
Queen's Ter *SHAM* SO14 ...... 13 H6
Queenstown Rd
　WSHM SO15...... 343 H2 🖾
Queen St *ASHV* GU12...... 7 M1
　EMRTH PO10 ...... 378 E8
　FBDG SP6...... 285 C7
　PSEA PO1 ...... 20 C1
　RWIN SO21 ...... 266 E3
Queens Vw *HLER* SO31 ...... 368 F2
Queensway *FRIM* GU16 ...... 91 K1
　HISD PO11 ...... 401 L5
　RGWD BH24 ...... 382 F1
Queen's Wy *SHAM* SO14 ...... 13 G6
　SSEA PO5 ...... 21 H6 🖾
The Queensway
　FHAM/PORC PO16 ...... 373 M8
Queenswood Av *CHAR* BH8...... 433 J7
Queenswood Dr *FERN* BH22 ...... 406 B1
Queenwood Ri *STOK* SO20 ...... 209 G2
Queenwood Rd *STOK* SO20 ...... 209 G2
Quennells HI *RFNM* GU10...... 158 B2
Querida Cl *HLER* SO31 ...... 346 B8 🖾
Quilter Cl *ITCH* SO19 ...... 345 H4 🖾
Quilter Rd *KEMP* RG22 ...... 104 B8
Quince La *WIMB* BH21 ...... 404 E2
Quince Tree Wy *HTWY* RG27 .... 86 A7
Quintin Cl *CHCH/BSGR* BH23 .... 436 D8
Quinton Cl *SSEA* PO5 ...... 21 H2
Quintrell Av *FHAM/PORC* PO16.. 373 L8
Quob Farm Cl *HEND* SO30 ...... 320 D5
Quob La *HEND* SO30 ...... 320 D5
The Quomp *RGWD* BH24 ...... 382 E1 🖾

R

Racecourse Vw *LYND* SO43 ...... 363 K2 🖾
Rachel Cl *ELGH* SO50 ...... 295 G6
Rack Cl *AND* SP10 ...... 9 J5
Rack Close La *ALTN* GU34 ...... 176 D5
Rackfield *HASM* GU27 ...... 228 A1
Rackstraw Rd *SHST* GU47 ...... 50 A7
　SHST GU47 ...... 70 A1
Racton Av *NEND* PO2 ...... 399 M1
Racton Rd *EMRTH* PO10 ...... 378 D7
Radar Rd *FARN* GU14 ...... 90 A7
Radcliffe Cl *FRIM* GU16...... 91 J1
Radclyffe Rd *FHAM/PORC* PO16.. 15 M3
Radford Cl *FNM* GU9 ...... 135 J1
Radford Gdns *BSTK* RG21 ...... 104 E6
Radical Ride *EWKG* RG40 ...... 48 C1
Radipole Rd *CFDH* BH17 ...... 430 D6
Radleigh Gdns *TOTT* SO40 ...... 316 A4
Radley Cl *HEND* SO30 ...... 321 H7 🖾
Radnor St *SSEA* PO5 ...... 21 H3
Radstock Rd *ITCH* SO19 ...... 344 C5
Radway Crs *WSHM* SO15 ...... 318 C8
Radway Rd *WSHM* SO15 ...... 318 C8
Raeburn Av *NALR* SO24 ...... 242 C3
Raeburn Dr *HEND* SO30 ...... 346 A1
Raeburn Wy *SHST* GU47 ...... 70 A2
Rae Rd *FARN* GU14 ...... 90 E7
Raf Gate Rd *FARN* GU14 ...... 90 E7 🖾
Ragdale *THLE* RG7 ...... 31 K5
Raghill *THLE* RG7 ...... 42 D7
Raglan Cl *ASHV* GU12 ...... 7 J4
　CHFD SO53 ...... 292 F4
　FRIM GU16 ...... 71 J8
Raglan Gdns *BWD* BH11 ...... 431 L6
Raglan St *SSEA* PO5 ...... 21 J2
Ragmore La *PSF* GU32 ...... 246 D3
Railside *THLE* RG7 ...... 29 J6
Rails La *HISD* PO11 ...... 425 M6
Railway Rd *LISS* GU33 ...... 225 J5
　NWBY RG14 ...... 3 C5
Railway Vw *PSEA* PO1 ...... 21 J1
Rainbow Cl *CHAM* RG24 ...... 106 B3
Rainham Cl *KEMP* RG22 ...... 126 E1
Rakemakers *ALTN* GU34 ...... 177 J1 🖾
Rake Rd *LIPH* GU30 ...... 250 C6
　LISS GU33 ...... 248 F4
Raleigh Cl *CHCH/BSGR* BH23 .... 450 E3
　NMIL/BTOS BH25 ...... 437 K5
　RGWD BH24 ...... 359 G8 🖾
Raleigh Wy *CBLY* GU15 ...... 71 J5
Raley Rd *HLER* SO31 ...... 370 E4
Ralph Rd *WIMB* BH21 ...... 429 J1
Ram Aly *STHA* RG19...... 39 M8
Ramalley La *CHFD* SO53 ...... 293 G1
Rambler Dr *LSOL/BMARY* PO13.. 421 G5
Ramblers Cl *ALDT* GU11 ...... 113 H1
Ramblers Wy *HORN* PO8 ...... 352 F3
Ramillies Cl *ALDT* GU11 ...... 113 H1
Ramley Rd *LYMN* SO41 ...... 439 K8
Rampart Gdns *HSEA* PO3 ...... 399 K3
Rampart Rd *WEND* SO18 ...... 344 B1
The Ramparts *AND* SP10 ...... 8 D7
The Ramparts *LYMN* SO41 ...... 440 B3
Rampton Av *WHCH* RG28 ...... 122 C4

Ramptons La *THLE* RG7 ...... 42 E2
Rampton's Meadow *TADY* RG26.. 62 A1
Ramsay Cl *CBLY* GU15 ...... 51 L3 🖾
Ramsay Pl
　LSOL/BMARY PO13 ...... 397 G6 🖾
Ramsay Rd *WINC* SO23 ...... 215 H1
Ramsdale Av *HAV* PO9 ...... 377 G3
Ramsdean Rd *PSF* GU32 ...... 274 C7
Ramsdell Cl *TADY* RG26 ...... 61 L1
Ramsdell Rd *TADY* RG26 ...... 60 B7
　TADY RG26 ...... 62 A7
Ramsey Rd *HISD* PO11 ...... 425 L5
Ramshill *EPSF* GU31 ...... 275 M4
Ramsholt Cl *OVTN* RG25 ...... 125 K7 🖾
Rances Wy *WINW* SO22 ...... 238 D3
Randall Cl *TOTT* SO40 ...... 316 B6
Randall Rd *CHFD* SO53 ...... 265 J6
Randalls HI *UPTN* BH16 ...... 428 D8
Randalls La *RGWD* BH24 ...... 384 B3
Randolph Dr *FARN* GU14 ...... 89 M5
Randolph Rd *NEND* PO2 ...... 399 J3
Randolph St *WSHM* SO15 ...... 343 G1
Ranelagh Gdns
　WSHM SO15...... 343 J1
Ranelagh Rd
　CHCH/BSGR BH23 ...... 451 L1
　HAV PO9...... 16 B4
　NEND PO2 ...... 399 J7
　WINC SO23 ...... 238 D2
Ranfurly Gdns *FAWY* SO45 ...... 367 G6
Range Gdns *ITCH* SO19 ...... 344 F5
Range Gn *NEND* PO2 ...... 399 G5
Range Ride *CBLY* GU15 ...... 70 C1
Range Rd *EWKG* RG40 ...... 48 E1
　FARN GU14 ...... 89 M7
Range Vw *SHST* GU47 ...... 50 B8
Rankine Cl *FNM* GU9...... 6 F9
Rannoch Cl *FARN* GU14 ...... 14 C2
Ransome Cl *FHAM/STUB* PO14... 395 K1
Ranvilles La *FHAM/STUB* PO14... 395 M1
Rapallo Cl *FARN* GU14 ...... 90 F4 🖾
Raphael Cl *BSTK* RG21 ...... 105 J5
Rapley Cl *CBLY* GU15 ...... 51 J8
Rapson Cl *CHAM* PO6 ...... 375 G7
Rareridge La *BPWT* SO32 ...... 297 K8
Ratcliffe Rd *FARN* GU14 ...... 70 C8
　FAWY SO45 ...... 367 K7 🖾
　HEND SO30 ...... 346 A1
Ratlake La *ROMY* SO51 ...... 264 E4
Rattigan Gdns *HLER* SO31 ...... 347 G8
Ravel Cl *KEMP* RG22 ...... 104 C7
Ravelin Cl *RFNM* GU10 ...... 133 J3 🖾
Raven Cl *LSOL/BMARY* PO13 .... 421 G2
　NTID SO52 ...... 114 C2
　YTLY GU46 ...... 68 E2 🖾
Raven Rd *HTWY* RG27 ...... 85 M7
　SHAM SO14 ...... 343 M2
Ravens Cl *FHAM/STUB* PO14 ...... 396 B5
Ravenscourt Rd *LYMN* SO41 ...... 440 B5
　SBNE BH6 ...... 449 H3
Ravens Cft *HTWY* RG27 ...... 86 B7 🖾
Ravenscroft Cl *ASHV* GU12 ...... 113 M5
　HLER SO31 ...... 345 K7
Ravenscroft Wy *BPWT* SO32 ...... 321 M7
Raven Sq *ALTN* GU34 ...... 176 E2
　ELGH SO50 ...... 293 J6 🖾
Ravens Wy *LYMN* SO41 ...... 454 C4
Ravenswood
　FHAM/STUB PO14 ...... 371 G5 🖾
Ravenswood Av *CWTH* RG45 ...... 49 H3
Ravenswood Dr *CBLY* GU15 ...... 71 K3
Ravensworth Rd *THLE* RG7 ...... 43 H7
Raven Wy *CHCH/BSGR* BH23 .... 450 F3
Ravine Rd *BOSC* BH5...... .
　CCLF BH13 ...... 446 E8
Rawlings Rd *HTWY* RG27 ...... 86 A8
Rawlinson Rd *CBLY* GU15 ...... 70 C2
Rayleigh Rd *BSTK* RG21 ...... 4 D8
Raymond Cl *FAWY* SO45 ...... 392 B5
　HEND SO30 ...... 320 D5
　VWD BH31 ...... 356 F2
Raymond Rd *CHAM* PO6 ...... 374 C7
　WSHM SO15...... 343 H1
Rayners Gdns *ROWN* SO16 ...... 319 J4 🖾
Raynes Rd *LSOL/BMARY* PO13 .. 420 D4
Readon Cl *EPSF* GU31 ...... 275 M4
Reading Rd *BLKW* GU17 ...... 69 L4
　CHAM RG24 ...... 5 J1
　CHAM RG24 ...... 83 K6
　EWKG RG40 ...... 47 J4
　FARN GU14 ...... 90 F7
　HTWY RG27 ...... 48 A8
　HTWY RG27 ...... 64 C8
　HTWY RG27 ...... 66 B8
　HTWY RG27 ...... 68 C1
　HTWY RG27 ...... 85 M6 🖾
　HTWY RG27 ...... 86 A6
　THLE RG7 ...... 31 J3
　THLE RG7 ...... 31 M4
　TLHT RG30 ...... 31 M4
　YTLY GU46 ...... 68 C1
Reading Rd North *FLET* GU13 ...... 88 D7
Reading Rd South *FLET* GU13 .... 110 F1
Reading Room La *BPWT* SO32 ... 322 C8
Read's Fld *ALTN* GU34 ...... 197 G6
Rebbeck Rd *LTDN* BH7 ...... 448 F3
Rebecca Cl *FLET* GU13 ...... 110 D5
The Recess *ELGH* SO50 ...... 294 A3
Record Rd *EMRTH* PO10 ...... 378 C7
Recreation Cl *FARN* GU14 ...... 70 C7 🖾
Recreation Rd *AND* SP10 ...... 9 K4
　BKME/WDN BH12 ...... 446 D2
　RFNM GU10 ...... 158 B5
　ODIM RG29 ...... 108 B6
　RAND SP11 ...... 92 E6
　THLE RG7 ...... 31 K6
Rectory Av *CHAM* PO6 ...... 374 D7
Rectory Cl *FHAM/STUB* PO14 .... 396 A5
　GPORT PO12 ...... 18 D7
　NWBY RG14 ...... 2 D6
　SHST GU47 ...... 49 J8 🖾
　TADY RG26 ...... 61 M2
Rectory Ct *HEND* SO30 ...... 346 D1
Rectory HI *RSAL* SP5 ...... 207 M7
Rectory La *RSAL* SP5 ...... 231 J5
Rectory La *BPWT* SO32 ...... 299 H3
　FBDG SP6 ...... 284 A7
　LIPH GU30 ...... 227 G1

RFNM GU10 157 G4
RWIN SO21 192 F8
STOK SO20 209 G2
TADY RG26 59 M8
Rectory Pl RAND SP11 117 J6
Rectory Rd DEAN RG23 102 D7
FARN GU14 90 F4
HAV PO9 16 E6
HTWY RG27 85 M8
PLE BH15 445 H2
THLE RG7 42 C1
Reculver Wy AND SP10 118 C5
Redan Cl CHCH/BSGR BH23 451 L1
Redan Gdns ASHV GU12 7 J2
Redan Rd ASHV GU12 7 J2
The Redan GPORT PO12 19 H9
Red Barn Av
FHAM/PORC PO16 374 A7
Red Barn La FHAM PO15 372 C4
Redbreast Rd
MOOR/WNTN BH9 432 E5
Redbridge Cswy WSHM SO15 317 G8
Redbridge Dr AND SP10 8 E8
Redbridge Gv HAV PO9 377 H5
Redbridge Hl ROWN SO16 317 L7
Redbridge La ALTN GU34 220 F2
CHAM RG24 5 M8
ROWN SO16 317 G6
Redbridge Rd WSHM SO15 317 J8
Redcar Av HSEA PO3 399 L7
Redcliffe Cl CHCH/BSGR BH23 435 G6
Redcote Cl WEND SO18 344 F1 1
Redcrest Gdns CBLY GU15 71 J3
Redcroft La HLER SO31 345 L7
Redenham Dro RAND SP11 93 M8
Redfield Ct NWBY RG14 3 M2
Redfields La RFNM GU10 110 D7
The Redfords TOTT SO40 316 D7
Redgauntlet EWKG RG40 48 B2 3
Redhearne Flds RFNM GU10 181 H6
Red Hl ALTN GU34 197 G3
HTWY RG27 66 D7
KSCL RG20 75 M2
RAND SP11 75 H6
Redhill ROWN SO16 318 D4
Redhill Av NBNE BH10 432 C6
Redhill Cl NBNE BH10 432 C6
ROWN SO16 318 D4
Redhill Crs MOOR/WNTN BH9 432 D5
Red Hill Crs ROWN SO16 318 D4
Redhill Dr NBNE BH10 432 C6
Redhill Rd HAV PO9 353 M7
Red Hill Wy ROWN SO16 318 D5
Redhoave Rd CFDH BH17 430 B6
Redhorn Cl UPTN BH16 444 B4 1
Red House Ct EPSF GU31 277 L4
Redhouse Park Gdns
LSOL/BMARY PO13 421 J1
Redlands BKME/WDN BH12 446 E3
Redlands Dr ITCH SO19 344 D2
Redlands Gv ENEY PO4 424 A4
Redlands La EMRTH PO10 378 D4
FHAM/STUB PO14 14 F6
RFNM GU10 133 J1
Red La BOR GU35 202 E1
OVTN RG25 152 B4
RSAL SP5 231 M1
THLE RG7 42 A3
Red Leaves BPWT SO32 323 K6
Red Lion La BSTK RG21 4 F9
FNM GU9 134 E7
OVTN RG25 100 F8
Red Ldg CHFD SO53 293 G5
Redlynch Cl HAV PO9 377 M4 1
Redmans Vw VWD BH31 356 B2
Redmayne CBLY GU15 71 M4 2
Redmoor Cl ITCH SO19 344 C2
Red Oaks Cl FERN BH22 405 M1
Red Oaks Dr FHAM PO15 370 F3
Redon Wy AND SP10 8 E2
Red Post La RAND SP11 117 K8
Red Rice Rd RAND SP11 142 B7
Redrise Cl FAWY SO45 391 M5
Redshank Cl CFDH BH17 429 K7
Redshank Rd HORN PO8 352 E1
Redvers Buller Rd ALDT GU11 112 F1
Redvers Rd CHCH/BSGR BH23 450 D1
Redward Rd ROWN SO16 317 L3
Redwing Cl KEMP RG22 126 F1
Redwing Ct ENEY PO4 424 A3 3
Redwing Gdns TOTT SO40 316 B8 7
Redwing Rd HORN PO8 328 B3
Redwood Cl FAWY SO45 367 H5
HEND SO30 320 B6
LYMN SO41 440 A3
RGWD BH24 382 F1
Redwood Dr FERN BH22 380 A8
FHAM/PORC PO16 373 M8
Redwood Gdns TOTT SO40 341 G1
Redwood Gv HAV PO9 377 L4
Redwood La ALTN GU34 174 F8
Redwood Rd UPTN BH16 428 E8
Redwoods Wy FLET GU13 111 G4
Redwood Wy ROWN SO16 318 F2
Reed Cl ALDT GU11 113 G2
Reed Dr TOTT SO40 342 D6
Reedmace Cl WVILLE PO7 376 E2 3
Reeds La LISS GU33 249 J2
Reed's Pl GPORT PO12 18 D1
Reeds Rd GPORT PO12 421 M1
The Reeds Rd RFNM GU10 159 G7
Rees Rd RWIN SO21 190 B6
Reeves Cl ROMY SO51 288 D5
Reeves Rd ASHV GU12 7 J3
Reeves Wy HLER SO31 345 K7 3
Regal Cl CHAM PO6 375 K8
Regency Gdns WVILLE PO7 376 B2 1
Regency Pl FHAM PO15 14 C5
Regent Cl FLET GU13 88 F8
RWIN SO21 266 B4
Regent Dr LTDN BH7 433 K8
Regent Pl SSEA PO5 20 F6 2
Regent Rd CHFD SO53 293 J2
Regents Ct HAV PO9 16 E7
Regents Ga HLER SO31 370 C3
Regent's Gv WSHM SO15 318 A8 2
Regent's Park Gdns
WSHM SO15 342 F1 2
Regent's Park Rd WSHM SO15 342 E1
Regents Pl SHST GU47 49 M8
Regent St FLET GU13 88 F8
PSEA PO1 423 G1
SHAM SO14 12 F3
Regent Wy FRIM GU16 71 J7
Regiment Cl FARN GU14 89 M5 4
Reginald Rd ENEY PO4 423 L5
Regnum Dr NWBY RG14 25 L3
Reid St CHCH/BSGR BH23 449 M1
Reith Wy AND SP10 118 A7
Relay Rd WVILLE PO7 352 B8
Reliant Cl CHFD SO53 293 G4 1
Rembrandt Cl BSTK RG21 105 J5
Rememberance Gdns
CHAM RG24 83 L6 2
Remembrance Rd NWBY RG14 2 A6
Rempstone Rd WIMB BH21 404 B7
Renault Dr BDST BH18 429 L7
Renda Rd FAWY SO45 392 A4
Renny Rd PSEA PO1 21 M2
Renoir Cl BSTK RG21 105 J5
Renouf Cl LYMN SO41 440 A5
Renown Cl CHFD SO53 293 G3
Renown Gdns HORN PO8 352 D3
Renown Wy CHAM RG24 83 L4 3
Repton Cl GPORT PO12 421 J4
Repton Gdns HEND SO30 321 J6
Reservoir La HEND SO30 345 L2
PSF GU32 275 L3
Reservoir Rd FARN GU14 90 A7
Rest-a-wyle Av HISD PO11 425 L3
Restormel Cl DEAN RG23 104 A2
Retreat Rd WIMB BH21 404 B4
The Retreat ELGH SO50 294 A4
SSEA PO5 21 H6
TOTT SO40 341 K3
Reuben Dr PLE BH15 444 C6
Reuben's Crs TADY RG26 61 L1
Revelstoke Av FARN GU14 90 E2
Revenge Cl ENEY PO4 424 A2 2
Rewlands Dr WINW SO22 214 B4
Reynards Cl TADY RG26 41 L8
Reynolds Cl BSTK RG21 105 J4
Reynolds Dl TOTT SO40 341 H3
Reynolds Gn SHST GU47 70 A2 2
Reynolds Rd ELGH SO50 295 J7
WSHM SO15 318 B8
Reyntiens Vw ODIM RG29 108 D5 2
Rhine Banks FARN GU14 90 A3
Rhinefield Cl BROC SO42 387 J6
ELGH SO50 294 E6 2
HAV PO9 377 G4 3
Rhinefield Ornamental Dr
BROC SO42 386 D3
Rhinefield Rd
NMIL/BTOS BH25 411 J6
Rhiners Cl LYMN SO41 412 F5
Rhododendron Rd FRIM GU16 71 L8
Rhyme Hall Ms FAWY SO45 392 F5 3
Ribble Cl BDST BH18 429 L6
CHFD SO53 293 J3
Ribble Ct ROWN SO16 317 K7
Ribble Pl FARN GU14 90 B2
Ribble Wy BSTK RG21 5 J8
Ricardo Crs CHCH/BSGR BH23 450 F2
Rice Gdns UPTN BH16 444 C4
Richard Cl FLET GU13 110 D1
UPTN BH16 444 A1 1
Richard Gv GPORT PO12 397 L7
Richards Cl ASHV GU12 113 K3 1
HLER SO31 370 F5
Richborough Dr AND SP10 118 B5
Richlans Rd HEND SO30 346 A2
Richmond Cl CHFD SO53 265 G7
FARN GU14 90 A5
FLET GU13 110 E2
FRIM GU16 71 J7
HISD PO11 425 J4
BOR GU35 201 J7 3
TOTT SO40 316 A7
Richmond Dr HISD PO11 425 H4
Richmond Gdns PTSW SO17 319 G7
WCLF BH2 22 E5
Richmond Hl WCLF BH2 22 E5
Richmond Hill Dr WCLF BH2 22 E5
Richmond Hill Rbt WCLF BH2 22 E4
Richmond La ROMY SO51 262 F7
Richmond Pk RWIN SO21 266 C4
Richmond Park Av CHAR BH8 448 A1
Richmond Park Crs CHAR BH8 448 B1
Richmond Park Rd CHAR BH8 448 B1
Richmond Pl PSEA PO1 20 E2
SSEA PO5 21 H7 1
Richmond Ri
FHAM/PORC PO16 374 A7
Richmond Rd BSTK RG21 4 D5
GPORT PO12 18 C4
LSOL/BMARY PO13 420 B2
PSTN BH14 446 B4
SHST GU47 50 B8
WSHM SO15 343 G2
Richmond St SHAM SO14 13 H5
Richmond Wood Rd
CHAR BH8 448 A1
Richville Rd ROWN SO16 317 M8
Ridding Cl WSHM SO15 318 A8
Riddings La STHA RG19 39 M6
Riders La HAV PO9 377 J4
Rideway Cl CBLY GU15 70 E4
Ridge Cl HORN PO8 328 B4
KEMP RG22 127 H3
Ridge Common La PSF GU32 275 H2
Ridgefield Gdns
CHCH/BSGR BH23 436 B8
Ridge La HEND SO30 347 H5
HTWY RG27 85 K6
ROMY SO51 290 A7
Ridge Moor Cl GSHT GU26 204 B3
Ridgemount Av ROWN SO16 318 E3
Ridgemount Gdns PLE BH15 444 D5 3
Ridges Cl RAND SP11 96 C8 1
The Ridge RSAL SP5 285 J4
Ridge Top La PSF GU32 274 F1
Ridgeway BDST BH18 429 M4
FERN BH22 406 C8
WINW SO22 238 B3
Ridgeway Cl CHAM PO6 374 D7 1
CHFD SO53 293 K3
ELGH SO50 295 H5 1
Ridgeway Hill Rd FNM GU9 134 F8
Ridgeway La LYMN SO41 440 B6
Ridgeway Rd FNM GU9 158 F1
The Ridgeway ALTN GU34 176 E6
FHAM/PORC PO16 373 J7
Ridgewood Cl FAWY SO45 367 G5 1
Ridgway HAV PO9 16 A5
The Ridings BPWT SO32 323 K4
ELGH SO50 294 F6
FRIM GU16 71 L5
LISS GU33 249 G4
NEND PO2 399 K5
Ridley Cl FAWY SO45 392 A4 3
FLET GU13 110 E1
Ridley Rd MOOR/WNTN BH9 432 D8
Ridleys Piece ODIM RG29 130 F4
Ridout Cl NBNE BH10 431 M7
Rifle Wy FARN GU14 89 M5 3
Rigby Rd SHAM SO14 319 G8
Riggs Gdns BWD BH11 431 K6
Rigler Rd PLE BH15 444 F7
Riley La CHAM RG24 106 A1
Riley Rd RWIN SO21 190 D6
Rimbault Cl ALDT GU11 113 G1 2
Rimbury Wy CHCH/BSGR BH23 434 E8
Rimes's La TADY RG26 61 J2
Rimington Rd HORN PO8 352 D5
Ringbury LYMN SO41 440 B2
Ringlet Wy WINC SO23 11 M7
Ringsgreen La PSF GU32 246 F5
Ringshall Gdns TADY RG26 63 K5
The Ring ROWN SO16 318 D1
Ringway East CHAM RG24 5 K3
Ringway North CHAM RG24 104 D1
Ringway South BSTK RG21 105 H5
Ringway West DEAN RG23 104 D1
KEMP RG22 104 D4
Ringwood Dr NBAD SO52 291 K3
Ringwood Rd
BKME/WDN BH12 431 H6
BLKW GU17 69 M2 1
BWD BH11 431 L2
CHCH/BSGR BH23 408 E8
CHCH/BSGR BH23 436 A2
ENEY PO4 423 M5
FARN GU14 90 F1
FBDG SP6 309 M8
FBDG SP6 333 K3
FERN BH22 380 F8
PSTN BH14 445 L2
RGWD BH24 381 K4
RGWD BH24 384 B3
TOTT SO40 340 E1
VWD BH31 356 D1
WIMB BH21 356 C8
WIMB BH21 380 F2
Ripley Gv HSEA PO3 399 L8
Ripon Gdns WVILLE PO7 352 F7
Ripon Rd BLKW GU17 69 J7
MOOR/WNTN BH9 432 E8
Ripplesmore Cl SHST GU47 49 L8
Ripplewood TOTT SO40 342 E7 2
Ripstone Gdns PTSW SO17 319 G5
The Rise BROC SO42 387 K7
CWTH RG45 49 J3
EWKG RG40 47 K6
WVILLE PO7 376 B6
Ritchie Ct ITCH SO19 344 F4
Ritchie Pl FERN BH22 380 B4 1
Ritchie Rd BWD BH11 431 M4
Rival Moor Rd EPSF GU31 276 A6
Rivar Rd MARL SN8 32 B6
River Cl ALTN GU34 197 G6
WIMB BH21 404 A2
Riverdale RFNM GU10 158 B1
Riverdale Av WVILLE PO7 376 E1
Riverdale Cl FBDG SP6 309 L6
Riverdale La CHCH/BSGR BH23 449 M2
Riverdene Pl WEND SO18 319 J8 2
River Gdns LYMN SO41 454 D4
River Gn HLER SO31 369 L6
Riverhead NALR SO24 219 H4
Riverhead Cl ENEY PO4 423 M3
River La FHAM PO15 372 A2
FNM GU9 158 B1
Riverlea Rd CHCH/BSGR BH23 449 M2
Rivermead Cl ROMY SO51 290 C1
Rivermead Gdns
CHCH/BSGR BH23 434 C6
Rivermead Rd CBLY GU15 70 E6
Rivermede BOR GU35 201 K4
River Pde AND SP10 9 L1 1
River Pk NWBY RG14 3 H3
River Rd YTLY GU46 68 E1
Rivers Cl FARN GU14 91 H7
Riversdale Cl ITCH SO19 344 C8 2
Riversdale Rd SBNE BH6 449 M4
Riverside ELGH SO50 294 C5
RGWD BH24 382 D2
Riverside Av
FHAM/PORC PO16 373 H5
LTDN BH7 434 A7
Riverside Cl CHAM RG24 106 A1
FARN GU14 90 C3
LISS GU33 248 E4
OVTN RG25 101 G8
TOTT SO40 340 A2
Riverside Gdns ROMY SO51 290 D2
Riverside Gn STOK SO20 210 F5
Riverside La SBNE BH6 449 L3
Riverside Rd FERN BH22 380 B6
Riverside Wy CBLY GU15 70 D5
River's St SSEA PO5 21 J3
River St EMRTH PO10 378 F4
Riverview TOTT SO40 341 K3
River View Cl STOK SO20 165 L4
River View Rd WEND SO18 319 J6
River Wk WEND SO18 319 K5
River Wy AND SP10 9 K1
CHCH/BSGR BH23 434 B6
HAV PO9 17 G1
R L Stevenson Av WBNE BH4 447 G5
Roads Hl HORN PO8 327 L7
Road Vw NEND PO2 399 G8
Robert Cecil Av WEND SO18 319 K4
Robert Mays Rd ODIM RG29 108 B6 3
Roberts Cl LYMN SO41 439 J7
WHAM PO17 348 E4
WINC SO23 191 G7
Robertsfield STHA RG19 26 C5
Roberts La CFDH BH17 444 F1
Robertson Cl NWBY RG14 25 L8 2
Robertson Rd NALR SO24 218 B4 2
Robertson Wy ASHV GU12 113 J7
Roberts Rd ASHV GU12 7 L3
CBLY GU15 70 D2
CFDH BH17 429 M7
FAWY SO45 367 K4
GPORT PO12 421 K2 3
LISS GU33 225 H6
LTDN BH7 448 F2
RAND SP11 92 D7
RWIN SO21 145 J8
TOTT SO40 341 K3
WSHM SO15 12 B1
Robert Wy FRIM GU16 91 J5
Robert Whitworth Dr
ROMY SO51 262 E7
Robina Cl WVILLE PO7 376 E1
Robin Cl ALTN GU34 176 F2
ASHV GU12 113 J2
KEMP RG22 103 M8
THLE RG7 31 L5 3
Robin Crs NMIL/BTOS BH25 437 H3
Robin Gdns HORN PO8 352 B4
TOTT SO40 316 B8
Robin Gv NMIL/BTOS BH25 437 K6
Robin Hill Dr CBLY GU15 71 K5
Robin Hood Cl FARN GU14 90 D1
Robinia Gn ROWN SO16 318 B3
Robin La SHST GU47 49 M8
Robins Cl FHAM/STUB PO14 396 A5
NWBY RG14 37 J1
Robins Grove Crs YTLY GU46 68 E2
Robins Hl HUNG RG17 34 B2
Robins La MIDH GU29 279 G1
Robins Meadow
FHAM/STUB PO14 371 G7
Robinson Rd
FHAM/STUB PO14 395 M7
Robinson Wy HSEA PO3 400 A5
BOR GU35 201 K6
Robin Sq ELGH SO50 293 H7
Robins Wy CHCH/BSGR BH23 451 G3
Robinswood Dr FERN BH22 380 B8
Robin Wy AND SP10 119 G6
Rochester Cl KEMP RG22 104 A8 4
Rochester Gv FLET GU13 88 E8
Rochester Rd BWD BH11 431 M4
ENEY PO4 423 K5
Rochester St SHAM SO14 13 L2
Rochford Rd BSTK RG21 4 C8
CHAM PO6 375 H8
Rockall Cl ROWN SO16 317 K3
Rockbourne Cl HAV PO9 377 G4 5
Rockbourne Gdns
NMIL/BTOS BH25 437 H8 1
Rockbourne La FBDG SP6 308 D1
Rockbourne Rd WINW SO22 214 C4
Rockdale Dr GSHT GU26 204 A5 1
Rockery Cl FAWY SO45 367 G4
The Rockery FARN GU14 90 A5
Rocket Rd FARN GU14 90 A7
Rockfield Wy SHST GU47 50 A8 4
Rockford Cl SBNE BH6 449 L5
Rock Gdns ALDT GU11 6 C3
Rockingham Rd NWBY RG14 2 C5
Rockingham Wy
FHAM/PORC PO16 373 M8
Rock La RFNM GU10 158 D3
Rockleigh Dr TOTT SO40 341 H4
Rockleigh Rd ROWN SO16 318 C5
Rockley Rd PLE BH15 444 D6
Rockmoor La RAND SP11 53 J6
Rockram Cl TOTT SO40 339 M1
Rockram Gdns FAWY SO45 367 G5 2
Rockrose Wy CHAM PO6 374 E6
Rockstone La SHAM SO14 343 L2
Rockstone Pl WSHM SO15 343 K2
Rockville Dr WVILLE PO7 376 C1
Rodbourne Cl LYMN SO41 439 H7
Rodfield La RWIN SO21 241 G5
Roding Cl BSTK RG21 5 J8
Rodlease La LYMN SO41 414 C6
Rodmel Ct FARN GU14 91 H7
Rodney Cl LSOL/BMARY PO13 421 G2
Rodney Dr CHCH/BSGR BH23 450 E2
Rodney Rd ENEY PO4 423 K3
Rodney Wy HORN PO8 352 F2
Rodway WIMB BH21 404 A4
Rodwell Cl NBNE BH10 432 A2
Roebuck Av FHAM PO15 372 B3
Roebuck Cl CHAM PO6 399 K1 3
NMIL/BTOS BH25 437 M5
Roebuts Cl NWBY RG14 25 J8
Roedeer Copse HASM GU27 228 B2
Roe Downs Rd ALTN GU34 196 E2
Roentgen Rd CHAM RG24 5 M4
Roeshot Crs CHCH/BSGR BH23 436 C7
Roewood Cl FAWY SO45 392 A5 2
Roewood Rd FAWY SO45 392 A5
Rogate Gdns
FHAM/PORC PO16 374 A7
Roger Penny Wy FBDG SP6 310 F5
Rogers Cl ELGH SO50 294 D4
GPORT PO12 421 M2
Rogers Ct ALTN GU34 176 E4
Rogers Md HISD PO11 401 K5
Rogers Rd ELGH SO50 294 D4
Rokeby Cl NWBY RG14 37 K1
Roke La ODIM RG29 108 F8
Roker Wy ELGH SO50 295 G7
Rokes Pl YTLY GU46 68 D2
Roland Cl HORN PO8 352 F2
Rollestone Rd FAWY SO45 391 M5
Rolls Dr SBNE BH6 450 A4
Roman Cl CHFD SO53 293 K1
Roman Dr ROWN SO16 318 D1
Roman Gdns FAWY SO45 367 H7 1
Roman Gv FHAM/PORC PO16 398 B2
Roman Landing SELS PO20 427 J6
Roman Ride CWTH RG45 49 G3
Roman Rd BDST BH18 429 J4
DEAN RG23 104 A3
FAWY SO45 367 G6
FAWY SO45 391 M2
ROWN SO16 292 D7
RWIN SO21 266 F3
STOK SO20 186 C5
Romans Fld THLE RG7 42 E7
Romans Ga THLE RG7 42 C7
Romans' Rd WINC SO23 238 E2
Roman Wy AND SP10 119 G4
DEAN RG23 103 M3
FAWY SO45 367 H7
FNM GU9 135 H4
HAV PO9 377 G6
NTHA RG18 26 D4
RWIN SO21 145 K8
The Romany FARN GU14 89 K7
Romayne Cl FARN GU14 90 D3
Romford Rd HLER SO31 370 B8
Romill Cl WEND SO18 320 A5
Romney Rd FARN GU14 90 B7
NBNE BH10 432 C4
Romsey Av FHAM/PORC PO16 373 L8
HSEA PO3 423 M2
Romsey Cl ALDT GU11 7 K
BLKW GU17 69 M2
CHAM RG24 82 F
ELGH SO50 293 M5
Romsey Rd ELGH SO50 293 M5
WINW SO22 10 C8
HORN PO8 328 B6
LYND SO43 363 K2
RAND SP11 143 H8
ROMY SO51 288 D6
ROMY SO51 315 K3
ROWN SO16 317 J3
RSAL SP5 259 G4
STOK SO20 184 C
STOK SO20 209 G3
STOK SO20 210 D7
TOTT SO40 314 E
Romyns Ct FHAM/STUB PO14 14 E
Rookcliff Wy LYMN SO41 454 B
Rookery Av FHAM PO15 371 G
HLER SO31 370 F
Rookery La FBDG SP6 283 L
STOK SO20 209 H
The Rookery EMRTH PO10 378 E
WHCH RG28 122 B3
Rookes Cl HORN PO8 352 F
Rookes La LYMN SO41 440 B
Rook Hill Rd CHCH/BSGR BH23 451 G
Rook La RWIN SO21 169 M
Rookley HLER SO31 369 G
Rooksbridge FAWY SO45 367 G5
Rooksbury Cft HAV PO9 377 L3
Rooksbury Rd AND SP10 8 D
Rooksdown Av CHAM RG24 82 B
Rooksdown La CHAM RG24 82 B
Rooks Down Rd WINW SO22 238 C
Rooksfield KSCL RG20 38 D
Rooksnest La HUNG RG17 34 D
Rooksway Gv
FHAM/PORC PO16 373 J
Rookswood ALTN GU34 176 E
KSCL RG20 24 C
Rookswood Cl HTWY RG27 86 A7
Rookwood Av SHST GU47 50 B
Rookwood Cl ELGH SO50 294 A2
Rookwood La ALTN GU34 196 B
SELS PO20 427 L
Rookwood Rd SELS PO20 427 L
Rookwood Vw WVILLE PO7 351 K
Roosevelt Crs BWD BH11 431 M
Rope Hl LYMN SO41 414 B
Ropers La UPTN BH16 444 C
Rope Wk STHA RG19 26 F
Ropley Cl ITCH SO19 344 E8
TADY RG26 61 K
Ropley Rd ALTN GU34 221 L
HAV PO9 377 M
LTDN BH7 449 H
Rorkes Drift FRIM GU16 91 J
Rosamund Av WIMB BH21 404 C
Rosary Gdns YTLY GU46 69 G2
Roscrea Dr SBNE BH6 450 A
Rosebank Cl ROWN SO16 317 K
Rosebay Cl ELGH SO50 321 H2
Rosebay Ct WVILLE PO7 376 D3
Rose Bay Gdns HTWY RG27 86 B6
Roseberry Cl KEMP RG22 127 G
Rosebery Av CHAM PO6 399 L
Rosebery Cl VWD BH31 357 G
Rosebery Crs ELGH SO50 294 A
Rosebery Rd NALR SO24 218 B
Rosebury Av FAWY SO45 367 L
Rose Cl FAWY SO45 367 L6
HEND SO30 321 H
KEMP RG22 104 A
Rosecrae Cl
NMIL/BTOS BH25 437 K4
Rose Crs PLE BH15 445 L
Rosedale ASHV GU12 7 J
Rosedale Av ROMY SO51 290 F
Rosedale Cl FHAM/STUB PO14 371 K
Rosedale Gdns STHA RG19 26 F
Rosedene Gdns FLET GU13 88 E
Rosedene La SHST GU47 70 B1
Rose Gdns FARN GU14 90 A
MOOR/WNTN BH9 432 E
Rose Hl HORN PO8 352 E
Rosehill Dr CHCH/BSGR BH23 409 M
Rosehip Wy CHAM RG24 105 L
Rose Hodson Pl DEAN RG23 104 B
Roselands HEND SO30 320 C8
HORN PO8 352 E
Roselands Cl ELGH SO50 295 C
Roselands Gdns PTSW SO17 318 F
Roseleigh Dr TOTT SO40 341 J
Rosemary Av ASHV GU12 91 K
Rosemary Cl FARN GU14 90 A
Rosemary Dr TADY RG26 61 L
Rosemary Gdns
BKME/WDN BH12 446 A
BLKW GU17 69 M
FHAM PO15 347 H
HEND SO30 346 A
Rosemary La BLKW GU17 69 M
RFNM GU10 158 E

PSEA PO1 .... 20 C2 ↗

Rosemary Rd
BKME/WDN BH12 .... 446 B1
Rosemary Rd HORN PO8 ...... 352 F4
Rosemoor Gv CHFD SO53 ...... 265 C9
Rosemount Rd WBNE BH4 .... 447 C6
Rosendale Rd CHFD SO53 .... 293 J4 ↗
Rose Rd SHAM SO14 .... 318 F8
TOTT SO40 .... 341 L2
The Rosery GPORT PO12 ...... 18 E9
Rosetta Rd ENEY PO4 .... 423 M4
Rose Wk FLET GU13 .... 88 E6
Rosewall Rd ROWN SO16 ...... 317 L5
Rosewarne Ct WINC SO23 ...... 10 F5
Rosewood LSOL/BMARY PO13 .. 397 J7
Rosewood Gdns HORN PO8 .... 328 B3
NMIL/BTOS BH25 .... 437 K4
TOTT SO40 .... 342 E7
Rosewood Rd BOR GU35 ...... 201 M3
Rosier Cl STHA RG19 .... 27 C1
Rosina Cl WVILLE PO7 .... 352 F8
Roslin Rd TWDS BH3 .... 447 K1
Roslin Rd South TWDS BH3 .... 447 J1
Rosoman Rd ITCH SO19 ...... 344 C4
Rossan Av HLER SO31 .... 394 B1
Ross Cl BSTK RG21 .... 104 F6 ↗
Ross Gdns ROWN SO16 .... 317 M6
Rossington Av WEND SO18 .... 344 D1
Rossington Wy WEND SO18 .... 344 D1
Rossini Cl KEMP RG22 .... 104 D8
Rossley Cl CHCH/BSGR BH23 .. 436 E6
Rosslyn Cl NBAD SO52 .... 291 M4
Rossmore Gdns ALDT GU11 .... 6 B4
Rossmore Rd
BKME/WDN BH12 .... 431 C8
Ross Rd RGWD BH24 .... 359 C8
Ross Wy LSOL/BMARY PO13 .. 420 D1
Rostron Cl WEND SO18 ...... 319 M5 ↗
Rosyth Rd WEND SO18 .... 344 D1
Rotary Cl WIMB BH21 .... 404 D1
Rotary Ct HLER SO31 .... 368 F2
Rothay Ct BSTK RG21 .... 5 J8
Rothbury Cl ITCH SO19 ...... 344 E4 ↗
TOTT SO40 .... 316 C7
Rothbury Pk
NMIL/BTOS BH25 .... 437 M6 ↗
Rotherbank Farm La
LISS GU33 .... 248 E2
Rother Cl EPSF GU31 .... 276 B4
SHST GU47 .... 49 M8
WEND SO18 .... 320 A7
Rothercombe La PSF GU32 .... 274 F3
Rother Dl ITCH SO19 .... 345 J5
Rotherfield Rd
CHCH/BSGR BH23 .... 436 E7
Rother La EPSF GU31 .... 278 D7
Rother Rd FARN GU14 .... 90 B2
Rotherwick La HAV PO9 ...... 377 M3
Rotherwick La HTWY RG27 .... 65 C8
Rotherwick La TADY RG26 .... 61 L1
Rothesay Dr CHCH/BSGR BH23.. 451 K1
Rothesay Rd GPORT PO12 .... 421 L1
TWDS BH3 .... 447 H2
Rothsbury Dr CHFD SO53 .... 293 G2
Rothschild Cl ITCH SO19 .... 344 C8
Rothville Pl CHFD SO53 ...... 265 G6 ↗
Rothwell Cl CHAM PO6 .... 374 E7 ↗
Rotten Green Rd HTWY RG27 .. 88 D2
Rotten Hl OVTN RG25 .... 123 K2
Rotterdam Dr
CHCH/BSGR BH23 .... 450 C1
Roughdown La FAWY SO45 .... 392 A7
Roumelia La BOSC BH5........ 448 D4
The Roundabouts LISS GU33 .. 248 F3 ↗
Roundaway La RAND SP11 .... 94 D6
Round Cl YTLY GU46 .... 69 J3
Roundcopse FAWY SO45 ...... 367 C5 ↗
Round End NWBY RG14 ...... 37 C3
Roundfield THLE RG7 .... 27 L2 ↗
Roundhaye Rd BDLH BH11 .... 431 K3
Round Hl FBDG SP6 .... 309 L7 ↗
Roundhill Cl WEND SO18 .... 319 M7
Roundhouse Dr TOTT SO40 .... 340 F2
Roundhouse Meadow
EMRTH PO10 .... 402 E1
Roundhuts Ri WINC SO23 .... 11 M7
Roundmead Rd BSTK RG21 .... 4 C9
Roundway CBLY GU15 .... 71 M2
WVILLE PO7 .... 352 D8
Roundway Cl CBLY GU15 .... 71 M2
Roundway Ct AND SP10 ...... 8 C5
Rounton Rd FLET GU13 ...... 110 E3
Routs Wy ROWN SO16 .... 317 K1
Rowallan Av
LSOL/BMARY PO13 .... 396 F7
Rowan Av HORN PO8 .... 352 F6
Rowan Cha RFNM GU10 ...... 158 D3 ↗
Rowan Cl BPWT SO32 .... 324 A4 ↗
CBLY GU15 .... 51 J8
CHCH/BSGR BH23 .... 436 B8
FLET GU13 .... 89 H7
HLER SO31 .... 345 K8
LSOL/BMARY PO13 .... 420 D3
LYMN SO41 .... 412 F4
RGWD BH24 .... 381 H4
ROMY SO51 .... 291 H2
ROWN SO16 .... 317 L5
RWIN SO21 .... 190 D4
TOTT SO40 .... 341 H2
Rowan Dl FLET GU13 .... 110 E3
Rowan Dr CFDH BH17 .... 429 J7
CHCH/BSGR BH23 .... 436 B8
CWTH RG45 .... 49 M1
NWBY RG14 .... 25 K3
VWD BH31 .... 356 A4
Rowan Gdns HEND SO30 .... 346 B2
Rowan Rd HAV PO9 .... 377 M5
TADY RG26 .... 61 M1
Rowans Cl FARN GU14 ...... 70 B7
Rowanside Cl BOR GU35 .... 202 F4
Rowans Pk LYMN SO41 ...... 440 B5
The Rowans CSHT GU26 .... 204 A6 ↗
TOTT SO40 .... 342 D7
Rowan Wy FHAM/STUB PO14 .. 372 A8
TLHT RG30 .... 31 L4
Rowbarrow Cl FHAM BH17 .. 430 A1
Rowborough Rd WEND SO18 .. 319 L8
Rowbury Rd HAV PO9 .... 377 H2

Rowcroft Cl ASHV GU12 ...... 113 K2
Rowcroft Rd WHIT RG2 ...... 47 J1
Rowdell Cottages NALR SO24 .. 220 B3
Rowden Cl ROMY SO51 ...... 288 D6
Rowe Ashe Wy HLER SO31 .. 370 D5 ↗
Rowena Rd SBNE BH6 .... 449 L3
Rowes La LYMN SO41 .... 441 M1
Rowhay La ALDT GU11 ...... 6 C5
Rowhill Av ALDT GU11 ...... 6 C6
Rowhill Crs ALDT GU11 ...... 6 C6
Rowhill Dr FAWY SO45 ...... 367 G5
Rowhills FNM GU9 .... 6 A6
Rowhills Cl FNM GU9 .... 6 C6
Rowin Cl HISD PO11 .... 426 B6
Rowland Av PLE BH15 ...... 5 K3
Rowland Cl CHAM PO6 ...... 374 C7 ↗
FHAM PO15 .... 14 E4
Rowlands Av
HORN PO8 .... 353 K2
Rowlands Cl CHFD SO53 .... 292 F4
THLE RG7 .... 42 F1
Rowlands Hl WIMB BH21 .... 404 A3
Rowlett Rd LYMN SO41 ...... 440 C5
Rowley Cl HEND SO30 ...... 321 L8 ↗
Rowley Dr HEND SO30 ...... 321 L8
Rowlings Rd WINW SO22 .... 214 C5
Rowner Cl LSOL/BMARY PO13 .. 397 G7
Rowner La LSOL/BMARY PO13 .. 397 G7
Rowner Rd LSOL/BMARY PO13 .. 396 F7
Rownhams Cl ROWN SO16 .... 317 K2
Rownhams La
ROMY SO51 .... 291 L7
ROWN SO16 .... 317 L1
Rownhams Rd CHAR BH8 .. 433 G5
HAV PO9 .... 377 H3
NBAD SO52 .... 291 M5
ROWN SO16 .... 317 L6
Rownhams Rd North
ROWN SO16 .... 317 L3
Rownhams Wy ROWN SO16 .. 317 K2
Rowse Cl ROMY SO51 .... 262 F2 ↗
The Row RSAL SP5 .... 285 K1
Row Wood La
LSOL/BMARY PO13 .... 396 F7
Roxbee Cox Rd FARN GU14 .. 89 K7
Roxburgh Cl CBLY GU15 .... 71 M1
Roxburghe Rd BOR GU35 .... 201 J6
Royal Cl DEAN RG23 .... 126 F3
Royal Crescent Rd SHAM SO14 .. 13 G2
Royale Cl ALDT GU11 ...... 7 K6 ↗
Royal Gdns HAV PO9 .... 353 L7
Royal Ga ENEY PO4 .... 423 M6
Royal Oak Rd NBNE BH10 .... 432 A3
Royal Sovereign Av
FHAM/STUB PO14 .... 396 D3
Royal Wy WVILLE PO7 ...... 376 L1
Royce Cl AND SP10 .... 118 A7
SELS PO20 .... 427 L7
Royce Wy SELS PO20 .... 427 L7
Royden La LSOL/BMARY PO13 .. 414 B5
Roydon Cl WINW SO22 ...... 238 C3
Roy's La BPWT SO32 .... 325 H6
Royster Cl CFDH BH17 ...... 430 A7
Royston Av ELGH SO50 ...... 293 M3
Royston Cl PTSW SO17 ...... 319 G7
Royston Dr WIMB BH21 .... 404 B3 ↗
Royston Pl NMIL/BTOS BH25.. 437 M8
Rozelle Cl WINW SO22 ...... 213 M3
Rozelle Rd PSTN BH14 ...... 446 B4
Rubens Cl BSTK RG21 ...... 105 J6
NMIL/BTOS BH25 .... 437 L4
Ruby Rd ITCH SO19 .... 344 C2
Rudd Hall Ri CBLY GU15 .... 71 C5
Rudd La ROMY SO51 ...... 234 C8
ROMY SO51 .... 262 J1
Rudgwick Cl
FHAM/PORC PO16 .... 373 M8 ↗
Rudland Cl STHA RG19 ...... 27 C6
Rudmore Sq NEND PO2 ...... 399 G8
Ruffield Cl WINW SO22 ...... 214 B5
Rufford Cl ELGH SO50 ...... 293 M2
FLET GU13 .... 110 F2
Rufford Gdns SBNE BH6 .... 449 K3
Rufus Cl CHFD SO53 .... 265 K8
ROWN SO16 .... 317 J2
Rufus Gdns TOTT SO40 ...... 341 G1
Rugby Cl SHST GU47 .... 50 B7 ↗
Rugby Rd CFDH BH17 .... 429 L7
SSEA PO5 .... 21 L3
Rumbridge Gdns TOTT SO40 .. 341 L1 ↗
Rumbridge St TOTT SO40 .... 341 K2
Rune Dr AND SP10 .... 118 E4
Runnymede FHAM PO15 ...... 372 B4
HEND SO30 .... 320 C7 ↗
Runnymede Av BWD BH11 .. 431 H2
Runton Rd BKME/WDN BH12 .. 446 E3
The Runway CHCH/BSGR BH23.. 451 C1
Runwick La RFNM GU10 ...... 134 A7
Rupert Rd NWBY RG14 ...... 25 J3
Rushall La WIMB BH21 ...... 428 E4
Rushcombe Wy WIMB BH21 .. 429 H2 ↗
Rushden Wy FNM GU9 ...... 135 G1
Rushes Rd PSF GU32 .... 275 K4
The Rushes BSTK RG21 .... 5 K8
TOTT SO40 .... 342 D6
Rushfield Rd LISS GU33 .... 248 E4
Rushford Warren
CHCH/BSGR BH23 .... 450 E4
Rushington Av TOTT SO40 .... 341 K2
Rushington La TOTT SO40 .... 341 J3
Rushmere La WVILLE PO7 .... 351 H1
Rushmere Rd SBNE BH6 .... 449 H1
Rushmoor Cl FLET GU13 .... 110 F1
Rushmoor Rd ALDT GU11 .. 112 B5
Ruskin Av MOOR/WNTN BH9.. 432 F5
Ruskin Cl BSTK RG21 ...... 105 J5
Ruskin Cl CWTH RG45 ...... 49 J4 ↗
ENEY PO4 .... 423 L4
Ruskin Wy HORN PO8 ...... 352 D4
Rusland Cl CHFD SO53 ...... 293 G1
Russell Cl LSOL/BMARY PO13.. 420 D1
Russell Cotes Rd BMTH BH1 .. 3 G7 ↗
Russell Ct BLKW GU17 ...... 70 A3 ↗
Russell Dr CHCH/BSGR BH23 .. 450 C2
ROMY SO51 .... 233 J8
Russell Gdns RGWD BH24 .. 381 M3 ↗

Russell Pl FHAM/PORC PO16 .. 15 J5
PTSW SO17 .... 319 G7
Russell Rd HAV PO9 .... 16 F1
LSOL/BMARY PO13 .... 420 D3
NWBY RG14 .... 2 B5
WINC SO23 .... 11 H3
Russell St GPORT PO12 ...... 421 L2
SHAM SO14 .... 13 J5
Russell Wy EPSW GU31 ...... 275 M6
Russel Rd NBNE BH10 ...... 432 A2
Russet Cl FERN BH22 ...... 406 D2
LYMN SO41 .... 440 D6
NALR SO24 .... 218 B4
RFNM GU10 .... 136 B1
Russet Gdns CBLY GU15 .... 71 C5
EMRTH PO10 .... 378 F8
Russet Gld ALDT GU11 ...... 6 A4
FNM GU9 .... 6 A4
THLE RG7 .... 31 L6
Russett Cl BPWT SO32 ...... 324 A4 ↗
Russett Rd ALTN GU34 ...... 176 F5
Russetts Dr FLET GU13 ...... 88 F8
Rustan Cl ELGH SO50 ...... 295 H2
HEND SO30 .... 345 M2 ↗
Rustic Gln FLET GU13 .... 110 E5
Ruth Cl FARN GU14 .... 89 M3
Rutherford Rd CHAM RG24 .. 5 J2
Rutland Cl ALDT GU11 ...... 112 D5
Rutland Gdns HLER SO31 .... 345 L7
FRIM GU16 .... 71 K7
HISD PO11 .... 425 C5
SBNE BH6 .... 449 K5
WEND SO18 .... 319 K7
Rutland Rd CHCH/BSGR BH23 .. 434 D7
MOOR/WNTN BH9 .... 432 F8
Rutland Wy WEND SO18 .... 319 M7
Ruxley Cl FAWY SO45 ...... 392 A4
Ryall Dr CFDH BH17 .... 430 B7
Ryan Cl FERN BH22 .... 406 A1
Ryan Gdns BWD BH11 ...... 431 C4
Ryan Mt SHST GU47 .... 49 K8
Rydal Cl CHAM PO6 .... 374 F7
CHCH/BSGR BH23 .... 434 B4
FARN GU14 .... 90 A5 ↗
BOR GU35 .... 201 J3
Rydal Dr FLET GU13 ...... 110 D3
Ryde Pl LSOL/BMARY PO13 .. 420 E4
Ryde Ter SHAM SO14 ...... 13 K5
Ryebeck Rd FLET GU13 .... 110 F3
Rye Cl FARN GU14 .... 89 H5
FARN GU14 .... 90 B2
NBAD SO52 .... 292 E2
Ryecroft FHAM/STUB PO14 .. 371 G6 ↗
Rye Cft FLET GU13 .... 110 D4
Ryecroft HAV PO9 .... 17 K4
Ryecroft Av BWD BH11 .... 431 J3
Ryecroft Gdns BLKW GU17 .. 70 B4 ↗
Rye Dl TOTT SO40 .... 341 C5
Ryedown La ROMY SO51 .... 289 H4
Ryefield Cl EPSF GU31 ...... 276 B5
Ryeland Cl FARN GU14 ...... 89 H3 ↗
Ryelaw Rd FLET GU13 ...... 110 F3
Rye Paddock La FAWY SO45 .. 392 F4
Rylandes Cl ROWN SO16 .... 317 L5
Ryle Rd FNM GU9 .... 134 E8
Ryon Cl AND SP10 .... 118 F4
Ryves Av YTLY GU46 .... 68 D3

S

Sabre Ct ALDT GU11 .... 6 B2
Sabre Rd EMRTH PO10 ...... 402 E5
Sackville St SSEA PO5 ...... 21 G4
Saddleback Rd CBLY GU15 .. 51 H8
Saddleback Wy FARN GU14 .. 89 G4
Saddle Cl WIMB BH21 ...... 405 G2 ↗
Saddlers Cl ELGH SO50 ...... 293 M4
RWIN SO21 .... 168 B4
Saddlers Scarp GSHT GU26 .. 203 K4
Saddlewood CBLY GU15 .... 70 F4
Sadlers La FAWY SO45 ...... 367 L7
Sadlers Rd HUNG RG17 ...... 33 J2
Sadlers Wk EMRTH PO10 .... 378 E8
Saffron Cl CHAM RG24 ...... 83 L4
NWBY RG14 .... 2 D3
Saffron Dr CHCH/BSGR BH23 .. 435 M8
Saffron Wy BWD BH11 ...... 431 H5
FHAM PO15 .... 347 H8
Sage Cl WVILLE PO7 .... 376 L2
Sagecroft Rd NTHA RG18 .... 26 F3
Sages La ALTN GU34 .... 245 H3
Sailor's La BPWT SO32 ...... 298 B1
Sainfoin La DEAN RG23 ...... 105 C8
Sainsbury Cl AND SP10 ...... 8 A8
St Agatha's Rd HLER SO31 .. 369 L4 ↗
St Alban's Av CHAR BH8 .... 448 A1
St Alban's Crs CHAR BH8 .... 448 A1
St Alban's Rd CHAR BH8 .... 448 A1
HAV PO9 .... 377 L4
SHAM SO14 .... 13 K1 ↗
St Aldhelm's Cl CCLF BH13 .. 446 E5
St Aldhelm's Rd CCLF BH13 .. 446 E6
St Andrew Cl HORN PO8 .... 328 B6
St Andrews CWTH RG45 .... 49 J3
NBAD SO52 .... 291 K3
ROMY SO51 .... 262 C2
St Andrews Pk ELGH SO50 .. 321 H2
St Andrew's Rd CHAM PO6 .. 376 D8
GPORT PO12 .... 18 F4
HISD PO11 .... 425 M6
KEMP RG22 .... 104 C5
BOR GU35 .... 201 C6
SHAM SO14 .... 13 H1
SSEA PO5 .... 21 J5
WIMB BH21 .... 429 J3
St Andrew's Wy FRIM GU16 .. 91 J1
St Anne's Av SBNE BH6 ...... 449 K3
St Annes Cl WINW SO22 .... 238 B3
RAND SP11 .... 142 E8
St Anne's Gdns ITCH SO19 .. 344 C6
LYMN SO41 .... 440 B5
St Anne's Gv
FHAM/STUB PO14 .... 396 C1
St Annes La BPWT SO32 .... 348 B1
St Annes Rd ITCH SO19 ...... 344 C6
UPTN BH16 .... 444 A1

Russell Pl FHAM/PORC PO16 .. 444 B4

UPTN BH16 .... 444 B4
St Ann's Cl AND SP10 ...... 8 F7
AND SP10 .... 9 C7 ↗
St Ann's Crs GPORT PO12 .. 421 L2
St Ann's Rd HORN PO8 ...... 353 C1
St Anthony's Rd WCLF BH2 .. 22 E2
St Aubin's Av ITCH SO19 .... 344 E3
St Aubins Cl ALTN GU34 .... 197 C6
St Aubin's Pk HISD PO11 .... 425 H5
St Aubyns La RGWD BH24 .. 359 J7
St Augustine Gdns
PTSW SO17 .... 319 J7 ↗
St Augustine Rd ENEY PO4 .. 423 K5
St Augustine's Cl ASHV GU12 .. 7 M3
St Augustin's Rd WCLF BH2 .. 22 E1
St Austell Cl ELGH SO50 .... 294 D5 ↗
St Barbara's Cl TADY RG26 .. 64 A6
St Barbara Wy NEND PO2 .. 399 K4 ↗
St Barbe Cl ROMY SO51 .... 290 F2 ↗
St Bartholomew's Gdns
SSEA PO5 .... 21 K5 ↗
St Benedict's Cl ALDT GU11 .. 6 L4
St Blaize Rd ROMY SO51 .... 263 C8 ↗
St Bonnet Dr BPWT SO32 .. 297 H8 ↗
St Brelades Av
BKME/WDN BH12 .... 431 H7
St Catherines WIMB BH21 .. 404 A4
St Catherine's Hl THLE RG7 .. 43 H3
St Catherine's Rd ELGH SO50 .. 293 M3
FRIM GU16 .... 71 K7
HISD PO11 .... 425 G5
SBNE BH6 .... 449 K5
WEND SO18 .... 319 K7
WINC SO23 .... 239 G2
St Catherine's Wy LTDN BH7 .. 436 A1
St Catherine St SSEA PO5 .. 21 K9
St Catherines Vw
HEND SO30 .... 345 L2 ↗
St Catherines Wy
FHAM/PORC PO16 .... 373 J7
St Chad's Av NEND PO2 .... 399 J6
St Christopher Av
FHAM/PORC PO16 .... 15 K2
St Christophers Cl ASHV GU12 .. 7 L1
KEMP RG22 .... 104 B5 ↗
NBAD SO52 .... 291 L4
St Christophers Pl FARN GU14 .. 90 C5 ↗
St Christopher's Rd FARN GU14 .. 90 D5
HASM GU27 .... 228 D2
HAV PO9 .... 377 C5
St Clair Rd CCLF BH13 ...... 457 K2
St Clares Av HAV PO9 ...... 377 H1
St Clements Cl ROMY SO51 .. 262 D8 ↗
St Clements Gdns BMTH BH1 .. 448 C3
St Clement's Rd BMTH BH1 .. 448 C3
PLE BH15 .... 446 A1
St Clement St WINC SO23 .. 10 F8
St Colman's Av CHAM PO6 .. 375 L8
St Cross Rd FNM GU9 ...... 134 F5 ↗
FRIM GU16 .... 91 K1
RFNM GU10 .... 133 J2
WINC SO23 .... 238 E2
St Cuthberts Cl HLER SO31 .. 370 F4 ↗
St Cuthberts La HLER SO31 .. 370 F4
St David's Cl FARN GU14 .... 70 C8
FNM GU9 .... 6 B8
ODIM RG29 .... 108 B6 ↗
TOTT SO40 .... 316 B7
St Davids Rd HLER SO31 .... 370 D5
HORN PO8 .... 328 B3
KEMP RG22 .... 104 D5
NWBY RG14 .... 2 D5
SSEA PO5 .... 21 K4
UPTN BH16 .... 444 A1
St Denys Rd PTSW SO17 .... 319 G7
PTSW SO17 .... 319 G7
St Donats Pl NWBY RG14 .. 2 F6
St Edmund Cl
FHAM/STUB PO14 .... 370 F7
St Edmund's Rd FHAM/STUB PO14 .. 318 A8
HLER SO31 .... 368 F1
SSEA PO5 .... 21 G6
St Edward's Rd GPORT PO12.. 18 F4
HLER SO31 .... 345 K7
SSEA PO5 .... 21 G6
St Elizabeth's Av WEND SO18 .. 344 F1
St Evox Cl ROWN SO16 ...... 317 L3
St Faith's Cl GPORT PO12 .. 18 C2
St Faith's Rd PSEA PO1 .... 423 H2
WINC SO23 .... 238 E3
St Francis Av WEND SO18 .. 320 A8
St Francis Cl FAWY SO45 .. 418 C1 ↗
St Francis Rd NEND PO2 .... 399 J4 ↗
St Francis Pl HAV PO9 ...... 377 J5
St Francis Rd FAWY SO45 .. 418 C1
GPORT PO12 .... 19 C9
St Gabriels Lea CHAM RG24 .. 83 M5
St Gabriel's Rd WEND SO18 .. 344 F1
St George Cl HLER SO31 .... 345 K7
St Georges Av CHAR BH8 .. 448 B1
BKME/WDN BH12 .... 430 F8
HAV PO9 .... 17 K4
NWBY RG14 .... 2 B6
St Georges Cl
CHCH/BSGR BH23 .... 409 M8
CHAR BH8 .... 433 G8
CHCH/BSGR BH23 .... 436 B8
FNM GU9 .... 135 L2 ↗
St Georges Crs FBDG SP6 .. 309 L6 ↗
St George's Dr FERN BH22 .. 406 A4
St George's Rd ASHV GU12 .. 7 G4
CBLY GU15 .... 71 C2
CHAM PO6 .... 375 K8
ENEY PO4 .... 423 L8
FBDG SP6 .... 309 L6
FNM GU9 .... 135 G7
FNM GU9 .... 135 L2
HISD PO11 .... 425 H5
HLER SO31 .... 370 D5
RFNM GU10 .... 135 L4
NTID SP9 .... 114 D2
PSEA PO1 .... 20 C3
St George's Sq PSEA PO1 .. 20 D2 ↗
St Georges Sq SHAM SO14 .. 13 G4
WINC SO23 .... 11 K9
St George's Wy PSEA PO1 .. 20 D2
St Giles Cl WINC SO23 ...... 11 K9
St Giles Wy HORN PO8 ...... 328 B3
St Helena Gdns WEND SO18 .. 319 L5

St Helena Wy
FHAM/PORC PO16 .... 374 A8
St Helen's Cl ENEY PO4 .... 423 K6
St Helens Crs SHST GU47 .. 49 L8 ↗
St Helens Pde ENEY PO4 .. 21 M9
St Helens Rd GPORT PO12 .. 421 L2
HISD PO11 .... 425 H5
St Helier Rd BKME/WDN BH12 .. 431 H7
St Hellen's Rd CHAM PO6 .. 376 B8
St Hermans Rd HISD PO11 .. 426 A6
St Hilda Av HORN PO8 ...... 328 B6
St Hubert Rd AND SP10 .... 8 D6
HORN PO8 .... 328 B6
St Ives End La RGWD BH24 .. 381 L3
St Ives Gdns WCLF BH2 .... 22 F2
St Ives Pk RGWD BH24 .... 381 L3
St Ives Wd RGWD BH24 .... 381 M3
St James' Av FNM GU9 .... 135 C4
St James Cl HORN PO8 .... 328 B4
St James' La WINW SO22 .. 10 D8
St James' Rd EMRTH PO10 .. 378 D8
FLET GU13 .... 88 E8
HEND SO30 .... 320 C6
LYMN SO41 .... 413 G6
WIMB BH21 .... 405 L2
St James's Cl WSHM SO15 .. 318 B7
St James's Park Rd
ROWN SO16 .... 318 B6
St James's Rd SSEA PO5 .. 21 G4
WSHM SO15 .... 318 B7
St James's Sq BOSC BH5 .. 448 E8
St James's St PSEA PO1 .. 20 E1 ↗
St James' Ter FNM GU9 .... 134 F5
WINW SO22 .... 10 E8
St James' Vls WINC SO23 .. 10 E9
St James Wy
FHAM/PORC PO16 .... 374 B8
St John Cl TADY RG26 ...... 63 M6
St John's Av WVILLE PO7 .. 376 C4
St John's Cl GPORT PO12 .. 18 E1
HISD PO11 .... 425 J5
HTWY RG27 .... 86 A7 ↗
ROWN SO16 .... 317 K1
WIMB BH21 .... 404 B4
St Johns Ct TOTT SO40 .... 342 D7
St Johns Dr TOTT SO40 .... 342 C7
St Johns Gdns ROMY SO51 .. 262 E8 ↗
St Johns Glebe ROWN SO16.. 317 L1
St Johns Gv FNM GU9 ...... 158 E1
St John's Hl WIMB BH21 .. 404 B3
St John's Piece DEAN RG23 .. 103 C8
St John's Rd AND SP10 .... 9 A4
BOSC BH5 .... 448 C4
CHAM PO6 .... 375 L8
CHCH/BSGR BH23 .... 449 M2
DEAN RG23 .... 103 C4
ELGH SO50 .... 294 A4
EMRTH PO10 .... 379 G7
FARN GU14 .... 90 B4
FNM GU9 .... 134 E8
HAV PO9 .... 377 C4
HEND SO30 .... 345 L4
HLER SO31 .... 370 F6
HTWY RG27 .... 87 J3
NMIL/BTOS BH25 .... 437 L1
NWBY RG14 .... 2 E7
PLE BH15 .... 445 J4
SHST GU47 .... 69 L1
STHA RG19 .... 26 F5
THLE RG7 .... 43 K3
WINC SO23 .... 11 K7
St John's St FAWY SO45 .... 367 L4
SHAM SO14 .... 11 J8
St Joseph's Crs CHAM RG24 .. 83 L6 ↗
St Joseph's Rd ALDT GU11 .. 6 F4
ASHV GU12 .... 7 G4
St Just Cl AMSY SP4 ...... 160 A3
FERN BH22 .... 405 M5
St Lawrence Rd ALTN GU34 .. 176 F4
ELGH SO50 .... 293 M4
SHAM SO14 .... 13 J6
St Ledger's Rd CHAR BH8 .. 448 C4
St Leonards RAND SP11 .... 140 A7 ↗
St Leonard's Av CHAM RG24 .. 83 M5
HISD PO11 .... 425 L5
St Leonards Cl FHAM PO15 .. 371 J5
St Leonard's Rd CHAR BH8 .. 448 A2
LYMN SO41 .... 415 M8
St Leonards Wy RGWD BH24.. 381 H3
St Lukes Cl HEND SO30 .... 321 H7 ↗
St Luke's Rd GPORT PO12 .. 421 L2
TWDS BH3 .... 447 L2
St Margaret's Av
CHCH/BSGR BH23 .... 449 M2
St Margaret's Cl WEND SO18.. 344 F1
St Margarets La
FHAM/STUB PO14 .... 371 J7
St Margarets Rd HISD PO11 .. 425 L5
PLE BH15 .... 445 H4
St Marks Cl FARN GU14 .... 90 F7 ↗
GPORT PO12 .... 18 D9
STHA RG19 .... 26 F5
St Marks Pl FNM GU9 ...... 134 E1 ↗
St Marks Rd LYMN SO41 .. 439 M5
BWD BH11 .... 431 M5
GPORT PO12 .... 18 D9
NEND PO2 .... 399 F7 ↗
St Martin's Cl ROWN SO16 .. 317 K5
WINC SO23 .... 11 K7
St Mary Gv LYMN SO41 .... 438 E6
St Mary's Av GPORT PO12 .. 18 D7
TADY RG26 .... 64 A6
St Marys Cl ALTN GU34 .... 176 E6
CHCH/BSGR BH23 .... 409 M8
RSAL SP5 .... 285 L3
SHST GU47 .... 49 M8
WINC SO23 .... 215 H3
St Mary's Ct BSTK RG21 .... 5 G8
St Mary's Meadow
RAND SP11 .... 141 M4 ↗
St Mary's Pl SHAM SO14 .. 13 H3
St Mary's Rd ASHV GU12 .. 7 K3
CBLY GU15 .... 70 F2 ↗
CHAR BH8 .... 448 C2
ELGH SO50 .... 294 C4
FERN BH22 .... 406 A3
FHAM/STUB PO14 .... 396 A4

HISD PO11 .... 425 K5
HLER SO31 .... 369 C2
HTWY RG27 .... 87 H1
KSCL RG20 .... 59 J6
LISS GU33 .... 248 E4
NWBY RG14 .... 2 F2
PLE BH15 .... 445 K4
PSEA PO1 .... 423 J2
SHAM SO14 .... 13 H1
SHAM SO14 .... 343 J2
THLE RG7 .... 43 K3
St Mary's Ter RWIN SO21 .... 266 F2 ☒
St Mary St WINW SO22 .... 238 C3
SHAM SO14 .... 13 J4
St Mary's Wy THLE RG7 .... 31 M5 ☒
St Matthews Cl SHAM SO14... .... 13 H1
St Matthew's Rd CHAM PO6 .... 375 K8
WINW SO22 .... 10 B2
St Michaels Av NTID SP9 .... 114 D3
St Michaels Cl FAWY SO45 .... 392 C7
FLET GU13 .... 89 H8
OVTN RG25 .... 125 K7
PLE BH15 .... 444 D5 ☒
VWD BH31 .... 356 D3 ☒
St Michaels Ct CHAM PO6 .... 374 F7 ☒
St Michael's Gdns WINC SO23 .... 10 F9
St Michael's Gv
FHAM/STUB PO14... .... 14 F8
FHAM/STUB PO14... .... 396 D1
St Michaels La THLE RG7 .... 31 C3
St Michael's Rd ASHV GU12 .... 7 G4
CBLY GU15 .... 70 E3 ☒
FARN GU14 .... 90 E2
HAV PO9 .... 377 C5
HLER SO31 .... 370 D6
KEMP RG22 .... 104 B5
NWBY RG14 .... 2 C6
PSEA PO1 .... 20 F3
SHST GU47 .... 49 L8
TOTT SO40 .... 316 E7
VWD BH31 .... 356 D3
WCLF BH2 .... 22 C6
WINC SO23 .... 238 C2
St Michael's St SHAM SO14 .... 12 F5
St Michaels Wy HORN PO8 .... 328 B6
St Monica Rd ITCH SO19 .... 344 E5
St Neot's Rd HTWY RG27 .... 67 J1
St Nicholas SO23 .... 215 G2
St Nicholas Av
LSOL/BMARY PO13 .... 421 G1
St Nicholas Cl FLET GU13 .... 88 E7
RAND SP11 .... 93 G6 ☒
St Nicholas Ct KEMP RG22 .... 104 C4
St Nicholas' Rd HAV PO9 .... 377 G5 ☒
NWBY RG14 .... 2 D5
St Nicholas St PSEA PO1 .... 20 D5
St Omer Barracks ALDT GU11 .... 113 G3
St Osmund's Rd PSTN BH14 .... 446 B5
St Patricks Av NTID SP9 .... 114 C3
St Patrick's La LISS GU33 .... 249 H3
St Patrick's Rd KEMP RG22 .... 104 D5
St Pauls Cl RFNM GU10 .... 136 C1 ☒
St Paul's Hl WINW SO22 .... 10 E6
St Paul's La BMTH BH1 .... 23 J4
St Paul's Pl BMTH BH1 .... 23 J4
St Pauls Rd BMTH BH1 .... 23 J3
HLER SO31 .... 370 C2
KEMP RG22 .... 104 D5
SSEA PO5 .... 20 F3
St Pauls Rbt BMTH BH1 .... 23 H3
St Paul's Sq PSEA PO5 .... 20 F4 ☒
St Peter's Av HISD PO11 .... 402 A6
St Peters Cl NTID SP9 .... 138 D1
St Peter's Gdns RFNM GU10 .... 158 C2 ☒
YTLY GU46 .... 68 C2
St Peter's Gv SSEA PO5 .... 21 J5
St Peters Md ASHV GU12 .... 113 L6
St Peters Pk ALDT GU11 .... 6 A5 ☒
St Peter's Rd BMTH BH1 .... 22 F5
HISD PO11 .... 402 A6
KEMP RG22 .... 104 D5
PSF GU32 .... 275 L5
PSTN BH14 .... 445 M4
St Peters Rbt BMTH BH1 .... 23 G6
St Peter's Sq EMRTH PO10 .... 378 D8
St Peter's St BPWT SO32 .... 297 H8
St Peter St WINC SO23 .... 11 C7
St Peter's Wy FRIM GU16 .... 91 J1
St Philip's Wy WEND SO18 .... 344 F1 ☒
St Piran's Av HSEA PO3 .... 423 L1
St Richards Rd RWIN SO14 .... 25 L3
St Ronan's Av ENEY PO4 .... 21 M7
St Ronan's Rd ENEY PO4 .... 21 M7
St Sebastian Crs
FHAM/PORC PO16 .... 15 K1
St Simon Cl HLER SO31 .... 370 F5 ☒
St Simon's La SSEA PO5... .... 21 K8
St Stephens Cl HASM GU27 .... 228 F1
St Stephens La VWD BH31 .... 356 E2
St Stephen's Rd WINW SO22 .... 10 B3
NEND PO2 .... 399 J8 ☒
WCLF BH2 .... 22 C4
St Stephen's Wy WCLF BH2 .... 22 E4
St Swithun Cl BPWT SO32 .... 297 G8 ☒
St Swithun's Cl ROMY SO51 .... 263 J7 ☒
St Swithun's Rd BMTH BH1 .... 23 K3
NEND PO2 .... 399 K4
St Swithun's Rd South
BMTH BH1 .... 23 K4
St Swithun St WINC SO23 .... 10 F9
St Theresas Cl HAV PO9 .... 377 C5
St Thomas Av HISD PO11 .... 425 H5
St Thomas Cl AND SP10 .... 118 D5
BSTK RG21 .... 4 D4
FHAM/PORC PO16 .... 15 J1
St Thomas Pk LYMN SO41 .... 440 B4
St Thomas's Rd GPORT PO12 .... 397 M8
St Thomas's Rd LYMN SO41 .... 440 B5
PSEA PO1 .... 20 C5
St Thomas St WINC SO23 .... 10 F9
St Tristan Cl HLER SO31 .... 370 F5
St Ursula Gv SSEA PO5 .... 21 J5 ☒
St Valerie Rd GPORT PO12 .... 18 F6
WCLF BH2 .... 22 E2
St Vigor Wy RWIN SO21 .... 266 E2
St Vincent Crs HORN PO8 .... 352 F2
St Vincent Rd GPORT PO12 .... 421 M2
SSEA PO5 .... 21 J7

St Vincent St SSEA PO5 .... 20 F3 ☒
St Winifred's Rd ROWN SO16 .... 318 B6
WCLF BH2 .... 22 E1
Salamanca CWTH RG45 .... 49 H3 ☒
Salcombe Av HSEA PO3 .... 399 L7
Salcombe Cl CHFD SO53 .... 293 G4
Salcombe Crs TOTT SO40 .... 341 J2
Salcombe Rd NWBY RG14 .... 2 A7
TOTT SO40 .... 341 J2
WSHM SO15 .... 342 F1
Salcot Rd WINC SO23 .... 11 G3
Salem St WSHM SO15 .... 318 B7
Salerno Cl ALDT GU11 .... 6 F1
Salerno Dr GPORT PO12 .... 18 B3
Salerno Pl PLE BH15 .... 444 C6 ☒
ROWN SO16 .... 318 B4
Salesian Vw FARN GU14 .... 91 H8
Salet Wy WVILLE PO7 .... 352 F7
Salisbury Av ALTN GU34 .... 176 F6
ELGH SO50 .... 294 A4 ☒
ODIM RG29 .... 108 B6 ☒
Salisbury Gdns KEMP RG22 .... 104 B4
Salisbury Gv FRIM GU16 .... 91 K5
Salisbury La STOK SO20 .... 162 B7
Salisbury Rd AND SP10 .... 8 B9
ASHV GU12 .... 113 K6
BLKW GU17 .... 69 M3 ☒
CHAM PO6 .... 399 L1
CHCH/BSGR BH23 .... 434 F2
ENEY PO4 .... 423 K6
FARN GU14 .... 90 F4
FBDG SP6 .... 309 M6
NALR SO24 .... 218 B3
NTID SP9 .... 138 D3
PSTN BH14 .... 446 B3
PTSW SO17 .... 318 F5
RAND SP11 .... 141 M7
RAND SP11 .... 161 K2
RAND SP11 .... 163 J2
RCWD BH24 .... 334 E7
ROMY SO51 .... 261 K8
RSAL SP5 .... 256 D7
STOK SO20 .... 208 F1
TOTT SO40 .... 316 D7
Salisbury St FBDG SP6 .... 309 L7
WIMB BH21 .... 306 D8
Salisbury Ter FRIM GU16 .... 91 K5
LSOL/BMARY PO13 .... 420 D3
Salmon Dr ELGH SO50 .... 294 E6
Salmond Rd RAND SP11 .... 118 A8
Salmons Rd ODIM RG29 .... 108 B6
Salterns Av ENEY PO4 .... 423 M3
Salterns Cl HISD PO11 .... 426 A5
Salterns Est FHAM/PORC PO16 .... 15 K9
Salterns La FAWY SO45 .... 392 F4
FHAM/PORC PO16 .... 396 F1
HISD PO11 .... 425 M5
HLER SO31 .... 369 L2
Salterns Rd FHAM/STUB PO14 .... 395 M8
PSTN BH14 .... 445 M5
Salterns Wy PSTN BH14 .... 446 A5
Salter Rd CCLF BH13 .... 457 C5
Salters Acres WINW SO22 .... 214 B6
Salters Heath Rd TADY RG26 .... 82 A2
Saltgrass La LYMN SO41 .... 454 F6
Saltings Rd UPTN BH16 .... 444 A2
The Saltings CHAM PO6 .... 400 C1
HAV PO9 .... 401 K2
Salt La BPWT SO32 .... 269 K5
Saltmarsh La HISD PO11 .... 425 J3
Saltmarsh Rd SHAM SO14 .... 13 K6
Saltmead PTSW SO17 .... 319 J7 ☒
Salt Meat La GPORT PO12 .... 422 B2
Saltram Rd FARN GU14 .... 91 H6
Salvia Cl WVILLE PO7 .... 376 E2 ☒
Salwey Rd HEND SO30 .... 346 B3
Samarkand Cl CBLY GU15 .... 71 L4
Samber Cl HLER SO31 .... 440 L4
Sampan Cl HLER SO31 .... 370 C7
Sampson Rd
FHAM/STUB PO14 .... 396 D2
PSEA PO1 .... 422 D2
Samson Cl LSOL/BMARY PO13... .... 421 H1
Samson Rd PLE BH15 .... 444 C5
Samuel Rd PSEA PO1 .... 423 K2
Sam Whites Hl RAND SP11 .... 142 D4
San Carlos Ap ALDT GU11... .... 7 K1
Sancreed Rd BKME/WDN BH12... 446 D1
Sandbanks Dr KEMP RG22 .... 127 G1 ☒
Sandbanks Rd PLE BH15 .... 445 L5
PSTN BH14 .... 445 M5
Sandbourne Rd CCLF BH13 .... 447 G7
PLE BH15 .... 445 J4
WBNE BH4 .... 447 H7
Sandcroft Cl GPORT PO12 .... 421 J5 ☒
Sandecotes Rd PSTN BH14 .... 446 B5
Sanderling Rd ENEY PO4 .... 424 A3
Sanderlings RCWD BH24 .... 383 G2 ☒
The Sanderlings HISD PO11 .... 425 L6 ☒
Sandford Av GPORT PO12 .... 421 H4
Sandford Cl KSCL RG20 .... 59 L6
MOOR/WNTN BH9 .... 433 L2
Sandford Ct ALDT GU11 .... 6 B3
Sandford Rd ALDT GU11 .... 6 D2 ☒
FNM GU9 .... 134 E1
TADY RG26 .... 41 K8
Sandford Wy BDST BH18 .... 429 K5
Sandheath Rd GSHT GU26 .... 203 M1
Sand Hl FARN GU14 .... 90 E1
Sandhill La LSOL/BMARY PO13... 420 E1
Sandhills Cl CHFD BH17 .... 430 B6
Sandhurst Dr WIMB BH21 .... 380 E1
Sandhurst La BLKW GU17 .... 69 L2
Sandhurst Rd CWTH RG45 .... 49 L5
WSHM SO15 .... 343 K2
YTLY GU46 .... 69 H2
San Diego Rd GPORT PO12 .... 421 M2
Sandisplatt
FHAM/STUB PO14 .... 372 A8 ☒
Sandle Copse FBDG SP6 .... 309 G7
Sandleford Ri NWBY RG14 .... 37 K1
Sandleford Rd HAV PO9 .... 377 H1
Sandleheath Rd FBDG SP6 .... 308 E8
Sandlewood Cl HORN PO8 .... 328 B3
TOTT SO40 .... 316 B8 ☒
Sandmartin Cl
NMIL/BTOS BH25 .... 452 E1

Sandown Cl ALTN GU34 .... 176 F6 ☒
BLKW GU17 .... 70 A3
GPORT PO12 .... 421 H5 ☒
Sandown Crs ALDT GU11 .... 7 G8
Sandown Dr FRIM GU16 .... 71 G6
Sandown Rd CHAM PO6... .... 399 J1
CHCH/BSGR BH23 .... 450 D2
WSHM SO15 .... 318 A7
Sandown Wy NWBY RG14 .... 3 J8
Sandpiper Cl CFDH BH17 .... 429 K7
HORN PO8 .... 352 E1
TOTT SO40 .... 342 C7
Sandpiper Rd ROWN SO16 .... 317 M3
Sandpit Hl KSCL RG20 .... 36 F5
Sandpit La LYMN SO41 .... 442 C4
THLE RG7 .... 46 E3
Sandport Gv
FHAM/PORC PO16 .... 397 M1
Sandringham Cl ALTN GU34 .... 176 C5 ☒
MOOR/WNTN BH9 .... 432 F4
NBAD SO52 .... 292 E4
Sandringham Gdns
MOOR/WNTN BH9 .... 432 F4
Sandringham La PSEA PO1 .... 21 L1 ☒
Sandringham Rd
FHAM/STUB PO14 .... 371 M8
PSEA PO1 .... 21 L1
PSF GU32 .... 275 L4
PSTN BH14 .... 446 A5
WEND SO18 .... 319 K7
Sandringham Wy FRIM GU16 .... 71 J8
Sandrock HASM GU27 .... 228 F2
Sandrock Hill Rd RFNM GU10 .... 158 C2
Sandsbury La PSF GU32 .... 275 G3
Sands Cl RFNM GU10 .... 136 A6
Sands Rd RFNM GU10 .... 135 M6
The Sands BOR GU35 .... 200 F6
Sandy Brow WVILLE PO7 .... 376 B4
Sandy Cl EPSF GU31 .... 276 B5
Sandycroft HLER SO31 .... 370 B8
Sandy Down LYMN SO41 .... 413 M4
Sandy Field Crs HORN PO8 .... 352 C5
Sandy Hill Rd FNM GU9 .... 134 D1
Sandyhurst Cl CFDH BH17 .... 430 A7
Sandy La BPWT SO32 .... 323 H7
CBLY GU15 .... 71 H2
CHCH/BSGR BH23 .... 434 C6
ELGH SO50 .... 295 G6
FARN GU14 .... 89 M2
FHAM/STUB PO14 .... 371 K8
FLET GU13 .... 110 F4
GSHT GU26 .... 204 C6
HASM GU27 .... 205 H7
HASM GU27 .... 227 M1
HTWY RG27 .... 87 J3
LISS GU33 .... 249 K5
LYND SO43 .... 363 K4
MIDH GU29 .... 279 M8
NBAD SO52 .... 292 A3 ☒
RFNM GU10 .... 158 F7
RFNM GU10 .... 181 K2
RGWD BH24 .... 381 K4
ROMY SO51 .... 262 F5
RSAL SP5 .... 285 K1
SBNE BH6 .... 449 G6
SHST GU47 .... 49 J7
TADY RG26 .... 42 A8
UPTN BH16 .... 428 A2
VWD BH31 .... 356 E2
WIMB BH21 .... 306 C6
Sandy Mead Rd CHAR BH8 .... 433 K7
Sandy Plot CHCH/BSGR BH23 .... 435 G7
Sandy Point Rd HISD PO11 .... 426 C7
Sandys Cl KEMP RG22 .... 104 D5
Sandys Rd KEMP RG22 .... 104 D4
Sandy Wy NBNE BH10 .... 432 C5
Sankey La FARN GU14 .... 89 J4
Sanross Cl FHAM/STUB PO14... 395 L7
Santina Cl FNM GU9 .... 112 A8
Saor Ms AND SP10 .... 8 F4
Sapley La OVTN RG25 .... 123 M1
Sapphire Cl WVILLE PO7 .... 376 E1 ☒
Sapphire Rdg WVILLE PO7 .... 376 E1
Saracen Cl LYMN SO41 .... 440 A7 ☒
Saracens Rd CHFD SO53 .... 293 L1
Sarah Cl LTDN BH7 .... 433 M8
Sarah Wy FARN GU14 .... 90 E4
Sargood Cl STHA RG19 .... 27 H6 ☒
Sarisbury Cl TADY RG26 .... 41 K8
Sark Rd BKME/WDN BH12 .... 431 H8
Sarnia Ct ROWN SO16 .... 317 K5
Sarson Cl RAND SP11 .... 141 G2
Sarson La RAND SP11 .... 141 G1
Sarum Av FERN BH22 .... 380 C4
Sarum Cl WINW SO22 .... 238 B1
Sarum Hl BSTK RG21 .... 4 D9
Sarum Rd CHFD SO53 .... 293 K2
WINW SO22 .... 10 A8
WINW SO22 .... 237 J1
TADY RG26 .... 41 K7
Sarum Vw WINW SO22 .... 238 A2
Sarum Wk LYMN SO41 .... 440 B2 ☒
Satchell La HLER SO31 .... 369 L5
Saturn Cl ROWN SO16 .... 317 L4
Saulfland Dr CHCH/BSGR BH23... 436 B8
Saunders La ROMY SO51 .... 261 K3
Saunders Ms ENEY PO4 .... 423 M6 ☒
Saunton Gdns FARN GU14 .... 90 D2 ☒
Savernake Cl
LSOL/BMARY PO13 .... 397 H6 ☒
ROMY SO51 .... 263 G7 ☒
Savile Crs BOR GU35 .... 201 J5
Saville Cl ELGH SO50 .... 294 C3
GPORT PO12 .... 18 A5
Saville Gdns CBLY GU15 .... 71 L3
FHAM/PORC PO16 .... 14 F7
Savoy Cl AND SP10 .... 9 J6
Savoy Gv BLKW GU17 .... 70 A5
Sawyer Cl WINW SO22 .... 214 B7 ☒
Saxby Cl THLE RG7 .... 31 L5
Saxholm Cl ROWN SO16 .... 318 L2
Saxholm Dl ROWN SO16 .... 318 L2
Saxholm Wy ROWN SO16... .... 318 L2
Saxley Ct HAV PO9 .... 377 G2
Saxonbury Rd SBNE BH6 .... 449 K2

Saxon Cl FHAM/PORC PO16 .... 373 M7
HLER SO31 .... 370 C7
HORN PO8 .... 328 B4
Saxon Ct STHA RG19 .... 26 D5 ☒
Saxon Cft FNM GU9 .... 134 F7 ☒
Saxon Gdns HEND SO30 .... 345 L3
Saxonhurst RSAL SP5 .... 284 F1
Saxonhurst Rd NBNE BH10 .... 432 B4
Saxon King Gdns SBNE BH6 .... 450 A4
Saxon Leas RSAL SP5 .... 206 F2
Saxon Pl LYMN SO41 .... 440 B2
Saxon Rd FAWY SO45 .... 392 D7
WINC SO23 .... 11 G5
WSHM SO15 .... 12 B1
Saxon Wy AND SP10 .... 118 E4
CHAM RG24 .... 105 L1
FBDG SP6 .... 333 L3 ☒
ROMY SO51 .... 291 G1
Sayers Cl FRIM GU16 .... 91 H1
NWBY RG14 .... 25 L8
Sayers Rd ELGH SO50 .... 294 C6
Sbac Tr ALDT GU11 .... 112 B2
Scafell Av FHAM/STUB PO14 .... 14 B8
Scallows La ROMY SO51 .... 288 C5
Scantabout Av CHFD SO53 .... 293 K1
Scant Road (West) RCCH PO18... 379 M6
Scarf Rd CFDH BH17 .... 445 L1
Scarlatti Rd KEMP RG22 .... 104 E8
Scarlet Oaks CBLY GU15 .... 71 H5
Scarlett's Rd ALDT GU11 .... 112 D5
Scholars' Wk CHAM PO6 .... 400 A1
School Cl CHFD SO53 .... 293 G3
LYMN SO41 .... 440 A6
RAND SP11 .... 73 H3
School Flds BOR GU35 .... 179 G7
School Hl BPWT SO32 .... 325 H2
CWTH RG45 .... 50 A4
RFNM GU10 .... 136 E4
RFNM GU10 .... 158 C2
SHST GU47 .... 49 K7
School La BWD BH11 .... 431 M3
CHCH/BSGR BH23 .... 410 C4
CHFD SO53 .... 292 F4
EMRTH PO10 .... 378 F3
HLER SO31 .... 369 L7
LISS GU33 .... 248 E4
LYMN SO41 .... 414 D8
LYMN SO41 .... 440 C4
LYMN SO41 .... 454 D2
MIDH GU29 .... 279 J7
NALR SO24 .... 219 G3
NALR SO24 .... 220 B4
RFNM GU10 .... 157 G3
RFNM GU10 .... 159 G2
PLE BH15 .... 445 H3
PSF GU32 .... 275 M2
RCCH PO18 .... 330 E6
RCCH PO18 .... 403 K1
RGUW GU3 .... 137 M4
RGWD BH24 .... 381 L3
RWIN SO21 .... 216 E1
STOK SO20 .... 162 E8
STOK SO20 .... 208 F1
THLE RG7 .... 31 J6
THLE RG7 .... 42 F7
THLE RG7 .... 46 B5
WIMB BH21 .... 380 D1
WINC SO23 .... 215 G3
WVILLE PO7 .... 351 H3
YTLY GU46 .... 68 E2
School Rd BPWT SO32 .... 324 E6
CHCH/BSGR BH23 .... 410 C4
FAWY SO45 .... 392 E5
GPORT PO12 .... 397 K7
GSHT GU26 .... 203 L5
HASM GU27 .... 228 C3
HAV PO9 .... 16 D5
HLER SO31 .... 345 L8
BOR GU35 .... 201 J4
RFNM GU10 .... 158 B5
ROMY SO51 .... 263 H7
ROMY SO51 .... 288 E6
RSAL SP5 .... 285 L4
RSAL SP5 .... 287 H8
RWIN SO21 .... 266 E2
THLE RG7 .... 30 C7
THLE RG7 .... 46 B4
TLHT RG30 .... 31 M2
TOTT SO40 .... 341 L2
WHAM PO17 .... 348 E5
Schooner Wy HLER SO31 .... 370 C7
Schroeder Cl BSTK RG21 .... 104 F6
Schubert Rd KEMP RG22 .... 104 D8
The Scimitars
FHAM/STUB PO14 .... 395 M5 ☒
Scivier's La BPWT SO32 .... 296 B6
Scotland Cl ASHV GU12 .... 113 K3
ELGH SO50 .... 295 K6
Scotland Farm Rd ASHV GU12 ... 113 K3
Scotland Hl SHST GU47 .... 49 J8
Scotland La HASM GU27 .... 228 E3
RSAL SP5 .... 286 F1
Scotlands Cl HASM GU27 .... 228 E3
Scotlands Dr HASM GU27 .... 228 E3 ☒
Scotney Ct HAV PO9 .... 377 M2 ☒
Scotney Rd BSTK RG21 .... 4 E3
Scott Cl BKME/WDN BH12 .... 431 K7
RWIN SO21 .... 396 A4
STOK SO20 .... 210 F6
Scotter Rd ELGH SO50 .... 294 C5
LTDN BH7 .... 449 G3
Scott Rd BKME/WDN BH12 .... 431 K8
ELGH SO50 .... 293 L6
HSEA PO3 .... 399 K3
ITCH SO19 .... 344 D7
PSEA PO1 .... 422 D2
Scott's Ct FARN GU14 .... 90 E1
Scott's Gn CHCH/BSGR BH23 .... 435 K8
Scotts Hills La
CHCH/BSGR BH23 .... 450 C2
Scratchface La HAV PO9 .... 376 F4
WVILLE PO7 .... 376 D4
Scrivens Md STHA RG19 .... 27 J5
Scrubbs La NALR SO24 .... 218 F5
Scullards La SHAM SO14 .... 12 F3
Scures Rd HTWY RG27 .... 85 L7

Seabird Wy FHAM/PORC PO16 .... 15 K9
Seabourne Rd BOSC BH5 .... 449 G2
Seabreeze Wy LYMN SO41 .... 453 M4 ☒
Seacombe Gn ROWN SO16 .... 317 J2
Seacombe Rd CCLF BH13 .... 457 G5
Sea Crest Rd
LSOL/BMARY PO13 .... 420 F8
Seacroft Av NMIL/BTOS BH25 .... 437 J8
Seafield Cl NMIL/BTOS BH25 .... 452 E1
Seafield Dr SBNE BH6 .... 449 K2
Seafield Park Rd
FHAM/STUB PO14 .... 395 K3
Seafield Rd CHCH/BSGR BH23 ... 451 H2
FHAM/PORC PO16 .... 397 M3
HSEA PO3 .... 399 L2
NMIL/BTOS BH25 .... 437 J8
ROWN SO16 .... 317 J6
SBNE BH6 .... 449 J4
Seafields EMRTH PO10 .... 378 C8
Seafire Wy FARN GU14 .... 112 A1
Seaford Cl HLER SO31 .... 345 K7 ☒
Seagarth La ROWN SO16 .... 318 C3
Seager's Ct PSEA PO1 .... 20 B5 ☒
Sea Grove Av HISD PO11 .... 425 L6
Seagrove Rd NEND PO2 .... 399 H1
Seagull Cl ENEY PO4 .... 423 L8
KEMP RG22 .... 103 L8 ☒
Seagull La EMRTH PO10 .... 378 D2
Seagull Rd CHAR BH8 .... 433 G2
The Seagulls
LSOL/BMARY PO13 .... 420 E4 ☒
Sea Kings FHAM/STUB PO14 ... 395 M6 ☒
Sea La LSOL/BMARY PO13 .... 396 A4
Seale La RFNM GU10 .... 136 A4
RGUW GU3 .... 137 J4
Seale Rd BSTK RG21 .... 4 F7
Seaman's La LYND SO43 .... 338 F7
Seamead FHAM/STUB PO14 .... 396 A4
Seamoor Rd CCLF BH13 .... 447 C6
WBNE BH4 .... 447 G5
Searing Wy TADY RG26 .... 41 K7
Searle Rd FNM GU9 .... 134 E3
Searles Cl NALR SO24 .... 218 C3 ☒
Searles Hl RWIN SO21 .... 266 F2
Searl's La HTWY RG27 .... 86 A4
Sea Rd BOSC BH5 .... 448 D6
ITCH SO19 .... 344 B4
LYMN SO41 .... 454 D4
NMIL/BTOS BH25 .... 437 J4
SBNE BH6 .... 449 L4
Seaton Av HSEA PO3 .... 399 L4
Seaton Cl CHCH/BSGR BH23 .... 436 F6
FHAM/STUB PO14 .... 396 A4
LYMN SO41 .... 440 C3 ☒
WEND SO18 .... 320 B8
Seaton Rd CBLY GU15 .... 70 E7
CHCH/BSGR BH23 .... 436 F7
Seatown Cl CFDH BH17 .... 430 E7
Seaview Av FHAM/PORC PO16 ... 374 C7
Sea View Rd BKME/WDN BH12... 445 M4
CHAM PO6 .... 376 A4
Seaview Rd CHCH/BSGR BH23 .... 437 G7
HISD PO11 .... 426 A4
NMIL/BTOS BH25 .... 452 C1
Seaward Av NMIL/BTOS BH25 .... 452 D1
SBNE BH6 .... 449 G4
Seaward Dr SELS SO20 .... 427 L1
Seaward Rd FAWY SO45 .... 367 M4
ITCH SO19 .... 344 C2
Seaway NMIL/BTOS BH25 .... 437 M8 ☒
Seaway Av CHCH/BSGR BH23 ... 451 H4
Seaway Crs ENEY PO4 .... 424 A4
Seaway Gv FHAM/PORC PO16... 398 A4
Seawinds LYMN SO41 .... 453 M3 ☒
Sebastian Gv WVILLE PO7 .... 352 E8 ☒
Sebastopol Rd ALDT GU11 .... 7 G2
Second Av CHAM PO6 .... 400 C2
EMRTH PO10 .... 379 H4
HAV PO9 .... 17 J2
THLE RG7 .... 41 M7
WSHM SO15 .... 342 B4
Second Marine Av
NMIL/BTOS BH25 .... 452 F1
Second St FAWY SO45 .... 368 C2
STHA RG19 .... 38 C7
Sedbergh Rd ROWN SO16 .... 317 J2
Sedgefield Cl CHAM PO6 .... 374 D7
TOTT SO40 .... 316 B3
Sedgefield Rd NWBY RG14 .... 3 J2
Sedge Gv NTHA RG18 .... 27 H2 ☒
Sedgeley Gv GPORT PO12 .... 397 L2
Sedgemead HLER SO31 .... 368 F3 ☒
Sedgemoor FARN GU14 .... 90 E2
Sedgewick Cl
LSOL/BMARY PO13 .... 397 G2
Sedgewick Rd ELGH SO50 .... 294 C2
ITCH SO19 .... 345 G2
Sedgley Cl SSEA PO5 .... 21 L7
Sedley Gdns BOR GU35 .... 200 F6
Segars La RWIN SO21 .... 266 E2
Segensworth Rd FHAM PO15 ... 371 K8
Sek Kong Cl STOK SO20 .... 162 E7
Selangor Av EMRTH PO10 .... 378 D7
Selborne Av ALDT GU11 .... 7 H2
HAV PO9 .... 377 H3
WEND SO18 .... 320 E2
Selborne Cl BLKW GU17 .... 69 M2 ☒
HTWY RG27 .... 86 A4
PSF GU32 .... 275 J1
Selborne Gdns FNM GU9 .... 158 D1 ☒
GPORT PO12 .... 397 L2
Selborne Pl WINW SO22 .... 238 C3 ☒
Selborne Rd ALTN GU34 .... 176 F7
LISS GU33 .... 224 A2
Selborne Wy BOR GU35 .... 200 F6
Selborne Dr ELGH SO50 .... 293 M4
Selbourne Rd HAV PO9 .... 377 H3
TOTT SO40 .... 316 C8
Selbourne Ter PSEA PO1 .... 21 M4 ☒
Selby Cl BDST BH18 .... 429 L3
Seldon Cl WINW SO22 .... 238 A4
Seldown Br PLE BH15 .... 445 J3
Seldown La PLE BH15 .... 445 J2
Seldown Rd PLE BH15 .... 445 J3
Selfridge Av SBNE BH6 .... 450 A4

Selhurst Wy ELGH SO50 .... 295 H7
Seliot Cl PLE BH15 .... 445 J3
Selkirk Cl WIMB BH21 .... 404 C7
Sellwood Rd HLER SO31 .... 369 G3
Sellwood Wy
  NMIL/BTOS BH25 .... 437 H8
Selsdon Av ROMY SO51 .... 263 G8
Selsey Av ENEY PO4 .... 423 J4
  GPORT PO12 .... 397 K8
Selsey Cl HISD PO11 .... 426 D6
  ROWN SO16 .... 317 K6
Selsmore Av HISD PO11 .... 426 A6
Selsmore Rd HISD PO11 .... 425 L5
Selworth La BPWT SO32 .... 325 G5
Selworthy Cl PSTN BH14 .... 445 M6
Selwyn Dr YTLY GU46 .... 68 C2
Selwyn Gdns ELGH SO50 .... 293 M3
Sengana Cl HEND SO30 .... 346 B2
Seniac Rd ROMY SO51 .... 291 G1
Sennen Pl CHAM PO6 .... 398 E1
Sentinel Cl WVILLE PO7 .... 352 F7
September Cl HEND SO30 .... 320 C7
Seremban Cl STOK SO20 .... 162 F3
Serle Cl TOTT SO40 .... 340 F1
Serle Gdns TOTT SO40 .... 341 H1
Sermon Rd WINW SO22 .... 214 A7
Serpentine Rd
  FHAM/PORC PO16 .... 15 J2
  PLE BH15 .... 445 H5
  SSEA PO5 .... 20 F8
  SSEA PO5 .... 21 G7
  WVILLE PO7 .... 376 A1
Setley Gdns CHAR BH8 .... 433 J3
Seton Cl HTWY RG27 .... 85 L8
Setters Cl RWIN SO21 .... 266 E8
Set Thorns Rd LYMN SO41 .... 413 G6
Settle Cl ROWN SO16 .... 318 A3
Settlers Rd PSEA PO1 .... 423 H2
The Sett YTLY GU46 .... 68 E3
Sevenoaks Dr LTDN BH7 .... 433 L8
Sevenoaks Rd CHAM PO6 .... 375 J8
Seventh St STHA RG19 .... 38 C3
Severals Rd MIDH GU29 .... 279 L8
The Severals CHAM RG24 .... 82 D5
Severn Cl CHAM PO6 .... 374 F7
  FHAM/PORC PO16 .... 373 L8
  NTHA RG18 .... 26 E3
  SHST GU47 .... 49 M8
Severn Ct AND SP10 .... 9 L4
Severn Gdns DEAN RG23 .... 103 C2
Severn Rd FARN GU14 .... 90 B2
  FERN BH22 .... 406 E2
  ROWN SO16 .... 317 K8
Severn Wy BSTK RG21 .... 5 K8
  HEND SO30 .... 320 C7
Seville Crs AND SP10 .... 9 L3
Seward Ri ROMY SO51 .... 263 H8
Seymour Cl CHFD SO53 .... 293 K3
  NEND PO2 .... 423 H1
  TOTT SO40 .... 316 B7
Seymour Dr CBLY GU15 .... 51 L8
Seymour La NBAD SO52 .... 291 L4
Seymour Rd KEMP RG22 .... 104 B6
  BOR GU35 .... 202 F4
  LSOL/BMARY PO13 .... 420 D4
  RGWD BH24 .... 358 F7
  ROWN SO16 .... 318 B5
Shackleton Rd
  LSOL/BMARY PO13 .... 397 H8
Shadwell Rd NEND PO2 .... 399 J6
Shady Nook FNM GU9 .... 134 C2
Shaftesbury Av CHFD SO53 .... 293 H4
  PTSW SO17 .... 319 G7
  WVILLE PO7 .... 352 C1
Shaftesbury Cl FERN BH22 .... 380 D6
Shaftesbury Mt BLKW GU17 .... 69 M5
Shaftesbury Rd CHAR BH8 .... 448 B2
  FERN BH22 .... 380 D7
  PLE BH15 .... 445 J5
  SSEA PO5 .... 21 H6
Shaftesbury St FBDG SP6 .... 309 K7
Shaftsbury Rd GPORT PO12 .... 19 G4
Shaggs Meadow LYND SO43 ..... 363 K3
Shakespeare Av AND SP10 .... 8 A3
Shakespeare Dr TOTT SO40 ...... 316 C6
Shakespeare Gdns
  FARN GU14 .... 90 A3
  HORN PO8 .... 352 C5
Shakespeare Rd CHAM RG24 .... 5 G1
  ELGH SO50 .... 293 L5
  NTHA RG18 .... 26 F4
  PSEA PO1 .... 423 J2
  WIMB BH21 .... 404 A2
Shalbourne Ri CBLY GU15 .... 71 G3
Shalbourne Rd GPORT PO12 ..... 421 J1
Shalcombe HLER SO31 .... 369 G1
Shalden Rd ASHV GU12 .... 7 L1
Shaldon Cl ROWN SO16 .... 318 A4
Shaldon Rd HAV PO9 .... 377 M2
Shaldon Wy FLET GU13 .... 88 C8
Shales Rd WEND SO18 .... 344 F1
Shallow La LYMN SO41 .... 414 B8
The Shallows FBDG SP6 .... 310 B1
Shambehurst La HEND SO30 ...... 321 H7
Shamblehurst La North
  BPWT SO32 .... 321 J5
Shamblehurst La South
  HEND SO30 .... 321 H8
Shamrock Cl FRIM GU16 .... 71 G8
  GPORT PO12 .... 19 J4
Shamrock Rd ITCH SO19 .... 344 B5
Shamrock Wy FAWY SO45 .... 367 L3
Shanklin Cl ASHV GU12 .... 7 K4
Shanklin Crs WSHM SO15 .... 318 C7
Shanklin Rd ENEY PO4 .... 21 M4
  WSHM SO15 .... 318 C6
Shannon Cl FHAM PO15 .... 14 A3
Shannon Ct AND SP10 .... 9 M1
Shannon Rd
  FHAM/STUB PO14 .... 395 M4
  FHAM/STUB PO14 .... 396 D3
Shannon Wy CHFD SO53 .... 293 G2
Shapland Av BWD BH11 .... 431 J3
Shappen Hill La RGWD BH24 ..... 384 D6
Shapton Cl FAWY SO45 .... 391 M4
Shapwick Rd PLE BH15 .... 444 F7
Shard Cl VWD BH31 .... 356 E2

Sharf Rd BKME/WDN BH12 .... 446 F1
Sharlands Cl BDST BH18 .... 429 M5
Sharon Rd HEND SO30 .... 320 B6
Sharpley Cl FBDG SP6 .... 309 K5
Sharpness Cl
  FHAM/STUB PO14 .... 372 A8
Sharps Cl HSEA PO3 .... 399 M5
Sharps Rd HAV PO9 .... 377 M3
Sharvells Rd LYMN SO41 .... 454 B3
Shavard La BPWT SO32 .... 299 J3
Shaves La NMIL/BTOS BH25 ...... 437 L3
Shaw Cl AND SP10 .... 118 B8
  TOTT SO40 .... 341 H1
  WEND SO18 .... 319 M6
Shaw Farm Rd NWBY RG14 .... 25 L3
Shawfield La ASHV GU12 .... 113 J6
Shawfield Rd ASHV GU12 .... 113 J7
  HAV PO9 .... 17 H6
Shawford Cl ROWN SO16 .... 318 D4
  TOTT SO40 .... 340 F1
Shawford Gv HAV PO9 .... 377 G3
Shawford Rd CHAR BH8 .... 433 H5
  RWIN SO21 .... 266 E2
Shaw Hl MARL SN8 .... 92 A4
  NWBY RG14 .... 25 L3
Shaw La TADY RG26 .... 61 J2
Shaw Pk CWTH RG45 .... 49 L5
Shaw Pightle HTWY RG27 .... 85 L7
Shaw Rd NWBY RG14 .... 3 G1
  RGWD BH24 .... 359 G6
Sheardley La BPWT SO32 .... 299 L8
Shearer Rd PSEA PO1 .... 423 J1
Shear Hl EPSF GU31 .... 276 A3
Shears Rd ELGH SO50 .... 294 D5
Shearwater Av
  FHAM/PORC PO16 .... 373 J8
Shearwater Cl
  LSOL/BMARY PO13 .... 396 F6
Shearwater Dr CHAM PO6 .... 400 D1
Sheep Dro STOK SO20 .... 184 C4
Sheep Fair Cl AND SP10 .... 9 G5
Sheephatch La FARN GU10 .... 159 L3
Sheephouse FNM GU9 .... 134 F3
Sheep Pond La BPWT SO32 .... 298 F5
Sheep St PSF GU32 .... 275 L5
Sheepwash La KSCL SO20 .... 37 K6
  SELS SO20 .... 427 M5
  TADY RG26 .... 81 J2
  WVILLE PO7 .... 351 K8
Sheerlands Rd EWKG RG40 .... 47 L2
Sheffield Cl ELGH SO50 .... 294 C3
  FARN GU14 .... 90 C4
Sheffield Rd PSEA PO1 .... 21 L1
Shelbourne Cl CHAR BH8 .... 448 A5
Sheldon's La HTWY RG27 .... 85 M7
Sheldon Rd HTWY RG27 .... 85 M7
Shelley Av CHAM PO6 .... 374 C7
  CHCH/BSGR BH23 .... 451 H1
  FLET GU13 .... 88 F8
  WINW SO22 .... 10 A6
  RGWD BH24 .... 381 J3
  RWIN SO21 .... 216 D2
Shelley Ct CBLY GU15 .... 70 F3
Shelley Gdns BMTH BH1 .... 448 B5
  HORN PO8 .... 352 C5
Shelley La ROMY SO51 .... 289 K7
Shelley La BMTH BH1 .... 448 B5
  ELGH SO50 .... 293 L7
  ITCH SO19 .... 345 H2
  NTHA RG18 .... 26 F4
  PSTN BH14 .... 446 C3
  TOTT SO40 .... 316 C6
Shelley Rd East BMTH BH1 .... 448 D5
Shelleys La ALTN GU34 .... 177 K7
Shelley Wk YTLY GU46 .... 68 E3
Shell La ALTN GU34 .... 222 A5
Shelly Ri FARN GU14 .... 90 C1
Shelton Rd SBNE BH6 .... 449 H2
Shenley Cl FHAM PO15 .... 372 A6
Shepards Cl FHAM/STUB PO14 .. 372 A8
Shepherd Cl CHCH/BSGR BH23 .. 436 C7
  TOTT SO40 .... 339 M2
Shepherds Cl WINW SO22 .... 238 A4
Shepherds Down NALR SO24 ..... 218 D4
Shepherds Her Rd TOTT SO40 ... 316 A7
Shepherd's Hl HASM GU27 .... 228 F2
  RGWD BH24 .... 358 A2
Shepherds La RGWD BH24 .... 357 L2
  RWIN SO21 .... 265 L2
Shepherds Purse Cl
  HLER SO31 .... 370 D6
Shepherds Ri RAND SP11 .... 73 H3
Shepherds Rd TOTT SO40 .... 339 M2
  WINC SO23 .... 11 M7
Shepherds Rw AND SP10 .... 9 L6
Shepherds Spring La AND SP10 ... 9 H4
Shepherds Wk FARN GU14 .... 90 B1
Shepherds Wy CWTH RG45 .... 49 H1
  LIPH GU30 .... 227 G5
  LTDN BH7 .... 448 K1
  RFNM GU10 .... 159 M4
  ROWN SO16 .... 317 H3
Sheppard Cl HORN PO8 .... 352 E2
  WHCH RG28 .... 122 B4
Sheppard Rd BSTK RG21 .... 104 F6
Shepton Br BROC SO42 .... 589 M3
Sheraton Av KEMP RG22 .... 127 G5
Sheraton Cl BLKW GU17 .... 70 B4
Sherborn Cl CFDH BH17 .... 430 D7
Sherborne Cl ELGH SO50 .... 293 L2
Sherborne Dr FERN BH22 .... 406 A4
Sherborne Rd BSTK RG21 .... 4 C4
  CHAM RG24 .... 82 E6
  FARN GU14 .... 91 G8
  PTSW SO17 .... 319 G8
Sherborne Wy HEND SO30 .... 346 A2
Sherbrooke Cl WINC SO23 .... 191 H8
Sherfield Av HAV PO9 .... 377 L3
Sherfield English La
  ROMY SO51 .... 288 B2
  RSAL SP5 .... 288 A3

Sherfield English Rd RSAL SP5 .. 288 A5
Sherfield Rd TADY RG26 .... 63 L5
Sheridan Cl WINW SO22 .... 238 B3
  ITCH SO19 .... 345 G3
Sheridan Crs TADY RG26 .... 41 H7
Sheridan Gdns HLER SO31 .... 347 G8
  TOTT SO40 .... 341 H1
Sheridan Rd FRIM GU16 .... 71 J6
Sheringham Rd
  BKME/WDN BH12 .... 446 E3
  CHAM PO6 .... 375 H7
Sherlock Lea HTWY RG27 .... 68 B1
Shermin's Bank
  CHCH/BSGR BH23 .... 450 D3
Sherrardmead NWBY RG14 .... 25 L3
Sherrin Cl PLE BH15 .... 445 J3
Sherringham Cl FAWY SO45 ...... 392 F5
Sherwin Crs FARN GU14 .... 70 E8
Sherwood Av FERN BH22 .... 406 A5
  HEND SO30 .... 346 A4
  PSTN BH14 .... 445 L6
Sherwood Cl
  CHCH/BSGR BH23 .... 449 L1
  KEMP RG22 .... 127 H2
  LISS GU33 .... 248 F1
  ROWN SO16 .... 318 D5
Sherwood Dr VWD BH31 .... 356 F2
Sherwood Gdns HLER SO31 ...... 370 C4
Sherwood Rd CHFD SO53 .... 265 K7
  GPORT PO12 .... 18 D3
Sherwood Wy FAWY SO45 .... 418 C1
Shetland Cl CHAM PO6 .... 375 K7
  TOTT SO40 .... 316 A8
Shetland Hl HLER SO31 .... 370 F2
Shetland Rd CHAM RG24 .... 83 H5
Shetland Wy FARN GU14 .... 89 G4
Shillinglee WVILLE PO7 .... 376 C5
Shillingstone Dr
  MOOR/WNTN BH9 .... 432 F4
Shillito Rd BKME/WDN BH12 .... 446 C3
Shingle Bank Dr LYMN SO41 ..... 454 C4
Ship Aly FARN GU14 .... 90 F2
Shipbuilding Rd PSEA PO1 .... 422 F1
Shipcote La BPWT SO32 .... 297 H6
Ship La FARN GU14 .... 90 F2
Ship Leopard St PSEA PO1 .... 20 C2
Shipley Cl LIPH GU30 .... 226 E5
Shipley Rd RWIN SO21 .... 266 F1
Shipstal Cl UPTN BH16 .... 444 B4
Shipton Wy KEMP RG22 .... 104 B6
Shire Av FARN GU14 .... 89 H5
Shire Cl HLER SO31 .... 370 F1
  HORN PO8 .... 352 F7
Shire Ct ALDT GU11 .... 6 A2
Shires Cl RGWD BH24 .... 382 E4
Shires Md VWD BH31 .... 356 E2
The Shires HEND SO30 .... 345 L2
Shires Wy YTLY GU46 .... 49 G8
Shirley Av ENEY PO4 .... 424 A4
  WSHM SO15 .... 318 B8
Shirley Cl CHCH/BSGR BH23 ..... 409 M7
  FERN BH22 .... 380 C5
Shirley High St ROWN SO16 ..... 318 A8
Shirley Holms LYMN SO41 .... 413 K7
Shirley Park Rd ROWN SO16 ..... 318 A8
Shirley Rd BKME/WDN BH12 ..... 446 A5
  MOOR/WNTN BH9 .... 432 E7
  SSEA PO5 .... 21 L8
  WSHM SO15 .... 318 B8
Shoddesden La RAND SP11 .... 92 F8
  RAND SP11 .... 116 B2
Shoe La ALDT GU11 .... 112 D2
  BPWT SO32 .... 296 E2
Sholing Ct HAV PO9 .... 377 L4
Sholing Rd ITCH SO19 .... 344 C4
Shooters Hill Cl ITCH SO19 .... 344 F5
Shooters Wy BSTK RG21 .... 5 G4
Shoot Hl WHAM PO17 .... 350 B5
Shoot La LSOL/BMARY PO13 ..... 396 E8
Shop La HLER SO31 .... 345 J5
  NWBY RG14 .... 25 J2
Shore Av HSEA PO3 .... 423 K4
  UPTN BH16 .... 444 B2
Shore Cl UPTN BH16 .... 444 B4
Shore Crs BPWT SO32 .... 323 J1
Shorefield Crs LYMN SO41 .... 454 B3
Shorefield Rd LYMN SO41 .... 453 M2
  TOTT SO40 .... 342 D6
Shorefield Wy LYMN SO41 .... 454 A3
Shore Gdns UPTN BH16 .... 444 A2
Shorehaven CHAM PO6 .... 374 D8
Shore La BPWT SO32 .... 323 J1
  UPTN BH16 .... 444 A3
Shore Rd CCLF BH13 .... 457 J2
  FAWY SO45 .... 367 M4
  PSTN BH14 .... 457 J1
Shorewell HLER SO31 .... 369 G1
Shorewood Cl HLER SO31 .... 370 E7
Short Cl BKME/WDN BH12 .... 431 L8
Short Dale Rd ALDT GU11 .... 7 K9
Shortfield Rd RFNM GU10 .... 158 F7
Shortheath Crest FNM GU9 ...... 158 C2
Shortheath Rd THLE RG7 .... 31 G5
Shortheath Rd FNM GU9 .... 158 D2
Short Hl ROMY SO51 .... 263 H7
Short La RAND SP11 .... 117 M7
Short Rd FHAM/STUB PO14 ...... 395 L6
Short Rw PSEA PO1 .... 422 E2
Shorts Cl CHCH/BSGR BH23 ..... 435 C7
Shorts Rd ELGH SO50 .... 295 G6
Short St ALDT GU11 .... 6 E1
  RAND SP11 .... 92 E6
Shotterfield Ter LISS GU33 .... 248 E4
Shotters La ALTN GU34 .... 222 E2
Shottsford Rd PLE BH15 .... 445 H3
Shotts La LYMN SO41 .... 441 G4
Shraveshill Cl TOTT SO40 .... 316 C7
The Shrave ALTN GU34 .... 197 K4
Shrivenham Cl SHST GU47 .... 50 A8
Shrubbery Cl
  FHAM/PORC PO16 .... 398 A1
The Shrubbery FARN GU14 .... 90 A5
  GPORT PO12 .... 19 K1
Shrubb's Av LYMN SO41 .... 440 C5
Shrubbs Hill Gdns
  LYND SO43 .... 363 K4
Shrubbs Hill Rd LYND SO43 ...... 363 K4
Shrubbs La RFNM GU10 .... 158 C4

Shrubland Cl WEND SO18........... 320 A8
Shyshack La TADY RG26 .... 41 H7
Sibelius Cl KEMP RG22 .... 127 K1
Sibland Cl FHAM/STUB PO14 ...... 14 A8
Sickle Rd HASM GU27 .... 228 C3
Sickles Rd BOR GU35 .... 179 G6
Sidbury Circular Rd NTID SP9 ... 114 C1
Sidestrand Rd ALDT GU11 .... 112 B1
  NWBY RG14 .... 25 G8
The Sidings ALDT GU11 .... 112 F5
  HLER SO31 .... 369 H3
  RSAL SP5 .... 256 F8
Sidlaw Cl KEMP RG22 .... 103 M5
Sidlaws Rd FARN GU14 .... 90 A1
Sidlesham Cl HISD PO11 .... 426 D6
Sidmouth Av HSEA PO3 .... 399 L8
Sidmouth Rd AND SP10 .... 9 M5
Silchester Cl AND SP10 .... 8 C1
  WCLF BH2 .... 22 E3
Silchester Rd HSEA PO3 .... 423 M1
  TADY RG26 .... 41 L7
  TADY RG26 .... 62 D3
  TADY RG26 .... 63 G5
Silkin Gdns TOTT SO40 .... 341 H2
Silk Mill La OVTN RG25 .... 100 E8
Silkstead Av HAV PO9 .... 377 K2
Silkstead La RWIN SO21 .... 265 L3
Silkweavers Rd AND SP10 .... 9 J4
Sillen La HASM GU27 .... 280 F5
Silver Birch Av
  FHAM/STUB PO14 .... 14 C7
Silver Birch Cl
  BKME/WDN BH12 .... 446 F4
  FLET GU13 .... 110 E3
  LISS GU33 .... 248 F4
Silver Birches HLER SO31 .... 345 K8
Silver Birch Rd AND SP10 .... 8 C3
Silverdale FLET GU13 .... 110 F2
  NMIL/BTOS BH25 .... 437 M8
  NMIL/BTOS BH25 .... 453 G1
Silverdale Crs FBDG SP6 .... 333 L2
Silverdale Dr WVILLE PO7 .... 352 A6
Silverdale Rd TADY RG26 .... 41 K7
  WSHM SO15 .... 343 J1
Silver Dr FRIM GU16 .... 71 M5
Silverglades YTLY GU46 .... 68 F4
Silver Hl SHST GU47 .... 50 B8
  WINC SO23 .... 11 H8
Silver La THLE RG7 .... 30 D8
Silverlock Cl NEND PO2 .... 399 H8
Silver Park Cl FLET GU13 .... 111 G2
Silversands Gdns HISD PO11 ..... 425 M6
Silvers End FAWY SO45 .... 367 L7
Silver St LYMN SO41 .... 438 D4
  LYND SO43 .... 363 H3
  SSEA PO5 .... 20 F5
Silvers Wd TOTT SO40 .... 316 A8
Silverthorne Wy WVILLE PO7 .... 352 B8
Silvertrees EMRTH PO10 .... 378 D6
Silver Wy CHCH/BSGR BH23 .... 436 C8
Silverwood Cl WINW SO22 .... 238 C3
  WIMB BH21 .... 404 B6
Silverwood Dr CBLY GU15 .... 71 K1
Silvester Cl BSTK RG21 .... 5 H4
Silvester Rd HORN PO8 .... 352 C6
Silvester Wy FLET GU13 .... 110 D4
Silwood Cl WINW SO22 .... 238 C3
Simmondstone La RFNM GU10 .. 181 G6
Simmons Cl HEND SO30 .... 321 H8
Simmons Gn HISD PO11 .... 426 A5
Simms Farm La THLE RG7 .... 43 J4
Simnel St SHAM SO14 .... 12 F5
Simonds Rd RAND SP11 .... 92 D6
Simons Fld NTHA RG18 .... 27 J4
Simons Rd CHAM RG24 .... 83 K6
Simon Wy WEND SO18 .... 345 J1
Simpson Cl FHAM/PORC PO16 .. 374 B8
Simpson Rd NEND PO2 .... 399 G7
Sims Cl TADY RG26 .... 64 A6
Sinah La HISD PO11 .... 425 G5
Sinclair Rd ROWN SO16 .... 317 M3
Sine Cl FARN GU14 .... 70 E8
Singleton Dr NBNE BH10 .... 432 A6
Singleton Gdns HORN PO8 .... 328 C4
Singleton Wy TOTT SO40 .... 316 A8
Sinhurst Rd CBLY GU15 .... 70 E4
Sir Christopher Cl
  FAWY SO45 .... 367 M4
Sirdar Rd PTSW SO17 .... 319 H5
Sir Galahad Rd NBAD SO52 ...... 292 E2
Sir George's Rd WSHM SO15 ..... 343 H2
Sir Lancelot Cl NBAD SO52 .... 292 E2
Siskin Cl BPWT SO32 .... 296 F8
  FERN BH22 .... 405 M1
  ROWN SO16 .... 317 M3
Siskin Gv WVILLE PO7 .... 376 E2
Sissinghurst Cl ITCH SO19 .... 344 E7
Sissinghurst Rd
  FHAM/PORC PO16 .... 397 M1
Six Acre La HUNG RG17 .... 32 C2
Six Oaks Rd NBAD SO52 .... 291 M3
Sixpenny Cl BKME/WDN BH12 .. 446 E1
  HLER SO31 .... 370 E7
Sixth Av CHAM PO6 .... 375 J8
Sixth St STHA RG19 .... 38 C3
Sizer Wy FAWY SO45 .... 366 F5
Skates La TADY RG26 .... 62 A3
Skew Rd RAND SP11 .... 140 A5
Skilman Dr STHA RG19 .... 27 J5
Skinner's Green La KSCL SO20 .... 36 C2
Skinner St PLE BH15 .... 445 H7
Skipper Wy LSOL/BMARY PO13 .. 420 D3
Skippetts La East BSTK RG21 .... 105 H5
Skippetts La West BSTK RG21 ... 105 G6
Skippons Ct NWBY RG14 .... 36 C1
Skipton Cl BDST BH18 .... 429 L6
Skipton Rd CHFD SO53 .... 293 J4
Sky End La LYMN SO41 .... 438 E6
Skylark Mdw FHAM PO15 .... 371 K3
Skylark Ri WHCH RG28 .... 122 A2
Skylings NWBY RG14 .... 3 J2
Skys Wood Rd NBAD SO52 .... 292 E1
Slab La ROMY SO51 .... 288 C5
  RSAL SP5 .... 284 F1
Slade Cl LYMN SO41 .... 438 E5

Slade La EPSF GU31 .... 277 H4
Slades Farm Rd NBNE BH10 ...... 432 A7
Slades Hl FAWY SO45 .... 392 D6
Slade's La NBNE BH10 .... 432 A8
Slater Cl TOTT SO40 .... 316 A8
Sleepbrook Cl VWD BH31 .... 356 C2
Sleepers Delle Gdns
  WINW SO22 .... 238 D2
Sleepers' Hl WINW SO22 .... 238 C2
Sleepers Hill Gdns
  WINW SO22 .... 238 C2
Slepe Crs BKME/WDN BH12 ...... 431 K8
Slessor Cl RAND SP11 .... 142 A1
Slim Cl ALDT GU11 .... 113 H1
Slim Rd CBLY GU15 .... 70 E1
Slindon Cl HORN PO8 .... 328 C3
Slindon St PSEA PO1 .... 21 H1
Slingsby Cl PSEA PO1 .... 20 F5
Slinn Rd CHCH/BSGR BH23 ...... 450 D1
Slipper Rd EMRTH PO10 .... 402 E1
Slip Wy PLE BH15 .... 445 H8
Sloane Av FAWY SO45 .... 392 B4
Sloane Ct FAWY SO45 .... 392 D6
Sloane Pk BPWT SO32 .... 348 B1
Sloe Tree Cl HLER SO31 .... 371 G6
Smallcutts Av EMRTH PO10 ...... 379 H7
Smallfield Dr HTWY RG27 .... 86 B7
Smallridge KSCL SO20 .... 36 F7
Smannell Rd RAND SP11 .... 119 J4
Smay Down La MARL SN8 .... 52 A5
Smeaton Rd AND SP10 .... 118 A6
Smeaton St NEND PO2 .... 399 G6
Smeeton Rd
  LSOL/BMARY PO13 .... 420 D2
Smith Cl FAWY SO45 .... 392 D6
Smithe Cl ELGH SO50 .... 293 M5
Smithfield La BOR GU35 .... 180 D7
Smith Gv HEND SO30 .... 346 A3
Smith La EMRTH PO10 .... 403 G7
Smith's Fld ROMY SO51 .... 262 F3
Smiths La BPWT SO32 .... 323 L8
Smith's Md OVTN RG25 .... 125 L7
Smith St GPORT PO12 .... 18 D5
Smithy Cl ALTN GU34 .... 177 J1
Smithy La BOR GU35 .... 180 B6
  NMIL/BTOS BH25 .... 437 K2
The Smithy TADY RG26 .... 63 L5
  WVILLE PO7 .... 351 J4
Smugglers La North
  CHCH/BSGR BH23 .... 436 A8
Smugglers La South
  CHCH/BSGR BH23 .... 436 C8
Smugglers' Wy RFNM GU10 ...... 136 B8
Smugglers Wood Rd
  CHCH/BSGR BH23 .... 436 A7
Smythe Rd ITCH SO19 .... 345 H5
Snailing La LISS GU33 .... 224 C7
  LISS GU33 .... 248 A2
Snail's La RGWD BH24 .... 358 C6
Snake La KSCL SO20 .... 24 D2
Snakemoor La BPWT SO32 .... 321 K3
Snapdragon Cl HLER SO31 .... 370 D6
Snape Cl LSOL/BMARY PO13 .... 397 G8
Snellgrove Cl TOTT SO40 .... 316 A8
Snellgrove Pl TOTT SO40 .... 316 B6
Snipe La HASM GU27 .... 228 D7
Snoddington Rd RAND SP11 ...... 139 J1
Snode Hl ALTN GU34 .... 175 M5
Snooks La LYMN SO41 .... 440 F2
Snowberry Crs HAV PO9 .... 377 M5
Snowdon Cl STHA RG19 .... 27 G6
Snowdon Dr FHAM/STUB PO14 .. 14 C8
Snowdon Rd FARN GU14 .... 90 B1
  WBNE BH4 .... 447 H4
Snowdrop Cl KEMP RG22 .... 103 M8
Snowdrop Copse NTHA RG18 ...... 27 J4
Snowdrop Gdns
  CHCH/BSGR BH23 .... 435 M7
Soake Rd WVILLE PO7 .... 351 M5
Soalwood La PSF GU32 .... 246 E7
Soame's La NALR SO24 .... 220 D5
Sobers Sq AND SP10 .... 119 H5
Soberton Rd CHAR BH8 .... 448 C1
  HAV PO9 .... 377 J5
Soke Hl ALTN GU34 .... 196 D8
Soke Rd THLE RG7 .... 42 C7
The Soke NALR SO24 .... 218 C1
Soiartron Rd FARN GU14 .... 90 D5
Solby's Rd BSTK RG21 .... 4 C8
Soldiers Ri EWKG RG40 .... 49 G1
Soldridge Cl HAV PO9 .... 377 M2
Soldridge Rd ALTN GU34 .... 196 D5
Solent Av ITCH SO19 .... 345 J2
  LYMN SO41 .... 440 D5
Solent Cl CHFD SO53 .... 293 K2
  LYMN SO41 .... 440 D5
Solent Dr FAWY SO45 .... 367 K4
  HISD PO11 .... 425 K6
  HLER SO31 .... 394 B2
  KEMP RG22 .... 127 G1
  NMIL/BTOS BH25 .... 452 F1
  HLER SO31 .... 370 E1
Solent Mdw HLER SO31 .... 369 L7
Solent Rd CHAM PO6 .... 376 A8
  CHCH/BSGR BH23 .... 436 F6
  FAWY SO45 .... 367 J8
  FHAM/STUB PO14 .... 395 L7
  HAV PO9 .... 16 C5
  SBNE BH6 .... 449 M5
Solent Vw FHAM/PORC PO16 .... 373 M7
Solent Wy BROC SO42 .... 391 G3
  BROC SO42 .... 416 F1
  FHAM/STUB PO14 .... 395 L7
  GPORT PO12 .... 19 J7
  GPORT PO12 .... 421 J5
  HAV PO9 .... 16 A7
  HSEA PO3 .... 424 B2
  LSOL/BMARY PO13 .... 420 E5
  LYMN SO41 .... 440 C6
  PSEA PO1 .... 20 D2
  SSEA PO5 .... 13 G7
Solly Cl BKME/WDN BH12 .... 446 D1
Solomons La BPWT SO32 .... 323 L6
Solomon Wy PLE BH15 .... 444 C6
Solona Cl CHFD SO53 .... 293 L1
Somborne Dr HAV PO9 .... 377 K3

Somborne Park Rd *STOK* SO20 .. 187 H7
Somerby Rd *PLE* BH15 .... 445 J2
Somerford Av
  CHCH/BSGR BH23 .... 435 M8
Somerford Cl *ITCH* SO19 .... 344 E2 🔢
Somerford Rd
  CHCH/BSGR BH23 .... 450 E1
Somerford Wy
  CHCH/BSGR BH23 .... 450 D1
Somerley Rd
  MOOR/WNTN BH9 .... 447 M1
Somerley Vw *RGWD* BH24 ..... 358 E8 🔢
Somers Cl *WINW* SO22 .... 238 C3
Somerset Av *BOR* GU35 .... 201 J5
  WEND SO18 .... 345 G1
Somerset Crs *CHFD* SO53 .... 293 H5
Somerset Rd
  CHCH/BSGR BH23 .... 449 K1
  FARN GU14 .... 90 F7
  LTDN BH7 .... 448 E3
  PTSW SO17 .... 319 H6
  SSEA PO5 .... 21 K9
Somerset Ter *WSHM* SO15 ..... 342 F2
Somers Rd *SSEA* PO5 .... 21 K3
Somers Rd North *PSEA* PO1 .... 21 K2
Somerton Av *WEND* SO18 ...... 344 F1
Somerton Cl
  NMIL/BTOS BH25 .... 438 B5 🔢
Somerton Gv *STHA* RG19 .... 26 F6
Somervell Cl *GPORT* PO12 .... 18 D8
Somerville Crs *YTLY* GU46 .... 69 H2
Somerville Rd *RGWD* BH24 ...... 359 G8
  WCLF BH2 .... 22 B6
  WINC SO23 .... 191 H7
Somme Rd *RAND* SP11 .... 92 C8
Sonnet Wy *WVILLE* PO7 .... 352 F8 🔢
Sonning Cl *KEMP* RG22 .... 126 E1
Sonninge Cl *SHST* GU47 .... 50 A8 🔢
Soper Gv *BSTK* RG21 .... 4 E5
Sopers La *BPWT* SO32 .... 297 H8
  CHCH/BSGR BH23 .... 449 M2
Sopley Cl *NMIL/BTOS* BH25 .... 437 K8
Sopley Ct *HAV* PO9 .... 377 M2 🔢
Sopwith Cl *STOK* SO20 .... 210 F6
Sopwith Crs *WIMB* BH21 .... 404 C6
Sopwith Pk *AND* SP10 .... 118 A7
Sopwith Wy *HLER* SO31 .... 346 C8
Sorrel Cl *NWBY* RG14 .... 26 A3
  ROMY SO51 .... 263 H7
  THLE RG7 .... 31 L5 🔢
  WVILLE PO7 .... 376 A2
Sorrel Dr *FHAM* PO15 .... 371 H1
Sorrel Gdns *WIMB* BH21 .... 429 K6
Sorrell Cl *HLER* SO31 .... 370 D6
Sorrell's Cl *CHAM* RG24 .... 83 L5
Sorrell Wy *CHCH/BSGR* BH23 . 435 M8
Sotherington La *ALTN* GU34 ... 223 L2
South Acre *EPSF* GU31 .... 305 G5
Southampton Cl *BLKW* GU17 .. 69 M2 🔢
Southampton Hl
  FHAM/STUB PO14........... 371 K7
Southampton Rd *BROC* SO42 .. 413 L1
  CHAM PO6 .... 374 D8
  ELGH SO50 .... 293 M8
  FAWY SO45 .... 367 L5
  FBDG SP6 .... 310 A7
  FHAM PO15 .... 371 G3
  FHAM/PORC PO16 .... 15 J4
  FHAM/STUB PO14........... 371 H6
  LYMN SO41 .... 440 B3
  LYND SO43 .... 364 A2
  RGWD BH24 .... 358 E8
  ROMY SO51 .... 290 F2
  TOTT SO40 .... 339 M1
Southampton St *FARN* GU14 ... 90 E8
  WSHM SO15 .... 343 K2 🔢
South Atlantic Dr *ALDT* GU11 .. 112 F5
South Av *FAWY* SO45 .... 392 C5
  FNM GU9 .... 135 G2
  NEND PO2 .... 399 J4
  NMIL/BTOS BH25 .... 437 M6
South Baddesley Rd
  LYMN SO41 .... 440 F4
South Bay *EMRTH* PO10.......... 402 E5
South Beta Rd *FARN* GU14 ...... 90 E6
Southbourne Av *CHAM* PO6 .... 399 M1
  EMRTH PO10 .... 378 F8
  FAWY SO45 .... 392 A4
Southbourne Coast Rd
  SBNE BH6 .... 449 K5
Southbourne Gv *SBNE* BH6..... 449 G4
Southbourne Overcliff Dr
  SBNE BH6 .... 449 H5
Southbourne Rd *LYMN* SO41... 440 A5
  SBNE BH6 .... 449 G3
Southbrook Cl *CFDH* BH17....... 430 E6
  HAV PO9 .... 16 E7
Southbrook Pl *RWIN* SO21 .... 169 M5 🔢
Southbrook Rd *HAV* PO9 .... 16 E8
Southby Dr *FLET* GU13 .... 89 G7
South Charford Dro *FBDG* SP6.. 283 M4
Southcliff
  LSOL/BMARY PO13 .... 420 C1 🔢
Southcliffe Rd
  CHCH/BSGR BH23 .... 451 G2
  NMIL/BTOS BH25 .... 437 H8
Southcliff Rd *SHAM* SO14 ...... 343 L1
South Cliff Rd *WCLF* BH2 .... 22 E8
South Cl *GPORT* PO12 .... 18 B7
  HAV PO9 .... 17 G6
  NALR SO24 .... 218 A3
  ROMY SO51 .... 263 H7 🔢
Southcote Dr *CBLY* GU15 .... 71 K3 🔢
Southcote Rd *BMTH* BH1 .... 23 L3
South Ct *HLER* SO31 .... 369 J6
Southcroft Rd *GPORT* PO12 ..... 18 A1
South Cross St *GPORT* PO12 .... 19 K3
Southdene Rd *CHFD* SO53 ...... 293 H3
Southdown Rd *CHAM* PO6 ...... 375 L8
  HORN PO8 .... 328 B5
  RWIN SO21 .... 266 C2
  STHA RG19 .... 26 C4 🔢
  TADY RG26 .... 41 K7
Southdowns *NALR* SO24 .... 194 C7
South Downs Wy *BPWT* SO32 .. 270 C4
  EPSF GU31 .... 305 K7
  HORN PO8 .... 302 B5

South View Rd
  CHCH/BSGR BH23 .... 449 M2
  WINW SO22 .... 238 A5
Southview Rd *BOR* GU35........ 202 E3
South View Ter *RAND* SP11 ...... 97 M8
South Wk *ASHV* GU12 .... 7 M1
Southwark Cl *YTLY* GU46 .... 68 F2
South Wy *AND* SP10 .... 119 K6
Southway *CBLY* GU15 .... 70 E4
  FHAM PO15 .... 371 J5
Southways *FHAM/STUB* PO14... 396 B6
South Weirs *BROC* SO42 .... 413 H1
Southwell Park Rd *CBLY* GU15 .. 70 E3
South West Coast Pth
  SWGE BH19 .... 457 G8
South Western Crs *PSTN* BH14 .. 446 A5
Southwick Av
  FHAM/PORC PO16 .... 374 C7
Southwick Cl *WINW* SO22 ..... 214 C4 🔢
Southwick Ct
  FHAM/STUB PO14........... 396 E2 🔢
Southwick Hill Rd *CHAM* PO6 .. 375 J7
Southwick Rd *CHAM* PO6 ...... 375 G6
  SBNE BH6 .... 449 H2
  WHAM PO17 .... 349 G5
  WVILLE PO7 .... 351 J4
Southwood Av
  CHCH/BSGR BH23 .... 436 E7
  FERN BH22 .... 406 A3
Southwood Cl
  CHCH/BSGR BH23 .... 436 E7
  FERN BH22 .... 406 A3
South Wood Gdns *HLER* SO31 .. 370 D5
Southwood Gdns *THLE* RG7 ..... 31 K5
Southwood La *FARN* GU14 .... 89 K8
Southwood Rd *ALTN* GU34 ..... 154 A8
  FARN GU14 .... 69 H7
  FARN GU14 .... 90 B4
  HISD PO11 .... 426 A6
  NEND PO2 .... 399 J4
Sovereign Crs
  FHAM/STUB PO14........... 370 E7
Sovereign Dr *CBLY* GU15 .... 71 L1
  ENEY PO4 .... 424 B3 🔢
  HEND SO30 .... 346 B2
Sovereign La *WVILLE* PO7 ...... 376 C5
Sovereign Wy *ELGH* SO50 ...... 293 L2
Sowcroft La *ODIM* RG29 .... 154 F3
Sowden Cl *HEND* SO30 .... 345 M1
Sowley La *LYMN* SO41 .... 441 L3
Spackman Rd *STHA* RG19 .... 27 G6
Spain La *ALTN* GU34 .... 152 D5
The Spain *PSF* GU32 .... 275 K5
Spalding Rd *ITCH* SO19 .... 345 H3
Spaniard's La *ROMY* SO51 ..... 290 C5
Sparkford Cl *WINW* SO22 .... 238 D2
Sparkford Rd *WINW* SO22 ...... 238 D2
Spa Rd *SHAM* SO14 .... 12 F4
Sparrow Cl *HORN* PO8 .... 352 D4
Sparrow Ct
  LSOL/BMARY PO13 .... 420 D1 🔢
Sparrowgrove Rd *RWIN* SO21.. 266 B4
Sparrowhawk Cl
  RFNM GU10 .... 111 G8 🔢
Sparrow Sq *ELGH* SO50 .... 293 J6
Sparsholt Cl *HAV* PO9 .... 377 G3
Sparsholt Rd *ITCH* SO19 .... 344 D8
  RWIN SO21 .... 237 G5
Spartan Cl *EMRTH* PO10......... 402 A4
  FHAM/STUB PO14........... 396 A3
Spartina Dr *LYMN* SO41 .... 440 C2
Sparvells *HTWY* RG27 .... 48 B8 🔢
Spats La *BOR* GU35.............. 180 C8
Speakers Corner Rbt
  SHAM SO14 .... 13 G4
Spear Rd *SHAM* SO14 .... 13 F8
Speckled Wood Rd *CHAM* RG24 .. 83 G7
Specks La *ENEY* PO4 .... 423 L4
Speedwell Cl *HLER* SO31 .... 370 D6 🔢
Speedwell Wy *NTHA* RG18 ...... 27 J4
Speen Hill Cl *NWBY* RG14 .... 2 A2
Speen La *NWBY* RG14 .... 2 B2
Speen Lodge Ct *NWBY* RG14 .... 2 A1
Speen Pl *NWBY* RG14 .... 2 A1
Speggs Wk *HEND* SO30 .... 346 A2
Speltham Hl *WVILLE* PO7 .... 326 C6
Spencer Cl *ALTN* GU34........... 197 G5
  FLET GU13 .... 111 H3
  FRIM GU16 .... 91 H2
  HISD PO11 .... 425 L5 🔢
  TADY RG26 .... 42 B7 🔢
Spencer Ct *FHAM/STUB* PO14.. 396 C6
Spencer Dr *LSOL/BMARY* PO13 .. 420 D3
Spencer Gdns *HORN* PO8 .... 352 C5
Spencer Rd *BMTH* BH1 .... 23 M3
  CCLF BH13 .... 446 D8
  ELGH SO50 .... 293 K6
  EMRTH PO10 .... 378 C4
  ENEY PO4 .... 423 K6
  ITCH SO19 .... 345 H2
  NMIL/BTOS BH25 .... 437 L5
  NWBY RG14 .... 37 G2
Spenlow Cl *NEND* PO2 .... 399 H8 🔢
Spenser Cl *ALTN* GU34........... 176 F3
  HLER SO31 .... 370 B8 🔢
Sperrin Cl *KEMP* RG22 .... 104 A5
Spetisbury Cl
  MOOR/WNTN BH9 .... 432 F5
Spicer La *BWD* BH11 .... 431 J3
Spicers *ALTN* GU34............... 176 F5
Spicer's Hl *TOTT* SO40 .... 341 K3
Spicer St *PSEA* PO1 .... 423 G2
Spicer's Wy *TOTT* SO40 .... 341 J2
Spicewood *FHAM* PO15 .... 14 C4
Spiers Cl *TADY* RG26 .... 42 A8
Spiers La *NALR* SO24 .... 172 D5
Spinacre *NMIL/BTOS* BH25...... 437 M8
Spindle Cl *HAV* PO9 .... 17 L1
  WIMB BH21 .... 429 K6
Spindle Warren *HAV* PO9 .... 17 L1
Spindlewood Cl
  NMIL/BTOS BH25 .... 437 L7 🔢
  ROWN SO16 .... 318 F2
Spindlewood Wy *TOTT* SO40.. 342 D8
Spinnaker Cl *HISD* PO11 .... 425 J4 🔢
  LSOL/BMARY PO13 .... 421 H1 🔢
Spinnaker Dr *NEND* PO2 .... 399 H4

Spinnaker Gra *HISD* PO11 .... 402 A4
Spinnaker Vw *CHAM* PO6 .... 376 E7
Spinners Ct *FERN* BH22 .... 380 C7 🔢
Spinney Cl *HORN* PO8 .... 352 C5
  RGWD BH24 .... 381 H4
Spinney Dl *FAWY* SO45 .... 367 M6
Spinney Gdns *FAWY* SO45 ...... 367 M6 🔢
Spinneys La *FERN* BH22 .... 406 B3
The Spinney *CBLY* GU15 .... 71 M2
  ELGH SO50 .... 294 F6
  FHAM/PORC PO16 .... 373 K7
  FLET GU13 .... 88 C8 🔢
  GSHT GU26 .... 203 K4
  HASM GU27 .... 202 F8
  HORN PO8 .... 352 C2
  HTWY RG27 .... 85 M6
  LSOL/BMARY PO13 .... 397 H7 🔢
  NALR SO24 .... 243 H3
  RGWD BH24 .... 381 K2
  ROWN SO16 .... 318 E2
  RWIN SO21 .... 266 B1
  TOTT SO40 .... 316 B7
  WVILLE PO7 .... 351 K5
  YTLY GU46 .... 68 F1
Spinney Wk *WEND* SO18 .... 319 L5
Spinney Wy *NMIL/BTOS* BH25.. 437 L2
Spitalfields Rd *ALTN* GU34 ..... 176 E4
Spitalhatch *ALTN* GU34......... 177 G5
Spitfire End *WINC* SO23 .... 215 J8 🔢
Spitfire Loop *ELGH* SO50 .... 319 L1
Spitfire Wy *FARN* GU14.......... 90 B8
  HLER SO31 .... 369 K6
Spithead Av *GPORT* PO12 ...... 422 A7
Spittlefields *RGWD* BH24 .... 382 F1
Spoil La *RFNM* GU10 .... 136 C1
Spokane Cl *ALDT* GU11 .... 6 D5
Spouts La *ROMY* SO51 .... 288 C2
Sprat's Hatch La *HTWY* RG27 .. 109 K1
  ODIM RG29 .... 109 J3
Spray Leaze *RAND* SP11 .... 93 G6
Spray Rd *MARL* SN8 .... 33 H5
Spriggs Cl *STHA* RG19 .... 27 G6
Springbank Rd *LTDN* BH7 .... 433 K8
Spring Cl *CHAM* RG24 .... 82 C5
  ELGH SO50 .... 295 H6
  ITCH SO19 .... 344 D4
  VWD BH31 .... 356 D3
Spring Crs *PTSW* SO17 .... 319 G8
Springcroft
  LSOL/BMARY PO13 .... 396 F3
Springcross Av *BLKW* GU17 .... 70 A4 🔢
Springdale Av *BDST* BH18 ...... 429 K3
Springdale Gv *WIMB* BH21 ..... 429 J4
Springdale Rd *BDST* BH18 ...... 429 K4
  WIMB BH21 .... 429 H4
Springfarm Rd *HASM* GU27 .... 228 D3
Springfield *DEAN* RG23 .... 103 G6
Springfield Av
  CHCH/BSGR BH23 .... 434 B6
  FAWY SO45 .... 392 B4
  HTWY RG27 .... 87 H1
  SBNE BH6 .... 449 M4
Springfield Cl *AND* SP10 .... 119 J8
  HAV PO9 .... 376 F6
  LYMN SO41 .... 440 E5
  VWD BH31 .... 356 D3
Springfield Crs *PSTN* BH14 ..... 446 A4
  RSAL SP5 .... 285 J2
Springfield Dr *TOTT* SO40 ...... 341 J2 🔢
Springfield Gdns
  NMIL/BTOS BH25 .... 438 B6 🔢
Springfield Gv *FAWY* SO45 ..... 392 B4
Springfield La *FLET* GU13 .... 88 D7
  NWBY RG14 .... 25 K8
Springfield Rd *ASHV* GU12 ..... 113 K3
  CBLY GU15 .... 71 K3
  PSTN BH14 .... 445 M3
  TADY RG26 .... 42 B7
  VWD BH31 .... 356 D3
Springfields Cl *RWIN* SO21 ..... 266 E7
Springfield Wy
  FHAM/STUB PO14........... 396 A7
Springford Cl *ROWN* SO16 ..... 318 A4
Springford Crs *ROWN* SO16 .... 318 A5
Springford Gdns *ROWN* SO16 .. 318 A4
Springford Rd *ROWN* SO16 .... 318 A5
Spring Garden La *GPORT* PO12 .. 19 H2
Spring Gdns *BKME/WDN* BH12 .. 446 C3
  CBLY GU15 .... 71 K3
  EMRTH PO10 .... 378 D8
  FARN GU14 .... 90 D1 🔢
  NALR SO24 .... 218 A4
  NBAD SO52 .... 291 L3
  PSEA PO1 .... 20 F2 🔢
Spring Gv *HLER* SO31 .... 345 L7
Spring Hill La *RAND* SP11 .... 97 L6
Springhill Rd *CHFD* SO53 .... 293 H2
Spring Hills *ITCH* SO19 .... 345 G4
Spring La *BPWT* SO32 .... 324 A3
  ELGH SO50 .... 294 C5
  FNM GU9 .... 134 D1
  KSCL RG20 .... 57 J2
  NMIL/BTOS BH25 .... 438 B6
  RWIN SO21 .... 266 E7
  THLE RG7 .... 41 M2
  THLE RG7 .... 43 K1
  THLE RG7 .... 45 J3
Spring La West *FNM* GU9 ...... 134 D2
Springles La *FHAM* PO15 .... 371 L3
Spring Ms *AND* SP10 .... 9 J8
Spring Pl *ROMY* SO51 .... 290 D1 🔢
Spring Rd *BMTH* BH1 .... 23 M2
  FAWY SO45 .... 367 L4
  HLER SO31 .... 370 C2
  ITCH SO19 .... 344 D2
  LYMN SO41 .... 440 E5
The Springs *THLE* RG7 .... 44 A8
Spring St *PSEA* PO1 .... 21 G1
The Spring *WVILLE* PO7 .... 351 K5
Spring V *BPWT* SO32 .... 323 M4
  HORN PO8 .... 352 F4
Springvale Av *LTDN* BH7 .... 433 K8
Springvale Rd *WINC* SO23 ...... 215 G2
Springwater Rd *BWD* BH11 .... 431 L5
Spring Wy *NALR* SO24 .... 218 B4
Springwell La *HTWY* RG27 ...... 67 J8
Springwood Av *WVILLE* PO7 ... 376 D2

Spring Wood La *THLE* RG7 .... 31 K5
Spring Woods *FLET* GU13 .... 110 E1
  SHST GU47 .... 49 M7
Spruce Av *BOR* GU35 .... 201 G5
  WVILLE PO7 .... 376 E1
Spruce Cl *AND* SP10 .... 142 B1 🔢
  CFDH BH17 .... 429 J7
  HLER SO31 .... 370 B8
  RWIN SO21 .... 190 D3
Spruce Dr *ITCH* SO19 .... 345 J3
  TOTT SO40 .... 316 A8
Spruce Wy *FLET* GU13............ 89 J7
Spur Cl *WIMB* BH21 .... 405 G2 🔢
Spurcroft Rd *STHA* RG19 .... 27 G6
Spurgeon Rd *LTDN* BH7 .... 449 G2
Spur Hill Av *PSTN* BH14 .... 446 C5
Spurlings Rd *WHAM* PO17 ...... 373 H4
Spur Rd *CHAM* PO6 .... 376 A1
  PSTN BH14................... 446 C4
  WVILLE PO7 .... 376 C1
Spurs Ct *ALDT* GU11 .... 6 B2
The Spur *GPORT* PO12 .... 18 A8
  WHAM PO17 .... 348 E4
Spybush La *NALR* SO24 .... 172 B7
Spurgeon Rd *LTDN* BH7 .... 449 G2
Squarefield Gdns *HTWY* RG27 .. 86 B5 🔢
The Square *EMRTH* PO10 .... 378 F5 🔢
  EPSF GU31 .... 305 C4
  FAWY SO45 .... 392 F5 🔢
  GPORT PO12 .... 397 M8
  LYMN SO41 .... 440 E5
  PSF GU32 .... 275 L5
  ROMY SO51 .... 261 G4
  STOK SO20 .... 184 F2 🔢
  WHAM PO17 .... 348 E5
  WINC SO23 .... 11 G8
Squarey Cl *RSAL* SP5 .... 284 C2
Squires Hill La *RFNM* GU10 .... 159 M3
Squires Wk *ITCH* SO19 .... 344 C7
Squirrel Cl *ELGH* SO50 .... 294 E6 🔢
  SHST GU47 .... 49 L8
Squirrel Dr *ITCH* SO19 .... 344 E5
Squirrel La *FARN* GU14 .... 90 D3
Squirrels Drey *CWTH* RG45 ..... 49 J3 🔢
Squirrels Wk *FAWY* SO45 .... 367 K6
Stable Cl *FHAM/STUB* PO14 .... 371 H6
  HTWY RG27 .... 85 L7
  THLE RG7 .... 31 K5
Stable Ct *NWBY* RG14 .... 25 L3
Stable Rd *BOR* GU35 .... 201 H2
Stables Rd *NTID* SP9 .... 114 D4
Stable Vw *YTLY* GU46 .... 69 G1
Stacey Cl *BKME/WDN* BH12 .... 446 B1
Stacey Ct *HAV* PO9 .... 377 H1
Stacey Gdns *CHAR* BH8 .... 433 K6
Staff College Rd *CBLY* GU15 .... 70 E2
Stafford Rd *BMTH* BH1 .... 23 H5
  PSF GU32 .... 275 L3
  SSEA PO5 .... 21 J6
  WSHM SO15 .... 343 H1
Staff Rd *ASHV* GU12 .... 7 K2
  ROMY SO51 .... 234 A2
Stagbrake Cl *FAWY* SO45 .... 391 M5 🔢
Stag Cl *ELGH* SO50 .... 294 E6
  NMIL/BTOS BH25 .... 437 J4
Stag Hl *KEMP* RG22 .... 104 C6
Stagshorn Rd *HORN* PO8 .... 353 C2 🔢
Stags La *RWIN* SO21 .... 267 M3
Stagswood *VWD* BH31 .... 356 B2
Stag Wy *FHAM* PO15 .... 372 B3
Stainer Cl *ITCH* SO19 .... 345 H5
Stainers La *RWIN* SO21 .... 190 A4
Staith Cl *ITCH* SO19 .... 345 G3
Stake La *FARN* GU14 .... 90 D4
Stakes Hill Rd *WVILLE* PO7 ..... 376 C1
Stakes La *BPWT* SO32 .... 296 D6
  BPWT SO32 .... 297 L1
Stakes Rd *WVILLE* PO7 .... 376 B4
Stalbridge Dr *FERN* BH22 .... 406 B4
Stalbridge Rd *HAV* PO9 .... 377 M4
Stalham Rd *BKME/WDN* BH12 .. 446 C2
Stallard Cl *EMRTH* PO10 .... 378 C7
Stallards La *RGWD* BH24 .... 382 C1
Stalybridge Cl *HLER* SO31 ...... 370 E2
Stamford Av *FRIM* GU16 .... 71 J7 🔢
  HISD PO11 .... 425 J5
Stamford Rd *SBNE* BH6 .... 449 J3
Stamford St *PSEA* PO1 .... 423 H2
Stamford Wy *ELGH* SO50 .... 295 H7 🔢
Stamshaw Rd *NEND* PO2 .... 399 H7
Stanbridge La *ROMY* SO51...... 262 A5
Stanbridge Rd *HAV* PO9 .... 377 M4
Stanbury Cl *RAND* SP11 .... 116 B8
Stanbury Rd *RAND* SP11 .... 116 B8
Stancomb Broad La
  ALTN GU34 .... 196 B6
Stancombe La *ALTN* GU34 ..... 154 B7
  ALTN GU34 .... 196 C5
Standard Wy *FHAM/PORC* PO16.. 15 M1
Standen Rd *ROWN* SO16 .... 317 H3
Standford Hl *BOR* GU35.......... 201 M7
Standford La *BOR* GU35.......... 201 M5
Standford St *SHAM* SO14 .... 13 K4 🔢
Standing Hl *RSAL* SP5 .... 207 K8
Stanfield *TADY* RG26 .... 41 L8
Stanfield Rd *BKME/WDN* BH12.. 446 C1
  FERN BH22 .... 406 A2
  MOOR/WNTN BH9 .... 432 D2
Stanford Cl *CHAM* PO6 .... 375 H8
Stanford Ct *HAV* PO9 .... 377 M3 🔢
Stanford Ri *LYMN* SO41 .... 412 F6
Stanford Rd *KEMP* RG22 .... 127 J1
Stanham Cl *RWIN* SO21 .... 190 C6
Stanhope Rd *CBLY* GU15 .... 70 C4
  PSEA PO1 .... 21 H5
Stanier Wy *HEND* SO30 .... 321 H6
Stanley Av *HSEA* PO3 .... 399 M8
Stanley Cl *FHAM* PO15 .... 14 C5
  GPORT PO12 .... 397 L7
  VWD BH31 .... 356 E3
Stanley Dr *FARN* GU14 .... 89 M5 🔢
Stanley Green Rd *PLE* BH15 .... 445 H3
Stanley La *SSEA* PO5 .... 21 H7
Stanley Rd *BMTH* BH1 .... 23 L2
  CHCH/BSGR BH23 .... 436 E8
  EMRTH PO10 .... 378 A4
  FAWY SO45 .... 392 B4
  LYMN SO41 .... 440 D6

NEND PO2 .... 399 G7
NWBY RG14 .... 3 G6
PLE BH15 .... 445 H7
PTSW SO17 .... 319 H7
TOTT SO40 .... 316 C7
Stanley St *SSEA* PO5 .... 21 H7
Stanmore Gdns *THLE* RG7 .... 43 J3
Stanmore La *WINW* SO22 .... 238 B2
Stannington Cl
NMIL/BTOS BH25 .... 437 M6
Stannington Crs *TOTT* SO40 .... 316 E8
Stannington Wy *TOTT* SO40 .... 316 E8
Stanpit *CHCH/BSGR* BH23 .... 450 D3
Stanstead Cl *HAV* PO9 .... 354 A6
Stanstead Rd *ELGH* SO50 .... 293 L4
Stansted Crs *HAV* PO9 .... 377 M2
Stansted Rd *SSEA* PO5 .... 21 K4
Stanswood Rd *FAWY* SO45 .... 418 F4
HAV PO9 .... 377 H2
Stanton Dr *FLET* GU13 .... 88 D8
Stanton Rd *NBNE* BH10 .... 432 A6
PSF GU32 .... 275 K4
WSHM SO15 .... 342 D1
Stanwater La *MIDH* GU29 .... 279 H4
Stapehill Crs *WIMB* BH21 .... 404 F3
Stapehill Rd *WIMB* BH21 .... 405 K3
Staple Ash La *PSF* GU32 .... 274 B1
Staple Cl *WVILLE* PO7 .... 352 B7
Staple Close La *PLE* BH15 .... 445 H2
Staplecross La
CHCH/BSGR BH23 .... 435 H8
Stapleford Av *FERN* BH22 .... 406 D2
Stapleford Cl *ROMY* SO51 .... 263 G6
Stapleford La *BPWT* SO32 .... 321 L3
Staple Gdns *WINC* SO23 .... 10 F7
Staplehurst Cl *ITCH* SO19 .... 344 E8
Staplers Reach
LSOL/BMARY PO13 .... 396 F7
Stapleton Cl *NWBY* RG14 .... 36 F2
Stapleton Rd *HSEA* PO3 .... 399 L8
Staplewood La *TOTT* SO40 .... 342 B7
Stapley La *NALR* SO24 .... 220 C6
Stares Cl *LSOL/BMARY* PO13 .... 421 G1
Star Hl *RFNM* GU10 .... 181 G6
Star Hill Dr *RFNM* GU10 .... 181 G5
Starina Gdns *WVILLE* PO7 .... 352 F8
Star La *ASHV* GU12 .... 113 J6
KSCL RG20 .... 56 C2
Starlight Farm Cl *VWD* BH31 .... 356 E1
Starling Cl *KEMP* RG22 .... 103 L8
Starling Sq *ELGH* SO50 .... 293 J6
Star Post Rd *CBLY* GU15 .... 51 H8
Starting Gates *NWBY* RG14 .... 3 J8
Station Ap *ALTN* GU34 .... 197 G5
AND SP10 .... 8 E4
ASHV GU12 .... 113 K1
BDST BH18 .... 429 L4
NALR SO24 .... 218 C3
PSEA PO1 .... 20 C2
RAND SP11 .... 92 E5
RAND SP11 .... 161 L1
Station Cl *RWIN* SO21 .... 216 D2
WHAM PO17 .... 348 E4
Station Hl *ELGH* SO50 .... 294 A5
FNM GU9 .... 134 F6
HEND SO30 .... 347 G1
HLER SO31 .... 369 M1
NALR SO24 .... 219 L3
OVTN RG25 .... 101 G6
RWIN SO21 .... 216 D2
WINC SO23 .... 10 F6
Station La *CHFD* SO53 .... 293 H2
Station Rd *ALDT* GU11 .... 7 G2
ALTN GU34 .... 176 F4
BPWT SO32 .... 323 H1
BPWT SO32 .... 325 H1
CHAM PO6 .... 400 A2
CHCH/BSGR BH23 .... 436 C5
CHCH/BSGR BH23 .... 449 M1
DEAN RG23 .... 102 E6
EPSF GU31 .... 275 L4
FARN GU14 .... 90 E4
FBDG SP6 .... 333 K2
FERN BH22 .... 380 B5
FHAM/PORC PO16 .... 374 B8
FRIM GU16 .... 70 F7
GPORT PO12 .... 421 K1
HISD PO11 .... 425 J4
HLER SO31 .... 368 F3
HSEA PO3 .... 399 L8
HTWY RG27 .... 85 M7
ITCH SO19 .... 344 E5
KSCL RG20 .... 36 D5
BOR GU35 .... 201 H3
LIPH GU30 .... 226 E6
LISS GU33 .... 248 E4
LYMN SO41 .... 412 F6
NALR SO24 .... 218 C2
RFNM GU10 .... 156 F4
NMIL/BTOS BH25 .... 437 L6
NTID SP9 .... 114 E3
NWBY RG14 .... 2 E6
NWBY RG14 .... 25 G3
OVTN RG25 .... 101 G8
OVTN RG25 .... 128 A1
PSF GU32 .... 272 B4
PSF GU32 .... 275 K4
PSTN BH14 .... 446 A5
RAND SP11 .... 161 L1
RGWD BH24 .... 411 J2
ROMY SO51 .... 290 D1
ROWN SO16 .... 316 F3
STHA RG19 .... 27 H5
STOK SO20 .... 165 L5
THLE RG7 .... 28 F6
THLE RG7 .... 44 B3
VWD BH31 .... 356 B1
WHAM PO17 .... 348 E4
WHCH RG28 .... 122 B2
WIMB BH21 .... 404 B5
WINC SO23 .... 10 E6
WSHM SO15 .... 317 H8
Station Rd East *ASHV* GU12 .... 113 J1
Station Rd North *TOTT* SO40 .... 341 L1
Station Rd South
TOTT SO40 .... 341 M1
Station St *LYMN* SO41 .... 440 D4
PSEA PO1 .... 21 G1
Station Ter *WIMB* BH21 .... 404 B4
Station Vw *ASHV* GU12 .... 91 K8
Station Yd *FBDG* SP6 .... 333 J2
Staunton Av *HISD* PO11 .... 425 H5
Staunton Rd *HAV* PO9 .... 16 C3
Staunton St *PSEA* PO1 .... 423 G2
Staunton Wy *HAV* PO9 .... 16 C2
HAV PO9 .... 377 J5
HORN PO8 .... 302 E8
Stavedown Rd *RWIN* SO21 .... 190 B4
Stead Cl *HISD* PO11 .... 425 M5
Stedham La *MIDH* GU29 .... 279 K5
Steele Cl *CHFD* SO53 .... 293 J4
Steeles Rd *ALDT* GU11 .... 112 E4
Steels Dro *FBDG* SP6 .... 310 D1
Steels La *FBDG* SP6 .... 308 B4
Steel St *SSEA* PO5 .... 20 F5
Steep Cl *FHAM/PORC* PO16 .... 374 A7
Steepdene *PSTN* BH14 .... 446 A5
Steeple Cl *CFDH* BH17 .... 430 B5
Steeple Dr *ALTN* GU34 .... 176 E4
Steepleton Rd *BDST* BH18 .... 430 A5
Steeple Wy *FHAM/STUB* PO14 .... 371 H5
Steepways *GSHT* GU26 .... 203 L2
Steerforth Cl *NEND* PO2 .... 423 H1
Steerforth Copse *SHST* GU47 .... 50 B6
Steinbeck Cl *FHAM* PO15 .... 347 G8
Stein Rd *EMRTH* PO10 .... 379 H6
Stem La *NMIL/BTOS* BH25 .... 437 J3
Stenbury Dr *OVTN* RG25 .... 151 G8
Stenbury Wy *HLER* SO31 .... 369 G1
Stephen Cl *HORN* PO8 .... 352 F6
Stephendale Rd *FNM* GU9 .... 135 G4
Stephen Martin Gdns
FBDG SP6 .... 309 K6
Stephen Rd *FHAM* PO15 .... 14 F5
Stephen's Cl *THLE* RG7 .... 43 J2
Stephens Firs *THLE* RG7 .... 43 J2
Stephenson Cl *AND* SP10 .... 118 B7
GPORT PO12 .... 18 C8
NTHA RG18 .... 26 F4
Stephenson Rd *TOTT* SO40 .... 316 C6
WHIT RG2 .... 47 K1
Stephenson Wy *HEND* SO30 .... 321 G5
Stephens Rd *TADY* RG26 .... 41 M8
THLE RG7 .... 43 J2
Steplake Rd *ROMY* SO51 .... 288 C1
Step Ter *WINW* SO22 .... 10 D7
Sterling Pk *AND* SP10 .... 118 B7
Sterte Av *PLE* BH15 .... 445 G4
Sterte Cl *PLE* BH15 .... 445 H4
Sterte Rd *PLE* BH15 .... 445 H4
Steuart Rd *WEND* SO18 .... 344 B1
Stevens Dro *STOK* SO20 .... 210 B3
Stevens Gn *RAND* SP11 .... 97 M7
Stevens Hl *YTLY* GU46 .... 69 H3
Stevenson Crs *PSTN* BH14 .... 446 C5
Stevenson Rd *RWIN* SO21 .... 145 H6
Stevensons Cl *WIMB* BH21 .... 404 A4
Steventon Rd *OVTN* RG25 .... 125 K7
WEND SO18 .... 345 G1
Stewart Cl *CHAR* BH8 .... 23 M1
Stewart Rd *CHAR* BH8 .... 448 A2
Stewarts Gn *WVILLE* PO7 .... 326 B5
Stewarts Wy *FERN* BH22 .... 406 C1
Stibbs Wy *CHCH/BSGR* BH23 .... 410 A7
Stile Gdns *HASM* GU27 .... 228 C2
Stiles Dr *AND* SP10 .... 119 J8
Stillions Cl *ALTN* GU34 .... 176 F5
Stillmore Rd *BWD* BH11 .... 431 H5
Stilwell Cl *YTLY* GU46 .... 69 H2
Stinchar Dr *CHFD* SO53 .... 292 F3
Stinsford Cl *MOOR/WNTN* BH9 .... 432 F4
Stinsford Rd *CFDH* BH17 .... 430 B7
Stirling Av *WVILLE* PO7 .... 376 D1
Stirling Cl *FARN* GU14 .... 90 D5
FRIM GU16 .... 71 H6
NMIL/BTOS BH25 .... 437 M5
TOTT SO40 .... 316 F8
Stirling Crs *HEND* SO30 .... 321 H7
TOTT SO40 .... 316 F8
Stirling Rd *MOOR/WNTN* BH9 .... 447 K1
Stirling St *NEND* PO2 .... 399 H8
Stirling Wy *CHCH/BSGR* BH23 .... 451 G2
FARN GU14 .... 112 A1
NTHA RG18 .... 26 F4
Stirrup Cl *UPTN* BH16 .... 444 C1
WIMB BH21 .... 405 G2
Stirrup Pightle *NWBY* RG14 .... 37 L1
Stoatley Hollow *HASM* GU27 .... 204 D8
Stoatley Ri *HASM* GU27 .... 204 D8
Stockbridge Cl *CHAM* RG24 .... 84 A4
HAV PO9 .... 377 M3
Stockbridge Dr *ALDT* GU11 .... 7 K9
Stockbridge Rd *WINW* SO22 .... 10 C5
RAND SP11 .... 163 M5
ROMY SO51 .... 262 B1
RWIN SO21 .... 168 B4
RWIN SO21 .... 188 F8
STOK SO20 .... 210 F5
Stockbridge Wy *YTLY* GU46 .... 69 G4
Stocker Cl *BSTK* RG21 .... 104 F6
Stocker Pl
LSOL/BMARY PO13 .... 397 H6
Stockers Av *WINW* SO22 .... 10 A3
Stockheath La *HAV* PO9 .... 16 C2
Stockheath Rd *HAV* PO9 .... 377 K4
Stockheath Wy *HAV* PO9 .... 377 K5
Stockholm Dr *HEND* SO30 .... 346 A3
Stock La *RSAL* SP5 .... 287 K3
Stockley Cl *FAWY* SO45 .... 392 A5
Stocks La *ALTN* GU34 .... 244 F7
BPWT SO32 .... 299 M4
Stockton Av *FLET* GU13 .... 88 E5
Stockton Cl *HEND* SO30 .... 346 B1
Stockton Pk *FLET* GU13 .... 88 E6
Stockwood Ri *CBLY* GU15 .... 71 J3
Stockwood Wy *FNM* GU9 .... 6 D7
Stoddart Av *ITCH* SO19 .... 344 D2
Stodham La *EPSF* GU31 .... 248 D8
LISS GU33 .... 248 D6
Stoke Charity Rd *RWIN* SO21 .... 190 F5
Stoke Common Rd *ELGH* SO50 .... 294 D3
Stoke Gdns *GPORT* PO12 .... 18 F4
Stoke Hts *ELGH* SO50 .... 295 G5
Stoke Hl *RAND* SP11 .... 97 G5
Stoke Hills *FNM* GU9 .... 134 F5
Stoke La *RAND* SP11 .... 96 F3
Stoken La *HTWY* RG27 .... 86 E1
Stoke Park Rd *ELGH* SO50 .... 294 D4
Stoke Rd *GPORT* PO12 .... 18 F4
RAND SP11 .... 96 E8
ROWN SO16 .... 317 M7
WINC SO23 .... 11 H1
Stokes Av *PLE* BH15 .... 445 H4
Stokesay Cl *FAWY* SO45 .... 367 L8
Stokes Bay Rd *GPORT* PO12 .... 421 H6
Stokes La *STHA* RG19 .... 40 F7
Stoke Wood Cl *ELGH* SO50 .... 295 G6
Stoke Wood Rd *TWDS* BH3 .... 447 L1
Stonechat Cl *EPSF* GU31 .... 276 B6
Stonechat Dr *TOTT* SO40 .... 316 A8
Stonechat Rd *HORN* PO8 .... 352 E2
Stone Cl *AND* SP10 .... 8 C9
RSAL SP5 .... 206 F2
Stone Copse *NTHA* RG18 .... 26 B1
Stone Crop Cl *HLER* SO31 .... 370 C7
Stonecrop Cl *WIMB* BH21 .... 429 J6
Stonedene Cl *BOR* GU35 .... 202 E4
Stone Gdns *CHAR* BH8 .... 433 L6
Stonegate *CBLY* GU15 .... 71 M2
Stoneham Cemetery Rd
WEND SO18 .... 319 L4
Stoneham Cl *PSF* GU32 .... 275 J4
ROWN SO16 .... 319 J3
Stoneham La *ELGH* SO50 .... 293 K8
ROWN SO16 .... 319 J3
Stoneham Pk *PSF* GU32 .... 275 J4
Stoneham Wy *ELGH* SO50 .... 319 K3
Stonehill Pk *BOR* GU35 .... 202 E4
Stonehill Rd *BOR* GU35 .... 202 F4
Stonehills *FAWY* SO45 .... 393 G6
Stonehouse Ri *FRIM* GU16 .... 71 H7
Stonehouse Rd *LIPH* GU30 .... 227 G4
Stone La *GPORT* PO12 .... 18 F4
GPORT PO12 .... 18 F5
Stoneleigh Av *LYMN* SO41 .... 438 D4
Stoneleigh Cl
FHAM/PORC PO16 .... 373 M8
Stoneleigh Ct *FRIM* GU16 .... 71 J7
Stoners Cl *LSOL/BMARY* PO13 .... 396 F5
Stone Sq *HAV* PO9 .... 377 K4
Stone St *ASHV* GU12 .... 7 M5
SSEA PO5 .... 20 F5
Stoney Bottom *GSHT* GU26 .... 203 M5
Stoney Cl *YTLY* GU46 .... 69 G4
Stoney Cross *RAND* SP11 .... 92 E6
Stoneyfield *THLE* RG7 .... 29 K2
Stoneyfields *FNM* GU9 .... 135 H7
Stoney La *ALTN* GU34 .... 197 G4
WINW SO22 .... 10 A2
NWBY RG14 .... 26 A2
STHA RG19 .... 27 H5
Stony La *CHCH/BSGR* BH23 .... 434 F6
FBDG SP6 .... 307 M4
PSEA PO1 .... 422 E2
Stony La South
CHCH/BSGR BH23 .... 450 B2
Stonymoor Cl *FAWY* SO45 .... 392 A5
Stookes Wy *YTLY* GU46 .... 68 E4
Stopples La *LYMN* SO41 .... 438 D4
Storrington Rd *HORN* PO8 .... 328 C3
Story La *BDST* BH18 .... 429 M4
Stourbank Rd
CHCH/BSGR BH23 .... 449 M2
Stourcliffe Av *SBNE* BH6 .... 449 H4
Stour Cl *PSF* GU32 .... 275 K6
WEND SO18 .... 319 M5
WIMB BH21 .... 405 H4
Stourcroft Dr
CHCH/BSGR BH23 .... 434 B6
Stourfield Rd *BOSC* BH5 .... 449 G4
Stourhead Cl *AND* SP10 .... 8 B7
FARN GU14 .... 91 G4
Stourpaine Rd *CFDH* BH17 .... 430 B6
Stour Rd *CHAR* BH8 .... 448 C2
CHCH/BSGR BH23 .... 449 M1
DEAN RG23 .... 103 G7
Stourvale Av
CHCH/BSGR BH23 .... 434 B8
Stourvale Gdns *CHFD* SO53 .... 293 J3
Stourvale Rd *SBNE* BH6 .... 449 G3
Stour Valley Wy *FERN* BH22 .... 406 B8
MOOR/WNTN BH9 .... 433 G2
SBNE BH6 .... 449 K1
WIMB BH21 .... 404 A4
Stour Wy *CHCH/BSGR* BH23 .... 434 B6
Stourwood Av *SBNE* BH6 .... 449 H4
Stourwood Rd *SBNE* BH6 .... 449 J4
Stouts La *CHCH/BSGR* BH23 .... 409 M7
Stovold's Wy *ALDT* GU11 .... 6 C5
Stowe Cl *HEND* SO30 .... 321 J7
Stowe Rd *ENEY* PO4 .... 423 M4
Stradbrook *LSOL/BMARY* PO13 .... 396 F7
Stragwyne Cl *NBAD* SO52 .... 291 L2
The Straight Mile *ROMY* SO51 .... 263 K7
Strand *SHAM* SO14 .... 13 G4
Strand St *PLE* BH15 .... 445 G7
The Strand *HISD* PO11 .... 426 A7
Stratfield Av *TADY* RG26 .... 61 L1
Stratfield Dr *CHFD* SO53 .... 265 G7
Stratfield Pl
NMIL/BTOS BH25 .... 437 J5
Stratfield Rd *BSTK* RG21 .... 4 E2
Stratfield Saye Rd *TADY* RG26 .... 63 M3
Stratford Pl *ELGH* SO50 .... 294 A4
LYMN SO41 .... 440 B3
Stratford Rd *ASHV* GU12 .... 91 J8
WVILLE PO7 .... 352 E8
Strathfield Rd *AND* SP10 .... 142 E3
Strathmore Dr *VWD* BH31 .... 356 F2
Strathmore Rd *GPORT* PO12 .... 19 H3
NBNE BH10 .... 432 E4
Stratton Cl *CHAM* PO6 .... 375 G8
RWIN SO21 .... 170 F4
Stratton La *RWIN* SO21 .... 171 H7
Stratton Rd *BSTK* RG21 .... 104 E6
MOOR/WNTN BH9 .... 433 G4
WINC SO23 .... 11 K9
WSHM SO15 .... 318 B7
Stratton Wk *FARN* GU14 .... 90 D1
Strauss Rd *KEMP* RG22 .... 104 B8
Stravinsky Rd *KEMP* RG22 .... 104 E8
Strawberry Flds *TADY* RG26 .... 63 L5
Strawberry Hl *HLER* SO31 .... 370 D5
NWBY RG14 .... 2 D2
Stream Farm Cl *RFNM* GU10 .... 159 G1
Streamleaze
FHAM/STUB PO14 .... 371 G7
Streamside *FLET* GU13 .... 88 F8
Stream Valley Rd *RFNM* GU10 .... 158 F2
Street End *HTWY* RG27 .... 88 A4
NBAD SO52 .... 292 A3
Streets La *RGWD* BH24 .... 383 G4
The Street *ALTN* GU34 .... 178 D1
CHAM RG24 .... 105 M2
FLET GU13 .... 110 C3
HTWY RG27 .... 85 K3
MIDH GU29 .... 279 K7
RFNM GU10 .... 136 C3
RFNM GU10 .... 158 B2
RFNM GU10 .... 180 B2
RFNM GU10 .... 180 F1
ODIM RG29 .... 107 L5
ODIM RG29 .... 131 J5
RGUW GU3 .... 137 L4
RSAL SP5 .... 206 C2
RSAL SP5 .... 230 B1
RSAL SP5 .... 258 F4
TADY RG26 .... 63 J6
THLE RG7 .... 41 K1
THLE RG7 .... 43 L3
THLE RG7 .... 45 M2
Streetway Rd *RAND* SP11 .... 161 K2
Strettons Copse *LIPH* GU30 .... 250 E5
Stride Av *HSEA* PO3 .... 423 M2
Strides La *RGWD* BH24 .... 382 D1
Strides Wy *TOTT* SO40 .... 340 F1
Strode Gdns *RGWD* BH24 .... 381 M3
Strode Rd *NEND* PO2 .... 399 G6
Strokins Rd *KSCL* RG20 .... 59 J5
Strongs Cl *ROMY* SO51 .... 263 G8
Stroud Cl *CHAM* RG24 .... 83 K6
WIMB BH21 .... 404 E2
Strouden Av *CHAR* BH8 .... 432 F7
Strouden Ct *HAV* PO9 .... 377 H1
Stroud End *PSF* GU32 .... 275 G4
Strouden Rd
MOOR/WNTN BH9 .... 432 E7
Stroud La *CHCH/BSGR* BH23 .... 450 D2
HTWY RG27 .... 110 B3
Stroudley Av *CHAM* PO6 .... 400 A2
Stroudley Rd *CHAM* RG24 .... 5 M3
Stroudley Wy *HEND* SO30 .... 321 J6
Stroud Park Av
CHCH/BSGR BH23 .... 450 D1
Strouds Meadow *NTHA* RG18 .... 26 F1
The Strouds *THLE* RG7 .... 29 J2
Stroudwood La *BPWT* SO32 .... 295 M5
RWIN SO21 .... 295 M3
Stroudwood Rd *HAV* PO9 .... 377 L5
Struan Ct *RGWD* BH24 .... 381 L2
Struan Dr *RGWD* BH24 .... 381 L2
Struan Gdns *RGWD* BH24 .... 381 K2
Stuart Cl *FARN* GU14 .... 90 D3
FHAM/STUB PO14 .... 396 A6
UPTN BH16 .... 444 A1
Stuart Crs *WINW* SO22 .... 238 D3
Stuart Rd *CHCH/BSGR* BH23 .... 436 F8
NWBY RG14 .... 36 F2
Stubbington Av *BOR* GU35 .... 201 H7
NEND PO2 .... 399 J7
Stubbington Gn
FHAM/STUB PO14 .... 396 A5
Stubbington La
FHAM/STUB PO14 .... 396 A8
Stubbington Wy *ELGH* SO50 .... 295 J7
Stubbs Ct *AND* SP10 .... 8 F2
Stubbs Court Ct *AND* SP10 .... 8 F2
Stubbs Dro *HEND* SO30 .... 346 B1
Stubbs Folly *SHST* GU47 .... 70 A1
Stubbs Moor Rd *FARN* GU14 .... 90 C3
Stubbs Rd *BSTK* RG21 .... 105 H6
ITCH SO19 .... 345 G6
Stuckton Rd *FBDG* SP6 .... 309 M8
Studland Cl *ROWN* SO16 .... 317 J7
Studland Dr *LYMN* SO41 .... 454 A3
Studland Rd
LSOL/BMARY PO13 .... 420 C2
ROWN SO16 .... 317 J7
WBNE BH4 .... 447 H7
Studley Av *FAWY* SO45 .... 392 A5
Studley Cl *CHCH/BSGR* BH23 .... 437 G8
Studley Ct *NMIL/BTOS* BH25 .... 437 H8
Stukeley Rd *BSTK* RG21 .... 104 E4
Sturdee Cl *FRIM* GU16 .... 71 H7
Sturt Av *HASM* GU27 .... 228 C3
Sturt Rd *FNM* GU9 .... 134 E1
FRIM GU16 .... 91 J3
HASM GU27 .... 228 D4
Sudbury Rd *CHAM* PO6 .... 375 H8
Suetts La *BPWT* SO32 .... 323 L1
Suffield La *RGUW* GU3 .... 137 J8
Suffolk Av *CHCH/BSGR* BH23 .... 434 D6
WSHM SO15 .... 343 H1
Suffolk Cl *CHFD* SO53 .... 293 H6
WIMB BH21 .... 405 G2
Suffolk Dr *CHFD* SO53 .... 293 H6
FHAM PO15 .... 370 F1
HLER SO31 .... 370 F1
Suffolk Rd *AND* SP10 .... 8 F7
ENEY PO4 .... 423 L5
WCLF BH2 .... 22 A5
Suffolk Rd South *WBNE* BH4 .... 22 A4
Sulhamstead Hl *THLE* RG7 .... 30 F2
Sulhamstead Rd *THLE* RG7 .... 31 J4
Sullivan Cl *CHAM* PO6 .... 374 C8
FARN GU14 .... 90 E4
Sullivan Rd *CBLY* GU15 .... 70 D3
ITCH SO19 .... 345 H5
KEMP RG22 .... 104 D7
Sullivan Wy *WVILLE* PO7 .... 376 C3
Sultan Rd *EMRTH* PO10 .... 378 D7
NEND PO2 .... 423 G1
Sumar Cl *FHAM/STUB* PO14 .... 396 B3
Summercroft Wy *FERN* BH22 .... 380 C5
Summer Down La *DEAN* RG23 .... 102 D3
Summer Fld *WIMB* BH21 .... 404 E4
Summerfield Gdns
ROWN SO16 .... 319 J3
Summerfield La *RFNM* GU10 .... 158 D6
Summerfield Rd *SELS* PO20 .... 427 L6
Summerfields *CHAM* RG24 .... 83 M4
FHAM/STUB PO14 .... 370 F7
LTDN BH7 .... 448 E1
Summer Flds *VWD* BH31 .... 356 D4
Summer Gdns *CBLY* GU15 .... 71 M3
Summerhill Rd *HORN* PO8 .... 352 D5
Summerlands Rd *ELGH* SO50 .... 295 H6
Summer La *BROC* SO42 .... 391 J7
Summerleigh Wk
FHAM/STUB PO14 .... 396 B3
Summers Av *BWD* BH11 .... 431 M2
Summers La *CHCH/BSGR* BH23 .... 435 H7
Summers St *SHAM* SO14 .... 343 M2
Summertrees Ct
NMIL/BTOS BH25 .... 438 B4
Summit Av *FARN* GU14 .... 89 M5
Summit Cl *EWKG* RG40 .... 48 C2
Summit Wy *WEND* SO18 .... 319 L7
Sumner Rd *EPSF* GU31 .... 303 J3
FNM GU9 .... 134 F5
Sunbeam Wy *GPORT* PO12 .... 18 F6
Sun Brow *HASM* GU27 .... 228 C3
Sunbury Cl *BOR* GU35 .... 201 K5
Sunbury Ct *FHAM* PO15 .... 372 C4
Sunderland Pl *NTHA* RG18 .... 26 F4
Sunderton La *HORN* PO8 .... 328 A4
Sundew Cl *CHCH/BSGR* BH23 .... 436 A7
NMIL/BTOS BH25 .... 438 B4
Sundew Rd *WIMB* BH21 .... 429 J6
Sundridge Cl *CHAM* PO6 .... 375 J8
Sunflower Cl *KEMP* RG22 .... 126 F1
Sun Gdns *THLE* RG7 .... 31 K7
Sun Hill Crs *NALR* SO24 .... 218 C4
Sun La *NALR* SO24 .... 218 C4
THLE RG7 .... 45 L6
Sunley Cl *NWBY* RG14 .... 37 G2
Sunningdale *FAWY* SO45 .... 367 K6
Sunningdale Cl *ELGH* SO50 .... 294 E6
LSOL/BMARY PO13 .... 397 G7
Sunningdale Crs *NBNE* BH10 .... 432 A4
Sunningdale Gdns
WEND SO18 .... 344 F1
Sunningdale Rd
FHAM/PORC PO16 .... 398 B1
HSEA PO3 .... 423 L2
Sunnybank *RAND* SP11 .... 141 K2
Sunnybank Rd *FARN* GU14 .... 90 A2
WIMB BH21 .... 404 F2
Sunnydell La *FNM* GU9 .... 158 D2
Sunnydown Rd *WINW* SO22 .... 237 M5
Sunnyfield Ri *HLER* SO31 .... 345 L7
Sunnyfield Rd
NMIL/BTOS BH25 .... 437 L8
Sunnyheath *HAV* PO9 .... 377 J4
Sunny Hill Rd *ALDT* GU11 .... 112 A6
BKME/WDN BH12 .... 446 C3
Sunnyhill Rd *SBNE* BH6 .... 449 G3
Sunnylands Av *SBNE* BH6 .... 449 L4
Sunny Md *DEAN* RG23 .... 103 G8
Sunnymead Dr *WVILLE* PO7 .... 352 A6
Sunnymoor Rd *BWD* BH11 .... 431 L7
Sunnyside *FLET* GU13 .... 88 D6
Sunnyside Cl *AND* SP10 .... 118 C6
Sunnyside Rd
BKME/WDN BH12 .... 446 C2
BOR GU35 .... 202 F4
Sunny Wk *PSEA* PO1 .... 20 B1
Sunny Wy *TOTT* SO40 .... 341 K1
Sun Ray Est *SHST* GU47 .... 49 J8
Sunridge Cl *BKME/WDN* BH12 .... 446 F2
Sunset Av *TOTT* SO40 .... 316 D8
Sunset Rd *TOTT* SO40 .... 316 D8
Sunshine Av *HISD* PO11 .... 425 M6
Sun St *PSEA* PO1 .... 20 D2
Sunvale Av *HASM* GU27 .... 228 A2
Sunvale Cl *HASM* GU27 .... 228 A2
ITCH SO19 .... 344 F5
Sunwood Rd *HAV* PO9 .... 377 H3
Surbiton Rd *CBLY* GU15 .... 51 K7
ELGH SO50 .... 294 A3
Surrey Av *CBLY* GU15 .... 70 D4
Surrey Cl *CHCH/BSGR* BH23 .... 434 D6
TOTT SO40 .... 341 H3
Surrey Gdns *WBNE* BH4 .... 447 H4
Surrey Rd *BKME/WDN* BH12 .... 446 F3
CHFD SO53 .... 293 H5
ITCH SO19 .... 344 B6
WBNE BH4 .... 447 H4
Surrey Rd South *WBNE* BH4 .... 447 H4
Surrey St *PSEA* PO1 .... 21 G1
Sussex Border Pth
EMRTH PO10 .... 402 D5
EPSF GU31 .... 304 E3
HASM GU27 .... 229 J7
HAV PO9 .... 354 B4
HORN PO8 .... 329 H4
LIPH GU30 .... 226 E8
LISS GU33 .... 249 L2
Sussex Cl *MOOR/WNTN* BH9 .... 432 F4
Sussex Gdns *EPSF* GU31 .... 275 L6
FARN GU14 .... 89 G4
Sussex Pl *SSEA* PO5 .... 21 G6
Sussex Rd *CHFD* SO53 .... 293 J5
EPSF GU31 .... 275 M6
SHAM SO14 .... 13 G3
SSEA PO5 .... 21 G6
Sussex St *WINC* SO23 .... 10 F7
Sutherland Av *BDST* BH18 .... 429 J3
Sutherland Cl *BOR* GU35 .... 201 J7
ROMY SO51 .... 263 G7
Sutherland Rd *ENEY* PO4 .... 21 M5
ROWN SO16 .... 317 L3
Sutherlands *NWBY* RG14 .... 37 H1
Sutherlands Ct *CHFD* SO53 .... 293 H2
Sutherlands Wy *CHFD* SO53 .... 293 G1
Sutton Cl *CFDH* BH17 .... 430 E6
HORN PO8 .... 352 B5
HSEA PO3 .... 399 M4
Sutton Fld *BOR* GU35 .... 201 H7
Sutton Gdns *WINC* SO23 .... 11 G7
Sutton Pl *BROC* SO42 .... 387 L7
Sutton Rd *BSTK* RG21 .... 4 E4
CBLY GU15 .... 51 K7
HORN PO8 .... 352 B5
MOOR/WNTN BH9 .... 432 F7
NWBY RG14 .... 25 G3
TOTT SO40 .... 316 C7
Sutton Wood La *NALR* SO24 .... 195 K8
Swains Cl *TADY* RG26 .... 41 L8
Swains Rd *TADY* RG26 .... 41 L8

Swaledale Gdns FARN GU14 ...... 89 G4
Swale Dr CHFD SO53 .... 292 F1
Swale Rd FARN GU14 .... 90 A2
Swallow Cl ALTN GU34 .... 176 F2
  CFDH BH17 .... 429 K8
  HAV PO9 .... 17 J1
  KEMP RG22 .... 103 L8
  NTID SP9 .... 114 E2
  TOTT SO40 .... 340 F1
  YTLY GU46 .... 68 E2
Swallow Ct
  LSOL/BMARY PO13 .... 420 D1
Swallow Dr LYMN SO41 .... 454 E4
Swallowfield Rd THLE RG7 ...... 46 D1
Swallowfields AND SP10 .... 119 G6
Swallow Sq ELGH SO50 .... 293 J6
Swanage Cl ITCH SO19 .... 344 C5
Swanage Rd
  LSOL/BMARY PO13 .... 420 C2
Swan Barn Rd HASM GU27 .... 229 G2
Swan Cl EMRTH PO10 .... 378 E8
  HLER SO31 .... 370 B1
Swancote FHAM/PORC PO16 .... 373 K8
Swan Ct HTWY RG27 .... 87 J2
Swan Dr THLE RG7 .... 29 L5
Swan La SHST GU47 .... 69 L2
  WINC SO23 .... 10 F6
Swanley Cl ELGH SO50 .... 293 M3
Swan Md RGWD BH24 .... 383 G2
Swan Ms ODIM RG29 .... 108 B4
Swanmore Av ITCH SO19 .... 344 F5
Swanmore Cl WINW SO22 .... 214 C4
Swanmore Rd BPWT SO32 .... 323 L1
  HAV PO9 .... 377 H1
  LTDN BH7 .... 449 L2
Swansbury Dr CHAR BH8 .... 433 L6
Swan St KSCL RG20 .... 59 H7
  PSF GU32 .... 275 K5
Swanton Gdns CHFD SO53 .... 293 G1
Swan Wy FLET GU13 .... 110 C1
Swanwick La HLER SO31 .... 346 B8
Swanwick Shore Rd
  HLER SO31 .... 370 B1
Swarraton Rd HAV PO9 .... 377 L4
Sway Ct HAV PO9 .... 377 M3
Sway Gdns CHAR BH8 .... 433 H6
Sway Rd BROC SO42 .... 413 K1
  LYMN SO41 .... 439 J5
  NMIL/BTOS BH25 .... 457 M2
Swaythling Rd HAV PO9 .... 377 H2
  HEND SO30 .... 320 A6
Swedish Houses TADY RG26 ...... 61 M1
The Sweep RGWD BH24 .... 382 D1
Sweetbriar Cl CWTH RG45 .... 49 K1
Sweetbriar Gdns
  WVILLE PO7 .... 376 D3
Sweethills Crs HLER SO31 ...... 346 F8
Sweetzer's Piece THLE RG7 ..... 43 H2
Swelling Hl ALTN GU34 .... 220 F2
Sweyns Lease BROC SO42 .... 416 A2
Swift Cl AND SP10 .... 119 G6
  CFDH BH17 .... 429 K8
  ELGH SO50 .... 293 M6
  WINW SO22 .... 238 C3
  HORN PO8 .... 352 L1
  LSOL/BMARY PO13 .... 420 D1
Swift Gdns ITCH SO19 .... 344 B7
Swift Hollow ITCH SO19 .... 344 B7
Swift Rd EMRTH PO10 .... 402 E5
  FNM GU9 .... 134 E1
  ITCH SO19 .... 344 B7
Swift's Cl RFNM GU10 .... 135 L7
Swinburn Gdns HORN PO8 .... 352 D4
Swincombe Ri WEND SO18 .... 320 A4
Swingate Rd FNM GU9 .... 134 F8
Swing Swang La CHAM RG24 ...... 5 L3
Swiss Cl RFNM GU10 .... 158 C4
Swiss Rd WVILLE PO7 .... 376 C1
Switchback La RFNM GU10 .... 158 C4
Swivelton La WHAM PO17 .... 373 L5
Sword Cl GPORT PO12 .... 421 K4
  HORN PO8 .... 328 A3
Swordfish Wy FARN GU14 .... 112 B1
Sword Sands Rd HSEA PO3 .... 424 A1
Sycamore Av CHFD SO53 .... 265 K7
Sycamore Cl CFDH BH17 .... 429 K7
  FHAM/STUB PO14 .... 371 G7
  FRIM GU16 .... 71 H7
  HLER SO31 .... 345 K8
  HORN PO8 .... 352 C5
  LSOL/BMARY PO13 .... 397 J7
  LYMN SO41 .... 454 B3
  NBAD SO52 .... 291 L3
  NTID SP9 .... 114 F2
  ROMY SO51 .... 291 H2
  SHST GU47 .... 69 L1
  TLHT RG30 .... 31 L3
Sycamore Crs FLET GU13 .... 110 D2
  STOK SO20 .... 163 G4
Sycamore Dr ASHV GU12 .... 113 J1
  FAWY SO45 .... 391 M3
  FRIM GU16 .... 71 H6
  HISD PO11 .... 425 J4
  RFNM GU10 .... 158 D2
  WINC SO23 .... 191 G8
Sycamore Ri NWBY RG14 .... 25 M2
Sycamore Rd BPWT SO32 .... 297 K8
  FARN GU14 .... 90 F6
  FAWY SO45 .... 367 K5
  LYMN SO41 .... 438 D4
  ROWN SO16 .... 317 M6
The Sycamores BLKW GU17 .... 69 L3
  FARN GU14 .... 91 G5
Sycamore Wy DEAN RG23 .... 104 C1
Sydenham Ter PSEA PO4 .... 21 K2
The Sydings NWBY RG14 .... 25 G3
Sydling Cl CFDH BH17 .... 430 F6
Sydmanton Cl ROMY SO51 .... 290 F2
Sydmonton Ct HAV PO9 .... 377 M2
Sydney Av HLER SO31 .... 369 G4
Sydney Cl CWTH RG45 .... 49 M1
  RAND SP11 .... 115 J1
Sydney Rd BDST BH18 .... 429 L5
  CHCH/BSGR BH23 .... 434 C7
  ELGH SO50 .... 294 C4
  GPORT PO12 .... 18 F3
  BOR GU35 .... 201 J5
  WSHM SO15 .... 318 A7

Sydney Smith Av FARN GU14 ..... 90 E7
Syers Rd LISS GU33 .... 248 E4
Sylmor Gdns
  MOOR/WNTN BH9 .... 432 E6
Sylvan Cl ITCH SO19 .... 345 G2
Sylvan Cl LYMN SO41 .... 438 F6
  RCWD BH24 .... 381 H4
Sylvan Dr NBAD SO52 .... 291 L4
Sylvan La HLER SO31 .... 369 L6
Sylvan Rdg SHST GU47 .... 49 K7
Sylvan Rd BKME/WDN BH12 .... 446 A2
The Sylvans FAWY SO45 .... 367 H5
Sylvan Vw WVILLE PO7 .... 376 D2
Sylvan Wy FLET GU13 .... 110 E3
Sylvester Cl NWBY RG14 .... 25 H3
Sylvia Crs TOTT SO40 .... 316 D7
Symes Rd PLE BH15 .... 444 C4
  ROMY SO51 .... 291 G1
Symonds Cl CHFD SO53 .... 293 J4
Symonds St WINC SO23 .... 11 G9
Sympson Rd TADY RG26 .... 42 A7
Syon Pl FARN GU14 .... 91 G4
Sywell Crs HSEA PO3 .... 399 M4

T

Tadburn Cl CHFD SO53 .... 293 J3
  ROMY SO51 .... 290 F1
Tadburn Rd ROMY SO51 .... 290 F2
Tadden Wk BDST BH18 .... 429 K6
Tadfield Rd ROMY SO51 .... 290 F1
Tadham Pl STHA RG19 .... 26 F6
Tadley Common Rd TADY RG26 .... 41 M7
Tadley Hl TADY RG26 .... 61 M1
Tadpole La RFNM GU10 .... 111 G7
Tagdell La HORN PO8 .... 327 L8
Taiping Rd STOK SO20 .... 162 F4
Tait Cl CFDH BH17 .... 445 K1
Tait Pl LSOL/BMARY PO13 .... 397 H7
Talbot Cl SHAM SO14 .... 13 K1
Talbot Av TWDS BH3 .... 447 K1
Talbot Cl FRIM GU16 .... 91 K4
  HAV PO9 .... 377 C5
  NWBY RG14 .... 25 H3
  ROWN SO16 .... 318 E4
Talbot Dr BKME/WDN BH12 .... 431 M8
  CHCH/BSGR BH23 .... 436 D6
Talbot Hill Rd
  MOOR/WNTN BH9 .... 432 B8
Talbot Mdw BKME/WDN BH12 ...... 431 M8
Talbot Rd NBNE BH10 .... 432 A7
Talbot Rd ENEY PO4 .... 21 M4
  FAWY SO45 .... 367 H7
  FNM GU9 .... 134 E8
  HAV PO9 .... 16 A1
  MOOR/WNTN BH9 .... 432 B8
Talgarth Dr FARN GU14 .... 91 G6
Talisman Cl CWTH RG45 .... 49 G3
Talland Rd FHAM/STUB PO14 ..... 370 F7
Tallis Gdns KEMP RG22 .... 104 D7
Talmey Cl CHAM RG24 .... 83 K5
Tamar Cl FERN BH22 .... 406 C2
  FHAM/PORC PO16 .... 373 L7
Tamar Down WVILLE PO7 .... 376 L1
Tamar Dr DEAN RG23 .... 103 G7
Tamar Gv FAWY SO45 .... 367 J5
Tamarisk Cl ENEY PO4 .... 424 A5
  FHAM/STUB PO14 .... 396 A7
  KEMP RG22 .... 127 H3
  WVILLE PO7 .... 376 E3
Tamarisk Ct NTHA RG18 .... 27 J4
Tamarisk Gdns WEND SO18 .... 319 K8
Tamarisk Rd HEND SO30 .... 345 M1
Tamella Rd HEND SO30 .... 346 C2
Tammys Turn
  FHAM/STUB PO14 .... 371 M8
Tamorisk Dr TOTT SO40 .... 341 G2
Tamworth Dr FARN GU14 .... 89 G4
Tamworth Rd HSEA PO3 .... 423 L2
Tanfield La WHAM PO17 .... 348 D5
Tanfield Pk WHAM PO17 .... 348 D5
Tangier La BPWT SO32 .... 322 E1
Tangier Rd HSEA PO3 .... 423 L1
Tanglewood EWKG RG40 .... 48 D1
  FHAM/PORC PO16 .... 15 G1
  TOTT SO40 .... 342 E7
Tanglewood Cl WVILLE PO7 ...... 376 A4
Tangmere Cl CHCH/BSGR BH23 .... 451 L2
Tangmere Dr ROWN SO16 .... 317 L4
Tangway CHAM RG24 .... 83 L4
Tangyes Cl FHAM/STUB PO14 ..... 396 B5
Tanhouse Cl HEND SO30 .... 346 A3
Tanhouse La ALTN GU34 .... 176 D5
  HEND SO30 .... 346 B3
Tan Howse Cl LTDN BH7 .... 433 M8
Tankerdale La PSF GU32 .... 248 B8
Tanker Rd FARN GU14 .... 90 A4
Tankerton Cl CHAM RG24 .... 375 J8
Tankerville Rd ITCH SO19 ...... 344 B5
Tank Rd CBLY GU15 .... 70 C3
Tanner's Brook Wy
  WSHM SO15 .... 342 D2
Tanners Cl THLE RG7 .... 31 J7
Tanners La FBDG SP6 .... 308 E5
  FHAM/STUB PO14 .... 396 C2
  HASM GU27 .... 228 F1
  LYMN SO41 .... 441 L4
  ROMY SO51 .... 261 J8
  WVILLE PO7 .... 351 K3
Tanner's Rdg WVILLE PO7 .... 376 C5
Tanners Rd NBAD SO52 .... 291 M4
The Tanners
  FHAM/STUB PO14 .... 371 G7
Tanner St WINC SO23 .... 11 H8
Tanners Wy DEAN RG23 .... 103 G6
Tansy Cl WVILLE PO7 .... 376 M4
Tansy Meadow NBAD SO52 .... 292 E4
The Tanyards CHFD SO53 .... 265 C7
Taplin Dr HEND SO30 .... 321 H8
Taplings Cl WINW SO22 .... 10 A1
Taplings Rd WINW SO22 .... 10 A1
Taplin's Farm La HTWY RG27 .... 87 K5
Taranto Rd ROWN SO16 .... 318 D4
Tarbat Cl SHST GU47 .... 50 A8
Tarbery Crs HORN PO8 .... 353 G1

Target Rd NEND PO2 .... 399 G5
Tarius Cl LSOL/BMARY PO13 ..... 397 H6
Tarleton Rd CHAM PO6 .... 374 F7
Tarn Cl FARN GU14 .... 90 B6
Tarn Dr CFDH BH17 .... 429 K7
Tarn La NWBY RG14 .... 2 C9
Tarn Ri HORN PO8 .... 328 B6
Tarn Rd GSHT GU26 .... 204 A5
Tarragon Cl FARN GU14 .... 89 M4
Tarragon Wy THLE RG7 .... 31 L5
Tarrant Cl CFDH BH17 .... 430 C6
Tarrant Gdns HAV PO9 .... 16 B1
Tarrant Rd MOOR/WNTN BH9 ...... 432 F5
Tasker Dr RAND SP11 .... 142 B3
Tasman Cl CHCH/BSGR BH23 ...... 434 D8
  SHAM SO14 .... 13 K8
Tasmania Cl CHAM RG24 .... 83 H6
Taswell Rd SSEA PO5 .... 21 K8
Tatchbury La TOTT SO40 .... 315 L7
Tate Rd WSHM SO15 .... 317 H8
Tates Rd FAWY SO45 .... 367 M5
  FAWY SO45 .... 367 M6
Tatnam Rd PLE BH15 .... 445 H4
Tattenham Rd BSGR SO42 .... 387 K8
Tattershall Crs
  FHAM/PORC PO16 .... 397 M1
Tatwin Cl ITCH SO19 .... 345 H3
Tatwin Crs ITCH SO19 .... 345 H3
Taunton Dr WEND SO18 .... 344 F1
Tavells Cl TOTT SO40 .... 342 C7
Tavell's La TOTT SO40 .... 342 C7
Taverner Cl BSTK RG21 .... 5 J4
Taverners Cl ITCH SO19 .... 345 H5
Tavistock Cl ROMY SO51 .... 263 G7
Tavistock Gdns FARN GU14 ...... 90 E1
  HAV PO9 .... 17 J5
Tavistock Rd FLET GU13 .... 88 C8
Tavy Cl CFDH SO53 .... 293 G2
Taw Dr CFDH SO53 .... 293 C1
Tawny Gv ALTN GU34 .... 196 F6
Tawny Owl Cl
  FHAM/STUB PO14 .... 395 M4
Tay Cl FARN GU14 .... 90 B2
Taylor Dr CHAR BH8 .... 433 H4
  TADY RG26 .... 63 M6
Taylors La BOR GU35 .... 201 L3
Teachers Wy FAWY SO45 .... 391 M4
Teal Cl FHAM/PORC PO16 .... 373 K8
  HISD PO11 .... 425 M5
  TOTT SO40 .... 341 C1
Teal Crs KEMP RG22 .... 126 E1
Teasel Cl RAND SP11 .... 92 E7
Teasel Wy FERN BH22 .... 380 C7
Teazle Cl EPSF GU31 .... 276 B6
Tebourba Dr GPORT PO12 .... 18 C5
Tebourba Wy WSHM SO15 .... 342 D1
Tedder Cl BWD BH11 .... 431 M5
  RAND SP11 .... 142 A1
Tedder Gdns BWD BH11 .... 431 M5
Tedder Rd BWD BH11 .... 431 M5
  LSOL/BMARY PO13 .... 397 H5
  WEND SO18 .... 319 M8
Tedder Wy TOTT SO40 .... 341 H1
Teddington Rd ENEY PO4 .... 423 L4
Tees Cl CHFD SO53 .... 292 F1
  FARN GU14 .... 90 B2
Teg Down Meads WINW SO22 ...... 214 A7
Tegg Down Nr NALR SO24 .... 219 K5
Teignmouth Rd GPORT PO12 ...... 421 K1
  HSEA PO3 .... 399 L8
Tekels Av CBLY GU15 .... 71 G4
Tekels Wy CBLY GU15 .... 71 J5
Telconia Cl BOR GU35 .... 202 F4
Telegraph La ALTN GU34 .... 197 J5
  EPSF GU31 .... 305 K6
Telegraph Rd HEND SO30 .... 320 D8
Telephone Rd ENEY PO4 .... 21 M3
Telford Gdns HEND SO30 .... 321 J6
Telford Rd NEND PO2 .... 399 J5
Teme Crs ROWN SO16 .... 317 K8
Teme Rd ROWN SO16 .... 317 K8
Tempest Av WVILLE PO7 .... 352 E8
Templar Cl BKME/WDN BH12 ...... 431 K7
  SHST GU47 .... 49 K8
Templars Mede CHFD SO53 .... 293 G5
Templars Wy NBAD SO52 .... 292 E4
Templecombe Rd ELGH SO50 ...... 294 E7
Temple Gdns ITCH SO19 .... 344 D6
Temple La PSF GU32 .... 273 J8
Templemere
  FHAM/STUB PO14 .... 396 A1
Temple Rd ITCH SO19 .... 344 D6
  LISS GU33 .... 248 F2
Temple's Cl RFNM GU10 .... 135 M7
Templeton Cl NEND PO2 .... 399 J5
Tenby Cl WEND SO18 .... 319 M8
Tenby Dr CHFD SO53 .... 292 F4
Tenby Rd FRIM GU16 .... 71 K8
Tench Wy ROMY SO51 .... 262 E8
Tennyson Cl BPWT SO32 .... 297 K8
Tennyson Gdns
  FHAM/PORC PO16 .... 15 G4
Tennyson Rd ELGH SO50 .... 293 L6
  MOOR/WNTN BH9 .... 432 D6
  NEND PO2 .... 399 K8
  NTHA RG18 .... 26 F7
  PSTN BH14 .... 445 M5
  PTSW SO17 .... 319 G8
  TOTT SO40 .... 316 C6
  WIMB BH21 .... 404 A2
Tennyson's La HASM GU27 .... 229 H4
Tennyson Wy KEMP RG22 .... 104 D5
Tensing Cl FHAM/PORC PO16 ..... 15 G1
Tenterton Av ITCH SO19 .... 344 F7
Terence Rd WIMB BH21 .... 429 G3
Terminus Ter SHAM SO14 .... 13 J6
Tern Cl FAWY SO45 .... 367 M6
Tern Ct SBNE BH6 .... 449 J2
Terrace Rd WCLF BH2 .... 22 D6
The Terrace CBLY GU15 .... 70 C3
  CWTH RG45 .... 50 A3
Terrier Cl HEND SO30 .... 321 H5
Terrington Av
  CHCH/BSGR BH23 .... 436 C7

Terriote Cl CHFD SO53 .... 293 H1
Terwick La EPSF GU31 .... 278 D8
Tesimond Dr YTLY GU46 .... 68 D3
Test Cl PSF GU32 .... 275 K7
Testbourne Av TOTT SO40 .... 341 H1
Testbourne Cl TOTT SO40 .... 341 H1
Testbourne Rd TOTT SO40 .... 341 H1
Test La ROWN SO16 .... 317 G7
Test Rd STOK SO20 .... 165 M5
Test Rd SHAM SO14 .... 343 M8
  WHCH RG28 .... 122 B4
Testlands Av ROWN SO16 .... 317 G7
Testwood Crs TOTT SO40 .... 316 C6
Testwood La TOTT SO40 .... 316 C7
Testwood Pl TOTT SO40 .... 316 F8
Testwood Rd HAV PO9 .... 377 H3
  WSHM SO15 .... 342 F2
Tethering Dro FBDG SP6 .... 285 J5
Tetney Cl ROWN SO16 .... 317 K5
Teviot Rd CHFD SO53 .... 292 F3
Tewkesbury Av FHAM PO15 .... 372 A5
  GPORT PO12 .... 421 L1
Tewkesbury Cl CHAM RG24 .... 83 G7
  CHAM PO6 .... 375 H8
Texas Dr WINW SO22 .... 238 A6
Thackeray Rd PTSW SO17 .... 319 G8
Thackham's La HTWY RG27 .... 86 E3
The Thakerays STHA RG19 .... 27 G6
Thames Ct AND SP10 .... 119 J6
  BSTK RG21 .... 5 J7
Thames Dr FHAM PO15 .... 372 B4
Thamesmead Cl
  GPORT PO12 .... 421 K1
Thames Rd NTHA RG18 .... 26 E3
Thames St PLE BH15 .... 445 G7
Thatchers La
  CHCH/BSGR BH23 .... 409 K6
  LYMN SO41 .... 415 K8
Theal Cl SHST GU47 .... 50 A8
Theale Rd TLHT RG30 .... 31 L2
Theatre Ms SSEA PO5 .... 21 K7
Theatre Rd FARN GU14 .... 90 E8
The Itchen Br ITCH SO19 .... 13 M6
Theobalds Wy FRIM GU16 .... 71 M5
Theobold Rd
  CHCH/BSGR BH23 .... 407 L8
Theseus Rd LSOL/BMARY PO13 .... 420 B1
Thetchers Cl NMIL/BTOS BH25 ... 437 M3
Thetford Gdns CHFD SO53 .... 292 F1
Thibet Rd SHST GU47 .... 49 M8
The Thicket FHAM/PORC PO16 .... 373 L8
  LSOL/BMARY PO13 .... 397 J7
  ROMY SO51 .... 291 H2
  SSEA PO5 .... 21 J6
  WVILLE PO7 .... 376 B6
Third Av CHAM PO6 .... 375 J8
  HAV PO9 .... 17 H3
  WSHM SO15 .... 342 D2
Third St STHA RG19 .... 27 H8
Thirlmere ELGH SO50 .... 293 L6
Thirlmere Cl FARN GU14 .... 90 B4
  FHAM/STUB PO14 .... 396 B4
  BOR GU35 .... 180 D2
Thirlmere Crs FLET GU13 .... 110 D3
Thirlmere Rd ROWN SO16 .... 317 K6
Thirlstane Firs CHFD SO53 ..... 293 G4
Thirsk Ct ASHV GU12 .... 7 M1
Thirt Wy STOK SO20 .... 166 B7
Thistlebarrow Rd LTDN BH7 ..... 448 D2
Thistledown HORN PO8 .... 352 F3
Thistledown Cl AND SP10 .... 8 D3
Thistledowne Gdns
  EMRTH PO10 .... 378 F8
Thistle Rd HEND SO30 .... 345 M2
  NBAD SO52 .... 292 E3
Thomas Cl TOTT SO40 .... 341 H2
Thomas Lewis Wy
  PTSW SO17 .... 319 C8
Thomas Rd NBAD SO52 .... 291 M4
Thompson Dr STHA RG19 .... 27 H6
Thompson's La RWIN SO21 .... 295 L1
  WVILLE PO7 .... 351 G3
Thorburn Cha SHST GU47 .... 70 B2
Thoresby Ct
  NMIL/BTOS BH25 .... 437 J5
Thornbrake Rd GPORT PO12 ...... 19 H5
Thornbury Av FAWY SO45 .... 392 C4
  WSHM SO15 .... 343 J1
Thornbury Cl CWTH RG45 .... 49 G3
  FHAM/STUB PO14 .... 372 A8
Thornbury Hts CHFD SO53 .... 265 K7
Thornbury Rd SBNE BH6 .... 449 M4
Thornbury Wd CHFD SO53 .... 265 L7
Thorncliffe Cl NEND PO2 .... 399 K8
Thorn Cl ELGH SO50 .... 293 M3
  EPSF GU31 .... 276 B6
  RFNM GU10 .... 158 C7
Thorncombe Cl CFDH BH17 .... 430 C6
Thorn Crs ALTN GU34 .... 197 G6
Thorncroft Rd PSEA PO4 .... 21 M2
Thorndike Cl ROWN SO16 .... 317 M6
Thorn Dr ALTN GU34 .... 197 G6
Thorne Cl CWTH RG45 .... 49 K1
  VWD BH31 .... 356 C1
Thorneley Rd KSCL RG20 .... 59 J6
Thorness Cl ROWN SO16 .... 317 H7
Thorney Cl FHAM/STUB PO14 ..... 14 A8
Thorney Old Pk EMRTH PO10 ..... 403 H7
Thorney Rd EMRTH PO10 .... 402 F5
Thornfield Dr
  CHCH/BSGR BH23 .... 436 D7
Thornfield Gn BLKW GU17 .... 70 D5

Thornford Rd STHA RG19 .... 38 E4
Thorngate Wy GPORT PO12 .... 19 K3
Thornham Rd EMRTH PO10 .... 402 F2
Thornham Rd
  NMIL/BTOS BH25 .... 438 B5
Thornhill Av ITCH SO19 .... 345 H4
Thornhill Cl FAWY SO45 .... 392 D6
Thornhill Park Rd WEND SO18 ... 345 H1
Thornhill Rd ALDT GU11 .... 113 G4
  FAWY SO45 .... 392 D6
  ROWN SO16 .... 318 C4
Thorni Av FHAM PO15 .... 372 A5
Thorn La ALTN GU34 .... 197 H6
Thornleigh Rd ITCH SO19 .... 344 C6
Thornley Rd NBNE BH10 .... 432 B4
Thorn Rd CFDH BH17 .... 430 A5
  RFNM GU10 .... 158 C3
Thorns La SLO SO41 .... 442 D1
Thornton Av HLER SO31 .... 370 A4
Thornton Cl CHAM PO6 .... 375 M6
  WIMB BH21 .... 429 G3
Thornton End ALTN GU34 .... 177 H2
Thornton Rd GPORT PO12 .... 397 M4
Thornycroft Av ITCH SO19 ...... 344 B6
Thornyhurst Rd FRIM GU16 ...... 91 K4
Thorold Rd CHFD SO53 .... 265 K7
  FNM GU9 .... 134 F5
  WEND SO18 .... 319 K7
Thorpe Gdns ALTN GU34 .... 176 C4
Threadgill Wy NTID SP9 .... 138 B1
Three Acre Dr
  NMIL/BTOS BH25 .... 437 K8
Three Acre Rd NWBY RG14 .... 25 J8
Three Acres WVILLE PO7 .... 351 L5
Three Castles Pth HTWY RG27 ... 67 K3
  NALR SO24 .... 172 F8
  NALR SO24 .... 194 C1
  ODIM RG29 .... 107 L6
  OVTN RG25 .... 106 F7
  RWIN SO21 .... 193 H8
  RWIN SO21 .... 215 H4
Three Cross Rd WIMB BH21 ...... 380 C2
Threefield La SHAM SO14 .... 13 H5
Three Firs Wy THLE RG7 .... 31 H7
Three Gates La HASM GU27 ...... 229 G1
Three Horse Shoes La
  ALTN GU34 .... 244 D6
Three Oaks ITCH SO19 .... 345 J3
Three Stiles Rd FNM GU9 .... 134 C5
Three Tun Cl PSEA PO1 .... 20 D2
Thresher Cl HORN PO8 .... 353 G7
Threshers Cnr FARN GU14 .... 89 H4
Throgmorton Rd YTLY GU46 ...... 68 D3
Throop Cl CHAR BH8 .... 433 L1
Throop Rd CHAR BH8 .... 433 J4
Throopside Av
  MOOR/WNTN BH9 .... 433 H4
Thrush Cl THLE RG7 .... 31 L5
Thrush Rd BKME/WDN BH12 .... 431 G7
Thrush Wk HORN PO8 .... 352 C4
Thruxton Rd HAV PO9 .... 377 C3
Thuillier Rd RWIN SO21 .... 145 H6
Thumwood CHAM RG24 .... 83 L5
Thundery Hl RFNM GU10 .... 136 C4
Thurbans Rd FNM GU9 .... 158 D1
Thurbern Rd NEND PO2 .... 399 J6
Thurmell Cl HEND SO30 .... 346 A4
Thurmond Crs WINW SO22 .... 238 B2
Thurmond Rd WINW SO22 .... 238 B2
Thursby Rd CHCH/BSGR BH23 ..... 436 D6
Thursley Rd RFNM GU10 .... 181 M5
Thurston Cl CHFD SO53 .... 293 J1
Thurston Pl BSTK RG21 .... 104 F2
Thurstons ALTN GU34 .... 178 D2
Thwaite Rd BKME/WDN BH12 ...... 447 C3
Thyme Av FNM GU9 .... 347 H8
Thyme Cl CHAM RG24 .... 83 M4
Thyme Ct FARN GU14 .... 89 M3
Tides Reach WEND SO18 .... 319 J8
Tiberius Cl DEAN RG23 .... 104 B1
Tiberius Rd AND SP10 .... 119 C5
Tichborne Cl BLKW GU17 .... 70 A3
Tichborne Down NALR SO24 ...... 218 B5
Tichborne Gv HAV PO9 .... 377 H3
Tichborne Rd ELGH SO50 .... 293 L8
  WEND SO18 .... 320 C8
Tichborne Wy
  LSOL/BMARY PO13 .... 397 H7
Tichbourne Cl FRIM GU16 .... 71 J5
Tickenor Dr EWKG RG40 .... 48 C1
Tickleford Dr ITCH SO19 .... 344 E7
Tickner Cl HEND SO30 .... 346 B3
Ticonderoga Gdns ITCH SO19 .... 344 C7
Tidemill Cl CHCH/BSGR BH23 .... 434 E8
Tides Wy TOTT SO40 .... 342 D6
Tideway Gdns ENEY PO4 .... 424 A4
Tidworth Rd HAV PO9 .... 377 K4
  RAND SP11 .... 92 E6
Tiffany Cl LYMN SO41 .... 438 D4
Tiffield Cl HSEA PO3 .... 400 A4
Tigwells Fld ODIM RG29 .... 130 F4
Tilbrook Rd WSHM SO15 .... 317 M8
Tilburg Rd CHCH/BSGR BH23 ..... 450 C1
Tilbury's Cl BOR GU35 .... 201 J5
Tilden Rd RWIN SO21 .... 266 B3
Tile Barn Cl FARN GU14 .... 90 D2
Tilebarn La BROC SO42 .... 413 K2
Tilford Rd FNM GU9 .... 135 G7
  GSHT GU26 .... 204 C3
  HORN PO8 .... 352 D2
  RFNM GU10 .... 159 M5
Tilford St RFNM GU10 .... 159 M5
Tillington Gdns HORN PO8 ...... 328 C4
Tilmore Gdns PSF GU32 .... 275 L3
Tilmore Rd PSF GU32 .... 275 L3
Tilney Cl ALTN GU34 .... 176 D4
Timber Bank FRIM GU16 .... 91 K3
Timbercroft Cl ALTN GU34 ...... 196 F7
Timberlake Rd BSTK RG21 .... 4 E8
Timberland Wy WVILLE PO7 ...... 376 B4
Timberley La RSAL SP5 .... 285 M2
Timberley Pl CWTH RG45 .... 49 H4
Timbermill Ct HASM GU27 .... 228 C2
The Timbers FHAM PO15 .... 372 A7
Timor Cl HLER SO31 .... 346 F4

Timothy Cl *NBNE* BH10 .... **432** B3
Timpson Rd *PSEA* PO1 .... **423** J2
Timsbury Crs *HAV* PO9 .... **16** C1
Timsbury Dr *ROWN* SO16 .... **317** L6
Timson Cl *TOTT* SO40 .... **341** G2
Tincleton Gdns
    MOOR/WNTN BH9 .... **432** F4
Tindal Cl *YTLY* GU46 .... **69** G2
Tindale Rd *ROWN* SO16 .... **317** K6
Tinker Aly *ELGH* SO50 .... **319** M1
Tinneys Cl *RSAL* SP5 .... **285** J4
Tintagel Cl *AND* SP10 .... **118** C5
    DEAN RG23 .... **104** B2
Tintagel Dr *FRIM* GU16 .... **71** J7
Tintagel Wy *CHAM* PO6 .... **398** F1
Tintern Cl *CHAM* RG24 .... **4** B1
    CHAM PO6 .... **374** D7
Tintern Gv *WSHM* SO15 .... **12** C1
Tintern Rd *GPORT* PO12 .... **18** D5
Tipner Gn *NEND* PO2 .... **399** G5
Tipner La *NEND* PO2 .... **398** F5
Tipner Rd *NEND* PO2 .... **399** G6
Tipper La *EPSF* GU31 .... **305** G5
Tippet Gdns *KEMP* RG22 .... **104** E8
Tiptoe Rd *NMIL/BTOS* BH25 .... **412** A7
Tiptree Cl *ELGH* SO50 .... **293** M3
Tisted Ct *HAV* PO9 .... **377** M3
Titchfield Cl *TADY* RG26 .... **61** M1
Titchfield Hl *FHAM/STUB* PO14.. **371** L8
Titchfield La *FHAM* PO15 .... **348** A8
    WHAM PO17 .... **348** A7
Titchfield Park Rd *FHAM* PO15.. **371** H5
Titchfield Rd
    FHAM/STUB PO14.. .... **395** L1
Tithe Barn *LYMN* SO41 .... **440** C3
Tithelands La *NALR* SO24 .... **243** L4
Tithe Meadow *KEMP* RG22 .... **127** H3
The Tithe *WVILLE* PO7 .... **351** K5
Tithewood Cl *CHFD* SO53 .... **265** G6
Tittymouse La *RAND* SP11 .... **117** H6
Titus Gdns *WVILLE* PO7 .... **352** E8
Tiverton Rd *DEAN* RG23 .... **104** B3
Tivoli Cl *CHFD* SO53 .... **293** L1
Toad La *BLKW* GU17 .... **70** B4
Tobago Rd *CHAM* RG24 .... **83** G7
Tobruk Cl *RAND* SP11 .... **119** G1
Tobruk Rd *RAND* SP11 .... **115** J2
Toby St *PSEA* PO1 .... **423** G2
Todmore *LISS* GU33 .... **224** D5
Tokar St *ENEY* PO4 .... **423** L6
Tokio Rd *HSEA* PO3 .... **399** L7
Toledo Gv *ITCH* SO19 .... **345** M3
Tolefrey Gdns *NBAD* SO52 .... **292** E2
Tollard Cl *BKME/WDN* BH12 .... **431** J4
Tollbar Wy *HEND* SO30 .... **320** F8
Tollerford Rd *CFDH* BH17 .... **430** B6
Tollgate *CHFD* SO53 .... **293** H6
Tollgate Cl *DEAN* RG23 .... **103** C5
Tollgate Rd *AND* SP10 .... **8** B2
    HLER SO31 .... **346** B8
Tollway *CHAM* RG24 .... **83** M5
Tolpuddle Cl
    MOOR/WNTN BH9 .... **432** F4
Tolpuddle Wy *YTLY* GU46 .... **69** J3
Tolstoi Rd *PSTN* BH14 .... **445** M4
Tomlin Cl *STHA* RG19 .... **27** H6
Tomlins Av *FRIM* GU16 .... **71** J6
Tomlins Cl *TADY* RG26 .... **61** L1
Tomlinscote Wy *FRIM* GU16 .... **71** K6
Tomlinson Dr *EWKG* RG40 .... **48** D2
Tonbridge La *RGWD* BH24 .... **335** L8
Tonbridge St *SSEA* PO5 .... **21** H7
Tonge Rd *BWD* BH11 .... **431** M2
Tongham Mdw *RFNM* GU10 .. **136** C1
Tongham Rd *ASHV* GU12 .... **7** L6
    RFNM GU10 .... **135** M4
Tonnant Cl
    FHAM/STUB PO14.. .... **396** B7
Toogoods Wy *ROWN* SO16.. .... **317** J3
Toomer Cl *FAWY* SO45 .... **592** D6
Toothill Rd *ROMY* SO51 .... **291** H7
Topaz Gr *WVILLE* PO7 .... **352** F8
Topiary Gdns *HLER* SO31 .... **370** F4
The Topiary *CHAM* RG24.. .... **83** M8
    FARN GU14 .... **90** B5
Toplady Pl *FNM* GU9 .... **134** F1
Top La *RGWD* BH24 .... **382** E1
Top Terrace Rd *FARN* GU14 .... **90** D8
Torbay Rd *PSTN* BH14.. .... **446** B5
Torberry Dr *EPSF* GU31 .... **276** A4
Torch Cl *ELGH* SO50 .... **295** G6
Tor Cl *FHAM/PORC* PO16 .... **373** D7
Torcross Cl *ITCH* SO19 .... **344** C6
Torfrida Ct *ENEY* PO4 .... **424** A1
Tormead *FAWY* SO45 .... **367** K5
Tornay Gv *NBAD* SO52 .... **291** L4
Toronto Pl *GPORT* PO12 .... **18** F2
Toronto Rd *NEND* PO2 .... **423** J1
Torquay Av *GPORT* PO12 .... **397** C8
    WSHM SO15 .... **318** B8
Torque Cl *ITCH* SO19 .... **345** M4
Torre Cl *RAND* SP11 .... **293** M2
Torridge Gdns *WEND* SO18 .... **320** A5
Torrington Cl *ITCH* SO19 .... **344** E4
    BOR GU35 .... **201** M3
Torrington Rd *NEND* PO2 .... **399** J5
Tor Rd *FNM* GU9 .... **134** C6
Tortworth Cl *FHAM/STUB* PO14.. **14** A8
Tor Wy *EPSF* GU31 .... **275** M5
Torwood Gdns *ELGH* SO50 .... **294** B7
Tosson Cl *ROWN* SO16 .... **317** K8
Tote La *MIDH* GU29 .... **279** K2
Totford La *RFNM* GU10 .... **137** H5
Totland Cl *FARN* GU14 .... **90** D2
    ROWN SO16 .... **317** K8
Totland Rd *CHAM* PO6 .... **399** J1
    LSOL/BMARY PO13 .... **397** C6
Totmel Rd *CFDH* BH17 .... **430** E6
Totnes Cl *ELGH* SO50 .... **293** L1
Tottehale Cl *NBAD* SO52 .... **291** L5
Tottenham Cl *TADY* RG26 .... **63** H3
Tottenham Rd *PSEA* PO1 .... **423** J2
Tottenham Wk *SHST* GU47 .... **50** D1
Totterdown *THLE* RG7 .... **31** J7
Totters La *HTWY* RG27 .... **86** E7
Totton By-pass *TOTT* SO40 .... **341** L2
Tournai Cl *ALDT* GU11 .... **113** H1
Tournerbury La *HISD* PO11 .... **425** L4

Tourney Rd *BWD* BH11 .... **431** H2
Tovey Pl *WINC* SO23 .... **191** H8
Tower Cl *AND* SP10 .... **118** C5
    GPORT PO12 .... **421** H5
Tower Gdns *HAV* PO9 .... **401** K2
Tower Hl *FARN* GU14 .... **90** D5
Tower La *ELGH* SO50 .... **294** B6
    WIMB BH21 .... **404** B2
Tower Pl *HEND* SO30 .... **320** C7
Tower Rd *BMTH* BH1 .... **448** D3
    CCLF BH13 .... **447** G7
    ENEY PO4 .... **423** K5
    GSHT GU26 .... **204** B4
    LIPH GU30 .... **226** E4
    SO23 .... **10** F6
Tower Rd West *CCLF* BH13 .... **446** F7
Towers Dr *CWTH* RG45 .... **49** L4
Towers Farm *WIMB* BH21 .... **429** H1
Tower St *ALTN* GU34 .... **176** D6
    EMRTH PO10 .... **378** E8
    PSEA PO1 .... **20** B5
    WINC SO23 .... **10** F7
Town Cl *NALR* SO24 .... **220** C4
Towngate Br *PLE* BH15 .... **445** H6
Town Hall Rd *HAV* PO9 .... **16** F5
Townhill Wy *WEND* SO18 .... **319** M7
Town La *EPSF* GU31 .... **276** A3
Town Mill La *WHCH* RG28 .... **122** C3
Town Quay *SHAM* SO14 .... **12** F7
Townsend Cl *BSTK* RG21 .... **4** B9
Townsend La *FBDG* SP6 .... **280** D4
Townside Pl *CBLY* GU15 .... **71** G2
Townsville Rd
    MOOR/WNTN BH9 .... **432** F6
Towpath Md *ENEY* PO4 .... **424** A4
Toynbee Cl *ELGH* SO50 .... **293** M5
Toynbee Rd *ELGH* SO50 .... **293** M5
Tozer Cl *BWD* BH11 .... **431** K6
Trafalgar Ct *FHAM/STUB* PO14.. **396** D1
    FNM GU9 .... **134** E7
Trafalgar Pl *PSEA* PO1 .... **423** J2
Trafalgar Rd
    MOOR/WNTN BH9 .... **447** L1
    WINC SO23 .... **343** G2
Trafalgar Sq *GPORT* PO12 .... **18** E1
Trafalgar St *WINC* SO23 .... **10** F8
Trafalgar Wy *CBLY* GU15 .... **70** C4
    FAWY SO45 .... **367** M7
    STOK SO20 .... **186** E6
Trafford Rd *FRIM* GU16 .... **71** G8
Trafford Wy *ELGH* SO50 .... **295** G7
Trampers La *WHAM* PO17 .... **349** L7
Tranby Rd *ITCH* SO19 .... **344** C4
Tranmere Cl *LYMN* SO41 .... **440** D6
Tranmere Rd *ENEY* PO4 .... **423** M5
Transport Rd *FARN* GU14 .... **90** E7
Travis La *SHST* GU47 .... **69** M1
Treadwheel Rd *HORN* PO8.. .... **353** L2
Treagore Rd *TOTT* SO40 .... **316** B7
Trearnan Cl *ROWN* SO16.. .... **317** L8
Treble Cl *WINW* SO22 .... **238** A4
Trebor Av *FNM* GU9 .... **135** G7
Tredegar Rd *ENEY* PO4.. .... **423** K5
Tree Av *HASM* GU27 .... **204** C8
Treebys Cl *CHCH/BSGR* BH23.. **435** H7
Treeside *CHCH/BSGR* BH23 .... **436** A6
Treeside Av *TOTT* SO40 .... **341** L1
Treeside Dr *FNM* GU9 .... **6** A8
Treeside Rd *WSHM* SO15 .... **318** B8
Tree Tops Av *CBLY* GU15 .... **51** K8
Trefoil Cl *HTWY* RG27 .... **87** H1
    WVILLE PO7 .... **376** D1
Trefoil Dro *NTHA* RG18 .... **27** J4
Trefoil Wy *CHCH/BSGR* BH23.. **436** A8
Tregaron Av *CHAM* PO6 .... **399** M1
Tregolls Dr *FARN* GU14 .... **90** F5
Tregonwell Rd *WCLF* BH2 .... **22** D6
Trellis Dr *CHAM* RG24 .... **83** M8
Treloar Rd *HISD* PO11 .... **426** C7
Tremayne Wk *CBLY* GU15 .... **71** M4
Tremona Rd *ROWN* SO16 .... **318** A5
Trenchard Rd *RAND* SP11 .... **142** A1
Trenley Cl *FAWY* SO45 .... **392** A5
Trent Cl *FARN* GU14 .... **90** B2
    WEND SO18 .... **319** L7
Trent Ct *AND* SP10 .... **9** M1
Trent Crs *NTHA* RG18 .... **26** E3
Trentham Av *LTDN* BH7 .... **433** M8
Trentham Cl *LTDN* BH7 .... **433** M8
Trenton Cl *FRIM* GU16 .... **71** K6
Trent Rd *WEND* SO18 .... **319** L7
Trent Wy *BSTK* RG21 .... **5** K8
    FERN BH22 .... **406** E2
    LSOL/BMARY PO13 .... **420** D2
Tresham Crs *YTLY* GU46 .... **68** D2
Tresillian Gdns *WEND* SO18 .... **320** A6
Tresillian Wy *CHCH/BSGR* BH23.. **436** F6
Trevis Rd *ENEY* PO4 .... **424** A4
Trevone Cl *TOTT* SO40 .... **341** J3
Trevor Rd *ENEY* PO4 .... **21** M6
Trevose Cl *CHFD* SO53 .... **293** J4
    LSOL/BMARY PO13 .... **397** G2
Trevose Crs *CHFD* SO53 .... **293** J3
Trevose Wy *FHAM/STUB* PO14.. **370** F7
Triangle La *FHAM/STUB* PO14.. **395** J4
The Triangle *NWBY* RG14 .... **37** L1
    RSAL SP5 .... **259** G4
    WCLF BH2 .... **22** C6
Tribe Rd *GPORT* PO12 .... **18** D2
Tricketts La *FERN* BH22 .... **406** D2
Trigon Rd *PLE* BH15 .... **445** J1
Trimaran Cl *HLER* SO31 .... **370** D4
Trimaran Rd *HLER* SO31 .... **370** C7
Trimmers Cl *FNM* GU9 .... **134** F1
Trimmers Wd *GSHT* GU26 .... **204** A2
Trimm's Dro *FBDG* SP6 .... **284** D8
Trinidad Cl *CHAM* RG24 .... **83** G7
Trinidad Crs *BKME/WDN* BH12.. **431** H4
Trinity Cl *GSHT* GU47 .... **50** B6
Trinity Ct *GPORT* PO12 .... **19** L4
Trinity Flds *FNM* GU9 .... **134** D2
Trinity Hl *ALTN* GU34 .... **174** D7

    FNM GU9 .... **134** D2
Trinity Ri *RAND* SP11 .... **117** L4
Trinity Rd *ALTN* GU34 .... **174** D7
    BMTH BH1 .... **23** H1
    SHAM SO14 .... **13** H1
Trinity St *FHAM/PORC* PO16 .... **15** J5
Tristan Cl *FHAM* PO15 .... **419** J1
Triumph Cl *FHAM* PO15 .... **14** B1
Triumph Rd *FHAM/STUB* PO14.. **396** D3
Troak Cl *CHCH/BSGR* BH23.. **435** J8
Trojan Wy *WVILLE* PO7 .... **376** D5
Troon Rd *CHAM* PO6 .... **376** A7
Troon Rd *WIMB* BH21 .... **429** L3
Trosnant Rd *HAV* PO9 .... **16** C2
Trotton Rd *EPSF* GU31 .... **278** C8
Trotts La *TOTT* SO40 .... **342** A4
Trotwood Cl *SHST* GU47 .... **50** B6
Trout Cl *HASM* GU27 .... **228** B2
Trout Wk *NWBY* RG14 .... **25** L3
Trowbridge Cl *ROWN* SO16 .... **317** K2
Trowe's La *THLE* RG7 .... **45** G4
Truman Rd *BWD* BH11 .... **431** M2
Trunk Rd *FARN* GU14 .... **89** M4
Truro Ri *ELGH* SO50 .... **294** D5
Truro Rd *CHAM* PO6 .... **374** D8
Truscott Av *MOOR/WNTN* BH9.. **447** M1
Trussell Cl *WINW* SO22 .... **10** A1
Trussell Crs *WINW* SO22 .... **10** A1
Trust *HTWY* RG27 .... **85** L7
Tubb's La *KSCL* RG20 .... **56** C2
    TADY RG26 .... **61** M8
Tuckers Cl *PLE* BH15 .... **444** E7
Tucks Cl *CHCH/BSGR* BH23.. **409** L4
Tuckton Cl *SBNE* BH6 .... **449** J4
Tuckton Rd *SBNE* BH6 .... **449** J4
Tudor Av *EMRTH* PO10 .... **378** C4
Tudor Cl *FBDG* SP6 .... **333** L3
    FHAM/PORC PO16 .... **373** M7
    GSHT GU26 .... **204** A6
    HISD PO11 .... **425** K6
    LSOL/BMARY PO13 .... **397** H8
    TOTT SO40 .... **316** B8
Tudor Ct *FHAM/STUB* PO14.. **396** D1
    PLE BH15 .... **445** K2
Tudor Crs *CHAM* PO6 .... **399** K2
Tudor Dr *YTLY* GU46 .... **69** G3
Tudor Gdns *HEND* SO30 .... **345** L3
Tudor Rd *BDST* BH18 .... **429** M4
    NWBY RG14 .... **2** F7
Tudor Wy *FLET* GU13 .... **110** F4
    WINC SO23 .... **191** G8
Tudor Wood Cl *ROWN* SO16 .... **318** A1
Tuffin Cl *ROWN* SO16 .... **317** H3
Tukes Av *LSOL/BMARY* PO13.. **396** F4
Tulip Cl *KEMP* RG22 .... **126** F1
Tulip Gdns *HAV* PO9 .... **377** G6
    HLER SO31 .... **370** D5
Tulip Rd *ROWN* SO16 .... **319** H4
Tulls La *BOR* GU35 .... **202** A6
Tumulus Cl *ITCH* SO19 .... **345** K4
Tunball La *MARL* SN8 .... **72** B1
Tunbridge Crs *LIPH* GU30 .... **226** E3
Tunbridge La *LIPH* GU30 .... **226** E2
Tunnel Rd *FARN* GU14 .... **90** A7
Tunstall Rd *CHAM* PO6 .... **375** H7
    ITCH SO19 .... **345** J4
Tunworth Ct *HAV* PO9 .... **377** M3
Tunworth Ms *TADY* RG26 .... **41** M8
Tunworth Rd *OVTN* RG25 .... **106** D4
Tuppenny La *EMRTH* PO10 .... **379** D4
Turbary Cl *BKME/WDN* BH12.. **431** J8
Turbary Ct *UPTN* BH16 .... **429** G8
Turbary Gdns *TADY* RG26 .... **41** L7
Turbary Park Av *BWD* BH11.. **431** K5
Turbary Rd *BKME/WDN* BH12.. **446** C1
    FERN BH22 .... **406** D7
Turf Hill Rd *CBLY* GU15 .... **51** J8
Turin Ct *AND* SP10 .... **119** G4
Turks La *PSTN* BH14 .... **445** M7
    THLE RG7 .... **43** J4
Turk St *ALTN* GU34 .... **176** E5
Turlin Rd *UPTN* BH16 .... **444** E4
Turner Av *LSOL/BMARY* PO13.. **397** J7
Turner Cl *BSTK* RG21 .... **105** K4
Turner Pl *SHST* GU47 .... **70** A2
Turners Dr *STHA* RG19 .... **27** H5
Turners Farm Crs
    LYMN SO41 .... **438** E6
Turner's Green La *HTWY* RG27.. **88** B4
The Turnery *STHA* RG19 .... **26** F5
Turnfields *STHA* RG19 .... **27** G5
Turnpike Down *WINC* SO23 .... **11** M7
Turnpike Rd *NTHA* RG18 .... **26** B4
    NWBY RG14 .... **3** M1
Turnpike Wy *DEAN* RG23 .... **102** F6
    HEND SO30 .... **320** C7
Turnstone End *YTLY* GU46 .... **68** E2
Turnstone Gdns *ROWN* SO16.. **318** A3
Turnworth Cl *BDST* BH18 .... **430** A5
Turtle Cl *FHAM/STUB* PO14.. **395** M4
Tuscan Wk *CHFD* SO53 .... **293** K2
Tuscany Wy *WVILLE* PO7 .... **352** F8
The Tussocks *TOTT* SO40 .... **342** D6
Tutland Rd *NBAD* SO52 .... **291** L4
Tutor Cl *HLER* SO31 .... **369** K5
Tutts La *ROMY* SO51 .... **288** D4
Tweedale Rd
    MOOR/WNTN BH9 .... **433** G5
Tweed Cl *CHFD* SO53 .... **292** F1
    FARN GU14 .... **90** B2
Tweed La *LYMN* SO41 .... **414** B8
Tweedsmuir Cl *FARN* GU14 .... **90** A5
    KEMP RG22 .... **104** A4
Twelve Acre Crs *FARN* GU14 .... **90** A3
Twemlow Av *PSTN* BH14 .... **445** L6
Tweseldown Rd *FLET* GU13 .... **111** G4
Twiggs End Cl *HLER* SO31 .... **370** D4
Twiggs La *TOTT* SO40 .... **366** B2
Twiggs Lane End *TOTT* SO40.. **366** A3
Twin Oaks Cl *BDST* BH18 .... **429** M5
Twisell Thorne *FLET* GU13 .... **110** D4
Two Gate La *OVTN* RG25 .... **124** A1
Two Gate Meadow *OVTN* RG25.. **101** G8
Two Rivers Wy *NWBY* RG14.. **3** M3
Twyford Av *NEND* PO2 .... **399** H7
    WSHM SO15 .... **318** B7
Twyford Cl *CHAM* PO6 .... **399** M1
Twyford La *RFNM* GU10 .... **158** E2

Twyford Rd *ELGH* SO50 .... **294** A2
Twyford Wy *CFDH* BH17 .... **430** E6
Twynham Av
    CHCH/BSGR BH23 .... **449** M2
Twynham Cl *RSAL* SP5 .... **284** E2
Twynham Rd *SBNE* BH6 .... **449** K5
Twynhams Hl *WHAM* PO17 .... **323** M8
Tydehams *NWBY* RG14 .... **37** H1
Tyfield *CHAM* RG24 .... **82** D5
Tyler Dr *WHIT* RG2 .... **47** H1
Tylers Cl *LYMN* SO41 .... **440** A8
The Tyleshades *ROMY* SO51 .... **290** F2
Tylney La *HTWY* RG27 .... **85** J7
Tylston Meadow *LIPH* GU30 .... **226** E3
Tyne Cl *CHFD* SO53 .... **292** F3
    FARN GU14 .... **90** B2
Tyne Ct *AND* SP10 .... **119** J6
Tynedale Cl *GPORT* PO12 .... **397** K8
    MOOR/WNTN BH9 .... **433** C4
Tyneham Av *BKME/WDN* BH12.. **430** F8
Tyne Wy *HEND* SO30 .... **320** D6
    NTHA RG18 .... **26** E3
Tyrell Rd *CHFD* SO53 .... **293** H1
Tyrells Cl *RGWD* BH24 .... **384** C4
Tyrrell Gdns *CHAR* BH8 .... **433** L6
Tyrrells Ct *CHCH/BSGR* BH23.. **409** M7
Tyseley Rd *SSEA* PO5 .... **21** H3
Tytherley Gn *CHAR* BH8 .... **433** H6
Tytherley Rd *RSAL* SP5 .... **207** H2
    WEND SO18 .... **320** B8

U

Uddens Dr *WIMB* BH21 .... **405** J2
Ullswater Av *FARN* GU14 .... **90** B5
Ullswater Cl *FNM* GU9 .... **134** D2
    BOR GU35 .... **201** J3
    STHA RG19 .... **26** D5
Ullswater Gv *NALR* SO24 .... **218** C4
Ullswater Rd *ROWN* SO16 .... **317** K7
    WIMB BH21 .... **404** A6
Undercliff Dr *BMTH* BH1 .... **23** H7
Undercliff Rd *BOSC* BH5.. .... **448** C5
Underdown Av *WVILLE* PO7 .... **376** B6
Underhill La *FNM* GU9 .... **158** E1
Undershore *LYMN* SO41 .... **440** E4
Underwood Av *ASHV* GU12 .... **113** H7
Underwood Cl *ROWN* SO16 .... **318** D4
Underwood Rd *ELGH* SO50 .... **294** C4
    HASM GU27 .... **228** C1
    ROWN SO16 .... **318** D4
Unicorn Rd *LSOL/BMARY* PO13.. **420** B1
Union Cl *SHST* GU47 .... **50** B6
Union La *BPWT* SO32 .... **298** F6
    KSCL RG20 .... **59** J5
Union Pl *PSEA* PO1 .... **423** H2
Union Ri *LISS* GU33 .... **225** J6
Union Rd *FNM* GU9 .... **134** F6
    HAV PO9 .... **16** D4
    SHAM SO14 .... **343** M2
Union St *FARN* GU14 .... **90** D4
    FHAM/PORC PO16 .... **15** M6
    PSEA PO1 .... **20** D1
    WINC SO23 .... **11** J7
Union Ter *ALDT* GU11 .... **6** E2
University Crs *PTSW* SO17 .... **319** G5
University Pkwy *ROWN* SO16.. **292** B7
University Rd *PTSW* SO17 .... **318** F5
Unwin Cl *ITCH* SO19 .... **344** B7
Upfallow *CHAM* RG24 .... **105** M1
Upham St *BPWT* SO32 .... **296** B4
Uphill Rd *WINW* SO22 .... **214** A3
Upland La *LISS* GU33 .... **247** M1
Upland Rd *CBLY* GU15 .... **71** G1
Uplands Av *NMIL/BTOS* BH25.. **437** L8
Uplands Cl *FERN* BH22 .... **380** E8
    HASM GU27 .... **205** G8
    SHST GU47 .... **49** L8
Uplands La *FHAM/PORC* PO16.. **15** J3
Uplands La *ALTN* GU34 .... **196** F7
Uplands Rd *CHAM* PO6 .... **376** A7
    CHAR BH8 .... **433** C6
    FERN BH22 .... **380** D6
    FNM GU9 .... **135** H7
    WINW SO22 .... **10** C1
Uplands Wy *PTSW* SO17 .... **318** F6
Uplyme Cl *CFDH* BH17 .... **430** E6
Upnor Cl *RAND* SP11 .... **115** J1
Upper Arundel St *PSEA* PO1 .... **21** H1
Upper Banister St
    WSHM SO15 .... **343** K2
Upper Barn Copse *ELGH* SO50.. **295** G5
Upper Bere Wd *WVILLE* PO7 .... **376** D2
Upper Bourne La *RFNM* GU10.. **158** D3
Upper Bourne V *RFNM* GU10.. **158** D3
Upper Broadmoor Rd
    CWTH RG45 .... **49** M3
Upper Brook Dr *HLER* SO31 .... **370** C5
Upper Brook St *WINC* SO23 .... **11** H7
Upper Brownhill Rd
    ROWN SO16 .... **317** L5
Upper Bugle St *SHAM* SO14.. **12** F5
Upper Charles St *CBLY* GU15 .... **70** F2
Upper Chestnut Dr *BSTK* RG21.. **104** E5
Upper Chobham Rd *CBLY* GU15.. **71** L4
    FRIM GU15 .... **71** K5
Upper Church La *FNM* GU9 .... **134** E6
Upper Church Rd *BPWT* SO32.. **348** C1
Upper College Ride *CBLY* GU15.. **51** H8
Upper Common Rd
    LYMN SO41 .... **439** K4
Upper Cornaway La
    FHAM/PORC PO16 .... **373** M8
Upper Crabbick La
    WVILLE PO7 .... **351** C2
Upper Crescent Rd
    NBAD SO52 .... **291** L4
Upper Deacon Rd *ITCH* SO19.. **344** F2
Upper Dro *AND* SP10 .... **118** D8
Upper Elms Rd *ALDT* GU11 .... **6** E3
Upper Farm Rd *DEAN* RG23.. **102** F8

Upper Golf Links Rd
    BDST BH18 .... **429** M3
Upper Gordon Rd *CBLY* GU15 .... **71** G3
    CHCH/BSGR BH23 .... **436** E7
Upper Grove Rd *ALTN* GU34.. **176** E6
Upper Hale Rd *FNM* GU9 .... **134** E1
Upper Heyshott *EPSF* GU31.. **275** M5
Upper High St *WINW* SO22 .... **10** E6
Upper Hinton Rd *BMTH* BH1 .... **22** F6
Upper House Ct *WHAM* PO17.. **348** E5
Upper Lamborough La
    NALR SO24 .... **242** D2
Upper Lanham La *NALR* SO24.. **195** J1
Upper Market St *ELGH* SO50 .... **294** A5
Upper Mead Cl *ELGH* SO50 .... **295** J6
Upper Moors Rd *ELGH* SO50 .... **266** E5
    RWIN SO21 .... **266** E8
Upper Mt *HASM* GU27 .... **205** J7
    LISS GU33 .... **248** D5
Upper Mullin's La *FAWY* SO45.. **367** J5
Upper Neatham Mill La
    ALTN GU34 .... **177** H2
Upper New Rd *HEND* SO30 .... **320** C7
Upper Northam Cl *HEND* SO30.. **345** L2
Upper Northam Dr
    HEND SO30 .... **345** J2
Upper Northam Rd
    HEND SO30 .... **345** L1
Upper Norwich Rd *WCLF* BH2.. **22** B6
Upper Old Park La *FNM* GU9.. **134** C3
Upper Old St
    FHAM/STUB PO14.. .... **395** M4
Upper Park Cl *CBLY* GU15 .... **71** G3
Upper Piece *WVILLE* PO7 .... **351** L5
Upper Pinewood Rd
    ASHV GU12 .... **113** M5
Upper Rd *BKME/WDN* BH12.. **446** B2
Upper St Helens Rd
    HEND SO30 .... **345** M4
Upper St Michael's Rd
    ALDT GU11 .... **7** G5
Upper Shaftesbury Av
    PTSW SO17 .... **319** G6
Upper Sherborne Rd *BSTK* RG21.. **4** C2
Upper Shirley Av *WSHM* SO15.. **318** B7
Upper Soldridge Rd
    ALTN GU34 .... **196** C6
Upper South Vw *FNM* GU9 .... **134** F5
Upper Spinney *HLER* SO31 .... **370** A8
Upper St *FLET* GU13 .... **88** E7
Upper Terrace Rd *FARN* GU14.. **90** D8
    WCLF BH2 .... **22** D6
Upper Toothill Rd *ROWN* SO16.. **291** K7
Upper Union St *ALDT* GU11 .... **6** D2
Upper Union Ter *ALDT* GU11 .... **6** E2
Upper Verran Rd *CBLY* GU15 .... **71** G5
Upper Wardown *EPSF* GU31 .... **276** A4
Upper Wy *FNM* GU9 .... **134** E4
Upper Weston La *ITCH* SO19.. **344** E6
Upper Weybourne La
    FNM GU9 .... **112** A8
Upper Wht *FHAM/PORC* PO16.. **15** L7
Uppleby Rd *BKME/WDN* BH12.. **446** B2
Upron Field Cl *KEMP* RG22 .... **127** G1
Up St *OVTN* RG25 .... **125** K7
Upton Cl *FARN* GU14 .... **91** G3
    HAV PO9 .... **377** H1
    UPTN BH16 .... **444** A1
Upton Ct *UPTN* BH16 .... **444** B1
Upton Crs *BSTK* RG21 .... **4** D3
    ROWN SO16 .... **317** H1
Upton Grey Cl *WINW* SO22 .... **214** C5
Upton Grey Rd *OVTN* RG25 .... **107** J7
Upton Heath Est *UPTN* BH16.. **444** C1
Upton La *ROWN* SO16 .... **317** G3
Upton Rd *CFDH* BH17 .... **444** D1
Upton Wy *BDST* BH18 .... **429** J5
Upwey Av *PLE* BH15 .... **444** D5
Urquhart Rd *STHA* RG19 .... **27** G7

V

Vadne Gdns *GPORT* PO12 .... **421** M2
Vaggs La *LYMN* SO41 .... **438** C2
Vale Cl *RFNM* GU10 .... **158** F4
Vale Dr *WEND* SO18.. .... **319** L7
Vale Gv *GPORT* PO12 .... **421** L1
Valencia Wy *AND* SP10 .... **9** K3
Valentine Av *ITCH* SO19 .... **345** G5
Valentine Cl *FHAM* PO15 .... **372** A5
Valentine Ct *WVILLE* PO7 .... **352** E8
Valerian Cl *ELGH* SO50 .... **321** H2
Valerian Rd *HEND* SO30 .... **346** A2
Vale Rd *ASHV* GU12 .... **113** K3
    BMTH BH1 .... **448** C4
    CBLY GU15 .... **70** D4
    PSTN BH14 .... **446** A4
    RSAL SP5 .... **285** J2
    WINC SO23 .... **239** G2
The Vale *DEAN* RG23 .... **102** F7
    FAWY SO45 .... **367** K5
    HLER SO31 .... **370** F6
    HORN PO8 .... **328** B7
    SSEA PO5 .... **21** H8
Valetta Pk *EMRTH* PO10 .... **378** C8
Valetta Rd *EMRTH* PO10 .... **403** H7
Valette Rd *MOOR/WNTN* BH9.. **432** D8
Vale View Dr *THLE* RG7 .... **45** G3
Vale Wy *WINC* SO23 .... **191** G7
Vale Wood Dr *RFNM* GU10 .... **159** G4
Vale Wood La *GSHT* GU26 .... **203** M4
Valewood Rd *HASM* GU27 .... **228** F4
Valiant Gdns *NEND* PO2 .... **399** H4
Valiant Rd *EMRTH* PO10 .... **403** H7
Valiant Wy *CHCH/BSGR* BH23.. **451** C1
    FARN GU14 .... **90** A8
Valley Cl *CHCH/BSGR* BH23.. **392** D7
    FAWY SO45 .... **392** D7
    RSAL SP5 .... **285** J2
    RWIN SO21 .... **266** D4
    WVILLE PO7 .... **376** A5
Valleydene *FAWY* SO45 .... **367** K6
Valley Hi *WINW* SO22 .... **214** B3
Valley La *CHCH/BSGR* BH23.. **410** C4
    FNM GU9 .... **158** F1
Valley Md *RAND* SP11 .... **142** B3

Valley Park Dr *HORN* PO8 ...... 328 C5
Valley Ri *HLER* SO31 ...... 370 C4
RAND SP11 ...... 142 D4
Valley Rd *CHAR* BH8 ...... 433 K5
CHFD SO53 ...... 293 H1
FRIM GU16 ...... 71 L8
WINW SO22 ...... 214 A3
NWBY RG14 ...... 2 A9
NWBY RG14 ...... 25 C8
THLE RG7 ...... 31 K5
TOTT SO40 ...... 341 K3
Valley Side *LIPH* GU30 ...... 226 E3
The Valley *WINW* SO22 ...... 238 C2
Valley Vw *BKME/WDN* BH12 ...... 447 G1
SHST GU47 ...... 69 K1
Valley Wk *BPWT* SO32 ...... 269 H6
Valley Wy *TADY* RG26 ...... 42 B7
Vallis Cl *PLE* BH15 ...... 445 J7
Valmeade Cl *HTWY* RG27 ...... 86 A7
Valroy Cl *CBLY* GU15 ...... 71 G2
Valsheba Dr *FHAM/STUB* PO14 ...... 395 M7
Vampire Wy *CHFD* SO53 ...... 265 C7
Vanburgh Gdns *KEMP* RG22 ...... 127 G1
Vanburgh Wy *CHFD* SO53 ...... 265 C7
Van Dyck Cl *BSTK* RG21 ...... 105 K5
Vanguard Hl *WINW* SO22 ...... 214 B2
Vanguard Rd *CHAR* BH8 ...... 433 J7
WEND SO18 ...... 319 M8
Vanners La *KSCL* RG20 ...... 36 A3
Vanstone Rd
LSOL/BMARY PO13 ...... 397 H8
Vardy Cl *ITCH* SO19 ...... 345 H5
Varna Rd *BOR* GU35 ...... 201 M8
WSHM SO15 ...... 343 G3
Varney Cl *FARN* GU14 ...... 90 B3
Varos Cl *GPORT* PO12 ...... 421 L2
Varsity Rd *EMRTH* PO10 ...... 403 H7
Vaudrey Cl *WSHM* SO15 ...... 318 B7
Vaughan Cl *ITCH* SO19 ...... 345 J3
Vaughan Rd *FAWY* SO45 ...... 367 G4
Vaughans *ALTN* GU34 ...... 176 H3
Vauxhall Wy *PSF* GU32 ...... 275 K5
Veal's La *TOTT* SO40 ...... 366 F1
Vear's La *RWIN* SO21 ...... 266 F8
Vecta Cl *CHCH/BSGR* BH23 ...... 451 H2
Vectis Cl *ITCH* SO19 ...... 345 H5
Vectis Rd *GPORT* PO12 ...... 421 J5
NMIL/BTOS BH25 ...... 452 C1
Vectis Wy *CHAM* PO6 ...... 399 K1
Velder Av *ENEY* PO4 ...... 423 L3
Vellan Ct *ROWN* SO16 ...... 317 H7
Velmead Cl *FLET* GU13 ...... 111 G1
Velmead Rd *FLET* GU13 ...... 110 F1
Velmore Rd *CHFD* SO53 ...... 293 G4
Velsheda Ct *FAWY* SO45 ...... 367 L3
Velvet Lawn Rd
NMIL/BTOS BH25 ...... 437 K4
Venator Pl *WIMB* BH21 ...... 404 A2
Venerable Rd
FHAM/STUB PO14 ...... 396 E3
Vengeance Rd
LSOL/BMARY PO13 ...... 420 C1
Venice Cl *WVILLE* PO7 ...... 352 E8
Venice Ct *AND* SP10 ...... 119 H5
Venning Av *BWD* BH11 ...... 431 J3
Ventnor Rd *ENEY* PO4 ...... 21 M4
LSOL/BMARY PO13 ...... 396 F5
Ventnor Ter *ASHV* GU12 ...... 7 J4
Ventnor Wy *FHAM/PORC* PO16 ...... 373 J7
Ventry Cl *CCLF* BH13 ...... 446 E4
Ventura Pl *UPTN* BH16 ...... 444 C2
Venture Rd *ROWN* SO16 ...... 292 C7
Verbena Crs *HORN* PO8 ...... 352 F4
Verbena Wy *HEND* SO30 ...... 346 B2
Verden Wy *AND* SP10 ...... 118 E5
Verdi Cl *KEMP* RG22 ...... 104 C8
Verdon Av *HLER* SO31 ...... 369 J5
Verger Cl *FHAM/STUB* PO14 ...... 371 G5
Verity Crs *CFDH* BH17 ...... 430 E7
Vermont Cl *ROWN* SO16 ...... 318 E4
Vermont Woods *EWKG* RG40 ...... 48 B1
Vernalls Cl *NBNE* BH10 ...... 432 B3
Vernalls Gdns *NBNE* BH10 ...... 432 B3
Verner Cl *BOR* GU35 ...... 202 B4
Verne Rd *VWD* BH31 ...... 356 C3
The Verne *FLET* GU13 ...... 110 F3
Verney Cl *BWD* BH11 ...... 431 M5
Verney Rd *BWD* BH11 ...... 431 L5
Vernham Rd *WINW* SO22 ...... 10 B2
Verno La *CHCH/BSGR* BH23 ...... 436 A6
Vernon Av *ENEY* PO4 ...... 423 L4
Vernon Cl *GPORT* PO12 ...... 18 D2
Vernon Hl *BPWT* SO32 ...... 297 H6
Vernon Rd *GPORT* PO12 ...... 18 D2
HSEA PO3 ...... 399 L6
Verona Av *SBNE* BH6 ...... 449 J3
Verona Rd *CHFD* SO53 ...... 293 H4
Veronica Cl *KEMP* RG22 ...... 126 F1
Veronica Dr *FLET* GU13 ...... 110 C3
Verran Rd *CBLY* GU15 ...... 71 G5
Verulam Pl *BMTH* BH1 ...... 22 F5
Verulam Rd *PLE* BH15 ...... 445 L4
SHAM SO14 ...... 343 M1
Verwood Crs *SBNE* BH6 ...... 449 M4
Verwood Rd *HAV* PO9 ...... 377 M2
RGWD BH24 ...... 357 L2
WIMB BH21 ...... 356 D2
Veryan *FHAM* PO15 ...... 14 C6
Vesey Cl *FARN* GU14 ...... 90 D3
Vespasian Gdns *CHAM* RG24 ...... 82 B8
Vespasian Rd *AND* SP10 ...... 119 G4
WEND SO18 ...... 344 B1
Vespasian Wy *CHFD* SO53 ...... 293 K1
Vesta Wy *CHFD* SO53 ...... 293 K1
Vestry Cl *AND* SP10 ...... 8 F5
Vetch Cl *CHCH/BSGR* BH23 ...... 435 M8
Vetch Flds *HTWY* RG27 ...... 86 B7
Viables La *BSTK* RG21 ...... 105 C7
Vian Cl *LSOL/BMARY* PO13 ...... 397 G4
Vian Pl *WINC* SO23 ...... 191 H8
Vian Rd *WVILLE* PO7 ...... 376 B2
Vicarage Cl *EWKG* RG40 ...... 48 C2
FNM GU9 ...... 159 G1
Vicarage Dr *HEND* SO30 ...... 345 M3
Vicarage Gdns *FLET* GU13 ...... 110 E4
GSHT GU26 ...... 203 M5
LYMN SO41 ...... 438 E6
Vicarage Hl *ALTN* GU34 ...... 176 E5

FNM GU9 ...... 159 G1
HTWY RG27 ...... 87 J3
Vicarage La *BPWT* SO32 ...... 324 B2
FHAM/STUB PO14 ...... 396 A5
FNM GU9 ...... 134 C6
FNM GU9 ...... 134 F1
FNM GU9 ...... 159 G1
HASM GU27 ...... 228 C2
HTWY RG27 ...... 65 L7
LYMN SO41 ...... 438 E6
NALR SO24 ...... 220 A4
TOTT SO40 ...... 315 C2
WVILLE PO7 ...... 326 C5
YTLY GU46 ...... 68 F1
Vicarage Pk *RSAL* SP5 ...... 285 J2
Vicarage Rd *ALTN* GU34 ...... 176 D6
BFOR GU20 ...... 51 M5
BLKW GU17 ...... 70 B4
MOOR/WNTN BH9 ...... 432 C7
PLE BH15 ...... 445 H3
RSAL SP5 ...... 285 M3
TOTT SO40 ...... 342 D7
VWD BH31 ...... 356 D2
YTLY GU46 ...... 68 F1
Vicarage Wy *CHCH/BSGR* BH23 ...... 435 H6
Vice La *ROMY* SO51 ...... 313 M4
Viceroy Rd *ITCH* SO19 ...... 344 K5
Vickers Cl *CHAR* BH8 ...... 433 M6
Vickers Rd *ASHV* GU12 ...... 113 J5
Vickery Wy *CHCH/BSGR* BH23 ...... 435 J8
Victena Rd *ELGH* SO50 ...... 295 H6
Victoria Av *CBLY* GU15 ...... 70 D3
HISD PO11 ...... 425 K5
MOOR/WNTN BH9 ...... 432 C7
WVILLE PO7 ...... 375 M5
Victoria Cl *HLER* SO31 ...... 370 E7
WIMB BH21 ...... 429 H4
Victoria Ct *AND* SP10 ...... 9 G6
Victoria Crs *BKME/WDN* BH12 ...... 446 C2
Victoria Dr *BLKW* GU17 ...... 69 M4
Victoria Gdns *FBDG* SP6 ...... 309 J7
FERN BH22 ...... 406 B2
NWBY RG14 ...... 2 F1
RGWD BH24 ...... 382 C2
Victoria Gld *HLER* SO31 ...... 369 G3
Victoria Gv *SSEA* PO5 ...... 21 K6
Victoria Hill Rd *FLET* GU13 ...... 88 D7
Victoria Park Rd
MOOR/WNTN BH9 ...... 432 C7
Victoria Pl *BMTH* BH1 ...... 23 M1
GPORT PO12 ...... 18 F4
LYMN SO41 ...... 440 C6
Victoria Rd *ALDT* GU11 ...... 6 F2
ALTN GU34 ...... 176 E4
BKME/WDN BH12 ...... 446 B3
BMTH BH1 ...... 23 M2
BPWT SO32 ...... 297 G8
CHCH/BSGR BH23 ...... 450 D3
ELGH SO50 ...... 294 A3
EMRTH PO10 ...... 378 C7
FARN GU14 ...... 90 E4
FBDG SP6 ...... 309 J7
FERN BH22 ...... 406 B2
FLET GU13 ...... 88 D7
FNM GU9 ...... 159 G1
HISD PO11 ...... 401 K6
HLER SO31 ...... 368 E2
ITCH SO19 ...... 344 B7
LYMN SO41 ...... 454 A4
PSEA PO1 ...... 422 D2
SHST GU47 ...... 50 B7
THLE RG7 ...... 43 J1
WINC SO23 ...... 10 F5
WVILLE PO7 ...... 376 C1
Victoria Rd East *ALTN* GU34 ...... 176 F4
Victoria Rd North *SSEA* PO5 ...... 21 L3
Victoria Rd South *SSEA* PO5 ...... 21 J7
Victoria Sq *LSOL/BMARY* PO13 ...... 420 C2
Victoria St *BSTK* RG21 ...... 4 E7
GPORT PO12 ...... 19 G2
PSEA PO1 ...... 423 G1
SHAM SO14 ...... 13 L2
Victoria Tr *ALDT* GU11 ...... 112 A1
Victor Pl *THLE* RG7 ...... 28 F5
Victor Rd *EMRTH* PO10 ...... 403 H7
HSEA PO3 ...... 423 K1
STHA RG19 ...... 27 H5
Victor St *WSHM* SO15 ...... 318 B8
Victor Wy *FARN* GU14 ...... 89 M8
Victory Av *HORN* PO8 ...... 352 E2
Victory Cl *CHFD* SO53 ...... 293 C3
Victory Crs *WSHM* SO15 ...... 342 F2
Victory Gn *NEND* PO2 ...... 399 G6
Victory Rd *FHAM/STUB* PO14 ...... 396 B6
PSEA PO1 ...... 20 C2
WSHM SO15 ...... 342 F2
Victory Rbt *BSTK* RG21 ...... 4 D7
Victory Sq *WSHM* SO15 ...... 342 F2
Viewside Cl *WIMB* BH21 ...... 429 C3
Vigo La *YTLY* GU46 ...... 68 F5
Vigo Rd *AND* SP10 ...... 9 L3
Viking Cl *FAWY* SO45 ...... 392 D8
FHAM/STUB PO14 ...... 395 M5
ROWN SO16 ...... 317 K3
SBNE BH6 ...... 449 M4
The Vikings *ROMY* SO51 ...... 291 C3
Viking Wy *AND* SP10 ...... 119 G4
CHCH/BSGR BH23 ...... 450 F3
HORN PO8 ...... 328 C4
SBNE BH6 ...... 449 M4
Villa Gdns *WVILLE* PO7 ...... 352 C8
Village Cl *FHAM/STUB* PO14 ...... 396 A6
Village Gn *GPORT* PO12 ...... 18 B7
Village St *ALTN* GU34 ...... 175 G3
PSF GU32 ...... 276 A2
STOK SO20 ...... 165 M4
The Village *EWKG* RG40 ...... 48 B5
Village Wy *YTLY* GU46 ...... 69 G1
Ville De Paris Rd
FHAM/STUB PO14 ...... 396 E3
Villette Cl *CHCH/BSGR* BH23 ...... 434 E7
Villiers Rd *FAWY* SO45 ...... 367 K8
SSEA PO5 ...... 21 H8
WSHM SO15 ...... 343 G1
Villiers Wy *FARN* GU14 ...... 36 F2
Vimoutiers Ct *FBDG* SP6 ...... 309 K7
Vince Cl *BWD* BH11 ...... 431 M3
Vincent Av *ROWN* SO16 ...... 318 B6

Vincent Cl *NMIL/BTOS* BH25 ...... 437 L6
Vincent Dr *AND* SP10 ...... 9 K6
Vincent Gv *FHAM/PORC* PO16 ...... 399 J1
Vincent Rd *NMIL/BTOS* BH25 ...... 437 K5
NTHA RG18 ...... 27 H4
WSHM SO15 ...... 318 B8
Vincent's Gv *WSHM* SO15 ...... 318 B8
Vincent St *WSHM* SO15 ...... 318 A8
Vincent's Wk *SHAM* SO14 ...... 13 G4
Vindomis Cl *ALTN* GU34 ...... 177 J1
Vine Bank *WEND* SO18 ...... 320 B8
Vine Cl *ALDT* GU11 ...... 112 D2
HLER SO31 ...... 370 B5
LTDN BH7 ...... 448 F1
Vine Coppice *WVILLE* PO7 ...... 376 C4
Vine Farm Rd
BKME/WDN BH12 ...... 431 M8
Vinegar Hl *LYMN* SO41 ...... 454 C3
Vine House Cl *FRIM* GU16 ...... 91 K5
Vineries Cl *WIMB* BH21 ...... 404 D2
The Vineries *WIMB* BH21 ...... 404 D2
Vine Rd *ROWN* SO16 ...... 317 M5
Vinery Gdns *ROWN* SO16 ...... 318 A6
Vinery Rd *ROWN* SO16 ...... 318 B6
Vineside *LSOL/BMARY* PO13 ...... 397 J7
Vine St *ALDT* GU11 ...... 6 E3
Vine Tree Cl *TADY* RG26 ...... 62 A1
Vine Wy *RFNM* GU10 ...... 158 D3
Vineyard Cl *ITCH* SO19 ...... 344 B5
The Vineyards *NBAD* SO52 ...... 291 M4
Viney Av *ROMY* SO51 ...... 263 G8
Viney Rd *LYMN* SO41 ...... 440 C7
Vinnells La *PSF* GU32 ...... 272 C1
Vinneys Cl *CHCH/BSGR* BH23 ...... 435 G6
Vinson La *OVTN* RG25 ...... 123 L1
Vinson Rd *LISS* GU33 ...... 248 F4
Violet Av *FHAM/STUB* PO14 ...... 395 M6
Violet Cl *KEMP* RG22 ...... 126 F1
NBAD SO52 ...... 292 F2
Violet Gv *NTHA* RG18 ...... 27 H3
Violet La *NMIL/BTOS* BH25 ...... 437 L4
TADY RG26 ...... 60 F2
Violet Rd *ROWN* SO16 ...... 318 F4
Virginia Gdns *FARN* GU14 ...... 90 F6
Virginia Park Rd *GPORT* PO12 ...... 421 K2
Viscount Dr *CHCH/BSGR* BH23 ...... 451 G2
Viscount Wk *BWD* BH11 ...... 431 H2
WIMB BH21 ...... 431 G3
Vita Rd *NEND* PO2 ...... 399 J5
Vitre Gdns *LYMN* SO41 ...... 440 C6
Vivaldi Cl *KEMP* RG22 ...... 127 K1
Vivash Rd *PSEA* PO1 ...... 21 L2
Vivian Cl *FLET* GU13 ...... 111 G2
Vivian Rd *BSTK* RG21 ...... 5 H3
Vixen Cl *FHAM/STUB* PO14 ...... 395 M6
Vixen Wk *NMIL/BTOS* BH25 ...... 437 M3
Vokes Cl *ITCH* SO19 ...... 344 F3
Vulcan Cl *WSHM* SO15 ...... 342 D2
Vulcan Rd *EMRTH* PO10 ...... 403 H7
WSHM SO15 ...... 342 D2
Vulcan Wy *FARN* GU14 ...... 89 M8
SHST GU47 ...... 69 K1
Vyne Cl *ALTN* GU34 ...... 176 E3
Vyne Meadow *CHAM* RG24 ...... 82 E4
Vyne Rd *BSTK* RG21 ...... 4 E5
CHAM RG24 ...... 82 E4
Vyse La *SHAM* SO14 ...... 12 F6

W

Wade Court Rd *HAV* PO9 ...... 17 G6
Wade La *HAV* PO9 ...... 17 G8
Wade Rd *CHAM* RG24 ...... 5 M1
Wadham *SHST* GU47 ...... 50 C7
Wadham Rd *NEND* PO2 ...... 399 H6
Wadhurst Gdns *ITCH* SO19 ...... 344 E8
Wadhurst Rd *HEND* SO30 ...... 346 A2
The Wad *SELS* SO20 ...... 427 K7
Wadwick Bottom *RAND* SP11 ...... 97 L5
Waggoners Wy *GSHT* GU26 ...... 203 K4
Waggoners Wells Rd
GSHT GU26 ...... 203 K6
Wagner Cl *KEMP* RG22 ...... 104 D8
Wagon La *HTWY* RG27 ...... 86 A6
Wagtail Dr *NMIL/BTOS* BH25 ...... 437 K6
Wagtail Rd *HORN* PO8 ...... 352 E2
Wagtail Wy *FHAM/PORC* PO16 ...... 373 K8
Wainscott Rd *ENEY* PO4 ...... 423 L6
Wainsford Cl *LYMN* SO41 ...... 439 M5
Wainsford Plantation
LYMN SO41 ...... 439 J8
Wainsford Rd *LYMN* SO41 ...... 439 J6
Wainwright Cl *CHAM* PO6 ...... 400 A2
Wait End Rd *WVILLE* PO7 ...... 376 C2
Wakefield Ct *WEND* SO18 ...... 319 M7
Wakefield Rd *WEND* SO18 ...... 319 M7
Wakeford Cl *TADY* RG26 ...... 42 B7
Wakefords Copse *FLET* GU13 ...... 111 G5
Wakefords Pk *FLET* GU13 ...... 111 G5
Wakefords Wy *HAV* PO9 ...... 377 M2
Wakely Rd *BWD* BH11 ...... 431 M3
Walberton Av *CHAM* PO6 ...... 375 L8
Walburton Wy *HORN* PO8 ...... 328 C4
Walcheren Pl *PLE* BH15 ...... 444 B5
Walcott Av *CHCH/BSGR* BH23 ...... 434 D7
Waldegrave Cl *ITCH* SO19 ...... 344 B7
Walden Gdns *HORN* PO8 ...... 352 F1
Walden Rd *NEND* PO2 ...... 399 G6
Walditch Gdns *CFDH* BH17 ...... 430 C6
Waldon Gdns *WEND* SO18 ...... 320 A6
Waldorf Hts *BLKW* GU17 ...... 70 A4
Waldren Cl *PLE* BH15 ...... 445 J6
Wales St *WINC* SO23 ...... 11 J7
Walford Cl *WIMB* BH21 ...... 404 A2
Walford Rd *CHAM* PO6 ...... 375 G8
Walhampton Hl *LYMN* SO41 ...... 440 F4
Walker Gdns *HEND* SO30 ...... 321 H7
Walker Pl *LSOL/BMARY* PO13 ...... 397 H7
Walker Rd *NEND* PO2 ...... 399 G6
Walkers Cl *ELGH* SO50 ...... 295 J6
Walkers La North *FAWY* SO45 ...... 392 D7
Walker's La South *FAWY* SO45 ...... 392 D8
Walker's Rdg *CBLY* GU15 ...... 71 H3

Walkford La *NMIL/BTOS* BH25 ...... 437 H5
Walkford Rd *CHCH/BSGR* BH23 ...... 437 G6
Walkford Wy
CHCH/BSGR BH23 ...... 436 F7
Walkwood Av *LTDN* BH7 ...... 433 M8
Wallace La *BROC* SO42 ...... 416 A2
Wallace Rd *BDST* BH18 ...... 429 L5
ITCH SO19 ...... 344 D7
NEND PO2 ...... 399 K8
Walldown Rd *BOR* GU35 ...... 201 J8
Walled Meadow *AND* SP10 ...... 9 K6
Waller Dr *NWBY* RG14 ...... 26 B3
Wallington Ct
FHAM/STUB PO14 ...... 396 D2
Wallington Dr *CHFD* SO53 ...... 264 F8
Wallington Hl
FHAM/PORC PO16 ...... 15 L4
Wallington Rd *CBLY* GU15 ...... 51 K7
NEND PO2 ...... 399 K7
Wallington Shore Rd
FHAM/PORC PO16 ...... 15 M4
Wallington Wy
FHAM/PORC PO16 ...... 15 L4
Wallins Copse *CHAM* RG24 ...... 83 L6
Walliscott Rd *BWD* BH11 ...... 431 L7
Wallisdean Av
FHAM/STUB PO14 ...... 14 E8
HSEA PO3 ...... 423 M1
Wallisdown Rd
BKME/WDN BH12 ...... 431 H6
Wallis Dr *TADY* RG26 ...... 64 A6
Wallis Gdns *WVILLE* PO7 ...... 352 C7
Wallis Rd *BSTK* RG21 ...... 105 G5
NBNE BH10 ...... 431 M7
WVILLE PO7 ...... 352 C7
Wall La *THLE* RG7 ...... 42 F6
Wallop Dr *KEMP* RG22 ...... 126 F2
Wallop Dro *STOK* SO20 ...... 184 C4
Wallop Rd *RAND* SP11 ...... 162 A1
STOK SO20 ...... 161 M4
Walmer Cl *CWTH* RG45 ...... 49 M3
ELGH SO50 ...... 293 M1
FRIM GU16 ...... 91 J1
Walmer Rd *PSEA* PO1 ...... 21 M2
Walnut Av *WEND* SO18 ...... 319 K3
Walnut Cl *ALDT* GU11 ...... 6 F6
ALTN GU34 ...... 176 E3
CHFD SO53 ...... 265 H6
NMIL/BTOS BH25 ...... 437 K5
ROWN SO16 ...... 317 L7
YTLY GU46 ...... 69 G4
Walnut Dr *FHAM/STUB* PO14 ...... 395 M6
Walnut Gv *WINW* SO22 ...... 10 B5
ROWN SO16 ...... 317 L8
Walnut Tree Cl *HISD* PO11 ...... 425 K5
RWIN SO21 ...... 190 C4
Walnut Tree Dr *EMRTH* PO10 ...... 379 J5
Walnut Tree Rd *AND* SP10 ...... 8 E7
Walnwright Gdns *HEND* SO30 ...... 321 H5
Walpole La *HLER* SO31 ...... 370 C1
Walpole Rd *BMTH* BH1 ...... 448 C3
WINW SO22 ...... 238 B3
GPORT PO12 ...... 19 H3
Walrus Rd *FARN* GU14 ...... 90 A8
Walsall Rd *HSEA* PO3 ...... 423 L2
Walsford Rd *WBNE* BH4 ...... 447 K5
Walsingham Cl *CHAM* PO6 ...... 375 H7
Walsingham Dene *LTDN* BH7 ...... 433 K8
Walsingham Gdns *WEND* SO18 ...... 319 K5
Waltham Cl *BPWT* SO32 ...... 298 F6
FHAM/PORC PO16 ...... 374 A6
SHST GU47 ...... 50 A7
Waltham Ct *OVTN* RG25 ...... 101 C8
Waltham Crs *ROWN* SO16 ...... 318 A4
Waltham La *OVTN* RG25 ...... 124 D4
Waltham Rd *LTDN* BH7 ...... 449 G1
OVTN RG25 ...... 124 A1
Waltham St *SSEA* PO5 ...... 20 F3
Walton Cl *GPORT* PO12 ...... 18 D4
WVILLE PO7 ...... 376 B4
Walton Ct *FHAM* PO15 ...... 372 B4
Walton Pl *WINW* SO22 ...... 238 C2
Walton Rd *CHAM* PO6 ...... 400 A2
GPORT PO12 ...... 18 D4
ITCH SO19 ...... 345 H4
NBNE BH10 ...... 432 A6
PLE BH15 ...... 445 M2
Waltons Av *FAWY* SO45 ...... 392 B4
Walton Wy *NWBY* RG14 ...... 3 J1
Walworth Rd *RAND* SP11 ...... 119 L6
Wanborough Hl *RGUW* GU3 ...... 137 M2
Wandesford Pl *GPORT* PO12 ...... 397 L2
Wandle Cl *ASHV* GU12 ...... 113 K7
Wandsdyke Cl *FRIM* GU16 ...... 71 J8
Wangfield La *BPWT* SO32 ...... 322 B7
Wansbeck Cl *CHFD* SO53 ...... 293 C3
Wansey Gdns *NWBY* RG14 ...... 26 A3
Wanstead Cl *RGWD* BH24 ...... 358 F8
Wantage Rd *SHST* GU47 ...... 50 A8
Wapiti Wy *FARN* GU14 ...... 90 A8
Warbler Cl *HORN* PO8 ...... 352 E1
ROWN SO16 ...... 318 A2
UPTN BH16 ...... 428 F8
Warbleton Rd *CHAM* RG24 ...... 83 M5
Warblington Av *HAV* PO9 ...... 17 K5
Warblington Cl *CHFD* SO53 ...... 293 C5
TADY RG26 ...... 61 M1
Warblington Rd *EMRTH* PO10 ...... 402 C1
Warblington St *PSEA* PO1 ...... 20 D4
Warborne La *LYMN* SO41 ...... 440 E1
Warbrook La *HAV* PO9 ...... 377 M3
Warbrook La *HTWY* RG27 ...... 47 K8
Warburton Cl *ITCH* SO19 ...... 345 J4
Warburton Rd *CFDH* BH17 ...... 430 C8
ITCH SO19 ...... 345 H3
Ward Cl *AND* SP10 ...... 9 G1
Ward Crs *EMRTH* PO10 ...... 378 C5
Warden Cl *HEND* SO30 ...... 320 C7
Wardens Cl *HISD* PO11 ...... 425 K3
Wardle Rd *ELGH* SO50 ...... 294 C1
Ward Rd *ENEY* PO4 ...... 423 L6
Wardroom Rd *NEND* PO2 ...... 398 F2
Wareham Rd *WIMB* BH21 ...... 428 F5
Warehouse Rd *STHA* RG19 ...... 38 C3
Warfield Av *WVILLE* PO7 ...... 376 C1
Warfield Crs *WVILLE* PO7 ...... 376 C1
Wargrove Dr *SHST* GU47 ...... 50 A8
The Warings *THLE* RG7 ...... 29 K1

Warland Wy *WIMB* BH21 ...... 429 J1
Warlock Cl *ITCH* SO19 ...... 345 H5
Warmwell Cl *CFDH* BH17 ...... 430 C6
Warner Ct *AND* SP10 ...... 8 F5
Warnes La *RGWD* BH24 ...... 384 D6
Warnford Cl *GPORT* PO12 ...... 18 B4
Warnford Crs *HAV* PO9 ...... 377 H3
Warnford Rd *LTDN* BH7 ...... 449 G1
Warren Av *CHCH/BSGR* BH23 ...... 450 E3
CHFD SO53 ...... 293 C3
ENEY PO4 ...... 423 M3
HSEA PO3 ...... 399 L4
ROWN SO16 ...... 317 M6
Warren Cl *CHFD* SO53 ...... 293 C3
FLET GU13 ...... 111 G1
HISD PO11 ...... 425 C4
HTWY RG27 ...... 87 J3
BOR GU35 ...... 200 F6
RGWD BH24 ...... 382 B3
ROWN SO16 ...... 317 M6
SHST GU47 ...... 49 K8
THLE RG7 ...... 31 K6
Warren Cnr *RFNM* GU10 ...... 133 M1
Warren Crs *ROWN* SO16 ...... 317 M6
Warren Dr *RAND* SP11 ...... 141 L5
RGWD BH24 ...... 382 B2
Warren Edge Rd *SBNE* BH6 ...... 449 L5
EWKG RG40 ...... 48 A3
PSF GU32 ...... 247 H3
RGWD BH24 ...... 382 B3
RWIN SO21 ...... 240 D8
Warren Pk *LYMN* SO41 ...... 453 M2
Warren Pl *TOTT* SO40 ...... 316 B6
Warren Ri *FRIM* GU16 ...... 71 H5
Warren Rd *LISS* GU33 ...... 225 J6
LISS GU33 ...... 248 F1
NWBY RG14 ...... 37 G2
WBNE BH4 ...... 447 C6
WINC SO23 ...... 11 M6
Warren Side *EPSF* GU31 ...... 305 C5
Warrens La *RSAL* SP5 ...... 256 D4
The Warren *ALDT* GU11 ...... 6 D3
FAWY SO45 ...... 391 M3
FNM GU9 ...... 6 A6
TADY RG26 ...... 41 K8
Warrington Ms *ALDT* GU11 ...... 6 A5
Warrior Cl *CHFD* SO53 ...... 293 G4
Warrys Cl *FAWY* SO45 ...... 367 L8
Warsash Cl *HAV* PO9 ...... 377 J2
Warsash Gv
LSOL/BMARY PO13 ...... 397 G6
Warsash Rd *FHAM/STUB* PO14 ...... 371 J7
HLER SO31 ...... 370 B7
Warspite Cl *NEND* PO2 ...... 399 H4
Warton Cl *BROC* SO42 ...... 416 A2
Warton Rd *BSTK* RG21 ...... 5 G5
Warwick Av *NMIL/BTOS* BH25 ...... 437 M5
Warwick Cl *ALDT* GU11 ...... 7 J6
CBLY GU15 ...... 71 L5
CHFD SO53 ...... 292 F4
LSOL/BMARY PO13 ...... 420 E4
WINC SO23 ...... 11 G3
Warwick Crs *SSEA* PO5 ...... 21 H4
Warwick Dr *NWBY* RG14 ...... 3 H8
Warwick Rd *ASHV* GU12 ...... 91 J7
DEAN RG23 ...... 104 B2
FARN GU14 ...... 90 A8
LTDN BH7 ...... 448 F3
TOTT SO40 ...... 316 E8
WSHM SO15 ...... 318 C6
Wasdale Cl *HORN* PO8 ...... 328 B6
Wash Brook *HTWY* RG27 ...... 85 M6
Washbrook Rd *CHAM* PO6 ...... 375 H8
Washford La *BOR* GU35 ...... 201 L4
Washington Av *BMTH* BH1 ...... 448 C2
Washington Rd *EMRTH* PO10 ...... 378 D7
NEND PO2 ...... 399 H8
Wash Water *KSCL* RG20 ...... 36 D5
Wasing La *THLE* RG7 ...... 41 G2
Watchetts Dr *CBLY* GU15 ...... 70 F6
Watchetts Lake Cl *CBLY* GU15 ...... 71 G5
Watchetts Rd *CBLY* GU15 ...... 70 E5
Watch La *WHCH* RG28 ...... 99 M7
Watchmoor Rd *CBLY* GU15 ...... 70 D4
Watcombe Rd *SBNE* BH6 ...... 449 J3
Waterbeech Dr *HEND* SO30 ...... 321 H8
Waterberry Dr *WVILLE* PO7 ...... 352 A7
Watercress Meadow
NALR SO24 ...... 218 A4
Waterditch Rd
CHCH/BSGR BH23 ...... 435 K5
Water End La *CHAM* RG24 ...... 106 C1
Waterford Cl *LYMN* SO41 ...... 440 D5
Waterford Gdns
CHCH/BSGR BH23 ...... 451 M1
Waterford La *LYMN* SO41 ...... 440 D5
Waterford Pl
CHCH/BSGR BH23 ...... 451 M1
Waterford Rd
CHCH/BSGR BH23 ...... 436 F8
NMIL/BTOS BH25 ...... 438 A5
Waterhouse La *WSHM* SO15 ...... 342 F2
Waterhouse Md *SHST* GU47 ...... 70 A1
Waterhouse Wy *WSHM* SO15 ...... 342 F1
Wateridge Rd *BSTK* RG21 ...... 5 G2
Water La *FARN* GU14 ...... 90 D1
FAWY SO45 ...... 367 J4
FNM GU9 ...... 135 J4
NALR SO24 ...... 219 H4
RAND SP11 ...... 142 E4
SBNE BH6 ...... 449 J1
STHA RG19 ...... 37 M1
TOTT SO40 ...... 316 C8
WINC SO23 ...... 11 J7
Waterilly Cl *BSTK* RG21 ...... 5 K8
Waterloo Gdns *ENEY* PO4 ...... 424 D1
Waterloo Av *DEAN* RG23 ...... 104 B1
Waterloo Cl *CBLY* GU15 ...... 71 L1
HORN PO8 ...... 352 B5
Waterloo Ct *AND* SP10 ...... 9 K6
Waterloo Rd *ASHV* GU12 ...... 7 J4
CFDH BH17 ...... 430 A8
CWTH RG45 ...... 49 K4
GPORT PO12 ...... 19 H9
HAV PO9 ...... 16 F3
LYMN SO41 ...... 440 D4

MOOR/WNTN BH9 447 L1
WIMB BH21 428 F2
WSHM SO15 343 G2
Waterloo St SSEA PO5 21 H3
Waterloo Ter WSHM SO15 343 K2
Waterloo Wy RGWD BH24 382 E2 3
Watermain Rd RGWD BH24 407 L3
Waterman Cl BOR GU35 201 L6
Watermans La FAWY SO45 367 J7
Watermead Rd CHAM PO6 400 C1 1
Watermill Rd
CHCH/BSGR BH23 434 E8
Watermills Cl AND SP10 8 F9
Water Rede FLET GU13 110 D5
Water Ridges DEAN RG23 103 G8
Water's Edge HEND SO30 345 M2
Waters Edge Gdns
EMRTH PO10 378 D8
Watersedge Rd CHAM PO6 374 E8 2
Waters Gn BROC SO42 387 L6 2
Waters Green Ct BROC SO42 387 L6 3
Watership Dr RGWD BH24 383 H2
Waterside CHCH/BSGR BH23 450 E4
FAWY SO45 367 K3
Waterside Cl BOR GU35 201 K4
RGWD BH24 358 F7
Waterside Ct ALTN GU34 176 F4 2
FARN GU14 89 G5
Waterside Gdns
FHAM/PORC PO16 373 H7 1
Waterside La
FHAM/PORC PO16 398 C2
Waterside Rd ROMY SO51 262 F7 3
Watersmeet
FHAM/PORC PO16 396 F2
The Waters WHAM PO17 372 C3
Water Tower Rd BDST BH18 430 A4
Water Wy BSTK RG21 5 K7
Waterworks Rd CHAM PO6 376 B8
PSF GU32 275 M2
RWIN SO21 266 B4
Watery La AND SP10 9 K2
CHCH/BSGR BH23 435 L7
FLET GU13 110 D5
KSCL RG20 35 J3
Watkin Rd BOSC BH5 448 E4
HEND SO30 321 K6 1
Watley Cl ROWN SO16 317 J3
Watley La RWIN SO21 213 J4
RWIN SO21 267 G2
Watling End KEMP RG22 127 G1
Watson Acre AND SP10 8 C4
Watson Wk TOTT SO40 341 G1 3
Watson Wy DEAN RG23 104 C1
Watt Cl AND SP10 118 B7
Watton Cl CHAR BH8 433 L6
Watton La BPWT SO32 299 J6
Watton Rd FAWY SO45 392 A5
Watts Cl ROWN SO16 317 K6
Watts Common Rd ALDT GU11 112 B1
Watts Rd FARN GU14 90 C3
HEND SO30 346 A1
PSEA PO1 423 H1
Wavell Av CFDH BH17 429 L7
Wavell Cl KEMP RG22 104 D6
Wavell Rd BWD BH11 431 M4
LSOL/BMARY PO13 397 H5
WEND SO18 344 E1
Wavell Wy WINW SO22 238 B3
Wavendon Av
NMIL/BTOS BH25 437 J8
Waveney Cl
LSOL/BMARY PO13 420 D2 2
Waveney Gn ROWN SO16 317 K7
Waverley Av BSTK RG21 104 F6
FLET GU13 88 E5
HLER SO31 369 G2
Waverley Cl CBLY GU15 71 J4
FBDG SP6 309 L5
ODIM RG29 108 E5
ROMY SO51 263 G7 5
Waverley Ct HLER SO31 369 G3 2
Waverley Crs PLE BH15 445 J3
Waverley Dr ASHV GU12 113 K2
CBLY GU15 71 H3
RWIN SO21 190 D4
Waverley Gdns ASHV GU12 113 K2 1
Waverley Gv ENEY PO4 21 L8
Waverley La FNM GU9 135 M8
Waverley Rd CHAM PO6 376 A8
FARN GU14 91 G5
FBDG SP6 309 L5
NMIL/BTOS BH25 437 M6
SSEA PO5 21 L7
WSHM SO15 12 A1
The Waverleys NTHA RG18 27 G4 1
Wayfarer Cl ENEY PO4 424 A3 4
HLER SO31 370 D7
Wayfarers LSOL/BMARY PO13 421 H1
Wayfarer's Wk BPWT SO32 270 B7
DEAN RG23 126 D5
HAV PO9 377 G6
HORN PO8 301 K6
KSCL RG20 54 E1
KSCL RG20 78 E2
NALR SO24 172 B4
NALR SO24 242 B2
NALR SO24 270 A3
RAND SP11 55 J4
WVILLE PO7 375 M6
Waylands Pl HEND SO30 345 L4
Wayman Rd FARN GU14 70 B8
WIMB BH21 429 J2 2
Wayne Rd BKME/WDN BH12 446 A2
Waynflete Cl BPWT SO32 297 H8
Waynflete La FNM GU9 134 C6
Waynflete Pl WINW SO22 238 C2 2
Ways End CBLY GU15 71 H4
Wayside HLER SO31 346 B8
Wayside Cl LYMN SO41 454 C3
Wayside Rd DEAN RG23 104 A3
RGWD BH24 381 J7
SBNE BH6 449 K4
Wayte St CHAM PO6 399 K1
Waytown Cl CFDH BH17 430 B7
Weald Cl HLER SO31 370 E4
Weapon Rd FARN GU14 90 E6
Weardale Rd CHFD SO53 293 J4
Weatherby Gdns HTWY RG27 87 J2 5
Weathermore La ALTN GU34 197 J6
Weavers Cl AND SP10 9 J4
FERN BH22 380 C7 2
Weavers Gdns RFNM GU10 158 C1 3
Weavers Gn HAV PO9 17 L1
Weavers Pl CHFD SO53 265 G8
Weavills Rd ELGH SO50 294 F6
Webb Cl CHAM RG24 83 K6
HISD PO11 425 L6
Webb La HISD PO11 425 L6
Webb Rd FHAM/PORC PO16 398 B2
Webbs Acre STHA RG19 27 J6
Webbs Cl RGWD BH24 381 H2
Webbs Farm Cl WHCH RG28 122 B5
Webbs Gn BPWT SO32 325 G5
Webbs La THLE RG7 29 L1
Webburn Gdns WEND SO18 319 M5 3
Webster Rd WINW SO22 214 A7
Wedgewood Cl FAWY SO45 392 A4
FHAM/STUB PO14 396 A6 1
Wedgewood Wy WVILLE PO7 352 C6
Wedgwood Dr PSTN BH14 445 M6
Wedman's La HTWY RG27 85 L1
Wedmore Cl WINW SO22 237 M5
Weeke Cl RSAL SP5 284 C1 1
Weeke Manor Cl WINW SO22 10 A3
Weir Av FARN GU14 90 D5
Weir Cl FARN GU14 90 D5
Weir Rd FARN GU14 89 K6
HTWY RG27 87 G4
The Weir WHCH RG28 122 B5
Welbeck Av PTSW SO17 319 G6
Welbeck Cl FARN GU14 90 C4
Welch Rd ENEY PO4 21 M8
GPORT PO12 421 L1
Welch Wy ROWN SO16 317 K3
Welchwood Cl HORN PO8 352 D2
Weldon Av BWD BH11 431 J3
Weldon Cl FLET GU13 111 G3
Welland Gdns WEND SO18 320 A6
Welland Gn ROWN SO16 317 K8
Welland Rd WIMB BH21 404 B4
Wellands Rd LYND SO43 363 K3 3
Wella Rd KEMP RG22 104 E6
Wellbrooke Gdns CHFD SO53 293 G1
Wellburn Cl SHST GU47 69 L1
Well Cl CBLY GU15 70 E4
NMIL/BTOS BH25 437 K7
OVTN RG25 125 K7
Well Copse Cl HORN PO8 328 B7
Weller Dr CBLY GU15 70 F5
EWKG RG40 47 K2
Wellers Cl TOTT SO40 340 F1
Wellesley Av CHCH/BSGR BH23 451 G1
Wellesley Cl ASHV GU12 113 J1
BAGS GU19 51 M5
WVILLE PO7 376 C1
Wellesley Dr CWTH RG45 49 H3
Wellesley Gdn FNM GU9 134 F1
Wellesley Rd ALDT GU11 112 A5
AND SP10 9 G9
FARN GU14 90 A8
RFNM GU10 181 L2
Welles Rd CHFD SO53 293 J2
Well House Cl FBDG SP6 283 G5
Well House La WINW SO22 214 D3
HTWY RG27 46 E5
Wellhouse Rd ALTN GU34 175 L6
Wellington Av ALDT GU11 6 F1
CHCH/BSGR BH23 451 H1
FLET GU13 89 G6
BOR GU35 201 H6
WEND SO18 344 F1
Wellington Cl FAWY SO45 367 H7
HORN PO8 353 H2
NWBY RG14 25 M3 3
SHST GU47 49 M8
Wellington Crs TADY RG26 41 G7
Wellington Gv
FHAM/PORC PO16 398 A1
Wellingtonia Av EWKG RG40 48 E4
Wellington La FNM GU9 135 G1
Wellington Pk HEND SO30 320 F7
Wellington Rd AND SP10 8 E3
CHAR BH8 23 G1
CWTH RG45 49 M4
PSTN BH14 446 B5
SHST GU47 49 L8
WEND SO18 319 J6
Wellington St ALDT GU11 6 F1
SSEA PO5 21 G3
Wellington Ter DEAN RG23 104 B1
SHST GU47 49 M8 1
Wellington Wy FARN GU14 112 A1
WVILLE PO7 376 C1 2
Well La ALTN GU34 132 A8
ALTN GU34 156 A2
BPWT SO32 324 A1
FBDG SP6 310 D6
HASM GU27 229 G2
HLER SO31 369 L6
PLE BH15 445 H4
Wellmans Meadow KSCL RG20 59 H5
Well Meadow HAV PO9 377 J2
NWBY RG14 25 L3
Wellowbrook Cl CHFD SO53 292 F2 2
Wellow Cl HAV PO9 16 B1
WEND SO18 345 G1
Wellow Dro ROMY SO51 288 D1
Wellow Gdns
FHAM/STUB PO14 371 G6
Wellow Wood Rd ROMY SO51 260 C8
Well Rd RFNM GU10 133 H2
Wells Cottages FNM GU9 158 D1 5
Wellsfield SELS PO20 427 L7
Wellsmoor FHAM/STUB PO14 371 G5
Wells Pl ELGH SO50 293 M6
Wells's La WHCH RG28 122 A4
Well St KSCL RG20 57 K4
Wellswood Gdns HAV PO9 354 A5
Wellsworth La HAV PO9 354 A5
Welsh La THLE RG7 45 K6
Welshman's Rd THLE RG7 42 E3
Welton Ct BSTK RG21 4 C7
Wembley Gv CHAM PO6 399 L2 1
Wendan Rd NWBY RG14 2 D9
Wendover Cl
NMIL/BTOS BH25 437 K7 4
Wendover Dr FRIM GU16 71 M5
Wendover Rd HAV PO9 16 C3
Wenlock Wy STHA RG19 27 G6 7
Wensley Dr FLET GU13 88 F5 2
Wensley Gdns EMRTH PO10 378 D5
Wentwood Gdns
NMIL/BTOS BH25 438 B6
Wentworth Av BOSC BH5 448 F4
Wentworth Cl ASHV GU12 113 K1
BOSC BH5 448 F5
CWTH RG45 49 J2
FNM GU9 6 C9
YTLY GU46 69 G3 3
Wentworth Ct NWBY RG14 3 G7
Wentworth Crs ASHV GU12 113 K2
Wentworth Dr BDST BH18 429 L3
HORN PO8 352 F1
Wentworth Gdns ALTN GU34 176 D4
FAWY SO45 392 B6 1
ITCH SO19 344 F7 1
Wentworth Gra WINW SO22 238 D2
Wentworth Gv FAWY SO45 392 B5
Wesermarsch Rd HORN PO8 352 E4
Wesley Cl CHAR BH8 23 M1
ITCH SO19 345 H4
Wesley Gv HSEA PO3 399 K5
Wesley Rd PSTN BH14 446 B3
WIMB BH21 404 B3
WINC SO23 215 H1
Wessex Av NMIL/BTOS BH25 437 L6
ODIM RG29 108 C7
Wessex Cl BSTK RG21 104 F5
CHCH/BSGR BH23 451 H1
FAWY SO45 392 D7
Wessex Crs ODIM RG29 108 C7
Wessex Dr WINW SO22 10 C2
ODIM RG29 108 C7
Wessex Est RGWD BH24 358 F8
Wessex Gdns AND SP10 8 F4
FHAM/PORC PO16 397 M1
ROMY SO51 291 G1
Wessex La WEND SO18 319 J4
Wessex Pl FNM GU9 134 F7
Wessex Rd FARN GU14 90 C6
HORN PO8 328 B5
PSTN BH14 445 M5
RGWD BH24 358 F8
Wessex Wy CHAR BH8 433 L7
RWIN SO21 266 F8
WBNE BH4 447 G4
WCLF BH2 22 C4
West Ashling Rd RCCH PO18 379 M5
West Av FNM GU9 135 G2
WIMB BH21 356 B8
West Bargate SHAM SO14 12 F4 1
West Battery Rd NEND PO2 398 F7
Westbeams Rd LYMN SO41 412 F6
Westborn Rd FHAM/PORC PO16 15 K5
Westbourne Av EMRTH PO10 378 E6
FAWY SO45 392 A4
Westbourne Cl EMRTH PO10 378 E6 1
WBNE BH4 447 H5
Westbourne Crs PTSW SO17 318 E7
Westbourne Park Rd
WBNE BH4 447 G6
Westbourne Rd EMRTH PO10 378 E5
NEND PO2 399 K8
SHST GU47 70 B1
Westbroke Gdns ROMY SO51 262 E7 3
West Brook Cl DEAN RG23 103 G8
Westbrook Cl HLER SO31 370 E3
Westbrooke Cl AND SP10 9 H6
HORN PO8 352 E2
Westbrooke Rd ALTN GU34 176 D5
Westbrook Gv WVILLE PO7 376 B3
Westbrook Rd
FHAM/PORC PO16 398 B2
Westbrook Wy WEND SO18 319 K4 3
Westburn ALTN GU34 156 B4
Westbury Av FLET GU13 89 J8
Westbury Cl CHAM PO6 374 F7 3
CHCH/BSGR BH23 435 L1
CHCH/BSGR BH23 436 B7
CWTH RG45 49 L2
FLET GU13 89 H8
NMIL/BTOS BH25 437 L8
Westbury Ct HEND SO30 346 A3
Westbury Gdns FLET GU13 89 J8
FNM GU9 135 H4 2
Westbury Rd RGWD BH24 382 F1
WSHM SO15 342 D1
Westbury Wy ASHV GU12 7 L1
Westby Rd BOSC BH5 448 D4
Westcliff Cl LSOL/BMARY PO13 420 C1
West Cliff Gdns WCLF BH2 22 C8
West Cliff Rd WBNE BH4 447 H6
WCLF BH2 22 C7
West Cl FNM GU9 135 G1
LYMN SO41 439 M6
VWD BH31 356 B2
West Common FAWY SO45 418 B1
Westcot Rd FAWY SO45 391 M5 3
Westcroft Pk BDST BH18 430 A4
Westcroft Rd GPORT PO12 18 A1
Westdean Ct BSTK RG21 4 B9
Westdeane Ct BSTK RG21 4 B9
Westdown Rd BWD BH11 431 L3
West Downs Cl
FHAM/PORC PO16 372 E4
West Dr ELGH SO50 294 C4
West End TADY RG26 82 C3
West End Cl WINW SO22 10 D7
West End Gv FNM GU9 134 D6
West End La ALTN GU34 196 A4
RFNM GU10 158 B7
Westend Rd ITCH SO19 344 E1
West End Rd THLE RG7 43 H3
Westend Rd WEND SO18 320 B8
West End Rd HEND SO30 345 K4
WEND SO18 319 M8
West End Ter WINW SO22 10 D7
Westerdale STHA RG19 26 F5
Westerdale Dr FRIM GU16 71 L5
Westerham Cl CHAM PO6 375 J8
Westerham Rd CCLF BH13 447 G5
Westering ROMY SO51 263 H7 2
ROMY SO51 263 H8 2
Westerley Cl HLER SO31 370 C7 5
Western Av AND SP10 9 H7
CCLF BH13 446 D6
EMRTH PO10 378 B8
NBNE BH10 432 B4
NMIL/BTOS BH25 437 H8
NWBY RG14 2 E1
Western Cl NBNE BH10 432 B3
Western District Cut
WSHM SO15 343 H1 1
Western End NWBY RG14 2 A6 1
Western Esp SHAM SO14 12 D2
Western La ODIM RG29 108 C6
Western Pde EMRTH PO10 402 C1
SSEA PO5 20 F6
Western Rd ALDT GU11 6 B3
AND SP10 9 G6
CCLF BH13 446 E8
CHAM PO6 399 J2
CHFD SO53 265 K7
FHAM/PORC PO16 15 J6
WINW SO22 10 D6
HAV PO9 16 C3
HEND SO30 320 C7
BOR GU35 201 H2
LISS GU33 248 E4
LYMN SO41 440 B4
Western Wy FHAM/PORC PO16 15 H6
GPORT PO12 421 J5
KEMP RG22 104 C6
Westfield Av FHAM/STUB PO14 14 F8
HISD PO11 425 J5
Westfield Cl ELGH SO50 321 H1
HLER SO31 369 J6
West Field Cl TADY RG26 42 A8
Westfield Common
HLER SO31 369 H6 1
Westfield Crs CHFD SO53 293 H5
NTHA RG18 26 E4
Westfield Dr BPWT SO32 324 C6
Westfield Dro NALR SO24 241 M8
Westfield Gdns
CHCH/BSGR BH23 435 M7
Westfield La RFNM GU10 158 B2
Westfield Rd BSTK RG21 105 H5
CBLY GU15 70 E6
CHFD SO53 293 H5
ENEY PO4 423 L5
WINW SO22 214 A3
GPORT PO12 18 B2
LYMN SO41 440 D6
NTHA RG18 26 D3
SBNE BH6 449 K4
TOTT SO40 316 E8
West Field Rd WINC SO23 191 H8
Westfield Rd WSHM SO15 342 E1
Westfield Wy NWBY RG14 2 A6
West Fryerne YTLY GU46 69 G1
Westgate FHAM/STUB PO14 396 A7
Westgate Pk WBNE BH4 447 G5
Westgate Rd NWBY RG14 2 A6
Westgate St SHAM SO14 12 F6
Westglade FARN GU14 90 A4 1
West Gn YTLY GU46 68 E1
West Green Rd HTWY RG27 86 E2
Westgrove FBDG SP6 309 K7 3
Westham Cl CFDH BH17 430 C5
West Ham Cl KEMP RG22 104 B4
West Ham La KEMP RG22 104 A4
West Haye Rd HISD PO11 426 B7
West Hayes LYMN SO41 440 D5
Westheath Rd BDST BH18 429 M4
West Heath Rd FARN GU14 90 C4
West Hill Dr FAWY SO45 367 K3
WINW SO22 10 C7
West Hill Pk WINW SO22 10 B7
West Hill Pl WCLF BH2 22 C6
West Hill Rd WCLF BH2 22 C7
West Hill Rd North RWIN SO21 190 D3
West Hill Rd South RWIN SO21 190 D4
West Hoe La BPWT SO32 297 L8
West Horton La ELGH SO50 294 E7
Westland NTHA RG18 26 E4 1
Westland Dr WVILLE PO7 376 C4
Westland Gdns GPORT PO12 18 C6
Westlands Ct
CHCH/BSGR BH23 409 L8
Westlands Gv
FHAM/PORC PO16 398 A1
Westlands Rd NWBY RG14 2 F9
West La HISD PO11 425 J3
LYMN SO41 439 J7 2
NBAD SO52 291 K3
Westley Cl WINW SO22 10 A4
Westley Gv FHAM/STUB PO14 14 E7
Westley La RWIN SO21 213 H4
Westlyn Rd TADY RG26 42 B7
Westman Rd WINW SO22 10 A2
West Marlands Rd SHAM SO14 12 F2
Westmead FARN GU14 90 E5
Westmead Cl HISD PO11 425 H5
Westmead Dr NWBY RG14 25 J8
West Meade LIPH GU30 250 E6
West Mills NWBY RG14 2 D4
Westminister Rd LYMN SO41 454 A4
Westminster Cl FLET GU13 88 F6 1
KEMP RG22 127 G1 3
Westminster Gdns
FHAM/STUB PO14 371 G5 5
Westminster Ga WINW SO22 238 A3 1
Westminster Rd CCLF BH13 447 G7
Westminster Rd East
CCLF BH13 447 G7
West Moors Rd FERN BH22 406 B1
WIMB BH21 380 C1
Westmorland Dr CBLY GU15 71 L5
Westmorland Wy CHFD SO53 293 K3
Weston Av ENEY PO4 423 M4
Weston Cl ITCH SO19 344 D7
Weston Ct RAND SP11 96 A8
Weston Crs WEND SO18 345 G1
Weston Down Rd RWIN SO21 169 K3
Weston Dr BMTH BH1 23 K5
Weston Grove Rd ITCH SO19 344 B6
Weston La ITCH SO19 344 C7
PSF GU32 275 G8
ROWN SO16 316 F4
RSAL SP5 206 E3
Weston Rd ELGH SO50 293 M5
EPSF GU31 275 M5
OVTN RG25 129 M5
WIMB BH21 404 D1 3
West Overcliff Dr WBNE BH4 447 H6
Westover La RGWD BH24 382 B2
Westover Rd BMTH BH1 22 F6
FLET GU13 89 G7
HSEA PO3 399 M8
LYMN SO41 454 C4
ROWN SO16 317 G8
West Pk RAND SP11 117 G2
West Park Dr FBDG SP6 308 C3
West Park La FBDG SP6 308 B3
West Park Rd WSHM SO15 12 E2
West Portway AND SP10 118 A6
West Quay Rd PLE BH15 445 G6
WSHM SO15 12 D3
Westray Cl BSTK RG21 5 J4
Westridge KSCL RG20 56 B4
Westridge Rd PTSW SO17 319 G7
West Rd BOSC BH5 449 G4
CBLY GU15 71 G3
CHCH/BSGR BH23 409 L8
EMRTH PO10 378 C8
FARN GU14 70 D8
FAWY SO45 367 H7
HEND SO30 345 K2
ITCH SO19 344 C6
LYMN SO41 453 M3
RWIN SO21 167 J1
SHAM SO14 13 G7
WHAM PO17 374 E2
Westrow Gdns WSHM SO15 343 J1
Westrow Rd WSHM SO15 343 J1
Westside Cl KEMP RG22 104 C5 1
West Strd SELS PO20 427 J8
West St AND SP10 9 G5
BPWT SO32 325 G3
EMRTH PO10 378 D8
FAWY SO45 367 K3
FBDG SP6 309 K7
FHAM/PORC PO16 15 L6
FHAM/PORC PO16 374 B8
FHAM/STUB PO14 371 K8
FNM GU9 134 C7
HASM GU27 228 F2
HAV PO9 16 B4
KSCL RG20 57 H4
NALR SO24 218 C2
NWBY RG14 2 D3
ODIM RG29 108 B6
PLE BH15 445 G6
PSEA PO1 20 B5
RGWD BH24 382 C1
SHAM SO14 12 F5
TADY RG26 42 A8
WHAM PO17 374 C2
WVILLE PO7 326 B7
West Undercliff Prom
WBNE BH4 447 H7
West View Dr STOK SO20 165 M5
West View Rd
CHCH/BSGR BH23 450 D2
Westview Rd WINW SO22 213 M6
West View Rd BOR GU35 202 F4
PLE BH15 445 H4
Westward Rd HEND SO30 321 H8
West Wy BDST BH18 429 K5
LYMN SO41 440 A6
MOOR/WNTN BH9 432 F6
Westway FHAM PO15 371 J5
Westway Cl ROWN SO16 317 J2
Westways CHAM PO6 376 D8
FHAM/STUB PO14 396 B6
Westways Cl ROWN SO16 317 J3 1
Westwood Av FERN BH22 406 A2
Westwood Cl EMRTH PO10 378 E5
Westwood Gdns CHFD SO53 265 K8
Westwood La RGUW GU3 137 L1
Westwood Rd HLER SO31 368 F1
LYND SO43 363 K2
NEND PO2 399 J4
NWBY RG14 3 H9
PTSW SO17 318 E8
Westwood Vw NALR SO24 242 D7
Wetherby Cl CFDH BH17 429 L6
Wetherby Gdns AND SP10 118 D6
FARN GU14 90 F8 3
TOTT SO40 316 B8
Wetherdown EPSF GU31 275 M5
Wey Bank ALTN GU34 157 H5
Weybank Cl FNM GU9 134 F5 4
Weybourne Rd FNM GU9 135 H3
Weybridge Md YTLY GU46 69 H1
Weybrook Ct TADY RG26 82 C4
Wey Cl ASHV GU12 113 K7
CBLY GU15 70 E3
Weycombe Rd HASM GU27 204 F8
Weydon Hill Cl FNM GU9 134 E8 2
Weydon Hill Rd FNM GU9 134 E8
Weydon La FNM GU9 134 D8
Weydon Mill La FNM GU9 134 E7
Weydown Rd HASM GU27 228 E1
Wey Hl HASM GU27 228 D2
Weyhill Cl FHAM/PORC PO16 374 A7
HAV PO9 377 H3 5
TADY RG26 61 L1
Weyhill Gdns RAND SP11 117 J6
Weyhill Rd AND SP10 8 E6
RAND SP11 117 M7
Weyland Cl LIPH GU30 226 F3
Wey Lodge Cl LIPH GU30 227 G4 2
Weyman's Av NBNE BH10 432 A2
Weymans Dr NBNE BH10 432 A2
Weymouth Av GPORT PO12 397 K8
Weymouth Rd PSTN BH14 446 B3
Weysprings HASM GU27 228 C1
Weysprings Cl BSTK RG21 5 J7
Weywood Cl FNM GU9 6 C8
Weywood La FNM GU9 6 B8
Whaddon Cha
FHAM/STUB PO14 395 M6
Whaddon Ct HAV PO9 377 G2
Whaddon La RWIN SO21 267 M7
Whale Island Wy NEND PO2 399 G7
Whalesmead Cl ELGH SO50 294 E7

Whalesmead Rd ELGH SO50 294 E7
Whaley Rd NEND PO2 398 F7
Wharf Cl BKME/WDN BH12 446 D2
Wharfdale Rd
BKME/WDN BH12 446 C2
WBNE BH4 447 H4
Wharfenden Wy FRIM GU16 91 J2
Wharf Hl WINC SO23 239 G2
Wharf Rd ASHV GU12 113 K4
FRIM GU16 91 J2
NEND PO2 399 G8
NWBY RG14 2 F4
Wharfside THLE RG7 29 M5
Wharf St NWBY RG14 2 E4
Wharf Wy FRIM GU16 91 J2
Wharncliffe Gdns
CHCH/BSGR BH23 451 M1
Wharncliffe Rd BMTH BH1 448 C4
CHCH/BSGR BH23 451 M1
ITCH SO19 344 B5
Whartons La TOTT SO40 341 G4
Whatleigh Cl PLE BH15 445 H7
Wheat Cl NBAD SO52 292 E2
Wheatcroft Dr WEND SO18 320 A7 5
Wheatcroft Rd
LSOL/BMARY PO13 420 D2
Wheatear Dr EPSF GU31 276 B5 2
Wheatears Dr ROMY SO51 288 D5
Wheatland Cl WINW SO22 238 C3
Wheatlands FHAM/STUB PO14 371 G4
Wheatlands Av HISD PO11 426 C7
Wheatlands Crs HISD PO11 426 C7 1
Wheatlands NWBY RG14 36 E2
Wheatley La ALTN GU34 178 F1
Wheaton Rd LTDN BH7 448 F3
Wheatsheaf Ct HEND SO30 345 M2 5
Wheatsheaf Dr HORN PO8 352 B5
Wheatstone Rd ENEY PO4 21 M6
Wheeler Cl GPORT PO12 421 M2
THLE RG7 31 L5 6
WHCH RG28 122 C4
Wheeler Hl HTWY RG27 86 B7
Wheelers Green Wy STHA RG19 27 H6
Wheelers La BWD BH11 431 G3
Wheelers Wk FAWY SO45 392 C8
Wheelwrights La GSHT GU26 203 K4
Whernside Cl ROWN SO16 317 L8 5
Wherwell Ct HAV PO9 377 M3 10
Whetstone Rd FARN GU14 89 M4
Whichers Cl HAV PO9 353 M8
Whichers Gate Rd HAV PO9 353 M8
Whimbrel Cl ENEY PO4 424 A3
Whinchat Cl FHAM PO15 372 A4
HTWY RG27 87 H1
ROWN SO16 318 A2
Whincroft Cl FERN BH22 406 C1
Whincroft Dr FERN BH22 406 C2
Whinfield Rd FAWY SO45 367 J7
Whin Holt FLET GU13 110 F2
Whins Cl CBLY GU15 70 E4
Whins Dr CBLY GU15 70 E4
Whinwhistle Rd ROMY SO51 289 G6
Whippingham Cl CHAM PO6 375 H8
Whistler Cl BSTK RG21 105 J5
Whistler Gv SHST GU47 70 A2
Whistler Rd ITCH SO19 345 G5
Whistlers Cl CHCH/BSGR BH23 409 M7
Whistlers La THLE RG7 42 E7
Whitaker Crs LYMN SO41 440 A5
Whitby Av BDST BH18 429 L6
Whitby Cl FARN GU14 91 H7 1
Whitby Crs BDST BH18 429 L6
Whitby Rd LYMN SO41 454 A4
Whitchurch Av BDST BH18 430 A5
Whitchurch Cl ALDT GU11 7 L9
Whitcombe Cl TOTT SO40 341 J1 2
Whitcombe Gdns HSEA PO3 423 K2
White Acres Rd FRIM GU16 91 J4
White Av LISS GU33 225 H6
White Barn Crs LYMN SO41 438 E5
Whitebeam Cl
FHAM/STUB PO14 14 C7
HORN PO8 353 G3 1
RWIN SO21 266 F8
White Beam Ri HORN PO8 328 B3
Whitebeam Rd HEND SO30 346 B2
Whitebeams Gdns
FARN GU14 89 M5 7
Whitebeam Wy NBAD SO52 291 M3
VWD BH31 356 F3
Whitechimney Rw
EMRTH PO10 378 F5
White City CWTH RG45 50 A3
Whitecliff Crs PSTN BH14 445 M6
Whitecliffe Av HSEA PO3 423 L1
Whitecliff Rd PSTN BH14 445 L6
White Cliff Rd PSTN BH14 445 M6
White Cloud Pk ENEY PO4 423 K5 1
White Cottage Cl FNM GU9 135 G2
Whitecross Cl CFDH BH17 430 C5
Whitecross Gdns NEND PO2 399 K5
Whitedell La WHAM PO17 373 H4
White Dirt La HORN PO8 328 A6
Whitedown ALTN GU34 176 D6
Whitedown La ALTN GU34 176 C6
Whitedown Rd TADY RG26 41 J8
White Farm Cl NBNE BH10 432 B8
White Farm La MARL SN8 53 G3
Whitefield Rd FAWY SO45 392 A5
NMIL/BTOS BH25 437 L5
PSTN BH14 445 M6
White Gates BPWT SO32 322 A3
Whitehall CHCH/BSGR BH23 450 A3
Whitehall Rd STOK SO20 187 M8
Whitehart Flds RGWD BH24 359 G8 5
White Hart La BSTK RG21 5 G9
FHAM/PORC PO16 397 M1
TADY RG26 61 K8
TOTT SO40 314 E8
White Hart Rd ELGH SO50 295 H7
GPORT PO12 18 F4 5
PSEA PO1 20 C5
Whitehaven
FHAM/PORC PO16 397 M1
HORN PO8 353 H2
Whitehayes Cl
CHCH/BSGR BH23 435 H6
Whitehayes Rd
CHCH/BSGR BH23 435 G7
Whitehead Cl CHAM RG24 105 L1 2
White Heather Ct FAWY SO45 367 L3
White Hl KSCL RG20 57 G6
KSCL RG20 58 C5
ODIM RG29 132 A6
Whitehill Cl CBLY GU15 71 G1
Whitehill La NALR SO24 218 E4
Whitehill Rd BOR GU35 201 L7
Whitehorn Dr RSAL SP5 287 J8
White Horse Dr PLE BH15 445 H3
White Horse La EWKG RG40 47 M3
WVILLE PO7 351 L2
White House Cl KEMP RG22 104 C6
Whitehouse Gdns PSF GU32 275 K3
White House Gdns
WSHM SO15 342 E2
YTLY GU46 68 F1 2
Whitehouse Rd WIMB BH21 404 B6
White House Wk FNM GU9 135 G1 2
White Knights
NMIL/BTOS BH25 452 E1
White Ladies Cl HAV PO9 17 G5
Whitelands CHCH/BSGR BH23 410 B5
Whitelands Rd NTHA RG18 26 F4
White La ASHV GU12 113 M7
RFNM GU10 136 F1
OVTN RG25 107 J6
RWIN SO21 238 F8
TADY RG26 102 B2
Whitelaw Rd WSHM SO15 342 F1
Whiteleaf La WVILLE PO7 326 B1
Whitelegg Wy NBNE BH10 432 C3
Whiteley La FHAM PO15 371 K4
HLER SO31 347 G7
Whiteley Wy FHAM PO15 371 H2
White Lion Wy YTLY GU46 69 G1
Whitemoor La TOTT SO40 315 K4
Whitemoor Rd BROC SO42 387 H6
Whitenap Cl ROMY SO51 291 G2
Whitenap La ROMY SO51 291 H2
White Oak Wy RAND SP11 142 B4
White Post La RFNM GU10 158 D4
White Rd CBLY GU15 70 C2
ELGH SO50 294 C4
White Rose La FNM GU9 158 E1
Whites Cl HTWY RG27 85 L7 5
Whites Hl RWIN SO21 267 L4
THLE RG7 31 H4
Whiteshoot RSAL SP5 285 L4
STOK SO20 209 G1
Whiteshoot Hl RSAL SP5 285 K4
Whiteshute La WINC SO23 238 D4
Whites La FAWY SO45 392 F5 10
Whites Rd FARN GU14 91 H7
ITCH SO19 344 E3
Whitestone Cl ROWN SO16 317 L8 4
Whitestones KEMP RG22 127 H2 3
White Swan Rd PSEA PO1 20 F2
Whitethorn Cl ASHV GU12 113 L7
Whitethorn Rd HISD PO11 425 M5 1
Whitewater Ri FAWY SO45 367 K6
HTWY RG27 86 B6 6
Whitewater Rd ODIM RG29 108 B4
Whiteways WIMB BH21 404 C2
The White Wy BPWT SO32 270 E6
Whitewood CHAM RG24 83 L5
Whitfield Cl HASM GU27 204 F7 1
Whitfield Pk RGWD BH24 381 M3
Whitfield Rd HASM GU27 204 F8
Whithedwood Av WSHM SO15 318 C8
Whithers La BROC SO42 416 A2
Whitlet Cl FNM GU9 134 E7 2
Whitley Cl EMRTH PO10 378 F3
Whitley Rd HORN PO8 352 D2
YTLY GU46 69 G4
Whitley Wy FARN GU14 90 B7
NMIL/BTOS BH25 437 M3
Whitmarsh La CHAM RG24 84 A5
Whitmoor Vale Rd GSHT GU26 203 J1
Whitmore Cl SHST GU47 50 A8
Whitmore Gn FNM GU9 135 H2
Whitmore V GSHT GU26 203 J2
Whitmore Vale Rd GSHT GU26 203 L4
Whitney Rd CHAM RG24 5 L4
Whitsbury Rd FBDG SP6 309 L5
HAV PO9 377 L3
Whitstable Rd CHAM PO6 375 J8
Whittington Cl FAWY SO45 367 K6
Whittington Ct EMRTH PO10 378 D8
Whittle Av FHAM PO15 371 G3
Whittle Cl EWKG RG40 48 B1
SHST GU47 49 K7 5
Whittle Crs FARN GU14 90 C1
Whittle Rd AND SP10 118 A7
WIMB BH21 405 K1
Whittles Wy PLE BH15 445 G6
Whitwell HLER SO31 369 G1 7
Whitwell Rd ENEY PO4 21 L9
Whitworth Cl GPORT PO12 18 D3
Whitworth Crs WEND SO18 319 J8
Whitworth Rd GPORT PO12 18 D3
NEND PO2 399 K8
WEND SO18 319 J8
WHIT RG2 47 K1
Whynot La AND SP10 8 D5
Whyte Av ASHV GU12 7 L7
Whyte Cl FAWY SO45 391 M5
Whyteways ELGH SO50 293 L4
Wick Cl NMIL/BTOS BH25 437 J6
Wick Dr NMIL/BTOS BH25 437 J6
Wicket Hl RFNM GU10 158 D2
Wicket Rd NBNE BH10 432 A3
The Wicket FAWY SO45 367 K6
Wickfield Av CHCH/BSGR BH23 450 A2
Wickham Cl ALTN GU34 176 C6
FLET GU13 110 D3
TADY RG26 41 L8
Wickham Dr WIMB BH21 429 H4
Wickham Pl FLET GU13 110 D2
Wickham Rd BPWT SO32 324 F4
CBLY GU15 51 H8
FHAM/PORC PO16 15 J1
FLET GU13 110 D2
WHAM PO17 372 F4
Wickham St PSEA PO1 20 C1
Wick Hill La EWKG RG40 48 D2
Wick La CHCH/BSGR BH23 450 A3
RSAL SP5 255 M8
SBNE BH6 449 M3
Wicklea Rd SBNE BH6 450 A4
Wicklow Cl KEMP RG22 104 A5
Wicklow Dr CHFD SO53 292 F3
Wickor Cl EMRTH PO10 378 E6
Wickor Wy EMRTH PO10 378 D5
Wicor Mill La
FHAM/PORC PO16 397 M2
Wicor Pth FHAM/PORC PO16 398 C2
Widbury Rd LYMN SO41 440 A6
Widden Cl LYMN SO41 412 F6
Widdicombe Av PSTN BH14 446 D6
Widecombe Dr FAWY SO45 367 J4
Wide La ELGH SO50 319 L1
WEND SO18 319 K3
Wide Lane Cl BROC SO42 387 K7 5
Widgeon Cl GPORT PO12 421 M1
ROWN SO16 318 A2
Widgeons ALTN GU34 176 E3
Widget Cl BWD BH11 431 M6
Widlers La BPWT SO32 296 D2
Widley Ct FHAM/STUB PO14 396 D2
Widley Court Dr CHAM PO6 399 L1
Widley Gdns WVILLE PO7 376 B5
Widley Rd CHAM PO6 375 L8
NEND PO2 399 G6
Widley Wk CHAM PO6 375 K6
Widmore Rd KEMP RG22 104 B6
Widworthy Dr BDST BH18 429 K3
Wield Cl HAV PO9 377 G4
Wield Rd ALTN GU34 174 A5
Wigan Crs HAV PO9 376 F6
Wigan Rd FARN GU14 90 A8
Wights Wk KEMP RG22 127 G1 7
Wight Wk FERN BH22 406 C6
Wigmore Rd TADY RG26 41 J7
Wilberforce Cl WINW SO22 238 B2 5
Wilberforce Rd GPORT PO12 19 G9
SSEA PO5 21 G5 5
Wild Arum Wy NBAD SO52 292 E3
Wild Briar EWKG RG40 48 C1
Wildburn Cl TOTT SO40 316 B6
Wild Cherry Wy NBAD SO52 292 F2 5
Wilde Cl TOTT SO40 341 H1 6
Wildern Cl HLER SO31 370 D5 2
Wilderness Hts WEND SO18 320 B7
Wilderness Rd FRIM GU16 71 H6
Wildern La HEND SO30 321 G8
Wilders Cl FRIM GU16 71 G5
Wilderton Rd CCLF BH13 446 E5
Wilderton Rd West CCLF BH13 446 E4
Wildfell Cl CHCH/BSGR BH23 434 E7
Wild Herons HTWY RG27 86 B7 5
Wildmoor La HTWY RG27 84 B2
Wildown Gdns SBNE BH6 449 L5
Wildown Rd SBNE BH6 449 M5
Wild Ridings FHAM/STUB PO14 371 M8
Wild Rose Crs HLER SO31 370 C6
Wildwood Gdns YTLY GU46 68 F4
Wilfred Rd BOSC BH5 448 E4
Wilfred Wy STHA RG19 27 J5
Wilkins Cl HORN PO8 328 A2
Wilkinson Dr CHAR BH8 433 L6
Wilks Cl ROWN SO16 317 H3
Willems Av ALDT GU11 6 D1
Willersley Cl CHAM PO6 375 G7
Will Hall Cl ALTN GU34 176 C6
William Cl CHCH/BSGR BH23 436 E6
FHAM/STUB PO14 396 B7
STHA RG19 27 G6
William Farthing Cl ALDT GU11 6 E2
William Macleod Wy
ROWN SO16 317 M8
William Price Gdns
FHAM/PORC PO16 15 J3
William Rd LTDN BH7 448 E1
LYMN SO41 440 C3 4
Williams Cl FAWY SO45 392 B5
LSOL/BMARY PO13 421 H1
Williamson Cl HASM GU27 205 J7 2
RAND SP11 92 D6
Williams Rd HSEA PO3 399 M5
William St SHAM SO14 13 M1
Williams Wy FLET GU13 89 H7
William Wy ALTN GU34 176 F3 2
Willington Cl CBLY GU15 70 E2 1
Willis Av NBAD SO52 292 A4
Willis La ALTN GU34 197 J7
Willis Rd GPORT PO12 19 H3
PSEA PO1 21 G1
ROWN SO16 319 J3
Willis Wy CFDH BH17 445 G2
Willis Wy WINC SO23 215 H3
Willoughby Cl ALTN GU34 176 D4
Willoughby Wy DEAN RG23 104 C2
Willow Av FBDG SP6 309 K6
Willow Cl FRIM GU16 91 H4
HAV PO9 17 G5
HEND SO30 320 D6 5
BOR GU35 201 K5
LIPH GU30 227 G5 2
NWBY RG14 2 D8
RGWD BH24 381 H4
TLHT RG30 31 L3
UPTN BH16 444 C3
Willow Ct FRIM GU16 71 G7
ROWN SO16 317 M5
Willow Crs FARN GU14 90 E1
Willowdale Cl PSF GU32 274 E4
Willowdene Cl HAV PO9 376 F4
NMIL/BTOS BH25 438 A5
Willow Dr CHCH/BSGR BH23 449 M3
RGWD BH24 382 E3
TOTT SO40 342 D8
WIMB BH21 405 G2
Willowford YTLY GU46 69 G2
Willow Gdns EMRTH PO10 378 F4
LIPH GU30 227 G5
NBAD SO52 291 L3
Willow Gn RWIN SO21 266 F8
Willow Gv AND SP10 8 F7
ELGH SO50 295 J6
Willow Herb Cl HLER SO31 370 C6
Willow La BLKW GU17 70 A4
CHCH/BSGR BH23 410 B5
Willow Md CHAR BH8 433 H4
Willowmead Cl NWBY RG14 36 F3
Willow Pk ASHV GU12 113 J6
PSTN BH14 445 L5
Willow Pl GPORT PO12 18 F1
Willow Rd BPWT SO32 323 K1
KSCL RG20 38 C6
LISS GU33 248 E4
TADY RG26 41 L8
Willows End SHST GU47 49 L8 4
The Willows AND SP10 8 E8
RFNM GU10 135 M4
NMIL/BTOS BH25 437 M8
WVILLE PO7 351 J4
Willow Tree Av HORN PO8 352 F6
Willow Tree Gdns
FHAM/STUB PO14 14 C7
Willow Tree Ri BWD BH11 431 M6
Willow Tree Wk ITCH SO19 344 F5
Willow Wy ASHV GU12 113 H8
CHCH/BSGR BH23 449 M3
DEAN RG23 104 C1
FERN BH22 406 B1
FNM GU9 135 G2
HTWY RG27 64 C7
SHST GU47 49 J7
STOK SO20 163 G4
Willow Wood Rd HISD PO11 425 L5 2
Wills Cl WIMB BH21 429 H4
Wills Rd BKME/WDN BH12 446 E3
Wills Wy ROMY SO51 290 F2
Wilmer Rd ELGH SO50 293 M6
Wilmington Cl WEND SO18 319 L5
Wilmot Cl ELGH SO50 294 D3
Wilmott Cl GPORT PO12 18 A2
Wilmott La GPORT PO12 18 A2
Wilmott Wy DEAN RG23 104 C2
Wilmot Wy CBLY GU15 71 J5
Wilmur Crs PLE BH15 445 K2
Wilsom Cl ALTN GU34 176 F5
Wilsom Rd ALTN GU34 177 G5
Wilson Gv SSEA PO5 21 K5
Wilson Rd ASHV GU12 7 M4
BMTH BH1 448 C3
FARN GU14 90 C5 5
NEND PO2 399 G6
PSTN BH14 446 B4
Wilsons Rd BOR GU35 202 E3
Wilson St SHAM SO14 13 L1
Wilton Av WSHM SO15 343 J2
Wilton Cl CHCH/BSGR BH23 434 B7
Wilton Ct FARN GU14 91 G5
Wilton Crs WSHM SO15 318 C7
Wilton Dr HORN PO8 352 E3
Wilton Gdns
NMIL/BTOS BH25 437 K5 5
WSHM SO15 318 C7
Wilton Pl BSTK RG21 4 B8
SSEA PO5 21 H7
Wilton Rd CBLY GU15 70 E5
LTDN BH7 448 E3
WSHM SO15 318 C7
Wilton Ter SSEA PO5 21 J7 3
Wiltshire Av CWTH RG45 49 L2
Wiltshire Gdns
CHCH/BSGR BH23 409 K8
Wiltshire Rd CHCH/BSGR BH23 409 K8
CHFD SO53 293 J5
Wiltshire St SSEA PO5 20 F3
Wilverley Av CHAR BH8 433 K6
HAV PO9 377 L4
Wilverley Pl FAWY SO45 392 C7
Wilverley Rd BROC SO42 387 K7
NMIL/BTOS BH25 411 K5
Wimbledon Cl CBLY GU15 51 J7
Wimbledon Pk Rd SSEA PO5 21 K8
Wimbledon Rd CBLY GU15 51 J7
Wimborne Rd BWD BH11 431 M2
ENEY PO4 423 L4
MOOR/WNTN BH9 432 D4
NBNE BH10 432 E4
PLE BH15 445 H2
TWDS BH3 447 L1
UPTN BH16 428 B4
WCLF BH2 22 F3
WIMB BH21 404 C2
Wimborne Rd East FERN BH22 406 B2
WIMB BH21 405 L2
Wimborne Rd West
WIMB BH21 404 E4
Wimbushes EWKG RG40 48 A2
Wimpole St PSEA PO1 423 H2
Wimpson Gdns ROWN SO16 317 L7
Wimpson La ROWN SO16 317 K8
Wincanton Cl ALTN GU34 176 F6
Wincanton Wy WVILLE PO7 352 F7
Winchcombe Cl FLET GU13 88 F7
Winchcombe Rd BSTK RG21 4 C9
CHAM PO6 374 F7
NWBY RG14 2 F5
Winchester By-pass
RWIN SO21 168 A7
WINC SO23 215 H3
WINC SO23 215 H5
Winchester Gdns AND SP10 9 H9
Winchester Hl ROMY SO51 263 G8
RWIN SO21 168 B5
Winchester Rd ALTN GU34 176 D7
ALTN GU34 197 H5
ASHV GU12 113 K5
BPWT SO32 296 C5
BPWT SO32 321 K5
BSTK RG21 104 F5
CHFD SO53 293 J2
DEAN RG23 126 D4
ELGH SO50 295 H4
KEMP RG22 126 F1
KSCL RG20 79 H1
NALR SO24 217 M3
NEND PO2 399 J8
RFNM GU10 181 L1
NMIL/BTOS BH25 438 A3
PSF GU32 274 A3
RAND SP11 142 F4
RAND SP11 166 B2
ROMY SO51 263 J7 2
ROMY SO51 290 F1
ROWN SO16 317 M7
RWIN SO21 170 A7
RWIN SO21 266 C1
STOK SO20 166 A3
STOK SO20 211 G5
WHAM PO17 348 D3
WHCH RG28 122 B5
Winchester St AND SP10 9 J6
BSTK RG21 4 E9
FARN GU14 90 F8
HEND SO30 321 M8
OVTN RG25 101 G8
WHCH RG28 122 B4
WSHM SO15 343 K2
Winchester Wy BLKW GU17 69 M2 5
TOTT SO40 341 G1 5
Winchfield Cl ITCH SO19 344 E8 5
Winchfield Ct HTWY RG27 87 M7 1
Winchfield Crs HAV PO9 377 G4
Wincombe Dr FERN BH22 406 B4
Windbury Rd ROWN SO16 317 K6
Windermere Av
FHAM/STUB PO14 396 B4
KEMP RG22 103 M6
ROWN SO16 317 J6
Windermere Cl FARN GU14 90 B5 2
Windermere Gdns
NALR SO24 218 C4 5
TOTT SO40 316 D8
Windermere Rd BOR GU35 201 J3
NEND PO2 399 K5
TWDS BH3 447 M2
WEND SO18 320 A7
Windermere Wy FNM GU9 134 D2
STHA RG19 26 D5
Windfield Dr ROMY SO51 263 G8 7
Windham Rd BMTH BH1 23 L2
Winding Wood Dr CBLY GU15 71 L4
Windmill Cl HORN PO8 328 B3
LYMN SO41 454 C3
RGWD BH24 382 B4
Windmill Copse FAWY SO45 367 K7 5
Windmill Cnr THLE RG7 43 K2
Windmill Dr BOR GU35 202 E2
Windmill Fld WVILLE PO7 351 L4
Windmill Flds ALTN GU34 197 G5
Windmill Gv FHAM/PORC PO16 397 M2
Windmill Hl ALTN GU34 176 F6
Windmill La HLER SO31 345 L6
RAND SP11 96 B1
RGWD BH24 382 B4
THLE RG7 28 D3
Windmill Rd ASHV GU12 7 J3
THLE RG7 43 K2
Windover Cl ITCH SO19 345 G2
Windrush Gdns WVILLE PO7 376 B1
Windrush Hts SHST GU47 49 L8 5
Windrush Rd ROWN SO16 317 K7
Windrush Wy FAWY SO45 367 L5
Windsor Cl ALTN GU34 176 C5 5
LYMN SO41 438 C4
RGWD BH24 381 K3
Windsor Ct ELGH SO50 294 C4 2
Windsor Crs FNM GU9 134 E2
Windsor Gdns ASHV GU12 113 J7 2
KEMP RG22 126 F2
Windsor Ga ELGH SO50 293 M2
Windsor Pk ALTN GU34 176 E6
Windsor Ride CBLY GU15 50 D8
EWKG RG40 48 D1
Windsor Ri NWBY RG14 3 J9
Windsor Rd ALTN GU34 197 G4
AND SP10 8 F5
BOSC BH5 448 D4
CHAM PO6 399 K1
CHCH/BSGR BH23 434 C8
FARN GU14 90 A8
FHAM/PORC PO16 398 B1
GPORT PO12 18 D3
BOR GU35 201 L3
NALR SO24 218 B4
PSF GU32 275 L5
PSTN BH14 446 A5
WVILLE PO7 352 B6
Windsor Wk BOR GU35 201 L3
Windsor Wy ALDT GU11 7 G2
FBDG SP6 333 L2
FRIM GU16 71 J8
Windwhistle La RSAL SP5 257 L1
Winfield Wy EMRTH PO10 378 D4 1
Winfrith Crs BKME/WDN BH12 431 J8
Winfrith Wy ROWN SO16 317 J3
Wingate Ct ALDT GU11 6 D1
Wingate Dr ITCH SO19 344 F3
Wingate Rd ODIM RG29 131 J5
TOTT SO40 316 C8
Wingfield Av
CHCH/BSGR BH23 436 B7
PLE BH15 445 J2
Wingfield St PSEA PO1 423 H1
Wingrove Rd TOTT SO40 341 G5 1
Wings Cl FNM GU9 134 E2 5
Wings Rd FNM GU9 134 E2
Winifred Cl ELGH SO50 295 H5 2
Winifred Rd PLE BH15 445 K3
WVILLE PO7 352 C8
Winkfield Rw HORN PO8 352 F3
Winklebury Wy DEAN RG23 104 A3
Winkle St SHAM SO14 12 F7
Winkton Cl CHCH/BSGR BH23 435 G5
HAV PO9 16 B1
Winkworth La THLE RG7 41 M6
Winnall Cl WINC SO23 11 M5
Winnall Manor Rd WINC SO23 11 M7
Winnall Valley Rd WINC SO23 11 L6
Winnards Cl FERN BH22 406 C6
Winnards Pk HLER SO31 370 B5
Winnham Dr
FHAM/PORC PO16 373 L7
Winnington FHAM PO15 372 B4
Winn Rd PTSW SO17 318 F8
Winscombe Av HORN PO8 352 E6
Winsford Av ELGH SO50 294 F7
Winsford Cl ELGH SO50 294 F7 1
Winsford Gdns ELGH SO50 294 F7 2
Winslade Rd WINW SO22 214 B4
HAV PO9 377 H3 5
Winsley Av SBNE BH6 449 H4
Winsor Cl HISD PO11 426 B7
Winsor La TOTT SO40 315 J8

Winsor Rd TOTT SO40 ..... 339 M1
TOTT SO40 ..... 341 L2
Winspit Cl PLE BH15 ..... 444 D5
ROWN SO16 ..... 317 H3
Winstanley Rd NEND PO2 ..... 399 G7
Winston Av BKME/WDN BH12.. 446 F2
TADY RG26 ..... 62 A1
Winston Churchill Av SSEA PO5 .. 21 H3
Winston Cl ELGH SO50 ..... 293 M4
FRIM GU16 ..... 91 J2
HISD PO11 ..... 425 J5
ROWN SO16 ..... 317 G4
Winstone Crs NBAD SO52 ..... 291 M5
Winston Gdns
BKME/WDN BH12 ..... 446 F2
Winston Ri ALTN GU34 ..... 197 G5
Winston Rd MOOR/WNTN BH9 .. 432 E5
Winston Wk RFNM GU10 ..... 158 F2
Winston Wy RGWD BH24 ..... 358 F8
STHA RG19 ..... 26 C4
Winterbourne Rd
CHAM PO6 ..... 374 D7
PLE BH15 ..... 445 J4
ROMY SO51 ..... 263 H7
Winterdyne Ms AND SP10 ..... 8 E6
Winterhayes Cl CFDH BH17 ..... 430 E5
Winterhill Rd CHAM PO6 ..... 375 H5
Winter Rd ENEY PO4 ..... 423 L8
Winters Cl FAWY SO45 ..... 392 B5
Winters Hl BPWT SO32 ..... 296 D8
Winterslow Dr HAV PO9 ..... 377 J2
Winters Rd BPWT SO32 ..... 323 M8
Winterthur Wy BSTK RG21 ..... 4 D7
Winterton Dr NWBY RG14 ..... 25 G3
Winton Cha AND SP10 ..... 119 J8
Winton Cl LYMN SO41 ..... 440 D5
NTID SP9 ..... 114 E4
Winton Crs YTLY GU46 ..... 69 G3
Winton Hl STOK SO20 ..... 186 F5
Winton Rd ALDT GU11 ..... 6 E4
FNM GU9 ..... 135 G4
NEND PO2 ..... 399 K6
PSF GU32 ..... 275 L6
Winton St SHAM SO14 ..... 13 H2
Winton Wy NBNE BH10 ..... 432 B7
NMIL/BTOS BH25 ..... 437 M3
Wiremead La RAND SP11 ..... 140 F2
Wisbech Wy LYMN SO41 ..... 438 D5
Wisborough Rd SSEA PO5 ..... 21 K7
Wise's Firs THLE RG7 ..... 31 G5
Wishanger La BOR GU35 ..... 180 E6
Wishart Gdns
MOOR/WNTN BH9 ..... 432 F3
Wishmoor Cl CBLY GU15 ..... 51 H3
Wishmoor Rd CBLY GU15 ..... 51 H3
Wish Pl SSEA PO5 ..... 21 L7
Wisley Gdns FARN GU14 ..... 90 A6
Wisley Rd AND SP10 ..... 8 C7
Wistaria La YTLY GU46 ..... 68 F3
Wisteria Dr BOR GU35 ..... 201 J6
VWD BH31 ..... 357 G4
Wisteria Gdns HAV PO9 ..... 377 M4
Witan Cl AND SP10 ..... 119 G4
Witan Ct WHCH RG28 ..... 122 A2
Witchampton Cl HAV PO9 ..... 377 L3
Witchampton Rd BDST BH18 ..... 429 K6
Witham Cl CHFD SO53 ..... 292 F2
Witherbed La FHAM PO15 ..... 371 H4
Withermoor Rd
MOOR/WNTN BH9 ..... 432 C8
Wither Ri DEAN RG23 ..... 102 F6
Witherslack Cl BOR GU35 ..... 202 F4
Withies Rd LSOL/BMARY PO13 .. 397 H8
The Withies RSAL SP5 ..... 207 M8
Withingham Rd CCLF BH13 ..... 446 A5
Withybed Wy NTHA RG18 ..... 27 H3
Withy Cl ROMY SO51 ..... 262 E8
Wittensford La LYND SO43 ..... 314 B8
Wittering Rd HISD PO11 ..... 426 D6
ROWN SO16 ..... 317 L3
Wittmead Rd FRIM GU16 ..... 91 M2
Witton Hl NALR SO24 ..... 218 C4
Witt Rd ELGH SO50 ..... 295 H6
RSAL SP5 ..... 207 G2
Witts Hl WEND SO18 ..... 319 M8
Wivelrod Rd ALTN GU34 ..... 175 H4
Wiverley Cl LYMN SO41 ..... 439 M6
Winton Cl WINW SO22 ..... 10 E3
Woburn Av FARN GU14 ..... 91 G4
Woburn Cl ELGH SO50 ..... 293 M2
FRIM GU16 ..... 71 K7
Woburn Rd ROWN SO16 ..... 318 A3
Wode Cl HORN PO8 ..... 328 B5
Wodehouse Rd ITCH SO19 ..... 344 C4
Wokingham Rd CWTH RG45 ..... 49 L5
Woking Rd PSTN BH14 ..... 446 B4
Wolfe Cl WINW SO22 ..... 238 B3
Wolfe Rd ASHV GU12 ..... 7 K3
Wolfmere La LISS GU33 ..... 224 F6
Wolf's La ALTN GU34 ..... 176 D8
Wollaston Rd SBNE BH6 ..... 449 L5
Wollaton Rd FERN BH22 ..... 406 A5
Wolseley Rd ALDT GU11 ..... 6 E1
BKME/WDN BH12 ..... 446 C2
WSHM SO15 ..... 343 G1
Wolsey Wy LYMN SO41 ..... 440 A4
Wolsingham Wy STHA RG19 ..... 27 G6
Wolterton Rd
BKME/WDN BH12 ..... 446 E1
Wolverley Rd ROWN SO16 ..... 318 C1
Wolversdene Cl AND SP10 ..... 9 L7
Wolversdene Gdns AND SP10 ..... 9 K7
Wolverdene Rd AND SP10 ..... 9 K7
AND SP10 ..... 9 M7
Wolverton La TADY RG26 ..... 60 C7
Wolverton Rd HAV PO9 ..... 377 J3
LTDN BH7 ..... 448 E3
SHAM SO14 ..... 13 K1
TADY RG26 ..... 60 B6
Wolverton Wy SHAM SO14 ..... 13 J1
Wolvesey Pl CFDH SO53 ..... 292 F4
Wonston Rd RWIN SO21 ..... 168 C5
Wonston Ct HAV PO9 ..... 377 M2
Wonston La RWIN SO21 ..... 190 B1
Wonston Rd ROWN SO16 ..... 318 A4
Woodacre Gdns FERN BH22 ..... 406 C4
Wood Barn Rd FHAM PO15 ..... 14 A5
Woodberry La EMRTH PO10 ..... 378 D1

HAV PO9 ..... 354 B7
Woodbine Cl SHST GU47 ..... 69 L1
Woodbine La KSCL RG20 ..... 37 J7
Woodbourne FNM GU9 ..... 6 B7
Woodbourne Cl FHAM PO15 ..... 14 A6
LISS GU33 ..... 248 F4
YTLY GU46 ..... 69 G2
Woodbridge Dr CBLY GU15 ..... 71 G1
Woodbridge Rd BLKW GU17 ..... 69 L3
Woodbury Av CHAR BH8 ..... 433 K6
HAV PO9 ..... 16 E7
PSF GU32 ..... 275 K3
Woodbury Cl
CHCH/BSGR BH23 ..... 434 C5
Woodbury Gv HORN PO8 ..... 352 D3
Woodbury Rd KEMP RG22 ..... 127 G5
Wood Cl ITCH SO19 ..... 345 G5
KEMP RG22 ..... 127 G5
Woodcock Cl NTID SP9 ..... 114 E2
Woodcock La LYMN SO41 ..... 438 F5
Woodcocks Crs LTDN BH7 ..... 448 F1
Woodcot Crs HAV PO9 ..... 377 L2
Woodcote Dr UPTN BH16 ..... 444 A2
Woodcote La BPWT SO32 ..... 296 F1
FHAM/STUB PO14 ..... 396 E6
Woodcote Rd MARL SN8 ..... 52 F1
PTSW SO17 ..... 319 H5
Woodcot Gdns FARN GU14 ..... 90 A4
Woodcott Ter ASHV GU12 ..... 7 L5
Woodcroft La HORN PO8 ..... 352 D3
Woodcroft Rd FARN GU10 ..... 158 C3
Wood End CWTH RG45 ..... 49 J4
Woodend Rd FRIM GU16 ..... 91 M1
MOOR/WNTN BH9 ..... 447 K1
Wood End Rd RGWD BH24 ..... 383 J3
Wood End Wy NBAD SO52 ..... 291 F1
Wooden House La LYMN SO41 .. 414 F6
Wooderson Cl ELGH SO50 ..... 295 G5
Woodfern FBDG SP6 ..... 310 C6
Woodfield BOR GU35 ..... 179 G7
Woodfield Av CHAM PO6 ..... 376 C7
Woodfield Dr WINW SO22 ..... 238 A2
Woodfield Gdns
CHCH/BSGR BH23 ..... 436 B7
Woodfield Park Rd
EMRTH PO10 ..... 378 F7
Woodfield Rd BWD BH11 ..... 431 L3
Woodford Cl RGWD BH24 ..... 382 F1
Woodford Rd BMTH BH1 ..... 23 L4
Woodgarston Dr KEMP RG22 ..... 126 F1
Woodgason La HISD PO11 ..... 402 A7
Woodgate FARN GU14 ..... 89 H5
Wood Glade Cl TOTT SO40 ..... 342 D7
Woodgreen Av HAV PO9 ..... 16 B2
Woodgreen Dr BWD BH11 ..... 431 H4
Woodgreen Rd WINW SO22 ..... 214 C4
Woodhall Wy FHAM PO15 ..... 14 D1
Woodhayes Av
CHCH/BSGR BH23 ..... 436 C6
Wood Hill La ODIM RG29 ..... 131 J4
Woodhouse La HAV PO9 ..... 354 A4
HEND SO30 ..... 321 K8
HORN PO8 ..... 353 L2
STHA RG19 ..... 40 B5
Woodhouse Rd HORN PO8 ..... 353 K1
Woodington Cl HAV PO9 ..... 377 L2
Woodington Rd ROMY SO51 .. 289 H4
Woodland Av BOSC BH5 ..... 448 F4
Woodland Cl ROMY SO51 ..... 289 G6
WEND SO18 ..... 345 H1
Woodland Dr RFNM GU10 ..... 158 C2
Woodland Dro RWIN SO21 ..... 266 F5
Woodland Ms HEND SO30 ..... 320 C7
Woodland Ri FLET GU13 ..... 110 D3
Woodlands CHAM RG24 ..... 83 M4
Woodlands Av
RSAL SP5 ..... 206 E1
TADY RG26 ..... 64 A6
Woodlands Cl ASHV GU12 .. 113 K3
CHFD SO53 ..... 265 J6
FARN GU14 ..... 70 B7
FAWY SO45 ..... 367 J7
HLER SO31 ..... 370 D2
LSOL/BMARY PO13 ..... 421 G2
SHST GU47 ..... 50 C7
Woodlands Crs PLE BH15 ..... 444 E5
Woodlands Dr HLER SO31 ..... 369 H2
Woodlands Dro TOTT SO40 ..... 340 D5
Woodlands Gdns WVILLE PO7 .. 376 B3
Woodlands La HASM GU27 ..... 228 C1
HISD PO11 ..... 425 J3
LISS GU33 ..... 249 G6
RCCH PO18 ..... 355 J4
Woodlands Rd BROC SO42 ..... 413 K1
CBLY GU15 ..... 70 E3
FARN GU14 ..... 90 A2
NMIL/BTOS BH25 ..... 452 D1
TADY RG26 ..... 41 G7
TOTT SO40 ..... 340 C7
The Woodlands BOR GU35 ..... 201 J7
WINC SO23 ..... 215 H2
Woodland St PSEA PO1 ..... 423 J2
Woodlands Wk FARN GU14 ..... 70 B7
Woodlands Wy AND SP10 ..... 9 L5
HAV PO9 ..... 377 K4
HLER SO31 ..... 345 K8
NBAD SO52 ..... 291 K4
NMIL/BTOS BH25 ..... 437 M2
RGWD BH24 ..... 381 K4
WSHM SO15 ..... 318 E8
Woodland Vw HLER SO31 ..... 345 K8
HORN PO8 ..... 352 D2
FERN BH22 ..... 406 D1
Woodland Wy
CHCH/BSGR BH23 ..... 436 B8

LYMN SO41 ..... 454 B4
Wood La BWD BH11 ..... 431 J2
FARN GU14 ..... 90 D5
FLET GU13 ..... 89 H7
HTWY RG27 ..... 107 H3
LYMN SO41 ..... 454 B4
NALR SO24 ..... 243 J3
RFNM GU10 ..... 136 C4
THLE RG7 ..... 45 H3
WHAM PO17 ..... 374 E1
Woodlane Cl NALR SO24 ..... 243 J3
Woodlark Gdns EPSF SO31 ..... 276 B5
Wood Lawn Cl
NMIL/BTOS BH25 ..... 437 K8
Woodlea Cl WINW SO22 ..... 10 C2
Woodlea Gdns HEND SO30 ..... 320 D7
Woodlea Wy ROMY SO51 ..... 264 E6
Woodleaze Cl BDST BH18 ..... 429 M2
Woodleigh FLET GU13 ..... 88 F8
Woodleigh Cl HAV PO9 ..... 378 A5
Woodley Cl ROMY SO51 ..... 263 H6
Woodley Gdns LYMN SO41 ..... 440 B3
Woodley La ROMY SO51 ..... 262 F7
Woodley Rd GPORT PO12 ..... 19 G5
ITCH SO19 ..... 344 B5
Woodley Wy ROMY SO51 ..... 263 H6
Woodling Crs FBDG SP6 ..... 310 C6
Woodlinken Cl VWD BH31 ..... 356 F4
Woodlinken Dr VWD BH31 ..... 356 F4
Woodlinken Wy VWD BH31 ..... 356 F4
Wood Ldg TOTT SO40 ..... 316 A7
Woodman Dr RWIN SO21 ..... 213 J6
Woodmancote La
EMRTH PO10 ..... 379 J4
Woodmancote Rd ENEY PO4 .... 423 L4
Woodman La RWIN SO21 ..... 213 K5
Woodmere Cft BPWT SO32 ..... 126 E1
Woodmill La WEND SO18 ..... 319 J5
Wood Moor EWKG RG40 ..... 48 C6
Woodmoor Cl TOTT SO40 ..... 342 E7
Woodpath SSEA PO5 ..... 21 H6
Woodpecker Cl HAV PO9 ..... 17 J4
KEMP RG22 ..... 103 L8
BOR GU35 ..... 201 J6
RFNM GU10 ..... 111 G8
VWD BH31 ..... 356 D3
Woodpecker Copse
HLER SO31 ..... 370 F5
Woodpecker Dr CFDH BH17 ..... 429 J8
WINW SO22 ..... 214 B6
TOTT SO40 ..... 342 C7
Woodpecker Wy ELGH SO50 ..... 293 C7
Wood Rdg NWBY RG14 ..... 37 H1
Wood Rd CBLY GU15 ..... 70 E7
FNM GU9 ..... 134 F1
CSHT GU26 ..... 204 A2
TOTT SO40 ..... 340 F6
Woodroffe Dr KEMP RG22 ..... 104 B7
Woodrow WVILLE PO7 ..... 351 J4
Woodrush Crs HLER SO31 ..... 370 C6
Woodsedge WVILLE PO7 ..... 376 E3
Woodside BLKW GU17 ..... 69 M5
CBLY GU15 ..... 70 C1
NWBY RG14 ..... 37 G1
LSOL/BMARY PO13 ..... 396 F5
ROWN SO16 ..... 292 D6
Woodside Av ELGH SO50 ..... 293 L3
LYMN SO41 ..... 440 C7
Woodside Cl FERN BH22 ..... 406 C2
BOR GU35 ..... 201 J5
THLE RG7 ..... 27 M3
THLE RG7 ..... 43 K2
TOTT SO40 ..... 342 C7
Woodside Crs BOR GU35 ..... 201 J5
ROWN SO16 ..... 292 C6
Woodside Gdns CHAM RG24 ..... 83 L4
FLET GU13 ..... 89 H6
TOTT SO40 ..... 341 G6
Woodside La ALTN GU34 ..... 197 M4
LYMN SO41 ..... 440 C6
Woodside Pk BOR GU35 ..... 201 J5
Woodside Rd ALDT GU11 ..... 112 C1
BOSC BH5 ..... 449 G4
ELGH SO50 ..... 293 K4
FERN BH22 ..... 406 C2
FNM GU9 ..... 6 A8
NBAD SO52 ..... 291 L4
PSTN BH14 ..... 446 B5
PTSW SO17 ..... 319 G8
Woodside Wy HEND SO30 ..... 345 L3
Woods La OVTN RG25 ..... 127 L1
Woodstock Av HORN PO8 ..... 352 E5
Woodstock Cl FHAM PO15 ..... 14 C1
HEND SO30 ..... 346 B3
Woodstock Dr PTSW SO17 ..... 318 F7
Woodstock La RGWD BH24 ..... 382 E2
Woodstock Rd GPORT PO12 ..... 19 G4
HAV PO9 ..... 377 G6
Woodstocks FARN GU14 ..... 90 F2
Wood St ASHV GU12 ..... 113 K2
Woods View Rd
MOOR/WNTN BH9 ..... 432 B8
Woodthorpe Gdns HLER SO31 .. 370 D2
Woodvale FHAM PO15 ..... 14 A4
Woodvale Gdns
NMIL/BTOS BH25 ..... 438 A4
Woodview Cl ROWN SO16 ..... 318 F2
Woodville Cl BLKW GU17 ..... 69 L3
Woodville Dr PSEA PO1 ..... 20 E5
Woodville Rd FAWY SO45 ..... 392 F5
HAV PO9 ..... 376 F6
Woodward Cl GPORT PO12 ..... 18 A4
Woodway CBLY GU15 ..... 70 E3
Woofferton Rd CHAM PO6 ..... 374 E7
Woolbeding La MIDH GU29 ..... 279 L5
Wooldridge Crs ODIM RG29 .. 108 B8
Woolfield La ALTN GU34 ..... 246 A1
PSF GU32 ..... 275 H8
Woolford Cl WINW SO22 ..... 238 B2
Woolford Wy DEAN RG23 ..... 104 C2
Wool Gv AND SP10 ..... 9 L6
Woolhampton Hl THLE RG7 ..... 28 F6
Woollards Rd ASHV GU12 ..... 113 K4
Woolmead Rd FNM GU9 ..... 5 J3
Woolmer Ct HAV PO9 ..... 377 M3
Woolmer Hill Rd HASM GU27.... 227 M1
Woolmer La LIPH GU30 ..... 202 F8

RGWD BH24 ..... 358 D6
Woolmer Rd LISS GU33 ..... 225 G5
Woolmer St EMRTH PO10 ..... 378 C4
Woolner Av CHAM PO6 ..... 375 L8
PSF GU32 ..... 275 L4
Wool Rd BKME/WDN BH12 ..... 430 F8
Wools Br RGWD BH24 ..... 381 J4
Woolsbridge Rd RGWD BH24 .. 381 G2
Woolslope Cl FERN BH22 ..... 380 C7
Woolslope Gdns FERN BH22 .. 380 D7
Woolslope Rd FERN BH22 ..... 380 D7
Wootton HAV PO9 ..... 377 G2
HLER SO31 ..... 344 F8
Wootton Farm Rd
NMIL/BTOS BH25 ..... 411 J6
Wootton Gdns BMTH BH1 ..... 23 G5
HLER SO31 ..... 344 F8
Wootton Mt BMTH BH1 ..... 23 H5
Wootton Rough
NMIL/BTOS BH25 ..... 411 M8
Wootton St HAV PO9 ..... 399 K1
Worbarrow Gdns
BKME/WDN BH12 ..... 431 G8
Worcester Av KEMP RG22 ..... 104 A8
Worcester Pl FARN GU14 ..... 90 E1
Worcester Pl ITCH SO19 ..... 344 F6
LYMN SO41 ..... 440 D6
Wordsworth Av CHAM PO6 ..... 374 C7
CHAR BH8 ..... 433 J7
YTLY GU46 ..... 68 E4
Wordsworth Cl BPWT SO32 ..... 297 K8
CHAM RG24 ..... 5 G1
WINW SO22 ..... 10 B6
Wordsworth Pl HLER SO31 ..... 346 F7
Wordsworth Rd NTHA RG18 ..... 26 F4
ROWN SO16 ..... 318 D7
Worgret Rd PLE BH15 ..... 445 K1
Workhouse La PSF GU32 ..... 273 J7
Workman's La HLER SO31 ..... 394 C3
Workshop Rd WVILLE PO7 ..... 374 E6
Worldham Hl ALTN GU34 ..... 177 M7
Worrell Dr BKME/WDN BH12 ..... 431 G8
Worrell Dr HAV PO9 ..... 377 M2
Wormersley Rd STHA RG19 ..... 38 A1
Worsley Rd FRIM GU16 ..... 91 J1
SSEA PO5 ..... 21 H6
Worsley St ENEY PO4 ..... 423 L6
Worthing Av GPORT PO12 ..... 397 K8
Worthing Rd SSEA PO5 ..... 21 K8
Worthington Crs PSTN BH14 .... 445 M5
Worthy Ct HAV PO9 ..... 377 M3
Worthy La WINC SO23 ..... 2 E3
Worthy Rd NMIL/BTOS BH25 .. 437 L5
WINC SO23 ..... 11 G3
Worting Rd BSTK RG21 ..... 4 B9
DEAN RG23 ..... 103 K4
KEMP RG22 ..... 103 M7
Wortley Rd CHCH/BSGR BH23 .. 451 M1
Wote St BSTK RG21 ..... 4 F9
Wouldham Cl RAND SP11 ..... 115 J1
Wraxhall Cl CFDH BH17 ..... 430 B7
Wraysbury Park Dr
EMRTH PO10 ..... 378 D4
Wrecclesham Hl RFNM GU10 .. 158 D4
Wrecclesham Rd FNM GU9 ..... 158 E2
Wrekin Cl KEMP RG22 ..... 104 A5
The Wrekin FARN GU14 ..... 91 H7
Wren Cl ALTN GU34 ..... 176 F5
CHCH/BSGR BH23 ..... 451 G3
WINW SO22 ..... 238 C3
NMIL/BTOS BH25 ..... 457 K6
RGWD BH24 ..... 383 G2
THLE RG7 ..... 31 G3
YTLY GU46 ..... 68 E2
Wren Crs BKME/WDN BH12 ..... 447 G3
Wren Gdns FBDG SP6 ..... 333 M2
Wren Rd ELGH SO50 ..... 293 K4
Wren Wy FARN GU14 ..... 90 C1
FHAM/PORC PO16 ..... 373 K8
Wrexham Gr HORN PO8 ..... 328 A6
Wrights Cl RWIN SO21 ..... 190 C4
Wright's Hl ITCH SO19 ..... 344 E6
Wrights Wy RWIN SO21 ..... 190 C4
Wroxham Rd
BKME/WDN BH12 ..... 446 E3
Wryneck Cl ROWN SO16 ..... 318 A2
Wurford Dr STHA RG19 ..... 27 J5
Wyatts Cl WIMB BH21 ..... 429 H2
Wyatts La WIMB BH21 ..... 429 G2
Wyborn Cl HISD PO11 ..... 425 L6
Wych La LSOL/BMARY PO13 ..... 396 F4
WCLF BH2 ..... 22 D3
Wychwood Cl ASHV GU12 ..... 113 K2
WCLF BH2 ..... 22 E2
Wychwood Dr FAWY SO45 ..... 418 C1
Wychwood Gv CHFD SO53 ..... 265 K8
Wyck La ALTN GU34 ..... 177 M6
Wycliffe Rd MOOR/WNTN BH9 .. 432 D8
WEND SO18 ..... 319 M7
Wycote Rd LSOL/BMARY PO13 .. 396 F4
Wye Ct AND SP10 ..... 9 M1
Wyeford Cl HAV PO9 ..... 377 M2
Wyelands Av WIMB BH21 ..... 405 H3
Wykeham Cl ROWN SO16 ..... 318 D4
Wykeham Ct ODIM RG29 ..... 108 C8
Wykeham Dr DEAN RG23 ..... 103 M4
Wykeham Fld WHAM PO17 ..... 348 C5
Wykeham Pl WINW SO22 ..... 238 C3
LYMN SO41 ..... 440 D6
Wykeham Rd FNM GU9 ..... 134 F5
HLER SO31 ..... 368 F2
NEND PO2 ..... 399 J7
Wykwood LIPH GU30 ..... 227 G4
Wylde Green La LISS GU33 ..... 248 F3
Wylds La PSF GU32 ..... 275 H8
Wyllie Rd NEND PO2 ..... 399 H4
Wylie Rd WEND SO18 ..... 320 B6
Wylye Rd NTID SP9 ..... 114 E1
Wymering Ct FARN GU14 ..... 91 G5
Wymering La CHAM PO6 ..... 375 J8

Wymering Manor Cl
CHAM PO6 ..... 375 J8
Wymering Rd NEND PO2 ..... 399 J8
Wyncombe Rd BOSC BH5 ..... 449 G3
Wyndcliffe Rd ENEY PO4 ..... 21 M6
Wyndham Cl
CHCH/BSGR BH23 ..... 436 F6
HORN PO8 ..... 352 F4
YTLY GU46 ..... 69 G1
Wyndham Ms PSEA PO1 ..... 20 D5
Wyndham Pl WSHM SO15 ..... 12 D1
Wyndham Rd AND SP10 ..... 8 D8
CHCH/BSGR BH23 ..... 436 F6
NWBY RG14 ..... 26 A3
PSTN BH14 ..... 446 A5
Wyndham St ASHV GU12 ..... 7 J3
Wynfields FRIM GU16 ..... 91 J5
Wynford Rd MOOR/WNTN BH9 .. 432 C5
PSTN BH14 ..... 446 B5
Wynne Cl BDST BH18 ..... 429 K4
Wynne Gdns FLET GU13 ..... 111 G3
Wynter Cl LTDN BH7 ..... 448 E1
Wynter Rd WEND SO18 ..... 320 A8
Wynton Wy FHAM PO15 ..... 372 A5
Wynyards Gap NBAD SO52 ..... 291 L4
Wyre Cl CHFD SO53 ..... 293 G2
Wyvern Cl ASHV GU12 ..... 113 J3
BKME/WDN BH12 ..... 446 C1
CHFD SO53 ..... 293 J2

Y

Yaldhurst Ct HAV PO9 ..... 377 M2
Yaldhurst La LYMN SO41 ..... 439 M4
Yale Cl SHST GU47 ..... 50 C6
Yapton St PSEA PO1 ..... 21 G1
Yarborough Rd SSEA PO5 ..... 21 G4
Yardlea Cl HAV PO9 ..... 353 M7
Yardley Cl HSEA PO3 ..... 400 A4
Yardley Rd HEND SO30 ..... 345 M3
Yarmley La RSAL SP5 ..... 206 D2
Yarmouth Gdns WSHM SO15 ..... 318 A7
Yarmouth Rd
BKME/WDN BH12 ..... 446 E2
Yarnhams Cl ALTN GU34 ..... 197 G6
Yarrell Md LYMN SO41 ..... 439 M4
Yarrells Cl UPTN BH16 ..... 444 E5
Yarrells La UPTN BH16 ..... 444 B2
Yarrow Cl CHCH/BSGR BH23 ..... 435 M8
Yarrow Rd BKME/WDN BH12 ..... 430 E8
Yarrow Wy HLER SO31 ..... 370 C6
Yateley Cl HAV PO9 ..... 377 G3
Yateley Rd YTLY GU46 ..... 69 J1
Yatesbury Cl FNM GU9 ..... 158 C1
Yates Copse NTHA RG18 ..... 26 B3
Yaverland HLER SO31 ..... 369 G2
Yeatminster Rd CFDH BH17 ..... 430 D6
Yellowhammer Rd
KEMP RG22 ..... 126 E2
Yellowhammers ALTN GU34 ..... 176 E2
Yelverton Av FAWY SO45 ..... 367 L7
Yelverton Rd WCLF BH2 ..... 22 E5
Yeo Ct ENEY PO4 ..... 424 A5
Yeomans HTWY RG27 ..... 68 B1
Yeomans Cl FARN GU14 ..... 90 D3
RFNM GU10 ..... 113 J8
Yeomans Fld RCCH PO18 ..... 379 M7
Yeomans La KSCL RG20 ..... 37 K7
LIPH GU30 ..... 226 D4
Yeomans Pl BOR GU35 ..... 202 B3
Yeomans Rd CHAR BH8 ..... 433 J5
Yeomans Wy CBLY GU15 ..... 71 H3
CHAR BH8 ..... 433 J5
TOTT SO40 ..... 316 E8
Yeovil Cha WEND SO18 ..... 320 A8
Yeovil Cl FARN GU14 ..... 91 G7
Yeovil Rd SHST GU47 ..... 50 B7
Yeovilton Cl LYMN SO41 ..... 439 J7
Yerville Gdns LYMN SO41 ..... 438 D5
Yetminster Rd FARN GU14 ..... 91 G7
Yew Cl KSCL RG20 ..... 59 K6
Yew Ga NWBY RG14 ..... 25 J3
Yew La NMIL/BTOS BH25 ..... 438 A4
Yew Rd WEND SO18 ..... 319 M8
Yewside LSOL/BMARY PO13 ..... 397 J7
The Yews HORN PO8 ..... 353 H1
Yewtree Cl FAWY SO45 ..... 367 L8
Yew Tree Cl DEAN RG23 ..... 103 G8
ELGH SO50 ..... 295 H5
FARN GU14 ..... 89 M5
HEND SO30 ..... 345 M2
RAND SP11 ..... 142 F7
RSAL SP5 ..... 206 E2
TADY RG26 ..... 65 M6
WIMB BH21 ..... 404 A3
Yew Tree Dr FHAM PO15 ..... 347 G8
HLER SO31 ..... 370 F1
Yew Tree Gdns WVILLE PO7 ..... 351 J4
Yew Tree La OVTN RG25 ..... 125 K7
RSAL SP5 ..... 208 A5
Yewtree La ROWN SO16 ..... 317 H5
Yew Tree Pl LISS GU33 ..... 248 F4
Yew Tree Rd HISD PO11 ..... 401 L8
Yew Tree Wk FRIM GU16 ..... 71 H7
Yoells Crs HORN PO8 ..... 352 D2
Yoells La HORN PO8 ..... 352 D2
Yokesford Hl ROMY SO51 ..... 262 D3
Yolland Cl FNM GU9 ..... 134 F1
Yonge Cl ELGH SO50 ..... 294 A5
York Av NMIL/BTOS BH25 ..... 437 M5
York Buildings SHAM SO14 ..... 13 G4
York Cl CHCH/BSGR BH23 ..... 449 L1
ELGH SO50 ..... 321 J1
KEMP RG22 ..... 104 A8
BOR GU35 ..... 201 J6
NBAD SO52 ..... 292 E4
NWBY RG14 ..... 3 G6
PSF GU32 ..... 275 J5
SHAM SO14 ..... 344 A2
TOTT SO40 ..... 316 F8
York Crs ALDT GU11 ..... 6 D4
LSOL/BMARY PO13 ..... 420 E4
York Dro RSAL SP5 ..... 287 H8
WEND SO18 ..... 344 F1
Yorke St SSEA PO5 ..... 20 F4
Yorke Wy HLER SO31 ..... 369 J5

York Gdns *FHAM/PORC* PO16 .... 398 B2
York La *HTWY* RG27 .... 87 H3
York Ms *ALTN* GU34 .... 176 F4
York Pl *CBLY* GU15 .... 71 G1
   LTDN BH7 .... 448 F3
   PSEA PO1 .... 422 F2
York Rd *ALDT* GU11 .... 6 D4
   ASHV GU12 .... 113 K5
   BMTH BH1 .... 23 K4

CBLY GU15 .... 71 G1
CFDH BH17 .... 429 L7
ELGH SO50 .... 293 M7
FARN GU14 .... 90 F7
FNM GU9 .... 134 F8
NWBY RG14 .... 3 G6
WSHM SO15 .... 343 G1
Yorktown Rd *SHST* GU47 .... 69 M1
York Wy *SHST* GU47 .... 49 K8

Yorkwood *LISS* GU33 .... 248 E4
Youlden Cl *CBLY* GU15 .... 71 K3
Youlden Dr *CBLY* GU15 .... 71 K3
Young Crs *STHA* RG19 .... 3 M9
Youngs Dr *ASHV* GU12 .... 113 J6
Youngs Paddock *RSAL* SP5 .. 206 F2 E1
Youngs Rd *ALTN* GU34 .... 176 E4
   BWD BH11 .... 431 L3
Yves Ms *SSEA* PO5 .... 21 J7 E1

Z

Zamek Cl *BWD* BH11 .... 431 L3
Zetland Rd *CHAM* PO6 .... 400 B1
   GPORT PO12 .... 18 E2
Zeus La *WVILLE* PO7 .... 376 D5
Zinnia Cl *KEMP* RG22 .... 126 F2
   NBNE BH10 .... 432 C6

Zion Rd *RAND* SP11 .... 161 J3
Zouch Av *NTID* SP9 .... 114 D1
Zouch Cl *NTID* SP9 .... 114 D1
Zouch Farm Rd *NTID* SP9 ... 114 D1

Index - featured places

The AA - Fanum House
   BSTK RG21 .... 5 K6
Abbey Business Park
   FNM GU9 .... 135 K8
Abbey Chiropractic Clinic
   ROMY SO51 .... 290 D1
Abbey Mead Surgery
   ROMY SO51 .... 290 C1
The Abbey School
   FNM GU9 .... 135 G7
Abbotsford Farm
   Business Centre
   ALTN GU34 .... 197 J5
Abbotswood Junior School
   TOTT SO40 .... 341 H1
Abbotts Ann Primary School
   RAND SP11 .... 141 L4
ABC Cinema
   BMTH BH1 .... 22 F6
Abraham Gallery
   SSEA PO5 .... 21 H6
Abro Industrial Estate
   ALDT GU11 .... 113 G5
Acorn Business Centre
   CHAM PO6 .... 375 H8
Ad Astra County First School
   CFDH BH17 .... 430 C7
Adelaide Medical Centre
   AND SP10 .... 9 K5
Adeline Road Surgery
   BOSC BH5 .... 448 D4
Admiral Lord Nelson School
   HSEA PO3 .... 399 M7
AFC Newbury
   Football Ground
   NWBY RG14 .... 3 G3
Airborne Forces Museum
   ALDT GU11 .... 112 D3
Albany Business Centre
   WHAM PO17 .... 372 F1
Alderman Quilley
   Secondary School
   ELGH SO50 .... 293 L7
Aldermaston C of E School
   THLE RG7 .... 41 J1
Aldermoor Health Centre
   ROWN SO16 .... 318 B4
Alderney Middle School
   BKME/WDN BH12 .... 431 H7
Aldershot & Farnham
   County Court
   ALDT GU11 .... 7 G2
Aldershot Health Centre
   ALDT GU11 .... 6 D1
Aldershot Military
   Historical Trust & Museum
   ALDT GU11 .... 112 F1
Aldershot Town Football Club
   ALDT GU11 .... 7 H2
Alexander House
   Business Centre
   ALDT GU11 .... 7 G2
Alexandra Surgery
   ALDT GU11 .... 6 D1
Allen Gallery
   ALTN GU34 .... 176 E5
All Hallows RC
   Secondary School
   FNM GU9 .... 6 C8
Allington Manor
   Business Centre
   ELGH SO50 .... 320 D1
All Saints C of E
   First School
   NFNM GU10 .... 159 M5
All Saints C of E Junior School
   FLET GU13 .... 88 C8
All Saints C of E
   Primary School
   RSAL SP5 .... 258 G5
All Saints Community
   Primary School
   WINC SO23 .... 239 G2
Alma Road Surgery
   PTSW SO17 .... 318 F8
Alma Road Surgery
   ROMY SO51 .... 290 E1
The Alpha Business Park
   SHAM SO14 .... 343 M1
Alresford County
   Junior School
   NARL SO24 .... 218 C3
Alresford Golf Club
   NARL SO24 .... 218 B5
The Alresford Surgery
   NARL SO24 .... 218 C2
Alton Business Centre
   ALTN GU34 .... 177 G5
Alton College
   ALTN GU34 .... 176 E3
Alton Convent School
   ALTN GU34 .... 176 F2
Alton County Infant School
   ALTN GU34 .... 176 F4
Alton Health Centre
   ALTN GU34 .... 176 F4
Alton Rugby Club
   ALTN GU34 .... 176 F2
Alton Town Football Club
   ALTN GU34 .... 176 F3

Alverstoke C of E
   Junior School
   GPORT PO12 .... 18 C6
Alverstoke County
   Infant School
   GPORT PO12 .... 18 C8
Amery Hill Secondary School
   ALTN GU34 .... 176 E4
Amesbury School
   GSHT GU26 .... 204 B7
Amey Industrial Estate
   PSF GU32 .... 275 K5
A M F Bowling
   ITCH SO19 .... 344 M1
A M F Bowling
   PSEA PO1 .... 21 H1
Ampfield Primary School
   ROMY SO51 .... 264 B4
Amport C of E (aided)
   Primary School
   RAND SP11 .... 140 F3
Anchor Business Centre
   CHFD SO53 .... 293 G2
Andover Football Club
   AND SP10 .... 118 B6
Andover Golf Club
   AND SP10 .... 9 H9
Andover Museum & the
   Museum of the Iron Age
   AND SP10 .... 9 J4
Andover Road Retail Park
   FUFL SO22 .... 10 E5
The Andrew Isaacs Practice
   BMTH BH1 .... 23 J4
Andrews Endowed
   Primary School
   ALTN GU34 .... 177 H2
Anne Dale County Junior &
   Infant School
   FHAM/STUB PO14 .... 396 A6
Anstey County Junior School
   ALTN GU34 .... 176 E4
Anton County Infant School
   AND SP10 .... 9 G9
Anton County Junior School
   AND SP10 .... 9 G9
Anton Trading Estate
   AND SP10 .... 9 G8
The Anvil Concert Hall
   BSTK RG21 .... 4 E7
Apple Industrial Estate
   FHAM PO15 .... 371 G3
Applemore College
   FAWY SO45 .... 367 G6
Applemore Recreation Centre
   FAWY SO45 .... 367 G5
Appleshaw School
   RAND SP11 .... 117 G1
Arch Farm Industrial Estate
   FBDG SP6 .... 309 K5
Arena Leisure Centre
   CBLY GU15 .... 70 E2
The Ark School
   THLE RG7 .... 30 C7
Army Golf Club
   ALDT GU11 .... 112 B2
The Arnewood Practice
   NMIL/BTOS BH25 .... 437 L5
Arnwood School
   NMIL/BTOS BH25 .... 437 K7
Arnhem Barracks
   ALDT GU11 .... 112 D5
Arrow Industrial Estate
   FARN GU14 .... 90 C2
The Art Gallery
   EMRTH PO10 .... 378 F4
Art Space School
   PSEA PO1 .... 423 G1
Arundel Court Junior &
   Infant School
   PSEA PO1 .... 423 H2
Ashdown Family &
   Health Centre
   NTID SP9 .... 114 E2
Ashdown School
   CFDH BH17 .... 430 C7
Ashford Hill Primary School
   STHA RG19 .... 40 B7
Ash Grange CP School
   ASHV GU12 .... 113 G6
Ashley County Infant School
   NMIL/BTOS BH25 .... 438 B5
Ashley Heath Industrial Estate
   WIMB BH21 .... 381 G1
Ashley Junior School
   NMIL/BTOS BH25 .... 438 A5
Ash Manor School
   ASHV GU12 .... 113 J8
Ashurst Hospital
   TOTT SO40 .... 340 F7
Ash Vale Health Centre
   ASHV GU12 .... 113 L4
Associated Football Club
   TOTT SO40 .... 316 F8
Atherley House Surgery
   WSHM SO15 .... 343 H2
The Atherley School
   ROWN SO16 .... 317 G2
Avenue Clinic
   WSHM SO15 .... 343 K2
Avenue Shopping Centre
   WCLF BH2 .... 22 D5

Avington Park
   RWIN SO21 .... 216 D3
Avonbourne Girls School
   LTDN BH7 .... 448 F1
Avon Castle
   RGWD BH24 .... 382 B5
Avonlea Preparatory School
   RGWD BH24 .... 358 F8
Awbridge County School
   ROMY SO51 .... 261 J3
Baddesley Park
   Industrial Estate
   NBAD SO52 .... 292 A4
Baden Powell &
   St Peters C of E (VC) School
   PSTN BH14 .... 446 A5
Badger Farm Surgery
   FUFL SO22 .... 238 B4
Badgerswood Surgery
   LIND GU35 .... 202 A3
Badshot Lea County
   First School
   FNM GU9 .... 135 K2
Balksbury County
   Infant School
   AND SP10 .... 8 B7
Balksbury Industrial Estate
   RAND SP11 .... 142 D3
Ballard College
   NMIL/BTOS BH25 .... 437 L5
Ballard Lake
   Preparatory School
   NMIL/BTOS BH25 .... 437 L4
Banister School
   WSHM SO15 .... 343 K1
Bargate Museum
   SHAM SO14 .... 13 G4
Bargate Shopping Centre
   SHAM SO14 .... 13 G4
Barncroft Infant School
   HAV PO9 .... 377 H4
Barncroft Junior School
   HAV PO9 .... 377 G4
Barratt Industrial Park
   FHAM PO15 .... 371 G3
Bartley C of E Middle School
   TOTT SO40 .... 339 M1
Bartley Wood Business Park
   HTWY RG27 .... 86 B8
Barton Industrial Estate
   NARL SO24 .... 173 L7
Barton Peveril College
   ELGH SO50 .... 293 L7
Barton Stacey C of E
   Primary School
   RWIN SO21 .... 145 K8
Barton Surgery
   NMIL/BTOS BH25 .... 437 L7
Basing County Infants School
   CHAM RG24 .... 106 A2
Basingstoke Business Centre
   KEMP RG22 .... 104 D6
Basingstoke College of
   Technology
   BSTK RG21 .... 4 C8
Basingstoke County Court
   BSTK RG21 .... 5 H7
Basingstoke &
   Deane Borough Council
   CHAM RG24 .... 5 L2
Basingstoke Ice Rink
   KEMP RG22 .... 104 C3
Basingstoke &
   North Hants Cricket Club
   BSTK RG21 .... 105 G5
Basingstoke Rugby Club
   KEMP RG22 .... 104 A7
Basingstoke Sports Centre
   BSTK RG21 .... 4 E7
Basingstoke Town
   Football Club
   KEMP RG22 .... 104 D6
Bassett Green Junior School
   ROWN SO16 .... 319 G4
Baycroft School
   FHAM/STUB PO14 .... 396 B6
Bay House School
   GPORT PO12 .... 421 J6
Baytree Gallery
   NARL SO24 .... 218 B2
BBC South TV & Radio Solent
   WSHM SO15 .... 12 E1
Beacon Hill County
   Primary School
   GSHT GU26 .... 203 M2
The Bear Museum
   EPSF GU31 .... 275 L6
Bearwood County
   Primary School
   WIMB BH21 .... 431 H4
Beaucroft School
   WIMB BH21 .... 404 C7
Beaufort Road Surgery
   SBNE BH6 .... 449 H3
Beaulieu CP School
   BROC SO42 .... 390 D7
Beaumont County
   Junior School
   ALDT GU11 .... 6 C2
Beaver Industrial Estate
   LIPH GU30 .... 226 F5

Bedales School
   PSF GU32 .... 275 K1
Bedenham County Junior &
   Infant School
   LSOL/BMARY PO13 .... 397 H5
Beech Down County
   Primary School
   KEMP RG22 .... 104 C8
Beechnut Industrial Estate
   ALDT GU11 .... 7 H3
Beechwood Middle School
   WEND SO18 .... 344 D1
Belbins Business Park
   ROMY SO51 .... 262 F5
Belgrave Industrial Estate
   PTSW SO17 .... 319 H6
Bellemoor Secondary School
   ROWN SO16 .... 318 C6
Belle Vue County
   Infant School
   ASHV GU12 .... 7 L2
Benham Park
   KSCL RG20 .... 24 D4
Berkshire Business Centre
   STHA RG19 .... 27 K6
Berkshire County Council
   NWBY RG14 .... 2 B8
Berkshire County Council
   NWBY RG14 .... 2 D3
Berkshire County Council
   NWBY RG14 .... 2 E7
Berrywood Primary School
   HEND SO30 .... 321 J7
Bethany C of E (VA)
   Junior School
   BMTH BH1 .... 448 C3
Bevois Town Primary School
   SHAM SO14 .... 343 L1
Bicknell Boys
   Residential School
   LTDN BH7 .... 448 F1
Bidbury Junior &
   Infant School
   HAV PO9 .... 16 A2
Bilton Industrial Estate
   CHAM RG24 .... 83 J7
Binsted C of E Primary School
   ALTN GU34 .... 178 C1
Binswood View
   Business Centre
   ALTN GU34 .... 200 C4
Birchwood Medical Centre
   CFDH BH17 .... 429 K8
Bishop Challoner RC Secondary
   School
   KEMP RG22 .... 104 B5
Bishops Waltham County Infant
   School
   BPWT SO32 .... 297 J8
Bishopswood Co Junior School
   TADY RG26 .... 41 L8
Bishopwood Co Infant School
   TADY RG26 .... 61 L1
Bitterne C of E First School
   ITCH SO19 .... 344 D1
Bitterne C of E Infant School
   ITCH SO19 .... 344 D2
Bitterne Health Centre
   WEND SO18 .... 344 E1
Bitterne Leisure Centre
   WEND SO18 .... 344 E1
Bitterne Manor Primary School
   ITCH SO19 .... 344 B1
Bitterne Middle School
   ITCH SO19 .... 344 D2
Bitterne Park Clinic
   WEND SO18 .... 319 K8
Bitterne Park Junior &
   Infant School
   WEND SO18 .... 319 J6
Bitterne Park Secondary School
   WEND SO18 .... 319 K6
Bitterne Park Surgery
   WEND SO18 .... 319 K8
Blackbrook Business Park
   FHAM PO15 .... 14 C5
Blackfield Health Centre
   FAWY SO45 .... 392 B6
Blackfield Junior &
   Infant School
   FAWY SO45 .... 392 C7
Blackmoor Golf Club
   LIND GU35 .... 200 F7
Blackwater & Hawley
   Leisure Centre
   BLKW GU17 .... 70 A5
Blackwater Industrial Estate
   BLKW GU17 .... 70 B4
Blackwater Trading Estate
   ASHV GU12 .... 113 H8
Bladon Gallery
   RAND SP11 .... 74 D8
Blands Infant School
   THLE RG7 .... 31 J6
Blue Fish Zoo
   BMTH BH1 .... 22 E6
The Boatyard Industrial Estate
   FHAM/PORC PO16 .... 15 H8
Bohunt Community School
   LIPH GU30 .... 226 E4
Bohunt Manor
   LIPH GU30 .... 226 E5

The Bold Gallery
   CHCH/BSGR BH23 .... 450 A1
Bordon County Junior &
   Infant School
   LIND GU35 .... 201 H4
Bordon Trading Estate
   LIND GU35 .... 200 F3
Boscombe Dental
   Health Centre
   BOSC BH5 .... 448 E4
Boscombe Manor
   Medical Centre
   BOSC BH5 .... 448 E4
Bosmere Junior School
   HAV PO9 .... 16 E5
Botley Junior & Infant School
   HEND SO30 .... 346 E1
Botley Park Hotel &
   Country Club
   BPWT SO32 .... 321 L6
Boundaries Surgery
   ALTN GU34 .... 197 H5
Boundary Oak School
   WHAM PO17 .... 372 F3
The Bourne Community
   College
   EMRTH PO10 .... 379 G7
Bourne County First School
   NFNM GU10 .... 159 G1
Bourne Mill Industrial Estate
   FNM GU9 .... 135 H5
Bournemouth Borough Council
   BMTH BH1 .... 23 K5
Bournemouth Business Centre
   BMTH BH1 .... 23 J4
Bournemouth College
   BMTH BH1 .... 23 M4
Bournemouth County Council
   BMTH BH1 .... 23 J4
Bournemouth County Court
   BMTH BH1 .... 23 H4
Bournemouth
   International Airport
   CHCH/BSGR BH23 .... 407 K8
Bournemouth
   Magistrates Court
   BMTH BH1 .... 23 H5
Bournemouth Mosque
   MOOR/WNTN BH9 .... 432 D8
The Bournemouth
   Nuffield Hospital
   BMTH BH1 .... 23 G1
Bournemouth & Poole College
   BMTH BH1 .... 23 H5
Bournemouth & Poole College
   BMTH BH1 .... 23 J5
Bournemouth & Poole College
   PSTN BH14 .... 445 L3
Bournemouth & Poole
   College of Further Education
   PSTN BH14 .... 445 L4
Bournemouth School for Boys
   CHAR BH8 .... 433 G7
Bournemouth School for Girls
   CHAR BH8 .... 433 G6
Bournemouth Sports Club
   CHCH/BSGR BH23 .... 407 G7
Bournemouth University
   BKME/WDN BH12 .... 432 A8
Bournemouth University
   BMTH BH1 .... 23 J5
Bournemouth University
   BMTH BH1 .... 23 K5
Bourne Tennis Club
   FNM GU9 .... 134 F8
Boveridge House School
   WIMB BH21 .... 307 H6
Boyatt Shopping Centre
   ELGH SO50 .... 293 M3
Boyatt Wood Surgery
   ELGH SO50 .... 293 L3
Braemore C of E
   Primary School
   FBDG SP6 .... 284 A8
Braishfield CP School
   ROMY SO51 .... 263 J2
Bramley C of E Primary School
   TADY RG26 .... 63 L4
Bramshaw Golf Club
   LYND SO43 .... 313 M7
Branksome Heath
   Middle School
   BKME/WDN BH12 .... 446 B2
Bransgore Primary School
   CHCH/BSGR BH23 .... 410 A8
Breamore House
   FBDG SP6 .... 283 M5
Brickfield Trading Estate
   CHFD SO53 .... 293 G3
Brick Kiln Industrial Estate
   TADY RG26 .... 41 M7
Brickyards Industrial Estate
   PSF GU32 .... 247 M7
Bridge Gallery
   WSHM SO15 .... 343 K2
Bridgemary Community School
   LSOL/BMARY PO13 .... 397 G6
The Bridge Shopping Centre
   PSEA PO1 .... 21 K1
Brighton Hill Community School
   KEMP RG22 .... 104 C7

Brimpton School
 THLE RG7 .... 40 C2
Bristow County First School
 CBLY GU15 .... 70 E6
Broad Chalke Primary School
 RSAL SP5 .... 252 B1
Broadlands House
 ROMY SO51 .... 290 D3
Broadmoor County Primary School
 CWTH RG45 .... 50 A4
Broadmoor Hospital
 CWTH RG45 .... 50 A4
Broadstone First School
 BDST BH18 .... 429 M4
Broadstone Middle School
 BDST BH18 .... 430 A3
Brockenhurst College
 BROC SO42 .... 387 L6
Brockenhurst Primary School
 BROC SO42 .... 387 K7
Brockhurst County Infant School
 GPORT PO12 .... 421 K1
Brockhurst County Junior School
 GPORT PO12 .... 421 L2
Brockhurst Medical Centre
 GPORT PO12 .... 421 K1
Brokenhurst Manor Golf Club
 BROC SO42 .... 413 J2
Brompton Gallery
 SHAM SO14 .... 13 H2
Brookes Hill Industrial Estate
 TOTT SO40 .... 316 A4
Brookfield Secondary School
 HLER SO31 .... 370 C4
Brookham School
 LIPH GU30 .... 227 H6
Brookside Business Centre
 THLE RG7 .... 46 A2
The Brook Trading Estate
 ASHV GU12 .... 113 H5
Brookwood Industrial Estate
 ELGH SO50 .... 293 L5
Broughton County Primary School
 STOK SO20 .... 209 G1
The Brownhill Surgery
 CHFD SO53 .... 293 J1
Browning Barracks
 ALDT GU11 .... 112 D3
Brownsea Open Air Theatre
 CFDH BH17 .... 429 L8
Broxhead Trading Estate
 LIND GU35 .... 201 L2
Brune Park Community School
 LSOL/BMARY PO13 .... 397 J8
Buckholme School
 PSTN BH14 .... 445 M4
Buckland Medical Centre
 NEND PO2 .... 399 H8
Bucklebury C of E Primary School
 THLE RG7 .... 27 M2
Burdwood Surgery
 STHA RG19 .... 27 H6
The Burgate School
 FBDG SP6 .... 309 L5
Burgess Road Surgery
 ROWN SO16 .... 319 H4
Burghclere CP School
 KSCL RG20 .... 57 K2
Burghfield Health Centre
 THLE RG7 .... 31 L5
Buriton Business Park
 EPSF GU31 .... 303 H1
Buriton CP School
 EPSF GU31 .... 303 J3
Burley CP School
 RGWD BH24 .... 384 E6
Burley Golf Club
 RGWD BH24 .... 384 F5
Burnham Copse Junior School
 TADY RG26 .... 41 K7
Burnside Surgery
 FLET GU13 .... 88 F7
Burrfields Retail Park
 HSEA PO3 .... 399 M7
Burridge Social & Sports Club
 HLER SO31 .... 346 F6
Bursledon C of E Junior & Infant School
 HLER SO31 .... 345 L4
Bursledon Windmill Museum
 HLER SO31 .... 345 L6
Burton Primary School
 CHCH/BSGR BH23 .... 435 G5
Buryfields Infant School
 ODIM RG29 .... 108 D6
Bury Hill
 RAND SP11 .... 142 C4
Business Centre
 SHAM SO14 .... 13 J7
The Business Centre
 BSTK RG21 .... 5 G8
The Business Centre
 RSAL SP5 .... 285 J1
The Business Centre
 THLE RG7 .... 40 C2
The Butts County Primary School
 ALTN GU34 .... 176 C6
Byngs Business Park
 WVILLE PO7 .... 351 M6
By Pass Football Club
 ROMY SO51 .... 290 E2
Cadnam Surgery
 TOTT SO40 .... 339 L1
Calleva Roman Antiquity and Museum
 THLE RG7 .... 42 E7
Calmore County Junior & Infant School
 TOTT SO40 .... 316 B6
Calmore Industrial Estate
 TOTT SO40 .... 316 D6

Calmore Sports Club
 TOTT SO40 .... 315 M6
Calshot Castle
 FAWY SO45 .... 393 M7
Calthorpe Park School
 FLET GU13 .... 88 B8
Camberley County Infant School
 CBLY GU15 .... 70 E3
Camberley Cricket Club
 CBLY GU15 .... 71 G5
Camberley Health Centre
 CBLY GU15 .... 70 E5
Camberley Heath Golf Club
 CBLY GU15 .... 71 K4
Camberley Magistrates Court
 CBLY GU15 .... 71 G2
Camberley Rugby Football Club
 CBLY GU15 .... 70 F5
Camberley Town Football Club
 CBLY GU15 .... 70 E5
Cambridge Military Hospital
 ALDT GU11 .... 112 E5
Cameleon Theatre
 WSHM SO15 .... 343 H2
Camelsdale County First School
 HASM GU27 .... 228 C3
Campbell Surgery
 SSEA PO5 .... 21 K5
Camp Road Industrial Estate
 FARN GU14 .... 91 G8
Cams Hill School
 FHAM/PORC PO16 .... 373 J8
Canada House Business Centre
 NMIL/BTOS BH25 .... 438 A6
Candover Gallery
 NARL SO24 .... 218 C2
Canford Heath First School
 CFDH BH17 .... 445 K1
Canford Heath Middle School
 CFDH BH17 .... 445 J1
Canford School
 WIMB BH21 .... 404 E6
Cantell Secondary School
 ROWN SO16 .... 318 F4
The Canute Surgery
 ITCH SO19 .... 344 C5
The Carpet Gallery
 WBNE BH4 .... 447 H5
Carter Community School
 PLE BH15 .... 444 E6
Carvers Trading Estate
 RGWD BH24 .... 382 E1
Carwarden House School
 CBLY GU15 .... 71 K5
Castle County Primary School
 FHAM/PORC PO16 .... 398 B1
Castle Court School
 WIMB BH21 .... 428 F1
Castledown Comprehensive School
 RAND SP11 .... 92 B7
Castle Hill Junior School
 DEAN RG23 .... 104 A3
Castle Industrial Park
 NWBY RG14 .... 25 M3
Castle Primary School
 RAND SP11 .... 92 F6
Castle School
 NWBY RG14 .... 25 J2
Catherine Corbett Clinic
 HAV PO9 .... 16 F3
Catherington C of E Controlled Infant School
 HORN PO8 .... 328 A7
The Cedar School
 ROWN SO16 .... 317 K4
Cedars School
 THLE RG7 .... 41 K1
Central Business Park
 BMTH BH1 .... 23 M2
Central Estate
 ALDT GU11 .... 7 H2
Central Trading Estate
 SHAM SO14 .... 13 L3
Centurion Industrial Park
 SHAM SO14 .... 344 A1
Century Galleries
 HTWY RG27 .... 87 J2
Chalkridge School
 KEMP RG22 .... 104 D7
Chamberlayne Park School
 ITCH SO19 .... 344 E7
Chandlers Ford Infant School
 CHFD SO53 .... 293 J1
Chantry Centre Shopping Precinct
 AND SP10 .... 9 H5
Chapel House Gallery
 OVTN RG25 .... 126 C7
Charles Dickens Junior & Infant School
 PSEA PO1 .... 423 H2
Charles Kingsley School
 HTWY RG27 .... 47 M8
Charlton Hill Surgery
 AND SP10 .... 8 D2
Charlton Road Health Centre
 AND SP10 .... 8 D2
Chase Community Hospital
 LIND GU35 .... 201 J6
Chawton House Surgery
 LYMN SO41 .... 440 C5
Chawtown Primary School
 ALTN GU34 .... 198 C1
Chesil Theatre
 WINC SO23 .... 11 J9
Cheswycks School
 FRIM GU16 .... 91 L3
Chevron Business Park
 FAWY SO45 .... 391 M2
Chineham Park Primary School
 CHAM RG24 .... 5 J2
Christchurch Infant School
 CHCH/BSGR BH23 .... 449 M1
Christchurch Junior School
 CHCH/BSGR BH23 .... 449 L1
Christchurch Medical Centre
 HAV PO9 .... 378 A5

Christchurch Ski & Leisure Centre
 CHCH/BSGR BH23 .... 407 M5
Christ the King RC Primary School
 BWD BH11 .... 431 L3
Churchers College
 EPSF GU31 .... 275 M4
Churchers College Junior School
 PSF GU31 .... 275 K5
Church Grange & Bramblys Grange Health Centre
 BSTK RG21 .... 4 D9
Church Grange Lychpit Surgery
 CHAM RG24 .... 105 L1
Churchill Yard Industrial Estate
 WVILLE PO7 .... 352 C7
Church of England Primary School
 AND SP10 .... 9 J6
Church of England School
 THLE RG7 .... 29 G4
City Business Centre
 WINC SO23 .... 11 G5
City Grove Trading Estate
 ELGH SO50 .... 293 K4
City Industrial Park
 WSHM SO15 .... 12 C3
City Museum
 PSEA PO1 .... 20 E5
City Museum & Art Gallery
 PSEA PO1 .... 20 E5
City Offices
 WINC SO23 .... 11 H3
The City of Portsmouth Boys School
 NEND PO2 .... 399 J4
The City of Portsmouth Girls School
 PSEA PO1 .... 423 J2
City of Portsmouth Sports Club
 NEND PO2 .... 399 H5
Civil Service Sports Ground
 ENEY PO4 .... 423 K3
Civil Service Sports Ground
 HSEA PO3 .... 399 L5
Clanfield Junior School
 HORN PO8 .... 328 A1
Clanfield Surgery
 HORN PO8 .... 328 B4
Clarendon County Junior & Infant School
 NTID SP9 .... 114 C1
Clatford Primary School
 RAND SP11 .... 142 C7
Clayfields Sports Centre
 FAWY SO45 .... 367 H4
Clayton Barracks
 ALDT GU11 .... 113 G4
The Clere Secondary School
 KSCL RG20 .... 57 K1
Clewborough House Preparatory School
 CBLY GU15 .... 71 K2
Cliddesden Primary School
 OVTN RG25 .... 127 M3
Cliffdale Primary School
 NEND PO2 .... 399 K6
Clift Surgery
 TADY RG26 .... 63 K4
The Clinic
 FNM GU9 .... 134 F6
Club House
 OVTN RG25 .... 126 D6
The Club House
 LISS GU33 .... 249 L6
Cluster Industrial Estate
 HSEA PO3 .... 423 L5
The Coast Clinic
 FAWY SO45 .... 392 F5
Colden Common Primary School
 RWIN SO21 .... 266 E7
Coliseum Business Centre
 CBLY GU15 .... 70 D5
College Art School
 WINC SO23 .... 238 E2
College Park Infant School
 NEND PO2 .... 399 K5
Collingwood Business Park
 FHAM/STUB PO14 .... 396 F2
Collingwood College
 CBLY GU15 .... 51 K8
Coltwood Business Centre
 ALDT GU11 .... 7 G2
Commercial Business Centre
 CHFD SO53 .... 293 H2
The Community Hospital
 ALTN GU34 .... 176 C7
Comprehensive
 YTLY GU46 .... 68 F4
Compton All Saints C of E Primary School
 RWIN SO21 .... 238 C8
Compton & Upmarden C of E Primary School
 RCCH PO18 .... 330 D4
The Connaught School
 ASHV GU12 .... 136 B1
Continental Ferry Port
 NEND PO2 .... 399 G3
Contour Gallery
 LIPH GU30 .... 226 E4
Copnor Infant School
 HSEA PO3 .... 399 L7
Copnor Junior School
 NEND PO2 .... 399 K7
Copythorne First School
 TOTT SO40 .... 315 G6
Cordwalles County Middle School
 CBLY GU15 .... 51 J8
Corfe Hills School
 WIMB BH21 .... 429 K2
Corhampton Golf Club
 BPWT SO32 .... 298 D4

Cornerways Surgery
 RGWD BH24 .... 381 J4
Corpus Christie School
 BOSC BH5 .... 448 E3
Corpus Christi RC Primary School
 NEND PO2 .... 399 H7
Cosham Health Centre
 CHAM PO6 .... 399 K1
Cottage Grove Primary School
 SSEA PO5 .... 21 H5
County and Magistrates Court
 PSEA PO1 .... 21 G3
County Primary School
 NTID SP9 .... 138 C1
Courthill First School
 PSTN BH14 .... 446 C1
Court Lane Junior & Infant School
 CHAM PO6 .... 399 L1
Court Moor School
 FLET GU13 .... 110 E1
Cove County Infant School
 FARN GU14 .... 90 B2
Cove County Junior School
 FARN GU14 .... 90 B3
Cove County Secondary School
 FARN GU14 .... 90 B3
Cove Cricket Club
 FARN GU14 .... 90 B4
Cove Manor County Junior & Infant School
 FARN GU14 .... 90 C2
Cowplain School
 HORN PO8 .... 352 C6
Coxmoor Farm Light Industrial Estate
 NFNM GU10 .... 110 A6
Cranbourne Secondary School
 BSTK RG21 .... 104 E5
Craneswater Junior School
 ENEY PO4 .... 21 M7
Crawley Ridge First School
 CBLY GU15 .... 71 J2
Crescent Primary School
 ELGH SO50 .... 293 M5
The Crestwood Community School
 ELGH SO50 .... 293 L3
Cricklade College
 AND SP10 .... 9 H4
Cricklade Theatre
 AND SP10 .... 9 G4
Crofton School
 FHAM/STUB PO14 .... 396 C6
Crondall CP School
 NFNM GU10 .... 133 H2
Crookham C of E Infants School
 FLET GU13 .... 110 E4
Crookham County Junior School
 FLET GU13 .... 111 G4
The Crookhorn Community School
 WVILLE PO7 .... 376 D4
Crow Arch Lane Industrial Estate
 RGWD BH24 .... 382 E3
Crowthorne Business Centre
 CWTH RG45 .... 49 M1
Crowthorne C of E Primary School
 CWTH RG45 .... 49 L3
Cumberland Business Centre
 SSEA PO5 .... 21 K2
Cumberland Infant School
 ENEY PO4 .... 423 L5
Cupernham County Junior & Infants School
 ROMY SO51 .... 263 G7
Curdridge Primary School
 BPWT SO32 .... 322 C7
Curtis Museum
 ALTN GU34 .... 176 E4
Cutlers Gallery
 BMTH BH1 .... 22 F5
Daneshill East Industrial Estate
 CHAM RG24 .... 5 L5
Daneshill Industrial Estate
 CHAM RG24 .... 5 M4
Daneshill School
 HTWY RG27 .... 65 J4
David Hart Business Centre
 RSAL SP5 .... 256 D8
Dawkins Business Centre
 PLE BH15 .... 444 C5
D Day Museum
 SSEA PO5 .... 423 G7
Deacon Trading Estate
 ELGH SO50 .... 294 B6
Dean Court (Bournemouth FC)
 LTDN BH7 .... 448 E2
Deanery School
 SHAM SO14 .... 13 J5
Deane's Almshouses
 BSTK RG21 .... 105 G4
Dean Farm Estate
 WHAM PO17 .... 372 E3
Dean Surgery
 NARL SO24 .... 219 M4
Delta Business Park
 FHAM/PORC PO16 .... 396 F1
Denmead Health Centre
 WVILLE PO7 .... 351 J3
Denmead Infant School
 WVILLE PO7 .... 351 L4
Denmead Junior School
 WVILLE PO7 .... 351 K4
Derby Road Surgery
 NEND PO2 .... 399 H7
Derry Down Health Clinic
 RAND SP11 .... 97 M7
Devonshire Infant School
 ENEY PO4 .... 21 M4
Devonshire Infant School
 ENEY PO4 .... 423 K4

Devonshire Practice
 ENEY PO4 .... 423 M5
Discover Bible School
 WSHM SO15 .... 343 G2
Diva Gallery
 ODIM RG29 .... 108 D5
Dockyard Apprentice Exhibition
 PSEA PO1 .... 20 B1
Dogmersfield C of E Primary School
 HTWY RG27 .... 109 M1
Donnington Castle
 NWBY RG14 .... 25 H1
Dorset County Council
 BMTH BH1 .... 23 H4
Dorset County Council
 FERN BH22 .... 406 B3
Dorset County Council
 WIMB BH21 .... 404 A3
Dorset County Council
 WIMB BH21 .... 405 K1
Dorset Health Authority
 FERN BH22 .... 406 B3
Dorset Healthcare NHS Trust
 WEND SO18 .... 345 G1
Dorset Magistrates Court
 BMTH BH1 .... 23 G4
Dorset Medical Centre
 SHAM SO14 .... 13 G2
Douai School
 THLE RG7 .... 29 G3
Dove House School
 BSTK RG21 .... 4 F4
Down House
 RSAL SP5 .... 257 J8
Downton C of E Primary School
 RSAL SP5 .... 256 D8
Downton County Secondary School
 RSAL SP5 .... 284 D1
Downton Industrial Estate
 RSAL SP5 .... 256 D8
Dr Gregs Surgery
 NTID SP9 .... 114 E2
Dr Hughes & Partners
 RGWD BH24 .... 382 D1
Dr Munroe & Partners
 TOTT SO40 .... 316 G8
Droxford Junior School
 BPWT SO32 .... 298 F7
Droxford Primary School
 BPWT SO32 .... 298 F7
Dunhurst School
 PSF GU32 .... 275 K2
Dunston Park School
 NTHA RG18 .... 27 G4
Dunwood Manor Golf Club
 ROMY SO51 .... 261 J6
Durley Primary School
 BPWT SO32 .... 321 M2
Duriston Court School
 NMIL/BTOS BH25 .... 452 F1
Eagle House School
 PSTN BH14 .... 445 M3
Eagle House School
 SHST GU47 .... 49 K6
East Barn Surgery
 CHAM RG24 .... 83 L8
East Berkshire Golf Club
 CWTH RG45 .... 49 H3
East Dorset Area Health Authority
 FERN BH22 .... 406 B3
Eastern Industrial Centre
 CHAM PO6 .... 400 A2
Eastfield House Surgery
 NWBY RG14 .... 2 E6
East Hants District Council
 PSF GU32 .... 275 K5
Eastleigh Borough Council
 ELGH SO50 .... 293 L5
Eastleigh College of Further Education
 ELGH SO50 .... 293 M6
Eastleigh Football Club
 ELGH SO50 .... 319 K1
Eastleigh Health Centre
 ELGH SO50 .... 293 M5
Eastleigh Museum
 ELGH SO50 .... 293 M6
Eastleigh Rugby Club
 ELGH SO50 .... 294 B5
East Meon Controlled Primary School
 PSF GU32 .... 273 J7
Eastney Health Centre
 ENEY PO4 .... 423 L5
Eastney Swimming Baths
 ENEY PO4 .... 424 A6
Easton Lane Business Park
 WINC SO23 .... 11 L6
East Shore School
 HSEA PO3 .... 423 M2
East Street Shopping Centre
 SHAM SO14 .... 13 H4
Ebblake Industrial Estate
 RGWD BH24 .... 357 H4
Eccossis Hospital Products
 RAND SP11 .... 116 F6
Edgebarrow School
 CWTH RG45 .... 49 L5
Edgebarrow Sports Centre
 CWTH RG45 .... 49 M5
Edgeborough School
 NFNM GU10 .... 158 F5
Eggars School
 ALTN GU34 .... 177 G2
Eling County Infant School
 TOTT SO40 .... 341 L2
Elliott Industrial Park
 ASHV GU12 .... 113 H6
Elm House Surgery
 NTID SP9 .... 114 D1
Elmhurst Business Park
 GPORT PO12 .... 18 F3

Elmrise Junior & Infant School
BWD BH11 .... 431 K4
Elson County Infant School
GPORT PO12 .... 397 L8
Elson County Junior School
GPORT PO12 .... 397 L8
Elstree School
THLE RG7 .... 29 G4
Embley Park School
ROMY SO51 .... 289 K2
Emsworth Museum
EMRTH PO10 .... 378 D7
Emsworth Primary School
EMRTH PO10 .... 378 C7
Emsworth Surgery
EMRTH PO10 .... 378 D8
Enborne C of E School
KSCL RG20 .... 36 B2
Enborne Lodge (Sch)
NWBY RG14 .... 36 E3
English Gallery
HAV PO9 .... 354 A6
Enterprise Industrial Estate
ASHV GU12 .... 113 J1
Enterprise Industrial Estate
HORN PO8 .... 328 B8
The Epiphany School
MOOR/WNTN BH9 .... 432 F4
Eversley Cricket Club
HTWY RG27 .... 48 C8
Evingar Industrial Estate
WHCH RG28 .... 122 A2
Fairfax Industrial Estate
ASHV GU12 .... 113 H6
Fairfield Infant School
HAV PO9 .... 17 G4
Fairfields Primary School
BSTK RG21 .... 105 G4
Fairisle Junior & Infant School
ROWN SO16 .... 317 K4
Fairlands Montessori School
BPWT SO32 .... 348 C1
Fair Oak Junior & Infant School
ELGH SO50 .... 295 J7
Fairway Business Centre
HSEA PO3 .... 400 A5
Falkland CP School
NWBY RG14 .... 37 G2
Fareham Borough Council
FHAM PO15 .... 371 H3
Fareham Borough Council
FHAM/PORC PO16 .... 15 K5
Fareham Borough Council
FHAM/PORC PO16 .... 397 L1
Fareham College
FHAM/STUB PO14 .... 14 D6
The Fareham Gallery
FHAM/PORC PO16 .... 15 J6
Fareham Leisure Centre
FHAM/PORC PO16 .... 15 H4
Fareham Megabowl
FHAM/STUB PO14 .... 396 F3
Fareham Park C of E Controlled Junior School
FHAM PO15 .... 372 A5
Fareham Park Infant School
FHAM PO15 .... 372 A5
Far Horizons Gallery
PSF GU32 .... 275 K5
Farleigh House Sch
OVTN RG25 .... 127 K6
Farleigh School
RAND SP11 .... 142 A8
Farley Hill Primary School
THLE RG7 .... 46 F3
Farleys All Saints Primary School
RSAL SP5 .... 206 B8
Farmhouse Gallery
KSCL RG20 .... 56 E1
Farnborough Business Centre
FARN GU14 .... 90 C6
Farnborough College of Technology
ASHV GU12 .... 7 H4
Farnborough College of Technology
FARN GU14 .... 90 E8
Farnborough College of Technology
FARN GU14 .... 90 F6
Farnborough Grange County Junior School
FARN GU14 .... 70 C8
Farnborough Hill School
FARN GU14 .... 90 F3
Farnborough Recreation Centre
FARN GU14 .... 90 E5
Farnborough Rugby Football Club
FARN GU14 .... 90 D2
Farnborough Town Football Club
FARN GU14 .... 70 D8
Farnham Business Centre
FNM GU9 .... 134 D7
Farnham Business Centre
FNM GU9 .... 134 F5
Farnham Business Park
FNM GU9 .... 134 D7
Farnham Castle
FNM GU9 .... 134 F5
Farnham College
FNM GU9 .... 134 F7
Farnham Golf Club
NFNM GU10 .... 136 A6
Farnham Hospital
FNM GU9 .... 135 H5
Farnham Museum
FNM GU9 .... 134 E6
Farnham Retail Park
FNM GU9 .... 135 H5
Farringdon Industrial Centre
ALTN GU34 .... 198 B6
Farringdon Industrial Estate
ALTN GU34 .... 198 B6

Fawley Business Centre
FAWY SO45 .... 392 E5
Fawley County First School
FAWY SO45 .... 392 E5
Fenwick Hospital
LYND SO43 .... 363 J2
Ferndown First School
FERN BH22 .... 406 A3
Ferndown Medical Centre
FERN BH22 .... 406 B3
Ferndown Middle School
FERN BH22 .... 405 M3
Ferndown Sports Centre
FERN BH22 .... 405 M2
Ferndown Town Council
FERN BH22 .... 406 A2
Ferndown Upper School
FERN BH22 .... 405 M2
Fernhill Comprehensive School
FARN GU14 .... 70 C7
Fernhill Primary School
FARN GU14 .... 70 C7
Fernhurst Junior School
ENEY PO4 .... 423 K4
Fernside Business Park
WIMB BH21 .... 405 L1
Finchampstead C of E Primary School
EWKG RG40 .... 48 B5
Finchampstead Sports Club
EWKG RG40 .... 48 B5
Finns Industrial Park
NFNM GU10 .... 110 A6
Fir Tree CP School
NTHA RG18 .... 26 B4
Fish Farm
RSAL SP5 .... 256 F5
Flanders Industrial Park
HEND SO30 .... 321 G8
Fleet Business Park
FLET GU13 .... 111 G5
Fleet Community Hospital
FLET GU13 .... 88 D6
Fleet Police Station
FLET GU13 .... 88 E8
Fleming Park Leisure Centre
ELGH SO50 .... 293 K5
Flying Bull Junior & Infant School
NEND PO2 .... 399 H8
Focus 303 Business Centre
AND SP10 .... 119 J7
Folly Hill County Infant School
FNM GU9 .... 134 D2
Fordingbrdge Junior & Infant School
FBDG SP6 .... 309 L5
Fordingbridge Hospital
FBDG SP6 .... 309 L7
Forest Edge School
TOTT SO40 .... 341 J1
Forest End Surgery
WVILLE PO7 .... 376 B1
Forest Gate Surgery
TOTT SO40 .... 341 G1
Forestside Medical Practice
FAWY SO45 .... 367 J8
Forest Surgery
LIND GU35 .... 201 J5
Fort Brockhurst
LSOL/BMARY PO13 .... 397 K7
Fort Cumberland
ENEY PO4 .... 424 C5
Fort Hill School
DEAN RG23 .... 104 B2
Forthill Surgery
DEAN RG23 .... 104 B2
Forton Road Surgery
GPORT PO12 .... 421 M2
Fort Wallington Industrial Estate
FHAM/PORC PO16 .... 373 H6
Fosters Business Park
HTWY RG27 .... 107 J1
Foundry Lane Middle & Primary School
WSHM SO15 .... 318 A8
Foxhills County First School
TOTT SO40 .... 341 H4
France Hill School
CBLY GU15 .... 70 F6
Francis Bailey School
STHA RG19 .... 27 H5
Freeground Junior & Infant School
HEND SO30 .... 346 B2
Freemantle Business Centre
WSHM SO15 .... 343 G3
Frensham C of E First School
NFNM GU10 .... 159 G8
Frensham Heights School
NFNM GU10 .... 158 D6
Frensham Pond Sailing Club
NFNM GU10 .... 180 F3
Friarsgate Medical Centre
WINC SO23 .... 11 H8
Frimley C of E First & Middle School
FRIM GU16 .... 91 H1
Frimley Green Medical Centre
FRIM GU16 .... 91 J2
Frimley Park Hospital
FRIM GU16 .... 71 G6
Frobisher Industrial Centre
ROMY SO51 .... 262 C7
Frogmore Community School
BLKW GU17 .... 69 J3
Frogmore County Infant School
BLKW GU17 .... 69 L4
Frogmore Junior School
BLKW GU17 .... 69 L3
Front Lawn GM Junior School
HAV PO9 .... 377 K2
Front Lawn Infant School
HAV PO9 .... 377 K3
Froxfield Endowed Controlled Infant School
PSF GU32 .... 246 D6

Fryern Junior & Infant School
CHFD SO53 .... 293 K2
The Fryern Surgery
CHFD SO53 .... 293 K1
The Futcher School
CHAM PO6 .... 376 A8
The Gallery
LYMN SO41 .... 412 F7
The Gallery
SHST GU47 .... 49 M8
The Gallery
SSEA PO5 .... 21 H7
Garlands County Junior School
THLE RG7 .... 31 K5
Garrison Theatre
NTID SP9 .... 114 C2
Gasholders
SHAM SO14 .... 13 K2
Gatcombe Park Infant School
NEND PO2 .... 399 K4
George & Dragon Surgery
EMRTH PO10 .... 378 F5
George Street School Branch Clinic
PSEA PO1 .... 423 K1
Gillies Health Centre
KEMP RG22 .... 104 C8
Glenfield Infant School
WEND SO18 .... 344 D1
Glenhurst School
HAV PO9 .... 17 G4
Glenmoor School for Girls
NBNE BH10 .... 432 B7
Glenwood School
EMRTH PO10 .... 378 C7
Global Adventure Sailing Club
FNM GU9 .... 134 E6
Goldfield Gallery
BPWT SO32 .... 325 H7
Goldfield Gallery
PSEA PO1 .... 20 D5
Goldsmith Infant School
ENEY PO4 .... 21 M5
Golf Club Bungalow
ALTN GU34 .... 154 D7
Gomer County Junior & Infant School
GPORT PO12 .... 421 J5
Goodway Sea School
GPORT PO12 .... 397 L8
Goodwyn Gallery
PSEA PO1 .... 21 L1
Gordleton Industrial Estate
LYMN SO41 .... 439 K3
Gorse Ride Junior School
EWKG RG40 .... 48 B1
Gosport Health Centre
GPORT PO12 .... 18 C4
Gosport Ice Rink
LSOL/BMARY PO13 .... 397 J7
Gosport Museum
GPORT PO12 .... 19 K3
Gosport War Memorial Hospital
GPORT PO12 .... 18 C4
Grange Comprehensive School
CHCH/BSGR BH23 .... 435 J8
Grange County Junior & Infant School
LSOL/BMARY PO13 .... 421 G1
Grange Farm Business Park
BPWT SO32 .... 323 H8
The Grange Park
NARL SO24 .... 193 K3
Grateley Business Park
RAND SP11 .... 161 K1
Grateley Junior & Infant School
RAND SP11 .... 139 M8
Gratton Surgery
RWIN SO21 .... 168 B4
Gravatom Business Centre
BPWT SO32 .... 297 G8
Grayshott Clinic
GSHT GU26 .... 203 L4
Grayshott Council Office
GSHT GU26 .... 204 A5
Grayshott Primary School
GSHT GU26 .... 203 L5
Grayshott Surgery
GSHT GU26 .... 204 A5
Grayswood C of E School
HASM GU27 .... 205 J6
Greatbridge Business Park
ROMY SO51 .... 262 C7
Greatham Primary School
LISS GU33 .... 224 E6
Greenacres School
FUFL SO22 .... 10 E3
Green Croft School
FARN GU14 .... 91 G2
Greenfields Junior School
HTWY RG27 .... 87 H3
Greenham Road Retail Park
NWBY RG14 .... 2 F6
The Gregg School
WEND SO18 .... 319 M5
Greggs School
PTSW SO17 .... 318 F7
Gresham Industrial Estate
ASHV GU12 .... 113 H6
Grey House Private School
HTWY RG27 .... 87 J2
Grey Welles Surgery
HAV PO9 .... 377 K4
Group Practice
NTID SP9 .... 114 E3
Group Surgery
ROWN SO16 .... 319 J4
Grovebell Industrial Estate
NFNM GU10 .... 158 C1
Grove County Primary School
FRIM GU16 .... 71 H6
Grove Medical Practice
WSHM SO15 .... 343 G1
Gudge Heath Surgery
FHAM PO15 .... 14 B2

Guildford Road Industrial Estate
FNM GU9 .... 135 G5
Guillemont County Junior School
FARN GU14 .... 89 M1
Gundrymoor Trading Estate
WIMB BH21 .... 380 D3
Gurdwara Sikh Temple
SHAM SO14 .... 343 L2
Hackwood Ho
OVTN RG25 .... 105 J8
Hadleigh Practice
WIMB BH21 .... 429 G1
Hale County First & Middle School
FNM GU9 .... 134 E1
Hale Primary School
FBDG SP6 .... 285 H5
Hall of Aviation
SHAM SO14 .... 13 K6
Halterworth CP School
ROMY SO51 .... 291 H1
Hamble County Primary School
HLER SO31 .... 369 J4
Hamble County Secondary School
HLER SO31 .... 369 J3
Hambledon Cricket Club
WVILLE PO7 .... 326 D3
Hambledon Infant School
WVILLE PO7 .... 326 C5
Hambrook Business Centre
RCCH PO18 .... 379 M4
Hammond County Junior & Infant School
FHAM/STUB PO14 .... 396 A6
Hammond Industrial Estate
FHAM/STUB PO14 .... 396 B7
Hampreston Primary School
WIMB BH21 .... 405 J5
The Hampshire Clinic
CHAM RG24 .... 5 M5
Hampshire County Council - Basing House
CHAM RG24 .... 105 M2
Hampshire County Council
ELGH SO50 .... 293 K5
Hampshire County Council
ELGH SO50 .... 294 A5
Hampshire County Council
FHAM/PORC PO16 .... 15 K5
Hampshire County Council
GPORT PO12 .... 19 G2
Hampshire County Council
HAV PO9 .... 17 G5
Hampshire County Council
LYMN SO41 .... 440 C3
Hampshire County Council
RGWD BH24 .... 382 E2
Hampshire County Council
TOTT SO40 .... 341 G4
Hampshire County Council
BSTK RG21 .... 4 F8
Hampshire County Council - Chute House
BSTK RG21 .... 4 E7
Hampshire County Council
WINC SO23 .... 10 E7
Hampshire County Cricket Club
WSHM SO15 .... 318 E8
Hampshire Gallery
BMTH BH1 .... 23 H4
Hampshire Golf Club
RAND SP11 .... 143 G5
Hamwic College
SHAM SO14 .... 13 J4
Hamworthy Community Clinic
PLE BH15 .... 444 D5
Hamworthy First School
PLE BH15 .... 444 E7
Hamworthy Middle School
PLE BH15 .... 444 E7
Hanway Group Practice
NEND PO2 .... 399 J7
Hanway Surgery
PSEA PO1 .... 423 H1
Harbridge School
RGWD BH24 .... 334 B8
Hardley School
FAWY SO45 .... 392 A3
Harefield Clinic
WEND SO18 .... 344 E1
Harefield Junior & Infant School
WEND SO18 .... 320 A8
Harestock Infant School
FUFL SO22 .... 214 C7
Harriet Costello School
BSTK RG21 .... 5 H9
Harrison County Primary School
FHAM/PORC PO16 .... 15 K4
Harrow Way Community School
AND SP10 .... 8 B1
Hartley Park Farm Business Centre
ALTN GU34 .... 199 J4
Hart Plain Infant School
HORN PO8 .... 352 C6
Hart Plain Junior School
WVILLE PO7 .... 352 C6
Hart Sports Centre
FLET GU13 .... 88 B8
Haselworth County Primary School
GPORT PO12 .... 18 F5
Haslemere District Hospital
HASM GU27 .... 229 G1
Haslemere Health Centre
HASM GU27 .... 229 G1
Haslemere Museum
HASM GU27 .... 229 G1
Haslemere Preparatory School
HASM GU27 .... 229 G3
Hassocks Wood Industrial Estate
CHAM RG24 .... 5 M3

Hatch Ride Primary School
CWTH RG45 .... 49 L1
Hatch Warren County Infant School
KEMP RG22 .... 127 H1
Hatch Warren County Junior School
KEMP RG22 .... 127 H1
Hatch Warren Retail Park
KEMP RG22 .... 126 F2
Hatch Warren Surgery
KEMP RG22 .... 126 F2
Hatherden C of E Primary School
RAND SP11 .... 95 H7
Havant Business Centre
HAV PO9 .... 16 A6
Havant College
HAV PO9 .... 16 D1
Havant Leisure Centre
HAV PO9 .... 16 E2
Havant Museum
HAV PO9 .... 16 F5
Havant Retail Park
HAV PO9 .... 376 F7
Havant Rugby Football Club
HAV PO9 .... 16 A2
Havant Sports Club
HAV PO9 .... 16 E3
Havant Town Football Club
HAV PO9 .... 377 L3
Havant War Memorial Hospital
HAV PO9 .... 16 D3
Hawley CP School
BLKW GU17 .... 70 B5
Hawley Lane Industrial Estate
FARN GU14 .... 70 E8
Hawley Place School
BLKW GU17 .... 70 A7
The Hawthorns School
KEMP RG22 .... 104 B7
Hayeswood County First School
WIMB BH21 .... 404 E2
Hayling Billy Business Centre
HISD PO11 .... 425 H4
Hayling Island Health Centre
HISD PO11 .... 425 L5
Haymarket Theatre
BSTK RG21 .... 4 E9
Haymoor Middle School
CFDH BH17 .... 430 C7
Hayward Business Centre
HAV PO9 .... 377 M5
Hazel Wood First School
TOTT SO40 .... 341 G1
Headlands Business Park
RGWD BH24 .... 358 E6
Headley Park Country Club
LIND GU35 .... 180 A7
Heath End County Secondary School
FNM GU9 .... 135 H2
Heatherlands First School
BKME/WDN BH12 .... 446 C3
Heatherside Surgery
CBLY GU15 .... 71 H7
Heathfield Infant & Middle School
ITCH SO19 .... 345 G6
Heathfield School
FHAM/STUB PO14 .... 372 A8
Heath Hill Surgery
CWTH RG45 .... 49 L4
Heathlands Primary School
BWD BH11 .... 431 L5
Hedge End Business Centre
HEND SO30 .... 321 G8
Hedge End Retail Park
HEND SO30 .... 345 L1
Hedge End Town Council
HEND SO30 .... 345 M2
Henbury View First School
WIMB BH21 .... 429 G2
Henry Beaufort School
FUFL SO22 .... 214 D5
Henry Cort Community School
FHAM PO15 .... 371 M5
The Heritage Centre & Museum
TOTT SO40 .... 341 M2
Herne County Junior School
EPSF GU31 .... 275 M4
The Herne Farm Leisure Centre
EPSF GU31 .... 275 M4
The Herons Swimming and Fitness Centre
HASM GU27 .... 228 C2
Highbury College
CHAM PO6 .... 399 L3
Highbury College
PSEA PO1 .... 21 H1
Highbury College of Technology
PSEA PO1 .... 422 F2
Highbury Primary School
CHAM PO6 .... 399 L2
Highclere Castle
KSCL RG20 .... 56 E6
Highcliffe Castle Golf Club
CHCH/BSGR BH23 .... 451 K1
Highcliffe County Junior School
CHCH/BSGR BH23 .... 436 E7
Highcliffe GM Comprehensive School
CHCH/BSGR BH23 .... 436 B7
Highcliffe Medical Centre
CHCH/BSGR BH23 .... 436 D8
Highcroft Industrial Estate
HORN PO8 .... 328 B8
Highfield C of E (A) Primary School
PTSW SO17 .... 318 F6
Highfield School
LIPH GU30 .... 227 H6

Highgrove Industrial Park
 HSEA PO3 .... 399 M5
Highlands Medical Centre
 FHAM PO15 .... 14 A2
Highlands Medical Centre
 FHAM PO15 .... 372 A5
Hightown Industrial Estate
 RGWD BH24 .... 382 F2
Hightown Primary School
 ITCH SO19 .... 345 J4
Hillbourne First School
 CFDH BH17 .... 429 L6
Hillbourne Middle School
 CFDH BH17 .... 429 L6
Hill House School
 LYMN SO41 .... 414 B7
Hill Lane Surgery
 WSHM SO15 .... 343 J1
Hill Park Clinic
 FHAM PO15 .... 14 D1
Hillside County First School
 VWD BH31 .... 356 E1
Hillside Industrial Estate
 HORN PO8 .... 328 B8
Hill View First School
 NBNE BH10 .... 432 C5
Hill View Junior School
 NBNE BH10 .... 432 C5
Hiltingbury County Junior &
 Infant School
 CHFD SO53 .... 265 H7
Hindhead Golf Club
 GSHT GU26 .... 203 L2
Hindu Temple
 SHAM SO14 .... 343 M2
Hiscock Gallery
 SSEA PO5 .... 21 H7
H M Coroners Court
 BMTH BH1 .... 23 H4
HMS Victory
 PSEA PO1 .... 422 D2
Holbrook County Junior &
 Infant School
 LSOL/BMARY PO13 .... 397 G5
Holbrook Recreation Centre
 LSOL/BMARY PO13 .... 397 J7
Holbury County JMI School
 FAWY SO45 .... 392 A5
Hollybrook First School
 ROWN SO16 .... 318 C5
Hollybrook Middle School
 ROWN SO16 .... 318 C5
Hollycombe School
 LIPH GU30 .... 250 F4
Holly Lodge CP School
 ASHV GU12 .... 91 J8
Holly Tree Surgery
 NFNM GU10 .... 158 D4
Holmwood Health Centre
 TADY RG26 .... 41 K7
Holybourne Theatre
 ALTN GU34 .... 177 H2
Holy Cross Hospital
 HASM GU27 .... 228 C1
Holy Family RC Primary School
 ROWN SO16 .... 317 H6
Home Farm School
 THLE RG7 .... 29 G5
Homefield School
 CHCH/BSGR BH23 .... 435 G4
Homeopathic Surgery
 NMIL/BTOS BH25 .... 452 E1
Homewood Chiropractic
 Health Centre
 FHAM/PORC PO16 .... 15 K4
Hook County Junior School
 HTWY RG27 .... 86 A7
Hook Infant School
 HTWY RG27 .... 86 A7
Hook with Warsash
 Primary School
 HLER SO31 .... 370 B8
The Hop Kiln
 FNM GU9 .... 134 E7
Hordle C of E GM
 Primary School
 LYMN SO41 .... 438 E5
Hordle House School
 LYMN SO41 .... 453 M3
Horndean C of E Junior School
 HORN PO8 .... 353 G1
Horndean Community School
 HORN PO8 .... 352 F1
Horndean Football Club
 HORN PO8 .... 352 F1
Horndean Health Centre
 HORN PO8 .... 353 H1
Horndean Infant School
 HORN PO8 .... 353 G1
Horris Hill Preparatory School
 KSCL RG20 .... 37 H5
The Hospital
 CBLY GU15 .... 50 D8
Houndmills Industrial Estate
 BSTK RG21 .... 104 D1
Hounsdown School
 TOTT SO40 .... 341 K4
Hulbert Junior School
 WVILLE PO7 .... 376 D2
Hunter Simmonds Gallery
 CCLF BH13 .... 447 G4
Hurstbourne Tarrant School
 RAND SP11 .... 96 D2
The Hurst Community School
 TADY RG26 .... 41 G7
Hyde (C of E Controlled)
 Primary School
 FBDG SP6 .... 335 H3
Hythe CP School
 FAWY SO45 .... 367 L4
Hythe Medical Centre
 FAWY SO45 .... 367 K6
Ian Walker Odiham Gallery
 ODIM RG29 .... 108 D5
Icknield School
 AND SP10 .... 119 J6
Imax Cinema
 BMTH BH1 .... 22 F7

Industrial Estate
 DEAN RG23 .... 126 E4
Inhurst House School
 STHA RG19 .... 40 F7
Inkpen Primary School
 HUNG RG17 .... 34 A2
International Centre &
 Leisure Pool
 WCLF BH2 .... 22 E8
Isambard Brunel Junior School
 NEND PO2 .... 399 J8
Isle of Wight
 Car Ferry Terminal
 PSEA PO1 .... 20 C4
Itchen Abbas Cp School
 RWIN SO21 .... 216 E2
Itchen College
 ITCH SO19 .... 344 E3
Jellicoe Theatre
 PSTN BH14 .... 445 L3
Jenner House Surgery
 FARN GU14 .... 90 B4
The Jigsaw School
 FRIM GU16 .... 91 H5
J M L Trading Estate
 WSHM SO15 .... 12 C2
John Hanson
 Community School
 AND SP10 .... 8 E6
John Hunt of
 Everest Community School
 CHAM RG24 .... 83 H7
John Rankin County
 Infants School
 NWBY RG14 .... 25 G8
John Rankin Junior
 NWBY RG14 .... 25 G8
Jubilee Business Centre
 WVILLE PO7 .... 352 C8
Jubilee Surgery
 FHAM/STUB PO14 .... 371 K8
Kanes Hill Primary School
 ITCH SO19 .... 345 J2
Keble Memorial
 Primary School
 RWIN SO21 .... 265 G2
Kelseys Doctors Surgery
 LISS GU33 .... 248 E4
Kempshott County
 Infant School
 KEMP RG22 .... 103 M8
Kempshott County
 Junior School
 KEMP RG22 .... 103 M8
Kennet Secondary School
 STHA RG19 .... 27 H5
The Kerridge Industrial Estate
 ALTN GU34 .... 176 F4
Kimpton Primary School
 RAND SP11 .... 116 C7
King Alfred College
 FUFL SO22 .... 10 B8
King Alfreds College of Higher
 Education
 FUFL SO22 .... 10 C9
King Edward VI School
 WSHM SO15 .... 318 D8
King Richard School
 CHAM PO6 .... 374 D8
The Kings Centre
 ALDT GU11 .... 6 F1
Kingsclere Health Centre
 KSCL RG20 .... 59 J6
Kingsclere Primary School
 KSCL RG20 .... 59 J6
Kings Copse Primary School
 HEND SO30 .... 346 A3
Kings Furlong Infant School
 BSTK RG21 .... 104 E5
Kings Furlong Junior School
 BSTK RG21 .... 104 E5
Kingsgrove Industrial Estate
 FARN GU14 .... 90 D5
Kings Junior School
 SBNE BH6 .... 449 L3
Kingsland Market
 SHAM SO14 .... 13 H3
Kingsleigh First School
 NBNE BH10 .... 432 A5
Kingsleigh Junior School
 NBNE BH10 .... 432 A5
Kingsleigh Secondary School
 NBNE BH10 .... 432 A5
Kingsley Business Park
 LIND GU35 .... 179 H7
Kings Park Primary School
 BMTH BH1 .... 448 D2
The Kings Primary School
 HEND SO30 .... 320 C5
Kings School
 BSTK RG21 .... 4 D9
Kings School
 ELGH SO50 .... 295 G7
Kings School
 FUFL SO22 .... 238 A2
Kings Somborne C of E School
 STOK SO20 .... 210 E6
Kings Theatre
 SSEA PO5 .... 21 K6
Kingstons Industrial Estate
 ASHV GU12 .... 113 H6
Kingsworthy Primary School
 WINC SO23 .... 215 H2
Kin Hon Clinic
 SSEA PO5 .... 20 F3
Kinson Primary School
 BWD BH11 .... 431 M3
Knights Enham Infants
 Infant School
 AND SP10 .... 118 F5
Knights Enham Junior School
 AND SP10 .... 118 F5
Knightwood Primary School
 NBAD SO52 .... 292 C1
Lacey Lodge School
 HSEA PO3 .... 423 M2
Lake Road Health Centre
 PSEA PO1 .... 423 J2

Lakeside Business Park
 SHST GU47 .... 69 K1
Lakeside Country Club
 FRIM GU16 .... 91 L2
Lakeside County
 Primary School
 FRIM GU16 .... 71 J7
Landford C of E
 Primary School
 RSAL SP5 .... 287 J4
Langdown County
 Infants School
 FAWY SO45 .... 367 M6
Langdown County
 Junior School
 FAWY SO45 .... 367 M5
Langrish CP School
 PSF GU32 .... 274 F5
Langside School
 BKME/WDN BH12 .... 431 L8
Langstone Infant School
 HSEA PO3 .... 423 J2
Langstone Junior School
 HSEA PO3 .... 423 J1
Lankhills School
 WINC SO23 .... 10 F1
Lansdowne Clinic
 BMTH BH1 .... 23 H2
Lee on Solent Health Centre
 LSOL/BMARY PO13 .... 420 C2
Lee-on-the-solent
 Infant School
 LSOL/BMARY PO13 .... 420 D3
Lee-on-the-solent
 Junior School
 LSOL/BMARY PO13 .... 420 D3
Leesland C of E Infant School
 GPORT PO12 .... 18 E3
Leesland C of E Junior School
 GPORT PO12 .... 18 E3
Leigh House Hospital
 CHFD SO53 .... 265 G8
Leisure Centre
 AND SP10 .... 9 H4
Leisure Centre
 HAV PO9 .... 16 F2
Leisure Centre
 SHAM SO14 .... 343 L2
Lido Sports Club
 WINC SO23 .... 11 G5
The Lilley Clinic
 HUNG RG17 .... 32 E2
Lilliput First School
 PSTN BH14 .... 446 B8
Limington House School
 KEMP RG22 .... 104 C5
Liner Industrial Estate
 WSHM SO15 .... 343 G2
Linsford Business Park
 FRIM GU16 .... 91 J5
Linwood School
 MOOR/WNTN BH9 .... 447 M1
Liphook County Infant School
 LIPH GU30 .... 226 E4
Liphook Golf Club
 LIPH GU30 .... 226 D8
Liphook Junior School
 LIPH GU30 .... 226 D4
Liss Business Centre
 LISS GU33 .... 248 D3
Liss County Infant &
 Junior School
 LISS GU33 .... 248 E5
Littledown Leisure Centre
 LTDN BH7 .... 433 L8
Littlefield School
 LIPH GU30 .... 227 G6
Little Green School
 RCCH PO18 .... 330 D4
Lockerley C of E (a)
 Primary School
 ROMY SO51 .... 232 F7
Locksheath County
 Infants & Primary School
 HLER SO31 .... 370 E7
Locks Road Surgery
 HLER SO31 .... 370 E6
Lockswood Surgery
 HLER SO31 .... 370 E5
Loddon Business Centre
 CHAM RG24 .... 5 M4
London Road School
 ODIM RG29 .... 108 D5
Longbridge Industrial Park
 SHAM SO14 .... 13 K6
Longdown Estates
 TOTT SO40 .... 341 J8
Longfellow Parade Clinic
 CHAM RG24 .... 5 H1
Longfleet C of E VC
 Combined School
 PLE BH15 .... 445 K4
Longparish School
 RAND SP11 .... 145 G4
Longspee School
 CFDH BH17 .... 445 J1
Longsutton Primary School
 ODIM RG29 .... 131 J5
Lord Mayor Treloar
 College Lower School
 ALTN GU34 .... 156 A6
Lord Mayor Treloar
 College Upper School
 ALTN GU34 .... 177 G1
Lordshill Health Centre
 ROWN SO16 .... 317 L4
Lord Wandsworth College
 ODIM RG29 .... 131 K6
Lorraine County First School
 CBLY GU15 .... 51 K8
L S U College of
 Higher Education
 WSHM SO15 .... 343 K1
Lucia Foster Welch College
 SHAM SO14 .... 13 J6
Ludgershall Health Centre
 RAND SP11 .... 92 E6

Ludgershall Sports Club
 RAND SP11 .... 92 D6
Ludlow Infant School
 ITCH SO19 .... 344 C5
Ludlow Middle School
 ITCH SO19 .... 344 C4
Lulworth Business Centre
 TOTT SO40 .... 316 D6
Lydlynch County First School
 TOTT SO40 .... 341 J1
Lymington Community
 Hospitals
 LYMN SO41 .... 440 C4
Lymington County Junior &
 Infant School
 LYMN SO41 .... 440 B4
Lymington Farm
 Industrial Estate
 ALTN GU34 .... 196 F5
Lymington Hospital
 LYMN SO41 .... 440 B4
Lymington Recreation Centre
 LYMN SO41 .... 440 A5
Lyndhurst Infant School
 LYND SO43 .... 363 K3
Lyndhurst Junior School
 NEND PO2 .... 399 K7
Lyndhurst School
 CBLY GU15 .... 70 E3
Lyndhurst Surgery
 LYND SO43 .... 363 K3
Lytchett Minster
 Upper School
 UPTN BH16 .... 428 C8
Magpies Sports Club
 WIMB BH21 .... 356 D8
Mainline Business Centre
 LISS GU33 .... 248 E4
The Malls/the Walks
 Shopping Centre
 BSTK RG21 .... 4 F7
Malmesbury Park School
 CHAR BH8 .... 23 J1
Malmesbury Park School
 CHAR BH8 .... 448 A2
Malvern Business Centre
 ROWN SO16 .... 318 C6
Manor Farm Business Centre
 NFNM GU10 .... 136 C3
Manorfield Infant School
 KEMP RG22 .... 127 K1
Manor Infant School
 FAWY SO45 .... 392 A3
Manor Infant School
 PSEA PO1 .... 423 J1
Manor Road Surgery
 VWD BH31 .... 356 C2
Mansbridge Primary School
 WEND SO18 .... 319 K4
The Manse Health Centre
 AND SP10 .... 9 J5
Mansel Infant & Junior Schools
 ROWN SO16 .... 317 J6
Mansfield Business Park
 ALTN GU34 .... 196 F5
Maple Business Park
 WIMB BH21 .... 405 K1
Maple Ridge School
 BSTK RG21 .... 4 E4
Marchwood C of E
 Infant School
 TOTT SO40 .... 342 C8
Marchwood Junior School
 TOTT SO40 .... 342 D7
Marchwood Priory Hospital
 TOTT SO40 .... 366 E1
Maritime Museum
 BROC SO42 .... 417 H4
Mark Way School
 AND SP10 .... 9 M4
Marlands Shopping Centre
 SHAM SO14 .... 12 F3
Marlborough County
 Infant School
 ALDT GU11 .... 112 F1
Marnel Infant & Junior Schools
 CHAM RG24 .... 83 H7
Marsh Farm Business Centre
 NFNM GU10 .... 110 C7
The Martin Kemp Welch School
 BKME/WDN BH12 .... 431 H8
Marwell Zoological Park
 RWIN SO21 .... 267 L8
Marycourt Co-educational
 School
 GPORT PO12 .... 18 D9
Mary Rose Exhibition
 PSEA PO1 .... 20 B1
Mary Rose Ship Hall
 PSEA PO1 .... 20 D2
Mason Manor Primary School
 ROWN SO16 .... 317 L8
Mayfield Avenue
 Industrial Park
 RAND SP11 .... 116 F6
Mayfield County
 Junior & Infant School
 FARN GU14 .... 90 D2
Mayfield Gallery
 MOOR/WNTN BH9 .... 432 D6
Mayfield School
 ALTN GU34 .... 177 G3
Mayflower Theatre
 WSHM SO15 .... 12 D1
Mayhill County Junior School
 ODIM RG29 .... 108 D6
May's Bounty
 BSTK RG21 .... 105 G5
Mayville High School
 SSEA PO5 .... 21 K8
Meadowlands Infant School
 HORN PO8 .... 352 C3
Meadowlands Junior School
 HORN PO8 .... 352 C3
The Meadow School
 LIND GU35 .... 201 M4

Mecca Leisure Bingo and
 Social Club
 AND SP10 .... 9 G6
Medina Primary School
 CHAM PO6 .... 399 J1
Medstead School
 ALTN GU34 .... 196 E2
Mengham Infant School
 HISD PO11 .... 425 L4
Mengham Junior School
 HISD PO11 .... 425 L4
Meoncross School
 FHAM/STUB PO14 .... 396 B4
Meon Infant School
 ENEY PO4 .... 423 M4
Meon Junior School
 ENEY PO4 .... 423 M3
Meonstoke School
 BPWT SO32 .... 299 H4
Meon Valley Golf &
 Country Club
 BPWT SO32 .... 323 J8
Meon Valley Police Station
 BPWT SO32 .... 297 J8
Merdon Junior School
 CHFD SO53 .... 293 J1
Meredith Infant School
 NEND PO2 .... 399 J8
Meridian TV Studios
 SHAM SO14 .... 344 A2
Merton County Junior School
 CHAM RG24 .... 4 C1
Micheldever Primary School
 RWIN SO21 .... 169 M5
Middle Hill Health Clinic
 ALDT GU11 .... 112 D5
Middle Park Medical Centre
 HAV PO9 .... 377 G4
Milestone Transport Museum
 KEMP RG22 .... 104 B3
Milford C of E School
 LYMN SO41 .... 454 D2
Millbrook Clinic
 ROWN SO16 .... 317 K8
Millbrook Community School
 ROWN SO16 .... 317 K5
Millbrook Secondary School
 ROWN SO16 .... 317 K5
Millbrook Trading Estate
 WSHM SO15 .... 342 C1
Mill Chase County
 Secondary School
 LIND GU35 .... 201 L5
Millers Dale Surgery
 CHFD SO53 .... 265 G8
Millhouse Business Centre
 ITCH SO19 .... 344 B4
Millstream Trading Estate
 RGWD BH24 .... 382 D3
Milton Park Infant School
 ENEY PO4 .... 423 M4
Milton Park Junior School
 ENEY PO4 .... 423 M4
M L S College
 BMTH BH1 .... 22 E5
Monks Brook Industrial Park
 CHFD SO53 .... 293 G3
Moordown C of E
 Primary School
 MOOR/WNTN BH9 .... 432 D7
Moorgreen Hospital
 HEND SO30 .... 320 E6
Moorings Way Infant School
 ENEY PO4 .... 424 A2
Moorlands College
 CHCH/BSGR BH23 .... 434 F2
Moorlands Infant School
 WEND SO18 .... 319 M7
Moor Park College
 NFNM GU10 .... 135 K7
More House School
 NFNM GU10 .... 158 F6
Morelands Primary School
 WVILLE PO7 .... 376 C6
Moreton House School
 PSF GU32 .... 275 K5
Morgans Vale &
 Woodfalls Primary School
 RSAL SP5 .... 285 J7
Morland Surgery
 TADY RG26 .... 61 L1
Mortimers Farm
 Industrial Estate
 ROMY SO51 .... 315 K2
Mortimer Surgery
 THLE RG7 .... 43 J2
Mottisfont Abbey
 ROMY SO51 .... 233 L5
Mottisfont Club House
 ROMY SO51 .... 233 K6
Mountbatten Business Centre
 WSHM SO15 .... 12 B1
Mountbatten Secondary School
 ROMY SO51 .... 291 H2
The Mount Hospital
 ELGH SO50 .... 294 C3
Mount Pleasant
 Industrial Estate
 SHAM SO14 .... 343 M1
Mount Pleasant Junior School
 SHAM SO14 .... 343 M1
Moyles Court School
 RGWD BH24 .... 359 G2
Mudeford County
 Primary School
 CHCH/BSGR BH23 .... 450 D2
Mudeford Junior School
 CHCH/BSGR BH23 .... 450 E2
Murrell Green Business Park
 HTWY RG27 .... 86 D2
Muscliff C Primary School
 MOOR/WNTN BH9 .... 433 G5
Museum of Army Flying
 STOK SO20 .... 162 F5
Music Gallery
 MOOR/WNTN BH9 .... 432 F8
Mylen Business Centre
 AND SP10 .... 8 D3

Mytchett County First School
FRIM GU16 .... 91 J4

National Motor Museum
BROC SO42 .... 390 D6

National Museum of Artillery
WHAM PO17 .... 373 M5

The Natural Health Centre
NWBY RG14 .... 37 G2

Natural Sciences Museum
ENEY PO4 .... 423 K7

Nelson Industrial Park
HEND SO30 .... 321 G7

Nethercliffe School
FUFL SO22 .... 10 D5

Netley Abbey Infant School
HLER SO31 .... 368 F1

Netley Court School
HLER SO31 .... 368 F3

Netley Marsh C of E
Controlled Infant School
TOTT SO40 .... 340 E1

Neville Lovett Community
School
FHAM/STUB PO14 .... 14 E8

New Ashgate Gallery
FNM GU9 .... 134 E6

Newbridge Junior School
NEND PO2 .... 423 K1

Newbury Business Park
NWBY RG14 .... 3 J2

Newbury College of Further
Education
NWBY RG14 .... 2 C1

Newbury District Council
NWBY RG14 .... 3 G6

Newbury District Council
WHCH RG28 .... 122 B2

Newbury District Hospital
NWBY RG14 .... 2 D7

Newbury District Museum &
Tourist Information Centre
NWBY RG14 .... 2 F4

Newbury Retail Park
NWBY RG14 .... 37 L1

Newbury Rugby
Football Club Ltd
NWBY RG14 .... 37 J2

Newbury Town Council
NWBY RG14 .... 2 E4

The New Chineham Surgery
CHAM RG24 .... 83 L6

New Forest District Council
NMIL/BTOS BH25 .... 437 L6

New Forest District Council
RGWD BH24 .... 382 D2

New Forest Golf Club
LYND SO43 .... 363 M2

New Forest Museum &
Visitors Centre
LYND SO43 .... 363 L3

New Greenham Park
Leisure Centre
STHA RG19 .... 38 D4

Newlands CP School
YTLY GU46 .... 68 F3

Newlands Infant &
Middle School
ROWN SO16 .... 317 K7

New Milton Junior School
NMIL/BTOS BH25 .... 437 L7

New Milton Recreation Centre
NMIL/BTOS BH25 .... 437 K6

New Milton Sports Club
NMIL/BTOS BH25 .... 438 A5

New Milton Town Council
NMIL/BTOS BH25 .... 437 L6

Newport County
Junior & Infant School
ASHV GU12 .... 7 L4

New Scotland Hill CP School
SHST GU47 .... 49 K6

New Street Football Club
RAND SP11 .... 118 C3

New Street Medical Centre
AND SP10 .... 9 K3

New Theatre Royal
PSEA PO1 .... 20 F2

The Newton Health Clinic
SHAM SO14 .... 343 L2

Newton Toney School
AMSY SP4 .... 160 A3

Newtown Soberton County
Primary School
WHAM PO17 .... 349 M2

Newtown Surgery
LIPH GU30 .... 226 E6

Nightingale County Junior &
Infant School
ELGH SO50 .... 293 J7

Nightingale Surgery
ROMY SO51 .... 262 F8

Nomansland & Hamptworth
C of E Primary School
RSAL SP5 .... 287 G8

Norman Court School
RSAL SP5 .... 207 K6

The Norman Gate School
(acorns)
AND SP10 .... 9 M3

Northam Business Centre
SHAM SO14 .... 344 A2

Northam Primary School
SHAM SO14 .... 13 L1

North Baddesley County Infants
School
NBAD SO52 .... 292 A4

North Baddesley Junior School
NBAD SO52 .... 292 A4

Northbrook Industrial Estate
ROWN SO16 .... 318 B6

Northcroft Surgery
NWBY RG14 .... 2 D4

Northern County Junior &
Infant School
FHAM/PORC PO16 .... 374 A7

Northern Parade Clinic
NEND PO2 .... 399 J4

Northern Parade Infant
School
NEND PO2 .... 399 J5

Northern Parade Junior
School
NEND PO2 .... 399 J5

North Farnborough County
Infant School
FARN GU14 .... 91 G3

North Hampshire Hospital
CHAM RG24 .... 82 D8

North Hants Golf Club
FARN GU14 .... 88 F4

North Lane Practice
ASHV GU12 .... 113 H7

Northtown Trading Estate
ASHV GU12 .... 113 H7

Northview Gallery
HLER SO31 .... 346 A8

North Waltham Business
Centre
OVTN RG25 .... 126 A6

North Waltham School
OVTN RG25 .... 125 K7

Norwood CP School
ELGH SO50 .... 293 M5

Nova Business Park
NMIL/BTOS BH25 .... 437 J6

Nuffield Theatre
PTSW SO17 .... 318 F5

Nursling C of E Primary School
ROWN SO16 .... 317 J3

Nursling Industrial Estate
ROWN SO16 .... 317 G5

Oakdale South Road
Middle School
PLE BH15 .... 445 J5

Oak Farm Community School
FARN GU14 .... 90 D2

Oakfield Primary School
TOTT SO40 .... 316 D8

Oaklands Community School
ROWN SO16 .... 317 J3

Oaklands County Junior &
Infant School
CWTH RG45 .... 49 K2

Oaklands RC School
WVILLE PO7 .... 376 D3

Oakley C of E Junior School
DEAN RG23 .... 102 F7

Oakley County Infant School
DEAN RG23 .... 102 F7

Oak Lodge School
FAWY SO45 .... 367 G5

Oakmead College of
Technology
BWD BH11 .... 431 K3

Oak Park Golf Club
NFNM GU10 .... 133 K2

Oakridge County Junior School
BSTK RG21 .... 4 C3

Oakwood First School
ROWN SO16 .... 318 A3

Oakwood Junior School
ROWN SO16 .... 318 A3

Oakwood School
HTWY RG27 .... 87 J3

Oatlands House Health Clinic
ROWN SO16 .... 318 B6

Oceanographic Centre
SHAM SO14 .... 13 K8

Odeon Cinema
BMTH BH1 .... 22 F6

Odeon Cinema
NEND PO2 .... 399 H7

Odeon Cinema
WSHM SO15 .... 12 D4

Odiham Castle
ODIM RG29 .... 108 A4

Odiham Cottage Hospital
ODIM RG29 .... 108 D6

The Odiham Health Centre
ODIM RG29 .... 108 C5

Oil Refinery
FAWY SO45 .... 392 D4

O Jays Industrial Park
HSEA PO3 .... 399 L6

Old Anchor Inn Surgery
ELGH SO50 .... 294 B5

Old Basing Surgery
CHAM RG24 .... 106 A3

Old Dames School
FBDG SP6 .... 285 H5

Oldfield Gallery
SSEA PO5 .... 21 H5

The Old Fire Station Surgery
ITCH SO19 .... 344 C5

Old Hambledonians
Cricket Club
HORN PO8 .... 301 K6

Old Thorns Golf &
Country Club
LIPH GU30 .... 226 A5

Olivers Battery Primary School
FUFL SO22 .... 238 B5

The Omni Business Centre
ALTN GU34 .... 177 G5

On Line Gallery
WSHM SO15 .... 343 K2

Orchard County Infant &
Junior School
FAWY SO45 .... 367 J6

Orchard Lea Junior &
Infant Schools
FHAM PO15 .... 372 C4

Oriel Business Park
ALTN GU34 .... 177 G5

Orion Business Centre
WEND SO18 .... 319 K3

The Osborn Clinic
FHAM/PORC PO16 .... 15 L5

Osborne Practice Surgery
SSEA PO5 .... 21 G7

Osborn Way Industrial Estate
HTWY RG27 .... 85 M8

Otterbourne Primary School
RWIN SO21 .... 266 A6

Our Lady & St Joseph RC
Primary School
LYMN SO41 .... 440 D4

Our Ladys Preparatory
School
CWTH RG45 .... 49 K3

Overbridge Surgery
KEMP RG22 .... 104 D4

Overton C of E Primary
School
OVTN RG25 .... 100 E7

Overton Gallery
OVTN RG25 .... 100 F8

Overton Surgery
OVTN RG25 .... 101 G8

Owlsmoor Primary School
SHST GU47 .... 50 B7

Owslebury CP School
RWIN SO21 .... 267 M4

Padnell Infant School
HORN PO8 .... 352 E6

Padnell Junior School
HORN PO8 .... 352 F5

Padworth College
THLE RG7 .... 30 B7

Palace House
BROC SO42 .... 390 C7

Palmerston Business Park
FHAM/STUB PO14 .... 396 E1

Park Community School
HAV PO9 .... 377 G3

Park Gate Business Centre
HLER SO31 .... 370 F2

Park Gate Junior School
HLER SO31 .... 370 F3

Park House Primary School
HAV PO9 .... 377 G3

Park House School
NWBY RG14 .... 37 H2

Parklands Business Park
WVILLE PO7 .... 351 K5

Park Lane Medical Centre
HAV PO9 .... 377 H5

Park Primary School
ALDT GU11 .... 7 J7

Parkstone Grammar School
for Girls
CFDH BH17 .... 429 M8

Park View Infant School
KEMP RG22 .... 104 B6

Park View Junior School
KEMP RG22 .... 104 B5

Parkway Retail Park
BMTH BH1 .... 23 J2

Parley First School
FERN BH22 .... 406 B5

Parsons Down Infant School
STHA RG19 .... 26 E5

Parsons Down Junior School
STHA RG19 .... 26 D5

The Pascoe Practice
PSEA PO1 .... 20 E4

Passfield Mill Business Park
LIPH GU30 .... 202 A7

Paulsgrove Industrial Centre
CHAM PO6 .... 374 F8

Paulsgrove Primary School
CHAM PO6 .... 374 F8

Pavilion
BMTH BH1 .... 23 G3

Pavilion Theatre
BMTH BH1 .... 22 E6

Pavillion Theatre
BMTH BH1 .... 22 F7

Peacock Trading Estate
ELGH SO50 .... 293 L3

Peel Common County Junior &
Infant School
LSOL/BMARY PO13 .... 396 E6

Pegham Industrial Park
FHAM PO15 .... 371 M2

Pendulum Gallery
ALTN GU34 .... 199 K8

Penhale Infant School
PSEA PO1 .... 21 M1

Pennington County Junior &
Infant School
LYMN SO41 .... 440 A5

Perins County Secondary
School
NARL SO24 .... 218 B3

Peter Dyer Gallery
SSEA PO5 .... 21 H7

Petersfield Business Park
PSF GU32 .... 275 J5

Petersfield Community
Hospital
PSF GU32 .... 275 K5

Petersfield County Infant
School
EPSF GU31 .... 275 L5

Petersfield Golf Club
PSF GU32 .... 248 B8

Petersfield Rugby
Football Club
EPSF GU31 .... 276 C4

Petersfield School
PSF GU32 .... 275 K6

Petersfield Swimming Pool
EPSF GU31 .... 275 L5

Petersfield Town Council
EPSF GU31 .... 275 M5

Petersfield Town
Football Club
EPSF GU31 .... 275 M4

Petersgate Infant School
HORN PO8 .... 328 B4

Peter Symonds College
FUFL SO22 .... 10 E4

The Pheasant Hotel
AMSY SP4 .... 182 D6

Phoenix Industrial Park
ELGH SO50 .... 294 B6

Pierreponte School
NFNM GU10 .... 159 H7

Pier Theatre
BMTH BH1 .... 22 F8

Pilgrims School
WINC SO23 .... 11 H9

Pilgrims Way Infants School
FNM GU9 .... 134 E8

Pinehill Surgery
LIND GU35 .... 201 J6

Pineridge County First School
CBLY GU15 .... 51 K7

Pinewood Infants School
FARN GU14 .... 90 A1

Pipers Industrial Estate
STHA RG19 .... 27 J7

Pipers Wood Industrial Park
WVILLE PO7 .... 352 A8

Pitmore School
CHFD SO53 .... 265 L8

Plaza Theatre
ROMY SO51 .... 290 E1

Pokesdown Primary School
BOSC BH5 .... 449 G3

The Polygon School
WSHM SO15 .... 343 J2

Poole Grammar School
CFDH BH17 .... 430 B6

Poole Road Medical Centre
WBNE BH4 .... 22 A6

Poole Technical High School
PLE BH15 .... 445 H4

Portcastrian R F C
SBNE BH6 .... 449 K2

Portchester Castle
FHAM/PORC PO16 .... 398 C3

Portchester Community
School
FHAM/PORC PO16 .... 398 A1

Portchester Health Centre
FHAM/PORC PO16 .... 374 A8

Portchester School
LTDN BH7 .... 448 F1

Portesbery School
CBLY GU15 .... 71 G2

Portsdown Group Practice
WVILLE PO7 .... 376 C5

Portsmouth City Council
CHAM PO6 .... 374 F7

Portsmouth City Council
CHAM PO6 .... 375 K8

Portsmouth City Council
CHAM PO6 .... 399 J1

Portsmouth City Council
HAV PO9 .... 377 K4

Portsmouth City Council
PSEA PO1 .... 20 D5

Portsmouth City Council
PSEA PO1 .... 423 J1

Portsmouth City Council
SSEA PO5 .... 21 G6

Portsmouth City Council
SSEA PO5 .... 21 H2

Portsmouth City Council
SSEA PO5 .... 21 J5

Portsmouth County Court
PSEA PO1 .... 21 G2

Portsmouth Crown Court
PSEA PO1 .... 21 G3

Portsmouth Grammar School
PSEA PO1 .... 20 E4

Portsmouth High School
SSEA PO5 .... 20 F6

Portsmouth Natural
Health Centre
SSEA PO5 .... 20 F4

Portsmouth Rugby
Football Club
HSEA PO3 .... 399 L4

Portsmouth Sixth
Form College
HSEA PO3 .... 424 A1

Portswood Primary School
PTSW SO17 .... 319 H6

Portswood Road Surgery
PTSW SO17 .... 319 G7

Portway County Infants School
AND SP10 .... 8 A4

Portway Junior School
AND SP10 .... 118 B8

Potley Hill County
Primary School
BLKW GU17 .... 69 K3

Potters Gate Primary School
FNM GU9 .... 134 D6

Poulner Junior & Infant School
RGWD BH24 .... 359 G6

The Practice Doctors Surgery
FHAM/PORC PO16 .... 15 H5

Premier Business Park
FHAM/STUB PO14 .... 14 C7

Preston Candover
Primary School
OVTN RG25 .... 151 L2

Preston Ho
OVTN RG25 .... 151 J7

Priestlands County
Secondary School
LYMN SO41 .... 440 D4

Priets House Museum
WIMB BH21 .... 404 A4

Princes Hall
ALDT GU11 .... 6 E1

Princes Mead School
RWIN SO21 .... 215 K2

Princess Anne Hospital
ROWN SO16 .... 318 A4

Prior Heath School
CBLY GU15 .... 71 K3

Priory C of E VA
Primary School
CHCH/BSGR BH23 .... 450 A1

The Priory Primary School
TADY RG26 .... 62 A7

Priory School
SSEA PO5 .... 21 L3

Private Medical Centre
BMTH BH1 .... 23 G5

Prospect Business Centre
NARL SO24 .... 218 B4

Purbrook Cricket Club
WVILLE PO7 .... 375 M4

Purbrook Junior &
Infant School
WVILLE PO7 .... 376 B2

Purbrook Park School
WVILLE PO7 .... 376 B5

Puttenham C of E School
RGUW GU3 .... 137 L4

Queen Alexandra Hospital
CHAM PO6 .... 375 J7

Queen Marys College
BSTK RG21 .... 105 G5

Queens Enclosure
Primary School
WVILLE PO7 .... 352 D7

Queens Road Surgery
NEND PO2 .... 399 J8

Raceview Business Centre
NWBY RG14 .... 3 H5

Rachel Madocks School
HORN PO8 .... 352 B4

Rake C of E Controlled
First School
LISS GU33 .... 249 L3

Ranvilles Junior &
Infant School
FHAM/STUB PO14 .... 372 A6

Red Barn County
Primary School
FHAM/PORC PO16 .... 373 M8

Redbridge Community School
ROWN SO16 .... 317 J8

Redbridge Primary School
ROWN SO16 .... 317 J8

Redfields Industrial Estate
FLET GU13 .... 110 E5

Redfields Industrial Park
FLET GU13 .... 110 D6

Red Funnel Ferry Terminal
SHAM SO14 .... 12 F7

Red Gallery
SSEA PO5 .... 21 J7

Red House Museum & Gardens
CHCH/BSGR BH23 .... 450 A3

Redlands County
Primary School
FHAM/PORC PO16 .... 15 H9

Red Lodge School
ROWN SO16 .... 318 D4

Redlynch C of E
Primary School
RSAL SP5 .... 285 M3

Redwood Park School
CHAM PO6 .... 399 M2

Regents Park Girls School
ROWN SO16 .... 317 J4

Regents Park Surgery
WSHM SO15 .... 318 A8

Regional Film Theatre
SHAM SO14 .... 13 J8

Retail Park
NWBY RG14 .... 3 J3

Rex Industrial Estate
CHFD SO53 .... 293 H3

Richard Aldworth
Community School
KEMP RG22 .... 104 C6

Richard Martin
Gallery & Bookshop
GPORT PO12 .... 19 H4

Richmond Surgery
FLET GU13 .... 110 E2

Riders Junior & Infant School
HAV PO9 .... 377 H3

Ridgemede Junior School
BPWT SO32 .... 297 J8

Ridgeway House
Special School
ITCH SO19 .... 344 C3

Ridgeway School
FNM GU9 .... 158 F1

Ringwood C of E
Infant School
RGWD BH24 .... 382 E1

Ringwood County
Junior School
RGWD BH24 .... 382 E2

Ringwood Recreation Centre
RGWD BH24 .... 382 E1

Ringwood School
RGWD BH24 .... 382 E1

Ringwood Town Council
RGWD BH24 .... 382 E2

Ringwood Trading Estate
RGWD BH24 .... 382 E2

Ringwood Waldorf School
RGWD BH24 .... 381 M2

Riverpark Industrial Estate
NWBY RG14 .... 3 J3

River Park Leisure Centre
WINC SO23 .... 11 H5

Riverside Business Park
FNM GU9 .... 134 F5

Riverside Business Park
LYMN SO41 .... 440 D4

Riverside Close Surgery
LISS GU33 .... 248 D4

Riverside Park
Industrial Estate
FNM GU9 .... 135 G5

Riverside School
WVILLE PO7 .... 376 D5

Riverwey Industrial Park
ALTN GU34 .... 177 G4

Robert King Gallery
LYMN SO41 .... 440 B5

Robert Mays School
ODIM RG29 .... 108 B5

Rogate C of E
Controlled School
EPSF GU31 .... 277 L4

Romans Business Park
FNM GU9 .... 135 G5

Roman Way Primary School
AND SP10 .... 118 F4

Romsey Abbey C of E
Primary School
ROMY SO51 .... 290 C1

Romsey County Junior School
  ROMY SO51...................... 262 F8
Romsey Cricket Club
  ROMY SO51...................... 290 E2
Romsey Hospital
  ROMY SO51...................... 290 F1
Romsey Industrial Estate
  ROMY SO51...................... 262 D7
Romsey Infant School
  ROMY SO51...................... 290 E1
Romsey Rugby Football Club
  ROMY SO51...................... 290 E2
The Romsey School
  ROMY SO51...................... 262 D8
Romsey Sports Centre
  ROMY SO51...................... 290 E2
Rookesbury Park School
  WHAM PO17...................... 349 H4
Ropley C of E Primary School
  NARL SO24...................... 220 B3
Rowledge C of E First School
  NFNM GU10...................... 158 A5
Rowmans House
Industrial Estate
  ROWN SO16...................... 317 K2
Rowner County Infant School
  LSOL/BMARY PO13.............. 397 H7
Rowner County Junior School
  LSOL/BMARY PO13.............. 397 H7
Rowner Health Centre
  LSOL/BMARY PO13.............. 397 G8
Rowner Swimming Centre
  LSOL/BMARY PO13.............. 421 G2
Royal Army Medical Corps
  ALDT GU11...................... 113 G4
Royal Hampshire
County Hospital
  FUFL SO22...................... 10 B8
Royal Hampshire
Regiment Museum
  WINC SO23...................... 10 F8
Royal Hospital Haslar
  GPORT PO12...................... 19 K7
Royal Marines Museum
  ENEY PO4...................... 423 M6
Royal Naval Museum
  PSEA PO1...................... 20 A1
Royal Navy Submarine Museum
Offices
  GPORT PO12...................... 19 L6
The Royal School
  HASM GU27...................... 204 D6
Royal South Hants Hospital
  SHAM SO14...................... 343 L2
Royal Winchester Golf Club
  FUFL SO22...................... 238 A1
Ruckstall County
Primary School
  BSTK RG21...................... 105 J5
Rushcombe County
First School
  WIMB BH21...................... 429 H2
Rushington Business Park
  TOTT SO40...................... 341 J3
Rushmoor Borough Council
  FARN GU14...................... 90 E5
Russell Cotes Art Gallery &
Museum
  BMTH BH1...................... 23 G7
Russell Hicks & Temple
  ROMY SO51...................... 290 D1
St Albans C of E Primary School
  HAV PO9...................... 377 L5
St Aldhelms C of E
Combined School
  BKME/WDN BH12.............. 446 F2
St Andrews Surgery
  ELGH SO50...................... 293 M6
St Annes Catholic
Primary School
  KEMP RG22...................... 104 C5
St Annes School
  LSOL/BMARY PO13.............. 420 C1
St Anns Hospital
  CCLF BH13...................... 457 K2
St Anthonys RC Primary School
  FHAM/STUB PO14.............. 371 H6
St Barbe Museum
  LYMN SO41...................... 440 C4
St Bartholomews C of E
School
  HASM GU27...................... 204 F8
St Bartholomews
(Joint School)
  NWBY RG14...................... 2 B7
St Bartholomews School
  NWBY RG14...................... 2 B8
St Bedes Catholic Primary
School
  CHAM RG24...................... 82 F7
St Bedes C of E Primary School
  WINC SO23...................... 11 H6
St Benedicts Convent School
  RAND SP11...................... 117 M5
St Bernadettes RC
Primary School
  FARN GU14...................... 90 D3
St Catherines RC
Primary School
  WIMB BH21...................... 404 E2
St Catherines Road
Junior School
  ELGH SO50...................... 293 M3
St Catherines School
  CBLY GU15...................... 70 F4
St Christophers Hospital
  FHAM/PORC PO16.............. 15 L2
St Christophers School
  WEND SO18...................... 319 K8
St Clements C of E School
  BMTH BH1...................... 448 C3
St Cuthmans School
  MIDH GU29...................... 279 K2
St Denys Primary School
  PTSW SO17...................... 319 H7
St Edmunds Catholic School
  PSEA PO1...................... 21 J1

St Edmunds School
  GSHT GU26...................... 204 A5
St Edward Comprehensive
School
  PLE BH15...................... 445 L1
St Edwards School
  ROMY SO51...................... 258 M7
St Faiths Primary School
  WINC SO23...................... 238 E3
St Francis Primary School
  NBAD SO52...................... 292 E3
St Francis School
  FHAM/STUB PO14.............. 372 A7
St Gabriels School
  KSCL RG20...................... 37 L2
St Georges Beneficial C of E
Primary School
  PSEA PO1...................... 20 D2
St Georges Business Centre
  PSEA PO1...................... 20 D2
St Georges Catholic
Boys School
  ELGH SO50...................... 319 H2
St Georges Hospital
  LYMN SO41...................... 454 B4
St Georges Industrial Estate
  CBLY GU15...................... 70 E5
St Georges Industrial Estate
  ENEY PO4...................... 423 L3
St Georges University School of
Medicine
  WINC SO23...................... 11 G7
St Ives CP School
  RGWD BH24...................... 381 L3
St James C of E
Primary School
  EMRTH PO10...................... 378 C6
St James C of E
Primary School
  LTDN BH7...................... 449 G3
St James C of E (VC)
First School
  FBDG SP6...................... 333 L2
St James Hospital
  ENEY PO4...................... 423 M3
St James Primary School
  HEND SO30...................... 320 E6
St Johns Cathedral
  PSEA PO1...................... 422 F2
St Johns Cathedral
Primary School
  PSEA PO1...................... 21 K1
St Johns C of E First School
  NFNM GU10...................... 181 H7
St Johns C of E Infant School
  HLER SO31...................... 371 G6
St Johns C of E Primary School
  GPORT PO12...................... 421 M1
St Johns C of E Primary School
  HAV PO9...................... 353 M8
St Johns College
  SSEA PO5...................... 21 J6
St Johns School
  BSTK RG21...................... 104 F5
St Johns School
  NWBY RG14...................... 2 D9
St Johns School
  THLE RG7...................... 43 K3
St Johns School
  WIMB BH21...................... 404 B4
St John the Baptist RC
Primary School
  AND SP10...................... 8 B6
St John the Baptist School
  BPWT SO32...................... 323 K6
St Josephs Gm RC
Primary School
  ALDT GU11...................... 6 F6
St Josephs RC Primary School
  NWBY RG14...................... 3 H1
St Josephs RC School
  BKME/WDN BH12.............. 446 D1
St Josephs RC School
  CHCH/BSGR BH23.............. 435 L8
St Josephs RC Junior School
  ALDT GU11...................... 6 F5
St Judes Catholic
Primary School
  FHAM/STUB PO14.............. 14 C6
St Judes C of E Primary School
  PSEA PO1...................... 20 E5
St Katherines C of E
Primary School
  SBNE BH6...................... 450 A4
St Lawrence C of E
(Controlled) Primary School
  ALTN GU34...................... 176 D4
St Leonards Hospital
  RGWD BH24...................... 381 G7
St Lukes C of E School
  MOOR/WNTN BH9.............. 432 D8
St Lukes C of E School
  SSEA PO5...................... 21 H2
St Lukes Surgery
  HEND SO30...................... 321 G7
St Marks C of E County
Infant School
  CHCH/BSGR BH23.............. 436 D7
St Marks C of E Junior School
  WSHM SO15...................... 343 H1
St Marks C of E Primary School
  FARN GU14...................... 91 G8
St Marks C of E Primary School
  NBNE BH10...................... 432 A7
St Marks Primary School
  KEMP RG22...................... 127 G3
St Martins East Woodhay C of E
Primary School
  KSCL RG20...................... 55 K1
St Mary Bourne School
  RAND SP11...................... 97 L6
St Marys C of E Junior School
  CHAM RG24...................... 106 A2
St Marys C of E Junior School
  NTHA RG18...................... 27 G4
St Marys C of E Primary School
  SHAM SO14...................... 13 J2

St Marys C of E Primary School
  SHAM SO14...................... 13 K2
St Marys College
  WEND SO18...................... 319 K8
St Marys First School
  FERN BH22...................... 380 B5
St Marys Hospital
  HSEA PO3...................... 423 L2
St Marys Primary School
  ALTN GU34...................... 175 M2
St Marys Primary School
  TLHT RG30...................... 31 M2
St Marys RC Primary School
  GPORT PO12...................... 18 C1
St Marys RC School
  PLE BH15...................... 445 K3
St Marys School
  THLE RG7...................... 44 A3
St Marys Surgery
  AND SP10...................... 9 J4
St Marys Surgery
  SHAM SO14...................... 13 J3
St Matthews C of E
Primary School
  LIND GU35...................... 200 F8
St Michaels Abbey
  FARN GU14...................... 90 F3
St Michaels C of E Controlled
Secondary School
  ALDT GU11...................... 7 J6
St Michaels C of E Infant School
  ALDT GU11...................... 7 H6
St Michaels C of E
Primary School
  SHST GU47...................... 49 H8
St Michaels C of E School
  WCLF BH2...................... 22 B6
St Michaels Middle School
  WIMB BH21...................... 404 C1
St Michaels School
  KSCL RG20...................... 57 J2
St Monica Infant School
  ITCH SO19...................... 344 E5
St Monica Middle School
  ITCH SO19...................... 344 E5
St Neots Preparatory
School Ltd
  HTWY RG27...................... 47 H8
St Nicholas C of E School
  NWBY RG14...................... 2 D6
St Nicholas School
  NFNM GU10...................... 110 D6
St Omer Barracks
  ALDT GU11...................... 113 G4
St Patricks RC Primary School
  ITCH SO19...................... 344 C5
St Patricks RC School
  FARN GU14...................... 91 G4
St Pauls C of E First School
  NFNM GU10...................... 136 D1
St Pauls Hospital
  FUFL SO22...................... 10 E6
St Pauls RC Primary School
  CHAM PO6...................... 374 F8
St Peter's Church
  BMTH BH1...................... 22 F6
St Peters C of E Middle School
  FNM GU9...................... 158 C2
St Peters Gm C of E School
  YTLY GU46...................... 69 G2
St Peters Junior School
  FARN GU14...................... 90 F4
St Peters School
  FUFL SO22...................... 238 A3
St Peters School
  LTDN BH7...................... 433 M8
St Peters School
  SBNE BH6...................... 449 L4
St Polycarps RC Primary School
  FNM GU9...................... 135 G7
St Swithuns RC Primary School
  SSEA PO5...................... 21 K8
St Swithuns School
  RWIN SO21...................... 215 J8
St Swithun Wells RC
Primary School
  CHFD SO53...................... 293 J3
St Thomas Clinic
  LYMN SO41...................... 440 B5
St Thomas Infant School
  KSCL RG20...................... 36 B8
St Thomas Mores RC
Primary School
  HAV PO9...................... 16 A1
St Vincent College
  GPORT PO12...................... 18 F1
St Walburgas RC
Primary School
  MOOR/WNTN BH9.............. 432 F6
Salesian College
  FARN GU14...................... 91 G7
Salterns School
  TOTT SO40...................... 316 F8
Sampson Business Park
  CBLY GU15...................... 70 E5
The Samuel Cody School
  ALDT GU11...................... 112 E1
The Sanatorium Canford
School
  WIMB BH21...................... 404 E7
Sandford Springs Golf Club
  TADY RG26...................... 59 M6
Sandhurst College
Town County Junior School
  SHST GU47...................... 50 B8
Sandhurst School
  SHST GU47...................... 50 A8
Sandhurst Sports Club
  SHST GU47...................... 69 M1
Sandhurst Surgery
  SHST GU47...................... 69 L1
Sandleford Hospital
  NWBY RG14...................... 25 K8
Sandleheath Industrial Estate
  FBDG SP6...................... 309 G5
Sandle Manor School
  FBDG SP6...................... 309 J6

Sarisbury Green C of E
Primary School
  HLER SO31...................... 370 C3
Sarisbury Infant School
  HLER SO31...................... 370 C4
Sarum Road Hospital
  FUFL SO22...................... 238 B1
Saxon Shore Infant School
  CHAM PO6...................... 374 C8
Saxonwood School for the
Handicapped
  DEAN RG23...................... 82 A8
Scantabout Primary School
  CHFD SO53...................... 293 L1
Scaplens Court Museum
  PLE BH15...................... 445 G7
Selborne Primary School
  ALTN GU34...................... 199 J8
Shakespeare Business Centre
  ELGH SO50...................... 294 A4
Shakespeare County
Infant School
  ELGH SO50...................... 293 M4
Shalbourne C of E School
  MARL SN8...................... 32 B4
Shamblehurst CP School
  HEND SO30...................... 321 H8
Sharps Copse Junior &
Infant School
  HAV PO9...................... 377 M3
Shawcross Industrial Park
  HSEA PO3...................... 399 L3
Shaw-cum-donnington School
  NWBY RG14...................... 25 K2
Shawfield County
Infant School
  ASHV GU12...................... 113 K5
Sheet CP School
  PSF GU32...................... 276 A2
Shelley Museum
  BOSC BH5...................... 448 E4
Shepherds Down School
  RWIN SO21...................... 266 B2
Shepherd Spring
Medical Centre
  AND SP10...................... 119 G5
Shepherds Spring
County Infants School
  AND SP10...................... 119 G5
Sherborne House School
  CHFD SO53...................... 265 J8
Sherborne St John
Primary School
  CHAM RG24...................... 82 D4
The Ship House Surgery
  LIPH GU30...................... 226 E5
Shirley Business Park
  WSHM SO15...................... 343 G1
Shirley First & Middle School
  WSHM SO15...................... 318 B7
The Shirley Health Centre
  WSHM SO15...................... 343 G1
Shirley Swimming Pool
  WSHM SO15...................... 343 G1
Shirley Warren Primary School
  ROWN SO16...................... 317 M6
Sholing First School
  ITCH SO19...................... 344 E4
Sholing Girls School
  ITCH SO19...................... 344 E4
Sholing Infants School
  ITCH SO19...................... 344 E3
Sholing Middle School
  ITCH SO19...................... 344 E3
Shottermill County
Middle School
  HASM GU27...................... 228 C1
Sidings Industrial Estate
  HLER SO31...................... 369 H3
Sikh Temple
  SSEA PO5...................... 21 J4
Silchester Primary School
  THLE RG7...................... 42 E7
Simcoe Clinic
  WSHM SO15...................... 343 J1
Sinclair First & Junior School
  ROWN SO16...................... 317 M3
Siskin County Junior &
Infant School
  LSOL/BMARY PO13.............. 421 H2
The Sixth Form College
  FARN GU14...................... 90 E1
Slades Farm Special School
  NBNE BH10...................... 432 B7
Smannell & Enham
Primary School
  RAND SP11...................... 119 K1
Solent Business Centre
  WSHM SO15...................... 342 F2
Solent Industrial Centre
  WSHM SO15...................... 343 G1
Solent Industrial Estate
  HEND SO30...................... 321 G7
Solent Infant School
  CHAM PO6...................... 376 B8
Solent Junior School
  CHAM PO6...................... 376 B8
Solent Peoples Theatre
  ITCH SO19...................... 345 G5
Somerford County
Infant School
  CHCH/BSGR BH23.............. 450 D1
Somerford County
Junior School
  CHCH/BSGR BH23.............. 450 D1
Somers Park Primary School
  SSEA PO5...................... 21 J2
Somers Town Health Centre
  SSEA PO5...................... 21 J3
Sopley CP School
  CHCH/BSGR BH23.............. 409 G7
Southampton Airport Parkway
Station
  ELGH SO50...................... 319 L2
Southampton Central Mosque
  SHAM SO14...................... 343 M2
Southampton City College
  SHAM SO14...................... 13 J4

Southampton City Council
  PTSW SO17...................... 319 H6
Southampton City Council
  ROWN SO16...................... 317 H6
Southampton City Council
  ROWN SO16...................... 318 A7
Southampton City Council
  ROWN SO16...................... 318 C3
Southampton City Council
  SHAM SO14...................... 12 F5
Southampton City Council
  SHAM SO14...................... 12 F6
Southampton City Council
  SHAM SO14...................... 13 J2
Southampton City Council
  SHAM SO14...................... 13 K3
Southampton City Council
  WSHM SO15...................... 12 C2
Southampton Football Club
  WSHM SO15...................... 343 J2
Southampton General Hospital
  ROWN SO16...................... 318 A5
Southampton Institute &
Millais Gallery
  WSHM SO15...................... 13 G1
Southampton
Magistrates Court
  WSHM SO15...................... 343 L2
Southampton & New Forest
Magistrates Courts
  WSHM SO15...................... 12 D1
Southampton Sports Centre
  ROWN SO16...................... 318 C4
Southampton Sports Club
  ROWN SO16...................... 317 H6
Southampton Technical College
  SHAM SO14...................... 13 M5
Southampton University
  ROWN SO16...................... 292 B7
South Baddesley C of E
Primary School
  LYMN SO41...................... 441 H2
Southbourne County Junior &
Infant School
  EMRTH PO10...................... 379 J8
Southbourne Surgery
  EMRTH PO10...................... 379 J8
Southdown School
  RWIN SO21...................... 266 B2
The South Downs College
  WVILLE PO7...................... 376 E5
Southern Electric Museum
  CHCH/BSGR BH23.............. 450 A1
South Farnborough County
Junior School
  FARN GU14...................... 91 G6
South Farnborough
Infant School
  FARN GU14...................... 91 G8
South Farnham Middle School
  FNM GU9...................... 135 H7
South Ham Medical Centre
  KEMP RG22...................... 104 B5
South Hants Country Club
  WHAM PO17...................... 349 L7
Southlands School
  LYMN SO41...................... 440 C1
Southlea Surgery
  ALDT GU11...................... 7 H7
South Parade Pier
  PSEA PO1...................... 423 J7
Southsea Castle Museum
  SSEA PO5...................... 423 G7
Southsea Infant School
  SSEA PO5...................... 21 L7
South West Health Authority
  HEND SO30...................... 345 M4
Southwick Park Naval
Recreation Centre
  WHAM PO17...................... 374 E3
South Wonston
Primary School
  RWIN SO21...................... 190 C4
Southwood Golf Club
  FARN GU14...................... 90 B6
Sparsholt College Hampshire
  RWIN SO21...................... 212 F4
Sparsholt Primary School
  RWIN SO21...................... 213 J5
Spectrum Sports Club
  SBNE BH6...................... 449 H4
Speenhamland Cp School
  NWBY RG14...................... 2 D1
Spitfire Court Surgery
  SHAM SO14...................... 13 M6
Springdale First School
  BDST BH18...................... 429 J4
Springfield School
  CHAM PO6...................... 400 A1
Springhill RC Primary School
  WSHM SO15...................... 343 J2
Springlake Country Club
  ASHV GU12...................... 113 H4
Spurcroft Primary School
  STHA RG19...................... 27 G6
Staff College
  CBLY GU15...................... 70 F1
Stag Business Park
  RGWD BH24...................... 382 E3
Stakes Hill Infant School
  WVILLE PO7...................... 376 D2
Stakes Lodge Surgery
  WVILLE PO7...................... 376 E2
Stamshaw Infant School
  NEND PO2...................... 399 H6
Stamshaw Junior School
  NEND PO2...................... 399 G5
Stamshaw & Tipner
Leisure Centre
  NEND PO2...................... 399 G6
Stanbridge Earls School
  ROMY SO51...................... 262 A5
Stanley Green First School
  PLE BH15...................... 445 H2
Stanmore Primary School
  FUFL SO22...................... 238 D3
Stanton Industrial Estate
  WSHM SO15...................... 342 E1

Stapehill Abbey
WIMB BH21 .... 405 J3
Station Industrial Estate
FLET GU13 .... 89 G5
Station Road Surgery
FRIM GU16 .... 71 G8
Station Theatre
HISD PO11 .... 425 H4
Staunton Park
Community School
HAV PO9 .... 377 M1
Stedham CP School
MIDH GU29 .... 279 J7
Steep School
PSF GU32 .... 275 K1
Stephen's Castle
VWD BH31 .... 332 E8
Sterling Industrial Estate
NWBY RG14 .... 3 G5
Stockbridge CP School
STOK SO20 .... 186 F5
Stockcross School
KSCL RG20 .... 24 B2
Stoke Gallery
GPORT PO12 .... 18 F5
Stoke Park County
Junior School
ELGH SO50 .... 294 D5
Stoke Park Infant School
ELGH SO50 .... 294 D6
Stokewood Surgery
ELGH SO50 .... 294 F6
Stourfield First School
SBNE BH6 .... 449 J2
Stratfield Saye
THLE RG7 .... 65 G1
Stroud School
ROMY SO51 .... 263 K8
Stubbs Industrial Estate
ALDT GU11 .... 113 H3
Summerbee First School
CHAR BH8 .... 433 G7
Summerbee Junior School
CHAR BH8 .... 433 G7
Summerbee Secondary School
CHAR BH8 .... 433 H7
Sun Hill Infant School
NARL SO24 .... 218 C4
Sunnyside Doctors Surgery
PSEA PO1 .... 21 L1
Sun Valley Business Park
WINC SO23 .... 11 M5
Super Bowl
BMTH BH1 .... 23 G5
Super Bowl
WSHM SO15 .... 342 D1
Superstore
BMTH BH1 .... 23 J3
Superstore
BSTK RG21 .... 4 A8
Superstore
SHAM SO14 .... 12 E2
Superstore
SHAM SO14 .... 12 E3
Surrey Hampshire Borders
Nhs Trust
BSTK RG21 .... 5 G8
Surrey House First School
ITCH SO19 .... 345 G5
Surrey House Health Centre
ITCH SO19 .... 345 G5
Swallowfield Medical Practice
THLE RG7 .... 45 M1
Swanmore Business Park
BPWT SO32 .... 323 L3
Swanmore C of E School
BPWT SO32 .... 324 A2
Swanmore County
Secondary School
BPWT SO32 .... 323 M3
Swan Street Surgery
PSF GU32 .... 275 K5
Swanwick Business Park
HLER SO31 .... 370 B1
Sway Park Industrial Estate
LYMN SO41 .... 412 F7
Sway St Lukes Primary School
LYMN SO41 .... 412 F6
Swaythling Clinic
PTSW SO17 .... 319 H5
Swaythling Primary School
PTSW SO17 .... 319 G5
Sylvan First School
BKME/WDN BH12 ...... 446 A2
Synagogue
BMTH BH1 .... 23 G5
The Synagogue
PTSW SO17 .... 343 K1
Tadley CP School
TADY RG26 .... 61 M2
Tadley Police Station
TADY RG26 .... 41 L7
Talavera County Junior &
Infant School
ALDT GU11 .... 112 E5
Talbot Heath School
WBNE BH4 .... 447 H3
Talbot House
Preparatory School
MOOR/WNTN BH9 ...... 432 C8
Talbot School
BKME/WDN BH12 ...... 431 M8
Talisman Business Centre
HLER SO31 .... 370 F2
Tankerville School
ELGH SO50 .... 294 A5
Tanners Brook Infant School
WSHM SO15 .... 342 D1
Tanners Brook Junior School
ROWN SO16 .... 342 D1
Tatchbury Manor House
TOTT SO40 .... 315 L7
Tatchbury Mount Hospital
TOTT SO40 .... 315 M6
Tauntons College
WSHM SO15 .... 318 D7

Tavistock County
Infant School
FLET GU13 .... 88 C8
Tempus Business Centre
BSTK RG21 .... 4 A4
Tennis Club
FLET GU13 .... 110 E5
Terminus Industrial Estate
PSEA PO1 .... 21 J2
Testbourne Community School
WHCH RG28 .... 122 C5
Test Vale Surgery
TOTT SO40 .... 316 E8
Test Valley Business Centre
TOTT SO40 .... 317 G6
Test Valley County
Secondary School
STOK SO20 .... 186 C5
Testwood School
TOTT SO40 .... 316 E7
Thatcham Bowling Club
NTHA RG18 .... 27 G4
Thatcham Health Centre
NTHA RG18 .... 26 F4
Thatcham Town Council
NTHA RG18 .... 26 F4
Thatcham Town Football Club
STHA RG19 .... 27 J8
Thornden School
CHFD SO53 .... 265 L8
Thorney County
Primary School
EMRTH PO10 .... 402 E6
Thorneycroft Industrial Estate
BSTK RG21 .... 4 A4
Thorngrove School
KSCL RG20 .... 56 B1
Thornhill Clinic
ITCH SO19 .... 345 H3
Thornhill First School
ITCH SO19 .... 345 G4
Thornhill Junior School
ITCH SO19 .... 345 G3
Thornhill Park Surgery
ITCH SO19 .... 345 H2
Three Legged Cross
Country First School
WIMB BH21 .... 356 C7
Tidworth Garrison Golf Club
NTID SP9 .... 114 B4
Tidworth Health Centre
NTID SP9 .... 114 E2
Tiptoe CP School
LYMN SO41 .... 412 B8
Titchfield County
Primary School
FHAM/STUB PO14 ...... 371 K7
Tomlinscote School
FRIM GU16 .... 71 J6
Totton College
TOTT SO40 .... 316 C8
Totton College
TOTT SO40 .... 341 J3
Totton Recreation Centre
TOTT SO40 .... 316 C8
Tower Hill CP School
FARN GU14 .... 90 C5
Tower Industrial Estate
ELGH SO50 .... 294 B6
Townhill Infant School
WEND SO18 .... 319 M6
Townhill Middle School
WEND SO18 .... 319 M6
Townhill Park Health Clinic
WEND SO18 .... 319 M6
Townhill Surgery
WEND SO18 .... 320 A1
The Toynbee School
CHFD SO53 .... 293 J3
Treadgold Museum
PSEA PO1 .... 20 D1
Trinidad First School
BKME/WDN BH12 ...... 431 G8
Trinity Business Centre
TOTT SO40 .... 316 D6
Trinity Industrial Estate
WSHM SO15 .... 342 D1
Trinity School
NWBY RG14 .... 25 L3
Trojans Sports Club
ELGH SO50 .... 319 H1
Tudor House Museum
SHAM SO14 .... 12 F5
Tunworth Ho
OVTN RG25 .... 106 D8
Turlin Moor First School
UPTN BH16 .... 444 B4
Turlin Moor Middle School
UPTN BH16 .... 444 B4
Turnpike Business Park
FHAM/PORC PO16 ...... 15 K3
Turnpike Gallery
PSF GU32 .... 275 L5
Tweseldown Infant School
FLET GU13 .... 111 G4
Two Riversmeet
Leisure Centre
CHCH/BSGR BH23 ...... 450 B2
Twyford C of E
Primary School
RWIN SO21 .... 266 C2
Twyford School
RWIN SO21 .... 266 F2
Twyford Surgery
RWIN SO21 .... 266 E7
Twynham
Comprehensive School
CHCH/BSGR BH23 ...... 449 M2
Tylney Park Golf Club
HTWY RG27 .... 85 J4
Ufton Nervet
Parochial Primary School
THLE RG7 .... 30 F4
Unicorn Trading Estate
HASM GU27 .... 228 E1
Union Buildings Playschool
ALDT GU11 .... 112 D5

United Services Cricket Ground
PSEA PO1 .... 20 D3
United Services Rugby Club
PSEA PO1 .... 20 E2
University of Portsmouth
ENEY PO4 .... 423 M4
University of Portsmouth
HISD PO11 .... 424 D4
University of Portsmouth
PSEA PO1 .... 20 D1
University of Portsmouth
PSEA PO1 .... 20 D4
University of Portsmouth
PSEA PO1 .... 20 E2
University of Portsmouth
PSEA PO1 .... 20 E3
University of Portsmouth
PSEA PO1 .... 21 K2
University of Portsmouth
SSEA PO5 .... 20 F6
University of Portsmouth
SSEA PO5 .... 21 G3
University of Portsmouth
SSEA PO5 .... 21 H4
University of Southampton
PTSW SO17 .... 319 G5
University of Southampton
ROWN SO16 .... 318 E5
University Practice
SSEA PO5 .... 20 F4
Upham School
BPWT SO32 .... 296 D3
Uplands County
Primary School
FHAM/PORC PO16 ...... 15 G2
Uplands CP School
SHST GU47 .... 49 L8
Uplands School
PSTN BH14 .... 446 B5
Upton Grey Ho
OVTN RG25 .... 129 M2
Upton Health Centre
UPTN BH16 .... 444 B1
Venture Industrial Park
LSOL/BMARY PO13 ...... 397 H5
Vermont School
ROWN SO16 .... 318 D4
Vernham Dean School
RAND SP11 .... 73 J3
Verwood C of E First School
VWD BH31 .... 356 C3
Verwood C of E School
VWD BH31 .... 356 C3
Verwood Industrial Estate
VWD BH31 .... 356 F2
Verwood Leisure Centre
VWD BH31 .... 356 D2
Verwood Sports Centre
VWD BH31 .... 356 E2
Verwood Town Council
VWD BH31 .... 356 D1
Viables Industrial Estate
KEMP RG22 .... 104 F7
Vicarage Lane Clinic
HASM GU27 .... 228 C2
Vickers Business Centre
CHAM PO6 .... 82 D8
Victoria Cottage Hospital
EMRTH PO10 .... 378 D8
Victoria Park
Swimming Centre
PSEA PO1 .... 20 F1
Victor Street Surgery
WSHM SO15 .... 318 A7
Victory Business Centre
PSEA PO1 .... 21 L2
Victory Retail Park
PSEA PO1 .... 423 G1
Victory Trading Estate
HSEA PO3 .... 399 M6
Vigo County Infant School
AND SP10 .... 9 M3
Vigo County Junior School
AND SP10 .... 9 M3
Village Medical Practice
FERN BH22 .... 380 B6
The Vine School
BPWT SO32 .... 322 C8
Vintage Motorcycle Museum
NMIL/BTOS BH25 ...... 437 J3
Virgin Cinemas
SHAM SO14 .... 13 J7
Wallisdean County
Infant School
FHAM/STUB PO14 ...... 14 D7
Wallisdean County
Junior School
FHAM/STUB PO14 ...... 14 E7
Wallop CP School
STOK SO20 .... 184 D1
Walsh C of E First &
Middle School
ASHV GU12 .... 113 J7
Waltham Business Park
BPWT SO32 .... 323 M4
Warblington School
HAV PO9 .... 17 J4
War Memorial Hospital
AND SP10 .... 8 D1
War Memorial Hospital
LYMN SO41 .... 454 D4
Warren Avenue
Industrial Estate
ENEY PO4 .... 423 M3
Warren Park Primary School
HAV PO9 .... 377 H1
Warrior Business Centre
CHAM PO6 .... 400 C1
Watchetts County
Middle School
CBLY GU15 .... 70 F6
Waterfront Garden Surgery
FAWY SO45 .... 367 L3
Waterfront Museum
PLE BH15 .... 445 G7
Waterloo Industrial Estate
HEND SO30 .... 321 G7

The Waterloo School
WVILLE PO7 .... 376 C1
Waterlooville Football Club
WVILLE PO7 .... 352 C8
Waterlooville Health Centre
WVILLE PO7 .... 352 B6
Watermill Theatre &
Restaurant
KSCL RG20 .... 24 E1
Watermill Theatre
STHA RG19 .... 38 C3
The Waterside Health Centre
FAWY SO45 .... 367 L6
Waterside School
FHAM/PORC PO16 ...... 398 F5
The Wavell School
ALDT GU11 .... 112 E1
Waverley Abbey C of E School
NFNM GU10 .... 159 M3
Webb Peploe House Surgery
LYMN SO41 .... 440 C5
Weeke CP School
FUFL SO22 .... 10 A2
Weford County Infants School
LIND GU35 .... 201 L4
Wellington Business Park
CWTH RG45 .... 49 H4
Wellington College
CWTH RG45 .... 49 K5
Wellington Shopping Centre
ALDT GU11 .... 6 F2
Wellington Sports Centre
CWTH RG45 .... 49 J4
Wellington Sports Club
ELGH SO50 .... 319 J1
Wellow County Primary School
ROMY SO51 .... 288 E5
Wellum House Dental
Health Centre
AND SP10 .... 9 J7
Wentworth College
BOSC BH5 .... 448 F4
Wessex Bowl
KEMP RG22 .... 104 B3
Wessex Downs Golf Club
THLE RG7 .... 29 H4
Wessex Nuffield Hospital
CHFD SO53 .... 265 L7
Wessex Nuffield Hospital
ELGH SO50 .... 294 A5
Wessex Regional
Health Authority
HEND SO30 .... 321 G7
Wessex Superbowl
CHAM PO6 .... 376 E7
West Berkshire Council
NWBY RG14 .... 2 D5
West Berkshire District Council
NWBY RG14 .... 2 D3
West Berkshire District Council
NWBY RG14 .... 2 E4
West Berkshire District Council
NWBY RG14 .... 2 E5
West Berkshire District Council
NWBY RG14 .... 3 G2
Westbourne County
Primary School
EMRTH PO10 .... 378 F4
Westbourne Galleries
CCLF BH13 .... 447 G5
Westbourne Surgery
EMRTH PO10 .... 378 F5
West Cliff Medical Centre
WCLF BH2 .... 22 C8
Westend County Infant School
ALDT GU11 .... 6 D3
West End Surgery
HEND SO30 .... 320 D6
Western Community Hospital
ROWN SO16 .... 317 M7
Western Downland
Primary School
FBDG SP6 .... 308 C4
Western Downland School
FBDG SP6 .... 282 E7
Western Primary School
FUFL SO22 .... 10 B6
Westfield County Junior School
YTLY GU46 .... 68 E3
Westfield Junior School
CHAM PO6 .... 374 C8
The Westgate School
FUFL SO22 .... 10 C5
West Hill Park School
FHAM/STUB PO14 ...... 371 J8
Westlands Medical Centre
FHAM/PORC PO16 ...... 398 A1
West March Business Centre
AND SP10 .... 9 J1
West Meon Controlled
Primary School
PSF GU32 .... 272 A3
West Moors Group Practice
FERN BH22 .... 380 B6
West Moors Middle School
FERN BH22 .... 380 D7
Weston Park Boys School
ITCH SO19 .... 344 F7
Weston Park First School
ITCH SO19 .... 344 F7
Weston Park Junior School
ITCH SO19 .... 344 F7
Weston Shore First School
ITCH SO19 .... 344 D8
Westover Gallery
BMTH BH1 .... 22 F6
Westover Primary School
HSEA PO3 .... 399 M8
West Point Business Park
AND SP10 .... 118 A7
West Portway
Industrial Estate
RAND SP11 .... 117 M7
West Quay Retail Park
WSHM SO15 .... 12 D3
West Quay Shopping Centre
SHAM SO14 .... 12 E3

West Suuex County Council
CBLY GU15 .... 70 A3
West Tytherley Primary School
RSAL SP5 .... 207 M13
West Wittering
Parochial School
SELS PO20 .... 427 K7
Westwood Business Park
TOTT SO40 .... 316 E6
Weybourne County
Infant School
FNM GU9 .... 6 A3
Weydon County
Secondary School
FNM GU9 .... 158 C1
Weydown Industrial Estate
HASM GU27 .... 228 E1
Weyford County Junior School
LIND GU35 .... 201 L4
Wherwell School
RAND SP11 .... 166 A1
Whitchurch C of E
Primary School
WHCH RG28 .... 122 C4
Whitchurch Medical Centre
WHCH RG28 .... 122 A4
Whitedown Special School
ALTN GU34 .... 176 D6
White Hart Gallery
OVTN RG25 .... 100 F5
White Hart Industrial Estate
BLKW GU17 .... 70 B3
Whitelands Park CP School
NTHA RG18 .... 26 F3
Whiteley County
Primary School
FHAM PO15 .... 371 G1
The Whiteley Surgery
HLER SO31 .... 346 F8
Whiteparish Surgery
RSAL SP5 .... 258 C2
Whitewater C of E (Controlled)
Primary School
HTWY RG27 .... 85 K3
Wickham C of E
Controlled Primary School
WHAM PO17 .... 348 D3
Wickham Park Golf Club
WHAM PO17 .... 348 C4
Wickham Riding School
WHAM PO17 .... 349 J2
Wickham Surgery
WHAM PO17 .... 348 C4
Wick 1 Industrial Estate
NMIL/BTOS BH25 ...... 437 J5
Wick 2 Industrial Estate
NMIL/BTOS BH25 ...... 437 J6
Wicor County Primary School
FHAM/PORC PO16 ...... 373 L8
Wildern Clinic
HEND SO30 .... 346 A1
The Wildern School
HEND SO30 .... 346 A1
Wildground County
Infant School
FAWY SO45 .... 367 K7
Wildground County
Junior School
FAWY SO45 .... 367 K7
William Cobbett County
Junior School
FNM GU9 .... 6 B5
William Gilpin C of E
Primary School
LYMN SO41 .... 414 C2
Willink Leisure Centre
THLE RG7 .... 31 J6
Willink School
THLE RG7 .... 31 J6
Willis Museum
BSTK RG21 .... 4 F9
Willments Industrial Estate
ITCH SO19 .... 344 B3
Willowdene Play School
CHAM PO6 .... 83 L6
Wimbledon Park Sports Centre
SSEA PO5 .... 21 K8
Wimborne Industrial Estate
WIMB BH21 .... 404 A3
Wimborne Junior &
Infant School
ENEY PO4 .... 423 J2
Winchcombe CP Infant School
NWBY RG14 .... 25 L3
Winchcombe Junior School
NWBY RG14 .... 2 E1
Winchester Agricultural
Museum
WINC SO23 .... 11 G5
Winchester City Museum
WINC SO23 .... 11 G6
Winchester College
WINC SO23 .... 238 F2
The Winchester Gallery
ROWN SO16 .... 318 E3
Winchester Lawn Tennis Club
FUFL SO22 .... 10 B3
Winchester Recreation Centre
WINC SO23 .... 11 H6
Winchester Road
Industrial Estate
BSTK RG21 .... 104 E5
Winchester Rugby
Football Club
WINC SO23 .... 11 J4
Winchester School of Art
WINC SO23 .... 11 J6
Winklebury Infant School
DEAN RG23 .... 104 C2
Winklebury Junior School
DEAN RG23 .... 104 C2
Winklebury Medical Centre
DEAN RG23 .... 104 B2
Winnall CP School
WINC SO23 .... 11 L1
Winnall Farm Industrial Estate
WINC SO23 .... 11 K6

Winterslow Primary School
    RSAL SP5 .... 206 E2
Winton Play School
    AND SP10 .... 9 L4
The Winton School
    AND SP10 .... 119 J8
The Wishing Well Gallery
    CHCH/BSGR BH23 .... 409 M7
The Wishing Well Gallery
    RGWD BH24 .... 384 E5
Wispers School
    HASM GU27 .... 204 F7
Wolverdene School
    AND SP10 .... 9 K7
Wolvesey Palace
    WINC SO23 .... 11 H9

Woodhill Preparatory School
    CHFD SO53 .... 293 J1
Woodhills School
    HEND SO30 .... 346 D1
Woodlands Community School
    WEND SO18 .... 320 C8
Woodlea Primary School
    LIND GU35 .... 201 J7
Wool House Maritime Museum
    SHAM SO14 .... 12 F6
Woolmer Hill School
    HASM GU27 .... 228 A1
Woolmer Surgery
    LIND GU35 .... 201 J5
Woolsbridge Industrial Estate
    WIMB BH21 .... 380 F2

Woolsbridge
    Small Business Centre
    WIMB BH21 .... 380 E2
Woolston First School
    ITCH SO19 .... 344 C6
Woolston School
    ITCH SO19 .... 344 D5
Woolton Hill County
    Junior School
    KSCL RG20 .... 56 B1
Wordsworth Infant School
    WSHM SO15 .... 318 B7
Worldham Park Golf Club
    ALTN GU34 .... 177 H6
Worting County Infant School
    DEAN RG23 .... 103 M4

Worting County Junior School
    KEMP RG22 .... 104 A4
Wykeham Gallery
    STOK SO20 .... 186 E5
Wykeham House School
    FHAM/PORC PO16 .... 15 M5
Wykeham Industrial Estate
    WINC SO23 .... 11 L4
Wynford Farm Industrial Estate
    ROMY SO51 .... 262 E4
The Wyvern Community
    Secondary School
    ELGH SO50 .... 295 H7
Yarrells Preparatory School
    UPTN BH16 .... 444 A1

Yateley County Infant School
    YTLY GU46 .... 69 G2
Yateley Health Centre
    YTLY GU46 .... 69 G2
Yateley Manor
    Preparatory School
    YTLY GU46 .... 69 G1
Yateley School
    YTLY GU46 .... 68 F3
Yeoman Industrial Park
    TOTT SO40 .... 317 G6
Youngs Industrial Estate
    THLE RG7 .... 41 J4